CALIFORNIA CAMPING

TOM STIENSTRA

formerly published as
Foghorn Outdoors California Camping

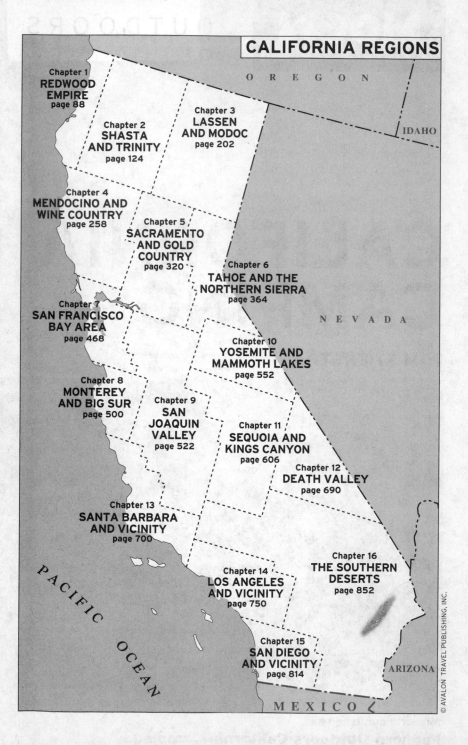

CALIFORNIA REGIONS

OREGON

IDAHO

NEVADA

ARIZONA

Chapter 1
REDWOOD
EMPIRE
page 88

Chapter 2
SHASTA
AND TRINITY
page 124

Chapter 3
LASSEN
AND MODOC
page 202

Chapter 4
MENDOCINO AND
WINE COUNTRY
page 258

Chapter 5
SACRAMENTO
AND GOLD
COUNTRY
page 320

Chapter 6
TAHOE AND THE
NORTHERN SIERRA
page 364

Chapter 7
SAN FRANCISCO
BAY AREA
page 468

Chapter 10
YOSEMITE AND
MAMMOTH LAKES
page 552

Chapter 8
MONTEREY
AND BIG SUR
page 500

Chapter 9
SAN
JOAQUIN
VALLEY
page 522

Chapter 11
SEQUOIA AND
KINGS CANYON
page 606

Chapter 12
DEATH VALLEY
page 690

Chapter 13
SANTA BARBARA
AND VICINITY
page 700

Chapter 16
THE SOUTHERN
DESERTS
page 852

Chapter 14
LOS ANGELES
AND VICINITY
page 750

Chapter 15
SAN DIEGO
AND VICINITY
page 814

PACIFIC OCEAN

MEXICO

© AVALON TRAVEL PUBLISHING, INC.

Contents

Chapter 1 **Redwood Empire** 85

Chapter 2 **Shasta and Trinity** 121

Silver Lake
Stampede Lake
Stanislaus National Forest
Stanislaus River
Stumpy Meadows Lake
Sugar Pine Point State Park
Tahoe National Forest

Tahoe State Recreation Area
Topaz Lake
Truckee River
Turtle Rock Park
Walker River
Woods Lake
Yuba River

Chapter 7 **San Francisco Bay Area**. 465

Including:
Angel Island
Anthony Chabot Regional Park
Big Basin Redwoods State Park
Butano State Park
China Camp State Park
Coyote Lake County Park
Del Valle Regional Park
Half Moon Bay
Half Moon Bay State Beach
Henry Cowell Redwoods State Park
Henry W. Coe State Park
Joseph D. Grant County Park

Marin Headlands
Memorial County Park
Mount Diablo State Park
Mount Tamalpais State Park
Point Reyes National Seashore
Portola Redwoods State Park
Samuel P. Taylor State Park
San Francisco Presidio
San Pablo Bay
Sanborn-Skyline County Park
Sunol Regional Wilderness
Tomales Bay
Uvas Canyon County Park

Chapter 8 **Monterey and Big Sur**. 497

Including:
Andrew Molera State Park
Arroyo Seco River
Big Sur
Carmel River
Fremont Peak State Park
Hollister Hills State Vehicular
   Recreation Area
Laguna Seca Recreation Area
Limekiln State Park
Los Padres National Forest

Manresa Uplands State
McAlpine Lake and Park
Monterey Bay
New Brighton State Beach
Pfeiffer Big Sur State Park
Pinnacles National Monument
Pinto Lake Park
San Lorenzo County Park
Seacliff State Beach
Sunset State Beach

Giant Sequoia National Forest
Giant Sequoia National Monument
Hensley Lake
Hume Lake
Huntington Lake
Inyo National Forest
Isabella Lake
John Muir Wilderness
Kaweah River
Kern River
Kings Canyon National Park
Kings River
Lake Edison
Lake Ming

Lake Sabrina
Lake Success
Millerton Lake State
 Recreation Area
Mono Hot Springs
Mount Whitney
Mountain Home State Forest
North Lake
Pine Flat Lake
San Joaquin River
Shaver Lake
Sierra National Forest
South Lake
Tule River

How to Use This Book

ABOUT THE CAMPGROUND PROFILES

The campgrounds are listed in a consistent, easy-to-read format to help you choose the ideal camping spot. If you already know the name of the specific campground you want to visit, or the name of the surrounding geological area or nearby feature (town, national or state park, forest, mountain, lake, river, etc.), look it up in the index and turn to the corresponding page. Here is a sample profile:

Campground name and number →

Icons noting activities and facilities at or nearby the campground

1 SOMEWHERE USA CAMPGROUND

General location of the campground in relation to the nearest major town or landmark →

Scenic rating: 10

south of Somewhere USA Lake

Rating of scenic beauty on a scale of 1-10 with 10 the highest rating

Map the campground can be found on and page number the map can be found on →

Map 1.2, page 4   **BEST** (

Each campground in this book begins with a brief overview of its setting. The description typically covers ambience, information about the attractions, and activities popular at the campground.

Symbol indicating that the campground is listed among the author's top picks

Campsites, facilities: This section notes the number of campsites for tents and RVs and indicates whether hookups are available. Facilities such as restrooms, picnic areas, recreation areas, laundry, and dump stations will be addressed, as well as the availability of piped water, showers, playgrounds, stores, and other amenities. The campground's pet policy and wheelchair accessibility is also mentioned here.

Reservations, fees: This section notes whether reservations are accepted, and provides rates for tent sites and RV sites. If there are additional fees for parking or pets, or discounted weekly or seasonal rates, they will also be noted here.

Directions: This section provides mile-by-mile driving directions to the campground from the nearest major town or highway.

Contact: This section provides an address, phone number, and website, if available, for the campground.

ABOUT THE ICONS

The icons in this book are designed to provide at-a-glance information on activities, facilities, and services available on-site or within walking distance of each campground.

- 🏃 Hiking trails
- 🚴 Biking trails
- 🏊 Swimming
- 🎣 Fishing
- 🚤 Boating
- 🛶 Canoeing and/or kayaking
- ❄ Winter sports

- ♨ Hot springs
- 🐕 Pets permitted
- 🎠 Playground
- ♿ Wheelchair accessible
- 5️⃣ 5 Percent Club
- 🚐 RV sites
- ⛺ Tent sites

ABOUT THE SCENIC RATING

Each campground profile employs a scenic rating on a scale of 1 to 10, with 1 being the least scenic and 10 being the most scenic. A scenic rating measures only the overall beauty of the campground and environs. The scenic rating, whether a 1 or a 10, does not take into account noise level, facilities, maintenance, recreation options, or campground management. The setting of a campground with a lower scenic rating may simply not be as picturesque as that of a higher rated campground. However other factors, such as noise or recreation access, can still affect your camping trip.

If the noise levels or cleanliness of a campground—even a high-rated one—are unacceptable, it's best to contact the campground manager with your concerns. But because these elements can change from day to day, or simply with a new employee hired, these issues are not factored into the ratings. Consider both the scenic rating and the profile description before deciding which campground is perfect for you.

MAP SYMBOLS

══════ Expressway	(80) Interstate Freeway	✗ Airfield
────── Primary Road	(101) U.S. Highway	✗ Airport
────── Secondary Road	(29) State Highway	○ City/Town
- - - - - - Unpaved Road	(66) County Highway	▲ Mountain
·········· Ferry	Lake	♠ Park
—·—·— National Border	Dry Lake	⅄ Pass
—··— State Border	Seasonal Lake	◉ State Capital

ABOUT THE MAPS

This book is divided into chapters based on major regions in the state; an overview map of these regions precedes the table of contents. Each chapter begins with a map of the region, which is further broken down into detail maps. Campgrounds are noted on the detail maps by number.

Reference to adjacent region

Detail map number and page number

Grid line divides region into detail maps

Locates region within state

Region border

Detail map 11.5 shown on next page

INTRODUCTION

Author's Note

Going on a camping trip can be like trying to put hiking boots on an octopus. You've tried it too, eh? Instead of a relaxing and fun trip full of adventure, it turns into a scenario called "You Against the World." You might as well try to fight a volcano.

But it doesn't have to be that way, and that's what this book is all about. If you give it a chance, the information herein can put the mystery, excitement, and fun back into your camping vacations—and remove the snarls, confusion, and occasional, volcanic temper explosions that keep people at home, locked away from the action.

Mystery? There are hundreds of hidden, rarely used campgrounds listed and mapped in this book that most people have never dreamed of. *Excitement?* At many of them, you'll find the sizzle with the steak: the hike to a great lookout or the big fish at the end of your line. *Fun?* The *Camping Tips* section of this book can help you take the futility out of your trips and put the fun back in. Add it up, put it in your cash register, and you can turn a camping trip into the satisfying adventure it's meant to be, whether it's just an overnight quickie or a monthlong expedition.

It's estimated that 95 percent of American vacationers use only 5 percent of the country's available recreation areas. With this book, you can leave the herd, wander, and be free. You can join the inner circle, the 5 Percenters who know the great hidden areas used by so few people. To join the 5 Percent Club, take a hard look at the maps for the areas you wish to visit and the corresponding campground listings. As you study the camps, you'll start to feel a sense of excitement building, a feeling that you are about to unlock a door and venture into a world that is rarely viewed. When you feel that excitement, act on it. Parlay that energy into a great trip.

The campground maps and listings can serve in two ways: 1) If you're on the road late in the day and you're stuck for a spot for the night, you can likely find one nearby; or 2) if you are planning a trip, you can tailor a vacation to fit exactly into your plans rather than heading off and hoping—maybe praying—it turns out all right.

For the latter, you may wish to obtain additional maps, particularly if you are venturing into areas governed by the U.S. Forest Service or Bureau of Land Management. Both are federal agencies that offer low-cost maps detailing all hiking trails, lakes, streams, and backcountry camps reached via logging roads. The *Resources* section at the back of this book details how to obtain these and other maps.

Backcountry camps listed in this book are often in primitive and rugged settings but provide the sense of isolation that you may want from a trip. They also provide good jump-off points for backpacking trips, if that's your calling. These camps are often free, and I have listed hundreds of them.

At the other end of the spectrum are the developed parks for RVs. They offer a home away from home, with everything from full hookups to a grocery store and laundry room. These spots are just as important as the remote camps with no facilities. Instead of isolation, an RV park provides a place to shower and get outfitted for food and clean clothes. For RV cruisers, it's a place to stay in high style while touring the area. RV parks range in price $12–25 per night, depending on location, and an advance deposit may be necessary in summer.

Somewhere between the two extremes—the remote, unimproved camps and the lavish RV parks—are hundreds and hundreds of campgrounds that provide a compromise: beautiful settings and some facilities, with a small overnight fee. Piped water, vault toilets, and picnic tables tend to come with the territory. Fees for these sites are usually in the $6–15 range, with the higher-priced sites located near population centers. Because they offer a bit of both worlds, they are in high demand. Reservations are usually advised, and at state parks, particularly during the summer season, you can expect company. This doesn't mean you need to forgo them in hopes of a less confined environment. For one thing, most state parks have set up quotas so that visitors don't feel as if they've been squeezed in with a shoehorn. For another, the same parks are often uncrowded during the off-season and on weekdays.

Before your trip, you'll want to get organized, and that's when you must start putting boots on that giant octopus. The trick to organization for any task is breaking it down to its key components and then solving each element independent of the others. Remember the octopus. Grab a moving leg, jam on a boot, and make sure it's on tight before reaching for another leg. Do one thing at a time, in order, and all will get done quickly and efficiently.

In the *Camping Tips* section that follows, I have isolated the different elements of camping, and you should do the same when planning for your trip. There are separate sections on each of the primary ingredients for a successful trip: 1) Food and cooking gear; 2) Clothing and weather protection; 3) Hiking and foot care and how to choose the right boots and socks; 4) Sleeping gear; 5) Combating bugs and some commonsense first-aid; 6) Catching fish, avoiding bears, and camp fun; 7) Outdoors with kids; and 8) Weather prediction. I've also included sections on boat-in and desert camping and ethics in the outdoors, as well as a camping gear checklist.

Now you can become completely organized for your trip in just one week, spending just a little time each evening on a given component. Getting organized is an unnatural act for many. By splitting up the tasks, you take the pressure out of planning and put the fun back in.

As a full-time outdoors writer, the question I am asked more than any other is: "Where are you going this week?" All of the answers are in this book.

KEEP IT WILD

"Enjoy America's country and leave no trace." That's the motto of the Leave No Trace program, and I strongly support it. Promoting responsible outdoor recreation through education, research, and partnerships is its mission. Look for the Keep It Wild Tips, developed from the policies of Leave No Trace, throughout the Camping Tips portion of this book. This copyrighted information has been reprinted with permission from the Leave No Trace Center for Outdoor Ethics. For more information or materials, please visit www.LNT.org or call 303/442-8222 or 800/332-4100.

Best Campgrounds

The most common emails I get are those where readers ask me to plan their adventures and to rate campgrounds as launch points for specific activities. While I can't respond to all emails, I do often rate the top 10 campgrounds in California for scenery, hiking, fishing, boating, water sports, rafting, and family activities.

I've organized the following selections by activity, then rated them 1 through 10, starting with my pick for the best. These are among America's preeminent campgrounds, so if you plan a trip to any be sure to plan your stay far in advance. Here are my picks for 2007–2008:

◖ Best Scenic Destinations

1. **Bridalveil Creek and Equestrian and Group Camp (Glacier Point),** Yosemite and Mammoth Lakes, page 564.
2. **Emerald Bay State Park and Boat-In,** Tahoe and the Northern Sierra, page 429.
3. **Manresa Uplands State Beach Walk-in,** Monterey and Big Sur, page 504.
4. **Sardine Lake,** Tahoe and the Northern Sierra, page 380.
5. **Gaviota State Park/El Capitán State Beach,** Santa Barbara and Vicinity, pages 721 and 722.
6. **Sabrina near Lake Sabrina in Inyo National Forest,** Sequoia and Kings Canyon, page 636.
7. **Santa Rosa Island Boat-In in Channel Islands National Park,** Santa Barbara and Vicinity, page 744.
8. **Mary Smith on Lewiston Lake,** Shasta and Trinity, page 191.
9. **Steep Ravine Environmental Campsites,** San Francisco Bay Area, page 477.
10. **Salt Point State Park,** Mendocino and Wine Country, page 299.

◖ Best for Hikes with Views

1. **Yosemite Creek (hike to Yosemite Point in Yosemite National Park),** Yosemite and Mammoth Lakes, page 559.
2. **Canyon View (hike to Lookout Peak in Kings Canyon National Park),** Sequoia and Kings Canyon, page 649.
3. **Mount San Jacinto State Park: Wilderness Walk-In Camps (climb San Jacinto Peak),** Los Angeles and Vicinity, page 803.
4. **Whitney Trailhead Walk-In (climb Mount Whitney),** Sequoia and Kings Canyon, page 666.
5. **Angel Island State Park Walk-In/Boat-In (hike to Mount Livermore),** San Francisco Bay Area, page 481.
6. **Manker Flats (climb Mount Baldy in Angeles National Forest),** Los Angeles and Vicinity, page 774.
7. **D. L. Bliss State Park (hike Rubicon Trail),** Tahoe and the Northern Sierra, page 429.
8. **Panther Meadows Walk-In (climb Mount Shasta),** Shasta and Trinity, page 145.
9. **Tuolumne Meadows (hike PCT to Grand Canyon of the Tuolumne),** Yosemite and Mammoth Lakes, page 557.
10. **Summit Lake: North, South, and Equestrian (climb Lassen Peak),** Lassen and Modoc, page 231.

❰ Best Family Destinations

1. **Historic Camp Richardson Resort,** Tahoe and the Northern Sierra, page 430.
2. **Lake Siskiyou Camp-Resort,** Shasta and Trinity, page 148.
3. **Lake Alpine Campground,** Tahoe and the Northern Sierra, page 455.
4. **Convict Lake,** Yosemite and Mammoth Lakes, page 594.
5. **Summit Lake: North, South, and Equestrian in Lassen Volcanic National Park,** Lassen and Modoc, page 231.
6. **MacKerricher State Park,** Mendocino and Wine Country, page 268.
7. **Serrano on Big Bear Lake,** Los Angeles and Vicinity, page 795.
8. **Prairie Creek Redwoods State Park,** Redwood Empire, pages 102–103.
9. **Gaviota State Park/El Capitán State Beach,** Santa Barbara and Vicinity, pages 721 and 722.
10. **Dorst Creek in Sequoia National Park,** Sequoia and Kings Canyon, page 652.

❰ Best Boat-In Campgrounds

1. **Emerald Bay State Park and Boat-In on Emerald Bay in Lake Tahoe,** Tahoe and the Northern Sierra, page 429.
2. **Lake Sonoma Recreation Area,** Mendocino and Wine Country, page 298.
3. **Greens Creek Boat-In on Shasta Lake,** Shasta and Trinity, page 184.
4. **Ridgeville Boat-In Camp on Trinity Lake,** Shasta and Trinity, page 172.
5. **Bullards Bar Reservoir,** Sacramento and Gold Country, pages 335 and 337.
6. **Catalina Island Boat-In,** Los Angeles and Vicinity, page 765.
7. **Jackson Point Boat-In at Jackson Meadow Reservoir,** Tahoe and the Northern Sierra, page 388.
8. **Brannan Island State Recreation Area,** Sacramento and Gold Country, page 347.
9. **Santa Rosa Island Boat-In,** Santa Barbara and Vicinity, page 744.
10. **Stone Lagoon Boat-In,** Redwood Empire, page 104.

❰ Best for Fishing

1. **Snug Harbor Resort in the Sacramento River Delta,** Sacramento and Gold Country, page 348.
2. **Hirz Bay on Shasta Lake,** Shasta and Trinity, page 179.
3. **North Shore/South Shore San Antonio on Lake San Antonio,** Santa Barbara and Vicinity, pages 707–708.
4. **Agnew Meadows and Equestrian Camp on the Middle Fork San Joaquin River,** Yosemite and Mammoth Lakes, page 584.
5. **Cachuma Lake Recreation Area,** Santa Barbara and Vicinity, page 732.
6. **Clear Lake State Park,** Mendocino and Wine Country, page 293.
7. **Lower Twin Lake,** Yosemite and Mammoth Lakes, page 574.
8. **Hermit Gulch on Catalina Island,** Los Angeles and Vicinity, page 766.
9. **Ah-Di-Nah on McCloud River,** Shasta and Trinity, page 157.
10. **Lake Oroville Boat-In and Floating Camps,** Sacramento and Gold Country, page 332.

❰ Best for White-Water Rafting

1. **Lumsden on the main stem of the Tuolumne River,** San Joaquin Valley, pages 534–535.
2. **Matthews Creek on the Salmon River,** Shasta and Trinity, page 139.
3. **Fairview on the Kern River,** Sequoia and Kings Canyon, page 671.
4. **Tree of Heaven on the Upper Klamath River,** Shasta and Trinity, page 142.
5. **Camp Lotus on the South Fork American River,** Sacramento and Gold Country, page 351.
6. **Kirch Flat on the Upper Kings River,** Sequoia and Kings Canyon, page 640.
7. **Merced Recreation Area on the Merced River,** Yosemite and Mammoth Lakes, page 565.
8. **Elk Creek Campground and RV Park / Dillon Creek on the Klamath River (Happy Camp to Green Riffle),** Shasta and Trinity, pages 130 and 134.
9. **Auburn State Recreation Area on the Middle Fork American River,** Sacramento and Gold Country, pages 341–342.
10. **Hobo on the Lower Kern,** Sequoia and Kings Canyon, page 682.

❰ Best for Waterskiing

1. **Havasu Landing Resort and Casino on Lake Havasu,** The Southern Deserts, page 881.
2. **Eddos Harbor and RV Park in the San Joaquin Delta,** Sacramento and Gold Country, page 349.
3. **Moabi Regional Park on the Colorado River,** The Southern Deserts, page 880.
4. **Holiday Harbor Resort on Shasta Lake,** Shasta and Trinity, page 184.
5. **Lake Nacimiento Resort,** Santa Barbara and Vicinity, page 708.
6. **Lake Perris State Recreation Area,** Los Angeles and Vicinity, page 786.
7. **Lake Piru Recreation Area,** Los Angeles and Vicinity, page 754.
8. **Lake Elsinore Campground and Recreation Area,** Los Angeles and Vicinity, page 789.
9. **Los Alamos near Pyramid Lake,** The Southern Deserts, page 868.
10. **Snug Harbor Resort in the Sacramento River Delta,** Sacramento and Gold Country, page 348.

❰ Best Island Campgrounds

1. **Catalina Island Boat-In,** Los Angeles and Vicinity, page 765.
2. **Santa Cruz Island Boat-In,** Santa Barbara and Vicinity, page 744.
3. **Two Harbors on Catalina,** Los Angeles and Vicinity, page 763.
4. **Santa Rosa Island Boat-In,** Santa Barbara and Vicinity, page 744.
5. **Angel Island State Park Walk-In/Boat-In,** San Francisco Bay Area, page 481.
6. **Anacapa Island Boat-In and Hike-In,** Santa Barbara and Vicinity, page 745.
7. **San Miguel Island Boat-In and Hike-In,** Santa Barbara and Vicinity, page 743.
8. **Little Harbor Hike-In on Catalina,** Los Angeles and Vicinity, page 764.
9. **Parson's Landing Hike-In on Catalina,** Los Angeles and Vicinity, page 763.
10. **Brannan Island State Recreation Area,** Sacramento and Gold Country, page 347.

Camping Tips

FOOD AND COOKING GEAR

It was a warm, crystal clear day, the kind of day when, if you had ever wanted to go sky-diving, you would go skydiving. That was exactly the case for my old pal Foonsky, who had never before tried the sport. But a funny thing happened after he jumped out of the plane and pulled on the rip cord: His parachute didn't open.

In total free fall, Foonsky watched the earth below getting closer and closer. Not one to panic, he calmly pulled the rip cord on the emergency parachute. Again, nothing happened. No parachute, no nothing.

The ground was getting ever closer, and as he tried to search for a soft place to land, Foonsky detected a small object shooting up toward him, growing larger as it approached. It looked like a camper.

Figuring this was his last chance, Foonsky shouted as they passed in midair, "Hey, do you know anything about parachutes?"

The other fellow just yelled back as he headed off into space, "Do you know anything about lighting camping stoves?"

Well, Foonsky got lucky and his parachute opened. As for the other guy, well, he's probably in orbit like a NASA weather satellite. If you've ever had a mishap while lighting a camping stove, you know exactly what I'm talking about.

When it comes to camping, all gear is not created equal. Nothing is more important than lighting your stove easily and having it reach full heat without feeling as if you're playing with a short fuse to a miniature bomb. If your stove does not work right, your trip can turn into a disaster, regardless of how well you have planned the other elements. In addition, a bad stove will add an underlying sense of foreboding to your day. You will constantly have the inner suspicion that your darn stove is going to foul up again.

Camping Stoves

If you are buying a camping stove, remember this one critical rule: Do not leave the store with a new stove unless you have been shown exactly how to use it.

Know what you are getting. Many stores that specialize in outdoor recreation equipment now staff experienced campers/employees who will demonstrate the use of every stove they sell. While they're at it, they'll also describe the stoves' respective strengths and weaknesses.

An innovation by Peak 1 is a two-burner backpacking stove that allows you to boil water and heat a pot of food simultaneously. While that has long been standard for car campers using Coleman's legendary camp stove, it was previously unheard of for wilderness campers in high-elevation areas.

A stove that has developed a cultlike following is the little Sierra, which burns small twigs and pinecones, then uses a tiny battery-driven fan to develop increased heat and cooking ability. It's an excellent alternative for long-distance backpacking trips, as it solves the problem of carrying a fuel bottle, especially on expeditions for which large quantities of fuel would otherwise be needed. Some tinkering with the flame (a very hot one) is required, and they are legal and functional only in the alpine zone where dry wood is available. Also note that in years with high fire danger, the U.S. Forest Service enacts rules prohibiting open flames, and fires are also often prohibited above an elevation of 10,000 feet.

For expeditions, I prefer a small, lightweight stove that uses white gas so I can closely gauge fuel consumption. My pal Foonsky uses one with a butane bottle because it lights so easily. We have contests to see who can boil a pot of water faster, and the difference is usually negligible. Thus,

Stoves are available in many styles and burn a variety of fuels. These are three typical examples. Top left: **White gas stoves** are the most popular because they are inexpensive and easy to find; they do require priming and can be explosive. Top right: **Gas canister stoves** burn propane, butane, isobutane, and mixtures of the three. These are the easiest to use but have two disadvantages: 1) Because the fuel is bottled, determining how much fuel is left can be difficult. 2) The fuel is limited to above-freezing conditions. Bottom: **Liquid fuel stoves** burn Coleman fuel, denatured alcohol, kerosene, and even gasoline; these fuels are economical and have a high heat output, but most must be primed.

other factors are important when choosing a stove.

Of these, ease of cleaning the burner is the most important. If you camp often, especially with a smaller stove, the burner holes will eventually become clogged. Some stoves have a built-in cleaning needle: a quick twist of the knob and you're in business. Others require disassembly and a protracted cleaning session using special tools. If a stove is difficult to clean, you will tend to put off the tiresome chore, and your stove will sputter and pant while you watch that pot of water sitting there, staying cold.

Before making a purchase, have the salesperson show you how to clean the burner head. Except in the case of large, multi-burner family-style camping stoves, which rarely require cleaning, this run-through can do more to determine the long-term value of a stove than any other factor.

Fuels for Camping Stoves

White gas and butane have long been the most popular camp fuels, but a newly developed fuel could dramatically change that.

LPG (liquid petroleum gas) comes in

cartridges for easy attachment to a stove or lantern. At room temperature, LPG is delivered in a combustible gaseous form. When you shake the cartridge, the contents sound liquid; that is because the gas liquefies under pressure, which is why it is so easy to use. Large amounts of fuel can be compressed into small canisters.

While convenience has always been the calling card for LPG, recent innovations have allowed it to become a suitable choice for winter and high-altitude mountaineering expeditions, and it now comes close to matching white gas performance specs. For several years now, Camping Gaz, Coleman, Epi (Coleman), Markill, MSR, Primus, and other makers have been mixing propane, butane, and isobutane to improve performance capabilities.

The industry has leaped two important hurdles that stood in the way of LPG's popularity. Coleman, working in cooperation with the U.S. Postal Service, has developed a program in which three-packs of 170-gram Coleman Max fuel cartridges can be shipped by mail to any address or post office in the 50 states and Puerto Rico. Also, each Coleman Max fuel cartridge is now made of aluminum and comes with a special device that allows the consumer to puncture the cartridge safely once the fuel is gone and then toss it into any aluminum recycling container.

The following summaries detail the benefits and drawbacks of other available fuels:

• **Butane:** You don't have to worry about explosions when using stoves that burn bottled butane fuel. Butane requires no pouring, pumping, or priming, and butane stoves are the easiest to light. Just turn a knob and light—that's it. On the minus side, because it comes in bottles, you never know precisely how much fuel you have left. And when a bottle is empty, you have a potential piece of litter. (Never litter. Ever.)

The other problem with butane is that it just plain does not work well in cold weather or when there is little fuel left in the cartridge. Since you cannot predict mountain weather

in spring or fall, you might wind up using more fuel than originally projected. That can be frustrating, particularly if your stove starts wheezing when there are still several days left to go. In addition, with most butane cartridges, if there is any chance of the temperature falling below freezing, you often have to sleep with the cartridge to keep it warm. Otherwise, forget about using it come morning.

• **Butane/Propane:** This blend offers higher octane performance than butane alone, solving the cold temperature doldrums somewhat. However, propane burns off before butane, so there's a performance drop as the fuel level in the cartridge lowers.

• **Coleman Max Performance Fuel:** This fuel offers a unique approach to solving the consistent burn challenge facing all pressurized gas cartridges: operating at temperatures at or below 0°F. Using a standard propane/butane blend for high-octane performance, Coleman gets around the drop-off in performance other cartridges experience by using a version of fuel injection. A hose inside the cartridge pulls liquid fuel into the stove, where it vaporizes—a switch from the standard approach of pulling only a gaseous form of the fuel into a stove. By drawing liquid out of the cartridge, Coleman gets around the tendency of propane to burn off first and allows each cartridge to deliver a consistent mix of propane and butane to the stove's burners throughout the cartridge's life.

• **Denatured alcohol:** Though this fuel burns cleanly and quietly and is virtually explosion-proof, it generates much less heat than pressurized or liquid gas fuels.

• **Kerosene:** Never buy a stove that uses kerosene for fuel. Kerosene is smelly and messy, generates low heat, needs priming, and is virtually obsolete as a camp fuel in the United States. As a test, I once tried using a kerosene stove. I could scarcely boil a pot of water. In addition, some kerosene leaked out when the stove was packed, ruining everything it touched. The smell of kerosene never did go away. Kerosene remains popular in Europe only because most campers there haven't yet heard much about white gas. When they do, they will demand it.

• **Primus Tri-Blend:** This blend is made up of 20 percent propane, 70 percent butane, and 10 percent isobutane and is designed to burn with more consistent heat and efficiency than standard propane/butane mixes.

• **Propane:** Now available for single-burner stoves using larger, heavier cartridges to accommodate higher pressures, propane offers the very best performance of any of the pressurized gas canister fuels.

• **White gas:** White gas is the most popular camp fuel in the United States because it is inexpensive and effective—not to mention, sold at most outdoor recreation stores and many supermarkets. It burns hot, has virtually no smell, and evaporates quickly when spilled. If you are caught in wet, miserable weather and can't get a fire going, you can use white gas as an emergency fire starter; however, if you do so, use it sparingly and never on an open flame.

White gas is a popular fuel both for car campers who use the large, two-burner stoves equipped with a fuel tank and a pump and for hikers who carry a lightweight backpacking stove. On the latter, lighting can require priming with a gel called priming paste, which some people dislike. Another problem with white gas is that it can be extremely explosive.

As an example, I once almost burned my beard completely off in a mini-explosion while lighting one of the larger stoves designed for car camping. I was in the middle of cooking dinner when the flame suddenly shut down. Sure enough, the fuel tank was empty, and after refilling it, I pumped the tank 50 or 60 times to regain pressure. When I lit a match, the sucker ignited from three feet away. The resulting explosion was like a stick of dynamite going off, and immediately the smell of burning beard was in the air. In a flash, my once thick, dark beard had been reduced to a mass of little, yellow, burned curlicues.

My error? After filling the tank, I forgot to shut the fuel cock off while pumping up the pressure in the tank. As a result, the stove burners were slowly emitting the gas/air mixture as I pumped the tank, filling the air above the stove. Then, strike a match from even a few feet away and ka-boom!

Building Fires

One summer expedition took me to the Canadian wilderness in British Columbia for a 75-mile canoe trip on the Bowron Lake Circuit, a chain of 13 lakes, six rivers, and seven portages. It is one of the greatest canoe trips in the world, a loop that ends just a few hundred feet from its starting point. But at the first camp at Kibbee Lake, my stove developed a fuel leak at the base of the burner, and the nuclear-like blast that followed just about turned Canada into a giant crater.

As a result, we had to complete the final 70 miles of the trip without a stove, cooking instead on open fires each night. The problem was compounded by the weather. It rained eight of the 10 days. Rain? In Canada, raindrops the size of silver dollars fall so hard they actually bounce on the lake surface. We had to stop paddling a few times to empty the rainwater out of the canoe. At the end of the day, we'd make camp and then face the critical decision: either make a fire or go to bed cold and hungry.

Equipped with an ax, at least we had a chance for success. Although the downed wood was soaked, I was able to make my own fire-starting tinder from the chips of split logs; no matter how hard it rains, the inside of a log is always dry.

In miserable weather, matches don't stay lit long enough to get tinder started. Instead, we used either a candle or the little waxlike fire-starter cubes that remain lit for several minutes. From those, we could get the tinder going. Then we added small, slender strips of wood that had been axed from the interior of the logs. When the flame reached a foot high,

KEEP IT WILD TIP 1: CAMPFIRES

1. Fire use can scar the backcountry. If a fire ring is not available, use a lightweight stove for cooking.
2. Where fires are permitted, use existing fire rings away from large rocks or overhangs.
3. Don't char rocks by building new rings.
4. Gather sticks from the ground that are no larger than the diameter of your wrist.
5. Don't snap branches of live, dead, or downed trees, which can cause personal injury and also scar the natural setting.
6. Put the fire "dead out" and make sure it's cold before departing. Remove all trash from the fire ring and sprinkle dirt over the site.
7. Remember that some forest fires can be started by a campfire that appears to be out. Hot embers burning deep in the pit can cause tree roots to catch fire and burn underground. If you ever see smoke rising from the ground, seemingly from nowhere, dig down and put the fire out.

we added the logs, their dry interior facing in. By the time the inside of the logs had caught fire, the outside was drying from the heat. It wasn't long before a royal blaze was brightening the rainy night.

That's a worst-case scenario, and I hope you will never face anything like it. Nevertheless, being able to build a good fire and cook on it can be one of the more satisfying elements of a camping trip. At times, just looking into the flames can provide a special satisfaction at the end of a good day.

However, never expect to build a fire for every meal or, in some cases, even to build one at all. Many state and federal campgrounds have been picked clean of downed wood. During the fire season, the danger of forest fires can force rangers to prohibit fires altogether. In either case, you must use your camp stove or go hungry.

But when you can build a fire and the resources for doing so are available, it will enhance the quality of your camping experience. Of the campgrounds listed in this book, those where you are permitted to build fires will usually have fire rings. In primitive areas where you can make your own fire, you should dig a ring eight inches deep, line the edges with rock, and clear all the needles

and twigs in a five-foot radius. The next day, when the fire is dead, you can scatter the rocks, fill over the black charcoal with dirt, and then spread pine needles and twigs over it. Nobody will even know you camped there. That's the best way I know to keep a secret spot a real secret.

When you start to build a campfire, the first thing you will notice is that no matter how good your intentions, your fellow campers will not be able to resist moving the wood around. Watch. You'll be getting ready to add a key piece of wood at just the right spot, and your companion will stick his mitts in, confidently believing he has a better idea. He'll shift the fire around and undermine your best-thought-out plans.

So I enforce a rule on camping trips: One person makes the fire while everybody else stands clear or is involved with other camp tasks, such as gathering wood, getting water, putting up tents, or planning dinner. Once the fire is going strong, then it's fair game; anyone adds logs at his or her discretion. But in the early, delicate stages of the campfire, it's best to leave the work to one person.

Before a match is ever struck, you should gather a complete pile of firewood. Then, start small, with the tiniest twigs you can find, and slowly add larger twigs as you go, crisscrossing them like a miniature tepee. Eventually, you will get to the big chunks that produce high heat. The key is to get one piece of wood burning into another, which then burns into another, setting off what I call the chain of flame. Conversely, single pieces of wood set apart from each other will not burn.

On a dry summer evening at a campsite where plenty of wood is available, about the only way you can blow the deal is to get impatient and try to add the big pieces too quickly. Do that and you'll get smoke, not flames, and it won't be long before every one of your fellow campers is poking at your fire. It will drive you crazy, but they just won't be able to help it.

Cooking Gear

I like traveling light, and I've found that all I need for cooking is a pot, small frying pan, metal pot grabber, fork, knife, cup, and matches. If you want to keep the price of food low and also cook customized dinners each night, a small pressure cooker can be just the ticket. (See *Keeping the Price Down* in this chapter.) I store all my gear in one small bag that fits into my pack. If I'm camping out of my four-wheel-drive rig, I can easily keep track of the little bag of cooking gear. Going simple, not complicated, is the key to keeping a camping trip on the right track.

You can get more elaborate by buying complete kits with plates, a coffeepot, large pots, and other cookware, but what really counts is having a single pot that makes you happy. It needs to be just the right size, not too big or small, and stable enough so it won't tip over, even if it is at a slight angle on a fire, filled with water at a full boil. Mine is just six inches wide and 4.5 inches deep. It holds better than a quart of water and has served me well for several hundred camp dinners.

The rest of your cook kit is easy to complete. The frying pan should be small, light-gauge aluminum, and Teflon-coated, with a fold-in handle so it's no hassle to store. A pot grabber is a great addition. This little aluminum gadget clamps to the edge of pots and allows you to lift them and pour water with total control and without burning your fingers. For cleanup, take along a plastic scrubber and a small bottle filled with dish soap, and you're in business.

A sierra cup, a wide aluminum cup with a wire handle, is an ideal item to carry because you can eat out of it as well as use it for drinking. This means no plates to scrub after dinner, so washing up is quick and easy. In addition, if you go for a hike, you can clip its handle to your belt.

If you opt for a more formal setup, complete with plates, glasses, silverware, and the like, you can end up spending more time preparing and cleaning up after meals than enjoying the country you are exploring. In addition, the more equipment you bring, the more loose ends you will have to deal with, and loose ends can cause plenty of frustration. If you have a choice, go simple.

Remember what Thoreau said: "A man is rich in proportion to what he can do without."

Food and Cooking Tricks

On a trip to the Bob Marshall Wilderness in western Montana, I woke up one morning, yawned, and said, "What've we got for breakfast?"

The silence was ominous. "Well," finally came the response, "we don't have any food left."

"What!?"

"Well, I figured we'd catch trout for meals every other night."

On the return trip, we ended up eating wild berries, buds, and, yes, even roots (not too tasty). When we finally landed the next day at a suburban pizza parlor, we nearly ate the wooden tables.

Running out of food on a camping trip can do more to turn reasonable people into violent grumps than any other event. There's no excuse for it, not when figuring meals can be done precisely and with little effort. You should not go out and buy a bunch of food, throw it in your rig, and head off for yonder. That leaves too much to chance. And if you've ever been really hungry in the woods, you know it's worth a little effort to guard against a day or two of starvation. Here's a three-step solution:

1. Draw up a general meal-by-meal plan and make sure your companions like what's on it.
2. Tell your companions to buy any specialty items (such as a special brand of coffee) on their own and not to expect you to take care of everything.
3. Put all the food on your living room floor and literally plan out every day of your trip, meal by meal, putting the food in plastic bags as you go. That way, you will know exact food quotas and you won't go hungry.

Fish for your dinner? There's one guarantee as far as that goes: If you expect to catch fish for meals, you will most certainly get skunked. If you don't expect to catch fish for meals, you will probably catch so many they'll be coming out of your ears. I've seen it a hundred times.

Keeping the Price Down

"There must be some mistake," I said with a laugh. "Whoever paid $750 for camp food?"

But the amount was as clear as the digital numbers on the cash register: $753.27.

"How is this possible?" I asked the clerk.

"Just add it up," she responded, irritated.

Then I started figuring. The freeze-dried backpack dinners cost $6 apiece. A small pack of beef jerky went for $2, the beef sticks for $.75, granola bars for $.50. Multiply it all by four hungry men, including Foonsky, for 21 days. This food was to sustain us on a major expedition—four guys hiking 250 miles over three weeks from Mount Whitney to Yosemite Valley.

The dinners alone cost close to $500. Add in the usual goodies—candy, coffee, dried fruit, granola bars, jerky, oatmeal, soup, and

Tang—and I felt as if an earthquake had struck when I saw the tab.

A lot of campers have received similar shocks. In preparation for their trips, campers shop with enthusiasm. Then they pay the bill in horror.

Well, there are solutions, lots of them. You can eat gourmet-style in the outback without having your wallet cleaned out. But it requires do-it-yourself cooking, more planning, and careful shopping. It also means transcending the push-button, I-want-it-now attitude that so many people can't leave behind when they go to the mountains.

The secret is to bring along a small pressure cooker. A reader in San Francisco, Mike Bettinger, passed this tip on to me. Little pressure cookers weigh about two pounds, which may sound like a lot to backpackers and backcountry campers. But when three or four people are on a trip, it actually saves weight.

The key is that it allows campers to bring items that are normally difficult to cook at high altitudes, such as brown and white rice; red, black, pinto, and lima beans; and lentils. You pick one or more for a basic staple and then add a variety of freeze-dried ingredients to make a complete dish. Packets of garlic, meat, onions, shallots, and vegetables are available. Sun-dried tomatoes, for instance, reconstitute wonderfully in a pressure cooker. Add herbs, spices, and maybe a few rainbow trout and you will be eating better out of a backpack than most people do at home.

"In the morning, I have used the pressure cooker to turn dried apricots into apricot sauce to put on the pancakes we made with sourdough starter," Bettinger said. "The pressure cooker is also big enough for washing out cups and utensils. The days when backpacking meant eating terrible freeze-dried food are over. It doesn't take a gourmet cook to prepare these meals, only some thought beforehand."

Now when Foonsky, Mr. Furnai, Rambob, and I sit down to eat such a meal, we don't call it "eating." We call it "hodgepacking" or "time to pack your hodge." After a particularly

HOW TO MAKE BEEF JERKY IN YOUR OWN KITCHEN

Start with a couple of pieces of meat: lean top round, sirloin, or tritip. Cut them into 3/16-inch strips across the grain, trimming out the membrane, gristle, and fat. Marinate the strips for 24 hours in a glass dish. The fun begins in picking a marinade. Try two-thirds teriyaki sauce, one-third Worcestershire sauce. You can customize the recipe by adding pepper, ground mustard, bay leaf, red wine vinegar, garlic, and, for the brave, Tabasco sauce.

After a day or so, squeeze out each strip of meat with a rolling pin, lay them in rows on a cooling rack over a cookie sheet, and dry them in the oven at 125°F for 12 hours. Thicker pieces can take as long as 18–24 hours.

That's it. The hardest part is cleaning the cookie sheet when you're done. The easiest part is eating your own homemade jerky while sitting at a lookout on a mountain ridge. The do-it-yourself method for jerky may take a day or so, but it is cheaper and can taste better than any store-bought jerky.

—my thanks to Jeff Patty for this recipe

long day on the trail, you can do some serious hodgepacking.

If your trip is a shorter one, say for a weekend, consider bringing more fresh food to add some sizzle to the hodge. You can design a hot soup/stew mix that is good enough to eat at home.

Start by bringing a pot of water to a full boil, and then add pasta, ramen noodles, or macaroni. While it simmers, cut in a potato, carrot, onion, and garlic clove, and cook for about 10 minutes. When the vegetables have softened, add in a soup mix or two, maybe some cheese, and you are just about in business. But you can still ruin it and turn your hodge into slodge. Make sure you read the directions on the soup mix to determine cooking time. It can vary widely. In addition, make sure you stir the whole thing up; otherwise, you will get those hidden dry clumps of soup mix that taste like garlic sawdust.

How do I know? Well, it was up near Kearsage Pass in the Sierra Nevada, where, feeling half-starved, I dug into our nightly hodge. I will never forget that first bite—I damn near gagged to death. Foonsky laughed at me, until he took his first bite (a nice big one) and then turned green.

Another way to trim food costs is to make your own beef jerky, the trademark staple of campers for more than 200 years. A tiny packet of beef jerky costs $2, and for that 250-mile expedition, I spent $150 on jerky alone. Never again. Now we make our own and get big strips of jerky that taste better than anything you can buy.

If all this still doesn't sound like your idea of a gourmet but low-cost camping meal, well, you are forgetting the main course: rainbow trout. Remember: If you don't plan on catching them for dinner, you'll probably snag more than you can finish in one night's hodgepacking.

Some campers go to great difficulties to cook their trout, bringing along frying pans, butter, grills, tinfoil, and more, but all you need is some seasoned salt and a campfire.

Rinse the gutted trout, and while it's still wet, sprinkle on a good dose of seasoned salt, both inside and out. Clear any burning logs to the side of the campfire, then lay the trout right on the coals, turning it once so both sides are cooked. Sound ridiculous? Sound like you are throwing the fish away? Sound like the fish will burn up? Sound like you will have to eat the campfire ash? Wrong on all counts. The fish cooks perfectly, the ash doesn't stick, and after cooking trout this way, you may never fry trout again.

If you can't convince your buddies, who may insist that trout should be fried, then make sure you have butter to fry them in, not oil. Also make sure you cook them all the way through, so the meat strips off the backbone in two nice, clean fillets. The fish should end up looking like one that Sylvester the Cat just drew out of his mouth—only the head, tail, and a perfect skeleton.

You can supplement your eats with sweets, nuts, freeze-dried fruits, and drink mixes. In any case, make sure you keep the dinner menu varied. If you and your buddies look into your dinner cups and groan, "Ugh, not this again," you will soon start dreaming of cheeseburgers and french fries instead of hiking, fishing, and finding beautiful campsites.

If you are car camping and have a big ice chest, you can bring virtually anything to eat and drink. If you are on the trail and don't mind paying the price, the newest freeze-dried dinners provide another option.

Some of the biggest advances in the outdoors industry have come in the form of freeze-dried dinners. Some of them are almost good enough to serve in restaurants. Sweet-and-sour pork over rice, tostadas, Burgundy chicken—it sure beats the poopy goop we used to eat, like the old soupy chili-mac dinners that tasted bad and looked so unlike food that consumption was nearly impossible, even for my dog, Rebel. Foonsky usually managed to get it down, but just barely.

To provide an idea of how to plan a menu, consider what my companions and I ate while hiking 250 miles on California's John Muir Trail:

• Breakfast: instant soup, oatmeal (never get plain), one beef or jerky stick, coffee or hot chocolate.

• Lunch: one beef stick, two jerky sticks, one granola bar, dried fruit, half cup of pistachio nuts, Tang, one small bag of M&Ms.

• Dinner: instant soup, one freeze-dried dinner (split between two people), one milk bar, rainbow trout.

What was that last item? Rainbow trout? Right! Unless you plan on it, you can catch them every night.

CLOTHING AND WEATHER PROTECTION

What started as an innocent pursuit of the perfect campground evolved into one heck of a predicament for Foonsky and me.

We had parked at the end of a logging road and then bushwhacked our way down a canyon to a pristine trout stream. On my first cast—a little flip into the plunge pool of a waterfall—I caught a 16-inch rainbow trout, a real beauty that jumped three times. Magic stuff.

Then, just across the stream, we saw it: The Perfect Camping Spot. On a sandbar on the edge of the forest, there lay a flat spot, high and dry above the river. Nearby was plenty of downed wood collected by past winter storms that we could use for firewood. And, of course, this beautiful trout stream was bubbling along just 40 yards from the site.

But nothing is perfect, right? To reach it, we had to wade across the river, although it didn't appear to be too difficult. The cold water tingled a bit, and the river came up surprisingly high, just above the belt. But it would be worth it to camp at The Perfect Spot.

Once across the river, we put on some dry clothes, set up camp, explored the woods, and fished the stream, catching several nice trout for dinner. But late that afternoon, it started raining. What? Rain in the summertime? Nature makes its own rules. By the next morning, it was still raining, pouring like a Yosemite waterfall from a solid gray sky.

That's when we noticed The Perfect Spot wasn't so perfect. The rain had raised the river level too high for us to wade back across. We were marooned, wet, and hungry.

"Now we're in a heck of a predicament," said Foonsky, the water streaming off him.

Getting cold and wet on a camping trip with no way to warm up is not only unnecessary and uncomfortable, it can be a fast ticket to hypothermia, the number one killer of campers in the woods. By definition, hypothermia is a condition in which body temperature is lowered to the point that it causes illness. It is particularly dangerous because the afflicted are usually unaware it is setting in. The first sign is a sense of apathy, then a state of confusion, which can lead eventually to collapse (or what appears to be sleep), then death.

You must always have a way to get warm and dry in short order, regardless of any conditions you may face. If you have no way of getting dry, then you must take emergency steps to prevent hypothermia. (See the steps detailed in *First Aid and Insect Protection* in this chapter.)

But you should never reach that point. For starters, always have spare sets of clothing tucked away so no matter how cold and wet you might get, you have something dry to put on. On hiking trips, I always carry a second set of clothes, sealed to stay dry, in a plastic garbage bag. I keep a third set waiting back at the truck.

If you are car camping, your vehicle can cause an illusory sense of security. But with an extra set of dry clothes stashed safely away, there is no illusion. The security is real. And remember, no matter how hot the weather is when you start your trip, always be prepared for the worst. Foonsky and I learned the hard way.

So both of us were soaking wet on that sandbar. With no other choice, we tried holing up in the tent for the night. A sleeping bag with Quallofil or another polyester fiberfill can retain warmth even when wet, because the fill is hollow and retains its loft. So as miserable as it was, the night passed without incident.

The rain stopped the next day and the river dropped a bit, but it was still rolling big and angry. Using a stick as a wading staff, Foonsky crossed about 80 percent of the stream before he was dumped, but he made a jump for it and managed to scramble to the riverbank. He waved for me to follow. "No problem," I thought.

It took me 20 minutes to reach nearly the same spot where Foonsky had been dumped. The heavy river current was above my belt and pushing hard. Then, in the flash of an instant, my wading staff slipped on a rock. I teetered in the river current and was knocked over like a bowling pin. I became completely submerged. I went tumbling down the river, heading right toward the waterfall. While underwater, I looked up at the surface, and I can remember how close it seemed yet how out of control I was. Right then, this giant hand appeared, and I grabbed it. It was Foonsky. If it weren't for that hand, I would have sailed right over the waterfall.

My momentum drew Foonsky right into the river, and we scrambled in the current, but I suddenly sensed the river bottom under my knees. On all fours, the two of us clambered ashore. We were safe.

"Thanks, ol' buddy," I said.

"Man, we're wet," he responded. "Let's get to the rig and get some dry clothes on."

The Art of Layering

The most important element for enjoying the outdoor experience in any condition is to stay dry and warm. There is no substitute. You must stay dry and you must stay warm.

Thus comes the theory behind layering, which suggests that as your body temperature fluctuates or the weather shifts, you simply peel off or add available layers as needed—and have a waterproof shell available in case of rain.

The introduction of a new era of outdoor clothing has made it possible for campers to turn choosing clothes into an art form. Like art, it's much more expensive than throwing on a pair of blue jeans, a T-shirt, and some flannel, but, for many, it is worth the price.

In putting together your ideal layering system, there are some general considerations. What you need to do is create a system that effectively combines elements of breathability, durability, insulation, rapid drying, water repellence, wicking, and wind resistance, while still being lightweight and offering the necessary freedom of movement, all with just a few garments.

The basic intent of a base layer is to manage moisture. Your base layer will be the first article of clothing you put on and the last to come off. Since your own skin will be churning out the perspiration, the goal of this second skin is to manage the moisture and move it away from you. The best base layers are made of bicomponent knits, that is, blends of polyester and cotton, which provide wicking and insulating properties in one layer.

The way it works is that the side facing your skin is water-hating, while the side away from your skin is water-loving; thus, it pulls or "wicks" moisture through the material. You'll stay dry and happy, even with only one layer on, something not possible with old single-function weaves. The best include Capilene, Driclime, Lifa, Polartec 100, and Thermax. The only time that cotton should become a part of your base layer is if you wish to keep cool, not warm, such as in a hot desert climate where evaporative cooling becomes your friend, not your enemy.

Stretch fleece and microdenier pile also provide a good base layer, though they can be used as a second layer as well. Microdenier pile can be worn alone or layered under or over other pieces; it has excellent wicking capability as well as more windproof potential.

The next layer should be a light cotton shirt or a long-sleeved cotton/wool shirt, or both, depending on the coolness of the day. For pants, many just wear blue jeans when camping, but blue jeans can be hot and tight, and once wet, they tend to stay that way. Putting on wet blue jeans on a cold morning is a torturous way to start the day. (I tell you this from experience, since I have suffered that fate

a number of times.) A better choice is pants made from a cotton/canvas mix, which are available at outdoors stores. They are light, have a lot of give, and dry quickly. If the weather is quite warm, shorts that have some room to them can be the best choice.

Finally, you should top the entire ensemble off with a thin, windproof, water-resistant layer. You want this layer to breathe like crazy, yet not be so porous that rain runs through it like floodwater through a leaking dike. Patagonia's Velocity shell is one of the best. Its outer fabric is treated with DWR (durable water-repellent finish), and the coating is by Gore. Patagonia calls it Pneumatic (Gore now calls it Activent, while Marmot, Moonstone, and North Face all offer their own versions). Though condensation will still build up inside, it manages to get rid of enough moisture.

It is critical to know the difference between "water-resistant" and "waterproof." (This is covered under the *Rain Gear* section in this chapter.)

But hey, why does anybody need all this fancy stuff just to go camping? Fair question. Like the introduction of Gore-Tex years ago, all this fabric and fiber mumbo jumbo has its skeptics, including me. You don't have to opt for this aerobic-function fashion statement; it is unnecessary on many camping trips. But the fact is you must be ready for anything when you venture into the outdoors. Truth be told, the new era of outdoor clothing works, and it works better than anything that has come before.

Regardless of what you choose, weather should never be a nuisance or cause discomfort. Instead it should provide a welcome change of pace.

Hats

Another word of advice: Always pack along a warm hat for those times when you need to seal in warmth. You lose a large percentage of heat through your head. I almost always wear a wide-brimmed hat, something like those that the legendary outlaws wore 150 years ago. There's actually logic behind it: My hat is made of waterproof canvas, is rigged with a lariat (it can be cinched down when it's windy), and has a wide brim that keeps the tops of my ears from being sunburned (years ago, they burned to a red crisp on a trip when I was wearing a baseball hat). But to be honest, I like how I look in it, kind of like my pal Waylon Jennings.

Vests and Parkas

In cold weather, you should take the layer system one step further with a warm vest and a parka jacket. Vests are especially useful because they provide warmth without the bulkiness of a parka. The warmest vests and parkas are either filled with down or Quallofil, or they are made with a cotton/wool mix. Each has its respective merits and problems. Down fill provides the most warmth for the amount of weight, but becomes useless when wet, closely resembling a wet dishrag. Quallofil keeps much of its heat-retaining quality even when wet, but it is expensive. Vests made of cotton/wool mixes are the most attractive and also are quite warm, but they can be as heavy as a ship's anchor when wet.

Sometimes, the answer is combining a parka with a vest. One of my best camping companions wears a good-looking cotton/wool vest and a parka filled with Quallofil. The vest never gets wet, so weight is not a factor.

Rain Gear

One of the most miserable nights of my life was on a camping trip for which I hadn't brought my rain gear or a tent. Hey, it was early August, the temperature had been in the 90s for weeks, and if anybody had said it was going to rain, I would have told him to consult a brain doctor. But rain it did. And as I got wetter and wetter, I kept saying to myself, "Hey, it's summer, it's not supposed to rain." Then I remembered one of the 10 commandments of camping: Forget your rain gear and you can guarantee it will rain.

To stay dry, you need some form of water-repellent shell. It can be as simple as a $5 poncho made out of plastic or as elaborate as a $300 Gore-Tex jacket-and-pants set. What counts is not how much you spend, but how dry you stay.

The most important thing to realize is that waterproof and water-resistant are completely different things. In addition, there is no such thing as rain gear that is both waterproof and breathable. The more waterproof a jacket is, the less it breathes. Conversely, the more breathable a jacket is, the less waterproof it becomes.

If you wear water-resistant rain gear in a downpour, you'll get soaked. Water-resistant rain gear is appealing because it breathes and will keep you dry in the light stuff, such as mist, fog, even a little splash from a canoe paddle. But in rain? Forget it.

So what is the solution?

I've decided that the best approach is a set of fairly light but 100 percent–waterproof rain gear. I recently bought a hooded jacket and pants from Coleman, and my assessment is that it is the most cost-efficient rain gear I've ever had. All I can say is, hey, it works: I stay dry, it doesn't weigh much, and it didn't cost a fortune.

You can also stay dry with any of the waterproof plastics and even heavy-duty rubber-coated outfits made for commercial anglers. But these are uncomfortable during anything but a heavy rain. Because they are heavy and don't breathe, you'll likely get soaked anyway (that is, from your own sweat), even if it isn't raining hard.

On backpacking trips, I still stash a super-lightweight, water-repellent slicker for day hikes and a poncho, which I throw over my pack at night to keep it dry. But, otherwise, I never go anywhere—*anywhere*—without my rain gear.

Some do just fine with a cheap poncho,

and note that ponchos can serve other uses in addition to a raincoat. Ponchos can be used as a ground tarp, as a rain cover for supplies or a backpack, or can be roped up to trees in a pinch to provide a quick storm ceiling if you don't have a tent. The problem with ponchos is that in a hard rain, you just don't stay dry. First your legs get wet, then they get soaked. Then your arms follow the same pattern. If you're wearing cotton, you'll find that once part of the garment gets wet, the water spreads until, alas, you are dripping wet, poncho and all. Before long, you start to feel like a walking refrigerator.

One high-cost option is buying a Gore-Tex rain jacket and pants. Gore-Tex is actually not a fabric, as is commonly believed, but a laminated film that coats a breathable fabric. The result is lightweight, water-repellent, breathable jackets and pants. They are perfect for campers, but they cost a fortune.

Some hiking buddies of mine have complained that the older Gore-Tex rain gear loses its water-repellent quality over time. However, manufacturers insist that this is the result of water seeping through seams, not leaks in the jacket. At each seam, tiny needles have pierced the fabric, and as tiny as the holes are, water will find a way through. An application of Seam Lock, especially at major seams around the shoulders of a jacket, can usually fix the problem.

If you don't want to spend the big bucks for Gore-Tex rain gear but want more rain protection than a poncho affords, a coated nylon jacket is the compromise that many choose. They are inexpensive, have the highest water-repellency of any rain gear, and are warm, providing a good outer shell for your layers of clothing. But they are not without fault. These jackets don't breathe at all, and if you zip them up tight, you can sweat a river.

My brother Rambob gave me a nylon jacket before a mountain-climbing expedition. I wore that $20 special all the way to the top with no complaints; it's warm and 100 percent waterproof. The one problem with

nylon comes when temperatures drop below freezing. It gets so stiff that it feels as if you are wearing a straitjacket. But at $20, it seems like a treasure, especially compared to a $180 Gore-Tex jacket.

There's one more jacket-construction term to know: DWR, or durable water-repellent finish. All of the top-quality jackets these days are DWR-treated. The DWR causes water to bead up on the shell. When the DWR wears off, even a once-waterproof jacket will feel like a wet dishrag.

Also note that ventilation is the key to coolness. The only ventilation on most shells is often the zipper. But waterproof jackets need additional openings. Look for mesh-backed pockets and underarm zippers, as well as cuffs, waists, and hems that can be adjusted to open wide. Storm flaps (the baffle over the zipper) that close with hook-and-loop material or snaps let you leave the zipper open for airflow into the jacket.

Other Gear

What are the three items most commonly forgotten on a camping trip? A hat, sunglasses, and lip balm.

A hat is crucial, especially when you are visiting high elevations. Without one you are constantly exposed to everything nature can give you. The sun will dehydrate you, sap your energy, sunburn your head, and in worst cases, cause sunstroke. Start with a comfortable hat. Then finish with sunglasses, lip balm, and sunscreen for additional protection. They will help protect you from extreme heat.

To guard against extreme cold, it's a good idea to keep a pair of thin ski gloves stashed away with your emergency clothes, along with a wool ski cap. The gloves should be thick enough to keep your fingers from stiffening up, but pliable enough to allow full movement so you don't have to take them off to complete simple tasks, like lighting a stove. An alternative to gloves is glovelets, which look like gloves with no fingers. In any case, just because the weather turns cold doesn't mean that your hands have to.

And if you fall into a river as Foonsky and I did—well, I hope you have a set of dry clothes waiting back at your rig. Oh, and a hand reaching out to you.

HIKING AND FOOT CARE

We had set up a nice little camp in the woods, and my buddy, Foonsky, was strapping on his hiking boots, sitting against a big Douglas fir.

"New boots," he said with a grin. "But they seem pretty stiff."

We decided to hoof it down the trail for a few hours, exploring the mountain wildlands that are said to hide Bigfoot and other strange creatures. After just a short while on the trail, a sense of peace and calm seemed to settle in. The forest provides the chance to be purified with clean air and the smell of trees, freeing you from all troubles.

But it wasn't long before a look of trouble was on Foonsky's face. And no, it wasn't from seeing Bigfoot.

"Got a hot spot on my toe," he said.

Immediately, we stopped. He pulled off his right boot, then his sock, and inspected the left side of his big toe. Sure enough, a blister had bubbled up, filled with fluid, but hadn't popped. From his medical kit, Foonsky cut a small piece of moleskin to fit over the blister and taped it to hold it in place. In a few minutes we were back on the trail.

A half hour later, there was still no sign of Bigfoot. But Foonsky stopped again and pulled off his other boot. "Another hot spot." On the little toe of his left foot was another small blister, over which he taped a Band-Aid to keep it from further chafing against the inside of his new boot.

In just a few days, ol' Foonsky, a strong, 6-foot-5, 200-plus-pound guy, was walking around like a sore-hoofed horse that had been loaded with a month's worth of supplies and ridden over sharp rocks. Well, it

wasn't the distance that had done Foonsky in; it was those blisters. He had them on eight of his 10 toes and was going through Band-Aids, moleskin, and tape like a walking emergency ward. If he'd used any more tape, he would've looked like a mummy from an Egyptian tomb.

If you've ever been in a similar predicament, you know the frustration of wanting to have a good time, wanting to hike and explore the area where you have set up a secluded camp, only to be held up by several blisters. No one is immune—all are created equal before the blister god. You can be forced to bow to it unless you get your act together.

What causes blisters? In almost all cases, it is the simple rubbing of a foot against the rugged interior of a boot. That can be worsened by several factors:

1. A very stiff boot or one in which your foot moves inside as you walk, instead of a boot that flexes as if it were another layer of skin.

2. Thin, ragged, or dirty socks. This is the fastest route to blisters. Thin socks will allow your feet to move inside your boots, ragged socks will allow your skin to chafe directly against the boot's interior, and dirty socks will wrinkle and fold, also rubbing against your feet instead of cushioning them.

3. Soft feet. By themselves, soft feet will not cause blisters, but in combination with a stiff boot or thin socks, they can cause terrible problems. The best way to toughen up your feet is to go barefoot. In fact, some of the biggest, toughest-looking guys you'll ever see, from Hells Angels to pro football players, have feet that are as soft as a baby's butt. Why? Because they never go barefoot and don't hike much.

The Perfect Boot

Every hiker eventually conducts a search for the perfect boot in the mission for ideal foot comfort and freedom from blisters. While there are many entries in this search—in fact, so many that it can be confusing—there is a way to find that perfect boot for you.

To stay blister-free, the most important factors are socks and boot flexibility. If there is any foot slippage from a thin sock or a stiff boot, you can rub up a blister in minutes. For instance, I never wear stiff boots and I always wear two fresh sets of SmartWools ($13 a pop).

My search for the perfect boot included discussions with the nation's preeminent long-distance hikers, Brian Robinson of Mountain View (7,200 miles in 2001) and Ray Jardine of Oregon (2,700 miles of Pacific Crest Trail in three months). Both believe that the weight of a boot (or athletic shoe, as they often use) is the defining factor when selecting hiking footwear. They both go as light as possible, believing that heavy boots will eventually wear you out by forcing you to pick up several pounds on your feet over and over again. A compatriot at the *San Francisco Chronicle,* outdoors writer Paul McHugh, offers the reminder that arch support may be even more vital, especially for people who hike less frequently and thus have not developed great foot strength as have Robinson and Jardine.

It is absolutely critical to stay away from very stiff boots and thin socks. Always wear the right style boots for what you have in mind and then protect your feet with carefully selected socks. If you are still so unfortunate as to get a blister or two, it means knowing how to treat them fast so they don't turn your walk into a sore-footed endurance test.

Selecting the Right Boots

When I hiked the John Muir Trail, I hiked 400 miles in three months—that is, 150 miles in a two-month general-training program, then 250 miles in three weeks from Mount Whitney to Yosemite Valley. In that span, I got just one blister, suffered on the fourth day of the 250-miler. I treated it immediately and suffered no more. One key is wearing the right boot, and for me, that means a boot that acts as a thick layer of skin that is flexible and pliable to my foot. I want my feet to fit snugly in them, with no interior movement.

There are four kinds of hiking footwear, most commonly known as: 1. Hiking boots; 2. Hunting boots; 3. Mountaineering boots; 4. Athletic shoes. Select the right one for you or pay the consequences.

One great trick when on a hiking vacation is to bring all four, and then for each hike, wear different footwear. This has many benefits. By changing boots, you change the points of stress for your feet and legs, greatly reducing soreness and the chance of creating a hot spot on a foot. It also allows you to go light on flat trails and heavy on steep trails, where additional boot weight can help with traction in downhill stretches.

HIKING BOOTS

Hiking boots can resemble low-cut leather/ Gore-Tex hunting boots or Gore-Tex walking shoes. They are designed for day walks or short backpacking trips. Some of the newer models are like rugged athletic shoes, designed with a Gore-Tex top for lightness and a Vibram sole for traction. These are perfect for people who like to walk but rarely carry a heavy backpack. Because they are flexible, they are easy to break in, and with fresh socks, they rarely cause blister problems. Because they are light, general hiking fatigue is greatly reduced.

On the negative side, because hiking boots are light, traction can be far from good on steep, slippery surfaces. In addition, they provide less than ideal ankle support, which can be a problem in rocky areas, such as along a stream where you might want to go trout fishing. Turn your ankle and your trip can be ruined.

For day hiking, they are the footwear of choice for most.

HUNTING BOOTS

Hunting boots are also called backpacking boots, super boots, or wilderness boots. They feature high ankle support, deep Vibram lug sole, built-in orthotics and arch support, and waterproof exterior. Many larger backpackers and those carrying heavy packs prefer them because of the additional support they provide. They also can stand up to hundreds of miles of wilderness use, constantly being banged against rocks and walked through streams while supporting 200 pounds.

On the negative side, hunting boots can be quite hot, weigh a ton, and if they get wet, take days to dry. Because they are heavy, they can wear you out. Often, the extra weight can add days to long-distance expeditions, cutting into the number of miles a hiker is capable of on a daily basis.

MOUNTAINEERING BOOTS

Mountaineering boots are identified by mid-range tops, laces that extend almost as far as the toe area, and ankle areas that are as stiff as a board. The lack of "give" is what endears them to mountaineers. Their stiffness is preferred when rock-climbing, walking off-trail on craggy surfaces, or hiking along the edge of streambeds where walking across small rocks can cause you to turn your ankle. Because these boots don't give on rugged, craggy terrain, they reduce ankle injuries and provide better traction.

The drawback to stiff boots is that if you don't have the proper socks and your foot starts slipping around in the boot, blisters will inevitably follow. If you just want to go for a walk or a good tromp with a backpack, then hiking shoes or hunting boots will serve you better.

ATHLETIC SHOES

Athletic shoes are built so well these days that they often can serve as good hiking footwear. They are frequently featherlight, so the long-term wear on your legs is minimal. For many short walks, they are ideal. For those with very strong feet and arches, they are popular even on multi-day trips that require only a small pack.

But there can be many problems with such a shoe. On steep sections, you can lose your footing, slip, and fall. If you stub your toe, you have little protection, and it hurts like heck. If you try to carry a backpack and don't have a strong arch, your arch can collapse or, at the minimum, overstress your ankles and feet. In addition, heavy socks usually are not a good fit in these lightweight shoes; if you go with a thin cotton sock and it folds over, you can rub up a blister in minutes.

AT THE STORE

There are many styles, brands, and price ranges to choose from. If you wander about comparing all their many features, you will get as confused as a kid in a toy store.

Instead, go into the store with your mind clear about what you want, find it, and buy it. If you want the best, expect to spend $85–150 for hiking boots, $100–175 for hunting boots, $140–200 for mountaineering boots, and $50–90 for athletic shoes. If you go much cheaper, well, then you are getting cheap footwear.

This is one area where you don't want to scrimp, so try not to yelp about the high cost. Instead, walk into the store believing you deserve the best, and that's exactly what you'll pay for.

You don't always get what you pay for, though. Once, I spent $250 for hiking boots custom-made in Germany. I wore them for close to 2,000 miles, yet they weighed four pounds each! Another time, trying to go light, I spent $185 on some low-cut hiking boots; they turned out to be miserable blister makers. Even after a year of trying to get my money's worth, I never felt they worked right on the trail. They now occupy a dark place deep in my closet.

If you plan to use the advice of a shoe salesperson, first look at what kind of boots he or she is wearing. If the salesperson isn't even wearing boots, then their advice may not be worth much. Most people I know who own quality boots, including salespeople, wear them almost daily if their jobs allow, since boots are the best footwear available. However, even

KEEP IT WILD TIP 2: TRAVEL LIGHTLY

1. Visit the backcountry in small groups.
2. Below tree line, always stay on designated trails.
3. Don't cut across switchbacks.
4. When traveling cross-country where no trails are available, follow animal trails or spread out with your group so no new routes are created.
5. Read your map and orient yourself with landmarks, a compass, and an altimeter. Avoid marking trails with rock cairns, tree scars, or ribbons.

these well-meaning folks can offer sketchy advice. Plenty of hikers claim to wear the world's greatest boot! Instead of asking how great the boot is, ask, "How many blisters did you get when you hiked 12 miles a day for a week?"

Enter the store with a precise use and style in mind. Rather than fish for suggestions, tell the salesperson exactly what you want, try two or three brands of the same style, and always try on both boots in a pair simultaneously so you know exactly how they'll feel. If possible, walk up and down stairs with them. Are they too stiff? Are your feet snug yet comfortable, or do they slip? Do they have that "right" kind of feel when you walk?

If you get the appropriate answers to those questions, then you're on your way to blister-free, pleasure-filled days of walking.

Socks

People can spend so much energy selecting the right kind of boots that they virtually overlook wearing the right kind of socks. One goes with the other.

Your socks should be thick enough to cushion your feet as well as fit snugly. Without good socks, you might tie your bootlaces too tight—and that's like putting a tourniquet on your feet. You should have plenty of clean socks on hand, or plan on washing what you have on your trip. As socks are worn, they become compressed, dirty, and damp. If they fold over, you'll rub up a blister in minutes.

My companions believe I go overboard when it comes to socks, that I bring too many and wear too many. But it works, so that's where the complaints stop. So how many do I wear? Well, it varies. On day hikes, I have found a sock called a SmartWool that makes my size 13s feel as if they're walking on pillows. I always wear two of them; that is, two on each foot.

Do not wear cotton socks. Your foot can get damp and mix with dirt, which can cause a hot spot to start on your foot. Eventually, you get blisters, lots of them.

SmartWool socks and other similar socks are a synthetic composite. They can partially wick moisture away from the skin.

The exterior sock can be wool or its equivalent. This will cushion your foot, provide that just-right snug fit in your boot, and give you some additional warmth and insulation in cold weather. It is critical to keep the sock clean. If you wear a dirty wool sock over and over again, it will compact, lose its cushion, and start wrinkling while you hike. Then your feet will catch on fire from the blisters that start popping up. Of course, when wearing multiple socks, especially a wool composite, you will likely need to go up a boot size so they fit comfortably.

A Few More Tips

If you are like most folks—that is, if the bottoms of your feet are rarely exposed and quite soft—you can take additional steps in their care. The best tip is keeping a fresh foot pad made of sponge rubber in your boot. But note that brand-new foot pads are often slippery for a few days, which can cause blisters. Just like new boots, they need to be broken in before an expedition.

Another cure for soft feet is to get out and walk or jog on a regular basis before your camping trip. On one trip on the Pacific Coast Trail, I ran into the long-distance master Jardine. He swore that going barefoot regularly is the best way to build up foot strength and arch support, while toughening up the bottom of your feet.

If you plan to use a foot pad and wear two heavy socks, you will need to use these items when sizing boots. It is an unforgiving error to wear thin cotton socks when buying boots and later try to squeeze all that stuff, plus your feet, into them. There just won't be enough room.

Treating Blisters

The key to treating blisters is fast work at the first sign of a hot spot. If you feel a hot spot, never keep walking, figuring that the problem will go away or that you will work through it. Wrong! Stop immediately and go to work.

Before you remove your socks, check to see if the sock has a wrinkle in it, a likely cause of the problem. If so, either change socks or pull them tight, removing the tiny folds, after taking care of the blister.

To take care of the blister, cut a piece of moleskin to cover the offending toe, securing the moleskin with white medical tape. If moleskin is not available, small Band-Aids can do the job, but these have to be replaced daily, and sometimes with even more frequency. At night, clean your feet and sleep without socks. That will allow your feet to dry and heal.

Tips in the Field

Two other items that can help your walking are an Ace bandage and a pair of gaiters.

For sprained ankles and twisted knees, an Ace bandage can be like an insurance policy to get you back on the trail and out of trouble. In many cases, a hiker with a twisted ankle or sprained knee has relied on a good wrap with a four-inch bandage for the added support to get home. Always buy the Ace bandages that come with the clips permanently attached, so you don't have to worry about losing them.

Gaiters are leggings made of Gore-Tex that fit from just below your knees, over your calves, and attach under your boots. They are of particular help when walking in damp areas or in places where rain is common. As your legs brush against ferns or low-lying plants, gaiters deflect the moisture. Without them, pants get soaking wet in short order.

Another tip: Should your boots become wet, never try to force-dry them. Some well-meaning folks will try to dry them quickly at the edge of a campfire or actually put the boots in an oven. While this may dry the boots, it can also loosen the glue that holds them together, ultimately weakening them until one day they fall apart in a heap.

A better bet is to treat the leather so the boots become water-repellent. Silicone-based liquids are the easiest to use and least greasy of the treatments available.

A final tip is to have another pair of lightweight shoes or moccasins that you can wear around camp and, in the process, give your feet the rest they deserve.

SLEEPING GEAR

On an eve long ago in the mountain pines, my dad, brother, and I had rolled out our sleeping bags and were bedded down for the night. After the pre-trip excitement, a long drive, an evening of trout fishing, and a barbecue, we were like three tired doggies who had played too much.

But as I looked up at the stars, I was suddenly wide awake. I was still wired. A half hour later? No change—wide awake.

And as little kids can do, I had to wake

up ol' Dad to tell him about it. "Hey, Dad, I can't sleep."

"This is what you do," he said. "Watch the sky for a shooting star and tell yourself that you cannot go to sleep until you see at least one. As you wait and watch, you will start getting tired, and it will be difficult to keep your eyes open. But tell yourself you must keep watching. Then you'll start to really feel tired. When you finally see a shooting star, you'll go to sleep so fast you won't know what hit you."

Well, I tried it that night and I don't even remember seeing a shooting star, I went to sleep so fast.

It's a good trick, and along with having a good sleeping bag, ground insulation, maybe a tent, or a few tricks for bedding down in a pickup truck or motor home, you can get a good night's sleep on every camping trip.

More than 20 years after that camping episode with my dad and brother, we made a trip to the planetarium at the Academy of Sciences in San Francisco to see a show on Halley's Comet. The lights dimmed, and the ceiling turned into a night sky, filled with stars and a setting moon. A scientist began explaining phenomenas of the heavens.

After a few minutes, I began to feel drowsy. Just then, a shooting star zipped across the planetarium ceiling. I went into such a deep sleep, it was like I was in a coma. I didn't wake up until the show was over, the lights were turned back on, and the people were leaving.

Feeling drowsy, I turned to see if Dad had liked the show. Oh yeah? Not only had he gone to sleep too, but he apparently had no intention of waking up, no matter what. Just like a camping trip.

Sleeping Bags

Question: What could be worse than trying to sleep in a cold, wet sleeping bag on a rainy night without a tent in the mountains?

Answer: Trying to sleep in a cold, wet sleeping bag on a rainy night without a tent in the mountains when your sleeping bag is filled with down.

Water will turn a down-filled sleeping bag into a mushy heap. Many campers do not like a high-tech approach, but a state-of-the-art polyfiber sleeping bag can keep you warm even when wet. That factor, along with temperature rating and weight, is key when selecting a sleeping bag.

A sleeping bag is a shell filled with heat-retaining insulation. By itself, it is not warm. Your body provides the heat, and the sleeping bag's ability to retain that heat is what makes it warm or cold.

The old-style canvas bags are heavy, bulky, cold, and, when wet, useless. With other options available, their function is limited. Anybody who sleeps outdoors or backpacks should choose otherwise. Use a sleeping bag filled with down or one of the quality poly-fills. Down is light, warm, and aesthetically pleasing to those who don't think camping and technology mix. If you choose a down bag, be sure to keep it double wrapped in plastic garbage bags on your trip to keep it dry. Once it's wet, you'll spend your nights howling at the moon.

The polyfiber-filled bags are not necessarily better than those filled with down, but they can be. Their one key advantage is that even when wet, some poly-fills can retain up to 85 percent of your body heat. This allows you to sleep and get valuable rest even in miserable conditions. In my camping experience, no matter how lucky you may be, there will come a time when you will get caught in an unexpected, violent storm and everything you've got will get wet, including your sleeping bag. That's when a poly-fill bag becomes priceless. You either have one and can sleep, or you don't have one and suffer. It is that simple. Of the synthetic fills, Quallofil made by DuPont is the industry leader.

But just because a sleeping bag uses a high-tech poly-fill doesn't necessarily make it a better bag. There are other factors.

Even with the warmest sleeping bag in the world, if you just lay it down on the ground and try to sleep, you will likely get as cold as a winter cucumber. That is because the cold ground will suck the warmth right out of your body. The solution? A sleeping pad.

The most important are a bag's temperature rating and weight. The temperature rating of a sleeping bag refers to how cold it can get outside before you start actually feeling cold. Many campers make the mistake of thinking, "I only camp in the summer, so a bag rated at 30 or 40°F should be fine." Later, they find out it isn't so fine, and all it takes is one cold night to convince them of that. When selecting the right temperature rating, visualize the coldest weather you might ever confront, and then get a bag rated for even colder weather.

For instance, if you are a summer camper, you may rarely experience a night in the low 30s or high 20s. A sleeping bag rated at 20°F would be appropriate, keeping you snug, warm, and asleep. For most campers, I advise bags rated at 0 or 10°F.

If you buy a poly-filled sleeping bag, never leave it squished in your stuff sack between camping trips. Instead, keep it on a hanger in a closet or use it as a blanket. One thing that can reduce a poly-filled bag's heat-retaining qualities is if the tiny hollow fibers that make up the fill lose their loft. You can avoid this with proper storage.

The weight of a sleeping bag can also be a key factor, especially for backpackers. When you have to carry your gear on your back, every ounce becomes important. Sleeping bags that weigh just three pounds are avail-able, although they are expensive. But if you hike much, it's worth the price to keep your weight to a minimum. For an overnighter, you can get away with a 4- or 4.5-pound bag without much stress. However, bags weighing five pounds and up should be left back at the car.

I have two sleeping bags: a seven-pounder that feels like a giant sponge, and a four-pounder. The heavy-duty model is for pickup-truck camping in cold weather and doubles as a blanket at home. The lightweight bag is for hikes. Between the two, I'm set.

Insulation Pads

Even with the warmest sleeping bag in the world, if you just lay it down on the ground and try to sleep, you will likely get as cold as a winter cucumber. That is because the cold ground will suck the warmth right out of your body. The solution is to have a layer of insulation between you and the ground. For this, you can use a thin Insulite pad, a lightweight Therm-a-Rest inflatable pad, a foam pad or mattress, an air bed, or a cot. Here is a capsule summary of each:

• **Insulite pads:** They are light, inexpensive, roll up quickly for transport, and can double as a seat pad at your camp. The negative side is that in one night, they will compress, making you feel like you are sleeping on granite.

• **Therm-a-Rest pads:** These are a real luxury

because they do everything an Insulite pad does, but they also provide a cushion. The negative side is that they are expensive by comparison, and if they get a hole in them, they become worthless without a patch kit.

• **Foam mattresses, air beds, and cots:** These are excellent for car campers. The new line of air beds, especially the thicker ones, are outstanding and inflate quickly with an electric motor inflator that plugs into a power plug or cigarette lighter in your vehicle. Foam mattresses are also excellent—in fact, the most comfortable of all—but their size precludes many from considering them. I've found that cots work great, too. I finally wore out an old wood one and replaced it immediately with one of the new high-tech, light metal ones. For camping in the back of a pickup truck with a camper shell, the cots with three-inch legs are best, of course.

A Few Tricks

When surveying a camp area, the most important consideration should be to select a good spot for sleeping. Everything else is secondary. Ideally, you want a flat area that is wind-sheltered and on ground soft enough to drive stakes into. Yeah, and I want to win the lottery, too.

Sometimes, the ground will have a slight slope to it. In that case, always sleep with your head on the uphill side. If you sleep parallel to the slope, every time you roll over, you'll find yourself rolling down the hill. If you sleep with your head on the downhill side, you'll get a headache that feels as if an ax is embedded in your brain.

When you've found a good spot, clear it of all branches, twigs, and rocks, of course. A good tip is to dig a slight indentation in the ground where your hip will fit. Since your body is not flat, but has curves and edges, it will not feel comfortable on flat ground. Some people even get severely bruised on the sides of their hips when sleeping on flat, hard ground. For that reason alone, they learn to hate camping. What a shame, especially when

the problem is solved easily with a Therma-Rest pad, foam insulation, an air bed, or a cot.

After the ground is prepared, throw a ground cloth over the spot, which will keep much of the morning dew off you. In some areas, particularly where fog is a problem, morning dew can be heavy and get the outside of your sleeping bag quite wet. In that case, you need overhead protection, such as a tent or some kind of roof, like a poncho or tarp with its ends tied to trees.

Tents and Weather Protection

All it takes is to get caught in the rain once without a tent and you will never go anywhere without one again. A tent provides protection from rain, wind, and mosquito attacks. In exchange, you can lose a starry night's view, though some tents now even provide moon roofs.

A tent can be as complex as a four-season, tubular-jointed dome with a rain fly or as simple as two ponchos snapped together and roped up to a tree. They can be as cheap as a $10 tube tent, which is nothing more than a hollow piece of plastic, or as expensive as a $500 five-person deluxe expedition dome model. They vary greatly in size, price, and assembly time. For those who camp infrequently and want to buy a tent without paying much, off-brand models are available at considerable price discounts. My experience in field-testing outdoor gear, though, is that these tents often rip at the seams if subjected to regular use. If you plan on getting a good one, plan on doing plenty of shopping and asking lots of questions. With a little bit of homework, you can get the right answers to these questions:

WILL IT KEEP ME DRY?

On many one-person and two-person tents, the rain fly does not extend far enough to keep water off the bottom sidewalls of the tent. In a driving rain, water can also drip from the rain fly and onto those sections of the tent. Eventually, the water can leak through to the inside, particularly through the seams.

You must be able to stake out your rain fly so it completely covers all of the tent. If you are tent shopping and this does not appear possible, then don't buy the tent. To prevent potential leaks, use a seam waterproofer, such as Seam Lock, a gluelike substance that can close potential leak areas on tent seams. For large umbrella tents, keep a patch kit handy. Note that as of 2003, Coleman tents are guaranteed to keep campers dry.

Another way to keep water out of your tent is to store all wet garments outside the tent, under a poncho. Moisture from wet clothes stashed in the tent will condense on the interior tent walls. If you bring enough wet clothes into the tent, by the next morning you'll feel as if you're camping in a duck blind.

HOW HARD IS IT TO PUT UP?

If a tent is difficult to erect in full sunlight, you can just about forget it at night, especially the first night out. Some tents can go up in just a few minutes, without requiring help from another camper. This might be the kind of tent you want.

The way to compare put-up times when shopping for tents is to count the number of connecting points from the tent poles to the tent and the number of stakes required. The fewer, the better. Think simple. My two-person-plus-a-dog tent has seven connecting points and, minus the rain fly, requires no stakes. It goes up in a few minutes.

My bigger family tent, which has three rooms with walls, so we can keep our two kids, Jeremy and Kris, isolated on each side, takes about a half hour to put up. That's without anybody's help. With their help, add about 15 minutes. Heh, heh.

Another factor is the tent poles themselves. Some small tents have poles that are broken into small sections that are connected by bungee cords. It takes only an instant to convert them to a complete pole.

Some outdoor shops have tents on display on their showroom floors. Before buying the tent, have the salesperson take the tent down and put it back up. If it takes him more than five minutes, or he says he doesn't have time, then keep looking.

IS IT ROOMY ENOUGH?

Don't judge the size of a tent on floor space alone. Some tents that are small on floor space can give the illusion of roominess with a high ceiling. You can be quite comfortable and snug in them.

But remember that a one-person or two-person tent is just that. A two-person tent has room for two people plus gear. That's it. Don't buy a tent expecting it to hold more than it is intended to.

HOW MUCH DOES IT WEIGH?

If you're a hiker, this becomes the preeminent question. If it's much more than six or seven pounds, forget it. A 12-pound tent is bad enough, but get it wet and it's like carrying a piano on your back. On the other hand, weight is scarcely a factor if you camp only where you can take your car. My dad, for instance, used to have this giant canvas umbrella tent that folded down to a neat little pack that weighed about 500 pounds.

Family Tents

It is always worth spending the time and money to buy a tent you and your family will be happy with.

Many excellent family tents are available for $125–175, particularly from Cabela's, Coleman, Eureka!, North Face, Remington, and Sierra Designs. Guide-approved expedition tents for groups cost more, generally $350–600. Here is a synopsis of some of best tents available:

CABELA'S ALASKAN VESTIBULE

800/237-4444
www.cabelas.com
$129–250

The new Alaskan Vestibule series is based around a dome tent that can be connected by a tube to another dome tent. In use, it looks like a giant caterpillar, with dome tents that sleep four, or six to eight, on each end of a connector tube. It allows privacy without having to buy separate tents. A favorite for both families and professionals.

CABELA'S THREE-ROOM CABIN
800/237-4444
www.cabelas.com
$270

This beautiful forest-green, three-room tent features a 10- by 20-foot floor available in different configurations with removable interior walls. Three doors mean everybody doesn't tromp through the center room for access to the side rooms. It will stand up to wind, rain, and frequent use.

COLEMAN MODIFIED DOME
800/835-3278
www.coleman.com
$70–230

Coleman Modified Dome tents are available in six different single- and multi-room designs. The pole structure is unique, with all four upright poles and one ridgepole shock-corded together for an integrated system that makes setup extremely fast and easy. Yet, because of the ridgepole's engineering, the tent has passed tests in high winds. Mesh panels in the ceiling are a tremendous plus for ventilation.

COLEMAN WEATHERMASTER
800/835-3278
www.coleman.com
$150–200

The Weathermaster series features tents with multiple rooms, walls, and ample headroom, and they are guaranteed to keep rain out. The 17- by 9-foot model sleeps six to eight, has a 76-inch ceiling, and has zippered dividers. Since the dividers are removable, you can configure the tent in multiple layouts. The frame is designed with poles adjustable to three different heights to accommodate uneven ground.

EUREKA! ZEUS 4EXO
800/572-8822
website: www.EurekaTent.com
$200–300

The Eureka! Zeus is the best new tent yet created in the 21st century. It features three poles, goes up quickly, and has strategically placed mesh panels and multiple hooded vents. The result is maximum airflow and little condensation build-up, even with four people. It comes in three sizes. It weighs nine pounds and provides 64 square feet of space, with a center peak of four feet, eight inches.

KELTY NIRVANA
800/423-2320
www.kelty.com
$325

The Nirvana is a top-of-the-line tent based on a sleek dome profile. This is a great package, with mesh sides, tops, and doors, along with a full awning fly and coverage for weather protection. Clip sleeves and rubber-tipped poles for easy slide during setup are nice bonuses.

Bivouac Bags

If you like going solo and choose not to own a tent at all, a bivy bag, short for bivouac bag and pronounced "bivvy" as in dizzy, not "bivy" as in ivy, can provide the extremely lightweight weather protection you require. A bivy bag is a water-repellent shell in which your sleeping bag fits. It is light and tough, and for some is the perfect alternative to a heavy tent. My own bivy weighs 31 ounces and cost me $240; it's made by OR (Outdoor Research), and I just plain love the thing on expeditions. On the downside, however, it can be a bit difficult getting settled just right in it, and some say they feel claustrophobic in such

With the world going high-tech, **tents** of today vary greatly in complexity, size, price, and put-up time. And they wouldn't be fit for this new millennium without offering options such as moon roofs, rain flies, and tent wings. Be sure to buy the one that's right for your needs.

close quarters. Once you get used to a bivy, spend a night in a tent; the tent will feel like a room at the Mirage.

The idea of riding out a storm in a bivy can be quite worrisome. You can hear the rain hitting you, and sometimes even feel the pounding of the drops through the bivy bag. For some, it can be unsettling to try to sleep under such circumstances. On the other hand, I've always looked forward to it. In cold weather, a bivy also helps keep you warm. I've had just one miserable night in mine. That was when my sleeping bag was a bit wet when I started the night. By the middle of the night, the water was condensing from the sleeping bag on the interior walls of the bivy, and then soaking the bag, like a storm cycle. The night hit only about 45°F but I just about froze

to death anyway. Otherwise, I've used it on multi-week expeditions with great results: warm, dry quarters and deep, restful sleeps by night, and a pack lightened without carrying a tent by day.

Pickup Truck Campers

If you own a pickup truck with a camper shell, you can turn it into a self-contained campground with a little work. This can be an ideal way to go: It's fast, portable, and you are guaranteed a dry environment.

But that does not necessarily mean it is a warm environment. In fact, without insulation from the metal truck bed, it can be like trying to sleep on an iceberg. The metal truck bed will get as cold as the air temperature, which is often much colder than the ground temperature. Without insulation, it can be much

KEEP IT WILD TIP 3: CAMP WITH CARE

1. Choose an existing, legal site. Restrict activities to areas where vegetation is compacted or absent.
2. Camp at least 75 steps (200 feet) from lakes, streams, and trails.
3. Always choose sites that won't be damaged by your stay.
4. Preserve the feeling of solitude by selecting camps that are out of view when possible.
5. Don't dig trenches or build structures or furniture.

colder in your camper shell than it would be on the open ground.

When I camp in my rig, I use a large piece of foam for a mattress and insulation. The foam measures four inches thick, 48 inches wide, and 76 inches long. It makes for a bed as comfortable as anything one might ask for. In fact, during the winter, if I don't go camping for a few weeks because of writing obligations, I sometimes will throw the foam on the floor, lay down the old sleeping bag, light a fire, and camp right in my living room. It's in my blood, I tell you. Air beds and cots are also extremely comfortable and I've used both many times. Whatever you choose, just make sure you have a comfortable sleeping unit. Good sleep makes for great camping trips.

RVs

The problems RVers encounter come from two primary sources: lack of privacy and light intrusion.

The lack of privacy stems from the natural restrictions of where a land yacht can go. Without careful use of the guide section of this book, motor-home owners can find themselves in parking-lot settings, jammed in with plenty of neighbors. Because RVs often have large picture windows, you lose your privacy, causing some late nights; then, come daybreak, light intrusion forces an early wake up. As a result, you get shorted on your sleep.

The answer is to carry inserts to fit over the inside of your windows. These close off the outside and retain your privacy. And if you don't want to wake up with the sun at daybreak, you don't have to. It will still be dark.

FIRST AID AND INSECT PROTECTION

Mountain nights don't get any more perfect, I thought as I lay in my sleeping bag.

The sky looked like a mass of jewels and the air tasted sweet and smelled of pines. A shooting star fireballed across the sky, and I remember thinking, "It just doesn't get any better."

Just then, as I was drifting into sleep, a mysterious buzz appeared from nowhere and deposited itself inside my left ear. Suddenly awake, I whacked my ear with the palm of my hand, hard enough to cause a minor concussion. The buzz disappeared. I pulled out my flashlight and shined it on my palm, and there, lit in the blackness of night, lay the squished intruder: a mosquito, dead amid a stain of blood.

Satisfied, I turned off the light, closed my eyes, and thought of the fishing trip planned for the next day. Then I heard them. It was a squadron of mosquitoes making landing patterns around my head. I tried to grab them with an open hand, but they dodged the assault and flew off. Just 30 seconds later, another landed in my left ear. I promptly dispatched the invader with a rip of the palm.

Now I was completely awake, so I got out

of my sleeping bag to retrieve some mosquito repellent. But en route, several of the buggers swarmed and nailed me in the back and arms. After I applied the repellent and settled snugly again in my sleeping bag, the mosquitoes would buzz a few inches from my ear. After getting a whiff of the poison, they would fly off. It was like sleeping in a sawmill.

The next day, drowsy from little sleep, I set out to fish. I'd walked but 15 minutes when I brushed against a bush and felt a stinging sensation on the inside of my arm, just above the wrist. I looked down: A tick had his clamps in me. I ripped it out before he could embed his head into my skin.

After catching a few fish, I sat down against a tree to eat lunch and just watch the water go by. My dog, Rebel, sat down next to me and stared at the beef jerky I was munching as if it were a T-bone steak. I finished eating, gave him a small piece, patted him on the head, and said, "Good dog." Right then, I noticed an itch on my arm where a mosquito had drilled me. I unconsciously scratched it. Two days later, in that exact spot, some nasty red splotches started popping up. Poison oak. By petting my dog and then scratching my arm, I had transferred the oil residue of the poison oak leaves from Rebel's fur to my arm.

When I returned home, Foonsky asked me about the trip.

"Great," I said. "Mosquitoes, ticks, poison oak. Can hardly wait to go back."

"Sorry I missed out," he answered.

Mosquitoes, No-See-Ums, Horseflies

On a trip to Canada, Foonsky and I were fishing a small lake from the shore when suddenly a black horde of mosquitoes could be seen moving across the lake toward us. It was like when the French army looked across the Rhine and saw the Wehrmacht coming. There was a buzz in the air. We fought them off for a few minutes, then made a fast retreat to the truck and jumped in, content the buggers had been foiled. But in some way still unknown to us,

the mosquitoes gained entry to the truck. In 10 minutes, we squished 15 of them as they attempted to plant their oil drills into our skins. Just outside the truck, the black horde waited for us to make a tactical error, such as rolling down a window. It finally took a miraculous hailstorm to squelch the attack.

When it comes to mosquitoes, no-see-ums, gnats, and horseflies, there are times when there is nothing you can do. However, in most situations, you can muster a defense to repel the attack.

The first key with mosquitoes is to wear clothing too heavy for them to drill through. Expose a minimum of skin, wear a hat, and tie a bandanna around your neck, preferably one that has been sprayed with repellent. If you try to get by with just a cotton T-shirt, you will be declared a federal mosquito sanctuary.

So, first, your skin must be well covered, with only your hands and face exposed. Second, you should have your companion spray your clothes with repellent. Third, you should dab liquid repellent directly on your skin.

At night, the easiest way to get a good sleep without mosquitoes buzzing in your ear is to sleep in a bug-proof tent. If the nights are warm and you want to see the stars, new tent models are available that have a skylight covered with mosquito netting. If you don't like tents on summer evenings, mosquito netting rigged with an air space at your head can solve the problem. Otherwise, prepare to get bitten, even with the use of mosquito repellent.

If your problems are with no-see-ums or biting horseflies, then you need a slightly different approach.

No-see-ums are tiny black insects that look like nothing more than a sliver of dirt on your skin. Then you notice something stinging, and when you rub the area, you scratch up a little no-see-um. The results are similar to mosquito bites, making your skin itch, splotch, and, when you get them bad, swell. In addition to using the techniques described to repel mosquitoes, you should go one step further.

The problem is that no-see-ums are tricky little devils. Somehow, they can actually get under your socks and around your ankles, where they will bite to their hearts' content all night long while you sleep, itch, sleep, and itch some more. The best solution is to apply a liquid repellent to your ankles, then wear clean socks.

Horseflies are another story. They are rarely a problem, but when they get their dander up, they can cause trouble you'll never forget.

One such episode occurred when Foonsky and I were paddling a canoe along the shoreline of a large lake. This giant horsefly, about the size of a fingertip, started dive-bombing the canoe. After 20 minutes, it landed on Foonsky's thigh. He immediately slammed it with an open hand, then let out a blood-curdling "Yeeeee-ow!" that practically sent ripples across the lake. When Foonsky whacked it, the horsefly had somehow turned around and bit him on the hand, leaving a huge red welt.

In the next 10 minutes, that big fly strafed the canoe on more dive-bomb runs. I finally got my canoe paddle, swung it as if it were a baseball bat, and nailed that horsefly as if I'd hit a home run. It landed about 15 feet from the boat, still alive and buzzing in the water. While I was trying to figure what it would take to kill this bugger, a large rainbow trout surfaced and snatched it out of the water, finally avenging the assault.

If you have horsefly or yellow jacket problems, you'd best just leave the area. One, two, or a few can be dealt with. More than that and your fun camping trip will be about as fun as being roped to a tree and stung by an electric shock rod.

On most trips, you will spend time doing everything possible to keep from getting bitten by mosquitoes or no-see-ums. When your attempts fail, you must know what to do next, and fast, especially if you are among those ill-fated campers who get big, red lumps from a bite inflicted from even a microscopic mosquito.

A fluid called After Bite or a dab of ammonia should be applied immediately to the bite. To start the healing process, apply a first-aid gel (not a liquid), such as the one made by Campho-Phenique.

DEET

What is DEET? You're not likely to find the word DEET on any repellent label. That's because DEET stands for N,N diethyl-m-toluamide. If the label contains this scientific name, the repellent contains DEET. Despite fears of DEET-associated health risks and the increased attention given natural alternatives, DEET-based repellents are still acknowledged as by far the best option when serious insect protection is required.

What are the health risks associated with using DEET? A number of deaths and a number of medical problems have been attributed in the press to DEET in recent years—events that those in the DEET community vehemently deny as being specifically DEET-related, pointing to reams of scientific documentation as evidence. It does seem logical to assume that if DEET can peel paint, melt nylon, destroy plastic, wreck wood finishes, and damage fishing line, then it must be hell on the skin—perhaps worse.

On one trip, I had a small bottle of mosquito repellent in the same pocket as a Swiss army knife. Guess what happened? The mosquito repellent leaked a bit and literally melted the insignia right off the knife. DEET will also melt synthetic clothes. That is why, in bad mosquito country, I'll expose a minimum of skin, just hands and face (with full beard), apply the repellent only to my cheeks and the back of my hands, and perhaps wear a bandanna sprinkled with a few drops as well. That does the trick, with a minimum of exposure to the repellent.

Although nothing definitive has been published, a growing number in the scientific community believe that repeated applications of products containing low percentages of DEET can be potentially dangerous. It is theorized that this actually puts

KEEP IT WILD TIP 4: SANITATION

If no refuse facility is available:
1. Deposit human waste in "cat holes" dug 6–8 inches deep. Cover and disguise the cat hole when finished.
2. Deposit human waste at least 75 paces (200 feet) from any water source or camp.
3. Use toilet paper sparingly. When finished, carefully burn it in the cat hole, then bury it.
4. If no appropriate burial locations are available, such as in popular wilderness camps above tree line in granite settings, then all human refuse should be double-bagged and packed out.
5. At boat-in campsites, chemical toilets are required. Chemical toilets can also solve the problem of larger groups camping for long stays at one location where no facilities are available.
6. To wash dishes or your body, carry water away from the source and use small amounts of biodegradable soap. Scatter dishwater after all food particles have been removed.
7. Scour your campsites for even the tiniest piece of trash and any other evidence of your stay. Pack out all the trash you can, even if it's not yours. Finding cigarette butts, for instance, provides special irritation for most campers. Pick them up and discard them properly.
8. Never litter. Never. Or you become the enemy of all others.

consumers at a greater risk for absorbing high levels of DEET into the body than if they had just used one application of a 30–50 percent DEET product with an efficacy of 4–6 hours. Also being studied is the possibility that low levels of DEET, which might not otherwise be of toxicological concern, may become hazardous if they are formulated with solvents or diluters (considered inert ingredients) that may enhance the absorption rate.

"NATURAL" REPELLENTS

Are natural alternatives a safer choice than DEET? To imply that essential oils are completely safe because they are natural products is not altogether accurate. Essential oils, while derived from plants that grow naturally, are chemicals too. Some are potentially hazardous if ingested, and most are downright painful if they find their way into the eyes or onto mucus membranes.

For example, pennyroyal is perhaps the most toxic of the essential oils used to repel insects and can be deadly if taken internally. Other oils used include cedarwood, citronella (perhaps the most common, it's extracted from an aromatic grass indigenous to Southern Asia), eucalyptus, and peppermint.

Three citronella-based products—Avon's Skin-So-Soft, Buzz Away (manufactured by Quantum), and Natrapel (manufactured by Tender)—have received EPA registration and approval for sale as repellents against flies, gnats, midges, and mosquitoes.

How effective are natural repellents? While there are numerous studies cited by those on both the DEET and citronella sides of the fence, the average effective repelling time of a citronella product appears to range from 1.5 to two hours. Tests conducted at Cambridge University, England, comparing Natrapel to DEET-based Skintastic (a low-percentage

DEET product) found citronella to be just as effective in repelling mosquitoes. The key here is effectiveness and the amount of time until reapplication.

Citronella products work for up to two hours and then require reapplication (the same holds true for other natural formulations). Products using a low-percentage level of DEET also require reapplication every two hours to remain effective. So, if you're going outside for only a short period in an environment where insect bites are more an irritant than a hazard, you would do just as well to go natural.

What other chemical alternatives are there? Another line of defense against insects is the chemical permethrin, used on clothing, not on skin. Permethrin-based products are designed to repel and kill arthropods or crawling insects, making them a preferred repellent for ticks. The currently available products remain effective—repelling and killing chiggers, mosquitoes, and ticks—for two weeks and through two launderings.

Ticks

Ticks are nasty little vermin that will wait in ambush, jump on unsuspecting prey, and then crawl to a prime location before filling their bodies with their victim's blood.

I call them Dracula bugs, but by any name they can be a terrible camp pest. Ticks rest on grass and low plants and attach themselves to those who brush against the vegetation (dogs are particularly vulnerable). Typically, they can be found no more than 18 inches above ground, and if you stay on the trails, you can usually avoid them.

There are two common species of ticks. The common coastal tick is larger, brownish in color, and prefers to crawl around before putting its clamps on you. The feel of any bug crawling on your skin can be creepy, but consider it a forewarning of assault; you can just pick the tick off and dispatch it. The coastal tick's preferred destination is usually the back of your neck, just where the hairline starts.

The other species, the wood tick, is small and black, and when he puts his clamps in, it's immediately painful. When a wood tick gets into a dog for a few days, it can cause a large red welt. In either case, ticks should be removed as soon as possible.

If you have hiked in areas infested with ticks, it is advisable to shower as soon as possible, washing your clothes immediately. If you just leave your clothes in a heap, a tick can crawl out and invade your home. They like warmth, and one way or another, they can end up in your bed. Waking up in the middle of the night with a tick crawling across your chest can be unsettling, to put it mildly.

Once a tick has its clampers in your skin, you must determine how long it has been there. If it has been a short time, the most painless and effective method for removal is to take a pair of sharp tweezers and grasp the little devil, making certain to isolate the mouth area, then pull him out. Reader Johvin Perry sent in the suggestion to coat the tick with Vaseline, which will cut off its oxygen supply, after which it may voluntarily give up the hunt.

If the tick has been in longer, you may wish to have a doctor extract it. Some people will burn a tick with a cigarette or poison it with lighter fluid, but neither is advisable. No matter how you do it, you must take care to remove all of the tick, especially its clawlike mouth.

The wound, however small, should then be cleansed and dressed. First, apply liquid peroxide, which cleans and sterilizes, and then apply a dressing coated with a first-aid gel, such as First-Aid Cream, Campho-Phenique, or Neosporin.

Lyme disease, which can be transmitted by the bite of a deer tick, is rare but common enough to warrant some attention. To prevent tick bites, some people tuck their pant legs into their hiking socks and spray tick repellent, called Permamone, on their pants.

The first symptom of Lyme disease is a

bright red, splotchy rash that develops around the bite area. Other possible early symptoms include headache, nausea, fever, and/or a stiff neck. If any of these happen, or if you have any doubts, you should see your doctor immediately. If you do get Lyme disease, don't panic. Doctors say it is easily treated in the early stages with simple antibiotics. If you are nervous about getting Lyme disease, carry a small plastic bag with you when you hike. If a tick manages to get his clampers into you, put the tick in the plastic bag after you pull it out. Then give it to your doctor for analysis to see if the tick is a carrier of the disease.

During the course of my hiking and camping career, I have removed ticks from my skin hundreds of times without any problems. However, if you are worried about ticks, you can buy a tick removal kit from any outdoors store. These kits allow you to remove ticks in such a way that their toxins are guaranteed not to enter your bloodstream.

If you are particularly wary of ticks or perhaps even have nightmares of them, wear long pants that are tucked into your socks, as well as a long-sleeved shirt tucked securely into your pants and held with a belt. Clothing should be light in color, making it easier to see ticks, and tightly woven so ticks have trouble hanging on. On one hike with my mom, Eleanor, I brushed more than 100 ticks off my blue jeans in less than an hour, while she did not pick up a single one on her polyester pants.

Perform tick checks regularly, especially on the back of the neck. The combination of DEET insect repellents applied to the skin and permethrin repellents applied directly to clothing is considered to be the most effective line of defense against ticks.

Poison Oak

After a nice afternoon hike, about a five-miler, I was concerned about possible exposure to poison oak, so I immediately showered and put on clean clothes. Then I settled into a chair with my favorite foamy elixir to watch the end of a baseball game. The game went 18 innings; meanwhile, my dog, tired from the hike, went to sleep on my bare ankles.

A few days later, I had a case of poison oak. My feet looked as though they had been on fire and put out with an ice pick. The lesson? Don't always trust your dog, give him a bath as well, and beware of extra-inning ball games.

You can get poison oak only from direct contact with the oil residue from the plant's leaves. It can be passed in a variety of ways, as direct as skin-to-leaf contact or as indirect as leaf to dog, dog to sofa, sofa to skin. Once you have it, there is little you can do but feel horribly itchy. Applying Caladryl lotion or its equivalent can help because it contains antihistamines, which attack and dry the itch.

My pal Furniss offers a tip that may sound crazy but seems to work. You should expose the afflicted area to the hottest water you can stand, then suddenly immerse it in cold water. The hot water opens the skin pores and gets the "itch" out, and the cold water then quickly seals the pores.

In any case, you're a lot better off if you don't get poison oak to begin with. Remember that poison oak can disguise itself. In the spring, it is green; then it gradually turns reddish in the summer. By fall, it becomes a bloody, ugly-looking red. In the winter, it loses its leaves altogether and appears to be nothing more than the barren, brown sticks of a small plant. However, at any time and in any form, its contact with skin can quickly lead to infection.

Some people are more easily afflicted than others, but if you are one of the lucky few who aren't, don't cheer too loudly. While some people can be exposed to the oil residue of poison oak with little or no effect, the body's resistance can gradually be worn down with repeated exposure. At one time, I could practically play in the stuff and the only symptom would be a few little bumps on the inside of my wrist. Now, more than 15 years later, my resistance has broken down. If I merely brush against poison oak now, in a few days the exposed area can look as if it were used for a track meet.

So regardless of whether you consider yourself vulnerable or not, you should take heed to reduce your exposure. That can be done by staying on trails when you hike and making sure your dog does the same. Remember, the worst stands of poison oak are usually brush-infested areas just off the trail. Also protect yourself by dressing so your skin is completely covered, wearing long-sleeved shirts, long pants, and boots. If you suspect you've been exposed, immediately wash your clothes and then wash yourself with aloe vera, rinsing with a cool shower.

And don't forget to give your dog a bath as well.

Sunburn

The most common injury suffered on camping trips is sunburn, yet some people wear it as a badge of honor, believing that it somehow enhances their virility. Well, it doesn't. Neither do suntans. Too much sun can lead to serious burns or sunstroke.

Both are easy enough to avoid. Use a high-level sunscreen on your skin, apply lip balm, and wear sunglasses and a hat. If any area gets burned, apply first-aid cream, which will soothe and provide moisture to the parched skin.

The best advice is not to get even a suntan. Those who tan are involved in a practice that can eventually ruin their skin and possibly lead to cancer.

Giardia and Cryptosporidium

You have just hiked in to your backwoods spot, you're thirsty and a bit tired, but you smile as you consider the prospects. Everything seems perfect—there's not a stranger in sight, and you have nothing to do but relax with your pals.

You toss down your gear, grab your cup, dip it into the stream, and take a long drink of that ice-cold mountain water. It seems crystal pure and sweeter than anything

Avoiding Poison Oak: Remember the old Boy Scout saying: "Leaves of three, let them be."

you've ever tasted. It's not till later that you find out it can be just like drinking a cup of poison.

Whether you camp in the wilderness or not, if you hike, you're going to get thirsty. And if your canteen runs dry, you'll start eyeing any water source. Stop! Do not pass Go. Do not drink.

By drinking what appears to be pure mountain water without first treating it, you can ingest a microscopic protozoan called *Giardia lamblia*. The ensuing abdominal cramps can make you feel like your stomach and intestinal tract are in a knot, ready to explode. With that comes long-term diarrhea that is worse than even a bear could imagine.

Doctors call the disease giardiasis, or giardia for short, but it is difficult to diagnose. One friend of mine who contracted giardia was told he might have stomach cancer before the proper diagnosis was made.

Drinking directly from a stream or lake does not mean you will get giardia, but you are taking a giant chance. There is no reason to assume such a risk, potentially ruining your trip and enduring weeks of misery.

A lot of people are taking that risk. I made a personal survey of campers in the Yosemite National Park wilderness, and found that roughly only one in 10 was equipped with some kind of water-purification system. The result, according to the Public Health Service, is that an average of 4 percent of all backpackers and campers suffer giardiasis. According to the Parasitic Diseases Division of the Center for Infectious Diseases, the rates range from 1 percent to 20 percent across the country.

But if you get giardia, you are not going to care about the statistics. "When I got giardia, I just about wanted to die," said Henry McCarthy, a California camper. "For about 10 days, it was the most terrible thing I have ever experienced. And through the whole thing, I kept thinking, 'I shouldn't have drunk that water, but it seemed all right at the time.'"

That is the mistake most campers make. The stream might be running free, gurgling over boulders in the high country, tumbling into deep, oxygenated pools. It looks pure. Then in a few days, the problems suddenly start. Drinking untreated water from mountain streams is a lot like playing Russian roulette. Sooner or later the gun goes off.

FILTERS

There's really no excuse for going without a water filter: Handheld filters are getting more compact, lighter, easier to use, and often less expensive. Having to boil water or endure chemicals that leave a bad taste in the mouth has been all but eliminated.

With a filter, you just pump and drink. Filtering strains out microscopic contaminants, rendering the water clear and somewhat pure. How pure? That depends on the size of the filter's pores—what manufacturers call pore-size efficiency. A filter with a pore-size efficiency

of one micron or smaller will remove protozoa, such as *Giardia lamblia* and cryptosporidium, as well as parasitic eggs and larva, but it takes a pore-size efficiency of less than 0.4 micron to remove bacteria. All but one of the filters recommended here do that.

A good backcountry water filter weighs less than 20 ounces, is easy to grasp, simple to use, and a snap to clean and maintain. At the very least, buy one that will remove protozoa and bacteria. (A number of cheap, pocket-sized filters remove only *Giardia lamblia* and cryptosporidium. That, in my book, is risking your health to save money.) Consider the flow rate, too: A liter per minute is good.

All filters will eventually clog—it's a sign that they've been doing their job. If you force water through a filter that's becoming difficult to pump, you risk injecting a load of microbial nasties into your bottle. Some models can be back-washed, brushed, or, as with ceramic elements, scrubbed to extend their useful lives. And if the filter has a pre-filter to screen out the big stuff, use it: It will give your filter a boost in mileage, which can then top out at about 100 gallons per disposable element. Any of the filters reviewed here will serve well on an outing into the wilds, providing you always play by the manufacturer's rules. They cost about $35–75, up to more than $200, depending on the volume of water they are constructed to filter.

• **Basic Designs Ceramic:** The Basic Designs Ceramic Filter Pump weighs eight ounces and is as stripped-down a filter as you'll find. The pump is simple, easy to use, and quite reliable. The ceramic filter effectively removes protozoa and bacteria, making it ideal and cost effective for backpacking—but it won't protect against viruses. Also, the filter element is too bulbous to work directly from a shallow water source; as with the PentaPure, you'll have to decontaminate a pot, cup, or bottle to transfer your unfiltered water. It's a great buy, though, for anyone worried only about *Giardia lamblia* and cryptosporidium.

• **First Need Deluxe:** The 15-ounce First Need

Water filters are a wise investment since all wilderness water should be considered contaminated. Make sure the filter can be easily cleaned or has a replaceable cartridge. The filter pores must be 0.4 micron or less to remove bacteria.

Deluxe from General Ecology does something no other handheld filter will do: It removes protozoa, bacteria, and viruses without using chemicals. Such effectiveness is the result of a fancy three-stage matrix system. Unfortunately, if you drop the filter and unknowingly crack the cartridge, all the little nasties can get through. General Ecology's solution is to include a bottle of blue dye that indicates breaks. The issue hasn't scared off too many folks, though: The First Need has been around since 1982. Additional cartridges cost $30. A final note: The filter pumps smoothly and puts out more than a liter per minute. A favorite of mine.

• **Katadyn U.S.A. Mini Filter:** The Mini Filter is a much more compact version of Katadyn's venerable Pocket Filter. This one weighs just eight ounces, ideal for the minimalist backcountry traveler, and it effectively removes protozoa and bacteria. A palm-of-the-hand-size filter, however, makes it challenging to put any kind of power behind the pump's tiny handle, and the filtered water comes through at a paltry half-liter per minute. It also requires more cleaning than most filters—though the

good news is that the element is made of long-lasting ceramic. Ironically, one option lets you buy the Mini Filter with a carbon element instead of the ceramic. The pumping is easier, the flow rate is better, and the price is way down ($99), but I'd only go that route if you'll be pumping from clear mountain streams.

• **MSR MiniWorks:** Like the WalkAbout, the bargain-priced MiniWorks has a bigger and more expensive water-filtering brother. But in this case, the differences are harder to discern: The new 14.3-ounce MiniWorks looks similar to the $140 WaterWorks II and, like the WaterWorks, is fully field-maintainable, while guarding against protozoa, bacteria, and chemicals. But the Mini is the best-executed, easiest-to-use ceramic filter on the market, and it attaches directly to a standard one-quart Nalgene water bottle. Too bad it takes 90 seconds to filter that quart.

• **MSR WaterWorks II Ceramic:** At 17.4 ounces, the WaterWorks II isn't light, but for the same price as the Katadyn, you get a better flow rate (90 seconds per liter), an easy pumping action, and—like the original Mini Filter—a long-lasting ceramic cartridge. This filter is a good match for the person who encounters a lot of dirty water—its three-stage filter weeds out protozoa, bacteria, and chemicals—and is mechanically inclined. The MSR can be completely disassembled in the field for troubleshooting and cleaning. (If you're not so mechanically endowed, take the filter apart at home only, as the potential for confusion is somewhat high.) By the way, the company has corrected the clogging problem that plagued a previous version of the WaterWorks.

• **PentaPure Oasis:** The PentaPure Oasis Water Purification System from WTC/Ecomaster offers drinkable water with a twist: You squeeze and sip instead of pumping. Weighing 6.5 ounces, the system packages a three-stage filter inside a 21-ounce-capacity sport bottle with an angled and sealing drinking nozzle, ideal for mountain bikers. The filter removes and/or kills protozoa, bacteria, and viruses, so it's also suitable for world travel. It's certainly convenient: Just fill the bottle with untreated water, screw on the cap, give it a firm squeeze (don't expect the easy flow of a normal sport bottle; there's more work being done), and sip. The Oasis only runs into trouble if the water source is shallow; you'll need a cup for scooping.

• **PUR Explorer:** The Explorer offers protection from all the bad guys—viruses as well as protozoa and bacteria—by incorporating an iodine matrix into the filtration process. An optional carbon cartridge ($20) neutralizes the iodine's noxious taste. The Explorer is also considered a trusty veteran among water filters because of its smooth pumping action and nifty back-washing feature: With a quick twist, the device switches from filtering mode to self-cleaning mode. It may be on the heavy side (20 ounces) and somewhat pricey, but the Explorer works very well on iffy water anywhere.

• **SweetWater WalkAbout:** The WalkAbout is perfect for the day hiker or backpacker who obsesses on lightening the load. The filter weighs just 8.5 ounces, is easily cleaned in the field, and removes both protozoa and bacteria:

a genuine bargain. There are some trade-offs, however, for its diminutiveness. Water delivery is a tad slow at just under a liter per minute, but redesigned filter cartridges ($12.50) are now good for up to 100 gallons.

The big drawback with filters is that if you pump water from a mucky lake, the filter can clog in a few days. Therein lies the weakness. Once plugged up, it is useless, and you have to replace it or take your chances. One trick to extend the filter life is to fill your cook pot with water, let the sediment settle, then pump from there. As an insurance policy, always have a spare filter canister on hand.

BOILING WATER

Except for water filtration, this is the only treatment that you can use with complete confidence. According to the federal Parasitic Diseases Division, it takes a few minutes at a rolling boil to be certain you've killed *Giardia lamblia*. At high elevations, boil for 3–5 minutes. A side benefit is that you'll also kill other dangerous bacteria that live undetected in natural waters.

But to be honest, boiling water is a thorn for most people on backcountry trips. For one thing, if you boil water on an open fire, what should taste like crystal-pure mountain water tastes instead like a mouthful of warm ashes. If you don't have a campfire, it wastes stove fuel. And if you are thirsty *now,* forget it. The water takes hours to cool.

The only time boiling always makes sense, however, is when you are preparing dinner. The ash taste will disappear in whatever freeze-dried dinner, soup, or hot drink you make.

WATER-PURIFICATION PILLS

Pills are the preference for most backcountry campers, and this can get them in trouble. At just $3–8 per bottle, which can figure up to just a few cents per canteen, they do come cheap. In addition, they kill most of the bacteria, regardless of whether you use iodine crystals or potable aqua iodine tablets. The problem is they just don't always kill *Giardia lamblia,* and that is the one critter worth worrying about on your trip. That makes water-treatment pills unreliable and dangerous.

Another key element is the time factor. Depending on the water's temperature, organic content, and pH level, these pills can take a long time to do the job. A minimum wait of 20 minutes is advised. Most people don't like waiting that long, especially when they're hot and thirsty after a hike and thinking, "What the heck, the water looks fine."

And then there is the taste. On one trip, my water filter clogged and we had to use the iodine pills instead. It doesn't take long to get tired of iodine-tinged water. Mountain water should be one of the greatest tasting beverages of the world, but the iodine kills that.

No Treatment

This is your last resort and, using extreme care, can be executed with success. One of my best hiking buddies, Michael Furniss, is a nationally renowned hydrologist, and on wilderness trips he has shown me the difference between safe and dangerous water sources.

Long ago, people believed that just finding water running over a rock was a guarantee of its purity. Imagine that. What we've learned is that the safe water sources are almost always small springs in high, craggy mountain areas. The key is making sure no one has been upstream from where you drink. We drink untreated water only when we can see the source, such as a spring.

Furniss mentioned that another potential problem in bypassing water treatment is that even in settings free of *Giardia lamblia,* you can still ingest other bacteria that cause stomach problems.

Hypothermia

No matter how well planned your trip might be, a sudden change in weather can turn it into a puzzle for which there are few answers. Bad weather or an accident can set in motion a dangerous chain of events.

Such a chain of episodes occurred for my brother Rambob and me on a fishing trip one fall day just below the snow line. The weather had suddenly turned very cold, and ice was forming along the shore of the lake. Suddenly, the canoe became terribly imbalanced, and, just that quickly, it flipped. The little life vest seat cushions were useless, and using the canoe as a paddleboard, we tried to kick our way back to shore where my dad was going crazy at the thought of his two sons drowning before his eyes.

It took 17 minutes in that 38-degree water, but we finally made it to shore. When they pulled me out of the water, my legs were dead, not strong enough even to hold up my weight. In fact, I didn't feel so much cold as tired, and I just wanted to lie down and go to sleep.

I closed my eyes, and my brother-in-law, Lloyd Angal, slapped me in the face several times, then got me on my feet and pushed and pulled me about.

In the celebration over our making it to shore, only Lloyd had realized that hypothermia was setting in. Hypothermia is the condition in which the temperature of the body is lowered to the point that it causes poor reasoning, apathy, and collapse. It can look like the afflicted person is just tired and needs to sleep, but that sleep can be the first step toward a coma.

Ultimately, my brother and I shared what little dry clothing remained. Then we began hiking around to get muscle movement, creating internal warmth. We ate whatever munchies were available because the body produces heat by digestion. But most important, we got our heads as dry as possible. More body heat is lost through wet hair than any other single factor.

A few hours later, we were in a pizza parlor replaying the incident, talking about how only a life vest can do the job of a life vest. We decided never again to rely on those little flotation seat cushions that disappear when the boat flips.

We had done everything right to prevent

hypothermia: Don't go to sleep, start a physical activity, induce shivering, put dry clothes on, dry your head, and eat something. That's how you fight hypothermia. In a dangerous situation, whether you fall in a lake or a stream or get caught unprepared in a storm, that's how you can stay alive.

After being in that ice-bordered lake for almost 20 minutes and then finally pulling ourselves to the shoreline, we discovered a strange thing. My canoe was flipped rightside up and almost all of its contents were lost: tackle box, flotation cushions, and cooler. But remaining were one paddle and one fishing rod, the trout rod my grandfather had given me for my 12th birthday.

Lloyd gave me a smile. "This means that you are meant to paddle and fish again," he said with a laugh.

Getting Unlost

I could not have been more lost. There I was, a guy who is supposed to know about these things, transfixed by confusion, snow, and hoofprints from a big deer.

I discovered that it is actually quite easy to get lost. If you don't get your bearings, getting found is the difficult part. This occurred on a wilderness trip where I'd hiked in to a remote lake and then set up a base camp for a deer hunt.

"There are some giant bucks up on that rim," confided Mr. Furnai, who lives near the area. "But it takes a mountain man to even get close to them."

That was a challenge I answered. After four-wheeling it to the trailhead, I tromped off with pack and rifle, gut-thumped it up 100 switchbacks over the rim, then followed a creek drainage up to a small but beautiful lake. The area was stark and nearly treeless, with bald granite broken only by large boulders. To keep from getting lost, I marked my route with piles of small rocks to act as directional signs for the return trip.

But at daybreak the next day, I stuck my head out of my tent and found eight inches of snow on the ground. I looked up into a gray sky filled by huge, cascading snowflakes. Visibility was about 50 yards, with fog on the mountain rim. "I better get out of here and get back to my truck," I said to myself. "If my truck gets buried at the trailhead, I'll never get out."

After packing quickly, I started down the mountain. But after 20 minutes, I began to get disoriented. You see, all the little piles of rocks I'd stacked to mark the way were now buried in snow, and I had only a smooth white blanket of snow to guide me. Everything looked the same, and it was snowing even harder now.

Five minutes later, I started chewing on some jerky to keep warm, then suddenly stopped. Where was I? Where was the creek drainage? Isn't this where I was supposed to cross over a creek and start the switchbacks down the mountain?

Right then, I looked down and saw the tracks of a huge deer, the kind Mr. Furnai had talked about. What a predicament: I was lost and snowed in and seeing big hoofprints in the snow. Part of me wanted to abandon all safety and go after that deer, but a little voice in the back of my head won out. "Treat this as an emergency," it said.

The first step in any predicament is to secure your present situation, that is, to make sure it does not get any worse. I unloaded my rifle (too easy to slip, fall, and have a misfire), took stock of my food (three days' worth), camp fuel (plenty), and clothes (rain gear keeping me dry). Then I wondered, "Where the hell am I?"

I took out my map, compass, and altimeter, then opened the map and laid it on the snow. It immediately began collecting snowflakes. I set the compass atop the map and oriented it to north. Because of the fog, there was no way to spot landmarks, such as prominent mountaintops, to verify my position. Then I checked the altimeter, which read 4,900 feet. Well, the elevation at my lake was 5,320 feet. That was critical information.

HIGHEST POINT

SHEER CLIFF

80
70
60
50
40
30
20
10
0

BRUSH
OR FOREST

BEACH

RIDGE ENDS
IN CLIFF
(Vs point down)

STREAM
RUNNING DOWNHILL
TO SEA
(Vs point up)

The **topographical map** is easier to read than many believe. Lines close together mean steep gradients; lines farther apart mean gentle gradients; V-shaped sets of lines pointing to higher elevations mean gulleys or stream-beds; V-shaped sets of lines pointing to lower elevations mean ridges.

I scanned the elevation lines on the map and was able to trace the approximate area of my position, somewhere downstream from the lake, yet close to a 4,900-foot elevation. "Right here," I said, pointing to a spot on the map with my finger. "I should pick up the switch-back trail down the mountain somewhere off to the left, maybe just 40 or 50 yards away."

Slowly and deliberately, I pushed through the light, powdered snow. In five minutes, I suddenly stopped. To the left, across a 10-foot depression in the snow, appeared a flat spot that veered off to the right. "That's it! That's the crossing."

In minutes, I was working down the switch-backs, on my way, no longer lost. I thought of the hoofprints I had seen, and now that I knew my position, I wanted to head back and spend the day hunting. Then I looked up at the sky, saw it filled with falling snowflakes, and en-visioned my truck buried deep in snow. Alas, this time logic won out over dreams.

In a few hours, now trudging through more than a foot of snow, I was at my truck at a spot called Doe Flat, and next to it was a giant, all-terrain U.S. Forest Service vehicle and two rangers.

"Need any help?" I asked them.

They just laughed. "We're here to help you," one answered. "It's a good thing you filed a trip plan with our district office in Gasquet. We wouldn't have known you were out here."

"Winter has arrived," said the other. "If we don't get your truck out now, it will be stuck here until next spring. If we hadn't found you, you might have been here until the end of time."

They connected a chain from the rear axle of their giant rig to the front axle of my truck and started towing me out, back to civiliza-tion. On the way to pavement, I figured I had gotten some of the more important lessons of my life. Always file a trip plan and have plenty of food, fuel, and a camp stove you can rely on. Make sure your clothes, weather gear, sleeping bag, and tent will keep you dry and warm. Always carry a compass, altimeter, and map with elevation lines, and know how to use them, practicing in good weather to get the feel of it.

To keep from getting lost (above tree line or in sparse vegetation), mark your route with **trail ducks,** small piles of rock that act as directional signs for the return trip.

And if you get lost and see the hoofprints of a giant deer, well, there are times when it is best to pass them by.

CATCHING FISH, AVOIDING BEARS, AND HAVING FUN

Feet tired and hot, stomachs growling, we stopped our hike for lunch beside a beautiful little river pool that was catching the flows from a long but gentle waterfall. My brother Rambob passed me a piece of jerky. I took my boots off, then slowly dunked my feet into the cool, foaming water.

I was gazing at a towering peak across a canyon when suddenly, Wham! There was a quick jolt at the heel of my right foot. I pulled my foot out of the water to find that, incredibly, a trout had bitten it.

My brother looked at me as if I had antlers growing out of my head. "Wow!" he exclaimed. "That trout almost caught himself an outdoors writer!"

It's true that in remote areas trout sometimes bite on almost anything, even feet. On one high-country trip, I caught limits of trout using nothing but a bare hook. The only problem is that the fish will often hit the splitshot sinker instead of the hook. Of course, fishing isn't usually that easy. But it gives you an idea of what is possible.

America's wildlands are home to a remarkable abundance of fish and wildlife. Deer browse with little fear of man, bears keep an eye out for your food, and little critters, such as squirrels and chipmunks, are daily companions. Add in the fishing, and you've got yourself a camping trip.

Your camping adventures will evolve into premium outdoor experiences if you can work in a few good fishing trips, avoid bear problems, and occasionally add a little offbeat fun with some camp games.

Trout and Bass

He creeps up on the stream as quietly as an Indian scout, keeping his shadow off the water. With his little spinning rod he'll zip his lure within an inch or two of its desired mark, probing along rocks, the edges of riffles, pocket water, or wherever he can find a change in river habitat. Rambob is trout fishing, and he's a master at it.

In most cases, he'll catch a trout on his first or second cast. After that, it's time to move up the river, giving no spot much more than five minutes' due. Stick and move, stick and move, stalking the stream like a bobcat zeroing in on an unsuspecting rabbit. He might keep a few trout for dinner, but mostly he releases what he catches. Rambob doesn't necessarily fish for food. It's the feeling that comes with it.

You don't need a million dollars' worth of fancy gear to catch fish. What you need is the right outlook, and that can be learned. That goes regardless of whether you are fishing for trout or bass, the two most popular fisheries in the United States. Your fishing tackle selection should be as simple and clutter-free as possible.

At home, I've got every piece of fishing tackle you might imagine, more than 30 rods and many tackle boxes, racks and cabinets filled with all kinds of stuff. I've got one lure that looks like a chipmunk and another that resembles a miniature can of beer with hooks. If I hear of something new, I want to try it and usually do. It's a result of my lifelong fascination with the sport.

But if you just want to catch fish, there's an easier way to go. And when I go fishing, I take that path. I don't try to bring everything. It would be impossible. Instead, I bring a relatively small amount of gear. At home, I scan my tackle boxes for equipment and lures, make my selections, and bring just the essentials. Rod, reel, and tackle will fit into a side pocket of my backpack or a small carrying bag.

So what kind of rod should be used on an outdoor trip? For most camper/anglers, I suggest the use of a light, multipiece spinning rod that will break down to a small size. The lowest-priced, quality six-piece rod on the market is the Daiwa 6.5-foot pack rod, number 6752, which is made of a graphite/glass composite that gives it the quality of a much more expensive model. And it comes in a hard plastic carrying tube for protection. Other major rod manufacturers, such as Fenwick, offer similar premium rods. It's tough to miss with any of them.

The use of graphite/glass composites in fishing rods has made them lighter and more sensitive, yet stronger. The only downside to graphite as a rod material is that it can be brittle. If you rap your rod against something, it can crack or cause a weak spot. That weak spot can eventually snap under even light pressure, like setting a hook or casting. Of course, a bit of care will prevent that from ever occurring.

If you haven't bought a fishing reel in some time, you will be surprised at the quality and price of micro spinning reels on the market. The reels come tiny and strong, with rear-control drag systems. Among others, Abu, Cardinal, Shimano, Sigma all make premium reels. They're worth it. With your purchase, you've just bought a reel that will last for years and years.

The one downside to spinning reels is that after long-term use, the bail spring will weaken. As a result, after casting and beginning to reel, the bail will sometimes not flip over and allow the reel to retrieve the line. Then you have to do it by hand. This can be incredibly frustrating, particularly when stream fishing, where instant line pickup is essential. The solution is to have a new bail spring installed every few years. This is a cheap, quick operation for a tackle expert.

You might own a giant tackle box filled with lures but, on your fishing trip, you are better off to fit just the essentials into a small container. One of the best ways to do that is to use the Plano Micro-Magnum 3414, a tiny two-sided tackle box for trout anglers that fits into a shirt pocket. In mine, I can fit 20 lures in one side of the box and 20 flies, splitshot, and snap swivels in the other. For bass lures, which are bigger, you need a slightly larger box, but the same principle applies.

There are more fishing lures on the market than you can imagine, but a few special ones can do the job. I make sure these are in my box on every trip. For trout, I carry a small black Panther Martin spinner with yellow spots, a small gold Kastmaster, a yellow Roostertail, a gold Z-Ray with red spots, a Super Duper, and a Mepps Lightning spinner.

You can take it a step further using insider's wisdom. My old pal Ed "the Dunk" showed me his trick of taking a tiny Dardevle spoon, spray painting it flat black, and dabbing five tiny red dots on it. It's a real killer, particularly in tiny streams where the trout are spooky.

The best trout catcher I've ever used on rivers is a small metal lure called a Met-L Fly. On days when nothing else works, it can be like going to a shooting gallery. The problem is that the lure is nearly impossible to find. Rambob and I consider the few we have remaining so valuable that if the lure is snagged on a rock, a cold swim is deemed mandatory for its retrieval. These lures are as hard to find in tackle shops as trout can be to catch without one.

For bass, you can also fit all you need into a small plastic tackle box. I have fished with many bass pros, and all of them actually use just a few lures: a white spinner bait, a small jig called a Gits-It, a surface plug called a Zara Spook, and plastic worms. At times, like when the bass move into shoreline areas during the spring, shad minnow imitations like those made by Rebel or Rapala can be dynamite. My favorite is the one-inch, blue-silver Rapala. Every spring as the lakes

begin to warm and the fish snap out of their winter doldrums, I like to float and paddle around in my small raft. I'll cast that little Rapala along the shoreline and catch and release hundreds of bass, bluegill, and sunfish. The fish are usually sitting close to the shoreline, awaiting my offering.

Fishing Tips

There's an old angler's joke about how you need to think like a fish. But if you're the one getting zilched, you may not think it's so funny.

The irony is that it is your mental approach, what you see and what you miss, that often determines your fishing luck. Some people will spend a lot of money on tackle, lures, and fishing clothes, and that

Basic Steps to Cleaning a Fish: First, slit belly from anal vent to gills. Then sever lower junctions of gills. Next, pull out innards and gills. And last but not least, run thumbnail along cavity to clean out dark matter.

done, just saunter up to a stream or lake, cast out, and wonder why they are not catching fish. The answer is their mental outlook. They are not attuning themselves to their surroundings.

You must live on nature's level, not your own. Try this and you will become aware of things you never believed even existed. Soon you will see things that will allow you to catch fish. You can get a head start by reading about fishing, but to get your degree in fishing, you must attend the University of Nature.

On every fishing trip, regardless of what you fish for, try to follow three hard-and-fast rules:
1. Always approach the fishing spot so you will be undetected.
2. Present your lure, fly, or bait in a manner so it appears completely natural, as if no line was attached.
3. Stick and move, hitting one spot, working it the best you can, then moving to the next.

APPROACH

No one can just walk up to a stream or lake, cast out, and start catching fish as if someone had waved a magic wand. Instead, give the fish credit for being smart. After all, they live there.

Your approach must be completely undetected by the fish. Fish can sense your presence through sight and sound, though these factors are misinterpreted by most people. By sight, fish rarely actually see you; more often, they see your shadow on the water or the movement of your arm or rod while casting. By sound, they don't necessarily hear you talking, but they do detect the vibrations of your footsteps along the shore, a rock being kicked, or the unnatural plunking sound of a heavy cast hitting the water. Any of these elements can spook them off the bite. In order to fish undetected, you must walk softly, keep your shadow off the water, and keep your casting motion low. All of these key elements become easier at sunrise or sunset, when shadows are

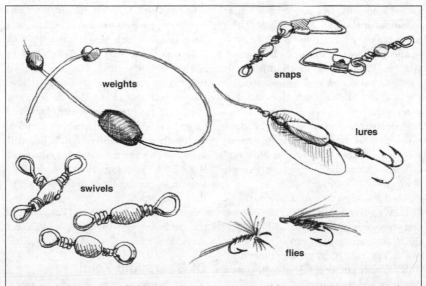

While camping, the only **fishing tackle** you should bring is the essentials: several varying weights, about 20 lures, and about 20 flies, splitshot, and snap swivels. These should all fit into a container just bigger than a deck of cards.

on the water. At midday, the sun is at its peak, causing a high level of light penetration in the water. This can make the fish skittish to any foreign presence.

Like a hunter, you must stalk the spots. When my brother Rambob sneaks up on a fishing spot, he is like a burglar sneaking through an unlocked window.

Presentation

Your lure, fly, or bait must appear in the water as if no line were attached, so it looks as natural as possible. My pal Mo Furniss has skin-dived in rivers to watch what the fish see when somebody is fishing.

"You wouldn't believe it," he said. "When the lure hits the water, every trout within 40 feet, like 15, 20 trout, will do a little zigzag. They all see the lure and are aware something is going on. Meanwhile, onshore the guy casting doesn't get a bite and thinks there aren't any fish in the river."

If your offering is aimed at fooling a fish into striking, it must appear as part of the natural habitat, like an insect just hatching or a small fish looking for a spot to hide. That's where you come in.

After you have sneaked up on a fishing spot, you should zip your cast upstream and start your retrieval as soon as it hits the water. If you let the lure sink to the bottom and then start the retrieval, you have no chance. A minnow, for instance, does not sink to the bottom, then start swimming. On rivers, the retrieval should be more of a drift, as if the "minnow" is in trouble and the current is sweeping it downstream.

When fishing on trout streams, always hike and cast upriver and retrieve as the offering drifts downstream in the current. This is effective because trout will sit almost motionless, pointed upstream, finning against the current. This way, they can see anything coming their direction, and if a potential food morsel arrives, all they need to do is move over a few inches, open their mouths, and they've got an easy lunch. Thus, you must cast upstream.

Conversely, if you cast downstream, your retrieval will bring the lure from behind the fish, where he cannot see it approaching. And I've never seen a trout that had eyes in its tail. In addition, when retrieving a downstream lure, the river current will tend to sweep your lure inshore to the rocks.

Finding Spots

A lot of anglers don't catch fish, and a lot of hikers never see any wildlife. The key is where they are looking.

The rule of the wild is that fish and wildlife will congregate wherever there is a distinct change in the habitat. This is where you should begin your search. To find deer, for instance, forget probing a thick forest, but look for where it breaks into a meadow or a clear-cut has splayed a stand of trees. That's where the deer will be.

In a river, it can be where a riffle pours into a small pool, a rapid plunges into a deep hole and flattens, a big boulder in the middle of a long riffle, a shoreline point, a rock pile, a submerged tree. Look for the changes. Conversely, long, straight stretches of shoreline will not hold fish—the habitat is lousy.

On rivers, the most productive areas are often where short riffles tumble into small oxygenated pools. After sneaking up from the downstream side and staying low, you should zip your cast so the lure plops gently into the white water just above the pool. Start your retrieval instantly; the lure will drift downstream and plunk into the pool. Bang! That's where the trout will hit. Take a few more casts and then head upstream to the next spot.

With a careful approach and lure presentation and by fishing in the right spots, you have the ticket to many exciting days on the water.

Of Bears and Food

The first time you come nose-to-nose with a bear can make your skin quiver.

Even the sight of mild-mannered black bears, the most common bear in America,

The rule of the wild is that wildlife will congregate wherever there is a distinct change in habitat. To find where fish are hiding, look where a riffle pours into a small pond, where a rapid plunges into a deep hole and flattens, and around submerged trees, rock piles, and boulders in the middle of a long riffle.

minimum 10 feet

minimum diameter
1 inch

minimum diameter
4 inch

heavy stick

minimum 22 feet to ground

minimum 20 feet to food bags

food wrapped in
plastic bags

In an area frequented by bears, a good **bear-proof food hang** is a must. Food should be stored in a plastic bag 10 feet from the trunk of the tree and at least 20 feet from the ground.

can send shock waves through your body. They weigh 250–400 pounds and have large claws and teeth that are made to scare campers. When they bound, the muscles on their shoulders roll like ocean breakers.

Bears in camping areas are accustomed to sharing the mountains with hikers and campers. They have become specialists in the food-raiding business. As a result, you must be able to bear-proof your camp or be able to scare the fellow off. Many campgrounds provide bear- and raccoon-proof food lockers. In most wilderness areas, bear-proof food canisters are required. Never leave your food or trash in your car!

If you are staying at one of the backpack sites listed in this book, there will be no food lockers available. Your car will not be there, either. The solution is to make a bear-proof food hang, suspending all of your food wrapped in a plastic garbage bag from a rope in midair, 10 feet from the trunk of a tree and 20 feet off the ground. (Counterbalancing two bags with a rope thrown over a tree limb is very effective, but finding an appropriate limb can be difficult.)

The food hang is accomplished by tying a rock to a rope, then throwing it over a high but sturdy tree limb. Next, tie your food bag to the rope and hoist it in the air. When you are satisfied with the position of the food bag, tie off the end of the rope to

GRIZZLY BEAR TERRITORY

If you are hiking in a wilderness area in Canada or Alaska that may have grizzlies, it is necessary to wear bells on your pack (grizzlies are not a problem in California, but you do not want to attract the native bears either). That way the bear will hear you coming and likely get out of your way. Keep talking, singing, or maybe even debating the country's foreign policy, but do not fall into a silent hiking vigil. And if a breeze is blowing in your face, you must make even more noise (a good excuse to rant and rave about the government's domestic affairs). Noise is important because your smell will not be carried in the direction you are hiking. As a result, the bear will not smell you coming.

If a bear can hear you and smell you, it will tend to get out of the way and let you pass without your knowing it was even close by. The exceptions are if you are carrying fish or lots of sweets in your pack or if you are wearing heavy, sweet deodorants or makeup. All of these are bear attractants.

another tree. In an area frequented by bears, a good food bag is a necessity—nothing else will do.

I've been there. On one trip, my pal Foonsky and my brother Rambob left to fish. I was stoking up an evening campfire when I felt the eyes of an intruder on my back. I turned around and saw a big bear heading straight for our camp. In the next half hour, I scared the bear off twice, but then he got a whiff of something sweet in my brother's pack.

The bear rolled into camp like a truck, grabbed the pack, ripped it open, and plucked out the Tang and the Swiss Miss. The 350-pounder then sat astride a nearby log and lapped at the goodies like a thirsty dog drinking water.

Once a bear gets his mitts on your gear, he considers it his. I took two steps toward the pack, and that bear jumped off the log and galloped across the camp right at me. Scientists say a man can't outrun a bear, but they've never seen how fast I can go up a granite block with a bear on my tail.

Shortly thereafter, Foonsky returned to find me perched on top of the rock and demanded to know how I could let a bear get our Tang. It took all three of us, Foonsky, Rambob, and me, charging at once and shouting like madmen, to clear the bear out of camp and send him off over the ridge. We learned never to let food sit unattended.

The Grizzly

When it comes to grizzlies, well, my friends, you need what we call an attitude adjustment. Or that big ol' bear may just decide to adjust your attitude for you, making your stay at the park a short one.

Grizzlies are nothing like black bears. They are bigger, stronger, have little fear, and take what they want. Some people believe there are many different species of this critter, such as Alaskan brown, silvertip, cinnamon, and Kodiak, but the truth is they are all grizzlies. Any difference in appearance has to do with diet, habitat, and life habits, not speciation. By any name, they all come big.

The first thing you must do is determine if there are grizzlies in the area where you are camping. That can usually be done by asking local rangers. If you are heading into Yellowstone or Glacier National Park, or the Bob Marshall Wilderness of Montana, well, you don't have to ask. They're out there, and they're the biggest and potentially most dangerous critters you could run into.

BLACK BEAR

No Hump

Straight Profile

3¾ in.   3½ in.

7 in.

Grizzly bears are distinguished from **black bears** by a pronounced shoulder hump and a concave facial profile. Grizzlies are generally brown and average 10 to 11 feet in length, while black bears (which can also be brown) attain lengths of five to seven feet.

Hump

Dish Face Profile

GRIZZLY BEAR

5½ in.   5¼ in.

9¾ in.

Note: Color of bears can't be used for identification.

One general way to figure the size of a bear is from his footprint. Take the width of the footprint in inches, add one to it, and you'll have an estimated length of the bear in feet. For instance, a nine-inch footprint equals a 10-foot bear. Any bear that big is a grizzly. In fact, most grizzly footprints average about 9–10 inches across, and black bears (though they may be brown in color) tend to have footprints only 4.5–6 inches across.

Most encounters with grizzlies occur when hikers fall into a silent march in the wilderness with the wind in their faces, and they walk around a corner and right into a big, unsuspecting grizzly. If you do this and see a big hump just behind its neck, don't think twice. It's a grizzly.

And then what should you do? Get up a tree, that's what. Grizzlies are so big that their claws cannot support their immense weight,

and thus they cannot climb trees. And although young grizzlies can climb, they rarely want to get their mitts on you.

If you do get grabbed, every instinct in your body will tell you to fight back. Don't believe it. Play dead. Go limp. Let the bear throw you around a little. After awhile, you'll become unexciting play material and the bear will get bored. My grandmother was grabbed by a grizzly in Glacier National Park and, after a few tosses and hugs, was finally left alone to escape.

Some say it's a good idea to tuck your head under his chin, since that way the bear will be unable to bite your head. I'll take a pass on that one. If you are taking action, any action, it's a signal that you are a force to be reckoned with, and he'll likely respond with more aggression. And bears don't lose many wrestling matches.

What grizzlies really like to do, believe it or not, is to pile a lot of sticks and leaves on you. Just let them, and keep perfectly still. Don't fight them; don't run. And when you have a 100 percent chance (not 98 or 99) to dash up a nearby tree, that's when you let fly. Once safely in a tree, you can hurl down insults and let your aggression out.

In a wilderness camp, there are special precautions you should take. Always hang your food at least 100 yards downwind of camp and get it high; 30 feet is reasonable. In addition, circle your camp with rope and hang the bells from your pack on it. Thus, if a bear walks into your camp, he'll run into the rope, the bells will ring, and everybody will have a chance to get up a tree before ol' griz figures out what's going on. Often, the unexpected ringing of bells is enough to send him off in search of a quieter environment.

You see, more often than not, grizzlies tend to clear the way for campers and hikers. So be smart, don't act like bear bait, and always have a plan if you are confronted by one.

My pal Foonsky had such a plan during a wilderness expedition in Montana's northern Rockies. On our second day of hiking, we started seeing scratch marks on the trees 13–14 feet off the ground.

"Mr. Griz made those," Foonsky said. "With spring here, the grizzlies are coming out of hibernation and using the trees like a cat uses a scratch board to stretch the muscles."

The next day, I noticed Foonsky had a pair of track shoes tied to the back of his pack. I just laughed.

"You're not going to outrun a griz," I said. "In fact, there's hardly any animal out here in the wilderness that man can outrun."

Foonsky just smiled.

"I don't have to outrun a griz," he said. "I just have to outrun you!"

Fun and Games

"Now what are we supposed to do?" the young boy asked his dad.

"Yeah, Dad, think of something," said another son.

Well, Dad thought hard. This was one of the first camping trips he'd taken with his sons and one of the first lessons he received was that kids don't appreciate the philosophic release of mountain quiet. They want action and lots of it. With a glint in his eye, Dad searched around the camp and picked up 15 twigs, breaking them so each was four inches long. He laid them in three separate rows, three twigs in one row, five twigs in another, and seven in the other.

"OK, this game is called 3-5-7," said Dad. "You each take turns picking up sticks. You are allowed to remove all or as few as one twig from a row, but here's the catch: You can pick only from one row per turn. Whoever picks up the last stick left is the loser."

I remember this episode well because those two little boys were my brother Bobby, as in Rambobby, and I. And to this day, we still play 3-5-7 on campouts, with the winner getting to watch the loser clean the dishes. What I have learned in the span of time since that original episode is that it does not matter what your age is: Campers need options for camp fun.

Some evenings, after a long hike or ride, you feel too worn out to take on a serious romp downstream to fish or a climb up to a ridge for a view. That is especially true if you have been in the outback for a week or more. At that point, a lot of campers will spend their time resting and gazing at a map of the area, dreaming of the next day's adventure, or just take a seat against a rock, watching the colors of the sky and mountain panorama change minute by minute. But kids in the push-button video era, and a lot of adults too, want more. After all, "I'm on vacation. I want some fun."

There are several options, such as the 3-5-7 twig game, and they should be just as much a part of your trip planning as arranging your gear.

For kids, plan on games, the more physically challenging the competition, the better. One of the best games is to throw a chunk of wood into a lake and challenge the kids to hit it by throwing rocks. It wreaks havoc on the fishing, but it can keep kids totally absorbed for some time. Target practice with a wrist-rocket slingshot—firing rocks at small targets, like pinecones set on a log—is also all-consuming for kids.

You can also set kids off on little missions near camp, such as looking for the footprints of wildlife, searching out good places to have a "snipe hunt," picking up twigs to get the evening fire started, or having them take the water purifier to a stream to pump some drinking water into a canteen. The latter is an easy, fun, yet important task that will allow kids to feel a sense of equality they often don't get at home.

For adults, the appeal should be more to the intellect. A good example is star and planet identification, and while you are staring into space, you're bound to spot a few asteroids or shooting stars. A star chart can make it easy to find and identify many distinctive stars and constellations, such as Pleiades (the Seven Sisters), Orion, and others from the zodiac, depending on the time of year. With a little research, this can add a unique perspective to your trip. You could point to Polaris, one of the most easily identified of all stars, and note that navigators in the 1400s used it to find their way. Polaris, of course, is the North Star and is at the end of the handle of the Little Dipper. Pinpointing Polaris is quite easy. First find the Big Dipper and then find the outside stars of the ladle of the Big Dipper. They are called the "pointer stars" because they point right at Polaris.

A tree identification book can teach you a few things about your surroundings. It is also a good idea for one member of the party to research the history of the area you have chosen and another to research the geology. With shared knowledge, you end up with a deeper love of wild places.

Another way to add some recreation into your trip is to bring a board game, a number of which have been miniaturized

for campers. The most popular are chess, checkers, and cribbage. The latter comes with an equally miniature set of playing cards. And if you bring those little cards, that opens a vast set of other possibilities. With kids along, for instance, just take three queens out of the deck and you can play Old Maid.

But there are more serious card games, and they come with high stakes. Such occurred on one high-country trip where Foonsky, Rambob, and I sat down for a late-afternoon game of poker. In a game of seven-card stud, I caught a straight on the sixth card and felt like a dog licking on a T-bone. Already, I had bet several Skittles and peanut M&Ms on this promising hand.

Then I examined the cards Foonsky had face up. He was showing three sevens, and acting as happy as a grizzly with a pork chop—or a full house. He matched my bet of two peanut M&Ms, then raised me three SweetTarts, one Starburst, and one sour apple Jolly Rancher. Rambob folded, but I matched Foonsky's bet and hoped for the best as the seventh and final card was dealt.

Just after Foonsky glanced at that last card, I saw him sneak a look at my grape stick and beef jerky stash.

"I raise you a grape stick," he said.

Rambob and I both gasped. It was the highest bet ever made, equivalent to a million dollars laid down in Las Vegas. Cannons were going off in my chest. I looked hard at my cards. They looked good, but were they good enough?

Even with a great hand like I had, a grape stick was too much to gamble, my last one with 10 days of trail ahead of us. I shook my head and folded my cards. Foonsky smiled at his victory.

But I still had my grape stick.

Old Tricks Don't Always Work

Most people are born honest, but after a few camping trips, they usually get over it.

KEEP IT WILD TIP 5: KEEP THE WILDERNESS WILD

1. Let nature's sound prevail. Avoid loud voices and noises.
2. Leave radios and tape players at home. At drive-in camping sites, never open car doors with music playing.
3. Careful guidance is necessary when choosing any games to bring for children. Most toys, especially any kind of gun toys with which children simulate shooting at each other, shouldn't be allowed on a camping trip.
4. Control pets at all times or leave them with a sitter at home.
5. Treat natural heritage with respect. Leave plants, rocks, and historical artifacts where you find them.

I remember some advice I got from Rambob, normally an honest soul, on one camping trip. A giant mosquito had landed on my arm and he alerted me to an expert bit of wisdom.

"Flex your arm muscles," he commanded, watching the mosquito fill with my blood. "He'll get stuck in your arm, then he'll explode."

For some reason, I believed him. We both proceeded to watch the mosquito drill countless holes in my arm.

Alas, the unknowing face sabotage from their most trusted companions on camping trips. It can arise at any time, usually in the form of advice from a friendly, honest-looking face, as if to say, "What? How can you doubt me?" After that mosquito episode, I was a little more skeptical of my dear old brother. Then the next day, when another mosquito was nailing me in the back of the neck, out came this gem:

"Hold your breath," he commanded. I instinctively obeyed. "That will freeze the mosquito," he said, "then you can squish him."

But in the time I wasted holding my breath, the little bugger was able to fly off without my having the satisfaction of squishing him. When he got home, he probably told his family, "What a dummy I got to drill today!"

Over the years, I have been duped numerous times with dubious advice:

On a grizzly bear attack: "If he grabs you, tuck your head under the grizzly's chin; then he won't be able to bite you in the head." This made sense to me until the first time I saw a nine-foot grizzly 40 yards away. In seconds, I was at the top of a tree, which suddenly seemed to make the most sense.

On coping with animal bites: "If a bear bites you in the arm, don't try to jerk it away. That will just rip up your arm. Instead, force your arm deeper into his mouth. He'll lose his grip and will have to open it to get a firmer hold, and right then you can get away." I was told this in the Boy Scouts. When I was 14, I had a chance to try it out when a friend's dog bit me as I tried to pet it. What happened? When I shoved my arm deeper into his mouth, he bit me three more times.

On cooking breakfast: "The bacon will curl up every time in a camp frying pan. So make sure you have a bacon stretcher to keep it flat." As a 12-year-old Tenderfoot, I spent two hours looking for the bacon stretcher until I figured out the camp leader had forgotten it. It wasn't for several years that I learned that there is no such thing.

On preventing sore muscles: "If you haven't hiked for a long time and you are facing a rough climb, you can keep from getting sore muscles in your legs, back, and shoulders by practicing the 'Dead Man's Walk.' Simply let your entire body go slack, and then take slow, wobbling steps. This will clear your muscles of lactic acid, which causes them to be so sore after a rough hike." Foonsky pulled this one on me. Rambob and I both bought it and tried it while we were hiking up Mount Whitney, which requires a 6,000-foot elevation gain in six miles. In one 45-minute period, about 30 other hikers passed us and looked at us as if we were suffering from some rare form of mental aberration.

Fish won't bite? No problem: "If the fish are not feeding or will not bite, persistent anglers can still catch dinner with little problem. Keep casting across the current, and eventually, as they hover in the stream, the line will feed across their open mouths. Keep reeling and you will hook the fish right in the side of the mouth. This technique is called 'lining.' Never worry if the fish will not bite, because you can always line 'em." Of course, heh, heh, heh, that explains why so many fish get hooked in the side of the mouth.

On keeping bears away: "To keep bears away, urinate around the borders of your campground. If there are a lot of bears in the area, it is advisable to go right on your sleeping bag." Yeah, surrrrrre.

On disposing of trash: "Don't worry about packing out trash. Just bury it. It will regenerate into the earth and add valuable minerals." Bears, raccoons, skunks, and other critters will dig up your trash as soon as you depart, leaving one huge mess for the next camper. Always pack out everything.

Often the advice comes without warning. That was the case after a fishing trip with a female companion, when she outcaught me two to one, the third such trip in a row. I explained this to a shopkeeper, and he nodded, then explained why.

"The male fish are able to detect the female scent on the lure, and thus become aroused into striking."

Of course! That explains everything!

Getting Revenge

I was just a lad when Foonsky pulled the old snipe-hunt trick on me. It took nearly 30 years to get revenge.

You probably know about snipe hunting. The victim is led out at night in the woods by a group, and then is left holding a bag.

"Stay perfectly still and quiet," Foonsky explained. "You don't want to scare the snipe. The rest of us will go back to camp and let the woods settle down. Then when the snipe are least expecting it, we'll form a line and charge through the forest with sticks, beating bushes and trees, and we'll flush the snipe out right to you. Be ready with the bag. When we flush the snipe out, bag it. But until we start our charge, make sure you don't move or make a sound or you will spook the snipe and ruin everything."

I sat out there in the woods with my bag for hours, waiting for the charge. I waited, waited, and waited. Nothing happened. No charge, no snipe. It wasn't until well past midnight that I figured something was wrong. When I finally returned to camp, everybody was sleeping.

Well, I tell ya, don't get mad at your pals for the tricks they pull on you. Get revenge. About 25 years later, on the last day of a camping trip, the time finally came.

"Let's break camp early," Foonsky suggested to Mr. Furnai and me. "Get up before dawn, eat breakfast, pack up, and be on the ridge to watch the sun come up. It will be a fantastic way to end the trip."

"Sounds great to me," I replied. But when Foonsky wasn't looking, I turned his alarm clock ahead three hours. So when the alarm sounded at the appointed 4:30 A.M. wake-up time, Mr. Furnai and I knew it was actually only 1:30 A.M.

Foonsky clambered out of his sleeping bag and whistled with a grin. "Time to break camp."

"You go ahead," I answered. "I'll skip breakfast so I can get a little more sleep. At the first sign of dawn, wake me up, and I'll break camp."

"Me, too," said Mr. Furnai.

Foonsky then proceeded to make some coffee, cook a breakfast, and eat it, sitting on a log in the black darkness of the forest, waiting for the sun to come up. An hour later, with still no sign of dawn, he checked his clock. It now read 5:30 A.M. "Any minute now we should start seeing some light," he said.

He made another cup of coffee, packed his gear, and sat there in the middle of the night, looking up at the stars, waiting for dawn. "Anytime now," he said. He ended up sitting there all night long.

Revenge is sweet. Before a fishing trip at a lake, I took Foonsky aside and explained that the third member of the party, Jimbobo, was hard of hearing and very sensitive about it. "Don't mention it to him," I advised. "Just talk real loud."

Meanwhile, I had already told Jimbobo the same thing. "Foonsky just can't hear very good."

We had fished less than 20 minutes when Foonsky got a nibble.

"GET A BITE?" shouted Jimbobo.

"YEAH!" yelled back Foonsky, smiling. "BUT I DIDN'T HOOK HIM!"

"MAYBE NEXT TIME!" shouted Jimbobo with a friendly grin.

Well, they spent the entire day yelling at each other from the distance of a few feet. They never did figure it out. Heh, heh, heh.

That is, I thought so, until we made a trip salmon fishing. I got a strike that almost knocked my fishing rod out of the boat. When I grabbed the rod, it felt as if Moby Dick were on the other end. "At least a 25-pounder," I said. "Maybe bigger."

The fish dove, ripped off line, and then bulldogged. "It's acting like a 40-pounder," I announced, "Huge, just huge. It's going deep. That's how the big ones fight."

Some 15 minutes later, I finally got the "salmon" to the surface. It turned out to be a coffee can that Foonsky had clipped on the line with a snap swivel. By maneuvering the boat, he made the coffee can fight like a big fish.

This all started with a little old snipe hunt years ago. You never know what your pals will try next. Don't get mad. Get revenge.

CAMPING OPTIONS
Boat-In Seclusion

Most campers would never think of trading in their cars, pickup trucks, or RVs for a boat, but people who go by boat on a camping trip enjoy virtually guaranteed seclusion and top-quality outdoor experiences.

Camping with a boat is a do-it-yourself venture in living under primitive circumstances. Yet at the same time, you can bring along any luxury item you wish, from giant coolers, stoves, and lanterns to portable gasoline generators. Weight is almost never an issue.

Many outstanding boat-in campgrounds in beautiful surroundings are available in California. The best are on the shores of lakes accessible by canoe or skiff, and at offshore islands reached by saltwater cruisers. Several boat-in camps are detailed in this book.

If you want to take the adventure a step further and create your own boat-in camp, perhaps near a special fishing spot, this is a go-for-it deal that provides the best way possible to establish your own secret campsite. But most people who set out freelance style forget three critical items for boat-in camping: a shovel, a sunshade, and an ax. Here is why these items can make a key difference in your trip:

• **Shovel:** Many lakes and virtually all reservoirs have steep, sloping banks. At reservoirs subject to drawdowns, what was lake bottom in the spring can be a campsite in late summer. If you want a flat area for a tent site, the only answer is to dig one out yourself. A shovel gives you that option.

• **Sunshade:** The flattest spots to camp along lakes often have a tendency to support only sparse tree growth. As a result, a natural shield from sun and rain is rarely available. What? Rain in the summer? Oh yeah, don't get me started. A light tarp, set up with poles and staked ropes, solves the problem.

• **Ax:** Unless you bring your own firewood, which is necessary at some sparsely wooded reservoirs, there is no substitute for a good, sharp ax. With an ax, you can almost always find dry firewood, since the interior of an otherwise wet log will be dry. When the weather turns bad is precisely when you will most want a fire. You may need an ax to get one going.

In the search to create your own personal boat-in campsite, you will find that the flattest areas are usually the tips of peninsulas and points, while the protected back ends of coves are often steeply sloped. At reservoirs, the flattest areas are usually near the mouths of the feeder streams and the points are quite steep. On rivers, there are usually sandbars on the inside of tight bends that make for ideal campsites.

Almost all boat-in campsites developed by government agencies are free of charge, but you are on your own. Only in extremely rare cases is piped water available.

Any way you go, by canoe, skiff, or power cruiser, you end up with a one-in-a-million campsite you can call your own.

Desert Outings

It was a cold, snowy day in Missouri when 10-year-old Rusty Ballinger started dreaming about the vast deserts of the West.

"My dad was reading aloud from a Zane Grey book called *Riders of the Purple Sage,*" Ballinger said. "He would get animated when he got to the passages about the desert. It wasn't long before I started to have the same feelings."

That was in 1947. Ballinger, now in his 60s, has spent a good part of his life exploring the West, camping along the way. "The deserts are the best part. There's something about the uniqueness of each little area you see," Ballinger said. "You're constantly surprised. Just the time of day and the way the sun casts a different color. It's like the lady you care about. One time she smiles, the next time she's pensive. The desert is like that. If you love nature, you can love the desert. After awhile, you can't help but love it."

A desert adventure is not just an antidote

for a case of cabin fever in the winter. Whether you go by RV, pickup truck, car, or on foot, it provides its own special qualities.

If you go camping in the desert, your approach has to be as unique as the setting. For starters, don't plan on any campfires, but bring a camp stove instead. And unlike in the mountains, do not camp near a water hole. That's because an animal, such as a badger, coyote, or desert bighorn, might be desperate for water, and if you set up camp in the animal's way, you may be forcing a confrontation.

In some areas, there is a danger of flash floods. An intense rain can fall in one area, collect in a pool, then suddenly burst through a narrow canyon. If you are in its path, you could be injured or drowned. The lesson? Never camp in a gully.

"Some people might wonder, 'What good is this place?'" Ballinger said. "The answer is that it is good for looking at. It is one of the world's unique places."

CAMP ETHICS AND POLITICS

The perfect place to set up a base camp turned out to be not so perfect. In fact, according to Doug Williams of California, it did not even exist.

Williams and his son, James, had driven deep into Angeles National Forest, prepared to set up camp and then explore the surrounding area on foot. But when they reached their destination, no campground existed.

"I wanted a primitive camp in a national forest where I could teach my son some basics," said the senior Williams. "But when we got there, there wasn't much left of the camp, and it had been closed. It was obvious that the area had been vandalized."

It turned out not to be an isolated incident. A lack of outdoor ethics practiced by a few people using the unsupervised campgrounds available on national forestland has caused the U.S. Forest Service to close a few of them and make extensive repairs to others.

food cache
(hang downwind)

escape tree

minimum 100 feet

minimum 100 feet

minimum 200 feet

6-8 inch "cat hole" for
depositing human waste

minimum 200 feet

In setting up camp, always be mindful of potential ecological disturbances. Pitch tents and dispose of human waste at least 200 feet from the water's edge. In grizzly bear territory, increase the distance between your tent and your cooking area, food-hang, and the water's edge threefold. In other words, if you're in grizzly country, do all your cooking 100 yards (not feet) downwind of your sleeping area. If you can establish an escape tree nearby, all the better.

"There have been sites closed, especially in Angeles and San Bernardino National Forests in Southern California," said David Flohr, regional campground coordinator for the U.S. Forest Service. "It's an urban type of thing, affecting forests near urban areas, and not just Los Angeles. They get a lot of urban users and they bring with them a lot of the same ethics they have in the city. They get drinking and they're not afraid to do things. They vandalize and run. Of course, it is a public facility, so they think nobody is getting hurt."

But somebody is getting hurt, starting with the next person who wants to use the campground. And if the ranger district budget doesn't have enough money to pay for repairs, the campground is then closed for the next arrivals. Just ask Doug and James Williams.

In an era of considerable fiscal restraint for the U.S. Forest Service, vandalized campgrounds could face closure instead of repair. Williams had just a taste of it, but Flohr, as camping coordinator, gets a steady diet.

"It starts with behavior," Flohr said. "General rowdiness, drinking, partying, and then vandalism. It goes all the way from the felt-tip pen things (graffiti) to total destruction, blowing up toilet buildings with dynamite. I have seen toilets destroyed totally with shotguns. They burn up tables, burn barriers. They'll burn up signs for firewood, even the shingles right off the roofs of the bathrooms. They'll shoot anything, garbage cans, signs. It can get a little hairy. A favorite is to remove the stool out of a toilet building. We've had people fall in the open hole."

The National Park Service had similar problems some years back, especially with rampant littering. Park Director Bill Mott responded by creating an interpretive program

KEEP IT WILD TIP 6: RESPECT OTHER USERS

1. Horseback riders have priority over hikers. Step to the downhill side of the trail and talk softly when encountering horseback riders.
2. Hikers and horseback riders have priority over mountain bikers. When mountain bikers encounter other users even on wide trails, they should pass at an extremely slow speed. On very narrow trails, they should dismount and get off to the side so hikers or horseback riders can pass without having their trip disrupted.
3. Mountain bikes aren't permitted on most single-track trails and are expressly prohibited in designated wilderness areas and all sections of the Pacific Crest Trail. Mountain bikers breaking these rules should be confronted and told to dismount and walk their bikes until they reach a legal area.
4. It's illegal for horseback riders to break off branches that may be in the path of wilderness trails.
5. Horseback riders on overnight trips are prohibited from camping in many areas and are usually required to keep stock animals in specific areas where they can do no damage to the landscape.

that attempts to teach visitors the wise use of natural areas, and to have all park workers set examples by picking up litter and reminding others to do the same.

The U.S. Forest Service has responded with a similar program, making brochures available that detail the wise use of national forests. The four most popular brochures are titled: "Rules for Visitors to the National Forest," "Recreation in the National Forests," "Is the Water Safe?" and "Backcountry Safety Tips." These include details on campfires, drinking water from lakes or streams, hypothermia, safety, and outdoor ethics. They are available free by writing to Public Affairs, U.S. Forest Service, 630 Sansome St., San Francisco, CA 94111.

Flohr said even experienced campers sometimes cross over the ethics line unintentionally. The most common example, he said, is when campers toss garbage into the outhouse toilet, rather than packing it out in a plastic garbage bag.

"They throw it in the vault toilet bowls, which just fills them up," Flohr said. "That creates an extremely high cost to pump it. You know why? Because some poor guy has to pick that stuff out piece by piece. It can't be pumped."

At most backcountry sites, the U.S. Forest Service has implemented a program called "Pack it in, pack it out," even posting signs that remind all visitors to do so. But a lot of people don't do it, and others may even uproot the signs and burn them for firewood.

On a trip to a secluded lake near Carson Pass in the Sierra Nevada, I arrived at a small, little-known camp where the picnic table had been spray painted and garbage had been strewn about. A pristine place, the true temple of God, had been defiled.

Getting Along with Fellow Campers

The most important thing about a camping, fishing, or hunting trip is not where you go, how many fish you catch, or how many shots you fire. It often has little to do with how beautiful the view is, how easily the campfire lights, or how sunny the days are.

Oh yeah? Then what is the most important factor? The answer: The people you are with. It is that simple.

Who would you rather camp with? Your enemy at work or your dream mate in a good mood? Heh, heh. You get the idea. A camping trip is a fairly close-knit experience, and you can make lifetime friends or lifelong enemies in the process. That is why your choice of companions is so important. Your own behavior is equally consequential.

Yet most people spend more time putting together their camping gear than considering why they enjoy or hate the company of their chosen companions. Here are 10 rules of behavior for good camping mates:

1. **No whining:** Nothing is more irritating than being around a whiner. It goes right to the heart of adventure, since often the only difference between a hardship and an escapade is simply whether or not an individual has the spirit for it. The people who do can turn a rugged day in the outdoors into a cherished memory. Those who don't can ruin it with their incessant sniveling.

2. **Activities must be agreed upon:** Always have a meeting of the minds with your companions over the general game plan. Then everybody will possess an equal stake in the outcome of the trip. This is absolutely critical. Otherwise they will feel like merely an addendum to your trip, not an equal participant, and a whiner will be born (see number one).

3. **Nobody's in charge:** It is impossible to be genuine friends if one person is always telling another what to do, especially if the orders involve simple camp tasks. You need to share the space on the same emotional plane, and the only way to do that is to have a semblance of equality, regardless of differences in experience. Just try ordering your mate around at home for a few days. You'll quickly see the results, and they aren't pretty.

4. **Equal chances at the fun stuff:** It's fun to build the fire, fun to get the first cast at the best fishing spot, and fun to hoist the bagged food for a bear-proof food hang. It is not fun to clean the dishes, collect firewood, or cook every night. So obviously, there must be an equal distribution of the fun stuff and the not-fun stuff, and everybody on the trip must get a shot at the good and the bad.

5. **No heroes:** No awards are bestowed for achievement in the outdoors, yet some guys treat mountain peaks, big fish, and big game as if they are prizes in a trophy competition. Actually, nobody cares how wonderful you are, which is always a surprise to trophy chasers. What people care about is the heart of the adventure, the gut-level stuff.

6. **Agree on a wake-up time:** It is a good idea to agree on a general wake-up time before closing your eyes for the night, and that goes regardless of whether you want to sleep in late or get up at dawn. Then you can proceed on course regardless of what time you crawl out of your sleeping bag in the morning, without the risk of whining (see number one).

7. **Think of the other guy:** Be self-aware instead of self-absorbed. A good test is to count the number of times you say, "What do you think?" A lot of potential problems can be solved quickly by actually listening to the answer.

8. **Solo responsibilities:** There are a number of essential camp duties on all trips, and while they should be shared equally, most should be completed solo. That means that when it is time for you to cook, you don't have to worry about me changing the recipe on you. It means that when it is my turn to make the fire, you keep your mitts out of it.

9. **Don't let money get in the way:** Of course everybody should share equally in trip expenses, such as the cost of food, and it should be split up before you head out yonder. Don't let somebody pay extra, because that person will likely try to control the trip. Conversely, don't let somebody weasel out of paying a fair share.

10. **Accordance on the food plan:** Always have complete agreement on what you plan to eat each day. Don't figure that just because you like Steamboat's Sludge, everybody else will, too, especially youngsters. Always, always, always check for food allergies, such as nuts, onions, or cheese, and make sure each person brings his or her own personal coffee brand. Some people drink only decaffeinated; others might gag on anything but Burma monkey beans.

Obviously, it is difficult to find companions who will agree on all of these elements. This is why many campers say that the best camping buddies they'll ever have are their mates, who know all about them and like them anyway.

OUTDOORS WITH KIDS

How do you get a youngster excited about the outdoors? How do you compete with the television and remote control? How do you prove to a kid that success comes from persistence, spirit, and logic, which the outdoors teaches, and not from pushing buttons?

The answer is in the Ten Camping Commandments for Kids. These are lessons that will get youngsters excited about the outdoors and that will make sure adults help the process along, not kill it. I've put this list together with the help of my own kids, Jeremy and Kris, and their mother, Stephani. Some of the commandments are obvious, some are not, but all are important:

1. Take children to places where there is a guarantee of action. A good example is camping in a park where large numbers of wildlife can be viewed, such as squirrels, chipmunks, deer, and even bears. Other good choices include fishing at a small pond loaded with bluegill or hunting in a spot where a kid can shoot a .22 at pinecones all day. Boys and girls want action, not solitude.

2. Enthusiasm is contagious. If you aren't excited about an adventure, you can't expect a child to be. Show a genuine zest for life in the outdoors, and point out everything as if it is the first time you have ever seen it.

3. Always, always, always be seated when talking to someone small. This allows the adult and child to be on the same level. That is why fishing in a small boat is perfect for adults and kids. Nothing is worse for youngsters than having a big person look down at them and give them orders. What fun is that?

4. Always *show* how to do something, whether it is gathering sticks for a campfire, cleaning a trout, or tying a knot. Never tell—always show. A button usually clicks to "off" when a kid is lectured. But kids can learn behavior patterns and outdoor skills by watching adults, even when the adults are not aware they are being watched.

5. Let kids be kids. Let the adventure happen, rather than trying to force it within some preconceived plan. If they get sidetracked watching pollywogs, chasing butterflies, or sneaking up on chipmunks, let them be. A youngster can have more fun turning over rocks and looking at different kinds of bugs than sitting in one spot, waiting for a fish to bite.

6. Expect short attention spans. Instead of getting frustrated about it, use it to your advantage. How? By bringing along a bag of candy and snacks. Where there is a lull in the camp activity, out comes the bag. Don't let them know what goodies await, so each one becomes a surprise.

7. Make absolutely certain the child's sleeping bag is clean, dry, and warm. Nothing is worse than discomfort when trying to sleep, but a refreshing sleep makes for a positive attitude the next day. In addition, kids can become quite scared of animals at night. A parent should not wait for any signs of this, but always play the part of the outdoor guardian, the one who will take care of everything.

8. Kids quickly relate to outdoor ethics. They will enjoy eating everything they kill, building a safe campfire, and picking up all their litter, and they will develop a sense of pride that goes with it. A good idea is to bring extra plastic garbage bags to pick up any trash you come across. Kids long remember when they do something right that somebody else has done wrong.

9. If you want youngsters hooked on the outdoors for life, take a close-up photograph of them holding up fish they have caught, blowing on the campfire, or completing other camp tasks. Young children can forget how much

fun they had, but they never forget if they have a picture of it.

10. The least important word you can ever say to a kid is "I." Keep track of how often you are saying "Thank you" and "What do you think?" If you don't say them very often, you'll lose out. Finally, the most important words of all are: "I am proud of you."

PREDICTING WEATHER

Foonsky climbed out of his sleeping bag, glanced at the nearby meadow, and scowled hard.

"It doesn't look good," he said. "Doesn't look good at all."

I looked at my adventure companion of 20 years, noting his discontent. Then I looked at the meadow and immediately understood why: *"When the grass is dry at morning light, look for rain before the night."*

"How bad you figure?" I asked him.

"We'll know soon enough, I reckon," Foonsky answered. *"Short notice, soon to pass. Long notice, long it will last."*

When you are out in the wild, spending your days fishing and your nights camping, you learn to rely on yourself to predict the weather. It can make or break you. If a storm hits the unprepared, it can quash the trip and possibly endanger the participants. But if you are ready, a potential hardship can be an adventure.

You can't rely on TV weather forecasters, people who don't even know that when all the cows on a hill are facing north, it will rain that night for sure. God forbid if the cows are all sitting. But what do you expect from TV's talking heads?

Foonsky made a campfire, started boiling some water for coffee and soup, and we started to plan the day. In the process, I noticed the smoke of the campfire: It was sluggish, drifting and hovering.

"You notice the smoke?" I asked, chewing on a piece of homemade jerky.

"Not good," Foonsky said. "Not good." He knew that sluggish, hovering smoke indicates rain.

"You'd think we'd have been smart enough to know last night that this was coming," Foonsky said. "Did you take a look at the moon or the clouds?"

"I didn't look at either," I answered. "Too busy eating the trout we caught." You see, if the moon is clear and white, the weather will be good the next day. But if there is a ring around the moon, the number of stars you can count inside the ring equals the number of days until the next rain. As for clouds, the high, thin ones—called cirrus—indicate a change in the weather.

We were quiet for a while, planning our strategy, but as we did so, some terrible things happened: A chipmunk scampered past with his tail high, a small flock of geese flew by very low, and a little sparrow perched on a tree limb quite close to the trunk.

"We're in for trouble," I told Foonsky.

"I know, I know," he answered. "I saw 'em, too. And come to think of it, no crickets were chirping last night either."

"Damn, that's right!"

These are all signs of an approaching storm. Foonsky pointed at the smoke of the campfire and shook his head as if he had just been condemned. Sure enough, now the smoke was blowing toward the north, a sign of a south wind. *"When the wind is from the south, the rain is in its mouth."*

"We'd best stay hunkered down until it passes," Foonsky said.

I nodded. "Let's gather as much firewood now as we can, get our gear covered up, then plan our meals."

"Then we'll get a poker game going."

As we accomplished these camp tasks, the sky clouded up, then darkened. Within an hour, we had gathered enough firewood to make a large pile, enough wood to keep a fire going no matter how hard it rained. The day's meals had been separated out of the food bag so it wouldn't have to be retrieved during the storm. We buttoned two ponchos together, staked two of the corners with ropes to the ground, and tied the other two with ropes to different tree limbs to create a slanted roof/shelter.

As the first raindrop fell with that magic sound on our poncho roof, Foonsky was just starting to shuffle the cards.

"Cut for deal," he said.

Just as I did so, it started to rain a bit harder. I pulled out another piece of beef jerky and started chewing on it. It was just another day in paradise.

Weather lore can be valuable. Here is the list I have compiled over the years:

When the grass is dry at morning light,
Look for rain before the night.

Short notice, soon to pass.
Long notice, long it will last.

When the wind is from the east,
Tis fit for neither man nor beast.

When the wind is from the south,
The rain is in its mouth.

When the wind is from the west,
Then it is the very best.

Red sky at night, sailors' delight.
Red sky in the morning, sailors take warning.

When all the cows are pointed north,
Within a day rain will come forth.

Onion skins very thin, mild winter coming in.
Onion skins very tough, winter's going to be very rough.

When your boots make the squeak of snow,
Then very cold temperatures will surely show.

If a goose flies high, fair weather ahead.
If a goose flies low, foul weather will come instead.

Small signs provided by nature and wildlife can also be translated to provide a variety of weather information:

• A thick coat on a woolly caterpillar means a big, early snow is coming.

• Chipmunks will run with their tails up before a rain.

• Bees always stay near their hives before a rainstorm.

• When the birds are perched on large limbs near tree trunks, an intense but short storm will arrive.

• On the coast, if groups of seabirds are flying a mile inland, look for major winds.

• If crickets are chirping very loudly during the evening, the next day will be clear and warm.

• If the smoke of a campfire at night rises in a thin spiral, good weather is assured for the next day.

• If the smoke of a campfire at night is sluggish, drifting and hovering, it will rain the next day.

• If there is a ring around the moon, count the number of stars inside the ring, and that is how many days until the next rain.

• If the moon is clear and white, the weather will be good the next day.

• High, thin clouds, or cirrus, indicate a change in the weather.

• Oval-shaped lenticular clouds indicate high winds.

• Two levels of clouds moving in different directions indicate changing weather soon.

• Huge, dark, billowing clouds, called cumulonimbus, suddenly forming on warm afternoons in the mountains mean that a

KEEP IT WILD TIP 7: PLAN AHEAD AND PREPARE

1. Learn about the regulations and issues that apply to the area you're visiting.
2. Avoid heavy-use areas.
3. Obtain all maps and permits.
4. Bring extra garbage bags to pack out any refuse you come across.

short but intense thunderstorm with lightning can be expected.

• When squirrels are busy gathering food for extended periods, it means good weather is ahead in the short term, but a hard winter is ahead in the long term.

And God forbid if all the cows are sitting down....

CAMPING GEAR CHECKLIST

Cooking Gear

- Camp stove and fuel
- Dish soap and scrubber
- Fire-starter cubes
- Heavy-duty paper plates
- Ice chest and drinks
- Itemized food, separated by groups
- Knife, fork, cup
- Large, heavy-duty garbage bags
- Matches stored in resealable (such as Ziploc) bags
- One lighter for each camper
- Paper towels
- Plastic spatula and stir spoon
- Pot grabber or pot holder
- Salt, pepper, spices
- Two pots and no-stick pan
- Water jug or lightweight plastic "cube"

Optional Cooking Gear
- Aluminum foil
- Ax or hatchet
- Barbecue tongs
- Can opener
- Candles
- Dustpan
- Grill or hibachi
- Plastic clothespins
- Tablecloth
- Whisk broom
- Wood or charcoal for barbecue

Clothing

- Cotton/canvas pants
- Gore-Tex parka or jacket
- Gore-Tex rain pants
- Lightweight, breathable shirt
- Lightweight fleece jacket
- Medium-weight fleece vest
- Polypropylene underwear
- Rain jacket and pants, or poncho
- Sunglasses
- Waterproofed, oilskin wide-brimmed hat

Optional Clothing
- Gloves
- Shorts
- Ski cap
- Swimsuit

Hiking Gear

- Backpack or daypack
- Hiking boots
- Fresh bootlaces
- Innersole or foot cushion (for expeditions)
- Moleskin and medical tape
- SmartWool (or equivalent) socks
- Water-purification system

Optional Hiking Gear
- Backup lightweight shoes or moccasins
- Gaiters
- Water-repellent boot treatment

Sleeping Gear

- Ground tarp
- Sleeping bag
- Tent or bivy bag
- Therm-a-Rest pad
- Air bed
- Cot
- Catalytic heater

Optional Sleeping Gear
- Air bed
- Cot
- Catalytic heater

- Foam pad for truck bed
- Mosquito netting
- Mr. Heater and propane tank (for use in pickup truck camper shell)
- Pillow (even in wilderness)
- RV windshield light screen
- Seam Lock for tent stitching

First Aid

- Ace bandage
- After-Bite for mosquito bites (before you scratch them)
- Aspirin
- Biodegradable soap
- Caladryl for poison oak
- Campho-Phenique gel for bites (after you scratch them)
- Mosquito repellent
- Lip balm
- Medical tape to affix pads
- Neosporin for cuts
- Roller gauze
- Sterile gauze pads
- Sunscreen
- Tweezers

Optional First Aid

- Athletic tape for sprained ankle
- Cell phone or coins for phone calls
- Extra set of matches
- Mirror for signaling
- Thermometer

Fishing/Recreation Gear

- All required permits and licenses
- Fishing reel with fresh line
- Fishing rod
- Knife
- Leatherman tool or needle-nose pliers
- Small tackle box with flies, floats, hooks, lures, snap swivels, and splitshot

Optional Recreation Gear

- Backpacking cribbage board
- Deck of cards
- Folding chairs
- Guidebooks
- Hammock
- Mountain bike
- Reading material

Other Necessities

- Duct tape
- Extra plastic garbage bags
- Flashlight and batteries
- Lantern and fuel
- Maps
- Nylon rope for food hang
- Spade for cat hole
- Toilet paper
- Toothbrush and toothpaste
- Towelettes
- Wristwatch

Other Optional Items

- Altimeter
- Assorted bungee cords
- Binoculars
- Camera with fresh battery and digital card or film
- Compass
- Feminine hygiene products
- GPS unit
- Handkerchief
- Notebook and pen

REDWOOD EMPIRE

BEST CAMPGROUNDS

《 Family Destinations
Prairie Creek Redwoods State Park, **pages**
  102-103

《 Boat-In Campgrounds
Stone Lagoon Boat-In, **page 104**

Visitors come from around the world to the Redwood
Empire for one reason: to see the groves of giant redwoods, the tallest trees in the
world. On a perfect day in the redwoods here, refracted sunlight beams through
the forest canopy, creating a solemn, cathedral-like effect. It feels as if you are
standing in the center of the earth's pure magic.

But the redwood forests are only one of the attractions to this area. The
Smith River canyon, Del Norte and Humboldt Coasts, and the remote edge of
the Siskiyou Wilderness in Six Rivers National Forest all make this region like
none other in the world.

On sunny days in late summer, some visitors are incredulous that so few
people live in the Redwood Empire. The reason is the same one that explains why
the trees grow so tall: rain in the winter – often for weeks at a time – and fog in
the summer. If the sun does manage to appear, it's an event almost worthy of
calling the police to say you've spotted a large, yellow Unidentified Flying Object.
So most folks are content to just visit.

Three stellar areas should be on your must-see list for outstanding days
of adventure here: the redwood parks from Trinidad to Klamath River, the Smith
River Recreation Area, and the Lost Coast.

I've hiked every trailhead from Trinidad to Crescent City and believe
that the hikes here feature some of the best adventuring day trips in Northern
California. A good place to start is Prairie Creek Redwoods State Park, where
you can see fantastic herds of Roosevelt elk. Then head over to the beach by
hiking Fern Canyon, where you walk for 20 minutes at the bottom of a canyon
adjacent to vertical walls covered with ferns, and then continue north on the
Coastal Trail, where you'll pass through pristine woodlands and fantastic ex-
panses of untouched beaches. All the trails through the redwoods north of the
Klamath River are winners; it's just a matter of matching your level of ambition
to the right hike.

The Smith River Recreation Area is equally gorgeous. The Smith is one of the last major free-flowing rivers in America. Wild, pristine, and beautiful, it's set in a series of gorges and bordered by national forest. The centerpiece is Jedediah Smith Redwoods State Park and its grove of monster-sized redwoods. South Fork Road provides an extended tour into Six Rivers National Forest along the South Fork Smith River, with the option of visiting many of the largest trees in Jedediah Smith Redwoods State Park. The turnoff is on U.S. 199 just northeast of the town of Hiouchi. Turn right, cross two bridges, and you will arrive at a fork in the road. Turning left at the fork will take you along the South Fork Smith River and deep into Six Rivers National Forest. Turning right at the fork will take you to a series of trailheads for hikes into redwoods. Of these, the best is the Boy Scout Tree Trail.

The Lost Coast is often overlooked by visitors because of the difficulty in reaching it; your only access is via a slow, curvy road through the Mattole River Valley, past Petrolia, and out to a piece of coast. The experience is like being in suspended animation — your surroundings peaceful and pristine, with a striking lack of people. One of the best ways to capture the sensation is to drive out near the mouth of the Mattole, then hike south on the Coastal Trail long enough to get a feel for the area.

Compared to other regions in California, this corner of the state is somewhat one-dimensional. The emphasis here is primarily on exploring the redwoods and the coast, and to some extent, the Smith River. Most of the campgrounds here are designed with that in mind.

Many private campgrounds are set on U.S. 101 as well as near the mouths of the Smith and Klamath Rivers. These make fine base camps for fishing trips when the salmon are running. The state and national park campgrounds in the redwoods are in high demand, and reservations are often necessary in the peak vacation season. On the opposite end of the spectrum are primitive and remote settings, in Six Rivers National Forest, the Lost Coast, and even a few surprise nuggets in Redwood National Park.

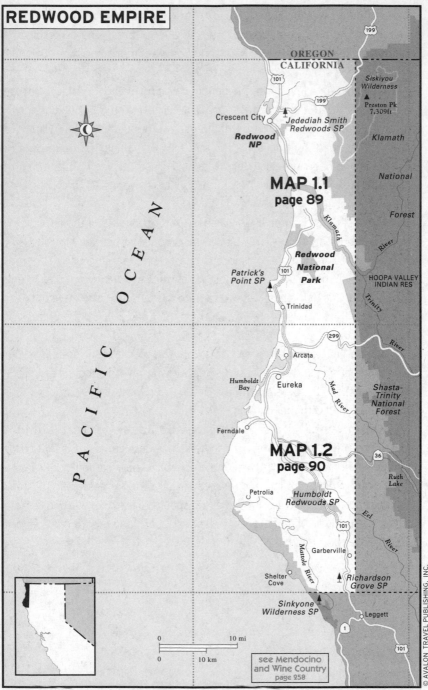

REDWOOD EMPIRE

OREGON
CALIFORNIA

Siskiyou
Wilderness

▲ Preston Pk
7,309ft

199

101

199

Crescent City
Jedediah Smith
Redwoods SP

*Redwood
NP*

Klamath

National

Forest

MAP 1.1
page 89

Klamath

*Redwood
National
Park*

Patrick's
Point SP

101

HOOPA VALLEY
INDIAN RES

Trinity

● Trinidad

299

River

● Arcata

Shasta-
Trinity
National
Forest

Humboldt
Bay

● Eureka

Mad River

MAP 1.2
page 90

Ferndale ●

36

Ruth
Lake

Petrolia ●

*Humboldt
Redwoods SP*

Eel

101

River

Mattole River

Garberville ●

Shelter
Cove ●

▲ *Richardson
Grove SP*

Leggett ●

*Sinkyone
Wilderness SP*

1

101

PACIFIC OCEAN

0   10 mi
0   10 km

see Mendocino
and Wine Country
page 258

© AVALON TRAVEL PUBLISHING, INC.

Map 1.1

Campgrounds 1-35
Pages 91-108

Map 1.2

Campgrounds 36-58
Pages 109-120

© AVALON TRAVEL PUBLISHING, INC.

1 SALMON HARBOR RV RESORT

🛶 � 🐕 🚐 ⛺

Scenic rating: 6

on the Smith River

Map 1.1, page 89

If location is everything, this privately operated campground rates high for salmon and steelhead anglers in the fall. It is set near the mouth of the Smith River, where salmon enter and school in the deep river holes in October. The fish are big, often in the 20-pound range, occasionally surpassing even 40 pounds. Year-round this is a good layover for RV cruisers looking for a spot near the Oregon border. It is actually an RV parking area with hookups, set within a mobile home park. Salmon Harbor Resort overlooks the ocean, with good beachcombing and driftwood and agate hunting nearby. Note that most sites are filled for the entire summer, but several sites are kept open for overnight campers.

Campsites, facilities: There are 93 sites for tents or RVs up to 40 feet; most sites have full hookups (30 and 50 amps) and are pull-through. Picnic tables and fire grills are provided. Drinking water, restrooms with flush toilets and showers, cable TV, coin laundry, storage sheds, modem hookups, and a recreation room are available. A grocery store, ice, gas, propane, a restaurant, boat ramp, fish cleaning station, RV storage, snack bar and a bar are available within three miles. Leashed pets are permitted.

Reservations, fees: Reservations are accepted at 800/332-6139. Sites are $28 per night, $1.50 per person for more than two people. Monthly rates are available. Open year-round.

Directions: From Crescent City, drive north on U.S. 101 for 13 miles to the town of Smith River. Continue three miles north on U.S. 101 to the Salmon Harbor Road exit. Turn left on Salmon Harbor Road, drive a short distance, and look for Salmon Harbor Resort at the end of the road.

Contact: Salmon Harbor RV Resort, 707/487-3341 or 800/332-6139, www.salmonharborrvresort.com.

2 SHIP ASHORE RESORT

🛶 � 🐕 🚐 ⛺

Scenic rating: 7

on the Smith River

Map 1.1, page 89

This is a famous spot for Smith River anglers in late fall and all through winter, when the tales get taller as the evening gets late. In the summer, the resort has become quite popular with people cruising the coast on U.S. 101. The park is set on five acres of land adjacent to the lower Smith River. Note that in addition to the 120 RV sites, another 80 sites have mobile homes. The salmon and steelhead seem to come in one size here—big—but they can be as elusive as Bigfoot. If you want to hear how big these fish can be, just check into the Captain's Galley restaurant any fall or winter evening. Salmon average 15–25 pounds, occasionally bigger, with 50-pounders caught each year, and steelhead average 10–14 pounds, with bigger fish occasionally hooked as well.

Campsites, facilities: There are 120 sites for RVs, and a separate area for 10–15 tents. Most RV sites have full hookups (30 amps); some sites are pull-through. Two houses and motel rooms are also available. Picnic tables are provided. Restrooms with flush toilets and showers, boat dock, boat ramp, coin laundry, propane, and a restaurant are available. A grocery store is two miles away. Leashed pets are permitted, with a maximum of two pets.

Reservations, fees: Reservations are not accepted. Sites are $9–16 per night, $1 per person per night for more than two people. Some credit cards accepted. Open year-round.

Directions: From Crescent City, drive north on U.S. 101 for 16 miles, three miles past the town of Smith River, to the Ship Ashore sign at Chinook Street. At Chinook Street, turn left and drive a short distance (less than half a block) to the motel lobby to register.

Contact: Ship Ashore Resort, 707/487-3141, fax 707/487-7070, www.ship-ashore.com.

3 TOLOWA DUNES STATE PARK, WALK-IN AND EQUESTRIAN

🚶 🚴 🛶 🎣 🐕 ⛺

Scenic rating: 9

near Crescent City

Map 1.1, page 89

This park is one of the great discoveries available to people who love the outdoors. The walk-in sites are extremely secluded, quiet, and sheltered, set off little spur trails from the main access trail/road. With forested rolling hills, a benign climate, and a combination of marshes, sandy soil, and proximity to the ocean, the Smith River and Lake Earl are not only pretty and pleasant, but they attract a wide variety of bird life. This is a 5,000-acre park contains an ocean beach, a river, open and vegetated sand dunes, wood ridges, a large but shallow lake, and some of the best wetlands along the Northern California coast. These wetlands are an important stopover for waterfowl on the Pacific Flyway. The access trail to and from camp provides an outstanding bike trip along the adjacent wildlife area. The campgrounds are not set near Lake Earl, but the lake is accessible with a short drive. Lakes Earl and Tolowa are connected by a curving piece of water, with Tolowa to the west and Earl to the east. Tolowa borders coastal sand dunes and, after heavy rainfall, sometimes runs into the ocean. That is how sea-run cutthroat trout and flounder enter the brackish waters, caught rarely at the narrows between the lakes. Lakes Earl and Tolowa offer 7.5 miles of ocean frontage, 15 miles of horseback-riding trails, numerous hiking trails, opportunities for canoeing and kayaking, and the bonus of having the Smith River nearby to the north. Spring and early summer bring great wildflower displays. The Tolowa people, for whom the park is named, are the most recent Native Americans to occupy the area. Note that mosquitoes are heavy in spring and summer.

Campsites, facilities: There are six primitive sites and a ride-in horse camp with 16 individual corrals and food lockers. There is no drinking water, but picnic tables are provided. Pit toilets are available. Fire rings are provided for the walk-in sites and fire pits for the horse camp. Garbage must be packed out. Leashed pets are permitted.

Reservations, fees: Reservations are not accepted. Walk-in sites are $12 per night. In the horse camp, there is a $5 fee per night per horse and rider, and a group rate of $75 per night for 15 or more riders. Registration is required at Del Norte Coast Redwoods State Park, Jedediah Smith Redwoods State Park, or Crescent City Information Center. Open year-round.

Directions: In Crescent City, drive on U.S. 101 to the lighted intersection at Northcrest Drive. Turn left (northwest) and drive about five miles (Northcrest becomes Lake Earl Drive) to Lower Lake Road. Turn left and drive 2.5 miles. Turn left on Kellogg Road and drive 0.5 mile. A small metal gate, for which the combination is given at registration, and parking area large enough for a few cars is the access point on the right side of the road.

For the horse camp: In Crescent City, turn northwest on Northcrest Drive and drive five miles to Lower Lake Road. At Lower Lake Road, turn left and drive about seven miles to Pala Road. At Pala Road, turn left and drive to the parking area. The horse camp is about a mile southwest of the Pala Road parking lot.

For trail and walk-in beach access: In Crescent City, turn northwest on Northcrest Drive and continue 1.5 miles to Old Mill Road. Turn west (left) on Old Mill Road and drive three miles (stay on paved road) to Sand Hill Road. For the state park trailhead, turn left at Sand Hill Road and drive 0.25 mile to the trail entrance. For Fish and Game trail and walk-in beach access, continue on Old Mill Road to the locked gate at the road's end (about 100 yards past the

Sand Hill Road turnoff). The trail begins at the parking lot.

For the Lake Earl boat launch: In Crescent City, turn northwest on Northcrest Drive and drive about 3.5 miles to Lake View Road. At Lake View Road, turn left and drive a mile to the road's end at Lake Earl.

For the drive-in beach access: From Crescent City, turn northwest on Northcrest Drive and drive north for about five miles to Lower Lake Road. At Lower Lake Road, turn left and drive 2.5 miles to Kellogg Road. At Kellogg Road, turn left and drive 1.5 miles to the beach parking lot at the end of the road.

For picnicking and bird-watching: In Crescent City, turn northwest on Northcrest Drive and drive north for about five miles to Lower Lake Road. At Lower Lake Road, turn left and drive about seven miles to Pala Road on the left. Note: Refer to trail notes and walk-in beach access.

Contact: Tolowa Dunes State Park, 707/464-6101 (ext. 5151), www.parks.ca.gov.

4 CRESCENT CITY REDWOODS KOA
🚶 🚣 🐕 🚲 🚐 ⛺

Scenic rating: 6

five miles north of Crescent City

Map 1.1, page 89

This KOA camp is on the edge of a recreation wonderland, a perfect jump-off spot for a vacation. The park covers 17 acres, with 11 acres of redwood forest. A few farm animals live here, and guests are allowed to feed them. In addition, there are three golf courses nearby. The camp is only two miles from Redwood National Park, Jedediah Smith Redwoods State Park, and the Smith River National Recreation Area. It is also only a 10-minute drive to the beach and Tolowa Dunes Wildlife Area to the east and to Crescent City Harbor to the south.

Campsites, facilities: There are 44 tent sites and 30 sites with full hookups (30 and 50

amps) for RVs of any length. Seventeen cabins and one cottage are also available. Picnic tables and fire grills are provided. A dump station, restrooms with flush toilets and showers, a coin laundry, free Wi-Fi, playground, propane, convenience store, ice, firewood, recreation room, pool table, table tennis, horseshoes, go-carts, and volleyball are available. Leashed pets are permitted.

Reservations, fees: Reservations are accepted at 800/562-5754. Sites are $20–39 per night, $2.50–3.50 per person per night for more than two people. Some credit cards accepted. Open year-round.

Directions: From Crescent City, take U.S. 101 north for five miles to the campground entrance on the right (east) side of the road.

Contact: Crescent City Redwoods KOA, 707/464-5744, www.crescentcitykoa.com.

5 JEDEDIAH SMITH REDWOODS STATE PARK
🚶 🚴 🏊 🚣 🐕 ♿ 🚐 ⛺

Scenic rating: 10

on the Smith River

Map 1.1, page 89

This is a beautiful park set along the Smith River, where the campsites are sprinkled amid a grove of old-growth redwoods. Reservations are usually a necessity during the summer. This park covers 10,000 acres on both sides of the Smith River, a jewel and California's last major free-flowing river. There are 20 miles of hiking and nature trails. The park has hiking trails that lead right out of the campground; one is routed along the beautiful Smith River, and another heads through forest, across U.S. 199, and hooks up with Simpson-Reed Interpretive Trail. In the summer, interpretive programs are available. There is also a good put-in spot at the park for river access in a drift boat, canoe, or raft. The fishing is best for steelhead from mid-January through March. In the summer, a seasonal footbridge connects the campground with more extensive trails. The best hikes are on the south side of the Smith River, accessible via Howland Hill Road, including the Boy Scout Tree Trail and Stout Grove (for access, see next listing, *Hiouchi Hamlet RV Resort*). Note that in winter, 100 inches of cumulative rainfall is common.

Campsites, facilities: There are 106 sites for tents or RVs up to 36 feet (no hookups) and trailers up to 31 feet, five hike-in/bike-in sites, and one group site for up to 15 vehicles and 50 people. Picnic tables, fire grills, and food lockers are provided. Drinking water, flush toilets, and a dump station are available. There is a visitors center with exhibits and a nature store. Propane gas and groceries are available within one mile. Some facilities are wheelchair-accessible. Leashed pets are permitted only in the campground and on roads.

Reservations, fees: Reservations are accepted ($7.50 reservation fee) at 800/444-PARK (800/444-7275) or www.reserveamerica.com. Sites are $15–20 per night, $6 per night for each additional vehicle, $100 per night for the group site, and $3 per person per night for hike-in, bike-in sites. Open year-round.

Directions: From Crescent City, drive north on U.S. 101 for four miles to the junction with U.S. 199. Turn east at U.S. 199 and drive five miles. Turn right at the well-signed entrance station.

Contact: Redwood National and State Parks, 707/464-6101, fax 707/464-1812, www.parks.ca.gov.

6 HIOUCHI HAMLET RV RESORT
🏔️ 🚵 🐕 ♿ 🚲 ⛺

Scenic rating: 7

near the Smith River

Map 1.1, page 89

This park is out of the wind and fog you get on the coast and set instead in the heart of the forest country. It makes a good base camp for a steelhead trip in winter. Insiders know that right next door, the fried chicken at the Hamlet's market is always good for a quick hit. An excellent side trip is to drive just east of Hiouchi on U.S. 199, turn right, and cross over two bridges, where you will reach a fork in the road. Turn left for a great scenic drive along the South Fork Smith River or turn right to get backdoor access to Jedediah Smith Redwoods State Park and three great trailheads for hiking in the redwoods. My favorite of the latter is the Boy Scout Tree Trail. Note that about one-fourth of the RV sites are filled with long-term renters, and many other sites fill up quickly with summer vacationers.

Campsites, facilities: There are 120 sites with full hookups (30 and 50 amps) for RVs of any length and six tent sites. Some sites are pull-through. Two park-model cabins and six furnished apartments are also available. Restrooms with flush toilets and showers, a dump station, coin laundry, Wi-Fi, high-speed modem hookups, cable TV, recreation room, horseshoe pits, grocery store, propane, and deli are available. A motel and café are nearby. A golf course is available within four miles. Some facilities are wheelchair-accessible. Leashed pets are permitted.

Reservations, fees: Reservations are accepted at 800/722-9468. Sites are $26.70–28.90 per night, $2 per person per night for more than two people. Some credit cards accepted. Open year-round.

Directions: From Crescent City, drive five miles north on U.S. 101 to U.S. 199. Turn east (right) on U.S. 199 and drive about five miles (just past the entrance to Jedediah Smith Redwoods State Park) to the town of Hiouchi. In Hiouchi, turn left at the well-signed campground entrance.

Contact: Hiouchi Hamlet RV Resort 707/458-3321, fax 707/458-3521.

7 PANTHER FLAT

🚶 🏊 🎣 🐕 ♿ 🚐 ⛺

Scenic rating: 8

on the Smith River in Six Rivers National
Forest

Map 1.1, page 89

This is an ideal alternative to the often-crowded
Jedediah Smith Redwoods State Park. The
park provides easy road access since it is set
right along U.S. 199, the two-laner that runs
beside the Smith River. This is the largest and
one of the feature campgrounds in the Smith
River National Recreation Area, with excellent
prospects for salmon and steelhead fishing in
the fall and winter respectively, and outstanding hiking and backpacking in the summer. A
0.25-mile interpretive trail and viewing area
is one mile north of the campground, off U.S.
199. A great nearby hike is Stony Creek Trail,
an easy walk along the North Fork Smith
River; the trailhead is in nearby Gasquet on
Stoney Creek Road. Redwood National Park is
a short drive to the west. The Siskiyou Wilderness is a short drive to the southeast via forest
roads detailed on Forest Service maps. The
wild and scenic Smith River system provides
fishing, swimming, sunbathing, kayaking for
experts, and beautiful scenery.
Campsites, facilities: There are 39 sites for
tents or RVs up to 40 feet (no hookups). Picnic
tables and fire grills are provided. Drinking
water and restrooms with flush toilets and coin
showers are available. Propane gas, groceries,
and coin laundry are available nearby. Some
facilities are wheelchair-accessible. Leashed
pets are permitted.
Reservations, fees: Reservations are accepted
($9 reservation fee) at 877/444-6777 or www
.ReserveUSA.com. Sites are $15 per night, $5
per night for each additional vehicle. Open
year-round.
Directions: From Crescent City, drive north
on U.S. 101 for three miles to the junction
with U.S. 199. At U.S. 199, turn east and
drive 14.5 miles to Gasquet. From Gasquet,
continue for 2.3 miles east on U.S. 199 and
look for the entrance to the campground on
the left side of the highway.
Contact: Smith River National Recreation
Area, Six Rivers National Forest, 707/457-
3131, fax 707/457-3794.

8 GRASSY FLAT

🎣 🐕 ♿ 🚐 ⛺

Scenic rating: 4

on the Smith River in Six Rivers National
Forest

Map 1.1, page 89

This is one in a series of three easy-to-reach
Forest Service camps set near U.S. 199 along
the beautiful Middle Fork of the Smith River.
It's a classic wild river, popular in the summer
with kayakers, and the steelhead come huge in
the winter for the crafty few. The camp itself is
set directly across from a CalTrans waste area,
and if you hit it when the crews are working, it
can be noisy here. Most of the time, however,
it is peaceful and quiet.
Campsites, facilities: There are four walk-
in tent sites and 15 sites for tents or RVs up
to 30 feet (no hookups). Picnic tables and
fire grills are provided. Drinking water and
vault toilets are available. Propane gas and
groceries are available nearby. Some facilities are wheelchair-accessible. Leashed pets
are permitted.
Reservations, fees: Reservations are accepted
($9 reservation fee) at 877/444-6777 or www
.ReserveUSA.com. Sites are $10 per night, $5
per night for each additional vehicle. Open
late May through mid-September.
Directions: From Crescent City, drive north
on U.S. 101 for three miles to the junction
with U.S. 199. Turn east on U.S. 199 and
drive 14.5 miles to Gasquet. From Gasquet,
continue east on U.S. 199 for 4.4 miles and
look for the campground entrance on the right
side of the road.
Contact: Smith River National Recreation
Area, Six Rivers National Forest, 707/457-
3131, fax 707/457-3794.

9 PATRICK CREEK
🧍🛶🐕♿🚐⛰️

Scenic rating: 8

in Six Rivers National Forest

Map 1.1, page 89

This is one of the prettiest spots along U.S. 199, where Patrick Creek enters the upper Smith River. It is also a historic California Conservation Corps site that was built in the 1930s. This section of the Smith looks something like a large trout stream, rolling green past a boulder-lined shore, complete with forest canopy. There are small cutthroat trout in summer and salmon and steelhead in fall and winter. A big plus for this camp is its nearby access to excellent hiking in the Siskiyou Wilderness, especially the great day hike to Buck Lake. It is essential to have a map of Six Rivers National Forest, both for driving directions to the trailhead and for the hiking route. You can buy maps at the information center for the Smith River National Recreation Area on the north side of U.S. 199 in Gasquet. Patrick Creek Lodge, on the opposite side of the highway from the campground, has a restaurant and bar. A paved trail connects the campground to Patrick Creek Lodge.

Campsites, facilities: There are 13 sites for tents or RVs up to 35 feet (no hookups). Picnic tables and fire grills are provided. Drinking water and flush toilets are available. Some facilities are wheelchair-accessible, including a fishing area. Leashed pets are permitted.

Reservations, fees: Reservations are accepted ($9 reservation fee) at 877/444-6777 or www.ReserveUSA.com. Sites are $14 per night, $5 per night for each additional vehicle. Open May to early September.

Directions: From Crescent City, drive north on U.S. 101 for three miles to the junction with U.S. 199. Turn east on U.S. 199 and drive 14.5 miles to Gasquet. From Gasquet, continue east on U.S. 199 for 7.5 miles and look for the campground entrance on the right side of the road.

Contact: Smith River National Recreation Area, Six Rivers National Forest, 707/457-3131, fax 707/457-3794.

10 BAYSIDE RV PARK
🛶🚐🏠🐕🚐

Scenic rating: 6

in Crescent City

Map 1.1, page 89

If you are towing a boat, you just found your personal heaven: This RV park is directly adjacent to the boat docking area in Crescent City Harbor. There are several walks in the immediate area, including exploring the harbor and ocean frontage. For a quick change of scenery, it is only a 15-minute drive to Redwood National Park and Jedediah Smith Redwoods State Park along U.S. 199 to the north. Note that about 20 sites are filled with long-term renters, and most of the spaces book up for the entire season.

Campsites, facilities: There are 110 sites for RVs up to 34 feet. Most sites have full hookups (30 amps) and/or are pull-through. No tents. Picnic tables are provided. Restrooms with flush toilets and showers, cable TV, Wi-Fi, and a coin laundry are available. A restaurant is adjacent to the park. Leashed pets are permitted.

Reservations, fees: Reservations are accepted at 800/446-9482. Sites are $18–22 per night, $3 per person per night for more than two people. Open year-round.

Directions: From U.S. 101 at the southern end of Crescent City, drive to Citizen Dock Road and continue one-half block south to the park office.

Contact: Bayside RV Park, 707/464-9482.

11 VILLAGE CAMPER INN RV PARK
🧍🏠🚐⛰️

Scenic rating: 7

in Crescent City

Map 1.1, page 89

Woods and water, that's what attracts visitors to California's north coast. Village Camper Inn provides nearby access to big woods and big water. This RV park is on 20 acres of wooded land, about a 10-minute drive away from the giant redwoods along U.S. 199. In addition, you find some premium beachcombing for driftwood and agates a mile away on the spectacular rocky beaches just west of town. Note that about half of the sites fill up for the entire summer season.

Campsites, facilities: There are 135 sites for RVs of any length, and a separate area for tents. Most RV sites have full hookups (30 and 50 amps); some sites are pull-through. Picnic tables are provided. Drinking water, a dump station, restrooms with flush toilets and showers, coin laundry, modem access and cable TV are available. Leashed pets are permitted, with certain restrictions.

Reservations, fees: Reservations are accepted. Sites are $22.50 per night, $2 per person per night for more than two people. Some credit cards accepted. Open year-round.

Directions: From Crescent City, drive north on U.S. 101 to the Parkway Drive exit. Take that exit and drive 0.5 mile to the campground on the right.

On U.S. 101, driving south in Crescent City: Drive south on U.S. 101 to the Washington Boulevard exit. Turn left on Washington Boulevard and drive one block to Parkway Drive. Turn left on Parkway and drive one block to the campground on the right.

Contact: Village Camper Inn RV Park, 707/464-3544.

12 SUNSET HARBOR RV PARK

Scenic rating: 4

in Crescent City

Map 1.1, page 89

People camp here with their RVs to be close to the action in Crescent City and to the nearby harbor and beach frontage. For starters, drive a few minutes to the northwest side of town, where the sea is sprinkled with gigantic rocks

and boulders, for dramatic ocean views and spectacular sunsets. For finishers, go down to the west side of town for great walks along the ocean parkway or south to the harbor and adjacent beach, which is long and expansive. About half of the sites are filled with long-term renters.

Campsites, facilities: There are 69 sites with full hookups (30 and 50 amps) for RVs up to 40 feet. No tents. Picnic tables are provided at some sites. Restrooms with flush toilets and showers, cable TV, coin laundry, and a recreation room are available. A grocery store is available nearby. Some facilities are wheelchair-accessible. Leashed pets are permitted.

Reservations, fees: Reservations are accepted. Sites are $26 per night, $2 per person per night for more than two people. Monthly rates are available. Some credit cards accepted. Open year-round.

Directions: In Crescent City on U.S. 101, drive to King Street. At King Street, turn east and drive one block to the park entrance at the end of the road.

Contact: Sunset Harbor RV Park, 707/464-3423.

13 NICKEL CREEK WALK-IN

Scenic rating: 8

in Redwood National Park

Map 1.1, page 89

This camp is set 100 yards from the beach on a bluff, right near the mouth of Nickel Creek. One of the least-known national park campgrounds in the whole state, Nickel Creek Walk-In provides a backpacking-type experience, yet it requires only a short walk. In return for the effort, you get seclusion and beach frontage, with seashore walks and tidepool exploration available.

Campsites, facilities: There are five hike-in tent sites. There is no drinking water. Picnic tables, food lockers and fire pits are provided.

Composting toilets are available. Garbage must be packed out. No pets are allowed.

Reservations, fees: Reservations are not accepted. There is no fee for camping. Open year-round.

Directions: From Crescent City, drive south on U.S. 101 for two miles to Enderts Beach Road. Turn right on Enderts Beach Road and drive about a mile to the trailhead at the end of the road. From the trailhead, hike in 0.5 mile to the campground.

Contact: Redwood National and State Parks, 707/464-6101, fax 707/464-1812, www.nps .gov/redw.

14 DEL NORTE COAST REDWOODS STATE PARK

Scenic rating: 8

near Crescent City

Map 1.1, page 89

The campsites are set in a series of loops in the forest, so while there are a lot of camps, you still feel a sense of privacy here. In addition to redwoods, there are also good stands of alders, along with a rambling stream fed by several creeks. It makes for a very pretty setting, with four loop trails available right out of the camp. This park covers 6,400 acres, featuring 50 percent old-growth coastal redwoods and eight miles of wild coastline. Topography is fairly steep, with elevations ranging from sea level to 1,277 feet. This range is oriented in a north-to-south direction, with steep cliffs adjacent to the ocean. That makes most of the rocky seacoast generally inaccessible except by Damnation Trail and Footsteps Rock Trail. The best coastal access is at Wilson Beach or False Klamath Cove, where there is a half-mile of sandy beach bordered by excellent tide pools. The forest interior is dense, with redwoods and tanoaks, madrones, red alders, bigleaf maples, and California bay. One reason for the lush growth is what rangers call the "nurturing" coastal climate. Nurturing, in this case, means rain like you wouldn't believe in the winter—often more than 100 inches in a season—and lots of fog in the summer. Interpretive programs are conducted here. Insider's note: Hike-in and bike-in campers beware. There is a 900-foot elevation change over the course of two miles between the U.S. 101 access road and the campground.

Campsites, facilities: There are 38 tent sites and 107 sites for tents or RVs up to 31 feet (no hookups). Hike-in/bike-in sites are also available. Picnic tables, fire pits, and food lockers are provided. Drinking water, a dump station, and restrooms with flush toilets and coin showers are available. Some facilities are wheelchair-accessible. Leashed pets are permitted only in the campground.

Reservations, fees: Reservations are accepted ($7.50 reservation fee) at 800/444-PARK (800/444-7275) or www.reserveamerica.com. Sites are $15–20 per night, $4 per night for each additional vehicle, $3 per person per night for hike-in/bike-in sites. Open May to mid-September.

Directions: From Crescent City, drive seven miles south on U.S. 101 to a signed access road for Del Norte Coast Redwoods State Park. Turn left at the park entrance.

Contact: Redwood National and State Parks, 1111 2nd Street, Crescent City, CA 95531, 707/464-6101, fax 707/464-1812, www.nps .gov/redw.

15 BIG FLAT

Scenic rating: 7

on Hurdygurdy Creek in Six Rivers National Forest

Map 1.1, page 89

This camp provides an ideal setting for those who know of it, which is why it gets quite a bit of use for a relatively remote camp. Set along Hurdygurdy Creek, near where the creek enters the South Fork of the Smith River, it provides nearby access to South Kelsey Trail, an outstanding hiking route whether you are walking for a few hours or backpacking for days. In the summer, it is a good layover for rafters or kayakers paddling the South Fork of the Smith River.

Campsites, facilities: There are 25 sites for tents or RVs up to 22 feet (no hookups). Picnic tables and fire grills are provided. Vault toilets and food lockers are available. There is no drinking water and garbage must be packed out. Some facilities are wheelchair-accessible. Leashed pets are permitted.

Reservations, fees: Reservations are not accepted. Sites are $8 per night, $5 per night for each additional vehicle. Open May to early September.

Directions: From Crescent City, drive north on U.S. 101 for three miles to the junction with U.S. 199. Turn east on U.S. 199 and drive five miles to Hiouchi. Continue just past Hiouchi to South Fork Road. Turn right and cross two bridges. At the Y, turn left on South Fork Road and drive about 14 miles to Big Flat Road/County Road 405. Turn left and drive 0.25 mile to the campground entrance road (Forest Road 15N59) on the left. Turn left and drive a short distance to the camp on the left.

Contact: Smith River National Recreation Area, Six Rivers National Forest, 707/457-3131, fax 707/457-3794.

16 DEMARTIN

Scenic rating: 8

in Redwood National Park

Map 1.1, page 89

For hikers on the Pacific Coastal Trail, this camp is ideal for an overnight spot. It is set in a grassy prairie area on a bluff overlooking the ocean along the DeMartin section of the trail, aside Wilson Creek. Sound good? You can chase the waves, hike the Coastal Trail, or just hunker down and let the joy of a peaceful spot renew your spirit.

Campsites, facilities: There are 10 tent sites. Picnic tables, fire pits and caches for food storage are provided. Composting toilets are available. There is no drinking water. Garbage must be packed out. No pets are allowed.

Reservations, fees: Reservations are not accepted. There is no fee for camping. Open year-round.

Directions: From Crescent City, drive south for approximately 18 miles on U.S. 101 to Wilson Creek Road. At Wilson Creek Road, turn left and drive 0.25 mile to the trailhead at the end of the road. From the trailhead, marked Coastal Trail, hike in about 2.5 miles to the campground.

Contact: Redwood National and State Parks, 707/464-6101, fax 707/464-1812, www.nps .gov/redw.

17 MYSTIC FOREST RV PARK

Scenic rating: 6

near the Klamath River

Map 1.1, page 89

The park features gravel roads, redwood trees, and grassy sites amid a 50-acre park designed primarily for RVs with a separate area for tents. A bonus here is the 18-hole miniature golf course. The Trees of Mystery is less than a mile away and features a nearly 50-foot-tall Paul Bunyan. The park is about 1.5 miles away from the ocean and 3.5 miles from the Klamath River. Jet-boat tours are available on the Klamath River.

Campsites, facilities: There are 30 sites with full hookups (30 amps) for RVs of any length and 14 tent sites. Some of the RV sites are pull-through. Picnic tables and fire rings are provided. Drinking water, restrooms with flush toilets and showers, playground, recreation room, horseshoes, miniature golf, a coin laundry, modem access, convenience store and gift shop, group facilities, and firewood are available. Some facilities are wheelchair-accessible. Leashed pets are permitted.

Reservations, fees: Reservations are accepted. Sites are $16–24 per night, $3 per person per night for more than two people. Group rates available. Some credit cards accepted. Open year-round.

Directions: From Eureka, drive north on U.S. 101 to Klamath and continue north for four miles. Look for the entrance sign on the left side of the road. If you reach the Trees of Mystery, you have gone a mile too far north.

Contact: Mystic Forest RV Park, 707/482-4901, fax 707/482-0704, www.mysticforestrv .com.

18 CHINOOK RV RESORT
🎣 🚐 🐕 🏕 🔺

Scenic rating: 7

on the Klamath River

Map 1.1, page 89

The camping area at this park consists of grassy RV sites that overlook the Klamath River. Chinook RV Resort is one of the more well-known parks on the lower Klamath. A boat ramp and fishing supplies are available.

Campsites, facilities: There are 70 sites with full hookups (30 and 50 amps) for RVs of any length and a grassy area for tents. Some RV sites are pull-through. An apartment is also available. Picnic tables and fire grills are provided. Restrooms with flush toilets and showers, cable television, modem access, coin laundry, recreation room, propane, convenience store, RV supplies, boat ramp, boat rentals, and a tackle shop are available. Leashed pets are permitted.

Reservations, fees: Reservations are accepted. RV sites are $25–27 per night, tents are $16 per night, $2 per person per night for more than two people. Some credit cards accepted. Open year-round.

Directions: From Eureka, drive north on U.S. 101 to Klamath. After crossing the bridge at the Klamath River, continue north on U.S. 101 for a mile to the campground on the left.

Contact: Chinook RV Resort, 707/482-3511, fax 707/482-0493, www.chinookrvresort .com.

19 CAMP MARIGOLD
🚶 🏊 🐕 🚐 🔺

Scenic rating: 7

near the Klamath River

Map 1.1, page 89

Camp Marigold is surrounded by wonder: Redwood National Park, towering redwoods, Pacific Ocean beaches, driftwood, agates, fossilized rocks, blackberries, Fern Canyon, Lagoon Creek Park, and the Trees of Mystery. Fishing is available nearby, in season, for several species, including king salmon, steelhead, redtail perch, and candlefish. The camp has 3.5 acres of landscaped gardens with hiking trails.... get the idea? Well, there's more: It is only two miles to the Klamath River, in case you can't find enough to do already. A few sites are filled with long-term renters.

Campsites, facilities: There are 40 sites for tents or RVs up to 35 feet (full hookups). Twelve park-model cabins are also available. Picnic tables and barbecues are provided. Restrooms with showers, cable TV, group facilities, and a coin laundry are available. Small leashed pets are permitted.

Reservations, fees: Reservations are recommended. Sites are $10–15 per night, $5 per night per person for more than two people. Monthly rates available. Some credit cards accepted. Open year-round.

Directions: From Eureka, drive 60 miles north on U.S. 101 to the campground at 16101 U.S. 101, four miles north of the Klamath River Bridge, on the right side of the road. The camp is a mile south of the Trees of Mystery.

Contact: Camp Marigold, 707/482-3585 or 800/621-8513.

20 FLINT RIDGE WALK-IN

Scenic rating: 7

in Redwood National Park

Map 1.1, page 89

This little-known camp is on a grassy bluff overlooking the ocean along the Flint Ridge section of the Pacific Coastal Trail. From the parking area at the trailhead, it's only a five-minute walk to reach a meadow surrounded by a thicket of wild blackberries, alders, and redwoods, with the ocean looming huge to the west, but there is no trail to the beach from here. The parking area, by the way, is an excellent perch to watch for the "puff-of-smoke" spouts from passing whales. A hike out of camp is routed into the forest; it's a two-mile climb to reach a hill filled solid with redwoods. The only problem is that there is no real destination—just in and then back.

Campsites, facilities: There are 11 hike-in tent sites. Picnic tables, fire pits and food lockers are provided. Composting toilets are available. There is no drinking water. You must pack out garbage. No pets are allowed.

Reservations, fees: Reservations are not accepted. There is no fee for camping. Open year-round.

Directions: From Eureka, drive north on U.S. 101 to the Klamath River. Just before reaching the bridge at the Klamath River, take the Coastal Drive exit and head west up the hill for four miles to a dirt parking area on the right side of the road. Park here. The campground trailhead is adjacent to the parking area on the east side of the road. Hike 0.25 mile to the camp.

Contact: Redwood National and State Parks, 707/464-6101, fax 707/464-1812, www.nps .gov/redw.

21 KLAMATH'S CAMPER CORRAL

Scenic rating: 6

on the Klamath River

Map 1.1, page 89

This 50-acre resort offers 3,000 feet of Klamath River frontage, grassy tent sites, berry picking, access to the ocean, and hiking trails nearby. And, of course, in the fall it has salmon and steelhead, the main attraction on the lower Klamath. A boat launch is about 1.5 miles from the resort. Nature trails are on the property, and there is room for bike riding. River swimming is popular in summer. A nightly campfire is usually available. Organized recreation is available in summer. A free pancake breakfast is offered to campers on Sundays.

Campsites, facilities: There are 140 sites for RVs of any length and 60 tent sites. Many RV sites have full or partial hookups (30 amps) and are pull-through. Picnic tables and fire rings are provided at the tent sites. Drinking water, restrooms with flush toilets and showers, a seasonal heated swimming pool, recreation hall, general store, playground, dump station, coin laundry, cable TV, ice, firewood, bait and tackle, fish-cleaning station, fishing guide service, group facilities, arcade, basketball, volleyball, badminton, shuffleboard, horseshoes, table tennis, croquet, and tetherball are available. Leashed pets are permitted.

Reservations, fees: Reservations are accepted at 800/701-7275. Sites are $16–29.95 per night, $2 per night for each additional vehicle, $2 per person per night for more than two people. Weekly and monthly rates are available. Some credit cards accepted. Open April through October.

Directions: From Eureka, drive north on U.S. 101 to Klamath. Just after crossing the Klamath River/Golden Bear Bridge, take the Terwer Valley/Highway 169 exit. At the stop sign, turn left, drive under the highway and continue a short distance west to the campground.

Contact: Klamath's Camper Corral, 707/482-5741, www.campercorral.net.

22 STEELHEAD LODGE

🏊 🚣 �'= 🏍 ⛴ 🏕

Scenic rating: 6

on the Klamath River

Map 1.1, page 89

Many anglers use this park as headquarters when the salmon and steelhead get going in August. The park has grassy sites near the Klamath River.

Campsites, facilities: There are 24 sites for tents or RVs of any length (full hookups); some sites are pull-through. Picnic tables are provided. Drinking water, restrooms with flush toilets and showers, and ice are available. A bar, restaurant, and motel are also available. Some facilities are wheelchair-accessible. Leashed pets are permitted.

Reservations, fees: Reservations are required. RV sites are $20 per night, and tent sites are $10 per night. Some credit cards accepted. Open year-round.

Directions: From Eureka, drive north on U.S. 101 to Klamath and the junction with Highway 169. Turn east on Highway 169 and drive 3.2 miles to Terwer Riffle Road. Turn right (south) on Terwer Riffle Road and drive one block to Steelhead Lodge on the right.

Contact: Steelhead Lodge, 707/482-8145.

23 TERWER PARK

🏍 🚣 🚲 🚐 🏍 🚐 🏕

Scenic rating: 7

on the Klamath River

Map 1.1, page 89

This RV park is situated near the Terwer Riffle, one of the better shore-fishing spots for steelhead and salmon on the lower Klamath River. You get grassy sites, river access, and some fair trails along the Klamath. When the salmon arrive in late August and September, Terwer Riffle can be loaded with fish, as well as boaters and shore anglers—a wild scene. Note that at this park, tent campers are separated from the RV park, with tent camping at a grassy area near the river. Some sites are taken by monthly renters.

Campsites, facilities: There are 35 sites with full hookups (30 amps) for RVs up to 34 feet, and a separate tent area. Several sites are pull-through. Five cabins are also available. Picnic tables are provided. Restrooms with flush toilets and showers are available. A pulley boat launch is available nearby. Leashed pets are permitted.

Reservations, fees: Reservations are accepted. Sites are $17–20 per night, $5 per night for each additional vehicle. Weekly and monthly rates available. Open April through October.

Directions: From Eureka, drive north on U.S. 101 to Klamath and the junction with Highway 169. Turn east on Highway 169 and drive 3.5 miles to Terwer Riffle Road. Turn right on Terwer Riffle Road and drive two blocks, then bear right on Terwer Riffle Road and continue five blocks (about 0.5 mile) to the park at the end of the road (641 Terwer Riffle Road).

Contact: Terwer Park, 707/482-3855.

24 PRAIRIE CREEK REDWOODS STATE PARK: GOLD BLUFF BEACH

🏍 🚣 🏍 🚐 🏕

Scenic rating: 8

in Prairie Creek Redwoods State Park

Map 1.1, page 89   **BEST (**

The campsites here are set in a sandy, exposed area with man-made windbreaks with a huge, expansive beach on one side and a backdrop of 100- to 200-foot cliffs on the other side. You can walk for miles at this beach, often without seeing another soul, and there is a great trail routed north through forest, with many hidden little waterfalls. In addition, Fern Canyon

Trail, one of the best 30-minute hikes in California, is at the end of Davison Road. Hikers walk along a stream in a narrow canyon, its vertical walls covered with magnificent ferns. There are some herds of elk in the area, often right along the access road. These camps are rarely used in the winter because of the region's heavy rain and winds. The expanse of beach here is awesome, covering 10 miles of huge, pristine ocean frontage. (See next listing, *Elk Prairie*, for more information about Prairie Creek Redwoods.)

Campsites, facilities: There are 26 sites for tents or RVs up to 24 feet (no hookups). No trailers or vehicles wider than eight feet. Fire grills, food lockers, and picnic tables are provided. Drinking water and restrooms with flush toilets and cold showers are available. Leashed pets are permitted.

Reservations, fees: Reservations are not accepted. Sites are $14–15 per night, $6 per night for each additional vehicle. Open year-round, weather permitting.

Directions: From Eureka, drive north on U.S. 101 for 45 miles to Orick. At Orick, continue north on U.S. 101 for three miles to Davison Road. Turn left (west) on Davison Road and drive six miles to the campground on the left. Note: No vehicles more than 24 feet long or more than eight feet wide are permitted on gravel Davison Road, which is narrow and very bumpy.

Contact: Prairie Creek Redwoods State Park, 707/464-6101; Visitors Center 707/465-7354, www.parks.ca.gov.

25 PRAIRIE CREEK REDWOODS STATE PARK: ELK PRAIRIE

🚶 🚵 🐎 ♿ 🚐 ⛺

Scenic rating: 9

in Prairie Creek Redwoods State Park

Map 1.1, page 89   BEST (

A small herd of Roosevelt elk wander free in this remarkable 14,000-acre park. Great opportunities for photographs abound, with a group of about five elk often found right along the highway and access roads. Where there are meadows, there are elk; it's about that simple. An elky here, an elky there, making this one of the best places to see wildlife in California. Remember that these are wild animals, they are huge, and they can be unpredictable; in other words, enjoy them, but don't harass them or get too close. This park consists of old-growth coastal redwoods, prairie lands, and 10 miles of scenic, open beach (Gold Bluff Beach). The interior of the park can be reached by 75 miles of hiking, biking, and nature trails, including a trailhead for a great bike ride at the visitors center. There are many additional trailheads and a beautiful tour of giant redwoods along the Drury Scenic Parkway. A visitors center and summer interpretive programs with guided walks and junior ranger programs are available. The forest understory is very dense due to moisture from coastal fog. Western azalea and rhododendron blooms, peaking in May and June, are best seen from the Rhododendron Trail. From November through May, always bring your rain gear. Summer temperatures range 40–75°F; winter temperatures range 35–55°F.

Campsites, facilities: There are 76 sites for tents or RVs up to 27 feet (no hookups), and one hike-in/bike-in site. Picnic tables, fire rings, and bear-proof food lockers are provided. Drinking water and restrooms with flush toilets and coin showers are available. Some facilities are wheelchair-accessible. Leashed pets are permitted.

Reservations, fees: Reservations are accepted during the summer ($7.50 reservation fee) at 800/444-PARK (800/444-7275) or www.reserveamerica.com. Sites are $15–20 per night, $6 per night for each additional vehicle, $3 per person per night for hike-in/bike-in site. Open year-round.

Directions: From Eureka, drive 45 miles north on U.S. 101 to Orick. At Orick, continue north on U.S. 101 for five miles to the Newton B. Drury Scenic Parkway. Take the exit for the Newton B. Drury Scenic Parkway and drive north for a mile to the park. Turn left at the park entrance.

Contact: Prairie Creek Redwoods State Park, 707/464-6101; Elk Prairie Campground 707/465-7347; Visitors Center 707/465-7354; www.parks.ca.gov.

26 STONE LAGOON BOAT-IN
🏕️ 🛶 🚤 ⛴️ 5% ⛺

Scenic rating: 10

in Humboldt Lagoons State Park

Map 1.1, page 89   BEST (

Virtually nobody knows about this ideal spot for canoeists. While Stone Lagoon is directly adjacent to U.S. 101, the camp is set in a cove that is out of sight of the highway. That makes it a secret spot for many. It is a great place to explore by canoe or kayak, especially paddling upstream to the lagoon's inlet creek. After setting up camp, it is possible to hike to a secluded sand spit and stretch of beachfront. You may see elk in this area on the rare occasion. The water is usually calm in the morning but often gets choppy from afternoon winds. Translation: Get your paddling done early on Stone Lagoon. There is also good fishing for cutthroat trout here. The early 1900s saw several dairy ranches established along Stone Lagoon's shore; however, today's regenerated marshland habitat is home to a wide range of marsh flora, as well as birdlife and other creatures.

Campsites, facilities: There are six primitive tent sites accessible by boat only. There is no drinking water. Picnic tables, food lockers, and fire rings are provided. Pit toilets are available. Garbage must be packed out. No pets are allowed.

Reservations, fees: Reservations are not accepted. Sites are $12 per night, $6 per night for each additional vehicle. Open year-round.

Directions: From Eureka, drive 41 miles north on U.S. 101 (15 miles north of Trinidad) to Stone Lagoon. At Stone Lagoon, turn left at the visitor information center. The boat-in campground is in a cove directly across the lagoon from the visitors center. The campsites are dispersed in an area covering about 300 yards in the landing area.

Contact: Humboldt Lagoons State Park, Trinidad Sector 707/677-3132, www.parks.ca.gov; Humboldt County Parks, 707/445-7652.

27 DRY LAGOON WALK-IN
🏕️ 🚤 5% ⛺

Scenic rating: 8

in Humboldt Lagoons State Park

Map 1.1, page 89

This is a walk-in camp; that is, you need to walk about 200 yards from the parking area to reach the campsites. This makes it a dream for members of the 5 Percent Club, because many tourists are unwilling to walk at all. It is beautiful here, set in the woods, with ocean views and beach access. In the early 1900s, Dry Lagoon was drained by farmers and several types of crops were attempted. The farming projects were colossal failures and the lagoon was allowed to refill. This spot receives 60 inches of rain, on the average, in winter, with spring and fall pleasant. In summer, it can be foggy, cool, and damp, so bring warm, layered clothing. The park has a visitors center and bookstore. A highlight here is a three-mile segment of the Coastal Trail.

Campsites, facilities: There are six primitive tent sites. Picnic tables, fire rings, and food lockers are provided. Pit toilets are available. There is no drinking water. Garbage must be packed out. No pets are allowed.

Reservations, fees: Reservations are not accepted. Sites are $12 per night, $6 per night for each additional vehicle. All campers must register at the Patrick's Point State Park entrance station to obtain the combination to the gate lock. Open year-round.

Directions: From Eureka, drive north on U.S. 101 for 22 miles to Trinidad. At Trinidad, continue north on U.S. 101 for 13 miles to

Dry Lagoon Road. Turn left and drive approximately one mile to the gate at the end of the road. Open gate combination (see previous note) and drive 0.25 mile to the trailhead. Park and walk 200 yards to the camp.
Contact: Humboldt Lagoons State Park, Trinidad Sector 707/677-3132, www.parks.ca.gov; Humboldt County Parks, 707/445-7652.

28 BIG LAGOON COUNTY PARK
🏊 💺 � 🏕 🚻 ♿ 🚐 ⛰️

Scenic rating: 7

north of Trinidad overlooking the Pacific Ocean

Map 1.1, page 89

This is a remarkable, huge lagoon that borders the Pacific Ocean. It provides good boating, excellent exploring, fair fishing, and good duck hunting in the winter. It's a good spot to paddle a canoe around on a calm day. A lot of out-of-towners cruise by, note the lagoon's proximity to the ocean, and figure it must be saltwater. Wrong! Not only is it freshwater, but it provides a long shot for anglers trying for rainbow trout. One reason not many RV drivers stop here is that most of them are drawn farther north (another eight miles) to Freshwater Lagoon.
Campsites, facilities: There are 25 sites for tents or RVs of any length (no hookups). Picnic tables and fire grills are provided. Drinking water and restrooms with flush toilets and coin showers are available. A boat ramp is also available. Some facilities are wheelchair-accessible. Leashed pets are permitted.
Reservations, fees: Reservations are not accepted. Sites are $15 per night per vehicle, $3 per night for a second vehicle, $3 per person per night for hike-in/bike-in, $1 per pet per night. Open year-round.
Directions: From Eureka, drive 22 miles north on U.S. 101 to Trinidad. At Trinidad, continue north on U.S. 101 for eight miles to Big Lagoon Park Road. Turn left (west) at

Big Lagoon Park Road and drive two miles to the park.
Contact: Humboldt County Public Works, 707/445-7651, www.co.humboldt.ca.us; Humboldt Lagoons State Park Visitor Center, 707/488-2041.

29 PATRICK'S POINT STATE PARK
🥾 💺 🏕 🏠 ♿ 🚐 ⛰️

Scenic rating: 9

near Trinidad

Map 1.1, page 89

This pretty park covers 640 acres of coastal headlands and it is filled with Sitka spruce, dramatic ocean lookouts, and several beautiful beaches, including one with agates, one with tidepools, and another with an expansive stretch of beachfront leading to a lagoon. You can best see it on the Rim Trail, which has many little cut-off routes to the lookouts and down to the beaches. The campground is sheltered in the forest, and while it is often foggy and damp in the summer, it is always beautiful. A Native American village, constructed by the Yurok tribe, is also here. At the north end of the park, a short hike to see the bizarre "Octopus Trees" is a good side trip, with trees that are growing atop downed logs, their root systems exposed like octopus tentacles; the trail here loops through a grove of old-growth Sitka spruce. In addition, there are several miles of pristine beach to the north that extends to the lagoons. Interpretive programs are available. The forest here is dense, with spruce, hemlock, pine, fir, and red alder covering an ocean headland. Night and morning fog are common almost year-round, and there are periods where it doesn't lift for days. This area gets 60 inches of rain per year on the average. For camping, plan on making reservations.
Campsites, facilities: There are 85 sites for tents or RVs (no hookups), 39 sites for RVs up to 31 feet, and one group site for up to 100

people. Fire grills, storage lockers, and picnic tables are provided. Drinking water and restrooms with flush toilets and coin showers are available. Some facilities are wheelchair-accessible. Leashed pets are permitted at campsites, but not on trails or beaches.

Reservations, fees: Reservations are accepted ($7.50 reservation fee) at 800/444-PARK (800/444-7275) or www.reserveamerica.com. Sites are $15–20 per night, $6 per night for each additional vehicle, $200 per night for the group site. Open year-round.

Directions: From Eureka, drive north on U.S. 101 for 22 miles to Trinidad. At Trinidad, continue north on U.S. 101 for 5.5 miles to Patrick's Point Drive. Take that exit and at the stop sign, turn left and drive 0.5 mile to the park entrance.

Contact: Patrick's Point State Park, 707/677-3570, www.parks.ca.gov.

30 SOUNDS OF THE SEA RV PARK
🏃 🎣 🐾 🚙

Scenic rating: 6

in Trinidad

Map 1.1, page 89

The Trinidad area, about 20 miles north of Eureka, is one of the great places on this planet. Nearby Patrick's Point State Park is one of the highlights, with a Sitka spruce forest, beautiful coastal lookouts, a great easy hike on the Rim Trail, and access to several secluded beaches. To the nearby south at Trinidad Head is a small harbor and dock, with deep-sea and salmon fishing trips available. A breezy beach is to the immediate north of the Seascape Restaurant. A bonus at this privately operated RV park is good berry picking in season.

Campsites, facilities: There are 70 sites with full hookups (30 and 50 amps) for RVs; some sites are pull-through. No tents. Four park-model cabins are also available. Picnic tables and fire rings are provided at most sites.

Restrooms with showers, cable TV, Wi-Fi, exercise room and indoor spa (fee), bicycle rentals, dump station, coin laundry, convenience store, gift shop, propane, firewood, and ice are available. Leashed pets are permitted.

Reservations, fees: Reservations are accepted at 877/489-6360. Sites are $18–38 per night, $3–5 per person per night for more than two people. Some credit cards accepted. Open year-round.

Directions: From Eureka, drive north on U.S. 101 for 28 miles to Trinidad. In Trinidad, continue north on U.S. 101 for five miles to the Patrick's Point exit. Take the Patrick's Point exit, turn left, and drive 0.5 mile to the park.

Contact: Sounds of the Sea RV Park, 707/677-3271.

31 SYLVAN HARBOR RV PARK AND CABINS
🏃 🎣 🐾 🚙

Scenic rating: 8

in Trinidad

Map 1.1, page 89

This park is designed as an RV park and fish camp, with cleaning tables and canning facilities available on-site. It is a short distance from the boat hoist at Trinidad Pier. Beauty surrounds Sylvan Harbor on all sides for miles. Visitors come to enjoy the various beaches, go agate hunting, or look for driftwood on the beach. Nearby Patrick's Point State Park is an excellent getaway side trip. This is one of several privately operated parks in the Trinidad area, offering a choice of shaded or open sites. (For more information about recreation options nearby, see previous listing, *Sounds of the Sea.*)

Campsites, facilities: There are 73 sites with full hookups (30 amps) for RVs up to 35 feet. No tents. A storage shed and cable TV are provided. Three cabins are available. Restrooms with showers, fish-cleaning stations, fish smokers, canning facilities, coin laundry, and propane are available. Leashed pets are permitted.

Reservations, fees: Reservations are accepted for cabins only. Sites are $22 per night, $2 per person per night for more than two people. Monthly rates available during the summer. Open year-round.

Directions: From Eureka, drive north on U.S. 101 for 28 miles to the Trinidad exit. Take that exit to Main Street. Turn left on Main Street and drive 0.1 mile under the freeway to Patrick's Point Drive. Turn right on Patrick's Point Drive and drive one mile to the campground on the right at 875 Patrick's Point Drive.

Contact: Sylvan Harbor RV Park and Cabins, 707/677-9988, www.sylvanharbor.com.

32 VIEW CREST LODGE, COTTAGES, AND CAMPGROUND

🏃 🏊 🐕 🚐 ⛺

Scenic rating: 8

in Trinidad

Map 1.1, page 89

View Crest Campground is one of the premium spots in Trinidad, with pretty cottages available as well as campsites for RVs and tents. A bonus here is the remarkable flights of swallows, many of which have nests at the cottages. Recreation options include deep-sea and salmon fishing at Trinidad Harbor to the nearby south, and outstanding easy hiking at Patrick's Point State Park to the nearby north.

Campsites, facilities: There are 36 sites with full hookups (20 and 30 amps) for RVs of any length, and a separate area for tents. Some sites are pull-through. Twelve cottages are also available. Picnic tables and fire rings are provided. Restrooms with showers, cable TV, a coin laundry, and firewood are available. Leashed pets are permitted only in the campground.

Reservations, fees: Reservations are accepted. Sites are $16–25 per night, $1 per person per night for more than two people. Monthly rates available. Some credit cards accepted. Open year-round.

Directions: From Eureka, drive north on U.S. 101 for 28 miles to Trinidad. Take the Patrick's Point State Park exit. Continue north for five miles to Patrick's Point Drive. Turn left and drive 0.9 mile to the lodge on the left.

Contact: View Crest Lodge, Cottages, and Campground, 707/677-3393, www.viewcrest-lodge.com.

33 MIDWAY RV PARK

🏃 🏊 🏕 🐕 ♿ 🚐

Scenic rating: 6

in Trinidad

Map 1.1, page 89

This is one of several privately developed campgrounds in Trinidad. In the summer, salmon fishing can be excellent just off Trinidad Head. In the fall, rock fishing is the way to go, and in winter, crabbing is tops. Patrick's Point State Park provides a nearby side-trip option to the north. Note that some sites have long-term renters, and most of the remaining sites fill up for the entire summer season. It can be difficult to get a space here for overnight camping during the summer.

Campsites, facilities: There are 73 sites with full hookups (30 amps) for RVs up to 40 feet. No tents. Picnic tables are provided. Restrooms with showers, cable TV, club room, propane, coin laundry, and fish-cleaning station are available. Some facilities are wheelchair-accessible. Leashed pets are permitted.

Reservations, fees: Reservations are recommended in the summer. Sites are $25–28 per night. Some credit cards accepted. Open year-round.

Directions: From Eureka, drive north on U.S. 101 for 28 miles to the Trinidad exit. Take that exit to Main Street. Turn left on Main Street and drive 0.1 mile under the freeway to Patrick's Point Drive. Turn right on Patrick's Point Drive and drive 0.5 mile to Midway

Drive. Turn right and drive 0.1 mile to the campground at 51 Midway Drive.

Contact: Midway RV Park, tel./fax 707/677-3934.

34 EMERALD FOREST

Scenic rating: 5

in Trinidad

Map 1.1, page 89

This campground is set on 12 acres of redwoods, often dark and wet, with the ocean at Trinidad Head only about a five-minute drive away. The campground owners emphasize that they are a vacation and overnight park only, and not a mobile home or long-term park.

Campsites, facilities: There are 45 sites with full or partial hookups (30 amps) for RVs up to 45 feet, and 30 tent sites. Some sites are pull-through. There are also 19 cabins. Picnic tables, fire rings, and barbecues are provided. Restrooms, showers, free cable TV in RV sites, playground, convenience store, ice, firewood, coin laundry, group facilities, fish-cleaning station, dump station, propane, telephone and modem hookups, Wi-Fi, volleyball, horseshoes, badminton, and video arcade are available. Leashed pets are permitted, except in the tent sites or cabins.

Reservations, fees: Reservations are recommended in the summer. Sites are $26–38 per night, $2.50–3 per person per night for more than two people. Winter rates available. Some credit cards accepted. Open year-round.

Directions: From Eureka, drive north on U.S. 101 for 28 miles to the Trinidad exit. Take that exit to Main Street. Turn left on Main Street and drive 0.1 mile under the freeway to Patrick's Point Drive. Turn right on Patrick's Point Drive and drive 0.9 mile north to the campground at 753 Patrick's Point Drive.

Contact: Emerald Forest, 707/677-3554, fax 707/677-0963, www.rvintheredwoods.com.

35 HIDDEN CREEK

Scenic rating: 5

in Trinidad

Map 1.1, page 89

To tell you the truth, there really isn't much hidden about this RV park, but you might be hard-pressed to find year-round Parker Creek. Regardless, it is still in a pretty location in Trinidad, with the Trinidad pier, adjacent harbor, restaurants, and beach all within a drive of just a minute or two. Deep-sea fishing for salmon, lingcod, and rockfish is available on boats out of Trinidad Harbor. Crab and albacore tuna are also caught here, and there's beachcombing for agates and driftwood on the beach to the immediate north. Note that half of the sites are filled with long-term renters.

Campsites, facilities: There are 56 sites with full or partial hookups (30 and 50 amps) for RVs up to 40 feet, and a grassy area for tents. Six park-model cabins are also available. Picnic tables are provided. Cable TV, restrooms with showers, fish-cleaning station, ice, picnic area, and a dump station are available. Leashed pets are permitted.

Reservations, fees: Reservations are recommended in the summer. Sites are $14–29 per night, $2 per person per night for more than two people. Long-term rates available. Open year-round.

Directions: From Eureka, drive north on U.S. 101 for 28 miles to Trinidad. Take the Trinidad exit to the stop sign. Turn right at Westhaven Drive and drive a short distance to the RV park on the left at 199 North Westhaven.

Contact: Hidden Creek RV Park, 707/677-3775.

36 CLAM BEACH COUNTY PARK

Scenic rating: 7

near McKinleyville

Map 1.2, page 90

Here awaits a beach that seems to stretch on forever, one of the great places to bring a lover, dog, children, or, hey, all three. While the campsites are a bit exposed, making winds out of the north a problem in the spring, the direct beach access largely makes up for it. The park gets its name from the fair clamming that is available, but you must come equipped with a clam gun or special clam shovel, and then be out when minus low tides arrive at daybreak. Most people just enjoy playing tag with the waves, taking long romantic walks, or throwing sticks for the dog.

Campsites, facilities: There are 12 sites for tents and a parking lot for 15 RVs of any length (no hookups). Picnic tables and fire rings are provided. Drinking water and vault toilets are available. Propane gas, grocery store, and a coin laundry are available in McKinleyville. Leashed pets are permitted.

Reservations, fees: Reservations are not accepted. Sites are $10 per night per vehicle, $3 per person per night for hike-in/bike-in, $1 per pet per night. Open year-round.

Directions: From Eureka, drive north on U.S. 101 to McKinleyville. Continue past McKinleyville to the Clam Beach Park exit. Take that exit and turn west at the sign for Clam Beach. Drive two blocks to the campground, which is adjacent to Little River State Beach.

Contact: Humboldt County Public Works, 707/445-7651, www.co.humboldt.ca.us.

37 MAD RIVER RAPIDS RV PARK

Scenic rating: 7

in Arcata

Map 1.2, page 90

This park is near the farmlands on the outskirts of town, in a pastoral, quiet setting. There is a great bike ride nearby on a trail routed along the Mad River, and it is also excellent for taking a dog for a walk. Nearby Arcata is a unique town, a bit of the old and a bit of the new, and the Arcata Marsh at the north end of Humboldt Bay provides a scenic and easy bicycle trip, as well as an excellent destination for hiking, sightseeing, and birdwatching. About half of the sites are filled with long-term renters.

Campsites, facilities: There are 92 sites with full hookups (30 and 50 amps) for RVs of any length; some sites are pull-through. No tents. Picnic tables are provided. Fire grills are provided at two sites. Restrooms with showers, cable TV, Wi-Fi, a dump station, recreation room, tennis courts, fitness room, playground, basketball courts, jogging trail, arcade, table tennis, horseshoe pits, heated swimming pool, spa, group facilities, restaurant and bar, convenience store, RV supplies, and coin laundry are available. A motel is adjacent to the park. Some facilities are wheelchair-accessible. Leashed pets are permitted.

Reservations, fees: Reservations are accepted at 800/822-7776. Sites are $33 per night. Some credit cards accepted. Weekly and monthly rates available. Open year-round.

Directions: From the junction of U.S. 101 and Highway 299 in Arcata, drive 0.25 mile north on U.S. 101 to the Guintoli Lane/Janes Road exit. Take that exit and turn left (west) on Janes Road and drive two blocks to the park on the left.

Contact: Mad River Rapids RV Park, 707/822-7275, www.madriverrv.com.

38 EUREKA KOA

🚶 🚲 🏊 ⛵ 🏕 🎣 ♿ 🚐 ⛺

Scenic rating: 2

in Eureka

Map 1.2, page 90

This is a year-round KOA camp for U.S. 101 cruisers looking for a layover spot in Eureka. A bonus here is a few of those little KOA Kamping Kabins, the log-style jobs that win on cuteness alone. The closest significant recreation option is the Arcata Marsh on Humboldt Bay, a richly diverse spot with good trails for biking and hiking or just parking and looking at the water. Another option is excellent salmon fishing in June, July, and August.

Campsites, facilities: There are 140 sites with full or partial hookups (30 and 50 amps) for RVs of any length, 26 tent sites, and eight hike-in/bike-in sites. Most RV sites are pull-through. Ten camping cabins and two cottages are also available. Picnic tables and fire pits are provided. Drinking water, restrooms with flush toilets and showers, cable TV, playground, recreation room, heated swimming pool, two spas, convenience store, coin laundry, dump station, propane, ice, firewood, fax machine, and Wi-Fi are available. Some facilities are wheelchair-accessible. Leashed pets are permitted.

Reservations, fees: Reservations are accepted at 800/562-3136. Sites are $26–45 per night, $3 per person per night for more than two people, $20 per night for hike-in/bike-in sites, $2 per pet per night, $2 per night for each additional vehicle. Some credit cards accepted. Open year-round.

Directions: From Eureka, drive north on U.S. 101 for four miles to KOA Drive (well signed on east side of highway). Turn right on KOA Drive and drive a short distance to the end of the road.

Contact: Eureka KOA, 707/822-4243, fax 707/822-0126, www.koa.com.

39 SAMOA BOAT LAUNCH COUNTY PARK

🏊 ⛵ 🏕 🎣 🚐 ⛺

Scenic rating: 7

on Humboldt Bay

Map 1.2, page 90

The nearby vicinity of the boat ramp, with access to Humboldt Bay and the Pacific Ocean, makes this a star attraction for campers towing their fishing boats. Near the campground you get good beachcombing and clamming at low tides and a chance to see a huge variety of seabirds, highlighted by egrets and herons. There's a reason: Directly across the bay is the Humboldt Bay National Wildlife Refuge. Adjacent to the park is the Samoa Dunes Recreation Area, which is popular with ATV enthusiasts who are allowed to ride on the beach. This park is set near the famed all-you-can-eat, logger-style Samoa Cookhouse. The park is on the bay, not on the ocean.

Campsites, facilities: There are 20 sites for tents or RVs of any length (no hookups). Overflow camping is also available in a parking lot for tents or RVs of any length. Picnic tables and fire grills are provided. Drinking water and restrooms with flush toilets and coin showers are available. A boat ramp, grocery store, propane, and a coin laundry are available in Eureka (about five miles away). Leashed pets are permitted.

Reservations, fees: Reservations are not accepted. Sites are $14 per night per vehicle, $3 per person per night for hike-in/bike-in, $3 per night for each additional vehicle, $1 per pet per night. Open year-round.

Directions: From U.S. 101 in Eureka, turn west on Highway 255 and drive two miles until it dead-ends at New Navy Base Road. At New Navy Base Road, turn left and drive five miles to the end of the Samoa Peninsula and the campground entrance.

Contact: Humboldt County Public Works, 707/445-7651, www.co.humboldt.ca.us.

40 E-Z LANDING RV PARK AND MARINA

Scenic rating: 6

on Humboldt Bay

Map 1.2, page 90

This is a good base camp for salmon trips in July and August when big schools of king salmon often teem just west of the entrance of Humboldt Bay. A nearby boat ramp with access to Humboldt Bay is a bonus. It's not the prettiest camp in the world, with quite a bit of asphalt, but most people use this camp as a simple parking spot for sleeping and getting down to the business of the day: fishing. This spot is ideal for ocean fishing, clamming, beachcombing, and boating. There are a few long-term and seasonal renters here.

Campsites, facilities: There are 45 sites with full hookups (30 amps) for RVs; some sites are pull-through. Tent camping is allowed in vacant RV sites. Restrooms with flush toilets and showers, marine gas, ice, coin laundry, bait, and boat slips are available. Some facilities are wheelchair-accessible. Leashed pets are permitted.

Reservations, fees: Reservations are accepted. RV sites are $20 per night, $15 per night for tent sites. Some credit cards accepted. Open year-round.

Directions: From Eureka, drive 3.5 miles south on U.S. 101 to King Salmon Avenue. Turn west (right) on King Salmon Avenue (it becomes Buhne Drive) and drive for 0.5 mile to where the road turns. Turn left (south) on Buhne Drive and go 0.5 mile to the park on the left (1875 Buhne Drive).

Contact: E-Z Landing RV Park and Marina, 707/442-1118, fax 707/442-1999.

41 JOHNNY'S MARINA AND RV PARK

Scenic rating: 5

on Humboldt Bay

Map 1.2, page 90

This is a good base camp for salmon fishing during the peak season—always call, since the season changes each year as set by the Department of Fish and Game. Mooring for private boats is available, a nice plus for campers trailering boats. Other recreation activities include beachcombing, clamming, and perch fishing from shore. The owners have run this place since 1948. Note that a number of sites are filled with long-term renters.

Campsites, facilities: There are 53 sites with full hookups (30 and 50 amps) for RVs up to 38 feet. No tents. Flush toilets and a dump station are available; there are no showers. A coin laundry and boat dock are available. Leashed pets are permitted.

Reservations, fees: Reservations are accepted. Sites are $23 per night, $1 per person per night for more than two people. Open year-round.

Directions: From Eureka, drive 3.5 miles south on U.S. 101 to King Salmon Avenue. Turn west (right) on King Salmon Avenue (it becomes Buhne Drive). Continue about 0.5 mile to the park on the left (1821 Buhne Drive).

Contact: Johnny's Marina and RV Park, 707/442-2284, fax 707/443-4608.

42 VAN DUZEN COUNTY PARK: SWIMMER'S DELIGHT

Scenic rating: 6

on the Van Duzen River

Map 1.2, page 90

This campground is set near the headwaters of the Van Duzen River, one of the Eel River's major tributaries. The river is subject to tremendous fluctuations in flows and height, so low in the fall that it is often temporarily closed to fishing by the Department of Fish and Game, so high in the winter that only fools would stick their toes in. For a short period in late spring, it provides a benign run for rafting and canoeing, putting in at Grizzly Creek and taking out at Van Duzen. In October, you'll find an excellent salmon fishing spot where the Van Duzen enters the Eel.

Campsites, facilities: There are 30 sites for tents or RVs of any length; some sites have partial hookups (30 amps). Picnic tables and fire grills are provided. Drinking water and restrooms with flush toilets and coin showers are available. A grocery store and coin laundry are available nearby. Some facilities are wheelchair-accessible. Leashed pets are permitted in the campground, but not on the beach.

Reservations, fees: Reservations are not accepted. Sites are $15–20 per night, $3 per person per night for hike-in/bike-in, $3 per night for each additional vehicle, $1 per pet per night. Open year-round.

Directions: From Eureka, drive south on U.S. 101 to the junction of Highway 36 at Alton. Turn east on Highway 36 and drive 12 miles to the campground.

Contact: Humboldt County Public Works, 707/445-7651, www.co.humboldt.ca.us.

43 GRIZZLY CREEK REDWOODS STATE PARK

🏃 ⛵ 🐕 ♿ 🚐 ⛺

Scenic rating: 8

near Bridgeville

Map 1.2, page 90

Most summer vacationers hit the campgrounds on the Redwood Highway, that is, U.S. 101. However, this camp is just far enough off the beaten path to provide some semblance of seclusion. It is set in redwoods, quite beautiful, with fair hiking and good access to the adjacent Van Duzen River. The park encompasses only a few acres, yet it is very intimate. There

are 4.5 miles of hiking trails, a visitors center with exhibits, and a bookstore. The Cheatham Grove in this park is an exceptional stand of coast redwoods. Fishing is catch-and-release only with barbless hooks. Nearby attractions include the Victorian village of Ferndale and Fort Humboldt to the north, Humboldt Redwoods State Park to the south, and Ruth Lake to the more distant east. Insider's tip: Half of the park borders Highway 36, and you can hear highway noise from some campsites.

Campsites, facilities: There are 10 tent sites, nine sites for tents or small RVs, 11 sites for RVs up to 30 feet or trailers up to 24 feet, and one hike-in/bike-in site. No hookups. Picnic tables, food lockers, and fire grills are provided. Drinking water and restrooms with flush toilets and showers are available. A grocery store is available within 3.5 miles. Some facilities are wheelchair-accessible. Leashed pets are permitted in the campground, but not on trails or beach area.

Reservations, fees: Reservations are accepted ($7.50 reservation fee) at 800/444-PARK (800/444-7275) or www.reserveamerica.com. Sites are $20 per night, $6 per night for each additional vehicle, $3 per person per night for hike-in/bike-in site. Open year-round.

Directions: From Eureka, drive south on U.S. 101 to the junction of Highway 36 at Alton. Turn east on Highway 36 and drive about 17 miles to the campground on the right.

Contact: Grizzly Creek Redwoods State Park, 707/777-3683, www.parks.ca.gov.

44 MATTOLE

🏃 🛶 🐕 ♿ 5% 🚐 ⛺

Scenic rating: 8

north of Garberville on the Pacific Ocean

Map 1.2, page 90

This is a little-known camp set at the mouth of the Mattole River, right where it pours into the Pacific Ocean. It is beautiful and isolated. An outstanding hike leads to the Punta Gorda Lighthouse. Hike from the campground to the ocean and head south. It's a level walk, and at low tide, there's a chance to observe tidepool life. Perch fishing is good where the Mattole flows into the ocean, best during low tides. In the winter, the Mattole often provides excellent steelhead fishing. Check the Department of Fish and Game regulations for closed areas. Be sure to have a full tank on the way out—the nearest gas station is quite distant.

Campsites, facilities: There are 14 sites for tents or RVs up to 16 feet (no hookups). Picnic tables and fire rings are provided. Vault toilets are available. No drinking water is available. Some facilities are wheelchair-accessible. Leashed pets are permitted.

Reservations, fees: Reservations are not accepted. Sites are $8 per night. Open year-round.

Directions: From U.S. 101 north of Garberville, take the South Fork-Honeydew exit and drive west to Honeydew. At Honeydew and Mattole Road, turn right on Mattole Road and drive toward Petrolia. At the second bridge over the Mattole River, one mile before Petrolia, turn west on Lighthouse Road and drive five miles to the campground at the end of the road.

Contact: Bureau of Land Management, Arcata Field Office, 707/825-2300, fax 707/825-2301; Department of Fish & Game, Low-Flow Fishing Information, 707/442-4502.

45 A. W. WAY COUNTY PARK
🚶 🛶 🐕 🚐 ⛺

Scenic rating: 8

on the Mattole River

Map 1.2, page 90

This secluded camp provides a home for visitors to the "Lost Coast," the beautiful coastal stretch of California far from any semblance of urban life. The highlight here is the Mattole River, a great steelhead stream when flows are suitable between January and mid-March. Nearby is excellent hiking in the King Range National Conservation Area. For the great hike out to the abandoned Punta Gorda

Lighthouse, drive to the trailhead on the left side of Lighthouse Road (see the previous listing, *Mattole*). This area is typically bombarded with monsoon-level rains in winter.

Campsites, facilities: There are 35 sites for tents or RVs of any length (no hookups). Overflow camping is also available. Picnic tables and fire grills are provided. Drinking water, restrooms with flush toilets, and cold showers are available. A grocery store, coin laundry, and propane gas are available nearby. Leashed pets are permitted.

Reservations, fees: Reservations are not accepted. Sites are $15 per night per vehicle, $3 per person per night for hike-in/bike-in, $3 per night for each additional vehicle, $1 per pet per night. Open year-round.

Directions: From Garberville, drive north on U.S. 101 to the South Fork-Honeydew exit. Turn west on South Fork-Honeydew Road and drive 31 miles (the road changes between pavement, gravel, and dirt, and is steep and curvy) to the park entrance on the left side of the road. The park is 7.5 miles east of the town of Petrolia. (South Fork-Honeydew Road can be difficult for larger vehicles.)

Contact: Humboldt County Public Works, 707/445-7651, www.co.humboldt.ca.us.

46 HUMBOLDT REDWOODS STATE PARK: ALBEE CREEK
🚶 🏊 🛶 🐕 ♿ 🚐 ⛺

Scenic rating: 8

in Humboldt Redwoods State Park

Map 1.2, page 90

Humboldt Redwoods State Park is a massive sprawl of forest that is known for some unusual giant trees in the Federation Grove and Big Tree Area. The park covers nearly 53,000 acres, including more than 17,000 acres of old-growth coast redwoods. It has 100 miles of hiking trails, many excellent, both short and long. The camp is set in a redwood grove, and the smell of these trees has a special magic.

Nearby Albee Creek, a benign trickle most of the year, can flood in the winter after heavy rains. Seasonal interpretive programs, campfire talks, nature walks, and junior ranger programs are available.

Campsites, facilities: There are 40 sites for tents or RVs up to 33 feet and trailers up to 24 feet (no hookups). Picnic tables, fire grills, and food lockers are provided. Drinking water, restrooms with flush toilets and showers, and firewood are available. Some facilities are wheelchair-accessible. Leashed pets are permitted.

Reservations, fees: Reservations are accepted ($7.50 reservation fee) at 800/444-PARK (800/444-7275) or www.reserveamerica.com. Sites are $20 per night, $6 per night for each additional vehicle, $3 per person per night for hike-in/bike-in. Open Memorial Day weekend to mid-October.

Directions: From Eureka, drive south on U.S. 101 about 11 miles to the Honeydew exit (if you reach Weott, you have gone two miles too far). At Mattole Road, turn west and drive five miles to the campground on the right.

Contact: Humboldt Redwoods State Park, 707/946-2472 or 707/946-2409, fax 707/946-2326, www.parks.ca.gov.

47 HUMBOLDT REDWOODS STATE PARK: BURLINGTON

🚶 🏊 🎣 🐾 ♿ 🚐 ⛺

Scenic rating: 7

in Humboldt Redwoods State Park

Map 1.2, page 90

This camp is one of the centerpieces of Humboldt Redwoods State Park. Humboldt is California's largest redwood state park and also includes the largest remaining contiguous old-growth coast redwood forest in the world: the Rockefeller Forest. The trees here are thousands of years old and have never been logged; they are as pristine now as 200 years ago. This camp is often at capacity during the tourist months. You get shady campsites with big redwood

stumps that kids can play on. There's good hiking on trails routed through the redwoods, and in winter, steelhead fishing is often good on the nearby Eel River. The park has 100 miles of trails, but it is little half-mile Founders Grove Nature Trail that has the quickest payoff and requires the least effort. The average rainfall here is 65 inches per year, with most occurring between October and May. Morning and evening fog in the summer keeps the temperature cool in the river basin.

Campsites, facilities: There are 57 sites for tents or RVs up to 33 feet (no hookups) and trailers up to 24 feet, and three hike-in/bike-in sites. Picnic tables, fire grills, and food lockers are provided. Drinking water, restrooms with flush toilets and showers and firewood are available. Some facilities are wheelchair-accessible. Leashed pets are permitted.

Reservations, fees: Reservations are accepted ($7.50 reservation fee) at 800/444-PARK (800/444-7275) or www.reserveamerica.com. Sites are $20 per night, $6 per night for each additional vehicle, $3 per person per night for hike-in/bike-in sites. Open year-round.

Directions: From Eureka, drive south on U.S. 101 for 45 miles to the Weott/Newton Road exit. Turn right on Newton Road and continue to the T junction where Newton Road meets the Avenue of the Giants. Turn left on the Avenue of the Giants and drive two miles to the campground entrance on the left.

Contact: Humboldt Redwoods State Park, 707/946-1811 or 707/946-2409, fax 707/946-2326, www.parks.ca.gov.

48 HUMBOLDT REDWOODS STATE PARK: HIDDEN SPRINGS

🚶 🏊 🎣 🐾 🚐 ⛺

Scenic rating: 7

in Humboldt Redwoods State Park

Map 1.2, page 90

This camp gets heavy use from May through September, but the campsites have been situated in a way that offers relative seclusion. Side trips include good hiking on trails routed through redwoods and a touring drive on Avenue of the Giants. The park has more than 100 miles of hiking trails, many of them amid spectacular giant redwoods, including Bull Creek Flats Trail and Founders Grove Nature Trail. Bears are occasionally spotted by mountain bikers on rides out to the park's outskirts. In winter, nearby High Rock on the Eel River is one of the better shoreline fishing spots for steelhead. (For more information on Humboldt Redwoods, see previous listings for *Albee Creek* and *Burlington* campgrounds.)

Campsites, facilities: There are 154 sites for tents or RVs up to 33 feet (no hookups) and trailers up to 24 feet. Picnic tables, fire grills, and food lockers are provided. Drinking water, restrooms with flush toilets and showers and firewood are available. A grocery store and coin laundry are available within one mile in Myers Flat. Leashed pets are permitted.

Reservations, fees: Reservations are accepted ($7.50 reservation fee) at 800/444-PARK (800/444-7275) or www.reserveamerica.com. Sites are $20 per night, $6 per night for each additional vehicle. Open mid-April through Labor Day weekend.

Directions: From Eureka, drive south 50 miles on U.S. 101 to the Myers Flat/Avenue of the Giants exit. Continue south and drive less than a mile to the campground entrance on the left.

Contact: Humboldt Redwoods State Park, 707/943-3177 or 707/946-2409, fax 707/946-2326, www.parks.ca.gov.

49 GIANT REDWOODS RV AND CAMP
🏃 ♨ ⛵ 🐾 🚵 🚐 ⛺

Scenic rating: 8

on the Eel River

Map 1.2, page 90

This privately operated park is set in a grove of redwoods and covers 23 acres, much of it fronting the Eel River. Trip options include the scenic drive on Avenue of the Giants.

Campsites, facilities: There are 26 tent sites and 57 sites for RVs of any length. Many of the RV sites have full or partial hookups (30 amps) and are pull-through. Picnic tables and fire rings are provided. Restrooms with showers, modem hookups, a convenience store, ice, coin laundry, playground, dog "freedom area," and a recreation room are available. Leashed pets are permitted.

Reservations, fees: Reservations are recommended in the summer. Sites are $25.30–37.40 per night, $3 per person per night for more than two people, $2 per pet per night. Seventh night free. Some credit cards accepted. Open year-round, with limited facilities in winter.

Directions: From Eureka, drive south 50 miles on U.S. 101 to the Myers Flat/Avenue of the Giants exit. Turn right on Avenue of the Giants and make a quick left onto Myers Avenue. Drive 0.25 mile on Myers Avenue to the campground entrance.

Contact: Giant Redwoods RV and Camp, 707/943-3198, www.giantredwoodsrvcamp.com.

50 DEAN CREEK RESORT
🏃 ♨ ⛵ 🐾 🚵 ♿ 🚐 ⛺

Scenic rating: 7

on the South Fork of the Eel River

Map 1.2, page 90

This year-round RV park is set on the South Fork of the Eel River. This is a very family-oriented resort. In the summer, it makes a good base camp for a redwood park adventure, with Humboldt Redwoods State Park (well north of here) providing 100 miles of hiking trails, many routed through awesome stands of giant trees. In the winter heavy rains feed the South Fork Eel, inspiring steelhead upstream on their annual winter journey. Fishing is good in this area, best by shore at nearby High Rock. Bank access is good at several other spots. Note that there is catch-and-release fishing only; check fishing regulations. Contact information for fishing guides is available at the resort, and they offer winter steelhead fishing specials. An excellent side trip is to drive three miles south to the Avenue of the Giants, a tour through giant redwood trees. The campground also offers volleyball, shuffleboard, badminton, and horseshoes. You get the idea.

Campsites, facilities: There are 64 sites with full or partial hookups (30 and 50 amps) for tents or RVs of any length; some sites are pull-through. Picnic tables and fire grills are provided. Restrooms with showers, recreation room, coin laundry, motel, convenience store, modem and Wi-Fi access, RV supplies, firewood, ice, giant spa, sauna, seasonal heated swimming pool, dump station, amphitheater, group facilities, arcade, basketball, tetherball, shuffleboard, volleyball, mini golf, and a playground are available. Some facilities are wheelchair-accessible. Leashed pets are permitted.

Reservations, fees: Reservations are recommended in the summer at 877/923-2555. Sites are $26–36 per night, $3.50 per person per night for more than two people, $1.50 per pet per night, $1.50 per night for each additional vehicle. Some credit cards accepted. Open year-round.

Directions: From Eureka, drive 60 miles south on U.S. 101 to the Redwood Drive exit. Exit onto Redwood Drive and continue about one-half block to the motel/campground entrance on the right; check in at the motel.

Contact: Dean Creek Resort, 707/923-2555, www.deancreekresort.com.

51 HORSE MOUNTAIN

Scenic rating: 6

in the King Range

Map 1.2, page 90

Few people know of this spot. The campground is set along the northwest flank of Horse Mountain. A primitive road (Saddle Mountain Road) leads west from the camp and then goes left at the Y, up to Horse Mountain (1,929 feet), which offers spectacular ocean and coastal views on clear days. If you turn right at the Y, the road leads to the trailhead for the King Crest Trail near Saddle Mountain (3,290 feet). This hike is an ambitious climb to King Peak (4,087 feet), rewarding hikers with a fantastic panorama, including Mount Lassen poking above the Yolla Bolly Wilderness to the east.

Campsites, facilities: There are nine sites for tents only. Picnic tables and fire rings are provided. Vault toilets are available. No drinking water is available. Leashed pets are permitted.

Reservations, fees: Reservations are not accepted. Sites are $5 per night. Open year-round.

Directions: From Eureka, drive 60 miles south on U.S. 101 to the Redway/Shelter Cove exit. Take that exit and drive 2.5 miles north on Redwood Road to Briceland-Thorne Road. Turn right on Briceland-Thorne Road (which will become Shelter Cove Road) and drive 17 miles to King Peak Road (Horse Mountain). Turn right and continue six miles to the campground on the right.

Contact: Bureau of Land Management, Arcata Field Office, 707/825-2300, fax 707/825-2301.

52 TOLKAN

Scenic rating: 6

in the King Range

Map 1.2, page 90

This remote camp is set at 1,840 feet, a short drive south of Horse Mountain. (For nearby side-trip options, see the previous listing for *Horse Mountain*.)

Campsites, facilities: There are nine sites for tents or RVs up to 20 feet (no hookups). Picnic tables and fire rings are provided. Vault toilets are available. No drinking water is available.

Some facilities are wheelchair-accessible. Leashed pets are permitted.

Reservations, fees: Reservations are not accepted. Sites are $5 per night. Open year-round.

Directions: From Eureka, drive 60 miles south on U.S. 101 to the Redway exit. Take the Redway/Shelter Cove exit onto Redwood Drive into the town of Redway. Drive 2.5 miles (look on the right for the King Range Conservation Area sign) to Briceland-Thorne Road. Turn right on Briceland-Thorne Road (which will become Shelter Cove Road) and drive 17 miles to King Peak (Horse Mountain) Road. Turn right on King Peak Road and continue 3.5 miles to the campground on the right.

Contact: Bureau of Land Management, Arcata Field Office, 707/825-2300, fax 707/825-2301.

53 SHELTER COVE CAMPGROUND AND DELI

🏃 🎣 🚐 🏕 🚗 ⛰

Scenic rating: 8

in Shelter Cove overlooking the Pacific Ocean

Map 1.2, page 90

This is a prime oceanside spot to set up a base camp for deep-sea fishing, whale-watching, tidepool gazing, beachcombing, and hiking. While this is a prime recreation area, the campground itself is rather uninspiring. Long-term renters occupy some of the campsites. A wide boat ramp makes it perfect for campers who have trailered boats and don't mind the long drive. Reservations are strongly advised here. The park's backdrop is the King Range National Conservation Area, offering spectacular views. The deli is well known for its fish-and-chips. The salmon, halibut, and rockfish fishing is quite good here in the summer; always call first for current regulations and seasons, which change every year. Clamming is best during winter's low tides, and hiking in the King Mountain Range during the summer. Seasonal abalone

diving and shore fishing for redtail perch are also available. There is heavy rain in winter. Insider's tip: Two miles north is one of the only black-sand beaches in the continental United States.

Campsites, facilities: There are 103 sites for tents or RVs; many have full hookups (30 amps); some sites are pull-through. Picnic tables and fire rings are provided. Restrooms with showers, dump station, coin laundry, grocery store, deli, propane, ice, and RV supplies are available. A boat ramp and marina are across the street. Leashed pets are permitted.

Reservations, fees: Reservations are recommended. Sites are $26–37 per night, $5 per person per night for more than two people, $1 per pet per night. Some credit cards accepted. Open year-round.

Directions: From Eureka, drive 60 miles south on U.S. 101 to the Redway/Shelter Cove exit. Take that exit and drive 2.5 miles north on Redwood Road to Briceland-Thorne Road (which will become Shelter Cove Road). Turn right (west) and drive 18 miles (following the truck/RV route signs) to Upper Pacific Drive. Turn left (south) on Upper Pacific Drive and proceed (it becomes Machi Road) 0.5 mile to the park on the right.

Contact: Shelter Cove Campground and Deli, 707/986-7474, fax 707/986-7101.

54 BENBOW LAKE STATE RECREATION AREA

🏃 🏊 🎣 🚐 🏕 🚗 ⛰

Scenic rating: 7

on the Eel River

Map 1.2, page 90

This camp is set along the South Fork of the Eel River, with easy access from U.S. 101. It gets heavy use in the summer. In theory, Benbow Lake is created each summer when the river is dammed on a temporary basis, creating a 26-acre lake for swimming and light boating (no motors). This seasonal dam is projected to be installed in mid-June and kept in place until mid-September. However, there is no guarantee this will occur. If you're making a vacation planned around lake recreation, always call first. In the winter, this stretch of river can be quite good for catch-and-release steelhead fishing. Warning: Blue-green algae warnings are sometimes posted here in late summer; the algae can be dangerous to dogs.

Campsites, facilities: There are 77 sites for tents or RVs up to 30 feet; two sites have full hookups (30 amps). Picnic tables, food lockers, and fire grills are provided. Drinking water and restrooms with flush toilets and coin showers are available. A boat ramp (no motors) and seasonal boat rentals are available nearby. There is a dump station at the park entrance. Supplies and a coin laundry are available in Garberville. Leashed pets are permitted at campsites only.

Reservations, fees: Reservations are accepted ($7.50 reservation fee) at 800/444-PARK (800/444-7275) or www.reserveamerica.com. Sites are $20–28 per night, $6 per night for each additional vehicle. Open May through September, weather permitting.

Directions: From the junction of U.S. 101 and Highway 1 in Leggett, drive north on U.S. 101 past Richardson Grove State Park to the Benbow Drive exit (two miles south of Garberville). Take that exit and drive 2.7 miles to the park entrance.

Contact: Benbow Lake State Recreation Area, 707/923-3238; Richardson Grove State Park, 707/247-3318, www.parks.ca.gov.

55 BENBOW VALLEY RV RESORT AND GOLF COURSE

Scenic rating: 7

on the Eel River

Map 1.2, page 90

This is an RV park set along U.S. 101 and the South Fork Eel River, with both a pretty nine-hole regulation golf course and little Benbow Lake providing nearby recreation. It takes on a dramatically different character in the winter, when the highway is largely abandoned, the river comes up, and steelhead migrate upstream to the stretch of water here. Cooks Valley and Benbow provide good shore fishing access. Note that fishing restrictions for steelhead are extremely severe and subject to constant change; always check with DFG before fishing for steelhead. (See the previous listing, *Benbow Lake State Recreation Area*, for a note on the status of Benbow Lake.)

Campsites, facilities: There are 112 sites with full hookups (30 and 50 amps), including four "VIP" sites for RVs of any length. Many sites are pull-through. No tents. Cottages, park-model cabins, and trailer rentals are also available. Picnic tables and cable TV are provided. Restrooms with showers, coin laundry, convenience store, snack bar, playground, recreation room, seasonal heated swimming pool, seasonal spa, Wi-Fi, modem access, fax and copy services, group facilities, organized activities, shuffleboard, table tennis, horseshoes, game room, RV supplies, and a nine-hole golf course are available. A boat dock and boat rentals (in summer) are available within 100 feet at Benbow Lake. Leashed pets are permitted. A doggy playground and pet wash are available.

Reservations, fees: Reservations are accepted at 866/236-2697. Sites are $42–47 per night, $4 per person per night for more than two people, $4 per night for each additional vehicle, $3 per pet per night. Some credit cards accepted. Open year-round.

Directions: From the junction of U.S. 101 and Highway 1 in Leggett, drive north on U.S. 101 past Richardson Grove State Park to the Benbow Drive exit (two miles south of Garberville). Take that exit and turn right at the stop sign. Drive a short distance to the end of the road and Benbow Drive. Bear left on Benbow Drive and continue a short distance to the resort on the left.

Contact: Benbow Valley RV Resort and Golf Course, 707/923-2777, www.benbowrv .com.

56 RICHARDSON GROVE STATE PARK: MADRONE AND HUCKLEBERRY
🏃 🏊 🛶 🐾 ♿ 🚐 ⛺

Scenic rating: 8

in Richardson Grove State Park

Map 1.2, page 90

The highway cuts a swath right through Richardson Grove State Park, and everyone slows to gawk at the tallest trees in the world, one of the most impressive groves of redwoods you can drive through in California. To explore further, there are several campgrounds available at the park, as well as a network of outstanding hiking trails. The best of these are short Redwood Exhibit Trail, Settlers Loop, and Toumey Trail. The park is one of the prettiest and most popular state parks, making reservations a necessity from Memorial Day through Labor Day weekend. When arriving from points south on U.S. 101, this is the first park in the Redwood Empire where you will encounter significant old-growth redwood. There are nine miles of hiking trails, fishing in the winter for steelhead, and several trees of significant note.

Campsites, facilities: At Madrone Camp, there are 40 sites for tents or RVs up to 30 feet. At Huckleberry, there are 36 sites for tents or RVs up to 30 feet. No hookups. Picnic tables, food lockers, and fire grills are provided. Drinking water and restrooms with flush toilets and coin showers are available. A minimart and dump station (three miles away) are available nearby. Some facilities are wheelchair-accessible. Leashed pets are permitted at campsites only.

Reservations, fees: Reservations are accepted ($7.50 reservation fee) at 800/444-PARK (800/444-7275) or www.reserveamerica.

com. Sites are $15–20 per night, $6 per night for each additional vehicle. Open year-round, but subject to occasional winter closures.

Directions: From the junction of U.S. 101 and Highway 1 in Leggett, drive north on U.S. 101 for 16 miles (past Piercy) to the park entrance along the west (left) side of the road (eight miles south of Garberville).

Contact: Richardson Grove State Park, 707/247-3318, www.parks.ca.gov.

57 RICHARDSON GROVE STATE PARK: OAK FLAT
🏃 🏊 🛶 🐾 🚐 ⛺

Scenic rating: 8

in Richardson Grove State Park

Map 1.2, page 90

Oak Flat is on the eastern side of the Eel River in the shade of forest and provides easy access to the river. The campground is open only in the summer. (For side-trip information, see the previous listing, *Madrone and Huckleberry.*)

Campsites, facilities: There are 100 sites for tents or RVs up to 24 feet (no hookups) and trailers up to 18 feet. Picnic tables, food lockers, and fire grills are provided. Drinking water, restrooms with flush toilets and coin showers, and Wi-Fi are available. A grocery store and propane gas are available nearby. Leashed pets are permitted.

Reservations, fees: Reservations are accepted ($7.50 reservation fee) at 800/444-PARK (800/444-7275) or www.reserveamerica.com. Sites are $15–20 per night, $6 per night for each additional vehicle. Open mid-June to mid-September, weather permitting.

Directions: From the junction of U.S. 101 and Highway 1 in Leggett, drive north on U.S. 101 for 16 miles (past Piercy) to the park entrance on the west (left) side of the road (eight miles south of Garberville).

Contact: Richardson Grove State Park, 707/247-3318, www.parks.ca.gov.

58 RICHARDSON GROVE CAMPGROUND AND RV PARK

🏃 🏊 🐕 🚴 🚐 ⛺

Scenic rating: 7

on the Eel River

Map 1.2, page 90

This private camp provides a nearby alternative to Richardson Grove State Park, complete with cabin rentals. The state park, with its grove of giant redwoods and excellent hiking, is the primary attraction. The RV park is family-oriented, with volleyball and basketball courts and horseshoe pits. The adjacent South Fork Eel River may look like a trickle in the summer, but there are some good swimming holes. It also provides good steelhead fishing in January and February, with especially good shore fishing access here as well as to the south in Cooks Valley (check DFG regulations before fishing). This campground is owned and operated by the Northern California/Nevada District Assemblies of God. Because of their nonprofit status, several cabins and a dorm are no longer available for rent.

Campsites, facilities: There are 98 sites for tents or RVs; some sites are pull-through and many have full or partial hookups (30 amps). Two log cabins are also available. Picnic tables and fire rings are provided. Restrooms with showers, dump station, Wi-Fi, modem access, playground, coin laundry, convenience store, group facilities, propane, and ice are available. Leashed pets are permitted.

Reservations, fees: Reservations are recommended in the summer. Sites are $17–25 per night. Weekly, winter, and group rates available. Some credit cards accepted. Open year-round.

Directions: From the junction of U.S. 101 and Highway 1 in Leggett, drive north on U.S. 101 for 15 miles (one mile before reaching Richardson Grove State Park) to the camp entrance on the west side (left) of the road.

Contact: Richardson Grove Campground and RV Park, 707/247-3380, fax 707/247-9806, www.redwoodfamilycamp.com.

SHASTA AND TRINITY

© KEN DECAMP

BEST CAMPGROUNDS

At 14,162 feet, Mount Shasta rises like a diamond in a field of coal. Its sphere of influence spans a radius of 125 miles, and its shadow is felt everywhere in the region. This area has much to offer with giant Shasta Lake, the Sacramento River above and below the lake, the McCloud River, and the wonderful Trinity Divide country with its dozens of pretty backcountry lakes and several wilderness areas. This is one of the best regions anywhere for an outdoor adventure – especially hiking, fishing, powerboating, rafting, and exploring.

In this area, you can find campgrounds that are truly remote, set near quiet wilderness, and that offer the potential for unlimited adventures. Of all the regions in this book, this is the easiest one in which to find a campground in a secluded setting near great recreation opportunities. That is the main reason people visit.

There are hundreds of destinations, but the most popular are Shasta Lake, the Trinity Alps and their surrounding lakes and streams, and the Klamath Mountains, known as "Bigfoot Country" by the locals.

Shasta Lake is one of America's top recreation lakes and the boating capital of the west. It is big enough to handle all who love it. The massive reservoir boasts 370 miles of shoreline; more than a dozen each of campgrounds, boat launches, and marinas; lakeshore lodging; and 400 houseboat rentals and cabin rentals. A remarkable 22 species of fish live in the lake. Many of the campgrounds feature lake views. In addition, getting here is easy – a straight shot off I-5.

At the charmed center of this beautiful region are the Trinity Alps, where lakes are sprinkled everywhere. It's also home to the headwaters for feeder streams to the Trinity River, Klamath River, New River, Wooley Creek, and others. Trinity Lake provides outstanding boating and fishing, and just downstream, smaller Lewiston Lake offers a quiet alternative. One advantage to Lewiston Lake is that it is always full of water, even all summer long, making for a very pretty scene. Downstream of Lewiston, the Trinity River provides low-cost rafting and outstanding shoreline access along Highway 299 for fishing for salmon and steelhead.

The neighboring Klamath Mountains are well known as Bigfoot Country. If you drive up the Forest Service road at Bluff Creek, just off Highway 96 upstream of Weitchpec, you can even find the spot where the famous Bigfoot movie was shot in the 1960s. Well, I haven't seen Bigfoot, but I have discovered tons of outdoor recreation. This remote region features miles of the Klamath and Salmon Rivers, as well as the Marble Mountain Wilderness. Options include canoeing, rafting, and fishing for steelhead on the Klamath River, or hiking into your choice of more than 100 wilderness lakes.

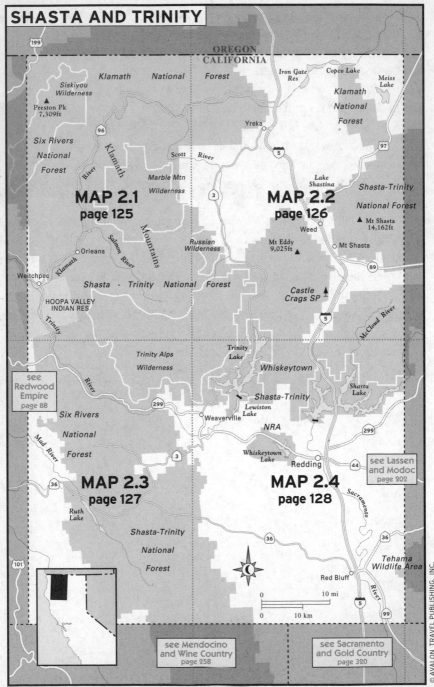

SHASTA AND TRINITY

OREGON
CALIFORNIA

199

Siskiyou
Wilderness

▲ Preston Pk
7,309ft

Klamath   National   Forest

Six Rivers
National
Forest

96

Klamath River

Scott   River

Marble Mtn
Wilderness

Iron Gate
Res

Copco Lake

Meiss
Lake

Klamath
National
Forest

Yreka

5

97

Lake
Shastina

MAP 2.1
page 125

3

Russian
Wilderness

Mt Eddy
9,025ft ▲

MAP 2.2
page 126

Weed

Mt Shasta

Shasta-Trinity
National Forest

▲ Mt Shasta
14,162ft

89

Orleans

Salmon River

Mountains

Weitchpec

Klamath

Shasta - Trinity   National   Forest

HOOPA VALLEY
INDIAN RES

Trinity

Castle
Crags SP

McCloud River

5

Trinity Alps
Wilderness

Trinity
Lake

Whiskeytown

Shasta
Lake

see
Redwood
Empire
page 88

River

299

Shasta-Trinity

Weaverville

Lewiston
Lake

NRA

299

Six Rivers

Mad River

36

National

Forest

3

Whiskeytown
Lake

Redding

44

see Lassen
and Modoc
page 202

MAP 2.3
page 127

Ruth
Lake

Sacramento

MAP 2.4
page 128

36

Shasta-Trinity

National

Forest

36

101

Tehama
Wildlife Area

Red Bluff

River

99

5

0   10 mi

0   10 km

© AVALON TRAVEL PUBLISHING, INC.

see Mendocino
and Wine Country
page 258

see Sacramento
and Gold Country
page 320

Map 2.1

Campgrounds 1-26
Pages 130-142

Map 2.2

Campgrounds 27-58

Pages 142-158

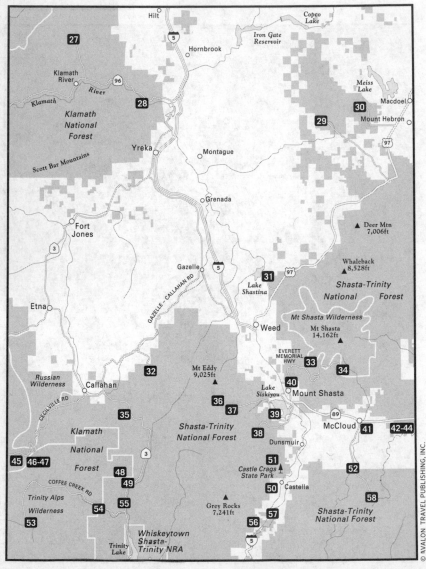

© AVALON TRAVEL PUBLISHING, INC.

Map 2.3

Campgrounds 59-79
Pages 158-167

2.1
2.4

1 2
3 4

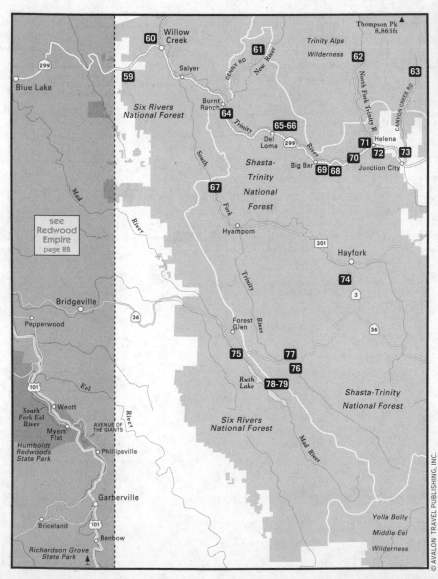

Thompson Pk ▲
8,863ft

Trinity Alps
Wilderness

60 Willow
Creek

61

DENNY RD

New River

Salyer

62

North Fork Trinity R.

CANYON CREEK RD.

63

299

59

Blue Lake

Six Rivers
National Forest

Burnt
Ranch

64

Trinity

65-66

Del
Loma

299

River

Helena

71

72

73

Shasta-
Trinity

National

Forest

South

Fork

Big Bar

69 68

70

Junction City

Mad

River

see
Redwood
Empire
page 88

67

Hyampom

301

Hayfork

Bridgeville

36

Trinity

River

74

3

Pepperwood

Forest
Glen

36

75

77

76

101

Eel

Weott

South
Fork Eel
River

Myers
Flat

River

AVENUE OF
THE GIANTS

Ruth
Lake

78-79

Shasta-Trinity
National Forest

Humboldt
Redwoods
State Park

Phillipsville

Six Rivers
National Forest

Mad River

Garberville

Briceland

101

Benbow

Yolla Bolly

Middle Eel

Wilderness

Richardson Grove
State Park

Map 2.4

Campgrounds 127-148
Pages 188-198

for numbers
80-99 see Map 2.4
Trinity Lake Detail
page 129

for numbers
100-126 see Map 2.4
Shasta Lake Detail
page 129

Shasta-Trinity National Forest

Trinity
Center

Sacramento
River

McCloud
River

Squaw Creek

Stuart Fork

Trinity Mountains

Trinity
Lake

Whiskeytown
Shasta-Trinity
NRA

Shasta
Lake

Pit River

Trinity Dam

127

133-136

Weaverville **132**

130-131

128

129 Douglas
City

Lewiston
Lake

Lewiston

Whiskeytown
Lake

137

138

139

Whiskeytown
Shasta-Trinity
NRA

Shasta
Dam

Shasta Lake

299

140-141

Redding

142

273

44

Anderson

Cottonwood

Sacramento River

HARRISON GULCH RD

143

144 Platina

Shasta-
Trinity
National
Forest

36

36

145

Tehama
Wildlife
Area

147

148

Yolla Bolly
Middle Eel
Wilderness

Red Bluff

146

99

Tehama

Los
Molinos

© AVALON TRAVEL PUBLISHING, INC.

Map 2.4

TRINITY LAKE DETAIL

Campgrounds 80-99
Pages 167-175

Map 2.4

SHASTA LAKE DETAIL

Campgrounds 100-126
Pages 175-188

1 WEST BRANCH

Scenic rating: 6

in Klamath National Forest

Map 2.1, page 125

Note: At the time of publication, this campground was closed because of road damage; check current status. This is a virtually unknown, low-charge camp, set in a canyon near Indian Creek. This is deep in Klamath National Forest at 2,200 feet in elevation. The best side trip here is the winding four-mile drive on a bumpy dirt road to Kelly Lake, little known and little used. A remote Forest Service station is on the opposite side of Indian Creek Road from the campground. It is a 20-minute drive from the town of Happy Camp.

Campsites, facilities: There are 12 sites for tents or RVs up to 25 feet (no hookups). Picnic tables and fire grills are provided. Vault toilets are available. There is no drinking water. There is a dump station in Happy Camp. Garbage must be packed out. Some facilities are wheelchair-accessible. Leashed pets are permitted.

Reservations, fees: Reservations are not accepted. Sites are $10 per night. Open May through October.

Directions: From Happy Camp on Highway 96, turn north on Indian Creek Road (a paved road) and drive 14.5 miles to the camp on the right side of the road.

Contact: Klamath National Forest, Happy Camp and Oak Knoll Ranger Districts, 530/493-2243, fax 530/493-1794.

2 CURLY JACK

Scenic rating: 7

on the Klamath River in Klamath National Forest

Map 2.1, page 125

This campground is set at 1,000 feet in elevation on the Klamath River, providing opportunities for fishing, light rafting, and kayaking. What's special about Curly Jack, though, is that the water is generally warm enough through the summer for swimming.

Campsites, facilities: There are 16 sites for tents or RVs up to 22 feet, with some specially designed sites for RVs up to 45 feet, and three group sites for tents or RVs up to 22 feet that can accommodate up to 30 people each. No hookups. Fire grills and picnic tables are provided. Drinking water and vault toilets are available. Some facilities are wheelchair-accessible. Leashed pets are permitted.

Reservations, fees: Reservations are not accepted for individual sites but are required for group sites ($9 reservation fee) at 877/444-6777 or www.ReserveUSA.com. Sites are $10 per night, $30 per night for a group site. Open year-round, with limited winter facilities.

Directions: From the town of Happy Camp on Highway 96, turn south on Elk Creek Road and drive about one mile. Turn right on Curly Jack Road and drive one block to the campground entrance on the right.

Contact: Klamath National Forest, Happy Camp and Oak Knoll Ranger Districts, 530/493-2243, fax 530/493-1794.

3 ELK CREEK CAMPGROUND AND RV PARK

Scenic rating: 8

on the Klamath River

Map 2.1, page 125   BEST (

Elk Creek Campground is a year-round RV park set where Elk Creek pours into the Klamath River. It is a beautiful campground, with sites right on the water in a pretty, wooded setting. The section of the Klamath River nearby is perfect for inflatable kayaking and rafting. Guided trips are available, with a wide scope of white water available, rated all the way from the easy Class I stuff all the way to the Class V to hell-and-back rapids. In addition, the water is quite warm in the summer and flows are maintained throughout the year, making it ideal for water sports. A swimming hole gets use in summer. The park is popular with anglers and hunters.

Campsites, facilities: There are 34 sites for RVs of any length, some with full or partial hookups (30 and 50 amps); some sites are pull-through. There is a separate area for tents. Three cabins and three rental trailers are available. Picnic tables and fire grills are provided. Restrooms with showers, cable TV, Wi-Fi, recreation room with billiards and table tennis, horseshoes, beach, coin laundry, dump station, propane, and firewood are available. Leashed pets are permitted.

Reservations, fees: Reservations are recommended. RV sites are $20–24 per night, $15 per night for tent sites. Weekly, monthly, and group rates are available. Some credit cards accepted. Open year-round.

Directions: From Highway 96 in the town of Happy Camp, turn south on Elk Creek Road and drive 0.75 mile to the campground on the right.

Contact: Elk Creek Campground and RV Park, 530/493-2208, fax 530/493-2029, www .elkcreekcampground.com.

4 FORT GOFF

Scenic rating: 7

in Klamath National Forest

Map 2.1, page 125

This small, primitive campground is set right along the Klamath River, an ideal location for both fishing and rafting. Many of the most productive shoreline fishing spots on the Klamath River are in this area, with fair trout fishing in summer, good steelhead fishing in the fall and early winter, and a wild card for salmon in late September. There are pullouts along Highway 96 for parking, with short trails/scrambles down to the river. This is also a good spot for rafting, especially in inflatable kayaks, and commercial rafting operations

have trips (Class II+ and III) available on this stretch of river. On the opposite side of Highway 96 (within walking distance to the west) is a trailhead for a hike that is routed along Little Fort Goff Creek, an uphill tromp for five miles to Big Camp and Boundary National Recreation Trail. The creek also runs near the camp, and the elevation is 1,300 feet.

Campsites, facilities: There are five walk-in tent sites. Picnic tables and fire grills are provided. Vault toilets are available. There is no drinking water and garbage must be packed out. Supplies are available in Seiad Valley. Leashed pets are permitted.

Reservations, fees: Reservations are not accepted. There is no fee for camping. Open May through October.

Directions: From Yreka, drive north on I-5 to the junction with Highway 96. At Highway 96, turn west and drive to Seiad Valley. At Seiad Valley, continue west on Highway 96 for five miles to the campground on the left side of the road. Walk a very short distance to the campsites.

Contact: Klamath National Forest, Happy Camp and Oak Knoll Ranger Districts, 530/493-2243, fax 530/493-1794.

5 GRIDER CREEK

Scenic rating: 6

in Klamath National Forest

Map 2.1, page 125

This obscure little camp is used primarily by hikers, since a trailhead for the Pacific Crest Trail is available, and by deer hunters in the fall. The camp is set at 1,400 feet along Grider Creek. Access to the PCT is provided from a bridge across the creek. From here, the Pacific Crest Trail is routed uphill along Grider Creek into the Marble Mountain Wilderness, about an 11-mile ripper to Huckleberry Mountain at 6,303 feet. There are no lakes along the route, only small streams and feeder creeks.

Campsites, facilities: There are 10 sites for

tents or RVs up to 16 feet (no hookups). Picnic tables and fire grills are provided. Vault toilets, horse corrals, and a loading ramp are available. No drinking water is provided. Garbage must be packed out. Some facilities are wheelchair-accessible. Leashed pets are permitted.

Reservations, fees: Reservations are not accepted. There is no fee for camping. Two vehicles maximum per site. Open May through October.

Directions: From Yreka, drive north on I-5 to the junction with Highway 96. At Highway 96, turn west and drive to Walker Creek Road/Forest Road 46N64, one mile before Seiad Valley. Turn left to enter Walker Creek Road and stay to the right as it runs adjacent to the Klamath River to Grider Creek Road. At Grider Creek Road, turn left and drive south for three miles to the camp entrance.

Contact: Klamath National Forest, Happy Camp and Oak Knoll Ranger Districts, 530/493-2243, fax 530/493-1794.

⑥ O'NEIL CREEK

Scenic rating: 7

in Klamath National Forest

Map 2.1, page 125

This camp is set near O'Neil Creek at 1,500 feet in elevation, and though it's not far from the Klamath River, access to the river is not easy. To fish or raft, most people will use this as a base camp, then drive out for recreation during the day. That creates a predicament for RV owners, who lose their campsites every time they drive off. During the fall hunting season, this is a good base camp for hunters branching out into the surrounding national forest. There are also historic mining sites nearby.

Campsites, facilities: There are 11 sites for tents or RVs up to 22 feet (no hookups). Picnic tables and fire grills are provided. Drinking water and vault toilets are available. Garbage must be packed out. Supplies can be obtained in Seiad Valley. Leashed pets are permitted.

Reservations, fees: Reservations are not accepted. Sites are $10 per night. Open May through October.

Directions: From Yreka drive north on I-5 to the junction with Highway 96. Turn west on Highway 96 and drive past Hamburg, continuing west for three miles to the campground.

Contact: Klamath National Forest, Happy Camp and Oak Knoll Ranger Districts, 530/493-2243, fax 530/493-1794.

⑦ SARAH TOTTEN

Scenic rating: 7

on the Klamath River in Klamath National Forest

Map 2.1, page 125

This is one of the more popular Forest Service camps on the Klamath River, and it's no mystery why. In the summer, its placement is perfect for rafters (Class II+ and III), who camp here and use it as a put-in spot. In fall and winter, anglers arrive for the steelhead run. It's in the "banana belt," or good-weather area of the Klamath, in a pretty grove of oak trees. Fishing is often good here for salmon in early October and for steelhead from November through spring, providing there are fishable water flows.

Campsites, facilities: There are eight sites for tents or RVs up to 22 feet, and two group sites for tents or RVs up to 22 feet that can accommodate up to 30 people each. No hookups. Picnic tables and fire grills are provided. Drinking water and vault toilets are available. A small grocery store is nearby. Some facilities are wheelchair-accessible. Leashed pets are permitted.

Reservations, fees: Reservations are not accepted for individual sites but are required for the group sites ($9 reservation fee) at 877/444-6777 or www.ReserveUSA.com. Sites are $10 for per night, $30 per night for group sites. Open May through October.

Directions: From Yreka, drive north on I-5 to

the junction with Highway 96. At Highway 96, turn west and drive to Horse Creek, continuing west for five miles to the campground on the right side of the road. If you reach the town of Hamburg, you have gone 0.5 mile too far.

Contact: Klamath National Forest, Happy Camp and Oak Knoll Ranger Districts, 530/493-2243, fax 530/493-1794.

8 SULPHUR SPRINGS

Scenic rating: 8

on Elk Creek in Klamath National Forest

Map 2.1, page 125

This hidden spot is set along Elk Creek on the border of the Marble Mountain Wilderness. The camp is at a trailhead that provides access to miles and miles of trails that follow streams into the backcountry of the wilderness area. It is a 12-mile backpack trip one way and largely uphill to Spirit Lake, one of the prettiest lakes in the entire wilderness. Sulphur Springs Camp is set at 2,300 feet. The nearby hot springs (which are actually lukewarm) provide a side attraction. There are also some swimming holes nearby in Elk Creek, but these aren't hot springs, so expect the water to be cold.

Campsites, facilities: There are six walk-in tent sites. Picnic tables and fire grills are provided. Vault toilets are available. No drinking water is available. Garbage must be packed out. Leashed pets are permitted.

Reservations, fees: Reservations are not accepted. There is no fee for camping. Open late May through early October.

Directions: From Yreka, drive north on I-5 to the junction with Highway 96. At Highway 96, turn west and drive to Happy Camp. In Happy Camp, turn south on Elk Creek Road and drive 14 miles to the campground.

Contact: Klamath National Forest, Happy Camp and Oak Knoll Ranger Districts, 530/493-2243, fax 530/493-1794.

9 NORCROSS

Scenic rating: 7

near Happy Camp in Klamath National Forest

Map 2.1, page 125

Set at 2,400 feet in elevation, this camp serves as a staging area for various trails that provide access into the Marble Mountain Wilderness. There is also access to the popular Kelsey Trail and to swimming and fishing activities.

Campsites, facilities: There are six sites for tents or RVs up to 25 feet (no hookups). Picnic tables and fire pits are provided. Vault toilets, a horse corral, stock water, and a loading ramp are available. No drinking water is available. Garbage must be packed out. Some facilities are wheelchair-accessible. Leashed pets are permitted.

Reservations, fees: Reservations are not accepted. There is no fee for camping. Open May through October.

Directions: From Yreka on I-5, drive west on Highway 96 to the town of Happy Camp. In Happy Camp, turn south onto Elk Creek Road and drive 16 miles to the campground.

Contact: Klamath National Forest, Happy Camp and Oak Knoll Ranger Districts, 530/493-2243, fax 530/493-1794.

10 BRIDGE FLAT

Scenic rating: 7

in Klamath National Forest

Map 2.1, page 125

This camp is set at 2,000 feet along the Scott River. Though commercial rafting trips are only rarely available here, the river is accessible during the early spring for skilled rafters and kayakers, with a good put-in and take-out spot four miles downriver; others begin their trip at the Buker bridge or the Kelsey Creek bridge (popular swimming hole here). For backpackers a trailhead for the Kelsey Trail is nearby, leading into the Marble Mountain

Wilderness. A fish-spawning area is located on Kelsey Creek, upriver from camp.

Campsites, facilities: There are four sites for tents or RVs up to 22 feet (no hookups). Picnic tables and fire grills are provided. Vault toilets are available. There is no drinking water. Garbage must be packed out. Some facilities are wheelchair-accessible. Leashed pets are permitted.

Reservations, fees: Reservations are not accepted. There is no fee for camping. Open May through September.

Directions: From Redding, drive north on I-5 to Yreka. In Yreka, turn southwest on Highway 3 and drive 16.5 miles to Fort Jones. In Fort Jones, turn right on Scott River Road and drive 21 miles to the campground on the right side of the road, just after crossing a bridge.

Contact: Klamath National Forest, Scott River and Salmon River Ranger Districts, 530/468-5351, fax 530/468-1290.

11 INDIAN SCOTTY

Scenic rating: 7

on the Scott River in Klamath National Forest

Map 2.1, page 125

This popular camp provides direct access to the adjacent Scott River. Because it is easy to reach (no gravel roads) and shaded, it gets a lot of use. The camp is set at 2,400 feet. The levels, forces, and temperatures on the Scott River fluctuate greatly from spring to fall. In the spring, it can be a raging cauldron, but cold from snowmelt. Come summer it quiets, with some deep pools providing swimming holes. By fall, it can be reduced to a trickle. Keep your expectations flexible according to the season.

Campsites, facilities: There are 28 sites and a group site (parking lot) for tents or RVs up to 38 feet (no hookups). Picnic tables and fire grills are provided. Drinking water and vault toilets are available. There is a playground in the group-use area. Leashed pets are permitted.

Reservations, fees: Reservations are not accepted for individual sites but are required for the group site ($9 reservation fee) at 800/444-6777 or www.ReserveUSA .com. Individual sites are $10 per night, and the group site is $30 per night. Open May through October.

Directions: From Redding, drive north on I-5 to Yreka. In Yreka, turn southwest on Highway 3 and drive 16.5 miles to Fort Jones. In Fort Jones, turn right on Scott River Road and drive 14 miles to a concrete bridge and the adjacent signed campground entrance on the left.

Contact: Klamath National Forest, Scott River and Salmon River Ranger Districts, 530/468-5351, fax 530/468-1290.

12 DILLON CREEK

Scenic rating: 7

on the Klamath River in Klamath National Forest

Map 2.1, page 125   BEST (

This is a prime base camp for rafting or a steelhead fishing trip. A put-in spot for rafting is adjacent to the camp, with an excellent river run available from here on down past Presido Bar to the takeout at Ti-Bar. If you choose to go on, make absolutely certain to pull out at Green Riffle river access and takeout, or risk death at Ishi Pishi Falls. The water is warm here in the summer, and there are also many excellent swimming holes in the area. In addition, this is a good stretch of water for steelhead fishing from September to February, best in early winter from Dillon Beach to Ti-Bar. The elevation is 800 feet.

Campsites, facilities: There are 21 sites for tents or RVs up to 30 feet (no hookups). Picnic tables, food lockers, and fire grills are provided. Drinking water and vault toilets are available. There is a dump station in Happy Camp 25 miles north of the campground and at Aikens Creek nine miles west of the town of Orleans. Some facilities are wheelchair-accessible. Leashed pets are permitted.

Reservations, fees: Reservations are not accepted. Sites are $10 per night, $5 per night for each additional vehicle. Open mid-May to early November.

Directions: From Yreka, drive north on I-5 to the junction with Highway 96. At Highway 96, turn west and drive to Happy Camp. Continue south from Happy Camp for 35 miles and look for the campground on the right side of the road.

Coming from the west, from Somes Bar, drive 15 miles northeast on Highway 96.

Contact: Six Rivers National Forest, Orleans Ranger District, 530/627-3291, fax 530/627-3401.

13 LOVERS CAMP

Scenic rating: 5

in Klamath National Forest

Map 2.1, page 125

Lovers Camp isn't set up for lovers at all, but for horses and backpackers. This is a trailhead camp set at 4,300 feet at the edge of the Marble Mountain Wilderness, one of the best in the entire wilderness for packers with horses. The trail here is routed up along Canyon Creek to the beautiful Marble Valley at the foot of Black Marble Mountain. The most common destination is Sky High Lakes, a good one-day huff-and-puff away. Now there's a place for lovers.

Campsites, facilities: There are eight walk-in tent sites. Picnic tables and fire grills are provided. Vault toilets are available. There are also facilities for stock unloading and a corral. There is no drinking water, but water is available for stock. Garbage must be packed out. Some facilities are wheelchair-accessible. Leashed pets are permitted.

Reservations, fees: Reservations are not accepted. There is no fee for camping. Open May through October.

Directions: From Redding, drive north on I-5 to Yreka. In Yreka, turn southwest on Highway 3 and drive to Fort Jones and Scott River Road. Turn right on Scott River Road and drive 18 miles to Forest Road 43N45. Turn left (south) on Forest Road 43N45 and drive nine miles to the campground at the end of the road.

Contact: Klamath National Forest, Scott River and Salmon River Ranger Districts, 530/468-5351, fax 530/468-1290.

14 MARBLE MOUNTAIN RANCH

Scenic rating: 6

near the Klamath River

Map 2.1, page 125

The lodge is set just across the road from the Klamath River, an ideal location as headquarters for a rafting trip in the summer or a steelhead fishing trip in the fall. This ranch is considered a vacation destination, with most people staying for a week. The majority of people staying at the ranch are on a package deal with cabin lodging, but campers can participate in meals and organized activities if they make reservations. Commercial rafting or kayaking trips on the Klamath River and Trinity River are available here, with guided trips offered by the ranch. This piece of river is beautiful and fresh with lots of wildlife and birds, yet not dangerous. However, be absolutely certain to take out at Green Riffle boat access before reaching Ishi Pishi Falls, which cannot be run. There's a full pack station at the ranch for guided trail rides lasting from one hour to overnight. Riding lessons are available. Wilderness pack trips, salmon and steelhead drift-boat fishing, and nature walks are also available. In addition, there is a sporting clays trap course. Hiking trails and swimming holes are available on the property. This is a popular ranch for family reunions, conferences, and weddings.

Campsites, facilities: There are 30 tent sites and 10 sites with full hookups (30 amps) for RVs of any length; some sites are pull-through. Eleven housekeeping cabins and two houses are also available. Picnic tables and fire grills are provided. Restrooms with showers, drinking water, coin laundry, ice, firewood, recreation room, swimming pool, spa, fitness room, deli and gift shop, swimming and fishing pond, petting zoo, playground, horseshoe pits, and volleyball and basketball courts are available.

Reservations, fees: Reservations are recommended. RV sites are $20 per night, $5 per person per night for tent sites, $2 per person per night for more than two people. Some credit cards accepted. Open year-round, weather permitting.

Directions: From the junction of U.S. 101 and Highway 299 near Arcata, turn east on Highway 299 and drive to Willow Creek. In Willow Creek, turn north (left) on Highway 96 east and drive to Somes Bar. At Somes Bar, continue for 7.5 miles to Mile Marker 7.6 and Marble Mountain Ranch on the right.

Contact: Marble Mountain Ranch, 530/469-3322 or 800/KLAMATH (800/552-6284), fax 530/469-3321, www.marblemountain-ranch.com.

15 OAK BOTTOM ON THE SALMON RIVER

🚶 ⛵ 🎣 🐕 ♿ 🚐 ⛺

Scenic rating: 7

in Klamath National Forest

Map 2.1, page 125

This camp is just far enough off Highway 96 that it gets missed by zillions of out-of-towners every year. It is set across the road from the lower Salmon River, a pretty, clean, and cold stream that pours out of the surrounding wilderness high country. Swimming is very good in river holes, though the water is cold, especially when nearby Wooley Creek is full of snowmelt pouring out of the Marble

Mountains to the north. In the fall, there is good shoreline fishing for steelhead, though the canyon bottom is shaded almost all day and gets very cold.

Campsites, facilities: There are 26 sites for tents or RVs up to 25 feet (no hookups). Picnic tables and fire grills are provided. Drinking water and vault toilets are available. There is a dump station at the Elk Creek Campground in Happy Camp and at Aikens Creek, 13 miles southwest of the town of Orleans. Supplies are available in Somes Bar. Some facilities are wheelchair-accessible. Leashed pets are permitted.

Reservations, fees: Reservations are not accepted. Sites are $10 per night, $5 per night for each additional vehicle. Open April to mid-October, weather permitting.

Directions: From the junction of U.S. 101 and Highway 299 near Arcata, turn east on Highway 299 and drive to Willow Creek. In Willow Creek, turn north (left) on Highway 96 east and drive to Somes Bar-Etna Road (0.25 mile before Somes Bar). Turn right on Somes Bar-Etna Road and drive two miles to the campground on the left side of the road.

Contact: Six Rivers National Forest, Orleans Ranger District, 530/627-3291, fax 530/627-3401.

16 FISH LAKE

⛵ 🎣 🐕 ♿ 5% 🚐 ⛺

Scenic rating: 8

in Six Rivers National Forest

Map 2.1, page 125

This is a pretty little lake that provides good fishing for stocked rainbow trout from the season opener on Memorial Day weekend through July. The camp gets little pressure in other months. It's in the heart of Bigfoot Country, with numerous Bigfoot sightings reported near Bluff Creek. No powerboats are permitted on the lake, but it's too small for that anyway, being better suited for a canoe, float tube, raft, or pram. The elevation is 1,800 feet.

The presence here of Port-Orford-cedar root disease, spread by spores in the mud, forces closure from October through May in some years; call for current status.

Campsites, facilities: There are 24 sites for tents or RVs up to 20 feet (no hookups). Picnic tables and fire grills are provided. Drinking water and vault toilets are available. Some facilities are wheelchair-accessible. Leashed pets are permitted.

Reservations, fees: Reservations are not accepted. Sites are $10 per night, $5 per night for each additional vehicle. Open late May through early October, weather permitting.

Directions: From I-5 in Redding, turn west on Highway 299 and drive to Willow Creek. In Willow Creek, turn north (left) on Highway 96 east and drive to Weitchpec, continuing seven miles north on Highway 96 to Fish Lake Road/Bluff Creek Road. Turn left on Fish Lake Road/Bluff Creek Road and drive five miles (stay to the right at the Y) to Fish Lake.

Contact: Six Rivers National Forest, Orleans Ranger District, 530/627-3291, fax 530/627-3401.

17 E-NE-NUCK

Scenic rating: 7

in Six Rivers National Forest

Map 2.1, page 125

The campground gets its name from a Karuk chief who lived in the area in the late 1800s. It's a popular spot for anglers; Bluff Creek and the Klamath are within walking distance and Fish Lake is eight miles to the west. Bluff Creek is the legendary site where the Bigfoot film of the 1960s was shot. While it was finally admitted that the film was a phony, it still put Bluff Creek on the map. A unique feature at this campground is a smokehouse for lucky anglers.

Campsites, facilities: There are 11 sites for tents or RVs up to 30 feet (no hookups). Picnic tables, fire rings, and cast-iron firebox stoves are provided. Drinking water, vault toilets, and a smokehouse are available. Some facilities are wheelchair-accessible. Leashed pets are permitted.

Reservations, fees: Reservations are not accepted. Sites are $10 per night, $5 for each additional vehicle. Open late June through October.

Directions: From the junction of U.S. 101 and Highway 299 near Arcata, turn east on Highway 299 and drive to Willow Creek. In Willow Creek, turn north (left) on Highway 96 east and drive to Weitchpec, continuing on Highway 96 for about five miles to the campground. E-Ne-Nuck is just beyond Aikens Creek West campground.

Contact: Six Rivers National Forest, Orleans Ranger District, 530/627-3291, fax 530/627-3401.

18 AIKENS CREEK WEST

Scenic rating: 7

on the Klamath River in Six Rivers National Forest

Map 2.1, page 125

The Klamath River is warm and green here in summer, and this camp provides an ideal put-in spot for a day of easy rafting, especially for newcomers in inflatable kayaks. The camp is set at 340 feet in elevation along the Klamath. From here to Weitchpec is an easy paddle, with the take-out on the right side of the river just below the confluence with the Trinity River. The river is set in a beautiful canyon with lots of birds and enters the Yurok Indian Reservation. The steelhead fishing can be good in this area from August through mid-November. Highway 96 is a scenic but slow cruise.

Campsites, facilities: There are dispersed sites for tents or RVs of any length (no hookups). Picnic tables and fire grills are provided. Vault toilets, drinking water and a dump station are available. There are reduced services in winter, and all garbage must be packed out. Leashed pets are permitted.

Reservations, fees: Sites are $10 per night, $5 per night for each additional vehicle; no fees during the winter. Open year-round, weather permitting.

Directions: From the junction of U.S. 101 and Highway 299 near Arcata, turn east on Highway 299 and drive to Willow Creek. In Willow Creek, turn north (left) on Highway 96 east and drive to Weitchpec, continuing on Highway 96 for five miles to the campground on the right side of the road.

Contact: Six Rivers National Forest, Orleans Ranger District, 530/627-3291, fax 530/627-3401.

19 KLAMATH RIVERSIDE RV PARK AND CAMPGROUND

🚶 🏊 🎣 ⛴ 🐕 🎣 🚐 ⛺

Scenic rating: 8

on the Klamath River

Map 2.1, page 125

Klamath Riverside RV Park and Campground is an option for RV cruisers touring Highway 96—designated the Bigfoot Scenic Byway—and looking for a place in Orleans. The camp has large grassy sites set amid pine trees, right on the river. There are spectacular views of Mount Orleans and the surrounding hills. A 12-foot Bigfoot statue is on the property. Through the years, I've seen many changes at this park. It has been transformed from a dusty fishing spot to a park more resembling a rural resort that attracts hikers, cyclists, gold panners, river enthusiasts, anglers, and hunters. One big plus is that the park offers guided trips during the season for fishing.

Campsites, facilities: There are 12 tent sites and 45 sites with full hookups (30 and 50 amps) for RVs of any length; some sites are pull-through. Two cabins and six rental trailers are also available. Picnic tables and fire rings are provided. Restrooms with showers, seasonal swimming pool, a spa, group pavilion,

fish-cleaning station, coin laundry, horseshoes, playground, modem access, pay phone, and RV storage are available. Guided drift-boat fishing in season is available. Leashed pets are permitted.

Reservations, fees: Reservations are accepted. Sites are $18–24 per night, $5 per person per night for more than two people. Group, weekly, and monthly rates available. Open year-round.

Directions: From the junction of U.S. 101 and Highway 299 near Arcata, drive east on Highway 299 to Willow Creek, turn north (left) on Highway 96 east and drive past Weitchpec to Orleans. This campground is at the west end of the town of Orleans on Highway 96 on the right.

Contact: Klamath Riverside RV Park and Campground, 530/627-3239 or 800/627-9779, fax 530/627-3755, www.klamathriversidervpark.com.

20 PEARCH CREEK

🚶 🏊 🎣 🐕 🚐 ⛺

Scenic rating: 7

on the Klamath River in Six Rivers National Forest

Map 2.1, page 125

This is one of the premium Forest Service camps on the Klamath River because of its easy access from the highway and easy access to the river. The camp is set on Pearch Creek, about a quarter mile from the Klamath at a deep bend in the river. Indeed, the fishing is often excellent for one- to five-pound steelhead from August through November. The elevation is 400 feet.

Campsites, facilities: There are 10 sites for tents or RVs up to 22 feet (no hookups). Picnic tables and fire grills are provided. Drinking water and vault toilets are available. A grocery store, coin laundry, and propane gas are available within one mile. Leashed pets are permitted.

Reservations, fees: Reservations are not

accepted. Sites are $10 per night, $5 per night for each additional vehicle. Open late May to early November.
Directions: From I-5 in Redding, turn west on Highway 299 and drive to Willow Creek. In Willow Creek, turn north (left) on Highway 96 east, drive past Weitchpec, and continue to Orleans. In Orleans, continue for one mile and look for the campground entrance on the right side of the road.
Contact: Six Rivers National Forest, Orleans Ranger District, 530/627-3291, fax 530/627-3401.

21 IDLEWILD

🏃 🚣 🛶 🏕 🚐 ⛺

Scenic rating: 8

on the North Fork of the Salmon River in Klamath National Forest

Map 2.1, page 125

This is one of the prettiest drive-to camps in the region, set on the North Fork of the Salmon River, a beautiful, cold, clear stream and a major tributary to the Klamath River. Most campers use the camp for its nearby trailhead (two miles north on a dirt Forest Service road out of camp). The hike here is routed to the north, climbing alongside the Salmon River for miles into the Marble Mountain Wilderness (wilderness permits are required). It's a rugged 10-mile, all-day climb to Lake of the Island with several other lakes (highlighted by Hancock Lake) to the nearby west, accessible on weeklong trips. The elevation is 2,600 feet.
Campsites, facilities: There are 18 sites for tents or RVs up to 22 feet (no hookups). Picnic tables and fire grills are provided. Drinking water and vault toilets are available, with limited winter facilities. Leashed pets are permitted.
Reservations, fees: Reservations are not accepted. Sites are $10 per night, with no fee during the winter. Open year-round.
Directions: From Yreka, turn southwest on

Highway 3 and drive to Etna. In Etna, turn west on Etna-Somes Bar Road (Main Street in town) and drive about 16 miles to the campground on the right side of the road. Note: A shorter, more scenic, and more complex route is available from Gazelle (north of Weed on Old Highway 99). Take Gazelle-Callahan Road west over the summit and continue north to Etna.
Contact: Klamath National Forest, Salmon River and Scott River Ranger Districts, 530/468-5351, fax 530/468-1290.

22 MATTHEWS CREEK

🚣 🛶 🏕 🚐 ⛺

Scenic rating: 8

on the Salmon River in Klamath National Forest

Map 2.1, page 125   **BEST (**

This camp is set in a dramatic river canyon, with the beautiful South Fork of the Salmon River nearby. Rafters call it the "Cal Salmon," and good put-in and take-out spots are found every few miles all the way to the confluence with the Klamath. In early summer the water is quite cold from snowmelt, but by midsummer it warms up significantly. The best fishing for steelhead on the Salmon is in December and January in the stretch of river downstream from the town of Forks of Salmon or upstream in the South Fork (check regulations for closed areas). In winter the mountain rims shield the canyon floor from sunlight and it gets so cold you'll feel like a human glacier. The elevation is 1,700 feet.
Campsites, facilities: There are 12 sites for tents or RVs up to 16 feet (no hookups). Picnic tables and fire grills are provided. Drinking water and vault toilets are available, with limited winter facilities. Leashed or controlled pets are permitted.
Reservations, fees: Reservations are not accepted. Sites are $10 per night. Open May through October.
Directions: From the junction of U.S. 101 and

Highway 299 near Arcata, head east on Highway 299 and drive to Willow Creek. In Willow Creek, turn north on Highway 96 and drive past Orleans to Somes Bar. At Somes Bar, turn east on Salmon River Road/Forest Road 2B01 and drive to the town of Forks of Salmon. Turn right on Cecilville Road/Forest Road 1002 and drive about nine miles to the campground. Cecilville Road is very narrow.

Contact: Klamath National Forest, Salmon River and Scott River Ranger Districts, 530/468-5351, fax 530/468-1290.

23 EAST FORK

Scenic rating: 6

on the Salmon River in Klamath National Forest

Map 2.1, page 125

This is one of the more spectacular areas in the fall when the leaves turn different shades of gold. It's set at 2,600 feet along the Salmon River, just outside the town of Cecilville. Directly adjacent to the camp is Forest Road 37N02, which leads to a Forest Service station four miles away, and to a trailhead for the Trinity Alps Wilderness three miles beyond that. Note to steelhead anglers: Check the Department of Fish and Game regulations for closed areas on the Salmon River.

Campsites, facilities: There are nine sites for tents or RVs up to 16 feet (no hookups). Picnic tables and fire grills are provided. Vault toilets are available. No drinking water is available. Garbage must be packed out. Leashed pets are permitted.

Reservations, fees: Reservations are not accepted. There is no fee for camping. Open May through October.

Directions: From Weed, drive north on I-5 to the Edgewood exit. Take the Edgewood exit, turn left at the stop sign, and drive a short distance under the freeway to another stop sign at Old Highway 99. Turn right (north)

and drive six miles to Gazelle and Gazelle-Callahan Road. Turn left (west) on Gazelle-Callahan Road, and drive to Callahan and Cecilville Road. Turn left (southwest) on Cecilville Road and drive about 30 miles to the campground on the right side of the road. If you reach the town of Cecilville, you have gone two miles too far.

Contact: Klamath National Forest, Salmon River and Scott River Ranger Districts, 530/468-5351, fax 530/468-1290.

24 SHADOW CREEK

Scenic rating: 7

in Klamath National Forest

Map 2.1, page 125

This tiny spot, secluded and quiet, is along little Shadow Creek where it enters the East Fork Salmon River, adjacent to a deep bend in the road. An unusual side trip is to take the Forest Service road out of camp (turn north off Cecilville Road) and follow it as it winds back and forth, finally arriving at Grouse Point, 5,409 feet in elevation, for a view of the western slopes of the nearby Russian and Trinity Alps Wilderness Areas. There are three trailheads six miles to the east of the camp: Fish Creek, Long Gulch, and Trail Gulch. Note: The river adjacent to the campground is a spawning area and is closed to salmon and steelhead fishing, but you can take trout.

Campsites, facilities: There are five sites for tents or RVs up to 16 feet (no hookups). Picnic tables and fire grills are provided. Vault toilets are available. No drinking water is available. Garbage must be packed out. Leashed pets are permitted.

Reservations, fees: Reservations are not accepted. There is no fee for camping. Open May through October.

Directions: From Weed, drive north on I-5 to the Edgewood exit. Take the Edgewood exit, turn left at the stop sign, and drive a short distance under the freeway to another stop sign at Old Highway 99. Turn right (north) and drive six miles to Gazelle and Gazelle-Callahan Road. Turn left (west) and drive to Callahan and Cecilville Road. Turn left (southwest) on Cecilville Road and drive about 25 miles to the campground on the left side of the road.

Contact: Klamath National Forest, Salmon River and Scott River Ranger Districts, 530/468-5351, fax 530/468-1290.

25 TISH TANG

Scenic rating: 8

in Six Rivers National Forest

Map 2.1, page 125

This campground is adjacent to one of the best swimming holes in all of Northern California. By late July the adjacent Trinity River is warm and slow, perfect for tubing, a quick dunk, and paddling a canoe. There is a large gravel beach, and some people will bring along their shorty lawn chairs and just take a seat on the edge of the river in a few inches of water. Though Tish Tang is a good put-in spot for rafting in the late spring and early summer, the flows are too slow and quiet for most rafters to even ruffle a feather during the summer. The elevation is 300 feet.

Campsites, facilities: There are 40 sites for tents or RVs up to 22 feet (no hookups). Picnic tables and fire grills are provided. Drinking water and vault toilets are available, and there is a camp host. Leashed pets are permitted.

Reservations, fees: Reservations are accepted at 530/625-4284. Sites are $10 per night, $3 per night for each additional vehicle, $15 per night for double sites. Open late May through September.

Directions: From the junction of U.S. 101 and Highway 299 near Arcata, turn east on Highway 299 and drive to Willow Creek. In Willow Creek, turn north (left) on Highway 96 east

and drive eight miles north to the campground entrance on the right side of the road.

Contact: Hoopa Valley Tribal Council, Forestry Department, 530/625-4284, fax 530/625-4230.

26 MILL CREEK LAKE HIKE-IN

Scenic rating: 4

on the border of the Trinity Alps Wilderness

Map 2.1, page 125

In 1999, a forest fire affected this area and it now is surrounded by many tree skeletons. Recovery is occurring and in time this will again become something of a secret camp. Mill Creek Lake is a secret three-acre lake set at 5,000 feet on the edge of the Trinity Alps Wilderness. Reaching it requires a two-mile hike from the wilderness boundary, with the little lake set just north of North Trinity Mountain (6,362 feet). This is a rare chance to reach a wilderness lake with such a short walk, backpacking without having to pay the penalty of days of demanding hiking. The lake features excellent swimming, with warmer water than in higher and more remote wilderness lakes, and decent fishing for rainbow trout.

Campsites, facilities: There are three primitive tent sites at locations around the lake. Fire rings are provided. No drinking water or toilets are available. Garbage must be packed out. Leashed pets are permitted.

Reservations, fees: Reservations are not accepted. There is no fee for camping. A free wilderness permit is required from the U.S. Forest Service. Open year-round, weather permitting.

Directions: From the junction of U.S. 101 and Highway 299 near Arcata, turn east on Highway 299 and drive to Willow Creek. In Willow Creek turn north (left) on Highway 96 east and drive into the Hoopa Valley to Mill Creek Road. Turn east (right) on Mill Creek Road, and drive approximately 12 miles to the national forest boundary and Forest

Road 10N02. Turn right on Forest Road 10N02 and drive about 3.5 miles, where you will reach another junction. Turn left at the signed junction to the Mill Creek Lake Trailhead and drive a short distance to the parking area. A one-hour walk is then required to reach the lake.

Contact: Six Rivers National Forest, Lower Trinity Ranger District, 530/629-2118, fax 530/629-2102.

27 BEAVER CREEK

Scenic rating: 8

in Klamath National Forest

Map 2.2, page 126

This camp is set along Beaver Creek, a feeder stream to the nearby Klamath River, with two small creeks entering Beaver Creek on the far side of the river near the campground. It is quiet and pretty. There are several historic mining sites in the area; you'll need a map of Klamath National Forest (available for a fee at the district office) to find them. In the fall, this campground is usually taken over by deer hunters. The elevation is 2,400 feet.

Campsites, facilities: There are eight sites for tents or RVs up to 16 feet (no hookups). Picnic tables and fire grills are provided. Vault toilets are available. There is no drinking water. Garbage must be packed out. Leashed pets are permitted.

Reservations, fees: Reservations are not accepted. There is no fee for camping. Open May through October.

Directions: From Yreka, drive north on I-5 to Highway 96. Turn west on Highway 96 and drive approximately 15 miles (if you reach the town of Klamath River, you have gone 0.5 mile too far) to Beaver Creek Road. Turn right on Beaver Creek Road/Forest Road 11 and drive four miles to the campground.

Contact: Klamath National Forest, Happy Camp and Oak Knoll Ranger Districts, 530/493-2243, fax 530/493-1796.

28 TREE OF HEAVEN

Scenic rating: 7

in Klamath National Forest

Map 2.2, page 126   BEST (

This outstanding riverside campground provides excellent access to the Klamath River for fishing, rafting, and hiking. The best deal is to put in your raft, canoe, or drift boat upstream at the ramp below Iron Gate Reservoir, then make the all-day run down to the take-out at Tree of Heaven. This section of river is an easy paddle (Class II, II+, and III) and also provides excellent steelhead fishing in the winter. A 0.25 mile paved interpretive trail is near the camp. On the drive in from the highway, you can watch the landscape turn from high chaparral to forest.

Campsites, facilities: There are 20 sites for tents or RVs up to 35 feet (no hookups). Picnic tables and fire grills are provided. Drinking water and vault toilets are available. A river access spot for put-in and take-out for rafts and drift boats is available. Some facilities are wheelchair-accessible. Leashed pets are permitted.

Reservations, fees: Reservations are accepted ($9 reservation fee) at 877/444-6777 or www .ReserveUSA.com. Sites are $10 per night. Open year-round.

Directions: From Yreka, drive north on I-5 to Highway 96. Turn west on Highway 96 and drive seven miles to the campground entrance on the left side of the road.

Contact: Klamath National Forest, Happy Camp and Oak Knoll Ranger Districts, 530/493-2243, fax 530/493-1796.

29 MARTINS DAIRY

Scenic rating: 8

on the Little Shasta River in Klamath National Forest

Map 2.2, page 126

This camp is set at 6,000 feet, where the deer get big and the country seems wide open. A large meadow is nearby, directly across the road from this remote camp, with fantastic wildflower displays in late spring. This is one of the prettiest camps around in the fall, with dramatic color from aspens, elderberries, and willows. It also makes a good base camp for hunters in the fall. Before heading into the surrounding backcountry, obtain a map (fee) of Klamath National Forest, at the Goosenest Ranger Station on Highway 97, on your way in to camp.

Campsites, facilities: There are eight sites for tents or RVs up to 30 feet (no hookups) and a horse campsite. Picnic tables and fire grills are provided. Drinking water and vault toilets are available. Leashed pets are permitted.

Reservations, fees: Reservations are not accepted. Sites are $8 per night. Open late May to early October, weather permitting.

Directions: From Weed and I-5, turn north on U.S. 97 (Klamath Falls exit) and drive to Grass Lake. Continue about seven miles to Forest Road 70/46N10 (if you reach Hebron Summit, you have driven about a mile too far). Turn left, drive about 10 miles to a Y, take the left fork, and drive three miles (including a very sharp right turn) to the campground on the right side of the road. A map of Klamath National Forest is advised.

Contact: Klamath National Forest, Goosenest Ranger District, 530/398-4391, fax 530/398-5749.

30 JUANITA LAKE

Scenic rating: 7

in Klamath National Forest

Map 2.2, page 126

Small and relatively unknown, this camp is set along the shore of Juanita Lake at 5,100 feet. Swimming is not recommended because the water is cold and mucky, and mosquitoes can be abundant as well. It is stocked with rainbow trout, brown trout, bass, and catfish, but a problem with golden shiners has cut into the lake's fishing productivity. It's a small lake

and forested, set near the Butte Valley Wildlife Area in the plateau country just five miles to the northeast. The latter provides an opportunity to see waterfowl and, in the winter, bald eagles. Campers will discover a network of Forest Service roads in the area, providing an opportunity for mountain biking. There are designated fishing areas and a paved trail around the lake that is wheelchair-accessible and spans approximately 1.25 miles.

Campsites, facilities: There are 23 sites for tents or RVs up to 32 feet (no hookups), and a group tent site that can accommodate up to 50 people. Picnic tables and fire grills are provided. Drinking water and vault toilets are available. Boating is allowed, but no motors are permitted on the lake. Many facilities are wheelchair-accessible. Leashed pets are permitted.

Reservations, fees: Reservations are not accepted for individual sites but are required for the group site at 530/398-4391. Individual sites are $10 per night, and the group site is $30 per night. Open late May to mid-October, weather permitting.

Directions: From Weed and I-5, turn north on U.S. 97 (Klamath Falls exit) and drive approximately 37 miles to Ball Mountain Road. Turn left on Ball Mountain Road and drive 2.5 miles, veer right at the fork, and continue to the campground entrance at the lake.

Contact: Klamath National Forest, Goosenest Ranger District, 530/398-4391, fax 530/398-5749.

31 LAKE SHASTINA

Scenic rating: 7

near Klamath National Forest and Weed

Map 2.2, page 126

Lake Shastina is set at the northern foot of Mount Shasta at 3,000 feet in elevation. It offers spectacular views, good swimming on hot summer days, waterskiing, and all water sports. There is fishing for catfish and bass in the spring and summer, an occasional opportunity for crappie, and good fishing for trout in late winter and spring. One reason the views of Mount Shasta are so good is that this is largely high sagebrush country with few trees. As such, it can get very dusty, windy, and in the winter, nasty cold. When the lake is full, the wind is down, and the weather is good, there are few complaints. But that is only rarely the case. The lake level is often low, with the water drained for hay farmers to the north. This is one of the few lakes in Northern California that has property with lakeside housing. Lake Shastina Golf Course is nearby.

Campsites, facilities: There is a small primitive area for tents or RVs of any length (no hookups). There is one faucet, but you should bring your own water just in case. A vault toilet is available and a boat launch is available nearby; the boat ramp is nonfunctional when the lake level drops below the concrete ramp. Garbage service available May to September only. There is a 14-day limit for camping. Supplies can be obtained five miles away in Weed. Leashed pets are permitted.

Reservations, fees: Reservations are not accepted. There is no fee for camping. Open May through September.

Directions: From Weed and I-5, turn north on U.S. 97 (Klamath Falls exit) and drive about five miles to Big Springs Road. Turn left (west) on Big Springs Road and drive about two miles to Jackson Ranch Road. Turn left (west) on Jackson Ranch Road and drive 0.5 mile to Emerald Isle Road (watch for the signed turnoff). Turn right and drive one mile to the campground.

Contact: Siskiyou County Public Works, 530/842-8250.

32 KANGAROO LAKE WALK-IN

🚶 🏞 🏊 🐕 ♿ 🚐 ⛺

Scenic rating: 10

in Klamath National Forest

Map 2.2, page 126

A remote paved road leads right to Kangaroo Lake, set at 6,500 feet, providing a genuine rarity: a beautiful and pristine mountain lake with a campground, good fishing for brook and rainbow trout, and an excellent trailhead for hikers. The lake is small, 25 acres, but deep at 100 feet. No boat motors are allowed. The walk to the campsites is very short, 1–3 minutes, with many sites very close. Reaching the lake requires another five minutes, but a paved wheelchair-accessible trail is available. In addition, a switchbacked ramp for wheelchairs makes it one of the best wheelchair-accessible fishing areas in California. For hiking, a trail rises steeply out of the campground and connects to the Pacific Crest Trail, from which you turn left to gain a dramatic lookout of Northern California peaks as well as the lake below.

Campsites, facilities: There are 18 walk-in sites for tents, and RVs up to 25 feet (no hookups) are allowed in the parking lot. Picnic tables and fire grills are provided. Drinking water and vault toilets are available. Some facilities are wheelchair-accessible, including a nearby fishing pier. Leashed pets are permitted.

Reservations, fees: Reservations are not accepted. Sites are $10 per night. Open June through October, weather permitting.

Directions: From Weed, drive north on I-5 and take the Edgewood exit. At the stop sign, turn left and drive a short distance under the freeway to the stop sign at Old Highway 99. Turn right (north) on Old Highway 99 and drive six miles to Gazelle and Gazelle-Callahan Road. Turn left at Gazelle-Callahan Road and drive over the summit. From the summit, continue about five miles to Rail Creek Road. Turn left at Rail Creek Road and drive approximately eight miles to where the road dead-ends near the campground. Walk approximately 30–150 yards to reach the campsites.

Contact: Klamath National Forest, Scott River and Salmon River Ranger Districts, 530/468-5351, fax 530/468-1290.

33 McBRIDE SPRINGS

🏃 🐕 ♿ 🚐 ⛺

Scenic rating: 8

in Shasta-Trinity National Forest

Map 2.2, page 126

This camp is set at 4,880 feet on the slopes of the awesome Mount Shasta (14,162 feet), California's most majestic mountain. Stargazing is fantastic here, and during full moons, an eerie glow is cast on the adjoining high mountain slopes. A good side trip is to drive to the end of Everitt Memorial Highway, which tops out above 7,800 feet. You get great lookouts to the west and a jump-off point for a Shasta expedition or day hike to Panther Meadows.

Campsites, facilities: There are nine sites for tents or RVs up to 16 feet (no hookups). Picnic tables and fire grills are provided. Drinking water (from a single well with a hand pump at the north end of the campground) and vault toilets are available. Supplies and a coin laundry are available in the town of Mount Shasta. Some facilities are wheelchair-accessible. Leashed pets are permitted.

Reservations, fees: Reservations are not accepted. Sites are $10 per night. Open Memorial Day weekend through October, weather permitting.

Directions: From Redding drive north on I-5 to the town of Mount Shasta and the Central Mount Shasta exit. Take that exit and drive to the stop sign and Lake Street. Turn right and continue on Lake Street through town; once out of town, the road becomes Everitt Memorial Highway. Continue on Everitt Memorial Highway for four miles to the campground entrance on the left side of the road.

Contact: Shasta-Trinity National Forest, Mount Shasta Ranger District, 530/926-4511, fax 530/926-5120.

34 PANTHER MEADOWS WALK-IN

🏃 🐕 ⛺

Scenic rating: 9

in Shasta-Trinity National Forest

Map 2.2, page 126   BEST (

This quiet site, on the slopes of Mount Shasta at 7,500 feet, features access to the pristine Panther Meadows, a high mountain meadow set just below tree line. It's a sacred place, regardless of your religious orientation. The hiking is excellent here, with a short hike out to Gray Butte (8,119 feet) for a perfect look to the south of Castle Crags, Mount Lassen, and the Sacramento River Canyon. A three-night maximum stay is enforced to minimize long-term impacts.

Campsites, facilities: There are 10 walk-in tent sites (trailers not allowed). Picnic tables and fire grills are provided. Vault toilets are available. No drinking water is available. Garbage must be packed out. Supplies are available in the town of Mount Shasta. Leashed pets are permitted.

Reservations, fees: Reservations are not accepted. There is no fee for camping. Open mid-June to mid-October, weather permitting.

Directions: From Redding, drive north on I-5 to the town of Mount Shasta and the Central Mount Shasta exit. Take that exit and drive to the stop sign and Lake Street. Turn right and continue on Lake Street through town; once out of town, Lake Street becomes Everitt Memorial Highway. Continue on Everitt Memorial Highway for about 12 miles (passing the Bunny Flat parking area) to the campground parking area on the right. Park and walk a short distance to the campsites. Note: When the gate is closed just past Bunny Flat, the walk in is 1.5 miles from the Bunny Flat parking area.

Contact: Shasta-Trinity National Forest, Mount Shasta Ranger District, 530/926-4511, fax 530/926-5120.

35 SCOTT MOUNTAIN

Scenic rating: 7

in Shasta-Trinity National Forest

Map 2.2, page 126

This camp is a jump-off point for hikers, with the Pacific Crest Trail passing right by here. If you hike southwest, it leads into the Scott Mountains and skirts the northern edge of the Trinity Alps Wilderness. Another option here is driving on Forest Road 40N08, which begins directly across from camp and Highway 3. On this road, it's only two miles to Big Carmen Lake, a small, largely unknown and pretty little spot. Campground elevation is 5,300 feet. A Forest Service map is advisable.

Campsites, facilities: There are five tent sites. Picnic tables and fire grills are provided. Vault toilets are available. No drinking water is available. Garbage must be packed out. Leashed pets are permitted.

Reservations, fees: Reservations are not accepted. There is no fee for camping. Open May through October, weather permitting.

Directions: From Weed, drive north on I-5 and take the Edgewood exit. At the stop sign, turn left and drive a short distance under the freeway to the stop sign at Old Highway 99. Turn right (north) and drive six miles to Gazelle and Gazelle-Callahan Road. Turn left at Gazelle-Callahan Road and drive to Callahan and Highway 3. Turn south on Highway 3 and drive to Scott Mountain Summit and look for the campground on the right side of the road.

Contact: Klamath National Forest, Shasta-Trinity National Forest, Weaverville Ranger District, 530/623-2121, fax 530/623-6010.

36 TOAD LAKE WALK-IN

Scenic rating: 9

in Shasta-Trinity National Forest

Map 2.2, page 126

If you want the remote beauty and splendor of an alpine lake on the Pacific Crest Trail, yet you don't want to walk far to get there, this is the place. Toad Lake is no easy trick to get to, with a bone-jarring ride for the last half hour, followed by a 15-minute walk, but it's worth the effort. It's a beautiful little lake, just 23.5 acres, set at 6,900 feet in the Mount Eddy Range, with lakeside sites, excellent swimming, fair fishing for small trout, and great hiking. The best of the latter is a 45-minute hike out of the Toad Lake Basin; follow the trail counterclockwise around the lake and up to the top of the ridge for hiking on the Pacific Crest Trail.

Campsites, facilities: There are six walk-in tent sites. A vault toilet is available. No drinking water is available. Garbage must be packed out. Leashed pets are permitted.

Reservations, fees: Reservations are not accepted. There is no fee for camping. Open May through October, weather permitting.

Directions: From the town of Mount Shasta on I-5, take the Central Mount Shasta exit and drive to the stop sign. Turn west and drive less than a mile to Old Stage Road. Turn left and drive 0.25 mile to a Y intersection at W. A. Barr Road. Bear right and drive past Box Canyon Dam and the entrance to Lake Siskiyou, and continue up the mountain (the road becomes Forest Road 26). Just past a concrete bridge, turn right on Forest Road 41N53 and drive 0.2 mile to a fork and Toad Lake Road. Turn left onto Toad Lake Road (a dirt road) and continue for 11 miles to the parking area. The road is bumpy and twisty, and the final half-mile to the trailhead is rocky and rough. High-clearance or four-wheel-drive vehicles are recommended. Walk in about 0.5 mile to the lake and campsites. Note: Access roads may be closed because of flooding; call ahead for status.

Contact: Shasta-Trinity National Forest, Mount Shasta Ranger District, 530/926-4511, fax 530/926-5120.

37 GUMBOOT LAKE

Scenic rating: 9

in Shasta-Trinity National Forest

Map 2.2, page 126

This pretty spot at 6,080 feet in elevation provides a few small camps set beside a small yet beautiful high mountain lake, the kind of place many think you can reach only with long hikes. Not so with Gumboot. In addition, the fishing is good here, with rainbow trout in the 12-inch class. The lake is small, almost too small for even a canoe, and better suited to a pram, raft, or float tube. No motors of any kind are permitted, including electric motors. When the fishing gets good, it can get crowded, with both out-of-towners and locals making casts from the shoreline. An option is hiking 10 minutes through forest to Upper Gumboot Lake, which is more of a pond with small trout. Another excellent hike is available here, tromping off-trail beyond Upper Gumboot Lake and up the back slope of the lake to the Pacific Crest Trail, then turning left and scrambling to a great lookout of Mount Shasta in the distance and Gumboot in the foreground.

Campsites, facilities: There are four sites for tents or RVs up to 16 feet (no hookups), and across the creek there are four walk-in tent sites. Picnic tables are provided. Vault toilets are available. No drinking water is available. Garbage must be packed out. Some facilities are wheelchair-accessible. Leashed pets are permitted.

Reservations, fees: Reservations are not accepted. There is no fee for camping. Open May through October, weather permitting.

Directions: From the town of Mount Shasta on I-5, take the Central Mount Shasta exit and drive to the stop sign. Turn west and continue less than a mile to Old Stage Road. Turn left and drive 0.25 mile to a Y intersection at W. A. Barr Road. Bear right on W. A. Barr Road and drive past Box Canyon Dam and the Lake Siskiyou Campground entrance. Continue 10 miles to a fork, signed for Gumboot Lake. Bear left and drive 0.5 mile to the lake and campsites. Note: Access roads may be closed because of flooding: call for current status.

Contact: Shasta-Trinity National Forest, Mount Shasta Ranger District, 530/926-4511, fax 530/926-5120.

38 CASTLE LAKE

Scenic rating: 10

in Shasta-Trinity National Forest

Map 2.2, page 126

Castle Lake is a beautiful spot, a deep blue lake set in a granite bowl with a spectacular wall on the far side. The views of Mount Shasta are great, fishing is good (especially ice fishing in winter), canoeing or floating around on a raft is a lot of fun, and there is a terrific hike that loops around the left side of the lake, rising to the ridge overlooking the lake for dramatic views. Locals use this lake for ice-skating in winter. The campground is not right beside the lake, to ensure the pristine clear waters remain untouched, but is rather just a short distance downstream along Castle Lake Creek. The lake is only 47 acres, but 120 feet deep. The elevation is 5,280 at the camp, and 5,450 feet at the lake.

Campsites, facilities: There are six sites for tents or RVs up to 16 feet (no hookups). Picnic tables and fire grills are provided. Vault toilets are available. No drinking water is available. Garbage must be packed out. Leashed pets are permitted.

Reservations, fees: Reservations are not accepted. There is no fee for camping. Open May through October, weather permitting.

Directions: From the town of Mount Shasta on I-5, take the Central Mount Shasta exit and drive to the stop sign. Turn west and drive less than a mile to Old Stage Road. Turn left and drive 0.25 mile to a Y intersection at W. A. Barr Road. Bear right on W. A. Barr Road and drive past Box Canyon Dam. Turn left at Castle Lake Road and drive seven miles to the campground access road on the left. Turn left and drive a short distance to the campground. Note: Castle Lake is another 0.25 mile up the road; there are no legal campsites along the lake's shoreline.

Contact: Shasta-Trinity National Forest, Mount Shasta Ranger District, 530/926-4511, fax 530/926-5120.

39 LAKE SISKIYOU CAMP-RESORT

Scenic rating: 9

near Mount Shasta

Map 2.2, page 126   BEST (

This is a true gem of a lake, a jewel set at the foot of Mount Shasta at 3,181 feet. The lake level is almost always full (because it was built for recreation, not water storage) and offers a variety of quality recreation options, with great swimming, low-speed boating, and fishing. The campground complexes are huge, yet they are tucked into the forest so visitors don't get their styles cramped. The water in this 435-acre lake is clean and fresh. There is an excellent beach and swimming area, the latter protected by a buoy line. In spring, the fishing is good for trout, and then as the water warms, for smallmouth bass. A good boat ramp and boat rentals are available, and a 10-mph speed limit is strictly enforced, keeping the lake pristine and quiet. The City of Mount Shasta holds its July 4 fireworks display above the lake.

Campsites, facilities: There are 150 sites with full or partial hookups (30 and 50 amps) for RVs of any length, including some pull-through sites, and 225 additional sites for tents, seven of which are group areas. There are also 20 cabins and 10 park-model cabins. Picnic tables and fire grills are provided. Drinking water, restrooms with flush toilets and showers, playground, propane, convenience store, gift shop, deli, coin laundry, and a dump station are available. There are also a marina, boat rentals (canoes, kayaks, pedal boats, motorized boats), free boat launching, fishing dock, fish-cleaning station, boat slips, swimming beach, horseshoes, volleyball, group facilities, and a recreation room. A free movie plays every night in the summer. Some facilities are wheelchair-accessible. Leashed pets are permitted at the campground only.

Reservations, fees: Reservations are accepted. Sites are $20–29 per night, $3 per person per night for more than two people, $5 per night for each additional vehicle, $2 per pet per night. Some credit cards accepted. Open April through October, weather permitting.

Directions: From the town of Mount Shasta on I-5, take the Central Mount Shasta exit and drive to the stop sign. Turn west and drive less than a mile to Old Stage Road. Turn left and drive 0.25 mile to a Y intersection at W. A. Barr Road. Bear right on W. A. Barr Road and drive past Box Canyon Dam. Two miles farther, turn right at the entrance road for Lake Siskiyou Campground and Marina and drive a short distance to the entrance station.

Contact: Lake Siskiyou Camp-Resort, 530/926-2618 or 888/926-2618, www.lakesis.com.

40 KOA MOUNT SHASTA

Scenic rating: 7

in Mount Shasta City

Map 2.2, page 126

Despite this KOA camp's relative proximity to the town of Mount Shasta, the extended driveway, wooded grounds, and view of Mount Shasta offer some feeling of seclusion.

There are many excellent side trips. The best is driving up Everitt Memorial Highway, which rises up the slopes of Mount Shasta to the tree line at Bunny Flat, where you can take outstanding, short day hikes with great views to the south of the Sacramento River Canyon and Castle Crags. In the winter, you can play in the snow, including heading up to Bunny Flat for snowplay or to the Mount Shasta Board and Ski Park for developed downhill and cross-country skiing. An ice skating rink is in Mount Shasta. One of the biggest events of the year in Mount Shasta is the Fourth of July Run For Fun (billed as the largest small-town foot race anywhere) and associated parade and fireworks display at nearby Lake Siskiyou.

Campsites, facilities: There are 47 sites with full or partial hookups (20, 30, and 50 amps) for RVs of any length, 50 additional sites with partial hookups for tents or RVs, and four camping cabins. All sites are pull-through. Picnic tables are provided, and fire grills are provided at tent sites only. Restrooms with showers, a playground, propane gas, a convenience store, recreation room with arcade, horseshoe pit, shuffleboard, a seasonal swimming pool, high-speed modem access and Wi-Fi, and coin laundry are available. Leashed pets are permitted.

Reservations, fees: Reservations are accepted at 800/562-3617. Sites are $20–38 per night, $3–4 per person per night for more than two people. Some credit cards accepted. Open year-round.

Directions: From Redding, drive north on I-5 to the town of Mount Shasta. Continue past the first Mount Shasta exit and take the Central Mount Shasta exit. At the stop sign, turn right (east) on Lake Street and drive 0.6 mile to Mount Shasta Boulevard. Turn left and drive 0.5 mile to East Hinckley Boulevard. Turn right (signed KOA) on East Hinckley, drive a very short distance, then turn left at the entrance to the extended driveway for KOA Mount Shasta.

Contact: KOA Mount Shasta, 530/926-4029, www.koa.com.

41 McCLOUD DANCE COUNTRY RV PARK

🕺 🛶 ❄ 🐕 ♿ 🚐 ⛰

Scenic rating: 6

in McCloud

Map 2.2, page 126

McCloud Dance Country RV Park is very popular with square dancers in the summer. The town of McCloud is the home of McCloud Dance Country Hall, a large dance hall dedicated to square and round dancing. The park used to be affiliated with the dance hall, but now the park is open to the public. The park is sprinkled with old-growth pine trees and bordered by Squaw Valley Creek, a pretty stream. The RV sites are grassy and manicured, many shaded. McCloud River's three waterfalls are accessible from the McCloud River Loop, five miles south of the park on Highway 89. Mount Shasta Board and Ski Park also offers summer activities such as biking, a rock-climbing structure, and chairlift rides to great views of the surrounding forests. The ski park access road is six miles west of McCloud off Highway 89 at Snowman's Hill Summit. The McCloud River Railroad runs an excursion and a dinner train on summer weekends out of McCloud; reservations are available in town. If you're lucky you might see "Old Engine No. 25," one of the few remaining steam engines in service. (For more information, see the next listing, *Fowler's Camp.*)

Campsites, facilities: There are 136 sites with full or partial hookups (30 and 50 amps) for RVs of any length, a grassy area for dispersed tent camping, and seven cabins. There are a few long-term rentals. Picnic tables are provided. Drinking water, restrooms with hot showers (heated bathhouse), a central barbecue and campfire area, cable TV, pay telephone, coin laundry, dump station, propane, horseshoes, fish-cleaning station, and two pet walks are available. Some facilities are wheelchair-accessible. Large groups are welcome. Leashed pets are permitted, except in cabins.

Reservations, fees: Reservations are recommended. Sites are $15.74–25 per night, $1.50–3 per person per night for more than two people. Some credit cards accepted. Open year-round.

Directions: From Redding, drive north on I-5 and continue just past Dunsmuir to the junction with Highway 89. Turn east on Highway 89 and drive nine miles to McCloud and Squaw Valley Road. Turn right on Squaw Valley Road and then turn immediately left into the park entrance.

Contact: McCloud Dance Country RV Park, 530/964-2252, www.mccloudrvpark.com.

42 FOWLER'S CAMP

Scenic rating: 10

on the McCloud River in Shasta-Trinity National Forest

Map 2.2, page 126

This campground is set beside the beautiful McCloud River at 3,400 feet, providing the chance for an easy hike to two waterfalls, including one of the most dramatic in Northern California. From the camp, the trail is routed upstream through forest, a near-level walk for only 15 minutes, then arrives at awesome Middle Falls, a wide-sweeping and powerful cascade best viewed in April. By summer, the flows subside and warm to the point that some people will swim in the pool at the base of the falls. The trail is also routed from camp downstream to Lower Falls, an outstanding swimming hole in midsummer. Fishing the McCloud River here is fair, with trout stocks made from Lakim Dam on downstream to the camp. If this camp is full, Cattle Camp and Algoma (see next listings) offer overflow areas.

Campsites, facilities: There are 38 sites and one double site for tents or RVs up to 30 feet (no hookups). Picnic tables and fire grills are provided. Drinking water and vault toilets are available. Some facilities are wheelchair-accessible. Leashed pets are permitted.

Reservations, fees: Reservations are not accepted. Sites are $12 per night. Open late April through October.

Directions: From Redding, drive north on I-5 and continue just past Dunsmuir to the junction with Highway 89. Turn east on Highway 89 and drive 12 miles to McCloud. From McCloud, continue driving on Highway 89 for five miles to the campground entrance road on the right. Turn right and drive a short distance to a Y intersection, then turn left at the Y to the campground.

Contact: Shasta-Trinity National Forest, McCloud Ranger District, 530/964-2184, fax 530/964-2938.

43 ALGOMA

Scenic rating: 7

on the McCloud River in Shasta-Trinity National Forest

Map 2.2, page 126

This little-known, undeveloped spot along the McCloud River at 3,800 feet in elevation is quite dusty in August. It is an alternative to Fowler's Camp and Cattle Camp. (See the previous and the next entries for side-trip options.) A dirt road out of Algoma Camp (turn right at the junction) follows along the headwaters of the McCloud River, past Cattle Camp to Upper Falls. There is a parking area for a short walk to view Middle Falls and on to Fowler's Camp and Lower Falls.

Campsites, facilities: There are eight sites for tents or RVs up to 27 feet (no hookups). Picnic tables and fire grills are provided. No drinking water or toilets are available. Leashed pets are permitted.

Reservations, fees: Reservations are not accepted. There is no fee for camping. Open late April to October, weather permitting.

Directions: From Redding, drive north on I-5 and continue just past Dunsmuir to the junction with Highway 89. Turn east on Highway 89 and drive to McCloud. From McCloud, continue driving on Highway 89 for 14 miles to the campground entrance road on the right (signed). Turn right and drive one mile to the campground by the bridge.

Contact: Shasta-Trinity National Forest, McCloud Ranger District, 530/964-2184, fax 530/964-2938.

44 CATTLE CAMP

Scenic rating: 5

on the McCloud River in Shasta-Trinity National Forest

Map 2.2, page 126

This campground, at 3,700 feet, is ideal for RV campers who want a rustic setting, or as an overflow area if the more attractive Fowler's Camp is filled. A small swimming hole in the McCloud River is near the camp, although the water is typically cold. There are several good side trips in the area, including fishing on the nearby McCloud River, visiting the three waterfalls near Fowler's Camp, and exploring the north slopes of Mount Shasta (a map of Shasta-Trinity National Forest details the back roads).

Campsites, facilities: There are 19 individual sites and four double sites for tents or RVs up to 32 feet (no hookups). Picnic tables and fire grills are provided. Drinking water and vault toilets are available. Some facilities are wheelchair-accessible. Leashed pets are permitted.

Reservations, fees: Reservations are not accepted. Sites are $12 per night. Open late April to October, weather permitting.

Directions: From Redding, drive north on I-5 and continue just past Dunsmuir to the junction with Highway 89. Turn east on Highway 89 and drive to McCloud. From McCloud, continue driving on Highway 89 for 11 miles to the campground entrance road on the right. Turn right and drive 0.5 mile to the campground on the left side of the road.

Contact: Shasta-Trinity National Forest, McCloud Ranger District, 530/964-2184, fax 530/964-2938.

45 TRAIL CREEK

Scenic rating: 7

in Klamath National Forest

Map 2.2, page 126

This simple and quiet camp is set beside Trail Creek, a small tributary to the upper Salmon River, at an elevation of 4,700 feet. A trailhead is about a mile to the south, accessible via a Forest Service road, providing access to a two-mile trail routed along Fish Creek and leading to little Fish Lake. From Fish Lake the trail climbs steeply, switchbacking at times, for another two miles to larger Trail Gull Lake, a very pretty spot set below Deadman Peak (7,741 feet).

Campsites, facilities: There are 12 sites for tents or RVs up to 22 feet (no hookups). Picnic tables and fire grills are provided. Drinking water and vault toilets are available. Leashed pets are permitted.

Reservations, fees: Reservations are not accepted. Sites are $10 per night. Open May through October.

Directions: From Weed, drive north on I-5 to the Edgewood exit. Take the Edgewood exit, turn left at the stop sign, and drive a short distance under the freeway to another stop sign at Old Highway 99. Turn right (north) and drive six miles to Gazelle and Gazelle-Callahan Road. Turn left (west) on Gazelle-Callahan Road and continue to Callahan and Cecilville Road. Turn left (southwest) on Cecilville Road and drive 17 miles to the campground.

Contact: Klamath National Forest, Scott River Ranger District, 530/468-5351, fax 530/468-1290.

46 HIDDEN HORSE

Scenic rating: 7

in Klamath National Forest

Map 2.2, page 126

Hidden Horse provides an alternate horse camp to nearby Carter Meadows. The horse camps are in close proximity to the Pacific Crest Trail, which passes through the area and serves as access to the Russian Wilderness to the north and the Trinity Alps Wilderness to the south. Trail Creek and East Fork campgrounds are nearby. The elevation is 6,000 feet.

Campsites, facilities: There are six sites for tents or RVs up to 35 feet (no hookups). Picnic tables and fire grills are provided. Drinking water and vault toilets are available. A horse-mounting ramp and corrals are also available. There is no designated water for stock available, so bring a bucket. Some facilities are wheelchair-accessible. Leashed pets are permitted.

Reservations, fees: Reservations are not accepted. Sites are $10 per night. Open June through October, weather permitting.

Directions: From Weed, drive north on I-5 to the Edgewood exit. Take the Edgewood exit, turn left at the stop sign, and drive a short distance under the freeway to Old Highway 99. Turn right (north) and drive six miles to Gazelle and Gazelle-Callahan Road. Turn left (west) on Gazelle-Callahan Road, and continue to Callahan and Cecilville Road. Turn left (southwest) on Cecilville Road and drive 11 miles to Carter Meadows Horse Camp. Continue 0.25 mile to the campground on the left.

Contact: Klamath National Forest, Scott River and Salmon River Ranger Districts, 530/468-5351, fax 530/468-1290.

47 CARTER MEADOWS GROUP HORSE CAMP

🚶 🛶 🐕 🚐 ⛺

Scenic rating: 7

in Klamath National Forest

Map 2.2, page 126

Carter Meadows offers an extensive trail network for riding and hiking. The Pacific Crest Trail passes through the area and serves as access to the Russian Wilderness to the

north and the Trinity Alps Wilderness to the south. Stream fishing is another option here. Trail Creek and East Fork campgrounds are nearby.

Campsites, facilities: There is one disbursed group equestrian site for tents or RVs up to 35 feet (no hookups) that can accommodate up to 25 people and 25 horses. Group barbecues and picnic tables are provided. Drinking water, vault toilets, and 13 horse corrals are available. Leashed pets are permitted.

Reservations, fees: Reservations are required ($9 reservation fee) at 800/444-6777 or www.ReserveUSA.com. The camp is $30 per night. Open mid-May through October, weather permitting.

Directions: From Weed, drive north on I-5 to the Edgewood exit. Take the Edgewood exit, turn left at the stop sign, and drive a short distance under the freeway to Old Highway 99. Turn right (north) and drive six miles to Gazelle and Gazelle-Callahan Road. Turn left (west) on Gazelle-Callahan Road, and continue to Callahan and Cecilville Road. Turn left (southwest) on Cecilville Road and drive 11 miles to the campground.

Contact: Klamath National Forest, Scott River and Salmon River Ranger Districts, 530/468-5351, fax 530/468-1290.

48 HORSE FLAT

🚶 🐕 🚐 ⛺

Scenic rating: 6

on Eagle Creek in Shasta-Trinity National Forest

Map 2.2, page 126

This camp is used by commercial pack operations as well as horse owners preparing for trips into the Trinity Alps. A trail starts right out of camp and is routed deep into the Trinity Alps Wilderness. It starts at 3,200 feet in elevation, then climbs all the way along Eagle Creek to Eagle Peak, where it intersects with the Pacific Crest Trail, then drops over the ridge to little Telephone Lake, a nine-mile hike. Note: Horse owners should call for the conditions of the corral and trail before making the trip.

Campsites, facilities: There are 16 sites for tents or RVs up to 16 feet (no hookups). Picnic tables and fire grills are provided. Vault toilets are available. No drinking water is available. Horse corrals are available. Garbage must be packed out. Leashed pets are permitted.

Reservations, fees: Reservations are not accepted. There is no fee for camping. Open mid-May through October.

Directions: From Redding, drive west on Highway 299 to Weaverville and Highway 3. Turn right (north) on Highway 3 and drive to Trinity Center at the north end of Trinity Lake. From Trinity Center, continue north on Highway 3 for 16.5 miles to Eagle Creek Campground (on the left) and Forest Road 38N27. Turn left on Forest Road 38N27 and drive two miles to the campground.

Contact: Shasta-Trinity National Forest, Weaverville Ranger Station, 530/623-2121, fax 530/623-6010.

49 EAGLE CREEK

Scenic rating: 7

in Shasta-Trinity National Forest

Map 2.2, page 126

This campground is set where little Eagle Creek enters the north Trinity River. Some campers use it as a base camp for a fishing trip, with the rainbow trout often abundant but predictably small in this stretch of water. The elevation is 2,800 feet.

Campsites, facilities: There are 17 sites for tents or RVs up to 35 feet (no hookups). Picnic tables and fire grills are provided. Drinking water and vault toilets are available. Leashed pets are permitted.

Reservations, fees: Reservations are not accepted. Sites are $9 per night. Open mid-May through October.

Directions: From Redding, drive west on Highway 299 to Weaverville and Highway 3. Turn right (north) on Highway 3 and drive to Trinity Center at the north end of Trinity Lake. From Trinity Center, continue north on Highway 3 for 16.5 miles to the campground on the left side of the road.

Contact: Shasta-Trinity National Forest, Weaverville Ranger Station, 530/623-2121, fax 530/623-6010.

50 RAILROAD PARK RV AND CAMPGROUND

Scenic rating: 7

south of Dunsmuir

Map 2.2, page 126

The resort adjacent to the RV park and campground was designed in the spirit of the railroad, when steam trains ruled the rails. The property features old stage cars (available for overnight lodging) and a steam locomotive. The railroad theme does not extend to the campground, however. What you'll find at the park is a classic campground set amid tall trees. There is a swimming hole in Little Castle Creek alongside the park. Many good side trips are available in the area, including excellent hiking and sightseeing at Castle Crags State Park (where there is a series of awesome granite spires) and outstanding trout fishing on the upper Sacramento River. At night, the sound of occasional passing trains soothes some, wakes others.

Campsites, facilities: There are 21 sites with full or partial hookups (30 amps) for RVs of any length, 31 sites with no hookups for tents or RVs. Some sites are pull-through. Cabins and a motel are next door at the resort. Picnic tables and fire rings are provided. Restrooms with showers, ice, coin laundry, group barbecue pit, game room, and horseshoes are available. A restaurant and lounge are within walking distance. Some facilities are wheelchair-accessible. Leashed pets are permitted.

Reservations, fees: Reservations are accepted. Sites are $20–27 per night, $3 per person per night for more than two people, $3 per night for each additional vehicle. Some credit cards accepted. Open April through November, weather permitting.

Directions: From Redding, drive north on I-5 for 45 miles to Exit 728 for Cragview Drive/Railroad Park Road. Take that exit and drive to the stop sign and Railroad Park Road. Turn left and drive under the freeway and continue to the campground on the left.

Contact: Railroad Park RV and Campground, 530/235-0420 or 530/235-4440, www.rrpark.com

51 CASTLE CRAGS STATE PARK

Scenic rating: 9

on the Sacramento River

Map 2.2, page 126

This park is named for the awesome granite spires that tower 6,000 feet above the park. Beyond to the north is giant Mount Shasta (14,162 feet), making for a spectacular natural setting. The campsites are set in forest, shaded, very pretty, and sprinkled along a paved access road. But not a year goes by when people don't write in complaining of the highway noise from I-5 echoing in the Sacramento River Canyon, as well as of the occasional passing freight trains in the night. Pristine quiet, this campground is not. At the end of the access road is a parking area for the two-minute walk to the Crags Lookout, a beautiful view. Nearby is the trailhead (at 2,500 feet elevation) for hikes up the Crags, featuring a 5.4-mile round-trip that rises to the base of Castle Dome at 4,800 feet, the leading spire on the crag's ridge. Again, road noise echoing up the canyon provides a background once you clear the tree line. Trout fishing is good in the nearby Sacramento River but requires driving, walking,

and exploring to find the best spots. There are also some good swimming holes, but the water is cold. This is a popular state park, with reservations often required in summer, but with your choice of any campsite even in late spring.

Campsites, facilities: There are 52 sites for tents only, three sites for RVs up to 27 feet (no hookups), an overflow area with 12 sites and limited facilities, six walk-in environmental sites (100-yard walk required) with limited facilities, and a hike-in/bike-in site. Picnic tables, food lockers, and fire grills or fire rings are provided. Drinking water, restrooms with flush toilets and showers, and firewood are available. Leashed pets are permitted at campsites only.

Reservations, fees: Reservations are accepted ($7.50 reservation fee) at 800/444-PARK (800/444-7275) or www.reserveamerica.com. Sites are $13–20 per night, $9 per night for walk-in environmental sites, $6 per night for each additional vehicle. The hike-in/bike-in site is $3 per person per night. Open year-round.

Directions: From Redding, drive north on I-5 for 45 miles to the Castle Crags State Park exit. Take that exit, turn west, and drive a short distance to the well-signed park entrance on the right side of the road.

Contact: Castle Crags State Park, 530/235-2684, fax 530/235-1965, www.parks.ca.gov.

52 FRIDAY'S RV RETREAT AND McCLOUD FLY FISHING RANCH

Scenic rating: 7

near McCloud

Map 2.2, page 126

Friday's RV Retreat and McCloud Fly Fishing Ranch offers great recreation opportunities for every member of the family. The property features a small private fishing lake, two casting ponds, 1.5 miles of Squaw Valley Creek frontage, and five miles of hiking trails. The ranch specializes in fly-fishing packages, with both lodging and fly-fishing for one price. However, campers are welcome to stay here. In addition, the McCloud River's wild trout section is a 45-minute drive to the south, the beautiful McCloud Golf Course (nine holes) is within a five-minute drive, and a trailhead for the Pacific Crest Trail is also only five minutes away. Lake McCloud is three miles away and offers fishing and water-sports options. The park covers 400 wooded and grassy acres. Owner Bob Friday is quite a character, and he figured out that if he planted giant rainbow trout in the ponds for catch-and-release fishing, fly fishers would stop to catch a monster and take a photograph, and then tell people they caught the fish on the McCloud River, where they are smaller and elusive. Also available is the dinner and excursion train that runs out of McCloud on summer weekends. (See *Ah-Di-Na* and *McCloud Dance Country RV Park* listings in this chapter for other information and side-trip options.)

Campsites, facilities: There are 30 sites with full hookups (30 and 50 amps) for RVs of any length, a large, grassy area for dispersed tent camping, and two cabins. Most RV sites are pull-through. Picnic tables and fire pits are provided. Drinking water, restrooms with showers and flush toilets, coin laundry, pay phone, propane gas, and a recreation room are available. A fly-fishing school is available by arrangement. Some facilities are wheelchair-accessible. Leashed pets are permitted.

Reservations, fees: Reservations are recommended. Sites are $16–24 per night, $3.50 per person per night for more than two people. Monthly rates available. Open early May through September.

Directions: From Redding, drive north on I-5 and continue just past Dunsmuir to the junction with Highway 89. Bear right on Highway 89 and drive nine miles to McCloud and Squaw Valley Road. Turn right

at Squaw Valley Road and drive six miles to the park entrance on the right.

Contact: Friday's RV Retreat and McCloud Fly Fishing Ranch, 530/964-2878.

53 BIG FLAT

Scenic rating: 8

on Coffee Creek in Klamath National Forest

Map 2.2, page 126

This is a great jump-off spot for a wilderness backpacking trip into the adjacent Trinity Alps. An 11-mile hike will take you into the beautiful Caribou Lakes Basin for lakeside campsites, excellent swimming, dramatic sunsets, and fair trout fishing. The trail is routed out of camp, crosses the stream, then climbs a series of switchbacks to the ridge. From here it gets easier, rounding a mountain and depositing you in the basin. Bypass Little Caribou, Lower Caribou, and Snowslide Lakes, and instead head all the way to Caribou, the biggest and best of the lot. Big Flat is set at 5,000 feet in elevation along Coffee Creek, and on the drive in, you'll see big piles of boulders along the stream, evidence of past gold mining activity.

Campsites, facilities: There are nine sites for tents or RVs up to 16 feet (no hookups). Picnic tables and fire grills are provided. Vault toilets are available. No drinking water is available. Garbage must be packed out. Leashed pets are permitted.

Reservations, fees: Reservations are not accepted. There is no fee for camping. Open May through October, weather permitting.

Directions: From Redding, turn east on Highway 299 and drive to Weaverville. In Weaverville, turn right (north) on Highway 3 and drive just past the north end of Trinity Lake to Coffee Creek Road/Forest Road 104, adjacent to a Forest Service ranger station. Turn left on Coffee Creek Road and drive 21 miles to the campground at the end of the road.

Contact: Klamath National Forest, Salmon

River Ranger District, 530/468-5351, fax 530/468-1290.

54 GOLDFIELD
🚶 🐕 🚐 ⛺

Scenic rating: 6

in Shasta-Trinity National Forest

Map 2.2, page 126

For hikers, this camp makes a perfect first stop after a long drive. You wake up, get your gear organized, and then take the trailhead to the south. It is routed along Boulder Creek, and with a left turn at the junction (about four miles in) will take you to Boulder Lake (another two miles), set inside the edge of the Trinity Alps Wilderness. Former 49er coach George Seifert first told me about the beauty of this place and how perfectly this campground is situated for the hike. Campground elevation is 3,000 feet.

Campsites, facilities: There are six sites for tents or RVs up to 16 feet (no hookups). Picnic tables and fire grills are provided. Vault toilets and hitching posts for horses are available. No drinking water is available. Garbage must be packed out. Leashed pets are permitted.

Reservations, fees: Reservations are not accepted. There is no fee for camping. Open year-round.

Directions: From Redding, head east on Highway 299 and drive to Weaverville. Turn right (north) on Highway 3 and drive just past the north end of Trinity Lake to Coffee Creek Road/Forest Road 104 (a Forest Service ranger station is nearby). Turn left on Coffee Creek Road/Forest Road 104 and drive 6.5 miles to the campground on the left side of the road.

Contact: Shasta-Trinity National Forest, Weaverville Ranger Station, 530/623-2121, fax 530/623-6010.

55 TRINITY RIVER
🚶 🛶 🐕 🚐 ⛺

Scenic rating: 7

in Shasta-Trinity National Forest

Map 2.2, page 126

This camp offers easy access off Highway 3, yet it is fairly secluded and provides streamside access to the upper Trinity River. It's a good base camp for a fishing trip when the upper Trinity is loaded with small trout. The elevation is 2,500 feet.

Campsites, facilities: There are seven sites for tents or RVs up to 35 feet (no hookups). Picnic tables and fire grills are provided. Drinking water and vault toilets are available. Leashed pets are permitted.

Reservations, fees: Reservations are not accepted. Sites are $9 per night. Open May through October.

Directions: From Redding, drive west on Highway 299 to Weaverville and Highway 3. Turn right (north) on Highway 3 and drive to Trinity Center at the north end of Trinity Lake. From Trinity Center, continue north on Highway 3 for 9.5 miles to the campground on the left side of the road.

Contact: Shasta-Trinity National Forest, Weaverville Ranger Station, 530/623-2121, fax 530/623-6010.

56 BEST IN THE WEST RESORT
🚶 🏊 🛶 🐕 🎣 🚐 ⛺

Scenic rating: 3

near Dunsmuir

Map 2.2, page 126

This is a good layover spot for RV cruisers looking to take a break. The proximity to Castle Crags State Park, the Sacramento River, and Mount Shasta make the location a winner. Meers Creek runs through the property, and the local area has outstanding swimming holes on the Sacramento River. Trains make regular runs every night in the Sacramento

River Canyon and the noise is a problem for some visitors.

Campsites, facilities: There are 12 sites with full hookups (30 and 50 amps) for RVs, a separate grassy area for dispersed tent camping, eight cabins, and a lodge. Picnic tables are provided. Restrooms with showers, cable TV, coin laundry, and playground are available. Leashed pets are permitted.

Reservations, fees: Reservations are accepted. Sites are $17–21 per night. Monthly rates available. Open year-round.

Directions: From Redding, drive north on I-5 for about 40 miles to the Sims Road exit. Take the Sims Road exit and drive one block west on Sims Road to the resort on the left.

Contact: Best in the West Resort, 530/235-2603, www.eggerbestwest.com.

57 SIMS FLAT

🚶 🏊 🛶 🏕 ♿ 🚐 ⛺

Scenic rating: 7

on the Sacramento River

Map 2.2, page 126

The upper Sacramento River is again becoming one of the best trout streams in the West with easy and direct access off an interstate highway. This camp is a good example. Sitting beside the upper Sacramento River at an elevation of 1,600 feet, it provides access to some of the better spots for trout fishing, particularly from late April through July. The trout population has recovered since the devastating spill from a train derailment that occurred in 1991, and there's good trout fishing in this area. There is a wheelchair-accessible interpretive trail. If you want to literally get away from it all, there is a trailhead about three miles east on Sims Flat Road that climbs along South Fork, including a terrible, steep, one-mile section near the top, eventually popping out at Tombstone Mountain. The noise from passing trains can be a shock for newcomers.

Campsites, facilities: There are 20 sites for tents or RVs up to 24 feet (no hookups). Picnic tables

and fire grills are provided. Drinking water and flush and vault toilets are available. A nearby seasonal grocery store is open intermittently. Supplies are available to the north in Castella and Dunsmuir. Some facilities are wheelchair-accessible. Leashed pets are permitted.

Reservations, fees: Reservations are not accepted. Sites are $12 per night. Open late April through October.

Directions: From Redding, drive north on I-5 for about 40 miles to the Sims Road exit. Take the Sims Road exit (on the east side of the highway) and drive south for a mile (crossing the railroad tracks and a bridge) to the campground on the right.

Contact: Shasta-Trinity National Forest, Mount Shasta Ranger District, 530/926-4511, fax 530/926-5120.

58 AH-DI-NA

🚶 🏊 🛶 🏕 🚐 ⛺

Scenic rating: 9

on the McCloud River in Shasta-Trinity National Forest

Map 2.2, page 126   **BEST (**

This is the perfect base camp for trout fishing on the lower McCloud River, with campsites just a cast away from one of the prettiest streams in California. Downstream of the camp is a special two-mile stretch of river governed by the Nature Conservancy, where all fish must be released, no bait is permitted, single, barbless hooks are mandated, and only 10 rods are allowed on the river at any one time. Wildlife is abundant in the area, the Pacific Crest Trail passes adjacent to the camp, and an excellent nature trail is also available along the river in the McCloud Nature Conservancy.

Campsites, facilities: There are 16 sites for tents or RVs up to 16 feet (no hookups). Picnic tables and fire grills are provided. Drinking water and flush toilets are available. Garbage must be packed out. Leashed pets are permitted.

Reservations, fees: Reservations are not accepted. Sites are $8 per night. Open late April through October, weather permitting.

Directions: From Redding, drive north on I-5 past Dunsmuir to the junction with Highway 89. Turn right and drive nine miles to McCloud and Squaw Valley Road. Turn right on Squaw Valley Road and drive to Lake McCloud. Turn right at Lake McCloud and continue along the lake to a signed turn-off on the right side of the road (at a deep cove in the lake). Turn right (the road turns to dirt) and drive four miles to the campground entrance on the left side of the road. Turn left and drive a short distance to the campground.

Contact: Shasta-Trinity National Forest, McCloud Ranger District, 530/964-2184, fax 530/964-2938.

59 EAST FORK WILLOW CREEK

Scenic rating: 9

on Willow Creek

Map 2.3, page 127

This is a beautiful spot along Willow Creek. Set at a 2,000-foot elevation, it's one of the prettiest campgrounds in the area. While you can dunk into the cold creek, it's not really a good swimming area. Fishing is prohibited here.

Campsites, facilities: There are 10 sites for tents or RVs up to 20 feet (no hookups). Picnic tables and fire rings are provided. Vault toilets are available. No drinking water is available. Leashed pets are permitted.

Reservations, fees: Reservations are not accepted. Sites are $8 per night, $5 per night for each additional vehicle. Open late May through September, weather permitting.

Directions: From the junction of U.S. 101 and Highway 299 near Arcata, turn east on Highway 299 and drive 32 miles (six miles west of Willow Creek) and look for the camp's

entrance road (well signed) on the right (south) side of the road.

Contact: Six Rivers National Forest, Lower Trinity Ranger District, 530/629-2118, fax 530/629-2102.

60 BOISE CREEK

Scenic rating: 7

in Six Rivers National Forest

Map 2.3, page 127

This camp features a 0.25-mile-long trail down to Willlow Creek and nearby access to the Trinity River. If you have ever wanted to see Bigfoot, you can do it while camping here because there's a giant wooden Bigfoot on display in nearby Willow Creek. After your Bigfoot experience, your best bet during summer is to head north on nearby Highway 96 (turn north in Willow Creek) to the campground at Tish Tang, where there is excellent river access, swimming, and rafting in the late summer's warm flows. The Trinity River also provides good salmon and steelhead fishing during fall and winter, respectively. Note that fishing is prohibited in nearby Willow Creek.

Campsites, facilities: There are 17 sites for tents or RVs up to 35 feet (no hookups). Picnic tables and fire grills are provided. No drinking water. Vault toilets are available, and a camp host is on-site. A grocery store, gas station, restaurant, and propane gas are available nearby. Some facilities are wheelchair-accessible. Leashed pets are permitted.

Reservations, fees: Reservations are not accepted. Sites are $10 per night, $5 per night for each additional vehicle. Open year-round.

Directions: From the intersection of U.S. 101 and Highway 299 near Arcata, drive 38 miles east on Highway 299 and look for the campground entrance on the left side of the road. If you reach the town of Willow Creek, you have gone 1.5 miles too far.

Contact: Six Rivers National Forest, Lower Trinity Ranger District, 530/629-2118, fax 530/629-2102.

61 DENNY
🏃 🏊 ⛵ 🐎 5% 🚐 ⛺

Scenic rating: 6

on the New River in Shasta-Trinity National Forest

Map 2.3, page 127

This is a secluded and quiet campground along the New River, a tributary to the Trinity River and a designated Wild and Scenic River. The stream here is OK for swimming but too cold to even dip a toe in until late summer. If you drive north from the camp on Denny Road, you will find several trailheads for trips into the Trinity Alps Wilderness. The best of them is at the end of the road, where there is a good parking area, with a trail that is routed along the East Fork New River up toward Limestone Ridge. Note that the stretch of river near the camp is closed to fishing year-round. The campground is set at 1,400 feet.

Campsites, facilities: There are five sites for tents or RVs up to 22 feet (no hookups). Picnic tables and fire grills are provided. Vault toilets are available. No drinking water is available. Garbage must be packed out. Leashed pets are permitted. Supplies are available about one hour away in Salyers Bar.

Reservations, fees: Reservations are not accepted. There is no fee for camping. Open year-round.

Directions: From the junction of U.S. 101 and Highway 299 near Arcata, turn east on Highway 299 and drive to Willow Creek. In Willow Creek, continue east on Highway 299 and, after reaching Salyer, continue for four miles to Denny Road/County Road 402. Turn north (left) on Denny Road and drive about 14 miles on a paved but very windy road to the campground.

Contact: Shasta-Trinity National Forest, Big Bar Ranger Station, 530/623-6106, fax 530/623-6123.

62 HOBO GULCH
🏃 ⛵ 🐎 🚐 ⛺

Scenic rating: 7

on the North Fork of the Trinity River in Shasta-Trinity National Forest

Map 2.3, page 127

Only the ambitious need apply. This is a trailhead camp set on the edge of the Trinity Alps Wilderness, and the reason only the ambitious show up is that it is a 20-mile uphill haul all the way to Grizzly Lake, set at the foot of the awesome Thompson Peak (8,663 feet), with no other lakes available en route. The camp is set at 2,200 feet along the North Fork of the Trinity River. The adjacent slopes of the wilderness are known for little creeks, woods, and a few pristine meadows, and are largely devoid of lakes.

Campsites, facilities: There are 10 sites for tents or RVs up to 16 feet (no hookups). Picnic tables and fire grills are provided. Vault toilets are available. No drinking water is available. Garbage must be packed out. Supplies can be obtained in Junction City, about one hour away. Leashed pets are permitted.

Reservations, fees: Reservations are not accepted. There is no fee for camping. Open year-round.

Directions: From Redding, turn on Highway 299 west and drive west past Weaverville, and continue 13 miles to Helena and County East Fork Road. Turn right on County East Fork Road and drive four miles to Hobo Gulch Road. At Hobo Gulch Road, turn left (north) and drive 16 miles (very rough road) to the end of the road at the campground.

Contact: Shasta-Trinity National Forest, Big Bar Ranger Station, 530/623-6106, fax 530/623-6123.

63 RIPSTEIN

Scenic rating: 8

on Canyon Creek in Shasta-Trinity National Forest

Map 2.3, page 127

This is one of the great trailhead camps for the neighboring Trinity Alps. It is set at 3,000 feet on the southern edge of the wilderness and is a popular spot for a late-night arrival followed by a backpacking trip the next morning. Waiting are the Canyon Creek Lakes via a six-mile uphill hike along Canyon Creek. The destination is extremely beautiful—two alpine lakes set in high granite mountains. The route passes Canyon Creek Falls, a set of two different waterfalls, about 3.5 miles out. This is one of the most popular backpacking destinations in Northern California. Seasonal guided rafting trips on Canyon Creek are also available.

Campsites, facilities: There are 10 sites for tents or RVs up to 22 feet (no hookups). Picnic tables and fire grills are provided. Vault toilets are available. No drinking water is available. Garbage must be packed out. Supplies can be obtained 25 minutes away in Junction City. Leashed pets are permitted.

Reservations, fees: Reservations are not accepted. There is no fee for camping. Open year-round.

Directions: From Redding, turn on Highway 299 west and drive west to Junction City and Canyon Creek Road. Turn right on Canyon Creek Road and drive 15 miles to the campground on the left side of the road.

Contact: Shasta-Trinity National Forest, Big Bar Ranger Station, 530/623-6106, fax 530/623-6123; Trinity River Rafting Company, 530/623-3033.

64 BURNT RANCH

Scenic rating: 7

on the Trinity River in Shasta-Trinity National Forest

Map 2.3, page 127

This campground is set on a bluff above the Trinity River and is one of its most compelling spots. This section of river is very pretty, with deep, dramatic canyons nearby. The elevation is 1,000 feet. Note that the trail to Burnt Ranch Falls is not maintained and is partially on private land—the landowners will not take kindly to anyone trespassing.

Campsites, facilities: There are 16 sites for tents or RVs up to 25 feet (no hookups). Picnic tables and fire grills are provided. Drinking water and vault toilets are available. Garbage must be packed out. Supplies can be obtained in Hawkins Bar about one hour away. Leashed pets are permitted.

Reservations, fees: Reservations are not accepted. Sites are $8 per night. Open year-round, weather permitting.

Directions: From Redding, take Highway 299 west and drive past Weaverville to Burnt Ranch. In Burnt Ranch, continue 0.5 mile and look for the campground entrance on the right side of the road.

Contact: Shasta-Trinity National Forest, Big Bar Ranger Station, 530/623-6106, fax 530/623-6123; Trinity River Rafting Company, 530/623-3033.

65 DEL LOMA RV PARK AND CAMPGROUND

Scenic rating: 7

on the Trinity River

Map 2.3, page 127

RV cruisers looking for a layover spot near the Trinity River will find just that at Del Loma. Shady sites and sandy beaches are available here along the Trinity. Rafting and tubing trips are popular in this area during the summer. Salmon fishing is best in the fall, steelhead fishing in the winter. This camp is popular for family reunions and groups. Salmon fishing can be sensational on the Trinity in the fall and some anglers will book a year in advance to make certain they get a spot. About two-thirds of the sites are rented for extended periods.

Campsites, facilities: There are 41 sites, including two pull-through, with full hookups (50 amps) for RVs and tents, five park-model cabins, and two apartments. Picnic tables and fire grills are provided. Restrooms with flush toilets and showers, a dump station, convenience store, clubhouse, heated pool, deli, Wi-Fi, RV supplies, firewood, coin laundry, recreation room, volleyball, tetherball, 18-hole mini golf, and horseshoe pits are available. Leashed pets are permitted.

Reservations, fees: Reservations are accepted at 800/839-0194. Sites are $23 per night, $2 per person per night for more than two people. Group and monthly rates available. Some credit cards accepted. Open year-round.

Directions: From the junction of U.S. 101 and Highway 299 in Arcata, turn east on Highway 299 and drive to Burnt Ranch. From Burnt Ranch, continue 10 miles east on Highway 299 to the town of Del Loma and look for the campground entrance on the right.

Contact: Del Loma RV Park and Campground, 530/623-2834 or 800/839-0194, www.dellomarv.com.

66 HAYDEN FLAT/GROUP

Scenic rating: 7

on the Trinity River in Shasta-Trinity National Forest

Map 2.3, page 127

This campground is split into two pieces, with most of the sites grouped in a large, shaded area across the road from the river and a few on the river side. A beach is available along the river; it is a good spot for swimming as well as a popular put-in and take-out for rafters. The elevation is 1,200 feet.

Campsites, facilities: There are 36 sites for tents or RVs up to 25 feet (no hookups); it can also be used as a group camp with a three-site minimum. Picnic tables and fire grills are provided. Drinking water and vault toilets are available. Some facilities are wheelchair-accessible. Leashed pets are permitted.

Reservations, fees: Reservations are not accepted for individual sites but are required for group sites at 530/623-6106. Sites are $10 per night, $30 minimum per night for groups. Open year-round.

Directions: From the junction of U.S. 101 and Highway 299 in Arcata, head east on Highway 299 and drive to Burnt Ranch. From Burnt Ranch, continue 10 miles east on Highway 299 and look for the campground entrance. If you reach the town of Del Loma, you have gone 0.5 mile too far.

Contact: Shasta-Trinity National Forest, Big Bar Ranger Station, 530/623-6106, fax 530/623-6123.

67 BIG SLIDE

Scenic rating: 7

on the South Fork of the Trinity River in Shasta-Trinity National Forest

Map 2.3, page 127

This camp is literally out in the middle of nowhere. Free? Of course it's free. Otherwise, someone would actually have to show up now and then to collect. It's a tiny, secluded, little-visited spot set along the South Fork of the Trinity River. The elevation is 1,250 feet.

Campsites, facilities: There are eight sites for tents or RVs up to 16 feet (no hookups). Picnic tables and fire grills are provided. Vault toilets are available. No drinking water is available. Leashed pets are permitted.

Reservations, fees: Reservations are not accepted. There is no fee for camping. Open late May to early October, weather permitting.
Directions: From Redding, turn on Highway 299 west and drive west over the Buckhorn Summit to the junction with Highway 3 near Douglas City. Turn south on Highway 3 and drive to Hayfork. From Hayfork, turn right on County Road 301 and drive about 20 miles to the town of Hyampom. In Hyampom, turn right on Lower South Fork Road/County Road 311 and drive five miles on County Road 311 to the campground on the right.
Contact: Shasta-Trinity National Forest, Hayfork Ranger Station, 530/628-5227, fax 530/628-5212.

68 SKUNK POINT GROUP CAMP

Scenic rating: 7

on the Trinity River in Shasta-Trinity National Forest

Map 2.3, page 127

This is an ideal site for groups on rafting trips. You get easy access to the nearby Trinity River with a streamside setting and privacy for the group. A beach on the river is nearby. In the spring, this section of river offers primarily Class II rapids (only more difficult during high water), but most of it is rated Class I. By late summer, the water is warm and benign, ideal for families. Guided rafting trips and inflatables are available for hire and rent in nearby Big Flat. The camp elevation is 1,200 feet.
Campsites, facilities: There are two group tent sites that can accommodate up to 30 people each. Picnic tables and fire grills are provided. Vault toilets are available. No drinking water is available. Some facilities are wheelchair-accessible. Leashed pets are permitted.
Reservations, fees: Reservations are required at 530/623-6106. The fee is $30 per night per site. Open year-round.

Directions: From Redding, turn on Highway 299 west, and drive west past Weaverville, Junction City, and Helena, and continue for about seven miles. Look for the campground entrance on the left side of the road. If you reach the town of Big Bar, you have gone two miles too far.
Contact: Shasta-Trinity National Forest, Big Bar Ranger Station, 530/623-6106, fax 530/623-6123; Trinity River Rafting Company, 530/623-3033.

69 BIG BAR

Scenic rating: 6

near the Trinity River in Shasta-Trinity National Forest

Map 2.3, page 127

You name it, you got it—a quiet, small campground with easy access, and good fishing nearby (in the fall). In addition, there is a good put-in spot for inflatable kayaks and rafts. It is an ideal piece of water for newcomers, with Trinity River Rafting offering inflatable rentals for as low as $35. The elevation is 1,200 feet. If the shoe fits....
Campsites, facilities: There are three sites for tents or RVs up to 20 feet (no hookups). Picnic tables and fire grills are provided. Vault toilets are available. No drinking water is available. Garbage must be packed out. Supplies are available one mile away in Big Bar. Leashed pets are permitted.
Reservations, fees: Reservations are not accepted. There is no fee for camping. Open year-round.
Directions: From Redding, turn on Highway 299 west and drive west to Weaverville. Continue on Highway 299 for 25 miles to the ranger station one mile east of Big Bar, and look for Corral Bottom Road (across from the ranger station). Turn left on Corral Bottom Road and drive 0.25 mile to the campground on the left.
Contact: Shasta-Trinity National Forest,

Big Bar Ranger Station, 530/623-6106, fax 530/623-6123; Trinity River Rafting, 530/623-3033, www.trinityriverrafting.com.

70 BIG FLAT

Scenic rating: 6

on the Trinity River in Shasta-Trinity National Forest

Map 2.3, page 127

This level campground is set off Highway 299, just across the road from the Trinity River. The sites are close together, and it can be hot and dusty in midsummer. No problem. That is when you will be on the Trinity River, taking a rafting or kayaking trip—as low as $35 to rent an inflatable kayak from Trinity River Rafting in nearby Big Bar. It's fun, exciting, and easy (newcomers are welcome).

Campsites, facilities: There are 10 sites for tents or RVs up to 22 feet (no hookups). Picnic tables and fire grills are provided. Drinking water and vault toilets are available. Some facilities are wheelchair-accessible. Leashed pets are permitted.

Reservations, fees: Reservations are not accepted. Sites are $8 per night. Open year-round.

Directions: From Redding, turn on Highway 299 west, and drive west past Weaverville, Junction City, and Helena, and continue for about seven miles. Look for the campground entrance on the right side of the road. If you reach the town of Big Bar, you have gone three miles too far.

Contact: Shasta-Trinity National Forest, Big Bar Ranger Station, 530/623-6106, fax 530/623-6123; Trinity River Rafting Company, 530/623-3033, www.trinityriverrafting.com.

71 PIGEON POINT AND GROUP

Scenic rating: 7

on the Trinity River in Shasta-Trinity National Forest

Map 2.3, page 127

In the good old days, huge flocks of bandtail pigeons flew the Trinity River Canyon, swooping and diving in dramatic shows. Nowadays you don't see too many pigeons, but this camp still keeps its namesake. It is better known for its access to the Trinity River, with a large beach for swimming. The elevation is 1,100 feet.

Campsites, facilities: There are 10 sites for tents or RVs up to 22 feet and one group site for tents or RVs up to 16 feet that can accommodate up to 50 people. No hookups. Picnic tables and fire grills are provided. Vault toilets are available. No drinking water is available. Supplies can be obtained within 10 miles in Big Bar or Junction City. Some facilities are wheelchair-accessible. Leashed pets are permitted.

Reservations, fees: Reservations are not accepted for individual sites but are required for the group site at 530/623-6106. Sites are $12 per night, and $50 per night for the group site. Open year-round.

Directions: From Redding, turn on Highway 299 west and drive west to Weaverville. Continue west on Highway 299 to Helena and continue 0.5 mile to the campground on the left (south) side of the road.

Contact: Shasta-Trinity National Forest, Big Bar Ranger Station, 530/623-6106, fax 530/623-6123.

72 BIGFOOT CAMPGROUND AND RV PARK

Scenic rating: 8

on the Trinity River

Map 2.3, page 127

This private RV park is set along the Trinity River and has become one of the most popular spots on the Trinity River. Rafting and fishing trips are a feature, along with cabin rentals. It is also a popular layover for Highway 299 cruisers but provides the option for longer stays with rafting, gold panning, and in the fall and winter, fishing for salmon and steelhead, respectively. RV sites are exceptionally large, and a bonus is that a storage area is available. A three-acre site for tent camping is set along the river.

Campsites, facilities: There are 46 sites with full or partial hookups (30 and 50 amps) for RVs of any length, a separate area for tent camping, and four cabins. Tent camping is not allowed during the winter. Picnic tables and barbecues are provided. Restrooms with flush toilets and coin showers, coin laundry, convenience store, dump station, propane gas, solar-heated swimming pool (summer only), and horseshoe pits are available. Modem hookups, television hookups, fishing licenses, and a tackle shop are also available. Some facilities are wheelchair-accessible. Leashed pets are permitted.

Reservations, fees: Reservations are recommended from June through October. Sites are $18–24 per night, $2 per night per person for more than two people. Some credit cards accepted. Open year-round.

Directions: From Redding, turn on Highway 299 west and drive west to Junction City. Continue west on Highway 299 for three miles to the camp on the left.

Contact: Bigfoot Campground and RV Park, 530/623-6088 or 800/422-5219, www.bigfootrvcabins.com.

73 JUNCTION CITY

Scenic rating: 7

on the Trinity River

Map 2.3, page 127

Some of the Trinity River's best fall salmon fishing is in this area in September and early October, with steelhead following from mid-

October into the winter. That makes it an ideal base camp for a fishing or camping trip.

Campsites, facilities: There are 22 sites for tents or RVs up to 40 feet (no hookups). Picnic tables, fire grills, and bearproof food lockers are provided. Drinking water and vault toilets are available. Groceries and propane gas are available within two miles in Junction City. Some facilities are wheelchair-accessible. Leashed pets are permitted.

Reservations, fees: Reservations are not accepted. Sites are $10 per night per vehicle. Open May through November.

Directions: From Redding, turn on Highway 299 west and drive west to Junction City. At Junction City, continue west on Highway 299 for 1.5 miles to the camp on the right.

Contact: Bureau of Land Management, Redding Field Office, 530/224-2100, fax 530/224-2172.

74 PHILPOT

Scenic rating: 7

on the North Fork of Salt Creek in Shasta-Trinity National Forest

Map 2.3, page 127

It's time to join the 5 Percent Club; that is, the 5 percent of the people who know the little-used, beautiful spots in California. This is one of those places, set on the North Fork of Salt Creek on national forest land. The elevation is 2,600 feet. Remember: 95 percent of the people use just 5 percent of the available open space. Why would anyone come here? To join the 5 Percent Club, that's why. Note: The road is too rough for many vehicles, and the sites are too small for most RVs. Trailers and RVs are not recommended.

Campsites, facilities: There are six sites for tents only. Picnic tables and fire grills are provided. Vault toilets are available. No drinking water is available. Garbage must be packed out. Leashed pets are permitted.

Reservations, fees: Reservations are not accepted. There is no fee for camping. Open late May to early November, weather permitting.

Directions: From Redding, turn on Highway 299 west and drive west over the Buckhorn Summit, and continue to the junction with Highway 3 near Douglas City. Turn left (south) on Highway 3 and drive to Hayfork. From Hayfork, continue southwest on Highway 3 for eight miles to County Road 353 (Rattlesnake Creek Road). Turn right and drive one mile to Forest Road 30N31. Turn right and drive 0.5 mile to the campground on the left. Trailers and RVs are not recommended.

Contact: Shasta-Trinity National Forest, Hayfork Ranger Station, 530/628-5227, fax 530/628-5212.

75 MAD RIVER

🏊 🚣 🎣 🐾 🚐 ⛺

Scenic rating: 7

in Six Rivers National Forest

Map 2.3, page 127

Note that this campground has been closed for a couple of years because of road work and was scheduled to reopen by the time of publication; check current status. This Forest Service campground is set along an alluvial flood terrace, a unique landscape for this region, featuring a forest of manzanita and Douglas fir. It is often hot, always remote, in a relatively unknown section of Six Rivers National Forest at an elevation of 2,600 feet. The headwaters of the Mad River pour right past the campground, about two miles downstream from the Ruth Lake Dam. People making weekend trips to Ruth Lake sometimes end up at this little-used camp. Ruth Lake is a designated Watchable Wildlife Site and is the only major recreation lake within decent driving range of Eureka, offering a small marina with boat rentals and a good boat ramp for access to trout and bass fishing and waterskiing. Swimming and all water sports are allowed at Ruth Lake.

Campsites, facilities: There are 40 sites for tents or RVs up to 22 feet (no hookups). Picnic tables and fire grills are provided. Drinking water and vault toilets are available. Leashed pets are permitted.

Reservations, fees: Reservations are not accepted. Sites are $12 per night, $5 per night for each additional vehicle. Open late May to mid-September.

Directions: From Eureka, drive south on U.S. 101 to Alton. Turn east on Highway 36 and drive about 50 miles to the town of Mad River. Turn southeast on Lower Mad River Road and drive four miles to the camp on the right side of the road.

Contact: Six Rivers National Forest, Mad River Ranger District, 707/574-6233, fax 707/574-6273.

76 HELLS GATE

🚶 🏊 🚣 🎣 🐾 ♿ 🚐 ⛺

Scenic rating: 7

on the South Fork of the Trinity River in Shasta-Trinity National Forest

Map 2.3, page 127

This is a pretty spot bordering the South Fork of the Trinity River. The prime feature is for hikers. The South Fork National Recreation Trail begins at the campground and follows the river for many miles. Additional trails branch off and up into the South Fork Mountains. This area is extremely hot in summer. The elevation is 2,300 feet. It gets moderate use and may even fill on three-day weekends. Insider's note: If Hells Gate is full, there are seven primitive campsites at Scott's Flat Campground, 0.5 mile beyond Hells Gate, that can accommodate RVs up to 20 feet.

Campsites, facilities: There are 15 sites for tents or RVs up to 16 feet (no hookups). Picnic tables and fire grills are provided. Drinking water and vault toilets are available. Some facilities are wheelchair-accessible. Leashed pets are permitted.

Reservations, fees: Reservations are not accepted. Sites are $6 per night. Open late May to early November, weather permitting.

Directions: From Red Bluff, turn west on Highway 36 (very twisty) and drive past Platina to the junction with Highway 3. Continue west on Highway 36 for 10 miles to the campground entrance on the left side of the road. If you reach Forest Glen, you have gone a mile too far.

Contact: Shasta-Trinity National Forest, Hayfork Ranger Station, 530/628-5227, fax 530/628-5212.

77 FOREST GLEN

Scenic rating: 7

on the South Fork of the Trinity River in Shasta-Trinity National Forest

Map 2.3, page 127

If you get stuck for a spot in this region, this camp almost always has sites open, even during three-day weekends. It is on the edge of a forest near the South Fork of the Trinity River. If you hit it wrong, during a surprise storm, a primitive shelter is available at the nearby Forest Glen Guard Station—a historic cabin that sleeps eight and rents out from the Forest Service for $35 a night.

Campsites, facilities: There are 15 sites for tents or RVs up to 15 feet (no hookups). Picnic tables and fire grills are provided. Vault toilets are available. No drinking water is available. Some facilities are wheelchair-accessible. Leashed pets are permitted.

Reservations, fees: Reservations are not accepted. Sites are $6 per night. Open late May to early November, weather permitting.

Directions: From Red Bluff, turn west on Highway 36 (very twisty) and drive past Platina to the junction with Highway 3. Continue west on Highway 36 for 11 miles to Forest Glen. The campground is at the west end of town on the right side of the road.

Contact: Shasta-Trinity National Forest, Hayfork Ranger Station, 530/628-5227, fax 530/628-5212.

78 FIR COVE CAMP

Scenic rating: 7

on Ruth Lake in Six Rivers National Forest

Map 2.3, page 127

This spot is situated along Ruth Lake adjacent to Bailey Cove. The elevation is 2,600 feet, and the lake covers 1,200 acres. Swimming and all water sports are allowed on Ruth Lake, and there are three boat ramps. In the summer the warm water makes this an ideal place for families to spend some time swimming. Fishing is decent for rainbow trout in the spring and for bass in the summer.

Campsites, facilities: There 19 sites for tents or RVs up to 22 feet (no hookups). Picnic tables and fire grills are provided. Drinking water and vault toilets are available. Some facilities are wheelchair-accessible. Leashed pets are permitted.

Reservations, fees: Reservations are not accepted. Sites are $12 per night, $5 per night for each additional vehicle. Open late May through mid-September.

Directions: From Eureka, drive south on U.S. 101 to Alton and the junction with Highway 36. Turn east on Highway 36 and drive about 50 miles to the town of Mad River. Turn right at the sign for Ruth Lake/Lower Mad River Road and drive 12 miles to the campground on the right side of the road.

Contact: Six Rivers National Forest, Mad River Ranger District, 707/574-6233, fax 707/574-6273.

79 BAILEY CANYON

Scenic rating: 7

on Ruth Lake in Six Rivers National Forest

Map 2.3, page 127

Ruth Lake is the only major lake within a reasonable driving distance of U.S. 101, although some people might argue with you over how reasonable this twisty drive is. Regardless, you end up at a camp along the east shore of Ruth Lake, where fishing for trout or bass and waterskiing are popular. What really wins out is that it is hot and sunny all summer, the exact opposite of the fogged-in Humboldt coast. The elevation is 2,600 feet.

Campsites, facilities: There are 25 sites for tents or RVs up to 22 feet (no hookups). Picnic tables and fire grills are provided. Drinking water and vault toilets are available. A boat ramp and small marina are available nearby. Some facilities are wheelchair-accessible. Leashed pets are permitted.

Reservations, fees: Reservations are not accepted. Sites are $12 per night, $5 per night for each additional vehicle. Open late May to mid-September.

Directions: From Eureka, drive south on U.S. 101 to Alton and the junction with Highway 36. Turn east on Highway 36 and drive about 50 miles to the town of Mad River. Turn right at the sign for Ruth Lake/Lower Mad River Road and drive 13 miles to the campground on the right side of the road.

Contact: Six Rivers National Forest, Mad River Ranger District, 707/574-6233, fax 707/574-6273.

80 TRINITY LAKE KOA

🏃 🚴 ⛵ 🏄 🚙 🐕 🎣 ♿ 🚐 ⛺

Scenic rating: 8

on Trinity Lake

Map 2.4 Trinity Lake Detail, page 129

This huge resort (some may remember this as the former Wyntoon Resort) is an ideal family vacation destination. Set in a wooded area covering 90 acres on the north shore of Trinity Lake, it provides opportunities for fishing, boating, swimming, and waterskiing, with access within walking distance. The lake boasts a wide variety of fish, including smallmouth bass and rainbow trout. The tent sites are spread out on 20 forested acres. The lake sits at the base of the dramatic Trinity Alps, one of the most beautiful regions in the state.

Campsites, facilities: There are 77 tent sites, 136 sites with full hookups (30 and 50 amps) for RVs of any length, and 19 cottages. Some RV sites are pull-through. Picnic tables and fire rings are provided. Drinking water, restrooms with showers, a coin laundry, a playground, seasonal heated pool, dump station, gasoline, convenience store, ice, snack bar, fish-cleaning area, boat rentals and slips are available. Some facilities are wheelchair-accessible. Leashed pets are permitted, with certain restrictions.

Reservations, fees: Reservations are accepted. Sites are $28–35 per night, $3–5 per person per night for more than two people. Some credit cards accepted. Open year-round.

Directions: From Redding, drive west on Highway 299 to Weaverville and Highway 3. Turn right (north) on Highway 3 and drive approximately 30 miles to Trinity Lake. At Trinity Center, continue 0.5 mile north on Highway 3 to the resort on the right.

Contact: Trinity Lake KOA, 530/266-3337 or 800/715-3337, www.koa.com.

81 PREACHER MEADOW

🏃 🐕 🚐 ⛺

Scenic rating: 7

in Shasta-Trinity National Forest

Map 2.4 Trinity Lake Detail, page 129

The view of the Trinity Alps can be excellent here from the right vantage point. Otherwise, compared to all the other camps in the area so close to Trinity Lake, it has trouble matching up in the quality department. If the lakeside camps are full, this camp provides an overflow option. The winter of 2000 was one of the strangest on record, where a localized wind storm knocked down 66 trees at this campground.

Campsites, facilities: There are 45 sites for tents or RVs up to 40 feet (no hookups). Picnic tables and fire grills are provided. Drinking water and vault toilets are available. Supplies, a coin laundry, and a small airport are available nearby. Leashed pets are permitted.

Reservations, fees: Reservations are not accepted. Sites are $11 per night. Open mid-May through October.

Directions: From Redding, drive west on Highway 299 to Weaverville at Highway 3. Turn right (north) on Highway 3 and drive to Trinity Lake. Continue toward Trinity Center and look for the campground entrance on the left side of the road (if you reach Trinity Center you have gone two miles too far).

Contact: Shasta-Trinity National Forest, Weaverville Ranger Station, 530/623-2121, fax 530/623-6010.

82 JACKASS SPRINGS
🚶 🏊 🎣 🚤 🐴 🚐 ⛺

Scenic rating: 6

near Trinity Lake in Shasta-Trinity National Forest

Map 2.4 Trinity Lake Detail, page 129

If you're poking around for a more secluded campsite on this end of the lake, halt your search and pick the best spot you can find at this campground, since it's the only one in this area of Trinity Lake. The campground is 0.5 mile from Trinity Lake, but you can't see the lake from the camp. It is most popular in the fall as a base camp for deer hunters. The elevation is 2,500 feet.

Campsites, facilities: There are 21 sites for tents or RVs up to 32 feet (no hookups). Picnic tables and fire grills are provided. Vault toilets are available. No drinking water is available. Garbage must be packed out. Leashed pets are permitted.

Reservations, fees: Reservations are not accepted. There is no fee for camping. Open year-round, weather permitting.

Directions: From Redding, drive west on Highway 299 to Weaverville and the junction with Highway 3. Turn right (north) on Highway 3 and drive 29 miles to Trinity Center. Continue five miles past Trinity Center to County Road 106. Turn right on County Road 106 and drive 12 miles to the Jackass

Springs/County Road 119 turnoff. Turn right on County Road 119 and drive five miles to the campground near the end of the road.

Contact: Shasta-Trinity National Forest, Weaverville Ranger Station, 530/623-2121, fax 530/623-6010.

83 BRIDGE CAMP
🚶 🐴 🚐 ⛺

Scenic rating: 8

on Stuarts Fork in Shasta-Trinity National Forest

Map 2.4 Trinity Lake Detail, page 129

This remote spot is an ideal jump-off point for backpackers. It's at the head of Stuarts Fork Trail, about 2.5 miles from the western shore of Trinity Lake. The trail leads into the Trinity Alps Wilderness, along Stuarts Fork, past Oak Flat and Morris Meadows, and up to Emerald Lake and the Sawtooth Ridge. It is a long and grueling climb, but fishing is excellent at Emerald Lake as well as at neighboring Sapphire Lake. There's a great view of the Alps from this camp. It is set at 2,700 feet and remains open year-round, but there's no piped water in the winter and it gets mighty cold up here.

Campsites, facilities: There are 10 sites for tents or RVs up to 20 feet (no hookups). Picnic tables and fire grills are provided. Drinking water (summer season), vault toilets, and horse corrals are available. Leashed pets are permitted.

Reservations, fees: Reservations are not accepted. Sites are $11 per night in the summer, $6 per night in the winter. Open year-round.

Directions: From Redding, drive west on Highway 299 to Weaverville. In Weaverville, turn right (north) on Highway 3 and drive 17 miles to Trinity Alps Road (at Stuarts Fork of Trinity Lake). Turn left at Trinity Alps Road and drive about two miles to the campground on the right side of the road.

Contact: Shasta-Trinity National Forest, Weaverville Ranger Station, 530/623-2121, fax 530/623-6010.

84 RUSH CREEK

Scenic rating: 4

in Shasta-Trinity National Forest, north of
Weaverville

Map 2.4 Trinity Lake Detail, page 129

This small, primitive camp provides overflow
space during busy holiday weekends when
the camps at Lewiston and Trinity Lakes are
near capacity. It may not be much, but hey,
at least if you know about Rush Creek you'll
never get stuck for a spot. The camp borders
Rush Creek and is secluded, but again, it's
nearly five miles to the nearest access point
to Trinity Lake.

Campsites, facilities: There are 10 sites for
tents or RVs up to 20 feet (no hookups). Picnic
tables and fire pits are provided. Vault toilets
are available. No drinking water is available.
Leashed pets are permitted.

Reservations, fees: Reservations are not
accepted. Sites are $6 per night. Open mid-
May to mid-September.

Directions: From Redding, drive west on
Highway 299 to Weaverville. In Weaverville,
turn right (north) on Highway 3 and drive
about eight miles to the signed turnoff on the
left side of the road. Turn left and drive 0.25
mile on the short spur road to the campground
on the left side of the road. If you get to Forest
Road 113, you've gone too far.

Contact: Shasta-Trinity National Forest,
Weaverville Ranger Station, 530/623-2121,
fax 530/623-6010.

85 STONEY POINT

Scenic rating: 7

on Trinity Lake in Shasta-Trinity National
Forest

Map 2.4 Trinity Lake Detail, page 129

This is a popular spot at Trinity Lake, easily
discovered and easily reached. Set near the
outlet of Stuarts Fork, it often fills up, but two
other campgrounds close by provide overflow
options. The elevation is 2,400 feet.

Campsites, facilities: There are 21 sites for
tents only. Picnic tables and fire grills are provided. Drinking water and flush toilets are
available, with limited facilities during the
winter season. Leashed pets are permitted.

Reservations, fees: Reservations are not
accepted. Sites are $12 per night in summer,
$6 per night in winter. Open year-round,
weather permitting.

Directions: From Redding, drive west on
Highway 299 to Weaverville. In Weaverville,
turn right (north) on Highway 3 and drive 14
miles (about 0.25 mile past the Stuarts Fork
Bridge) to the campground.

Contact: Shasta-Trinity National Forest,
Weaverville Ranger Station, 530/623-2121,
fax 530/623-6010.

86 PINEWOOD COVE RESORT

Scenic rating: 7

on Trinity Lake

Map 2.4 Trinity Lake Detail, page 129

This is a privately operated camp with full
boating facilities at Trinity Lake. If you don't
have a boat but want to get on Trinity Lake,
this can be a good starting point. A reservation
is advised during the peak summer season.
The elevation is 2,300 feet.

Campsites, facilities: There are 50 sites with
full or partial hookups (30 and 50 amps)
for RVs up to 40 feet, including 10 RV sites
rented for the entire season and wait-listed,
and 28 tent sites. There are also 15 park-
model cabins. Picnic tables and fire grills are
provided. Restrooms with showers, a coin
laundry, dump station, RV supplies, seasonal heated swimming pool, playground,
children's treehouse, volleyball, badminton,
free movies three nights a week in summer,
modem access, video rentals, recreation
room with billiards and video arcade,

convenience store, ice, fishing tackle, library, boat dock with 32 slips, beach, and canoe and kayak rentals are available. Some facilities are wheelchair-accessible. Leashed pets are permitted.

Reservations, fees: Reservations are recommended in the summer. Sites are $27.50–37.50 per night, $4 per person per night for more than two people, $4 per pet per night. Some credit cards accepted. Campground open mid-April through October.

Directions: From Redding, drive west on Highway 299 to Weaverville. In Weaverville, turn north (right) on Highway 3 and drive 14 miles to the campground entrance on the right.

Contact: Pinewood Cove Resort, 530/286-2201 or 800/988-5253, www.pinewoodcove .com.

87 STONEY CREEK GROUP CAMP

Scenic rating: 7

on Trinity Lake in Shasta-Trinity National Forest

Map 2.4 Trinity Lake Detail, page 129

A couple of camps sit on the northern shore of the Stuarts Fork arm of Trinity Lake. This is one of two designed for groups (the other is Fawn), and it is clearly the better. It is set along the Stoney Creek arm, a cove with a feeder creek, with the camp large but relatively private. A swimming beach nearby is a bonus. The elevation is 2,400 feet.

Campsites, facilities: This group tent site can accommodate up to 50 people. Picnic tables and fire grills are provided. Drinking water and flush toilets are available. Leashed pets are permitted.

Reservations, fees: Reservations are required ($9 reservation fee) at 877/444-6777 or www .ReserveUSA.com. The camp is $70 per night. Open early May through late September.

Directions: From Redding, drive west on

Highway 299 to Weaverville. In Weaverville, turn right (north) on Highway 3 and drive 14.5 miles (about a mile past the Stuarts Fork Bridge) to the campground.

Contact: Shasta-Trinity National Forest, Weaverville Ranger Station, 530/623-2121, fax 530/623-6010.

88 TANNERY GULCH

Scenic rating: 8

on Trinity Lake in Shasta-Trinity National Forest

Map 2.4 Trinity Lake Detail, page 129

This is one of the more popular Forest Service camps on the southwest shore of huge Trinity Lake. There's a nice beach near the campground, provided the infamous Bureau of Reclamation hasn't drawn the lake level down too far. It can be quite low in the fall. The elevation is 2,400 feet. Side note: This campground was named by the tannery that once operated in the area; bark from local trees was used in the tanning process.

Campsites, facilities: There are 72 sites and four double sites for tents or RVs up to 40 feet (no hookups). Picnic tables and fire grills are provided. Drinking water, flush and vault toilets, and a boat ramp are available. Leashed pets are permitted.

Reservations, fees: Reservations are accepted ($9 reservation fee) at 877/444-6777 or www .ReserveUSA.com. Sites are $16–22 per night, $5 per night for each additional vehicle. Open early May to late September.

Directions: From Redding, drive west on Highway 299 to Weaverville. In Weaverville, turn right (north) on Highway 3 and drive 13.5 miles north to County Road 172. Turn right on County Road 172 and drive 1.5 miles to the campground entrance.

Contact: Shasta-Trinity National Forest, Weaverville Ranger Station, 530/623-2121, fax 530/623-6010.

89 FAWN GROUP CAMP

Scenic rating: 7

on Trinity Lake in Shasta-Trinity National Forest

Map 2.4 Trinity Lake Detail, page 129

If you want Trinity Lake all to yourself, one way to do it is to get a group together and then reserve this camp near the shore of Trinity Lake. The elevation is 2,500 feet.

Campsites, facilities: There are two group sites for tents or RVs up to 37 feet (no hookups) that can accommodate up to 100 people each. Picnic tables and fire grills are provided. Drinking water and flush toilets are available. A marina is nearby. Leashed pets are permitted.

Reservations, fees: Reservations are required ($9 reservation fee) at 877/444-6777 or www .ReserveUSA.com. Sites are $85 per night. Open early May to late September.

Directions: From Redding, drive west on Highway 299 to Weaverville. In Weaverville, turn right (north) on Highway 3 and drive 15 miles to the campground.

Contact: Shasta-Trinity National Forest, Weaverville Ranger Station, 530/623-2121, fax 530/623-6010.

90 BUSHY TAIL AND BUSH TAIL GROUP

Scenic rating: 7

on Trinity Lake in Shasta-Trinity National Forest

Map 2.4 Trinity Lake Detail, page 129

This is a great spot for families and water sports enthusiasts. It's pretty here on Trinity Lake, and the nearby boat launch is a bonus. The elevation is 2,500 feet.

Campsites, facilities: There are 11 sites with partial hookups (30 amps) for tents or RVs up to 40 feet. The sites are single, double, and triple sizes. Picnic tables and fire grills

are provided. Drinking water and restrooms with flush toilets and coin showers are available. Supplies, a swimming beach, and a boat ramp are available nearby. Leashed pets are permitted.

Reservations, fees: Reservations are required ($9 reservation fee) at 877/444-6777 or www .ReserveUSA.com. Sites are $16–24 per night for single sites, $40 per night for double sites, and $56 per night for triple sites. Open mid May through late September.

Directions: From Redding, drive west on Highway 299 to Weaverville. In Weaverville, turn right (north) on Highway 3 and drive 16.2 miles (approximately 3.5 miles past the Stuarts Fork Bridge) to the campground entrance road on the right. Turn right and drive a short distance to the camp on the left side of the road.

Contact: Shasta-Trinity National Forest, Weaverville Ranger Station, 530/623-2121, fax 530/623-6010.

91 MINERSVILLE

Scenic rating: 7

on Trinity Lake in Shasta-Trinity National Forest

Map 2.4 Trinity Lake Detail, page 129

The setting is near lakeside, quite beautiful when Trinity Lake is fullest in the spring and early summer. This is a good camp for boaters, with a boat ramp in the cove a short distance to the north. But note that the boat ramp is not always functional. When the lake level drops to 65 feet below full, the ramp is not usable. The elevation is 2,400 feet.

Campsites, facilities: There are 14 sites for tents or RVs up to 36 feet (no hookups). Picnic tables and fire grills are provided. Drinking water, flush toilets, and a low-water boat ramp are provided. Leashed pets are permitted.

Reservations, fees: Reservations are not accepted. Sites are $15–24 per night, $7.50–12 per night during the winter season. Open year-round, with limited winter services.

Directions: From Redding, drive west on Highway 299 to Weaverville. Turn right (north) on Highway 3 and drive about 18 miles (if you reach the Mule Creek Ranger Station, you have gone 0.5 mile too far). Turn right at the signed campground access road and drive 0.5 mile to the camp.

Contact: Shasta-Trinity National Forest, Weaverville Ranger Station, 530/623-2121, fax 530/623-6010.

92 RIDGEVILLE BOAT-IN CAMP
🏊 🎣 🚐 🏕 5% ⛰

Scenic rating: 9

on Trinity Lake in Shasta-Trinity National Forest

Map 2.4 Trinity Lake Detail, page 129   BEST ☾

This is one of the ways to get a camping spot to call your own—go by boat. The camp is exposed on a peninsula, providing beautiful views. Prospects for waterskiing and trout or bass fishing are often outstanding. The early part of the season is the prime time here for boaters, before the furnace heat of full summer. A great view of the Trinity Alps is a bonus. The only downer is the typical lake drawdown at the end of summer and beginning of fall, when this boat-in camp is left a long traipse from water's edge.

Campsites, facilities: There are 21 tent sites. Picnic tables and fire grills are provided. Vault toilets are available. No drinking water is available. Garbage must be packed out. Boat ramps can be found near Clark Springs, Alpine View, or farther north at Trinity Center. Leashed pets are permitted.

Reservations, fees: Reservations are not accepted. There is no fee for camping. Open year-round.

Directions: From Redding, drive west on Highway 299 to Weaverville. In Weaver-

ville, turn right (north) on Highway 3 and drive seven miles to the Stuarts Fork arm of Trinity Lake. You'll find boat launches at Stuarts Fork. After launching, drive your boat to the mouth of Stuarts Fork. The campground is set on the western shore at the end of a peninsula at the entrance to that part of the lake.

Contact: Shasta-Trinity National Forest, Weaverville Ranger Station, 530/623-2121, fax 530/623-6010.

93 CLARK SPRINGS
🚶 🏊 🎣 🚣 🐕 🚐 ⛰

Scenic rating: 7

on Trinity Lake in Shasta-Trinity National Forest

Map 2.4 Trinity Lake Detail, page 129

This used to be a day-use-only picnic area, but because of popular demand, the Forest Service opened it for camping. That makes sense because people were bound to declare it a campground anyway, since it has a nearby boat ramp and a beach. The elevation is 2,400 feet.

Campsites, facilities: There are 21 sites for tents or RVs up to 25 feet (no hookups). Picnic tables and fire grills are provided. Drinking water and flush toilets are available, with limited facilities in the winter. Supplies are available in Weaverville. Leashed pets are permitted.

Reservations, fees: Reservations are not accepted. Sites are $11 per night. Open early April through October.

Directions: From Redding, drive west on Highway 299 to Weaverville. In Weaverville, turn right (north) on Highway 3 and drive 16.5 miles (about four miles past the Stuarts Fork Bridge) to the campground entrance road on the right.

Contact: Shasta-Trinity National Forest, Weaverville Ranger Station, 530/623-2121, fax 530/623-6010.

94 RIDGEVILLE ISLAND BOAT-IN CAMP

🏊 🎣 🚤 🐾 5% ⛺

Scenic rating: 9

on Trinity Lake in Shasta-Trinity National Forest

Map 2.4 Trinity Lake Detail, page 129

How would you like to be on a deserted island? You'll learn the answer from this tiny, little-known island with a great view of the Trinity Alps. It is one of several boat-in camps in the Trinity Lake region. The elevation is 2,400 feet. Note that the lake level at Trinity Lake is typically dropped significantly from September through October.

Campsites, facilities: There are three tent sites. Picnic tables and fire grills are provided. Vault toilets are available. No drinking water is available. Garbage must be packed out. Several boat ramps are available at campgrounds and private resorts at Trinity Lake. Leashed pets are permitted.

Reservations, fees: Reservations are not accepted. There is no fee for camping. Open year-round.

Directions: From Redding, drive west on Highway 299 to Weaverville. In Weaverville, turn right (north) on Highway 3 and drive seven miles to the Stuarts Fork arm of Trinity Lake. You'll find boat launches at Stuarts Fork. After launching, drive your boat to the campground set on a small island near Estrelita Marina, between Minersville and Mariner's Roost.

Contact: Shasta-Trinity National Forest, Weaverville Ranger Station, 530/623-2121, fax 530/623-6010.

95 MARINERS ROOST BOAT-IN CAMP

🏊 🎣 🚤 🐾 5% ⛺

Scenic rating: 8

on Trinity Lake in Shasta-Trinity National Forest

Map 2.4 Trinity Lake Detail, page 129

A perfect boat camp? This comes close at Trinity since it's positioned perfectly for boaters, with spectacular views of the Trinity Alps to the west, and it is an ideal spot for water-skiers. That is because it is on the western side of the lake's major peninsula, topped by Bowerman Ridge. Secluded and wooded, this area is set at 2,400 feet elevation.

Campsites, facilities: There are seven tent sites. Picnic tables and fire grills are provided. Vault toilets are available. No drinking water is available. Garbage must be packed out. Several boat ramps are available at campgrounds and private resorts at Trinity Lake. Leashed pets are permitted.

Reservations, fees: Reservations are not accepted. There is no fee for camping. Open year-round.

Directions: From Redding, drive west on Highway 299 to Weaverville. In Weaverville, turn right (north) on Highway 3 and drive seven miles to the Stuarts Fork arm of Trinity Lake. You'll find boat launches at Stuarts Fork. After launching, drive your boat to West Bowerman Ridge (near the point of the main arm of the lake) and look for the camp on the peninsula, just east and on the opposite shore of Ridgeville Island Boat-In Camp.

Contact: Shasta-Trinity National Forest, Weaverville Ranger Station, 530/623-2121, fax 530/623-6010.

96 HAYWARD FLAT

🥾 🏊 🎣 🚤 🐾 ♿ 🚐 ⛺

Scenic rating: 7

on Trinity Lake in Shasta-Trinity National Forest

Map 2.4 Trinity Lake Detail, page 129

When giant Trinity Lake is full of water, Hayward Flat is one of the prettiest places you could ask for. The camp has become one of the most popular Forest Service campgrounds on Trinity Lake because it sits right along the shore and offers a beach. The elevation is 2,400 feet.

Campsites, facilities: There are 98 sites for tents or RVs up to 40 feet (no hookups) and four double sites. Picnic tables and fire grills ided. Drinking water and flush toilets, and there is usually a camp host. Supplies and a boat ramp are available nearby. Some facilities are wheelchair-accessible. Leashed pets are permitted.

Reservations, fees: Reservations are accepted ($9 reservation fee) at 877/444-6777 or www .ReserveUSA.com. Sites are $16–22 per night, $5 per night for each additional vehicle. Open mid-May through mid-September.

Directions: From Redding, drive west on Highway 299 to Weaverville. In Weaverville, turn right (north) on Highway 3 and drive 19.5 miles, approximately three miles past the Mule Creek Ranger Station. Turn right at the signed access road for Hayward Flat and drive about three miles to the campground at the end of the road.

Contact: Shasta-Trinity National Forest, Weaverville Ranger Station, 530/623-2121, fax 530/623-6010.

97 ALPINE VIEW

Scenic rating: 9

on Trinity Lake in Shasta-Trinity National Forest

Map 2.4 Trinity Lake Detail, page 129

This is an attractive area, set on the shore of Trinity Lake at a creek inlet. The boat ramp nearby provides a bonus. It's a very pretty spot, with views to the west across the lake arm and to the Trinity Alps, featuring Granite Peak. The Forest Service occasionally runs tours from the campground to historic Bowerman Barn, which was built in 1894. The elevation is 2,400 feet.

Campsites, facilities: There are 53 sites for tents or RVs up to 32 feet (no hookups). Picnic tables and fire grills are provided. Drinking water and flush toilets are available. Some facilities are wheelchair-accessible. The Bowerman boat ramp is nearby. Leashed pets are permitted.

Reservations, fees: Reservations are not

accepted. Sites are $16–22 per night, $5 per night for each additional vehicle. Open mid-May through mid-September.

Directions: From Redding, drive west on Highway 299 to Weaverville. In Weaverville, turn right (north) on Highway 3 and drive 22.5 miles to Covington Mill (south of Trinity Center). Turn right (south) on Guy Covington Drive and drive three miles to the camp (one mile past Bowerman boat ramp) on the right side of the road.

Contact: Shasta-Trinity National Forest, Weaverville Ranger Station, 530/623-2121, fax 530/623-6010.

98 CAPTAIN'S POINT BOAT-IN CAMP

Scenic rating: 7

on Trinity Lake in Shasta-Trinity National Forest

Map 2.4 Trinity Lake Detail, page 129

The Trinity River arm of Trinity Lake is a massive piece of water, stretching north from the giant Trinity Dam for nearly 20 miles. This camp is the only boat-in camp along this entire stretch of shore, and it is situated at a prominent spot, where a peninsula juts well into the main lake body. This is a perfect boat-in site for water-skiers or anglers. The fishing is often excellent for smallmouth bass in the cove adjacent to Captain's Point, using grubs. The elevation is 2,400 feet.

Campsites, facilities: There are three tent sites. Picnic tables and fire grills are provided. Vault toilets are available. No drinking water is available. Garbage must be packed out. Several boat ramps are available at campgrounds and private resorts at Trinity Lake. Leashed pets are permitted.

Reservations, fees: Reservations are not accepted. There is no fee for camping. Open year-round.

Directions: From Redding, drive west on Highway 299 to Weaverville. In Weaverville, turn right (north) on Highway 3 and drive about seven miles to the signed turnoff on the right side of the road for the Trinity Alps Marina. Turn right and drive approximately 10 miles to the marina and boat ramp. Launch your boat and cruise north about four miles up the main Trinity River arm of the lake. Look for Captain's Point on the left side of the lake.

Contact: Shasta-Trinity National Forest, Weaverville Ranger Station, 530/623-2121, fax 530/623-6010.

99 CLEAR CREEK

Scenic rating: 6

in Shasta-Trinity National Forest

Map 2.4 Trinity Lake Detail, page 129

This is a primitive, little-known camp that gets little use. It is set near Clear Creek at 3,500 feet elevation. In fall hunters will occasionally turn it into a deer camp, with the adjacent slopes of Blue Mountain and Damnation Peak in the Trinity Divide country providing fair numbers of large bucks, three points or better. Trinity Lake is only seven miles to the west, but it seems as if it's in a different world.

Campsites, facilities: There are eight sites for tents or RVs up to 22 feet (no hookups). Picnic tables and fire grills are provided. Vault toilets are available. No drinking water is available. Garbage must be packed out. Leashed pets are permitted.

Reservations, fees: Reservations are not accepted. There is no fee for camping. Open year-round.

Directions: From Redding, drive west on Highway 299 for 17 miles to Trinity Mountain Road. Turn right (north) on Trinity Mountain Road and continue past the town of French Gulch for about 12 miles to East Side Road/County Road 106. Turn right on the gravel road and drive north for about 11 miles to the campground access road (dirt)

on right. Turn right on the access road and drive two miles to the campground.

Contact: Shasta-Trinity National Forest, Weaverville Ranger District, 530/623-2121, fax 530/623-6010.

100 LAKESHORE VILLA RV PARK

Scenic rating: 7

on Shasta Lake

Map 2.4 Shasta Lake Detail, page 129

This is a large campground with level, shaded sites for RVs, set near the northern Sacramento River arm of giant Shasta Lake. Most of the campers visiting here are boaters coming for the water sports, waterskiing, wakeboarding, or tubing. The sites are level and graveled.

Campsites, facilities: There are 92 sites with full or partial hookups (20, 30, and 50 amps) for RVs up to 45 feet; some sites are pull-through. There are also two RV rentals. No tents. Restrooms with showers, ice, dump station, cable TV, modem access, playground, group facilities, and a boat dock are available. Boat ramp, store, restaurant, and bar are nearby. Some facilities are wheelchair-accessible. Leashed pets are permitted.

Reservations, fees: Reservations are accepted. Sites are $25 per night. A few long-term rentals available. Some credit cards accepted. Open May through September.

Directions: From Redding, drive north on I-5 for 24 miles to Exit 702 for Lakeshore Drive/Antlers Road in Lakehead. Take that exit, turn left at the stop sign, and drive under the freeway to Lakeshore Drive. Turn left on Lakeshore Drive and drive 0.5 mile to the campground on the right.

Contact: Lakeshore Villa RV Park, 530/238-8688, www.american-rvresorts.com.

101 LAKESHORE INN AND RV

Scenic rating: 7

on Shasta Lake

Map 2.4 Shasta Lake Detail, page 129

Shasta Lake is a boater's paradise and an ideal spot for campers with boats. The nearest marina is 2.75 miles away. It is on the Sacramento River arm of Shasta Lake. Shasta Lake Caverns are 10 miles away, and Shasta Dam tours are available about 20 miles away.

Campsites, facilities: There are 40 sites with full or partial hookups (30 and 50 amps) for tents or RVs of any length; some sites are pull-through. Ten cabins are also available. Picnic tables are provided. Restrooms with showers, cable TV, dump station, seasonal swimming pool, playground, video arcade, coin laundry, seasonal bar and restaurant, and a small seasonal convenience store are available. Family barbecues are held on Sunday in season, 5 P.M.–9 P.M. Live music is scheduled most Friday and Saturday nights. Some facilities are wheelchair-accessible. Leashed pets are permitted in the campground only.

Reservations, fees: Reservations are recommended at 530/238-2003. Sites are $25–29 per night, $2 per person per night for more than two people, $1 per pet per night. Some credit cards accepted. Open year-round, with limited winter facilities.

Directions: From Redding, drive north on I-5 for 24 miles to Exit 702 for Lakeshore Drive/Antlers Road in Lakehead. Take that exit, turn left at the stop sign, and drive under the freeway to Lakeshore Drive. Turn left on Lakeshore Drive and drive one mile to the campground.

Contact: Lakeshore Inn and RV, 530/238-2003, www.shastacamping.com.

102 SHASTA LAKE RV RESORT AND CAMPGROUND

Scenic rating: 7

on Shasta Lake

Map 2.4 Shasta Lake Detail, page 129

Shasta Lake RV Resort and Campground is one of a series on the upper end of Shasta Lake with easy access off I-5 by car, then easy access by boat to premium trout or bass fishing as well as waterskiing and water sports.

Campsites, facilities: There are 53 sites with full hookups (30 amps) for RVs up to 40 feet, 21 tent sites, one trailer rental, and three cabins. Some sites are pull-through. Picnic tables, barbecues, and fire rings are provided. Restrooms with showers, seasonal convenience store, firewood, bait, coin laundry, playground, table tennis, horseshoes, trailer and boat storage, modem access, and a seasonal swimming pool are available. There is also a private dock with 36 boat slips. Leashed pets are permitted.

Reservations, fees: Reservations are accepted at 800/374-2782. Sites are $20–29 per night, $1 per pet per night. Some credit cards accepted. Open year-round.

Directions: From Redding, drive north on I-5 for 24 miles to the Lakeshore Drive/Antlers Road exit in Lakehead. Take that exit, turn left at the stop sign, and drive under the freeway to Lakeshore Drive. Turn left on Lakeshore Drive and drive 1.5 miles to the campground on the right.

Contact: Shasta Lake RV Resort and Campground, 530/238-2370, www.shastalakerv.com.

103 ANTLERS RV PARK AND CAMPGROUND

🏊 🎣 ⛴ 🏕 🏕 ♿ 🚐 ⛰

Scenic rating: 7

on Shasta Lake

Map 2.4 Shasta Lake Detail, page 129

Antlers Park is set along the Sacramento River arm of Shasta Lake at 1,215 feet. The park is set on 20 acres and has shady sites. This is a full-service spot for campers, boaters, and anglers, with access to the beautiful Sacramento River arm. The camp often fills in summer, including on weekdays.

Campsites, facilities: There are 70 sites with full hookups (30 and 50 amps) for RVs of any length (several are pull-through), 40 sites for tents, and several rental trailers. Picnic tables and fire rings or fire grills are provided. Tent sites also have food lockers. Restrooms with showers, seasonal convenience store and snack bar, ice, coin laundry, Sunday pancake breakfasts, video games, playground, volleyball court, table tennis, horseshoes, basketball, and seasonal swimming pool. Boat rentals, houseboats, moorage, and a complete marina with recreation room are available adjacent to the park. Some facilities are wheelchair-accessible. Leashed pets are permitted, with a limit of two.

Reservations, fees: Reservations are accepted. Sites are $22.50–33.50 per night, $4 per person per night for more than two people, $3 per pet per night. Some credit cards accepted. Open year-round.

Directions: From Redding, drive north on I-5 for 24 miles to the Lakeshore Drive/Antlers Road exit in Lakehead. Take that exit, turn right at the stop sign, and drive a short distance to Antlers Road. At Antlers Road, turn right and drive 1.5 miles south to the campground on the left.

Contact: Antlers RV Park and Campground, 530/238-2322 or 800/642-6849, www.antlersrvpark.com.

104 ANTLERS

🏊 🎣 ⛴ 🏕 ♿ 🚐 ⛰

Scenic rating: 7

on Shasta Lake in Shasta-Trinity National Forest

Map 2.4 Shasta Lake Detail, page 129

This spot is set on the primary Sacramento River inlet of giant Shasta Lake. Antlers is a well-known spot that attracts returning campers and boaters year after year. It is the farthest upstream marina/camp on the lake. Lake levels can fluctuate greatly from spring through fall, and the operators will move their docks to compensate. Easy access off I-5 is a big plus for boaters.

Campsites, facilities: There are 41 individual sites and 18 double sites for tents or RVs up to 30 feet (no hookups). Picnic tables, food lockers, and fire grills are provided. Drinking water and flush and vault toilets are available. A boat ramp, amphitheater with summer interpretive programs, grocery store, and coin laundry are available nearby. Some facilities are wheelchair-accessible. Leashed pets are permitted.

Reservations, fees: Reservations are accepted ($9 reservation fee) at 877/444-6777 or www.ReserveUSA.com. Sites are $18 per night, $30 per night for a double site, $5 per night for each additional vehicle. Open year-round.

Directions: From Redding, drive north on I-5 for 24 miles to the Lakeshore Drive/Antlers Road exit in Lakehead. Take that exit, turn right at the stop sign, and drive a short distance to Antlers Road. At Antlers Road, turn right and drive one mile south to the campground.

Contact: Shasta-Trinity National Forest, Shasta Lake Ranger District, 530/275-1587, fax 530/275-1512; Shasta Lake Visitor Center, 530/275-1589; Shasta Recreation Company, 530/275-8113.

105 LAKESHORE EAST

🚶 🏊 🛶 🚐 🏕️ ♿ 🚗 ⛺

Scenic rating: 7

on Shasta Lake in Shasta-Trinity National Forest

Map 2.4 Shasta Lake Detail, page 129

Lakeshore East is near the full-service community of Lakehead and is on the Sacramento arm of Shasta Lake. It's a nice spot, with a good boat ramp and marina nearby at Antlers or Sugarloaf.

Campsites, facilities: There are 20 individual sites and six double sites for tents or RVs up to 30 feet (no hookups). Picnic tables and fire grills are provided. Drinking water and flush toilets are available. A boat ramp, grocery store, and coin laundry are available nearby. Some facilities are wheelchair-accessible. Leashed pets are permitted.

Reservations, fees: Reservations are accepted ($9 reservation fee) at 877/444-6777 or www .ReserveUSA.com. Sites are $18 per night for a single site, $30 for a double site, $5 per night for each additional vehicle. Open year-round.

Directions: From Redding, drive north on I-5 for 24 miles to the Lakeshore Drive/Antlers Road exit at Lakehead. Take the Antlers exit, turn left at the stop sign, and drive under the freeway to Lakeshore Drive. Turn left on Lakeshore Drive and drive three miles. Look for the campground entrance on the left side of the road.

Contact: Shasta-Trinity National Forest, Shasta Lake Ranger District, 530/275-1587, fax 530/275-1512; Shasta Lake Visitor Center, 530/275-1589; Shasta Recreation Company, 530/275-8113.

106 GREGORY CREEK

🛶 🏕️ 🚗 ⛺

Scenic rating: 7

on Shasta Lake in Shasta-Trinity National Forest

Map 2.4 Shasta Lake Detail, page 129

This is one of the more secluded Forest Service campgrounds on Shasta Lake, and it has become extremely popular with the younger crowd. It is set just above lakeside, on the eastern shore of the northern Sacramento River arm of the lake. When the lake is fullest in the spring and early summer, this is a great spot. Note: This is a bald eagle nesting area and the campground is subject to closures for habitat protection.

Campsites, facilities: There are 18 sites for tents or RVs up to 16 feet (no hookups). Picnic tables and fire grills are provided. Drinking water and flush toilets are available. Leashed pets are permitted.

Reservations, fees: Reservations are not accepted. Sites are $14 per night, $5 per night for each additional vehicle. Open early August through September; call to verify current status.

Directions: From Redding, drive north on I-5 for 21 miles to the Salt Creek/Gilman Road exit. Take that exit and drive over the freeway to Gregory Creek Road. Turn right and drive 10 miles to the campground at the end of the road.

Contact: Shasta-Trinity National Forest, Shasta Lake Ranger District, 530/275-1587, fax 530/275-1512; Shasta Lake Visitor Center, 530/275-1589; Shasta Recreation Company, 530/275-8113.

107 HIRZ BAY GROUP CAMP

🚶 🏊 🛶 🚐 🏕️ 🚗 ⛺

Scenic rating: 8

on Shasta Lake in Shasta-Trinity National Forest

Map 2.4 Shasta Lake Detail, page 129

This is the spot for your own private party—providing you get a reservation—set on a point at the entrance of Hirz Bay on the McCloud River arm of Shasta Lake. A boat ramp is only 0.5 mile away on the camp access road, giving access to the McCloud River arm. This is an excellent spot to make a base camp for a fishing trip, with great trolling for trout in this stretch of the lake.

Campsites, facilities: There are two group sites for tents or RVs up to 30 feet (no hookups) that can accommodate 80–120 people each. Picnic tables and fire grills are provided. Drinking water, vault toilets, and a group picnic area are available. Leashed pets are permitted.

Reservations, fees: Reservations are required ($9 reservation fee) at 877/444-6777 or www .ReserveUSA.com. Sites are $80–110 per night. Open April to late September.

Directions: From Redding, drive north on I-5 for about 20 miles to the Salt Creek/Gilman exit. Turn right on Gilman Road/County Road 7H009 and drive northeast for 10 miles to the campground/boat launch access road. Turn right and drive 0.5 mile to the camp on the left side of the road. The group camp is past the family campground.

Contact: Shasta-Trinity National Forest, Shasta Lake Ranger District, 530/275-1587, fax 530/275-1512; Shasta Lake Visitor Center, 530/275-1589; Shasta Recreation Company, 530/275-8113.

108 HIRZ BAY

Scenic rating: 8

on Shasta Lake in Shasta-Trinity National Forest

Map 2.4 Shasta Lake Detail, page 129 **BEST**

This is one of two camps in the immediate area (the other is Hirz Bay Group Camp) that provides nearby access to a boat ramp (0.5 mile down the road) and the McCloud River arm of Shasta Lake. The camp is set on a point at the entrance of Hirz Bay. This is an excellent spot to make a base camp for a fishing trip, with great trolling for trout in this stretch of the lake.

Campsites, facilities: There are 37 individual sites and 10 double sites for tents or RVs up to 40 feet (no hookups). Picnic tables and fire grills are provided. Drinking water and flush and vault toilets are available. A camp host is usually available in the summer. A boat

ramp is nearby. Some facilities are wheelchair-accessible. Leashed pets are permitted.

Reservations, fees: Reservations are accepted ($9 reservation fee) at 877/444-6777 or www .ReserveUSA.com. Sites are $18 per night, $30 per night for a double site, $5 per night for each additional vehicle. Open year-round.

Directions: From Redding, drive north on I-5 for about 20 miles to the Salt Creek/Gilman exit. Turn right on Gilman Road/County Road 7H009 and drive northeast for 10 miles to the campground/boat launch access road. Turn right and drive 0.5 mile to the camp on the left side of the road.

Contact: Shasta-Trinity National Forest, Shasta Lake Ranger District, 530/275-1587, fax 530/275-1512; Shasta Lake Visitor Center, 530/275-1589; Shasta Recreation Company, 530/275-8113.

109 DEKKAS ROCK GROUP CAMP

Scenic rating: 8

on Shasta Lake in Shasta-Trinity National Forest

Map 2.4 Shasta Lake Detail, page 129

The few people who know about this camp love this little spot. It is an ideal group camp, set on a flat above the McCloud arm of Shasta Lake, shaded primarily by bays and oaks, with a boat ramp two miles to the south at Hirz Bay. The views are pretty here, looking across the lake at the limestone ridge that borders the McCloud arm. In late summer and fall when the lake level drops, it can be a hike from the camp down to water's edge.

Campsites, facilities: There is one group site for tents or RVs up to 16 feet (no hookups) that can accommodate up to 60 people. A central meeting area with preparation tables, picnic tables, two pedestal grills, and a large barbecue is provided. Drinking water and vault toilets are available. Leashed pets are permitted.

Reservations, fees: Reservations are

required ($9 reservation fee) at 877/444-6777 or www.ReserveUSA.com. The camp is $110 per night.

Directions: From Redding, drive north on I-5 for about 20 miles to the Salt Creek/Gilman exit. Turn right on Gilman Road/County Road 7H009 and drive northeast for 11 miles to the campground on the right side of the road.

Contact: Shasta-Trinity National Forest, Shasta Lake Ranger District, 530/275-1587, fax 530/275-1512; Shasta Lake Visitor Center, 530/275-1589; Shasta Recreation Company, 530/275-8113.

110 MOORE CREEK GROUP AND OVERFLOW

🏊 🛶 ⛴ 🐕 🚐 ⛺

Scenic rating: 8

on Shasta Lake in Shasta-Trinity National Forest

Map 2.4 Shasta Lake Detail, page 129

The McCloud arm of Shasta Lake is the most beautiful of the five arms at Shasta, with its emerald-green waters and limestone canyon towering overhead to the east. That beautiful setting is taken advantage of at this camp, with a good view of the lake and limestone, along with good trout fishing on the adjacent section of water. Moore Creek is rented as a group camp most of the summer, except during holidays when individual sites are available on a first-come, first-served basis.

Campsites, facilities: There are 12 sites for tents or RVs up to 16 feet (no hookups) that are usually rented as one group site for up to 90 people. Picnic tables and fire grills are provided. Drinking water and vault toilets are available. Leashed pets are permitted.

Reservations, fees: Reservations are required ($9 reservation fee) for the group site at 877/444-6777 or www.ReserveUSA.com. Sites are $14 per night for individual sites, $5 per night for each additional vehicle, $110 per night for group site. Open late May to early September.

Directions: From Redding, drive north on I-5 for about 20 miles to the Salt Creek/Gilman exit. Take that exit and turn right on Gilman Road/County Road 7H009 and drive northeast for 14 miles to the campground on the right side of the road.

Contact: Shasta-Trinity National Forest, Shasta Lake Ranger District, 530/275-1587, fax 530/275-1512; Shasta Lake Visitor Center, 530/275-1589; Shasta Recreation Company, 530/275-8113.

111 ELLERY CREEK

🏊 🛶 ⛴ 🐕 🚐 ⛺

Scenic rating: 7

on Shasta Lake in Shasta-Trinity National Forest

Map 2.4 Shasta Lake Detail, page 129

This camp is set at a pretty spot where Ellery Creek empties into the upper McCloud arm of Shasta Lake. Several sites are set on the pavement with an unobstructed view of the beautiful McCloud arm. This stretch of water is excellent for trout fishing in the summer, with bank-fishing access available two miles upstream at the McCloud Bridge. In the spring, there are tons of small spotted bass along the shore from the camp on upstream to the inlet of the McCloud River. Boat-launching facilities are available five miles south at Hirz Bay.

Campsites, facilities: There are 19 sites for tents or RVs up to 25 feet (no hookups). Picnic tables, food lockers, and fire grills are provided. Drinking water and vault toilets are available. Leashed pets are permitted.

Reservations, fees: Reservations are accepted ($9 reservation fee) at 877/444-6777 or www.ReserveUSA.com. Sites are $14 per night, $5 per night for each additional vehicle. Open early May through September.

Directions: From Redding, drive north on I-5 for about 20 miles to the Salt Creek/Gilman exit. Turn right on Gilman Road/County Road 7H009 and drive northeast for 15 miles to the campground on the right side of the road.

Contact: Shasta-Trinity National Forest, Shasta Lake Ranger District, 530/275-1587, fax 530/275-1512; Shasta Lake Visitor Center, 530/275-1589; Shasta Recreation Company, 530/275-8113.

112 PINE POINT AND GROUP CAMP

Scenic rating: 7

on Shasta Lake in Shasta-Trinity National Forest

Map 2.4 Shasta Lake Detail, page 129

Pine Point is a pretty little camp, set on a ridge above the McCloud arm of Shasta Lake amid oak trees and scattered ponderosa pines. The view is best in spring, when lake levels are generally highest. Boat-launching facilities are available at Hirz Bay; boaters park their boats on shore below the camp while the rest of their party arrives at the camp by car. That provides a chance not only for camping, but also for boating, swimming, waterskiing, and fishing. Note: From July through September, this campground can be reserved as a group site only. It is also used as a summer overflow camping area on weekends and holidays.

Campsites, facilities: There are 14 sites for tents or RVs up to 24 feet (no hookups), which can also be used as a group camp for up to 100 people. Picnic tables, food lockers, and fire rings are provided. Drinking water and vault toilets are available. Leashed pets are permitted.

Reservations, fees: Reservations are required ($9 reservation fee) for group site at 877/444-6777 or www.ReserveUSA.com. Sites are $14 per night, $5 per night for each additional vehicle, $110 per night for a group site. Open May to early September.

Directions: From Redding, drive north on I-5 for about 20 miles to the Salt Creek/Gilman exit. Turn right on Gilman Road/County Road 7H009 and drive northeast for 17 miles to the campground entrance road on the right.

Contact: Shasta-Trinity National Forest, Shasta Lake Ranger District, 530/275-1587, fax 530/275-1512; Shasta Lake Visitor Center, 530/275-1589; Shasta Recreation Company, 530/275-8113.

113 McCLOUD BRIDGE

Scenic rating: 7

on Shasta Lake in Shasta-Trinity National Forest

Map 2.4 Shasta Lake Detail, page 129

Even though reaching this camp requires a long drive, it remains popular. That is because the best shore-fishing access at the lake is available at nearby McCloud Bridge. It is common to see 15 or 20 people shore fishing here for trout on summer weekends. In the fall, big brown trout migrate through this section of lake en route to their upstream spawning grounds.

Campsites, facilities: There are 11 individual sites and three double sites for tents or RVs up to 16 feet (no hookups). Picnic tables and fire grills are provided. Drinking water, vault toilets, and a group picnic area are available. Some facilities are wheelchair-accessible. Leashed pets are permitted.

Reservations, fees: Reservations are not accepted. Sites are $18 per night, $30 per night for double sites, $5 per night for each additional vehicle. Open early May through September.

Directions: From Redding, drive north on I-5 for about 20 miles to the Salt Creek/Gilman exit. Turn right on Gilman Road/County Road 7H009 and drive northeast for 18.5 miles. Cross the McCloud Bridge and drive one mile to the campground entrance on the right.

Contact: Shasta-Trinity National Forest, Shasta Lake Ranger District, 530/275-1587, fax 530/275-1512; Shasta Lake Visitor Center, 530/275-1589; Shasta Recreation Company, 530/275-8113.

114 MADRONE CAMP

🚶‍♀️ 🎣 🐕 5% 🚗 ⛺

Scenic rating: 7

on Squaw Creek in Shasta-Trinity National Forest

Map 2.4 Shasta Lake Detail, page 129

Tired of people? Then you've come to the right place. This remote camp is set along Squaw Creek, a feeder stream of Shasta Lake, which lies to the southwest. It's way out there, far away from anybody. Even though Shasta Lake is relatively close, about 10 miles away, it is in another world. A network of four-wheel-drive roads provides a recreation option, detailed on a map of Shasta-Trinity National Forest.

Campsites, facilities: There are 10 sites for tents or RVs up to 16 feet (no hookups). Picnic tables and fire grills are provided. Vault toilets are available. No drinking water is available. Garbage must be packed out. Leashed pets are permitted.

Reservations, fees: Reservations are not accepted. There is no fee for camping. Open year-round.

Directions: From Redding, drive 31 miles east on Highway 299 to the town of Montgomery Creek. Turn left on Fenders Ferry Road/Forest Road 27 and drive 18 miles to the camp (the road starts as gravel and then becomes dirt). Note: The access road is rough and RVs are not advised.

Contact: Shasta-Trinity National Forest, Shasta Lake Ranger District, 530/275-1587, fax 530/275-1512; Shasta Lake Visitor Center, 530/275-1589.

115 GOOSENECK COVE BOAT-IN

🏊 🎣 🚤 🐕 ⛺

Scenic rating: 4

on Shasta Lake in Shasta-Trinity National Forest

Map 2.4 Shasta Lake Detail, page 129

You want a camp all to yourself? There's a good chance of that here at Gooseneck Cove. One reason is because it is well hidden, set well back in a cove on the west side of the Sacramento River arm of giant Shasta Lake. The other reason is there was some fire damage here in 1999, and some burned oaks and manzanita will take years to grow out. So there you have it, a chance any day of the year to have a campground all to yourself. The fishing on the Sacramento River arm of Shasta Lake is very good, both trolling for trout all summer, especially at the headwaters in midsummer, and for bass in the spring on plastic worms. Waterskiing is also excellent here, with water temperatures in the high 70s for most of summer.

Campsites, facilities: There are eight boat-in sites for tents. Picnic tables and fire grills are provided. Vault toilets are available. No drinking water is available. Garbage must be packed out. Small stores with supplies are available at Antlers. Leashed pets are permitted.

Reservations, fees: Reservations are not accepted. There is no fee for camping. A $8 fee is charged for boat launching. Open year-round.

Directions: From Redding, drive north on I-5 for 24 miles to the Lakeshore Drive/Antlers Road exit in Lakehead. Take that exit, turn left at the stop sign, and drive a short distance to Antlers Road. At Antlers Road, turn right and drive one mile south to the campground and nearby boat launch. Launch your boat and cruise seven miles south to the boat-in campground.

Contact: Shasta-Trinity National Forest, Shasta Lake Ranger District, 530/275-1587, fax 530/275-1512; Shasta Lake Visitor Center, 530/275-1589.

116 TRAIL IN RV PARK AND CAMPGROUND

🏊 🎣 🛶 🐴 ♿ 🚐 ⛺

Scenic rating: 7

near Shasta Lake

Map 2.4 Shasta Lake Detail, page 129

This is a privately operated campground near the Salt Creek arm of giant Shasta Lake. Open, level sites are available. Many of the sites are filled with long-term renters. The nearest boat launch is one mile away and the lake offers fishing, boating, and swimming. Its proximity to I-5 makes this a popular spot, fast and easy to reach, which is extremely attractive for drivers of RVs and trailers who want to avoid the many twisty roads surrounding Shasta Lake.

Campsites, facilities: There are 39 sites with full hookups (30 and 50 amps) for RVs of any length and four tent sites; some sites are pull-through. Picnic tables and fire grills are provided. Restrooms with showers, satellite TV hookups, seasonal heated swimming pool, playground, convenience store, ice, firewood, and coin laundry are available. Leashed pets are permitted.

Reservations, fees: Reservations are accepted. Sites are $28 per night for RV camping, $17 per night for tent camping, $2 per person per night for more than two people, $1 per pet per night. Monthly rates available. Some credit cards accepted. Open year-round.

Directions: From Redding, drive 22 miles north on I-5 to Exit 698/the Gilman Road/Salt Creek Road exit. Take that exit and turn left on Salt Creek Road and drive a short distance to Gregory Creek Road. Turn right and drive 0.25 mile to the campground on the right.

Contact: Trail In RV Park and Campground, tel./fax 530/238-8533.

117 NELSON POINT AND GROUP CAMP

🏊 🎣 🚣 🛶 🐕 🚐 ⛺

Scenic rating: 7

on Shasta Lake in Shasta-Trinity National Forest

Map 2.4 Shasta Lake Detail, page 129

This is an easy-to-reach campground, only a few minutes from I-5. It's set beside the Salt Creek inlet of Shasta Lake, deep in a cove. In low-water years, or when the lake level is low in the fall and early winter, this camp can seem quite distant from water's edge. This campground can be reserved as a group camp July through September.

Campsites, facilities: There are eight sites for tents or RVs up to 16 feet, and a group site for tents or RVs up to 16 feet that can accommodate up to 60 people. No hookups. Vault toilets, picnic tables, and fire grills are provided. No drinking water is available. A grocery store and coin laundry are nearby in Lakehead. Leashed pets are permitted.

Reservations, fees: Reservations are required for group sites only ($9 reservation fee) at 877/444-6777 or www.ReserveUSA.com. Sites are $9 per night, $5 per night for each additional vehicle, and $80 per night for a group site. Open May to early September.

Directions: From Redding, drive north on I-5 for about 20 miles to the Salt Creek Road/Gilman Road exit. Take that exit, turn left and drive 0.25 mile to Gregory Creek Road. Turn right and drive one mile to Conflict Point Road. Turn left and drive one mile to the campground on the left.

Contact: Shasta-Trinity National Forest, Shasta Lake Ranger District, 530/275-1587, fax 530/275-1512; Shasta Lake Visitor Center, 530/275-1589; Shasta Recreation Company, 530/275-8113.

118 HOLIDAY HARBOR RESORT

🏊 🎣 🚤 🐴 🚴 ♿ 🚐 ⛺

Scenic rating: 7

on Shasta Lake

Map 2.4 Shasta Lake Detail, page 129   BEST (

This camp is one of the more popular family-oriented, all-service resorts on Shasta Lake, which has the second-largest dam in the United States. It is set on the lower McCloud arm of the lake, which is extremely beautiful with a limestone mountain ridge off to the east. It is an ideal jump-off for all water sports, especially waterskiing, houseboating and boating, and fishing. A good boat ramp, boat rentals, and store with all the goodies are bonuses. The place is full service and even offers boat-launching service. Campers staying here also get a 15 percent discount on boat rentals. Another plus is the nearby side trip to Shasta Caverns, a privately guided adventure (fee charged) into limestone caves. This camp often fills in summer, even on weekdays.

Campsites, facilities: There are 28 sites with full hookups (50 amps) for RVs up to 40 feet, with tents allowed in several sites. Picnic tables and barbecues are provided. Restrooms with showers, general store, seasonal café, gift shop, coin laundry, marina, marine repair service, boat moorage, swim area, playground, propane gas, and houseboat and boat and personal watercraft rentals are available. Some facilities are wheelchair-accessible. Leashed pets are permitted.

Reservations, fees: Reservations are recommended. Sites are $21.50–34.25 per night, $5.25–7.25 per person per night for more than two people, $4–6 per night for each additional vehicle, and $7.50–9.50 per night for boat moorage. Some credit cards accepted. Open April through October.

Directions: From Redding, drive 18 miles north on I-5 to Exit 695 and the O'Brien Road/Shasta Caverns Road exit. Turn right (east) at Shasta Caverns Road and drive one mile to the resort entrance on the right; check in at the store (20061 Shasta Caverns Road).

Contact: Holiday Harbor Resort, 530/238-2383 or 800/776-2628, www.lakeshasta .com.

119 GREENS CREEK BOAT-IN

🏊 🎣 🚤 🐴 ⛺

Scenic rating: 10

on Shasta Lake in Shasta-Trinity National Forest

Map 2.4 Shasta Lake Detail, page 129   BEST (

This is one of my favorite spots on the planet on a warm spring day, maybe mid-April, but it is always special. This boat-in campsite provides an exceptional base camp and boat-in headquarters for a recreation paradise. The camp is set at the foot of dramatic limestone formations on the McCloud arm of Shasta Lake. By boat, this is one of the best fishing spots. The campsites are in a region well wooded, little traveled, with good opportunities in the evening to see wildlife.

Campsites, facilities: There are nine boat-in sites for tents. Picnic tables, bear lockers, and fire grills are provided. Vault toilets are available. No drinking water is available. Garbage must be packed out. Small stores with supplies are available at Holiday Harbor. Leashed pets are permitted.

Reservations, fees: Reservations are not accepted. There is no fee for camping. An $8 fee is charged for boat launching. Open year-round.

Directions: From Redding, drive north on I-5 over the Pit River Bridge at Shasta Lake to the O'Brien Road/Shasta Caverns Road exit. Turn east (right) on Shasta Caverns Road and drive 0.25 mile to a signed turnoff for Bailey Cove. Turn right and drive one mile to Bailey Cove boat ramp. Launch your boat and cruise four miles northeast up the McCloud Arm. Land your boat and pick your campsite. Note: The Bailey Cove boat ramp is not usable when the lake level drops more than 50 feet.

Contact: Shasta-Trinity National Forest, Shasta Lake Ranger District, 530/275-1587, fax 530/275-1512; Shasta Lake Visitor Center, 530/275-1589.

120 SKI ISLAND BOAT-IN

Scenic rating: 8

on Shasta Lake in Shasta-Trinity National Forest

Map 2.4 Shasta Lake Detail, page 129

Could there be any secrets left about Shasta Lake? You bet, with boat-in campsites providing the best of all worlds for people willing to rough it just a little. Ski Island is an outstanding place to set up camp, then boat, fish, ski, or explore this giant lake. It is on the Pit River arm of the lake about three miles upstream from the Pit River (I-5) bridge. The closest boat ramp to Ski Island is at Silverthorn Resort, which is in a cove on the Pit River arm of the lake. The closest public boat ramp is at Jones Valley, also on the Pit River arm. Here you will find this three-acre island with a boat-in campground and several little trails. It is well out of sight, and out of mind for most campers as well. One note: In wet weather, the reddish, iron-based soil on the island will turn the bottom of your boat rust-colored with even a minimum of tracking in.

Campsites, facilities: There are 23 boat-in sites for tents. Picnic tables and fire grills are provided. Vault toilets are available. No drinking water is available. Garbage must be packed out. Small stores with supplies are available at Silverthorn Resort and Jones Valley Resort. Leashed pets are permitted.

Reservations, fees: Reservations are not accepted. There is no fee for camping. An $8 fee is charged for boat launching. Open year-round.

Directions: From Redding, drive north on I-5 for three miles to Exit 682 for Oasis Road. Take that exit and drive to Oasis Road. Turn right on Oasis Road and drive 3.5 miles to Bear Mountain Road. Turn right and drive to Dry Creek Road. Turn left on Dry Creek Road and drive seven miles to a fork in the road. Bear right at the fork and drive to Jones Valley Boat Ramp (a left at the fork takes you to Silverthorn Resort). Launch your boat and head west (to the left) for four miles to Ski Island. Land and pick your campsite.

Contact: Shasta-Trinity National Forest, Shasta Lake Ranger District, 530/275-1587, fax 530/275-1512; Shasta Lake Visitor Center, 530/275-1589.

121 ARBUCKLE FLAT BOAT-IN

Scenic rating: 8

on Shasta Lake in Shasta-Trinity National Forest

Map 2.4 Shasta Lake Detail, page 129

How could anything be secluded on Northern California's most popular recreation lake? Well, here is your answer. Arbuckle Flat is a truly secluded boat-in campground well up the Pit River arm of the lake, set far back in a deep cove. You will feel a million miles away from all the fast traffic back at the main lake body. Specifically, it is five miles east of the Jones Valley Boat Ramp, set on the right (south) side of a deep cove. You pay a small price for this seclusion. After landing your boat, you must then carry your gear up a hill to the campsites. When the lake is low, this is like a march up Cardiac Hill. The landscape surrounding the campsites is peppered with oak. The fishing in the area is often good for bass, and where you find submerged trees, for crappie as well.

Campsites, facilities: There are 11 boat-in sites for tents. Picnic tables and fire grills are provided. Vault toilets are available. No drinking water is available. Garbage must be packed out. Small stores with supplies are available at Silverthorn Resort and Jones Valley Resort. Leashed pets are permitted.

Reservations, fees: Reservations are not

accepted. There is no fee for camping. A $8 fee is charged for boat launching. Open year-round.

Directions: From Redding, drive north on I-5 for three miles to Exit 682 for Oasis Road. Take that exit and drive to Oasis Road. Turn right on Oasis Road and drive 3.5 miles to Bear Mountain Road. Turn right and drive to Dry Creek Road. Turn left on Dry Creek Road and drive seven miles to a fork in the road. Bear right at the fork and drive to Jones Valley Boat Ramp (a left at the fork takes you to Silverthorn Resort). Launch your boat and head east (to the right) for five miles. The last major arm off to your right hides the campground at the back of the cove, in the oaks above the shore. Land and pick your campsite.

Contact: Shasta-Trinity National Forest, Shasta Lake Ranger District, 530/275-1587, fax 530/275-1512; Shasta Lake Visitor Center, 530/275-1589.

122 JONES VALLEY INLET
🚶 🚴 🏊 🛶 🚗 🏠 🐕 🚐 ⛺

Scenic rating: 4

on Shasta Lake in Shasta-Trinity National Forest

Map 2.4 Shasta Lake Detail, page 129

This is one of the few primitive camp areas on Shasta Lake, set on the distant Pit River arm of the lake. It is an ideal camp for hiking and biking, with nearby Clickapudi Trail routed for miles along the lake's shore, in and out of coves, and then entering the surrounding foothills and oak/bay woodlands. The camp is pretty, if a bit exposed, with two nearby resorts, Jones Valley and Silverthorn, providing boat rentals and supplies.

Campsites, facilities: There is an area for dispersed, primitive camping for tents or RVs up to 40 feet (no hookups). Portable toilets are available. No drinking water is available. Garbage must be packed out. A boat ramp at Jones Valley is two miles from camp. Groceries are available nearby. Leashed pets are permitted.

Reservations, fees: Reservations are not accepted. Sites are $6 per vehicle per night. Open year-round.

Directions: From Redding, turn east on Highway 299 and drive 7.5 miles just past the town of Bella Vista. At Dry Creek Road turn left and drive nine miles to a Y intersection. Bear right at the Y (left will take you to Silverthorn Resort) and drive a short distance to the campground entrance on the left side of the road.

Contact: Shasta-Trinity National Forest, Shasta Lake Ranger District, 530/275-1587, fax 530/275-1512; Shasta Lake Visitor Center, 530/275-1589; Shasta Recreation Company, 530/275-8113.

123 UPPER AND LOWER JONES VALLEY CAMPS
🚶 🚴 🏊 🛶 🚗 🏠 🐕 ♿ 🚐 ⛺

Scenic rating: 3

on Shasta Lake in Shasta-Trinity National Forest

Map 2.4 Shasta Lake Detail, page 129

Lower Jones is a small camp set along a deep cove in the remote Pit River arm of Shasta Lake. The advantage of Lower Jones Valley is that it is closer to the lake than Upper Jones Valley. Unfortunately, the Bear Fire of 2004 burned the trees and vegetation around these campgrounds. There is a trailhead at the camp that provides access to Clickapudi Trail, a great hiking and biking trail that traces the lake's shore, routed through woodlands. Two nearby resorts, Jones Valley and Silverthorn, provide boat rentals and supplies.

Campsites, facilities: There are 18 sites and three double sites for tents or RVs up to 16 feet (no hookups) in two adjacent campgrounds. Picnic tables and fire grills are provided. Drinking water, food lockers, and vault toilets are available. Some facilities are wheelchair-accessible. A boat ramp at Jones Valley is two miles from camp. Leashed pets are permitted.

Reservations, fees: Reservations are not accepted. Upper Jones sites are $14 per night, Lower Jones sites are $18 per night and $30 per night for a double site, $5 per night for each additional vehicle. Lower Jones is open year-round. Upper Jones is open May through September.

Directions: From Redding, turn east on Highway 299 and drive 7.5 miles just past the town of Bella Vista. At Dry Creek Road, turn left and drive nine miles to a Y intersection. Bear right at the Y (left will take you to Silverthorn Resort) and drive a short distance to the campground entrances, on the left side for Lower Jones and on the right side for Upper Jones.

Contact: Shasta-Trinity National Forest, Shasta Lake Ranger District, 530/275-1587, fax 530/275-1512; Shasta Lake Visitor Center, 530/275-1589; Shasta Recreation Company, 530/275-8113.

124 SHASTA

Scenic rating: 6

on the Sacramento River in Shasta-Trinity National Forest

Map 2.4 Shasta Lake Detail, page 129

Because campers must drive across Shasta Dam to reach this campground, general access was closed in 2002 for national security reasons. Call at least one week in advance (Bureau of Reclamation, Security Office, 530/275-4253) to get approval to cross the dam and make arrangements before planning a visit. The closed road also provides access to an adjacent OHV area, one of the few in the north state. Thus when open, this place is for quads and dirt bikes—loud and wild, and hey, it's a perfect spot for them. Because of past mining in the area, it's barren with almost no shade but the views of the river and Shasta Dam are incredible. Nearby dam tours are unique and memorable.

Campsites, facilities: There are 22 sites for tents or RVs up to 30 feet (no hookups). Picnic

tables and fire rings are provided. Drinking water and vault toilets are available. A boat ramp is nearby. Groceries and bait are available in Shasta Lake City. Leashed pets are permitted.

Reservations, fees: Reservations are not accepted. Sites are $10 per night, $5 per night for each additional vehicle. Open year-round.

Directions: From I-5 in Redding, drive north for three miles to the exit for the town of Shasta Lake City and Shasta Dam Boulevard. Take that exit and bear west on Shasta Dam Boulevard and drive three miles to Lake Boulevard. Turn right on Lake Boulevard and drive two miles. Cross Shasta Dam and continue four miles to the signed campground.

Contact: Bureau of Reclamation, Shasta Dam Visitor Center, 530/275-4463; Shasta-Trinity National Forest, Shasta Lake Ranger District, 530/275-1587, fax 530/275-1512; Shasta Lake Visitor Center, 530/275-1589.

125 FAWNDALE OAKS RV PARK

Scenic rating: 5

near Shasta Lake

Map 2.4 Shasta Lake Detail, page 129

This park is midway between Shasta Lake and Redding, so it's close to many recreational activities. Toward Redding, the options include Turtle Bay Exploration Park, WaterWorks Park, public golf courses, and Sacramento River trails, which are paved, making them accessible for wheelchairs and bicycles. Toward Shasta Lake, there are tours of Shasta Caverns, via a short drive to Holiday Harbor. The RV park is on 40 acres and has shaded sites.

Campsites, facilities: There are 10 tent sites and 15 sites with full hookups (30 and 50 amps) and cable TV for RVs up to 45 feet. Some sites are pull-through. A cabin and trailer are also available for rent. Picnic tables are provided and some sites have barbecues. Phone/modem hookups, coin laundry, boat and RV storage, a general store, picnic area, playground, seasonal swimming pool, club room, game room, propane, and group facilities are available. Some facilities are wheelchair-accessible. Leashed pets are permitted.

Reservations, fees: Reservations are accepted by telephone or website. RV sites are $23.50–27.50 per night for two people, tent sites are $17 per night for a family of four, $2 per person per night for any additional people, $1 per pet per night, $1 per night for each additional vehicle, $2 per night for phone/modem hookup. Weekly and monthly rates are available. Some credit cards accepted. Open year-round.

Directions: From Redding, drive north on I-5 for nine miles to the Fawndale Road exit (Exit 689). Take that exit and turn right (east) on Fawndale Road. Drive 0.5 mile to the second RV park at the end of the road at 15015 Fawndale Road.

Contact: Fawndale Oaks RV Park, 530/275-0764 or 888/838-2159, www.fawndaleoaksrv.com.

showers, coin laundry, modem access, convenience store, dump station, a seasonal swimming pool, recreation hall, arcade, table tennis, two playgrounds, volleyball, and horseshoe pit are available. Some facilities are wheelchair-accessible. A boat ramp is within three miles. Leashed pets are permitted.

Reservations, fees: Reservations are accepted at 800/952-0551. Tent sites are $14 per night, RV sites are $16–20 per night, $2 per person per night for more than two people, $2 per night for each additional vehicle. Weekly and monthly rates available. Some credit cards accepted. Open year-round.

Directions: From Redding, drive north on I-5 for three miles to Exit 682 for Oasis Road. Take that exit and drive to Oasis Road. Turn right on Oasis Road and drive 3.5 miles to Bear Mountain Road. Turn right on Bear Mountain Road and drive 3.5 miles to the campground on the left.

Contact: Bear Mountain RV Resort and Campground, 530/275-4728, www.camp-shasta.com.

126 BEAR MOUNTAIN RV RESORT AND CAMPGROUND

Scenic rating: 5

near Shasta Lake

Map 2.4 Shasta Lake Detail, page 129

This is a privately operated park in the remote Jones Valley area five miles from Shasta Lake. It is set on 52 acres. A hiking trail leaves from the campground, rises up a hill, and provides a great view of Redding. The resort emphasizes that there is no train noise here, as there often is at campgrounds closer to Shasta Lake.

Campsites, facilities: There are 70 sites with full or partial hookups (30 amps) for RVs up to 40 feet, 24 tent sites, and four park-model cabins. Some RV sites are pull-through. Picnic tables and fire rings are provided. Drinking water, restrooms with flush toilets and coin

127 EAST WEAVER

Scenic rating: 6

on the east branch of Weaver Creek in Shasta-Trinity National Forest

Map 2.4, page 128

This camp is set along East Weaver Creek. Another mile to the west on East Weaver Road, the road dead-ends at a trailhead, a good side trip. From here, the hiking trail is routed four miles, a significant climb, to tiny East Weaver Lake, set to the southwest of Monument Peak (7,771 feet elevation). The elevation at East Weaver is 2,700 feet.

Campsites, facilities: There are 11 sites for tents or RVs up to 25 feet (no hookups). Picnic tables and fire grills are provided. Drinking water and vault toilets are available. Supplies and a coin laundry are available in Weaverville. Leashed pets are permitted.

Reservations, fees: Reservations are not accepted. Sites are $10 per night, $6 per night in the winter. Open year-round.

Directions: From Redding, drive west on Highway 299 to Weaverville. In Weaverville, turn right (north) on Highway 3 and drive about two miles to East Weaver Road. Turn left on East Weaver Road and drive 3.5 miles to the campground.

Contact: Shasta-Trinity National Forest, Weaverville Ranger Station, 530/623-2121, fax 530/623-6010.

128 STEELBRIDGE

Scenic rating: 7

on the Trinity River

Map 2.4, page 128

Very few people know of this spot, yet it can be a prime spot for anglers and campers. It's one of the better stretches of water in the area for steelhead, with good shore-fishing access. The prime time is from October through December. In the summer, the shade of conifers will keep you cool. Don't forget to bring your own water. The elevation is 1,700 feet.

Campsites, facilities: There are nine sites for tents or RVs up to 20 feet (no hookups). Picnic tables and fire grills are provided. Vault toilets are available. No drinking water is available. Supplies are available within three miles in Douglas City. Some facilities are wheelchair-accessible. Leashed pets are permitted.

Reservations, fees: Reservations are not accepted. Sites are $5 per night. Open year-round, weather permitting.

Directions: From Redding, turn west on Highway 299 and drive over Buckhorn Summit, and continue toward Douglas City to Steel Bridge Road (if you reach Douglas City, you have gone 2.3 miles too far). At Steel Bridge Road, turn right and drive about four miles to the campground at the end of the road.

Contact: Bureau of Land Management,

Redding Field Office, 530/224-2100, fax 530/224-2172.

129 DOUGLAS CITY AND STEINER FLAT

Scenic rating: 7

on the Trinity River

Map 2.4, page 128

If you want to camp along this stretch of the main Trinity River, these camps are your best bet (they're along the river about two miles from each other). They are set off the main road, near the river, with good bank fishing access (the prime season is from mid-August through winter for salmon and steelhead). There's paved parking and two beaches at Douglas City Campground. Steiner Flat, a more primitive camp, provides better access for fishing. This can be a good base camp for an off-season fishing trip on the Trinity River or a lounging spot during the summer. The elevation is 1,700 feet.

Campsites, facilities: There are 20 sites for tents or RVs up to 28 feet at Douglas City with dispersed camping at Steiner Flat. No hookups. At Douglas City, picnic tables and fire grills are provided. Drinking water and restrooms with sinks and flush toilets are available. At Steiner Flat, no drinking water or toilets are available. Supplies are available within one mile in the town of Douglas City. Leashed pets are permitted.

Reservations, fees: Reservations are not accepted. Sites are $10 per night at Douglas City; no fee at Steiner Flat. Open mid-April through November.

Directions: From Redding, turn on Highway 299 west and drive west (toward Weaverville). Continue over the bridge at the Trinity River near Douglas City to Steiner Flat Road. Turn left on Steiner Flat Road and drive 0.5 mile to Douglas City campground on the left. To reach Steiner Flat, continue two more miles and look for the campground on the left.

Contact: Bureau of Land Management, Redding Field Office, 530/224-2100, fax 530/224-2172.

130 OLD LEWISTON BRIDGE RV RESORT

Scenic rating: 7

on the Trinity River

Map 2.4, page 128

This is a popular spot for calm-water kayaking, rafting, and fishing. Though much of the water from Trinity and Lewiston Lakes is diverted via tunnel to Whiskeytown Lake (en route to the valley and points south), enough escapes downstream to provide a viable stream here near the town of Lewiston. This upstream section below Lewiston Lake is prime in the early summer for trout, particularly the chance for a huge brown trout (special regulations in effect). A fishing shuttle service is available. The campground is in a hilly area but has level sites, with nearby Lewiston Lake also a major attraction. Some sites are occupied by long-term renters.

Campsites, facilities: There are 52 sites with full hookups (30 amps) for RVs up to 45 feet, a separate area for tents, and five rental trailers. Picnic tables are provided. Restrooms with showers, coin laundry, a grocery store, modem access, ice, bait and tackle, and propane gas refills are available. A group picnic area is available by reservation. A restaurant is within 0.5 mile. Leashed pets are permitted.

Reservations, fees: Reservations are accepted by phone or website. Sites are $26 per night for RVs, $14 per night per vehicle for tent campers, $2 per person per night for more than two people. Monthly rates available. Some credit cards accepted. Open year-round.

Directions: From Redding, turn on Highway 299 and drive west over Buckhorn Summit, and continue for five miles to Trinity Dam Boulevard. Turn right on Trinity Dam Boulevard and drive four miles to Lewiston, and

continue north to Rush Creek Road. Turn left (west) on Rush Creek Road and drive 0.25 mile to the resort on the left.

Contact: Old Lewiston Bridge RV Resort, 800/922-1924 or tel./fax 530/778-3894, www .lewistonbridgerv.com.

131 TRINITY RIVER LODGE RV RESORT

Scenic rating: 7

on the Trinity River

Map 2.4, page 128

For many, this privately operated park has an ideal location. You get level, grassy sites with shade trees along the Trinity River, yet it is just a short drive north to Lewiston Lake or a bit farther to giant Trinity Lake. Lake or river, take your pick. The resort covers nearly 14 acres, and about half the sites are rented for the entire summer.

Campsites, facilities: There are 60 sites with full hookups (30 and 50 amps) for RVs up to 40 feet, five tent sites, and one cottage. Restrooms with showers, a coin laundry, cable TV, modem access, recreation room, lending library, clubhouse, athletic field, propane gas, camp store, ice, firewood, boat and trailer storage, horseshoes, and picnic area are available. Some facilities are wheelchair-accessible. Leashed pets are permitted.

Reservations, fees: Reservations are recommended. Tent sites are $14.70 per night, and RV sites are $24 per night. Some credit cards accepted. Open year-round.

Directions: From Redding, turn on Highway 299 west and drive west over Buckhorn Summit, and continue for five miles to Trinity Dam Boulevard. Turn right on Trinity Dam Boulevard and drive four miles to Lewiston. Continue on Trinity Dam Boulevard to Rush Creek Road. Turn left on Rush Creek Road and drive 2.3 miles to the campground on the left.

Contact: Trinity River Lodge RV Resort,

530/778-3791 or 800/761-2769, www.trinityriverresort.com.

132 MARY SMITH

Scenic rating: 10

on Lewiston Lake in Shasta-Trinity National Forest

Map 2.4, page 128   **BEST (**

This is one of the prettiest spots you'll ever see, set along the southwestern shore of Lewiston Lake. When you wake up and peek out of your sleeping bag, the natural beauty of this serene lake can take your breath away. Hand-launched boats, such as canoes, are ideal here, and the lake speed limit is 10 mph. The lake has 15 miles of shoreline. Although swimming is allowed, the water is too cold for most people. Bird-watching is good in this area. The best fishing is from Lakeview Terrace and the tules on upstream to just below Trinity Dam. The elevation is 2,000 feet.

Campsites, facilities: There are 18 sites for tents only, some requiring a very short walk. Picnic tables and fire grills are provided. Drinking water and flush and vault toilets are available. Boat launching and rentals are available nearby at Pine Cove Marina. Supplies and a coin laundry are available in Lewiston. Leashed pets are permitted.

Reservations, fees: Reservations are not accepted. Sites are $11 per night. Open early May to mid-September.

Directions: From Redding, turn on Highway 299 west and drive west over Buckhorn Summit, and continue for five miles to Trinity Dam Boulevard. Turn right on Trinity Dam Boulevard and drive four miles to Lewiston, and then continue on Trinity Dam Boulevard for 2.5 miles to the campground.

Contact: Shasta-Trinity National Forest, Weaverville Ranger Station, 530/623-2121, fax 530/623-6010; Pine Cove Marina, 530/778-3770.

133 COOPER GULCH

Scenic rating: 8

on Lewiston Lake in Shasta-Trinity National Forest

Map 2.4, page 128

Here is a nice spot along a beautiful lake, featuring a short trail to Baker Gulch, where a pretty creek enters Lewiston Lake. The trout fishing is good on the upper end of the lake (where the current starts) and upstream. The lake speed limit is 10 mph. Swimming is allowed, although the water is cold because it flows in from the bottom of Trinity Lake. The lake is designated a wildlife-viewing area, with large numbers of waterfowl and other birds often spotted near the tules off the shore of Lakeview Terrace. Bring all of your own supplies and plan on hunkering down here for a while.

Campsites, facilities: There are five sites for tents or RVs up to 16 feet (no hookups). Picnic tables and fire grills are provided. Vault toilets and drinking water are available. Boat launching and rentals are nearby at Pine Cove Marina. Supplies and a coin laundry are available in Lewiston. Some facilities are wheelchair-accessible. Leashed pets are permitted.

Reservations, fees: Reservations are not accepted. Sites are $12 per night. Open early April to late October.

Directions: From Redding, turn on Highway 299 west and drive west over Buckhorn Summit, and continue for five miles to Trinity Dam Boulevard. Turn right on Trinity Dam Boulevard, drive four miles to Lewiston, and then continue on Trinity Dam Boulevard another four miles north to the campground.

Contact: Shasta-Trinity National Forest, Weaverville Ranger Station, 530/623-2121, fax 530/623-6010; Pine Cove Marina, 530/778-3770.

134 LAKEVIEW TERRACE RESORT

🚶 🎣 🚤 🚐 🏠 🛶 ♿ 🚗

Scenic rating: 8

on Lewiston Lake

Map 2.4, page 128

This might be your Golden Pond. It's a terraced RV park—with cabin rentals also available—that overlooks Lewiston Lake, one of the prettiest drive-to lakes in the region. Fishing for trout is excellent from Lakeview Terrace on upstream toward the dam. Lewiston Lake is perfect for fishing, with a 10-mph speed limit in effect (all the hot boats go to nearby Trinity Lake), along with excellent prospects for rainbow and brown trout. Other fish species include brook trout and kokanee salmon. The topper is that Lewiston Lake is always full to the brim, just the opposite of the up-and-down nightmare of its neighboring big brother, Trinity.

Campsites, facilities: There are 40 sites with full hookups (50 amps) for RVs up to 40 feet; some sites are pull-through. No tents. Cabins are also available. Picnic tables and barbecues are provided. Restrooms with showers, coin laundry, seasonal heated pool, propane gas, ice, horseshoes, playground, bait, and boat and patio-boat rentals are available. Supplies are available within five miles. Leashed pets are permitted.

Reservations, fees: Reservations are recommended. Sites are $24 per night, $3 per person per night for more than two people. Some credit cards accepted. Open year-round.

Directions: From Redding, turn on Highway 299 west and drive west over Buckhorn Summit, and continue for five miles to Trinity Dam Boulevard. Turn right on Trinity Dam Boulevard and drive 10 miles (five miles past Lewiston) to the resort on the left side of the road.

Contact: Lakeview Terrace Resort, 530/778-3803, fax 530/778-3960, www.lakeviewterraceresort.com.

135 TUNNEL ROCK

🚶 🎣 🚤 🚐 🏠 🚗 🛶

Scenic rating: 7

on Lewiston Lake in Shasta-Trinity National Forest

Map 2.4, page 128

This is a very small, primitive alternative to Ackerman, which is more developed and another mile up the road to the north. The proximity to the Pine Cove boat ramp and fish-cleaning station, less than two miles to the south, is a primary attraction. Pine Cove Marina is full service and rents fishing boats. The elevation is 1,700 feet.

Campsites, facilities: There are six sites for tents or RVs up to 15 feet (no hookups). Picnic tables and fire grills are provided. Vault toilets are available. No drinking water is available. Leashed pets are permitted.

Reservations, fees: Reservations are not accepted. Sites are $6 per night. Open year-round.

Directions: From Redding, turn on Highway 299 west and drive over Buckhorn Summit, and continue for five miles to County Road 105/Trinity Dam Road. Turn right on Trinity Dam Road and drive four miles to Lewiston, and then continue another seven miles north on Trinity Dam Boulevard to the campground.

Contact: Shasta-Trinity National Forest, Weaverville Ranger Station, 530/623-2121, fax 530/623-6010.

136 ACKERMAN

🎣 🚤 🚐 🏠 🚗 🛶

Scenic rating: 7

on Lewiston Lake in Shasta-Trinity National Forest

Map 2.4, page 128

Of the camps and parks at Lewiston Lake, Ackerman is closest to the lake's headwaters. This stretch of water below Trinity Dam is the best area for trout fishing on Lewiston Lake.

Nearby Pine Cove boat ramp, two miles south of the camp, offers the only boat launch on Lewiston Lake with docks and a fish-cleaning station—a popular spot for anglers. When the Trinity powerhouse is running, trout fishing is excellent in this area. The elevation is 2,000 feet.

Campsites, facilities: There are 66 sites for tents or RVs up to 40 feet (no hookups). Picnic tables and fire grills are provided. Drinking water, flush toilets, and a dump station are available. Leashed pets are permitted.

Reservations, fees: Reservations are not accepted. Sites are $12 per night, and $6 per night during the winter. Open year-round.

Directions: From Redding, turn on Highway 299 west and drive west over Buckhorn Summit, and continue for five miles to Trinity Dam Boulevard. Turn right on Trinity Dam Boulevard and drive four miles to Lewiston. Continue north on Trinity Dam Boulevard for eight miles to the campground.

Contact: Shasta-Trinity National Forest, Weaverville Ranger Station, 530/623-2121, fax 530/623-6010.

137 OAK BOTTOM

Scenic rating: 7

on Whiskeytown Lake

Map 2.4, page 128

The prettiest hiking trails at Whiskeytown Lake are at the far western end of the reservoir, and this camp provides excellent access to them. One hiking and biking trail skirts the north shoreline of the lake and is routed to the lake's inlet at the Judge Carr Powerhouse. The other, with the trailhead just a short drive to the west, is routed along Mill Creek, a pristine, clear-running stream with the trail jumping over the water many times. The campground sites seem a little close, but the camp is next to a beach area. There are junior ranger programs, and evening ranger programs at the Oak Bottom Amphitheater are available

several nights per week from mid-June through Labor Day. A self-guided nature trail is five miles away at the visitors center.

Campsites, facilities: There are 102 walk-in tent sites with picnic tables and fire grills. There are 22 sites for RVs up to 32 feet (no hookups) in the large parking area near the launch ramp. Drinking water, restrooms with flush toilets and coin showers, convenience store, ice, firewood, dump station, boat ramp, and boat rentals are available. Some facilities are wheelchair-accessible. Leashed pets are permitted.

Reservations, fees: Reservations are accepted in summer at 800/365-CAMP (800/365-2267) or http://reservations.nps.gov; reservations are not accepted in the off-season. Sites are $10–18 per night, plus a park use permit of $5 per day or $10 per week. Open year-round.

Directions: From Redding, turn on Highway 299 west and drive west for 15 miles (past the visitors center) to the campground entrance road on the left. Turn left and drive a short distance to the campground.

Contact: Whiskeytown National Recreation Area, 530/242-3400, fax 530/246-5154; Whiskeytown Visitor Center, 530/246-1225, www.nps.gov/whis.

138 DRY CREEK GROUP CAMP

Scenic rating: 7

on Whiskeytown Lake

Map 2.4, page 128

If you're in a group and take the time to reserve this spot, you'll be rewarded with some room and the quiet that goes along with it. This is the most remote drive-to camp at Whiskeytown Lake. A boat ramp is about two miles away (to the east) at Brandy Creek. You'll pass it on the way in. Note: Reservations are an absolute must, and are available five months in advance.

Campsites, facilities: There are two tents-only group sites that can accommodate 50 people each. Picnic tables and fire grills are provided. Drinking water and pit toilets are available. Leashed pets are permitted.

Reservations, fees: Reservations are accepted at 800/365-CAMP (800/365-2267) or http:// reservations.nps.gov. Sites are $75 per night, plus a park use permit of $5 per day or $10 per week. Open early April to mid-October.

Directions: From Redding, drive west on Highway 299 for 10 miles to the visitors center and Kennedy Memorial Drive. Turn left and drive six miles to the campground on the right side of the road.

Contact: Whiskeytown National Recreation Area, 530/242-3400, fax 530/246-5154; Whiskeytown Visitor Center, 530/246-1225, www.nps.gov/whis.

139 BRANDY CREEK

Scenic rating: 7

on Whiskeytown Lake

Map 2.4, page 128

For campers with boats, this is the best place to stay at Whiskeytown Lake, with a boat ramp less than a quarter mile away. Whiskeytown is popular for sailing and sailboarding, as it gets a lot more wind than other lakes in the region. Personal watercraft have been banned from this lake. Fishing for kokanee salmon is good in the early morning before the wind comes up; trout fishing is pretty good as well. The lake has 36 miles of shoreline.

Campsites, facilities: There are 37 sites with no hookups for RVs up to 35 feet. No tents. Drinking water and a dump station are available. Leashed pets are permitted.

Reservations, fees: Reservations are not accepted. Sites are $14 per night, $7 per night during off-season, plus a park use permit of $5 per day or $10 per week. Open year-round.

Directions: From Redding, drive west on Highway 299 for eight miles to the visitors

center and Kennedy Memorial Drive. Turn left at the visitors center (Kennedy Memorial Drive) and drive five miles to the campground entrance road on the right. Turn right and drive a short distance to the camp.

Contact: Whiskeytown National Recreation Area, 530/242-3400, fax 530/246-5154; Whiskeytown Visitor Center, 530/246-1225, www.nps.gov/whis.

140 PREMIER RV RESORT

Scenic rating: 2

in Redding

Map 2.4, page 128

If you're stuck with no place to go, this large park could be your savior. Nearby recreation options include a waterslide park and the Turtle Bay Museum and Exploration Park on the Sacramento River. The newest attraction is Sundial Bridge, with its glass walkway that allows users to look down into the river, a stunning feat of architecture—where the experience simulates walking on air. In addition, Whiskeytown Lake is nearby to the west and Shasta Lake to the north. A casino and several golf courses are nearby.

Campsites, facilities: There are 111 sites with full or partial hookups (30 and 50 amps) for RVs of any length, and two yurts. No tents. Picnic tables and fire grills are provided. Drinking water, restrooms with flush toilets and showers, playground, seasonal swimming pool, coin laundry, dump station, satellite TV hookups, modem access, a convenience store, propane gas, and recreation room are available. Some facilities are wheelchair accessible. Leashed pets are permitted.

Reservations, fees: Reservations are accepted. Sites are $39 per night, $3 per person per night for more than two people. Some credit cards accepted. Open year-round.

Directions: In Redding, drive north on I-5 to the Lake Boulevard/Burney-Alturas exit. Turn west (left) on Lake Boulevard and drive

0.25 mile to North Boulder Drive. Turn right (north) on North Boulder Drive and drive one block to the resort on the left.

Contact: Premier RV Resort, 530/246-0101 or 888/710-8450.

141 MARINA RV PARK

Scenic rating: 6

on the Sacramento River

Map 2.4, page 128

The riverside setting is a highlight here, with the Sacramento River providing relief from the dog days of summer. An easy, paved walking and bike trail is available nearby at the Sacramento River Parkway, providing river views and sometimes a needed breeze on hot summer evenings. It is also two miles away from the Turtle Bay Museum, and close to a movie theater. A golf driving range is nearby. This park includes an area with long-term RV renters.

Campsites, facilities: There are 42 sites with full or partial hookups (30 amps) for RVs up to 40 feet. Picnic tables, restrooms with showers, a coin laundry, small store, modem access, seasonal swimming pool, spa, boat ramp, and a dump station are available. Leashed pets are permitted.

Reservations, fees: Reservations are accepted. Sites are $29.70 per night, $2 per person per night for more than two people. Weekly and monthly rates available. Open year-round.

Directions: In Redding, turn west on Highway 44 and drive 1.5 miles to the exit for Convention Center/Marina Park Drive. Take that exit, turn left, and drive over the highway to a stoplight and Marina Park Drive. Turn left (south) on Marina Park Drive and drive 0.8 mile to the park on the left.

Contact: Marina RV Park, 530/241-4396.

142 SACRAMENTO RIVER RV RESORT

Scenic rating: 7

south of Redding

Map 2.4, page 128

This makes a good headquarters for a fall fishing trip on the Sacramento River, where the salmon come big from August through October. In the summer trout fishing is very good from this area as well, but a boat is a must. No problem; there's a boat ramp at the park. In addition, you can hire fishing guides who launch from here daily. The park is open year-round, and if you want to stay close to home, a three-acre pond with bass, bluegill, and perch is also available at the resort. You also get great long-distance views of Mount Shasta and Mount Lassen.

Campsites, facilities: There are 140 sites with full hookups (30 and 50 amps) for RVs of any length and 10 sites for tents in a shaded grassy area. Some RV sites are pull-through. Picnic tables, restrooms with showers, coin laundry, dump station, cable TV, modem access, bait, boat launch, playground, two tennis courts, golf driving range, and a large seasonal swimming pool are available. A clubhouse is available by reservation. Some facilities are wheelchair-accessible. Leashed pets are permitted.

Reservations, fees: Reservations are accepted. Sites are $16.50–27.40 per night. Some credit cards accepted. Open year-round.

Directions: From Redding, drive south on I-5 for five miles to the Knighton Road exit. Turn west (right) and drive a short distance to Riverland Drive. Turn left on Riverland Drive and drive two miles to the park at the end of the road.

Contact: Sacramento RV Resort, 530/365-6402, fax 530/365-2601, www.sacramento-riverrvresort.com.

143 DEERLICK SPRINGS

🥾 🚣 🐕 5% 🚐 ⛺

Scenic rating: 8

on Browns Creek in Shasta-Trinity National
Forest

Map 2.4, page 128

It's a long, twisty drive to this remote
and primitive camp set on the edge of the
Chanchelulla Wilderness in the transition
zone where the valley's oak grasslands give
way to conifers. This quiet little spot is set
along Browns Creek. A trailhead just north of
camp provides a streamside walk. The elevation is 3,100 feet.

Campsites, facilities: There are 13 sites for
tents or RVs up to 20 feet (no hookups). Picnic
tables and fire grills are provided. Vault toilets
are available. No drinking water is available.
Garbage must be packed out. Leashed pets
are permitted.

Reservations, fees: Reservations are not
accepted. There is no fee for camping. Open
May through October.

Directions: From Red Bluff, turn west on
Highway 36 (very twisty) and drive to the
Forest Service ranger station in Platina. In
Platina, turn right (north) on Harrison Gulch
Road and drive 10 miles to the campground
on the left.

Contact: Shasta-Trinity National Forest,
Yolla Bolly Ranger Station, 530/352-4211,
fax 530/352-4312.

144 BASIN GULCH

🥾 🐕 🚐 ⛺

Scenic rating: 5

in Shasta-Trinity National Forest

Map 2.4, page 128

This is one of two little-known campgrounds
in the vicinity that rarely gets much use. A
trail out of this camp climbs Noble Ridge,
eventually rising to a good lookout at 3,933
feet, providing sweeping views of the north
valley. Of course, you could also just drive

there, taking a dirt road out of Platina.
There are many backcountry Forest Service
roads in the area so your best bet is to get a
Shasta-Trinity National Forest map, which
details the roads. The elevation is 2,600 feet.
There is evidence in the area of a wildfire that
occurred in 2001.

Campsites, facilities: There are 13 sites for
tents or RVs up to 20 feet (no hookups). Picnic
tables and fire grills are provided. Vault toilets
are available. No drinking water is available.
Leashed pets are permitted.

Reservations, fees: Reservations are not
accepted. Sites are $6 per night. Open May
through October.

Directions: From Red Bluff, drive about 45
miles west on Highway 36 to the Yolla Bolly
District Ranger Station. From the ranger station, turn south on Stuart Gap Road and drive
two miles to the campground on the left.

Contact: Shasta-Trinity National Forest,
Yolla Bolly Ranger Station, 530/352-4211,
fax 530/352-4312.

145 BEND RV PARK AND
FISHING RESORT

🚣 🚤 🐕 🚐 ⛺

Scenic rating: 7

on the Sacramento River

Map 2.4, page 128

Here's a spot for RV cruisers to rest their
rigs for a while. Bend RV Park and Fishing
Resort is open year-round and is set beside
the Sacramento River. The salmon average
15–25 pounds in this area, and anglers typically have the best results from mid-August
through October. In recent years, the gates
of the Red Bluff Diversion Dam have been
raised in early September. When that occurs,
huge numbers of salmon charge upstream
from Red Bluff to Anderson, holding in each
deep river hole. Expect very hot weather in
July and August.

Campsites, facilities: There are 14 sites with
full or partial hookups (30 amps) for RVs up to

40 feet. In addition, there is a separate area for tents only. Picnic tables are provided. Drinking water, restrooms with showers and flush toilets, convenience store, bait and tackle, boat ramp, boat dock, coin laundry, and a dump station are available. Leashed pets are permitted.

Reservations, fees: Reservations are accepted. Sites are $21.50–24 per night, $3.50 per person per night for more than two people. Open year-round.

Directions: From I-5 in Red Bluff, drive four miles north on I-5 to the Jelly's Ferry Road exit. Take that exit and turn northeast on Jelly's Ferry Road and drive 2.5 miles to the resort at 21795 Bend Ferry Road.

Contact: Bend RV Park and Fishing Resort, 530/527-6289.

146 LAKE RED BLUFF

Scenic rating: 6

on the Sacramento River near Red Bluff

Map 2.4, page 128

Lake Red Bluff is created by the Red Bluff Diversion Dam on the Sacramento River, and waterskiing, bird-watching, hiking, and fishing are the most popular activities. A three-mile long paved trail parallels the river, and cycling and skating are allowed on the trail. It has become a backyard swimming hole for local residents in the summer when the temperatures reach the high 90s and low 100s almost every day. In early September, the Bureau of Reclamation raises the gates at the diversion dam to allow migrating salmon an easier course on the upstream journey, and in the process, Lake Red Bluff reverts to its former self as the Sacramento River.

Campsites, facilities: At Sycamore Camp, there are 30 sites for tents or RVs up to 35 feet (no hookups). There is also a tent-only group camp (Camp Discovery) that has 11 screened cabins and can accommodate up to 100 people. Drinking water, restrooms with coin showers and flush toilets, vault toilets, picnic areas, visitors center, two boat ramps, and a fish-viewing plaza are available. There are two large barbecues, electrical outlets, lockable storage, five large picnic tables, restroom with showers and sinks, and an amphitheater in the group camp area. Some facilities are wheelchair-accessible. Leashed pets are permitted.

Reservations, fees: Reservations are not accepted for individual sites but are required for the group camp at 530/527-1196. Sites are $12–24 per night for individual sites and the group camp is $150 per night. Open April through October.

Directions: From I-5 at Red Bluff, turn east on Highway 36 and drive 100 yards to the first turnoff at Sale Lane. Turn right (south) on Sale Lane and drive 2.5 miles to the campground at the end of the road.

Contact: Mendocino National Forest, Red Bluff Recreation Area, 530/527-2813, fax 530/527-1312; Discovery Center, 530/527-1196.

147 WHITE ROCK

Scenic rating: 4

in Shasta-Trinity National Forest

Map 2.4, page 128

There's a reason why there's no charge to camp here: Usually nobody's around. It's primitive, little known, and likely to be empty. If you don't want to see anybody, you've found the right place. The big attraction here is watching the turtles swim at nearby White Rock Pond. A trailhead is available nearby out of Stuart Gap, which provides access to the North Yolla Bolly Mountains.

Campsites, facilities: There are three tent sites. Picnic tables and fire grills are provided. Vault toilets are available. No drinking water is available. Garbage must be packed out. Leashed pets are permitted.

Reservations, fees: Reservations are not

accepted. There is no fee for camping. Open late June through mid-September, weather permitting.
Directions: From Red Bluff, drive about 45 miles west on Highway 36 to the Yolla Bolly ranger office. Continue west for about eight miles to Wild Mad River Road/Forest Road 30. Turn left on Forest Road 30 and drive nine miles to Pine Ridge Saddle Road/Forest Road 35. Turn left and drive nine miles (on a gravel road, very twisty) to the campground.
Contact: Shasta-Trinity National Forest, Yolla Bolly Ranger Station, 530/352-4211, fax 530/352-4312.

148 TOMHEAD SADDLE
🏃 🐕 5% 🚙 ⛺

Scenic rating: 4

in Shasta-Trinity National Forest
Map 2.4, page 128
This one is way out there in remote wildlands. Little known and rarely visited, it's primarily a jump-off point for ambitious backpackers. The camp is on the edge of the Yolla Bolly-Middle Eel Wilderness. A trailhead here is routed to the South Fork of Cottonwood Creek, a trek that entails hiking eight miles in dry, hot terrain. The elevation is 5,700 feet.
Campsites, facilities: There are five sites for tents or RVs up to 16 feet (no hookups). Picnic tables and fire grills are provided. Vault toilets are available. No drinking water is available. Garbage must be packed out. Leashed pets are permitted.
Reservations, fees: Reservations are not accepted. There is no fee for camping. Open late June to mid-September, weather permitting.
Directions: From I-5 in Red Bluff, turn west on Highway 36 and drive about 13 miles to Cannon Road. Turn left on Cannon Road and drive about five miles to Pettyjohn Road. Turn west on Pettyjohn Road, drive to Saddle Camp and Forest Road 27N06. Turn south on Forest Road 27N06 and drive three miles to the campground on the left. It is advisable to obtain a map of Shasta-Trinity National Forest.
Contact: Shasta-Trinity National Forest, Yolla Bolly Ranger Station, 530/352-4211, fax 530/352-4312.

LASSEN
AND MODOC

BEST CAMPGROUNDS

Hikes with Views
Summit Lake: North, South, and Equestrian, **page 231**

Family Destinations
Summit Lake: North, South, and Equestrian, **page 231**

Mount Lassen and its awesome volcanic past seem
to cast a shadow everywhere you go in this region. At 10,457 feet, the mountain's
domed summit is visible for more than 100 miles in all directions. It blew its top
in 1914, with continuing eruptions through 1918. Although now dormant, the
volcanic-based geology dominates the landscape everywhere you look.

Of all the areas covered in this book, this region has the least number
of romantic getaway spots. It caters instead primarily to outdoors enthusiasts.
And Lassen Volcanic National Park is one of the best places to lace up the hiking
boots or spool new line on a reel. It's often off the radar scope of vacationers,
making it one of the few national parks where you can enjoy the wilderness in
relative solitude.

The national park is easily explored along the main route, the Lassen
Park Highway. Along the way, you can pick a few trails for adventure. The best
hikes are the Summit Climb (moderate to challenging), best done first thing in
the morning, and Bumpass Hell (easy and great for kids) to see the sulfur vents
and boiling mud pots. Another favorite for classic alpine beauty is the Shadow
Lake Trail.

Unique features of the region include its pumice boulders, volcanic rock,
and spring-fed streams from the underground lava tubes. The highlights include
the best still-water canoeing and fly-fishing at Fall River, Big Lake, and Ahjumawi

State Park. Access at Ahjumawi is by canoe or powerboat only, a great boat-in campground with access to a matrix of clear, cold waters with giant trout.

Nearby is Burney Falls State Park, along with the Pit River and Lake Britton, which together make up one of Northern California's best recreation destinations for families. This is also one of the best areas for fly-fishing, especially at Hat Creek, Pit River, Burney Creek, and Manzanita Lake. For more beautiful settings, you can visit Lake Almanor and Eagle Lake, both of which provide lakeside campgrounds and excellent fishing and boating recreation.

And there's more. In remote Modoc County, you'll find Lava Beds National Monument and the South Warner Wilderness. Lava Beds is a stark, pretty, and often lonely place. It's sprinkled with small lakes full of trout, is home to large-antlered deer that migrate in after the first snow (and after the hunting season has closed), and features a unique volcanic habitat with huge flows of obsidian (dark, smooth, natural glass formed by the cooling of molten lava) and dacite (gray, craggy volcanic flow). Lava Beds National Monument boasts about 500 caves and lava tubes, including the 6,000-foot Catacomb Tunnel. Nearby is pretty Medicine Lake, formed in a caldera, which provides good trout fishing, hiking, and exploring.

It seems no matter where you go, there are so many campgrounds that you can always find a match for what you desire.

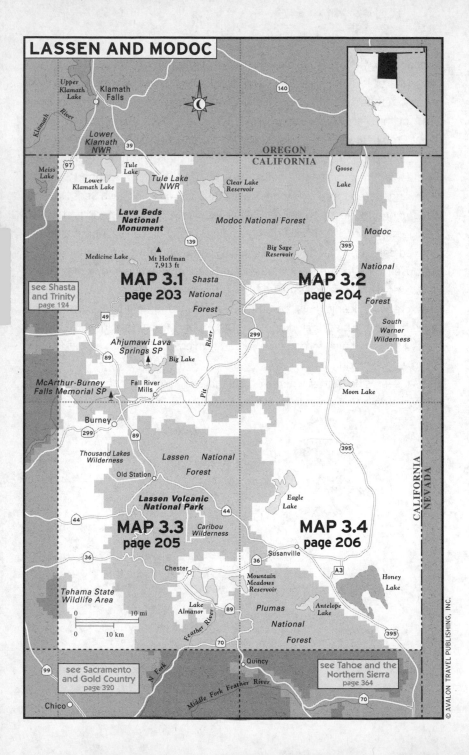

LASSEN AND MODOC

Upper Klamath Lake

Klamath Falls

Klamath River

140

Lower Klamath NWR

39

OREGON
CALIFORNIA

Meiss Lake

97

Tule Lake

Lower Klamath Lake

Tule Lake NWR

Clear Lake Reservoir

Goose Lake

Modoc National Forest

Modoc

395

Lava Beds National Monument

Medicine Lake

Mt Hoffman 7,913 ft

139

Big Sage Reservoir

National

see Shasta and Trinity
page 124

MAP 3.1
page 203

Shasta National Forest

MAP 3.2
page 204

Forest

South Warner Wilderness

49

Ahjumawi Lava Springs SP

River

Big Lake

299

89

McArthur-Burney Falls Memorial SP

Fall River Mills

Pit

Moon Lake

Burney

299

89

89

395

Thousand Lakes Wilderness

Lassen   National

Forest

Old Station

Lassen Volcanic National Park

44

Eagle Lake

44

MAP 3.3
page 205

Caribou Wilderness

MAP 3.4
page 206

CALIFORNIA
NEVADA

36

36

Susanville

A3

Chester

Mountain Meadows Reservoir

Honey Lake

Tehama State Wildlife Area

0   10 mi

0   10 km

Lake Almanor

89

Feather River

Plumas

Antelope Lake

National

395

70

Forest

see Sacramento and Gold Country
page 320

N Fork

Quincy

see Tahoe and the Northern Sierra
page 364

99

Chico

Middle Fork Feather River

70

Map 3.1

Campgrounds 1-16
Pages 207-214

Map 3.2

Campgrounds 17-33
Pages 215-222

© AVALON TRAVEL PUBLISHING, INC.

Map 3.3

Campgrounds 34-87
Pages 222-246

Map 3.4

Campgrounds 88-104
Pages 246-254

1 SHAFTER

Scenic rating: 4

in Klamath National Forest

Map 3.1, page 203

This is a little-used camp with trout fishing at nearby Butte Creek for small rainbows, primarily six- to eight-inchers. Little Orr Lake, about a 10-minute drive away on the southwest flank of Orr Mountain, provides fishing for bass and larger rainbow trout, 10- to 12-inchers, as well as a sprinkling of smaller brook trout. This camp is primitive and not well known, set in a juniper- and sage-filled landscape. The elevation is 4,300 feet. A great side trip is to the nearby Orr Mountain Lookout, where there are spectacular views of Mount Shasta. The road adjacent to the campground is paved, keeping the dust down—a Forest Service touch that is like gold in the summer.

Campsites, facilities: There are 10 sites for tents or RVs up to 28 feet (no hookups). Picnic tables and fire grills are provided. Drinking water and vault toilets are available. A boat ramp is available at Orr Lake. Garbage must be packed out. Leashed pets are permitted.

Reservations, fees: Reservations are not accepted. Sites are $6 per night. Open year-round, with limited services in winter.

Directions: From Redding, drive north on I-5 to Weed and the exit for Central Weed/Highway 97. Take that exit, turn right at the stop sign, drive through Weed and bear right (north) on Highway 97 and drive 40 miles to Ball Mountain Road. Turn right at Ball Mountain Road and drive 2.5 miles to a T with Old State Highway 97. Turn right and drive 4.25 miles (crossing railroad tracks) to the campground on the right side of the road.

Contact: Klamath National Forest, Goosenest Ranger District, 530/398-4391, fax 530/398-5749.

2 INDIAN WELL

Scenic rating: 9

in Lava Beds National Monument

Map 3.1, page 203

Lava Beds National Monument is a one-in-a-million spot with more than 500 lava tube caves, Schonchin Butte (a cinder cone with a hiking trail), Mammoth Crater, Native American petroglyphs and pictographs, battlefields and campsites from the Modoc War, and wildlife overlooks of Tule Lake. After winter's first snow, this is one of the best places in the West to photograph deer. Nearby is Klamath National Wildlife Refuge, the largest bald eagle wintering area in the lower 48. If you are new to the outdoors, an interpretive center is available to explain it all to you through informative displays. A visitors center is open year-round.

Campsites, facilities: There are 43 sites for tents or RVs up to 30 feet (no hookups). Picnic tables, fire rings, and cooking grills are provided. Drinking water and flush toilets are available. Some facilities are wheelchair-accessible. The town of Tulelake (30 miles north) is the nearest supply station. Leashed pets are permitted in the campground and roads only.

Reservations, fees: Reservations are not accepted. Sites are $10 per night plus $10 per vehicle park entrance fee. Open year-round.

Directions: From Redding, drive north on I-5 to the Central Weed/Highway 97 exit. Take that exit, turn right and continue for one mile to U.S. 97. Drive north on U.S. 97 for 54 miles to Highway 161. Turn east on Highway 161 and drive 20 miles to Hill Road. Turn right (south) and drive 18 miles to the visitors center and the campground entrance on the left. Turn left and drive 0.25 mile to the campground.

Contact: Lava Beds National Monument Visitor Center, 530/667-8113, www.nps.gov/labe.

❸ MEDICINE
👫 ≈ 🛶 🚤 🐕 ♿ 🚐 ⛺

Scenic rating: 7

on Medicine Lake in Modoc National Forest

Map 3.1, page 203

Lakeside campsites tucked away in conifers make this camp a winner. Medicine Lake, at 640 acres, was formed in the crater of an old volcano and is surrounded by lodgepole pine and fir trees. The lake is stocked with rainbow and brook trout in the summer, gets quite cold in the fall, and freezes over in winter. All water sports are permitted. Many side trips are possible, including nearby Bullseye and Blanche Lakes and Ice Caves (both signed and off the access road) and Lava Beds National Monument just 15 miles north. At 6,700 feet, temperatures can drop in summer and the season is short.

Campsites, facilities: There are 22 sites for tents or RVs up to 30 feet (no hookups). Picnic tables and fire grills are provided. Drinking water and vault toilets are available. Ranger-guided cave tours, walks and talks are available during the summer. A boat ramp is available nearby. A café and bar are available in Bartle; otherwise, no supplies are available within an hour's drive. Some facilities are wheelchair-accessible. Leashed pets are permitted.

Reservations, fees: Reservations are not accepted. Sites are $7 per vehicle per night. Open late May through early October, weather permitting.

Directions: From Redding, drive north on I-5 past Dunsmuir to Highway 89. Turn east on Highway 89 and drive 28 miles (just past Bartle) to Forest Road 15/Harris Springs Road. Turn left on Forest Road 15 and drive approximately five miles to the Y intersection with Forest Road 49/Medicine Lake Road. Turn right on Forest Road 49 and drive approximately 26 miles to the lake and campground access road.

Contact: Modoc National Forest, Doublehead Ranger District, 530/667-2246, fax 530/667-8609.

❹ A. H. HOGUE
👫 ≈ 🛶 🚤 🐕 ♿ 🚐 ⛺

Scenic rating: 7

on Medicine Lake in Modoc National Forest

Map 3.1, page 203

This camp was created in 1990 when the original Medicine Lake Campground was divided in half. (For more information, see the previous listing, *Medicine*.)

Campsites, facilities: There are 24 sites for tents or RVs up to 30 feet (no hookups). Picnic tables and fire grills are provided. Drinking water and vault toilets are available. A boat ramp is available nearby. Some facilities are wheelchair-accessible. Leashed pets are permitted. A café and bar are available in Bartle; otherwise, no supplies are available within an hour's drive.

Reservations, fees: Reservations are not accepted. Sites are $7 per vehicle per night. Open late May through early October, weather permitting.

Directions: From Redding, drive north on I-5 past Dunsmuir to Highway 89. Turn east on Highway 89 and drive 28 miles (just past Bartle) to Forest Road 15/Harris Springs Road. Turn left on Forest Road 15 and drive approximately five miles to the Y intersection with Forest Road 49/Medicine Lake Road. Turn right on Forest Road 49 and drive approximately 26 miles to the lake and campground access road.

Contact: Modoc National Forest, Doublehead Ranger District, 530/667-2246, fax 530/667-8609.

❺ HEMLOCK
👫 ≈ 🛶 🚤 🐕 ♿ 🚐 ⛺

Scenic rating: 7

on Medicine Lake in Modoc National Forest

Map 3.1, page 203

This is one in a series of campgrounds on Medicine Lake operated by the Forest Service. A special attraction at Hemlock is the natural sand beach. (For more information, see the *Medicine* listing in this chapter.)

Campsites, facilities: There are 19 sites for tents or RVs up to 22 feet (no hookups). Picnic tables and fire grills are provided. Drinking water and vault toilets are available. A boat ramp is available nearby. Some facilities are wheelchair-accessible. Leashed pets are permitted. A café and bar are available in Bartle; otherwise, no supplies are available within an hour's drive.

Reservations, fees: Reservations are not accepted. Sites are $7 per vehicle per night. Open late May to early October, weather permitting.

Directions: From Redding, drive north on I-5 past Dunsmuir to Highway 89. Turn east on Highway 89 and drive 28 miles (just past Bartle) to Forest Road 15/Harris Springs Road. Turn left on Forest Road 15 and drive approximately five miles to the Y intersection with Forest Road 49/Medicine Lake Road. Turn right on Forest Road 49 and drive approximately 26 miles to the lake and campground access road.

Contact: Modoc National Forest, Doublehead Ranger District, 530/667-2246, fax 530/667-8609.

6 HEADQUARTERS

Scenic rating: 7

on Medicine Lake in Modoc National Forest

Map 3.1, page 203

This is one of four campgrounds set beside Medicine Lake. There is no lake access from this camp because of private property between the lake and campground. The elevation is 6,700 feet. (For more information, see the *Medicine* listing in this chapter.)

Campsites, facilities: There are 10 sites for tents or RVs up to 16 feet (no hookups). Picnic tables and fire grills are provided. Drinking water and vault toilets are available. A boat ramp is available nearby. A café and bar are

available in Bartle; otherwise, no supplies are available within an hour's drive. Leashed pets are permitted.

Reservations, fees: Reservations are not accepted. Sites are $7 per vehicle per night. Open late May to early October, weather permitting.

Directions: From Redding, drive north on I-5 past Dunsmuir to Highway 89. Turn east on Highway 89 and drive 28 miles (just past Bartle) to Forest Road 15/Harris Springs Road. Turn left on Forest Road 15 and drive approximately five miles to the Y intersection with Forest Road 49/Medicine Lake Road. Turn right on Forest Road 49 and drive approximately 26 miles to the lake and campground access road.

Contact: Modoc National Forest, Doublehead Ranger District, 530/667-2246, fax 530/667-8609.

7 BULLSEYE LAKE

Scenic rating: 7

near Medicine Lake in Modoc National Forest

Map 3.1, page 203

This tiny lake gets overlooked every year, mainly because of its proximity to nearby Medicine Lake. Bullseye Lake is shallow, but because snow keeps it locked up until late May or early June, the water stays plenty cold for small trout through July. It is stocked with just 750 six- to eight-inch rainbow trout, not much to crow about—or to catch, for that matter. No boat motors are allowed. Nearby are some ice caves, created by ancient volcanic action. The place is small, quiet, and pretty, but most of all, small. This camp is set at an elevation of 6,500 feet.

Campsites, facilities: There are six sites for tents or RVs up to 22 feet (no hookups). Picnic tables and fire grills are provided. A vault toilet is available. No drinking water is available. Garbage must be packed out. Supplies are available in McCloud. A café and bar are available in Bartle; otherwise, no supplies are available within an hour's drive. Leashed pets are permitted.

Reservations, fees: Reservations are not accepted. There is no fee for camping. Open late May through October, weather permitting.

Directions: From Redding, drive north on I-5 past Dunsmuir to Highway 89. Turn east on Highway 89 and drive 28 miles (just past Bartle) to Forest Road 15/Harris Springs Road. Turn left on Forest Road 15 and drive approximately five miles to the Y intersection with Forest Road 49/Medicine Lake Road. Turn right on Forest Road 49 and drive approximately 24 miles (if you reach Medicine Lake, you have gone about two miles too far) to the Bullseye Lake access road. Turn right at the Bullseye Lake access road and drive a short distance past Blanche Lake, then turn right and drive a short distance to the lake.

Contact: Modoc National Forest, Doublehead Ranger District, 530/667-2246, fax 530/667-8609.

8 PAYNE SPRINGS
🚶 🐕 🚙 ⛺

Scenic rating: 8

near Medicine Lake in Modoc National Forest

Map 3.1, page 203

This camp is set by a small spring in a very pretty riparian area. It's small, but it is special.

Campsites, facilities: There are six dispersed sites for tents or RVs up to 20 feet (no hookups). Picnic tables and fire grills are provided. A vault toilet is available. No drinking water is available. Garbage must be packed out. A café and bar are available in Bartle. Supplies are available in Tionesta, a 30-minute drive, or McCloud. Leashed pets are permitted.

Reservations, fees: Reservations are not accepted. There is no fee for camping. Open late May through October, weather permitting.

Directions: From Redding, on I-5 drive past Dunsmuir to Highway 89. Turn east on Highway 89 and drive 28 miles (just past Bartle) to Forest Road 15/Harris Springs Road. Turn left on Forest Road 15 and drive approximately five miles to the Y intersection with Forest Road 49/Medicine Lake Road. Turn right on Forest Road 49 and drive 30 miles (0.2 mile past the Bullseye Lake access road) to the Payne Springs access road (if you reach Medicine Lake, you have gone too far). Turn left on the Payne Springs access road and drive a short distance to the campground.

Contact: Modoc National Forest, Doublehead Ranger District, 530/667-2246, fax 530/667-8609.

9 HARRIS SPRINGS
🚶 🐕 🚙 ⛺

Scenic rating: 3

in Shasta-Trinity National Forest

Map 3.1, page 203

This camp is a hidden spot in remote Shasta-Trinity National Forest, nestled in the long, mountainous ridge that runs east from Mount Shasta to Lava Beds National Monument. The camp is set at 4,800 feet, with a part-time fire station within a quarter mile on the opposite side of the access road. The area is best explored by four-wheel drive, venturing to a series of small buttes, mountaintops, and lookouts in the immediate area. A map of Shasta-Trinity National Forest is a must.

Campsites, facilities: There are 15 sites for tents or RVs up to 32 feet (no hookups). Picnic tables and fire grills are provided. There is no drinking water. Vault toilets are available. Garbage must be packed out. Leashed pets are permitted.

Reservations, fees: Reservations are not accepted. There is no fee for camping. Open late May to early October, weather permitting.

Directions: From Redding, drive north on I-5 past Dunsmuir to the junction with Highway

89. Turn east on Highway 89 and drive 28 miles (just past Bartle) to Forest Road 15/Harris Springs Road. Bear left on Forest Road 15 and drive five miles to the Y intersection with Harris Springs Road and Medicine Lake Road/Forest Road 49. Bear left at the Y, staying on Harris Springs Road/Forest Road 15, and drive 12 miles to a junction with a forest road signed for the Harris Springs Ranger Station. Turn right and drive a short distance, and look for the campground entrance on the right side of the road.

Contact: Shasta-Trinity National Forest, McCloud Ranger District, 530/964-2184, fax 530/964-2938.

10 COTTONWOOD FLAT

Scenic rating: 6

in Modoc National Forest

Map 3.1, page 203

The camp is wooded and shady, set at 4,700 feet in elevation in the rugged and remote Devil's Garden area of Modoc National Forest. The region is known for large mule deer, and Cottonwood Flat is well situated as a base camp for a hunting trip in the fall. The weather can get extremely cold early and late in the season.

Campsites, facilities: There are 10 sites for tents or RVs up to 16 feet (no hookups). Picnic tables and fire grills are provided. There is no drinking water. Vault toilets are available. Garbage must be packed out. Supplies are available within 10 miles in Canby. Leashed pets are permitted.

Reservations, fees: Reservations are not accepted. There is no fee for camping. Open May through October, weather permitting.

Directions: From Redding, drive east on Highway 299 for about 100 miles to Adin. Continue on Highway 299 for about 20 miles to the Canby Bridge at the Pit River and the junction with Forest Road 84. Turn left on Forest Road 84 and drive about eight miles to

Forest Road 42N95. Turn right and drive 0.5 mile to the campground entrance on the left side of the road. Note: The access road is not recommended for RVs longer than 16 feet.

Contact: Modoc National Forest, Devil's Garden Ranger District, 530/233-5811, fax 530/233-8709.

11 AHJUMAWI LAVA SPRINGS BOAT-IN

Scenic rating: 8

at Big Lake

Map 3.1, page 203

This is a one-of-a-kind boat-in camp set on Big Lake and connecting Horr Pond in the Fall River matrix of streams. Ahjumawi means "where the waters come together," named by the Pit River Native Americans who inhabit the area near the confluence of Big Lake, Tule River, Ja She Creek, Lava Creek, and Fall River. Together the waters form one of the largest freshwater springs in the world. Springs flowing from the lava are prominent along the shoreline. This is a place of exceptional and primeval scenery. Much of the land is covered by lava flows, including vast areas of jagged black basalt, along with lava tubes and spattercone and conic depressions. There are brilliant aqua bays, and for campers, peace and quiet. However, you may be joined on land by armies of mosquitoes in the spring; they're not so bad while you're on the water. Access is by boat only, ideal for canoes, and in addition, the lake is not well known outside of the region. Expert fly fishers try for giant but elusive rainbow trout, best in the early morning at the springs. Because of high water clarity, long leaders and perfect casts are essential. There are also nesting areas around the lake for bald eagles, ospreys, and blue herons, and this park is considered a stellar habitat for bird-watching. A series of connecting trails are accessible from camp. The park is a wilderness area, covering 6,000 acres, and most of it is extremely rugged lava rock. There are many signs of this area's ancient past, with bedrock mortars, ceremonial sites, and prehistoric fish traps. There are also great herds of mule deer that forage through much of the park. Bears also roam this area. Finally, there are magnificent views of Mount Shasta, Mount Lassen, and other peaks.

Campsites, facilities: There are nine boat-in sites. Picnic tables, food lockers, and fire pits are provided. Vault toilets are available. No drinking water is available; bring your own water. Garbage must be packed out. Leashed pets are permitted.

Reservations, fees: Reservations are not accepted. Sites are $9 per night. Open year-round, weather permitting.

Directions: From Redding, drive east on Highway 299 for 73 miles to McArthur. Turn left on Main Street and drive 3.5 miles (becomes a dirt road) to the Rat Farm boat launch at Big Lake. Launch boat and proceed by boat one to three miles to one of the nine boat-in campsites.

Contact: McArthur-Burney Falls Memorial State Park, 530/335-2777, www.parks .ca.gov.

fills completely, causing the lakeshore to be strewn with stumps and quite muddy after spring rains and snowmelt. A hot spring is available in Big Bend, about a 30-minute drive from camp.

Campsites, facilities: There are 25 sites for tents or RVs up to 24 feet (no hookups). Picnic tables and fire grills are provided. Vault toilets are available. No drinking water is available. A small boat ramp is available one mile from the camp. Garbage must be packed out. Leashed pets are permitted.

Reservations, fees: Reservations are not accepted. There is no fee for camping. Open year-round.

Directions: From Redding, drive east on Highway 299 for 37 miles to Big Bend Road/ County Road 7M01. Turn left and drive 17 miles to the town of Big Bend. Continue for five miles to the lake, bearing right at the T intersection, and continue for two miles (past the boat-launch turnoff) to the campground turnoff on the left side of the road. Turn left and drive one mile to the campground.

Contact: Shasta-Trinity National Forest, Shasta Lake Ranger District, 530/275-1587, fax 530/275-1512; Shasta Lake Visitor Center, 530/275-1589.

12 DEADLUN

Scenic rating: 7

on Iron Canyon Reservoir in Shasta-Trinity National Forest

Map 3.1, page 203

Deadlun is a pretty campground set in the forest, shaded and quiet, with a five-minute walk or one-minute drive to the Deadlun Creek arm of Iron Canyon Reservoir. Drive. If you have a canoe to launch or fishing equipment to carry, driving is the choice. Trout fishing is good here, both in April and May, then again in October and early November. One downer is that the shoreline is often very muddy here in March and early April. Because of an engineering error with the dam, the lake never

13 HAWKINS LANDING

Scenic rating: 7

on Iron Canyon Reservoir

Map 3.1, page 203

The adjacent boat ramp makes Hawkins Landing the better of the two camps at Iron Canyon Reservoir for campers with trailered boats (though Deadlun is far more secluded). Iron Canyon, with 15 miles of shoreline, provides good fishing for trout, has a resident bald eagle or two, and also has nearby hot springs in the town of Big Bend. One problem with this lake is the annual drawdown in late fall, which causes the shoreline to be extremely muddy in the spring. For this reason, swimming is lousy because there is no beach and lots of debris in the water. The lake usually rises high enough to make the boat ramp functional by mid-April. This camp is set at an elevation of 2,700 feet.

Campsites, facilities: There are 10 sites for tents or RVs up to 30 feet (no hookups). Picnic tables and fire grills are provided. Drinking water, vault toilets, and a small boat ramp are available. Supplies can be obtained in Big Bend. Leashed pets are permitted.

Reservations, fees: Reservations are not accepted. Sites are $10 per night, $1 per pet per night, $3 per night for each additional vehicle, $7 per night for additional RV. Open mid-May to Labor Day weekend, weather permitting.

Directions: From Redding, drive east on Highway 299 for 37 miles to Big Bend Road. At Big Bend Road turn left and drive 15.2 miles to the town of Big Bend. Continue for 2.1 miles to Forest Road 38N11. Turn left and drive 3.3 miles to the Iron Canyon Reservoir Spillway. Turn right and drive 1.1 miles to a dirt road. Turn left and drive 0.3 mile to the campground.

Contact: PG&E Land Projects, 916/386-5164, www.pge.com/recreation.

14 NORTHSHORE
🏊 🚣 🛥 🐾 🚙 ⛰

Scenic rating: 8

on Lake Britton

Map 3.1, page 203

This peaceful campground is set among the woodlands near the shore of Lake Britton, directly across the lake from McArthur-Burney Falls Memorial State Park. Boating and fishing are popular here, and once the water warms up in midsummer, swimming is also a winner. Boat rentals are available near the boat ramp. The lake has fair prospects for trout and is sometimes excellent for crappie. For side trips, the best trout fishing in the area is on the Pit River near Powerhouse Number

Three. A hot spring is available in Big Bend, about a 30-minute drive from camp. The elevation is 2,800 feet. Note: This is a bald eagle nesting area, and the area is subject to closure to protect the raptors.

Campsites, facilities: There are 30 sites for tents or RVs up to 30 feet (no hookups). Picnic tables and fire grills are provided. Drinking water and vault toilets are available. An unimproved boat ramp is available near the camp and an improved boat ramp is available in McArthur-Burney Falls State Park (about four miles away). Supplies can be obtained in Fall River Mills or Burney. Leashed pets are permitted.

Reservations, fees: Reservations are not accepted. Sites are $16 per night, $3 per night for each additional vehicle, $1 per pet per night. Open mid-May to mid-September, weather permitting.

Directions: From Redding, drive east on Highway 299 to Burney and then continue for five miles to Highway 89. Turn left (north) and drive 9.7 miles (past the state park entrance and over the Lake Britton Bridge) to Clark Creek Road. Turn left (west) and drive about a mile to the camp access road. Turn left and drive one mile to the camp.

Contact: PG&E Land Projects, 916/386-5164, www.pge.com/recreation.

15 McARTHUR-BURNEY FALLS MEMORIAL STATE PARK AND HORSE CAMP
🚶 🏊 🚣 🛥 🐾 🚻 🚙 ⛰

Scenic rating: 9

in McArthur-Burney Falls Memorial State Park

Map 3.1, page 203

Burney Falls is a 129-foot waterfall, a beautiful cascade split at the top by a little grove of trees, with small trickles oozing and falling out of the adjacent moss-lined wall. Since it is fed primarily by a spring, it runs strong and glorious most of the year, producing 100 million gallons of water every day. The

Headwaters Trail provides an outstanding hike, both to see the waterfall and Burney Creek, as well as for an easy adventure and fishing access to the stream. An excellent fly-fishing section of the Pit River is available below the dam. There are other stellar recreation options at this state park. At the end of the campground access road is a boat ramp for Lake Britton, with rentals available for canoes and paddleboats. This is a beautiful lake, with pretty canyon walls on its upper end, and good smallmouth bass (at rock piles) and crappie fishing (near the train trestle). There is also a good swimming beach. The Pacific Crest Trail is routed right through the park and provides an additional opportunity for a day hike, best explored downstream from the dam. Reservations for sites are essential during the summer. This park, originally formed by volcanic activity, features 910 acres of forest and five miles of stream and lake shore. The Headwaters horse camp is three miles from the main campground. Non-equestrian campers may stay at the horse camp, but only tents are allowed.

Campsites, facilities: There are 128 sites for tents or RVs up to 32 feet (no hookups), six horse-camp sites, and one hike-in/bike-in site. Picnic tables, food lockers, and fire grills are provided. Drinking water, restrooms with flush toilets and showers, and a dump station are available. Vault toilets and a small horse corral are available at the horse camp. Some facilities are wheelchair-accessible. A grocery/gift store and boat rentals are available in the summer. Leashed pets are permitted, except on the trails and the beach.

Reservations, fees: Reservations are accepted ($7.50 reservation fee) at 800/444-PARK (800/444-7275) or www.reserveamerica.com. Sites are $15–20 per night, $6 per night for each additional vehicle, $3 per person per night for hike-in/bike-in site. Horse camp is $9 per night and $2 per night per horse. Boat launching is $8 per day. Open year-round.

Directions: From Redding, drive east on Highway 299 to Burney and then continue for five miles to the junction with Highway 89. At Highway 89, turn north (left) and drive six miles to the campground entrance on the left side of the road.

Contact: McArthur-Burney Falls State Park, 530/335-2777, www.parks.ca.gov.

16 DUSTY CAMPGROUND

Scenic rating: 8

on Lake Britton

Map 3.1, page 203

This is one in a series of campgrounds near the north shore of Lake Britton. The lake has 18 miles of shoreline. (See *Northshore* listing in this chapter for more information.) The camp is set at an elevation of 2,800 feet. It provides an alternative to nearby McArthur-Burney Falls Memorial State Park, which is far more popular.

Campsites, facilities: There are seven sites for tents or RVs up to 30 feet (no hookups); two of the sites can accommodate groups of up to 25 people each. Fire rings are provided. Vault toilets are available. Drinking water is not available. Garbage must be packed out in winter. Some facilities are wheelchair-accessible. Leashed pets are permitted.

Reservations, fees: Reservations are not accepted. Sites are $6 per night, $3 per night for each additional vehicle, $1 per pet per night, and $12 per night for double sites. Open year-round.

Directions: From Redding, drive east on Highway 299 to Burney and continue for five miles to the junction with Highway 89. Turn left (north) and drive 7.5 miles (past the state park entrance and over the Lake Britton Bridge) to the campground access road on the right (it will be confusing because the campground is on the left). Turn right and drive 0.75 mile (in the process crossing the highway) to the campground.

Contact: PG&E Land Projects, 916/386-5164, www.pge.com/recreation.

17 CAVE LAKE

Scenic rating: 8

in Modoc National Forest

Map 3.2, page 204

A pair of lakes can be discovered out here in the middle of nowhere, with Cave Lake on one end and Lily Lake on the other. Together they make a nice set, very quiet, extremely remote, with good fishing for rainbow trout and brook trout. A canoe, pram, or float tube can be ideal. No motors are permitted. Of the two lakes, it is nearby Lily Lake that is prettier and provides the better fishing. Cave Lake is set at 6,600 feet. By camping here, you become a member of the 5 Percent Club; that is, the 5 percent of campers who know of secret, isolated little spots such as this one.

Campsites, facilities: There are six sites for tents or RVs up to 15 feet (no hookups); trailers are not advised because of the steep access road. Picnic tables and fire grills are provided. There is no drinking water. Vault toilets are available. Garbage must be packed out. Motors (including electric) are prohibited on the lake. Supplies are available in New Pine Creek and Davis Creek. Leashed pets are permitted.

Reservations, fees: Reservations are not accepted. There is no fee for camping. Open July through October, weather permitting.

Directions: From Redding, drive east on Highway 299 for 146 miles to Alturas and U.S. 395. Turn north on U.S. 395 and drive 40 miles to Forest Road 2 (if you reach the town of New Pine Creek on the Oregon/California border, you have driven a mile too far). Turn right on Forest Road 2 (a steep dirt road—trailers are not recommended) and drive six miles to the campground entrance on the left side of the road, just beyond the Lily Lake picnic area.

Contact: Modoc National Forest, Warner Mountain Ranger, 530/279-6116, fax 530/279-8309.

18 PLUM VALLEY

Scenic rating: 7

near the South Fork of Davis Creek in Modoc National Forest

Map 3.2, page 204

This secluded and primitive camp is set near the South Fork of Davis Creek, at 5,600 feet elevation. Davis Creek provides for catch-and-release, barbless hook, no-bait fishing. You can, however, keep the brown trout. There are no other campgrounds within 15 miles.

Campsites, facilities: There are 15 sites for tents or RVs up to 15 feet (no hookups). Picnic tables and fire grills are provided. Vault toilets are available. No drinking water is available. Garbage must be packed out. Supplies are available in Davis Creek, about 3.5 miles away. Leashed pets are permitted.

Reservations, fees: Reservations are not accepted. There is no fee for camping. Open May through September.

Directions: From Alturas drive north on U.S. 395 for 18 miles to the town of Davis Creek and County Road 11. Turn right on County Road 11 and drive two miles to a Y. Bear right on Forest Road 45N35 and drive one mile to the signed entrance to the campground on the left side of the road.

Contact: Modoc National Forest, Warner Mountain Ranger District, 530/279-6116, fax 530/279-8309; Department of Fish and Game fishing information, 530/225-2146.

19 RESERVOIR C

Scenic rating: 6

near Alturas in Modoc National Forest

Map 3.2, page 204

It is one great adventure to explore the "alphabet lakes" in the remote Devil's Garden area of Modoc County. Reservoir C and Reservoir F provide the best of the lot, but the success can go up and down like a yo-yo, just like the water levels in the lakes. Reservoir C is stocked with both Eagle Lake trout and brown trout. A sidelight to this area is the number of primitive roads that are routed through Modoc National Forest, perfect for four-wheel-drivers. The elevation is 4,900 feet.

Campsites, facilities: There are six sites for tents or RVs up to 22 feet (no hookups). Picnic tables and fire grills are provided. Vault toilets and a primitive boat ramp are available. No drinking water is available. Garbage must be packed out. Some facilities are wheelchair-accessible. Leashed pets are permitted.

Reservations, fees: Reservations are not accepted. There is no fee for camping. Open May through September.

Directions: From Alturas drive west on Highway 299 for three miles to Crowder Flat Road/County Road 73. Turn right on Crowder Flat Road and drive 9.5 miles to Triangle Ranch Road/Forest Road 43N18. Turn left on Triangle Ranch Road and drive seven miles to Forest Road 44N32. Turn right on Forest Road 44N32, drive 0.5 mile, turn right on the access road for the lake and campground, and drive 0.5 mile to the camp at the end of the road.

Contact: Modoc National Forest, Doublehead Ranger District, 530/667-2246, fax 530/667-8309.

are allowed, except for personal watercraft. Swimming is not recommended because of algae growth in midsummer, murky water, and muddy shoreline. Water levels can fluctuate greatly.

Campsites, facilities: There are six sites for tents or RVs up to 22 feet (no hookups). Picnic tables and fire grills are provided. Vault toilets are available. There is no drinking water. Some facilities are wheelchair-accessible. Garbage must be packed out. A boat ramp is available nearby. Leashed pets are permitted. Supplies can be obtained in Alturas, about eight miles away.

Reservations, fees: Reservations are not accepted. There is no fee for camping. Open May through September.

Directions: From Alturas, drive west on Highway 299 for three miles to Crowder Flat Road/County Road 73. Turn right on Crowder Flat Road and drive about five miles to County Road 180. Turn right on County Road 180 and drive four miles. Turn left at the access road for the campground and boat ramp and drive a short distance to the camp on the left side of the road.

Contact: Modoc National Forest, Doublehead Ranger District, 530/667-2246, fax 530/667-8309.

20 BIG SAGE RESERVOIR

Scenic rating: 5

in Modoc National Forest

Map 3.2, page 204

This is a do-it-yourself camp; that is, pick your own spot, bring your own water, and don't expect to see anybody else. This camp is set along Big Sage Reservoir—that's right, sagebrush country at 5,100 feet elevation. It is a big lake, covering 5,000 surface acres, and a boat ramp is adjacent to the campground. This is one of the better bass lakes in Modoc County. Catfish and crappie are also here. Water sports

21 CEDAR PASS

Scenic rating: 5

on Cedar Pass in Modoc National Forest

Map 3.2, page 204

Cedar Pass is at 5,600 feet, set on the ridge between Cedar Mountain (8,152 feet) to the north and Payne Peak (7,618) to the south, high in the north Warner Mountains. Bear Creek enters Thomas Creek adjacent to the camp; both are small streams, but it's a pretty spot.

Campsites, facilities: There are 17 sites for tents or RVs up to 16 feet (no hookups). Picnic tables and fire grills are provided. Vault toilets are available. No drinking water is available. Garbage must be packed out. Supplies can be obtained in Cedarville or Alturas. Leashed pets are permitted.

Reservations, fees: Reservations are not accepted. There is no fee for camping. Open late May through October, weather permitting.

Directions: From Redding drive east on Highway 299 to Alturas. In Alturas continue north on Highway 299/U.S. 395 for five miles to the split for Highway 299. Turn right on Highway 299 and drive about nine miles. Look for the signed entrance road on the right side of the road.

Contact: Modoc National Forest, Warner Mountain Ranger District, 530/279-6116, fax 530/279-8309.

22 STOUGH RESERVOIR
🏃 🏊 🎣 🏠 🚐 ⛰️

Scenic rating: 8

in Modoc National Forest

Map 3.2, page 204

Stough Reservoir looks like a large country pond where cattle might drink. You know why? Because it once actually was a cattle pond on a family ranch that has since been converted to Forest Service property. It is in the north Warner Mountains (not to be confused with the South Warner Wilderness), which features many back roads and remote four-wheel-drive routes. The camp is set at an elevation of 6,200 feet. Note that you may find this campground named "Stowe Reservoir" on some maps and in previous editions of this book. The name is now officially spelled "Stough Reservoir," after the family that originally owned the property.

Campsites, facilities: There are 14 sites for tents or RVs up to 22 feet (no hookups). Picnic tables and fire grills are provided. Drinking water and vault toilets are available. Garbage must be packed out. Leashed pets are permitted. Supplies can be obtained in Cedarville, six miles away.

Reservations, fees: Reservations are not accepted. There is no fee for camping. Open late May to early October, weather permitting.

Directions: From Redding, drive east on Highway 299 to Alturas. In Alturas, continue north on Highway 299/U.S. 395 for five miles to the split-off for Highway 299. Turn right on Highway 299 and drive about 12 miles (just past Cedar Pass). Look for the signed entrance road on the left side of the road. Turn left and drive one mile to the campground on the left side of the road.

Contact: Modoc National Forest, Warner Mountain Ranger District, 530/279-6116, fax 530/279-8309.

23 HOWARD'S GULCH
🏃 🏊 🏠 ♿ 🚐 ⛰️

Scenic rating: 6

near Duncan Reservoir in Modoc National Forest

Map 3.2, page 204

This is the nearest campground to Duncan Reservoir, three miles to the north and stocked with trout each year by the Department of Fish and Game. The camp is set in the typically sparse woods of Modoc National Forest, but a beautiful grove of aspen is three miles to the west on Highway 139, on the left side of the road. By the way, Highway 139 isn't much of a highway at all, but it is paved and will get you there. The elevation is 4,700 feet.

Campsites, facilities: There are 11 sites for tents or RVs up to 22 feet (no hookups). Picnic tables and fire grills are provided. Drinking water and vault toilets are available. Some facilities are wheelchair-accessible. Supplies are available within five miles in Canby. Leashed pets are permitted.

Reservations, fees: Reservations are not accepted. Sites are $6 per night. Open May through October, weather permitting.

Directions: From Redding, drive east on Highway 299 for about 100 miles to Adin.

Continue on Highway 299 for about 25 miles to Highway 139. Turn left (northwest) on Highway 139 and drive six miles to the campground on the left side of the road.

Contact: Modoc National Forest, Devil's Garden Ranger District, 530/233-5811, fax 530/233-8709.

24 PEPPERDINE

🚶‍♂️🐕5%🚐🏕️

Scenic rating: 5

in Modoc National Forest

Map 3.2, page 204

This camp is outstanding for hikers planning a backpacking trip into the adjacent South Warner Wilderness. The camp is at 6,680 feet, set along the south side of tiny Porter Reservoir, with a horse corral within walking distance. A trailhead out of camp provides direct access to the Summit Trail, the best hike in the South Warner Wilderness.

Campsites, facilities: There are five sites for tents or RVs up to 16 feet (no hookups). Picnic tables and fire grills are provided. Drinking water and vault toilets are available. Corrals are available with water for stock. Garbage must be packed out. Supplies are available in Cedarville or Alturas. Leashed pets are permitted.

Reservations, fees: Reservations are not accepted. There is no fee for camping. Open July through October, weather permitting.

Directions: In Alturas, drive south on U.S. 395 to the southern end of town and County Road 56. Turn left on County Road 56 and drive 13 miles to the Modoc Forest boundary and the junction with Parker Creek Road. Bear left on Parker Creek Road and continue for six miles to the signed campground access road on the right. Turn right and drive 0.5 mile to the campground on the left side of the road.

Contact: Modoc National Forest, Warner Mountain Ranger District, 530/279-6116, fax 530/279-8309.

25 UPPER RUSH CREEK

🚶‍♂️🛶🐕🚐🏕️

Scenic rating: 8

in Modoc National Forest

Map 3.2, page 204

Upper Rush Creek is a pretty campground, set along Rush Creek, a quiet, wooded spot that gets little use. It sits in the shadow of nearby Manzanita Mountain (7,036 feet elevation) to the east, where there is a Forest Service lookout for a great view. To reach the lookout, drive back toward Highway 299 and when you reach the paved road, County Road 198, turn left and drive 0.5 mile to Forest Road 22. Turn left on Forest Road 22 and head up the hill. One mile from the summit, turn left at a four-way junction and drive to the top. You get dramatic views of the Warm Springs Valley to the north and the Likely Flats to the east, looking across miles and miles of open country.

Campsites, facilities: There are 13 sites for tents or RVs up to 22 feet (no hookups), but Lower Rush Creek is better for trailers. Picnic tables and fire grills are provided. Drinking water is available intermittently; check current status. Vault toilets are available. Supplies can be obtained about nine miles away in Adin or Canby. Leashed pets are permitted.

Reservations, fees: Reservations are not accepted. Sites are $6 per night; no camping fee if there is no drinking water. Open May through October, weather permitting.

Directions: From Redding, turn east on Highway 299 and drive to Adin. Continue east on Highway 299 for about seven miles to a signed campground turnoff on the right side of the road. Turn right and drive to the junction with Forest Road 40N05. Turn left and drive 2.5 miles to the campground at the end of the road.

Contact: Modoc National Forest, Big Valley Ranger District, 530/299-3215, fax 530/299-8409.

26 LOWER RUSH CREEK

Scenic rating: 6

on Rush Creek in Modoc National Forest

Map 3.2, page 204

This is one of two obscure campgrounds set a short distance from Highway 299 on Rush Creek in southern Modoc County. Lower Rush Creek is the first camp you will come to, with flat campsites surrounded by an outer fence and set along Rush Creek. This camp is better suited for trailers than the one at Upper Rush Creek. It is little known and little used. It's set at 4,400 feet in elevation.

Campsites, facilities: There are 10 sites for tents or RVs up to 22 feet (no hookups). Picnic tables and fire grills are provided. Drinking water is available intermittently; check current status. Vault toilets are available. Supplies are available in Adin or Canby. Leashed pets are permitted.

Reservations, fees: Reservations are not accepted. Sites are $6 per night; no camping fee if there is no drinking water. Open May through October, weather permitting.

Directions: From Redding, turn east on Highway 299 and drive to Adin. Continue east on Highway 299 for about seven miles to a signed campground turnoff on the right side of the road. Turn right and drive to the junction with Forest Road 40N05. Turn left and drive one mile to the campground on the right.

Contact: Modoc National Forest, Big Valley Ranger District, 530/299-3215, fax 530/299-8409.

27 SOUP SPRINGS

Scenic rating: 8

in Modoc National Forest

Map 3.2, page 204

This is a beautiful, quiet, wooded campground at a trailhead into the South Warner Wilderness. Soup Creek originates at Soup Springs in the meadow adjacent to the campground. The trailhead here is routed two miles into the wilderness, where it junctions with the Mill Creek Trail. From here, turn left for a beautiful walk along Mill Creek and into Mill Creek Meadow, an easy yet pristine stroll that can provide a serene experience. The elevation is 6,800 feet.

Campsites, facilities: There are 14 sites for tents or RVs up to 22 feet (no hookups). Picnic tables and fire grills are provided. Drinking water and vault toilets are available. Corrals are also available. Supplies can be obtained in Likely. Leashed pets are permitted.

Reservations, fees: Reservations are not accepted. Sites are $6 per night. Open June through October, weather permitting.

Directions: From Alturas, drive south on U.S. 395 for 17 miles to the town of Likely, where you'll come to Jess Valley Road. Turn left on Jess Valley Road/County Road 64 and drive nine miles to the fork. Bear left on West Warner Road/Forest Road 5 and go 4.5 miles to Soup Loop Road. Turn right on Soup Loop Road/Forest Road 40N24 and continue on that gravel road for six miles to the campground entrance on the right.

Contact: Modoc National Forest, Warner Mountain Ranger District, 530/279-6116, fax 530/279-8309.

28 MILL CREEK FALLS

Scenic rating: 9

in Modoc National Forest

Map 3.2, page 204

This nice, wooded campground is a good base camp for a backpacking trip into the South Warner Wilderness. The camp is set on Mill Creek at 5,700 feet in elevation. To see Mill Creek Falls, take the trail out of camp and bear left at the Y. To enter the interior of the South Warner Wilderness, bear right at the Y, after which the trail passes Clear Lake, heads to Poison Flat and Poison Creek, and then reaches a junction. Left will take you to the Mill Creek Trail, right will take you up to the Summit Trail. Take your pick. You can't go wrong.

Campsites, facilities: There are 19 sites for tents or RVs up to 22 feet (no hookups). Picnic tables and fire grills are provided. Drinking water and vault toilets are available. Supplies are available in Likely. Leashed pets are permitted.

Reservations, fees: Reservations are not accepted. Sites are $10 per night. Open June through October, weather permitting.

Directions: From Alturas drive 17 miles south on U.S. 395 to the town of Likely, where you'll come to Jess Valley Road. Turn left on Jess Valley Road/County Road 64 and drive nine miles to the fork. Bear left on West Warner Road/Forest Road 5 and drive 2.5 miles to Forest Road 40N46. Turn right on Forest Road 40N46 and drive two miles to the campground entrance at the end of the road.

Contact: Modoc National Forest, Warner Mountain Ranger District, 530/279-6116, fax 530/279-8309.

29 EMERSON
🏃 🏊 🐕 5% 🚐 ⛺

Scenic rating: 6

in Modoc National Forest

Map 3.2, page 204

This tiny camp is virtually unknown, nestled at 6,000 feet on the eastern boundary of the South Warner Wilderness. Big alkali lakes and miles of the Nevada flats can be seen on the other side of the highway as you drive along the entrance road to the campground. A trailhead at this primitive setting is used by hikers and backpackers. Note that hitting the trail is a steep, sometimes wrenching climb for 4.5 miles to North Emerson Lake (poor to fair fishing). For many, this hike is a true butt-kicker.

Campsites, facilities: There are four sites for tents or RVs up to 16 feet (no hookups). Picnic

tables and fire grills are provided. Vault toilets are available. No drinking water is available. Garbage must be packed out. Supplies can be obtained in Eagleville. Leashed pets are permitted.

Reservations, fees: Reservations are not accepted. There is no fee for camping. Open July through October, weather permitting.

Directions: From Alturas, drive north on U.S. 395/Highway 299 for about five miles to the junction with Highway 299. Turn right on Highway 299 and drive to Cedarville and County Road 1. Turn south on County Road 1 and drive to Eagleville. From Eagleville, continue south on County Road 1 for 1.5 miles to Forest Road 40N43/County Road 40. Turn right and drive three miles to the campground at the end of the road. The access road is steep, narrow, and very slick in wet weather. Trailers are not recommended.

Contact: Modoc National Forest, Warner Mountain Ranger District, 530/279-6116, fax 530/279-8309.

30 ASH CREEK
🏊 🐕 🚐 ⛺

Scenic rating: 7

in Modoc National Forest

Map 3.2, page 204

This remote camp has stark beauty and is set at 4,800 feet along Ash Creek, a stream with small trout. This region of Modoc National Forest has an extensive network of backcountry roads, popular with deer hunters in the fall. The Ash Creek Wildlife Area is about 10 miles west of camp. Summer comes relatively late out here, and it can be cold and wet even in early June. Stash some extra clothes, just in case. That will probably guarantee nice weather.

Campsites, facilities: There are seven sites for tents or RVs up to 22 feet (no hookups). Picnic tables and fire grills are provided. Vault toilets are available. No drinking water is available. Garbage must be packed out. Supplies can be obtained in Adin. Leashed pets are permitted.

Reservations, fees: Reservations are not accepted. There is no fee for camping. Open May through October, weather permitting.

Directions: From Redding, turn east on Highway 299 and drive to Adin and Ash Valley Road. Turn right on Ash Valley Road/County Road 88/527 and drive eight miles. Turn left at the signed campground turnoff and drive a mile to the campground on the right side of the road.

Contact: Modoc National Forest, Big Valley Ranger District, 530/299-3215, fax 530/299-8409; Ash Creek Wildlife Area, 530/294-5824.

31 PATTERNSON

Scenic rating: 4

in Modoc National Forest

Map 3.2, page 204

This once-beautiful landscape was burned by the Blue Fire of 2001, which enveloped 35,000 acres in the South Warners. There are both positives and negatives. The positives are a chance for much wider and longer views previously impossible, as well as the opportunity to watch the evolution of the landscape in a post-fire setting, as has been the case in Yellowstone for years. The negatives are the tree skeletons. Regrowth of vegetation during the past several years is improving the situation, however. The most affected area is to the east, especially on East Creek Trail, which rises through the burned area to a high, barren mountain rim. Patterson is set across the road from Patterson Meadow at 7,200 feet in elevation. The camp is rarely open before July.

Campsites, facilities: There are five sites for tents or RVs up to 20 feet (no hookups). Picnic tables and fire grills are provided. Drinking water and vault toilets are available. Garbage must be packed out. Supplies are available

in Likely or Cedarville. Leashed pets are permitted.

Reservations, fees: Reservations are not accepted. There is no fee for camping. Open late July through October, weather permitting.

Directions: From Alturas drive 17 miles south on U.S. 395 to the town of Likely. Turn left on Jess Valley Road/County Road 64 and drive nine miles to the fork. Bear right on Forest Road 64 and drive for 16 miles to the campground on the left.

Contact: Modoc National Forest, Warner Mountain Ranger District, 530/279-6116, fax 530/279-8309.

32 BLUE LAKE

Scenic rating: 6

in Modoc National Forest

Map 3.2, page 204

You won't believe this: A few years ago, the Blue Fire burned 35,000 acres in this area, including the east and west slopes adjoining Blue Lake. Yet get this: The campground was untouched. It is a strange scene, a somewhat wooded campground (with some level campsites) near the shore of Blue Lake. The lake covers 160 acres and provides fishing for large brown trout and rainbow trout. A 5-mph speed limit assures quiet water for small boats and canoes. A trail circles the lake and takes less than an hour to hike. The elevation is 6,000 feet. Bald eagles have been spotted here. While their presence negates year-round use of six campsites otherwise available, the trade-off is an unprecedented opportunity to view the national bird.

Campsites, facilities: There are 48 sites for tents or RVs up to 22 feet (no hookups). Picnic tables and fire grills are provided. Drinking water and vault toilets are available. Some facilities are wheelchair-accessible, including a paved boat launch and fishing pier. Supplies are available in Likely. Leashed pets are permitted.

Reservations, fees: Reservations are not accepted. Sites are $7 per night. Open June through October, weather permitting.

Directions: From Alturas, drive south on U.S. 395 for seven miles to the town of Likely, where you'll come to Jess Valley Road. Turn left on Jess Valley Road/County Road 64 and drive nine miles to the fork. At the fork, bear right on Forest Road 64 and drive seven miles to Forest Road 38N30. Turn right on Forest Road 38N30 and drive two miles to the campground.

Contact: Modoc National Forest, Warner Mountain Ranger District, 530/279-6116, fax 530/279-8309.

33 WILLOW CREEK

Scenic rating: 7

in Modoc National Forest

Map 3.2, page 204

This remote camp and picnic area is set at 5,200 feet along little Willow Creek amid pine, aspen, and willows. On the north side of the campground is Lower McBride Springs.

Campsites, facilities: There are eight sites for tents or RVs up to 22 feet (no hookups). Picnic tables and fire grills are provided. Drinking water and vault toilets are available. A wheelchair-accessible toilet is at the picnic area next to the campground. Leashed pets are permitted.

Reservations, fees: Reservations are not accepted. Sites are $6 per night. Open May through October, weather permitting.

Directions: From Redding, drive east on Highway 299 to Adin and Highway 139. Turn right on Highway 139 and drive 14 miles to the campground on the left side of the road.

Contact: Modoc National Forest, Big Valley Ranger District, 530/299-3215, fax 530/299-8409.

34 PIT RIVER

Scenic rating: 6

on the Pit River

Map 3.3, page 205

Very few out-of-towners know about this hidden campground set along the Pit River. It can provide a good base camp for a fishing trip adventure. The best stretch of trout water on the Pit is near Powerhouse Number Three. In addition to fishing there are many other recreation options. A parking area and trail along Hat Creek are available where the Highway 299 bridge crosses Hat Creek. Baum Lake, Crystal Lake, and the Cassel section of Hat Creek are all within five miles of this camp.

Campsites, facilities: There are seven sites for tents or RVs up to 40 feet (no hookups), and one double site for up to eight people. Picnic tables and fire rings are provided. Vault toilets, wheelchair-accessible fishing pier, and small-craft launch ramp are available. No drinking water is available. Garbage must be packed out. There are supplies and a coin laundry in Fall River Mills. Some facilities are wheelchair-accessible. Leashed pets are permitted.

Reservations, fees: Reservations are not accepted. Sites are $8 per night, and $12 per night for the double site. Open mid-April to mid-November.

Directions: From Redding, drive east on Highway 299 to Burney and continue for five miles to the junction with Highway 89. At the junction, continue straight on Highway 299, cross the Pit River Bridge, and drive about three miles to Pit One Powerhouse Road. Turn right and drive down the hill to the Pit River Lodge. Turn right and drive 0.5 mile to the campground.

Contact: Bureau of Land Management, Alturas Field Office, 530/233-4666, fax 530/233-5696.

35 CASSEL

Scenic rating: 8

on Hat Creek

Map 3.3, page 205

This camp is set at 3,200 feet in the beautiful Hat Creek Valley. It is an outstanding location for a fishing trip base camp, with nearby Crystal Lake, Baum Lake, and Hat Creek (all set in the Hat Creek Valley) providing trout fishing. This section of Hat Creek is well known for its challenging fly-fishing. A good source of fishing information is Vaughn's Sporting Goods in Burney. Baum Lake is ideal for car-top boats with electric motors.

Campsites, facilities: There are 27 sites for tents or RVs up to 30 feet (no hookups). Picnic tables and fire grills are provided. Drinking water and vault toilets are available. Some facilities are wheelchair-accessible. Leashed pets are permitted.

Reservations, fees: Reservations are not accepted. Sites are $16 per night, $3 per night for each additional vehicle, $1 per pet per night. Open mid-April to mid-November, weather permitting.

Directions: From Redding, drive east on Highway 299 to Burney and continue for five miles to the junction with Highway 89. At the junction, continue straight on Highway 299 for two miles to Cassel Road. At Cassel Road, turn right and drive 3.6 miles to the campground entrance on the left.

Contact: PG&E Land Projects, 916/386-5164, www.pge.com/recreation.

36 HAT CREEK HEREFORD RANCH RV PARK AND CAMPGROUND

Scenic rating: 8

near Hat Creek

Map 3.3, page 205

This privately operated campground is set in a working cattle ranch. Campers are not allowed near the cattle pasture or cattle. Fishing is available in Hat Creek or in the nearby stocked trout pond. Swimming is also allowed in the pond. Sightseeing is excellent with Burney Falls, Lassen Volcanic National Park, and Subway Caves all within 30 miles.

Campsites, facilities: There are 40 tent sites and 40 RV sites with full or partial hookups (30 amps); some sites are pull-through. Picnic tables and fireplaces are provided. Restrooms with showers, a dump station, coin laundry, playground, modem hookups, wireless Internet access, and a convenience store are available. Some facilities are wheelchair-accessible. Leashed pets are permitted.

Reservations, fees: Reservations are recommended and can be made by telephone or website. Sites are $21.90–25.75 per night, $2 per night for more than two people, $1 per night per pet. Some credit cards accepted. Open April through October.

Directions: From Redding, drive east on Highway 299 to Burney and continue for five miles to the junction with Highway 89. Turn right (south) on Highway 89 and drive 12 miles to the second Doty Road Loop exit. Turn left and drive 0.5 mile to the park entrance on the right.

Contact: Hat Creek Hereford Ranch RV Park and Campground, 530/335-7171 or 877/459-9532, www.hatcreekrv.com.

37 HONN

♿🏊🎣🐕⛺

Scenic rating: 7

on Hat Creek in Lassen National Forest

Map 3.3, page 205

This primitive, tiny campground is set near the point where Honn Creek enters Hat Creek, at 3,400 feet elevation in Lassen National Forest. The creek is extremely pretty here, shaded by trees and flowing emerald green. The camp provides streamside access for trout fishing, though this stretch of creek is sometimes overlooked by the Department of Fish and Game in favor of stocking the creek at the more popular Cave and Bridge Campgrounds. (See listings in this chapter for more information.)

Campsites, facilities: There are six tent sites. Picnic tables and fire grills are provided. Vault toilets are available. Drinking water is not available. A grocery store, coin laundry, and propane gas are available nearby. Leashed pets are permitted.

Reservations, fees: Reservations are not accepted. Sites are $10 per night, $5 per night for each additional vehicle. Open late April through October, weather permitting.

Directions: From Redding, drive east on Highway 299 to Burney and continue for five miles to the junction with Highway 89. Turn right (south) on Highway 89 and drive 15 miles to the campground entrance on the left side of the road.

Contact: Lassen National Forest, Hat Creek Ranger District, 530/336-5521, fax 530/336-5758; Department of Fish and Game fishing information, 530/225-2146.

38 OLD COW MEADOWS

♿🏊🎣🐕♿5%🚐⛺

Scenic rating: 7

in Latour Demonstration State Forest

Map 3.3, page 205

Nobody finds this campground without this book. You want quiet? You don't want to be bugged by anybody? This tiny camp, virtually unknown, is set at 5,900 feet in a wooded area along Old Cow Creek. Recreation options include all-terrain-vehicle use on existing roads and walking the dirt roads that crisscross the area.

Campsites, facilities: There are three sites for tents or RVs up to 25 feet (no hookups). Picnic tables and fire grills are provided. Vault toilets and drinking water are available. Garbage must be packed out. Some facilities are wheelchair-accessible. Leashed pets are permitted.

Reservations, fees: Reservations are not accepted. There is no fee for camping. Open June through October, weather permitting.

Directions: In Redding, turn east on Highway 44 and drive about 9.5 miles to Millville Road. Turn left on Millville Road and drive 0.5 mile to the intersection of Millville Road and Whitmore Road. Turn right on Whitmore Road and drive 13 miles, through Whitmore, until Whitmore Road becomes Tamarac Road. Continue for one mile to a fork at Bateman Road. Take the right fork on Bateman Road, drive 3.5 miles (where the road turns to gravel), and then continue 12 miles to the entrance to the campground.

Contact: Latour Demonstration State Forest, 530/225-2438, fax 530/225-2514.

39 SOUTH COW CREEK MEADOWS

♿🐕♿5%🚐⛺

Scenic rating: 6

in Latour Demonstration State Forest

Map 3.3, page 205

This camp is set in a pretty, wooded area next to a small meadow along South Cow Creek. It's mostly used in the fall for hunting, with off-highway-vehicle use on the surrounding roads in the summer. The camp is set at 5,600 feet. If you want to get away from it all without leaving your vehicle, this is one way to do it. The creek is a reliable water source providing you use a water filtration pump.

Campsites, facilities: There are two sites for tents or RVs up to 30 feet (no hookups). Picnic tables and fire grills are provided. Vault toilets and drinking water are available. Garbage must be packed out. Some facilities are wheelchair-accessible. Leashed pets are permitted. **Reservations, fees:** Reservations are not accepted. There is no fee for camping. Open June through October, weather permitting. **Directions:** In Redding, turn east on Highway 44 and drive about 9.5 miles to Millville Road. Turn left on Millville Road and drive 0.5 mile to the intersection of Millville Road and Whitmore Road. Turn right on Whitmore Road and drive 13 miles, through Whitmore, until Whitmore Road becomes Tamarac Road. Continue for one mile to the fork at Bateman Road. Take the right fork on Bateman Road, drive 3.5 miles (where the road turns to gravel), and then continue for 11 miles to South Cow Creek Road. Turn right (east) and drive one mile to the campground. **Contact:** Latour Demonstration State Forest, 530/225-2438, fax 530/225-2514.

40 BRIDGE CAMP
🏕 🛶 🐕 🏞 🏕

Scenic rating: 7

on Hat Creek in Lassen National Forest

Map 3.3, page 205

This camp is one of four along Highway 89 in the area along Hat Creek. It is set at 4,000 feet elevation, with shaded sites and the stream within very short walking distance. Trout are stocked on this stretch of the creek, with fishing access available out of camp, as well as at Rocky and Cave Camps to the south and Honn to the north. In one weekend, anglers might hit all four. **Campsites, facilities:** There are 25 sites for tents or RVs up to 22 feet (no hookups). Picnic tables and fire grills are provided. There is no drinking water. Vault toilets are available. A grocery store and propane gas are available nearby. Leashed pets are permitted.

Reservations, fees: Reservations are not accepted. Sites are $10 per night, $5 per night for each additional vehicle. Open late April through October, weather permitting. **Directions:** From Redding, drive east on Highway 299 to Burney and continue for five miles to the junction with Highway 89. Turn right (south) on Highway 89 and drive 19 miles to the campground entrance on the right side of the road. If you reach Old Station, you have gone five miles too far. **Contact:** Lassen National Forest, Hat Creek Ranger District, 530/336-5521, fax 530/336-5758; Department of Fish and Game fishing information, 530/225-2146.

41 ROCKY CAMP
🏕 🛶 🐕 🏕

Scenic rating: 7

on Hat Creek in Lassen National Forest

Map 3.3, page 205

This is a small, primitive camp along Hat Creek on Highway 89. It's usually a second choice for campers if nearby Cave and Bridge Camps are full. Streamside fishing access is a plus here, with this section of stream stocked with rainbow trout. The elevation is 4,000 feet. (See *Cave Camp*, next listing, for more information.) **Campsites, facilities:** There are eight tent sites. Picnic tables and fire grills are provided. Vault toilets are available. No drinking water is available. A grocery store and propane gas are available nearby. Leashed pets are permitted. **Reservations, fees:** Reservations are not accepted. Sites are $10 per night, $5 per night for each additional vehicle. Open late April through October, weather permitting. **Directions:** From Redding, drive east on Highway 299 to Burney and continue for five miles to the junction with Highway 89. Turn right (south) on Highway 89 and drive 20 miles to the campground entrance on the right side of the road. If you reach Old Station, you have gone four miles too far.

Contact: Lassen National Forest, Hat Creek Ranger District, 530/336-5521, fax 530/336-5758; Department of Fish and Game fishing information, 530/225-2146.

42 CAVE CAMP

Scenic rating: 7

on Hat Creek in Lassen National Forest

Map 3.3, page 205

Cave Camp is set right along Hat Creek, with easy access off Highway 89 and an anglers' trail available along the stream. This stretch of Hat Creek is planted with rainbow trout twice per month by the Department of Fish and Game, starting with the opening of trout season on the last Saturday of April. Nearby side trips include Lassen Volcanic National Park, about a 15-minute drive to the south on Highway 89, and Subway Caves (turn left at the junction just across the road from the campground). A rare bonus at this camp is that wheelchair-accessible fishing is available.

Campsites, facilities: There are 46 sites for tents or RVs up to 22 feet (no hookups). Picnic tables and fire grills are provided. Drinking water and flush and vault toilets are available. Some facilities are wheelchair-accessible. Supplies can be obtained in Old Station. Leashed pets are permitted.

Reservations, fees: Reservations are not accepted. Sites are $16 per night, $5 per night for each additional vehicle. Open late April through October, weather permitting.

Directions: From Redding, drive east on Highway 299 to Burney and continue for five miles to the junction with Highway 89. Turn right (south) on Highway 89 and drive 23 miles to the campground entrance on the right side of the road. If you reach Old Station, you have gone one mile too far.

Contact: Lassen National Forest, Hat Creek Ranger District, 530/336-5521, fax 530/336-5758; Department of Fish and Game fishing information, 530/225-2146.

43 HAT CREEK

Scenic rating: 7

on Hat Creek in Lassen National Forest

Map 3.3, page 205

This is one in a series of Forest Service camps set beside beautiful Hat Creek, a good trout stream stocked regularly by the Department of Fish and Game. The elevation is 4,300 feet. The proximity to Lassen Volcanic National Park to the south is a big plus. Supplies are available in the little town of Old Station one mile to the north.

Campsites, facilities: There are 75 sites for tents or RVs up to 30 feet, and three group camps for tents or RVs up to 30 feet that can accommodate up to 50 people each. No hookups. Picnic tables and fire grills are provided. Drinking water and vault toilets are available. A grocery store, dump station, coin laundry, and propane gas are available nearby. Leashed pets are permitted.

Reservations, fees: Reservations are accepted for individual sites and required ($9 reservation fee) for group camps at 877/444-6777 or www.ReserveUSA.com. Sites are $17 per night, $5 per night for each additional vehicle, $85 per night for group camps. Open late April through October, weather permitting.

Directions: From Redding, drive east on Highway 44 to the junction with Highway 89 (near the entrance to Lassen Volcanic National Park). Turn left (north) on Highway 89 and drive about 12 miles to the campground entrance on the left side of the road. Turn left and drive a short distance to the campground.

Contact: Lassen National Forest, Hat Creek Ranger District, 530/336-5521, fax 530/336-5758; Department of Fish and Game fishing information, 530/225-2146.

44 NORTH BATTLE CREEK RESERVOIR

Scenic rating: 7

on Battle Creek Reservoir

Map 3.3, page 205

This little-known lake is at 5,600 feet in elevation, largely surrounded by Lassen National Forest. No gas engines are permitted on the lake, making it ideal for canoes, rafts, and car-top aluminum boats equipped with electric motors. When the lake level is up in early summer, it is a pretty setting with good trout fishing.

Campsites, facilities: There are 10 sites for tents or RVs up to 30 feet (no hookups) and five walk-in tent sites. Picnic tables and fire grills are provided. Drinking water and vault toilets are available. A car-top boat launch is available nearby. Leashed pets are permitted.

Reservations, fees: Reservations are not accepted. Sites are $13 per night, $3 per night for each additional vehicle, $1 per pet per night. Open mid-May to mid-September, weather permitting.

Directions: From Redding, drive east on Highway 44 to Viola. From Viola, continue east for 3.5 miles to Forest Road 32N17. Turn left on Forest Road 32N17 and drive five miles to Forest Road 32N31. Turn left and drive four miles to Forest Road 32N18. Turn right and drive 0.5 mile to the reservoir and the campground on the right side of the road.

Contact: PG&E Land Projects, 916/386-5164, www.pge.com/recreation.

45 BIG PINE CAMP

Scenic rating: 7

on Hat Creek in Lassen National Forest

Map 3.3, page 205

This campground is set on the headwaters of Hat Creek, a pretty spot amid ponderosa pines.

The elevation is 4,500 feet. A dirt road out of camp parallels Hat Creek, providing access for trout fishing. A great vista point is set on the highway, a mile south of the campground entrance road. It is only a 10-minute drive south to the Highway 44 entrance station for Lassen Volcanic National Park.

Campsites, facilities: There are 19 sites for tents or RVs up to 22 feet (no hookups). Picnic tables and fire grills are provided. Drinking water (at two hand pumps) and vault toilets are available. A dump station, grocery store, and propane gas are available nearby. Leashed pets are permitted.

Reservations, fees: Reservations are not accepted. Sites are $12 per night, $5 per night for each additional vehicle. Open late April through October, weather permitting.

Directions: From Redding, drive east on Highway 44 to the junction with Highway 89 (near the entrance to Lassen Volcanic National Park). Turn left (north) on Highway 89 and drive about eight miles (one mile past the vista point) to the campground entrance on the right side of the road. Turn right and drive 0.5 mile to the campground.

Contact: Lassen National Forest, Hat Creek Ranger District, 530/336-5521, fax 530/336-5758; Department of Fish and Game fishing information, 530/225-2146.

46 BUTTE CREEK

Scenic rating: 6

in Lassen National Forest

Map 3.3, page 205

This primitive, little-known spot is just three miles from the northern boundary of Lassen Volcanic National Park, set on little Butte Creek. The elevation is 5,600 feet. It is a four-mile drive south out of camp on Forest Road 18 to Butte Lake in Lassen Park and to the trailhead for a great hike up to the Cinder Cone (6,907 feet), with dramatic views of the Lassen wilderness.

Campsites, facilities: There are 20 sites for

tents or RVs up to 22 feet (no hookups). Vault toilets are available. No drinking water is available. Garbage must be packed out. Leashed pets are permitted.

Reservations, fees: Reservations are not accepted. There is no fee for camping. Open May through October, weather permitting.

Directions: From Redding, drive east on Highway 44 to the junction with Highway 89 (near the entrance to Lassen Volcanic National Park). Turn north on Highway 89 and drive to Highway 44. Turn east (right) on Highway 44 and drive 11 miles to Forest Road 18. Turn right at Forest Road 18 and drive three miles to the campground on the left side of the road.

Contact: Lassen National Forest, Eagle Lake Ranger District, 530/257-4188, fax 530/252-5803.

47 BOGARD
🏕️ 🛶 🐕 🚐 ⛺

Scenic rating: 6

in Lassen National Forest

Map 3.3, page 205

This little camp is set along Pine Creek, which flows through Pine Creek Valley at the foot of the Bogard Buttes. It is a relatively obscure camp that gets missed by many travelers. A bonus here are the beautiful aspens, breathtaking in fall. To the nearby west is a network of Forest Service roads, and beyond is the Caribou Wilderness.

Campsites, facilities: There are 11 sites for tents or RVs up to 25 feet (no hookups). Picnic tables and fire grills are provided. Drinking water and vault toilets are available. Leashed pets are permitted.

Reservations, fees: Reservations are not accepted. Sites are $13 per night. Open May through October, weather permitting.

Directions: From Redding, drive east on Highway 44 to the junction with Highway 89 (near the entrance to Lassen Volcanic National Park). Turn north on Highway 89 and drive to Highway 44. Turn east on Highway 44 and drive to the Bogard Work Center (about

seven miles past Poison Lake) and the adjacent rest stop. Continue east on Highway 44 for two miles to a gravel road on the right side of the road (Forest Road 31N26). Turn right on Forest Road 31N26 and drive two miles. Turn right on Forest Road 31N21 and drive 0.5 mile to the campground at the end of the road.

Contact: Lassen National Forest, Eagle Lake Ranger District, 530/257-4188, fax 530/252-5803.

48 CRATER LAKE
🏕️ 🛶 🐕 🚐 🏇 5% ⛺

Scenic rating: 8

in Lassen National Forest

Map 3.3, page 205

This hideaway is set near Crater Lake at 6,800 feet in remote Lassen National Forest, just below Crater Mountain (that's it up there to the northeast at 7,420 feet). This 27-acre lake provides trout fishing, boating, and, if you can stand the ice-cold water, a quick dunk on warm summer days.

Campsites, facilities: There are 17 sites for tents. Picnic tables and fire grills are provided. Drinking water and vault toilets are available. No gas motors are allowed on the lake. Leashed pets are permitted.

Reservations, fees: Reservations are not accepted. Sites are $13 per night. Open June through October, weather permitting.

Directions: From Redding, drive east on Highway 44 to the junction with Highway 89 (near the entrance to Lassen Volcanic National Park). Turn north on Highway 89 and drive to Highway 44. Turn east on Highway 44 (right) and drive to the Bogard Work Center and adjacent rest stop. Turn left at Forest Road 32N08 (signed Crater Lake) and drive one mile to a T intersection. Bear right and continue on Forest Road 32N08 for six miles (including two hairpin left turns) to the campground on the left side of the road. Note: Forest Road 32N08 is a rough washboard road.

Contact: Lassen National Forest, Eagle

Lake Ranger District, 530/257-4188, fax 530/252-5803.

49 MacCUMBER RESERVOIR

🏊 🚣 ⛴ 🐕 🚐 ⛺

Scenic rating: 7

on MacCumber Reservoir

Map 3.3, page 205

Here's a small lake, easy to reach from Redding, that is little known and rarely visited. MacCumber Reservoir is set at 3,500 feet and is stocked with rainbow trout each year, providing fair fishing. No gas motors are permitted here. That's fine—it guarantees quiet, calm water, ideal for car-top boats: prams, canoes, rafts, and small aluminum boats.

Campsites, facilities: There are seven sites for tents or RVs up to 30 feet (no hookups) and five walk-in tent sites. Picnic tables and fire grills are provided. Drinking water and vault toilets are available. Leashed pets are permitted.

Reservations, fees: Reservations are not accepted. Sites are $13 per night, $3 per night for each additional vehicle, $1 per pet per night. Open mid-April to mid-September, weather permitting.

Directions: In Redding, turn east on Highway 44 and drive toward Viola to Lake MacCumber Road (if you reach Viola, you have gone four miles too far). Turn left at Lake MacCumber Road and drive two miles to the reservoir and campground.

Contact: PG&E Land Projects, 916/386-5164, fax 916/923-7044, www.pge.com/recreation.

50 MANZANITA LAKE

🥾 🏊 🚣 ⛴ 🏕 ♿ 🚐 ⛺

Scenic rating: 9

in Lassen Volcanic National Park

Map 3.3, page 205

Manzanita Lake, set at 5,890 feet, is one of the prettiest lakes in Lassen Volcanic National Park and it has good catch-and-release trout fishing for experienced fly fishers in prams and other nonpowered boats. This is no place for a dad, mom, and a youngster to fish from shore with Power Bait because of the fishing regulations. Swimming is permitted, but there are few takers. Because of the great natural beauty of the lake, the campground is often crowded. Evening walks around the lake are beautiful. A museum, visitors center, and small store are available nearby. Ranger programs are offered in the summer.

Campsites, facilities: There are 179 sites for tents or RVs up to 35 feet (no hookups). Picnic tables, fire grills, and bearproof food lockers are provided. Drinking water and flush toilets are available. Propane gas, groceries, coin showers, a dump station, and a coin laundry are available nearby. A boat launch is also nearby (no motors are permitted on boats at Manzanita Lake). Some facilities are wheelchair-accessible. Leashed pets are permitted at campsites only.

Reservations, fees: Reservations are accepted ($9 reservation fee) at 877/444-6777 or www.ReserveUSA.com. Sites are $16 per night, $10 per vehicle park entrance fee. Some credit cards accepted. Open late May to late September, weather permitting (during the fall, it's open without drinking water until the camp is closed by snow).

Directions: From Redding, drive east on Highway 44 to the junction with Highway 89. Turn right (south) on Highway 89 and drive one mile to the entrance station to Lassen Volcanic National Park (the state highway becomes Lassen Park Highway/Main Park Road). Continue a short distance on Lassen Park Highway/Main Park Road to the campground entrance road. Turn right and drive 0.5 mile to the campground.

Contact: Lassen Volcanic National Park, 530/595-4444, fax 530/595-3262, www.nps.gov/lavo.

51 CRAGS

Scenic rating: 8

in Lassen Volcanic National Park

Map 3.3, page 205

Crags is sometimes overlooked as a prime spot at Lassen Volcanic National Park because there is no lake nearby. No problem, because even though this campground is small compared to the giant complex at Manzanita Lake, the campsites are more spacious, do not fill up as quickly, and many are backed by forest. In addition, Emigrant Trail runs out of camp, routing east and meeting pretty Lost Creek after a little more than a mile, a great short hike. Directly across from Crags are the towering Chaos Crags, topping out at 8,503 feet. The elevation here is 5,720 feet.

Campsites, facilities: There are 45 sites for tents or RVs up to 35 feet (no hookups). Picnic tables, fire rings, and bearproof food lockers are provided. Drinking water and vault toilets are available. Leashed pets are permitted in campground and on paved roads only.

Reservations, fees: Reservations are not accepted. Sites are $11 per night, $10 per vehicle park entrance fee. Open late June to early September.

Directions: From Redding, drive east on Highway 44 for 42 miles to the junction with Highway 89. Turn right and drive one mile to the entrance station at Lassen Volcanic National Park (the state highway becomes Lassen Park Highway/Main Park Road). Continue on Lassen Park Highway/Main Park Road for about five miles to the campground on the left side of the road.

Contact: Lassen Volcanic National Park, 530/595-4444, fax 530/595-3262, www.nps.gov/lavo.

52 BUTTE LAKE

Scenic rating: 9

in Lassen Volcanic National Park

Map 3.3, page 205

Butte Lake campground is situated in an open, volcanic setting with a sprinkling of lodgepole pine. The contrast of the volcanics against the emerald greens of the lake is beautiful and memorable. Cinder Cone Trail can provide an even better look. The trailhead is near the boat launch area, and it's a strenuous hike involving a climb of 800 feet over the course of two miles to the top of the Cinder Cone. The footing is often loose because of volcanic pebbles. At the rim, you can peer inside the Cinder Cone, as well as be rewarded with lake views and a long-distance vista. Trout fishing is poor at Butte Lake, as at nearly all the lakes at this national park, because trout have not been planted for years. The elevation is 6,100 feet, and the lake covers 212 acres.

Campsites, facilities: There are 101 sites for tents or RVs up to 35 feet (no hookups), one equestrian site, and six group tent sites that can accommodate 10–25 people each. Some sites are pull-through. Picnic tables, fire rings, and bearproof food lockers are provided. Drinking water and flush and vault toilets are available. A boat ramp is nearby. No motors are permitted on the lake. Some facilities are wheelchair-accessible. Leashed pets are permitted at campsites only.

Reservations, fees: Reservations are accepted for individual sites ($9 reservation fee) at 877/444-6777 or www.ReserveUSA.com. Reservations are required for equestrian and group sites at 530/335-7029. Sites are $14 per night, equestrian sites are $14 per night plus $4 per horse per night, group sites are $50 per night, $10 park entrance fee per vehicle. Open mid-June to mid-September, weather permitting.

Directions: From Redding, drive east on Highway 44 to the junction with Highway 89. Bear north on Highway 89/44 and drive

13 miles to Old Station. Just past Old Station, turn right (east) on Highway 44 and drive 10 miles to Forest Road 32N21/Butte Lake Road. Turn right and drive six miles to the campground.

Contact: Lassen Volcanic National Park, 530/595-4444, fax 530/595-3262, www .nps.gov/lavo.

53 MOUNT LASSEN/ SHINGLETOWN KOA

🚶 🏊 🎣 🐕 🐎 🚐 ⛺

Scenic rating: 6

near Lassen Volcanic National Park

Map 3.3, page 205

This popular KOA camp is 14 miles from the entrance of Lassen Volcanic National Park and has pretty, wooded sites. Location is always the critical factor on vacations, and this park is set up perfectly for launching trips to the nearby east. Hat Creek provides trout fishing along Highway 89, and just inside the Highway 44 entrance station at Lassen Park is Manzanita Lake, providing good fishing and hiking.

Campsites, facilities: There are 46 sites with full or partial hookups (30 and 50 amps) for tents or RVs up to 40 feet, including some pull-through sites, and five cabins. Picnic tables and fire grills are provided. Restroom with flush toilets and showers, playground, heated pool (summer only), dump station, convenience store, ice, firewood, coin laundry, video arcade and recreation room, dog run, and propane gas are available. Leashed pets are permitted.

Reservations, fees: Reservations are accepted with a deposit at 800/562-3403. Sites are $25–45 per night, $3–5 per person per night for more than two people. Some credit cards accepted. Open mid-March through November.

Directions: From Redding, turn east on Highway 44 and drive to Shingletown. In Shingletown, continue east for four miles

and look for the park entrance on the right (signed KOA).

Contact: Mount Lassen/Shingletown KOA, 530/474-3133, www.koa.com.

54 SUMMIT LAKE: NORTH, SOUTH, AND EQUESTRIAN

🚶 🏊 🎣 🚣 🚐 🐎 ♿ 🚙 ⛺

Scenic rating: 9

in Lassen Volcanic National Park

Map 3.3, page 205   **BEST (**

Summit Lake is a beautiful spot where deer often visit in the evening on the adjacent meadow just east of the campground. The lake is small, just 15 acres, and since trout plants were suspended it has been just about fished out. Summit Lake is the most popular lake for swimming in the park. Evening walks around the lake are perfect for families. A more ambitious trail is routed out of camp and leads past lavish wildflower displays in early summer to a series of wilderness lakes. The campgrounds are set at an elevation of 6,695 feet.

Campsites, facilities: There are 46 sites for tents or RVs up to 35 feet at North Summit, 48 sites for tents or RVs up to 30 feet at South Summit, and one equestrian site for tents or RVs up to 35 feet that can accommodate up to 10 people and eight horses. No hookups. Picnic tables, fire rings, and bearproof food lockers are provided. Drinking water and toilets (flush toilets on the north side, pit toilets on the south side, and vault toilets at the equestrian site) are available. Some facilities are wheelchair-accessible. Ranger programs are sometimes available in summer. Leashed pets are permitted at campsites only.

Reservations, fees: Reservations are accepted ($9 reservation fee) for individual sites at 877/444-6777 or www.ReserveUSA.com. Reservations are required for equestrian sites at 530/335-7029. Sites are $14 (South) to $16 (North) per night, $14 per night plus $4 per horse per night at the equestrian site, $10 park entrance fee per vehicle. Some credit cards accepted. Open late June to mid-September, weather permitting.

Directions: From Redding, drive east on Highway 44 to the junction with Highway 89. Turn south on Highway 89 and drive one mile to the entrance station to Lassen Volcanic National Park (where the state highway becomes Lassen Park Highway/Main Park Road). Continue on Lassen Park Highway/Main Park Road for 12 miles to the campground entrance on the left side of the road. The horse camp is located across the street from the other campsites.

Contact: Lassen Volcanic National Park, 530/595-4444, fax 530/595-3262, www.nps.gov/lavo.

55 SILVER BOWL
🏕🚣🛶🚐🐴🚗🏕

Scenic rating: 7

on Silver Lake in Lassen National Forest

Map 3.3, page 205

Silver Lake is a pretty lake set at 6,400 feet elevation at the edge of the Caribou Wilderness. There is an unimproved boat ramp at the southern end of the lake. It is occasionally planted by the Department of Fish and Game with Eagle Lake trout and brown trout, which provide a summer fishery for campers. A trailhead from adjacent Caribou Lake is routed west into the wilderness, with routes available both to Emerald Lake to the northwest, and Betty, Trail, and Shotoverin Lakes nearby to the southeast.

Campsites, facilities: There are 18 sites for tents or RVs up to 25 feet (no hookups). Picnic tables and fire grills are provided. Drinking water and vault toilets are available. Leashed pets are permitted.

Reservations, fees: Reservations are not accepted. Sites are $12 per night, $5 per night for each additional vehicle. Open late May through October, weather permitting.

Directions: From Red Bluff, drive east on Highway 36 to the junction with Highway

89. Continue east on Highway 36 past Lake Almanor to Westwood. In Westwood, turn left on County Road A21 and drive 12.5 miles to Silver Lake Road. Turn left on Silver Lake Road/County Road 110 and drive 8.5 miles north to Silver Lake. At Silver Lake, turn right and drive 0.75 mile to the campground.

Contact: Lassen National Forest, Almanor Ranger District, 530/258-2141, fax 530/258-5194.

56 ROCKY KNOLL
🏕🚣🛶🚐🐴🚗🏕

Scenic rating: 7

on Silver Lake in Lassen National Forest

Map 3.3, page 205

This is one of two camps at pretty Silver Lake, set at 6,400 feet elevation at the edge of the Caribou Wilderness. The other camp is Silver Bowl to the nearby north, which is larger and provides better access for hikers. This camp, however, is closer to the boat ramp, which is set at the south end of the lake. Silver Lake provides a good summer fishery for campers.

Campsites, facilities: There are 18 sites for tents or RVs up to 27 feet (no hookups). Picnic tables and fire grills are provided. Drinking water and vault toilets are available. Leashed pets are permitted.

Reservations, fees: Reservations are not accepted. Sites are $12 per night, $5 per night for each additional vehicle. Open late May to early November, weather permitting.

Directions: From Red Bluff, drive east on Highway 36 to the junction with Highway 89. Continue east on Highway 36 past Lake Almanor to Westwood. In Westwood, turn left on County Road A21 and drive 12.5 miles to Silver Lake Road. Turn left (west) on Silver Lake Road/County Road 110 and drive 8.5 miles to Silver Lake. At Silver Lake, turn left and drive 300 yards to the campground.

Contact: Lassen National Forest, Almanor Ranger District, 530/258-2141, fax 530/258-5194.

57 SOUTHWEST WALK-IN
🚶 🏕 🚐 ⛺

Scenic rating: 8

in Lassen Volcanic National Park

Map 3.3, page 205

Just taking the short walk required to reach this camp will launch you into an orbit beyond most of the highway cruisers visiting Lassen. In addition, the nearby trail to Bumpass Hell will put you into a different universe. The trail is about seven miles north of the campground on the Lassen Park Highway/Main Park Road on the right side of the road. The route will take you past steam vents and boiling mud pots, all set in prehistoric-looking volcanic rock. The 4.6-mile hike to Mill Creek Falls, the park's highest waterfall, begins at the campground. The Sulphur Works and Brokeoff Mountain trailheads are nearby. A visitors center also is nearby. Ranger-led programs are sometimes available. The elevation at the campground is 6,700 feet.

Campsites, facilities: There are 21 walk-in tent sites, and a large parking lot available for RVs of any length (no hookups). Picnic tables, fire rings, and bearproof food lockers are provided. Drinking water and restrooms with flush toilets are available in summer. Leashed pets are permitted in campground only.

Reservations, fees: Reservations are not accepted. Sites are $14 per night for tent campers, $10 per night for RV parking, plus $10 per vehicle park entrance fee. Open year-round, weather permitting.

Directions: From Red Bluff, take Highway 36 east for 48 miles to the junction with Highway 89. Turn left on Highway 89 (becomes Lassen Park Highway/Main Park Road) and drive to the park's entrance. Just after passing through the park entrance gate, look for the camp parking area on the right side of the road.

Contact: Lassen Volcanic National Park, 530/595-4444, fax 530/595-3262, www.nps.gov/lavo.

58 WARNER VALLEY
🚶 🛶 🏕 ♿ ⛺

Scenic rating: 9

on Hot Springs Creek in Lassen Volcanic National Park

Map 3.3, page 205

Lassen is one of the great national parks of the West, yet it gets surprisingly little use compared to Yosemite, Sequoia, and Kings Canyon National Parks. This campground gets overlooked because of its remote access out of Chester. The camp is set along Hot Springs Creek at 5,650 feet. The best hike here is the 2.5-mile walk out to the unique Devil's Kitchen geothermal area. Other options here are a 2.5-mile hike, with an 800-foot climb, to Drake Lake and a three-mile hike to Boiling Springs Lakes. It's also a good horseback-riding area. The Drakesbad Resort, where securing reservations is about as difficult as finding Bigfoot, is near the campground.

Campsites, facilities: There are 18 tent sites. RVs and trailers are not recommended because of road conditions. Picnic tables, food lockers, and fire rings are provided. Drinking water and pit toilets are available. Leashed pets are permitted in the campground only.

Reservations, fees: Reservations are not accepted. Sites are $14 per night, $10 per vehicle park entrance fee. Open June to late September, weather permitting, with no water from mid-September to snow closure.

Directions: From Red Bluff, take Highway 36 east for 44 miles to the junction with Highway 89 (do not turn left, or north, on Highway 89 to Lassen Volcanic National Park entrance, as signed). Continue east on Highway 36/89 to Chester and Feather River Drive. Turn left (north) on Feather River Drive (Warner Valley Road) and drive 0.75 mile to County Road 312. Bear left and drive six miles to Warner Valley Road. Turn right and drive 11 miles to the campground on the right. Note: The last 3.5 miles is unpaved and there is one steep hill that can be difficult to climb for large or underpowered RVs, or if you are towing a trailer.

Contact: Lassen Volcanic National Park, 530/595-4444, fax 530/595-3262, www .nps.gov/lavo.

59 JUNIPER LAKE
🏃 🛶 🎣 🐕 🏕 ⛺

Scenic rating: 10

in Lassen Volcanic National Park

Map 3.3, page 205

This pretty spot is on the eastern shore of Juniper Lake, at an elevation of 6,792 feet. It is far distant from the busy Lassen Park Highway/Main Park Road (Highway 89) corridor that is routed through central Lassen Volcanic National Park. From the north end of the lake, a great side trip is to make the half-mile, 400-foot climb to Inspiration Point, which provides a panoramic view of the park's backcountry. A two-mile hike up Mount Harkness begins from camp. Since no drinking water is provided, it is critical to bring a water purification pump or plenty of bottled water.

Campsites, facilities: There are 18 tent sites, an equestrian site, and two group tent sites that can accommodate 10–15 people each. No hookups. Picnic tables, fire rings, and bearproof food lockers are provided. Vault toilets are available. Drinking water is not available. Leashed pets are permitted in the campground only.

Reservations, fees: Reservations are not accepted for individual sites. Reservations are required for the group sites and the equestrian site at 530/335-7029. Sites are $10 per night, $30 per night for group sites, $10 per night for the equestrian site plus $4 per horse per night, $10 park entrance fee per vehicle. Open late June to late September, weather permitting.

Directions: From Red Bluff, take Highway 36 east for 44 miles to the junction with Highway 89 (do not turn left, or north, on Highway 89 to Lassen Volcanic National Park entrance,

as signed). Continue east on Highway 36/89 to Chester and Feather River Drive. Turn left (north) on Feather River Drive and drive 0.75 mile to the Y and the junction for County Road 318. Bear right (marked for Juniper Lake) on County Road 318 and drive 11 miles to the campground on the right, set along the east side of the lake. Note: This is a very rough dirt road; RVs and trailers are not recommended.

Contact: Lassen Volcanic National Park, 530/595-4444, fax 530/595-3262, www .nps.gov/lavo.

60 BATTLE CREEK
🏃 🎣 🐕 🚐 ⛺

Scenic rating: 7

on Battle Creek in Lassen National Forest

Map 3.3, page 205

This pretty spot offers easy access and streamside camping along Battle Creek. The trout fishing can be good in May, June, and early July, when the creek is stocked with trout by the Department of Fish and Game. Many people drive right by without knowing there is a stream here and that the fishing can be good. The elevation is 4,800 feet.

Campsites, facilities: There are 50 sites for tents or RVs up to 30 feet (no hookups). Picnic tables and fire grills are provided. Drinking water, flush and vault toilets, and a day-use picnic area are available. Supplies can be obtained in the town of Mineral. Leashed pets are permitted.

Reservations, fees: Reservations are not accepted. Sites are $18 per night, $5 per night for each additional vehicle. Open late April to early November, weather permitting.

Directions: From Red Bluff, turn east on Highway 36 and drive 39 miles to the campground (if you reach Mineral, you have gone two miles too far).

Contact: Lassen National Forest, Almanor Ranger District, 530/258-2141, fax 530/258 5194; Department of Fish and Game fishing information, 530/225-2146.

61 CHILDS MEADOW RESORT
🥾 🛶 🐕 🚐 ⛺

Scenic rating: 7

near Mill Creek

Map 3.3, page 205

Childs Meadow Resort is an 18-acre resort set at 5,000 feet elevation. It features many recreation options, including catch-and-release fishing one mile away at Mill Creek. There are also a number of trails nearby for horseback riding. The trailhead for Spencer Meadow Trail is just east of the resort along Highway 36. The trail provides a 12-mile route (one-way) to Spencer Meadow and an effervescent spring that is the source of Mill Creek.

Campsites, facilities: There are eight tent sites and 24 sites with full hookups (50 amps) for RVs of any length; most are pull-through. Cabins, park-model cabins, and a motel are also available. Picnic tables and fire rings are provided. Drinking water and restrooms with flush toilets and showers are available. A coin laundry, store, restaurant, group picnic area, meeting room, and horseshoes are on-site. Groups can be accommodated. Leashed pets are permitted.

Reservations, fees: Reservations are accepted at 888/595-3383. Sites are $15–25 per night, $5 per pet per night. Some credit cards accepted. Open mid-May through October, weather permitting.

Directions: From Red Bluff, drive east on Highway 36 for 43 miles to the town of Mineral. Continue east on Highway 36 for 10 miles to the resort on the left.

Contact: Childs Meadow Resort, 530/595-3383, www.childsmeadowresort.com.

62 DOMINGO SPRINGS
🥾 🛶 🐕 🚐 ⛺

Scenic rating: 7

in Lassen National Forest

Map 3.3, page 205

This camp is named after a spring adjacent to the site. It is a small fountain that pours into the headwaters of the North Fork Feather River, a good trout stream. The Pacific Crest Trail is routed from this camp north for four miles to Little Willow Lake and the southern border of Lassen Volcanic National Park. The elevation is 5,060 feet.

Campsites, facilities: There are 18 sites for tents or RVs up to 27 feet (no hookups). Picnic tables and fire grills are provided. Drinking water and vault toilets are available. Leashed pets are permitted.

Reservations, fees: Reservations are not accepted. Sites are $14 per night, $5 per night for each additional vehicle. Open late May to early November, weather permitting.

Directions: From Red Bluff, take Highway 36 east to Chester and Feather River Drive. Turn left on Feather River Drive and drive 0.75 mile to County Road 312. Bear left and drive five miles to the Y with County Road 311 and County Road 312. Bear left on County Road 311 and drive two miles to the campground entrance road on the left.

Contact: Lassen National Forest, Almanor Ranger District, 530/258-2141, fax 530/258-5194.

63 HIGH BRIDGE
🥾 🛶 🐕 🚐 ⛺

Scenic rating: 8

on the North Fork of the Feather River in Lassen National Forest

Map 3.3, page 205

This camp is set at an elevation of 5,200 feet, near where the South Cascades meets the North Sierra, and is ideal for many people. The result is that it is often full in July and August. The payoff includes a pretty, adjacent trout stream, the headwaters of the North Fork Feather. Trout fishing is often good here, including some rare large brown trout, a surprise considering the relatively small size of the stream. Nearby access to the Warner Valley/Drakesbad entrance of Lassen Volcanic National Park provides a must-do side trip. The area is wooded and the road dusty.

Campsites, facilities: There are 12 sites for tents or RVs up to 27 feet (no hookups). Picnic tables and fire grills are provided. Drinking water and vault toilets are available. Groceries and propane gas are available in Chester. Leashed pets are permitted.

Reservations, fees: Reservations are not accepted. Sites are $14 per night, $5 per night for each additional vehicle. Open late May to early November, weather permitting.

Directions: From Red Bluff, take Highway 36 east to Chester and Feather River Drive. Turn left on Feather River Drive and drive 0.75 mile to County Road 312. Bear left and drive five miles to the campground entrance road on the left.

Contact: Lassen National Forest, Almanor Ranger District, 530/258-2141, fax 530/258-5194; Department of Fish and Game fishing information, 530/225-2146.

64 HOLE-IN-THE-GROUND

🧍‍♂️ 🎣 🐕 🚐 ⛺

Scenic rating: 8

on Mill Creek in Lassen National Forest

Map 3.3, page 205

This is one of two campgrounds set along Mill Creek at 4,300 feet. Take your pick. The highlight here is a trail that follows along Mill Creek for many miles; it provides good fishing access. Rules mandate the use of artificials with a single barbless hook, and catch-and-release; check current fishing regulations. The result is a challenging but quality wild-trout fishery. Another option is to drive 0.5 mile to the end of the Forest Service road, where there is a parking area for a trail that is routed downstream along Mill Creek and into a state game refuge. To keep things easy, obtain a map of Lassen National Forest that details the recreational opportunities.

Campsites, facilities: There are 13 sites for tents or RVs up to 24 feet (no hookups). Picnic

tables and fire grills are provided. Drinking water and vault toilets are available. Supplies are available in Mineral. Leashed pets are permitted.

Reservations, fees: Reservations are not accepted. Sites are $12 per night, $5 per night for each additional vehicle. Open late April to early November, weather permitting.

Directions: From Red Bluff, drive 43 miles east on Highway 36 to the town of Mineral and the junction with Highway 172. Turn right on Highway 172 and drive six miles to the town of Mill Creek. In Mill Creek, turn south onto Forest Road 28N06 (signed) and drive five miles to the campground access road. Turn left and drive 0.25 mile to the camp.

Contact: Lassen National Forest, Almanor Ranger District, 530/258-2141, fax 530/258-5194.

65 MILL CREEK RESORT

🧍‍♂️ 🎣 🐕 🛶 ♿ 🚐 ⛺

Scenic rating: 7

on Mill Creek near Lassen National Forest

Map 3.3, page 205

This is a great area, surrounded by Lassen National Forest and within close range of the southern Highway 89 entrance to Lassen Volcanic National Park. It is set at 4,800 feet along oft-bypassed Highway 172. A highlight here is Mill Creek (to reach it, turn south on the Forest Service road in town and drive to a parking area at the end of the road along the stream), where there is a great easy walk along the stream and fair trout fishing. Note that about half the campsites are taken by long-term renters.

Campsites, facilities: There are 14 sites for tents or RVs up to 35 feet, eight with full hookups (30 amps). Nine one- and two-bedroom cabins are also available. Picnic tables and fire rings are provided. Drinking water, vault toilets, seasonal showers, coin laundry, playground, a small grocery store, and a restaurant are also available. Some facilities are wheelchair-accessible. Leashed pets are permitted.

Reservations, fees: Reservations are accepted. Sites are $15–25 per night. Campsites are open May through October. Cabins are available year-round.

Directions: From Red Bluff, drive 43 miles east on Highway 36 to the town of Mineral and the junction with Highway 172. Turn right and drive six miles to the town of Mill Creek. In Mill Creek, look for the sign for Mill Creek Resort on the right side of the road.

Contact: Mill Creek Resort, 530/595-4449 or 888/595-4449, www.millcreekresort.net.

66 GURNSEY CREEK GROUP CAMP
🧍🏊🐕🚐⛺

Scenic rating: 7

in Lassen National Forest

Map 3.3, page 205

This group camp is an ideal spot for a Scout troop. (See next listing, *Gurnsey Creek,* for more information.)

Campsites, facilities: There is one group camp for tents or RVs up to 30 feet (no hookups) that can accommodate up to 20 people. Picnic tables and fire grills are provided. Drinking water and vault toilets are available. A large community fireplace is centrally situated for group use. Supplies are available in Mineral or Chester. Leashed pets are permitted.

Reservations, fees: Reservations are required ($9 reservation fee) at 877/444-6777 or www .ReserveUSA.com. The camp is $112 per night for sites 31–37, $224 for sites 38–51, and $336 for sites 31–51, with a two-night minimum stay required. Open May through October, weather permitting.

Directions: From Red Bluff, drive east on Highway 36 for 55 miles (five miles east of Childs Meadow). Turn left at the campground entrance road and drive a short distance to the campground.

Contact: Lassen National Forest, Almanor

Ranger District, 530/258-2141, fax 530/258-5194.

67 GURNSEY CREEK
🧍🏊🐕🚐⛺

Scenic rating: 7

in Lassen National Forest

Map 3.3, page 205

This camp is set at 5,000 feet in Lassen National Forest, with extremely easy access off Highway 36. The camp is on the headwaters of little Gurnsey Creek, a highlight of the surrounding Lost Creek Plateau. Gurnsey Creek runs downstream and pours into Deer Creek, a good trout stream with access along narrow, winding Highway 32 to the nearby south.

Campsites, facilities: There are 30 sites for tents or RVs up to 30 feet (no hookups). Picnic tables and fire grills are provided. Drinking water and vault toilets are available. Supplies are available in Mineral. Leashed pets are permitted.

Reservations, fees: Reservations are not accepted. Sites are $14 per night. Open May to early November, weather permitting.

Directions: From Red Bluff, drive east on Highway 36 for 55 miles (five miles east of Childs Meadow). Turn left at the campground entrance road and drive a short distance to the campground.

Contact: Lassen National Forest, Almanor Ranger District, 530/258-2141, fax 530/258-5194.

68 LAST CHANCE CREEK
🧍🏊🐕🚐⛺

Scenic rating: 7

near Lake Almanor

Map 3.3, page 205

This secluded camp is set at 4,500 feet, adjacent to where Last Chance Creek empties into the north end of Lake Almanor. It is an unpublicized PG&E camp that is known primarily by locals and gets missed almost every time by out-of-towners. The adjacent lake area is a breeding ground in the spring for white pelicans, and the beauty of these birds in large flocks can be extraordinary.

Campsites, facilities: There are 12 sites for tents or RVs up to 30 feet (no hookups), and three group camps that can accommodate up to 100 people. Picnic tables and fire grills are provided. Drinking water and vault toilets are available. Leashed pets are permitted.

Reservations, fees: Reservations are not accepted for individual sites but are required for the group camps at 916/386-5164. Sites are $16 per night for individual sites, $3 per night for each additional vehicle, $60–120 per night for group sites, $1 per pet per night. Group sites require a two-night minimum stay and a three-night minimum on holidays. Open mid-May through September, weather permitting.

Directions: From Red Bluff, take Highway 36 east to Chester and continue for two miles over the causeway (at the north end of Lake Almanor). About 0.25 mile after crossing the causeway, turn left on the campground access road and drive 3.5 miles to the campground.

Contact: PG&E Land Projects, 916/386-5164, www.pge.com/recreation.

69 NORTH SHORE CAMPGROUND

Scenic rating: 7

on Lake Almanor

Map 3.3, page 205

This is a large, privately developed park on the northern shoreline of beautiful Lake Almanor. The park has 37 acres and a mile of shoreline. The camp is set amid pine tree cover, and most of the sites are lakefront or lakeview. About half of the sites are filled with seasonal renters. The lending library available here was once the original Chester jail, built in 1925. Alas, the jail itself busted out during a storm a few years

ago and was found washed ashore at this campground, which converted it to its new use.

Campsites, facilities: There are 34 tent sites and 94 sites with partial hookups (30 amps) for RVs up to 40 feet; a few are pull-through. Two log cabins are also available. Picnic tables and fire rings are provided. Drinking water, restrooms with showers and flush toilets, coin laundry, general store, playground, lending library, modem access, Wi-Fi, propane, dump station, fish-cleaning station, horseshoes, a boat ramp, boat dock, boat slips, and boat rentals are available. Leashed pets are permitted.

Reservations, fees: Reservations are accepted. Sites are $29–41 per night, $5 per person per night for more than two people (children under age 12 are free), $2 per pet per night. Monthly and seasonal rates available. Some credit cards accepted. Open April through October.

Directions: From Red Bluff, take Highway 36 east for 44 miles to the junction with Highway 89. Drive east on Highway 36/89; the camp is two miles past Chester on the right.

Contact: North Shore Campground, 530/258-3376, fax 530/258-2838, www.northshore-campground.com.

70 SOUTH ANTELOPE

Scenic rating: 6

near the eastern edge of the Ishi Wilderness

Map 3.3, page 205

This primitive campsite is for visitors who want to explore the Ishi Wilderness without an extensive drive (compared to other camps in the wilderness here). The South Fork of Antelope Creek runs west from the camp and provides an off-trail route for the ambitious. For easier hikes, trailheads along Ponderosa Way provide access into the eastern flank of the Ishi. The best nearby trail is Lower Mill Creek Trail, with the trailhead eight miles south at Black Rock.

Campsites, facilities: There are four sites for

tents only. Picnic tables and fire pits are provided. A vault toilet is available. No drinking water is available. Garbage must be packed out. Leashed pets are permitted.

Reservations, fees: Reservations are not accepted. There is no fee for camping. Open year-round.

Directions: From Red Bluff, drive east on Highway 36 for about 35 miles to the town of Paynes Creek and Plum Creek Road. Turn right (south) on Plum Creek Road and drive two miles to Ponderosa Way. Turn right (south) and continue for nine miles to the campground on the right. Note: The road is rough and only vehicles with high clearance are advised. No RVs or trailers are allowed.

Contact: Lassen National Forest, Almanor Ranger District, 530/258-2141, fax 530/258-5194.

71 BLACK ROCK
🏃 🐕 5% ⛰

Scenic rating: 7

on the eastern edge of the Ishi Wilderness

Map 3.3, page 205

This remote, primitive camp is set at the base of the huge, ancient Black Rock, one of the oldest geological points in Lassen National Forest. A bonus is that Mill Creek runs adjacent to the sites, providing a water source. This is the edge of the Ishi Wilderness, where remote hiking in solitude is possible without venturing to high mountain elevations; a campfire permit is required for overnight use by backpackers. A trailhead is available right out of the camp. The trail here is routed downstream along Mill Creek, extending five miles into the Ishi Wilderness, downhill all the way. Be prepared when hiking in this area because the heat can be almost intolerable at times, often passing the 100°F mark for days on end.

Campsites, facilities: There are six tent sites. Picnic tables and fire pits are provided. A vault toilet is available. No drinking water is

available. Mill Creek is adjacent to the camp and is a viable water source; remember to filter stream water. Garbage must be packed out. Leashed pets are permitted.

Reservations, fees: Reservations are not accepted. There is no fee for camping. Open year-round, weather permitting.

Directions: From Red Bluff, drive east on Highway 36 for about 35 miles to the town of Paynes Creek and Plum Creek Road. Turn right (south) on Plum Creek Road and drive two miles to Ponderosa Way. Turn right (south) and continue for 16 miles to the campground on the right. Note: The road is rough and only vehicles with high clearance are advised. No RVs or trailers are allowed.

Contact: Lassen National Forest, Almanor Ranger District, 530/258-2141, fax 530/258-5194.

72 ELAM
🎣 🐕 � ⛰

Scenic rating: 7

on Deer Creek in Lassen National Forest

Map 3.3, page 205

Of the campgrounds set on Deer Creek along Highway 32, Elam gets the most use. It is the first stopping point visitors arrive at while heading west on narrow, curvy Highway 32, and it has an excellent day-use picnic area available. The stream here is stocked with rainbow trout in late spring and early summer, with good access for fishing. It is a pretty area, set where Elam Creek enters Deer Creek. A Forest Service Information Center is nearby in Chester. If the camp has too many people to suit your style, consider other more distant and primitive camps downstream on Deer Creek. The elevation here is 4,600 feet.

Campsites, facilities: There are 11 sites for tents or RVs up to 30 feet (no hookups). Picnic tables and fire grills are provided. Drinking water and vault toilets are available. Leashed pets are permitted.

Reservations, fees: Reservations are not

accepted. Sites are $14 per night, $5 per night for each additional vehicle. Open mid-April through October, weather permitting.

Directions: From Red Bluff, take Highway 36 east for 44 miles to the junction with Highway 89. Continue east on Highway 36/89 to the junction with Highway 32. Turn south on Highway 32 and drive three miles to the campground on the right side of the road. Trailers are not recommended.

Contact: Lassen National Forest, Almanor Ranger District, 530/258-2141, fax 530/258-5194.

7.3 ALDER

Scenic rating: 7

on Deer Creek in Lassen National Forest

Map 3.3, page 205

Deer Creek is a great little trout stream that runs along Highway 32. Alder is one of three camps set along Highway 32 with streamside access; this one is at 3,900 feet elevation, set near where both Alder Creek and Round Valley Creek pour into Deer Creek. The stream's best stretch of trout water is from here on upstream to Elam.

Campsites, facilities: There are five tent sites. Trailers and RVs are not recommended. Picnic tables and fire grills are provided. Vault toilets are available. No drinking water is available. Leashed pets are permitted.

Reservations, fees: Reservations are not accepted. Sites are $10 per night, $5 for each additional vehicle. Open late March to early November, weather permitting.

Directions: From Red Bluff, take Highway 36 east for 44 miles to the junction with Highway 89. Continue east on Highway 36/89 to the junction with Highway 32. Turn south on Highway 32 and drive eight miles to the campground on the right side of the road.

Contact: Lassen National Forest, Almanor Ranger District, 530/258-2141, fax 530/258-5194.

7.4 POTATO PATCH

Scenic rating: 7

on Deer Creek in Lassen National Forest

Map 3.3, page 205

You get good hiking and fishing at this camp. It is set beside Deer Creek at 3,400 feet elevation, with good access for trout fishing. This is a wild trout stream in this area, and the use of artificials with a single barbless hook and catch-and-release are required along most of the river; check DFG regulations. An excellent angler's/swimmer's trail is available along the river.

Campsites, facilities: There are 32 sites for tents or RVs up to 27 feet (no hookups). Picnic tables and fire grills are provided. Drinking water and vault toilets are available. Leashed pets are permitted.

Reservations, fees: Reservations are not accepted. Sites are $14 per night, $5 per night for each additional vehicle. Open early April to early November, weather permitting.

Directions: From Red Bluff, take Highway 36 east for 44 miles to the junction with Highway 89. Continue east on Highway 36/89 to the junction with Highway 32. Turn south on Highway 32 and drive 11 miles to the campground on the right side of the road.

Contact: Lassen National Forest, Almanor Ranger District, 530/258-2141, fax 530/258-5194; Department of Fish and Game, 530/225-2146.

7.5 ROCKY POINT CAMPGROUND

Scenic rating: 7

on Lake Almanor

Map 3.3, page 205

What you get here is a series of four campgrounds along the southwest shore of Lake Almanor provided by PG&E as mitigation for its hydroelectric activities on the Feather River system. The camps are set upstream from the dam, with boat ramps available on each side of the dam. This is a pretty spot, with giant Almanor ringed by lodgepole pine and firs. The lake is usually full, or close to it, well into summer, with Mount Lassen set in the distance to the north—bring your camera. The lake is 13 miles long and all water sports are permitted. The lake level remains full most of the year and much of the shoreline is wooded. Though it can take a day or two to find the fish, once that effort is made, fishing is good for large trout and salmon in the spring and fall and for smallmouth bass in the summer.

Campsites, facilities: There are 131 sites for tents or RVs up to 30 feet (no hookups). Picnic tables and fire grills are provided. Drinking water, vault toilets, and a dump station are available. Some facilities are wheelchair-accessible. Leashed pets are permitted.

Reservations, fees: Reservations are not accepted. Sites are $18 per night, $3 per night for each additional vehicle, $1 per pet per night. Open May through September.

Directions: From Red Bluff, take Highway 36 east for 44 miles to the junction with Highway 89. Continue east on Highway 36/89 to Lake Almanor and the next junction with Highway 89 (two miles before reaching Chester). Turn right on Highway 89 and drive eight miles to the southwest end of Lake Almanor. Turn left at your choice of four campground entrances.

Contact: PG&E Land Projects, 916/386-5164, www.pge.com/recreation.

76 ALMANOR NORTH AND SOUTH

🚶 🚲 🏊 🛶 🎣 🐕 ♿ 🚐 ⛺

Scenic rating: 8

on Lake Almanor in Lassen National Forest

Map 3.3, page 205

This is one of Lake Almanor's best-known and most popular Forest Service campgrounds. It is set along the western shore of beautiful Almanor at 4,550 feet elevation, directly across from the beautiful Almanor Peninsula. There

is an excellent view of Mount Lassen to the north, along with gorgeous sunrises. A 10-mile recreation trail runs right through the campground and is excellent for biking or hiking. This section of the lake provides good fishing for smallmouth bass in the summer. Fishing in this lake is also good for rainbow trout, brown trout, and lake-raised salmon. There are two linked campgrounds, named North and South.

Campsites, facilities: There are 104 sites for tents or RVs up to 40 feet (no hookups), and a group camp for tents or RVs up to 40 feet that can accommodate up to 100 people. Picnic tables and fire grills are provided. Drinking water and vault toilets are available. A boat ramp and beach area are available nearby. Some facilities are wheelchair-accessible. Leashed pets are permitted.

Reservations, fees: Reservations are accepted for individual sites and required for the group camp ($9 reservation fee) at 877/444-6777 or www.ReserveUSA.com. Sites are $18 per night, $5 per night for each additional vehicle, and $100 per night for the group camp. Open May through October, weather permitting.

Directions: From Red Bluff, take Highway 36 east for 44 miles to the junction with Highway 89. Continue east on Highway 36/89 to Lake Almanor and the next junction with Highway 89 (two miles before reaching Chester). Turn right on Highway 89 and drive six miles to County Road 310. Turn left on County Road 310 and drive 0.25 mile to the campground.

Contact: Lassen National Forest, Almanor Ranger District, 530/258-2141, fax 530/258-5194.

77 SOLDIER CREEK

🛶 🐕 🚐 ⛺

Scenic rating: 7

on Soldier Creek in Lassen National Forest

Map 3.3, page 205

This camp is little known and primitive and is used primarily by anglers and hunters in season. The campsites here are shaded, set in forest on the edge of meadows, and near a stream. The latter is Soldier Creek, which is stocked with trout by the Department of Fish and Game; check fishing regulations. In the fall, early storms can drive deer through this area on their annual migration to their wintering habitat in the valley, making this a decent base camp for hunters. However, no early storms often mean no deer. The elevation is 4,890 feet.

Campsites, facilities: There are 15 sites for tents or RVs up to 25 feet (no hookups). Picnic tables and fire rings are provided. Vault toilets are available. No drinking water is available. Leashed pets are permitted.

Reservations, fees: Reservations are not accepted. Sites are $10 per night, $5 per night for each additional vehicle. Open late May to early November, weather permitting.

Directions: From Chester, drive south on Highway 89 for approximately six miles to Humboldt Road. Turn right on Humboldt Road and drive one mile, bear right at the fork, and continue five more miles to the intersection at Fanani Meadows. Turn right and drive one mile to the campground on the left.

Contact: Lassen National Forest, Almanor Ranger District, 530/258-2141, fax 530/258-5194.

with water from Almanor. What occurs is that pond smelt from Almanor get ground up in the Butt Lake powerhouse, providing a large amount of feed for trout at the head of the lake; that's why the trout often get huge at Butt Lake. The one downer here is that lake drawdowns are common, exposing tree stumps.

Campsites, facilities: There are 63 sites for tents or RVs up to 30 feet (no hookups), and an overflow camping area. Picnic tables and fire grills are provided. Drinking water, vault toilets, and a boat ramp are available. Some facilities are wheelchair-accessible. Leashed pets are permitted.

Reservations, fees: Reservations are not accepted. Sites are $18 per night, $3 per night for each additional vehicle, $1 per pet per night. Open May through October, weather permitting.

Directions: From Red Bluff, take Highway 36 east for 44 miles to the junction with Highway 89. Continue east on Highway 36/89 to Lake Almanor and the next junction with Highway 89 (two miles before reaching Chester). Turn right on Highway 89 and drive about seven miles to Butt Valley Road. Turn right on Butt Valley Road and drive 3.2 miles to the campground on the right side of the road.

Contact: PG&E Land Projects, 916/386-5164, www.pge.com/recreation.

78 PONDEROSA FLAT

Scenic rating: 7

on Butt Valley Reservoir

Map 3.3, page 205

This camp is set at the north end of Butt Valley Reservoir (more commonly called Butt Lake), the little brother to nearby Lake Almanor. It is a fairly popular camp, with the boat ramp a prime attraction, allowing campers/anglers a lakeside spot with easy access. Technically, Butt is the "afterbay" for Almanor, fed by a four-mile-long pipe

79 COOL SPRINGS

Scenic rating: 7

on Butt Valley Reservoir

Map 3.3, page 205

One of two camps at Butt Lake (officially known as Butt Valley Reservoir), Cool Springs is set about midway down the lake on its eastern shore, 2.5 miles south of Ponderosa Flat. Cool Springs Creek enters the lake near the camp. (See *Ponderosa Flat*, previous listing, for more information about Butt Lake.)

Campsites, facilities: There are 25 sites for

tents or RVs up to 30 feet (no hookups), and five walk-in tent sites. Picnic tables and fire grills are provided. Drinking water, vault toilets, and a boat ramp are available. Some facilities are wheelchair-accessible. Leashed pets are permitted.

Reservations, fees: Reservations are not accepted. Sites are $16 per night, $3 per night for each additional vehicle, $1 per pet per night. Open May through October, weather permitting.

Directions: From Red Bluff, take Highway 36 east for 44 miles to the junction with Highway 89. Continue east on Highway 36/89 to Lake Almanor and the next junction with Highway 89 (two miles before reaching Chester). Turn right on Highway 89 and drive about seven miles to Butt Valley Road. Turn right on Butt Valley Road and drive 5.7 miles to the campground on the right side of the road.

Contact: PG&E Land Projects, 916/386-5164, www.pge.com/recreation.

80 YELLOW CREEK
🏊 🐕 🚐 ⛺

Scenic rating: 8

in Humbug Valley

Map 3.3, page 205

Yellow Creek is one of Cal Trout's pet projects. It's a beautiful stream for fly fishers, demanding the best from skilled anglers. This camp is set at 4,400 feet in Humbug Valley and provides access to this stretch of water. An option is to fish Butt Creek, much easier fishing for small, planted rainbow trout, with access available along the road on the way in.

Campsites, facilities: There are 10 sites for tents or RVs up to 30 feet (no hookups). Picnic tables and fire grills are provided. Drinking water and vault toilets are available. Leashed pets are permitted.

Reservations, fees: Reservations are not accepted. Sites are $16 per night, $3 per night

for each additional vehicle, $1 per pet per night. Open May through September.

Directions: From Red Bluff, take Highway 36 east for 44 miles to the junction with Highway 89. Continue east on Highway 36/89 for eight miles to Humbug Road. Turn right and drive 0.6 mile and bear left to stay on Humbug Road. Continue for 1.2 miles and bear right (signed for Longville) to stay on Humbug Road. Continue for 5.4 miles to Humbug Valley and a road intersection. Turn left to stay on Humbug Road and drive 1.2 miles (passing the Soda Springs Historic Site) to a fork. Bear right to stay on Humbug Road and drive 0.3 mile to the campground.

Contact: PG&E Land Projects, 916/386-5164, www.pge.com/recreation.

81 BUTTE MEADOWS
🏊 🐕 🚐 ⛺

Scenic rating: 6

on Butte Creek in Lassen National Forest

Map 3.3, page 205

On hot summer days, when a cold stream sounds even better than a cold drink, Butte Meadows provides a hideout in the national forest east of Chico. This is a summer camp situated along Butte Creek, which is stocked with rainbow trout by the Department of Fish and Game. Nearby Doe Mill Ridge and the surrounding Lassen National Forest can provide a good side-trip adventure. The camp elevation is 4,600 feet.

Campsites, facilities: There are 13 sites for tents or RVs up to 25 feet (no hookups). Fire grills and picnic tables are provided. Drinking water and vault toilets are available. Supplies are available in Butte Meadows. Leashed pets are permitted.

Reservations, fees: Reservations are not accepted. Sites are $12 per night, $5 per night for each additional vehicle. Open late April to early November, weather permitting.

Directions: From Chico, drive about 15

miles northeast on Highway 32 to the town of Forest Ranch. Continue on Highway 32 for another nine miles. Turn right on Humboldt Road and drive five miles to Butte Meadows.

Contact: Lassen National Forest, Almanor Ranger District, 530/258-2141, fax 530/258-5194; Department of Fish and Game fishing information, 530/225-2146.

82 CHERRY HILL

Scenic rating: 7

on Butte Creek in Lassen National Forest

Map 3.3, page 205

The camp is set along little Butte Creek at the foot of Cherry Hill, just downstream from the confluence of Colby Creek and Butte Creek. It is also on the western edge of the alpine zone in Lassen National Forest. A four-mile drive to the north, much of it along Colby Creek, will take visitors to the Colby Mountain Lookout at 6,002 feet for a dramatic view of the Ishi Wilderness to the west. Nearby to the south is Philbrook Reservoir.

Campsites, facilities: There are six walk-in tent sites and 19 sites for tents or RVs up to 30 feet (no hookups). Picnic tables and fire grills are provided. Drinking water and vault toilets are available. Supplies are available in the town of Butte Meadows. Leashed pets are permitted.

Reservations, fees: Reservations are not accepted. Sites are $13 per night, $5 per night for each additional vehicle. Open late April to early November, weather permitting.

Directions: From Chico, drive northeast on Highway 32 for approximately 24 miles to the junction with Humboldt Road (well past the town of Forest Ranch). Turn right and drive five miles to Butte Meadows. Continue on Humboldt Road for three miles to the campground on the right side of the road.

Contact: Lassen National Forest, Almanor Ranger District, 530/258-2141, fax 530/258-5194.

83 PHILBROOK RESERVOIR

Scenic rating: 7

in Lassen National Forest

Map 3.3, page 205

Philbrook Reservoir is set at 5,600 feet on the western mountain slopes above Chico, on the southwest edge of Lassen National Forest. It is a pretty lake, though subject to late-season drawdowns, with a scenic lookout a short distance from camp. Swimming beaches and a picnic area are bonuses. The lake is loaded with small trout—a dink here, a dink there, a dink everywhere.

Campsites, facilities: There are 20 sites for tents or RVs up to 30 feet (no hookups), and an overflow camping area. Picnic tables and fire grills are provided. Drinking water and vault toilets are available. Trailer and car-top boat launches are available. Some facilities are wheelchair-accessible. Leashed pets are permitted.

Reservations, fees: Reservations are not accepted. Sites are $16 per night, $3 per night for each additional vehicle, $1 per pet per night. Open May through September.

Directions: At Orland on I-5, take the Highway 32/Chico exit and drive to Chico and the junction with Highway 99. Turn south on Highway 99 and drive to Skyway Road/Paradise (in south Chico). Turn east on Skyway Road, drive through Paradise, and continue for 27 miles to Humbug Summit Road. Turn right and drive two miles to Philbrook Road. Turn right and drive 3.1 miles to the campground entrance road. Turn right and drive 0.5 mile to the campground. Note: Access roads are unpaved and often rough.

Contact: PG&E Land Projects, 916/386-5164, www.pge.com/recreation.

84 QUEEN LILY

🚶 🏊 🎣 🐕 🚐 ⛺

Scenic rating: 7

on the North Fork of the Feather River in
Plumas National Forest

Map 3.3, page 205

The North Fork Feather River is a prime
destination for camping and trout fishing,
especially for families. This is one of three
camps along the river on Caribou Road. This
stretch of river is well stocked. Insider's note:
The first 150 yards of river below the dam at
Caribou typically have large but elusive trout.

Campsites, facilities: There are 12 sites for
tents or RVs up to 30 feet (no hookups). Picnic
tables and fire grills are provided. Drinking
water and vault toilets are available. A grocery
store and coin laundry are available within
three miles. Leashed pets are permitted.

Reservations, fees: Reservations are not
accepted. Sites are $18 per night. Open May
through September.

Directions: From Oroville, drive north on
Highway 70 to Caribou Road (two miles past
Belden). Turn left on Caribou Road and drive
about three miles to the campground on the
left side of the road.

Contact: Plumas National Forest, Mount
Hough Ranger District, 530/283-0555, fax
530/283-1821; Northwest Park Management,
530/283-5559.

85 NORTH FORK

🚶 🏊 🎣 🐕 🚐 ⛺

Scenic rating: 7

on the North Fork of the Feather River in
Plumas National Forest

Map 3.3, page 205

This camp is between Queen Lily to the
nearby north and Gansner Bar camp to the
nearby south, all three set on the North Fork
Feather River. The elevation is 2,600 feet.
Fishing access is good and trout plants are
decent, making for a good fishing/camping

trip. Note: All three camps are extremely
popular on summer weekends.

Campsites, facilities: There are 20 sites for
tents or RVs up to 32 feet (no hookups). Picnic
tables and fire grills are provided. Drinking
water and vault toilets are available. A grocery
store and coin laundry are available within
three miles. Leashed pets are permitted.

Reservations, fees: Reservations are not
accepted. Sites are $18 per night. Open May
through September.

Directions: From Oroville, drive north on
Highway 70 to Caribou Road (two miles past
Belden at Gansner Ranch Ranger Station).
Turn left on Caribou Road and drive about
two miles to the campground on the left side
of the road.

Contact: Plumas National Forest, Mount
Hough Ranger District, 530/283-0555, fax
530/283-1821; Northwest Park Management,
530/283-5559.

86 GANSNER BAR

🚶 🏊 🎣 🐕 ♿ 🚐 ⛺

Scenic rating: 7

on the North Fork of the Feather River in
Plumas National Forest

Map 3.3, page 205

Gansner Bar is the first of three camps along
Caribou Road, which runs parallel to the
North Fork Feather River. Of the three,
this one receives the highest trout stocks of
rainbow trout in the 10- to 12-inch class.
Caribou Road runs upstream to Caribou
Dam, with stream and fishing access along
almost all of it. The camps often fill on summer weekends.

Campsites, facilities: There are 14 sites for
tents or RVs up to 30 feet (no hookups). Picnic
tables and fire grills are provided. Drinking
water and vault toilets are available. A grocery
store and coin laundry are available within one
mile. Some facilities are wheelchair-accessible.
Leashed pets are permitted.

Reservations, fees: Reservations are not

accepted. Sites are $18 per night. Open April through October.

Directions: From Oroville, drive northeast on Highway 70 to Caribou Road (two miles past Belden). Turn left on Caribou Road and drive a short distance to the campground on the left side of the road.

Contact: Plumas National Forest, Mount Hough Ranger District, 530/283-0555, fax 530/283-1821; Northwest Park Management, 530/283-5559.

87 HALLSTED

Scenic rating: 7

on the North Fork of the Feather River in Plumas National Forest

Map 3.3, page 205

Easy highway access and a pretty trout stream right alongside have made this an extremely popular campground. It typically fills on summer weekends. Hallsted is set on the East Branch North Fork Feather River at 2,800 feet elevation. The river is stocked with trout by the Department of Fish and Game.

Campsites, facilities: There are 20 sites for tents or RVs up to 30 feet (no hookups). Picnic tables and fire grills are provided. Drinking water and vault toilets are available. A grocery store is available within a quarter mile. Some facilities are wheelchair-accessible. Leashed pets are permitted.

Reservations, fees: Reservations are accepted ($9 reservation fee) at 877/444-6777 or www .ReserveUSA.com. Sites are $18 per night. Open May through September.

Directions: From Oroville, drive northeast on Highway 70 to Belden. Continue past Belden for about 12 miles to the campground entrance on the right side of the road. Turn right and drive 0.25 mile to the campground.

Contact: Plumas National Forest, Mount Hough Ranger District, 530/283-0555, fax 530/283-1821; Northwest Park Management, 530/283-5559.

88 DODGE RESERVOIR

Scenic rating: 6

near Ravendale

Map 3.4, page 206

This camp is set at 5,735 feet near Dodge Reservoir, remote and little used. The lake covers 400 acres and is stocked with Eagle Lake trout. Those who know of this lake feel as if they know a secret, since the limit is two at Eagle Lake itself, yet it is five here. Small boats can be launched from the shoreline here, and though it can be windy, mornings are usually calm, ideal for canoes. The surrounding hillsides are sprinkled with sage and juniper. This camp is also popular with hunters who get drawn in the annual DFG lottery for tags for this zone. There is a very good chance that, along the entire length of road from the Madeline Plain into Dodge Reservoir, you'll see some wild horses. There's no sight quite like them. They are considered to be wild, but some will stay close to the road, while others will come no closer then 300 yards.

Campsites, facilities: There are 12 sites for tents or RVs up to 35 feet (no hookups). Picnic tables and fire pits are provided. A vault toilet is available. No drinking water is available. There is no developed boat ramp, but hand-launched boats are permitted. Leashed pets are permitted.

Reservations, fees: Reservations are not accepted. There is no fee for camping, but donations are encouraged. Open year-round, weather permitting.

Directions: From Susanville, drive north on U.S. 395 for 54 miles to Ravendale and County Road 502. Turn right on County Road 502 (Mail Route) and drive four miles, then bear left to stay on County Road 502. Continue four miles, then bear right to stay on County Road 502. Drive two miles to County Road 526. Continue straight onto County Road 526 and drive 4.5 miles to County Road 504. Turn left and drive two miles to County Road 506. Turn right and drive 7.5 miles to the access road for Dodge Reservoir. Turn left on the access road and drive one mile to the lake and camp. Note: The last mile of road before the turnoff to Dodge Reservoir can become impassable with just a small amount of rain or snow.

Contact: Bureau of Land Management, Eagle Lake Field Office, 530/257-0456, fax 530/257-4831.

89 NORTH EAGLE LAKE

Scenic rating: 7

on Eagle Lake

Map 3.4, page 206

This camp provides direct access in the fall to the best fishing area of huge Eagle Lake. When the weather turns cold, the population of big Eagle Lake trout migrates to its favorite haunts just outside the tules, often in water only 5–8 feet deep. A boat ramp is about 1.5 miles to the southwest on Stone Road. In the summer this area is quite exposed and the lake can be hammered by west winds, which can howl from midday to sunset. The elevation is 5,100 feet.

Campsites, facilities: There are 20 sites for tents or RVs up to 35 feet (no hookups). Picnic tables and fire grills are provided. Drinking water and vault toilets are available. A private dump station and boat ramp are available within 1.5 miles. Leashed pets are permitted.

Reservations, fees: Reservations are not accepted. Sites are $8 per night. Open Memorial Day to mid-November, weather permitting.

Directions: From Red Bluff, drive east on Highway 36 to Susanville. In Susanville, turn left (north) on Highway 139 and drive 29 miles to County Road A1. Turn left at County Road A1 and drive 0.5 mile to the campground on the right.

Contact: Bureau of Land Management, Eagle Lake Field Office, 530/257-0456, fax 530/257-4831.

90 RAMHORN SPRINGS

Scenic rating: 3

south of Ravendale

Map 3.4, page 206

This camp is not even three miles off the biggest state highway in northeastern California, yet it feels remote and is little known. It is way out in Nowhere Land, near the flank of Shinn Peak (7,562 feet). There are large numbers of antelope in the area, along with a sprinkling of large mule deer. Hunters lucky enough to get a deer tag can use this camp for their base in the fall. It is also popular for upland game hunters in search of sage grouse and chukar.

Campsites, facilities: There are 12 sites for tents or RVs up to 35 feet (no hookups). Picnic tables and fire grills are provided. Vault toilets and a horse corral are available. There is no drinking water, although spring water, which can be filtered, is available. Leashed pets are permitted.

Reservations, fees: Reservations are not accepted. There is no fee for camping, but donations are encouraged. Open year-round, weather permitting.

Directions: From Red Bluff, drive east on Highway 36 to Susanville. In Susanville, turn north on U.S. 395 and drive 45 miles to Post Camp Road. Turn right on Post Camp Road (unmarked except for small recreation sign) and drive 2.5 miles east to the campground.

Contact: Bureau of Land Management, Eagle Lake Field Office, 530/257-0456, fax 530/257-4831.

91 EAGLE LAKE RV PARK

Scenic rating: 7

near Susanville

Map 3.4, page 206

Eagle Lake RV Park has become something of a headquarters for anglers in pursuit of Eagle Lake trout, which typically range 18–22 inches. A nearby boat ramp provides access to Pelican Point and Eagle Point, where the fishing is often best in the summer. In the fall, the north end of the lake provides better prospects (see *North Eagle Lake* listing in this chapter). This RV park has all the amenities, including a small store. That means no special trips into town, just vacation time, lounging beside Eagle Lake, maybe catching a big trout now and then. One downer: The wind typically howls here most summer afternoons. When the whitecaps are too big to deal with and surface conditions become choppy, get off the water; it can be dangerous here. Resident deer, including bucks with spectacular racks, can be like pets here on late summer evenings.

Campsites, facilities: There are 69 RV sites with full hookups (30 amps), including some pull-through sites, a separate grassy area for tents only, and cabin and RV rentals. Picnic tables and fire grills are provided. Restrooms with showers, coin laundry, satellite TV hookups, dump station, convenience store, propane gas, diesel, bait and tackle, video rentals, RV supplies, firewood, and recreation room are available. A boat ramp, dock, and boat slips are available nearby. Some facilities are wheelchair-accessible. Leashed pets are permitted.

Reservations, fees: Reservations are recommended. Sites are $25–32.50 per night, $1 per pet per night. Some credit cards accepted. Open late May to early November, weather permitting.

Directions: From Red Bluff, drive east on Highway 36 toward Susanville. Just before reaching Susanville, turn left on County Road A1 and drive approximately 25 miles to County Road 518 near Spalding Tract. Turn right on County Road 518 and drive through a small neighborhood to The Strand (the lake frontage road). Turn right on The Strand and drive about eight blocks to Palmetto Way and the entrance to the store and the park entrance at 687-125 Palmetto Way. Register at the store.

Contact: Eagle Lake RV Park, 530/825-3133, www.eaglelakeandrv.com.

92 CHRISTIE

Scenic rating: 7

on Eagle Lake in Lassen National Forest

Map 3.4, page 206

This camp is set along the southern shore of Eagle Lake at 5,100 feet. Eagle Lake, with 100 miles of shoreline, is well known for its big trout (yea) and big winds (boo). The camp offers some protection from the north winds. Its location is also good for seeing osprey with the Osprey Management Area, which covers a six-mile stretch of shoreline, just two miles to the north above Wildcat Point. A nearby resort is a bonus. The nearest boat ramp is at Gallatin Marina. A five-mile-long paved trail runs from Christie to Aspen Grove Campground, perfect for hiking, cycling, and horseback riding.

Campsites, facilities: There are 69 individual sites and 10 double sites for tents or RVs up to 50 feet. No hookups. Picnic tables and fire grills are provided. Drinking water and flush toilets are available. Some facilities are wheelchair-accessible. A grocery store is nearby. A dump station is 2.5 miles away at Merrill Campground. Leashed pets are permitted.

Reservations, fees: Reservations are accepted ($9 reservation fee) at 877/444-6777 or www.ReserveUSA.com. Sites are $18 per night, $30 per night for double sites, $5 per night for each additional vehicle. Open May through October, weather permitting.

Directions: From Red Bluff, drive east on Highway 36 toward Susanville. Three miles before Susanville turn left on Eagle Lake Road/County Road A1 and drive 19.5 miles to the campground on the right side of the road.

Contact: Lassen National Forest, Eagle Lake Ranger District, 530/257-4188, fax 530/252-5803.

93 MERRILL

🚶 🏊 🎣 🚣 🏕 🐕 ♿ 🚐 ⛺

Scenic rating: 8

on Eagle Lake in Lassen National Forest

Map 3.4, page 206

This is one of the largest, most developed Forest Service campgrounds in the entire county. It is set along the southern shore of huge Eagle Lake at 5,100 feet. The nearest boat launch is at Gallatin Marina, where there is a developed swim beach.

Campsites, facilities: There are 173 individual sites and two double sites with full or partial hookups (30 and 50 amps) for tents or RVs up to 50 feet. Picnic tables and fire grills are provided. Drinking water and flush toilets are available. A dump station is nearby. Some facilities are wheelchair-accessible. A grocery store and boat ramp are available nearby. Leashed pets are permitted.

Reservations, fees: Reservations are accepted ($9 reservation fee) at 877/444-6777 or www .ReserveUSA.com. RV sites are $29–33 per night, double sites are $56 per night, tent sites are $18–19 per night. Open May through October, weather permitting.

Directions: From Red Bluff, drive east on Highway 36 toward Susanville. Three miles before Susanville, turn left on Eagle Lake Road/ County Road A1 and drive 17.5 miles to the campground on the right side of the road.

Contact: Lassen National Forest, Eagle Lake Ranger District, 530/257-4188, fax 530/252-5803.

94 ASPEN GROVE WALK-IN

🚶 🏊 🎣 🚣 🐕 ⛺

Scenic rating: 8

on Eagle Lake in Lassen National Forest

Map 3.4, page 206

Eagle Lake is one of the great trout lakes in California, producing the fast-growing and often huge Eagle Lake rainbow trout. All water sports are allowed and, with a huge lake and

100 miles of shoreline, there's plenty of room for everyone. Just be prepared for cold lake water. This camp is one of four at the south end of the lake and is a popular choice for anglers, with a boat ramp available adjacent to the campground. The one problem with Eagle Lake is the wind, which can whip the huge but shallow lake into a froth in the early summer. It is imperative that anglers/boaters get on the water early, and then get back to camp early, with the fishing for the day often done by 10:30 A.M. A bonus here is a good chance to see bald eagles and osprey. A five-mile-long paved, wheelchair-accessible recreation trail runs from this campground to Christie Campground, and then continues to other campgrounds.

Campsites, facilities: There are 28 tent sites. Picnic tables and fire grills are provided. Drinking water and flush toilets are available. A boat ramp is available nearby. There are no wheelchair facilities for campers. Leashed pets are permitted

Reservations, fees: Reservations are not accepted. Sites are $18 per night. Open May through September.

Directions: From Red Bluff, drive east on Highway 36 toward Susanville. Three miles before Susanville, turn left on Eagle Lake Road/County Road A1 and drive 15.5 miles to County Road 231. Turn right on County Road 231 and drive two miles to the campground on the left side of the road. Walk a short distance to the campsites.

Contact: Lassen National Forest, Eagle Lake Ranger District, 530/257-4188, fax 530/252-5803.

95 WEST EAGLE GROUP CAMPS

🚶 🏊 🎣 🚣 🏕 🐕 🚐 ⛺

Scenic rating: 9

on Eagle Lake in Lassen National Forest

Map 3.4, page 206

If you are coming in a big group to Eagle Lake, you'd better get on the telephone first and reserve this camp. Then you can have your own private slice of solitude along the southern shore of Eagle Lake. Bring your boat; the Gallatin Marina and a swimming beach are only about a mile away. The elevation is 5,100 feet.

Campsites, facilities: There are two group camps for tents or RVs up to 35 feet (no hookups) that can accommodate 75–100 people each. Picnic tables and fire grills are provided. Drinking water, flush toilets, and picnic areas are available. A grocery store, dump station, and boat ramp are nearby. Leashed pets are permitted.

Reservations, fees: Reservations are required ($9 reservation fee) at 877/444-6777 or www .ReserveUSA.com. The sites are $100–125 per night. Open May through October, weather permitting.

Directions: From Red Bluff, drive east on Highway 36 toward Susanville. Three miles before Susanville, turn left on Eagle Lake Road/County Road A1 and drive 15.5 miles to County Road 231. Turn right on County Road 231 and drive 0.25 mile to the campground on the left side of the road.

Contact: Lassen National Forest, Eagle Lake Ranger District, 530/257-4188, fax 530/252-5803.

96 EAGLE

Scenic rating: 8

on Eagle Lake in Lassen National Forest

Map 3.4, page 206

Eagle is set just up the road from Aspen Grove, which is more popular because of the boat ramp nearby. The elevation is 5,100 feet. (See *Aspen Grove Walk-In* listing in this chapter for information about Eagle Lake.)

Campsites, facilities: There are 50 individual sites and two double sites for tents or RVs up to 25 feet (no hookups). Picnic tables and fire grills are provided. Drinking water and flush toilets are available. Some facilities are wheelchair

accessible. There is a boat launch nearby at Gallatin Marina. Leashed pets are permitted.

Reservations, fees: Reservations are accepted ($9 reservation fee) at 877/444-6777 or www .ReserveUSA.com. Sites are $18 per night, double sites are $30 per night, $5 per night for each additional vehicle. Open May through October, weather permitting.

Directions: From Red Bluff, drive east on Highway 36 toward Susanville. Three miles before Susanville, turn left on Eagle Lake Road/County Road A1 and drive 15.5 miles to County Road 231. Turn right and drive 0.5 mile to the campground on the left side of the road.

Contact: Lassen National Forest, Eagle Lake Ranger District, 530/257-4188, fax 530/252-5803.

97 GOUMAZ

Scenic rating: 7

on the Susan River in Lassen National Forest

Map 3.4, page 206

This camp is set beside the Susan River, adjacent to historic Bizz Johnson Trail, a former route for a rail line that has been converted to a 25-mile trail. The trail runs from Susanville to Westwood, but this section provides access to many of its prettiest and most remote stretches as it runs in a half circle around Pegleg Mountain (7,112 feet) to the east. It is an outstanding route for biking, hiking, and horseback riding in the summer and cross-country skiing in the winter. Equestrian campers are welcome here. The elevation is 5,200 feet.

Campsites, facilities: There are six sites for tents or RVs up to 25 feet (no hookups). Picnic tables and fire grills are provided. Drinking water and vault toilets are available. Equestrian facilities include water troughs and tie-lines. Leashed pets are permitted.

Reservations, fees: Reservations are not accepted. Sites are $13 per night. Open May through October, weather permitting.

Directions: From Red Bluff, drive east on Highway 36 past Lake Almanor to the junction with Highway 44. Turn west on Highway 44 and drive six miles (one mile past the Worley Ranch) to Goumaz Road/Forest Road 30N08. Turn left on Goumaz Road and drive about five miles to the campground entrance road on the right.

Contact: Lassen National Forest, Eagle Lake Ranger District, 530/257-4188, fax 530/252-5803.

98 ROXIE PECONOM WALK-IN

Scenic rating: 5

in Lassen National Forest

Map 3.4, page 206

This small camp, at 4,800 feet in elevation, is set next to Willard Creek, a seasonal stream in eastern Lassen National Forest. It's shaded and quiet. The camp requires only about a 100-foot walk from the parking area. The best nearby recreation is the Bizz Johnson Trail, with a trailhead on Highway 36 (two miles east) at a parking area on the left side of the highway. This is an outstanding biking and hiking route.

Campsites, facilities: There are 10 walk-in tent sites. Picnic tables and fire rings are provided. Drinking water and vault toilets are available. Garbage must be packed out. Leashed pets are permitted.

Reservations, fees: Reservations are not accepted. There is no fee for camping. Open May through October, weather permitting.

Directions: From Red Bluff, drive east on Highway 36 past Lake Almanor and continue past Fredonyer Pass for three miles to Forest Road 29N03 on the right. Turn right and drive two miles to the campground parking area on the right. Park and walk 100 feet to the campground.

Contact: Lassen National Forest, Eagle Lake Ranger District, 530/257-4188, fax 530/252-5803.

99 BOULDER CREEK

Scenic rating: 7

at Antelope Lake in Plumas National Forest

Map 3.4, page 206

Antelope Lake is a pretty mountain lake circled by conifers with nice campsites and good trout fishing. It is set at 5,000 feet in remote eastern Plumas National Forest, far enough away so the marginally inclined never make the trip. Campgrounds are at each end of the lake (this one is just north of Lone Rock at the north end), with a boat ramp at Lost Cove on the east side of the lake. All water sports are permitted, and swimming is best near the campgrounds. The lake isn't huge, but it is big enough, with 15 miles of shoreline and little islands, coves, and peninsulas to give it an intimate feel.

Campsites, facilities: There are 70 sites for tents or RVs up to 40 feet (no hookups). Picnic tables and fire grills are provided. Drinking water and vault toilets are available. A dump station, boat ramp, and grocery store are nearby. Some facilities are wheelchair-accessible. Leashed pets are permitted.

Reservations, fees: Reservations are accepted ($9 reservation fee) at 877/444-6777 or www .ReserveUSA.com. Sites are $18–20 per night, double sites are $35 per night, $5 per night for each additional vehicle. Open May to early September.

Directions: From Red Bluff, drive east on Highway 36 to Susanville and U.S. 395. Turn south on U.S. 395 and drive about 10 miles (one mile past Janesville) to County Road 208. Turn right on County Road 208 (signed "Antelope Lake") and drive about 15 miles to a Y (one mile before Antelope Lake). Turn left at the Y and drive four miles to the campground entrance on the right side of the road (on the northwest end of the lake).

Contact: Plumas National Forest, Mount Hough Ranger District, 530/283-0555, fax 530/283-1821; Northwest Park Management, 530/283-5559.

100 LONE ROCK

Scenic rating: 9

at Antelope Lake in Plumas National Forest

Map 3.4, page 206

This camp provides an option to nearby Boulder Creek, to the immediate north at the northwest shore of Antelope Lake. (See the previous listing, *Boulder Creek*, for more information.) The elevation is 5,000 feet. Campfire programs are offered in the summer at the on-site amphitheater.

Campsites, facilities: There are 87 sites for tents or RVs up to 40 feet (no hookups). Picnic tables and fire grills are provided. Drinking water and vault toilets are available. A dump station, boat ramp, and grocery store are nearby. Some facilities are wheelchair-accessible. Leashed pets are permitted.

Reservations, fees: Reservations are accepted ($9 reservation fee) at 877/444-6777 or www.ReserveUSA.com. Sites are $18–20 per night. Open May through October.

Directions: From Red Bluff, drive east on Highway 36 to Susanville and U.S. 395. Go south on U.S. 395 and drive about 10 miles (one mile past Janesville) to County Road 208. Turn right on County Road 208 (signed Antelope Lake) and drive about 15 miles to a Y (one mile before Antelope Lake). Turn left at the Y and drive three miles to the campground entrance on the right side of the road (on the northwest end of the lake).

Contact: Plumas National Forest, Mount Hough Ranger District, 530/283-0555, fax 530/283-1821; Northwest Park Management, 530/283-5559.

101 LONG POINT

Scenic rating: 7

at Antelope Lake in Plumas National Forest

Map 3.4, page 206

Long Point is a pretty camp set on a peninsula that extends well into Antelope Lake, facing Lost Cove. The lake's boat ramp is at Lost Cove, a three-mile drive around the northeast shore. Trout fishing is often good here for both rainbow and brown trout, and there is a nature trail. A group campground is set within this campground.

Campsites, facilities: There are 38 sites for tents or RVs up to 30 feet, and four group sites for tents or RVs up to 35 feet that can accommodate up to 25 people each. No hookups. Picnic tables and fire grills are provided. Drinking water and vault toilets are available. A grocery store, boat ramp, and dump stations are nearby. Leashed pets are permitted.

Reservations, fees: Reservations are accepted for individual sites and required for the group sites ($9 reservation fee) at 877/444-6777 or www.ReserveUSA.com. Sites are $16–18 per night, double sites are $35 per night, $50 per night for group sites. Open May through October.

Directions: From Red Bluff, drive east on Highway 36 to Susanville and U.S. 395. Go south on U.S. 395 and drive about 10 miles (one mile past Janesville) to County Road 208. Turn right on County Road 208 (signed Antelope Lake) and drive about 15 miles to a Y (one mile before Antelope Lake). Turn right at the Y and drive one mile to the campground entrance on the left side of the road.

Contact: Plumas National Forest, Mount Hough Ranger District, 530/283-0555, fax 530/283-1821; Northwest Park Management, 530/283-5559.

102 HONEY LAKE CAMPGROUND

Scenic rating: 4

near Milford

Map 3.4, page 206

For newcomers, Honey Lake is a strange-looking place—a vast, shallow lake set on the edge of the desert of the Great Basin. The campground is set at 4,385 feet and covers 30 acres, most of it overlooking the lake. There are a few pine trees in the campground, and a waterfowl management area is along the north shore of the lake. This campground is popular with hunters. Equestrian facilities, including a corral and exercise ring, are available. Fishing for Eagle Lake trout is good here. The lake is 26 miles across, and on rare flat calm evenings, the sunsets are spectacular here.

Campsites, facilities: There are 63 pull-through sites for tents or RVs of any length, most with full or partial hookups (30 amps), plus 25 mobile homes and trailers available. Picnic tables are provided. Restrooms with showers, coin laundry, dump station, propane gas, restaurant, gift and grocery store, playground, ice, video rentals, and a recreation room are available. Some facilities are wheelchair-accessible. Leashed pets are permitted.

Reservations, fees: Reservations are not accepted. Sites are $14.50–29.95 per night, $3.50 per person per night for more than two people. Long-term rentals are available. Some credit cards accepted. Open year-round.

Directions: From Susanville on U.S. 395, drive 17 miles south (if you reach Milford, you have gone two miles too far) to the campground on the west side of the highway. It is 65 miles north of Reno.

Contact: Honey Lake Campground, 530/253-2508.

103 CONKLIN PARK

Scenic rating: 4

on Willow Creek in Plumas National Forest

Map 3.4, page 206

This camp is along little Willow Creek on the northeastern border of the Dixie Mountain State Game Refuge. Much of the area is recovering from a fire that burned during the summer of 1989. Although the area has greened up, there remains significant evidence of the fire. The campground is little known, primitive, rarely used, and is not likely to change any time soon. The elevation is 5,900 feet.

Campsites, facilities: There are nine sites for tents or RVs up to 25 feet (no hookups). Picnic tables and fire grills are provided. Vault toilets are available. No drinking water is available. Garbage must be packed out. Leashed pets are permitted.

Reservations, fees: Reservations are not accepted. There is no fee for camping. Open May through October, weather permitting.

Directions: From Susanville on U.S. 395, drive south for 24 miles to Milford. In Milford turn right (east) on County Road 336 and drive about four miles to a Y. Bear to the right on Forest Road 70/26N70 and drive three miles. Turn right at the bridge at Willow Creek, turn left on Forest Road 70 (now paved), and drive three miles to the camp entrance road on the left side.

Contact: Plumas National Forest, Beckwourth Ranger District, 530/836-2575, fax 530/836-0493.

104 MEADOW VIEW

Scenic rating: 6

near Little Last Chance Creek in Plumas National Forest

Map 3.4, page 206

This little-known, primitive camp is set along the headwaters of Little Last Chance Creek, along the eastern border of the Dixie Mountain State Game Refuge. The access road continues along the creek and connects with primitive roads that enter the interior of the game refuge. Side-trip options include Frenchman Lake to the south and the drive up to Dixie Mountain, at 8,323 feet in elevation. The camp elevation is 6,100 feet.

Campsites, facilities: There are six sites for

tents or RVs up to 30 feet (no hookups). Picnic tables and fire grills are provided. Vault toilets are available. No drinking water is available. Garbage must be packed out. Leashed pets are permitted.

Reservations, fees: Reservations are not accepted. There is no fee for camping. Open May through October, weather permitting.

Directions: From Reno, drive north on U.S. 395 for 43 miles to Doyle. At Doyle, turn west on Doyle Grade Road/County Road 331 (a dirt road most of the way) and drive seven miles to the campground.

Contact: Plumas National Forest, Beckwourth Ranger District, 530/836-2575, fax 530/836-0493.

MENDOCINO AND WINE COUNTRY

© KEN DECAMP

BEST CAMPGROUNDS

《 Scenic Destinations
Salt Point State Park, **page 299**

《 Family Destinations
MacKerricher State Park, **page 268**

《 Boat-In Campgrounds
Lake Sonoma Recreation Area, **page 298**

《 Fishing
Clear Lake State Park, **page 293**

For many people, this region offers the best

possible combination around of geography, weather, and outdoor activities. The Mendocino coast is dramatic and remote, with several stellar state parks for hiking, while Sonoma Valley, in the heart of wine country, produces some of the most popular wines in the world. Add in the self-indulgent options of mud baths and hot springs at Calistoga and a dash of mainstream recreation at Clear Lake, Lake Berryessa, or any other lake, and you have a capsule summary of why the Mendocino coast and the wine country have turned into getaway favorites.

But it's like two worlds, and the twain do not meet.

For many, this area is where people go for romance, fine cuisine, great wine, mineral springs, and anything else that comes to mind spur-of-the-moment. Such is a vacation in the Napa-Sonoma wine country, or on the beautiful Sonoma and Mendocino coast.

This region wouldn't be the best of both worlds if there weren't options on the other end of the spectrum. Campgrounds set up primarily for family recreation are available at Clear Lake, Lake Berryessa, and Blue Lakes. If the shoe fits – and for many, it does – you can have a great time fishing, boating, and waterskiing.

The coast features a series of romantic hideaways and excellent adventuring and hiking. The Fort Bragg area alone has three state parks, all with outstanding recreation, including several easy hikes, many amid redwoods and along pretty streams. Reservations are always required far in advance for a chance at getting a campsite at a state park on a summer weekend. Fort Bragg also offers excellent fishing out of Noyo Harbor.

The driving tour of Highway 1 along the coast here is the fantasy of many, and it can live up to that fantasy if you don't mind the twists and turns of the road. Along the way, there are dozens of hidden beaches and untouched coastline where you can stop and explore and maybe play tag with the waves. The prize spots are MacKerricher State Park, Salt Point State Park, and Anchor Bay.

MENDOCINO AND WINE COUNTRY

see Redwood Empire
page 88

see Shasta and Trinity
page 124

Red Bluff

Garberville

Yolla Bolly Middle Eel Wilderness

Leggett

Mendocino

National

Forest

Black Butte Lake

Stony Gorge Reservoir

see Sacramento and Gold Country
page 320

Laytonville

MAP 4.1
page 259

MAP 4.2
page 260

MacKerricher SP

Fort Bragg

Willits

Lake Pillsbury

Snow Mtn Wilderness

East Park Reservoir

Jackson State Forest

Mendocino

Navarro River

Ukiah

Lake Mendocino

Russian River

Clear Lake

Indian Valley Reservoir

Manchester State Park

Manchester

Boonville

Clear Lake SP

Clearlake

Cache Creek

Garcia R

Cobb

Middletown

Gualala

Lake Sonoma

Geyserville

Mt St Helena 4,343ft

Sothe-Napa Valley SP

Lake Berryessa

Armstrong Redwoods State Reserve

Healdsburg

MAP 4.3
page 261

MAP 4.4
page 262

Santa Rosa

P 313

Napa

Sonoma

Petaluma

PACIFIC

Point Reyes National Seashore

see San Francisco Bay Area
page 468

Vallejo

San Rafael

Oakland

SAN FRANCISCO

OCEAN

0   10 mi

0   10 km

© AVALON TRAVEL PUBLISHING, INC.

Map 4.1

Campgrounds 1-35
Pages 263-280

Map 4.2

Campgrounds 36-67
Pages 280-295

Yolla Bolly
Middle Eel
Wilderness

Flournoy A9 Corning 99

36 TOOMES CAMP RD

Thomes Creek Paskenta

37 I-5

Grindstone Creek

38

Newville Black Butte Lake 39

Chrome Orland 32 Hamilton City

40 Black Butte 7,448 ft 41

Mendocino

see Sacramento and Gold Country page 320

National Elk Creek 162

Gravel Ridge Stony Gorge Reservoir

Forest Willows 162

Eel River 42 45

44 Stony Creek I-5

45 43

46 Snow Mtn 48 Stonyford

47 Lake Pillsbury Wilderness 49 52

50-51 53 East Park Reservoir Delevan National Wildlife Refuge

54 55 57 Sacramento National Wildlife Refuge

58 56 Lodoga Maxwell

M1 59 60

61 Pacific Ridge North Fork Cache Creek Colusa 20

62 Upper Lake Bear Creek Williams Colusa National Wildlife Refuge

20 Nice

29 63 Indian Valley Reservoir 67 20

64 Lucerne

Clear Lake 66 Glenhaven 5

Lakeport 20 Clearlake Oaks

Clear Lake SP 65 Arbuckle

© AVALON TRAVEL PUBLISHING, INC.

Map 4.3

Campgrounds 68–86
Pages 295–306

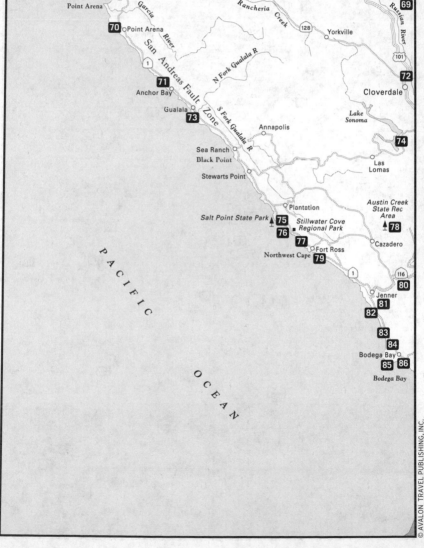

Map 4.4

Campgrounds 87-106

Pages 306-316

1 NADELOS AND WAILAKI

Scenic rating: 7

in the King Range

Map 4.1, page 259

Nadelos and Wailaki campgrounds are set a short distance apart at 1,840 feet near the South Fork Bear Creek at the southern end of the King Range National Conservation Area. This provides access to a rare geographic dynamic, where mountains and coast adjoin. Nearby Chemise Mountain, elevation 2,598 feet, is one of the highest points in California within two miles of the sea, and it provides a dramatic lookout on clear days.

Campsites, facilities: There are eight tent sites at Nadelos. There are 13 sites for tents or RVs up to 20 feet (no hookups) at Wailaki. Picnic tables and fire grills are provided. Drinking water and vault toilets are available. Some facilities are wheelchair-accessible. Leashed pets are permitted.

Reservations, fees: Reservations are not accepted. Sites are $8 per night. Open year-round.

Directions: From Eureka, drive 60 miles south on U.S. 101 to the Redway exit. Take the Redway/Shelter Cove exit onto Redwood Drive into the town of Redway. Drive 2.5 miles (look on the right for the King Range Conservation Area sign) to Briceland-Thorne Road. Turn right on Briceland-Thorne Road (which will become Shelter Cove Road) and drive 17 miles to Chemise Mountain Road. Turn left (south) on Chemise Mountain Road and drive one mile to Nadelos Campground on the right. To reach Wailaki Campground from Nadelos, continue 0.4 mile to the camp on the right.

Contact: Bureau of Land Management, Arcata Field Office, 707/825-2300, fax 707/825-2301, www.ca.blm.gov/arcata.

2 HAMMERHORN LAKE

Scenic rating: 7

near Covelo in Mendocino National Forest

Map 4.1, page 259

Obscure and hidden, this is a veritable dot of a lake, just five acres, set at 3,500 feet in Mendocino National Forest. The lake is too small for motorized boats, but swimming is allowed. There is a spring at the south end of the lake; go out of the camp and hike along the edge of the lake—you can hear the water running out of the pipe often before you see it. The lake is set near the border of the Yolla Bolly Wilderness, with Green Springs Trailhead a few miles away to the northeast. A great side trip is the drive up to Anthony Peak.

Campsites, facilities: There are nine sites for tents or RVs up to 16 feet (no hookups). Picnic tables and fire grills are provided. Drinking water, vault toilets, and fishing piers are available. Garbage must be packed out. Some facilities are wheelchair-accessible. Supplies are available in Covelo. Leashed pets are permitted.

Reservations, fees: Reservations are not accepted. Sites are $6 per night. Open April through December.

Directions: From Willits, drive north on U.S. 101 for 13 miles to Longvale and the junction with Highway 162. Turn northeast on Highway 162 and drive to Covelo. Continue east on Highway 162 for nine miles to the Eel River Bridge. After crossing the bridge, turn left on Forest Road M1 and drive about 17 miles to Forest Road M21. Turn right and drive one mile to the campground entrance.

Contact: Mendocino National Forest, Covelo Ranger District, 707/983-6118, fax 707/983-8004.

❸ SINKYONE WILDERNESS
❚❚❚ ❚❚ ❚❚ 5% ❚

Scenic rating: 10

in Sinkyone Wilderness State Park

Map 4.1, page 259

This is a great jump-off point for a backpacking trip in the Sinkyone Wilderness on the Lost Coast, one of the few wilderness areas where a trip can be made any month of the year. The terrain is primitive, steep, and often wet, but it provides a rare coastal wilderness experience. Starting at the northern trailhead at Orchard Camp, or the southern trailhead at the Usal Beach campground, it's an ambitious weekend tromp of 17 miles. This is a unique 7,367-acre park that is named after the Sinkyone tribe, who once lived in this area. It is called the Lost Coast because there are no highways that provide direct access. Regardless, it has become surprisingly popular for backpackers on the Coastal Trail. Annual rainfall is up to 80 inches per year, mostly between November and May. Summer temperatures range 45–75°F, with morning and evening fog common.

Campsites, facilities: At Usal Beach, there are 35 tent sites. Picnic tables and fire rings are provided. Pit toilets are provided. No drinking water is available. Between Bear Harbor and Jones Beach there are 23 tent sites with picnic tables, fire rings, and pit toilets. Drinking water is available at the Needle Rock Visitor Center (see directions below). Garbage service is provided at Usal Beach only; otherwise garbage must be packed out. Leashed pets are not permitted at campsites.

Reservations, fees: Reservations are not accepted. Sites are $10–15 per night, $3 per night for each additional vehicle, $2–3 per person per night for trail camping. Open year-round, weather permitting.

Directions: To reach the northern boundary of the Sinkyone Wilderness from U.S. 101 north of Garberville, take the Redway exit, turn west on Briceland Road, and drive 17 miles to Whitethorn. From Whitethorn continue six more miles to the four-corners fork. Drive straight ahead to the middle left fork and continue 3.5 miles on a dirt road to the Needle Rock Visitor Center (the last nine miles are unpaved).

To reach the southern boundary of the Sinkyone Wilderness from Leggett on U.S. 101, turn southwest on Highway 1 (toward Fort Bragg) and drive 14.66 miles to Mile Marker 90.88 at County Road 431. Turn right on County Road 431 (a dirt road, often unsigned) and drive six miles to the Usal Beach Campground. Note: The roads can be quite rough and impassable in wet weather. Trailers and RVs are not recommended.

Contact: Sinkyone Wilderness State Park, 707/986-7711 or 707/247-3318, fax 707/247-3300, www.parks.ca.gov.

❹ REDWOODS RIVER RESORT
❚❚❚ ❚❚ ❚❚ ❚❚ ❚❚ ❚❚ ❚❚ ❚

Scenic rating: 8

on the Eel River

Map 4.1, page 259

This resort is situated in a 21-acre grove of redwoods on U.S. 101 and features 1,500 feet of river access, including a sandy beach and two swimming holes. Many of the campsites are shaded. A hiking trail leads from the resort to the Eel River, a walk of just over a quarter mile. This is one in a series of both public and private campgrounds along the highway between Leggett and Garberville. Steelhead and salmon fishing are popular here in the winter, and the resort provides nearby access to state parks. The elevation is 700 feet.

Campsites, facilities: There are 14 tent sites and 27 sites with full hookups (30 amps) for RVs of any length; some sites are pull-through. Eight cabins and eight lodge rooms are also available. At campsites, picnic tables and fire rings are provided. Restrooms with showers, seasonal heated swimming pool, playground, recreation room, modem access, minimart, coin laundry, group kitchen, dump station, table tennis, basketball, volleyball, badminton, horseshoes, shuffleboard, group facilities, seasonal organized activities, and a seasonal evening campfire are available. Some facilities are wheelchair-accessible. Leashed pets are permitted, except in buildings.

Reservations, fees: Reservations are recommended in the summer. Sites are $22–35 per night, $3.75 per person per night for more than two people, $1.50 per pet per night. Off-season discounts available. Some credit cards accepted. Open year-round.

Directions: From the junction of U.S. 101 and Highway 1 in Leggett, drive north on U.S. 101 for seven miles to the campground entrance on the left.

Contact: Redwoods River Resort, 707/925-6249, www.redwoodriverresort.com.

5 STANDISH-HICKEY STATE RECREATION AREA: REDWOOD CAMPGROUND

Scenic rating: 8

on the Eel River in Standish-Hickey State Recreation Area

Map 4.1, page 259

This is one of three camps in Standish-Hickey State Recreation Area, and it is by far the most unusual. Reaching Redwood Campground requires driving over a temporary "summer bridge," which provides access to a pretty spot along the South Fork Eel River. In early September, out comes the bridge and up comes the river. The park covers 1,012 acres set in an inland river canyon; the South Fork Eel provides two miles of river frontage. Standish-Hickey is known as "the gateway to the tall trees country." The Grove Trail contains one of the few virgin stands of redwoods in this area. Note that two other campgrounds are available at this park, and that this camp is open only in summer. The elevation is 800 feet.

Campsites, facilities: There are 63 sites for tents or RVs up to 18 feet (no hookups). No trailers, including pop-up tent trailers, are permitted. Picnic tables, food lockers, and

fire rings are provided. Drinking water and restrooms with coin showers and flush toilets are available. Some facilities are wheelchair-accessible. Leashed pets are permitted.

Reservations, fees: Reservations are accepted ($7.50 reservation fee) at 800/444-PARK (800/444-7275) or www.reserveamerica.com. Sites are $20 per night, $6 per night for each additional vehicle. Open July through Labor Day weekend.

Directions: From the junction of U.S. 101 and Highway 1 in Leggett, drive north on U.S. 101 for one mile. The park entrance is on the west (left) side of the road.

Contact: Standish-Hickey State Recreation Area, 707/925-6482, fax 707/925-6402, www.parks.ca.gov.

6 STANDISH-HICKEY STATE RECREATION AREA: ROCK CREEK

Scenic rating: 8

on the Eel River in Standish-Hickey State Recreation Area

Map 4.1, page 259

This is one of two main campgrounds set in a mixed redwood grove at Standish-Hickey State Recreation Area (the other is Hickey). It is the classic state park camp, with numbered sites, flat tent spaces, picnic tables, and food lockers. There are 12 miles of hiking trails in the park. Hiking is only fair, but most people enjoy the short tromp down to the nearby South Fork Eel River. In the winter, steelhead migrate through the area. (See the previous listing, *Redwood Campground*, for more details on this park.)

Campsites, facilities: There are 35 sites for tents or RVs up to 27 feet (no hookups) and trailers to 24 feet, and one hike-in/bike-in site. Picnic tables, food lockers, and fire rings are provided. Drinking water and restrooms with coin showers and flush toilets are available. Some facilities are wheelchair-accessible. Leashed pets are permitted.

Reservations, fees: Reservations are accepted ($7.50 reservation fee) at 800/444-PARK (800/444-7275) or www.reserveamerica.com. Sites are $20 per night, $6 per night for each additional vehicle, $3 per person per night for the hike-in/bike-in site. Open year-round.

Directions: From the junction of U.S. 101 and Highway 1 in Leggett, drive north on U.S. 101 for one mile. The park entrance is on the west (left) side of the road.

Contact: Standish-Hickey State Recreation Area, 707/925-6482, fax 707/925-6402, www.parks.ca.gov.

7 STANDISH-HICKEY STATE RECREATION AREA: HICKEY
🚶 🚴 🏊 ⚓ 🐕 ♿ 🚐 ⛰️

Scenic rating: 8

on the Eel River in Standish-Hickey State Recreation Area

Map 4.1, page 259

This is an ideal layover for U.S. 101 cruisers yearning to spend a night in the redwoods. The park is best known for its campsites set amid redwoods and for the nearby South Fork Eel River with its steelhead fishing in the winter. The elevation is 800 feet. Insider's tip: There's a great swimming hole here in the summer. (See details about Standish-Hickey State Recreation Area in the *Redwood Campground* listing in this chapter.)

Campsites, facilities: There are 65 sites for tents or RVs up to 16 feet (no hookups) and trailers up to 24 feet. Picnic tables, food lockers, and fire rings are provided. Drinking water and restrooms with showers and flush toilets are available. A grocery store is available nearby. Some facilities are wheelchair-accessible. Leashed pets are permitted.

Reservations, fees: Reservations are accepted ($7.50 reservation fee) at 800/444-PARK (800/444-7275) or www.reserveamerica.com. Sites are $20 per night, $6 per night for each additional vehicle. Open year-round.

Directions: From the junction of U.S. 101 and Highway 1 in Leggett, drive north on U.S. 101 for one mile. The park entrance is on the west (left) side of the road.

Contact: Standish-Hickey State Recreation Area, 707/925-6482, fax 707/925-6402, www.parks.ca.gov.

8 LITTLE DOE
🚶 🏊 ⚓ 🚤 🐕 ♿ ⛰️ 🚐

Scenic rating: 5

near Howard Lake in Mendocino National Forest

Map 4.1, page 259

Little Howard Lake is tucked deep in the interior of Mendocino National Forest between Espee Ridge to the south and Little Doe Ridge to the north, at an elevation of 3,600 feet. For a drive-to lake, it is surprisingly remote and provides fair trout fishing, primitive camping, and an opportunity for car-top boating. The lake covers 15–20 acres, and swimming is allowed. Side trips include Hammerhorn Lake, about six miles away, and several four-wheel-drive roads that allow you to explore the area. A Forest Service map is recommended.

Campsites, facilities: There are 13 sites for tents or RVs up to 16 feet (no hookups). Picnic tables and fire pits are provided. Vault toilets are available. No drinking water is available. All garbage must be packed out. No gas motors allowed. Supplies are available in Covelo, 12 miles away. Some facilities are wheelchair-accessible. Leashed pets are permitted.

Reservations, fees: Reservations are not accepted. There is no fee for camping. Open April through December.

Directions: From Willits, drive north on U.S. 101 for 13 miles to Longvale and the junction with Highway 162. Turn northeast on Highway 162 and drive to Covelo. Continue east on Highway 162 and drive for nine miles to the Eel River Bridge. After crossing the bridge, turn left on Forest Road M1 and drive about 11 miles to the campground.

Contact: Mendocino National Forest, Covelo Ranger District, 707/983-6118, fax 707/983-8004.

9 EEL RIVER

Scenic rating: 8

in Mendocino National Forest

Map 4.1, page 259

This is a little-known spot, set in oak woodlands at the confluence of the Middle Fork of the Eel River and Black Butte River. The elevation is 1,500 feet, and it's often extremely hot in summer. Eel River is an ancient Native American campsite and a major archaeological site. For this reason restoration has been limited and at times the camp is overgrown and weedy. Who cares, though? After all, you're camping.

Campsites, facilities: There are 15 sites for tents or RVs up to 21 feet (no hookups). Picnic tables and fire grills are provided. Drinking water and vault toilets are available. Garbage must be packed out. Leashed pets are permitted.

Reservations, fees: Reservations are not accepted. Sites are $6 per night. Open April through December.

Directions: From Willits, drive north on U.S. 101 for 13 miles to Longvale and the junction with Highway 162. Turn northeast on Highway 162 and drive to Covelo. Continue east on Highway 162 for 13 miles to the campground.

Contact: Mendocino National Forest, Covelo Ranger District, 707/983-6118, fax 707/983-8004.

10 WESTPORT-UNION LANDING STATE BEACH

Scenic rating: 8

near Westport overlooking the Pacific Ocean

Map 4.1, page 259

The northern Mendocino coast is remote, beautiful, and gets far less people pressure than the Fort Bragg area. That is the key to its appeal. These state park campsites are on an ocean bluff. It can get windy here, but the reward is the view. This park covers more than three miles of rugged and scenic coastline. Splendid views, colorful sunsets, and tree-covered mountains provide great photo opportunities. Several small sandy beaches, and one large beach at the mouth of Howard Creek, provide some good spots for surf fishing. Several species of rockfish and abalone can be taken when tides and ocean conditions are right. But note that the surf here can surge, discouraging all but the hardy. The park was named for two early-day communities, Westport and Union Landing, settlements well known for lumber and rail ties. Insider's tip: This state beach formerly had 100 campsites, but some were closed to protect an endangered species, the Point Arena mountain beaver, and other sites are temporarily closed because a section of the state beach road eroded and fell into the ocean.

Campsites, facilities: There are 46 sites for tents or RVs of any length (no hookups); eight people maximum per site. Picnic tables and fire rings are provided. Drinking water and chemical flush toilets are available. A grocery store is nearby. Leashed pets are permitted.

Reservations, fees: Reservations are not accepted. Sites are $15 per night, $6 per night for each additional vehicle. Open year-round.

Directions: From Fort Bragg, drive north on Highway 1 to Westport. In Westport, continue north on Highway 1 for three miles to the campground entrance on the west side of the road.

Contact: California State Parks, Mendocino District, 707/937-5804, fax 707/937-2953, www.parks.ca.gov.

11 WESTPORT BEACH RV AND CAMPING

Scenic rating: 8

near Westport overlooking the Pacific Ocean

Map 4.1, page 259

Westport Beach RV and Camping is set above the beach near the mouth of Wages Creek, with both creekside sites and beach sites available. The 30-acre campground has a quarter mile of beach frontage. You will notice as you venture north from Fort Bragg that the number of vacationers in the area falls way off, providing a chance for quiet beaches and serene moments. The best nearby hiking is to the north out of the trailhead for the Sinkyone Wilderness.

Campsites, facilities: There are 75 sites with full hookups (20, 30, and 50 amps) for RVs of any length, 24 sites with no hookups for RVs of any length, 47 sites for tents only, and six group sites for tents or RVs (no hookups) that can accommodate 12–50 people each. Some RV sites are pull-through. A two-bedroom house is also available. Picnic tables and fire rings are provided at most sites. Drinking water, restrooms with coin showers and flush toilets, convenience store, coin laundry, telephone/modem access, playground, volleyball, shuffleboard, horseshoes, firewood, and ice are available. Some facilities are wheelchair-accessible. Leashed pets are permitted.

Reservations, fees: Reservations are accepted. Sites are $32–36 per night for RV sites, $22 per night per vehicle for tent and RV sites (including group sites) with no hookups, $3–5 per night per person for more than two people, $1 per pet per night. Monthly rates available. Some credit cards accepted. Open year-round.

Directions: From Fort Bragg, drive north on Highway 1 to Westport. In Westport, continue north on Highway 1 for 0.5 mile to the campground entrance on the west side of the highway.

Contact: Westport Beach RV and Camping, 707/964-2964, fax 707/964-8185, www.westportbeachrv.com.

12 CREEKSIDE CABINS AND RV RESORT

Scenic rating: 5

north of Willits

Map 4.1, page 259

The privately operated park is in a pretty valley, primarily oak/bay woodlands with a sprinkling of conifers. It was previously known as Hidden Valley Campground. The most popular nearby recreation option is taking the Skunk Train in Willits for the ride out to the coast at Fort Bragg. There are also two golf courses within six miles. Note that about half of the sites are occupied by long-term renters.

Campsites, facilities: There are 50 sites, including 35 with full or partial hookups (20 and 30 amps), for tents or RVs up to 38 feet. Picnic tables and fire grills are provided, and some sites provide satellite TV, telephone and Wi-Fi access. Restrooms with showers, ice, a coin laundry, and a dump station are available. Leashed pets are permitted.

Reservations, fees: Reservations are accepted. Sites are $18–33 per night, $3 per person per night for more than two people. Open year-round.

Directions: From Willits on U.S. 101, drive north for 6.5 miles on U.S. 101 to the campground on the east side (right) of the road at 29801 N. Highway 101.

Contact: Creekside Cabins and RV Resort, 707/459-2521.

13 MacKERRICHER STATE PARK

Scenic rating: 9

north of Fort Bragg overlooking the Pacific Ocean

Map 4.1, page 259   **BEST (**

MacKerricher is a beautiful park on the Mendocino coast, a great destination for adventure and exploration. The camps are set in a coastal forest, with gorgeous walk-in sites. Nearby is a small beach, great tidepools, a rocky point where harbor seals hang out in the sun, a small lake (Cleone) with trout fishing, a great bike trail, and outstanding short hikes. The short jaunt around little Cleone Lake has many romantic spots, often tunneling through vegetation, then emerging for lake views. The coastal walk to the point to see seals and tidepools is equally captivating. For wheelchair users, there is a wheelchair-accessible trail to Laguna Point and also a route on a raised boardwalk that runs halfway around Cleone Lake, a former tidal lagoon. This park covers more than 1,530 acres of beach, bluff, headlands, dune, forest, and wetlands. That diverse landscape provides habitat for more than 90 species of bird, most in the vicinity of Cleone Lake. The headland supplies a prime vantage point for whale-watching in winter and spring.

Campsites, facilities: There are 142 sites for tents or RVs up to 35 feet (no hookups), 10 walk-in sites, and two group sites for up to 40–60 people each. Picnic tables, fire rings, and food lockers are provided. Drinking water, restroom with flush toilets and coin showers, picnic area, Wi-Fi, and a dump station are available. A seasonal junior ranger program with nature walks, campfire programs, and exhibits is also available. Some facilities are wheelchair-accessible. Leashed pets are permitted.

Reservations, fees: Reservations are accepted ($7.50 reservation fee) at 800/444-PARK (800/444-7275) or www.reserveamerica.com. Sites are $25 per night, $6 per night for each additional vehicle. Group sites are $120–180 per night. Open year-round.

Directions: From Fort Bragg, drive north on Highway 1 for three miles to the campground entrance on the left side of the road.

Contact: MacKerricher State Park, 707/964-9112; Mendocino District, 707/937-5804, fax 707/937-2953, www.parks.ca.gov.

14 FORT BRAGG LEISURE TIME RV PARK

🚶 🚲 ⛵ 🐕 ♿ 🚐 ⛺

Scenic rating: 5

in Fort Bragg

Map 4.1, page 259

This privately operated park adjoins Jackson State Forest, with easy access for hiking and cycling trails. The park offers horseshoes, badminton, and a covered group picnic area. The drive from Willits to Fort Bragg on Highway 20 is always a favorite, a curving two-laner through redwoods, not too slow, not too fast, best seen from the saddle of a Harley-Davidson. At the end of it is the coast, and just three miles inland is this campground in the sunbelt, said to be out of the fog by breakfast. Within short drives are Noyo Harbor in Fort Bragg, Russian Gulch State Park, Mendocino to the south, and MacKerricher State Park to the north. In fact, there's so much in the area, you could explore for days. Note that about 10 percent of the sites are filled with permanent or long-term renters.

Campsites, facilities: There are 70 pull-through sites, many with full or partial hookups (30 amps), for tents or RVs up to 40 feet. Picnic tables and fire rings are provided. Restrooms with coin showers, satellite TV, modem access, dump station, fish-cleaning station, horseshoes, RV storage, and a coin laundry are available. Some facilities are wheelchair-accessible. Leashed pets are permitted.

Reservations, fees: Reservations are accepted at 800/700-8542. Sites are $21.50–32 per night, $1 per night for each additional vehicle, $2 per night for first pet, and $1 per night for additional pet. Monthly and seasonal rates available. Some credit cards accepted. Open year-round.

Directions: In Fort Bragg at the junction of Highway 1 and Highway 20, turn east on Highway 20 and drive 2.5 miles to the campground entrance on the right side of the road at 30801 Highway 20.

Contact: Fort Bragg Leisure Time RV Park, 707/964-5994.

15 POMO RV PARK AND CAMPGROUND

Scenic rating: 7

in Fort Bragg

Map 4.1, page 259

This park covers 17 acres of lush, native vegetation, including rhododendrons, near the ocean. It is one of several camps on the Fort Bragg and Mendocino coast, and groups are welcome. Nearby Noyo Harbor offers busy restaurants, deep-sea fishing, a boat ramp, harbor, and a nice walk out to the Noyo Harbor jetty. Huckleberry picking is also an option. Many of the RV spaces are quite wide at this park.

Campsites, facilities: There are 94 sites with full or partial hookups (30 and 50 amps) for RVs of any length, and 30 sites for tents. Some sites are pull-through. Picnic tables and fire rings are provided. Restrooms with coin showers, cable TV hookups, Wi-Fi, convenience store, firewood, ice, RV supplies, propane gas, coin laundry, dump station, fish-cleaning table, horseshoe pits, and large grass playing field are available. Some facilities are wheelchair accessible. Leashed pets are permitted.

Reservations, fees: Reservations are recommended in the summer. Sites are $24–35 per night, $3–5 per person per night for more than two people, $1 per pet per night. Open year-round.

Directions: In Fort Bragg at the junction of Highway 1 and Highway 20, drive south on Highway 1 for one mile to Tregoning Lane. Turn left (east) and drive a short distance to the park at the end of the road (17999 Tregoning Lane).

Contact: Pomo RV Park and Campground, 707/964-3373.

16 JACKSON DEMONSTRATION STATE FOREST, CAMP 1

Scenic rating: 7

near Fort Bragg

Map 4.1, page 259

Primitive campsites set in a vast forest of redwoods and Douglas fir are the prime attraction at Jackson Demonstration State Forest. Even though Highway 20 is a major connecting link to the coast in the summer, these camps get bypassed because they are primitive and largely unknown. Why? Because reaching them requires driving on dirt roads sometimes frequented by logging trucks, and there are few campground signs along the highway. This camp features lots of tree cover, with oaks, redwoods, and madrones. Most of the campsites are adjacent to the south fork of the north fork of the Noyo River, well known among locals, but completely missed by most others. A one-mile trail circles the campground; the trailhead is at the day-use area. A DFG hatchery is next to the campground, but note that no fishing is permitted in the river.

Campsites, facilities: There are 32 sites for tents or RVs up to 27 feet (no hookups), and one group site that can accommodate up to 150 people for tents or RVs up to 45 feet. Picnic tables and fire pits are provided. Vault toilets are available. No drinking water is available. Leashed pets are permitted.

Reservations, fees: Reservations are accepted only for the group site at 707/964-5674. There is no fee for camping. A camping permit is required and a campground map is needed. Both can be obtained from the State Department of Forestry and Fire Protection office at 802 North Main Street (Highway 1) in Fort Bragg. Open late May through September.

Directions: From Willits on U.S. 101, turn west on Highway 20 and drive 27 miles to Forest Road 350 (at Mile Marker 5.9). Turn right (north) and drive 1.3 miles to the campground.

Contact: Jackson Demonstration State Forest, 707/964-5674.

17 JACKSON DEMONSTRATION STATE FOREST, DUNLAP

🚶 🚴 🐴 5% 🚐 ⛺

Scenic rating: 6

near Fort Bragg

Map 4.1, page 259

A highlight of Jackson Demonstration Forest is a 50-foot waterfall on Chamberlain Creek. Set in a steep canyon at the east end of the forest, amid giant firs and redwoods, it can be reached with a 10-minute walk. There are also extensive logging roads that are good yet challenging for mountain biking. What to do first? Get a map from the State Forestry Department. For driving, the roads are extremely dusty in summer and muddy in winter.

Campsites, facilities: There are 30 sites for tents or RVs up to 16 feet (no hookups), including eight equestrian sites across the road at Big River Camp. Picnic tables and fire rings are provided. Vault toilets are available. No drinking water is available. Leashed pets are permitted.

Reservations, fees: Reservations are not accepted for individual sites, but are required for equestrian sites at 707/964-5674. There is no fee for camping. A camping permit is required and a campground map is needed. Both can be obtained from the State Department of Forestry and Fire Protection office at 802 North Main Street (Highway 1) in Fort Bragg. Open late May through September.

Directions: From Willits on U.S. 101, turn west on Highway 20 and drive 17 miles. At Mile Marker 16.9 (just past the Chamberlain Bridge) continue driving for about 0.25 mile to the Dunlap camp entrance on the left.

Contact: Jackson Demonstration State Forest, 707/964-5674, fax 707/964-0941.

18 WILLITS-UKIAH KOA

🚶 🏊 🛶 🏕 🐴 🚣 ♿ 🚐 ⛺

Scenic rating: 3

near Willits

Map 4.1, page 259

This is an ideal spot to park your RV if you plan on taking the Skunk Train west to Fort Bragg. A depot for the train is within walking distance of the campground, and tickets are available at KOA. The campground, which has a western theme, also offers nightly entertainment in summer. The elevation is 1,377 feet.

Campsites, facilities: There are 21 sites for tents and 50 sites with full or partial hookups (30 and 50 amps) for RVs of any length. Many sites are pull-through. Twelve cabins and two lodges are also available. Groups can be accommodated. Picnic tables and fire rings are provided. Drinking water, restrooms with flush toilets and showers, Wi-Fi, a playground, seasonal heated swimming pool, hay rides, mini golf, basketball, volleyball, fishing pond, convenience store, RV supplies, coin laundry, and a dump station are available. Some facilities are wheelchair accessible. Leashed pets are permitted, with certain restrictions.

Reservations, fees: Reservations are accepted at 800/562-8542. RV sites are $37–50 per night, tent sites are $33–37 per night, $3–4 per person per night for more than two people. Some credit cards accepted. Open year-round.

Directions: From Willits at the junction of U.S. 101 and Highway 20, turn west on Highway 20 and drive 1.5 miles to the campground on the right at 1600 Highway 20.

Contact: Willits-Ukiah KOA, 707/459-6179, fax 707/459-1489, www.koa.com.

19 POGIE POINT

Scenic rating: 7

on Lake Pillsbury in Mendocino National Forest

Map 4.1, page 259

This camp is set beside Lake Pillsbury in Mendocino National Forest, in the back of a cove at the lake's northwest corner. When the lake is full, this spot is quite pretty. A boat ramp is about a quarter mile to the south, a bonus. The elevation is 1,900 feet. (For more information about Lake Pillsbury, see the listing for *Fuller Grove* in this chapter.)

Campsites, facilities: There are 50 sites for tents or RVs up to 16 feet (no hookups). Picnic tables and fire grills are provided. Drinking water and vault toilets are available. Some facilities are wheelchair-accessible. Leashed pets are permitted.

Reservations, fees: Reservations are not accepted. Sites are $13 per night, $3 per night for each additional vehicle, $1 per pet per night. Open May through October.

Directions: From Ukiah on U.S. 101, drive north to the junction with Highway 20. Turn east (right) on Highway 20 and drive five miles. Turn northwest on East Potter Valley Road toward Lake Pillsbury. Drive 5.9 miles to the town of Potter Valley. Continue on east Potter Valley Road to Eel River Road. Turn right and drive 15 miles to the Eel River Information Kiosk at Lake Pillsbury. Continue for two miles to the campground access road. Turn right and drive a short distance to the campground.

Contact: Mendocino National Forest, Upper Lake Ranger District, 707/275-2361, fax 707/275-0676; PG&E Land Services, 916/386-5164, www.pge.com/recreation.

20 TROUT CREEK

Scenic rating: 7

near East Van Arsdale Reservoir

Map 4.1, page 259

Relatively few campers know about this spot. Most others looking over this area are setting up shop at nearby Lake Pillsbury to the east. But if you like to watch the water roll by, this could be your port of call since it sits at the confluence of Trout Creek and the Eel River (not far from the East Van Arsdale Reservoir). Boats can be hand-launched. Insider's tip: Nearby in Potter Valley to the south, the East Fork Russian River (Cold Creek) is stocked with trout during the summer. The elevation is 1,500 feet.

Campsites, facilities: There are 14 sites for tents or RVs up to 30 feet (no hookups), and three walk-in tent sites. Fire grills and picnic tables are provided. Drinking water and vault toilets are available. Leashed pets are permitted.

Reservations, fees: Reservations are not accepted. Sites are $13 per night, $3 per night for each additional vehicle, $1 per pet per night. Open May through September, weather permitting.

Directions: From Ukiah on U.S. 101, drive north to the junction with Highway 20. Turn east (right) on Highway 20 and drive five miles to East Potter Valley Road (M8/Eel River Road). Turn northwest on East Potter Valley Road toward Lake Pillsbury and drive 5.9 miles to the town of Potter Valley. Continue on east Potter Valley Road to Eel River Road. Turn right and drive 4.5 miles to the Eel River Bridge. From the bridge, continue two miles to the campground entrance.

Contact: PG&E Land Services, 916/386-5164, www.pge.com/recreation.

21 CASPAR BEACH RV PARK

Scenic rating: 8

near Mendocino

Map 4.1, page 259

This privately operated park has opportunities for beachcombing, kayaking, fishing, abalone and scuba diving, and good lookouts for whale-watching. The park is across the road from the ocean and somewhat wooded, with a small, year-round creek running behind it. The park is about midway between Fort Bragg and Mendocino, with Fort Bragg five miles to the north. Note that some of the sites are filled with long-term renters.

Campsites, facilities: There are 59 sites with full or partial hookups (30 amps) for RVs up to 50 feet, 30 tent sites, and two group tent sites that can accommodate up to 20 people each. Some sites are pull-through. Picnic tables and fire rings are provided. Cable TV, Wi-Fi, restrooms with flush toilets and coin showers, dump station, convenience store, firewood, playground, video arcade, video rentals, and a coin laundry are available. Some facilities are wheelchair accessible. Leashed pets are permitted.

Reservations, fees: Reservations are accepted. Sites are $25–35 per night, $3–5 per person per night for more than two people, $2 per pet per night. Group tent sites are $60 per night and $3–5 per person per night for more than six people. Monthly rates available. Some credit cards accepted. Open year-round.

Directions: From Mendocino on Highway 1, drive north for 3.5 miles to the Point Cabrillo exit. Turn west on Point Cabrillo Drive and continue 0.75 mile to the campground on the left at 14441 Point Cabrillo Drive.

From Fort Bragg on Highway 1, drive south for 4.5 miles to Point Cabrillo Drive (Mile Marker 54.6). Turn right and continue 0.75 mile to the campground.

Contact: Caspar Beach RV Park, 707/964-3306, fax 707/964-0526, www.casparbeachrvpark.com.

22 RUSSIAN GULCH STATE PARK

Scenic rating: 9

north of Mendocino near the Pacific Ocean

Map 4.1, page 259

Russian Gulch State Park is set near some of California's most beautiful coastline, but the camp speaks to the woods, not the water, with the campsites set in a wooded canyon. They include some of the prettiest and most secluded drive-in sites available on the Mendocino coast. There is a great hike here, an easy hour-long walk to Russian Gulch Falls, a wispy 36-foot waterfall that cascades into a rock basin. While it's always pretty, it's awesome in late winter. Much of the route is accessible by bicycle, with a bike rack available where the trail narrows and turns to dirt. In addition, there are many more miles of hiking trails and a few miles of trails for cycling. The park covers more than 1,100 acres with about 1.5 miles of ocean frontage, its rugged headlands thrusting into the Pacific. It rivals Point Lobos for coastal beauty. And yet the park is better known for its heavily forested canyon, Russian Gulch Creek Canyon, and a headland that features the Devil's Punchbowl, a 100-foot wide and 60-foot deep blowhole where one can look right in and watch the sea surge. Swim, dive, rock fish, or explore the tidepools on the beach.

Campsites, facilities: There are 30 sites for tents or RVs up to 24 feet (no hookups), one hike-in/bike-in site, four equestrian sites, and one group site for up to 40 people. Picnic tables, fire grills, and food lockers are provided. Drinking water, coin showers, and flush toilets are available. A seasonal junior ranger program with nature walks, campfire programs and exhibits is also available. A day-use picnic area, beach access, and recreation hall are available nearby. Some facilities are wheelchair-accessible. Leashed pets are permitted in the campground and on some trails.

Reservations, fees: Reservations are accepted

($7.50 reservation fee) at 800/444-PARK (800/444-7275) or www.reserveamerica.com. Equestrian sites can be reserved at 707/937-5804. Sites are $25 per night for individual and equestrian sites, $6 per night for each additional vehicle, $90 per night for the group site, and $3 per night per person for hike-in/bike-in site. Open mid-March through October, weather permitting, with a two-night maximum stay for hike-in/bike-in campers.

Directions: From Mendocino, drive two miles north on Highway 1 to the campground entrance on the west side of the highway.

Contact: Russian Gulch State Park, 707/937-4296; Mendocino District, 707/937-5804, fax 707/937-2953, www.parks.ca.gov.

23 VAN DAMME STATE PARK

Scenic rating: 10

near Mendocino

Map 4.1, page 259

The campsites at Van Damme are extremely popular, usually requiring reservations, but with a bit of planning your reward is a base of operations in a beautiful park with redwoods and a remarkable fern understory. The hike-in sites (about 1.75 miles to reach them) on Fern Canyon Trail are perfectly situated for those wishing to take one of the most popular hikes in the Mendocino area, with the trail crossing the Little River several times and weaving among old trees. Just across from the entrance of the park is a small but beautiful coastal bay with a pretty beach, ideal for launching sea kayaks. The park covers 1,831 acres. A sidelight is the Pygmy Forest, where mature cone-bearing cypress and pine trees are only six inches to eight feet tall. Another favorite is the Bog Trail, where skunk cabbage grows in abundance, most striking when seen in May and June. Ten miles of trails extend through the Little River's fern-rich canyon, and a paved road is popular with cyclists and joggers. Abalone divers explore the waters off

the beach. Kayak tours may be available at the beach parking lot in the summer.

Campsites, facilities: There are 74 sites for tents or RVs up to 35 feet (no hookups), 10 primitive environmental sites, one hike-in/bike-in site, and one group campsite for up to 50 people. Picnic tables, food lockers, and fire grills are provided. Drinking water, restrooms with flush toilets and coin showers, Wi-Fi, and a dump station are available. A seasonal junior ranger program with nature walks, campfire programs, and exhibits is also available. A grocery store and propane gas are available nearby. Some facilities are wheelchair-accessible. Leashed pets are permitted at campsites, but not in environmental sites.

Reservations, fees: Reservations are accepted ($7.50 reservation fee) at 800/444-PARK (800/444-7275) or www.reserveamerica.com. Sites are $25 per night, $6 per night for each additional vehicle, $15 per night for environmental sites, $111 per night for group site, $3 per night per person for hike-in/bike-in site. Open year-round.

Directions: From Mendocino on Highway 1, drive south for three miles to the town of Little River and the park entrance road on the left (east) side of the road.

Contact: Mendocino District, 707/937-5804, fax 707/937-2953, www.parks.ca.gov.

24 NAVARRO RIVER REDWOODS STATE PARK: NAVARRO BEACH CAMPGROUND

Scenic rating: 6

near the mouth of the Navarro River

Map 4.1, page 259

Navarro Beach is a primitive campground that can bail out drivers stuck for a night without a spot. It is small and open, with no tree cover, set near the ocean and the Navarro River. The camps are just south of the Navarro River Bridge.

Campsites, facilities: There 10 sites for tents or RVs up to 35 feet (no hookups). Picnic tables and fire grills are provided. No drinking water. Pit toilets are available. Leashed pets are permitted.

Reservations, fees: Reservations are not accepted. Sites are $15 per night, $6 per night for each additional vehicle. Open year-round.

Directions: Drive on U.S. 101 to the turnoff for Highway 128 (two miles north of Cloverdale). Turn west on Highway 128 and drive 55 miles to Highway 1. Turn south on Highway 1 and almost immediately, take the exit for Navarro Bluffs Road. Drive a short distance on Navarro Bluffs Road to the campground (on the south side of the Navarro River Bridge).

Contact: Navarro River Redwoods State Park, c/o Hendy Woods State Park, 707/895-3141; Mendocino District, 707/937-5804, fax 707/937-2953, www.parks.ca.gov.

25 NAVARRO RIVER REDWOODS STATE PARK: PAUL M. DIMMICK CAMPGROUND

🏊 🖐 🐾 🚐 ⛺

Scenic rating: 7

on the Navarro River in Navarro River Redwoods State Park

Map 4.1, page 259

A pretty grove of second-growth redwood trees and the nearby Navarro River are the highlights of this campground at Navarro River Redwoods State Park. It's a nice spot but, alas, lacks any significant hiking trails that could make it an overall spectacular destination; all the trailheads along Highway 128 turn out to be just little spur routes from the road to the river. That is because the park consists of an 11-mile "redwood tunnel" along the Navarro River in its course to the ocean. The river provides swimming in summer, but is better suited for easy kayaking and canoeing in later winter and early spring.

Campsites, facilities: There are 25 sites for

tents or RVs up to 30 feet (no hookups) and trailers up to 24 feet. Picnic tables and fire grills are provided. Drinking water (summer only) and vault (summer) or pit (winter) toilets are available. Leashed pets are permitted.

Reservations, fees: Reservations are not accepted. Sites are $15 per night, $6 per night for each additional vehicle. Open year-round, weather permitting.

Directions: From Cloverdale on U.S. 101, drive north for two miles to Highway 128. Turn west on Highway 128 and drive approximately 50 miles. Look for the signed campground entrance on the left side of the road at Mile Marker 8.

Contact: Navarro River Redwoods State Park, c/o Hendy Woods State Park, 707/895-3141; Mendocino District, 707/987-5804, fax 707/937-2953, www.parks.ca.gov.

26 BU-SHAY

🥾 🏊 ⛵ 🎣 🚐 🦌 🏕 👣 ♿ 🚍 ⛺

Scenic rating: 7

at Lake Mendocino

Map 4.1, page 259

Bu-Shay, on the northeast end of Lake Mendocino, is set on a point that provides a pretty southern exposure when the lake is full. The lake is five miles long and one mile wide. It offers fishing for striped bass, largemouth bass, smallmouth bass, crappie, catfish, and bluegill, as well as waterskiing and powerboating. A nearby visitors center features exhibits of local Native American history. The elevation is 750 feet, and the lake covers 1,750 acres and has 15 miles of shoreline. (For more information about Lake Mendocino, see the *Che-Ka-Ka* listing in this chapter.)

Campsites, facilities: There are 164 sites for tents or RVs up to 35 feet (no hookups). There are three group sites for up to 120 people each. Picnic tables, fire rings, and lantern holders are provided. Drinking water, restrooms with showers, playground (in the adjacent day-use area), group facilities, and a dump station are* available. The boat ramp is two miles from camp near Ky-En Campground. Some facilities are wheelchair-accessible. Leashed pets are permitted.

Reservations, fees: Reservations are accepted at 877/444-6777 or www.ReserveUSA.com. Sites are $20–25 per night, group sites are $140–200 per night. Boat launching is free with a camping pass. Open year-round, with limited winter facilities.

Directions: From Ukiah, drive north on U.S. 101 for five miles to the Highway 20 turnoff. Drive five miles east on Highway 20. Just after crossing the Russian River bridge, turn left (Inlet Road) and drive approximately one mile to the campground.

Contact: U.S. Army Corps of Engineers, Lake Mendocino, 707/462-7581, fax 707/462-3372.

27 KY-EN

Scenic rating: 7

at Lake Mendocino

Map 4.1, page 259

This camp is on the north shore of Lake Mendocino. With the access road off Highway 20 instead of U.S. 101 (as with Che-Ka-Ka), it can be overlooked by newcomers. A nearby boat ramp makes it especially attractive. (For more information, see *Bu-Shay*, the previous listing, and *Che-Ka-Ka*, the next listing.)

Campsites, facilities: There are 101 sites for tents or RVs up to 30 feet (no hookups). Picnic tables, fire grills, and lantern holders are provided. Restrooms with showers, playground (in the adjacent day-use area), a dump station, and a boat ramp are available. Some facilities are wheelchair-accessible. Leashed pets are permitted, except in some day-use areas

Reservations, fees: Reservations are accepted at 877/444-6777 or www.ReserveUSA.com. Sites are $20 per night. Boat launching is free with a camping pass. Open April to mid-October.

Directions: From Ukiah, drive north on U.S. 101 for five miles to the Highway 20 turnoff. Drive east on Highway 20 to Marina Drive. Turn right and drive 200 yards (past the boat ramp) to the campground.

Contact: U.S. Army Corps of Engineers, Lake Mendocino, 707/462-7581, fax 707/462-3372.

28 CHE-KA-KA

Scenic rating: 7

at Lake Mendocino

Map 4.1, page 259

Lake Mendocino is known for good striped-bass fishing, waterskiing, and boating. Nearby, upstream of the lake, is Potter Valley and the East Fork Russian River (also called Cold Creek), which provides trout fishing in the summer. A boat ramp adjacent to the dam is a bonus. The elevation is 750 feet. This campground sits beside the dam at the south end of Lake Mendocino, and the Kaweyo trailhead is nearby. Insider's tip: A newly installed 18-hole Frisbee-golf course is at the Che-Ka-Ka overlook.

Campsites, facilities: There are 21 sites for tents or RVs up to 35 feet (no hookups). Picnic tables, lantern hangers and fire grills are provided. Drinking water, vault toilets, and a playground are available. A boat ramp is available nearby. Leashed pets are permitted.

Reservations, fees: Reservations are accepted at 877/444-6777 or www.ReserveUSA.com. Sites are $16 per night. Boat launching is free with a camping pass. Open early April through September.

Directions: From Ukiah, drive north on U.S. 101 to Lake Mendocino Drive. Exit right on Lake Mendocino Drive and continue to the first stoplight. Turn left on North State Street and drive to the next stoplight. Turn right (which will put you back on Lake Mendocino Drive) and drive about two miles to

the signed entrance to the campground at Coyote Dam.

Contact: U.S. Army Corps of Engineers, Lake Mendocino, 707/462-7581, fax 707/462-3372.

29 MITI BOAT-IN/HIKE-IN

🏃 🏊 🛶 🚐 🐕 ⛺

Scenic rating: 7

on Lake Mendocino

Map 4.1, page 259

This is one of several campgrounds on the north end of Lake Mendocino. Boat ramps are at Kyen at the north end of the lake and at Che-Ka-Ka at the south end of the lake. The north ramp (Marina Drive off Highway 20) is open 24 hours; the south ramp closes at night.

Campsites, facilities: There are 15 boat-in/hike-in sites for tents only. Picnic tables, fire rings, and lantern holders are provided. Vault toilets are available. No drinking water is available. Garbage must be packed out. Leashed pets are permitted.

Reservations, fees: Reservations are not accepted. Sites are $5 per night, one-time $3 boat launch fee. Open April through September, weather permitting. (Some sites may be flooded in the spring.)

Directions: From Ukiah, drive north on U.S. 101 to the Highway 20 turnoff. For boat-in campers: Drive east on Highway 20 to Marina Drive. Turn right and drive to the north boat ramp of the lake. The campground is approximately one mile by water.

For hike-in campers: Drive five miles east on Highway 20. Just after crossing the Russian River bridge, turn left (Inlet Road) and drive approximately one mile to the Bu-Shay Ranger Station. Park and hike two miles to the campground.

Contact: U.S. Army Corps of Engineers, Lake Mendocino, 707/462-7581, fax 707/462-3372.

30 PINE ACRES BLUE LAKES RESORT

🏊 🛥 🚐 🏠 🚙 ⛺

Scenic rating: 8

on Upper Blue Lake

Map 4.1, page 259

The Blue Lakes are often overlooked because of their proximity to Clear Lake. These lovely lakes offer good fishing for trout, especially in spring and early summer on Upper Blue Lake. Other fish species are bass, crappie, catfish, and bluegill. With a 5-mph speed limit in place, quiet boating is the rule. Lake frontage sites are available, and other bonuses are a sandy beach and a good swimming area. A lawn area is available for tent camping. Note that the RV sites are spaced very close together.

Campsites, facilities: There are 30 sites with full or partial hookups (30 amps) for RVs up to 40 feet, a lawn area for dispersed tent camping, six cabins, and four lodge rooms. Two RV sites are pull-through. Picnic tables and barbecues are provided. Restrooms with flush toilets and coin showers, dump station, group facilities, boat rentals, boat launching, moorings, boat ramp, fish-cleaning station, horseshoes, convenience store, fishing supplies, and lake frontage sites are available. Leashed pets are permitted, with certain restrictions.

Reservations, fees: Reservations are accepted for RV sites, cabins, and lodge rooms, not for tent camping. Sites are $23–28 per night, $2 per person per night for more than two people, $3.50 per night for each additional vehicle, $5 per pet per night. Boat launching is free for campers. Some credit cards accepted. Open year-round.

Directions: From Ukiah, drive north on U.S. 101 for five miles to the junction with Highway 20. Turn east on Highway 20 and drive about 13 miles to Irvine Avenue. Turn right on Irvine Avenue and drive one block to the end of the road and Blue Lakes Road. Turn right and drive a short distance to the resort on the right at 5328 Blue Lakes Road.

Contact: Pine Acres Blue Lakes Resort, 707/275-2811, www.bluelakepineacres.com.

31 NARROWS LODGE RESORT

🏊 🎣 🚐 🐕 🚙 ⛺

Scenic rating: 8

on Upper Blue Lake

Map 4.1, page 259

One of several campgrounds in the immediate vicinity at Blue Lakes, this is a good fish camp with boat docks and a fish-cleaning station. The Blue Lakes are often overlooked because of their proximity to Clear Lake, but they are a quiet and pretty alternative, with good trout fishing in the spring and early summer, and decent prospects year-round. The lakes are long and narrow with a primarily forested shoreline, and the elevation is 1,400 feet.

Campsites, facilities: There are 48 sites with full or partial hookups (50 amps) for tents or RVs of any length, three park-model cabins, two cabins, and 14 motel rooms. Picnic tables are provided. Restrooms with flush toilets and showers, dump station, modem access, recreation room, boat rentals, pier, boat ramp, boat slips, fishing supplies, picnic area, and ice are available. Leashed pets are allowed.

Reservations, fees: Reservations are accepted at 800/476-2776. Sites are $23–25 per night, $3–4 per person per night for more than two people, $3 per pet per night. Some credit cards accepted. Open year-round.

Directions: From Ukiah, drive north on U.S. 101 for five miles to the junction with Highway 20. Turn east on Highway 20 and drive about 13 miles to Blue Lakes Road. Turn right and drive one mile to the resort (5690 Blue Lakes Road).

Contact: Narrows Lodge Resort, 707/275-2718 or 800/476-2776, www.thenarrows-resort.com.

32 HENDY WOODS STATE PARK

🏃 🚲 🏊 🐕 ♿ 🚙 ⛺

Scenic rating: 7

near Boonville

Map 4.1, page 259

This is a remarkable setting where the flora changes from open valley grasslands and oaks to a cloaked redwood forest with old growth, as if you had waved a magic wand. The campsites are set in the forest, with a great trail routed amid the old redwoods and up to the Hermit Hut (a fallen redwood stump covered with branches), where a hobo lived for 18 years. No, it wasn't me. There are two virgin redwood groves in the park: Big Hendy (80 acres with a self-guided discovery trail available) and Little Hendy (20 acres). The Navarro River runs the park's length, but note that fishing is forbidden in the park and that catch-and-release fishing is the law from the bridge at the park entrance on downstream; check regulations. The park is in the middle of the Anderson Valley wine district, which will at first seem an unlikely place to find an 845-acre redwood park, and is not as cold and foggy as the coastal redwood parks.

Campsites, facilities: There are 92 sites for tents or RVs up to 35 feet (no hookups), two hike-in/bike-in sites, and four cabins. Picnic tables, food lockers, and fire grills are provided. Drinking water, flush toilets, coin showers, and a dump station are available. A seasonal junior ranger program with nature walks, campfire programs, and exhibits is also available. A grocery store and propane gas station are available nearby. Some facilities are wheelchair-accessible. Leashed pets are permitted.

Reservations, fees: Reservations are accepted ($7.50 reservation fee) at 800/444-PARK (800/444-7275) or www.reserveamerica.com. Sites are $25 per night, $6 per night for each additional vehicle, $3 per person per night for hike-in/bike-in sites. Open year-round.

Directions: From Cloverdale on U.S. 101, turn northwest on Highway 128 and drive about 35 miles to Philo Greenwood Road. Turn left on Philo Greenwood Road and drive 0.5 mile to the park entrance on the left.

Contact: Hendy Woods State Park, 707/895-3141; Mendocino District, 707/937-5804, fax 707/937-2953, www.parks.ca.gov.

33 RED MOUNTAIN

Scenic rating: 3

near Ukiah

Map 4.1, page 259

Like Mayacmus (see next listing), this camp is set in the Cow Mountain area east of Ukiah. But be forewarned: It is a popular spot for off-highway motorcycles. If you don't like bikes, go to the other camp. Besides motorcycle trails, there are opportunities for hiking and hunting. Horseback riding is an option in the northern part of the recreation area.

Campsites, facilities: There are 10 tent sites. Picnic tables and fire grills are provided. No drinking water. Vault toilets are available. Leashed pets are permitted.

Reservations, fees: Reservations are not accepted. There is no fee for camping. Open year-round, weather permitting.

Directions: From U.S. 101 in Ukiah, turn east on Talmage Road and drive 1.5 miles to Eastside Road. Turn right and drive a short distance to Mill Creek Road. Turn left and drive seven miles to the campground entrance road on the right. Turn right and drive 0.25 mile to the campground.

Contact: Bureau of Land Management, Ukiah Field Office, 707/468-4000, fax 707/468-4027.

34 MAYACMUS

Scenic rating: 5

near Ukiah

Map 4.1, page 259

This campground is set within the Cow Mountain Recreation Area on the slopes of Cow Mountain, the oft-overlooked wild region east of Ukiah. The primitive area is ideal for hiking and horseback riding. In the fall, it is a popular hunting area as well, for the few who know of it. This section of the recreation area is quiet, with hiking on Mayacmus Trail providing access to Willow Creek, Mill Creek, and several overlooks of Clear Lake to the south. The flora is chaparral and oak/bay grasslands, and the weather is extremely hot in the summer. By the way, off-highway vehicles frequent the southern part of the recreation area, but are prohibited in this immediate region.

Campsites, facilities: There are 10 tent sites. Picnic tables and fire grills are provided (sometimes stolen or vandalized). Vault toilets are available. No drinking water is available. Garbage must be packed out. Some facilities are wheelchair-accessible. Leashed pets are permitted.

Reservations, fees: Reservations are not accepted. There is no fee for camping. Stay limit is 14 days. Open year-round, weather permitting.

Directions: From U.S. 101 in Ukiah, turn east on Talmage Road and drive 1.5 miles to Eastside Road. Turn right and drive 0.25 mile to Mill Creek Road. Turn left and drive three miles (just beyond Mill Creek County Park) to the sign for North Cow Mountain at Mendo Rock Road. Turn left and drive five miles to a Y intersection with the campground access road. Bear left and drive one mile to the campground.

Contact: Bureau of Land Management, Ukiah District, 707/468-4000, fax 707/468-4027.

35 MANCHESTER BEACH KOA

Scenic rating: 7

north of Point Arena at Manchester State Beach

Map 4.1, page 259

This is a privately operated KOA park set beside Highway 1 and near the beautiful Manchester State Beach. A great plus here is the cute little log cabins, complete with electric heat. They can provide a great sense of privacy, and after a good sleep, campers are ready to explore the adjacent state park.

Campsites, facilities: There are 57 tent sites and 43 sites with full or partial hookups (30 and 50 amps) for tents or RVs of any length. There are also two cottages and 27 cabins. Picnic tables, barbecues, and fire rings are provided. Drinking water, restrooms with flush toilets and showers, Wi-Fi and modem access, heated seasonal pool, spa, recreation room, playground, dump station, a convenience store, group facilities, ice, firewood, a coin laundry, and propane gas are available. Some facilities are wheelchair-accessible. Leashed pets are permitted, with certain breeds prohibited; call for details.

Reservations, fees: Reservations are accepted at 800/562-4188. Sites are $27–49 per night, $3–5 per person per night for more than two people. Some credit cards accepted. Open year-round.

Directions: From U.S. 101 in Petaluma, take the Washington Street exit. Turn west on Washington Street and drive through Petaluma (Washington Street becomes Bodega Highway) and continue for 17 miles to Highway 1. Continue straight (west) on Highway 1 for eight miles to Bodega Bay. Turn north on Highway 1 and drive 66 miles to Point Arena. Continue north on Highway 1 for about six miles to Kinney Road. Turn west (toward the ocean) and drive one mile to the campground at 44330 Kinney Road.

Contact: Manchester Beach KOA, 707/882-2375, fax 707/882-3104, www.manchesterbeachkoa.com.

36 WHITLOCK

Scenic rating: 4

in Mendocino National Forest

Map 4.2, page 260

This obscure Forest Service camp is often empty or close to it. It is set at 4,300 feet, where conifers have taken over from the valley grasslands to the nearby east. The camp is situated amid good deer range and makes a good hunting base camp in the fall, with a network of Forest Service roads in the area. It is advisable to obtain a Forest Service map.

Campsites, facilities: There are three sites for tents or RVs up to 16 feet (no hookups). Picnic tables, fire grills, and stoves are provided. Vault toilets are available. Drinking water is not available. Garbage must be packed out. Some facilities are wheelchair-accessible. Leashed pets are permitted.

Reservations, fees: Reservations are not accepted. There is no fee for camping. Open late May through October.

Directions: From Corning on I-5, turn west onto County Road A9/Corning Road and drive 20 miles to Paskenta and Toomes Camp Road/County Road 122. Turn right (north) on Toomes Camp Road/County Road 122 and drive 14 miles to the campground on the right.

Contact: Mendocino National Forest, Grindstone Ranger District, Paskenta Work Station, 530/833-5544, fax 530/833-5448.

37 WELLS CABIN

Scenic rating: 6

in Mendocino National Forest

Map 4.2, page 260

You'll join the 5 Percent Club when you reach this spot. It is one mile from Anthony Peak Lookout (6,900 feet) where, on a clear day, you can get great views all the way to the Pacific Ocean and sweeping views of the Sacramento

Valley to the east. This campground is hardly used during the summer and often provides a cool escape from the heat of the valley. The elevation is 6,300 feet.

Campsites, facilities: There are 25 sites for tents or small RVs up to 16 feet (no hookups). Picnic tables, stoves, and fire rings are provided. Vault toilets are available. Drinking water is not available. Garbage must be packed out. Leashed pets are permitted.

Reservations, fees: Reservations are not accepted. There is no fee for camping. Open late June through October, weather permitting.

Directions: From Corning on I-5, turn west on County Road A9 and drive 20 miles to Paskenta and Forest Road M4. Turn west on Forest Road M4 and drive to the junction with Forest Road 23N16. Turn right (north) and drive three miles to the campground.

Contact: Mendocino National Forest, Grindstone Ranger District, Paskenta Work Station, 530/833-5544, fax 530/833-5448.

38 BUCKHORN

Scenic rating: 7

on Black Butte Lake

Map 4.2, page 260

Black Butte Lake is set in the foothills of the north Sacramento Valley at 500 feet. It is one of the 10 best lakes in Northern California for crappie, best in spring. There can also be good fishing for largemouth, smallmouth, and spotted bass, channel catfish, bluegill, and sunfish. Recreation options include powerboating, sailboating, and sailboarding. A one-mile-long interpretive trail is available.

Campsites, facilities: There are 65 sites for tents or RVs up to 35 feet (no hookups). Picnic tables and fire grills are provided. Drinking water, restrooms with flush toilets and showers, dump station, fish-cleaning station, and a playground are available. A boat ramp is nearby. Some facilities are wheelchair-accessible. Leashed pets are permitted.

Reservations, fees: Reservations are accepted at 877/444-6777 or www.ReserveUSA.com. Sites are $15 per night, $10 per night from November through March. Open year-round.

Directions: From I-5 in Orland, take the Black Butte Lake exit. Drive about 15 miles west on Road 200/Newville Road to Buckhorn Road. Turn left and drive a short distance to the campground on the north shore of the lake.

Contact: Black Butte Lake, U.S. Army Corps of Engineers, 530/865-4781, fax 530/865-5283.

39 ORLAND BUTTES

Scenic rating: 7

on Black Butte Lake

Map 4.2, page 260

Black Butte Lake isn't far from I-5, but a lot of campers zoom right by it. The lake has 40 miles of shoreline at 500 feet in elevation. All water sports are allowed. The prime time to visit is in late spring and early summer, when the bass and crappie fishing can be quite good. Three self-guided nature trails are in the immediate area, including Paul Thomas Trail, a short 0.25-mile walk to an overlook. (See previous listing, *Buckhorn*, for more information.) Note: In late winter and early spring, this area is delightful as spring arrives. But from mid-June through August, expect very hot, dry weather.

Campsites, facilities: There are 35 sites for tents or RVs up to 35 feet (no hookups). Picnic tables and fire grills are provided. Drinking water, restrooms with showers, boat ramp, fish-cleaning station, and a dump station are available. Leashed pets are permitted.

Reservations, fees: Reservations are accepted at 877/444-6777 or www.ReserveUSA.com. Sites are $15 per night. Open April to early September.

Directions: From I-5 in Orland, take the

Black Butte Lake exit. Drive west on Road 200/Newville Road for six miles to Road 206. Turn left and drive three miles to the camp entrance on the right.

Contact: Black Butte Lake, U.S. Army Corps of Engineers, 530/865-4781, fax 530/865-5283.

40 MASTERSON GROUP CAMP

Scenic rating: 5

near Plaskett Lakes in Mendocino National Forest

Map 4.2, page 260

This is a group camp only. It is just 0.5 mile away from the Plaskett Lakes, two small lakes of three and four acres set at 6,000 feet and surrounded by a mixed conifer forest. No motors are permitted at either lake, and swimming is not recommended because it is mucky and weedy. It is advisable to obtain a map of Mendocino National Forest, which details nearby streams, lakes, and hiking trails. One notable trail is the Black Butte Trail. (For more information, see the next listing, *Plaskett Meadows*.)

Campsites, facilities: This group camp has 20 tent sites for up to 75 people. Fire grills and picnic tables are provided. Drinking water and vault toilets are available. Leashed pets are permitted.

Reservations, fees: Reservations are required at 530/963-3128. Sites are $50 per night. Open mid-May to mid-October.

Directions: In Willows on I-5, turn west on Highway 162 and drive toward the town of Elk Creek. Just after crossing the Stony Creek Bridge, turn north on County Road 306 and drive four miles to Alder Springs Road/Forest Highway 7. Turn left and drive 31 miles to the camp on the right.

Contact: Mendocino National Forest, Grindstone Ranger District, Stonyford Work Center, 530/963-3128, fax 530/963-3173.

41 PLASKETT MEADOWS

Scenic rating: 7

in Mendocino National Forest

Map 4.2, page 260

This is a little-known camp in the mountains near Plaskett Lakes, a pair of connected dot-sized mountain lakes that form the headwaters of little Plaskett Creek. Trout fishing is best at the westernmost of the two lakes. No motors are permitted in the lakes and swimming is not recommended. The camp is set at an elevation of 6,000 feet.

Campsites, facilities: There are 35 sites for tents or RVs up to 16 feet (no hookups). Fire grills and picnic tables are provided. Drinking water and vault toilets are available. Leashed pets are permitted.

Reservations, fees: Reservations are not accepted. Sites are $10 per night. Open mid-May to mid-October.

Directions: In Willows on I-5, turn west on Highway 162 and drive toward the town of Elk Creek. Just after crossing the Stony Creek Bridge, turn north on County Road 306 and drive four miles to Alder Springs Road/Forest Highway 7. Turn left and drive 31 miles to the campground on the left.

Contact: Mendocino National Forest, Grindstone Ranger District, Stonyford Work Center, 530/963-3128, fax 530/963-3173.

42 LOWER NYE

Scenic rating: 8

in Mendocino National Forest

Map 4.2, page 260

This camp is on the northern border of the Snow Mountain Wilderness. It is a good jump-off point for backpackers, or a spot for folks who don't want to be bugged by anybody. It is set at 3,300 feet on Skeleton Creek near the Eel River. It is advisable to obtain a detailed USGS topographic map.

Campsites, facilities: There are six sites for tents or RVs up to 16 feet (no hookups). Picnic tables and fire grills are provided. Vault toilets are available. No drinking water is available. Garbage must be packed out. Leashed pets are permitted.

Reservations, fees: Reservations are not accepted. There is no fee for camping. Open year-round, weather permitting.

Directions: From Ukiah on U.S. 101, drive north to the junction of Highway 20. Turn east on Highway 20 and drive to the town of Upper Lake and to Elk Mountain Road. Turn left on Elk Mountain Road (which becomes Forest Road M1) and drive 17 miles to Forest Road M-10/Bear Creek Road. Turn right (dirt road) on Forest Road M-10/Bear Creek Road and drive seven miles to Forest Road 18N04/Rice Creek Road. Turn north on Forest Road 18N04/Rice Creek Road and drive 14 miles to the campground.

Contact: Mendocino National Forest, Upper Lake Ranger District, 707/275-2361, fax 707/275-0676.

43 SUNSET CAMPGROUND
🚶 🏊 🎣 🚣 🛶 🐴 🚐 ⛺

Scenic rating: 7

on Lake Pillsbury in Mendocino National Forest

Map 4.2, page 260

This camp is on the northeast corner of Lake Pillsbury, and Pillsbury Pines boat launch and picnic area are less than a quarter mile to the south. Lakeshore Trail, an adjacent designated nature trail along the shore of the lake here, is accessible to hikers, equestrians and bicyclists. However, a section of the trail is covered with water when the lake is full. The surrounding national forest offers side-trip possibilities.

Campsites, facilities: There are 54 sites for tents or RVs up to 16 feet (no hookups). Picnic tables and fire grills are provided. Drinking water and vault toilets are available. A boat ramp is nearby. Leashed pets are permitted.

Reservations, fees: Reservations are not accepted. Sites are $13 per night, $3 per night for each additional vehicle, $1 per pet per night. Open May through October.

Directions: From Ukiah on U.S. 101, drive north to the junction with Highway 20. Turn east (right) on Highway 20 and drive five miles. Turn northwest on East Potter Valley Road toward Lake Pillsbury. Drive 5.9 miles to the town of Potter Valley. Continue on East Potter Valley Road to Eel River Road. Turn right and drive 15 miles to the Eel River Information Kiosk at Lake Pillsbury. Continue east for 4.1 miles to Lake Pillsbury and the junction with Hall Mountain Road. Turn right and drive three miles to the camp entrance.

Contact: Mendocino National Forest, Upper Lake Ranger District, 707/275-2361, fax 707/275-0676; PG&E Land Services, 916/386-5164, www.pge.com/recreation.

44 OAK FLAT
🚶 🏊 🎣 🚣 🛶 🐴 🚐 ⛺

Scenic rating: 6

near Lake Pillsbury in Mendocino National Forest

Map 4.2, page 260

This primitive camp provides an option if Lake Pillsbury's other camps are full. It is set at 1,850 feet near the north shore of Lake Pillsbury in the heart of Mendocino National Forest. Nearby trails leading into the backcountry are detailed on a Forest Service map.

Campsites, facilities: There are 12 sites for tents or RVs up to 16 feet (no hookups). Picnic tables and fire grills are provided. Vault toilets are available. No drinking water is available. Garbage must be packed out. A boat ramp is at the lake. Leashed pets are permitted.

Reservations, fees: Reservations are not accepted. There is no fee for camping. Open year-round.

Directions: From Ukiah on U.S. 101, drive north to the junction with Highway 20. Turn east (right) on Highway 20 and drive five miles to East Potter Valley Road. Turn northwest on East Potter Valley Road toward Lake Pillsbury and drive 5.9 miles to the town of Potter Valley. Continue on East Potter Valley Road to Eel River Road. Turn right and drive 15 miles to the Eel River Information Kiosk at Lake Pillsbury. Continue for four miles around the north end of the lake and look for the camp entrance on the right side of the road.

Contact: Mendocino National Forest, Upper Lake Ranger District, 707/275-2361, fax 707/275-0676.

45 NAVY CAMP

Scenic rating: 7

on Lake Pillsbury in Mendocino National Forest

Map 4.2, page 260

This camp is used primarily as an overflow area, and is usually open on busy weekends and holidays. When Lake Pillsbury is full of water, this is an attractive camp. However, when the lake level is down, as is common in the fall, it can seem as if the camp is on the edge of a dust bowl. The camp is set in the lake's north cove, sheltered from north winds. Although the camp is in a pretty setting, there is little shade and a lot of poison oak.

Campsites, facilities: There are 20 sites for tents or RVs up to 16 feet (no hookups). Picnic tables are provided. Drinking water and vault toilets are available. A boat ramp is nearby at Fuller Grove. Some facilities are wheelchair-accessible. Leashed pets are permitted.

Reservations, fees: Reservations are not accepted. Sites are $13 per night, $3 per night for each additional vehicle, $1 per pet per night. Open Memorial Day weekend through Labor Day weekend when needed for overflow camping.

Directions: From Ukiah on U.S. 101, drive north to the junction with Highway 20. Turn east (right) on Highway 20 and drive five miles to East Potter Valley Road. Turn northwest on

East Potter Valley Road toward Lake Pillsbury and drive 5.9 miles to the town of Potter Valley. Continue on East Potter Valley Road to Eel River Road. Turn right and drive 15 miles to the Eel River Information Kiosk at Lake Pillsbury. Continue for four miles around the north end of the lake and look for the campground entrance on the right side of the road. The campground is on the north shore, just west of Oak Flat Camp.

Contact: Mendocino National Forest, Upper Lake Ranger District, 707/275-2361, fax 707/275-0676.

46 FULLER GROVE AND FULLER GROVE GROUP CAMP

Scenic rating: 7

on Lake Pillsbury in Mendocino National Forest

Map 4.2, page 260

This is one of several campgrounds bordering Lake Pillsbury, which, at 2,000 acres, is by far the largest lake in Mendocino National Forest. Set at an elevation of 1,800 feet, Pillsbury is big and pretty when full, with 65 miles of shoreline. It has lakeside camping, good boat ramps, and in the spring, good fishing for trout, and in the warmer months, for bass. This camp is set along the northwest shore of the lake, with a boat ramp only about a quarter mile away to the north. There are numerous backcountry roads in the area, which provide access to a state game refuge to the north and the Snow Mountain Wilderness to the east.

Campsites, facilities: There are 30 sites for tents or RVs up to 16 feet (no hookups), and a group tent area for up to 60 people. Picnic tables and fire grills are provided. Drinking water and vault toilets are available. A boat ramp is nearby. Leashed pets are permitted.

Reservations, fees: Reservations are not

accepted for individual sites but are required for the group site at 916/386-5164. Sites are $13 per night for individual sites, $3 per night for each additional vehicle, $1 per pet per night, and $100 per night for the group site with a two-night minimum stay required. Open May through October.

Directions: From Ukiah on U.S. 101, drive north to the junction with Highway 20. Turn east (right) on Highway 20 and drive five miles to East Potter Valley Road. Turn northwest on East Potter Valley Road toward Lake Pillsbury and drive 5.9 miles to the town of Potter Valley. Continue on East Potter Valley Road to Eel River Road. Turn right and drive 15 miles to the Eel River Information Kiosk at Lake Pillsbury. Continue for 2.2 miles to the campground access road. Turn right and drive 0.25 mile to the campground; the group camp is adjacent to the boat ramp.

Contact: Mendocino National Forest, Upper Lake Ranger District, 707/275-2361, fax 707/275-0676; PG&E Land Services, 916/386-5164.

47 LAKE PILLSBURY RESORT

🏃 🏊 🛶 🏊 🐴 🚴 🚐 ⛺

Scenic rating: 6

on Lake Pillsbury in Mendocino National Forest

Map 4.2, page 260

This is a pretty spot beside the shore of Lake Pillsbury in the heart of Mendocino National Forest. It can be headquarters for a vacation involving boating, fishing, waterskiing, or exploring the surrounding national forest. A boat ramp, small marina, and full facilities make this place a prime attraction in a relatively remote location. This is the only resort on the lake that accepts reservations, and it has some lakefront sites.

Campsites, facilities: There are 41 sites for tents or RVs up to 26 feet (no hookups); two sites have full hookups (30 amps). Eight cabins are also available. Picnic tables and fire pits

are provided. Drinking water, restrooms with flush toilets and coin showers, playground, boat rentals, fuel, boat dock, fishing supplies, and small marina are available. Leashed pets are permitted.

Reservations, fees: Reservations are recommended. Sites are $22.75–30.25 per night, $8 per pet per night. Boat launching is $6 per day. Weekly rates available. Some credit cards accepted. Open May through October.

Directions: From Ukiah on U.S. 101, drive north to the junction with Highway 20. Turn east (right) on Highway 20 and drive five miles to East Potter Valley Road (toward Lake Pillsbury). Turn left (northwest) on East Potter Valley Road and drive 5.9 miles to the town of Potter Valley. Continue on East Potter Valley Road to Eel River Road. Turn right and drive 11 miles (unpaved road) to the stop sign. Turn right (still Eel River Road) and drive 0.2 mile to Kapranos Road. Turn left and drive about 1.5 miles to the resort at 2756 Kapranos Road.

Contact: Lake Pillsbury Resort, 707/743-9935, www.lprandm.com.

48 NORTH FORK

🏃 🐴 ⛺

Scenic rating: 2

on Stony Creek in Mendocino National Forest

Map 4.2, page 260

This primitive camp was largely wiped out by a forest fire. Facilities have been restored and regrown vegetation is improving the looks of the area. It is set at 1,700 feet at the confluence of the north, south, and middle forks of Stony Creek. There are many trailheads for hiking in the area, within a few miles of the Snow Mountain Wilderness, but none at this camp. There are great views of St. John Mountain and Snow Mountain. (See *Mill Creek* listing in this chapter for additional information.). OHV use is available from camp.

Campsites, facilities: There are 10 tent sites.

Picnic tables and stoves are provided. Vault toilets are available. No drinking water is available. Garbage must be packed out. Leashed pets are permitted.

Reservations, fees: Reservations are not accepted. There is no fee for camping. Open May through October.

Directions: From I-5 at Maxwell, turn west on Maxwell-Sites Road and drive to Sites. Turn left on Sites-Lodoga Road and continue to Lodoga and Lodoga-Stonyford Road. Turn right on Lodoga-Stonyford Road and loop around East Park Reservoir to reach Stonyford and Fouts Springs Road. Turn west on Fouts Springs Road/Forest Road M10 and drive about nine miles to Forest Road 18N03. Turn right on Forest Road 18N03 and drive two miles to the campground on the right.

Contact: Mendocino National Forest, Grindstone Ranger District, Stonyford Work Center, 530/963-3128, fax 530/963-3173.

49 FOUTS AND SOUTH FORK

🧍 🐕 ♿ 🚐 ⛺

Scenic rating: 1

on Stony Creek in Mendocino National Forest

Map 4.2, page 260

These two adjoining camps are in a designated off-highway-vehicle (OHV) area and are used primarily by dirt bikers. So if you're looking for quiet, these camps are not for you. The landscape was largely vanquished by forest fire, though facilities have been restored, including drinking water at Fouts. Several OHV trails are nearby—North Fork, South Fork, and Mill Creek—and campers can ride their OHVs directly out of camp. To the west is the Snow Mountain Wilderness and excellent hiking trails; to the south is an extensive Forest Service road and OHV trail network. The elevation is 1,700 feet.

Campsites, facilities: There are 11 dispersed sites for tents or RVs up to 16 feet at Fouts (no hookups); there are five dispersed tent sites at

South Fork. Picnic tables and fire grills are provided. Vault toilets and drinking water are available. Garbage must be packed out. Some facilities are wheelchair-accessible. Leashed pets are permitted.

Reservations, fees: Reservations are not accepted. There is no fee for camping. Open year-round, although trails may be closed during wet weather.

Directions: From I-5 at Maxwell, turn west on Maxwell-Sites Road and drive to Sites. Turn left on Sites-Lodoga Road and continue to Lodoga. Turn right on Lodoga-Stonyford Road and loop around East Park Reservoir to reach Stonyford. From Stonyford, turn west on Fouts Springs Road/County Road M10 and drive about eight miles. Turn right (north) on Forest Road 18N03 and drive one mile to the campgrounds on your right.

Contact: Mendocino National Forest, Grindstone Ranger District, Stonyford Work Center, 530/963-3128, fax 530/963-3173.

50 GRAY PINE GROUP CAMP

🧍 🐕 ♿ 🚐 ⛺

Scenic rating: 1

in Mendocino National Forest

Map 4.2, page 260

Similar to Fouts Campground, Gray Pine is set in an area of burned-out forest with many OHV trails nearby. It is near (but not on) Stony Creek. (See previous listing, *Fouts,* for additional information.)

Campsites, facilities: There is one group site for tents or RVs up to 26 feet (no hookups) that can accommodate up to 75 people. Picnic tables and fire rings are provided. Drinking water, a vault toilet, and a group barbecue grill are available. Leashed pets are permitted.

Reservations, fees: Reservations are required at 530/963-3128. The camp is $50 per night. Open year-round, weather permitting.

Directions: From I-5 at Maxwell, turn west on Maxwell-Sites Road and drive to Sites. Turn left on Sites-Lodoga Road and continue to Lodoga. Turn right on Lodoga-Stonyford Road and loop around East Park Reservoir to reach Stonyford. From Stonyford, turn west on Fouts Springs Road/County Road M10 and drive about nine miles. Turn right on Forest Road 18N03 and drive less than a mile to the campground on your right.

Contact: Mendocino National Forest, Grindstone Ranger District, Stonyford Work Center, 530/963-3128, fax 530/963-3173.

51 DAVIS FLAT
Scenic rating: 1

in Mendocino National Forest

Map 4.2, page 260

This camp was also a victim to the forest fire that swept through this area in August 2001. It is across the road from Fouts and South Fork campgrounds. All three are in a designated off-highway-vehicle area, so expect OHVers, especially in the winter; campers are allowed to ride their OHVs from the campground. This isn't the quietest camp around, but there is some good hiking in the area to the immediate west in the Snow Mountain Wilderness. The elevation is 1,700 feet.

Campsites, facilities: There are 60 dispersed sites for tents or RVs of any length (no hookups). Picnic tables and fire grills are provided. Drinking water and vault toilets are available. Garbage must be packed out. Some facilities are wheelchair-accessible. Leashed pets are permitted.

Reservations, fees: Reservations are not accepted. There is no fee for camping. Open year-round, weather permitting.

Directions: From I-5 at Maxwell, turn west on Maxwell-Sites Road and drive to Sites. Turn left on Sites-Lodoga Road and continue to Lodoga. Turn right on Lodoga-Stonyford Road and loop around East Park Reservoir to reach Stonyford. From Stonyford, turn west

on Fouts Springs Road/County Road M10 and drive about nine miles to Forest Road 18N03. Turn right and drive one mile to the campground on your left.

Contact: Mendocino National Forest, Grindstone Ranger District, Stonyford Work Center, 530/963-3128, fax 530/963-3173.

52 MILL CREEK
Scenic rating: 3

in Mendocino National Forest

Map 4.2, page 260

It's a strange experience at this camp, like a camping island. That is because this area, including five of the campsites, was burned by a forest fire. While most of the facilities have been restored and renewal is occurring, you are still amid the scene of a largely burned-out landscape. It is set beside Mill Creek near Fouts Springs at the southeastern boundary of the Snow Mountain Wilderness. A nearby trailhead, a mile to the west, provides a hiking route into the wilderness that connects along Trout Creek, a great little romp. Mill Creek is quite pretty in the late spring, but by late summer the flow drops way down. The elevation is 1,700 feet. Expect heavy off-highway-vehicle use from October through May; Fouts Springs/Davis Flat is an OHV staging area. OHV riders are allowed to ride from camp.

Campsites, facilities: There are six tent sites. Picnic tables, stoves, and barbecues are provided. Vault toilets are available. No drinking water is available. Garbage must be packed out. Leashed pets are permitted.

Reservations, fees: Reservations are not accepted. There is no fee for camping. Open year-round, weather permitting.

Directions: From I-5 at Maxwell, turn west on Maxwell-Sites Road and drive to Sites. Turn left on Sites-Lodoga Road and continue to Lodoga. Turn right on Lodoga-Stonyford Road and loop around East Park Reservoir to reach Stonyford. From Stonyford, turn west on Fouts Springs Road/Forest Road M10 and drive about 8.5 miles to the campground entrance on the right.

Contact: Mendocino National Forest, Grindstone Ranger District, Stonyford Work Center, 530/963-3128, fax 530/963-3173.

53 DIXIE GLADE HORSE CAMP

Scenic rating: 6

near the Snow Mountain Wilderness in Mendocino National Forest

Map 4.2, page 260

Got a horse who likes to tromp? No? Then take a pass on this one. Yes? Then sign right up, because this is a trailhead camp for people preparing to head north by horseback into the adjacent Snow Mountain Wilderness.

Campsites, facilities: There are eight sites for tents or RVs up to 26 feet (no hookups). Picnic tables and fire grills are provided. Vault toilets are available. No drinking water is available. Garbage must be packed out. Some facilities are wheelchair-accessible. A horse corral and hitching rack are available. Water in horse troughs is usually available; check current status. Leashed pets are permitted.

Reservations, fees: Reservations are not accepted. There is no fee for camping. Open year-round, weather permitting.

Directions: From I-5 at Maxwell, turn west on Maxwell-Sites Road and drive to Sites and Sites-Lodoga Road. Turn left on Sites-Lodoga Road and continue to Lodoga and Lodoga-Stonyford Road. Turn right on Lodoga-Stonyford Road and loop around East Park Reservoir to reach Stonyford and Fouts Spring Road. Turn west on Fouts Springs Road/County Road M10 and drive 13 miles to the camp on the right side of the road.

Contact: Mendocino National Forest, Grindstone Ranger District, Stonyford Work Center, 530/963-3128, fax 530/963-3173.

54 BEAR CREEK CAMPGROUND

Scenic rating: 7

in Mendocino National Forest

Map 4.2, page 260

This campground is a primitive spot out in the boondocks of Mendocino National Forest, set at 2,000 feet. It's a pretty spot, too, set beside Bear Creek near its confluence with Blue Slides Creek. Trout fishing can be good here. It's about a 10-minute drive to Summit Springs trailhead at the southern end of the Snow Mountain Wilderness. There are also numerous OHV roads in this region.

Campsites, facilities: There are 16 sites for tents or RVs up to 22 feet (no hookups). Picnic tables and fire grills are provided. Vault toilets are available. No drinking water is available. Garbage must be packed out. Leashed pets are permitted.

Reservations, fees: Reservations are not accepted. There is no fee for camping. Open year-round, weather permitting.

Directions: From Ukiah on U.S. 101, drive north to the junction with Highway 20 at Calpella. Turn east on Highway 20 and drive to the town of Upper Lake and Mendenhall Avenue. Turn left on Mendenhall Avenue (which becomes Forest Road M1) and drive one mile to the stop sign and Forest Road M-1/Elk Mountain Road. Bear left on Forest Road M-1/Elk Mountain Road and drive 16 miles (the latter stretch is extremely twisty) to Forest Road M-10. Turn right (east) and drive eight miles to the campground entrance road on the left. Turn left and continue 0.5 mile to the camp. Note: Approximately five miles along Forest Road M-10, the Rice Ford of the Eel River must be forded. Access can be dangerous and sometimes impossible when the water is high; call for road conditions. High-clearance vehicles are recommended.

Contact: Mendocino National Forest, Upper

Lake Ranger District, 707/275-2361, fax 707/275-0676.

55 MILL VALLEY
🏃 🐕 🚙 ⛺

Scenic rating: 5

near Letts Lake in Mendocino National Forest

Map 4.2, page 260

This camp is set beside Lily Pond, a little, teeny guy, with larger Letts Lake just a mile away. Since Lily Pond does not have trout and Letts Lake does, this camp gets far less traffic than its counterpart. The area is crisscrossed with numerous creeks, OHV routes, and Forest Service roads, making it a great adventure for owners of four-wheel drives who are allowed to drive their OHVs from the campground. The elevation is 4,200 feet.

Campsites, facilities: There are 15 sites for tents or RVs up to 18 feet (no hookups). Picnic tables and fire stoves are provided. Vault toilets and drinking water are available. Leashed pets are permitted.

Reservations, fees: Reservations are not accepted. Sites are $8 per night. Open mid-April through October, weather permitting.

Directions: From I-5 at Maxwell, turn west on Maxwell-Sites Road and drive to Sites and Sites-Lodoga Road. Turn left on Sites-Lodoga Road and continue to Lodoga and Lodoga-Stonyford Road. Turn right on Lodoga-Stonyford Road and loop around East Park Reservoir to reach Stonyford and Fouts Spring Road. Turn west on Fouts Springs Road/County Road M10 and drive about 16 miles into national forest (where the road becomes Forest Service 17N02) to the camp access road on the left. Turn left and drive 0.25 mile to the camp.

Contact: Mendocino National Forest, Grindstone Ranger District, Stonyford Work Center, 530/963-3128, fax 530/963-3173.

56 LETTS LAKE COMPLEX
🏊 🚣 🐕 ♿ 🚙 ⛺

Scenic rating: 9

in Mendocino National Forest

Map 4.2, page 260

An increasing popular spot is Letts Lake, a 35-acre, spring-fed lake set in a mixed conifer forest at 4,500 feet just south of the Snow Mountain Wilderness. There are four main loops, each with a separate campground: Main, Stirrup, Saddle, and Spillway. The complex is set on the east side of the lake. No motors are allowed at Letts Lake, making it ideal for canoes, rafts, and float tubes. Swimming is allowed, although the shoreline is rocky. This lake is stocked with rainbow trout in the early summer and is known also for black bass. It's a designated historical landmark, the site where the homesteaders known as the Letts brothers were murdered. While that may not impress you, the views to the north of the Snow Mountain Wilderness will. In addition, there are several natural springs that can be fun to hunt up. By the way, after such a long drive to get here, don't let your eagerness cause you to stop at Lily Pond (on the left, one mile before reaching Letts Lake), because there are no trout in it.

Campsites, facilities: There are four campgrounds with 44 sites for tents or RVs up to 20 feet (no hookups). Picnic tables and fire rings are provided. Drinking water and vault toilets are available. A picnic area is nearby. Some facilities, including a fishing pier, are wheelchair-accessible. Leashed pets are permitted.

Reservations, fees: Reservations are not accepted. Sites are $10 per night and there is a 14-day limit. Open May through October.

Directions: From I-5 at Maxwell, turn west on Maxwell-Sites Road and drive to Sites and Sites-Lodoga Road. Turn left on Sites-Lodoga Road and continue to Lodoga and Lodoga-Stonyford Road. Turn right on Lodoga-Stonyford Road and loop around East Park Reservoir to reach Stonyford and Fouts Spring Road. Turn west on Fouts Springs Road/County Road M10 and drive about 18 miles into national forest (where the road becomes Forest Service 17N02) to the campground on the east side of Letts Lake.

Contact: Mendocino National Forest, Grindstone Ranger District, Stonyford Work Center, 530/963-3128, fax 530/963-3173.

57 OLD MILL

Scenic rating: 5

near Mill Creek in Mendocino National Forest

Map 4.2, page 260

Little known and little used, this camp is set at 3,700 feet amid a mature stand of pine and fir on Trough Spring Ridge. It's at the site of—guess what? An old mill. Expect some OHV company as drivers of OHVs are allowed to ride from camp.

Campsites, facilities: There are eight sites for tents and two sites for tents or RVs up to 16 feet (no hookups). Note that the access road is poor for RVs. Picnic tables and fire rings are provided. Vault toilets are available. No drinking water is available. Garbage must be packed out. Leashed pets are permitted.

Reservations, fees: Reservations are not accepted. There is no fee for camping. Open May through October.

Directions: From I-5 at Maxwell, turn west on Maxwell-Sites Road and drive to Sites and Sites-Lodoga Road. Turn left on Sites-Lodoga Road and continue to Lodoga and Lodoga-Stonyford Road. Turn right on Lodoga-Stonyford Road and loop around East Park Reservoir to reach Stonyford and Fouts Spring Road. Turn west on Fouts Springs Road/County Road M10 and and drive about six miles to Forest Road M5. Turn left on Forest Road M5/Trough Springs Road and drive 7.5 miles on a narrow road to the campground on your right. (The access road is not recommended for RVs.)

Contact: Mendocino National Forest, Grindstone Ranger District, Stonyford Work Center, 530/963-3128, fax 530/963-3173.

58 DEER VALLEY CAMPGROUND

Scenic rating: 4

in Mendocino National Forest

Map 4.2, page 260

This one is way out there. It is used primarily in summer by OHV enthusiasts and in the fall by deer hunters. It is set at 3,700 feet in Deer Valley, about five miles from the East Fork of Middle Creek.

Campsites, facilities: There are 13 sites for tents or RVs up to 16 feet (no hookups). Picnic tables and fire grills are provided. Vault toilets are available. No drinking water is available. Garbage must be packed out. Leashed pets are permitted.

Reservations, fees: Reservations are not accepted. There is no fee for camping. Open year-round, weather permitting.

Directions: From Ukiah on U.S. 101, drive north to the junction with Highway 20. Turn east on Highway 20 and drive to the town of Upper Lake and Mendenhall Avenue. Turn left on Mendenhall Avenue (which becomes Forest Road M1) and drive 17 miles (the latter stretch is extremely twisty) to Forest Road 16N01. Turn right on Forest Road 16N01 and drive about four miles to the campground.

Contact: Mendocino National Forest, Upper Lake Ranger District, 707/275-2361, fax 707/275-0676.

59 CEDAR CAMP

Scenic rating: 6

in Mendocino National Forest

Map 4.2, page 260

This camp is set at 4,300 feet elevation, just below Goat Mountain (6,121 feet) to the west about a mile away. Why did anybody decide to build a campground way out here? Because a small spring starts nearby, creating a trickle that runs into the nearby headwaters of Little Stony Creek.

Campsites, facilities: There are five sites for tents or RVs up to 16 feet (no hookups). Note that the access road is poor for trailers. Picnic tables and fire grills are provided. A vault toilet is available. No drinking water is available. Garbage must be packed out. Leashed pets are permitted.

Reservations, fees: Reservations are not accepted. There is no fee for camping. Open mid-June through mid-October.

Directions: From I-5 at Maxwell, turn west on Maxwell-Sites Road and drive to Sites and Sites-Lodoga Road. Turn left on Sites-Lodoga Road and continue to Lodoga and Lodoga-Stonyford Road. Turn right on Lodoga-Stonyford Road and loop around East Park Reservoir to reach Stonyford and Fouts Spring Road. Turn west on Fouts Springs Road/County Road M10 and drive about six miles to County Road M5. Turn left on County Road M5 (Trough Springs Road) and drive 13 miles to the campground on your right.

Contact: Mendocino National Forest, Grindstone Ranger District, Stonyford Work Center, 530/963-3128, fax 530/963-3173.

60 LITTLE STONY CAMPGROUND

Scenic rating: 7

on Little Stony Creek in Mendocino National Forest

Map 4.2, page 260

This pretty spot is set in Little Stony Canyon, beside Little Stony Creek at 1,500 feet. Very few people know of the place, and you will find it is appropriately named: It is little, it is stony, and the little trout amid the stones fit right in. The camp provides streamside access and, with Goat Mountain Road running along most of the stream, it is easy to fish much of this creek in an evening. Expect heavy OHV use from fall through spring.

Campsites, facilities: There are eight sites for tents or RVs up to 16 feet, and two small group sites for up to eight people each. No hookups. Picnic tables and fire grills are provided. Vault toilets are available. No drinking water is available. Garbage must be packed out. A day-use area is nearby. Some facilities are wheelchair-accessible. Leashed pets are permitted.

Reservations, fees: Reservations are not accepted. There is no fee for camping. Open year-round.

Directions: From I-5 at Maxwell, turn west on Maxwell-Sites Road and drive to Sites. Turn left on Sites-Lodoga Road and continue to where the road crosses Stony Creek. Just after the bridge, turn left on Goat Mountain Road and drive four miles (a rough county road) to the campground on the left.

Contact: Mendocino National Forest, Grindstone Ranger District, Stonyford Work Center, 530/963-3128, fax 530/963-3173.

61 MIDDLE CREEK CAMPGROUND

Scenic rating: 6

in Mendocino National Forest

Map 4.2, page 260

This camp is not widely known, but it's known well enough as an off-highway-vehicle staging area. Some call it "CC Camp." It is set at 2,000 feet at the confluence of the West and East Forks of Middle Creek. An easy track for beginners on dirt bikes and OHVs is located here.

Campsites, facilities: There are 23 sites for tents or RVs up to 30 feet (no hookups). Picnic tables and fire grills are provided. Drinking water and vault toilets are available. Leashed pets are permitted.

Reservations, fees: Reservations are not accepted. Sites are $4 per night, $8 per night for a double site, $2 per night for each additional vehicle. Open year-round.

Directions: From Ukiah on U.S. 101, drive north to the junction with Highway 20. Turn east on Highway 20 and drive to the town of Upper Lake and Mendenhall Avenue. Turn left on Mendenhall Avenue (which becomes Forest Road M1) and drive eight miles to the camp on the right side of the road.

Contact: Mendocino National Forest, Upper Lake Ranger District, 707/275-2361, fax 707/275-0676.

62 KELLY'S FAMILY KAMPGROUND AND RV PARK

Scenic rating: 6

on Scotts Creek near Clear Lake

Map 4.2, page 260

This privately operated park is set beside Scotts Creek, within short driving range of Blue Lakes to the north on Highway 20 and the north end of Clear Lake to the south. The staff is friendly here, and the owner has been running the place for more than 30 years. A bonus is a 1.5-acre pond that can be used for swimming. Fishing is available 1.5 miles away at Blue Lakes.

Campsites, facilities: There are 75 sites for tents or RVs up to 40 feet, many with partial hookups (30 amps). Picnic tables, fire pits, and barbecues are provided. Restrooms with flush toilets and coin showers, dump station, coin laundry, ice, volleyball, basketball, horseshoes, and a small camp store are available. Leashed pets are permitted.

Reservations, fees: Reservations are accepted. Sites are $22–26 per night, $2 per night for each additional vehicle, $1 per pet per night. Open April through October.

Directions: From Ukiah on U.S. 101, drive north to the junction with Highway 20. Turn east and drive 14 miles (five miles from Upper Lake) to Scotts Valley Road. Turn right (south) and drive 1.5 miles to the park on the left (at 8220 Scotts Valley Road).

Contact: Kelly's Family Kampground and RV Park, 707/263-5754.

63 NICE HOLIDAY HARBOR RV PARK AND MARINA

Scenic rating: 7

on Clear Lake

Map 4.2, page 260

This is one of the most popular resorts at the north end of Clear Lake. It is ideal for boaters, with a marina, gas, and a major docking complex. Fishing for bass is good in this area along old docks and submerged pilings. Waterskiing just offshore is also good, with the north end of the lake often more calm than the water to points south. The elevation is about 2,000 feet. Unlike in several privately owned campgrounds in this area, no long-term rentals are permitted, a plus for vacationers. Note: At the time of publication, this resort was in the process of being sold; check current status.

Campsites, facilities: There are 30 sites with full or partial hookups (30 amps) for RVs of any length; some sites are pull-through. No tents. Picnic tables are provided. Restrooms with coin showers, recreation room, modem access, dump station, a coin laundry, and ice are available. An enclosed marina with 150 boat slips, boat ramp, and an adjacent beach are also available. Leashed pets are permitted.

Reservations, fees: Reservations are accepted. Sites are $22 per night, $3 per person per night for more than two people. Open year-round.

Directions: From north of Ukiah on U.S. 101, drive north to the junction with Highway 20. Turn east on Highway 20 and drive to the town of Nice and Howard Avenue. Turn right on Howard Avenue and drive 200 feet to the park at the end of the road at 3605 Lakeshore Boulevard.

Contact: Nice Holiday Harbor RV Park and Marina, 707/274-1136, www.niceholiday-harbor.com.

64 FANTASY COTTAGES BED AND BREAKFAST AND RV RESORT

Scenic rating: 6

on Clear Lake

Map 4.2, page 260

Lucerne is known for its harbor and its long stretch of well-kept public beaches along the shore of Clear Lake. The town offers a shopping district, restaurants, and cafés. In summer, crappie fishing is good at night from the boat docks.

Campsites, facilities: There are 16 sites with full hookups (30 amps) for RVs up to 45 feet and an area for tents. One RV site is pull-through. Two cottages are also available. Picnic tables and barbecues are provided. Restrooms with showers, dump station, coin laundry, pier, moorings, bait and tackle, fish-cleaning station, boat ramp, convenience store, wine-tasting room, picnic area, and ice are available. Leashed pets are permitted.

Reservations, fees: Reservations are accepted. Sites are $13–25 per night. Weekly and monthly rates available. Open year-round.

Directions: From north of Ukiah on U.S. 101 (or from Williams on I-5), turn on Highway 20 and drive to the east side of the town of Lucerne to the resort at 6720 East Highway 20.

Contact: Fantasy Cottages Bed and Breakfast and RV Resort, 707/274-7715, www.fantasy-cottagesresort.com.

65 CLEAR LAKE STATE PARK

Scenic rating: 9

in Kelseyville at Clear Lake

Map 4.2, page 260   **BEST**

If you have fallen in love with Clear Lake and its surrounding oak woodlands, it is difficult to find a better spot than at Clear Lake State Park. It is set on the western shore of Clear Lake, and though the oak woodlands flora means you can seem quite close to your camping neighbors, the proximity to quality boating, water sports, and fishing makes the lack of privacy worth it. Reservations are a necessity in summer. That stands to reason, with excellent bass fishing from boats beside a tule-lined shoreline near the park and good catfishing in the sloughs that run through the park. Some campsites have water frontage. The elevation is 1,500 feet. Clear Lake is the largest natural freshwater lake within California state borders, and it has 150 miles of shoreline. Despite its name, the lake is not clear but green, and in late summer, rather soupy with algae and water grass in certain areas. The high nutrients in the lake give rise to a flourishing aquatic food chain. With that comes the highest number of large bass of any lake in Northern California. A few short hiking trails are also available at the park. The self-guided Indian Nature Trail passes through the site of what was once a Pomo village. Rangers here are friendly, helpful, and provide reliable fishing information. Junior ranger programs and guided walks for bird and flower identification are also available.

Campsites, facilities: There are 147 sites for tents or RVs up to 35 feet (no hookups), two group sites for up to 40 people each, and two hike-in/bike-in sites. Picnic tables and fire rings are provided. Drinking water, restrooms with coin showers and flush toilets, and a dump station are available. A boat ramp, dock, fish-cleaning stations, boat battery charging station, visitors center, Wi-Fi, and swimming beach are available nearby. A grocery store, coin laundry, propane gas, restaurant, and gas station are available within three miles. Some facilities, including the boat ramp, are wheelchair-accessible. Leashed pets are permitted in the campgrounds.

Reservations, fees: Reservations are accepted ($7.50 reservation fee) at 800/444 PARK (800/444-7275) or www.reserveamerica.com. Sites are $20–30 per night, $6 per night for each additional vehicle, $66 per night for group site, $3 per person per night for hike-in/bike-in sites. Boat launching is $8 per day. Open year-round.

Directions: From Vallejo, drive north on Highway 29 to Lower Lake. Turn left on Highway 29 and drive seven miles to Soda Bay Road. Turn right on Soda Bay Road and drive 11 miles to the park entrance on the right side of the road.

From Kelseyville on Highway 29, take the Kelseyville exit and turn north on Main Street. Drive a short distance to State Street. Turn right and drive 0.25 mile to Gaddy Lane. Turn right on Gaddy Lane and drive about two miles to Soda Bay Road. Turn right and drive one mile to the park entrance on the left.

Contact: Clear Lake State Park, 707/279-4293, www.parks.ca.gov.

66 GLENHAVEN BEACH CAMP AND MARINA

Scenic rating: 6

on Clear Lake

Map 4.2, page 260

This makes a good base camp for boaters, water-skiers, and anglers. It is set on a peninsula on the eastern shore of Clear Lake, with nearby Indian Beach providing a good recreation and water-play spot. In addition, it is a short boat ride out to Anderson Island, Weekend Island, and Buckingham Point, where bass fishing can be excellent along shaded tules. Note that in addition to the campsites listed, there are another 22 sites occupied by long-term or permanent renters.

Campsites, facilities: There are 23 sites with full or partial hookups (30 amps) for RVs up to 35 feet and tents. Picnic tables and fire rings are provided. Drinking water, restrooms with showers and flush toilets, marina with gas, pier, mooring, convenience store, bait and tackle, boat ramp, boat and personal watercraft rentals, and a recreation room are available.

A boat ramp and boat rentals are available nearby. Leashed pets are permitted.

Reservations, fees: Reservations are accepted. Sites are $18–20 per night, $2 per person per night for more than two people. Some credit cards accepted. Open year-round.

Directions: From north of Ukiah on U.S. 101 (or I-5 at Williams), turn on Highway 20 and drive to Clear Lake and the town of Glenhaven (four miles northwest of Clearlake Oaks). In Glenhaven, continue on Highway 20 to the camp (lakeside) at 9625 East Highway 20.

Contact: Glenhaven Beach Camp and Marina, 707/998-3406.

67 BLUE OAK

Scenic rating: 7

at Indian Valley Reservoir

Map 4.2, page 260

Indian Valley Reservoir is kind of like an ugly dog that you love more than anything because inside beats a heart that will never betray you. The camp is out in the middle of nowhere in oak woodlands, about a mile from the dam. It is primitive and little known. For many, that kind of isolation is perfect. The lake has 41 miles of shoreline, is long and narrow, and set at 1,500 feet in elevation. The boat speed limit is 10 mph. While there are good trails nearby, it is the outstanding fishing for bass, bluegill, and some kokanee salmon at the lake every spring and early summer that is the key reason to make the trip. In addition, in the spring, there is a great variety of wildflowers in and around the campground. A detailed map is available from the BLM.

Campsites, facilities: There are six sites for tents or RVs up to 20 feet (no hookups). Picnic tables and fire grills are provided. Drinking water and vault toilets are available. Some facilities are wheelchair-accessible. Leashed pets are permitted.

Reservations, fees: Reservations are not accepted. There is no fee for camping. There is a 14-day stay limit. Open year-round, weather permitting.

Directions: From Williams on I-5, turn west on Highway 20 and drive 25 miles into the foothills to Walker Ridge Road. Turn north (right) on Walker Ridge Road (a dirt road) and drive north for about four miles to a "major" intersection of two dirt roads. Turn left and drive about 2.5 miles toward the Indian Valley Dam. The Blue Oak campground is just off the road on the right, about 1.5 miles from Indian Valley Reservoir.

Contact: Bureau of Land Management, Ukiah Field Office, 707/468-4000, fax 707/468-4027.

68 MANCHESTER STATE PARK

🚶 🛶 🐕 🚐 ⛺

Scenic rating: 8

near Point Arena

Map 4.3, page 261

Manchester State Park is a beautiful park on the Sonoma coast, set near the Garcia River with the town of Point Arena to the nearby north providing a supply point. If you hit it during one of the rare times when the skies are clear and the wind is down, the entire area will seem aglow in magical sunbeams. The park features 760 acres of beach, sand dunes, and grasslands, with 18,000 feet of ocean frontage and five miles of gentle sandy beach stretching southward toward the Point Arena Lighthouse. The curved beach catches a large amount of driftwood and other debris. Alder Creek Trail is a great hike here, routed north along beachfront to the mouth of Alder Creek and its beautiful coastal lagoon. This is where the San Andreas Fault heads off from land and into the sea. In winter, the main attraction is steelhead fishing in the Garcia River. Spring and early summer sees a variety of coastal wildflowers. The park provides habitat for tundra swans. The region near the park is grazing land for sheep and cattle. Sixteen campsites were closed in 2004 to protect an endangered species, the Point Arena mountain beaver.

Campsites, facilities: There are 18 sites for tents or RVs up to 32 feet, 10 environmental sites (a one-mile walk in), and one group site for up to 40 people and RVs up to 21 feet. No hookups. Picnic tables and fire grills are provided. Drinking water, vault toilets, and a dump station are available. The environmental sites have pit toilets, picnic tables and fire rings, but no drinking water, and garbage must be packed out. Leashed pets are permitted. No dogs in environmental sites.

Reservations, fees: Reservations are accepted only for the group site ($7.50 reservation fee) at 800/444-PARK (800/444-7275) or www.reserveamerica.com. Sites are $15 per night, $6 per night for each additional vehicle, $15 per night for environmental sites, $90 per night for group site. Open year-round.

Directions: On U.S. 101 north of Santa Rosa, turn west on River Road and drive 16 miles to Guerneville and Highway 116. Continue west on Highway 116 and drive about 20 miles to Highway 1 at Jenner. Turn north on Highway 1 and drive 55 miles to Point Arena. From Point Arena, continue north about five miles to Kinney Lane. Turn left and drive one mile to the campground entrance on the right.

Contact: Manchester State Park, 707/882-2463; Mendocino District, 707/937-5804, fax 707/937-2953, www.parks.ca.gov.

69 SHELDON CREEK

🚶 🛶 🐕 5% ⛺

Scenic rating: 3

near Hopland

Map 4.3, page 261

Only the locals know about this spot, and hey, there aren't a lot of locals around. The camp is set amid rolling hills, grasslands, and oaks along little Sheldon Creek. It is pretty and quiet in the spring when the hills have greened up, but hot in the summer.

Recreational possibilities include hiking, and in the fall, hunting.

Campsites, facilities: There are six sites for tents only. Picnic tables and fire grills are provided. Vault toilets are available. No drinking water is available. Garbage must be packed out. Leashed pets are permitted.

Reservations, fees: Reservations are not accepted. There is no fee for camping. Open year-round, weather permitting.

Directions: From Santa Rosa on U.S. 101, drive north to Hopland and the junction with Highway 175. Turn east on Highway 175 and drive three miles to Old Toll Road. Turn right on Old Toll Road and drive eight miles to the camp.

Contact: Bureau of Land Management, Ukiah Field Office, 707/468-4000, fax 707/468-4027.

70 ROLLERVILLE JUNCTION

Scenic rating: 7

near Point Arena

Map 4.3, page 261

This location makes it an attractive spot, with the beautiful Manchester State Beach, Alder Creek, and Garcia River all available nearby on one of California's most attractive stretches of coastline. Point Arena Lighthouse and a fishing pier are also nearby. The elevation of the camp is 220 feet. Insiders tip: More than 1,100 acres of public land across the road from this campground are available for exploring; this is prime ocean-frontage property bought from private owners.

Campsites, facilities: There are 34 sites with full hookups (30 and 50 amps) for RVs of any length, 10 tent sites, five sleeping cabins, and two park-model cabins. Some sites are pull-through. Picnic tables and fire rings are provided. Drinking water, restrooms with flush toilets and showers, spa, seasonal heated swimming pool, cable TV hookups, modem access, dump station, coin laun-

dry, seasonal café, convenience store, and propane gas are available. Some facilities are wheelchair-accessible. Leashed pets are permitted.

Reservations, fees: Reservations are accepted by telephone at 800/910-4317. Sites are $30–40 per night, $3–5 per person per night for more than two people. Some credit cards accepted. Open year-round.

Directions: On U.S. 101 north of Santa Rosa, turn west on River Road and drive 16 miles to Guerneville and Highway 116. Continue west on Highway 116 and drive about 20 miles to Highway 1 at Jenner. Turn north on Highway 1 and drive 55 miles to Point Arena. From Point Arena, continue north for 1.5 miles to Point Arena Lighthouse Road and the campground on the left (west side) at 22990 N. Highway 1.

Contact: Rollerville Junction, 707/882-2440, fax 707/882-3049.

71 ANCHOR BAY CAMPGROUND

Scenic rating: 8

near Gualala

Map 4.3, page 261

This is a quiet and beautiful stretch of California coast. The six-acre campground is on the ocean side of Highway 1 north of Gualala, with sites set at ocean level as well as amid trees—take your pick. Nearby Gualala Regional Park, six miles to the south, provides an excellent easy hike, the headlands-to-beach loop with coastal views, a lookout of the Gualala River, and many giant cypress trees. In winter, the nearby Gualala River attracts large but elusive steelhead.

Campsites, facilities: There are 37 sites for tents or RVs up to 40 feet; 12 sites have partial hookups (15 amps). Picnic tables and fire pits are provided. Drinking water, restrooms with flush toilets and coin showers, Wi-Fi, fish-cleaning room, dive-gear wash room, picnic area, and a dump station are available. Leashed pets are permitted, with certain restrictions, at a maximum of two per site.

Reservations, fees: Reservations are accepted ($10 reservation fee). Sites are $38–42 per night, $3–5 per person per night for more than two people, $20 per night for each additional vehicle, $3 per pet per stay. Boat launching is $5 per day. Some credit cards accepted. Open year-round.

Directions: On U.S. 101 north of Santa Rosa, turn west on River Road and drive 16 miles to Guerneville and Highway 116. Continue west on Highway 116 and drive about 13.1 miles to Highway 1 at Jenner. Turn north on Highway 1 and drive 38 miles to Gualala. Continue four miles north on Highway 1 to the campground on the left (west) side of the road.

Contact: Anchor Bay Campground, 707/884-4222, www.abcamp.com.

72 CLOVERDALE KOA

Scenic rating: 7

near the Russian River

Map 4.3, page 261

This KOA campground is set just above the Russian River in the Alexander Valley wine country, just south of Cloverdale. The park is both rustic and tidy. The hillside pool has a nice view. In addition, a fishing pond is stocked with largemouth bass, bluegill, and catfish. On moonless nights, this is a great place for stargazing. Bird-watching is another pastime in this area. The nearby Russian River is an excellent beginner's route in an inflatable kayak or canoe. The nearby winery in Asti makes for a popular side trip.

Campsites, facilities: There are 89 sites with full hookups (30 and 50 amps) for RVs of any length, 49 sites for tents, 18 cabins, and five lodges. Some sites are pull-through. Picnic tables and fire grills are provided. Restrooms with flush toilets and showers, Wi-Fi, solar-heated swimming pool, playground, dump

station, coin laundry, recreation room, mini golf, nature trails, catch-and-release fish pond, weekend entertainment in the summer, and a convenience and gift store are available. Some facilities are wheelchair-accessible. Leashed pets are permitted, with certain restrictions.

Reservations, fees: Reservations are accepted at 800/562-4042. Sites are $35–50 per night, $8 per person per night for more than two people, $8 per night for each additional vehicle. Some credit cards accepted. Open year-round.

Directions: From Cloverdale on U.S. 101, take the Central Cloverdale exit, which puts you on Asti Road. Drive straight on Asti Road to 1st Street. Turn right (east) and drive a short distance to River Road. Turn right (south) and drive four miles to Asti Ridge Road. Turn left and drive to the campground entrance.

In summer/fall: South of Cloverdale on U.S. 101, take the Asti exit to Asti Road. Turn right (south) on Asti Road and drive 1.5 miles to Washington School Road. Turn left (east) and drive 1.5 miles to Asti Ridge Road. Turn right and drive to the campground entrance. (Note: This route is usually open Memorial Day Weekend to late November, when a seasonal bridge is in place.) Both routes are well signed.

Contact: Cloverdale KOA, 707/894-3337, www.winecountrykoa.com.

73 GUALALA POINT REGIONAL PARK

Scenic rating: 8

at Sonoma County Regional Park

Map 4.3, page 261

This is a dramatic spot near the ocean, close to the mouth of the Gualala River. The campground is on the east side of the highway, about 0.3 mile from the ocean. A trail along the bluff provides an easy hiking adventure;

on the west side of the highway other trails to the beach are available.

Campsites, facilities: There are 19 sites for tents or RVs up to 25 feet (no hookups), six walk-in tent sites, and one hike-in/bike-in site. Picnic tables and fire rings are provided. Drinking water, restrooms with flush toilets and coin showers, dump station, and firewood are available. Some facilities are wheelchair-accessible. Leashed pets are permitted with valid rabies certificate.

Reservations, fees: Reservations are accepted ($7 reservation fee) on weekdays at 707/565-2267. Sites are $17 per night, $5 per person per night for hike-in/bike-in site, $6 per night for each additional vehicle, $1 per pet per night. Open year-round.

Directions: On U.S. 101 north of Santa Rosa, turn west on River Road and drive 16 miles to Guerneville and Highway 116. Continue west on Highway 116 and drive about 20 miles to Highway 1 at Jenner. Turn north on Highway 1 and drive 38 miles to Gualala. Turn right at the park entrance (a day-use area is on the west side of the highway).

Contact: Gualala Point Regional Park 707/785-2377, www.sonoma-county.org/parks.

74 LAKE SONOMA RECREATION AREA

🏃 🏊 🎣 🚤 🐕 ♿ 🚐 ⛺

Scenic rating: 8

near Healdsburg

| Map 4.3, page 261 | BEST (|

Lake Sonoma is one of the best weekend vacation sites for Bay Area campers. The developed campground (Liberty Glen) is fine for car campers, but the boat-in sites are ideal for folks who desire a quiet and pretty lakeside setting. This is a big lake, extending nine miles north on the Dry Creek arm and four miles west on the Warm Springs Creek arm. There is an adjacent 8,000-acre wildlife area that was set aside to protect nesting peregrine falcons, as well as 40 miles of hiking trails. The lake is set at an elevation of 450 feet, with 53 miles of shoreline and hundreds of hidden coves. A sandy swimming beach is available at Yorty Creek, but there is no lifeguard. The water-skier versus angler conflict has been resolved by limiting high-speed boats to specified areas. Laws are strictly enforced, making this lake excellent for either sport. Wildlife-watching includes wild pigs, wild turkeys, blacktail deer, and river otters. The best fishing is in the protected coves of the Warm Springs and Dry Creek arms of the lake. Fish species include bass, catfish, rainbow trout, crappie, and sunfish. The visitors center is adjacent to a public fish hatchery. Steelhead come to spawn from the Russian River between late December and late March.

Campsites, facilities: There are 109 primitive boat-in sites around the lake, several hike-in sites, and 95 tent and RV sites (no hookups). There are four group sites, two of which are boat-in; the other two are at Liberty Glen Campground 2.5 miles from the lake. Picnic tables, fire grills, vault toilets, lantern poles, and garbage bins are provided at the primitive sites, but no drinking water is available. At Liberty Glen, picnic tables, fire rings, lantern holders, and vault toilets are provided. A boat ramp and houseboat and boat rentals are available nearby. Saturday night campfire talks are held at an amphitheater during the summer. Some facilities are wheelchair-accessible. Campsites have limited facilities in winter. Leashed pets are permitted.

Reservations, fees: Reservations for the boat-in sites and group sites only are accepted at 877/444-6777 or www.ReserveUSA.com. Sites are $14 per night, $10–16 per night for primitive sites, $40–56 per night for group campsites. A camping permit is required from the visitors center for boat-in sites. Open year-round.

Directions: From Santa Rosa, drive north on U.S. 101 to Healdsburg. In Healdsburg, take the Dry Creek Road exit, turn left, and drive northwest for 11 miles. After you cross a small bridge, the visitors center will be on your right.

To reach the Yorty Creek Boat Ramp: On U.S. 101 at the south end of Cloverdale, take the Cloverdale Boulevard exit to Cloverdale Boulevard. Turn right on Cloverdale Boulevard and drive one block to Treadway Street. Turn left and drive two blocks to Foothill Boulevard. Turn right and drive 0.75 mile to Hot Springs Road. Turn left and drive about five miles to the boat launch. Note: Hot Springs Road is narrow with many hairpin turns. Trailers are prohibited, but the launch provides access for canoes, kayaks, and car-top boats to boat-in sites nearby.

Contact: U.S. Army Corps of Engineers, Lake Sonoma Visitor Center, 707/433-9483, fax 707/431-1031; headquarters, 707/431-0313, www.spn.usace.army.mil/LakeSonoma; Lake Sonoma Marina, 707/433-2200.

75 SALT POINT STATE PARK

🚶 🚴 🏊 🐎 ♿ 🚐 ⛺

Scenic rating: 9

near Fort Ross

Map 4.3, page 261   BEST (

This is a gorgeous piece of Sonoma coast, highlighted by Fisk Mill Cove, inshore kelp beds, outstanding short hikes, and abalone diving. In fact, this is one of the finest diving areas for red abalone in the state. There is also an underwater reserve for divers, which is a protected area. Unfortunately there are also diving accidents that are due to the occasional large surf, strong currents, and rocky shoreline. There are two campgrounds here, Gerstle Cove Campground and the much larger Woodside Campground. Great hikes include Bluff Trail and Stump Beach Trail (great views). During abalone season, this is one of the best and most popular spots on the Northern California coast. The Kruse Rhododendron Reserve is within the park and definitely worth the stroll. This is a 317-acre conservation reserve that features second-growth redwoods, Douglas firs, tan oak, and many rhododendrons, with five miles of hiking trails. After the fall rains, this area is popular for mushroom hunters (the Kruse Rhododendron Reserve is closed to mushroom picking). Mushroom hunters must park in the area open to picking and be limited to five pounds per day. Of course, this can be a dangerous hobby; only eat mushrooms you can identify as safe. But you knew that, right?

Campsites, facilities: At Gerstle Cove Campground, there are 30 sites for tents or RVs up to 31 feet (no hookups). At Woodside Campground, there are 79 sites for tents or RVs up to 31 feet (no hookups), 20 walk-in tent sites (about a 300-yard walk), 10 hike-in/bike-in sites, a group site that can accommodate up to 40 people, and a primitive overflow area for self-contained vehicles. Picnic tables and fire rings are provided. Drinking water and flush toilets are available. Summer interpretive programs are also available; firewood is available for purchase. The picnic area and one hiking trail are wheelchair-accessible. Leashed pets are permitted, except on trails.

Reservations, fees: Reservations are accepted ($7.50 reservation fee) at 800/444-PARK (800/444-7275) or www.reserveamerica.com. Sites are $25 per night, $6 per night for each additional vehicle, $15 per night for walk-in and overflow sites, $3 per person per night for hike-in/bike-in sites, $150 for the group site. Open year-round.

Directions: On U.S. 101 north of Santa Rosa, turn west on River Road and drive 16 miles to Guerneville and Highway 116. Continue west on Highway 116 and drive 13.1 miles to Highway 1 at Jenner. Turn north on Highway 1 and drive about 20 miles to the park entrance; Woodside Campground on the right and Gerstle Cove on the left.

Contact: Salt Point State Park, 707/847-3221; Russian River District, 707/865-2391, fax 707/865-2046, www.parks.ca.gov.

76 OCEAN COVE CAMPGROUND

Scenic rating: 8

near Fort Ross

Map 4.3, page 261

The highlights here are the campsites on a bluff overlooking the ocean. Alas, it can be foggy during the summer. A good side trip is to Fort Ross, with a stellar easy hike available on the Fort Ross Trail, which features a walk through an old colonial fort as well as great coastal views, excellent for whale-watching. There is also excellent hiking at Stillwater Cove Regional Park, just a mile to the south off Highway 1.

Campsites, facilities: There are 125 pull-through sites for tents or RVs of any length (no hookups). Picnic tables and fire grills are provided. Drinking water, chemical toilets, and coin showers are available. A boat launch, grocery store, fishing supplies, and diving-gear sales are available nearby. Leashed pets are permitted.

Reservations, fees: Reservations are not accepted. Sites are $17 per night per vehicle, $2 per pet per night, $8 per day for boat launching. Some credit cards accepted. Open April through November.

Directions: On U.S. 101 north of Santa Rosa, turn west on River Road and drive 16 miles to Guerneville and Highway 116. Continue west on Highway 116 and drive about 13 miles to Highway 1 at Jenner. Turn north on Highway 1 and drive 17 miles north on Highway 1 (five miles north of Fort Ross) to the campground entrance on the left.

Contact: Ocean Cove Campground, 707/847-3422, www.oceancove.org.

77 STILLWATER COVE REGIONAL PARK

Scenic rating: 8

near Fort Ross

Map 4.3, page 261

Stillwater Cove has a dramatic rock-strewn cove and sits on a classic chunk of Sonoma coast. The campground is sometimes overlooked, since it is a county-operated park and not on the state park reservation system. One of the region's great hikes is available here: Stockoff Creek Loop, with the trailhead at the day-use parking lot. In a little more than a mile, the trail is routed through forest with both firs and redwoods, and then along a pretty stream. To get beach access, you will need to cross Highway 1 and then drop to the cove.

Campsites, facilities: There are 23 sites for tents or RVs up to 30 feet (no hookups), and a hike-in/bike-in site. Picnic tables and fire rings are provided. Drinking water, restrooms with flush toilets and coin showers, firewood, and a dump station are available. Supplies can be obtained in Ocean Cove (one mile north) and Fort Ross. Some facilities are wheelchair-accessible. Leashed pets are permitted with a valid rabies certificate.

Reservations, fees: Reservations are accepted ($7 reservation fee) at 707/565-2267 on weekdays. Sites are $17 per night, $6 per night for each additional vehicle, $5 per person per night for the hike-in/bike-in site, and $1 per pet per night. Open year-round.

Directions: On U.S. 101 north of Santa Rosa, turn west on River Road and drive 16 miles to Guerneville and Highway 116. Continue west on Highway 116 and drive about 13 miles to Highway 1 at Jenner. Turn north on Highway 1 and drive 16 miles north on Highway 1 (four miles north of Fort Ross) to the park entrance.

Contact: Stillwater Cove Regional Park, Sonoma County, 707/847-3245; Sonoma County Regional Parks, 707/565-2041, www.sonoma-county.org/parks.

78 AUSTIN CREEK STATE RECREATION AREA

🚶 🛶 🐕 ♿ 🚐 ⛺

Scenic rating: 7

near the Russian River

Map 4.3, page 261

Austin Creek State Recreation Area and Armstrong Redwoods State Reserve are actually coupled, forming 7,000 acres of continuous parkland. Most visitors prefer the redwood park. The campground is called Bullfrog Pond, set near a pond with bluegill. The landscape features open woodlands and foothills with 22 miles of trails. The rugged topography provides a sense of isolation. The highlight at the recreation area is a system of hiking trails that lead to a series of small creeks: Schoolhouse Creek, Gilliam Creek, and Austin Creek. They involve pretty steep climbs, and in the summer it's hot here, with temperatures occasionally exceeding 100°F, so plan accordingly. Elevations range 150–1,900 feet on Marble Mine Ridge. All of the park's trails are open to horses and horseback-riding rentals are available in adjacent Armstrong Redwoods State Park. There are many attractive side-trip possibilities, including the adjacent Armstrong Redwoods, of course, but also canoeing on the Russian River (3.5 miles away), fishing (smallmouth bass in summer, steelhead in winter), and wine-tasting. Annual winter rainfall often exceeds 50 inches.

Campsites, facilities: There are 24 sites for tents or RVs up to 20 feet (no hookups), and three hike-in sites. (The access road is very steep and narrow.) Picnic tables and fire grills are provided. Drinking water and flush toilets are available. Some facilities are wheelchair-accessible. Leashed pets are permitted at the main campground only. There are also three primitive, hike-in, backcountry campsites (requiring a hike of 3.5–5.1 miles) with picnic tables, fire rings, and pit toilets, but no drinking water is available and no pets are permitted. Obtain a backcountry camping permit from the office.

Reservations, fees: Reservations are not accepted. Sites are $15 per night, $15 per night for hike-in sites, $6 per night for each additional vehicle. Open year-round, but expect occasional fire closures during the summer season.

Directions: On U.S. 101 north of Santa Rosa, turn west on River Road and drive 15 miles to Guerneville and Armstrong Woods Road. Turn right and drive 2.5 miles to the entrance of Armstrong Redwoods State Park. Check in at the kiosk, and continue 3.5 miles through Armstrong Redwoods to Austin Creek State Recreation Area and the campground. The final 2.5 miles are steep and narrow, and no trailers, towed vehicles, or vehicles over 20 feet are permitted.

Contact: Austin Creek State Recreation Area, 707/869-2015, fax 707/869-5629, www.parks .ca.gov.

79 FORT ROSS REEF

🚶 🛶 🐕 ♿ 🚐 ⛺

Scenic rating: 8

at Fort Ross State Historic Park

Map 4.3, page 261

Fort Ross is just as its name announces: an old fort, in this case, an old Russian fort from 1812. The campground is two miles south of the north entrance station, less than a quarter mile from the ocean. Some redwoods and pines provide cover, and some sites are open. The privacy and beauty of the campsites vary as much as in any state park camp in California. The sites at the end of the road fill up very quickly. Though the weather is relatively benign, tents are needed for protection against moisture from fog. From camp, a trail leads down to a beach, more rocky than sandy, and a one-mile trail leads to the fort. As a destination site, Fort Ross is known as a popular abalone diving spot, with the best areas below the campground and also at nearby Reef Terrace. It also provides good, easy hikes amid its 3,386 acres. The park features a museum in the visitors center, which is always a must-see for campers making the tour up Highway 1. Note: Mushroom picking is prohibited in this park.

Campsites, facilities: There are 20 sites for tents or RVs up to 18 feet (no hookups). Picnic tables, food lockers, and fire rings are provided. Drinking water and flush toilets are available. Supplies can be obtained nearby. A visitors center and guided tours and programs are available. Some facilities are wheelchair-accessible. Leashed pets are permitted.

Reservations, fees: Reservations are not accepted. Sites are $15 per night, $6 per night for each additional vehicle. Open April through November, weather permitting.

Directions: On U.S. 101 north of Santa Rosa, turn west on River Road and drive 16 miles to Guerneville and Highway 116. Continue west on Highway 116 and drive about 13 miles to Highway 1 at Jenner. Turn north on Highway 1 and drive 10 miles to the (Fort Ross Reef) campground entrance. To reach the main state park entrance, drive north for two miles.

Contact: Fort Ross State Historic Park, 707/847-3286 or 707/847-3708.

80 CASINI RANCH FAMILY CAMPGROUND

Scenic rating: 8

on the Russian River

Map 4.3, page 261

Woods and water—this campground has both, with sites set near the Russian River in both sun-filled and shaded areas. Its location on the lower river makes a side trip to the coast easy, with Sonoma Coast State Beach about a 15-minute drive to the nearby west. No long-term rentals available.

Campsites, facilities: There are 225 sites for tents or RVs of any length; many have full or partial hookups (30 amps); some sites are pull-through. Picnic tables and fire grills are provided. Restrooms with flush toilets and showers, playground, dump station, coin laundry, cable TV, Wi-Fi, game arcade, boat and canoe rentals, propane gas, group facilities, seasonal activities, and a convenience store are available. Some facilities are wheelchair-accessible. Leashed pets are permitted.

Reservations, fees: Reservations are accepted at 800/451-8400. Sites are $26–34 per night, $3 per person per night for more than two people, $1 per pet per night. Weekly and monthly rates available. Some credit cards accepted. Open year-round.

Directions: On U.S. 101 north of Santa Rosa, turn west on River Road and drive 16 miles to Guerneville and Highway 116. Continue west on Highway 116 and drive eight miles to Duncan Mills and Moscow Road. Turn left (southeast) on Moscow Road and drive 0.6 mile to the campground on the left.

Contact: Casini Ranch Family Campground Store, 707/865-2255, www.casiniranch.com.

81 SONOMA COAST STATE BEACH: POMO CANYON/ WILLOW CREEK WALK-IN

Scenic rating: 10

in Sonoma Coast State Beach

Map 4.3, page 261

This is a gorgeous camp, well hidden, and offering a great trailhead and nearby beach access. The camp is actually not on the coast at all, but on the east-facing slope of Pomo Canyon (just over the ridge from the coast), where the campsites are set within a beautiful second-growth redwood forest and among fern understory. A trail is routed through the redwoods (with many cathedral trees) and up to the ridge, where there are divine views of the mouth of the Russian River, Goat Rock, and the beautiful Sonoma coast. The trail continues for three miles, all the way to Shell Beach, where you can spend hours poking around and beachcombing. The camp's seclusion and proximity to the Bay Area make it a rare winner. Now get this: A camping option is provided at nearby Willow Creek hike-in sites. Willow Creek Campground is nestled in trees, adjacent to open meadow, next to the Russian River.

Campsites, facilities: At Pomo Canyon, there are 21 walk-in tent sites. Picnic tables, food lockers, and fire rings are provided. Drinking water and pit toilets are available. Some facilities are wheelchair-accessible. No pets are permitted. At Willow Creek, there are 11 hike-in sites. No drinking water. Pit toilets are available, otherwise no facilities. No pets are permitted.

Reservations, fees: Reservations are not accepted. Sites are $15 per night, $6 per night for each additional vehicle. Open April through November, weather permitting.

Directions: In Petaluma on U.S. 101, take the East Washington exit and turn west (this street becomes Bodega Avenue). Drive west through Petaluma and continue for 17 miles to Highway 1. Turn right (north) on Highway 1 and drive nine miles to Bodega Bay, then continue north for nine miles to Willow Creek Road. To reach Pomo Canyon Campground, turn right on Willow Creek Road and drive about three miles to the campground parking. Park and walk to the campsites, a one- to five-minute walk. To reach Willow Creek Campground, turn right on Willow Creek Road and drive 1.5 miles to the campground parking on the left. Hike up to 0.25 mile to reach the campsites.

Contact: Sonoma Coast State Beach, 707/875-3483, www.parks.ca.gov.

82 SONOMA COAST STATE BEACH: WRIGHTS BEACH

🏃 🏊 🏕 ♿ 🚗 ⛺

Scenic rating: 8

in Sonoma Coast State Beach

Map 4.3, page 261

This park provides for more than its share of heaven and hell. This state park campground is at the north end of a beach that stretches south for about a mile, yet to the north it is steep and rocky. The campsites are considered a premium because of their location next to the beach. Because the campsites are often full, a key plus is an overflow area available for self-contained vehicles. Sonoma Coast State Beach stretches from Bodega Head to Vista Trail for 17 miles, separated by rock bluffs and headlands that form a series of beaches. More than a dozen access points from the highway that allow you can reach the beach. There are many excellent side trips. The best is to the north, where you can explore dramatic Shell Beach (the turnoff is on the west side of Highway 1), or take Pomo Trail (the trailhead is on the east side of the highway, across from Shell Beach) up the adjacent foothills for sweeping views of the coast. That's the heaven. Now for the hell: Dozens of people have drowned here. Wrights Beach is not for swimming; rip currents, heavy surf, and surprise rogue waves can make even playing in the surf dangerous. Many rescues are made each year. The bluffs and coastal rocks can also be unstable and unsafe for climbing. Got it? 1. Stay clear of the water. 2. Don't climb the bluffs. Now it's up to you to get it right.

Campsites, facilities: There are 27 sites for tents or RVs up to 27 feet (no hookups), with a limit of eight people per site, and an overflow area for self-contained vehicles. Picnic tables, food lockers, and fire rings are provided. Drinking water and flush toilets are available. Showers are available at nearby Bodega Dunes Campground. Leashed pets are permitted in the campground and on the beach.

Reservations, fees: Reservations are recommended ($7.50 reservation fee) at 800/444-PARK (800/444-7275) or www.reserveamerica.com. Sites are $25–35 per night, $6 per night for each additional vehicle. Open year-round, weather permitting.

Directions: In Petaluma on U.S. 101, take the East Washington exit and turn west (this street becomes Bodega Avenue). Drive west through Petaluma and continue for 17 miles to Highway 1. Turn right (north) on Highway 1 and drive nine miles to Bodega Bay. From Bodega Bay, continue north for six miles to the campground entrance.

Contact: Sonoma Coast State Beach, 707/875-3483, www.parks.ca.gov.

83 BODEGA BAY RV PARK

Scenic rating: 8

in Bodega Bay

Map 4.3, page 261

Bodega Bay RV Park is one of the oldest RV parks in the state, and there are few north-state coastal destinations better than Bodega Bay. Excellent seafood restaurants are available within five minutes, and some of the best deep-sea fishing is available out of Bodega Bay Sportfishing. In addition, there is a great view of the ocean at nearby Bodega Head to the west. It is a 35-minute walk from the park to the beach.

Campsites, facilities: There are 85 sites, most with full hookups (30 and 50 amps), for RVs of any length; some sites are pull-through. No tents. Picnic tables are provided. Drinking water and restrooms with flush toilets and showers are available. Coin laundry, restaurant, group facilities, horseshoes, video arcade, boccie ball, Wi-Fi, and cable TV are available. Some facilities are wheelchair-accessible. Leashed pets are permitted.

Reservations, fees: Reservations are recommended at 800/201-6864. Sites are $35–39 per night, $3 per person per night for more than two people. Some credit cards accepted. Open year-round.

Directions: In Petaluma on U.S. 101, take the East Washington exit and turn west (this street becomes Bodega Avenue). Drive west through Petaluma and continue for 17 miles to Highway 1. Turn right (north) on Highway 1 and drive nine miles to Bodega Bay. In Bodega Bay, continue north for two miles to the RV park on the left at 2001 Highway 1.

Contact: Bodega Bay RV Park, 707/875-3701, www.bodegabayrvpark.com.

84 SONOMA COAST STATE BEACH: BODEGA DUNES

Scenic rating: 8

in Sonoma Coast State Beach

Map 4.3, page 261

Sonoma Coast State Beach features several great campgrounds, and if you like beaches, this one rates high. Bodega Dunes campground is set near Salmon Creek Beach, the closest beach to the campground and far safer than Wrights Beach. The beach stretches for miles, providing stellar beach walks and excellent beachcombing during low tides. For some campers, a foghorn sounding repeatedly through the night can make sleep difficult. The quietest sites here are among the dunes. A day-use area includes a wheelchair-accessible boardwalk that leads out to a sandy beach. In summer, campfire programs and junior ranger programs are often available. To the nearby south is Bodega Bay, with a major deep-sea sportfishing operation—crowned by often excellent salmon fishing; check current fishing regulations. The town of Bodega Bay offers a full marina and restaurants.

Campsites, facilities: There are 98 sites for tents or RVs up to 31 feet (no hookups), and one hike-in/bike-in site. Picnic tables, food lockers and fire grills are provided. Drinking water, restrooms with flush toilets and free showers, and a dump station are available. Laundry facilities, supplies, and horse rentals are available within one mile. Some facilities are wheelchair-accessible. Leashed pets are permitted at the campsites only.

Reservations, fees: Reservations are accepted ($7.50 reservation fee) at 800/444-PARK (800/444-7275) or www.reserveamerica.com. Sites are $25 per night, $6 per night for each additional vehicle, $3 per person per night for hike-in/bike-in site. Open year-round.

Directions: In Santa Rosa on U.S. 101, turn west on Highway 12 and drive 10 miles to Sebastopol (Highway 12 becomes Bodega Highway). Continue straight (west) for 10 miles to Bodega. Continue for 0.5 mile to Highway 1. Turn right (north) on Highway 1 and drive five miles to Bodega Bay. Continue 0.5 mile north to the campground entrance on the left (west).

Contact: Sonoma Coast State Beach, 707/875-3483, www.parks.ca.gov.

85 WESTSIDE REGIONAL PARK

Scenic rating: 7

on Bodega Bay

Map 4.3, page 261

This campground is on the west shore of Bodega Bay. One of the greatest boat launches on the coast is adjacent to the park on the south, providing access to prime fishing waters. Salmon fishing is excellent from mid-June through August; check current fishing regulations. A small, protected beach (for kids to dig in the sand and wade) is available at the end of the road beyond the campground. Hiking trails can be found at the state beach nearby.

Campsites, facilities: There are 47 sites for tents or RVs of any length (no hookups); most sites are pull-through. Picnic tables and fire grills are provided. Drinking water, restrooms with flush toilets and coin showers, fish-cleaning station, firewood, and a boat ramp are available. A dump station is available at Doran Regional Park. Supplies can be obtained in Bodega Bay. Some facilities are wheelchair-accessible. Leashed pets are permitted with valid rabies certificate.

Reservations, fees: Reservations are accepted ($7 reservation fee) on weekdays at 707/565-2267. Sites are $18 per night, $6 per night for each additional vehicle, $1 per pet per night. Open year-round.

Directions: In Petaluma on U.S. 101, take the East Washington exit and turn west (this street becomes Bodega Avenue). Drive west through Petaluma and continue for 17 miles to Highway 1 north. Merge right onto Highway 1 and drive north nine miles to Bodega Bay. In Bodega Bay, continue north to Eastshore Road. Turn left and drive one block to Bay Flat Road. Turn right and drive (becomes Westshore Road) two miles to the park on the left, 0.5 mile past Spud Point Marina.

Contact: Westside Regional Parks, Sonoma County Parks Department, 707/875-3540 or 707/565-2041, www.sonoma-county.org/parks.

86 DORAN REGIONAL PARK

Scenic rating: 7

on Bodega Bay

Map 4.3, page 261

This campground is set beside Doran Beach on Bodega Bay, which offers complete fishing and marina facilities. In season, it's also a popular clamming and crabbing spot. This park has a wide, somewhat sheltered sandy beach. Salmon fishing is often excellent during the summer at the Whistle Buoy offshore from Bodega Head, and rock fishing is good year-round offshore. Fishing is also available off the rock jetty in the park.

Campsites, facilities: There are 10 sites for tents and 128 sites for tents or RVs of any length (no hookups), one group tent site for up to 50 people, and one hike-in/bike-in site. Picnic tables and fire grills are provided. Drinking water, restrooms with flush toilets and coin showers, dump stations, fish-cleaning station, and a boat ramp are available. Some facilities are wheelchair-accessible. Supplies can be obtained in Bodega Bay. Leashed pets are permitted with a valid rabies certificate.

Reservations, fees: Reservations are accepted ($7 reservation fee and $30–50 reservation fee for the group site) on weekdays at 707/565-2267. Sites are $18 per night, $6 per night for each additional vehicle, $5 per person per night for hike-in/bike-in site, $1 per pet per night. The group site is $3 per person per night with a minimum of $72 and a maximum of 15 vehicles. Open year-round.

Directions: In Petaluma on U.S. 101, take the East Washington exit and turn west (this street becomes Bodega Avenue). Drive west through Petaluma and continue for 17 miles to Highway 1. Merge right (north) on Highway 1 and drive toward Bodega Bay and Doran Park Road. Turn left onto the campground entrance road. If you reach the town of Bodega Bay, you have gone a mile too far.

Contact: Sonoma County Parks Department, 707/875-3540 or 707/565-2041, www .sonoma-county.org/parks.

87 EDGEWATER RESORT AND RV PARK

Scenic rating: 7

on Clear Lake

Map 4.4, page 262

Soda Bay is one of Clear Lake's prettiest and most intimate spots, and this camp provides excellent access. It also provides friendly, professional service. Both waterskiing and fishing for bass and bluegill are excellent in this part of the lake. The resort has 600 feet of lake frontage, including 300 feet of swimming beach and a 230-foot fishing pier. This resort specializes in groups and family reunions. Wine-tasting, casinos, and golfing are nearby. Insider's tip: This park is very pet friendly and has occasional doggie socials.

Campsites, facilities: There are 61 sites with full hookups (20, 30, and 50 amps) for tents or RVs of any length, and eight cabins. Picnic tables and fire grills are provided. Restrooms with showers, cable TV, modem access, clubhouse, group facilities, general store, coin laundry, seasonal heated swimming pool, horseshoes, volleyball, and table tennis are available. A seasonal swimming beach, pet station, dog run, bait and tackle, boat ramp, fishing pier, boat docking, fish-cleaning station, and watercraft rentals are available on the premises. Firewood is available for purchase. Leashed pets are permitted.

Reservations, fees: Reservations are accepted at 800/396-6224. Sites are $30–40 per night, $5 per person per night for more than two people, $2.50 per pet per night. Boat launching is $5 per day. Winter discounts and weekly rates are available. Some credit cards accepted. Open year-round.

Directions: In Kelseyville on Highway 29, take the Merritt Road exit and drive on Merritt Road for two miles (it becomes Gaddy Lane) to Soda Bay Road. Turn right on Soda Bay Road and drive three miles to the campground entrance on the left at 6420 Soda Bay Road.

Contact: Edgewater Resort and RV Park, 707/279-0208, www.edgewaterresort.net.

88 SHAW'S SHADY ACRES

Scenic rating: 7

on Cache Creek

Map 4.4, page 262

Shaw's Shady Acres is set beside Cache Creek, just south of Clear Lake. Canoeing and kayaking are popular. The fishing for catfish is often quite good on summer nights in Cache Creek, a deep green, slow-moving water that looks more like a slough in a Mississippi bayou than a creek. Waterfront campsites with scattered walnut, ash, and oak trees are available. Clear Lake (the lake, not the town) is a short drive to the north, and a state park is across the creek. In addition to the campsites mentioned, there are an additional 36 long-term or permanent sites. Note: At the time of publication, this campground was in the process of being sold; check for current status.

Campsites, facilities: There are 13 sites, six with full hookups (30 amps), seven with partial hookups, for RVs up to 38 feet and tents. Picnic tables and barbecues are provided.

Restrooms with showers, dump station, fishing dock, fishing boat rentals, boat ramp, coin laundry, swimming pool (seasonal), recreation patio, fishing supplies, and a convenience store are available. Leashed pets are allowed, with certain restrictions.

Reservations, fees: Reservations are recommended. Sites are $22 per night, $3 per person per night for more than two people, $0.50 per pet per night. Boat launching is $1–3 per day. Open year-round.

Directions: From the town of Lower Lake, drive north on Highway 53 for 1.3 miles to Old Highway 53. Turn left on Old Highway 53 and then almost immediately you will arrive at Cache Creek Way. Turn left and drive 0.25 mile to the park entrance at 7805 Cache Creek Way.

Contact: Shaw's Shady Acres, 707/994-2236.

89 FUNTIME RV PARK AND WATERSPORTS

Scenic rating: 7

on Clear Lake

Map 4.4, page 262

This is one of several privately operated parks near the mouth of Cache Creek at the southern end of Clear Lake. Anderson Marsh State Park is nearby. Note that a mobile-home park is adjacent to the campground.

Campsites, facilities: There are 80 sites with full hookups (30 and 50 amps) for tents or RVs of any length, four park-model cabins, and two cabins. Most sites are pull-through. Picnic tables and barbecues are provided. Restrooms with flush toilets and showers, cable TV, modem access, boat rentals, pier, boat ramp, fish-cleaning station, seasonal swimming pool, wading pool, fishing supplies, coin laundry, arcade, and a convenience store are available. Some facilities are wheelchair-accessible. Leashed pets are permitted.

Reservations, fees: Reservations are accepted.

Sites are $17–30 per night, $3 per person per night for more than two people. Some credit cards accepted. Open year-round.

Directions: From the town of Lower Lake, drive north on Highway 53 for 1.3 miles to Old Highway 53. Turn left on Old Highway 53 and drive 1.2 miles to the resort entrance on the left.

Contact: Funtime RV Park, 707/994-6267, www.funtimervparks.com.

90 CACHE CREEK CANYON REGIONAL PARK

Scenic rating: 7

near Rumsey

Map 4.4, page 262

This is the best campground in Yolo County, yet it's known by few out-of-towners. It is set at 1,300 feet beside Cache Creek, which is the closest river to the Bay Area that provides white-water rafting opportunities. This section of river features primarily Class I and II water, ideal for inflatable kayaks and overnight trips. One rapid, Big Mother, is sometimes considered Class III, though that might be a stretch. Occasionally, huge catfish are caught in this area.

Campsites, facilities: There are 45 sites for tents or RVs up to 42 feet (no hookups), and three group sites that can accommodate 20–30 people. Picnic tables, barbecue pits, and fire rings are provided. Drinking water, restrooms with flush toilets, and a dump station are available. Some facilities are wheelchair-accessible. Leashed pets are permitted.

Reservations, fees: Reservations are accepted for group sites only at 530/666-8115. Sites are $19 per night, $5 per night for each additional vehicle, $2 per pet per night. Group sites are $165 per night. Off-season discounts available. Discount for Yolo County residents. Open year-round.

Directions: From Vacaville on I-80, turn north on I-505 and drive 21 miles to

Madison and the junction with Highway 16 west. Turn northwest on Highway 16 and drive northwest for about 35 miles to the town of Rumsey. From Rumsey, continue west on Highway 16 for five miles to the park entrance on the left at 1475 State Highway 16.

Contact: Cache Creek Canyon Regional Park, Yolo County, 530/666-8115, fax 530/666-8837, www.yolocounty.org.

91 BOGGS MOUNTAIN DEMONSTRATION STATE FOREST

Scenic rating: 5

near Middletown

Map 4.4, page 262

This overlooked spot is set in a state forest that covers 3,500 acres of pine and Douglas fir. There are two adjoining campgrounds here. This is a popular destination for the region's equestrians. There are numerous trails for horses, hikers, and bikers. Remember: Equestrians have the right of way over hikers and bikers, and hikers have the right of way over bikers. Got it? The International Mountain Biking Association has chosen this as one of the top 10 riding areas in the country. There is a 14-mile trail system available that started as a series of hand-built fire lines. Note that in early fall, this area is open to deer hunting. Boggs is one of nine state forests managed with the purpose of demonstrating economical forest management, which means there is logging along with compatible recreation.

Campsites, facilities: There are 22 sites for tents or RVs up to 22 feet (no hookups). No drinking water is available. Picnic tables and fire pits are provided. Vault toilets are available. Garbage must be packed out. Coin laundry, pizza parlor, and gas station are available within two miles. Horses are permitted. Leashed pets are permitted.

Reservations, fees: Reservations are not accepted. There is no fee for camping. Self-registration required. Open year-round.

Directions: From Vallejo, drive north on Highway 29 past Calistoga to Middletown and the junction with Highway 175. Turn left (north) on Highway 175 and drive seven miles (through the town of Cobb) to Forestry Road. Turn right and drive one mile to the campgrounds on the left.

Contact: Boggs Mountain Demonstration State Forest, 707/928-4378.

92 JELLYSTONE RV PARK

Scenic rating: 7

near Cobb Mountain

Map 4.4, page 262

This camp, formerly called Beaver Creek RV Park, has a trout creek, a pond with canoe and kayak rentals in summer, plus plenty of hiking and bird-watching opportunities. Kelsey Creek runs through the campground. In addition, horseback riding and hot-air balloon rides are available nearby. This camp is set near Highway 175 between Middletown and Clear Lake, and while there is a parade of vacation traffic on Highway 29, relatively few people take the longer route on Highway 175. Cobb Mountain looms nearby. Golf courses are in the vicinity.

Campsites, facilities: There are 97 sites with full hookups (30 and 50 amps) for RVs up to 40 feet, 10 tent sites, and four cabins. Most sites are pull-through. Picnic tables and fire rings are provided. Drinking water, restrooms with showers, group facilities, coin laundry, Wi-Fi and modem access, seasonal swimming pool, kayak and paddleboat rentals, boating pond, playground, horseshoes, miniature golf, recreation hall, picnic area, athletic field, basketball, volleyball, horseshoes, firewood, ice, propane, and a camp store are available. Some facilities are wheelchair-accessible. Leashed pets are permitted.

Reservations, fees: Reservations are accepted. Sites are $25–35 per night, $3–5 per person per night for more than two people. Some credit cards accepted. Open year-round.

Directions: From Vallejo, drive north on Highway 29 past Calistoga to Middletown and the junction with Highway 175. Turn north on Highway 175 (to Cobb) and drive 12 miles to Bottle Rock Road. Turn left and drive three miles to the campground entrance on the left side of the road at 14117 Bottle Rock Road.

Contact: Jellystone RV Park, 707/928-4322, www.jellystonecobbmtn.com.

93 LOWER HUNTING CREEK

Scenic rating: 4

near Lake Berryessa

Map 4.4, page 262

This little-known camp might seem as if it's out in the middle of nowhere for the folks who wind up here accidentally, and it turns out that it is. If you plan on spending a few days here, it's advisable to get information or a map of the surrounding area from the Bureau of Land Management before your trip. There are about 25 miles of trails for off-highway-vehicle exploration on the surrounding lands. In the fall, the area provides access for deer hunting with generally poor to fair results.

Campsites, facilities: There are five sites for tents or RVs up to 20 feet (no hookups) and an overflow area. Picnic tables and fire grills are provided. Shade shelters and vault toilets are available. No drinking water. Garbage must be packed out. Leashed pets are permitted.

Reservations, fees: Reservations are not accepted. There is no fee for camping. Open year-round.

Directions: In Lower Lake on Highway 29, turn southeast on Morgan Valley Road/Berryessa-Knoxville Road and drive 15 miles to

Devilhead Road. Turn south and drive two miles to the campground.

Contact: Bureau of Land Management, Ukiah District, 707/468-4000, fax 707/468-4027.

94 PUTAH CREEK RESORT

Scenic rating: 7

on Lake Berryessa

Map 4.4, page 262

This campground is set at 400 feet elevation on the northern end of Lake Berryessa. The lake is well known for powerboats and water sports. The Putah Creek arm provides very good bass fishing in the spring and trout trolling in the summer. In the fall, the trout come to the surface and provide excellent fishing at the mouth of Pope Creek or Putah Creek. The resort has a small, rustic motel. There is a two-week camping limit in season. Also, there is an area within this resort filled with long-term RV sites.

Campsites, facilities: There are 125 sites for tents, and 55 sites with full or partial hookups (30 and 50 amps) for RVs of any length; some sites are pull-through. Picnic tables and barbecues are provided. Vault toilets, dump station, coin laundry, two boat ramps, seasonal snack bar, motel, cocktail lounge, restaurant, propane gas, ice, and convenience store are available. Leashed pets are permitted, with some restrictions.

Reservations, fees: Reservations are accepted at 707/966-0794. Sites are $23–28 per vehicle per night, $2 per pet per night. Some credit cards accepted. Open year-round.

Directions: From Vallejo, drive north on I-80 to the Suisun Valley Road exit. Take Suisun Valley Road and drive north to Highway 121. Turn north on Highway 121 and drive five miles to Highway 128. Turn left on Highway 128 and drive five miles to Berryessa-Knoxville Road. Turn right and continue 13 miles to 7600 Knoxville Road.

Contact: Putah Creek Resort, 707/966-0775; store, 707/966-2116.

95 NAPA COUNTY FAIRGROUNDS

🚲 🎿 🐕 ♿ 🚐 ⛺

Scenic rating: 3

in Calistoga

Map 4.4, page 262

What this really is, folks, is just the county fairgrounds, converted to an RV park. It is open year-round, except when the county fair is in progress. Who knows, maybe you can win a stuffed animal. What is more likely, of course, is that you have come here for the health spas, with great natural hot springs, mud baths, and assorted goodies at the health resorts in Calistoga. The downtown is within walking distance. Nearby parks for hiking include Bothe-Napa Valley and Robert Louis Stevenson State Parks. Cycling, wine-tasting, and hot-air balloon rides are also popular.

Campsites, facilities: There are 78 sites with partial or full hookups (30 and 50 amps) for RVs, and a lawn area for tents. Some sites are pull-through. Group sites are available by reservation only with a 10-vehicle minimum. Restrooms with flush toilets and showers, picnic area, and a dump station are available. No fires are permitted. A nine-hole golf course is adjacent to the campground area. Some facilities are wheelchair-accessible. Leashed pets are permitted.

Reservations, fees: Reservations are accepted and required for groups at 707/942-5221 or by website. Sites are $10–27 per night. Some credit cards accepted. Open year-round.

Directions: From Napa on Highway 29, drive north to Calistoga, turn right on Lincoln Avenue, and drive four blocks to Fairway. Turn left and drive about four blocks to the end of the road to the campground.

Contact: Napa County Fairgrounds, 707/942-5111, fax 707/942-5125, www.napacountyfairgrounds.com.

96 WINDSORLAND RV PARK

🏊 🏠 🎣 ♿ 🚐 ⛺

Scenic rating: 3

near Santa Rosa

Map 4.4, page 262

This developed park is close to the Russian River, the wine country to the east, redwoods to the west, and Lake Sonoma to the northwest. But with a swimming pool, playground, and recreation room, many visitors are content to stay right here, spend the night, then head out on their vacation. Note that some sites are long-term rentals.

Campsites, facilities: There are 55 sites with full hookups (30 amps) for RVs up to 35 feet, and a separate area for tents. Restroom with flush toilets and showers, seasonal heated swimming pool, dump station, coin laundry, recreation room, picnic area, dog run, and a playground are available. Leashed pets are permitted.

Reservations, fees: Reservations are accepted at 800/864-3407. Sites are $27–30 per night. Monthly rates available. Open year-round.

Directions: From Santa Rosa on U.S. 101, drive north for nine miles to Windsor. Take the Windsor exit, turn left on Old Redwood Highway, and drive under the freeway to the stoplight. Turn right (still on Old Redwood Highway) and drive 0.25 mile to the park on the right (9290 Old Redwood Highway).

Contact: Windsorland RV Park, 707/838-4882.

97 BOTHE-NAPA VALLEY STATE PARK

🚶 🚲 🏊 🐕 ♿ 🚐 ⛺

Scenic rating: 7

near Calistoga

Map 4.4, page 262

It's always a stunner for newcomers to discover this beautiful park with redwoods and a pretty stream so close to the Napa Valley wine and spa country. Though the campsites are relatively exposed, they are set beneath a pretty oak/bay/madrone forest, with trailheads for hiking nearby. One trail is routed south from the day-use parking lot for 1.8 mile to the restored Bale Grist Mill, a giant waterwheel on a pretty creek. Weekend tours of the Bale Grist Mill are available in summer. Another, more scenic, route, the Redwood Trail, heads up Ritchey Canyon, amid redwoods and towering Douglas fir, and along Ritchey Creek, all of it beautiful and intimate. The park covers 2,000 acres. Most of it is rugged, with elevations ranging from 300 feet to 2,000 feet. In summer, temperatures can reach the 100s, which is why finding a redwood grove can be stunning. The park has more than 10 miles of trails. Those who explore will find that the forests are on the north-facing slopes while the south-facing slopes tend to be brushy. The geology here is primarily volcanic, yet the vegetation hides most of it. Bird-watchers will note that this is one of the few places where you can see six species of woodpeckers, including the star of the show, the pileated woodpecker (the size of a crow).

Campsites, facilities: There are 37 sites for tents or RVs up to 31 feet and trailers up to 24 feet (no hookups), nine walk-in (up to 50 feet) tent sites, one hike-in/bike-in site, and one group tent site for up to 30 people. Picnic tables and fire grills are provided. Drinking water, restrooms with flush toilets and coin showers, and a seasonal swimming pool are available. Some facilities are wheelchair-accessible. Supplies can be obtained four miles away in Calistoga. Leashed pets are permitted, but not on trails.

Reservations, fees: Reservations are accepted ($7.50 reservation fee) at 800/444-PARK (800/444-7275) or www.reserveamerica .com. Sites are $20–25 per night, $6 per night for each additional vehicle, $2 per person per night for hike-in/bike-in site, $66 per night for the group site, $1–3 pool fee (free for children five and under). Open year-round.

Directions: From Napa on Highway 29, drive north to St. Helena and continue north for five miles (one mile past the entrance to Bale Grist Mill State Park) to the park entrance road on the left.
Contact: Bothe-Napa Valley State Park, 707/942-4575, www.parks.ca.gov.

98 LAKE BERRYESSA MARINA RESORT

Scenic rating: 7

on Lake Berryessa

Map 4.4, page 262

With 165 miles of shoreline, Lake Berryessa is the Bay Area's backyard water-recreation headquarters—the number-one lake (in the greater Bay Area) for waterskiing, loafing, and fishing. All water sports are permitted, but the focus is on powerboating, wakeboarding, waterskiing, and tubing. This resort is set on the west shore of the main lake, one of several resorts at the lake. The addition of park-model cabins is a great plus here.

Campsites, facilities: There are 50 sites with full hookups (30 amps) for RVs up to 40 feet, an open area for tents, and 15 park-model cabins. Picnic tables are provided, and fire grills are also provided at the tent sites. Restrooms with flush toilets and showers, dump station, coin laundry, full-service marina, watercraft and houseboat rentals, and convenience store are available. Leashed pets are permitted at RV sites, but prohibited at tent sites and cabins.

Reservations, fees: Reservations are recommended. Sites are $25–30 per night, $4 per person per night for more than two people, $1 per pet per night. Boat launching is $5 per day. Some credit cards accepted. Open year-round.

Directions: From Vallejo, drive west on I-80 to the Suisun Valley Road exit. Take Suisun Valley Road and drive north to Highway 121. Turn north on Highway 121 and drive

five miles to Highway 128. Turn left on Highway 128 and drive five miles to Berryessa-Knoxville Road. Turn right and continue nine miles to 5800 Knoxville Road.
Contact: Lake Berryessa Marina Resort, 707/966-2161, www.lakeberryessa.com.

99 HILTON PARK FAMILY CAMPGROUND

🏊 🎣 🚤 🏇 🐾 🚐 ⛺

Scenic rating: 6

on the Russian River

Map 4.4, page 262

This lush, wooded park is set on the banks of the Russian River, with a choice of open or secluded sites. The highlight of the campground is a large, beautiful beach that offers access for swimming, fishing, and canoeing. You get a choice of many recreation options in the area.
Campsites, facilities: There are 37 tent sites, five sites with partial hookups (30 amps) for RVs up to 35 feet, and eight camping cottages. Picnic tables and fire rings are provided. Restrooms with coin showers, dishwashing area, arcade, playground, coin laundry, camp store, firewood, and ice are available. A beach is available nearby. Boat rentals are available within three miles. Leashed pets are permitted, with certain restrictions.
Reservations, fees: Reservations are recommended. Sites are $32–42 per night, $10 per person per night for more than two people, $5 per night for each additional vehicle, $5 per night per pet. Some credit cards accepted. Open May through October.
Directions: From U.S. 101 north of Santa Rosa, take the River Road/Guerneville exit. Drive west on River Road for 11.5 miles (one mile after the metal bridge) to the campground on the left side of the road (just before the Russian River Pub) at 10750 River Road.
Contact: Hilton Park Family Campground, 707/887-9206, www.hiltonparkcampground.com.

100 SCHOOLHOUSE CANYON CAMPGROUND

🚶 🏊 🚤 🏇 🏕 ♿ 🚐 ⛺

Scenic rating: 8

in the Russian River Valley

Map 4.4, page 262

This campground comprises 200 acres and river access along the Russian River, campsites in a grove of large redwoods, and a parklike setting on land originally homesteaded in the 1850s. A scenic hiking trail, two miles round-trip, is routed up to a ridge for some nice views of the countryside. This overlooks Korbel Winery and vineyards, with long-distance views of several counties. Touring the adjacent Korbel Winery is a popular side trip.
Campsites, facilities: There are 45 sites for tents or RVs up to 25 feet; some sites have partial hookups. Picnic tables and fire grills are provided. Drinking water, restrooms with flush toilets and coin showers, and firewood are available. Some facilities are wheelchair-accessible. Leashed pets are permitted.
Reservations, fees: Reservations are not accepted. Call for current prices. Open May through September.
Directions: From Santa Rosa, drive north on U.S. 101 about 2.5 miles and take the River Road/Guerneville exit. Drive to the stop sign, turn left on River Road, and drive 12.5 miles to the campground entrance (next to Korbel Winery) on the right.
Contact: Schoolhouse Canyon Campground, 707/869-2311.

101 SPRING LAKE REGIONAL PARK

🚶 🚤 🏇 ♿ 🚐 ⛺

Scenic rating: 6

at Spring Lake near Santa Rosa

Map 4.4, page 262

Spring Lake is one of the few lakes in the greater Bay Area that provides lakeside camping. No gas-powered boats are permitted on this small, pretty lake, which keeps things fun and quiet for everybody. An easy trail along the west shore of the lake to the dam, then into adjoining Howarth Park, provides a pleasant evening stroll. This little lake is where a 24-pound world-record bass was reportedly caught, a story taken as a hoax by nearly all anglers.

Campsites, facilities: There are 31 sites for tents or RVs up to 40 feet (no hookups), and one group site for up to 75 people and 15 vehicles. Several sites are pull-through. Picnic tables and fire grills are provided. Drinking water, restrooms with flush toilets and showers, dump station, boat ramp (no gas-powered motorboats), and boat rentals (in summer) are available. Some facilities are wheelchair-accessible. A grocery store, coin laundry, firewood, and propane gas are available within five minutes. Leashed pets are permitted.

Reservations, fees: Reservations are accepted (with a $7 reservation fee and $30–50 reservation fee for the group site) at 707/565-2267. Sites are $18 per night, $6 per night for each additional vehicle, group site is $3 per person per night with a $50 minimum, $1 per pet per night. There is a 10-day camping limit. Open daily from May through September and on weekends and holidays only during off-season.

Directions: From Santa Rosa on U.S. 101, turn east on Highway 12 and drive two miles to the junction with Hoen Avenue. Continue straight (east) onto Hoen Avenue and drive one mile (crossing Summerfield Road) to Newanga Avenue. Turn left and drive 0.5 mile to the park entrance at 5585 Newanga Avenue.

Contact: Spring Lake Regional Park, 707/539-8092; Sonoma County Parks, 707/565-2041, www.sonoma-county.org/parks.

102 SUGARLOAF RIDGE STATE PARK

Scenic rating: 5

near Santa Rosa

Map 4.4, page 262

Sugarloaf Ridge State Park is a perfect example of a place that you can't make a final judgment about from your first glance. Your first glance will lead you to believe that this is just hot foothill country, with old ranch roads set in oak woodlands for horseback riding and sweaty hiking or biking. A little discovery here, however, is that a half-mile walk off the Canyon Trail will lead you to a 25-foot waterfall, beautifully set in a canyon, complete with a redwood canopy. A shortcut to this waterfall is available off the south side of the park's entrance road. Otherwise, it can be a long, hot, and challenging hike. In all, there are 25 miles of trail here for hikers and equestrians. Hikers planning for a day of it should leave early, wear a hat, and bring plenty of water. Rangers report that some unprepared hikers have suffered heat stroke in summer, and many others have just plain suffered. In the off-season, when the air is cool and clear, the views from the ridge are eye-popping—visitors can see the Sierra Nevada, Golden Gate, and a thousand other points of scenic beauty from the top of Bald Mountain at 2,769 feet. For the less ambitious, a self-guided nature trail along Sonoma Creek begins at the campground.

Campsites, facilities: There are 47 sites for tents or RVs up to 27 feet (no hookups), and one group site for tents only for up to 50 people. Picnic tables, food lockers and fire grills are provided. Drinking water and flush toilets are available. Leashed pets are permitted in campsites only.

Reservations, fees: Reservations are recommended ($7.50 reservation fee) at 800/444-PARK (800/444-7275) or www.reserveamerica.com. Sites are $20 per night,

$6 per night for each additional vehicle, $111 per night for group site. Open year-round.

Directions: From Santa Rosa on U.S. 101, turn east on Highway 12 and drive seven miles to Adobe Canyon Road. Turn left and drive 3.5 miles to the park entrance at the end of the road.

Contact: Sugarloaf Ridge State Park, 707/833-5712, www.parks.ca.gov.

103 SPANISH FLAT RESORT

Scenic rating: 7

on Lake Berryessa

Map 4.4, page 262

This is one of several lakeside camps at Lake Berryessa. As at Lake Berryessa Marina Resort, the addition of park-model cabins has given this resort a nice touch. This is one of the most popular because many of the sites are on the waterfront. That makes it a natural gathering place for water-skiers and powerboaters, and on summer weekends, particularly holidays, it can get rowdy here. In fact, we've received notes from campers that they've had poor family experiences here. Berryessa, considered the Bay Area's backyard fishing hole, is the third-largest man-made lake in Northern California (Lakes Shasta and Oroville are larger). Trout fishing is good, and there are also bass and salmon. The elevation is approximately 500 feet. Note that there are an additional 180 RV sites filled with seasonal renters.

Campsites, facilities: There are 120 sites for tents or RVs up to 37 feet, two yurts, and 16 park-model cabins. Some sites have partial hookups (30 amps). Picnic tables and fire grills are provided. Restrooms with flush toilets and showers, drinking water, dump station, boat storage, picnic area, ATM, boat launch, full-service marina, boat rentals, and convenience store are available. A snack bar is open on summer weekends. Coin laundry, restaurant, and bar are available within one

mile. Some facilities are wheelchair-accessible. Leashed pets are permitted.

Reservations, fees: Reservations are accepted ($4 reservation fee). Sites are $25 per night, $50 per night for yurts, $5 per day for boat launching, $2 per pet per night. Some credit cards accepted. Open year-round.

Directions: From Vallejo, drive north on I-80 to the Suisun Valley Road exit. Take that exit and turn left onto Suisun Valley Road and drive north for approximately 17 miles to Highway 121. Turn north (right) on Highway 121 and drive seven miles to Highway 128. Turn north (left) on Highway 128 and drive five miles to Berryessa-Knoxville Road. Turn right on Berryessa-Knoxville Road and continue 4.5 miles to 4290 Knoxville Road.

Contact: Spanish Flat Resort, 707/966-7700; Spanish Flat Marina, 707/966-7708, www.spanishflatresort.com.

104 LAKE SOLANO PARK

Scenic rating: 6

near Lake Berryessa

Map 4.4, page 262

Lake Solano provides a low-pressure option to nearby Lake Berryessa. It is a long, narrow lake set below the outlet at Monticello Dam at Lake Berryessa, technically called the afterbay. Compared to Berryessa, life here moves at a much slower pace and some people prefer it. The water temperature at Lake Solano is also much cooler than at Berryessa. The lake has fair trout fishing in the spring, and it is known among Bay Area anglers as the closest fly-fishing spot for trout in the region. No motors, including electric motors, are permitted on boats at the lake. The park covers 177 acres along the river. A swimming pond is available in summer, and a children's fishing pond (trout and bass) is open year-round. The gate closes at night; check in before dusk.

Campsites, facilities: There are 50 sites with no hookups for tents or RVs, and 41 sites with full or partial hookups (30 amps) for tents or RVs up to 38 feet; some sites are pull-through. Picnic tables and fire grills are provided. Drinking water, restrooms with flush toilets and showers, two dump stations, picnic area, boat ramp (summer weekends only), and boat rentals are available. A grocery store is within walking distance, and firewood and ice are sold on the premises. Some facilities are wheelchair-accessible. Leashed pets are permitted in the campground only.

Reservations, fees: Reservations are recommended. Sites are $15–33 per night, $7 per night for each additional vehicle, $1 per pet per night. Holiday rates are higher. Some credit cards accepted. Open year-round.

Directions: In Vacaville, turn north on I-505 and drive 11 miles to the junction of Highway 128. Turn west on Highway 128 and drive about five miles (past Winters) to Pleasant Valley Road. Turn left on Pleasant Valley Road and drive to the park at 8685 Pleasant Valley Road (well signed).

Contact: Lake Solano Park, 530/795-2990, fax 530/795-1408, www.solanocounty.com.

105 NAPA VALLEY EXPOSITION RV PARK

Scenic rating: 2

in Napa

Map 4.4, page 262

This RV park is directly adjacent to the Napa Valley Exposition. When the fair is in operation in late July and early August, it is closed. The rest of the year it is simply a RV parking area, and it can come in handy.

Campsites, facilities: There are 45 sites with partial hookups (30 and 50 amps) for RVs of any length and a grassy area for at least 100 self-contained RVs. Some sites are pull-through. Picnic tables, restrooms with showers, coin laundry, and a dump station are available. A camp host is on-site. A grocery store and restaurant are within walking distance. Some facilities are wheelchair-accessible. Leashed pets are permitted.

Reservations, fees: Reservations are not accepted for individual sites, but are required for groups at 707/253-4900, ext. 102. Sites are $20 per night. Open year-round, except during the fair.

Directions: From Napa on Highway 29, drive to the Napa/Lake Berryessa exit. Take that exit and turn right (east) and drive about one mile to Silverado/Highway 121. Turn right and drive less than one mile to the fairgrounds entrance on the left.

Contact: Napa Valley Exposition, 707/253-4900, fax 707/253-4943, www.napavalleyexpo.com.

106 SAN FRANCISCO NORTH/PETALUMA KOA

Scenic rating: 3

near Petaluma

Map 4.4, page 262

This campground is less than a mile from U.S. 101, yet it has a rural feel in a 60-acre farm setting. It's a good base camp for folks who require some quiet mental preparation before heading south to the Bay Area or to the nearby wineries, redwoods, and the Russian River. The big plus here is that this KOA has the cute log cabins called "Kamping Kabins," providing privacy for those who want it. There are recreational activities and live music on Saturdays in summer. During October, a pumpkin patch and corn maze are open across the street from the park.

Campsites, facilities: There are 272 sites, most with full or partial hookups (30 and 50 amps) for RVs or tents, 34 cabins, and a lodge. Most sites are pull-through. Picnic tables and fire pits are provided. Restrooms with flush toilets and showers, cable TV hookups, modem access and free Wi-Fi, dump station, playground, recreation rooms, basketball, volleyball, heated seasonal swimming pool, spa, petting farm, shuffleboard, coin laundry, propane gas, and a convenience store are available. Some facilities are wheelchair-accessible. Leashed pets are permitted, with certain restrictions.

Reservations, fees: Reservations are accepted at 800/562-1233 or by website. Sites are $29.95–56 per night, $5–7 per person per night for more than two people. Some credit cards accepted. Open year-round.

Directions: From Petaluma on U.S. 101 north, take the Penngrove exit and drive west for 0.25 mile on Petaluma Boulevard to Stony Point Road. Turn right (north) on Stony Point Road and drive 0.25 mile to Rainsville Road. Turn left (west) on Rainsville Road and drive a short distance to the park entrance at 20 Rainsville Road.

Contact: San Francisco North/Petaluma KOA, 707/763-1492, www.koa.com.

SACRAMENTO AND GOLD COUNTRY

© KEN DECAMP

BEST CAMPGROUNDS

【 Boat-In Campgrounds
Bullards Bar Reservoir, **pages 335 and 337**
Brannan Island State Recreation Area,
    page 347

【 Fishing
Lake Oroville Boat-In and Floating Camps,
    page 332
Snug Harbor Resort, **page 348**

【 White-Water Rafting
Auburn State Recreation Area, **pages 341–342**
Camp Lotus, **page 351**

【 Waterskiing
Snug Harbor, **page 348**
Eddos Harbor and RV Park, **page 349**

【 Island Campgrounds
Brannan Island State Recreation Area, **page 347**

From a distance, this section of the Sacramento

Valley looks like flat farmland extending into infinity, with a sprinkling of cities and towns interrupting the view. But a closer look reveals a landscape filled with Northern California's most significant rivers – the Sacramento, Feather, Yuba, American, and Mokelumne. All of these provide water recreation, in both lakes and rivers, as well as serve as the lifeblood for a series of wildlife refuges.

This is an area for California history buffs, with Placerville KOA and nearby Malakoff Diggins State Historic Park in the center of some of the state's most extraordinary history: the gold rush era. Another good deal is the Lake Oroville Floating Camps, which can sleep 15 and cost $100 a night.

The highlight of the foothill country for lake recreation is the series of great lakes for water sports and fishing. These include Camanche, Rollins, Oroville, and many others. Note that the mapping I use for this region extends up to Bucks Lake, which is set high in Plumas National Forest, the northern start to the Gold Country.

Timing is everything in love and the great outdoors, and so it is in the

Central Valley and the nearby foothills. Spring and fall are gorgeous here, along with many summer evenings. But there are always periods of 100°F-plus temperatures in the summer.

But that's what gives the lakes and rivers such appeal, and in turn, why they are treasured. Take your pick: Lake Oroville in the northern Sierra, Folsom Lake outside Sacramento. . . the list goes on. On a hot day, jumping into a cool lake makes water more valuable than gold, a cold drink on ice worth more than silver. These have become top sites for boating-based recreation and fantastic areas for water sports and fishing.

In the Mother Lode country, three other lakes – Camanche, Amador, and Pardee – are outstanding for fishing. I rank three of this chapter's lakes among the top 10 lakes for fishing in the state – Lake Oroville and Camanche Lake make the list for bass and Lake Amador makes it for bluegill and catfish – no small feat considering the 381 other lakes they were up against.

For touring, the state capital and nearby Old Sacramento are favorites. Others prefer reliving the gold-mining history of California's past or exploring the foothill country, including Malakoff Diggins State Historic Park.

SACRAMENTO AND GOLD COUNTRY

see Lassen and Modoc
page 202

see Shasta and Trinity
page 124

Lassen National Forest

Susanville

Chester

Honey Lake

Tehama State Wildlife Area

Lake Almanor

Mtn Meadows Reservoir

Red Bluff

Antelope Lake

Bucks Lake Wilderness

Black Butte Lake

Quincy

Lake Davis

Plumas National Forest

Little Grass Valley Reservoir

Chico

Lake Oroville

see Tahoe and the Northern Sierra
page 364

MAP 5.1
page 321

MAP 5.2
page 322

Downieville

Truckee

Nevada City

Tahoe

Lake

National Forest

Colfax

Tahoe

Yuba City

Marysville

see Mendocino and Wine Country
page 258

Auburn

Cache Creek

Folsom Lake

Placerville

Lake Berryessa

SACRAMENTO

MAP 5.3
page 323

MAP 5.4
page 324

Calaveras Big Trees SP

Stanislaus NF

see San Francisco Bay Area
page 468

San Joaquin Delta

Camanche Res

New Hogan Reservoir

Sonora

Walnut Creek

Stockton

New Melones Reservoir

Modesto

Don Pedro Reservoir

see San Joaquin Valley
page 522

0   10 mi
0   10 km

Map 5.1

Campgrounds 1-3
Pages 325-326

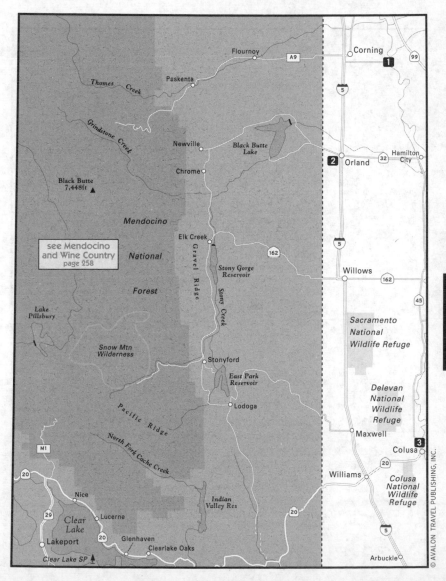

Map 5.2

Campgrounds 4-33
Pages 326-340

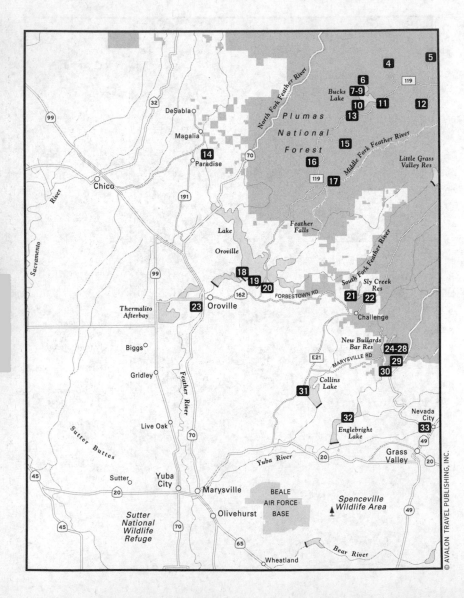

© AVALON TRAVEL PUBLISHING, INC.

Map 5.3

Campgrounds 34-53
Pages 340-350

Map 5.4

Campgrounds 54-68

Pages 351-359

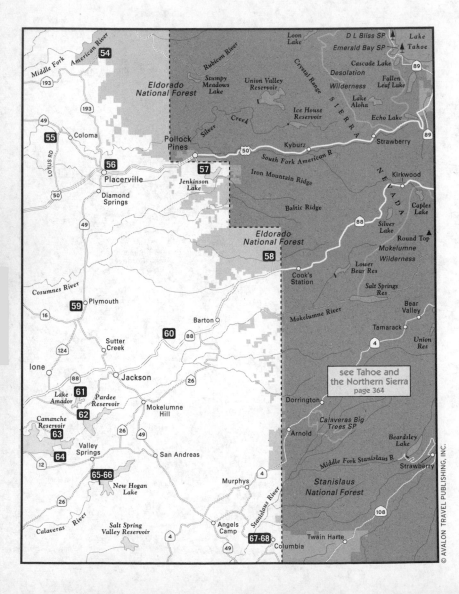

1 WOODSON BRIDGE STATE RECREATION AREA

Scenic rating: 7

on the Sacramento River

Map 5.1, page 321

This campground features direct access to the Sacramento River, and a boat ramp makes it an ideal spot for campers with trailered boats. The boat ramp is across the road in the county park, providing easy access for water sports. Waterskiing and personal watercraft are discouraged on this section of the river. This is a 328-acre preserve with a dense, native riparian forest, including some of the last virgin habitat on the 400-mile length of the Sacramento River. There are about two miles of hiking trails in the park; a sand and gravel beach is nearby. In June, the nearby Tehama Riffle is one of the best spots on the entire river for shad fishing. By mid-August, salmon start arriving, en route to their spawning grounds. Summer weather here is hot, with high temperatures commonly 85–100°F and up. In winter, it is home to bald eagles, and in summer, provides a nesting site for the yellow-billed cuckoo.

Campsites, facilities: There are 37 sites for tents or RVs up to 31 feet (no hookups) and five boat-in sites. One group site for up to 40 people is available. Picnic tables and fire grills are provided. Drinking water, coin showers, flush toilets, and boat launch (across the street) are available, and there is a camp host. Leashed pets are permitted.

Reservations, fees: Reservations are accepted ($7.50 reservation fee) at 800/444-PARK (800/444-7275) or www.reserveamerica.com. Sites are $11–14 per night, $6 per night for each additional vehicle, $6 per night for boat-in sites, $90 per night for the group camp. Open year-round.

Directions: From I-5 in Corning, take the South Avenue exit and drive six miles east to the campground on the left.

Contact: Woodson Bridge State Recreation Area, 530/839-2112; North Buttes District, 530/538-2200; Bidwell Mansion Visitor Center, 530/895-6144, www.parks.ca.gov.

2 OLD ORCHARD RV PARK

Scenic rating: 4

near Orland

Map 5.1, page 321

Most folks use this as a layover spot while on long trips up or down I-5 in the Central Valley. If you're staying longer than a night, there are two side trips that have appeal for anglers. Nearby Black Butte Lake to the west, with crappie in the early summer, and the Sacramento River to the east, with salmon in the late summer and early fall, can add some spice to your trip. The elevation is 250 feet. Some sites are filled with long-term renters.

Campsites, facilities: There are 52 pull-through sites with partial or full hookups (30 and 50 amps) for RVs of any length and six tent sites. Restrooms with showers, dump station, coin laundry, and modem access are available. Some facilities are wheelchair-accessible. Leashed pets are permitted.

Reservations, fees: Reservations are accepted. Sites are $15–24 per night, $2 per person per night for more than two people. Some credit cards accepted. Open year-round.

Directions: From I-5 at Orland, take the Chico/Highway 32 exit west (Exit 619). Drive west one block to County Road HH. Turn right on County Road HH and drive north one block to the park on the right at 4490 County Road HH.

Contact: Old Orchard RV Park, 877/481-9282, tel./fax 530/865-5335.

3 COLUSA-SACRAMENTO RIVER STATE RECREATION AREA

🛶 � 🐕 ♿ 🚻 ⛺

Scenic rating: 5

near Colusa

Map 5.1, page 321

This region of the Sacramento Valley is well known as a high-quality habitat for birds. This park covers 67 acres and features great bird-watching opportunities. Nearby Delevan and Colusa National Wildlife Refuges are outstanding destinations for wildlife-viewing as well, and they provide good duck hunting in December. In summer the nearby Sacramento River is a bonus with shad fishing in June and July, salmon fishing from August through October, sturgeon fishing in the winter, and striped-bass fishing in the spring. The landscape here features cottonwoods and willows along the Sacramento River.

Campsites, facilities: There are 10 sites for tents, four sites for tents or RVs up to 30 feet, and one group site for 10–40 people. No hookups. Picnic tables and barbecues are provided. Drinking water, restrooms with flush toilets and coin showers, boat ramp, Wi-Fi, and a dump station are available. Some facilities are wheelchair-accessible. A grocery store, restaurant, gas station, tackle shop, and coin laundry are nearby (within three blocks). Leashed pets are permitted.

Reservations, fees: Reservations for individual sites are accepted ($7.50 reservation fee) at 800/444-PARK (800/444-7275) or www.reserveamerica.com. Group reservations are accepted at 530/458-4927. Sites are $12–15 per night, $6 per night for each additional vehicle, $90 per night for the group site. Open year-round.

Directions: In Williams, at the junction of I-5 and Highway 20, drive east on Highway 20 for nine miles to the town of Colusa. Turn north (straight ahead) on 10th Street and drive two blocks, just over the levee, to the park.

Contact: Colusa-Sacramento River State Recreation Area, 530/458-4927, fax 530/458-8033; North Buttes District, 530/538-2200, www.parks.ca.gov.

4 SILVER LAKE

🏃 🛶 🐕 ⛺

Scenic rating: 8

in Plumas National Forest

Map 5.2, page 322

While tons of people go to Bucks Lake for the great trout fishing and lakeside camps, nearby Silver Lake gets little attention despite great natural beauty, good hiking, decent trout fishing, and a trailhead to the Bucks Lake Wilderness. The camp is at the north end of the lake, 5,800 feet elevation, a primitive and secluded spot. No powerboats (or swimming) are allowed on Silver Lake, which makes it ideal for canoes and rafts. The lake has lots of small brook trout. The Pacific Crest Trail is routed on the ridge above the lake, skirting past Mount Pleasant (6,924 feet) to the nearby west.

Campsites, facilities: There are eight tent sites. Picnic tables and fire grills are provided. Vault toilets are available. Garbage must be packed out. No drinking water is available. Leashed pets are permitted.

Reservations, fees: Reservations are not accepted. There is no fee for camping. Open May through October, weather permitting.

Directions: From Oroville, drive north on Highway 70 to the junction with Highway 89. Turn south on Highway 89/70 and drive 11 miles to Quincy and Bucks Lake Road. Turn right at Bucks Lake Road and drive west for nine miles to Silver Lake Road. Turn right and drive seven miles to the campground at the north end of the lake.

Contact: Plumas National Forest, Mount Hough Ranger District, 530/283-0555, fax 530/283-1821.

5 SNAKE LAKE

Scenic rating: 8

in Plumas National Forest

Map 5.2, page 322

Snake Lake is a rarity in the northern Sierra, a mountain lake that has bass, catfish, and bluegill. That is because it is a shallow lake, set at 5,800 feet in Plumas National Forest. The camp is on the west shore. Motors of up to 5 hp are allowed. A road that circles the lake provides a good bicycle route for youngsters. A side trip to the nearby north is Smith Lake, about a five-minute drive, with the Butterfly Valley Botanical Area bordering it.

Campsites, facilities: There are seven sites for tents only. Picnic tables and fire grills are provided. Vault toilets are available. No drinking water is available. Garbage must be packed out. Leashed pets are permitted.

Reservations, fees: Reservations are not accepted. There is no fee for camping. Open May through October, weather permitting.

Directions: From Oroville, drive north on Highway 70 to the junction with Highway 89. Turn south on Highway 89/70 and drive 11 miles to Quincy and Bucks Lake Road. Turn right at Bucks Lake Road and drive five miles to County Road 422. Turn right and drive two miles to the Snake Lake access road. Turn right and drive one mile to the campground on the right.

Contact: Plumas National Forest, Mount Hough Ranger District, 530/283-0555, fax 530/283-1821.

6 MILL CREEK

Scenic rating: 7

at Bucks Lake in Plumas National Forest

Map 5.2, page 322

When Bucks Lake is full, this is one of the prettiest spots on the lake. The camp is set deep in Mill Creek Cove, adjacent to where Mill Creek enters the northernmost point of Bucks Lake. A boat ramp is 0.5 mile away to the south, providing boat access to one of the better trout fishing spots at the lake. Unfortunately, when the lake level falls, this camp is left high and dry, some distance from the water. All water sports are permitted on this 1,800-acre lake. The elevation is 5,200 feet.

Campsites, facilities: There are 10 sites for tents or RVs up to 27 feet (no hookups) and two walk-in tent sites. Picnic tables and fire grills are provided. Drinking water and vault toilets are available. Groceries are available within five miles. Leashed pets are permitted.

Reservations, fees: Reservations are not accepted. Sites are $18–20 per night. Open mid-May through September, weather permitting.

Directions: From Oroville, drive north on Highway 70 to the junction with Highway 89. Turn south on Highway 89/70 and drive 11 miles to Quincy. In Quincy, turn right at Bucks Lake Road and drive 17 miles to Bucks Lake and the junction with Bucks Lake Dam Road/Forest Road 33. Turn right, drive around the lake, cross over the dam, and continue for about three miles to the campground.

Contact: Plumas National Forest, Mount Hough Ranger District, 530/283-0555, fax 530/283-1821; Northwest Park Management, 530/283-5559.

7 SUNDEW

Scenic rating: 7

on Bucks Lake in Plumas National Forest

Map 5.2, page 322

Sundew Camp is set on the northern shore of Bucks Lake, just north of Bucks Lake Dam. A boat ramp is about two miles north at Sandy Point Day Use Area at the Mill Creek Cove, providing access to one of the better trout spots on the lake. You want fish? At

Bucks Lake you can get fish—it's one of the state's top mountain trout lakes. Fish species include rainbow, brown, and Mackinaw trout. Sunrises are often spectacular from this camp, with the light glowing on the lake's surface.

Campsites, facilities: There are 19 sites for tents or RVs up to 35 feet (no hookups). Picnic tables and fire grills are provided. Drinking water and vault toilets are available. Leashed pets are permitted. There is a boat ramp two miles north of the camp.

Reservations, fees: Reservations are not accepted. Sites are $18–20 per night. Open mid-May through September, weather permitting.

Directions: From Oroville, drive north on Highway 70 to the junction with Highway 89. Turn south on Highway 89/70 and drive 11 miles to Quincy. In Quincy, turn right at Bucks Lake Road and drive 17 miles to Bucks Lake and the junction with Bucks Lake Dam Road/Forest Road 33. Turn right, drive around the lake, cross over the dam, continue for 0.5 mile, and turn right at the campground access road.

Contact: Plumas National Forest, Mount Hough Ranger District, 530/283-0555, fax 530/283-1821; Northwest Park Management, 530/283-5559.

8 HUTCHINS GROUP CAMP
Scenic rating: 6

near Bucks Lake in Plumas National Forest

Map 5.2, page 322

This is a prime spot for a Scout outing or for any other large group that would like a pretty spot. An amphitheater is available. It is set at 5,200 feet near Bucks and Lower Bucks Lakes. (For more information, see the previous entry, *Sundew,* and the next entries, *Lower Bucks* and *Haskins Valley.*)

Campsites, facilities: There are three group sites for tents or RV up to 35 feet (no hook-

ups) that can accommodate up to 25 people each. Picnic tables and fire grills are provided. Drinking water and vault toilets are available. A boat ramp is available. Leashed pets are permitted.

Reservations, fees: Reservations are required ($9 reservation fee) at 877/444-6777 or www.ReserveUSA.com. The camp is $60 per night. Open May through October.

Directions: From Oroville, drive north on Highway 70 to the junction with Highway 89. Turn south on Highway 89/70 and drive 11 miles to Quincy and Bucks Lake Road. Turn right at Bucks Lake Road and drive 17 miles to Bucks Lake and the junction with Bucks Lake Dam Road/Forest Road 33. Turn right, drive around the lake, cross over the dam, continue for a short distance, and turn right. Drive 0.5 mile, cross the stream (passing an intersection), and continue straight for 0.5 mile to the campground.

Contact: Plumas National Forest, Mount Hough Ranger District, 530/283-0555, fax 530/283-1821; Northwest Park Management, 530/283-5559.

9 LOWER BUCKS
Scenic rating: 7

on Lower Bucks Lake in Plumas National Forest

Map 5.2, page 322

This camp is on Lower Bucks Lake, which is actually the afterbay for Bucks Lake, set below the Bucks Lake Dam. It is a small, primitive, and quiet spot that is often overlooked because it is not on the main lake.

Campsites, facilities: There are six sites for tents or RVs up to 26 feet (no hookups). Picnic tables and fire rings are provided. Vault toilets are available. There is no drinking water. Leashed pets are permitted.

Reservations, fees: Reservations are not accepted. Sites are $16 per night. Open May through October.

Directions: From Oroville, drive north on Highway 70 to the junction with Highway 89. Turn south on Highway 89/70 and drive 11 miles to Quincy and Bucks Lake Road. Turn right at Bucks Lake Road and drive 17 miles to Bucks Lake and the junction with Bucks Lake Dam Road/Forest Road 33. Turn right and drive four miles around the lake, cross over the dam, drive 0.25 mile, and then turn left on the campground entrance road.

Contact: Plumas National Forest, Mount Hough Ranger District, 530/283-0555, fax 530/283-1821; Northwest Park Management, 530/283-5559.

10 HASKINS VALLEY
🏕🏊�m🏠🎣♿🚐⛺

Scenic rating: 7

on Bucks Lake

Map 5.2, page 322

This is the biggest and most popular of the campgrounds at Bucks Lake, a pretty alpine lake with excellent trout fishing and clean campgrounds. A boat ramp is available to the nearby north, along with Bucks Lodge. This camp is set deep in a cove at the extreme south end of the lake, where the water is quiet and sheltered from north winds. Bucks Lake, 5,200 feet elevation, is well documented for excellent fishing for rainbow and Mackinaw trout, with high catch rates of rainbow trout and lake records in the 16-pound class. Insider's tip: This is the best lake in the region for sailboarding.

Campsites, facilities: There are 65 sites for tents or RVs up to 30 feet (no hookups). Picnic tables and fire grills are provided. Drinking water and vault toilets are available. A dump station and boat ramp are available nearby. Some facilities are wheelchair-accessible. Leashed pets are permitted.

Reservations, fees: Reservations are not accepted. Sites are $18 per night, $3 per night for each additional vehicle, $1 per pet per night. Open May to early October, weather permitting.

Directions: From Oroville, drive north on Highway 70 to the junction with Highway 89. Turn south on Highway 89/70 and drive 11 miles to Quincy. In Quincy, turn right at Bucks Lake Road and drive 16.5 miles to the campground entrance on the right side of the road.

Contact: PG&E Land Services, 916/386-5164, www.pge.com/recreation.

11 WHITEHORSE
🏕🏊🚣🛶🏠🚐⛺

Scenic rating: 7

near Bucks Lake in Plumas National Forest

Map 5.2, page 322

This campground is set along Bucks Creek, about two miles from the boat ramps and south shore concessions at Bucks Lake. The trout fishing can be quite good at Bucks Lake. The elevation is 5,200 feet. (For more information, see the previous listing, *Haskins Valley.*)

Campsites, facilities: There are 20 sites for tents or RVs up to 27 feet (no hookups). Picnic tables and fire grills are provided. Drinking water and vault toilets are available. A grocery store and coin laundry are available within five miles. Leashed pets are permitted.

Reservations, fees: Reservations are not accepted. Sites are $16 per night. Open June through September.

Directions: From Oroville, drive north on Highway 70 to the junction with Highway 89. Turn south on Highway 89/70 and drive 11 miles to Quincy and Bucks Lake Road. Turn right at Bucks Lake Road and drive 14.5 miles to the campground entrance on the right side of the road.

Contact: Plumas National Forest, Mount Hough Ranger District, 530/283-0555, fax 530/283-1821; Northwest Park Management, 530/283-5559.

12 DEANES VALLEY

Scenic rating: 5

on Rock Creek in Plumas National Forest

Map 5.2, page 322

This secret spot is set on South Fork Rock Creek, deep in a valley at an elevation of 4,400 feet in Plumas National Forest. The trout here are very small natives. If you want a pure, quiet spot, great. If you want great fishing, not great. The surrounding region has a network of backcountry roads, including routes passable only by four-wheel-drive vehicles; to explore these roads, get a map of Plumas National Forest.

Campsites, facilities: There are seven sites for tents or RVs up to 24 feet (no hookups). Picnic tables and fire grills are provided. Vault toilets are available. No drinking water is available. Garbage must be packed out. Leashed pets are permitted.

Reservations, fees: Reservations are not accepted. There is no fee for camping. Open April through October, weather permitting.

Directions: From Oroville, drive north on Highway 70 to the junction with Highway 89. Turn south on Highway 89/70 and drive 11 miles to Quincy and Bucks Lake Road. Turn right at Bucks Lake Road and drive 3.5 miles to Forest Road 24N28. Turn left and drive seven miles to the campground on the left.

Contact: Plumas National Forest, Mount Hough Ranger District, 530/283-0555, fax 530/283-1821.

13 GRIZZLY CREEK

Scenic rating: 4

near Bucks Lake in Plumas National Forest

Map 5.2, page 322

This is an alternative to the more developed, more crowded campgrounds at Bucks Lake. It is a small, primitive camp set near Grizzly Creek at 5,400 feet in elevation. Nearby Bucks Lake provides good trout fishing, resorts, and boat rentals.

Campsites, facilities: There are eight sites for tents or RVs up to 35 feet (no hookups). Picnic tables and fire grills are provided. Drinking water and vault toilets are available. A boat ramp is available at Bucks Lake. A grocery store and coin laundry are available within five miles. Leashed pets are permitted.

Reservations, fees: Reservations are not accepted. Sites are $18 per night. Open June through October.

Directions: From Oroville, drive north on Highway 70 to the junction with Highway 89. Turn south on Highway 89/70 and drive 11 miles to Quincy and Bucks Lake Road. Turn right at Bucks Lake Road and drive 17 miles to Bucks Lake and the junction with Bucks Lake Dam Road/Forest Road 33. Turn right and drive one mile to the junction with Oroville-Quincy Road/Forest Road 36. Bear left and drive one mile to the campground on the right side of the road.

Contact: Plumas National Forest, Mount Hough Ranger District, 530/283-0555, fax 530/283-1821; Northwest Park Management, 530/283-5559.

14 QUAIL TRAILS VILLAGE RV AND MOBILE HOME PARK

Scenic rating: 4

near Paradise

Map 5.2, page 322

This is a rural motor-home campground, set near the west branch of the Feather River, with nearby Lake Oroville as the feature attraction. The Lime Saddle section of the Lake Oroville State Recreation Area is three miles away, with a beach, boat-launching facilities, and concessions. Note: About one-third of the sites are taken by long-term rentals here.

Campsites, facilities: There are 20 pull-through sites with full hookups (30 amps) for RVs of any length, and five tent sites. Picnic tables are provided. Restrooms with showers and coin laundry are available. Some facilities are wheelchair-accessible. Leashed pets up to 30 pounds are permitted.

Reservations, fees: Reservations are accepted. Sites are $15–25 per night. Weekly rates available. Open year-round.

Directions: From Oroville, drive north on Highway 70 for six miles to Pentz Road. Turn left and drive six miles south to the park on the left (5110 Pentz Road).

Contact: Quail Trails Village RV and Mobile Home Park, 530/877-6581, fax 530/876-0516, www.quailtrailsvillage.com.

15 LITTLE NORTH FORK

Scenic rating: 7

on the Middle Fork of the Feather River in Plumas National Forest

Map 5.2, page 322

Guaranteed quiet? You got it. This is a primitive camp in the outback that few know of. It is set along the Little North Fork of the Middle Fork of the Feather River at 4,000 feet. The surrounding backcountry of Plumas National Forest features an incredible number of roads, giving four-wheel-drive owners a chance to get so lost they'll need this camp. Instead, get a map of Plumas National Forest before venturing out.

Campsites, facilities: There are seven sites for tents or RVs up to 16 feet (no hookups). Picnic tables and fire grills are provided. Vault toilets are available. No drinking water is available. Garbage must be packed out. Leashed pets are permitted.

Reservations, fees: Reservations are not accepted. There is no fee for camping. Open May through October.

Directions: From Oroville, turn east on Highway 162/Oroville-Quincy Highway and drive 26.5 miles to the Brush Creek

Work Center. Continue northeast on Oroville-Quincy Highway for about six miles to County Road 60. Turn right and drive about eight miles to the campground entrance road on the left side of the road. Turn left and drive 0.25 mile to the campground. Note: This route is long, twisty, bumpy, and narrow for most of the way.

Contact: Plumas National Forest, Feather River Ranger District, 530/534-6500, fax 530/532-1210.

16 ROGERS COW CAMP

Scenic rating: 4

in Plumas National Forest

Map 5.2, page 322

First note that the Oroville-Quincy "Highway" is actually a twisty Forest Service road, a backcountry route that connects Oroville to Quincy and passes Lake Oroville and Bucks Lake in the process. The road is paved, but it can still put you way out there in no-man's-land, set in Plumas National Forest at 4,000 feet. You want quiet, you get it. You want water, you bring it yourself. The camp is set near the headwaters of Coon Creek. There are no other natural destinations in the area, and I'm not saying Coon Creek is anything to see. It's advisable to obtain a map of Plumas National Forest, which details all backcountry roads. There has been logging activity in the area.

Campsites, facilities: There are five sites for tents or RVs up to 16 feet (no hookups). Picnic tables and fire grills are provided. Vault toilets are available. No drinking water is available. Garbage must be packed out. Leashed pets are permitted.

Reservations, fees: Reservations are not accepted. There is no fee for camping. Open May through September.

Directions: In Oroville, drive east on Highway 162/Oroville-Quincy Highway for 26.5 miles to the Brush Creek Work Center. Continue on Oroville-Quincy Highway for eight miles to the campground entrance road on the left side of the road. Turn left and drive a short distance to the camp.

Contact: Plumas National Forest, Feather River Ranger District, 530/534-6500, fax 530/532-1210.

17 MILSAP BAR
🥾 🎣 🛶 🏕 5% 🚐 ⛰

Scenic rating: 8

on the Middle Fork of the Feather River in Plumas National Forest

Map 5.2, page 322

Among white-water river rafters, Milsap Bar is a well-known access point to the Middle Fork Feather River. This river country features a deep canyon, beautiful surroundings, and is formally recognized as the Feather Falls Scenic Area (named after the awesome 640-foot waterfall). Note that while no commercial raft companies are permitted to run this section of the Feather, private groups or individual use are permitted. The elevation is 1,600 feet.

Campsites, facilities: There are 20 sites for tents or RVs up to 16 feet (no hookups). Picnic tables and fire grills are provided. Vault toilets are available. No drinking water is available. Garbage must be packed out. Leashed pets are permitted.

Reservations, fees: Reservations are not accepted. There is no fee for camping. Open May through September.

Directions: In Oroville, drive east on Highway 162/Oroville-Quincy Highway for 26.5 miles to the Brush Creek Work Center and Bald Rock Road. Turn right on Bald Rock Road and drive for about 0.5 mile to Forest Road 22N62/Milsap Bar Road. Turn left and drive eight miles to the campground (a narrow, steep, mountain dirt road).

Contact: Plumas National Forest, Feather River Ranger District, 530/534-6500, fax 530/532-1210.

18 LAKE OROVILLE BOAT-IN AND FLOATING CAMPS
🥾 🎣 🛶 🏕 🐕 ⛰

Scenic rating: 10

on Lake Oroville

Map 5.2, page 322   **BEST (**

It doesn't get any stranger than this, and for those who have tried, it doesn't get any better. We're talking about the double-decker floating camps at Lake Oroville, along with the great boat-in sites. The floating camps look like giant patio boats. They sleep 15 people and they include picnic table, sink, food locker, garbage can, vault toilet, and propane barbecue. There are also a series of dispersed boat-in camps around the lake, which are particularly excellent in the spring and early summer, when the water level at the lake is high. In late summer, when the lake level drops, it can be a fair hike up the bank to the campsites, and in addition, if the water drops quickly, your boat can be left sitting on the bank; it can be quite an effort to get it back in the water. Oroville is an outstanding lake for water sports, with warm water and plenty of room, and also with excellent bass fishing, especially in the spring.

Campsites, facilities: There are four dispersed boat-in camps, one group boat-in site (Bloomer) for up to 75 people, and 10 boat-in floating camps. Picnic tables and fire grills are provided. Vault toilets are available. No drinking water is provided. Leashed pets are permitted, except on trails or beaches.

Reservations, fees: Reservations are accepted ($7.50 reservation fee) at 800/444-PARK (800/444-7275) or www.reserveamerica .com. Floating camps are $100 per night, individual boat-in sites are $12 per night, and the group boat-in site is $90 per night. Open year-round.

Directions: From Oroville, drive east on Oroville Dam Boulevard/Highway 162 (becomes the Olive Highway) for 5.5 miles to Canyon Drive. Turn left and drive two miles to Oroville Dam. Turn left and drive over the dam to the spillway parking lot at the end of the road. Register at the entrance station. Boats can be launched from this area.

Contact: Lake Oroville State Recreation Area, 530/538-2200; Lake Oroville Visitor Center, 530/538-2219, www.parks.ca.gov.

19 BIDWELL CANYON
🏃 🏊 ⚓ 🚤 🎣 🚐 ⛺

Scenic rating: 7

on Lake Oroville

Map 5.2, page 322

Bidwell Canyon is a major destination at giant Lake Oroville as the campground is near a major marina and boat ramp. It is set along the southern shore of the lake, on a point directly adjacent to the massive Oroville Dam to the west. Many campers use this spot for boating headquarters. Lake Oroville is created from the tallest earth-filled dam in the country, rising 770 feet above the streambed of the Feather River. It creates a huge reservoir when full. It is popular for waterskiing, as the water is warm enough in the summer for all water sports, and there is enough room for both anglers and water-skiers. Fishing is excellent for spotted bass. What a lake—there are even floating toilets here (imagine that!). It is very hot in midsummer, with high temperatures ranging from the mid-80s to the low 100s. The area has four distinct seasons—spring is quite beautiful with many wildflowers and greenery. A must-see is the view from the 47-foot tower using the high-powered telescopes, where there is a panoramic view of the lake, Sierra Nevada, valley, foothills, and the Sutter Buttes. The Feather River Hatchery is nearby.

Campsites, facilities: There are 75 sites with full hookups (30 amps) for tents or RVs up to 40 feet and trailers up to 31 feet (including boat trailers). Picnic tables and fire grills are provided. Drinking water, flush toilets, and coin showers are available. Boat rentals are available on the lake. A grocery store, boat ramp, marina with fuel and boat pumping station, snack bar, and propane gas are available within two miles. Leashed pets are permitted, except on trails or beaches.

Reservations, fees: Reservations are accepted ($7.50 reservation fee) at 800/444-PARK (800/444-7275) or www.reserveamerica.com. Sites are $19–24 per night, $4 per night for each additional vehicle. Open year-round.

Directions: From Oroville, drive east on Oroville Dam Boulevard/Highway 162 (becomes the Olive Highway) for 6.8 miles to Kelly Ridge Road. Turn left (north) on Kelly Ridge Road and drive 1.5 miles to Arroyo Drive. Turn right and drive 0.25 mile to the campground.

Contact: Lake Oroville State Recreation Area, 530/538-2200; Lake Oroville Visitor Center, 530/538-2219, www.parks.ca.gov.

20 LOAFER CREEK FAMILY, GROUP, AND EQUESTRIAN CAMPS
🏃 🏊 ⚓ 🚤 🐎 ♿ 🚐 ⛺

Scenic rating: 7

on Lake Oroville

Map 5.2, page 322

These are three different campground areas that are linked, designed for individual use, groups, and equestrians, respectively. The camps are just across the water at Lake Oroville from Bidwell Canyon, but campers come here for more spacious sites. It's also a primary option for campers with boats, with the Loafer Creek boat ramp one mile away. So hey, this spot is no secret. A bonus here includes an extensive equestrian trail system right out of camp.

Campsites, facilities: There are 137 sites for tents or RVs up to 40 feet (no hookups) and trailers to 31 feet (including boat trailers), 15 equestrian sites with a two-horse limit per site, and six group sites for up to 25 people each. Picnic tables and fire grills are provided. Drinking water, restrooms with flush toilets and coin showers, laundry tubs, Wi-Fi, and a dump station are available. A tethering and feeding station is near each site for horses, and a horse-washing station is provided. Some facilities are wheelchair-accessible. Propane, groceries, boat rentals, and a boat ramp are available nearby. Leashed pets are permitted, but not on trails or beaches.

Reservations, fees: Reservations are accepted ($7.50 reservation fee) at 800/444-PARK (800/444-7275) or www.reserveamerica.com. Sites are $13–18 per night for single sites, $4 per night for each additional vehicle, $60 per night for group sites, $30 per night for equestrian sites. Open year-round.

Directions: From Oroville, drive east on Oroville Dam Boulevard/Highway 162 (becomes the Olive Highway) for approximately eight miles to the signed campground entrance on the left.

Contact: Lake Oroville State Recreation Area, 530/538-2200; Lake Oroville Visitor Center, 530/538-2219, www.parks.ca.gov.

21 SLY CREEK

🏊 🎣 🚤 🏕 🚻 ♿ 🚐 ⛺

Scenic rating: 7

on Sly Creek Reservoir in Plumas National Forest

Map 5.2, page 322

Sly Creek Camp is set on Sly Creek Reservoir's southwestern shore near Lewis Flat, with a boat ramp about a mile to the north. Both camps at this lake are well situated for campers and anglers. This camp provides direct access to the lake's main body, with good trout fishing well upstream on the main lake arm. You get quiet water and decent fishing. The elevation is 3,530 feet.

Campsites, facilities: There are 26 sites for tents or RVs up to 40 feet (no hookups). Five walk-in tent cabins are also available. Picnic tables and fire grills are provided. Drinking water and vault toilets are available. A car-top boat launch and fish-cleaning stations are available on Sly Creek Reservoir. Some

facilities are wheelchair-accessible. Leashed pets are permitted.

Reservations, fees: Reservations are not accepted. Sites are $18 per night. Open late April to mid-October, weather permitting.

Directions: From Oroville, drive east on Highway 162/Oroville Dam Boulevard for about eight miles (becomes the Olive Highway) to Forbestown Road. Turn right and drive through Forbestown to Challenge and LaPorte Road. Turn left on LaPorte Road and drive 15 miles to Forest Road 16 (signed for Sly Creek Reservoir). Turn left on Forest Road 16 and drive 4.5 miles to the campground on the eastern end of the lake.

Contact: Plumas National Forest, Feather River Ranger District, 530/534-6500, fax 530/532-1210; Northwest Park Management, 530/283-5559.

22 STRAWBERRY

🏊 🎣 🚤 🏕 🐕 🚐 ⛺

Scenic rating: 7

on Sly Creek Reservoir in Plumas National Forest

Map 5.2, page 322

Sly Creek Reservoir is a long, narrow lake set in western Plumas National Forest. There are two campgrounds on opposite ends of the lake, with different directions to each. This camp is set in the back of a cove on the lake's eastern arm at an elevation of 3,530 feet, with a nearby boat ramp available. This is a popular lake for trout fishing in the summer. You must bring your own drinking water. The water source (such as at the fish-cleaning station) has a high mineral content and strong smell.

Campsites, facilities: There are 27 sites for tents or RVs up to 40 feet (no hookups). Picnic tables and fire grills are provided. There is no drinking water. Vault toilets are available. A car-top boat launch and fish-cleaning station are available on Sly Creek Reservoir. Leashed pets are permitted.

Reservations, fees: Reservations are not

accepted. Sites are $18 per night. Open late April to mid-October, weather permitting.
Directions: From Oroville, drive east on Highway 162/Oroville Dam Boulevard for about eight miles (becomes the Olive Highway) to Forbestown Road. Turn right and drive through Forbestown to Challenge and LaPorte Road. Turn left on LaPorte Road and drive 15 miles to Forest Road 16 (signed for Sly Creek Reservoir). Turn left on Forest Road 16 and drive two miles to the campground on the eastern end of the lake.
Contact: Plumas National Forest, Feather River Ranger District, 530/534-6500, fax 530/532-1210; Northwest Park Management, 530/283-5559.

23 DINGERVILLE USA
🥾 🏊 ⛴ ⛴ 🏠 ♿ 🚐

Scenic rating: 3

near Oroville

Map 5.2, page 322

You're right, they thought of this name all by themselves, needed no help. It is an RV park set in the Oroville foothill country—hot and dry in the summer, but with a variety of side trips available nearby. It is adjacent to a wildlife area and the Feather River and within short range of Lake Oroville and the Thermalito Afterbay for boating, water sports, and fishing. The RV park is a clean, quiet campground with easy access from the highway. Some of the sites are occupied by long-term renters.
Campsites, facilities: There are 29 pull-through sites with full hookups (30 and 50 amps) for RVs of any length. No tents. Picnic tables are provided. Restrooms with showers, modem access, cable TV, seasonal swimming pool, coin laundry, horseshoe pit, and a nine-hole executive golf course are available. Some facilities are wheelchair-accessible. Leashed pets are permitted.
Reservations, fees: Reservations are recommended. Sites are $27 per night. Some credit cards accepted. Open year-round.

Directions: From Oroville, drive south on Highway 70 to the second Pacific Heights Road turnoff. Turn right at Pacific Heights Road and drive less than one mile to the campground on the left.
From Marysville, drive north on Highway 70 to Palermo-Welsh Road. Turn left on Palermo-Welsh Road and drive to Pacific Heights Road. Turn left (north) on Pacific Heights Road and drive 0.5 mile to the campground entrance on the right.
Contact: Dingerville USA, 530/533-9343.

24 GARDEN POINT BOAT-IN
🏊 🚣 ⛴ 🐕 5️⃣ ⛰

Scenic rating: 8

on Bullards Bar Reservoir

Map 5.2, page 322   **BEST (**

Bullards Bar Reservoir is one of the few lakes in the Sierra Nevada to offer boat-in camping at developed boat-in sites and to allow boaters to create their own primitive sites anywhere along the lake's shoreline when permitted. A chemical toilet is required gear for boat-in shoreline camping at some sites. Garden Point Boat-In is on the western shore of the northern Yuba River arm. This lake provides plenty of recreation options, including good fishing for kokanee salmon, waterskiing, and many coves for playing in the water. All water sports are allowed.
Campsites, facilities: There are 30 tent sites accessible by boat only. Picnic tables and fire grills are provided. Vault toilets are available. No drinking water is available. Garbage must be packed out. Supplies and boat rentals are available at the Emerald Cove Marina. Leashed pets are permitted.
Reservations, fees: Reservations and a camping permit are required ($7.50 reservation fee) from Emerald Cove Marina at 530/692-3200. Sites are $17 per night, $34 per night for a double site. Open mid-April to mid-October, weather permitting.
Directions: From Marysville, drive northeast

on Highway 20 to Marysville Road. Turn north at Marysville Road (signed "Bullards Bar Reservoir") and drive about 12 miles to Old Marysville Road. Turn right and drive 14 miles to reach the Cottage Creek launch ramp and the marina (turn left just before the dam).

To reach the Dark Day boat ramp, continue over the dam and drive four miles, turn left on Dark Day Road, and continue to the ramp. From the boat launch, continue to the campground on the northwest side.

Contact: Emerald Cove Marina, 530/692-3200; Tahoe National Forest, Yuba River Ranger District, North, 530/288-3231, fax 530/288-0727; www.bullardsbar.com.

25 DARK DAY WALK-IN
🏃 🛶 ⛵ 🚤 🐕 ⛺

Scenic rating: 8

on Bullards Bar Reservoir

Map 5.2, page 322

Along with Schoolhouse, this is the only car-accessible camping area at Bullards Bar Reservoir with direct shoreline access. You park in a central area and then walk a short distance to the campground. The lake is a very short walk beyond that. Bullards Bar is a great camping lake, pretty, with 55 miles of shoreline and several lake arms and good fishing for kokanee salmon (as long as you have a boat). It is set at 2,000 feet in the foothills, like a silver dollar in a field of pennies. A bonus at Bullards Bar is that there is never a charge for day use, parking, or boat launching.

Campsites, facilities: There are 10 walk-in tent sites (some are double or triple sites). Picnic tables and fire pits are provided. Drinking water and vault toilets are available. Garbage must be packed out. A boat ramp is available nearby, and supplies and boat rentals are available at Emerald Cove Marina. Leashed pets are permitted.

Reservations, fees: Reservations and a camping permit are required ($7.50 reservation fee)

from Emerald Cove Marina at 530/692-3200. Sits are $17 per night, $34 per night for a double site, and $51 per night for a triple site. Open mid-April to mid-October, weather permitting.

Directions: From Marysville, drive northeast on Highway 20 to Marysville Road. Turn north at Marysville Road (signed "Bullards Bar Reservoir") and drive about 12 miles to Old Marysville Road. Turn right, drive 14 miles, and continue over the dam for four miles to Dark Day Road. Turn left and drive past the boat launch to the campground on the northwest side of the lake.

Contact: Emerald Cove Marina, 530/692-3200; Tahoe National Forest, Yuba River Ranger District, North, 530/288-3231, fax 530/288-0727; www.bullardsbar.com.

26 SHORELINE CAMP BOAT-IN
🏃 🛶 ⛵ 🚤 🐕 5% ⛺

Scenic rating: 8

on Bullards Bar Reservoir

Map 5.2, page 322

There are two boat-in campgrounds on Bullards Bar Reservoir, but another option is to throw all caution to the wind and just head out on your own, camping wherever you want. It is critical to bring a shovel to dig a flat site for sleeping, a large tarp for sun protection, and of course, plenty of water or a water purification pump. This is a big, beautiful lake, with good trolling for kokanee salmon. Rainbow trout are also here. Note: A portable chemical toilet and camping permit are required.

Campsites, facilities: Boaters may choose their own primitive campsite anywhere on the shore of Bullards Bar Reservoir, with a maximum of six people per site. Garbage must be packed out. Supplies and boat rentals are available at Emerald Cove Marina. Leashed pets are permitted.

Reservations, fees: Reservations and a camping permit are required ($7.50 reservation fee) from Emerald Cove Marina at 530/692-3200. Sites are $17 per night. Open mid-April to mid-October, weather permitting.

Directions: From Marysville, drive east on Highway 20 for 12 miles to Marysville Road. Turn left on Marysville Road (look for the sign for Bullards Bar Reservoir) and drive 12 miles to Old Marysville Road. Turn right on Old Marysville Road and drive 14 miles to the Cottage Creek Launch Ramp (turn left just before the dam). To reach the boat launch, continue to the campgrounds on the west side.

Contact: Emerald Cove Marina, 530/692-3200; Tahoe National Forest, Yuba River Ranger District, North, 530/288-3231, fax 530/288-0727; www.bullardsbar.com.

27 MADRONE COVE BOAT-IN

Scenic rating: 8

on Bullards Bar Reservoir

Map 5.2, page 322   **BEST (**

This is one of two boat-in campgrounds at Bullards Bar Reservoir. It is set on the main Yuba River arm of the lake, along the western shore. This is a premium boat-in site. The elevation is 2,000 feet.

Campsites, facilities: There are 10 tent sites, accessible by boat only. Picnic tables and fire grills are provided. Vault toilets are available. No drinking water is available. Garbage must be packed out. Supplies and boat rentals are available at the marina. Leashed pets are permitted.

Reservations, fees: Reservations and a camping permit are required ($7.50 reservation fee) from Emerald Cove Marina at 530/692-3200. Sites are $17 per night. Open mid-April to mid-October.

Directions: From Marysville, drive east on Highway 20 for 12 miles to Marysville Road (signed "Bullards Bar Reservoir"). Turn left at Marysville Road and drive 12 miles to Old Marysville Road. Turn right on Old

Marysville Road and drive 14 miles to reach the Cottage Creek Launch Ramp and the marina (turn left just before the dam). To reach the ramp, continue over the dam, drive four miles to Dark Day Road, turn left, and continue to the ramp. From the boat launch, continue to the campground on the west side.

Contact: Emerald Cove Marina, 530/692-3200; Tahoe National Forest, Yuba River Ranger District, North, 530/288-3231, fax 530/288-0727; www.bullardsbar.com.

28 SCHOOLHOUSE

Scenic rating: 7

on Bullards Bar Reservoir

Map 5.2, page 322

Bullards Bar Reservoir is one of the better lakes in the Sierra Nevada for camping, primarily because the lake levels tend to be higher here than at many other lakes. The camp is set on the southeast shore, with a trail available out of the camp to a beautiful lookout of the lake. Bullards Bar is known for good fishing for trout and kokanee salmon, waterskiing, and all water sports. A concrete boat ramp is to the south at Cottage Creek. Boaters should consider the special boat-in camps at the lake. The elevation is 2,200 feet.

Campsites, facilities: There are 56 sites with no hookups (one triple, 11 double, and 44 single sites) for tents or RVs of any length. Single sites accommodate six people, double sites accommodate 12, and triple sites hold up to 18 people. Picnic tables and fire rings are provided. Drinking water and flush and vault toilets are available. A boat ramp and boat rentals are nearby. Some facilities are wheelchair-accessible. Supplies are available in North San Juan, Camptonville, Dobbins, and at the marina. Leashed pets are permitted.

Reservations, fees: Reservations and a camping permit are required ($7.50 reservation fee) from Emerald Cove Marina at 530/692-3200. Sites are $17 per night, $34 per night for a double site, and $51 per night for a triple site. Open mid-April to mid-October.

Directions: From Marysville, drive east on Highway 20 for 12 miles to Marysville Road (signed "Bullards Bar Reservoir"). Turn left on Marysville Road and drive 12 miles to Old Marysville Road. Turn right on Old Marysville Road and drive 14 miles to the dam, then continue three miles to the campground entrance road on the left.

Contact: Emerald Cove Marina, 530/692-3200; Tahoe National Forest, Yuba River Ranger District North, 530/288-3231, fax 530/288-0727; www.bullardsbar.com.

29 HORNSWOGGLE GROUP CAMP

🏊 🛶 🚤 🐕 🚐 ⛺

Scenic rating: 7

on Bullards Bar Reservoir in Tahoe National Forest

Map 5.2, page 322

This camp is designed for group use. A concrete boat ramp is one mile north at the Dark Day Picnic Area. (For information about family campgrounds and boat-in sites, see the listings in this chapter for Bullards Bar Reservoir.)

Campsites, facilities: There are five 25-person group sites and one 50-person group site for tents or RVs up to 50 feet (no hookups). Picnic tables and fire grills are provided. Drinking water and flush and vault toilets are available. A boat ramp is nearby. Supplies and boat rentals are available at the marina. Leashed pets are permitted.

Reservations, fees: Reservations and a camping permit are required ($7.50 reservation fee) from Emerald Cove Marina at 530/692-3200. Sites are $60–100 per night. Open April to mid-October.

Directions: From Auburn, drive north on Highway 49 to Nevada City and continue for 17 miles through the town of North San Juan. Continue on Highway 49 for approximately

eight miles to Marysville Road. Turn left on Marysville Road and drive approximately five miles to the campground on the left.

Contact: Emerald Cove Marina, 530/692-3200; Tahoe National Forest, Yuba River Ranger District North, 530/288-3231, fax 530/288-0727; www.bullardsbar.com.

30 MOONSHINE CAMPGROUND

🏊 🛶 🐕 ♿ 🚐 ⛺

Scenic rating: 7

near the Yuba River and Bullards Bar Reservoir

Map 5.2, page 322

This campground features shaded sites and a swimming hole on the nearby Middle Fork Yuba River. Both are needed, with the weather hot here in the summer, at 1,430 feet in the Sierra foothills. Gold panning is available here. It's a seven-mile drive to a three-lane boat ramp at Dark Day Picnic Area at Bullards Bar Reservoir, the feature side trip. Malakoff Diggins State Historic Park is 15 miles away. A few of the sites are occupied by seasonal renters.

Campsites, facilities: There are 25 sites with partial hookups (30 amps), for tents or RVs up to 30 feet. Picnic tables and fire rings are provided. Drinking water, vault toilets, ice, and firewood are available. Some facilities are wheelchair-accessible. A grocery store, café, deli, and propane gas are available about three miles away in North San Juan. Leashed pets are permitted.

Reservations, fees: Reservations are required. Sites are $25–30 per night, $3 per night for air conditioning. Open May to early October, weather permitting.

Directions: From Auburn, drive north on Highway 49 to Nevada City and the exit for Downieville/Highway 49. Turn left and drive for 17 miles through the town of North San Juan. Continue on Highway 49 and cross a bridge over the Middle Fork Yuba River to

Moonshine Road (immediately after bridge crossing). Turn left on Moonshine Road and drive 0.75 mile to the campground on the left.

Contact: Moonshine Campground, 530/288-3585, www.moonshinecampground.com.

31 COLLINS LAKE RECREATION AREA

Scenic rating: 8

near Marysville on Collins Lake

Map 5.2, page 322

Collins Lake is set in the foothill country east of Marysville at 1,200 feet in elevation, ideal for the camper, boater, and angler. I counted 45 campsites set near the lakefront. This lake is becoming known as an outstanding destination for trophy-sized trout, especially in late spring through early summer, though fishing is often good year-round for know-hows. Other fish species are bass, crappie, bluegill, and catfish. The lake has 12 miles of shoreline and is quite pretty. In summer, warm water makes the lake exceptional for waterskiing (permitted from May to mid-October). There is a marina adjacent to the campground, and farther south is a 60-foot-wide swimming beach and boat ramp. Bonuses for anglers: No personal watercraft are allowed on the lake. A weekly fishing report is available at the camp's website. Insider's tip: Lakefront sites fill quickly; book early.

Campsites, facilities: There are 150 sites with full or partial hookups (30 amps) for RVs or tents, 60 sites with no hookups, five group tent sites, one RV group site, and a large overflow camping area. Some sites are pull-through. Four rental trailers and five cabins are also available. Picnic tables and barbecues are provided. Restrooms with flush toilets and coin showers, drinking water, portable toilets, dump station, playground, marina, boat ramp, boat rentals, berths, sandy swimming beach, beach volleyball, three group picnic areas, convenience store, coin laundry, firewood, ice, and propane gas are available. Some facilities are wheelchair-accessible. Leashed pets are permitted.

Reservations, fees: Reservations are accepted up to one year in advance ($8 reservation fee). Sites are $22–40 per night, $7 per night for each additional vehicle, $2 per pet per night. Group tent sites are $8 per person per night with a $75–150 per night minimum, and group RV sites are $10 per person per night with a $200 minimum per night. Boat launching is $6 per day. Weekly and monthly rates available. Some credit cards accepted. Open year-round.

Directions: From Marysville, drive east on Highway 20 for about 12 miles to Marysville Road/Road E-21. Turn left (north) and drive approximately 10 miles to the recreation area entrance road on the right. Turn right, drive 0.3 mile to the entrance station and store, and then continue to the campground. (For detailed directions from other areas, visit the website.)

Contact: Collins Lake Recreation Area, 530/692-1600 or 800/286-0576, www.collinslake.com.

32 ENGLEBRIGHT LAKE BOAT-IN

Scenic rating: 8

near Marysville

Map 5.2, page 322

Englebright Lake is an outstanding destination for boat-in camping, fishing, and waterskiing. Remember this place. It always seems to have plenty of water, and there are more developed boat-in campsites along its 19 miles of shoreline than at any other lake in California. The lake looks like a huge water snake, long and narrow, set in the Yuba/Nevada Canyon at 520 feet in elevation. In summer, it is a waterskiing mecca, with warm and calm water. All water sports are allowed. Trout fishing is good on the upper end of the lake, where waterskiing is prohibited year-round.

Campsites, facilities: There are 96 boat-in sites (no hookups) along the shores of Englebright Lake and a group camping area that accommodates 50 people. Picnic tables, fire grills, and lantern hangers are provided. Pit toilets are available. Two boat ramps are available on either side of Skippers Cove. Drinking water is available at the Narrows day-use area and at the marina. Boat rentals (including houseboats), mooring, fuel dock, and groceries are available at the marina. Leashed pets are permitted.

Reservations, fees: Reservations are accepted for groups only at 530/432-6427. Boat-in sites are $10 per night, $50–75 per night for group site. Open year-round.

Directions: From Auburn, drive north on Highway 49 to Grass Valley and the junction with Highway 20. Turn west on Highway 20 and drive to Mooney Flat Road (if you reach Smartville, you have gone a mile too far). Turn right on Mooney Flat Road and drive three miles to the entrance for the Narrows Recreation Area. Continue 0.5 mile to Joe Miller Road and the entrance to Skipper's Cove Marina on the left.

Contact: U.S. Army Corps of Engineers, Sacramento District, Englebright Lake, 530/432-6427 (reservations), fax 530/432-6418; Skippers Cove, concessionaire, 530/432-6302, www.englebrightlake.com.

33 NEVADA COUNTY FAIRGROUNDS

Scenic rating: 6

near Grass Valley

Map 5.2, page 322

The motto here is "California's Most Beautiful Fairgrounds," and that's right. The area is set at 2,300 feet in the Sierra foothills, with a good number of pines sprinkled about. The park is adjacent to the fairgrounds, and even though the fair runs for a week every August, the park is open year-round. However, check status before planning a trip because the campground is sometimes closed for scheduled activities. A caretaker at the park is available to answer any questions. Kids can fish at a small lake nearby. The Draft Horse Classic is held here every September and a country Christmas Faire is held Thanksgiving weekend.

Campsites, facilities: There are 130 sites with full or partial hookups (50 amps) for RVs of any length, and a open dirt and grassy area with no hookups available as an overflow area. No tents. Two dump stations, drinking water, restrooms with showers and flush toilets, and group facilities are available. Some facilities are wheelchair-accessible. Leashed pets are permitted.

Reservations, fees: Reservations are accepted. Sites are $21–26 per night. A seven-day limit is enforced. Some credit cards accepted. Open year-round.

Directions: From Auburn, drive north on Highway 49 to Grass Valley and the McKnight Way exit. Take that exit and turn left on McKnight Way and drive over the freeway to Freeman Lane (just past the shopping center on the left). Turn right on Freeman Lane and drive to the second stop sign and McCourtney Road. Continue straight on McCourtney Road and drive two blocks to the fairgrounds on the right. Continue to Gate 4.

Contact: Nevada County Fairgrounds, 530/273-6217, fax 530/273-1146, www.nevadacountyfair.com.

34 AUBURN GOLD COUNTRY RV PARK

Scenic rating: 4

near Auburn

Map 5.3, page 323

This year-round park is set at 1,250 feet and has all the amenities. Hey, a swimming pool is always a bonus in Auburn. Some may remember that this park was once a KOA campground. An 18-hole golf course is within one-half mile. The American River and Auburn State Recreation Area, which includes Clementine Lake, are nearby.

Campsites, facilities: There are 66 sites with full and partial hookups (30 and 50 amps) for RVs up to 40 feet, and 10 tent sites. Some sites are pull-through. Two cabins are also available. Picnic tables and fire rings are provided. Restrooms with flush toilets and showers, drinking water, dump station, a playground, seasonal heated swimming pool, spa, recreation room, fishing pond, basketball, horseshoes, convenience store, coin laundry, and propane gas are available. Some facilities are wheelchair-accessible. Leashed pets are permitted, with certain restrictions.

Reservations, fees: Reservations are accepted at 866/822-8362. Sites are $27–45 per night, $2.50–4.50 per person per night for more than two people. Some credit cards accepted. Open year-round.

Directions: From Auburn, drive north on Highway 49 for 3.5 miles to Rock Creek Road (one block past Bell Road). Turn right on Rock Creek Road and drive a short distance to the entrance on the left.

Contact: Auburn Gold Country RV Park, 530/885-0990.

35 AUBURN STATE RECREATION AREA: CLEMENTINE LAKE

🚶 🚵 🏊 🛶 ⛴ ⛺

Scenic rating: 8

near Auburn

Map 5.3, page 323   BEST (

This state park is a jewel in the valley foothill country, covering more than 42,000 acres along the North and Middle Forks of the American River. Formerly the domain of gold miners, the area is now home to wildlife as well as a wide variety of recreational opportunities. The Auburn SRA is composed of land set aside for the Auburn Dam, consisting of 40 miles along two forks of the American River. There is one boat-in campground at Clementine Lake. The lake is 3.5 miles long and very narrow. All water sports are allowed on the lake. The American River runs through the park, offering visitors opportunities to fish, boat, kayak, and raft. In addition, there are more than 100 miles of hiking, biking, and horseback-riding trails. Clementine Lake offers fishing (not stocked) and waterskiing, with a boat limit of 25 boats per day; the quota is reached every day on summer weekends. White-water rafting is extremely popular, with more than 30 private outfitters licensed for trips in sections of river through the park.

Campsites, facilities: There is a campground at Clementine Lake with 15 boat-in sites. Picnic tables and fire grills are provided. Pit toilets are available. No drinking water is available. Garbage must be packed out. No pets are permitted at Clementine Lake.

Reservations, fees: Reservations are accepted ($7.50 reservation fee) at 800/444-PARK (800/444-7275) or www.reserveamerica.com. Boat-in sites are $25 per night, $5 per night for each additional vehicle, $5 fee per stay for boat launching at Clementine Lake. Open Memorial Day weekend through Labor Day weekend.

Directions to Clementine Lake: From I-80 at Auburn, take the Auburn Ravine/Foresthill exit to Foresthill Road. Turn right and drive on Foresthill Road for two miles to Lake Clementine Road. Turn left and drive 2.5 miles to the boat launch. After launching, cruise by boat 1.5 miles northeast to the boat-in campgrounds.

Contact: Auburn State Recreation Area, 530/885-4527, fax 530/885-2798, www.parks.ca.gov.

36 AUBURN STATE RECREATION AREA: MINERAL BAR

🚶 🚴 🏊 🛶 🎣 🦌 🚐 🏕

Scenic rating: 8

near Colfax

Map 5.3, page 323　　　　**BEST (**

Mineral Bar Camp is situated in the Auburn State Recreation Area, a 42,000-acre park. This camp is near the American River. (For details about the Auburn State Recreation Area, see the previous listing, *Clementine Lake*.)

Campsites, facilities: There are 17 sites for tents or RVs up to 24 feet (no hookups). Picnic tables and fire grills are provided. Chemical toilets are available. No drinking water is available. Garbage must be packed out. Leashed pets are permitted.

Reservations, fees: Reservations are not accepted. Sites are $15 per night, $5 per night for each additional vehicle. Open year-round, with limited winter facilities.

Directions: From I-80 in Auburn, drive east for 15 miles to Colfax and the Canyon Way/Placer Hills Drive exit. Take that exit and turn left on Canyon Way and drive one mile to Iowa Hill Road. Turn right and drive three miles on a narrow paved road to the campground.

Contact: Auburn State Recreation Area, 530/885-4527, fax 530/885-2798, www .parks.ca.gov.

37 AUBURN STATE RECREATION AREA: RUCKY-A-CHUCKY

🚶 🚴 🏊 🛶 🎣 🦌 🏕

Scenic rating: 8

near Auburn

Map 5.3, page 323　　　　**BEST (**

Rucky-A-Chucky Camp is situated in the Auburn State Recreation Area, between Auburn and Foresthill. (For details about

the Auburn State Recreation Area, see the *Clementine Lake* listing in this chapter.)

Campsites, facilities: There are five sites for tents only. Picnic tables and fire grills are provided. Chemical toilets are available. No drinking water is available. Garbage must be packed out. Leashed pets are permitted.

Reservations, fees: Reservations are not accepted. Sites are $15 per night, $5 per night for each additional vehicle. Open year-round, weather permitting.

Directions: From I-80 in Auburn, take the Auburn Ravine/Foresthill Road exit to Foresthill Road. Turn right and drive for seven miles to Drivers Flat Road. Turn right and drive 2.8 miles on a dirt road to the campground on the right.

Contact: Auburn State Recreation Area, 530/885-4527, fax 530/885-2798, www .parks.ca.gov.

38 CAMPERS INN RV PARK AND GOLF COURSE

🏊 🦌 🏕 ♿ 🚐 🏕

Scenic rating: 1

near Dunnigan

Map 5.3, page 323

This private park has a rural valley atmosphere and provides a layover for drivers cruising I-5. The park has a par three golf course (nine holes), and it specializes in golf tournaments and group outings. The Sacramento River to the east is the closest body of water, but this section of river is hardly a premium side-trip destination. There are no nearby lakes.

Campsites, facilities: There are three tent sites and 72 sites with full or partial hookups (30 and 50 amps) for RVs of any length. Many sites are pull-through. Picnic tables are provided. Restrooms with flush toilets and showers, modem access, seasonal swimming pool, two clubhouses/meeting rooms, horseshoes, nine-hole golf course, coin laundry, propane gas, ice, and general store are available. Some facilities are wheelchair-accessible. Leashed pets are permitted.

Reservations, fees: Reservations are accepted. Sites are $18–29.50 per night. Some credit cards accepted. Open year-round.

Directions: From I-5 in Dunnigan, take the Dunnigan exit (just north of the I-505 cutoff). Drive west on County Road E4/Road 6 for a mile to County Road 88. Turn right and drive for 1.5 miles to the park.

Contact: Campers Inn RV Park and Golf Course, 530/724-3350 or 800/79-GOLF3 (800/794-6533), www.campersinnrv.com.

39 PENINSULA

🚶 🚴 ⛵ 🛶 ⛴ 🎣 🐕 ♿ 🚐 ⛺

Scenic rating: 6

in Folsom Lake State Recreation Area

Map 5.3, page 323

This is one of the big camps at Folsom Lake, but it is also more remote than the other camps, requiring a circuitous drive. It is set on the peninsula on the northeast shore, right where the North Fork American River arm of the lake enters the main lake area. A nearby boat ramp, marina, and boat rentals make this a great weekend spot. Fishing for bass and trout is often quite good in spring and early summer, and other species include catfish and perch. Waterskiing and wakeboarding are popular in the hot summer, and all water sports are allowed.

Campsites, facilities: There are 100 sites for tents or RVs up to 32 feet (no hookups). Picnic tables and fire grills are provided. Drinking water and restrooms with flush toilets are available. A bike path is available nearby. Boat rentals, moorings, snack bar, ice, and bait and tackle are available at the Folsom Lake Marina. Leashed pets are permitted.

Reservations, fees: Reservations are accepted ($7.50 reservation fee) at 800/444-PARK (800/444-7275) or www.reserveamerica.com. Sites are $15–20 per night $5–7 per night for each additional vehicle. Open year-round.

Directions: From Placerville, drive east on U.S. 50 to the Spring Street/Highway 49 exit. Turn north on Highway 49 (toward the town of Coloma) and continue 8.3 miles into the town of Pilot Hill and Rattlesnake Bar Road. Turn left on Rattlesnake Bar Road and drive nine miles to the end of the road and the park entrance.

Contact: Folsom Lake State Recreation Area, 916/988-0205, fax 916/988-9062, www.parks.ca.gov.

40 BEAL'S POINT

🚶 🚴 ⛵ 🛶 ⛴ 🐕 ♿ 🚐 ⛺

Scenic rating: 6

in Folsom Lake State Recreation Area

Map 5.3, page 323

Folsom Lake State Recreation Area is Sacramento's backyard vacation spot, a huge lake covering about 18,000 acres with 75 miles of shoreline, which means plenty of room for boating, waterskiing, fishing, and suntanning. This camp is set on the lake's southwest side, just north of the dam, with a boat ramp nearby at Granite Bay. The lake has a productive trout fishery in the spring, a fast-growing population of kokanee salmon, and good prospects for bass in late spring and early summer. By summer wakeboarders and water-skiers usually take over the lake each day by about 10 A.M. One problem with this lake is that a minor water drawdown can cause major amounts of shoreline to become exposed on its upper arms. There are opportunities for hiking, biking, running, picnics, and horseback riding. A 32-mile-long trail connects Folsom Lake with many Sacramento County parks before reaching Old Sacramento. This trail is outstanding for family biking and inline skating. Summers are hot and dry.

Campsites, facilities: There are 69 sites for tents or RVs up to 31 feet; some sites have full hookups (30 and 50 amps). Picnic tables and fire grills are provided. Drinking water, restrooms with flush toilets and showers, Wi-Fi, and a dump station are available. A bike path and horseback-riding facilities are available nearby. Some facilities are wheelchair-accessible. There are boat rentals, moorings, summer snack bar, ice, and bait and tackle available at the Folsom Lake Marina. Leashed pets are permitted.

Reservations, fees: Reservations are accepted April through September ($7.50 reservation fee) at 800/444-PARK (800/444-7275) or www.reserveamerica.com. Sites are $15–20 per night, $5–7 per night for each additional vehicle. Open year-round.

Directions: From Sacramento, drive east on U.S. 50 to the Folsom Boulevard exit. Take that exit to the stop sign and Folsom Boulevard. Turn left and continue north on Folsom Boulevard for 3.5 miles (road name changes to Folsom-Auburn Road) to the park entrance on the right.

Contact: Folsom Lake State Recreation Area, 916/988-0205, fax 916/988-9062; Beal's Point Campground, 916/791-1531, www.parks .ca.gov.

41 NEGRO BAR GROUP CAMP

Scenic rating: 6

in Folsom Lake State Recreation Area

Map 5.3, page 323

Lake Natoma is the afterbay for Folsom Lake, but it is nothing like Folsom Lake. Natoma is comparatively small with 13 miles of shoreline, very narrow instead of wide, with cold water instead of warm. This camp is set at the head of the lake on the northern shore, with an adjacent boat ramp available. Lake Natoma is popular for crew races, sailing, kayaking, and other aquatic sports. A 5-mph speed limit is enforced on the lake, and swimming is allowed. The Folsom Lake entrance is a 10-minute drive from Lake Natoma.

Campsites, facilities: There are three group tent sites that can accommodate 25–50 people each. Picnic tables and fire grills are provided. Drinking water and restrooms with flush toilets are available. A bike path and canoe and kayak rentals are available nearby. Leashed pets are permitted.

Reservations, fees: Reservations are accepted ($7.50 reservation fee) at 800/444-PARK (800/444-7275) or www.reserveamerica .com. Sites are $56–111 per night. Open year-round.

Directions: From I-80 north of Sacramento, take the Douglas Boulevard exit and head east for five miles to Auburn-Folsom Road. Turn right on Auburn-Folsom Road and drive south for six miles to Greenback Lane. Turn right on Greenback Lane and merge immediately into the left lane. The park entrance is approximately 0.2 mile on the left.

Contact: Folsom Lake State Recreation Area, 916/988-0205, fax 916/988-9062, www.parks .ca.gov.

42 SACRAMENTO WEST/ OLD TOWN KOA

Scenic rating: 2

in West Sacramento

Map 5.3, page 323

This is the choice of car and RV campers touring California's capital and looking for a layover spot. It is in West Sacramento not far from the Capitol building, the railroad museum, Sutter's Fort, Old Sacramento, Crocker Museum, and shopping.

Campsites, facilities: There are 95 pull-through sites with full or partial hookups (30 and 50 amps) for RVs up to 40 feet, and 27 tent sites. Twelve cabins are also available. Restrooms with flush toilets and showers, Wi-Fi, cable TV, playground, fishing pond, seasonal swimming pool, coin laundry, propane gas, and convenience store are available. Some facilities are wheelchair-accessible. Leashed pets are permitted, with certain restrictions.

Reservations, fees: Reservations are accepted at 800/562-2747. Sites are $30–45 per night. Some credit cards accepted. Open year-round.

Directions: From Sacramento, drive west on I-80 about four miles to the West Capitol Avenue exit. Exit and turn left onto West Capitol Avenue, going under the freeway to the second stoplight and the intersection with Lake Road. Turn left onto Lake Road and continue a half block to the camp on the right at 3951 Lake Road.

Contact: Sacramento West/Old Town KOA, 916/371-6771 or 800/545-KAMP (800/545-5267), www.koa.com.

43 VINEYARD RV PARK

Scenic rating: 2

in Vacaville

Map 5.3, page 323

This is one of two privately operated parks in the area set up primarily for RVs. It is in a eucalyptus grove, with clean, well-kept sites. If you are heading to the Bay Area, it is late in the day, and you don't have your destination set, this spot offers a chance to hole up for the night and formulate your travel plans. Note that about half of the sites are long-term rentals.

Campsites, facilities: There are 110 sites with full hookups (30 and 50 amps) for RVs of any length. No tents. Some sites are pull-through. Picnic tables are provided. Restrooms with flush toilets and showers, Wi-Fi, seasonal swimming pool, coin laundry, putting green, enclosed dog walk, and ice are available. Some facilities are wheelchair-accessible. Leashed pets are permitted, with certain restrictions.

Reservations, fees: Reservations are recommended at 866/447-8797. Sites are $44–48 per night, $2 per person per night for more than two people, $1 per pet per night. Some credit cards accepted. Open year-round.

From Vacaville on I-80, turn north on I-505 and drive three miles to Midway Road. Turn right (east) on Midway Road and drive 0.5 mile to the second campground on the left at 4985 Midway Road.

Contact: Vineyard RV Park, 707/447-8797, www.vineyardrvpark.com.

44 RANCHO SECO RECREATION AREA

Scenic rating: 6

near Sacramento

Map 5.3, page 323

There is a shortage of campgrounds close to Sacramento, so this one about 35 miles from the state capital comes in handy. This public facility has a 160-acre lake that is surrounded by 400 acres of open space and includes trails for walking and bicycling. In 2006, a seven-mile loop nature trail opened next to the lake. The centerpiece of this facility is the lake, which is especially popular for fishing and sailboarding. The lake is stocked with rainbow trout, and fishing derbies are held during the winter. Other fish species include bass, bluegill, redear sunfish, crappie, and catfish. Live bait is prohibited and only electric motors are allowed. A bonus is that the lake level remains constant year-round, and since the lake is fed by the Folsom South Canal, the water is warm in summer. Swimming is popular and there is a large sandy beach with summer lifeguard service. Pedal boats and kayaks can also be rented on weekends in summer. Tent sites are situated along the lake. The Amanda Blake Memorial Wildlife Refuge is here, and visitors can observe exotic captive wildlife that has been rescued from circuses and other performing groups. Migratory birds, including bald eagles, winter at the lake. What are those two large towers? They're remnants of the now-closed Rancho Seco nuclear power–generating station.

Campsites, facilities: There are 20 tent sites, 18 sites with partial hookups (30 amps) for RVs of any length, and two group tent sites that can accommodate up to 200 people each. A couple of sites are pull-through. Picnic tables and fire grills are provided. Drinking water, restrooms with coin showers, dump station, swimming beach, six fishing piers, picnic areas, coin laundry, fish-cleaning station, horseshoe pit, recreation room, seasonal general store, weekend boat rentals, and boat launch are available. Supplies are available in Galt. Some facilities are wheelchair-accessible, including some fishing piers. Leashed pets are permitted.

Reservations, fees: Reservations are accepted at 916/732-4913. Sites are $10–15 per night, and the group tent site is $45 per night for the first 20 people, plus $1.50 per person per night for additional campers. There is a 14-day maximum stay. Open year-round.

Directions: From Sacramento, drive south on Highway 99 for approximately 25 miles to the Twin Cities Road/Highway 104 exit. Take that exit and drive east for 13 miles, past the two towers, to the Rancho Seco Park exit. Turn right and continue to the lake and campground.

Contact: Rancho Seco Recreation Area, 209/748-2318, www.smud.org/about/recreation/rancho.html.

45 SANDY BEACH REGIONAL PARK

Scenic rating: 6

on the Sacramento River

Map 5.3, page 323

This is a surprisingly little-known park, especially considering it provides beach access to the Sacramento River. It is a popular spot for sunbathers in hot summer months, and the park has a sandy beach stretching for more than a half mile. Swimming is not allowed because there is no lifeguard; however, wading is permitted. Sailboarding and sailing are possible here. In winter, it is one of the few viable spots where you can fish from the shore for sturgeon; check fishing regulations. It also provides outstanding boating access to the Sacramento River, including one of the best fishing spots for striped bass in the fall, the Rio Vista Bridge.

Campsites, facilities: There are 42 sites with partial hookups (30 amps) for tents or RVs of any length. Picnic tables and fire pits are provided. Drinking water, restrooms with flush toilets and showers, a dump station, picnic areas, volleyball, horseshoes, firewood, and a boat ramp are available. A camp host is on-site. Some facilities are wheelchair-accessible. Supplies can be obtained nearby (within a mile). Leashed pets are permitted in the campground only.

Reservations, fees: Reservations are accepted. Sites are $21 per night, $7 per night for each additional vehicle, $1 per pet per night. Some credit cards accepted. Open year-round.

Directions: From I-80 in Fairfield, take the Highway 12 exit and drive southeast for 14 miles to Rio Vista and the intersection with Main Street. Turn right on Main Street and drive a short distance to 2nd Street. Turn right and drive 0.5 mile to Beach Drive. Turn left (west) and drive 0.5 mile to the park.

Contact: Sandy Beach Regional Park, 707/374-2097, fax 707/374-4972, www.solanocounty.com.

46 DELTA MARINA YACHT HARBOR AND RV

Scenic rating: 6

on the Sacramento River Delta

Map 5.3, page 323

This is a prime spot for boat campers. Summers are hot and breezy, and waterskiing is popular on the nearby Sacramento River. From November to March, the striped-bass fishing is quite good, often as close as just a half mile upriver at the Rio Vista Bridge. The boat launch at the harbor is a bonus, especially with night lighting. Some campsites have river frontage, and some sites are filled with long-term renters.

Campsites, facilities: There are 25 sites with full hookups (30 and 50 amps) for RVs up to 40 feet. No tents. Picnic tables and fire grills are provided. Restrooms with showers, cable TV, coin laundry, playground, boat ramp, fishing pier, marine repair service, pet restroom, restaurant, marine supplies and gift store, ice, and propane gas are available. Fuel is available 24 hours. Free boat launching for RV guests. Some facilities are wheelchair-accessible. Leashed pets are permitted.

Reservations, fees: Reservations are accepted. Sites are $25–35 per night. Two-week maximum stay in summer. Some credit cards accepted. Open year-round.

Directions: From Fairfield on I-80, take the Highway 12 exit and drive southeast for 14 miles to Rio Vista and the intersection with Main Street. Take the Main Street exit and drive a short distance to 2nd Street. Turn right on 2nd Street and drive to Marina Drive. Turn left on Marina Drive, and continue another short distance to the harbor.

Contact: Delta Marina Yacht Harbor and RV, 707/374-2315, fax 707/374-6471, www.deltamarina.com.

47 BRANNAN ISLAND STATE RECREATION AREA

Scenic rating: 7

on the Sacramento River

Map 5.3, page 323   **BEST (**

This state park is perfectly designed for boaters, set in the heart of the Delta's vast waterways. You get year-round adventure: waterskiing, wakeboarding, and fishing for catfish are popular in the summer, and in the winter the immediate area is often good for striped-bass fishing. The proximity of the campgrounds to the boat launch deserves a medal. What many people do is tow a boat here, launch it, keep it docked, and then return to their site and set up; this allows them to come and go as they please, boating, fishing, and exploring in the Delta. There is a six-lane boat ramp that provides access to a maze of waterways amid many islands, marshes, sloughs, and rivers. Day-use areas include the Windy Cove sailboarding area. Though striped bass in winter and catfish in summer are the most favored fish here, sturgeon, bluegill, perch, bullhead, and bass are also caught. Some sections of the San Joaquin Delta are among the best bass fishing spots in California. A hiking/biking trail circles the park.

Campsites, facilities: There are 102 sites for tents or RVs up to 36 feet, eight walk-in sites, and six group sites for up to 30 people each. No hookups. Picnic tables and fire grills are provided. Drinking water, restrooms with coin showers (at campground and boat launch), boat berths, dump station, Wi-Fi, and a boat launch are available. Some facilities are wheelchair-accessible. Supplies can be obtained three miles away in Rio Vista. Leashed pets are permitted.

Reservations, fees: Reservations are accepted ($7.50 reservation fee) at 800/444-PARK (800/444-7275) or www.reserveamerica.com. Sites are $15–20 per night, $5 per night for each additional vehicle, $66 per night for group sites. Boat launching is $5 per day. Open year-round.

Directions: In Fairfield on I-80, take the Highway 12 exit, drive southeast 14 miles to Rio Vista, and continue to Highway 160. Turn right on Highway 160 and drive three miles to the park entrance on the left.

Contact: Brannan Island State Recreation Area, 916/777-6671; Entrance Kiosk, 916/777-7701; Goldfield District Office, 916/988-0205, www.parks.ca.gov.

48 SNUG HARBOR RESORT

🚴 🏊 ⛵ 🛥 🐕 🚣 ♿ 🚐

Scenic rating: 7

near Rio Vista

Map 5.3, page 323   **BEST (**

This year-round resort is an ideal resting place for families who enjoy waterskiing, wakeboarding, boating, biking, swimming, and fishing. After the ferry ride, it is only a few minutes to Snug Harbor, a gated marina resort on eight acres with a campground, RV hookups, and a separate area with cabins and cottages. Some say that the waterfront sites with docks give the place the feel of a Louisiana bayou, yet everything is clean and orderly, including a full-service marina, a store, and all facilities—and an excellent location to explore the boating paradise of the Delta. Anglers will find good prospects for striped bass, black bass, blue gill, steelhead, sturgeon, and catfish. The waterfront sites with docks are a bonus.

Campsites, facilities: There are 38 waterfront sites with docks and full hookups (30 and 50 amps) for RVs of any length, 15 waterview sites with full hookups for RVs, six group sites for RVs, four tent trailers, and 20 park-model cabins. Barbecues or burn barrels are provided. Restrooms with showers, dump station, Wi-Fi, convenience store, swimming beach, children's play area, volleyball, croquet, bocce ball, badminton, horseshoes, boat launch, propane gas, and a full-service marina are available. Some facilities are wheelchair-accessible.

Reservations, fees: Reservations are recommended by website. Sites are $32–45 per night, $7.50 per night for each additional vehicle, $60–90 per night for group sites, $2 per pet per night. Boat launching is $10 per day. Call or check the website for tent trailer and cabin prices. Some credit cards accepted. Open year-round.

Directions: From the Bay Area, take I-80 to Fairfield and Highway 12. Turn east on Highway 12 and drive to Rio Vista and Front Street. Turn left on Front Street (before crossing the bridge) and drive under the bridge to River Road. Turn right on River Road and drive two miles to the Rio Vista/Real McCoy Ferry (signed Ryer Island). Take the ferry (free) across the Sacramento River to Ryer Island and Levee Road. Turn right on Levee Road and drive 4.5 miles to the Snug Harbor entrance on the right. For recorded directions from other areas, including Sacramento, call 916/775-1594.

Contact: Snug Harbor Resort, 916/775-1455, fax 916/775-1594, www.snugharbor.net.

49 WESTGATE LANDING COUNTY PARK

🏊 ⛵ 🛥 🐕 ♿ 🚐 ⛺

Scenic rating: 6

in the San Joaquin River Delta near Stockton

Map 5.3, page 323

Summer temperatures typically reach the high 90s and low 100s here, and this county park provides a little shade and boating access to the South Fork Mokelumne River. On hot summer nights, some campers will stay up late and night fish for catfish. Between storms in winter, the area typically gets smothered in dense fog. The sites are not pull-through but semicircles, which work nearly as well for RV drivers.

Campsites, facilities: There are 14 sites for tents or RVs up to 32 feet (no hookups). Picnic tables and barbecues are provided. Drinking water and flush toilets are available. Groceries and propane gas are nearby. A fishing pier, 24 boat slips, and boat docking are available. Some facilities are wheelchair-accessible. Leashed pets are permitted, with a limit of two.

Reservations, fees: Reservations are accepted ($10 reservation fee) at least two weeks in advance. Less than two weeks, sites are first-come, first-served. Sites are $15 per night, $5 per night for each additional vehicle, boat slips $15 per day, $1 per pet per night. Open year-round.

Directions: On I-5, drive to Lodi and Highway 12. Take Highway 12 west and drive about five miles to Glasscock Road. Turn right and drive about a mile to the park.
Contact: San Joaquin County Parks Department, 209/953-8800 or 209/331-7400, www.co.san-joaquin.ca.us/parks.

50 STOCKTON DELTA KOA

Scenic rating: 6

near Stockton

Map 5.3, page 323

Some people may remember this campground by its previous name: Tower Park Resort. This huge resort is ideal for boat-in campers who desire a full-facility marina. The camp is set on Little Potato Slough near the Mokelumne River. In the summer, this is a popular waterskiing area. Some hot weekends are like a continuous party. Note that tents are now allowed here.

Campsites, facilities: There are 300 sites with full hookups (30 amps) for RVs up to 45 feet, 20 tent sites, and five park-model cabins. Picnic tables are provided. Restrooms with showers, dump station, pavilion, banquet room, boat rentals, overnight boat slips, boat storage, double boat launch, playground, swimming pool, spa, horseshoes, gas station, restaurant, coin laundry, gift shop, store, ice, and propane gas are available. Some facilities are wheelchair-accessible. Leashed pets are permitted, with certain restrictions.
Reservations, fees: Reservations are available, with a three-night minimum on summer holidays. Sites are $30–54 per night, maximum six people per site. Some credit cards accepted. Open year-round.
Directions: On I-5, drive to Lodi and Highway 12. Take Highway 12 west and drive about five miles to Tower Park Way (before first bridge). Turn left and drive a short distance to the park.
Contact: Stockton Delta KOA, 209/369-

1041, fax 209/369-1301, www.koa.com or www.stocktondeltakoa.com.

51 EDDOS HARBOR AND RV PARK

Scenic rating: 6

on the San Joaquin River Delta

Map 5.3, page 323   **BEST**

This is an ideal spot for campers with boats. Eddos is set on the San Joaquin River and Gallagher Slough, upstream of the Antioch Bridge, in an outstanding region for fishing, powerboating, wakeboarding, and waterskiing. In summer, boaters have access to 1,000 miles of Delta waterways, with the best of them in a nearby spider web of rivers and sloughs off the San Joaquin to False River, Frank's Tract, and Old River. Hot weather and sheltered sloughs make this ideal for waterskiing. In the winter, a nearby fishing spot, as well as the mouth of the False River, attract striped bass. Many of the sites here are occupied by seasonal renters; plan well ahead for the summer.

Campsites, facilities: There are 44 sites with full hookups (15 amps) for RVs up to 40 feet. Picnic tables are provided. Restrooms with flush toilets and showers, launch ramp, boat storage, fuel dock, Wi-Fi, coin laundry, and a small grocery store are available. Some facilities are wheelchair-accessible. Leashed pets are permitted.
Reservations, fees: Reservations are recommended. Sites are $25 per night and $1 per pet per night. Monthly rates available. Some credit cards accepted. Open year-round.
Directions: In Fairfield on I-80, take the Highway 12 exit and drive 14 miles southeast to Rio Vista and continue three miles to Highway 160 (at the signal just after the bridge). Turn right on Highway 160 and drive three miles to Sherman Island/East Levee Road, at the end of the drawbridge. Turn left on East Levee Road and drive 5.5 miles to the campground along

the San Joaquin River. Note: If arriving by boat, the camp is adjacent to Light 21.

Contact: Eddos Harbor and RV Park, 925/757-5314.

52 LUNDBORG LANDING

🏊 🚣 🚤 🏇 🦮 👨‍🦽 🚙 ⛺

Scenic rating: 6

on the San Joaquin River Delta

Map 5.3, page 323

This park is set on Bethel Island in the heart of the California Delta. The boat ramp here provides immediate access to an excellent area for waterskiing, and it turns into a playland on hot summer days. In the fall and winter, the area often provides good striper fishing at nearby Frank's Tract, False River, and the San Joaquin River. The fishing for largemouth bass at Frank's Tract is rated among the best in North America. Catfishing in surrounding slough areas is also good year-round. The Delta Sportsman Shop at Bethel Island has reliable fishing information. Live webcams of Frank's Tract are available on the website. Note that some sites are occupied by long-term tenants.

Campsites, facilities: There are 70 sites with full hookups (30 and 50 amps) for RVs; some sites are pull-through and some sites allow tents. A large overflow area can handle up to 300 RVs and many tents. Several cabins are also available. Restrooms with showers, coin laundry, dump station, propane gas, modem access, playground, boat ramp, fishing pier, berthing, boat storage, fish-cleaning station, and full restaurant and bar are available. Some facilities are wheelchair-accessible. Leashed pets are permitted.

Reservations, fees: Reservations are accepted. Sites are $16–24 per night. Long-term rates available. Open year-round.

Directions: From Antioch, turn east on Highway 4 and drive to Oakley and East Cypress Road. Turn left on East Cypress Road, drive over the Bethel Island Bridge, and continue 0.5 mile to Gateway Road. Turn right on Gateway Road and drive two miles to the park entrance on the left (signed well, next to the tugboat).

Contact: Lundborg Landing, 925/684-9351, www.lundborglanding.com.

53 STOCKTON/LODI RV PARK

🏊 🏇 🦮 👨‍🦽 🚙 ⛺

Scenic rating: 3

in Lodi

Map 5.3, page 323

This former KOA camp is in the heart of the San Joaquin Valley. The proximity to I-5 and Highway 99 makes it work for long-distance vacationers looking for a spot to park the rig for the night. The San Joaquin Delta is 15 miles to the west, with best access provided off Highway 12 to Isleton and Rio Vista; it's also a pretty drive.

Campsites, facilities: There are 102 sites, most pull-through and many with full hook-ups (30 and 50 amps), for RVs of any length, 13 tent sites, and two cabins. Picnic tables are provided. Restrooms with showers, dump station, convenience store, propane gas, coin laundry, modem access, recreation room, seasonal swimming pool, bicycle rentals, and a playground are available. Some facilities are wheelchair-accessible. Leashed pets are permitted at campsites, with certain restrictions, but not in cabins.

Reservations, fees: Reservations are accepted at 800/562-1229. Sites are $26–34 per night, and $2–4 per night for more than two people. Some credit cards accepted. Open year-round.

Directions: On I-5, drive to Eight Mile Road (five miles north of Stockton). Turn east and drive five miles to the campground at 2851 East Eight Mile Road.

Contact: Stockton/Lodi RV Park, tel./fax 209/941-2573 or 209/334-0309 (from Lodi), www.stknlodirv.com.

54 DRU BARNER EQUESTRIAN CAMP

🥾 🐴 ♿ 🚐 ⛺

Scenic rating: 7

near Georgetown in Eldorado National Forest

Map 5.4, page 324

This camp, set at 3,200 feet in an area of pine and fir, is ideal for horses; there are miles of equestrian trails. Please note that wheat straw is not allowed at this campground. (For more information, see the listings for *Stumpy Meadows* and *Black Oak Group Camp* in the *Tahoe and Northern Sierra* chapter.)

Campsites, facilities: There are 48 sites for tents or RVs up to 35 feet (no hookups). Picnic tables and fire grills are provided. Drinking water and vault toilets are available. Five stock troughs are also available. Some facilities are wheelchair-accessible. Leashed pets are permitted.

Reservations, fees: Reservations are not accepted. Sites are $10 per night, $5 per night for each additional vehicle. Open year-round.

Directions: From Sacramento on I-80, drive east to the north end of Auburn and the exit for Elm Avenue. Take that exit and turn left on Elm Avenue and drive about 0.1 mile to High Street. Turn left on High Street and drive through the signal that marks the continuation of High Street as Highway 49 and drive 3.5 miles on Highway 49 to the bridge. Turn right over the bridge and drive 2.5 miles into the town of Cool and Georgetown Road/Highway 193. Turn left and drive 14 miles into Georgetown to a four-way stop at Main Street. Turn left on Main Street and drive 5.5 miles (the road becomes Georgetown-Wentworth Springs Road/Forest Road 1) to Bottle Hill Bypass Road. Turn left on Bottle Hill Bypass Road and drive about a mile to the campground on the left.

Contact: Eldorado National Forest, Georgetown Ranger District, 530/333-4312, fax 530/333-5522.

55 CAMP LOTUS

🥾 🚣 🏊 ♿ 🚐 ⛺

Scenic rating: 7

on the American River near Coloma

Map 5.4, page 324   **BEST (**

This is a great area with 0.5 mile of frontage on the South Fork of the American River. During spring and summer you'll see plenty of whitewater rafters and kayakers here because this is a popular place for outfitters to put in and take out. Several swimming holes are in the immediate vicinity. The camp is situated on 23 acres at 700 feet in elevation. There are a variety of trees at Camp Lotus, including pines, oaks, willows, and cottonwoods. Coloma, two miles away, is where you'll find the Marshall Gold Discovery Site. Gold was discovered there in 1848, and the site features displays and exhibits on gold rush–era mining methods and the history of the California gold rush. Wineries are nearby, and gold panning, hiking, and fishing are also popular. For details about whitewater rafting or kayaking on the American River, refer to my book *California Recreational Lakes and Rivers*.

Campsites, facilities: There are 26 tent sites and 10 sites with partial hookups (20 and 30 amps) for tents or RVs of any length. A cabin and three lodge rooms are also available for rent. Picnic tables and fire grills are provided. Drinking water, restrooms with showers, Wi-Fi, general store with deli, volleyball, horseshoes, and raft and kayak put-in and take-out areas are available. Groups can be accommodated. Limited supplies are available in Coloma. Some facilities are wheelchair-accessible. Dogs are not permitted.

Reservations, fees: Reservations are accepted and required for weekends. Sites are $7–9 per person per night with a minimum campsite fee of $21–27 per night. Some credit cards accepted. Open March through October.

Directions: From Sacramento, drive east on Highway 50 for approximately 30 miles (past Cameron Park) to Exit 37, the Ponderosa Road exit. Take that exit and drive north over the freeway to North Shingle Road. Turn right and drive 10 miles (the road becomes Lotus Road) to Bassi Road. Turn left and drive one mile to the campground entrance on the right.

Contact: Camp Lotus, 530/622-8672, www.camplotus.com.

56 PLACERVILLE KOA

Scenic rating: 5

near Placerville

Map 5.4, page 324

This is a classic KOA campground, complete with the cute little log cabins KOA calls "Kamping Kabins." The location of this camp is ideal for many, set near U.S. 50 in the Sierra foothills, the main route up to South Lake Tahoe. Nearby is Apple Hill, where from September to November it is a popular tourist attraction, when the local ranches and orchards sell produce and crafts, often with live music. In addition, the Marshall Gold Discovery Site is 10 miles north, where gold was discovered in 1848, setting off the 1849 gold rush. Whitewater rafting and gold panning are popular on the nearby American River.

Campsites, facilities: There are 70 sites with full or partial hookups (30 and 50 amps) for RVs of any length, 14 tent sites, including eight with electricity, 20 sites for tents or RVs, and eight cabins. Some sites are pull-through. Picnic tables and barbecues are provided. Restrooms with flush toilets and showers, drinking water, dump station, pay phone, cable TV, modem access, Wi-Fi, recreation room, seasonal swimming pool, spa (some restrictions apply), playground, video arcade, basketball courts, 18-hole miniature golf course, convenience store, snack bar, dog run, petting zoo, fishing pond, bike rentals, pavilion cooking facilities, volleyball court, and horseshoe pits are available. Some facilities are wheelchair-accessible. Leashed pets are permitted, with certain restrictions.

Reservations, fees: Reservations are accepted at 800/562-4197. Sites are $28–48 for RV sites, $25–30 for tent sites, $4 per person per night for more than two people. Some credit cards accepted. Open year-round.

Directions: From U.S. 50 west of Placerville, take the exit for Shingle Springs Drive/Exit 39 (and not the Shingle Springs/Ponderosa Road exit). Drive one block to Rock Barn Road. Turn left and drive 0.5 mile to the campground at the end of the road.

Contact: Placerville KOA, 530/676-2267, www.koa.com or www.koa-placerville.com.

57 SLY PARK RECREATION AREA

Scenic rating: 7

on Jenkinson Lake

Map 5.4, page 324

Jenkinson Lake is set at 3,500 feet in elevation in the lower reaches of Eldorado National Forest, with a climate that is perfect for waterskiing, wakeboarding, and fishing. The lake covers 640 acres and features eight miles of forested shoreline. Participants of these sports get along, with most water-skiers/wakeboarders motoring around the lake's main body, while anglers head upstream into the Hazel Creek arm of the lake for trout (in the spring) and bass (in the summer). Good news for anglers: Personal watercraft are not permitted. More good news: This is one of the better lakes in the Sierra for brown trout. There is a boat ramp at the campground, and another one located on the southwest end of the lake. The area also has several hiking trails, and the lake is good for swimming. There are nine miles of trails available for hiking, biking, and equestrians; an equestrian trail also circles the lake. A group camp is available for visitors with horses, complete with riding trails, hitching posts, and corrals. Note: No pets or babies with diapers are allowed in the lake.

Campsites, facilities: There are 164 sites

for tents or RVs up to 40 feet (no hookups). There are five group sites that can accommodate 50–100 people and an equestrian camp called Black Oak, which has 12 sites and two youth-group areas. Picnic tables, fire rings, and barbecues are provided. Drinking water, vault toilets, boat rentals, and firewood are available. Two boat ramps are available nearby. Some facilities are wheelchair-accessible. A grocery store, snack bar, dump station, bait, and propane gas are available nearby. Leashed pets are permitted.

Reservations, fees: Reservations are accepted at least seven days in advance ($8 reservation fee) at 530/644-2792. Sites are $20–25 per night, $200 per night for a group site, $100 per night for a youth group site, $10 per night for each additional vehicle. Boat launching is $6 per day. Reduced rates available in winter. Some credit cards accepted during the summer season. Open year-round.

Directions: From Sacramento, drive east on U.S. 50 to Pollock Pines and take the exit for Sly Park Road. Drive south for 4.5 miles to Jenkinson Lake and the campground entrance.

Contact: Sly Park Recreation Area, El Dorado Irrigation District, 530/644-2545, www.eid .org.

58 PIPI

🧑‍🤝‍🧑 ⛵ 🎣 🐕 ♿ 🚐 ⛺

Scenic rating: 7

on the Middle Fork of the Cosumnes River in Eldorado National Forest

Map 5.4, page 324

This place is far enough out of the way to get missed by most campers. It is beside the Middle Fork of the Cosumnes River at 4,100 feet. There are some good swimming holes in the area, but the water is cold and swift in early summer (after all, it's snowmelt). A trail/boardwalk along the river is wheelchair-accessible. Several sites border a pretty meadow in the back of the camp.

This is also a gateway to a vast network of Forest Service roads to the north in Eldorado National Forest.

Campsites, facilities: There are 51 sites for tents or RVs up to 42 feet (no hookups), including two double sites. Picnic tables and fire grills are provided. Drinking water and vault toilets are available. Some facilities are wheelchair-accessible. Leashed pets are permitted.

Reservations, fees: Reservations are accepted ($9 reservation fee) at 877/444-6777 or www .ReserveUSA.com. Sites are $18 per night, $36 per night for double site, $5 per night for each additional vehicle. Open May to mid-November, weather permitting.

Directions: From Jackson, drive east on Highway 88 to Pioneer and continue for nine miles to Omo Ranch Road. Turn left and drive 0.8 mile to North-South Road/Forest Road 6. Turn right and drive 5.9 miles to the campground on the right side of the road.

Contact: Eldorado National Forest, Amador Ranger District, 209/295-4251, fax 209/295-5998.

59 FAR HORIZONS 49ER VILLAGE RV RESORT

⛵ 🐕 🚴 ♿ 🚐

Scenic rating: 4

in Plymouth

Map 5.4, page 324

This is the granddaddy of RV parks, set on 23 acres in the heart of the Gold Country 40 miles east of Stockton and Sacramento. It is rarely crowded and offers warm pools and a huge spa. A bonus is the year-round heated, covered swimming pool. This resort is pet-friendly, and dogs receive a free milk bone at check-in. About one-fourth of the sites are occupied by annual renters. Wineries are nearby.

Campsites, facilities: There are 329 sites with full hookups (30 and 50 amps) for RVs up to 40 feet; some sites are pull-through. Eleven park-model cabins and a RV rental are also available. Restrooms with flush toilets and showers, cable TV, dump station, playground, two heated swimming pools, indoor spa, recreation room, TV lounge, recreation complex, modem access, Wi-Fi, business services, organized activities, café, gift shop, coin laundry, propane gas, and a general store are available. Some facilities are wheelchair-accessible. Leashed pets are permitted.

Reservations, fees: Reservations are recommended at 800/339-6981. Sites are $46–56 per night, $2 per night for each additional vehicle. Winter discounts are available. Some credit cards accepted. Open year-round.

Directions: From Sacramento, drive east on U.S. 50 to Watt Avenue. Turn south on Watt Avenue and drive to Highway 16. Turn left (east) on Highway 16/Jackson Road and drive approximately 30 miles to Highway 49 north/Jackson Road. Merge north on Highway 49 and drive two miles to the resort on the left side of the road at 18265 Highway 49. Note: This is a mile south of Main Street in Plymouth.

Contact: Far Horizons 49er Village RV Resort, 209/245-6981, www.49ervillage.com.

60 INDIAN GRINDING ROCK STATE HISTORIC PARK

Scenic rating: 7

near Jackson

Map 5.4, page 324

Visiting this park is like entering a time machine. It offers a reconstructed Miwok village with petroglyphs, bedrock mortars, a museum, a two-mile nature trail, and interpretive talks for groups, by reservation. Campers get free access to the museum. One unique element is that you will discover *Chaw-fe* (grinding rock) signs about the park. The camp is set at 2,500 feet in the Sierra foothills, about 12 miles from Jackson. It covers 135 acres and is nestled in a small valley among meadows and oak trees. The park contains the largest collection of bedrock mortars in North America; one segment of limestone contains 1,185 mortar holes. Ceremonies are scheduled several times a year by local Native Americans, including the Acorn Harvest Thanksgiving in September. Summers are warm and dry, with temperatures often exceeding 90°F. Spring and fall are ideal, with winters cool, often right on the edge of snow (a few times) and rain (mostly) during most storms.

Campsites, facilities: There are 23 sites for tents or RVs up to 27 feet (no hookups), and a group camp for up to 44 people that includes bark houses. Picnic tables, fire grills, and food lockers are provided. Drinking water and restrooms with flush toilets and coin showers are available. Some facilities are wheelchair-accessible. Leashed pets are permitted.

Reservations, fees: Reservations are accepted for the group camp only ($10 reservation fee), which includes bark houses. Sites are $18–20 per night, $6 per night for each additional vehicle, $75 per night for the group camp. Open year-round.

Directions: From Jackson, drive east on Highway 88 for 11 miles to Pine Grove-Volcano Road. Turn left on Pine Grove-Volcano Road and drive 1.75 miles to the campground on the left.

Contact: Indian Grinding Rock State Historic Park, 209/296-7488, www.parks.ca.gov.

61 LAKE AMADOR RECREATION AREA

Scenic rating: 7

near Stockton

Map 5.4, page 324

Lake Amador is set in the foothill country east of Stockton at an elevation of 485 feet, covering 400 acres with 13 miles of shoreline. Everything here is set up for fishing, with large trout stocks from winter through late spring and the chance for huge bass. The lake record bass weighed 17 pounds, 1.25 ounces. The Carson Creek arm and Jackson Creek arm are the top spots. Night fishing is available. Waterskiing and personal watercraft are prohibited, and the speed limit is 5 mph. A bonus is a swimming pond. About half of the sites are lakefront with full hookups.

Campsites, facilities: There are 150 sites for tents or RVs of any length, and 13 group sites for 5–30 vehicles each; some sites have full hookups (30 and 50 amps). Picnic tables and fire grills are provided. Drinking water, restrooms with showers, dump station, boat ramp, boat rentals, fishing supplies (including bait and tackle), café, convenience store, propane gas, swimming pond, and a playground are available. Some facilities are wheelchair-accessible. Leashed pets are permitted.

Reservations, fees: Reservations are accepted ($5 reservation fee) in the summer. Sites are $22–30 per night per vehicle, $3 per night for electricity. Boat launching is $6 per day and fishing is $8 per day. Winter rates are available. Some credit cards accepted. Open year-round.

Directions: From Stockton, turn east on Highway 88 and drive 24 miles to Clements. Just east of Clements, bear left on Highway 88 and drive nine miles to Jackson Valley Road. Turn right (well signed) and drive five miles to Lake Amador Drive. Turn right and drive over the dam to the campground office.

Contact: Lake Amador Recreation Area, 209/274-4739, www.lakeamador.com.

62 LAKE PARDEE MARINA

Scenic rating: 7

on Pardee Reservoir

Map 5.4, page 324

Many people think that Pardee is the prettiest lake in the Mother Lode country; it's a big lake covering 2,257 acres with 37 miles of shoreline. It is a beautiful sight in the spring when the lake is full and the surrounding hills are green and glowing. Waterskiing, personal watercraft, swimming, and all water/body contact are prohibited at the lake; it is set up expressly for fishing, with high catch rates for rainbow trout and kokanee salmon. During hot weather, attention turns to bass, both smallmouth and largemouth, as well as catfish and sunfish. The lake speed limit is 25 mph.

Campsites, facilities: There are 99 sites for tents or RVs up to 42 feet (no hookups), and 12 sites with full hookups (50 amps) for RVs. Picnic tables and fire grills are provided. Drinking water, restrooms with showers (in the hookup section), chemical toilets (in the no-hookup campground), dump station, full-service marina, fish-cleaning station, boat ramp, boat rentals, coin laundry, café, gas station, convenience store, propane gas, RV and boat storage, wading pool, and a seasonal swimming pool are available. Some facilities are wheelchair-accessible. Leashed pets are permitted.

Reservations, fees: Reservations are accepted. Sites are $19 per night, $10 per night for each additional vehicle, $2 per pet per night. Boat launching is $6.50 per day. Monthly and seasonal rates available. Fishing fee is charged. Some credit cards accepted. Open February through October.

Directions: From Stockton, drive east on Highway 88/Waterloo Road for 17 miles to the town of Clements. One mile east of Clements, bear left on Highway 88 and drive 11 miles to Jackson Valley Road. Turn right and drive 3.4 miles to a four-way stop sign at Buena Vista. Turn right and drive 3.1 miles to Stony Creek Road. Turn left and drive a mile to the campground on the right. (Driving directions from other areas are available on the marina's website.)

Contact: Lake Pardee Marina, 209/772-1472, fax 209/772-0985, www.pardeelakerecreation.com.

63 CAMANCHE LAKE NORTH

🧍 ☕ 🚣 🚤 🎣 🐎 ♿ 🚐 ⛰

Scenic rating: 7

on Camanche Lake

Map 5.4, page 324

The sites at North Shore feature grassy spots with picnic tables set above the lake, and though there are few trees and the sites seem largely exposed, the lake view is quite pretty. The lake will beckon you and is excellent for boating and all water sports, with a full-service marina available. The warm, clean waters make for good waterskiing and wakeboarding (in specified areas), and fishing for trout in spring, bass in early summer, and crappie, bluegill, and catfish in summer. There are five miles of hiking and equestrian trails.

Campsites, facilities: There are 219 sites for tents or RVs of any length (no hookups), and four group sites for 12–72 people. Nine cottages, four triplexes, and motel rooms are also available. Picnic tables and fire grills are provided. Restrooms with showers, drinking water, dump station, boat ramp, boat rentals, coin laundry, convenience store, café, and a playground are available. Some facilities are wheelchair-accessible. Leashed pets are permitted.

Reservations, fees: Reservations are accepted ($8.25 reservation fee) at 866/763-5121. Sites are $24 per night, $10 per night for each additional vehicle, $50–$212 per night for a group site, $3 per pet per night. Boat launching is $6.50 per day. Group rates are available. Some credit cards accepted. Open year-round.

Directions: From Stockton, drive east on Highway 88/Waterloo Road for 17 miles to Clements. One mile east of Clements, bear left on Highway 88 and drive six miles to Liberty Road/North Camanche Parkway. Turn right and drive six miles to Camanche Road. Turn right and drive to the Camanche North Shore entrance gate.

Contact: Camanche Lake North, 209/763-5121, fax 209/763-5789, www.camanche recreation.com.

64 CAMANCHE LAKE SOUTH AND EQUESTRIAN CAMP

☕ 🚣 🚤 🎣 🐎 ♿ 🚐 ⛰

Scenic rating: 7

on Camanche Lake

Map 5.4, page 324

Camanche Lake is a huge, multifaceted facility, covering 7,700 acres with 53 miles of shoreline, set in the foothills east of Lodi at 325 feet in elevation. It is the number-one recreation lake for waterskiing, wakeboarding, and personal watercraft (in specified areas), as well as swimming. In the spring and summer, it provides outstanding fishing for bass, trout, crappie, bluegill, and catfish. There are two campgrounds at the lake, and both have boat ramps nearby and full facilities. A new equestrian campground is open, and it's about one mile from the main campground area. This one at South Shore has a large, but exposed, overflow area for camping, a way to keep from getting stuck for a spot on popular weekends.

Campsites, facilities: There are 297 sites with no hookups for tents or RVs of any length, 99 sites with full hookups (30 and 50 amps) for RVs of any length, 25 double sites, five triple sites, two quad sites, seven equestrian sites, and one group site for 16–64 people. Seven cottages are also available. Additionally, Miners Camp has 108 RV sites with full hookups (30 and 50 amps), 63 of which are long-term rentals. Picnic tables and fire grills are provided. Drinking water, restrooms with flush toilets and showers, chemical toilets, dump station, trout pond, marina, boat ramp, boat rentals, coin laundry, amphitheater with seasonal movies, basketball, tennis courts, and a convenience store are available. Some facilities are wheelchair-accessible. Leashed pets are permitted.

Reservations, fees: Reservations are accepted ($8.25 reservation fee) at 866/763-5178. Sites are $36 per night, $35–106 per night for equestrian sites, $190 per night for group site, $10 per night for each additional vehicle, $6.50 per day boat launch fee, $3 per pet per night. Monthly rates available, with a six-month limit. Some credit cards accepted. Open year-round.

Directions: From Stockton, drive east on Highway 88/Waterloo Road for 17 miles to Clements. One mile east of Clements continue east on Highway 12 and drive six miles to South Camanche Parkway at Wallace. Continue straight and drive five miles to the entrance gate.

Contact: Camanche Lake South, 209/763-5178, www.camancherecreation.com.

65 OAK KNOLL AND GROUP CAMP

👫 ➿ 🛶 🚤 🐾 🚐 ⛰

Scenic rating: 7

at New Hogan Lake

Map 5.4, page 324

This is one of two camps at New Hogan Lake. The reservoir was created by an Army Corps of Engineers dam project on the Calaveras River. (See *Acorn Campground*, next listing, for more information.)

Campsites, facilities: There are 50 sites for tents or RVs of any length, and a group site for tents or RVs of any length that can accommodate up to 50 people. No hookups. Fire grills and picnic tables are provided. Drinking water and vault toilets are available. A dump station and a four-lane boat ramp (at Fiddleneck) are available nearby. A grocery store and propane gas are available within five miles. Leashed pets are permitted.

Reservations, fees: Reservations are accepted at 877/444-6777 or www.ReserveUSA.com. Sites are $10 per night, and the group site is $100 per night. Open May to early September.

Directions: From Stockton, drive east on Highway 26 for about 30 miles to Valley Springs and Hogan Dam Road. Turn right and drive 1.5 miles to Hogan Parkway. Turn left and drive one mile to South Petersburg Road. Turn left and drive 0.5 mile to the campground on the right (adjacent to Acorn Campground).

Contact: U.S. Army Corps of Engineers, Sacramento District, 209/772-1343, fax 209/772-9352.

66 ACORN CAMPGROUND AND BOAT-IN

👫 🚲 ➿ 🛶 🚤 🐾 🚐 ⛰

Scenic rating: 7

at New Hogan Lake

Map 5.4, page 324

New Hogan is a big lake in the foothill country east of Stockton, set at an elevation of 680 feet and covering 4,000 acres with 50 miles of shoreline. Acorn is on the lake and operated by the Army Corps of Engineers. Boaters might also consider boat-in sites near Deer Flat on the eastern shore, and there is a group camp at Coyote Point. Boating and waterskiing are popular here, and all water sports are allowed. It's a decent lake for fishing, with a unique opportunity for striped bass, and it's OK for largemouth bass. Other species are crappie, bluegill, and catfish. There are bicycle trails and an eight-mile equestrian trail. An interpretive trail below the dam is worth checking out. Insider's tip: This is a wintering area for bald eagles.

Campsites, facilities: There are 127 sites for tents or RVs of any length (no hookups) and 30 boat-in sites. Fire pits and picnic tables are provided. Drinking water, restrooms with flush toilets and coin showers, pay telephones, fish-cleaning station, amphitheater, and a dump station are available. A two-lane, paved boat ramp is nearby. Nature walks and ranger programs are sometimes available. Groceries, a restaurant, and propane gas are available within two miles. Leashed pets are permitted.

Reservations, fees: Reservations are accepted at 877/444-6777 or www.ReserveUSA.com. Sites are $12–16 per night, and boat-in sites are $10 per night. Some credit cards accepted. Open year-round, with reduced number of sites in winter; boat-in sites are open May through September.

Directions: From Stockton, drive east on Highway 26 for about 30 miles to Valley Springs and Hogan Dam Road. Turn right and drive 1.5 miles to Hogan Parkway. Turn left and drive one mile to South Petersburg Road. Turn left and drive 0.25 mile to the campground on the right.

Contact: U.S. Army Corps of Engineers, Sacramento District, 209/772-1343, fax 209/772-9352.

67 49ER RV RANCH

Scenic rating: 6

near Columbia

Map 5.4, page 324

This historic ranch/campground was originally built in 1852 as a dairy farm. Several original barns are still standing. The place has been brought up to date, of course, with a small store on the property providing last-minute supplies. Location is a plus, with the Columbia State Historic Park only 0.5 mile away, and the Stanislaus River arm of New Melones Lake within a five-minute drive. Live theater and wineries are nearby. The elevation is 2,100 feet. Note that there is a separate mobile home park on the premises.

Campsites, facilities: There are 42 sites with full hookups (30 and 50 amps) for trailers and RVs up to 40 feet. No tents. Picnic tables and cable TV are provided. Restrooms with showers, drinking water, coin laundry, convenience store, dump station, modem access, Wi-Fi, propane gas, and a large barn for group or club activities are available. Some facilities are wheelchair-accessible. Leashed pets are permitted.

Reservations, fees: Reservations are accepted by phone or website. Sites are $35.90 per night, $2.50 per person per night for more than two

people, $3 per night for each additional vehicle. Seasonal rates and group rates available. Open year-round.

Directions: From Sonora, turn north on Highway 49 and drive for 2.5 miles to Parrotts Ferry Road. Turn right and drive 1.7 miles to Columbia Street. Turn right and drive 0.4 mile to Pacific Street. Turn left and drive a block to Italian Bar Road. Turn right and drive 0.5 mile to the campground on the right.

Contact: 49er RV Ranch, tel./fax 209/532-4978, www.49rv.com.

68 MARBLE QUARRY RV PARK

Scenic rating: 6

near Columbia

Map 5.4, page 324

This is a family-oriented RV park set at 2,100 feet in the Gold Country, within nearby range of several adventures. A 0.25-mile trail leads directly to Columbia State Historic Park, and the Stanislaus River arm of New Melones Lake is only five miles away.

Campsites, facilities: There are 85 sites with full or partial hookups (30 and 50 amps) for RVs of any length, a small area for tents, and three sleeping cabins. A few sites are pull-through. Picnic tables are provided. Restrooms with showers, satellite TV, seasonal swimming pool, coin laundry, modem access, convenience store, dump station, playground, two clubhouses, reading/TV room, group facilities, and propane gas are available. Some facilities are wheelchair-accessible. Leashed pets are permitted.

Reservations, fees: Reservations are accepted. Sites are $33.50–36.50 per night for RV sites, $24 per night for tent sites, $3 per person per night for more than two people. Some credit cards accepted. Open year-round.

Directions: From Sonora, turn north on Highway 49 and drive 2.5 miles to Parrotts

Ferry Road (stop sign). Bear right on Parrotts Ferry Road and drive 1.5 miles to Columbia Street. Turn right and drive a short distance to Jackson Street. Turn right on Jackson Street and drive 0.25 mile (becomes Yankee Hill Road) to the campground on the right (at 11551 Yankee Hill Road).

Contact: Marble Quarry RV Park, 866/677-8464 or 209/532-9539, www.marblequarry .com.

TAHOE AND THE NORTHERN SIERRA

©TOM ZIKAS/NORTH LAKE TAHOE RESORT ASSOCIATION

BEST CAMPGROUNDS

Mount Tallac affords a view across Lake Tahoe

like no other: a cobalt-blue expanse of water bordered by mountains that span miles of Sierra wildlands. The beauty is stunning. Lake Tahoe is one of the few places on earth where people feel an emotional response just by looking at it. Yosemite Valley, the giant sequoias, the Grand Canyon, a perfect sunset on the Pacific Ocean... these are a few other sights that occasionally can evoke the same response. But Tahoe often seems to strike the deepest chord. It can resonate inside you for weeks, even after a short visit.

"What about all the people?" you ask. It's true that people come here in droves. But I found many spots that I shared only with the chipmunks. You can enjoy these spots, too, if you're willing to read my books, hunt a bit, and most important, time your trip to span Monday through Thursday.

This area has the widest range and number of campgrounds in California.

Tahoe and the Northern Sierra feature hundreds of lakes, including dozens you can drive to. The best for scenic beauty are Echo Lakes, Donner, Fallen Leaf, Sardine, Caples, Loon, Union Valley – well, I could go on and on. It is one of the most beautiful regions anywhere on earth.

The north end of the North Sierra starts near Bucks Lake, a great lake for trout fishing, and extends to Bear River Canyon (and Caples Lake, Silver Lake, and Bear River Reservoir). In between are the Lakes Basin Recreation Area (containing Gold, Sardine, Packer, and other lakes) in southern Plumas County, the Crystal Basin (featuring Union Valley Reservoir and Loon Lake, among others) in the Sierra foothills west of Tahoe, Lake Davis (with the highest catch rates for trout) near Portola, and the Carson River Canyon and Hope Valley south of Tahoe.

You could spend weeks exploring any of these places, having the time of your life, and still not get to Tahoe's magic. But it is Tahoe where the adventure starts for many, especially in the surrounding Tahoe National Forest and Desolation Wilderness.

One of California's greatest day trips from Tahoe is to Echo Lakes, where you can take a hikers' shuttle boat across the two lakes to the Pacific Crest Trail, then hike a few miles into Desolation Wilderness and Aloha Lakes. Yet with so many wonderful ways to spend a day in this area, this day trip is hardly a blip on the radar scope.

With so many places and so little time, this region offers what can be the ultimate adventureland.

TAHOE AND THE NORTHERN SIERRA

see Lassen and Modoc page 202

Honey Lake

Antelope Lake

Pyramid Lake

447

395

Plumas National Forest

Sutcliffe

Quincy

Lake Davis

446

70

445

Blairsden

80

Graeagle

49

Plumas-Eureka SP

Sierra City

89

Silver Spring

Truckee River

Reno

Lahontan Lake

49

Downieville

MAP 6.1
page 365

395

Yuba River

20

Tahoe

Truckee

80

Soda Springs

89

267

50

Emigrant Gap

National

Tahoe City

28

Carson City

ALT 95

Forest

28

Lake Tahoe

50

SIERRA

Loon Lake

see Sacramento and Gold Country page 320

Applegate

Desolation Wilderness

South Lake Tahoe

Yerington

ALT 95

Union Valley Reservoir

Strawberry

395

NEVADA

CALIFORNIA

Wellington

339

Placerville

50

Kyburz

S Fork American River

88

Kirkwood

Markleeville

338

Eldorado National Forest

49

MAP 6.2
page 366

NEVADA

Carson-Iceberg Wilderness

MAP 6.3
page 367

88

26

4

Dardanelle

108

395

Bridgeport

Stanislaus National

Forest

108

see Yosemite and Mammoth Lakes page 552

Mono Lake

see San Joaquin Valley page 522

New Melones Res

Sonora

Yosemite

National

120

108

120

Groveland

120

Park

Yosemite Village

0   10 mi

49

Don Pedro Reservoir

Lake McClure

0   10 km

© AVALON TRAVEL PUBLISHING, INC.

Map 6.1

Campgrounds 1-112
Pages 368-419

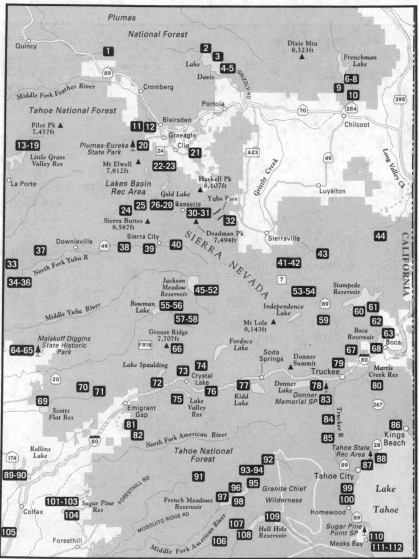

Plumas
National Forest

Quincy

1

2
3

Lake
Davis
4-5

Dixie Mtn
8,323ft ▲

Frenchman
Lake

6-8
9
10

GRIZZLY RD

Middle Fork Feather River

Cromberg

Portola

395

70

284

Chilcoot

Tahoe National Forest

Pilot Pk ▲
7,457ft

Blairsden

11 **12**

Graeagle

13-19

Plumas-Eureka ▲
State Park

20

Clio

24

21

A23

Grizzly Creek

49

Long Valley Ck

Little Grass
Valley Res

Mt Elwell ▲
7,812ft

22-23

Luyalton

La Porte

Lakes Basin
Rec Area

Gold Lake
Bassetts

Haskell Pk
8,107ft ▲

Yuba Pass

24 **25** **26-29**

30-31

32

44

Sierra Buttes ▲
8,587ft

Sierra City

Deadman Pk
7,494ft

Sierraville

CALIFORNIA

Downieville

37

49

38 **39**

40

43

33

North Fork Yuba R

SIERRA NEVADA

41-42

34-36

Jackson
Meadow
Reservoir

45-52

7

Stampede
Reservoir

Middle Yuba River

Bowman
Lake

55-56

53-54

89

60 **61**

57-58

Independence
Lake

62

Grouse Ridge
7,707ft

Mt Lola ▲
9,143ft

59

Boca
Reservoir

63

Malakoff Diggins
State Historic
Park

64-65

FR18

66

Fordyce
Lake

Soda
Springs

Donner
Summit ▲

67 **68**

Boca

Lake Spaulding

74

73

Crystal
Lake

79

Truckee

20

72

76

77

Donner
Lake

78

Martis
Creek Res

80

70 **71**

75

Lake
Valley
Res

Kidd
Lake

Donner
Memorial SP

83

267

69

Scotts
Flat Res

Emigrant
Gap

81

82

North Fork American River

84

Truckee R

86

Kings
Beach

Rollins
Lake

80

Tahoe National
Forest

92

85

28

88

174

89-90

91

93-94

95

Granite Chief
Wilderness

Tahoe State
Rec Area

87

101-103

FORESTHILL RD

French Meadows
Reservoir

96

97 **98**

99

Tahoe City

Lake

Sugar Pine
Res

104

MOSQUITO RIDGE RD

109

Homewood

100

Tahoe

105

Foresthill

107
106 **108**

Hell Hole
Reservoir

89

Sugar Pine
Point SP

110

Middle Fork American River

Meeks Bay

111-112

© AVALON TRAVEL PUBLISHING, INC.

Map 6.2

Campgrounds 113-169

Pages 419-445

© AVALON TRAVEL PUBLISHING, INC.

Map 6.3

Campgrounds 170-213

Pages 445-464

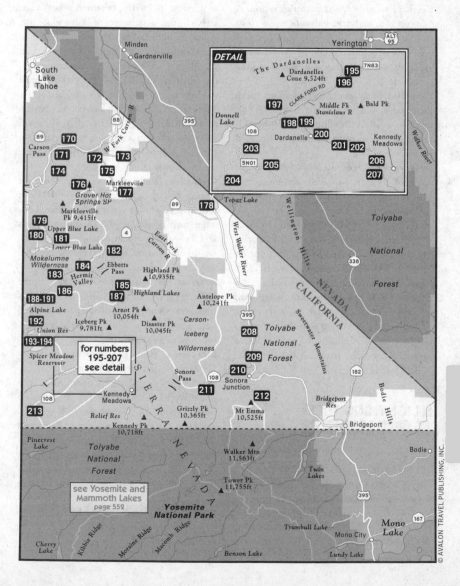

6.2

DETAIL

Minden

Gardnerville

Yerington

ALT 95

The Dardanelles

Dardanelles
Cone 9,524ft

7N83

195

196

South
Lake
Tahoe

395

88

Donnell
Lake

CLARK FORD RD

197

Middle Fk
Stanislaus R

Bald Pk

108

198 **199**

200

Dardanelle

Kennedy
Meadows

89

170

Carson
Pass

171

172 **173**

174

175

203

5N01 **205**

201 **202**

206

176

Markleeville

204

207

Grover Hot
Springs SP

177

Topaz Lake

Markleeville
Pk 9,415ft

89

178

Wellington Hills

Toiyabe

179

Upper Blue Lake

180 **181**

Lower Blue Lake

4

East Fork
Carson R

West Walker River

National

Mokelumne
Wilderness

182

CALIFORNIA

NEVADA

Forest

338

184

Ebbetts
Pass

Highland Pk
10,935ft

183

Hermit
Valley

186

185

187

Highland Lakes

Antelope Pk
10,241ft

188-191

Alpine Lake

Arnot Pk
10,054ft

Sweetwater Mountains

192

Iceberg Pk
9,781ft

Disaster Pk
10,045ft

Carson-

395

Union Res

Iceberg

Toiyabe

208

193-194

Wilderness

National

182

Spicer Meadow
Reservoir

**for numbers
195-207
see detail**

Sonora
Pass

108

209 Forest

Bodie Hills

108

213

Kennedy
Meadows

SIERRA NEVADA

Sonora
Junction

210

211

212

Bridgeport
Res

Relief Res

Grizzly Pk
10,365ft

Mt Emma
10,525ft

Bridgeport

Kennedy Pk
10,718ft

Pinecrest
Lake

Toiyabe

National

Forest

Walker Mtn
11,563ft

Bodie

Twin
Lakes

**see Yosemite and
Mammoth Lakes
page 552**

Tower Pk
11,755ft

**Yosemite
National Park**

395

167

Cherry
Lake

Kibbie Ridge

Moraine Ridge

Macomb Ridge

Benson Lake

Trumbull Lake

Mono City

Lundy Lake

Mono
Lake

1 BRADY'S CAMP
🏃 🛶 🏕 5% ⛰

Scenic rating: 4

on Pine Creek in Plumas National Forest

Map 6.1, page 365

Don't expect much company here. This is a tiny, little-known, primitive camp near Pine Creek, at roughly 7,000 feet in elevation. A side trip is to make the half-mile drive up to Argentine Rock (7,209 feet) for a lookout onto this remote forest country. To the east are many miles of national forest, accessible by vehicle.

Campsites, facilities: There are four tent sites. Picnic tables and fire grills are provided. Vault toilets are available. No drinking water is available. Garbage must be packed out. Leashed pets are permitted.

Reservations, fees: Reservations are not accepted. There is no fee for camping. Open May through October, weather permitting.

Directions: From Oroville, drive north on Highway 70 to the junction with Highway 89. Turn south on Highway 89/70 and drive 11 miles to Quincy. In Quincy, continue on Highway 89/70 for six miles to Squirrel Creek Road. Turn left and drive seven miles (after two miles bear right at the Y) to Forest Road 25N29. Turn left and drive one mile to the campground on the right side of the road.

Contact: Plumas National Forest, Mount Hough Ranger District, 530/283-0555, fax 530/283-1821.

2 LIGHTNING TREE
🏊 🛶 🏕 🐕 ♿ 🚐 ⛰

Scenic rating: 7

on Lake Davis in Plumas National Forest

Map 6.1, page 365

Lightning Tree campground is set near the shore of Lake Davis. Davis is a good-sized lake, with 32 miles of shoreline, set high in the northern Sierra at 5,775 feet. Lake Davis is one of the top mountain lakes in California for fishing, with large rainbow trout in the early summer and fall. This camp is perfectly situated for a fishing trip. It is at Lightning Tree Point on the lake's remote northeast shore, directly across the lake from Freeman Creek, one of the better spots for big trout. This lake is famous for the botched poisoning job (an attempt to wipe out nonnative northern pike) in the 1990s by the Department of Fish and Game, and then, in turn, the biggest trout plants in California history at a single lake: more than 1 million trout! Since pike have reappeared, the future of this lake is one of the biggest environmental time bombs in California. The Department of Fish and Game plans to poison this lake again. After that, they will stock the lake with trout and try to establish Davis as a blue-ribbon trout fishery. There are three boat ramps on the lake.

Campsites, facilities: There are 40 sites for tents or RVs up to 50 feet (no hookups). Vault toilets and drinking water are available. Garbage must be packed out. A dump station and a car-top boat launch are nearby. Some facilities are wheelchair-accessible. Leashed pets are permitted.

Reservations, fees: Reservations are accepted ($9 reservation fee) at 877/444-6777 or www .ReserveUSA.com. Sites are $9 per night, $16 per night for a double site. Open May to October, weather permitting.

Directions: From Truckee, turn north on Highway 89 and drive to Sattley and County Road A23. Turn right on County Road A23 and drive 13 miles to Highway 70. Turn left on Highway 70 and drive one mile to Grizzly Road. Turn right on Grizzly Road and drive about six miles to Lake Davis. Continue north on Lake Davis Road along the lake's east shore and drive about five miles to the campground entrance on the left side of the road.

Contact: Plumas National Forest, Beckwourth Ranger District, 530/836-2575, fax 530/836-0493; Thousand Trails, 530/832-1076.

3 GRASSHOPPER FLAT

Scenic rating: 7

on Lake Davis in Plumas National Forest

Map 6.1, page 365

Grasshopper Flat provides a nearby alternative to Grizzly at Lake Davis, with the nearby boat ramp at adjacent Honker Cove a primary attraction for campers with trailered boats for fishing. The camp is on the southeast end of the lake, at 5,800 feet elevation. Lake Davis is known for its large rainbow trout that bite best in early summer and fall. Swimming and powerboats are allowed, but no waterskiing or personal watercraft are allowed.

Campsites, facilities: There are 70 sites for tents or RVs up to 35 feet (no hookups). Picnic tables and fire grills are provided. Drinking water and restrooms with flush toilets and coin showers are available. A boat ramp, grocery store, and a dump station are nearby. Some facilities are wheelchair-accessible. Leashed pets are permitted.

Reservations, fees: Reservations are accepted ($9 reservation fee) at 877/444-6777 or www.ReserveUSA.com. Sites are $16 per night. Open May through October, weather permitting.

Directions: From Truckee, turn north on Highway 89 and drive to Sattley and County Road A23. Turn right on County Road A23 and drive 13 miles to Highway 70. Turn left on Highway 70 and drive one mile to Grizzly Road. Turn right on Grizzly Road and drive about six miles to Lake Davis. Continue north on Lake Davis Road for a mile (just past Grizzly) to the campground entrance on the left side of the road.

Contact: Plumas National Forest, Beckwourth Ranger District, 530/836-2575, fax 530/836-0493; Thousand Trails, 530/832-1076.

4 CROCKER

Scenic rating: 5

in Plumas National Forest

Map 6.1, page 365

Even though this camp is just four miles east of Lake Davis, it is little known and little used since there are three lakeside camps close by. This camp is set in Plumas National Forest at 5,900 feet elevation, and it is about a 15-minute drive north to the border of the Dixie Mountain State Game Refuge.

Campsites, facilities: There are 10 sites for tents or RVs up to 16 feet (no hookups). Picnic tables and fire grills are provided. Vault toilets are available. No drinking water is available. Garbage must be packed out. Leashed pets are permitted.

Reservations, fees: Reservations are not accepted. There is no fee for camping. Open May through October, weather permitting.

Directions: From Reno, drive north on U.S. 395 to the junction with Highway 70. Turn west on Highway 70 and drive to Beckwourth and County Road 111/Beckwourth-Genessee Road. Turn right on County Road 111 and drive six miles to the campground on the left side of the road.

Contact: Plumas National Forest, Beckwourth Ranger District, 530/836-2575, fax 530/836-0493; Thousand Trails, 530/832-1076.

5 GRIZZLY

Scenic rating: 7

on Lake Davis in Plumas National Forest

Map 6.1, page 365

This is one of the better developed campgrounds at Lake Davis and is a popular spot for camping anglers. Its proximity to the Grizzly Store, just over the dam to the south, makes getting last-minute supplies a snap. In addition, a boat ramp is to the north in Honker Cove, providing access to the southern reaches of the lake, including the island area, where trout trolling is good in early summer and fall. The elevation is 5,800 feet.

Campsites, facilities: There are 55 sites for tents or RVs up to 35 feet (no hookups). Picnic tables and fire grills are provided. Drinking water and flush toilets are available. A boat ramp, grocery store, and a dump station are nearby. Some facilities are wheelchair-accessible. Leashed pets are permitted.

Reservations, fees: Reservations are accepted ($9 reservation fee) at 877/444-6777 or www.ReserveUSA.com. Sites are $16 per night. Open May through October, weather permitting.

Directions: From Truckee, turn north on Highway 89 and drive to Sattley and County Road A23. Turn right on County Road A23 and drive 13 miles to Highway 70. Turn left on Highway 70 and drive one mile to Grizzly Road. Turn right on Grizzly Road and drive about six miles to Lake Davis. Continue north on Lake Davis Road for less than a mile to the campground entrance on the left side of the road.

Contact: Plumas National Forest, Beckwourth Ranger District, 530/836-2575, fax 530/836-0493; Thousand Trails, 530/832-1076.

6 BIG COVE

Scenic rating: 7

at Frenchman Lake in Plumas National Forest

Map 6.1, page 365

Big Cove is one of four camps at the southeastern end of Frenchman Lake, with a boat ramp available about a mile away near the Frenchman and Spring Creek camps. (For more information, see the *Frenchman* listing in this chapter.) A trail from the campground leads to the lakeshore. Another trail connects to the Spring Creek campground, a walk of 0.5 mile. The elevation is 5,800 feet.

Campsites, facilities: There are 38 sites for tents or RVs up to 50 feet (no hookups). Picnic tables and fire rings are provided. Drinking

water and flush toilets are available. Some facilities are wheelchair-accessible. A boat ramp and dump station are nearby. A grocery store and propane gas are available seven miles away. Leashed pets are permitted.

Reservations, fees: Reservations are accepted ($9 reservation fee) at 877/444-6777 or www.ReserveUSA.com. Sites are $16–32 per night. Open May through October, weather permitting.

Directions: From Reno, drive north on U.S. 395 to the junction with Highway 70. Turn west on Highway 70 and drive to Chilcoot and the junction with Frenchman Lake Road. Turn right on Frenchman Lake Road and drive nine miles to the lake and to a Y. At the Y, turn right and drive two miles to Forest Road 24N01. Turn left and drive a short distance to the campground entrance on the left side of the road (on the east side of the lake).

Contact: Plumas National Forest, Beckwourth Ranger District, 530/836-2575, fax 530/836-0493; Thousand Trails, 530/832-1076.

7 SPRING CREEK

Scenic rating: 7

on Frenchman Lake in Plumas National Forest

Map 6.1, page 365

Frenchman Lake is set at 5,800 feet elevation, on the edge of high desert to the east and forest to the west. The lake has 21 miles of shoreline and is surrounded by a mix of sage and pines. All water sports are allowed. This camp is on the southeast end of the lake, where there are three other campgrounds, including a group camp and a boat ramp. The lake provides good fishing for stocked rainbow trout—best in the cove near the campgrounds. Trails lead out from the campground: one heads 0.25 mile to the Frenchman campground; the other a 0.5-mile route to Big Cove campground.

Campsites, facilities: There are 35 sites for tents or RVs up to 35 feet (no hookups). Picnic tables and fire grills are provided. Drinking

water and vault toilets are available. Some facilities are wheelchair-accessible. A boat ramp and dump station are nearby. Leashed pets are permitted.

Reservations, fees: Reservations are accepted ($9 reservation fee) at 877/444-6777 or www.ReserveUSA.com. Sites are $16 per night. Open May through October, weather permitting.

Directions: From Reno, drive north on U.S. 395 to the junction with Highway 70. Turn west on Highway 70 and drive to Chilcoot and the junction with Frenchman Lake Road. Turn right on Frenchman Lake Road and drive nine miles to the lake and to a Y. At the Y, turn right and drive two miles to the campground on the left side of the road.

Contact: Plumas National Forest, Beckwourth Ranger District, 530/836-2575, fax 530/836-0493; Thousand Trails, 530/832-1076.

8 FRENCHMAN

Scenic rating: 7

on Frenchman Lake in Plumas National Forest

Map 6.1, page 365

This camp is on the southeast end of the lake, where there are three other campgrounds, including a group camp and a boat ramp. The best trout fishing is in the cove near the campgrounds and the two inlets, one along the west shore and one at the head of the lake. The proximity to Reno, only 35 miles away, keeps gambling in the back of the minds of many anglers. Because of water demands downstream, the lake often drops significantly by the end of summer. A trail from camp is routed 0.25 mile to the Spring Creek campground.

Campsites, facilities: There are 38 sites for tents or RVs up to 35 feet (no hookups). Picnic tables and fire grills are provided. Drinking water and vault toilets are available. A dump station and boat ramp are nearby. Leashed pets are permitted.

Reservations, fees: Reservations are accepted ($9 reservation fee) at 877/444-6777 or www.ReserveUSA.com. Sites are $16 per night. Open May through October, weather permitting.

Directions: From Reno, drive north on U.S. 395 to the junction with Highway 70. Turn west on Highway 70 and drive to Chilcoot and the junction with Frenchman Lake Road. Turn right on Frenchman Lake Road and drive nine miles to the lake and to a Y. At the Y, turn right and drive 1.5 miles to the campground on the left side of the road.

Contact: Plumas National Forest, Beckwourth Ranger District, 530/836-2575, fax 530/836-0493; Thousand Trails, 530/832-1076.

9 COTTONWOOD SPRINGS

Scenic rating: 7

near Frenchman Lake in Plumas National Forest

Map 6.1, page 365

Cottonwood Springs, elevation 5,800 feet, is largely an overflow camp at Frenchman Lake. It is the only camp at the lake with a group site. The more popular Frenchman, Big Cove, and Spring Creek camps are along the southeast shore of the lake near a boat ramp.

Campsites, facilities: There are 20 sites for tents or RVs up to 50 feet (no hookups), and two group sites for tents or RVs up to 35 feet that can accommodate 25–50 people each. Picnic tables and fire rings are provided. Drinking water and flush toilets are available. Some facilities are wheelchair-accessible. A boat ramp and dump station are nearby. Leashed pets are permitted.

Reservations, fees: Reservations are accepted for individual sites and are required for group sites ($9 reservation fee) at 877/444-6777 or www.ReserveUSA.com. Sites are $16 per night, $50–90 per night for groups. Open May through October, weather permitting.

Directions: From Reno, drive north on U.S. 395 to the junction with Highway 70. Turn west on Highway 70 and drive to Chilcoot and the junction with Frenchman Lake Road. Turn right on Frenchman Lake Road and drive nine miles to the lake and to a Y. At the Y, turn left and drive 1.5 miles to the campground on the right side of the road.

Contact: Plumas National Forest, Beckwourth Ranger District, 530/836-2575, fax 530/836-0493; Thousand Trails, 530/832-1076.

10 CHILCOOT

Scenic rating: 7

on Little Last Chance Creek in Plumas National Forest

Map 6.1, page 365

This small camp is set along Little Last Chance Creek at 5,400 feet in elevation, about three miles downstream from Frenchman Lake. The stream provides good trout fishing, but access can be difficult at some spots because of brush.

Campsites, facilities: There are 40 sites for tents or RVs up to 35 feet (no hookups), and five walk-in sites for tents only. Picnic tables and fire rings are provided. Drinking water and flush toilets are available. Some facilities are wheelchair-accessible. A boat ramp, grocery store, and dump station are nearby. Leashed pets are permitted.

Reservations, fees: Reservations are accepted ($9 reservation fee) at 877/444-6777 or www.ReserveUSA.com. Sites are $16 per night. Open May through October, weather permitting.

Directions: From Reno, drive north on U.S. 395 to the junction with Highway 70. Turn west on Highway 70 and drive to Chilcoot and the junction with Frenchman Lake Road. Turn right on Frenchman Lake Road and drive six miles to the campground on the left side of the road.

Contact: Plumas National Forest, Beckwourth Ranger District, 530/836-2575, fax 530/836-0493; Thousand Trails, 530/832-1076.

11 LITTLE BEAR RV PARK

Scenic rating: 7

on the Feather River

Map 6.1, page 365

This is a privately operated RV park set near the Feather River. Nearby destinations include Plumas-Eureka State Park and the Lakes Basin Recreation Area. The elevation is 4,300 feet. About half of the sites are taken by full-season rentals.

Campsites, facilities: There are 97 sites with full or partial hookups (20 and 30 amps) for RVs of any length, and 10 sleeping cabins. No tents are allowed. Picnic tables and fire rings are provided. Drinking water, restrooms with showers and flush toilets, coin laundry, convenience store, satellite TV, modem access, RV storage, propane, and ice are available. A dump station, clubhouse, table tennis, shuffleboard, and horseshoes are also available. Leashed pets are permitted.

Reservations, fees: Reservations are recommended. Sites are $24–26 per night, $4–8 per person per night for more than two people, $1 per pet per night. Weekly and monthly rates available. Open mid-April to late October.

Directions: In Truckee, drive north on Highway 89 to Graeagle. Continue north on Highway 89 for one mile to Little Bear Road. Turn left on Little Bear Road and drive a short distance to the campground on the right.

Contact: Little Bear RV Park, tel./fax 530/836-2774, www.littlebearrvpark.com.

12 MOVIN' WEST RV PARK

Scenic rating: 5

in Graeagle

Map 6.1, page 365

This RV park began life as a mobile home park and has become a very popular park for golfers. A nine-hole golf course is across the road, and five other golf courses are within five miles. About half of the sites are rented for the full summer. The elevation is 4,300 feet.

Campsites, facilities: There are 51 sites with full or partial hookups (30 amps) for RVs of any length, three tent sites, and two cabins. Some sites are pull-through. Picnic tables and fire rings are provided. Drinking water, restrooms with flush toilets and showers, pay phone, cable TV, modem access, and a coin laundry are available. Propane gas, a nine-hole golf course, swimming pond, horse stable, and mini golf are nearby. Leashed pets are permitted.

Reservations, fees: Reservations are recommended. Sites are $22.71–26.61 per night, $3–5 per person per night for more than two people. Open May through October.

Directions: From Truckee, drive northwest on Highway 89 about 50 miles to Graeagle. Continue just past Graeagle to County Road A14 (Graeagle-Johnsville Road). Turn left and drive 0.25 mile northwest to the campground on the left.

Contact: Movin' West RV Park, 530/836-2614.

13 BLACK ROCK WALK-IN AND OVERFLOW
🚶 ⛵ 🏊 🛶 🐎 🚐 ⛺

Scenic rating: 7

on Little Grass Valley Reservoir in Plumas National Forest

Map 6.1, page 365

This is the only campground on the west shore of Little Grass Valley Reservoir, with an adjacent boat ramp making it an attractive choice for anglers. The lake is set at 5,060 feet in Plumas National Forest and provides lakeside camping and decent fishing for rainbow trout and kokanee salmon. If you don't like the company, there are seven other camps to choose from at the lake, all on the opposite eastern shore.

Campsites, facilities: There are 20 walk-in

sites (a walk of a few yards to 0.1 mile) for tents or RVs up to 22 feet (no hookups). There is a parking lot for overflow camping for RVs up to 35 feet. Picnic tables and fire grills are provided. Drinking water, vault toilets, and a fish-cleaning station are available. A dump station, boat ramp, and grocery store are nearby. Leashed pets are permitted.

Reservations, fees: Reservations are not accepted. Sites are $18 per night. Open May through September, weather permitting.

Directions: From Oroville, drive east on Highway 162/Oroville Dam Boulevard for about eight miles (becomes the Olive Highway) to Forbestown Road. Turn right and drive through Forbestown to Challenge and La-Porte Road. Turn left on LaPorte Road and drive to LaPorte. Continue two miles past LaPorte to the junction with County Road 514/Little Grass Valley Road. Turn left and drive about five miles to the campground access road on the west side of the lake. Turn right on the access road and drive 0.25 mile to the campground.

Contact: Plumas National Forest, Feather River Ranger District, 530/534-6500, fax 530/532-1210; Northwest Management, 530/283-5559.

14 HORSE CAMP
🚶 ⛵ 🏊 🛶 🐎 ♿ 🚐 ⛺

Scenic rating: 7

on Little Grass Valley Reservoir in Plumas National Forest

Map 6.1, page 365

This camp is reserved for equestrians only and thus it gets low use. This is a high-country forested campground set near Little Grass Valley Reservoir, but there is no lake view because of tree cover. Several trails are accessible from the campground, including the Pacific Crest Trail and Lakeshore Trail, as well as access to Bald Mountain (6,255 feet). The elevation at camp is 5,060 feet.

Campsites, facilities: There are 10 sites

for tents or RVs up to 25 feet (no hookups) available for equestrian campers only. Picnic tables and fire grills are provided. Vault toilets are available. No drinking water is available. Hitching posts and a wheelchair-accessible mounting rack are available. A restaurant and deli are available five miles away in LaPorte. Leashed pets are permitted.

Reservations, fees: Reservations are accepted ($9 reservation fee) at 877/444-6777 or www .ReserveUSA.com. Sites are $18 per night. Open June through September.

Directions: From Oroville, drive east on Highway 162/Oroville Dam Boulevard for about eight miles (becomes the Olive Highway) to Forbestown Road. Turn right and drive through Forbestown to Challenge and LaPorte Road. Turn left on LaPorte Road and drive to LaPorte. Continue on County Road 512 (which becomes County Road 514/Little Grass Valley Road) for three miles to Forest Road 22N57. Turn right and drive four miles (cross the bridge) to the campground on the left.

Contact: Plumas National Forest, Feather River Ranger District, 530/534-6500, fax 530/532-1210; Northwest Management, 530/283-5559.

15 PENINSULA TENT

Scenic rating: 9

on Little Grass Valley Reservoir in Plumas National Forest

Map 6.1, page 365

This camp, at 5,060 feet in elevation, is exceptional in that most of the campsites provide views of Little Grass Valley Reservoir, a pretty lake in national forest. The fishing can be excellent, especially for rainbow trout, brown trout, and kokanee salmon. The camp gets moderate use, and it is a pretty site with tents sprinkled amid white fir and pine. This is a good family campground. A 13.5-mile hiking trail circles the lake.

Campsites, facilities: There are 25 sites for tents or RVs up to 25 feet (no hookups). Picnic tables and fire rings are provided. Drinking water and flush toilets are available. A boat launch, fish-cleaning station, and a swimming beach are available nearby. Leashed pets are permitted.

Reservations, fees: Reservations are not accepted. Sites are $18 per night. Open Memorial Day weekend through September, weather permitting.

Directions: From Oroville, drive east on Highway 162/Oroville Dam Boulevard for about eight miles (becomes the Olive Highway) to Forbestown Road. Turn right and drive through Forbestown to Challenge and LaPorte Road. Turn left on LaPorte Road and drive to LaPorte. Continue on County Road 512 (which becomes County Road 514/Little Grass Valley Road) for three miles to Forest Road 22N57. Continue on Forest Road 514 for one mile to the campground entrance on right. Turn right and drive 0.25 mile to the campground.

Contact: Plumas National Forest, Feather River Ranger District, 530/534-6500, fax 530/532-1210; Northwest Management, 530/283-5559.

16 RUNNING DEER

Scenic rating: 7

on Little Grass Valley Reservoir in Plumas National Forest

Map 6.1, page 365

Little Grass Valley Reservoir is a pretty mountain lake set at 5,060 feet in Plumas National Forest, providing lakeside camping, boating, and fishing for rainbow trout and kokanee salmon. Looking straight north from the camp is a spectacular view, gazing across the water and up at Bald Mountain, 6,255 feet in elevation. One of seven campgrounds on the eastern shore, this one is on the far northeastern end of the lake. A trailhead for the Pacific Crest

Trail is available nearby at little Fowler Lake about four miles north of Little Grass Valley Reservoir. Note that fish-cleaning stations are not available at Running Deer, but there is one nearby at Little Beaver.

Campsites, facilities: There are 40 sites for tents or RVs up to 40 feet (no hookups). Picnic tables and fire rings are provided. Drinking water and flush toilets are available. A fish-cleaning station, boat ramp, grocery store, and a dump station are nearby. Leashed pets are permitted.

Reservations, fees: Reservations are accepted ($9 reservation fee) at 877/444-6777 or www.ReserveUSA.com. Sites are $18–20 per night. Open late May through September.

Directions: From Oroville, drive east on Highway 162/Oroville Dam Boulevard for about eight miles (becomes the Olive Highway) to Forbestown Road. Turn right and drive through Forbestown to Challenge and LaPorte Road. Turn left on LaPorte Road and drive to LaPorte. Continue on County Road 512 (which becomes County Road 514/Little Grass Valley Road) for three miles to Forest Road 22N57. Turn right and drive three miles to the campground on the left.

Contact: Plumas National Forest, Feather River Ranger District, 530/534-6500, fax 530/532-1210; Northwest Management, 530/283-5559.

17 WYANDOTTE

Scenic rating: 8

on Little Grass Valley Reservoir in Plumas National Forest

Map 6.1, page 365

Of the eight camps on Little Grass Valley Reservoir, this is the favorite. It is set at 5,100 feet elevation on a small peninsula that extends well into the lake, with a boat ramp nearby. All water sports are allowed. (For more information, see the previous listing, *Running Deer.*)

Campsites, facilities: There are 28 individual sites and two double sites for tents or RVs up to 40 feet (no hookups). Picnic tables and fire rings are provided. Drinking water and flush toilets are available. A dump station, boat ramp, fish-cleaning station, and grocery store are nearby. Leashed pets are permitted.

Reservations, fees: Reservations are not accepted. Sites are $18–20 per night, $30 per night for a double site. Open late May to mid-October, weather permitting.

Directions: From Oroville, drive east on Highway 162/Oroville Dam Boulevard for about eight miles (becomes the Olive Highway) to Forbestown Road. Turn right and drive through Forbestown to Challenge and LaPorte Road. Turn left on LaPorte Road and drive to LaPorte. Continue two miles past LaPorte to the junction with County Road 514/Little Grass Valley Road. Turn left and drive one mile to a junction. Turn left and drive one mile to the campground entrance road on the right.

Contact: Plumas National Forest, Feather River Ranger District, 530/534-6500, fax 530/532-1210; Northwest Management, 530/283-5559.

18 LITTLE BEAVER

Scenic rating: 7

on Little Grass Valley Reservoir in Plumas National Forest

Map 6.1, page 365

This is one of eight campgrounds on Little Grass Valley Reservoir, set at 5,060 feet. Take your pick. (For more information, see the *Running Deer* listing in this chapter.)

Campsites, facilities: There are 120 sites for tents or RVs up to 40 feet (no hookups). Picnic tables and fire rings are provided. Drinking water and flush toilets are available. A grocery store, dump station, fish-cleaning station, and boat ramp are nearby. Some facilities are wheelchair-accessible. Leashed pets are permitted.

Reservations, fees: Reservations are not accepted. Sites are $18–20 per night. Open June to mid-September, weather permitting.
Directions: From Oroville, drive east on Highway 162/Oroville Dam Boulevard for about eight miles (becomes the Olive Highway) to Forbestown Road. Turn right and drive through Forbestown to Challenge and LaPorte Road. Turn left on LaPorte Road and drive to LaPorte. Continue two miles past LaPorte to the junction with County Road 514/Little Grass Valley Road. Turn left and drive one mile to a junction. Turn right and drive two miles to the campground entrance road on the left.
Contact: Plumas National Forest, Feather River Ranger District, 530/534-6500, fax 530/532-1210; Northwest Management, 530/283-5559.

19 RED FEATHER CAMP

Scenic rating: 7

on Little Grass Valley Reservoir in Plumas National Forest

Map 6.1, page 365

This camp is well developed and popular, set on the eastern shore of Little Grass Valley Reservoir, just south of Running Deer and just north of Little Beaver. Bears frequent this area, so be sure to properly store your food and avoid scented products. (For more information, see the *Running Deer* listing in this chapter.)
Campsites, facilities: There are 60 sites for tents or RVs up to 40 feet (no hookups). Picnic tables and fire rings are provided. Drinking water and flush toilets are available. A dump station, boat ramp, fish-cleaning station, and grocery store are nearby. Leashed pets are permitted.
Reservations, fees: Reservations are accepted ($9 reservation fee) at 877/444-6777 or www .ReserveUSA.com. Sites are $18–20 per night.

Open late June through September, weather permitting.
Directions: From Oroville, drive east on Highway 162/Oroville Dam Boulevard for about eight miles (becomes the Olive Highway) to Forbestown Road. Turn right and drive through Forbestown to Challenge and LaPorte Road. Turn left on LaPorte Road and drive to LaPorte. Continue two miles past LaPorte to the junction with County Road 514/Little Grass Valley Road. Turn left and drive one mile to a junction. Turn right and drive three miles to the campground entrance road on the left.
Contact: Plumas National Forest, Feather River Ranger District, 530/534-6500, fax 530/532-1210; Northwest Management, 530/283-5559.

20 PLUMAS-EUREKA STATE PARK

Scenic rating: 9

near Graeagle

Map 6.1, page 365

Plumas-Eureka State Park is a beautiful chunk of parkland, featuring great hiking, a pretty lake, and this well-maintained campground. For newcomers to the area, Jamison Camp at the southern end of the park makes for an excellent first stop. So does the nearby hike to Grass Lake, a first-class tromp that takes about two hours and features a streamside walk along Little Jamison Creek, with the chance to take a five-minute cutoff to see 40-foot Jamison Falls. A historic mine, park museum, blacksmith shop, stable, and stamp mill are also here, with campers allowed free admission to the museum. Other must-see destinations in the park include Eureka Lake, and from there, the 1,100-foot climb to Eureka Peak (formerly known as Gold Mountain), 7,447 feet, for a dramatic view of all the famous peaks in this region. Camp elevation is 5,200 feet. The park covers 5,500 acres. Fishing opportunities feature Madora and Eureka Lakes and Jamison Creek, best in May and June. The visitors center was originally constructed as a bunkhouse for miners. More than $8 million of gold was mined here.

Campsites, facilities: There are 67 sites for tents or RVs up to 30 feet (no hookups), and one group tent site for up to 50 people. Picnic tables, food lockers, and fire rings are provided. Drinking water and restrooms with flush toilets and free showers are available. Some facilities are wheelchair-accessible. A dump station is available nearby, and a grocery store, coin laundry, and propane gas are available within five miles. Leashed pets are permitted.

Reservations, fees: Reservations are accepted for the group site only. Sites are $20 per night, $6 per night for each additional vehicle, $200 per night for the group site. Open mid-May to mid-October, weather permitting.

Directions: In Truckee, drive north on Highway 89 to Graeagle. Just after passing Graeagle (one mile from the junction of Highway 70) turn left on County Road A14/Graeagle-Johnsville Road and drive west for about five miles to the park entrance on the left.

Contact: Plumas-Eureka State Park, 530/836-2380, fax 530/836-0498, www.parks .ca.gov.

21 CLIO'S RIVER'S EDGE RV PARK

🏊 🎣 🐕 ♿ 🚐

Scenic rating: 7

on the Feather River

Map 6.1, page 365

This is a giant RV park set adjacent to a pretty and easily accessible stretch of the Feather River. There are many possible side-trip destinations, including Plumas-Eureka State Park, Lakes Basin Recreation Area, and several nearby golf courses and a horseback-

riding facility. The elevation is about 4,500 feet. Many of the sites are rented for the entire summer season.

Campsites, facilities: There are 220 sites with full hookups (50 amps) for RVs of any length. Some sites are pull-through. No tents are allowed. Picnic tables are provided. Drinking water, restrooms with flush toilets and coin showers, coin laundry, modem access, and cable TV are available. Some facilities are wheelchair-accessible. A grocery store is within three miles. Leashed pets are permitted, with certain restrictions.

Reservations, fees: Reservations are accepted. Sites are $27–32 per night, $5 per person per night for more than two people, $1 per night for each additional vehicle not towed. Weekly and monthly rates available. Some credit cards accepted. Open mid-April through October.

Directions: From Truckee, drive north on Highway 89 toward Graeagle and Blairsden. Near Clio (4.5 miles south of Highway 70 at Blairsden), look for the campground entrance on the right (0.2 mile south of Graeagle).

Contact: Clio's River's Edge, tel./fax 530/836-2375, fax 530/836-2378, www .riversedgervpark.net.

22 LAKES BASIN GROUP CAMP

🚶 🐕 ⛺

Scenic rating: 8

in Plumas National Forest

Map 6.1, page 365

This is a Forest Service group camp that is ideal for Boy and Girl Scouts. It is set at 6,400 feet in elevation, just a short drive from the trailhead to beautiful Frazier Falls, and also near Gold Lake, Little Bear Lake, and 15 lakes set below nearby Mount Elwell.

Campsites, facilities: This group camp is for tents only and can accommodate up to 25 people. Picnic tables and fire grills are provided. Drinking water and vault toilets are available. Supplies are available in Graeagle. Leashed pets are permitted.

Reservations, fees: Reservations are required ($9 reservation fee) at 877/444-6777 or www .ReserveUSA.com. The camp is $50 per night. Open June through October, weather permitting.

Directions: From Truckee, drive north on Highway 89 toward Graeagle to the Gold Lake Highway (one mile before reaching Graeagle). Turn left on the Gold Lake Highway and drive about seven miles to the campground.

Contact: Plumas National Forest, Beckwourth Ranger District, 530/836-2575, fax 530/836-0493; Thousand Trails, 530/832-1076.

23 LAKES BASIN

Scenic rating: 8

in Plumas National Forest

Map 6.1, page 365

This camp is a great location for a base camp to explore the surrounding Lakes Basin Recreation Area. From nearby Gold Lake or Elwell Lodge, there are many short hikes to small pristine lakes. A must-do trip is the easy hike to Frazier Falls, only a mile round-trip to see the spectacular 176-foot waterfall, though the trail is crowded during the middle of the day. The trail to this waterfall is paved and is wheelchair-accessible. The camp elevation is 6,400 feet.

Campsites, facilities: There are 23 sites for tents or RVs up to 30 feet (no hookups). Picnic tables and fire grills are provided. Drinking water and vault toilets are available. Some facilities are wheelchair-accessible. Supplies are available in Graeagle. Leashed pets are permitted.

Reservations, fees: Reservations are accepted ($9 reservation fee) at 877/444-6777 or www .ReserveUSA.com. Sites are $16 per night and double sites are $32 per night. Open June through October, weather permitting.

Directions: From Truckee, drive north on Highway 89 toward Graeagle to the Gold Lake

Highway (one mile before reaching Graeagle). Turn left on the Gold Lake Highway and drive about seven miles to the campground.

Contact: Plumas National Forest, Beckwourth Ranger District, 530/836-2575, fax 530/836-0493; Thousand Trails, 530/832-1076.

24 PACKSADDLE

Scenic rating: 6

near Packer Lake in Tahoe National Forest

Map 6.1, page 365

Packsaddle is a Forest Service site about a half mile from Packer Lake, with an additional 15 lakes within a five-mile radius, and one of America's truly great hiking trails nearby. The trail to the Sierra Buttes features a climb of 2,369 feet over the course of five miles. It is highlighted by a stairway with 176 steps that literally juts into open space and crowned by an astounding view for hundreds of miles in all directions. Packer Lake, 6,218 feet, is at the foot of the dramatic Sierra Buttes and has lakefront log cabins, good trout fishing, and low-speed boating. The campground elevation is 6,000 feet.

Campsites, facilities: There are 15 sites for tents or RVs up to 35 feet (no hookups). Vault toilets and drinking water are available. Pack and saddle animals are permitted and corrals and hitching rails are available. Supplies are available in Bassetts and Sierra City. Some facilities are wheelchair-accessible. Leashed pets are permitted.

Reservations, fees: Reservations are not accepted. Sites are $18 per night, $5 per night for each additional vehicle. Open late May through September, weather permitting.

Directions: From Truckee, turn north on Highway 89 and drive 20 miles to Sierraville. At Sierraville, turn left on Highway 49 and drive about 10 miles to the Bassetts Store. Turn right on Gold Lake Road and drive 1.5 miles to Packer Lake Road. Turn left, drive a short distance, bear right at the fork, and drive 2.5 miles to the campground on the left.

Contact: Tahoe National Forest, Yuba River Ranger District, North, 530/288-3231, fax 530/288-0727; California Land Management, 650/322-1181.

25 BERGER CREEK

Scenic rating: 6

in Tahoe National Forest

Map 6.1, page 365

Berger Creek provides an overflow alternative to nearby Diablo, which is also extremely primitive. On busy summer weekends, when an open campsite can be difficult to find at a premium location in the Lakes Basin Recreation Area, these two camps provide a safety valve to keep you from being stuck for the night. Nearby are Packer Lake, the trail to the Sierra Buttes, Sardine Lakes, and Sand Pond, all excellent destinations. The elevation is 5,900 feet.

Campsites, facilities: There are 10 sites for tents or RVs up to 16 feet (no hookups). Picnic tables and fire grills are provided. Vault toilets are available. No drinking water is available. Garbage must be packed out. Supplies are available in Bassetts and Sierra City. Leashed pets are permitted.

Reservations, fees: Reservations are not accepted. Sites are $10 per night, $5 per night for each additional vehicle. Open June through October, weather permitting.

Directions: From Truckee, turn north on Highway 89 and drive 20 miles to Sierraville. At Sierraville, turn left on Highway 49 and drive about 10 miles to the Bassetts Store. Turn right on Gold Lake Road and drive 1.5 miles to Packer Lake Road. Turn left, drive a short distance, bear right at the fork, and drive two miles to the campground on the left.

Contact: Tahoe National Forest, Yuba River Ranger District, North, 530/288-3231, fax 530/288-0727; California Land Management, 650/322-1181.

26 SNAG LAKE

Scenic rating: 8

in Tahoe National Forest

Map 6.1, page 365

Snag Lake is an ideal little lake for camping anglers with canoes. There are no boat ramps and you can have the place virtually to yourself. It is set at 6,000 feet in elevation, an easy-to-reach lake in the Lakes Basin Recreation Area. Trout fishing is only fair, as in fair numbers and fair size, mainly rainbow trout in the 10- to 12-inch class. Note that campers here must provide their own drinking water.

Campsites, facilities: There are 12 sites for tents or RVs up to 16 feet (no hookups). Picnic tables and fire grills are provided. Vault toilets are available. No drinking water is available. Garbage must be packed out. Only hand boat launching is allowed. Supplies are available in Bassetts and Sierra City. Leashed pets are permitted.

Reservations, fees: Reservations are not accepted. There is no fee for camping. Open June through October, weather permitting.

Directions: From Truckee, turn north on Highway 89 and drive 20 miles to Sierraville. At Sierraville, turn left on Highway 49 and drive about 10 miles to the Bassetts Store. Turn right on Gold Lake Road and drive five miles to the campground on the left.

Contact: Tahoe National Forest, Yuba River Ranger District, North, 530/288-3231, fax 530/288-0727; California Land Management, 650/322-1181.

27 DIABLO

Scenic rating: 8

on Packer Creek in Tahoe National Forest

Map 6.1, page 365

This is a developed camping area set on Packer Creek, about two miles from Packer Lake. This area is extremely beautiful with several lakes nearby, including the Sardine Lakes and Packer Lake, and this camp provides an overflow area when the more developed campgrounds have filled.

Campsites, facilities: There are eight sites for tents or RVs up to 30 feet (no hookups). Picnic tables and fire rings are provided. Vault toilets are available. No drinking water is available. Supplies are available in Bassetts and Sierra City. Leashed pets are permitted.

Reservations, fees: Reservations are not accepted. Sites are $10 per night, $5 per night for each additional vehicle. Open June through October, weather permitting.

Directions: From Truckee, turn north on Highway 89 and drive 20 miles to Sierraville. At Sierraville, turn left on Highway 49 and drive about 10 miles to the Bassetts Store. Turn right on Gold Lake Road and drive 1.5 miles to Packer Lake Road. Turn left, drive a short distance, bear right at the fork, and drive one mile to the campground on the right side of the road.

Contact: Tahoe National Forest, Yuba River Ranger District, North, 530/288-3231, fax 530/288-0727; California Land Management, 650/322-1181.

28 SALMON CREEK
🏃 🏕 🚙 ⛺

Scenic rating: 9

in Tahoe National Forest

Map 6.1, page 365

This campground is set at the confluence of Packer and Salmon Creeks, 5,800 feet in elevation, with easy access off the Gold Lakes Highway. It is near the Lakes Basin Recreation Area, with literally dozens of small lakes within five miles, plus great hiking, fishing, and low-speed boating.

Campsites, facilities: There are 31 sites for tents or RVs up to 30 feet (no hookups). Picnic tables and fire grills are provided. Drinking water and vault toilets are available. Supplies and a coin laundry are available in Sierra City. Leashed pets are permitted.

Reservations, fees: Reservations are not accepted. Sites are $18 per night, $5 per night for each additional vehicle. Open June through October.

Directions: From Truckee, turn north on Highway 89 and drive 20 miles to Sierraville and Highway 49. Turn left on Highway 49 and drive about 10 miles to the Bassetts Store and Gold Lake Road. Turn right on Gold Lake Road and drive two miles to the campground on the left side of the road.

Contact: Tahoe National Forest, Yuba River Ranger District, North, 530/288-3231, fax 530/288-0727; California Land Management, 650/322-1181.

29 SARDINE LAKE
🏃 🏊 🏄 🚣 🎣 🚶 ♿ 🚐 ⛺

Scenic rating: 8

in Tahoe National Forest

Map 6.1, page 365   BEST (

Lower Sardine Lake is a jewel set below the Sierra Buttes, one of the prettiest settings in California. The campground is actually about a mile east of the lake. Nearby is beautiful Sand Pond Interpretive Trail. A great hike is routed along the shore of Lower Sardine Lake to a hidden waterfall (in spring) that feeds the lake, and ambitious hikers can explore beyond and discover Upper Sardine Lake. Trout fishing is excellent in Lower Sardine Lake, with a primitive boat ramp available for small boats. The speed limit and small size of the lake keeps boaters slow and quiet. A small marina and boat rentals are available.

Campsites, facilities: There are 29 sites for tents or RVs up to 22 feet (no hookups). Picnic tables and fire grills are provided. Drinking water and vault toilets are available. Some facilities are wheelchair-accessible. Limited supplies are available at the Sardine Lake Lodge or in Bassetts. Leashed pets are permitted.

Reservations, fees: Reservations are not accepted. Sites are $18 per night, $5 per night for each additional vehicle. Open June through October, weather permitting.

Directions: From Truckee, drive north on Highway 89 for 20 miles to Sierraville. Turn left on Highway 49 and drive about 10 miles to the Bassetts Store. Turn right on Gold Lake Road and drive 1.5 miles to Packer Lake Road. Turn left, drive a short distance, then bear left at the fork (signed) and drive 0.5 mile to the campground on the left.

Contact: Tahoe National Forest, Yuba River Ranger District, North, 530/288-3231, fax 530/288-0727.

30 CHAPMAN CREEK

Scenic rating: 8

on the North Yuba River in Tahoe National Forest

Map 6.1, page 365

This campground is set along Chapman Creek at 6,000 feet, just across the highway from where it enters the North Yuba River. A good side trip is to hike Chapman Creek Trail, which leads out of camp to Beartrap Meadow or to Haskell Peak (8,107 feet).

Campsites, facilities: There are 29 sites for tents or RVs up to 22 feet (no hookups). Picnic tables and fire grills are provided. Drinking water and vault toilets are available. Supplies are available in Bassetts. Leashed pets are permitted.

Reservations, fees: Reservations are not accepted. Sites are $18 per night, $5 per night for each additional vehicle. Open June through October, weather permitting.

Directions: From Truckee, turn north on Highway 89 and drive 20 miles to Sierraville. At Sierraville, turn left on Highway 49, drive over Yuba Pass, and continue for four miles to the campground on the right.

Contact: Tahoe National Forest, Yuba River Ranger District, North, 530/288-3231, fax 530/288-0727; California Land Management, 650/322-1181.

31 SIERRA

Scenic rating: 7

on the North Yuba River in Tahoe National Forest

Map 6.1, page 365

This is an easy-to-reach spot set along the North Yuba River, used primarily as an overflow area from nearby Chapman Creek (a mile upstream). Nearby recreation options include Chapman Creek Trail, several waterfalls (see *Wild Plum* listing in this chapter), and the nearby Lakes Basin Recreation Area to the north off the Gold Lake Highway. The elevation is 5,600 feet. Note: Bring your own drinking water.

Campsites, facilities: There are 16 sites for tents or RVs up to 22 feet (no hookups). Picnic tables and fire rings are provided. Vault toilets are available. No drinking water is available. Supplies are available in Bassetts. Leashed pets are permitted.

Reservations, fees: Reservations are not accepted. Sites are $10 per night, $5 per night for each additional vehicle. Open June through October, weather permitting.

Directions: From Truckee, turn north on Highway 89 and drive 20 miles to Sierraville. At Sierraville, turn left on Highway 49 and drive over Yuba Pass. Continue for five miles to the campground on the left side of the road.

Contact: Tahoe National Forest, Yuba River Ranger District, North, 530/288-3231, fax 530/288-0727; California Land Management, 650/322-1181.

32 YUBA PASS

Scenic rating: 6

in Tahoe National Forest

Map 6.1, page 365

This camp is set right at Yuba Pass at an elevation of 6,700 feet. In the winter, the surrounding area is a Sno-Park, which gives it an unusual look in summer. Yuba Pass is a popular bird-watching area in the summer.

Campsites, facilities: There are 20 sites for tents or RVs up to 22 feet (no hookups). Picnic tables and fire grills are provided. Vault toilets are available. There is no drinking water. Supplies are available at Bassetts. Leashed pets are permitted.

Reservations, fees: Reservations are not accepted. Sites are $18 per night, $5 per night for each additional vehicle. Open late June through October, weather permitting.

Directions: From Truckee, drive north on Highway 89 past Sattley to the junction with Highway 49. Turn west on Highway 49 and drive about six miles to the campground on the left side of the road.

Contact: Tahoe National Forest, Yuba River Ranger District, North, 530/288-3231, fax 530/288-0727; California Land Management, 650/322-1181.

33 CARLTON/CAL-IDA

🚶🏊🚣🐕🏕️♿🚐⛺

Scenic rating: 7

on the North Yuba River in Tahoe National Forest

Map 6.1, page 365

Carlton is on the North Yuba River, and Cal-Ida is across the road. Both are right next door to Fiddle Creek. (For more information, see the next listing, *Fiddle Creek*.)

Campsites, facilities: There are 30 sites at Carlton and 20 sites at Cal-Ida for tents or RVs up to 28 feet (no hookups). Picnic tables and fire grills are provided. Drinking water and vault toilets are available. Some facilities are wheelchair-accessible. Some supplies are available at the Indian Valley Outpost nearby. Leashed pets are permitted.

Reservations, fees: Reservations are not accepted. Sites are $18 per night. Open mid-April through November, weather permitting.

Directions: From Auburn, take Highway 49 north to Nevada City and continue on Highway 49 (the road jogs left, then narrows) to Camptonville. Continue northeast for nine miles to the campground entrance. The camping area at Carlton is one mile northeast of the Highway 49 bridge at Indian Valley. The camping area at Cal-Ida is just east of the Indian Valley Outpost on the Cal-Ida Road.

Contact: Tahoe National Forest, Yuba River Ranger District, North, 530/288-3231, fax 530/288-0727; California Land Management, 650/322-1181.

34 FIDDLE CREEK

🚶🏊🚣🐕♿⛺

Scenic rating: 7

on the North Yuba River in Tahoe National Forest

Map 6.1, page 365

This camp is situated on the North Yuba River along Highway 49 in a quiet, forested area. This is a beautiful river, one of the prettiest to flow westward out of the Sierra Nevada, with deep pools and miniature waterfalls. It is popular for rafting out of Goodyears Bar, and if you can stand the cold water, there are many good swimming holes along Highway 49. It's set at 2,200 feet. There are a series of campgrounds on this stretch of the Yuba River. Fiddle Creek Ridge Trail starts across the highway on Cal-Ida Road and is routed out to Indian Rock.

Campsites, facilities: There are 13 tent sites. Picnic tables and fire rings are provided. Drinking water and vault toilets are available. Limited supplies are available nearby at the Indian Valley Outpost. Some facilities are wheelchair-accessible, including a paved trail to the Yuba River. Leashed pets are permitted.

Reservations, fees: Reservations are not accepted. The fee is $18 per night, $5 per night for each additional vehicle. Open April to November, weather permitting.

Directions: From Auburn, take Highway 49 north to Nevada City and continue on Highway 49 (the road jogs left, then narrows) to Camptonville. Continue northeast for 9.5 miles to the campground entrance on the right.

Contact: Tahoe National Forest, Yuba River Ranger District, North, 530/288-3231, fax 530/288-0727; California Land Management, 650/322-1181.

35 INDIAN VALLEY

Scenic rating: 7

on the North Yuba River in Tahoe National Forest

Map 6.1, page 365

This is an easy-to-reach spot set at 2,200 feet beside the North Yuba River. Highway 49 runs adjacent to the Yuba River for miles eastward, providing easy access to the river in many areas. There are several other campgrounds in the immediate area (see the previous listings for *Fiddle Creek* and *Cal-Ida,* both within a mile).

Campsites, facilities: There are 17 sites for tents or RVs up to 22 feet (no hookups). Picnic tables and fire grills are provided. Drinking water and vault toilets are available. Limited supplies are available nearby at the Indian Valley Outpost. Some facilities are wheelchair-accessible. Leashed pets are permitted.

Reservations, fees: Reservations are not accepted. Sites are $18 per night, $5 per night for each additional vehicle. Open year-round.

Directions: From Auburn, take Highway 49 north to Nevada City and continue on Highway 49 (the road jogs left, then narrows) to Camptonville. Drive 10 miles to the camp entrance on the right.

Contact: Tahoe National Forest, Yuba River Ranger District, North, 530/288-3231, fax 530/288-0727; California Land Management, 650/322-1181.

36 ROCKY REST

Scenic rating: 7

on the North Yuba River in Tahoe National Forest

Map 6.1, page 365

This is one in a series of campgrounds set at streamside on the North Yuba River. The elevation is 2,200 feet. A footbridge crosses the North Yuba River and provides an outstanding seven-mile hike.

Campsites, facilities: There are 10 dispersed camping sites for tents and RVs up to 16 feet (no hookups). Picnic tables and fire grills are provided. Drinking water and vault toilets are available. Limited supplies are available at the Indian Valley Outpost nearby. Some facilities are wheelchair-accessible. Leashed pets are permitted.

Reservations, fees: Reservations are not accepted. Sites are $18 per night, $5 per night for each additional vehicle. Open mid-April through November, weather permitting.

Directions: From Auburn, take Highway 49 north to Nevada City and continue (the road jogs left, then narrows) to Camptonville. Continue on Highway 49 for 10 miles to the campground entrance on the right.

Contact: Tahoe National Forest, Yuba River Ranger District, North, 530/288-3231, fax 530/288-0727; California Land Management, 650/322-1181.

37 RAMSHORN

Scenic rating: 7

on the North Yuba River in Tahoe National Forest

Map 6.1, page 365

This camp is set on Ramshorn Creek, just across the road from the North Yuba River. It's one in a series of camps on this stretch of the beautiful North Yuba River. One mile east is a well-known access point for white-water rafting trips on the Yuba. The camp's elevation is 2,200 feet.

Campsites, facilities: There are 16 sites for tents or RVs up to 22 feet (no hookups). Picnic tables and fire grills are provided. Vault toilets and drinking water are available. Supplies are available in Downieville. Leashed pets are permitted.

Reservations, fees: Reservations are not accepted. Sites are $18, $5 per night for each additional vehicle per night. Open year-round.

Directions: From Auburn, take Highway 49 north to Nevada City and continue on Highway 49 (the road jogs left, then narrows) to Camptonville. Drive 15 miles north to the campground entrance on the left.

Contact: Tahoe National Forest, Yuba River Ranger District, North, 530/288-3231, fax 530/288-0727; California Land Management, 650/322-1181.

38 UNION FLAT

Scenic rating: 8

on the North Yuba River in Tahoe National Forest

Map 6.1, page 365

Of all the campgrounds on the North Yuba River along Highway 49, this one has the best swimming. The camp has a nice swimming hole next to it, and the water is cold. Recreational mining is also an attraction here. The elevation is 3,400 feet.

Campsites, facilities: There are 11 sites for tents or RVs up to 35 feet (no hookups). Picnic tables and fire grills are provided. Drinking water and vault toilets are available. Some facilities are wheelchair-accessible. Supplies are available in Downieville. Leashed pets are permitted.

Reservations, fees: Reservations are not accepted. Sites are $18 per night, $5 per night for each additional vehicle. Open May through October, weather permitting.

Directions: From Auburn, take Highway 49 north to Nevada City and continue (the road jogs left, then narrows) to Downieville. Drive six miles east to the campground entrance on the right.

Contact: Tahoe National Forest, Yuba River Ranger District, North, 530/288-3231, fax 530/288-0727; California Land Management, 650/322-1181.

39 LOGANVILLE

Scenic rating: 8

on the North Yuba River in Tahoe National Forest

Map 6.1, page 365

Sierra City is only two miles away, meaning you can make a quick getaway for a prepared meal or any food or drink you may need to add to your camp. Loganville is set on the North Yuba River, elevation 4,200 feet. It offers a good stretch of water in this region for trout fishing, with many pools set below miniature waterfalls.

Campsites, facilities: There are 20 sites for tents or RVs up to 22 feet (no hookups). Picnic tables and fire grills are provided. Drinking water and vault toilets are available. Supplies and a coin laundry are available in Sierra City. Leashed pets are permitted.

Reservations, fees: Reservations are not accepted. Sites are $18 per night, $5 per night for each additional vehicle. Open May through October, weather permitting.

Directions: From Auburn, take Highway 49 north to Nevada City and continue on Highway 49 (the road jogs left, then narrows) to Downieville. Drive 12 miles east to the campground entrance on the right (two miles west of Sierra City).

Contact: Tahoe National Forest, Yuba River Ranger District, North, 530/288-3231, fax 530/288-0727; California Land Management, 650/322-1181.

40 WILD PLUM

🚶 🛶 🐕 🚐 ⛺

Scenic rating: 8

on Haypress Creek in Tahoe National Forest

Map 6.1, page 365

This popular Forest Service campground is set on Haypress Creek at 4,400 feet. There are several hidden waterfalls in the area, which makes this a popular camp for the people who know of them. There's a scenic hike up Haypress Trail, which goes past a waterfall to Haypress Valley. Two other nearby waterfalls are Loves Falls (on the North Yuba on Highway 49 two miles east of Sierra City) and Hackmans Falls (remote, set in a ravine one mile south of Sierra City; no road access).

Campsites, facilities: There are 44 sites for tents or RVs up to 22 feet (no hookups). Picnic tables, food lockers, and fire grills are provided. Drinking water and vault toilets are available. Supplies and a coin laundry are available in Sierra City. Leashed pets are permitted.

Reservations, fees: Reservations are not accepted. Sites are $18 per night, $5 per night for each additional vehicle. Open May through October, weather permitting.

Directions: From Auburn, take Highway 49 north to Nevada City and continue (the road jogs left, then narrows) past Downieville to Sierra City at Wild Plum Road. Turn right on Wild Plum Road and drive two miles to the campground entrance road on the right.

Contact: Tahoe National Forest, Yuba River Ranger District, North, 530/288-3231, fax 530/288-0727; California Land Management, 650/322-1181.

41 COLD CREEK

🚶 🛶 🐕 🚐 ⛺

Scenic rating: 8

in Tahoe National Forest

Map 6.1, page 365

There are four small campgrounds along Highway 89 between Sierraville and Truckee, all within close range of side trips to Webber Lake, Independence Lake, and Sierra Hot Springs in Sierraville. Cold Creek is set just upstream of the confluence of Cottonwood Creek and Cold Creek, at 5,800 feet in elevation.

Campsites, facilities: There are 13 sites for tents or RVs up to 22 feet (no hookups). Picnic tables and fire rings are provided. Drinking water and vault toilets are available. Supplies are available in Sierraville. Leashed pets are permitted.

Reservations, fees: Reservations are accepted ($9 reservation fee) at 877/444-6777 or www .ReserveUSA.com. Sites are $15 per night, $3 per night for each additional vehicle. Open May through October.

Directions: From Truckee, drive north on Highway 89 for about 20 miles to the campground on the left side of the road. If you reach Sierraville, you have gone five miles too far.

Contact: Tahoe National Forest, Sierraville Ranger District, 530/994-3401, fax 530/994-3143; California Land Management, 650/322-1181.

42 COTTONWOOD CREEK

🚶 🛶 〰️ 🐕 ♿ 🚐 ⛺

Scenic rating: 7

in Tahoe National Forest

Map 6.1, page 365

This camp sits beside Cottonwood Creek at 5,800 feet elevation. An interpretive trail starts at the upper camp and makes a short loop, and there are several nearby side-trip options, including trout fishing on the Little Truckee River to the nearby south, visiting the Sierra Hot Springs out of Sierraville to the nearby north, or venturing into the surrounding Tahoe National Forest.

Campsites, facilities: There are 46 sites for tents or RVs up to 22 feet (no hookups). Picnic tables and fire rings are provided. Drinking water and vault toilets are available. Supplies are available in Sierraville. Some facilities are wheelchair-accessible. Leashed pets are permitted.

Reservations, fees: Reservations are

accepted ($9 reservation fee) at 877/444-6777 or www.ReserveUSA.com. Sites are $15 per night, $3 per night for each additional vehicle. Open mid-May to early October, weather permitting.

Directions: From Truckee, drive north on Highway 89 for about 20 miles to the campground entrance road on the right (0.5 mile past Cold Creek Camp).

Contact: Tahoe National Forest, Sierraville Ranger District, 530/994-3401, fax 530/994-3143; California Land Management, 650/322-1181.

43 BEAR VALLEY

Scenic rating: 7

on Bear Valley Creek in Tahoe National Forest

Map 6.1, page 365

The surrounding national forest land was largely burned by the historic Cottonwood Fire of 1994, but the camp itself was saved. It is at 6,700 feet in elevation, with a spring adjacent to the campground. The road leading southeast out of camp is routed to Sardine Peak Look-Out (8,134 feet), where there is a dramatic view of the region. There is an 18-mile loop OHV trail across the road from the campground.

Campsites, facilities: There are 10 sites for tents or RVs up to 16 feet (no hookups). Picnic tables and fire rings are provided. Vault toilets are available. There is no drinking water. Garbage must be packed out. Supplies are available in Sierraville. Leashed pets are permitted.

Reservations, fees: Reservations are not accepted. There is no fee for camping. Open May through October, weather permitting.

Directions: From Truckee, drive north on Highway 89 about 17 miles. Turn right on County Road 451 and drive northeast about six miles to the campground entrance on the right.

Contact: Tahoe National Forest, Sierraville Ranger District, 530/994-3401, fax 530/994-3143.

44 LOOKOUT

Scenic rating: 4

in Humboldt-Toiyabe National Forest

Map 6.1, page 365

This primitive camp is set in remote country near the California/Nevada border at 6,700 feet. It is a former mining site, and the highlight here is a quartz crystal mine a short distance from the campground. Stampede Lake provides a side-trip option, about 10 miles to the southwest, over the rough dirt Henness Pass Road.

Campsites, facilities: There are 18 sites for tents or RVs up to 35 feet (no hookups), and a group site for up to 16 people. Picnic tables and fire grills are provided. Vault toilets are available. There is no drinking water. Garbage must be packed out. Leashed pets are permitted.

Reservations, fees: Reservations are accepted for individual sites and are required for the group site at 775/882-2766. Sites are $6 per night and the group site is $25 per night. Open June through September.

Directions: From Truckee on I-80, drive east across the state line into Nevada to Verdi. Take the Verdi exit and drive north through town to Bridge Street and then to Old Dog Valley Road. Drive north on Old Dog Valley Road for 11 miles to the campground.

Contact: Humboldt-Toiyabe National Forest, Carson Ranger District, 775/882-2766, fax 775/884-8199.

45 SILVER TIP GROUP CAMP

Scenic rating: 7

at Jackson Meadow Reservoir in Tahoe National Forest

Map 6.1, page 365

This group camp is set on the southwest edge of Jackson Meadow Reservoir at 6,100 feet, in a pretty area with pine forest, high meadows, and the trademark granite look of the Sierra Nevada. A boat ramp and swimming beach are nearby at Woodcamp. (For more information, see the next listing, *Woodcamp.*)

Campsites, facilities: There are two group sites for tents or RVs up to 22 feet (no hookups) that can accommodate up to 25 people each. Picnic tables and fire rings are provided. Drinking water and vault toilets are available. Obtain supplies in Truckee or Sierraville. A boat ramp is nearby. Leashed pets are permitted.

Reservations, fees: Reservations are required ($9 reservation fee) at 877/444-6777 or www .ReserveUSA.com. The camps are $65–130 per night. Open June through October, weather permitting.

Directions: From Truckee, drive north on Highway 89 for 17 miles to Forest Road 7. Turn left on Forest Road 7 and drive 16 miles to Jackson Meadow Reservoir. At the lake, continue across the dam around the west shoreline and then turn left at the campground access road. The entrance is on the right just after the Woodcamp campground.

Contact: Tahoe National Forest, Sierraville Ranger District, 530/994-3401, fax 530/994-3143; California Land Management, 650/322-1181.

46 WOODCAMP
🚶🏊🛶🍴🐕🚐⛺

Scenic rating: 7

at Jackson Meadow Reservoir in Tahoe National Forest

Map 6.1, page 365

Woodcamp and Pass Creek are the best camps for boaters at Jackson Meadow Reservoir because each is directly adjacent to a boat ramp. That is critical because fishing is far better by boat here than from shore, with a good mix of both rainbow and brown trout. The camp is set at 6,700 feet along the lake's southwest shore, in a pretty spot with a swimming beach and short interpretive hiking trail nearby. All water sports are allowed. This is a beautiful

lake in the Sierra Nevada, complete with pine forest and a classic granite backdrop.

Campsites, facilities: There are 20 sites for tents or RVs up to 22 feet (no hookups). Picnic tables and fire rings are provided. Drinking water, flush and vault toilets, food lockers, and firewood (fee) are available. Supplies are available in Truckee or Sierraville. A boat ramp is adjacent to the camp and a dump station is nearby. Leashed pets are permitted.

Reservations, fees: Reservations are accepted ($9 reservation fee) at 877/444-6777 or www .ReserveUSA.com. Sites are $18 per night, $5 per night for each additional vehicle. Open June through October, weather permitting.

Directions: From Truckee, drive north on Highway 89 for 17 miles to Forest Road 7. Turn left on Forest Road 7 and drive 16 miles to Jackson Meadow Reservoir. At the lake, continue across the dam around the west shoreline and then turn left at the campground access road. The entrance is on the right just before the Woodcamp boat ramp.

Contact: Tahoe National Forest, Sierraville Ranger District, 530/994-3401, fax 530/994-3143; California Land Management, 650/322-1181.

47 FIR TOP
🚶🏊🛶🍴🐕🚐⛺

Scenic rating: 7

at Jackson Meadow Reservoir in Tahoe National Forest

Map 6.1, page 365

Jackson Meadow is a great destination for a short vacation, and that's why there are so many campgrounds available; it's not exactly a secret. This camp is set above the lake, less than a mile from a boat ramp near Woodcamp. (See the previous listing, *Woodcamp,* and the *Pass Creek* listing in this chapter for more information.) The elevation is 6,200 feet.

Campsites, facilities: There are 14 sites for tents or RVs up to 22 feet (no hookups). Picnic tables and fire rings are provided. Drinking water, flush and vault toilets, and food lockers are available. Supplies are available in Truckee or Sierraville. Leashed pets are permitted.

Reservations, fees: Reservations are accepted ($9 reservation fee) at 877/444-6777 or www.ReserveUSA.com. Sites are $18 per night, $5 per night for each additional vehicle. Open June through November, weather permitting.

Directions: From Truckee, drive north on Highway 89 for 17.5 miles to Forest Road 7. Turn left on Forest Road 7 and drive 16 miles to Jackson Meadow Reservoir. Continue across the dam and around the lake to the west side. Turn left at the campground access road. The campground entrance is on the right across from the entrance to the Woodcamp Picnic Area.

Contact: Tahoe National Forest, Sierraville Ranger District, 530/994-3401, fax 530/994-3143; California Land Management, 650/322-1181.

48 FINDLEY
🥾 🏊 🛶 🚤 🐕 ♿ 🚐 ⛺

Scenic rating: 7

at Jackson Meadow Reservoir in Tahoe National Forest

Map 6.1, page 365

Findley is set near Woodcamp Creek, 0.25 mile from where it pours into Jackson Meadow Reservoir. Though it is not a lakeside camp, it is quite pretty just the same, and within a mile of the boat ramp near Woodcamp. It is set at 6,300 feet. This is one of several camps at the lake.

Campsites, facilities: There are 14 sites for tents or RVs up to 22 feet (no hookups). Picnic tables and fire rings are provided. Drinking water, flush and vault toilets and food lockers are available. Supplies are available in Truckee or Sierraville. A boat ramp is nearby. Some facilities are wheelchair-accessible. Leashed pets are permitted.

Reservations, fees: Reservations are accepted

($9 reservation fee) at 877/444-6777 or www.ReserveUSA.com. Sites are $18 per night, $5 per night for each additional vehicle. Open May through October.

Directions: From Truckee, drive north on Highway 89 for 17 miles to Forest Road 7. Turn left on Forest Road 7 and drive 16 miles to Jackson Meadow Reservoir. Continue across the dam around the lake to the west side. Turn left at the campground access road and drive about 0.25 mile to the entrance on the left.

Contact: Tahoe National Forest, Sierraville Ranger District, 530/994-3401, fax 530/994-3143; California Land Management, 650/322-1181.

49 JACKSON POINT BOAT-IN
🏊 🛶 🚤 🐕 5% ⛺

Scenic rating: 10

at Jackson Meadow Reservoir in Tahoe National Forest

Map 6.1, page 365   **BEST** (

This is one of the few boat-in camps available anywhere in the high Sierra. The gorgeous spot is situated on the end of a peninsula that extends from the east shore of Jackson Meadow Reservoir. Small and primitive, it's the one place at the lake where you can gain entry into the 5 Percent Club. From the point, there is a spectacular view of the Sierra Buttes. Because the lake levels are kept near full all summer, this boat-in camp is doubly appealing. The elevation is 6,200 feet.

Campsites, facilities: There are 10 tent sites. Picnic tables and fire rings are provided. Vault toilets are available. No drinking water is available. Garbage must be packed out. Supplies are available in Truckee or Sierraville. Leashed pets are permitted.

Reservations, fees: Reservations are not accepted. There is no fee for camping. Open June through September, weather permitting.

Directions: From Truckee, drive north on Highway 89 for 17 miles to Forest Road 7. Turn left on Forest Road 7 and drive 16 miles to Jackson

Meadow Reservoir. Drive to Pass Creek and boat launch (on the left at the north end of the lake). Launch your boat and cruise 0.5 mile south to Jackson Point and the boat-in campsites.

Contact: Tahoe National Forest, Sierraville Ranger District, 530/994-3401, fax 530/994-3143; California Land Management, 650/322-1181.

50 PASS CREEK
🏃 🏊 🚣 ⛴ 🏕 🐕 🚐 🔺

Scenic rating: 7

at Jackson Meadow Reservoir in Tahoe National Forest

Map 6.1, page 365

This is the premium campground at Jackson Meadow Reservoir, a developed site with water, concrete boat ramp, swimming beach nearby at Aspen Creek Picnic Area, and access to the Pacific Crest Trail 0.5 mile to the east (you'll pass it on the way in). This lake has the trademark look of the high Sierra, and the bonus here is that lake levels are often kept higher than at other reservoirs on the western slopes of the Sierra Nevada. Trout stocks are excellent, with rainbow and brown trout planted each summer after ice-out. The elevation is 6,100 feet.

Campsites, facilities: There are 30 sites for tents or RVs up to 22 feet (no hookups). Picnic tables and fire rings are provided. Drinking water, flush and vault toilets, and food lockers are available. A dump station is nearby. A boat ramp is nearby. Supplies are available in Truckee or Sierraville. Leashed pets are permitted.

Reservations, fees: Reservations are accepted ($9 reservation fee) at 877/444-6777 or www .ReserveUSA.com. Sites are $18 per night, $5 per night for each additional vehicle. Open May through October, weather permitting.

Directions: From Truckee, drive north on Highway 89 for 17 miles to Forest Road 7. Turn left on Forest Road 7 and drive 16 miles to Jackson Meadow Reservoir; the campground is on the left at the north end of the lake.

Contact: Tahoe National Forest, Sierraville Ranger District, 530/994-3401, fax 530/994-3143; California Land Management, 650/322-1181.

51 EAST MEADOW
🏃 🏊 🚣 ⛴ 🏕 🐕 ♿ 🚐 🔺

Scenic rating: 7

at Jackson Meadow Reservoir in Tahoe National Forest

Map 6.1, page 365

This camp is in a beautiful setting on the northeast side of Jackson Meadow Reservoir, on the edge of a sheltered cove. The Pacific Crest Trail passes right by camp, providing access for a day trip, though no stellar destinations are on this stretch of the PCT. The nearest boat ramp is at Pass Creek, two miles away. The elevation is 6,200 feet.

Campsites, facilities: There are 46 sites for tents or RVs up to 40 feet (no hookups). Picnic tables and fire rings are provided. Drinking water, flush and vault toilets, food lockers, and firewood (fee) are available. A dump station and boat ramp are available near Pass Creek. Supplies are available in Truckee or Sierraville. Some facilities are wheelchair-accessible. Leashed pets are permitted.

Reservations, fees: Reservations are accepted ($9 reservation fee) at 877/444-6777 or www .ReserveUSA.com. The fee is $18 per night, $5 per night for each additional vehicle. Open May through October, weather permitting.

Directions: From Truckee, drive north on Highway 89 for 17 miles to Forest Road 7. Turn left on Forest Road 7 and drive 15 miles to the campground entrance road on the left (if you reach Pass Creek, you have gone too far). Turn left and drive a mile to the campground on the right.

Contact: Tahoe National Forest, Sierraville Ranger District, 530/994-3401, fax 530/994-3143; California Land Management, 650/322-1181.

52 ASPEN GROUP CAMP

Scenic rating: 7

at Jackson Meadow Reservoir in Tahoe
National Forest

Map 6.1, page 365

A boat ramp and easy access to adjacent Jackson Meadow Reservoir make this a premium group camp. The elevation is 6,100 feet.

Campsites, facilities: There are three group sites for tents or RVs up to 40 feet (no hookups) that can accommodate 25–50 people each. Picnic tables and fire grills are provided. Drinking water, vault toilets, food lockers, firewood (fee), and a campfire circle are available. A dump station is nearby. There is a boat ramp nearby at Pass Creek. Supplies are available in Truckee or Sierraville. Leashed pets are permitted.

Reservations, fees: Reservations are required ($9 reservation fee) at 877/444-6777 or www.ReserveUSA.com. Sites are $65–130 per night. Open mid-May through October, weather permitting.

Directions: From Truckee, drive north on Highway 89 for 17.5 miles to Forest Road 7. Turn left on Forest Road 7 and drive 16 miles (a mile past Pass Creek) to the campground entrance on the right.

Contact: Tahoe National Forest, Sierraville Ranger District, 530/994-3401, fax 530/994-3143; California Land Management, 650/322-1181.

53 UPPER LITTLE TRUCKEE

Scenic rating: 7

on the Little Truckee River in Tahoe National
Forest

Map 6.1, page 365

This camp is set along the Little Truckee River at 6,100 feet. The Little Truckee is a pretty trout stream, with easy access not only from this campground, but also from another three miles northward along Highway 89, then from another seven miles to the west along Forest Road 7, the route to Webber Lake. It is only about a 10-minute drive from this camp to reach Stampede Lake to the east.

Campsites, facilities: There are 26 sites for tents or RVs up to 30 feet (no hookups). Picnic tables and fire rings are provided. Drinking water and vault toilets are available. Supplies are available in Sierraville. Leashed pets are permitted.

Reservations, fees: Reservations are accepted ($9 reservation fee) at 877/444-6777 or www.ReserveUSA.com. Sites are $15 per night, $5 per night for each additional vehicle. Open mid-May through October, weather permitting.

Directions: From Truckee, drive north on Highway 89 for about 11 miles to the campground on the left, a short distance beyond Lower Little Truckee Camp.

Contact: Tahoe National Forest, Sierraville Ranger District, 530/994-3401, fax 530/994-3143; California Land Management, 650/322-1181.

54 LOWER LITTLE TRUCKEE

Scenic rating: 7

on the Little Truckee River in Tahoe National
Forest

Map 6.1, page 365

This pretty camp is set along Highway 89 and the Little Truckee River at 6,200 feet. (For more information, see the previous listing, *Upper Little Truckee*.)

Campsites, facilities: There are 15 sites for tents or RVs up to 20 feet (no hookups). Picnic tables and fire grills are provided. Drinking water and vault toilets are available. Supplies are available in Sierraville or Truckee. Leashed pets are permitted.

Reservations, fees: Reservations are accepted ($9 reservation fee) at 877/444-6777 or www

.ReserveUSA.com. Sites are $15 per night, $5 per night for each additional vehicle. Open May through October, weather permitting.

Directions: From Truckee, drive north on Highway 89 for about 12 miles to the campground on the left. If you reach Upper Little Truckee Camp, you have gone 0.5 mile too far.

Contact: Tahoe National Forest, Sierraville Ranger District, 530/994-3401, fax 530/994-3143; California Land Management, 650/322-1181.

55 JACKSON CREEK

Scenic rating: 7

near Bowman Lake in Tahoe National Forest

Map 6.1, page 365

This primitive campground is at 5,600 feet, adjacent to Jackson Creek, a primary feeder stream to Bowman Lake to the nearby west. There are several lakes within a five-mile radius, including Bowman Lake, Jackson Meadow Reservoir, Sawmill Lake (private), and Faucherie Lake. A trailhead is available a mile south (on the right side of the road) at the north end of Sawmill Lake. The trail is routed to a series of pretty Sierra lakes to the west of Haystack Mountain (7,391 feet).

Campsites, facilities: There are 14 primitive tent sites. Picnic tables and fire grills are provided. Vault toilets are available. No drinking water is available. Garbage must be packed out. Leashed pets are permitted.

Reservations, fees: Reservations are not accepted. There is no fee for camping. Open June through October, weather permitting.

Directions: From Sacramento, drive east on I-80 past Emigrant Gap to Highway 20. Turn west on Highway 20 and drive to Bowman Road/Forest Road 18. Turn right and drive about 16 miles to Bowman Lake (much of the road is quite rough), then con-

tinue for four miles east of the lake to the campground.

Contact: Tahoe National Forest, Yuba River Ranger District, South, 530/265-4531, fax 530/478-6109.

56 BOWMAN LAKE

Scenic rating: 8

in Tahoe National Forest

Map 6.1, page 365

Bowman is a sapphire jewel set in Sierra granite at 5,568 feet, extremely pretty and ideal for campers with car-top boats. Pine trees surround the lake, and the shoreline is sprinkled with large granite slabs. Swimming is allowed, and the boat speed limit is 10 mph. There is no boat ramp (you wouldn't want to trailer a boat on the access road anyway), but there are lots of small rainbow trout that are eager to please during the evening bite. The camp is set on the eastern end of the lake, just below where Jackson Creek pours in. The lake is flanked by Bowman Mountain (7,392 feet) and Red Hill (7,075 feet) to the south and Quartz Hill (7,025 feet) to the north.

Campsites, facilities: There are seven primitive tent sites. Vault toilets are available. No drinking water is available. Garbage must be packed out. Leashed pets are permitted.

Reservations, fees: Reservations are not accepted. There is no fee for camping. Open mid-June through October, weather permitting.

Directions: From Sacramento, drive east on I-80 past Emigrant Gap to Highway 20. Turn west on Highway 20 and drive to Bowman Road/Forest Road 18. Turn right and drive about 16 miles (much of the road is quite rough) to Bowman Lake and the campground on the right side of the road at the head of the lake.

Contact: Tahoe National Forest, Yuba River Ranger District, South, 530/265-4531, fax 530/478-6109; Big Bend Visitor Center, 530/426-3609, fax 530/426-1744.

57 FAUCHERIE LAKE GROUP CAMP

🏃 🏊 🚣 🚤 🐕 🚐 ⛺

Scenic rating: 7

near Bowman Lake in Tahoe National Forest

Map 6.1, page 365

Faucherie Lake is the kind of place that most people believe can only be reached by long, difficult hikes with a backpack. Guess again: Here it is, set in Sierra granite at 6,100 feet in elevation, quiet and pristine, a classic alpine lake. It is ideal for car-top boating and has decent fishing for both rainbow and brown trout. The boating speed limit is 10 mph. This is a group camp on the lake's northern shore, a prime spot, with the outlet creek nearby. Note: Road washouts may require four-wheel drive.

Campsites, facilities: There is one group camp for tents or RVs up to 22 feet (no hookups) that can accommodate up to 25 people. Picnic tables and fire grills are provided. Vault toilets are available. No drinking water is available. Garbage must be packed out. A boat ramp is nearby. Leashed pets are permitted.

Reservations, fees: Reservations are required ($9 reservation fee) at 877/444-6777 or www.ReserveUSA.com. The camp is $50 per night. Open June through October, weather permitting.

Directions: From Sacramento, drive east on I-80 past Emigrant Gap to Highway 20. Turn west on Highway 20 and drive to Bowman Road/Forest Road 18. Turn right and drive about 16 miles (much of the road is quite rough) to Bowman Lake and continue four miles to a Y. Bear right at the Y and drive about three miles to the campground at the end of the road.

Contact: Tahoe National Forest, Yuba River Ranger District, South, 530/265-4531, fax 530/478-6109; Big Bend Visitor Center, 530/426-3609, fax 530/426-1744.

58 CANYON CREEK

🏃 🏊 🏕 ⛺

Scenic rating: 6

near Faucherie Lake in Tahoe National Forest

Map 6.1, page 365

This pretty spot is at 6,000 feet in Tahoe National Forest, a mile from Sawmill Lake (which you pass on the way in) and a mile from pretty Faucherie Lake. It is set along Canyon Creek, the stream that connects those two lakes. Of the two, Faucherie provides better fishing and, because of that, there are fewer people at Sawmill. Take your pick. A trailhead is available at the north end of Sawmill Lake with a hike to several small alpine lakes, a great day or overnight backpacking trip.

Campsites, facilities: There are 20 sites for tents or RVs up to 16 feet (no hookups). Picnic tables and fire grills are provided. Vault toilets are available. No drinking water is available. Garbage must be packed out. Leashed pets are permitted.

Reservations, fees: Reservations are not accepted. There is no fee for camping. Open June through October, weather permitting.

Directions: From Sacramento, drive east on I-80 to Emigrant Gap. Take the off-ramp and head north on the short connector road to Highway 20. Turn west on Highway 20 and drive four miles to Bowman Road/Forest Road 18. Turn right and drive about 16 miles (nine of these miles are paved, but the rest is quite rough) to Bowman Lake and continue four miles to a Y. Bear right at the Y and drive about two miles to the campground on the right side of the road. (Occasionally the access route requires a four-wheel-drive vehicle.)

Contact: Tahoe National Forest, Yuba River Ranger District, South, 530/265-4531, fax 530/478-6109; Big Bend Visitor Center, 530/426-3609, fax 530/426-1744.

59 SAGEHEN CREEK

Scenic rating: 7

in Tahoe National Forest

Map 6.1, page 365

This is a small, primitive camp set at 6,500 feet beside little Sagehen Creek, just north of a miniature mountain range called the Sagehen Hills, which top out at 7,707 feet. Sagehen Creek provides an option when the camps along Highway 89 and at Stampede, Boca, and Prosser Creek have filled. In the fall, it is popular with campers as a base camp.

Campsites, facilities: There are 10 sites for tents or RVs up to 16 feet (no hookups). Picnic tables and fire grills are provided. Vault toilets are available. No drinking water is available. Garbage must be packed out. Leashed pets are permitted.

Reservations, fees: Reservations are not accepted. There is no fee for camping. Open June through October, weather permitting.

Directions: From Truckee, drive 8.5 miles north on Highway 89 to Sagehen Summit Road on the left. Turn left and drive four miles to the campground.

Contact: Tahoe National Forest, Truckee Ranger District, 530/587-3558, fax 530/587-6914.

60 LOGGER

Scenic rating: 7

at Stampede Lake in Tahoe National Forest

Map 6.1, page 365

Covering 3,400 acres and with 25 miles of shoreline, Stampede Lake is a huge lake by Sierra standards—the largest in the region after Lake Tahoe. It is set at 6,000 feet, surrounded by Sierra granite mountains and pines, and is big, and on days when the wind is down, quite beautiful. The campground is also huge, set along the lake's southern shore, a few minutes' drive from the Captain Roberts boat ramp.

This camp is ideal for campers, boaters, and anglers. The lake is becoming one of the top fishing lakes in California for kokanee salmon (which can be caught only by trolling), and it also has some large Mackinaw trout and a sprinkling of planter-sized rainbow trout. All water sports are allowed. One problem at Stampede is receding water levels from midsummer through fall, a real pain, which puts the campsites some distance from the lake. Even when the lake is full, there are only a few "lakeside" campsites. However, the boat ramp has been extended to assist boaters during drawdowns.

Campsites, facilities: There are 252 sites for tents or RVs up to 32 feet (no hookups). Picnic tables and fire rings are provided. Drinking water, vault toilets, and a dump station are available. A concrete boat ramp is available one mile from camp. Some facilities are wheelchair-accessible. Leashed pets are permitted.

Reservations, fees: Reservations are accepted ($9 reservation fee) at 877/444-6777 or www.ReserveUSA.com. Sites are $16 per night, $5 per night for each additional vehicle. Open May through October.

Directions: From Truckee, drive east on I-80 for seven miles to the Boca-Hirschdale/County Road 270 exit. Take that exit and drive north on County Road 270 for about seven miles (past Boca Reservoir) to the junction with County Road S261 on the left. Turn left and drive 1.5 miles to the campground on the right.

Contact: Tahoe National Forest, Truckee Ranger District, 530/587-3558, fax 530/587-6914; California Land Management, 530/544-0426.

61 EMIGRANT SPRINGS GROUP CAMP

Scenic rating: 7

at Stampede Lake in Tahoe National Forest

Map 6.1, page 365

Emigrant Group Camp is set at a beautiful spot on Stampede Lake, near a point along a cove on the southeastern corner of the lake. There is a beautiful view of the lake from the point, and a boat ramp is two miles to the east. Elevation is 6,000 feet. (See the previous entry, *Logger,* for more information.)

Campsites, facilities: There are three group sites for tents or RVs up to 32 feet (no hookups) that can accommodate 25–50 people each. Picnic tables and fire grills are provided. Drinking water and vault toilets are available. Bring your own firewood. A three-lane concrete boat ramp is available. Some facilities are wheelchair-accessible. Leashed pets are permitted.

Reservations, fees: Reservations are required ($9 reservation fee) at 877/444-6777 or www .ReserveUSA.com. The camp is $78–152 per night. Open May through September, weather permitting.

Directions: From Truckee, drive east on I-80 for seven miles to the Boca-Hirschdale/County Road 270 exit. Take that exit and drive north on County Road 270 for about seven miles (past Boca Reservoir) to the junction with County Road S261 on the left. Turn left and drive 1.5 miles to the campground access road on the right. Turn right and drive one mile to the camp on the left.

Contact: Tahoe National Forest, Truckee Ranger District, 530/587-3558, fax 530/587-6914; California Land Management, 530/544-0426.

62 BOYINGTON MILL
🏃‍♀️🚣🐕🚐🏕️

Scenic rating: 7

on the Little Truckee River in Tahoe National Forest

Map 6.1, page 365

Boyington Mill is a little Forest Service camp set between Boca Reservoir to the nearby south and Stampede Lake to the nearby north, along a small inlet creek to the adjacent Little Truckee River. Though open all summer, it is most often used as an overflow camp when

lakeside campsites at Boca, Stampede, and Prosser have already filled. The elevation is 5,700 feet.

Campsites, facilities: There are 10 sites for tents or RVs up to 32 feet (no hookups). Picnic tables and fire rings are provided. Vault toilets are available. No drinking water is available. Leashed pets are permitted.

Reservations, fees: Reservations are accepted at 877/444-6777 ($9 reservation fee) or www .ReserveUSA.com. Sites are $14 per night, $5 per night for each additional vehicle. Open May through October, weather permitting.

Directions: From Truckee, drive east on I-80 for seven miles. Take the Boca-Hirschdale exit and drive north on County Road 270 for four miles (past Boca Reservoir) to the campground.

Contact: Tahoe National Forest, Truckee Ranger District, 530/587-3558, fax 530/587-6914; California Land Management, 530/544-0426.

63 BOCA REST CAMPGROUND
🏊‍♀️🚣🚐🐕🚙🏕️

Scenic rating: 7

on Boca Reservoir in Tahoe National Forest

Map 6.1, page 365

The Boca Dam faces I-80, so the lake is out of sight of the zillions of highway travelers who would otherwise certainly stop here. Those who do stop find that the lake is very pretty, set at 5,700 feet in elevation and covering 1,000 acres with deep, blue water and 14 miles of shoreline. All water sports are allowed. This camp is on the lake's northeastern shore, not far from the inlet to the Little Truckee River. The boat ramp is some distance away.

Campsites, facilities: There are 31 sites for tents or RVs up to 22 feet (no hookups). Picnic tables and fire grills are provided. Drinking water and vault toilets are available. A hand-launch boat ramp is also available. A concrete boat ramp is three miles away on the southwest shore of Boca Reservoir. Leashed pets are permitted.

Reservations, fees: Reservations are accepted ($9 reservation fee) at 877/444-6777 or www .ReserveUSA.com. Sites are $14 per night, $5 per night for each additional vehicle. Open May through October, weather permitting.

Directions: From Truckee, drive east on I-80 for seven miles to the Boca-Hirschdale exit. Take that exit and drive north on County Road 270 for about 2.5 miles to the campground on the left side of the road.

Contact: Tahoe National Forest, Truckee Ranger District, 530/587-3558, fax 530/587-6914; California Land Management, 530/544-0426.

64 MALAKOFF DIGGINS STATE HISTORIC PARK

🧍 🐕 🚙 ⛺

Scenic rating: 7

near Nevada City

Map 6.1, page 365

This camp is set at 3,400 feet near a small lake in the park, but the main attraction of the area is its gold-mining past. A trip here is like a walk through history. Gold-mining efforts at this site washed away entire mountains with powerful streams of water, leaving behind enormous cliffs. This practice began in the 1850s and continued for many years. Several major gold-mining operations combined hydraulic mining with giant sluice boxes. Hydraulic mining was a scourge to the land, of course, and was eventually put to an end due to litigation between mine operators and landowners downstream. Though the remains of the state's biggest hydraulic mine are now closed to public viewing, visitors can view exhibits on mining life.

The park also contains a 7,847-foot bedrock tunnel that served as a drain. Although this tunnel is not open to the public, a shorter tunnel is available for viewing. The visitors center has exhibits on life in the old mining town of North Bloomfield. Tours of the numerous historic sites are available during the summer.

Campsites, facilities: There are 30 sites for tents or RVs up to 24 feet (no hookups), three cabins, and one group tent site for up to 50 people. Picnic tables and fire grills are provided. Drinking water and flush toilets (except mid-November through February) are available. Leashed pets are permitted.

Reservations, fees: Reservations are accepted Memorial Day through Labor Day ($7.50 reservation fee) at 800/444-PARK (800/444-7275) or www.reserveamerica.com. Sites are $11–15 per night, $6 per night for each additional vehicle, $111 per night for the group site. The cabins are $35 per night. Open year-round.

Directions: From Auburn, drive north on Highway 49 to Nevada City and continue 11 miles to the junction of Tyler Foote Crossing Road. Turn right and drive approximately 11 miles (in the process the road changes names to Cruzon Grade and Back Bone Road) to Der Bec Road. Turn right on Der Bec Road and drive one mile to North Bloomfield Road. Turn right and drive two miles to the entrance on the right. The route is well signed; the last two miles are quite steep.

Contact: California State Parks, Goldrush District, tel./fax 530/265-2740, www.parks .ca.gov.

65 SOUTH YUBA

🧍 🏊 🚤 🐕 ♿ 🚙 ⛺

Scenic rating: 7

near the Yuba River

Map 6.1, page 365

This little-known BLM camp is set next to where little Kenebee Creek enters the Yuba River. The Yuba is about a mile away, with some great swimming holes and evening trout-fishing spots to explore. A good side trip is to nearby Malakoff Diggins State Historic Park and the town of North Bloomfield (about a 10-minute drive to the northeast on North Bloomfield

Road), which is being completely restored to its 1850s character. Twelve-mile-long South Yuba Trail begins at the state park and features outstanding spring wildflower blooms. The elevation is 2,600 feet.

Campsites, facilities: There are 16 sites for tents or RVs up to 27 feet (no hookups). Picnic tables and fire grills are provided. Drinking water and vault toilets are available. Some facilities are wheelchair-accessible. Leashed pets are permitted.

Reservations, fees: Reservations are not accepted. Sites are $5 per night. Open April through October, weather permitting.

Directions: From Auburn, turn north on Highway 49, drive to Nevada City, and then continue on Highway 49 (the highway jogs left in town) a short distance to North Bloomfield Road. Turn right and drive 10 miles to the one-lane bridge at Edward's Crossing. Cross the bridge and continue 1.5 miles to the campground on the right side of the road (the road becomes quite rough). This route is not recommended for RVs or trailers.

Alternate route for RVs or vehicles with trailers: From Auburn turn north on Highway 49 to Nevada City and continue on Highway 49 (the highway jogs left in town) to Tyler Foote Crossing Road. Turn right and drive to Grizzly Hills Road (just past North Columbia). Turn right and drive two miles to North Bloomfield Road. Bear right on North Bloomfield Road and drive 0.5 mile to the campground on the left.

Contact: The Bureau of Land Management, Folsom Field Office, 916/985-4474, fax 916/985-3259.

66 GROUSE RIDGE
🏃 ☲ 🛶 🐕 ⛺

Scenic rating: 6

near Bowman Lake in Tahoe National Forest

Map 6.1, page 365

Grouse Ridge is set at 7,520 feet at the gateway to beautiful hiking country filled with small high Sierra lakes. The camp is primarily used as a trailhead and jump-off point, not as a destination itself. The closest hike is the 0.5-mile tromp up to Grouse Ridge Lookout, 7,707 feet, which provides a spectacular view to the north of this area and its many small lakes. As you hike north, the trail passes Round Lake (to the left) in the first mile and Middle Lake (on the right) two miles later, with opportunities to take cutoff trails on either side of the ridge to visit numerous other lakes.

Campsites, facilities: There are nine sites for tents only. Picnic tables and fire grills are provided. Vault toilets are available. No drinking water is available. Garbage must be packed out. Leashed pets are permitted.

Reservations, fees: Reservations are not accepted. There is no fee for camping. Open June through October, weather permitting.

Directions: From Sacramento, drive east on I-80 past Emigrant Gap to Highway 20. Turn west on Highway 20 and drive to Bowman Road/Forest Road 18. Turn north on Bowman Road and drive five miles to Grouse Ridge Road. Turn right on Grouse Ridge Road and drive six miles on rough gravel to the campground.

Contact: Tahoe National Forest, Yuba River Ranger District, South, 530/265-4531, fax 530/478-6109; Big Bend Visitor Center, 530/426-3609, fax 530/426-1744.

67 LAKESIDE
☲ 🛶 � 🐕 � ⛰

Scenic rating: 7

on Prosser Creek Reservoir in Tahoe National Forest

Map 6.1, page 365

This primitive camp is in a deep cove in the northwestern end of Prosser Creek Reservoir, near the lake's headwaters. It is a gorgeous lake, set at 5,741 feet, and a 10-mph speed limit keeps the fast boats out. The adjacent shore is decent for hand-launched, car-top boats, providing the lake level is up, and a concrete boat ramp is a mile down the road. Lots of trout are stocked here every year. The trout fishing is often quite good after the ice breaks up in late spring. Sound perfect? Unfortunately for many, the Prosser OHV Park is nearby and can be noisy.

Campsites, facilities: There are 30 sites for tents or RVs up to 33 feet (no hookups). Drinking water and vault toilets are available. A boat ramp is available nearby. Leashed pets are permitted.

Reservations, fees: Reservations are accepted ($9 reservation fee) at 877/444-6777 or www .ReserveUSA.com. Sites are $13 per night, $5 per night for each additional vehicle. Open June through October, weather permitting.

Directions: From Truckee, drive north on Highway 89 for three miles to the campground entrance road on the right. Turn right and drive less than a mile to the campground.

Contact: Tahoe National Forest, Truckee Ranger District, 530/587-3558, fax 530/587-6914; California Land Management, 530/544-0426.

68 BOCA

🏊 🚣 🛥️ 🐎 🚐 🔼

Scenic rating: 7

on Boca Reservoir in Tahoe National Forest

Map 6.1, page 365

Boca Reservoir is known as a "big fish factory," with some huge but rare brown trout and rainbow trout sprinkled among a growing fishery for kokanee salmon. The lake is set at 5,700 feet amid a few sparse pines. While the surrounding landscape is not in the drop-dead beautiful class, the lake can still seem a Sierra gem on a windless dawn out on a boat. It is within a few miles of I-80. The camp is the best choice for anglers/boaters, with a launch ramp set just down from the campground.

Campsites, facilities: There are 20 sites for tents or RVs up to 16 feet (no hookups). Picnic tables and fire grills are provided. Vault toilets are available. No drinking water is

available. A concrete boat ramp is north of the campground on Boca Reservoir. Truckee is the nearest place for telephones and supplies. Leashed pets are permitted.

Reservations, fees: Reservations are accepted ($9 reservation fee) at 877/444-6777 or www .ReserveUSA.com. Sites are $13 per night, $5 per night for each additional vehicle. Open May through October, weather permitting.

Directions: From I-80 in Truckee, take the exit for Highway 89-North. At the stoplight, turn left onto Highway 89-North and drive approximately one mile to Prosser Dam Road. Turn right and drive 4.5 miles to Prosser-Boca Road. Turn right and drive approximately four miles to the camp on the left.

Contact: Tahoe National Forest, Truckee Ranger District, 530/587-3558, fax 530/587-6914; California Land Management, 530/544-0426.

69 SCOTTS FLAT LAKE RECREATION AREA

🏊 🚣 🛥️ 🐎 🏕️ 👨‍🦽 🛒 🔼

Scenic rating: 8

near Grass Valley

Map 6.1, page 365

Scotts Flat Lake (at 3,100 feet in elevation) is shaped like a large teardrop and is one of the prettier lakes in the Sierra foothills, with 7.5 miles of shoreline circled by forest. Rules prohibiting personal watercraft keep the place sane. The camp is set on the lake's north shore, largely protected from spring winds and within short range of the marina and one of the lake's two boat launches. Trout fishing is good here in the spring and early summer. When the lake heats up, waterskiing and powerboating become more popular. Sailing and sailboarding are also good during afternoon winds.

Campsites, facilities: There are 187 sites for tents or RVs up to 35 feet (no hookups). Picnic tables and fire pits are provided. Restrooms with flush toilets and coin showers, coin laundry, and a dump station are provided. A general store, bait and tackle, boat rentals, boat ramp, and a playground are also available. Groups can be accommodated. Some facilities are wheelchair-accessible. Leashed pets are permitted.

Reservations, fees: Reservations are recommended in the summer at 530/265-5302. Sites are $23–28 per night, $6.25 per night for each additional vehicle, $3 per pet per night, with a 14-day maximum stay. Some credit cards accepted. Open year-round, weather permitting.

Directions: From Auburn, drive north on Highway 49 to Nevada City and the junction with Highway 20. Continue straight onto Highway 20 and drive five miles (east) to Scotts Flat Road. Turn right and drive four miles to the camp entrance road on the right (on the north shore of the lake).

Contact: Scotts Flat Lake Recreation Area, 530/265-5302 or 530/265-8861.

70 WHITE CLOUD

Scenic rating: 5

in Tahoe National Forest

Map 6.1, page 365

This camp is set along historic Pioneer Trail, which has turned into one of the top mountain-bike routes in the Sierra Nevada, easy and fast. The trail traces the route of the first wagon road opened by emigrants and gold seekers in 1850. It is best suited for mountain biking, with a lot of bikers taking the one-way downhill ride (with an extra car for a shuttle ride) from Bear Valley to Lone Grave. The Omega Overlook is the highlight, with dramatic views of granite cliffs and the Yuba River. The elevation is 4,200 feet.

Campsites, facilities: There are 46 sites for tents or RVs of any length (no hookups). Picnic tables and fire grills are provided. Drinking water, flush toilets, and vault toilets

are available. Some facilities are wheelchair-accessible. Leashed pets are permitted.

Reservations, fees: Reservations are accepted ($9 reservation fee) at 877/444-6777 or www.ReserveUSA.com. Sites are $18 per night, $5 per night for each additional vehicle. Open May through October, weather permitting.

Directions: From Sacramento, drive east on I-80 to Emigrant Gap. Take the off-ramp and then head north on the short connector road to Highway 20. Turn west on Highway 20 and drive about 15 miles to the campground entrance on the left.

Contact: Tahoe National Forest, Yuba River Ranger District, South, 530/265-4531, fax 530/478-6109; Big Bend Visitor's Center, 530/426-3609, fax 530/426-1744.

71 SKILLMAN FAMILY, EQUESTRIAN, AND GROUP CAMP

Scenic rating: 5

in Tahoe National Forest

Map 6.1, page 365

Skillman Group Camp is set at 4,400 feet, on a loop access road just off Highway 20, and historic Pioneer Trail runs right through it. (See the previous listing, *White Cloud*, for more information.)

Campsites, facilities: There are 16 sites for tents or RVs up to 25 feet (no hookups). This campground can also be used as a group camp for tents or RVs up to 25 feet and can accommodate up to 75 people. Picnic tables and fire grills are provided. Vault toilets and drinking water are available. Horse corrals, tie rails, troughs, and stock water are available. Leashed pets are permitted.

Reservations, fees: Reservations are not accepted for individual sites and are required for the group camp at 209/295-4512. Sites are $18 per night, double sites are $40 per night, and the group camp is $250 per night. Open May through October, weather permitting.

Directions: From Sacramento, drive east on I-80 past Emigrant Gap to Highway 20. Turn west on Highway 20 and drive 12 miles to the campground entrance on the left.

Contact: Tahoe National Forest, Yuba River Ranger District, South, 530/265-4531, fax 530/478-6109; Sierra Recreation Managers, 209/295-4512; Big Bend Visitor's Center, 530/426-3609, fax 530/426-1744.

72 LAKE SPAULDING

Scenic rating: 8

near Emigrant Gap

Map 6.1, page 365

Lake Spaulding is set at 5,000 feet in the Sierra Nevada, complete with huge boulders and a sprinkling of conifers. Its clear, pure, very cold water has startling effects on swimmers. The 772-acre lake is extremely pretty, with the Sierra granite backdrop looking as if it has been cut, chiseled, and smoothed. Just one problem: There's not much of a lake view from the campground, although there are a few sites with filtered views. In fact, the lake is about a quarter mile from the campground. The drive here is nearly a straight shot up I-80, so there will be plenty of company at the campground. All water sports are allowed, except personal watercraft. Fishing for kokanee salmon and rainbow trout is often good, as well as fishing for trout at the nearby South Fork Yuba River. There are many other lakes set in the mountain country to the immediate north that can make for excellent side trips, including Bowman, Weaver, and Faucherie Lakes.

Campsites, facilities: There are 25 sites (13 are walk-in) for tents or RVs up to 30 feet (no hookups) and an overflow area. Picnic tables and fire grills are provided. Drinking water, vault toilets, and picnic areas are available. A boat ramp is available nearby. Supplies are available in Nevada City. Some facilities are wheelchair-accessible. Leashed pets are permitted.

Reservations, fees: Reservations are not accepted. Sites are $18 per night, $5 per night for each additional vehicle, $1 per pet per night, $7 per day for boat launching. Open mid-May through September, weather permitting.

Directions: From Sacramento, drive east on I-80 past Emigrant Gap to Highway 20. Drive west on Highway 20 for 2.3 miles to Lake Spaulding Road. Turn right on Lake Spaulding Road and drive 0.5 mile to the campground.

Contact: PG&E Land Projects, 916/386-5164; Big Bend Visitor's Center, 530/426-3609, fax 530/426-1744, www.pge.com/recreation.

73 INDIAN SPRINGS

Scenic rating: 8

near the Yuba River in Tahoe National Forest

Map 6.1, page 365

The camp is easy to reach from I-80 yet is in a beautiful setting at 5,600 feet along the South Fork Yuba River. This is a gorgeous stream, running deep blue-green and pure through a granite setting, complete with giant boulders and beautiful pools. Trout fishing is fair. There is a small beach nearby where you can go swimming, though the water is cold. There are also several lakes in the vicinity.

Campsites, facilities: There are 35 sites for tents or RVs up to 26 feet (no hookups). Picnic tables and fire grills are provided. Drinking water and vault toilets are available. A grocery store and propane gas are available nearby. Some facilities are wheelchair-accessible. Leashed pets are permitted.

Reservations, fees: Reservations are not accepted. Sites are $18 per night, $5 per night for each additional vehicle. Open June through September, weather permitting.

Directions: From Sacramento, drive east on I-80 to Yuba Gap and continue for about three miles to the Eagle Lakes exit. Head north on Eagle Lakes Road for a mile to the campground on the left side of the road.

Contact: Tahoe National Forest, Yuba River Ranger District, South, 530/265-4531, fax 530/478-6109; Big Bend Visitor's Center, 530/426-3609, fax 530/426-1744.

7 4 WOODCHUCK

Scenic rating: 8

on Rattlesnake Creek in Tahoe National Forest

Map 6.1, page 365

This small camp is only a few miles from I-80, but it is quite obscure and little known to most travelers. It is set on Rattlesnake Creek at 6,300 feet in Tahoe National Forest, at the threshold of some great backcountry and four-wheel-drive roads that lead to many beautiful lakes. To explore, a map of Tahoe National Forest is a must.

Campsites, facilities: There are eight sites for tents. Picnic tables and fire grills are provided. Vault toilets are available. No drinking water is available. Garbage must be packed out. A grocery store and propane gas are available nearby. Leashed pets are permitted.

Reservations, fees: Reservations are not accepted. There is no fee for camping. Open June through October, weather permitting.

Directions: From Sacramento, drive east on I-80 to Yuba Gap and continue for about four miles to the Cisco Grove exit north. Take that exit, turn left on the frontage road, and drive a short distance to the stop sign and Rattlesnake Road/frontage road. Turn left on the frontage road/Rattlesnake Road and drive a short distance. Turn right and continue on Rattlesnake Road (gravel, steep, and curvy; trailers not recommended) and drive four miles to the campground on the right.

Contact: Tahoe National Forest, Yuba River Ranger District, South, 530/265-4531, fax 530/478-6109; Big Bend Visitor's Center, 530/426-3609, fax 530/426-1744.

7 5 LODGEPOLE

Scenic rating: 8

on Lake Valley Reservoir in Tahoe National Forest

Map 6.1, page 365

Lake Valley Reservoir is set at 5,786 feet and covers 300 acres. It is gorgeous when full, its shoreline sprinkled with conifers and boulders. The lake provides decent results for anglers, who have the best luck while trolling. A 15-mph speed limit prohibits waterskiing and personal watercraft, and that keeps the place quiet and peaceful. The camp is about a quarter mile from the lake's southwest shore and two miles from the boat ramp on the north shore. A trailhead from camp leads south up Monumental Ridge and to Monumental Creek (three miles, one-way) on the northwestern flank of Quartz Mountain (6,931 feet).

Campsites, facilities: There are 35 sites for tents or RVs up to 30 feet (no hookups). Picnic tables and fire grills are provided. Drinking water and vault toilets are available. A boat ramp is available nearby. Supplies can be obtained off I-80. Some facilities are wheelchair-accessible. Leashed pets are permitted.

Reservations, fees: Reservations are not accepted. Sites are $18 per night, $5 per night for each additional vehicle, $1 per pet per night. Open late May through September, weather permitting.

Directions: From I-80, take the Yuba Gap exit and drive south for 0.4 mile to Lake Valley Road. Turn right on Lake Valley Road and drive for 1.2 miles until the road forks. Bear right and continue for 1.5 miles to the campground entrance road to the right on another fork.

Contact: PG&E Land Projects, 916/386-5164, www.pge.com/recreation.

76 HAMPSHIRE ROCKS

🚶 🏊 ⛵ 🐕 ♿ 🚐 ⛺

Scenic rating: 8

on the Yuba River in Tahoe National Forest

Map 6.1, page 365

This camp sits along the South Fork of the Yuba River at 5,800 feet in elevation, with easy access off I-80 and a nearby Forest Service information center. Fishing for trout is fair. There are some swimming holes, but the water is often very cold. Nearby lakes that can provide side trips include Sterling and Fordyce Lakes (drive-to) to the north, and the Loch Leven Lakes (hike-to) to the south.

Campsites, facilities: There are 31 sites for tents or RVs up to 22 feet (no hookups) and four walk-in tent sites. Picnic tables and fire grills are provided. Drinking water and vault toilets are available. A convenience store, restaurant, and propane gas are available nearby. Some facilities are wheelchair-accessible. Leashed pets are permitted.

Reservations, fees: Reservations are accepted ($9 reservation fee) at 877/444-6777 or www .ReserveUSA.com. Sites are $18 per night, $5 per night for each additional vehicle. Open June through September, weather permitting.

Directions: From Sacramento, drive east on I-80 to Cisco Grove and continue for a mile to the Big Bend exit. Take that exit (remaining just south of the highway), then turn left on the frontage road and drive east for two miles to the campground on the right.

Contact: Tahoe National Forest, Yuba River Ranger District, South, 530/265-4531, fax 530/478-6109; Big Bend Visitor's Center, 530/426-3609, fax 530/426-1744.

77 KIDD LAKE GROUP CAMP

🏊 ⛵ ⛵ 🐕 ⛺

Scenic rating: 7

west of Truckee

Map 6.1, page 365

Kidd Lake is one of four lakes bunched in a series along the access road just south of I-80. It is set in the northern Sierra's high country, at 6,750 feet, and gets loaded with snow every winter. In late spring and early summer, always call ahead for conditions on the access road. The fishing is frustrating, consisting of a lot of tiny brook trout. Only car-top boats are permitted on Kidd Lake, with a primitive area available for launching. The camp is set just northeast of the lake, within walking distance of the shore. It features 10 small group sites that can accommodate 100 people when reserved together.

Campsites, facilities: There are 10 group tent sites for up to 10 people each. Picnic tables and fire grills are provided. Drinking water and vault toilets are available. Supplies are available in Truckee. Leashed pets are permitted.

Reservations, fees: Reservations are required at 916/386-5164 and must be reserved in increments of at least two sites. Sites are $20 per night, $1 per pet per night. Open June to mid-September, weather permitting.

Directions: From Sacramento, drive east on I-80 toward Truckee. Take the Norden/Soda Springs exit, drive a short distance, turn south on Soda Springs Road, and drive 0.8 mile to Pahatsi Road. Turn right and drive two miles. When the road forks, bear right and drive a mile to the campground entrance road on the left.

Contact: PG&E Land Projects, 916/386-5164, www.pge.com/recreation.

78 DONNER MEMORIAL STATE PARK

🧍 🚴 🏊 🛶 🛥 🐴 ♿ 🚐 ⛺

Scenic rating: 9

on Donner Lake

Map 6.1, page 365

The remarkable beauty of Donner Lake often evokes a deep, heartfelt response. Nearly everybody passing by from nearby I-80 has looked down and seen it. The lake is big, three miles long and 0.75 mile wide, gemlike blue, and set near the Sierra crest at 5,900 feet. The area is well developed, with a number of cabins and access roads, and this state park is the feature destination. Along the southeastern end of the lake, it is extremely pretty, but the campsites are set in forest, not along the lake. Fishing is good here (typically only in the early morning), trolling for kokanee salmon or rainbow trout, with big Mackinaw and brown trout providing wild cards. The park features more than three miles of frontage of Donner Creek and Donner Lake, with 2.5 miles of hiking trails. Donner Lake itself has 7.5 miles of shoreline. The lake is open to all water sports, but there is no boat launch at the park; a public ramp is available in the northwest corner of the lake. Campers get free admission to Emigrant Trail Museum.

Campsites, facilities: There are 150 sites for tents or RVs up to 28 feet (no hookups) and trailers up to 24 feet, and two hike-in/bike-in sites. Picnic tables and fire pits are provided. Drinking water, coin showers, vault toilets, picnic area, and interpretive trail are available. Supplies are available about one mile away in Truckee. Some facilities are wheelchair-accessible. Leashed pets are permitted.

Reservations, fees: Reservations are accepted ($7.50 reservation fee) at 800/444-PARK (800/444-7275) or www.reserveamerica.com. Sites are $25 per night, $6 per night for each additional vehicle, $3 per person per night for hike-in/bike-in sites. Open late May to mid-September, weather permitting.

Directions: From Auburn, drive east on I-80

just past Donner Lake to the Donner State Park exit. Take that exit and turn south (right) on Donner Pass Road and drive 0.5 mile to the park entrance on the left at the southeast end of the lake.

Contact: Donner Memorial State Park, 530/582-7892 or 530/582-7894. For boat-launching info, call 530/582-7720, www.parks.ca.gov.

79 COACHLAND RV PARK

🧍 🛶 🏊 🐴 👫 ♿ 🚐 🚐

Scenic rating: 6

in Truckee

Map 6.1, page 365

Truckee is the gateway to recreation at North Tahoe. Within minutes are Donner Lake, Prosser Creek Reservoir, Boca Reservoir, Stampede Lake, the Truckee River, and ski resorts. Squaw Valley is a short distance to the south off Highway 89, and Northstar is just off Highway 267. The park is set in a wooded area near I-80, providing easy access. The downtown Truckee area (with restaurants) is a half mile away. This is one of the few parks in the area that is open year-round. The elevation is 6,000 feet. One problem: Only 25 of the 131 sites are available for overnighters, with the rest taken by long-term rentals.

Campsites, facilities: There are 131 pull-through sites with full hookups (30 and 50 amps) for trailers or RVs up to 40 feet. No tents. Picnic tables are provided. Restrooms with showers, coin laundry, cable TV, modem access, Wi-Fi, playground, horseshoes, athletic field, tetherball, clubhouse, and propane are available. Some facilities are wheelchair-accessible. Leashed pets are permitted.

Reservations, fees: Reservations are recommended. Sites are $39 per night, $1.50–3 per person per night for more than two people, $2 per night for each additional vehicle. Monthly rates available. Major credit cards accepted. Open year-round.

Directions: From eastbound I-80 in Truckee,

take the 188A exit to Donner Pass Road. Turn north on Donner Pass Road and drive one block to Pioneer Trail. Turn left and drive a short distance to the park at 10100 Pioneer Trail on the left side of the road.

From westbound I-80 in Truckee, take the 188 exit to Highway 89. Turn right on Highway 89 and drive north one block to Donner Pass Road. Turn left and drive one block to Pioneer Trail. Turn right and continue to the park.

Contact: Coachland RV Park, 530/587-3071, fax 530/587-6976, www.coachlandrvpark .com.

80 MARTIS CREEK LAKE
🏊 🎣 🚣 🐕 ♿ 🚐 🅰

Scenic rating: 7

near Truckee

Map 6.1, page 365

If only this lake weren't so often windy in the afternoon, it would be heaven to fly fishers in float tubes. To some it's heaven anyway, with Lahontan cutthroat trout growing to 25 inches here. This is a special catch-and-release fishery where anglers are permitted to use only artificial lures with single, barbless hooks. The setting is somewhat sparse and open—a small lake, 70 acres, on the eastern edge of the Martis Valley. No motors are permitted at the lake, making it ideal (when the wind is down) for float tubes or prams. Sailing, sailboarding, and swimming are permitted. There is no boat launch, but small boats can be hand-launched. The lake level can fluctuate daily, which along with the wind, can be frustrating for those who show up expecting automatic perfection; that just isn't the way it is out there. At times, the lake level can even be very low. The elevation is 5,800 feet.

Campsites, facilities: There are 25 sites for tents or RVs up to 30 feet (no hookups). Some sites are pull-through. Picnic tables and fire grills are provided. Drinking water, vault toilets, tent pads, and pay phones are available. Some facilities are wheelchair-accessible.

Supplies are available six minutes away in Truckee. Leashed pets are permitted.

Reservations, fees: Reservations accepted for the wheelchair-accessible sites only at 530/587-8113. Sites are $12 per night. Open May to mid-November, weather permitting.

Directions: From Truckee, drive south on Highway 267 for about three miles (past the airport) to the lake entrance road on the left. Turn left and drive another 2.5 miles to the campground at the end of the road.

Contact: U.S. Army Corps of Engineers, Sacramento District, 530/587-8113, fax 530/432-6418.

81 NORTH FORK
🚶 🏊 🎣 🐕 🚐 🅰

Scenic rating: 7

on the North Fork of the American River in Tahoe National Forest

Map 6.1, page 365

This is gold-mining country, and this camp is set along the Little North Fork of the North Fork American River at 4,400 feet in elevation, where you might still find a few magic gold flecks. Unfortunately, they are probably fool's gold, not the real stuff. This feeder stream is small and pretty, and the camp is fairly remote and overlooked by most. It is set on the edge of a network of backcountry Forest Service roads. To explore them, a map of Tahoe National Forest is a must.

Campsites, facilities: There are 17 sites for tents or RVs up to 16 feet (no hookups). Picnic tables and fire grills are provided. Drinking water and vault toilets are available. Supplies are available at Emigrant Gap, Cisco Grove, and Soda Springs. Leashed pets are permitted.

Reservations, fees: Reservations are not accepted. Sites are $18 per night, $5 per night for each additional vehicle. Open June through October, weather permitting.

Directions: From Sacramento, drive east on I-80 to the Emigrant Gap exit. Take that exit and drive south a short distance to Texas

Hill Road/Forest Road 19. Turn right and drive about seven miles to the camp on the right.

Contact: Tahoe National Forest, Yuba River Ranger District, South, 530/265-4531, fax 530/478-6109; Big Bend Visitor's Center, 530/426-3609, fax 530/426-1744.

82 TUNNEL MILL GROUP CAMP

Scenic rating: 7

on the North Fork of the American River in Tahoe National Forest

Map 6.1, page 365

This is a good spot for a Boy or Girl Scout camp-out. It's a rustic, quiet group camp set all by itself along the (take a deep breath) East Fork of the North Fork of the North Fork of the American River (whew). (See *North Fork*, previous listing, for more recreation information.) The elevation is 4,400 feet.

Campsites, facilities: There are two group sites for tents or RVs up to 40 feet (no hook-ups) that can accommodate up to 30 people each. Picnic tables and fire grills are provided. Vault toilets are available. No drinking water is available. Supplies are available at the Nyack exit near Emigrant Gap. Leashed pets are permitted.

Reservations, fees: Reservations are required ($9 reservation fee) at 877/444-6777 or www.ReserveUSA.com. The camp is $90 per night. Open June through October, weather permitting.

Directions: From Sacramento, drive east on I-80 to the Emigrant Gap exit. Drive south for a short distance to Texas Hill Road/Forest Road 19. Turn right and drive about nine miles to the campground on the right side of the road.

Contact: Tahoe National Forest, Yuba River Ranger District, South, 530/265-4531, fax 530/478-6109; Big Bend Visitor's Center, 530/426-3609, fax 530/426-1744.

83 GRANITE FLAT

Scenic rating: 6

on the Truckee River in Tahoe National Forest

Map 6.1, page 365

This camp is set along the Truckee River at 5,800 feet. The area is known for a ton of traffic on adjacent Highway 89, as well as decent trout fishing and, in the spring and early summer, rafting. It is about a 15-minute drive to Squaw Valley or Lake Tahoe. A bike route is also available along the Truckee River out of Tahoe City.

Campsites, facilities: There are 68 sites for tents or RVs up to 40 feet (no hookups) and seven walk-in tent sites. Picnic tables and fire grills are provided. Drinking water and vault toilets are available. Some facilities are wheelchair-accessible. Leashed pets are permitted.

Reservations, fees: Reservations are accepted ($9 reservation fee) at 877/444-6777 or www.ReserveUSA.com. Sites are $15 per night, $5 per night for each additional vehicle. Open May through October, weather permitting.

Directions: From Truckee, drive south on Highway 89 for 1.5 miles to the campground entrance on the left.

Contact: Tahoe National Forest, Truckee Ranger District, 530/587-3558, fax 530/587-6914; California Land Management, 530/544-0426.

84 GOOSE MEADOWS

Scenic rating: 6

on the Truckee River in Tahoe National Forest

Map 6.1, page 365

There are three campgrounds set along the Truckee River off Highway 89 between Truckee and Tahoe City. Goose Meadows provides good fishing access with decent prospects, despite the high number of vehicles roaring past on the adjacent highway. This stretch of river is also popular for rafting. The elevation is 5,800 feet.

Campsites, facilities: There are 24 sites for tents or RVs up to 30 feet (no hookups). Picnic tables and fire grills are provided. Drinking water and vault toilets are available. Supplies are available in Truckee and Tahoe City. Some facilities are wheelchair-accessible. Leashed pets are permitted.

Reservations, fees: Reservations are accepted ($9 reservation fee) at 877/444-6777 or www.ReserveUSA.com. Sites are $13 per night, $5 per night for each additional vehicle. Open May through October, weather permitting.

Directions: From Truckee, drive south on Highway 89 for four miles to the campground entrance on the left (river) side of the highway.

Contact: Tahoe National Forest, Truckee Ranger District, 530/587-3558, fax 530/587-6914; California Land Management, 530/544-0426.

85 SILVER CREEK

Scenic rating: 8

on the Truckee River in Tahoe National Forest

Map 6.1, page 365

This pretty campground is set near where Silver Creek enters the Truckee River. The trout fishing is often good in this area. This is one of three campgrounds along Highway 89 and the Truckee River, between Truckee and Tahoe City. The elevation is 6,000 feet.

Campsites, facilities: There are 21 sites for tents or RVs up to 40 feet (no hookups) and seven walk-in tent sites. Picnic tables and fire grills are provided. Drinking water and vault toilets are available. Supplies are available in Truckee and Tahoe City. Some facilities are wheelchair-accessible. Leashed pets are permitted.

Reservations, fees: Reservations are

accepted ($9 reservation fee) at 877/444-6777 or www.ReserveUSA.com. Sites are $13 per night, $5 per night for each additional vehicle. Open June through September, weather permitting.

Directions: From Truckee, drive south on Highway 89 for six miles to the campground entrance on the river side of the highway.

Contact: Tahoe National Forest, Truckee Ranger District, 530/587-3558, fax 530/587-6914; California Land Management, 530/544-0426.

86 SANDY BEACH CAMPGROUND

Scenic rating: 8

on Lake Tahoe

Map 6.1, page 365

Sandy Beach Campground is set at 6,200 feet near the northwest shore of Lake Tahoe. A nearby boat ramp provides access to one of the better fishing areas of the lake for Mackinaw trout. A public beach is across the road. But the water in Tahoe is always cold, and though a lot of people will get suntans on beaches next to the lake, swimmers need to be members of the Polar Bear Club. A short drive to the east will take you past the town of Kings Beach and into Nevada, where there are some small casinos near the shore of Crystal Bay. Note that some sites fill up for the summer season.

Campsites, facilities: There are 27 sites with full or partial hookups (30 amps) for tents or RVs up to 40 feet. Some sites are pull-through. Picnic tables, barbecues, and fire rings are provided. Drinking water, restrooms with showers and flush toilets, a dump station, and coin laundry are available. A free public boat ramp is available half a block away. A grocery store and propane gas are available nearby. Leashed pets are permitted.

Reservations, fees: Reservations are recommended. Sites are $20–25 per night for up to six people with two vehicles, two-dog limit. For weeklong stays, seventh night is free. Some credit cards accepted. Open May through October.

Directions: From Truckee, drive south on Highway 267 to Highway 28. Turn right and drive one mile to the park on the right side of the road (entrance well signed).

Contact: Sandy Beach Campground, 530/546-7682.

87 TAHOE STATE RECREATION AREA

Scenic rating: 9

on Lake Tahoe

Map 6.1, page 365

This is a popular summer-only campground at the north shore of Lake Tahoe. The Tahoe State Recreation Area covers a large area just west of Highway 28 near Tahoe City. There are opportunities for hiking and horseback riding nearby (though not right at the park). It is also near shopping, restaurants, and unfortunately, traffic jams in Tahoe City. A boat ramp is two miles to the northwest at nearby Lake Forest, and bike rentals are available in Tahoe City for rides along Highway 89 near the shore of the lake. For a more secluded site nearby at Tahoe, get reservations instead for Sugar Pine Point State Park, 11 miles south on Highway 89.

Campsites, facilities: There are 25 sites for tents or RVs up to 27 feet (no hookups) and trailers up to 24 feet. Picnic tables, food lockers, barbecues, and fire pits are provided. Drinking water, vault toilets, and coin showers are available. Firewood, other supplies, and a coin laundry are available within walking distance. Leashed pets are permitted.

Reservations, fees: Reservations are accepted ($7.50 reservation fee) at 800/444-PARK (800/444-7275) or www.reserveamerica.com. Sites are $25 per night, $6 per night for each

additional vehicle. Open May through October, weather permitting.

Directions: From Truckee, drive south on Highway 89 through Tahoe City. Turn north on Highway 28 and drive 0.9 mile to the campground entrance on the right side of the road.

Contact: Tahoe State Recreation Area, 530/583-3074; Sierra District, 530/525-7232, www.parks.ca.gov.

88 LAKE FOREST CAMPGROUND

Scenic rating: 8

on Lake Tahoe

Map 6.1, page 365

The north shore of Lake Tahoe provides beautiful lookouts and excellent boating access. The latter is a highlight of this camp, with a boat ramp nearby. From here it is a short cruise to Dollar Point and around the corner north to Carnelian Bay, one of the better stretches of water for trout fishing. The elevation is 6,200 feet. There is a 10-day camping limit.

Campsites, facilities: There are 20 sites for tents or RVs up to 20 feet (no hookups). Picnic tables and fire grills are provided. Drinking water and vault toilets are available. Some facilities are wheelchair-accessible. A grocery store, coin laundry, and propane gas are available within four miles. Leashed pets are permitted.

Reservations, fees: Reservations are not accepted. Sites are $15 per night. Open April through October, weather permitting.

Directions: From Truckee, drive south on Highway 89 through Tahoe City to Highway 28. Bear north on Highway 28 and drive four miles to the campground entrance road (Lake Forest Road) on the right.

Contact: Tahoe City Public Utility District, Parks and Recreation, 530/583-3796, ext. 7, fax 530/583-8452.

89 ORCHARD SPRINGS RESORT

Scenic rating: 7

on Rollins Lake

Map 6.1, page 365

Orchard Springs Resort is set on the shore of Rollins Lake among pine, oak, and cedar trees in the Sierra Nevada foothills. The summer heat makes the lake excellent for waterskiing, boating, and swimming. Spring and fall are great for trout and bass fishing.

Campsites, facilities: There are 90 tent sites and 13 sites with full hookups (30 amps) for tents or RVs up to 40 feet. Two sites are pull-through. Two cabins and four camping cabins are also available. Picnic tables, fire rings, and barbecues are provided. Drinking water, restrooms with flush toilets and showers, launch ramp, boat rentals, slips, bait and tackle, swimming beach, group picnic area, lakeview restaurant, and a convenience store are available. Some facilities are wheelchair-accessible. Leashed pets are permitted.

Reservations, fees: Reservations are accepted. Sites are $29–39 per night, $15 per night for each additional vehicle unless towed, $5.75 per boat per night, $3 per pet per night. Some credit cards accepted. Open year-round.

Directions: From Auburn, drive northeast on I-80 for about 20 miles to the Colfax/Grass Valley exit. Take that exit and loop back over the freeway to the stop sign. Turn right and drive a short distance to Highway 174. Turn right and drive north on Highway 174 (a winding, two-lane road) for 3.7 miles (bear left at Giovanni's Restaurant) to Orchard Springs Road. Turn right on Orchard Springs Road and drive 0.5 mile to the road's end. Turn right at the gatehouse and continue to the campground.

Contact: Orchard Springs Resort, 530/346-2212 or 866/624-7497, www.osresort.com.

90 PENINSULA CAMPING AND BOATING RESORT

Scenic rating: 8

on Rollins Lake

Map 6.1, page 365

Peninsula Campground is set on a point that extends into Rollins Lake, flanked on each side by two sprawling lake arms. The resort has 280 acres and 1.5 miles of lake frontage. A bonus is that you can boat directly from some of the lakefront sites. If you like boating, waterskiing, or swimming, you'll definitely like this place in the summer. All water sports are allowed. This is a family-oriented campground with lots of youngsters on summer vacation. Fishing is available for rainbow and brown trout, small- and largemouth bass, perch, crappie, and catfish.

Campsites, facilities: There are 78 sites for tents or RVs up to 40 feet (no hookups), and three group sites for 16–40 people. Three cabins are also available. Picnic tables and fire pits are provided. Restrooms with flush toilets and showers, drinking water, modem access, Wi-Fi, dump station, boat rentals (fishing boats, patio boats, canoes, and kayaks), boat ramp, boat storage, limited fishing licenses, fish-cleaning station, swimming beach, horseshoes, volleyball, and a convenience store are available. Marine gas is available on the lake. Leashed pets are permitted, but call for current status.

Reservations, fees: Reservations are accepted by phone or website. Sites are $26–30 per night, $10 per night for each additional vehicle, $65–150 per night for a group site, $3 per pet per night. Maximum 14-day stay. Some credit cards accepted. Open mid-April to September.

Directions: From Auburn, drive northeast on I-80 for about 20 miles to the Colfax/Grass Valley exit. Take that exit and loop back over the freeway to the stop sign. Turn right and drive a short distance to Highway 174. Turn right and drive north on Highway 174 (a winding, two-lane road) for eight miles to You Bet Road. Turn right and drive 4.3 miles (turning right again to stay on You Bet Road), and continue another 3.1 miles to the campground entrance at the end of the road.

Contact: Peninsula Camping and Boating Resort, 530/477-9413 or 866/4MY-CAMP (866/469-2267), www.penresort.com.

91 ROBINSON FLAT

Scenic rating: 5

near French Meadows Reservoir in Tahoe National Forest

Map 6.1, page 365

This camp is set at 6,800 feet in remote Tahoe National Forest, on the eastern flank of Duncan Peak (7,116 feet), with a two-mile drive south to Duncan Peak Lookout (7,182 feet). A trail out of camp follows along a small stream, a fork to Duncan Creek, in Little Robinsons Valley. French Meadows Reservoir is 15 miles southeast. An equestrian camp with seven sites is also available.

Campsites, facilities: There are seven sites for tents or RVs up to 25 feet, plus an equestrian camp with seven sites for tents or RVs up to 45 feet. No hookups. Picnic tables and fire grills are provided. Drinking water and vault toilets are available. Garbage must be packed out. Supplies are available in Foresthill. Some facilities are wheelchair-accessible. Leashed pets are permitted.

Reservations, fees: Reservations are not accepted. There is no fee for camping. Open mid-May through October, weather permitting.

Directions: From Sacramento, drive east on I-80 to the north end of Auburn and the Foresthill Road exit. Take that exit and drive east to Foresthill (the road name changes to Foresthill Divide Road) and continue northeast (the road is narrow and curvy) for 27 miles to the junction with County Road 43. The campground is at the junction.

Contact: Tahoe National Forest, American River Ranger District, Foresthill Ranger Station, 530/367-2224, fax 530/367-2992.

92 TALBOT

Scenic rating: 7

on the Middle Fork of the American River in Tahoe National Forest

Map 6.1, page 365

Talbot camp is set at 5,600 feet along the Middle Fork of the American River, primarily used as a trailhead camp for backpackers heading into the Granite Chief Wilderness. The trail is routed along the Middle Fork American River, turning south into Picayune Valley, flanked by Needle Peak (8,971 feet), Granite Chief (9,886 feet), and Squaw Peak to the east, then beyond to connect with the Pacific Crest Trail. The nearby trailhead has stock trailer parking. Hitching rails are available at the trailhead.

Campsites, facilities: There are five tent sites. Picnic tables and fire grills are provided. Vault toilets are available. No drinking water is available. Garbage must be packed out. Supplies are available in Foresthill. The camp is within a state game refuge and no firearms are permitted. Leashed pets are permitted.

Reservations, fees: Reservations are not accepted. There is no fee for camping. Open June through October, weather permitting.

Directions: From Sacramento, drive east on I-80 to the north end of Auburn and the Foresthill Road exit. Take that exit and drive east to Foresthill and Mosquito Ridge Road (Forest Road 96). Turn right (east) and drive 40 miles (curvy) to Anderson Dam and to a junction. Turn left (still Mosquito Ridge Road) and then continue along the southern shoreline of French Meadows Reservoir for four miles (road turns into dirt) and continue four more miles to the campground.

Contact: Tahoe National Forest, American River Ranger District, Foresthill Ranger Station, 530/367-2224, fax 530/367-2992.

93 AHART

Scenic rating: 7

near French Meadows Reservoir in Tahoe National Forest

Map 6.1, page 365

This camp is a mile north of French Meadows Reservoir near where the Middle Fork of the American River enters the lake. It is on the Middle Fork and is primarily used for campers who would rather camp near this river than French Meadows Reservoir. Note: This is bear country in the summer.

Campsites, facilities: There are 12 sites for tents or RVs up to 40 feet (no hookups). Picnic tables and fire grills are provided. Vault toilets are available. No drinking water is available. Supplies are available in Foresthill. Some facilities are wheelchair-accessible. Leashed pets are permitted.

Reservations, fees: Reservations are not accepted. Sites are $16 per night, $5 per night for each additional vehicle. Open late May through October, weather permitting.

Directions: From Sacramento, drive east on I-80 to the north end of Auburn and the Foresthill Road exit. Take that exit and drive east to Foresthill and Mosquito Ridge Road (Forest Road 96). Turn right (east) and drive 40 miles (curvy) to Anderson Dam and to a junction. Turn left (still Mosquito Ridge Road) and then continue along the southern shoreline of French Meadows Reservoir for seven miles.

Contact: Tahoe National Forest, American River Ranger District, Foresthill Ranger Station, 530/367-2224, fax 530/367-2992.

94 GATES GROUP CAMP

Scenic rating: 7

on the North Fork of the American River in Tahoe National Forest

Map 6.1, page 365

This group camp is well secluded along the North Fork American River, just upstream from where it pours into French Meadows Reservoir. (For recreation options, see the *French Meadows* and *Lewis* listings in this chapter, and the next listing, *Coyote Group Camp.*)

Campsites, facilities: There are three group sites for tents or RVs of any length (no hookups) that can accommodate 25–75 people each. Picnic tables and fire grills are provided. Drinking water, vault toilets, central parking, and a campfire circle are available. Obtain supplies in Foresthill. Leashed pets are permitted.

Reservations, fees: Reservations are required ($9 reservation fee) at 877/444-6777 or www.ReserveUSA.com. Sites are $65–90 per night. Open mid-May through October, weather permitting.

Directions: From Sacramento, drive east on I-80 to the north end of Auburn and the Foresthill Road exit. Take that exit and drive east to Foresthill and Mosquito Ridge Road (Forest Road 96). Turn right (east) and drive 40 miles (curvy) to Anderson Dam and to a junction. Turn left (still Mosquito Ridge Road) and continue along the southern shoreline of French Meadows Reservoir for five miles to a fork at the head of the lake. Bear left at the fork (Forest Road 68) and drive a mile to the camp at the end of the road.

Contact: Tahoe National Forest, American River Ranger District, Foresthill Ranger Station, 530/367-2224, fax 530/367-2992.

95 COYOTE GROUP CAMP

👥 🏊 🛶 🎣 🐕 🚐 ⛺

Scenic rating: 6

on French Meadows Reservoir in Tahoe
National Forest

Map 6.1, page 365

This group camp is set right at the head of
French Meadows Reservoir, at 5,300 feet in
elevation. A boat ramp is two miles to the
south, just past Lewis on the lake's north
shore. (For recreation options, see the *Poppy
Hike-In/Boat-In* and *French Meadows* listings
in this chapter.)

Campsites, facilities: There are three group
sites for tents or RVs of any length (no hookups) that can accommodate 25–50 people
each. Picnic tables and fire grills are provided.
Drinking water and vault toilets are available.
A campfire circle and central parking area
are also available. Supplies are available in
Foresthill. Leashed pets are permitted.

Reservations, fees: Reservations are required
($9 reservation fee) at 877/444-6777 or www
.ReserveUSA.com. Sites are $65–90 per night.
Open mid-May through October.

Directions: From Sacramento, drive east on
I-80 to the north end of Auburn and the
Foresthill Road exit. Take that exit and drive
east to Foresthill and Mosquito Ridge Road
(Forest Road 96). Turn right (east) and drive
40 miles (curvy) to Anderson Dam and to
a junction. Turn left (still Mosquito Ridge
Road) and then continue along the southern
shoreline of French Meadows Reservoir for
five miles to a fork at the head of the lake.
Bear left at the fork and drive 0.5 mile to the
camp on the left side of the road.

Contact: Tahoe National Forest, American
River Ranger District, Foresthill Ranger
Station, 530/367-2224, fax 530/367-2992.

96 LEWIS

👥 🏊 🛶 🎣 🐕 ♿ 🚐 ⛺

Scenic rating: 7

on French Meadows Reservoir in Tahoe
National Forest

Map 6.1, page 365

This camp is not right at lakeside but is just
across the road from French Meadows Reservoir. It is still quite pretty, set along a feeder
creek near the lake's northwest shore. A boat
ramp is available only 0.5 mile to the south,
and the adjacent McGuire boat ramp area
has a trailhead that is routed along the lake's
northern shoreline. This lake is big (2,000
acres) and pretty, created by a dam on the
Middle Fork American River, with good fishing for rainbow trout.

Campsites, facilities: There are 40 sites for
tents or RVs up to 45 feet (no hookups). Picnic
tables and fire grills are provided. Drinking
water and vault toilets are available. A concrete
boat ramp is nearby. Supplies are available
in Foresthill. Some facilities are wheelchair-
accessible. Leashed pets are permitted.

Reservations, fees: Reservations are accepted
($9 reservation fee) at 877/444-6777 or www
.ReserveUSA.com. Sites are $16 per night, $5
per night for each additional vehicle. Open
mid-May to early September.

Directions: From Sacramento, drive east on
I-80 to the north end of Auburn and the Foresthill Road exit. Take that exit and drive east
to Foresthill and Mosquito Ridge Road (Forest
Road 96). Turn right (east) and drive 40 miles
(curvy) to Anderson Dam and to a junction.
Turn left (still Mosquito Ridge Road) and
then continue along the southern shoreline
of French Meadows Reservoir for five miles
to a fork at the head of the lake. Bear left at
the fork and drive 0.5 mile to the camp on the
right side of the road.

Contact: Tahoe National Forest, American
River Ranger District, Foresthill Ranger Station, 530/367-2224, fax 530/367-2992.

97 POPPY HIKE-IN/BOAT-IN
🥾 ⛵ 🛶 🚤 🐕 5% ⛰

Scenic rating: 10

on French Meadows Reservoir in Tahoe
National Forest

Map 6.1, page 365

This camp is on the north side of French
Meadows Reservoir, about midway along
the lake's shore. It can be reached only by
boat or on foot, supplying a great degree of
privacy compared to the other camps on this
lake. A trail that is routed along the north
shore of the reservoir runs right through the
camp, providing two different trailhead access points, as well as a good side-trip hike.
The lake is quite big, covering nearly 2,000
acres when full, at 5,300 feet in elevation
on a dammed-up section of the Middle Fork
American River. It is stocked with rainbow
trout but also has prime habitat for brown
trout, and big ones are sometimes caught
by surprise.

Campsites, facilities: There are 12 tent sites,
accessible by boat or by a mile-long foot trail
from McGuire boat ramp. Picnic tables and
fire grills are provided. Vault toilets are available. No drinking water is available. Garbage
must be packed out. Supplies are available in
Foresthill. Leashed pets are permitted.

Reservations, fees: Reservations are not
accepted. There is no fee for camping.
Open May through October, weather
permitting.

Directions: From Sacramento, drive east
on I-80 to the north end of Auburn and
the Foresthill Road exit. Take that exit
and drive east to Foresthill and Mosquito
Ridge Road (Forest Road 96). Turn right
(east) and drive 40 miles (curvy) to French
Meadows Reservoir Dam and to a junction.
Turn left (still Mosquito Ridge Road) and
continue for three miles to the lake and
campground.

Contact: Tahoe National Forest, American
River Ranger District, Foresthill Ranger Station, 530/367-2224, fax 530/367-2992.

98 FRENCH MEADOWS
🥾 ⛵ 🛶 🚤 🐕 ♿ 🚐 ⛰

Scenic rating: 7

on French Meadows Reservoir in Tahoe
National Forest

Map 6.1, page 365

The nearby boat launch makes this the choice
for boating campers. The camp is on French
Meadows Reservoir at 5,300 feet. It is set
on the lake's southern shore, with the boat
ramp about a mile to the south (you'll see
the entrance road on the way in). This is a
big lake set in remote Tahoe National Forest
in the North Fork American River Canyon
with good trout fishing. All water sports are
allowed. The lake level often drops in late
summer, and then a lot of stumps and boulders
start poking through the lake surface. This
creates navigational hazards for boaters and
water skiers, but it also makes it easier for the
anglers to know where to find the fish. If the
fish don't bite here, boaters should make the
nearby side trip to pretty Hell Hole Reservoir
to the south.

Campsites, facilities: There are 75 sites
for tents or RVs up to 45 feet (no hookups).
Picnic tables and fire grills are provided. Drinking water and vault toilets are
available. Some facilities are wheelchair-
accessible. A concrete boat ramp is nearby.
Supplies are available in Foresthill. Leashed
pets are permitted.

Reservations, fees: Reservations are available
($9 reservation fee) at 877/444-6777 or www
.ReserveUSA.com. Sites are $16 per night,
$5 per night for each additional vehicle.
Open late May through October, weather
permitting.

Directions: From Sacramento, drive east on
I-80 to the north end of Auburn and the Foresthill Road exit. Take that exit and drive east
to Foresthill and Mosquito Ridge Road (Forest
Road 96). Turn right (east) and drive 40 miles
(curvy) to Anderson Dam and to a junction.
Turn left (still Mosquito Ridge Road) and
then continue along the southern shoreline

of French Meadows Reservoir for four miles to the campground.
Contact: Tahoe National Forest, American River Ranger District, Foresthill Ranger Station, 530/367-2224, fax 530/367-2992.

99 WILLIAM KENT

Scenic rating: 8

near Lake Tahoe in the Lake Tahoe Basin

Map 6.1, page 365

William Kent camp is a little pocket of peace set near the busy traffic of Highway 89 on the western shore corridor. It is on the west side of the highway, meaning visitors have to cross the highway to get lakeside access. The elevation is 6,300 feet, and the camp is wooded with primarily lodgepole pines. The drive here is awesome or ominous, depending on how you look at it, with the view of incredible Lake Tahoe to the east, the third-deepest blue lake in North America and the 10th-deepest lake in the world. But you often have a lot of time to look at it, since traffic rarely moves quickly.
Campsites, facilities: There are 55 tent sites and 36 sites for RVs up to 40 feet (no hookups). Picnic tables, food lockers, and fire grills are provided. Drinking water, flush toilets, and a dump station are available. A grocery store, coin laundry, and propane gas are available nearby. Some facilities are wheelchair-accessible. Leashed pets are permitted.
Reservations, fees: Reservations are accepted ($9 reservation fee) at 877/444-6777 or www.ReserveUSA.com. Sites are $16 per night, $5 per night for each additional vehicle. Open late May to mid-October, weather permitting.
Directions: From Truckee, drive south on Highway 89 to Tahoe City. Turn south on Highway 89 and drive three miles to the campground entrance on the right side of the road.
Contact: Lake Tahoe Basin Management Unit, 530/543-2600, fax 530/543-2693; Taylor

Creek Visitor Center, 530/543-2674; California Land Management, 530/583-3642.

100 KASPIAN

Scenic rating: 7

on Lake Tahoe

Map 6.1, page 365

As gorgeous and as huge as Lake Tahoe is, there are relatively few camps or even restaurants with lakeside settings. This is one of the few. Kaspian is set along the west shore of the lake at 6,235 feet in elevation, near the little town of Tahoe Pines. A Forest Service road (03) is available adjacent to the camp on the west side of Highway 89, routed west into national forest (becoming quite rough) to a trailhead. From there you can hike up to Barker Peak (8,166 feet) for incredible views of Lake Tahoe, as well as access to the Pacific Crest Trail.
Campsites, facilities: There are nine walk-in sites for tents only. RVs up to 20 feet may use the parking lot on a space-available basis. Picnic tables and fire grills are provided. Drinking water, food lockers, and flush toilets are available. A grocery store, coin laundry, and propane gas are available nearby. Leashed pets are permitted.
Reservations, fees: Reservations are accepted ($9 reservation fee) at 877/444-6777 or www.ReserveUSA.com. Sites are $15 per night, $5 per night for each additional vehicle. Open May through September, weather permitting.
Directions: From Truckee, drive south on Highway 89 to Tahoe City. Turn south on Highway 89 and drive four miles to the campground (signed) on the west side of the road. The tent sites require a walk-in of 50–100 feet.
Contact: Lake Tahoe Basin Management Unit, 530/543-2600, fax 530/543-2693; Taylor Creek Visitor Center, 530/543-2674; California Land Management, 530/583-3642.

101 GIANT GAP

🚶 🏊 🚤 �- 🏕 ♿ 🚐 ⛺

Scenic rating: 7

on Sugar Pine Reservoir in Tahoe National
Forest

Map 6.1, page 365

This is a lakeside spot along the western
shore of Sugar Pine Reservoir at 4,000 feet
in elevation in Tahoe National Forest. For
boaters, there is a ramp on the south shore.
Note that a 10-mph speed limit is the law,
making this lake ideal for anglers in search of
quiet water. Other recreation notes: There's
a little less than a mile of paved trail, which
goes through the day-use area. Big Reservoir (also known as Morning Star Lake), five
miles to the east, is the only other lake in the
region and also has a campground. The trout
and bass fishing at Sugar Pine is fair—not
usually great, not usually bad. Swimming
is allowed; kayaking and canoeing are also
popular.
Campsites, facilities: There are 30 sites
for tents or RVs of any length (no hookups).
Picnic tables and fire grills are provided. Drinking water and vault toilets are
available. Some facilities are wheelchair-accessible. A dump station and boat ramp
are available on the south shore. Supplies
can be obtained in Foresthill. Leashed pets
are permitted.
Reservations, fees: Reservations are accepted
($9 reservation fee) at 877/444-6777 or www
.ReserveUSA.com. Sites are $16 per night, $32
per night for a double site, and $48 per night
for a triple site. Open May to mid-October,
weather permitting.
Directions: From Sacramento, drive east on
I-80 to the north end of Auburn and the
Foresthill Road exit. Take that exit and drive
east for 20 miles to Foresthill. Drive through
Foresthill (road changes to Foresthill Divide
Road) and continue for eight miles to Sugar
Pine Road. Turn left and drive five miles to
a fork. Turn right and drive one mile to the
campground.

Contact: Tahoe National Forest, American
River Ranger District, Foresthill Ranger Station, 530/367-2224, fax 530/367-2992.

102 SHIRTTAIL CREEK

🚶 🏊 🚤 �- 🏕 ♿ 🚐 ⛺

Scenic rating: 7

on Sugar Pine Reservoir in Tahoe National
Forest

Map 6.1, page 365

This camp is set near the little creek that feeds
into the north end of Sugar Pine Reservoir.
The boat ramp is all the way around the south
side of the lake, near Forbes Creek Group
Camp. (For recreation information, see the
previous listing, *Giant Gap*.)
Campsites, facilities: There are 30 sites for
tents or RVs of any length (no hookups, double
and triple sites are available). Picnic tables and
fire grills are provided. Drinking water and
vault toilets are available. Some facilities are
wheelchair-accessible. A dump station and
boat ramp are available on the south shore.
Supplies can be obtained in Foresthill. Leashed
pets are permitted.
Reservations, fees: Reservations are accepted
($9 reservation fee) at 877/444-6777 or www
.ReserveUSA.com. Sites are $16 for single
sites, $32 for double sites, $48 for triple site,
per night. Open May to mid-October, weather
permitting.
Directions: From Sacramento, drive east on
I-80 to the north end of Auburn and the
Foresthill Road exit. Take that exit and drive
east for 20 miles to Foresthill. Drive through
Foresthill (road changes to Foresthill Divide
Road) and continue for eight miles to Sugar
Pine Road. Turn left and drive five miles to the
campground access road. Turn right (signed)
and drive to the campground.
Contact: Tahoe National Forest, American
River Ranger District, Foresthill Ranger
Station, 530/367-2224, fax 530/367-2992.

103 BIG RESERVOIR/ MORNING STAR LAKE

🏊 🚣 🛥 ⛵ 🐕 ♿ 🚐 ⛺

Scenic rating: 7

on Big Reservoir in Tahoe National Forest

Map 6.1, page 365

Here's a quiet lake where only electric boat motors are allowed; no gas motors are permitted. That makes it ideal for canoeists, rowboaters, and tube floaters who don't like the idea of having to dodge water-skiers. The lake is stocked with rainbow trout; free fishing permits are required and can be obtained at the lake. Big Reservoir (also known as Morning Star Lake) is quite pretty with a nice beach and some lakefront campsites. The elevation is 4,000 feet.

Campsites, facilities: There are 100 sites for tents or RVs up to 40 feet (no hookups). Picnic tables and fire grills are provided. Drinking water, vault toilets, free showers, dump station, and firewood (fee) are available. There is a small store near the campground and supplies are also available in Foresthill. Some facilities are wheelchair-accessible. Leashed pets are permitted.

Reservations, fees: Reservations are accepted at 530/367-2129. Sites are $18–20 per night. Fishing fees are charged. Open May through October, weather permitting.

Directions: From Sacramento, drive east on I-80 to the north end of Auburn and the Foresthill Road exit. Take that exit and drive east for 20 miles to Foresthill. Drive through Foresthill (road changes to Foresthill Divide Road) and continue for eight miles to Sugar Pine Road. Turn left and drive about three miles to Forest Road 24 (signed Big Reservoir). Continue straight onto Forest Road 24 and drive about three miles to the campground entrance road on the right.

Contact: Tahoe National Forest, American River Ranger District, Foresthill Ranger Station, 530/367-2224, fax 530/367-2992; concessionaire: DeAnza Placer Gold Mining Company, 530/367-2129.

104 FORBES CREEK GROUP CAMP

🧍 🏊 🚣 🛥 🐕 ♿ 🚐 ⛺

Scenic rating: 7

on Sugar Pine Reservoir in Tahoe National Forest

Map 6.1, page 365

The boat launch is nearby, but note: A 10-mph speed limit is the law. That makes for quiet water, perfect for anglers, canoeists, and other small boats. A paved trail circles the 160-acre lake. (For more information see the *Giant Gap* listing in this chapter.)

Campsites, facilities: There are two group campsites, Madrone and Rocky Ridge, for tents or RVs up to 45 feet (no hookups) that can accommodate up to 50 people each. Picnic tables and fire grills are provided. Drinking water and vault toilets are available. Some facilities are wheelchair-accessible. A campfire circle, central parking area, dump station, and a boat ramp are available nearby. Supplies can be obtained in Foresthill. Leashed pets are permitted.

Reservations, fees: Reservations are accepted ($9 reservation fee) at 877/444-6777 or www.ReserveUSA.com. Sites are $100 per night. Open May to mid-October, weather permitting.

Directions: From Sacramento, drive east on I-80 to the north end of Auburn and the Foresthill Road exit. Take that exit and drive east for 20 miles to Foresthill. Drive through Foresthill (road changes to Foresthill Divide Road) and continue for eight miles to Sugar Pine Road/Forest Road 10. Turn left and drive five miles to the fork in the road (still Sugar Pine Road/Forest Road 10). Bear left and drive approximately 4.5 miles to the boat ramp (still Sugar Pine Road/Forest Road 10). Turn right, head up the hill, and drive approximately seven miles to the camp.

Contact: Tahoe National Forest, American River Ranger District, Foresthill Ranger Station, 530/367-2224, fax 530/367-2992.

105 BEAR RIVER CAMPGROUND

🚶 🏊 🎣 🐕 🚙 ⛰

Scenic rating: 7

near Colfax on Bear River

Map 6.1, page 365

This RV park is set in the Sierra foothills at 1,800 feet, near Bear River, and features riverfront campsites. The park covers 200 acres, offers five miles of hiking trails, and is set right on the Placer and Nevada County lines. It fills up on weekends and is popular with both locals and out-of-towners. In the spring, when everything is green, it can be a gorgeous landscape. Fishing is OK for rainbow and brown trout, smallmouth bass, and bluegill. Noncommercial gold panning is permitted, and some rafting is popular on the river. A 14-day maximum stay is enforced.

Campsites, facilities: There are 25 sites for tents or small RVs up to 40 feet (no hookups), and two group sites for tents or RVs up to 35 feet for 50–100 people. Picnic tables and fire rings are provided. Pit toilets are available. There is no drinking water. Supplies are available within five miles in Colfax or Bowman. Leashed pets are permitted.

Reservations, fees: Reservations are accepted ($5 reservation fee) only for the group sites at 530/886-4900. Sites are $10 per night, $2 per night for each additional vehicle, $1 per pet per night, and $40–75 per night for group sites. Open March through September.

Directions: From Sacramento, drive east on I-80 east of Auburn to West Weimar Crossroads exit. Take that exit on to Weimar Cross Road and drive north for 1.5 miles to Placer Hills Road. Turn right and drive 2.5 miles to Plum Tree Road. Turn left and drive one mile to the campground on the left. The access road is steep and narrow.

Contact: Bear River Campground, Placer County Facilities Services, 530/889-4900, fax 530/886-6809, www.placer.ca.gov.

106 MIDDLE MEADOWS GROUP CAMP

🐕 🚙 ⛰

Scenic rating: 7

on Long Canyon Creek in Eldorado National Forest

Map 6.1, page 365

This group camp is within range of several adventures. To the nearby east is Hell Hole Reservoir (you'll need a boat here to do it right), and to the nearby north is French Meadows Reservoir (you'll drive past the dam on the way in). Unfortunately, there isn't a heck of a lot to do at this camp other than watch the water flow by on adjacent Long Canyon Creek.

Campsites, facilities: There are two group sites for tents or RVs up to 16 feet (no hookups) that can accommodate 25–50 people each. Picnic tables and fire grills are provided. Drinking water and flush and vault toilets are available. Supplies can be obtained in Foresthill. Leashed pets are permitted.

Reservations, fees: Reservations are accepted ($9 reservation fee) at 877/444-6777 or www.ReserveUSA.com. Sites are $25–50 per night. Open mid-May to early November, weather permitting.

Directions: From Sacramento, drive east on I-80 to the north end of Auburn. Take the Elm Avenue exit and turn left at the first stoplight onto Elm Avenue. Drive 0.1 mile, turn left on High Street, and continue through the signal where High Street merges with Highway 49. Travel on Highway 49 for about 3.5 miles, turn right over the bridge, and drive about 2.5 miles into the town of Cool. Turn left on Georgetown Road/Highway 193 and drive about 14 miles into Georgetown. At the four-way stop turn left on Main Street (which becomes Wentworth Springs/Forest Road 1) and drive about 25 miles. Turn left on Forest Road 2 and drive 19 miles to the campground on the right.

Contact: Eldorado National Forest, Georgetown Ranger District, 530/333-4312, fax 530/333-5522.

107 BIG MEADOWS

🚶 🏊 🛶 🚤 🐕 🚐 ⛺

Scenic rating: 7

near Hell Hole Reservoir in Eldorado National Forest

Map 6.1, page 365

This camp sits on a meadow near the ridge above Hell Hole Reservoir, which is about two miles away. (For more information, see the next listing, *Hell Hole*.)

Campsites, facilities: There are 54 sites for tents or RVs of any length (no hookups). Picnic tables are provided. Drinking water and flush and vault toilets are available. Leashed pets are permitted.

Reservations, fees: Reservations are not accepted. Sites are $10 per night, $5 per night for each additional vehicle. Open mid-May to early November, weather permitting.

Directions: From Sacramento, drive east on I-80 to the north end of Auburn. Take the Elm Avenue exit and turn left at the first stoplight onto Elm Avenue. Drive 0.1 mile, turn left on High Street, and continue through the signal where High Street merges with Highway 49. Continue on Highway 49 for about 3.5 miles, turn right over the bridge, and drive about 2.5 miles into the town of Cool. Turn left on Georgetown Road/Highway 193 and drive about 14 miles into Georgetown. At the four-way stop turn left on Main Street (which becomes Wentworth Springs/Forest Road 1) and drive about 25 miles. Turn left on Forest Road 2 and drive 21 miles to the campground on the left.

Contact: Eldorado National Forest, Georgetown Ranger District, 530/333-4312, fax 530/333-5522.

108 HELL HOLE

🚶 🏊 🛶 🚤 🐕 ⛺

Scenic rating: 8

near Hell Hole Reservoir in Eldorado National Forest

Map 6.1, page 365

Hell Hole is a mountain temple with sapphire-blue water. For the most part, there is limited bank access because of its granite-sculpted shore, and that's why there are no lakeside campsites. This is the closest drive-to camp at Hell Hole Reservoir, about a mile away with a boat launch nearby. All water sports are allowed. Be sure to bring a boat and then enjoy the scenery while you troll for kokanee salmon, brown trout, Mackinaw trout, and a sprinkling of rainbow trout. This is a unique fishery compared to the put-and-take rainbow trout at so many other lakes. The lake has 15 miles of shoreline, and the elevation is 4,700 feet; the camp elevation is 5,200 feet. Note that afternoon winds can make the water choppy.

Campsites, facilities: There are 10 sites for tents only. Picnic tables and fire grills are provided. Drinking water and vault toilets are available. Supplies can be obtained in Georgetown. A boat launch is available nearby at the reservoir. Leashed pets are permitted.

Reservations, fees: Reservations are not accepted. Sites are $10 per night, $5 per night for each additional vehicle. Open mid-May to early November, weather permitting.

Directions: From Sacramento, drive east on I-80 to the north end of Auburn. Take the Elm Avenue exit and turn left at the first stoplight onto Elm Avenue. Drive 0.1 mile, turn left on High Street, and continue through the signal where High Street merges with Highway 49. Continue on Highway 49 for about 3.5 miles, turn right over the bridge, and drive about 2.5 miles into the town of Cool. Turn left on Georgetown Road/Highway 193 and drive about 14 miles into Georgetown. At the four-way stop turn left on Main Street (which becomes Wentworth Springs/Forest Road 1)

and drive about 25 miles. Turn left on Forest Road 2 and drive about 22 miles to the campground on the left.
Contact: Eldorado National Forest, Georgetown Ranger District, 530/333-4312, fax 530/333-5522.

109 UPPER HELL HOLE WALK-IN/BOAT-IN

🏃 ⛱ 🛶 🚤 🐕 5% 🏕

Scenic rating: 10

on Hell Hole Reservoir in Eldorado National Forest

Map 6.1, page 365

This is a beautiful spot, set on the southern shore at the upper end of Hell Hole Reservoir in remote national forest seen by relatively few people. Getting here requires a boat-in or 3.5-mile walk on a trail routed along the southern edge of the lake overlooking Hell Hole. The trail's short rises and falls can tire you out on a hot day—bring plenty of water. You arrive at this little trail camp, ready to explore onward the next day into the Granite Chief Wilderness, or just do nothing except enjoy adjacent Buck Meadow, the lake's headwaters, and the paradise you have discovered. Note that bears frequent this area, so store your food properly and avoid scented products.
Campsites, facilities: There are 15 tent sites, accessible by trail or boat only. Picnic tables and fire grills are provided. Vault toilets are available. No drinking water is available, so bring a water filter. Garbage must be packed out. A boat launch is available at the reservoir and the camp can be reached by boat, but low water levels during August and September can make passage difficult or impossible; call for current status. Supplies can be obtained in Georgetown. Leashed pets are permitted.
Reservations, fees: Reservations are not accepted. There is no fee for camping. Open May to early October, weather permitting.
Directions: From Sacramento, drive east on I-80 to the north end of Auburn. Take the Elm

Avenue exit and turn left at the first stoplight onto Elm Avenue. Drive 0.1 mile, turn left on High Street, and continue through the signal where High Street merges with Highway 49. Continue on Highway 49 for about 3.5 miles, turn right over the bridge, and drive about 2.5 miles into the town of Cool. Turn left on Georgetown Road/Highway 193 and drive about 14 miles into Georgetown. At the four-way stop turn left on Main Street (which becomes Wentworth Springs/Forest Road 1) and drive about 25 miles. Turn left on Forest Road 2 and drive about 23 miles (a mile past the Hell Hole Campground access road) to the parking area at the boat ramp. From the trailhead, hike 3.5 miles to the camp.
Contact: Eldorado National Forest, Georgetown Ranger District, 530/333-4312, fax 530/333-5522.

110 SUGAR PINE POINT STATE PARK

🏃 ⛱ 🛶 🎿 🐕 ♿ 🚲 🏕

Scenic rating: 10

on Lake Tahoe

Map 6.1, page 365

This is one of three beautiful and popular state parks on the west shore of Lake Tahoe. It is just north of Meeks Bay on General Creek, with almost two miles of lake frontage available, though the campground is on the opposite side of Highway 89. General Creek, a feeder stream to Lake Tahoe here, is one of the clearest streams imaginable. A pretty trail is routed seven miles along the creek up to Lost Lake, just outside the northern boundary of the Desolation Wilderness. This stream also provides trout fishing from mid-July to mid-September. This park contains one of the finest remaining natural areas at Lake Tahoe. The park features dense forests of pine, fir, aspen, and juniper, covering more than 2,000 acres of beautiful landscape. There are many hiking trails, a swimming beach, and in winter, 20 kilometers of cross-country skiing trails and heated restroom. There is also evidence of occupation by Washoe Indians, with bedrock mortars, or grinding rocks, near the Ehrman Mansion. The elevation is 6,200 feet.

Campsites, facilities: There are 175 sites for tents or RVs up to 32 feet and trailers up to 26 feet (no hookups). There are also 10 group sites for up to 40 people each. Picnic tables and fire rings are provided. Drinking water, restrooms with flush toilets and coin showers (except in winter), dump station, a day-use area, and nature center with bird display are available. A grocery store, coin laundry, and propane gas are available nearby. Some facilities are wheelchair-accessible. Leashed pets are permitted.

Reservations, fees: Reservations are accepted ($7.50 reservation fee) at 800/444-PARK (800/444-7275) or www.reserveamerica.com. Sites are $15–20 per night, $6 per night for each additional vehicle, $111 per night for a group site. Open year-round.

Directions: From Truckee, drive south on Highway 89 through Tahoe City. Continue south on Highway 89 and drive 9.3 miles to the campground (signed) on the right (west) side of the road.

Contact: Sugar Pine Point State Park, 530/525-7982; Sierra District, 530/525-7232, www.parks.ca.gov.

111 MEEKS BAY

Scenic rating: 9

on Lake Tahoe

Map 6.1, page 365

Meeks Bay is a beautiful spot along the western shore of Lake Tahoe. A bicycle trail is available nearby and is routed along the lake's shore, but it requires occasionally crossing busy Highway 89.

Campsites, facilities: There are 40 sites for tents or RVs up to 20 feet (no hookups). Picnic tables, food lockers, and fire grills are provided. Drinking water and flush toilets are available.

Coin laundry and groceries are available nearby. Leashed pets are permitted.

Reservations, fees: Reservations are accepted ($9 reservation fee) at 877/444-6777 or www.ReserveUSA.com. Sites are $17 per night, $5 per night for each additional vehicle. Open mid-May to mid-October, weather permitting.

Directions: In South Lake Tahoe at the junction of Highway 89 and U.S. 50, turn north on Highway 89 and drive 17 miles to the campground (signed) on the east side of Highway 89.

Contact: Lake Tahoe Basin Management Unit, 530/543-2600, fax 530/543-2693; Taylor Creek Visitor Center, 530/543-2674; California Land Management, 530/544-0426.

112 MEEKS BAY RESORT AND MARINA

Scenic rating: 7

on Lake Tahoe

Map 6.1, page 365

Prime access for boating makes this a camp of choice for the boater/camper at Lake Tahoe. This campground is extremely popular and often booked well ahead of time for July and August. A boat launch is on the premises, and access to Rubicon Bay and beyond to breathtaking Emerald Bay is possible, a six-mile trip one-way for boats. The resort is adjacent to a 20-mile paved bike trail, with a swimming beach also nearby. A 14-day stay limit is enforced.

Campsites, facilities: There are 10 sites with full hookups (50 amps) for RVs of any length, and 24 sites for tents. Some sites are pull-through. Lodge rooms, cabins, and a house are also available. Picnic tables and fire grills are provided. Restrooms with showers and flush toilets, coin laundry, snack bar, gift shop, and convenience store are available. A boat ramp, boat rentals (kayaks, canoes, and paddle boats), and boat slips are also available. No pets are allowed.

Reservations, fees: Reservations are accepted at 866/589-3411. Sites are $25–30 per night, $25 per night for boat slips. Some credit cards accepted. Open May through September.

Directions: In South Lake Tahoe at the junction of Highway 89 and U.S. 50, turn north on Highway 89 and drive 17 miles to the campground on the right at 7941 Emerald Bay Road.

Contact: Meeks Bay Resort and Marina, 530/525-6946, www.meeksbayresort.com.

113 STUMPY MEADOWS

Scenic rating: 7

on Stumpy Meadows Lake in Eldorado National Forest

Map 6.2, page 366

This is the camp of choice for visitors to Stumpy Meadows Lake. The first things visitors notice are the huge ponderosa pine trees, noted for their distinctive, mosaic-like bark. The lake is set at 4,400 feet in Eldorado National Forest and covers 320 acres with water that is cold and clear. The lake has both rainbow and brown trout, and in the fall provides good fishing for big browns (they move up into the head of the lake, near where Pilot Creek enters).

Campsites, facilities: There are 40 sites for tents or RVs of any length (no hookups). Two of the sites are double units. Picnic tables and fire grills are provided. Drinking water and vault toilets are available. A boat ramp is nearby. Leashed pets are permitted.

Reservations, fees: Reservations are accepted ($9 reservation fee) at 877/444-6777 or www.ReserveUSA.com. Sites are $16 per night, $28 per night for double-unit sites, $5 per night for each additional vehicle. Boat launching is $8 per day. Open April through October, weather permitting.

Directions: From Sacramento on I-80, drive east to the north end of Auburn. Turn left on Elm Avenue and drive about 0.1 mile. Turn left on High Street and drive through the signal that marks the continuation of High Street as Highway 49. Drive 3.5 miles on Highway 49, turn right over the bridge, and drive 2.5 miles into the town of Cool. Turn left on Georgetown Road/Highway 193 and drive 14 miles into Georgetown. At the four-way stop, turn left on Main Street, which becomes Georgetown-Wentworth Springs Road/Forest Road 1. Drive about 18 miles to Stumpy Meadows Lake. Continue about a mile and turn right into Stumpy Meadows campground.

Contact: Eldorado National Forest, Georgetown Ranger District, 530/333-4312, fax 530/333-5522.

114 BLACK OAK GROUP CAMP

Scenic rating: 7

near Stumpy Meadows Lake in Eldorado National Forest

Map 6.2, page 366

This group camp is set directly adjacent to Stumpy Meadows Campground. (See the previous listing, *Stumpy Meadows,* for more information.) The boat ramp for the lake is just south of the Mark Edson Dam, near the picnic area. The elevation is 4,400 feet.

Campsites, facilities: There are three group sites for tents and one group site for RVs of any length (no hookups) that can accommodate 25–75 people each. Picnic tables and fire grills are provided. Drinking water and vault toilets are available. A boat ramp is nearby. Leashed pets are permitted.

Reservations, fees: Reservations are accepted ($9 reservation fee) at 877/444-6777 or www.ReserveUSA.com. Sites are $65 per night. Boat launching is $8 per day. Open April to late September, weather permitting.

Directions: From Sacramento on I-80, drive east to the north end of Auburn. Turn left on

Elm Avenue and drive about 0.1 mile. Turn left on High Street and drive through the signal that marks the continuation of High Street as Highway 49. Drive 3.5 miles on Highway 49, turn right over the bridge, and drive 2.5 miles into the town of Cool. Turn left on Georgetown Road/Highway 193 and drive 14 miles into Georgetown. At the four-way stop, turn left on Main Street, which becomes Georgetown-Wentworth Springs Road/Forest Road 1. Drive about 18 miles to Stumpy Meadows Lake, and then continue for two miles to the north shore of the lake and the campground entrance road on the right.

Contact: Eldorado National Forest, Georgetown Ranger District, 530/333-4312, fax 530/333-5522.

115 GERLE CREEK

Scenic rating: 7

on Gerle Creek Reservoir in Eldorado National Forest

Map 6.2, page 366

This is a small, pretty, but limited spot set along the northern shore of little Gerle Creek Reservoir at 5,231 feet in elevation. The lake is ideal for canoes or other small boats because no motors are permitted and no boat ramp is available. That makes for quiet water. It is set in the Gerle Creek Canyon, which feeds into the South Fork Rubicon River. No trout plants are made at this lake, and fishing can be correspondingly poor. A wild brown trout population lives here, though. A network of Forest Service roads to the north can provide great exploring. A map of Eldorado National Forest is a must.

Campsites, facilities: There are 50 sites for tents or RVs up to 25 feet (no hookups). Picnic tables and fire grills are provided. Drinking water and vault toilets are available. Wheelchair-accessible trails and fishing pier are available nearby. Leashed pets are permitted.

Reservations, fees: Reservations accepted ($9 reservation fee) at 877/444-6777 or www.ReserveUSA.com. Sites are $18 per night, $5 per night for each additional vehicle. Open mid-May to mid-October, weather permitting.

Directions: From Placerville, drive east on U.S. 50 for 23 miles to Riverton and the junction with Ice House Road/Forest Road 3. Turn north and drive 27 miles (past Union Valley Reservoir) to a fork with Forest Road 30. Turn left, drive two miles, bear left on the campground entrance road, and drive a mile to the campground.

Contact: Eldorado National Forest, Pacific Ranger District, 530/644-2349, fax 530/647-5405.

116 SOUTH FORK GROUP CAMP

Scenic rating: 8

on the South Fork of the Rubicon River in Eldorado National Forest

Map 6.2, page 366

This primitive national forest camp sits alongside the South Fork Rubicon River, just over a mile downstream from the outlet at Gerle Creek Reservoir. Trout fishing is fair, the water tastes extremely sweet (always pump filter with a water purifier), and there are several side trips available. These include Loon Lake (eight miles to the northeast), Gerle Creek Reservoir (to the nearby north), and Union Valley Reservoir (to the nearby south). The elevation is 5,200 feet.

Campsites, facilities: There is a group camp for tents only that can accommodate up to 125 people. Picnic tables and fire grills are provided. Vault toilets are available. No drinking water is available. Garbage must be packed out. Leashed pets are permitted.

Reservations, fees: Reservations are required ($9 reservation fee) at 877/444-6777 or www.ReserveUSA.com. The camp is $100

per night. Open late May to early September.

Directions: From Placerville, drive east on U.S. 50 for 23 miles to Riverton and the junction with Ice House Road/Forest Road 3. Turn north and drive about 23 miles to the junction with Forest Road 13N28 (3.5 miles past Union Valley Reservoir). Bear left on Forest Road 13N28 and drive two miles to the campground entrance on the right.

Contact: Eldorado National Forest, Pacific Ranger District, 530/644-2349, fax 530/647-5405.

117 RED FIR GROUP CAMP

Scenic rating: 6

on Loon Lake in Eldorado National Forest

Map 6.2, page 366

This is a pretty, wooded camp, ideal for medium-sized groups. It is across the road from the 600-acre lake, offering a secluded, quiet spot. Lake access is a short hike away. All water sports are allowed on Loon Lake. (See the *Loon Lake Northshore* listing in this chapter for more information.) The elevation is 6,500 feet.

Campsites, facilities: This tents-only group site can accommodate up to 25 people. Drinking water, vault toilets, fire rings, and grills are available. Some facilities are wheelchair-accessible. Leashed pets are permitted.

Reservations, fees: Reservations are required ($9 reservation fee) at 877/444-6777 or www .ReserveUSA.com. The camp is $40 per night. Open mid-June to mid-October, weather permitting.

Directions: From Placerville, drive east on U.S. 50 for 23 miles to Riverton and the junction with Ice House Road/Forest Road 3. Turn left and drive 34 miles to a fork at the foot of Loon Lake. Turn left and drive three miles to the campground (just beyond the Loon Lake Northshore camp).

Contact: Eldorado National Forest, Pa-

cific Ranger District, 530/644-2349, fax 530/644-5405.

118 WENTWORTH SPRINGS FOUR-WHEEL DRIVE

Scenic rating: 7

near Loon Lake in Eldorado National Forest

Map 6.2, page 366

There is one reason people come here: to set up a base camp for an OHV adventure, whether they are the owners of four-wheel drives, all-terrain vehicles, or dirt bikes. A network of roads leads from this camp, passable only by these vehicles; these roads would flat-out destroy your average car. The camp is set deep in Eldorado National Forest, at 6,200 feet in elevation. While the north end of Loon Lake is a mile to the east, the road there is extremely rough (perfect, right?). The road is gated along the lake, preventing access to this camp for those who drive directly to Loon Lake.

Campsites, facilities: There are eight sites for tents only. Picnic tables and fire grills are provided. Vault toilets are available. No drinking water is available. Garbage must be packed out. Leashed pets are permitted.

Reservations, fees: Reservations are not accepted. There is no fee for camping. Open June through October, weather permitting.

Directions: From Placerville, drive east on U.S. 50 for 23 miles to Riverton and the junction with Ice House Road/Forest Road 3. Turn left and drive 30 miles to the junction with Forest Road 30. Bear left and drive 3.5 miles to Forest Road 33. Turn right and drive seven miles to the campground on the left side of the road. (The access road is suitable for four-wheel-drive vehicles and off-highway motorcycles only.)

Contact: Eldorado National Forest, Pacific Ranger District, 530/644-2349, fax 530/644-5405.

119 LOON LAKE NORTHSHORE

🚶 🏊 ⛴ 🐕 ♿ 🚐 ⛺

Scenic rating: 9

on Loon Lake in Eldorado National Forest

Map 6.2, page 366

The waterfront sites are in an extremely pretty setting on the northwestern shore of Loon Lake. There are few facilities, though, and no boat ramp; the boat ramp is near the Loon Lake campground and picnic area at the south end of the lake. (For more information about Loon Lake, see the next listings, *Loon Lake* and *Pleasant Hike-In/Boat-In.*)

Campsites, facilities: There are 15 sites for tents or RVs up to 35 feet (no hookups). Picnic tables and fire grills are provided. Vault toilets are available. There is no drinking water. Some facilities are wheelchair-accessible. Leashed pets are permitted.

Reservations, fees: Reservations are not accepted. Sites are $16 per night, $5 per night for each additional vehicle. Open June through September, weather permitting.

Directions: From Placerville, drive east on U.S. 50 for 23 miles to Riverton and the junction with Ice House Road/Forest Road 3. Turn left and drive 34 miles to a fork at the foot of Loon Lake. Turn left and drive three miles to the campground.

Contact: Eldorado National Forest, Pacific Ranger District, 530/644-2349, fax 530/644-5405.

120 LOON LAKE

🚶 🏊 🛶 🚐 🐕 ♿ 🚐 ⛺

Scenic rating: 9

in Eldorado National Forest

Map 6.2, page 366

Loon Lake is set near the Sierra crest at 6,400 feet, covering 600 acres with depths up to 130 feet. This is the lake's primary campground, and it is easy to see why, with a picnic area, beach (includes a small unit for changing clothes), and boat ramp adjacent to the camp. The lake provides good trout fishing, and the lake is stocked on a regular basis once the access road is clear of snow. Afternoon winds drive anglers off the lake but are cheered by sailboarders. An excellent trail is also available here, with the hike routed along the lake's eastern shore to Pleasant Hike-In/Boat-In, where there's a trailhead for the Desolation Wilderness.

Campsites, facilities: There are 53 sites for tents or RVs up to 40 feet, nine equestrian sites, and one group equestrian site for tents or RVs up to 40 feet that can accommodate up to 25 people. No hookups. Picnic tables and fire grills are provided. Drinking water and vault toilets are available. Tie lines are available for horses. A boat ramp and swimming beach are nearby. Some facilities are wheelchair-accessible. Leashed pets are permitted.

Reservations, fees: Reservations are accepted ($9 reservation fee) at 877/444-6777 or www .ReserveUSA.com. Sites are $18 per night, $34 per night for a double site, $5 per night for each additional vehicle. Open June to mid-October, weather permitting.

Directions: From Placerville, drive east on U.S. 50 for 23 miles to Riverton and the junction with Ice House Road/Forest Road 3. Turn left and drive 34 miles to a fork at the foot of Loon Lake. Turn right and drive one mile to the Loon Lake Picnic Area or boat ramp.

Contact: Eldorado National Forest, Pacific Ranger District, 530/644-2349, fax 530/644-5405.

121 PLEASANT HIKE-IN/ BOAT-IN

🚶 🏊 🛶 🚐 🐕 ⛺

Scenic rating: 9

on Loon Lake in Eldorado National Forest

Map 6.2, page 366

This premium Sierra camp, hike-in or boat-in only, is set on the remote northeast shore of Loon Lake at 6,378 feet in elevation. In many ways this makes for a perfect short vacation. After you reach the camp, a trail is available routed east for four miles past Buck Island Lake (6,436 feet) and Rockbound Lake (6,529 feet), set just inside the northern border of the Desolation Wilderness. When the trail is clear of snow, this makes for a fantastic day hike; a wilderness permit is required if staying overnight inside the wilderness boundary.

Campsites, facilities: There are 10 boat-in or hike-in tent sites. Picnic tables and fire rings are provided. Vault toilets are available. No drinking water is available. Garbage must be packed out. The camp is accessible by boat or trail only. Leashed pets are permitted.

Reservations, fees: Reservations are not accepted. There is no fee for camping. Open mid-June to mid-October, weather permitting.

Directions: From Placerville, drive east on U.S. 50 for 23 miles to Riverton and the junction with Ice House Road/Forest Road 3. Turn left and drive 34 miles to a fork at the foot of Loon Lake. Turn right and drive a mile to the Loon Lake Picnic Area or boat ramp. Either hike or boat 2.5 miles to the campground on the northeast shore of the lake.

Contact: Eldorado National Forest, Pacific Ranger District, 530/644-2349, fax 530/644-5405.

122 BIG SILVER GROUP CAMP

🚶 🚲 ♨ 🛶 🚤 🐕 ♿ 🚐 ⛺

Scenic rating: 7

on Big Silver Creek in Eldorado National Forest

Map 6.2, page 366

This camp was built along the Union Valley bike trail, less than a mile from Union Valley Reservoir. The paved bike trail stretches for miles both north and south of the campground and is wheelchair-accessible. It's a classic Sierra forest setting, with plenty of ponderosa pine on the north side of Big Silver Creek.

Campsites, facilities: There is one group site for tents or RVs up to 50 feet (no hookups) that can accommodate up to 50 people. Picnic tables and fire grills are provided. Vault toilets are available. No drinking water is available. There is also a group kitchen area with pedestal grills. Some facilities are wheelchair-accessible. Leashed pets are permitted.

Reservations, fees: Reservations are required ($9 reservation fee) at 877/444-6777 or www .ReserveUSA.com. The camp is $50 per night. Open late May to mid-October, weather permitting.

Directions: From Placerville, drive east on U.S. 50 for 23 miles to Riverton and the junction with Ice House Road/Forest Road 3. Turn left (north) and drive about 16 miles to the campground.

Contact: Eldorado National Forest, Pacific Ranger District, 530/644-2349, fax 530/647-5405.

123 WOLF CREEK AND WOLF CREEK GROUP

🚶 ♨ 🛶 🚤 🐕 ♿ 🚐 ⛺

Scenic rating: 9

on Union Valley Reservoir in Eldorado National Forest

Map 6.2, page 366

Wolf Creek Camp is on the north shore of Union Valley Reservoir. Listen up? Notice that it's quieter? Yep. That's because there are not as many water-skiers in the vicinity. Why? The nearest boat ramp is three miles away. The view of the Crystal Range from the campground is drop-dead gorgeous. The elevation is 4,900 feet.

Campsites, facilities: There are 42 sites for tents or RVs up to 40 feet, and three group sites for tents or RVs up to 40 feet that can accommodate up to 50 people each. No hookups. Picnic tables and fire grills are provided. Drinking water and vault toilets are available. Some facilities are wheelchair-accessible. A boat ramp is three miles away at the campground at Yellowjacket. Leashed pets are permitted.

Reservations, fees: Reservations are accepted for individual sites and required for group sites ($9 reservation fee) at 877/444-6777 or www .ReserveUSA.com. Sites are $18 per night for a single site, $34 per night for a double site, $5 per night for each additional vehicle. Group sites are $100–150 per night. Open mid-May to mid-October, weather permitting.

Directions: From Placerville, drive east on U.S. 50 for 23 miles to Riverton and the junction with Ice House Road/Forest Road 3. Turn left (north) and drive 19 miles to Forest Road 12N78/Union Valley Road (at the head of Union Valley Reservoir). Turn left (west) and drive two miles to the campground.

Contact: Eldorado National Forest, Pacific Ranger District, 530/644-2349, fax 530/647-5405.

124 CAMINO COVE
🏞️ 🏊 🚣 🛶 🎣 🐕 ♿ 🚐 ⛺

Scenic rating: 10

on Union Valley Reservoir in Eldorado National Forest

Map 6.2, page 366

Camino Cove Camp is the nicest spot at Union Valley Reservoir, a slam dunk. It is set at the north end of the lake on a peninsula, absolutely beautiful, a tree-covered landscape and yet with sweeping views of the Crystal Basin. The nearest boat ramp is 1.5 miles to the west at West Point. If this camp is full, there is a small camp at West Point, with just eight sites. The elevation is 4,900 feet.

Campsites, facilities: There are 32 sites for tents or RVs up to 30 feet (no hookups). Fire rings are provided. Vault toilets are available. No drinking water is available. Garbage must be packed out. A swimming beach is nearby and a boat ramp is 1.5 miles away at the campground at West Point. Some facilities are wheelchair-accessible. Leashed pets are permitted.

Reservations, fees: Reservations are not accepted. There is no fee for camping. Open early May through October, weather permitting.

Directions: From Placerville, drive east on U.S. 50 for 23 miles to Riverton and the junction with Ice House Road/Forest Road 3. Turn north on Ice House Road and drive seven miles to Peavine Ridge Road. Turn left and drive three miles to Bryant Springs Road. Turn right and drive five miles north past the West Point boat ramp, and continue 1.5 miles east to the campground entrance on the right.

Contact: Eldorado National Forest, Pacific Ranger District, 530/644-2349, fax 530/647-5405.

125 YELLOWJACKET
🏊 🚣 🛶 🐕 🚐 ⛺

Scenic rating: 8

on Union Valley Reservoir in Eldorado National Forest

Map 6.2, page 366

The camp is set at 4,900 feet on the north shore of gorgeous Union Valley Reservoir. A boat launch adjacent to the camp makes this an ideal destination for trout-angling campers with boats. Union Valley Reservoir, a popular weekend destination for campers from the Central Valley, is stocked with brook trout and rainbow trout by the Department of Fish and Game.

Campsites, facilities: There are 40 sites for tents or RVs up to 30 feet (no hookups). Picnic tables and fire rings are provided. Drinking water and vault toilets are available. A boat ramp and dump station are nearby. Leashed pets are permitted.

Reservations, fees: Reservations are accepted ($9 reservation fee) at 877/444-6777 or www.ReserveUSA.com. Sites are $18 per night, $5 per night for each additional vehicle. Open mid-May to mid-October, weather permitting.

Directions: From Placerville, drive east on

U.S. 50 for 23 miles to Riverton and the junction with Ice House Road/Forest Road 3. Turn left (north) and drive 19 miles to Forest Road 12N78/Union Valley Road (at the head of Union Valley Reservoir). Turn left (west) and drive one mile to Forest Road 12N33. Turn left (south) and drive 0.5 mile to the campground.

Contact: Eldorado National Forest, Pacific Ranger District, 530/644-2349, fax 530/647-5405.

126 WENCH CREEK AND WENCH CREEK GROUP

Scenic rating: 7

on Union Valley Reservoir in Eldorado National Forest

Map 6.2, page 366

Wench Creek is on the northeast shore of Union Valley Reservoir. (For more information, see the *Jones Fork* and *Peninsula Recreation Area* listings in this chapter.) The elevation is 4,900 feet.

Campsites, facilities: There are 100 sites for tents or RVs up to 25 feet (no hookups), and two group tent sites for up to 50 people each. Picnic tables and fire grills are provided. Drinking water and vault toilets are available. A boat ramp is three miles away at the Yellowjacket campground. Leashed pets are permitted.

Reservations, fees: Reservations are not accepted for individual sites, but are accepted for group sites ($9 reservation fee) at 877/444-6777 or www.ReserveUSA. com. Sites are $18 per night, $5 per night for each additional vehicle. The group sites are $100 per night. Open mid-May through September.

Directions: From Placerville, drive east on U.S. 50 for 23 miles to Riverton and the junction with Ice House Road/Forest Road 3. Turn left and drive 15 miles to the campground entrance road (four miles past the turnoff for Sunset Camp). Turn left and drive a mile to the campground at the end of the road.

Contact: Eldorado National Forest, Pacific Ranger District, 530/644-2349, fax 530/647-5405.

127 AZALEA COVE HIKE-IN/ BOAT-IN

Scenic rating: 7

on Union Valley Reservoir in Eldorado National Forest

Map 6.2, page 366

Union Valley Reservoir, at 4,900 feet in elevation, has 4.5 miles of bike trail on its shores, in addition to boating and fishing activities. The distance to the campsite is less than a half-mile by trail and approximately one mile by boat. (For additional information, see the previous listing, *Wench Creek,* and the next listing, *Peninsula Recreation Area.*)

Campsites, facilities: There are 10 sites for tents only. Picnic tables and fire grills are provided. Vault toilets are available. No drinking water is available. Garbage must be packed out. Some facilities are wheelchair-accessible. Leashed pets are permitted.

Reservations, fees: Reservations are not accepted. There is no fee for camping. Open mid-June to mid-October, weather permitting.

Directions: From Placerville, drive east on U.S. 50 for 23 miles to Riverton and the junction with Ice House Road/Forest Road 3. Turn left (north) and drive about 16 miles to the Big Silver Group Campground parking lot. Park and then hike or cycle approximately 0.5 mile to Azalea Cove Campground. To reach Azalea Cove Campground by boat, continue for three miles on Ice House Road to Forest Road 12N78. Turn left (west) and drive one mile to Forest Road 12N33. Turn left (south) and drive 0.5 mile to Yellowjacket Campground.

Park and boat approximately one mile to Azalea Cove Campground.

Contact: Eldorado National Forest, Pacific Ranger District, 530/644-2349, fax 530/647-5405.

128 PENINSULA RECREATION AREA

Scenic rating: 8

on Union Valley Reservoir in Eldorado National Forest

Map 6.2, page 366

The two campgrounds here, Sunset and Fashoda, are the prettiest of all the camps at Union Valley Reservoir, set at the eastern tip of the peninsula that juts into the lake at the mouth of Jones Fork. A nearby boat ramp (you'll see it on the left on the way in) is a big plus, along with a picnic area and beach. All water sports are allowed. The lake has decent trout fishing, with brook trout, brown trout, rainbow trout, Mackinaw, kokanee salmon, and smallmouth bass. The place is gorgeous, set at 4,900 feet in the Sierra Nevada.

Campsites, facilities: There are 131 sites for tents or RVs up to 50 feet (no hookups) at Sunset Camp and 30 walk-in tent sites at Fashoda Camp. Picnic tables, fire rings, and fire grills are provided. Drinking water, coin showers (at Fashoda), vault toilets, boat ramp, and a dump station are available. Some facilities are wheelchair-accessible. Leashed pets are permitted.

Reservations, fees: Reservations are required ($9 reservation fee) for the walk-in sites at 877/444-6777 or www.ReserveUSA.com. Sites are $18 per night, $34 per night for a double site, $5 per night for each additional vehicle. Open late May to early September, weather permitting.

Directions: From Placerville, drive east on U.S. 50 for 23 miles to Riverton and the junction with Ice House Road/Forest Road 3. Turn left and drive 14 miles to the campground entrance road (a mile past the turnoff for Jones Fork Camp). Turn left and drive 1.5 miles to the campground at the end of the road.

Contact: Eldorado National Forest, Pacific Ranger District, 530/644-2349, fax 530/647-5405.

129 JONES FORK

Scenic rating: 7

on Union Valley Reservoir in Eldorado National Forest

Map 6.2, page 366

The Crystal Basin Recreation Area is the most popular backcountry region for campers from the Sacramento area, and Union Valley Reservoir is the centerpiece. The area gets its name from the prominent granite Sierra ridge, which looks like crystal when it is covered with frozen snow. This is a big lake, set at 4,900 feet in elevation, with numerous lakeside campgrounds and three boat ramps providing access. This is the first camp you will arrive at, set at the mouth of the Jones Fork Cove.

Campsites, facilities: There are 10 sites for tents or RVs up to 25 feet (no hookups). Picnic tables and fire rings are provided. Vault toilets are available. No drinking water is available. Leashed pets are permitted.

Reservations, fees: Reservations are not accepted. Sites are $8 per night, $5 per night for each additional vehicle. Open June through October.

Directions: From Placerville, drive east on U.S. 50 for 23 miles to Riverton and the junction with Ice House Road/Forest Road 3. Turn left and drive 14 miles to the campground entrance road on the left (at the south end of Union Valley Reservoir). Turn left and drive 0.5 mile to the campground.

Contact: Eldorado National Forest, Pacific Ranger District, 530/644-2349, fax 530/647-5405.

130 SILVER CREEK GROUP

Scenic rating: 5

near Ice House Reservoir in Eldorado National Forest

Map 6.2, page 366

Silver Creek is a pretty spot at 5,200 feet in elevation. Ice House is only two miles north, and Union Valley Reservoir is four miles north. Either bring your own drinking water or bring a water filtration pump for stream water. Note: RVs and trailers are not allowed.

Campsites, facilities: There is one group tent site that can accommodate up to 50 people. Picnic tables and fire grills are provided. Vault toilets are available. No drinking water is available. Leashed pets are permitted.

Reservations, fees: Reservations are required ($9 reservation fee) at 877/444-6777 or www.ReserveUSA.com. The camp is $100 per night. Open June through October, weather permitting.

Directions: From Placerville, drive east on U.S. 50 for 23 miles to Riverton and the junction with Ice House Road/Forest Road 3. Turn left and drive about nine miles to the campground entrance road on the left (if you reach the junction with Forest Road 3, you have gone 0.25 mile too far). Turn left and drive 0.25 mile to the campground.

Contact: Eldorado National Forest, Pacific Ranger District, 530/644-2349, fax 530/647-5405.

131 ICE HOUSE UPPER AND LOWER

Scenic rating: 8

on Ice House Reservoir in Eldorado National Forest

Map 6.2, page 366

Along with Loon Lake and Union Valley Reservoir, Ice House Reservoir is a feature destination in the Crystal Basin Recreation Area. Ice House gets most of the anglers and Union Valley gets most of the campers. All water sports are allowed at Ice House, though. The camp here is set on the lake's northwestern shore, 5,500 feet in elevation, just up from the dam and adjacent to the lake's boat ramp. The lake, created by a dam on South Fork Silver Creek, covers 650 acres with the deepest spot about 130 feet deep. It is stocked with rainbow trout, brook trout, and brown trout. A 2.5-mile bike trail connects Ice House to Northwind and Strawberry Point campgrounds.

Campsites, facilities: There are 83 sites for tents or RVs up to 30 feet (no hookups). Picnic tables and fire grills are provided. Drinking water, vault toilets, boat ramp, and a dump station are available. Some facilities are wheelchair-accessible. Leashed pets are permitted.

Reservations, fees: Reservations are accepted ($9 reservation fee) at 877/444-6777 or www.ReserveUSA.com. Sites are $18 per night, $34 per night for a double site, $5 per night for each additional vehicle. Open mid-June to mid-October, weather permitting.

Directions: From Placerville, drive east on U.S. 50 for 23 miles to Riverton and the junction with Ice House Road/Forest Road 3. Turn left (north) and drive 11 miles to Forest Road 32/Ice House/Wrights Tie Road. Turn right (east) and drive 1.5 miles to the campground access road on the right.

Contact: Eldorado National Forest, Pacific Ranger District, 530/644-2349, fax 530/647-5405.

132 NORTHWIND

Scenic rating: 7

on Ice House Reservoir in Eldorado National Forest

Map 6.2, page 366

This camp sits on the north shore of Ice House Reservoir. It is slightly above the reservoir, offering prime views. A 2.5-mile bike trail connects Northwind with Ice House and Strawberry Point campgrounds. (See *Ice House,* previous listing, for more information.)

Campsites, facilities: There are nine sites for tents or RVs up to 40 feet (no hookups). Picnic tables and fire grills are provided. Vault toilets are available. No drinking water is available. Some facilities are wheelchair-accessible. Leashed pets are permitted.

Reservations, fees: Reservations are not accepted. Sites are $8 per night, $5 per night for each additional vehicle. Open May to mid-October, weather permitting.

Directions: From Placerville, drive east on U.S. 50 for 23 miles to Riverton and the junction with Ice House Road/Forest Road 3. Turn left (north) and drive 11 miles to Forest Road 32/Ice House/Wrights Tie Road. Turn right (east) and drive three miles (two miles past the boat ramp) to the campground access road on the right.

Contact: Eldorado National Forest, Pacific Ranger District, 530/644-2349, fax 530/647-5405.

133 STRAWBERRY POINT

Scenic rating: 7

on Ice House Reservoir in Eldorado National Forest

Map 6.2, page 366

This camp is set on the north shore of Ice House Reservoir, 5,400 feet in elevation. A 2.5-mile bike trail connects Strawberry Point with Northwind and Ice House campgrounds. (For more information, see the entry in this chapter for *Ice House.*)

Campsites, facilities: There are 10 sites for tents or RVs up to 40 feet (no hookups). Picnic tables and fire grills are provided. Vault toilets are available. No drinking water is available. Some facilities are wheelchair-accessible. Leashed pets are permitted.

Reservations, fees: Reservations are not accepted. Sites are $8 per night, $5 per night for each additional vehicle. Open May through December, weather permitting.

Directions: From Placerville, drive east on U.S. 50 for 23 miles to Riverton and the junction with Ice House Road/Forest Road 3. Turn left (north) and drive 11 miles to Forest Road 32/Ice House/Wrights Tie Road. Turn right (east) and drive three miles (three miles past the boat ramp) to the campground access road on the road.

Contact: Eldorado National Forest, Pacific Ranger District, 530/644-2349, fax 530/647-5405.

134 WRIGHTS LAKE

Scenic rating: 9

in Eldorado National Forest

Map 6.2, page 366

This high mountain lake (7,000 feet) has shoreline picnicking and good fishing and hiking. There is no boat ramp, and the rules do not permit motors, so it is ideal for canoes, rafts, prams, and people who like quiet. Swimming is allowed. Fishing is fair for both rainbow trout and brown trout. It is a classic alpine lake, though small (65 acres), with a trailhead for the Desolation Wilderness at its north end. From here it is only a three-mile hike to the beautiful Twin Lakes and Island Lake, set on the western flank of Mount Price (9,975 feet).

Campsites, facilities: There are 68 sites for tents or RVs up to 50 feet (no hookups). Picnic tables and fire grills are provided. Drinking water and vault toilets are available. Some facilities are wheelchair-accessible, including a boat dock. Leashed pets are permitted.

Reservations, fees: Reservations are accepted ($9 reservation fee) at 877/444-6777 or www .ReserveUSA.com. Sites are $18 per night, $36 per night for a double site, $5 per night for each additional vehicle. Open late June to mid-October, weather permitting.

Directions: From Placerville, drive east on U.S. 50 for 23 miles to Riverton and the junction with Ice House Road/Forest Road 3. Turn left (north) and drive 11 miles to Forest Road 32/Ice House/Wrights Tie Road. Turn right (east) and drive nine miles to Forest Road 4/Wrights Lake Road. Turn left (north) and drive two miles to the campground on the right side of the road.

Contact: Eldorado National Forest, Pacific Ranger District, 530/644-2349, fax 530/644-5405.

135 D. L. BLISS STATE PARK

🥾 🚵 🏊 🛶 🐾 🚐 ⛺

Scenic rating: 10

on Lake Tahoe

Map 6.2, page 366 **BEST (**

D. L. Bliss State Park is set on one of Lake Tahoe's most beautiful stretches of shoreline, from Emerald Point at the mouth of Emerald Bay on northward to Rubicon Point, spanning about three miles. The camp is at the north end of the park, the sites nestled amid pine trees, with 80 percent of the campsites within -0.5–1 mile of the beach. The park is named for a pioneering lumberman, railroad owner, and banker of the region, whose family donated this 744-acre parcel to California in 1929. There are two great easy hiking trails. Rubicon Trail is one of Tahoe's most popular easy hikes, a meandering path just above the southwest shore of Lake Tahoe, wandering through pine, cedar, and fir, with breaks for fantastic panoramas of the lake, as well as spots where you can see nearly 100 feet into the lake. Don't be surprised if you are joined by a chipmunk circus, many begging, sitting upright, hoping for their nut for the day. While this trail is beautiful and solitary at dawn, by noon it can be crowded with hikers and chipmunks alike. Another trail, a great hike for youngsters, is Balancing Rock Trail, just a 0.5-mile

romp, where after about 40 yards you arrive at this 130-ton, oblong granite boulder that is set on a tiny perch, and the whole thing seems to defy gravity. Some day it has to fall, right? Not yet. Rubicon Trail runs all the way past Emerald Point to Emerald Bay.

Campsites, facilities: There are 165 sites for tents or RVs up to 18 feet (no hookups) and trailers up to 15 feet, one hike-in or bike-in site, and a group site for up to 50 people. Picnic tables, fire grills, and food lockers are provided. Restrooms with coin showers and flush toilets are available. All water must sometimes be pump-filtered or boiled before use, depending on current water conditions. Some facilities are wheelchair accessible. Leashed pets are permitted at campsites only.

Reservations, fees: Reservations are accepted ($7.50 reservation fee) at 800/444-PARK (800/444-7275) or www.reserveamerica.com. Sites are $25–35 per night, $6 per night for each additional vehicle, $111 per night for group site, $6 per night for hike-in/bike-in site. Open late May to late September, weather permitting.

Directions: In South Lake Tahoe at the junction of Highway 89 and U.S. 50, turn north on Highway 89 and drive 10.5 miles to the state park turnoff on the right side of the road. Turn right (east) and drive to the park entrance. (If arriving from the north, drive from Tahoe City south on Highway 89 for 17 miles to the park entrance road).

Contact: D. L. Bliss State Park, 530/525-7277; Sierra District, 530/525-7232, www.parks.ca.gov.

136 EMERALD BAY STATE PARK AND BOAT-IN

🥾 🚵 🏊 🛶 🚤 🐾 🚐 ⛺

Scenic rating: 10

on Lake Tahoe

Map 6.2, page 366 **BEST (**

This is one of the most beautiful and popular state parks on the planet. The campground is set at Eagle Point, near the mouth of Emerald Bay on Lake Tahoe, a place of rare, divine beauty. Although the high number of people at Lake Tahoe, and at this park in particular, present inevitable problems, there is a remarkable solution: 20 boat-in sites. There may be no more beautiful place anywhere to run a boat than in Emerald Bay, with its deep cobalt-blue waters, awesome surrounding ridgelines, glimpses of Lake Tahoe out the mouth of the bay, and even a little island. The park also has several short hiking trails. Emerald Bay is a designated underwater park. It features Fanette Island, Tahoe's only island, and Vikingsholm, one of the greatest examples of Scandinavian architecture in North America; tours are available and very popular, and the hike here features a two-mile round-trip with 500-foot drop in elevation to the "castle." The boat-in camps are on the northern side of Emerald Bay at the site of the old Emerald Bay Resort.

Campsites, facilities: There are 100 sites for tents or RVs up to 21 feet (no hookups) and trailers up to 18 feet, one hike-in/bike-in site, and 22 boat-in sites. Picnic tables and fire grills are provided. Drinking water and restrooms with flush toilets and coin showers are available. At boat-in sites, drinking water and vault toilets are available. Leashed pets are permitted in the campground and on asphalt, but not on trails.

Reservations, fees: Reservations are accepted ($7.50 reservation fee) at 800/444-PARK (800/444-7275) or www.reserveamerica.com. Sites are $25 per night, $6 per night for each additional vehicle, $20 per night for boat-in sites, $6 per person per night for hike-in/bike-in sites. Open early June to mid-September, weather permitting.

Directions: In South Lake Tahoe at the junction of Highway 89 and U.S. 50, turn north on Highway 89 and drive 6.5 miles to the state park entrance turnoff on the right side of the road.

Contact: Emerald Bay State Park, 530/541-3030, or D. L. Bliss State Park, 530/525-7277, www.parks.ca.gov.

137 HISTORIC CAMP RICHARDSON RESORT

Scenic rating: 7

on Lake Tahoe

Map 6.2, page 366 · BEST (

Camp Richardson Resort is within minutes of boating, biking, gambling, and, in the winter, skiing and snowboarding. It's a take-your-pick deal. With cabins, restaurant, and live music (often nightly in summer) also on the property, this is a place that offers one big package. The campsites are set in the woods, not on the lake itself. From here you can gain access to an excellent bike route that runs for three miles, then loops around by the lake for another three miles, most of it flat and easy, all of it beautiful. Expect company. The elevation is 6,300 feet.

Campsites, facilities: There are 223 sites for tents, and 112 sites with full or partial hookups (30 amps) for RVs up to 35 feet. Some sites are pull-through. Cabins, duplex units, inn rooms, and hotel rooms are also available. Picnic tables and fire pits are provided. Restrooms with showers and flush toilets, drinking water, a dump station, group facilities, and a playground are available. A full-service marina, boat ramp, boat rentals, swimming beach, bike rentals, general store, restaurant, ice cream parlor, and propane gas are available nearby. Some facilities are wheelchair-accessible. No pets are allowed.

Reservations, fees: Reservations are accepted at 800/544-1801. Sites are $20–35 per night, $5 per night for each additional vehicle. Some credit cards accepted. Open June through October, with lodging available year-round.

Directions: In South Lake Tahoe at the junction of Highway 89 and U.S. 50, turn north on Highway 89 and drive 2.5 miles to the resort on the right side of the road.

Contact: Historic Camp Richardson Resort, 530/541-1801, www.camprichardson.com.

138 CAMP SHELLY

Scenic rating: 7

near Lake Tahoe in the Lake Tahoe Basin

Map 6.2, page 366

This campground is set near South Lake Tahoe within close range of an outstanding bicycle trail. The camp is set in the woods, with campfire programs available on Saturday night in summer. Nearby to the west is the drive to Inspiration Point and the incredible lookout of Emerald Bay, as well as the parking area for the short hike to Eagle Falls. Nearby to the east are Fallen Leaf Lake and the south shore of Lake Tahoe.

Campsites, facilities: There are 26 sites for tents or RVs up to 24 feet long and 10.5 feet high (no hookups). Picnic tables and fire grills are provided. Drinking water, restrooms with free showers and flush toilets, horseshoes, ping-pong, volleyball, and basketball are available. Some facilities are wheelchair-accessible. A boat ramp, groceries, and propane gas are available nearby at Camp Richardson. Leashed pets are permitted.

Reservations, fees: Reservations can be made in person, 9 A.M.–4 P.M. Monday–Friday, at the Robert Livermore Community Center, 4444 East Avenue, Livermore, CA 94550. Reservations can also be made by mail, fax, or at the campground office, which is intermittently staffed during the season. A reservation form can be downloaded from the website. Sites are $20–25 per night, ($12–18 for Livermore residents), $5 per night for each additional vehicle. Open mid-June through Labor Day weekend.

Directions: In South Lake Tahoe at the junction of U.S. 50 and Highway 89, turn north on Highway 89, drive 2.5 miles to Camp Richardson, and then continue for 1.3 miles to the sign for Mount Tallac. Turn left at the sign for Mount Tallac Trailhead/Camp Shelly and drive to the campground on the right.

Contact: Camp Shelly, 530/541-6985; Livermore Area Recreation and Park District, 925/373-5700, fax 925/447-2754, www.larpd.dst.ca.us.

139 FALLEN LEAF CAMPGROUND

Scenic rating: 7

in the Lake Tahoe Basin

Map 6.2, page 366

This is a large camp near the north shore of Fallen Leaf Lake, set at 6,337 feet. The lake is big (three miles long), quite deep (430 feet at its deepest point), and almost as blue as nearby Lake Tahoe. A concessionaire operates the campground. There are a variety of recreational opportunities, including boat rentals at the marina and horseback-riding rentals at Camp Richardson Resort. Fishing is best in the fall for kokanee salmon. Because Fallen Leaf Lake is circled by forest—much of it private property—you will need a boat to fish or explore the lake. A visitors center is north of the Fallen Leaf Lake turnoff on Highway 89.

Campsites, facilities: There are 75 sites for tents and 130 sites for tents or RVs up to 40 feet (no hookups). Picnic tables, food lockers, and fire grills are provided. Drinking water, vault toilets, and coin showers are available. A boat ramp, coin laundry, and supplies are available nearby. Some facilities are wheelchair-accessible. Leashed pets are permitted.

Reservations, fees: Reservations are accepted ($9 reservation fee) at 877/444-6777 or www.ReserveUSA.com. Sites are $20 per night, $5 per night for each additional vehicle. Open mid-May to mid-October, weather permitting.

Directions: In South Lake Tahoe at the junction of U.S. 50 and Highway 89, turn north on Highway 89 and drive two miles to the Fallen Leaf Lake turnoff. Turn left and drive 1.5 miles to the campground.

Contact: Lake Tahoe Basin Management Unit, 530/543-2600, fax 530/543-2693; Taylor Creek Visitor Center, 530/543-

2674; California Land Management, 530/544-0426; Fallen Leaf Lake Marina, 530/544-0787.

140 TAHOE VALLEY CAMPGROUND

Scenic rating: 5

near Lake Tahoe

Map 6.2, page 366

This is a massive, privately operated park near South Lake Tahoe. The nearby attractions include five golf courses, horseback riding, casinos and, of course, "The Lake." Note that about half of the sites are filled with seasonal renters.

Campsites, facilities: There are 305 sites with full or partial hookups (30 and 50 amps) for RVs of any length, and 77 sites for tents. Some sites are pull-through. Picnic tables and fire grills are provided. Restrooms with showers, cable TV, Wi-Fi, modem access, dump station, coin laundry, seasonal heated swimming pool, playground, tennis courts, grocery store, RV supplies, propane gas, ice, firewood, and a recreation room are available. Some facilities are wheelchair-accessible. Leashed pets are permitted.

Reservations, fees: Reservations are recommended. Sites are $36–46 per night. Monthly rates available. Some credit cards accepted. Open year-round.

Directions: Entering South Lake Tahoe on U.S. 50, drive east on U.S. 50 to Meyers. Continue on U.S. 50 about five miles beyond Meyers to the signed entrance on the right. Turn right on "C" Street and drive 1.5 blocks to the campground.

Contact: Tahoe Valley Campground, 530/541-2222, fax 530/541-1825.

141 CAMPGROUND BY THE LAKE

Scenic rating: 5

near Lake Tahoe

Map 6.2, page 366

This city-operated campground provides an option at South Lake Tahoe. It is set at 6,200 feet, across the road from the lake, with pine trees and views of the lake.

Campsites, facilities: There are 175 sites for tents or RVs up to 40 feet, and one group site for 30–50 people. Some sites have partial hookups (30 and 50 amps) and/or are pull-through. One cabin is also available. Picnic tables, barbecues, and fire grills are provided. Drinking water, restrooms with flush toilets and showers, dump station, playground, and a boat ramp (check current status) are available. An indoor ice-skating rink and a public indoor heated pool are available nearby (fee for access). Some facilities are wheelchair-accessible. Supplies and a coin laundry are nearby. Leashed pets are permitted.

Reservations, fees: Reservations are accepted ($3.50 reservation fee) at 530/542-6055. Sites are $22.50–30.50 per night, $4 per night for each additional vehicle, $150–250 per night for the group site, $1 per pet per night. Weekly rates available. Some credit cards accepted. Open April through October, with a 14-day maximum stay.

Directions: If entering South Lake Tahoe on U.S. 50, drive east on U.S. 50 to Rufus Allen Boulevard. Turn right and drive 0.25 mile to the campground on the right side of the road.

Contact: Campground by the Lake, 530/542-6096; City of South Lake Tahoe, Parks and Recreation Department, 530/542-6055, www.recreationintahoe.com.

142 KOA SOUTH LAKE TAHOE

Scenic rating: 5

near Lake Tahoe

Map 6.2, page 366

Like so many KOA camps, this one is on the outskirts of a major destination area, in this case, South Lake Tahoe. It is within close range of gambling, fishing, hiking, and bike rentals. The camp is set at 6,300 feet.

Campsites, facilities: There are 40 sites with full hookups (30 amps) for RVs up to 36 feet, and 16 sites with no hookups for tents and RVs. Some sites are pull-through. A lodge is also available. Picnic tables and fire grills are provided. Restrooms with showers, cable TV, Wi-Fi, dump station, recreation room, seasonal heated swimming pool, playground, coin laundry, convenience store, RV supplies, horseshoes, firewood, ice, and propane gas are available. Leashed pets are permitted.

Reservations, fees: Reservations are recommended at 800/562-3477. Sites are $36–53 per night, $4 per person per night for more than two people, $4 per night for each additional vehicle, $10–15 per boat per night, $4 per pet per night. Weekly and monthly rates available. Holiday rates are higher. Some credit cards accepted. Open April through mid-October.

Directions: From Sacramento, take U.S. 50 and drive east over the Sierra Nevada past Echo Summit to Meyers. As you enter Meyers, it will be the first campground on the right. Turn right and enter the campground.

Contact: KOA South Lake Tahoe, 530/577-3693, www.laketahoekoa.com.

143 SAND FLAT-AMERICAN RIVER

Scenic rating: 7

on the South Fork of the American River in Eldorado National Forest

Map 6.2, page 366

This first-come, first-served campground often gets filled up by U.S. 50 travelers. And why not? You get easy access, a well-signed exit, and a nice setting on the South Fork of the American River. The elevation is 3,900 feet. The river is very pretty here, but fishing is often poor. In winter, the snow level usually starts just a few miles uphill.

Campsites, facilities: There are 23 sites for tents or RVs of any length (no hookups) and six walk-in tent sites. Picnic tables and fire grills are provided. Drinking water and vault toilets are available. Groceries, restaurant, and gas are available nearby. Some facilities are wheelchair-accessible. Leashed pets are permitted.

Reservations, fees: Reservations are not accepted. Sites are $14 per night, $28 per night for a double site, $5 per night for each additional vehicle. Open May to late October, weather permitting.

Directions: From Sacramento, drive east on U.S. 50 to Placerville and then continue 28 miles to the campground on the right. (If you reach the Kyburz store, you have driven about one mile too far.)

Contact: Eldorado National Forest, Placerville Ranger District, 530/644-2324, fax 530/647-5315.

144 CHINA FLAT

Scenic rating: 7

on the Silver Fork of the American River in Eldorado National Forest

Map 6.2, page 366

China Flat sits across the road from the Silver Fork American River, with a nearby access road that is routed along the river for a mile. This provides access for fishing, swimming, gold panning, and exploring. The elevation is 4,800 feet. The camp feels far off the beaten path, even though it is only five minutes from that parade of traffic on U.S. 50.

Campsites, facilities: There are 18 sites for tents or RVs of any length (no hookups). Picnic tables and fire grills are provided. Drinking water and vault toilets are available. Some facilities are wheelchair-accessible. Leashed pets are permitted.

Reservations, fees: Reservations are not accepted. Sites are $14 per night, $28 per night for double sites, $5 per night for each additional vehicle. Open May through October, weather permitting.

Directions: From Sacramento, drive east on U.S. 50 to Kyburz and Silver Fork Road. Turn right and drive three miles to the campground on the right side of the road.

Contact: Eldorado National Forest, Placerville Ranger District, 530/644-2324, fax 530/647-5315.

145 CAPPS CROSSING GROUP CAMP

Scenic rating: 7

on the North Fork of the Cosumnes River in Eldorado National Forest

Map 6.2, page 366

This camp is set out in the middle of nowhere along the North Fork of the Cosumnes River. It's a primitive spot that doesn't get much use. This camp is in the western reaches of a vast number of backcountry Forest Service roads. A map of Eldorado National Forest is a must to explore them. The elevation is 5,200 feet.

Campsites, facilities: There is one group tent site for up to 40 people. Picnic tables and fire grills are provided. Drinking water and vault toilets are available. Leashed pets are permitted.

Reservations, fees: Reservations are required ($9 reservation fee) at 877/444-6777 or www.ReserveUSA.com. The camp is $55 per night. Open June through October, weather permitting.

Directions: From Sacramento, drive east on U.S. 50 to Placerville and continue for 12 miles to the Sly Park Road exit. Turn right and drive about six miles to the Mormon Emigrant Trail/Forest Road 5. Turn left on Mormon Emigrant Trail and drive about 13 miles to North-South Road/Forest Road 6. Turn right (south) on North-South Road and drive about six miles to the campground on the left side of the road.

Contact: Eldorado National Forest, Placerville Ranger District, 530/644-2324, fax 530/647-5315.

146 SILVER FORK

Scenic rating: 7

on the Silver Fork of the American River in Eldorado National Forest

Map 6.2, page 366

The tons of vacationers driving U.S. 50 along the South Fork American River always get frustrated when they try to fish or camp, because there are precious few opportunities for either. But, just 20 minutes off the highway, you can find both at Silver Fork Camp. The access road provides many fishing opportunities and the stream is stocked with rainbow trout by the state. The camp is set right along the river, at 5,500 feet in elevation, in Eldorado National Forest.

Campsites, facilities: There are 35 sites for tents or RVs of any length (no hookups) and four double sites. Picnic tables and fire grills are provided. Drinking water and vault toilets are available. Some of the facilities are wheelchair-accessible. Leashed pets are permitted.

Reservations, fees: Reservations are not accepted. Sites are $14 per night, $28 per night for double sites, $5 per night for each additional vehicle. Open May through October, weather permitting.

Directions: From Sacramento, drive east on U.S. 50 to Kyburz and Silver Fork Road. Turn right and drive eight miles to the campground on the right side of the road.

Contact: Eldorado National Forest, Placerville Ranger District, 530/644-6048, fax 530/647-5315.

147 KIRKWOOD LAKE

Scenic rating: 8

in Eldorado National Forest

Map 6.2, page 366

Little Kirkwood Lake is in a beautiful Sierra setting, with good shoreline access, fishing for small rainbow trout, and quiet water. Despite that, it is often overlooked in favor of nearby Silver Lake and Caples Lake along Highway 88. No boat motors are allowed, but swimming is permitted. Nearby Kirkwood Ski Resort stays open all summer and offers excellent opportunities for horseback riding, hiking, and meals. The elevation is 7,600 feet. Note: No trailers. The access road is too narrow.

Campsites, facilities: There are 12 sites for tents only. Picnic tables and fire grills are provided. Drinking water, vault toilets, and food lockers are available. Leashed pets are permitted.

Reservations, fees: Reservations are not accepted. Sites are $18 per night, $5 per night for each additional vehicle. Open June to mid-October, weather permitting.

Directions: From Jackson, drive east on Highway 88 for 60 miles (four miles past Silver Lake) to the campground entrance road on the left (if you reach the sign for Kirkwood Ski Resort, you have gone 0.5 mile too far). Turn left and drive 0.25 mile (road not suitable for trailers or large RVs) to the campground on the left.

Contact: Eldorado National Forest, Amador Ranger District, 209/295-4251, fax 209/295-5998.

148 CAPLES LAKE

Scenic rating: 8

in Eldorado National Forest

Map 6.2, page 366

Caples Lake, in the high country at 7,800 feet, is a pretty lake right along Highway 88. It covers 600 acres, has a 5-mph speed limit, and provides good trout fishing and excellent hiking terrain. Swimming is allowed. The camp is set across the highway (a little two-laner) from the lake, with the Caples Lake Resort and boat rentals nearby. There is a parking area at the west end of the lake, and from here you can begin a great 3.5-mile hike to Emigrant Lake, in the Mokelumne Wilderness on the western flank of Mount Round Top (10,310 feet).

Campsites, facilities: There are 30 sites for tents or RVs up to 35 feet (no hookups), and six walk-in tent sites (requiring a 200-foot walk). Picnic tables and fire grills are provided. Drinking water and vault toilets are available. Groceries, propane gas, boat ramp, and boat rentals are nearby. Some facilities are wheelchair-accessible. Leashed pets are permitted.

Reservations, fees: Reservations are not accepted. Sites are $20 per night, $5 per night for each additional vehicle, $40 per night for a double site. Open June to mid-October, weather permitting.

Directions: From Jackson, drive east on Highway 88 for 63 miles (one mile past the entrance road to Kirkwood Ski Area) to the camp entrance road on the left.

Contact: Eldorado National Forest, Amador Ranger District, 209/295-4251, fax 209/295-5998; Caples Lake Resort, 209/258-8888.

149 WOODS LAKE

Scenic rating: 9

in Eldorado National Forest

Map 6.2, page 366

Woods Lake is only two miles from Highway 88, yet it can provide campers the feeling of visiting a far-off land. It is a small but beautiful lake in the granite backdrop of the high Sierra, set at 8,200 feet near Carson Pass. Boats with motors are not permitted, making it ideal for canoes and rowboats. Trout fishing is fair. A great trailhead is available here, a three-mile loop hike to little Round Top Lake and Winnemucca Lake (twice the size of Woods Lake) and back. They are set on the northern flank of Mount Round Top (10,310 feet).

Campsites, facilities: There are 25 tent sites. Picnic tables and fire rings are provided. Drinking water and vault toilets are available. Groceries and propane gas are available within five miles. Some facilities are wheelchair-accessible. Leashed pets are permitted.

Reservations, fees: Reservations are not accepted. Sites are $20 per night, $5 per night for each additional vehicle, $40 per night for double site. Open late June through October, weather permitting.

Directions: From Jackson, drive east on Highway 88 to Caples Lake and continue for a mile to the Woods Lake turnoff on the right (two miles west of Carson Pass). Turn south and drive a mile to the campground on the right (trailers and RVs are not recommended).

Contact: Eldorado National Forest, Amador Ranger District, 209/295-4251, fax 209/295-5998.

150 SILVER LAKE WEST

Scenic rating: 9

on Silver Lake in Eldorado National Forest

Map 6.2, page 366

The Highway 88 corridor provides access to three excellent lakes: Lower Bear River Reservoir, Silver Lake, and Caples Lake. Silver Lake is difficult to pass by, with cabin rentals, pretty campsites, decent trout fishing, and excellent hiking. The lake is set at 7,200 feet in a classic granite cirque just below the Sierra ridge. This camp is on the west side of Highway 88, across the road from the lake. A great hike starts at the trailhead on the east side of the lake, a two-mile tromp to little Hidden Lake, one of several nice hikes in the area. In addition, horseback-riding rentals are available nearby at Plasse's Resort. Note that bears frequent this campground, so store food properly and avoid scented products.

Campsites, facilities: There are 42 sites for tents or RVs up to 30 feet (no hookups). Picnic tables, food lockers, and fire pits are provided. Vault toilets and drinking water are available. A boat ramp and boat rentals are nearby. Leashed pets are permitted. There is a maximum of six people and two pets per site.

Reservations, fees: Reservations are not accepted. Sites are $16 per night, $3 per night for each additional vehicle, $1 per pet per night. Open Memorial Day Weekend through October, weather permitting.

Directions: From Jackson, drive east on Highway 88 for 50 miles (to the north end of Silver Lake) to the campground entrance road on the left.

Contact: Eldorado Irrigation District, 530/644-1960, fax 530/647-5155.

151 SILVER LAKE EAST
🚶 🏊 🚣 🛶 🐕 🚐 ⛺

Scenic rating: 7

in Eldorado National Forest

Map 6.2, page 366

Silver Lake is an easy-to-reach alpine lake set at 7,200 feet, providing a beautiful setting, good trout fishing, and hiking. This camp is on the northeast side of the lake, with a boat ramp nearby. (See the previous listing, *Silver Lake West,* for more information.)

Campsites, facilities: There are 62 sites for tents or RVs up to 40 feet (no hookups). Picnic tables and fire grills are provided. Drinking water and vault toilets are available. A grocery store, boat rentals, boat ramp, and propane gas are nearby. Leashed pets are permitted.

Reservations, fees: Reservations are accepted ($9 reservation fee) at 877/444-6777 or www.ReserveUSA.com. Sites are $19 per night, $5 per night for each additional vehicle, $38 per night for a double site. Open June to mid-October, weather permitting.

Directions: From Jackson, drive east on Highway 88 for 50 miles (to the north end of Silver Lake) to the campground entrance road on the right.

Contact: Eldorado National Forest, Amador Ranger District, 209/295-4257, fax 209/295-5998; Silver Lake Resort, 209/258-8598.

152 BEAR RIVER GROUP CAMP
🚶 🏊 🚣 🛶 🐕 ⛺

Scenic rating: 6

on Bear River Reservoir in Eldorado National Forest

Map 6.2, page 366

This is a group camp set near Bear River Reservoir, a pretty lake that provides powerboating and trout fishing. (See the listing in this chapter for *South Shore,* which is just a mile from this camp.)

Campsites, facilities: There are three tent-only group sites that can accommodate 25–50 people each. Picnic tables and fire grills are provided. Drinking water, vault toilets, coin showers, food lockers, and wash racks are available. A grocery store, boat ramp, boat rentals, and propane gas are available nearby. Leashed pets are permitted.

Reservations, fees: Reservations are required ($9 reservation fee) at 877/444-6777 or www.ReserveUSA.com. The sites are $75–140 per night. Open mid-June to mid-September, weather permitting.

Directions: From Stockton, drive east on Highway 88 for about 80 miles to the lake entrance on the right side of the road (well signed). Turn right and drive five miles (past the dam) to the campground entrance on the left side of the road.

Contact: Eldorado National Forest, Amador Ranger District, 209/295-4251, fax 209/295-5994.

153 BEAR RIVER LAKE RESORT
🚶 🏊 🚣 🛶 🐕 🚴 ♿ 🚐 ⛺

Scenic rating: 8

on Bear River Reservoir

Map 6.2, page 366

Bear River Lake Resort is a complete vacation service lodge, with everything you could ask for. A lot of people have been asking in recent years, making this a popular spot that often requires a reservation. The resort also sponsors fishing derbies in the summer and sweetens the pot considerably by stocking exceptionally large rainbow trout. Other fish species include brown trout and Mackinaw trout. The resort is set at 6,000 feet. The lake freezes over in the winter. (See next listing, *South Shore,* for more information about Bear River Reservoir.)

Campsites, facilities: There are 150 sites with partial hookups (15 amps) for tents or RVs up to 35 feet, a group site for up to 60 people, and eight rental trailers. Picnic tables and fire pits are provided. Vault toilets, coin showers, drinking water, dump station, boat ramp, boat rentals, berthing, bait and tackle, fishing licenses, video arcade, playground, firewood, ice, propane gas, coin laundry, pay phone, restaurant and cocktail lounge, and a grocery store are available. Some facilities are wheelchair-accessible. Leashed pets are permitted at campsites, but not in lodging units.

Reservations, fees: Reservations are recommended. Sites are $29 per night, $5 per night for each additional vehicle, $240 per night for the group site, $5 one-time pet fee. Some credit cards accepted. Open April through October.

Directions: From Stockton, drive east on Highway 88 for about 80 miles to the lake entrance on the right side of the road, 42 miles east of Jackson. Turn right and drive 2.5 miles to a junction (if you pass the dam, you have gone 0.25 mile too far). Turn left and drive 0.5 mile to the campground entrance on the right side of the road.

Contact: Bear River Lake Resort, 209/295-4868.

154 SOUTH SHORE

Scenic rating: 7

on Bear River Reservoir in Eldorado National Forest

Map 6.2, page 366

Bear River Reservoir is set at 5,900 feet, which means it becomes ice-free earlier in the spring than its uphill neighbors to the east, Silver Lake and Caples Lake. It is a good-sized lake—725 acres—and cold and deep, too. All water sports are allowed. It gets double-barreled trout stocks, receiving fish from the state and from the operator of the lake's marina and lodge. This campground is on the lake's southern shore, just east of the dam. Explorers can drive south for five miles to Salt Springs Reservoir, which has a trailhead and parking area on the north

side of the dam for a great day hike along the lake.

Campsites, facilities: There are 22 sites for tents or RVs up to 35 feet (no hookups). Picnic tables and fire grills are provided. Drinking water and vault toilets are available. A boat ramp, grocery store, boat rentals, and propane gas are available at nearby Bear River Lake Resort. Some facilities are wheelchair-accessible. Leashed pets are permitted.

Reservations, fees: Reservations are accepted ($9 reservation fee) at 877/444-6777 or www .ReserveUSA.com. Sites are $20 per night, $40 per night for double site. Open mid-May to mid-October, weather permitting.

Directions: From Stockton, drive east on Highway 88 for about 80 miles to the lake entrance on the right side of the road (well signed). Turn right and drive four miles (past the dam) to the campground entrance on the right side of the road.

Contact: Eldorado National Forest, Amador Ranger District, 209/295-4251, fax 209/295-5998.

155 WHITE AZALEA

Scenic rating: 7

on the Mokelumne River in Eldorado National Forest

Map 6.2, page 366

Out here in the remote Mokelumne River Canyon are three primitive camps set on the Mokelumne's North Fork. White Azalea, 3,500 feet in elevation, is the closest of the three to Salt Springs Reservoir, the prime recreation destination. It's about a three-mile drive to the dam and an adjacent parking area for a wilderness trailhead for the Mokelumne Wilderness. This trail makes a great day hike, routed for four miles along the north shore of Salt Springs Reservoir to Blue Hole at the head of the lake.

Campsites, facilities: There are six tent sites. Portable toilets are provided. No drinking water is available. Garbage must be packed out. Leashed pets are permitted.

Reservations, fees: Reservations are not accepted. There is no fee for camping. Open year-round, weather permitting.

Directions: From Jackson, drive east on Highway 88 to Pioneer and then continue for 18 miles to Ellis Road/Forest Road 92 (78 miles from Jackson), at a signed turnoff for Lumberyard Campground. Turn right on Ellis Road and drive 12 miles to Salt Springs Road (Forest Road 9). Turn left, cross the Bear River, and continue for three miles to the campground on the right. The road is steep, narrow, and curvy in spots, not good for RVs or trailers.

Contact: Eldorado National Forest, Amador Ranger District, 209/295-4251, fax 209/295-5998.

156 MOORE CREEK

Scenic rating: 7

on the Mokelumne River in Eldorado National Forest

Map 6.2, page 366

This camp is set at 3,200 feet elevation on little Moore Creek, a feeder stream to the nearby North Fork Mokelumne River. It's one of three primitive camps within two miles. (See the previous listing, *White Azalea*, for more information.)

Campsites, facilities: There are eight tent sites. Picnic tables are provided. Portable toilets are available. No drinking water is available. Garbage must be packed out. Leashed pets are permitted.

Reservations, fees: Reservations are not accepted. There is no fee for camping. Open year-round, weather permitting.

Directions: From Jackson, drive east on Highway 88 to Pioneer and then continue for 18 miles to Ellis Road/Forest Road 92 (78 miles from Jackson), at a signed turnoff for Lumberyard Campground. Turn right

on Ellis Road and drive 12 miles to Salt Springs Road (Forest Road 9). Turn right and drive 2.5 miles, cross the bridge over the Mokelumne River, and turn right on the campground entrance road. Drive 0.25 mile to the campground on the right. The road is steep, narrow, and winding in spots—not good for RVs or trailers.

Contact: Eldorado National Forest, Amador Ranger District, 209/295-4251, fax 209/295-5998.

157 MOKELUMNE

Scenic rating: 7

on the Mokelumne River in Eldorado National Forest

Map 6.2, page 366

This primitive spot is set beside the Mokelumne River at 3,200 feet in elevation, one of three primitive camps in the immediate area. (See the *White Azalea* listing in this chapter for more information.) There are some good swimming holes nearby. Fishing is fair, with the trout on the small side.

Campsites, facilities: There are eight sites for tents only. Vault toilets are provided. No drinking water is available. Garbage must be packed out (it is occasionally serviced in summer). Leashed pets are permitted.

Reservations, fees: Reservations are not accepted. There is no fee for camping. Open year-round, weather permitting.

Directions: From Jackson, drive east on Highway 88 to Pioneer and then continue for 18 miles to Ellis Road/Forest Road 92 (78 miles from Jackson), at a signed turnoff for Lumberyard Campground. Turn right on Ellis Road and drive 12 miles to Salt Springs Road (Forest Road 9). Turn right and drive 2.5 miles to the campground on the left side of the road (at the Mokelumne River).

Contact: Eldorado National Forest, Amador Ranger District, 209/295-4251, fax 209/295-5998.

158 WA KA LUU HEP YOO
🚶🏊🐕♿5%🚐⛺

Scenic rating: 8

on the Stanislaus River in Stanislaus National Forest

Map 6.2, page 366

This is a riverside Forest Service campground that provides good trout fishing on the Stanislaus River and a put-in for whitewater rafting. The highlight for most is the fishing here—one of the best spots on the Stanislaus, stocked by Fish and Game, and good for rainbow, brook, and brown trout. It is four miles downstream of Dorrington and was first opened in 1999 as part of the Sourgrass Recreation Complex. There are cultural sites and preserved artifacts, such as grinding rocks. It is a pretty streamside spot, with ponderosa pine and black oak providing good screening. A wheelchair-accessible trail is available along the stream. The camp is set at an elevation of 3,900 feet, but it feels higher. By the way, I was told that the name of the campground means "wild river."

Campsites, facilities: There are 49 sites for tents or RVs up to 50 feet (no hookups) and four walk-in tent sites. Picnic tables and fire grills are provided. Drinking water and restrooms with flush and vault toilets are available. Some facilities are wheelchair-accessible. Leashed pets are permitted.

Reservations, fees: Reservations are not accepted. Sites are $16 per night, $5 per night for each additional vehicle. Free campfire permits are required. Open Memorial Day weekend through October, weather permitting.

Directions: From Angels Camp, drive east on Highway 4, past Arnold to Dorrington and Boards Crossing Road. Turn right and drive four miles to the campground on the left (just before the bridge that crosses the Stanislaus River).

Contact: Stanislaus National Forest, Calaveras Ranger District, 209/795-1381, fax 209/795-6849.

159 BIG MEADOW AND BIG MEADOW GROUP CAMP
🐕🚐⛺

Scenic rating: 5

in Stanislaus National Forest

Map 6.2, page 366

Big Meadow is set at 6,460 feet on the western slopes of the Sierra Nevada. There are a number of recreation attractions nearby, the most prominent being the North Fork Stanislaus River two miles to the south in a national forest (see *Sand Flat Four-Wheel Drive,* the next listing), with access available from a four-wheel-drive road just east of camp, or on Spicer Reservoir Road (see *Stanislaus River* listing in this chapter). Lake Alpine, a pretty lake popular for trout fishing, is nine miles east on Highway 4. Three mountain reservoirs—Spicer, Utica, and Union—are all within a 15-minute drive. Big Meadow is also a good base camp for hunting.

Campsites, facilities: There are 68 sites for tents or RVs up to 27 feet (no hookups), and one group tent site (requires a walk-in of 100 feet) that can accommodate up to 25 people. Picnic tables and fire grills are provided. Drinking water and vault toilets are available. Groceries, a coin laundry, and propane gas are within five miles. Leashed pets are permitted.

Reservations, fees: Reservations ($9 reservation fee) are accepted for individual sites and required for the group camp at 877/444-6777 or www.ReserveUSA.com. Sites are $15 per night, $5 per night for each additional vehicle, $65 per night for the group camp. Open June through October, weather permitting.

Directions: From Angels Camp on Highway 49, turn east on Highway 4 and drive about 30 miles (three miles past Ganns Meadows) to the campground on the right.

Contact: Stanislaus National Forest, Calaveras Ranger District, 209/795-1381, fax 209/795-6849.

160 SAND FLAT FOUR-WHEEL DRIVE

🥾 🛶 🐕 5% ⛺

Scenic rating: 7

on the Stanislaus River in Stanislaus National Forest

Map 6.2, page 366

This one is for four-wheel-drive cowboys who want to carve out a piece of the Sierra Nevada wildlands for themselves. It is set at 5,900 feet on the North Fork Stanislaus River, where there is decent fishing for small trout, with the fish often holding right where white water runs into pools. You won't get bugged by anyone at this tiny, primitive camp, named for the extensive sandy flat on the south side of the river. The access road is steep and often rough. Trailers are not allowed.

Campsites, facilities: There are 10 sites for tents only. Picnic tables and fire rings are provided. Vault toilets are available. No drinking water is available. Garbage must be packed out. Leashed pets are permitted.

Reservations, fees: Reservations are not accepted. There is no fee for camping. Free campfire permits are required. Open June through October, weather permitting.

Directions: From Angels Camp on Highway 49, turn east on Highway 4, drive about 25 miles (0.5 mile past Big Meadows) to a dirt/gravel road on the right. Turn right and drive two miles on a steep, unimproved road (four-wheel drive required).

Contact: Stanislaus National Forest, Calaveras Ranger District, 209/795-1381, fax 209/795-6849.

161 STANISLAUS RIVER

🛶 🐕 🚍 ⛺

Scenic rating: 8

in Stanislaus National Forest

Map 6.2, page 366

As you might figure from its name, this camp provides excellent access to the adjacent North Fork Stanislaus River. The elevation is 6,200 feet, with timbered sites and the river just south of camp.

Campsites, facilities: There are 25 sites for tents or RVs up to 35 feet (no hookups). Fire grills and picnic tables are provided. Drinking water and vault toilets are available. Supplies are available in Bear Valley. Leashed pets are permitted.

Reservations, fees: Reservations are not accepted. Sites are $8 per night. Open June through October, weather permitting.

Directions: From Angels Camp on Highway 49, turn east on Highway 4 and drive about 44 miles to Spicer Reservoir Road. Turn right and drive four miles to the campground on the right side of the road.

Contact: Stanislaus National Forest, Calaveras Ranger District, 209/795-1381, fax 209/795-6849.

162 BOARDS CROSSING

🛶 🐕 ⛺

Scenic rating: 8

on the North Fork of the Stanislaus River in Stanislaus National Forest

Map 6.2, page 366

One of the oldest campgrounds in the western United States, Boards Crossing is near a historic one-way bridge that crosses the North Fork Stanislaus River. It is a small, primitive camp set along the river at 3,800 feet in elevation, with Beaver Creek three miles to the east (continue on the access road after crossing the bridge). This place is just far enough off Highway 4 to be overlooked by most campers.

Campsites, facilities: There are five tent sites. Picnic tables and fire rings are provided. Vault toilets are available. No drinking water is available. Garbage must be packed out. You can buy groceries and propane gas within 10 miles. Leashed pets are permitted.

Reservations, fees: Reservations are not accepted. There is no fee for camping.

Campfire permits are required (free). Open June through October, weather permitting.
Directions: From Angels Camp, drive east on Highway 4 and pass Arnold to Dorrington and Boards Crossing Road on the right. Turn right and drive about four miles to the campground entrance road on the right. Turn right and drive about a mile to the campground on the right.
Contact: Stanislaus National Forest, Calaveras Ranger District, 209/795-1381, fax 209/795-6849.

163 GOLDEN PINES RV RESORT AND CAMPGROUND

Scenic rating: 6

near Arnold

Map 6.2, page 366

This is a privately operated park set at 5,800 feet on the slopes of the Sierra Nevada. The resort is surrounded by 400 acres of forest and has a self-guided nature trail. Nearby destinations include Stanislaus National Forest, the North Stanislaus River, and Calaveras Big Trees State Park (two miles away). The latter features 150 giant sequoias, along with the biggest stump you can imagine, and two easy hikes, one routed through the North Grove, another through the South Grove. The Bear Valley/Mount Reba ski resort is nearby. Note that about half the sites here are long-term vacation leases.

Campsites, facilities: There are 33 sites with full or partial hookups (30 amps) for RVs up to 42 feet, and 40 tent sites. Picnic tables, fire pits, and barbecues are provided. Drinking water, restrooms with showers, seasonal heated swimming pool, playground, horseshoes, table tennis, volleyball, group facilities, pay phone, coin laundry, and propane gas are available. Some facilities are wheelchair-accessible. Leashed pets are permitted.

Reservations, fees: Reservations are recommended. Sites are $20–35 per night, $2.50 per night for each additional vehicle, $2.50 one-time charge per pet. Some credit cards accepted. Open year-round.
Directions: From Angels Camp, turn northeast on Highway 4 and drive 22 miles to Arnold. Continue for seven miles to the campground entrance on the left.
Contact: Golden Pines RV Resort and Campground, 209/795-2820, www.golden-pinesrvresort.com.

164 NORTH GROVE

Scenic rating: 7

in Calaveras Big Trees State Park

Map 6.2, page 366

This is one of two campgrounds at Calaveras Big Trees State Park, the state park known for its two groves of giant sequoias (Sierra redwoods). The park covers 6,500 acres, preserving the extraordinary North Grove of giant sequoias. The grove includes the Discovery Tree. Through the years, additional acreage surrounding the grove has been added, providing a mixed conifer forest as a buffer around the giant sequoias. The trailhead for a hike on North Grove Loop is here; it's an easy 1.5-mile walk that is routed among 150 sequoias; the sweet fragrance of the huge trees fills the air. These trees are known for their massive diameter, not for their height, as is the case with coastal redwoods. Another hike, a five-miler, is in the South Grove, where the park's two largest sequoias (the Agassiz Tree and the Palace Hotel Tree) can be seen on a spur trail. A visitors center is open during peak periods, offering exhibits on the giant sequoia and natural history. The North Fork Stanislaus River runs near Highway 4, providing trout-fishing access. The Stanislaus (near the bridge) and Beaver Creek (about 10 miles away) are stocked with trout in late spring and early summer. In the winter, this is a popular spot for cross-country skiing and snowshoeing. The elevation is 4,800 feet.

Campsites, facilities: There are 51 sites for tents, 48 sites for RVs up to 30 feet (no hookups), five hike-in environmental sites, and two group sites for 40–60 people each. Fire grills, food lockers, and picnic tables are provided. Drinking water, restrooms with flush toilets and coin showers, firewood, and a dump station are available. Some facilities are wheelchair-accessible, including a nature trail and exhibits. No bicycles are allowed on the paths, but they are permitted on fire roads and paved roads. Leashed pets are permitted, but not on trails.

Reservations, fees: Reservations are accepted ($7.50 reservation fee) at 800/444-PARK (800/444-7275) or www.reserveamerica.com. Sites are $25 per night, $6 per night for each additional vehicle, $90–135 per night for group sites, and $15 per night for environmental sites. Open year-round, with 12 sites available in winter.

Directions: From Angels Camp, drive east on Highway 4 for 23 miles to Arnold and then continue another four miles to the park entrance on the right.

Contact: Calaveras Big Trees State Park, 209/795-2334; Columbia State Park, 209/532-0150, www.parks.ca.gov.

165 OAK HOLLOW
🚶 🚴 🏊 ⚓ ❄ 🐕 ♿ 🚐 ⛺

Scenic rating: 7

in Calaveras Big Trees State Park

Map 6.2, page 366

This is one of two campgrounds at Calaveras Big Trees State Park. (See the previous listing, *North Grove,* for recreation information.)

Campsites, facilities: There are 23 sites for tents only, and 18 sites for RVs up to 30 feet (no hookups). Picnic tables, fire rings, and food lockers are provided. Drinking water and restrooms with flush toilets and coin showers are available. A dump station is available four

miles away at North Grove. You can buy supplies in Dorrington or Arnold. Some facilities are wheelchair-accessible, including a nature trail and exhibits. Leashed pets are permitted in the campground, but not on trails.

Reservations, fees: Reservations are accepted ($7.50 reservation fee) at 800/444-PARK (800/444-7275) or www.reserveamerica.com. Sites are $25 per night, $6 per night for each additional vehicle. Open March through November.

Directions: From Angels Camp, drive east on Highway 4 for 23 miles to Arnold and then continue four miles to the park entrance on the right. Continue another four miles to the campground on the right.

Contact: Calaveras Big Trees State Park, 209/795-2334; Columbia State Park, 209/532-0150, www.parks.ca.gov.

166 BEARDSLEY
🚶 🏊 ⚓ 🚤 🦌 🚐 ⛺

Scenic rating: 6

at Beardsley Reservoir in Stanislaus National Forest

Map 6.2, page 366

This lake is set in a deep canyon with a paved ramp, nice picnic area, and a fair beach. It is often an outstanding fishery early in the season for brown trout, and then once planted, good for limits of hatchery fish during the evening bite. In winter and spring, as soon as the gate is opened to the boat ramp access road, the fishing is best when the wind blows. This lake allows powerboats and all water sports. The water is generally warm enough for swimmers by midsummer. The camp is set at 3,400 feet, but because it is near the bottom of the lake canyon, it actually feels much higher in elevation. Since the lake is a reservoir, it is subject to severe drawdowns. Bonus: There is more fishing nearby on the Middle Fork of the Stanislaus.

Campsites, facilities: There are 16 sites for tents or RVs up to 22 feet (no hookups). Fire rings are provided. Vault toilets are available.

No drinking water is available. Garbage must be packed out. Leashed pets are permitted.

Reservations, fees: Reservations are not accepted. There is no fee for camping. Open May through October, weather permitting (the road is often gated at the top of the canyon, when the boat ramp road at lake level is iced over).

Directions: From Sonora, drive east on Highway 108 for about 25 miles to Strawberry and the turnoff for Beardsley Reservoir/Forest Road 52. Turn left and drive seven miles to Beardsley Dam. Continue for 0.25 mile past the dam to the campground.

Contact: Stanislaus National Forest, Summit Ranger District, 209/965-3434, fax 209/965-3372.

167 FRASER FLAT

Scenic rating: 7

on the South Fork of the Stanislaus River in Stanislaus National Forest

Map 6.2, page 366

This camp is set along the South Fork of the Stanislaus River at an elevation of 4,800 feet. If the fish aren't biting, a short side trip via Forest Service roads will route you north into the main canyon of the Middle Fork Stanislaus. A map of Stanislaus National Forest is required for this adventure.

Campsites, facilities: There are 38 sites for tents or RVs up to 30 feet (no hookups). Picnic tables and fire grills are provided. Drinking water, vault toilets, and a wheelchair-accessible fishing pier are available. Some facilities are wheelchair-accessible. A grocery store and propane gas are nearby. Leashed pets are permitted.

Reservations, fees: Reservations are not accepted. Sites are $15 per night, $5 per night for each additional vehicle. Open May through October, weather permitting.

Directions: From Sonora, drive east on Highway 108 to Long Barn. Continue east for six miles to Spring Gap Road/Forest Road

4N01. Turn left and drive three miles to the campground on the left side of the road.

Contact: Stanislaus National Forest, Mi-Wok Ranger District, 209/586-3234, fax 209/586-0643.

168 HULL CREEK

Scenic rating: 7

in Stanislaus National Forest

Map 6.2, page 366

This obscure camp borders little Hull Creek (too small for trout fishing) at 5,600 feet elevation in Stanislaus National Forest. This is a good spot for those wishing to test out four-wheel-drive vehicles, with an intricate set of Forest Service roads available to the east. To explore that area, a map of Stanislaus National Forest is essential.

Campsites, facilities: There are 18 sites for tents or RVs up to 22 feet (no hookups). Picnic tables and fire grills are provided. Drinking water and vault toilets are available. Leashed pets are permitted.

Reservations, fees: Reservations are not accepted. Sites are $5 per night. Open May through October, weather permitting.

Directions: From Sonora, drive east on Highway 108 to Long Barn and the Long Barn Fire Station and a signed turnoff for the campground at Road 31/Forest Road 3N01. Turn right and drive 12 miles to the campground on the left side of the road.

Contact: Stanislaus National Forest, Mi-Wok Ranger District, 209/586-3234, fax 209/586-0643.

169 SUGARPINE RV PARK

Scenic rating: 5

in Twain Harte

Map 6.2, page 366

Twain Harte is a beautiful little town, right at the edge of the snow line in winter, and right where pines take over the alpine landscape. This park is at the threshold of mountain country, with Pinecrest, Dodge Ridge, and Beardsley Reservoir nearby. It sits on 15 acres and features several walking paths. Note that only 17 of the RV sites are available for overnight campers; the other sites are rented as annual vacation leases. RVs and mobile homes are also for sale at the park.

Campsites, facilities: There are 78 sites with full hookups (20, 30, and 50 amps) for RVs up to 40 feet, 15 tent sites, and three park-model cabins. Picnic tables are provided. Restrooms with showers, cable TV, modem access, playground, seasonal swimming pool, horseshoes, volleyball, badminton, tetherball, basketball, coin laundry, group facilities, and a convenience store are available. Some facilities are wheelchair-accessible. Leashed pets are permitted.

Reservations, fees: Reservations are accepted. Sites are $20–32 per night, $1 per pet per night, $3 per night for each additional vehicle, with exception for towed vehicles. Some credit cards accepted. Open year-round.

Directions: From Sonora, drive east on Highway 108 for 17 miles to the park on the right side of the road, three miles east of Twain Harte.

Contact: Sugarpine RV Park, 209/586-4631.

170 KIT CARSON
🚶 🏊 🐕 🚐 ⛺

Scenic rating: 8

on the West Fork of the Carson River in Humboldt-Toiyabe National Forest

Map 6.3, page 367

This is one in a series of pristine, high-Sierra camps set along the West Fork of the Carson River. There's good trout fishing, thanks to regular stocks from the Department of Fish and Game. This is no secret, however, and the area from the Highway 89 bridge on downstream gets a lot of fishing pressure. The elevation is 6,900 feet.

Campsites, facilities: There are 12 sites for tents or RVs up to 22 feet (no hookups). Picnic tables and fire grills are provided. Drinking water and vault toilets are available. Leashed pets are permitted.

Reservations, fees: Reservations are not accepted. Sites are $12 per night. Open late-May to mid-September, weather permitting.

Directions: From Sacramento, drive east on U.S. 50 to the junction with Highway 89. Turn south on Highway 89 and drive over Luther Pass to the junction with Highway 88. Turn left and drive a mile to the campground on the left side of the road.

From Jackson, drive east on Highway 88 over Carson Pass and to the junction with Highway 89 and then continue for a mile to the campground on the left side of the road.

Contact: Humboldt-Toiyabe National Forest, Carson Ranger District, 775/882-2766, fax 775/884-8199.

171 SNOWSHOE SPRINGS
🚶 🏊 🐕 🚐 ⛺

Scenic rating: 8

on the West Fork of the Carson River in Humboldt-Toiyabe National Forest

Map 6.3, page 367

Take your pick of this or the other three streamside camps on the West Fork of the Carson River. This one is at 6,100 feet. Trout are plentiful but rarely grow very large.

Campsites, facilities: There are 19 sites for tents or RVs up to 16 feet (no hookups). Picnic tables and fire grills are provided. Drinking water and vault toilets are available. Leashed pets are permitted.

Reservations, fees: Reservations are not accepted. Sites are $12 per night. Open late May to mid-September.

Directions: From Sacramento, drive east on U.S. 50 to the junction with Highway 89. Turn south on Highway 89 and drive over Luther Pass to the junction with Highway 88. Turn left (east) and drive two miles to the campground on the right side of the road.

From Jackson, drive east on Highway 88 over Carson Pass to the junction with Highway 89 and continue for two miles to the campground on the right side of the road.

Contact: Humboldt-Toiyabe National Forest, Carson Ranger District, 775/882-2766, fax 775/884-8199.

172 CRYSTAL SPRINGS

Scenic rating: 8

on the West Fork of the Carson River in Humboldt-Toiyabe National Forest

Map 6.3, page 367

For many people, this camp is an ideal choice. It is set at an elevation of 6,000 feet, right alongside the West Fork of the Carson River. This stretch of water is stocked with trout by the Department of Fish and Game. Crystal Springs is easy to reach, just off Highway 88, and supplies can be obtained in nearby Woodfords or Markleeville. Grover Hot Springs State Park makes a good side-trip destination.

Campsites, facilities: There are 20 sites for tents or RVs up to 22 feet (no hookups). Picnic tables and fire grills are provided. Drinking water and vault toilets are available. Some facilities are wheelchair-accessible. Leashed pets are permitted.

Reservations, fees: Reservations are not accepted. Sites are $12 per night. Open late April to early October, weather permitting.

Directions: From Sacramento, drive east on U.S. 50 to the junction with Highway 89. Turn south on Highway 89 and drive over Luther Pass to the junction with Highway 88. Turn left (east) and drive 4.5 miles to the campground on the right side of the road.

From Jackson, drive east on Highway 88 over Carson Pass to the junction with Highway 89 and continue for 4.5 miles to the campground on the right side of the road.

Contact: Humboldt-Toiyabe National Forest, Carson Ranger District, 775/882-2766, fax 775/884-8199.

173 INDIAN CREEK RECREATION AREA

Scenic rating: 10

near Indian Creek Reservoir and Markleeville

Map 6.3, page 367

This beautiful campground is set amid sparse pines near Indian Creek Reservoir, elevation 5,600 feet. The campground is popular and often fills to capacity. This is an excellent lake for trout fishing, and the nearby Carson River is managed as a trophy trout fishery. The lake covers 160 acres, with a maximum speed for boats on the lake set at 5 mph. Sailing, sailboarding, and swimming are allowed. There are several good hikes in the vicinity as well. The best is a short trek, a one-mile climb to Summit Lake, with scenic views of the Indian Creek area. Summers are dry and warm here, with high temperatures typically in the 80s, and nights cool and comfortable. (There is little shade in the summer at the group site.) Bears provide an occasional visit. The lake freezes over in winter. It is about 35 miles to Carson City, Nevada, and two miles to Markleeville.

Campsites, facilities: There are 19 sites for tents or RVs up to 30 feet (no hookups), 10 walk-in sites for tents only, and a group tent site for up to 40 people. Picnic tables and fire grills are provided. Drinking water and restrooms with flush toilets and showers are available. A boat ramp is nearby. Some facilities are wheelchair accessible. Leashed pets are permitted.

Reservations, fees: Reservations are not accepted for individual sites but are required for the group tent site at 775/885-6000. Sites are $20 per night, double sites are $32 per night, $14–20 per night for walk-in sites, $5 per night for each additional vehicle, $50 per night for group site. Open late April to mid-October, weather permitting.

Directions: From Sacramento, drive east on U.S. 50 over Echo Summit to Meyers and Highway 89. Turn south on Highway 89 and drive to Highway 88. Turn left (east) on Highway 88/89 and drive six miles to Woodfords and Highway 89. Turn right (south) on Highway 89 and drive about four miles to Airport Road. Turn left on Airport Road and drive four miles to Indian Creek Reservoir. At the fork, bear left and drive to the campground on the west side of the lake.

From Markleeville, drive north on Highway 89 for about four miles to Airport Road. Turn right on Airport Road and drive about four miles to Indian Creek Reservoir. At the fork, bear left and drive to the campground on the west side of the lake.

Contact: Bureau of Land Management, Carson City Field Office, 775/885-6000, fax 775/885-6147.

174 HOPE VALLEY

Scenic rating: 7

near the Carson River in Humboldt-Toiyabe National Forest

Map 6.3, page 367

The West Fork of the Carson River runs right through Hope Valley, a pretty trout stream with a choice of four streamside campgrounds. Trout stocks are made near the campgrounds during summer. The campground at Hope Valley is just east of Carson Pass, at 7,300 feet in elevation, in a very pretty area. A trailhead for the Pacific Crest Trail is three miles south of the campground. The primary nearby destination is Blue Lakes, about a 10-minute drive away. Insider's note: Little Tamarack Lake, set just beyond the turnoff for Lower Blue Lake, is excellent for swimming.

Campsites, facilities: There are 20 sites for tents or RVs up to 22 feet and a group site for tents or RVs up to 22 feet that can accommodate up to 16 people. No hookups. Picnic tables and fire grills are provided. Drinking water and vault toilets are available. Leashed pets are permitted.

Reservations, fees: Reservations ($9 reservation fee) are accepted for individual sites and are required for the group site at 877/444-6777 or www.ReserveUSA.com. Sites are $13 per night, $25 per night for the group camp. Open June through September.

Directions: From Sacramento, drive east on U.S. 50 to the junction with Highway 89. Turn south on Highway 89 and drive over Luther Pass to the junction with Highway 88. Turn right (west) and drive two miles to Blue Lakes Road. Turn left (south) and drive 1.5 miles to the campground on the right side of the road.

From Jackson, drive east on Highway 88 over Carson Pass and continue east for five miles to Blue Lakes Road. Turn right (south) and drive 1.5 miles to the campground on the right side of the road.

Contact: Humboldt-Toiyabe National Forest, Carson Ranger District, 775/882-2766, fax 775/884-8199.

175 TURTLE ROCK PARK

Scenic rating: 5

near Woodfords

Map 6.3, page 367

Because it is administered at the county level, this pretty, wooded campground, set at 6,000 feet, gets missed by a lot of folks. Most vacationers want the more pristine beauty of the nearby camps along the Carson River. But it doesn't get missed by mountain bikers, who travel here every July for the "Death Ride," a wild ride over several mountain passes. The camp always fills for this event. (If it snows, it closes, so call ahead if you're planning an autumn visit.) Nearby side trips include Grover Hot Springs and the hot springs in Markleeville.

Campsites, facilities: There are 28 sites for tents or RVs up to 34 feet (no hookups). Picnic tables and fire grills are provided. Drinking water, vault toilets, and showers are available. A recreation building is available for rent. A camp host is on-site. Some facilities are wheelchair-accessible. Coin laundry, groceries, and propane gas are available within two miles. Leashed pets are permitted.

Reservations, fees: Reservations are not accepted. Sites are $10 per night, $3 per night for each additional vehicle. Monthly rates available. Open May to mid-October, weather permitting.

Directions: From Sacramento, drive east on U.S. 50 to the junction with Highway 89. Turn south on Highway 89 and drive over Luther Pass to the junction with Highway 88. Turn left (east) and drive to Woodfords and the junction with Highway 89. Turn south on Highway 89 and drive 4.5 miles to the park entrance on the right side of the road.

Contact: Alpine County Public Works, 530/694-2140.

176 GROVER HOT SPRINGS STATE PARK

Scenic rating: 8

near Markleeville

Map 6.3, page 367

This is a famous spot for folks who like the rejuvenating powers of hot springs. Some say they feel a glow about them for weeks. When touring the South Tahoe/Carson Pass area, many vacationers take part of a day to make the trip to the hot springs. This park is set in alpine meadow at 5,900 feet on the east side of the Sierra at the edge of the Great Basin, and surrounded by peaks that top 10,000 feet. The hot springs are green because of the mineral deposits at the bottom of the pools. The landscape is primarily pine forest and sagebrush. It is well known for the great fluctuations in weather, from serious blizzards to intense, dry heat, and from mild nights to awesome rim-rattling thunderstorms. High winds are occasional but legendary. During thunderstorms, the hot springs pools close because of the chance of lightning strikes. Yet they remain open in snow, even blizzards, when it can be a euphoric experience to sit in the steaming water. Note that the pools are closed for maintenance for two weeks in September. A forest fire near here remains in evidence. A 2.4-mile round-trip hike starts from the campground and continues to a series of small waterfalls. Side-trip options include a nature trail in the park and driving to the Carson River (where the water is a mite cooler) and fishing for trout.

Campsites, facilities: There are 26 sites for tents, and 50 sites for tents or RVs up to 27 feet (no hookups) and trailers up to 24 feet. Picnic tables, fire grills, and food lockers are provided. Restrooms with flush toilets and coin showers (summer only), drinking water, hot springs pool with wheelchair access, and heated swimming pool are available. A grocery store is four miles away, and a coin laundry is within 10 miles. Leashed pets are permitted.

Reservations, fees: Reservations are accepted ($7.50 reservation fee) at 800/444-PARK (800/444-7275) or www.reserveamerica.com. Sites are $20–25 per night, $6 per night for each additional vehicle, pool fees are $2–5 per person per day. Open year-round, with reduced facilities in winter.

Directions: From Sacramento, drive east on U.S. 50 to the junction with Highway 89. Turn south on Highway 89 and drive over Luther Pass to the junction with Highway 88. Turn left and drive to Woodfords and the junction with Highway 89. Turn right (south) and drive six miles to Markleeville and the junction with Hot Springs Road. Turn right and drive four miles to the park entrance.

Contact: Grover Hot Springs State Park, 530/694-2248; Sierra District, 530/525-7232, www.parks.ca.gov.

177 MARKLEEVILLE

Scenic rating: 7

on Markleeville Creek in Humboldt-Toiyabe National Forest

Map 6.3, page 367

This is a pretty, streamside camp set at 5,500 feet along Markleeville Creek, a mile from the East Fork of the Carson River. The trout here are willing, but alas, are dinkers. This area is the transition zone where high mountains to the west give way to the high desert to the east. The hot springs in Markleeville and Grover Hot Springs State Park provide good side trips.

Campsites, facilities: There are 10 sites for tents or RVs up to 20 feet (no hookups). Trailers are not recommended because of road conditions. Picnic tables and fire grills are provided. Drinking water and vault toilets are available. A grocery store and restaurant are nearby. Leashed pets are permitted.

Reservations, fees: Reservations are not accepted. Sites are $12 per night. Open late April through September, weather permitting.

Directions: From Sacramento, drive east on U.S. 50 to the junction with Highway 89. Turn south on Highway 89 and drive over Luther Pass to the junction with Highway 88. Turn left and drive to Woodfords and the junction with Highway 89. Turn south, drive six miles to Markleeville, and continue for 0.5 mile to the campground on the left side of the highway.

Contact: Humboldt-Toiyabe National Forest, Carson Ranger District, 775/882-2766, fax 775/884-8199.

178 TOPAZ LAKE RV PARK

Scenic rating: 6

on Topaz Lake, near Markleeville

Map 6.3, page 367

Topaz Lake, set at 5,000 feet, is one of the hidden surprises for California anglers. The surprise is the size of the rainbow trout, with one of the highest rates of 15- to 18-inch trout of any lake in the mountain country. All water sports are allowed on this 2,400-acre lake, and there is a swimming area. The campground itself is attractive, with a number of shade trees. The setting is on the edge of barren high desert, which also serves as the border between California and Nevada. Wind is a problem for small boats, especially in the early summer. Some of the sites here are rented for the entire season.

Campsites, facilities: There are 54 sites with full hookups (30 amps) for RVs up to 40 feet. Some sites are pull-through. Tents are allowed with RVs only. Picnic tables and cable TV are provided. Restrooms with coin showers, coin laundry, propane gas, small grocery store, fish-cleaning station, and modem access are available. A 40-boat marina with courtesy launch and boat-trailer storage is available at lakeside. Some facilities are wheelchair-accessible. Leashed pets are permitted.

Reservations, fees: Reservations are accepted. Sites are $24–26 per night, $2 per person for more than two people. Monthly rates available. Some credit cards accepted. Open March to early October, weather permitting.

Directions: From Carson City, drive south on U.S. 395 for 45 miles to Topaz Lake and the campground on the left side of the road.

From Bridgeport, drive north on U.S. 395 for 45 miles to the campground on the right side of the road (0.3 mile south of the California/Nevada border).

Contact: Topaz Lake RV Park, 530/495-2357, fax 530/495-2118.

179 UPPER BLUE LAKE DAM AND EXPANSION

Scenic rating: 7

near Carson Pass

Map 6.3, page 367

These two camps are set across the road from each other along Upper Blue Lake, and are two of five camps in the area. The trout fishing is usually quite good here in early summer. (See *Lower Blue Lake* listing in this chapter for more information.) These camps are three miles past the Lower Blue Lake campground. The elevation is 8,400 feet.

Campsites, facilities: There are 10 sites at Upper Blue Lake Dam and 15 sites at the expansion area for tents or RVs up to 25 feet. Picnic tables and fire grills are provided at Upper Blue Lake Dam only. Drinking water and vault toilets are available. Some facilities are wheelchair-accessible. Leashed pets are permitted.

Reservations, fees: Reservations are not accepted. Sites are $16 per night, $5 per night for each additional vehicle, $1 per pet per night. Open June to mid-September, weather permitting.

Directions: From Sacramento, drive east on U.S. 50 to the junction with Highway 89. Turn south on Highway 89 and drive over Luther Pass to the junction with Highway 88. Turn right and drive 2.5 miles to Blue Lakes Road. Turn left and drive 12 miles to the junction at the south end of Lower Blue Lake. Turn right and drive three miles to the Upper Blue Lake Dam campground on the left side of the road or the expansion area on the right.

From Jackson, drive east on Highway 88 over Carson Pass and continue east for five miles to Blue Lakes Road. Turn right (south) and drive 12 miles to a junction at the south end of Lower Blue Lake. Turn right and drive three miles to the Upper Blue Lake Dam campground on the left side of the road or the expansion area on the right.

Contact: PG&E Land Projects, 916/386-5164, www.pge.com/recreation.

180 MIDDLE CREEK AND EXPANSION

Scenic rating: 7

near Carson Pass and Blue Lakes

Map 6.3, page 367

This tiny, captivating spot, set along the creek that connects Upper and Lower Blue Lakes, provides a take-your-pick deal for anglers. PG&E has expanded this facility and now offers a larger camping area about 200 yards from the original campground. (See the next listing, *Lower Blue Lake*, for more information.) The elevation is 8,200 feet.

Campsites, facilities: There are five sites for tents or RVs up to 30 feet at Middle Creek and 25 sites for tents or RVs up to 45 feet at the expansion area. No hookups. Picnic tables and fire grills are provided. Drinking water and vault toilets are available at the expansion area. Some facilities are wheelchair-accessible. Leashed pets are permitted.

Reservations, fees: Reservations are not accepted. Sites are $16 per night, $5 per night for each additional vehicle, $1 per pet per night. Open June through September, weather permitting.

Directions: From Sacramento, drive east on U.S. 50 to the junction with Highway 89. Turn south on Highway 89 and drive over Luther Pass to the junction with Highway 88. Turn right and drive 2.5 miles to Blue Lakes Road. Turn left and drive 12 miles to a junction at the south end of Lower Blue Lake. Turn right and drive 1.5 miles to the Middle Creek campground on the left side of the road and continue another 200 yards to reach the expansion area.

From Jackson, drive east on Highway 88 over Carson Pass and continue east for five miles to Blue Lakes Road. Turn right (south) and drive 12 miles (road becomes dirt) to a junction at the south end of Lower Blue Lake. Turn right and drive 1.5 miles to the Middle Creek campground on the left side of the road and continue another 200 yards to reach the expansion area.

Contact: PG&E Land Projects, 916/386-5164, www.pge.com/recreation.

181 LOWER BLUE LAKE

🚶 🏊 🎣 🚴 🐎 🚐 ⛺

Scenic rating: 7

near Carson Pass

Map 6.3, page 367

This is the high country, 8,400 feet, where the terrain is stark and steep and edged by volcanic ridgelines, and where the deep blue-green hue of lake water brightens the landscape. Lower Blue Lake provides a popular trout fishery, with rainbow, brook, and cutthroat trout all stocked regularly. The boat ramp is adjacent to the campground. The access road crosses the Pacific Crest Trail, providing a route to a series of small, pretty, hike-to lakes just outside the edge of the Mokelumne Wilderness.

Campsites, facilities: There are 17 sites for tents or RVs to 25 feet (no hookups). Picnic tables and fire grills are provided. Drinking water and vault toilets are available. Leashed pets are permitted.

Reservations, fees: Reservations are not accepted. Sites are $16 per night, $5 per night for each additional vehicle, $1 per pet per night, 14-day occupancy limit. Open June through September, weather permitting.

Directions: From Sacramento, drive east on U.S. 50 to the junction with Highway 89. Turn south on Highway 89 and drive over Luther Pass to the junction with Highway 88. Turn right and drive 2.5 miles to Blue Lakes Road. Turn left and drive 12 miles to a junction at the south end of Lower Blue Lake. Turn right and drive a short distance to the campground on the left side of the road.

From Jackson, drive east on Highway 88 over Carson Pass and continue east for five miles to Blue Lakes Road. Turn right (south) and drive 12 miles to a junction at the south

end of Lower Blue Lake. Turn right and drive a short distance to the campground on the left.

Contact: PG&E Land Projects, 916/386-5164, www.pge.com/recreation.

182 SILVER CREEK

🎣 🐎 ♿ 🚐 ⛺

Scenic rating: 6

in Humboldt-Toiyabe National Forest

Map 6.3, page 367

This pretty spot, set near Silver Creek, has easy access from Highway 4 and, in years without washouts, good fishing in early summer for small trout. It is in the remote high Sierra, east of Ebbetts Pass. A side trip to Ebbetts Pass features Kinney Lake, Pacific Crest Trail access, and a trailhead at the north end of the lake (on the west side of Highway 4) for a mile hike to Lower Kinney Lake. No bikes are permitted on the trails. The elevation is 6,800 feet.

Campsites, facilities: There are 22 sites for tents or RVs up to 22 feet (no hookups). Picnic tables and fire grills are provided. Drinking water and vault toilets are available. Some facilities are wheelchair-accessible. Leashed pets are permitted.

Reservations, fees: Reservations are accepted ($9 reservation fee) at 877/444-6777 or www.ReserveUSA.com. Sites are $13 per night. Open late May to early September, weather permitting.

Directions: From Angels Camp, drive east on Highway 4 all the way over Ebbetts Pass and continue for about six miles to the campground.

From Markleeville, drive south on Highway 89 to the junction with Highway 4. Turn west on Highway 4 (steep and winding) and drive about five miles to the campground.

Contact: Humboldt-Toiyabe National Forest, Carson Ranger District, 775/882-2766, fax 775/884-8199.

183 MOSQUITO LAKE

🚶 ≋ 🛶 🏕 🚐 ⛺

Scenic rating: 10

at Mosquito Lake in Stanislaus National Forest

Map 6.3, page 367

Mosquito Lake is in a pristine Sierra setting at 8,260 feet, presenting remarkable beauty for a place that can be reached by car. Most people believe that Mosquito Lake is for day-use only, and that's why they get crowded into nearby Lake Alpine Campground. But it's not just for day-use, and this camp is often overlooked because it is about a mile west of the little lake. The lake is small, a pretty emerald green, and even has a few small trout in it. The camp provides a few dispersed sites.

Campsites, facilities: There are eight sites for tents or RVs up to 16 feet (no hookups). Picnic tables and fire grills are provided. Vault toilets are available. No drinking water is available. Garbage must be packed out. Leashed pets are permitted.

Reservations, fees: Reservations are not accepted. Sites are $5 per night. A free campfire permit is required from the district office. Open June through September, weather permitting.

Directions: From Angels Camp, drive east on Highway 4 to Lake Alpine and continue for about six miles to the campground on the left side of the road.

Contact: Stanislaus National Forest, Calaveras Ranger District, 209/795-1381, fax 209/795-6849.

184 HERMIT VALLEY

🚶 🛶 🏕 🚐 ⛺

Scenic rating: 8

in Stanislaus National Forest

Map 6.3, page 367

This tiny, remote, little-known spot is set near the border of the Mokelumne Wilderness near where Grouse Creek enters the Mokelumne River, at 7,100 feet in elevation. Looking north, there is a good view into Deer Valley. A primitive road, 0.5-mile west of camp, is routed through Deer Valley north for six miles to the Blue Lakes. On the opposite (south) side of the road from the camp there is a little-traveled hiking trail that is routed up Grouse Creek to Beaver Meadow and Willow Meadow near the border of the Carson-Iceberg Wilderness.

Campsites, facilities: There are 25 sites for tents or RVs up to 16 feet (no hookups). Vault toilets are available. No drinking water is available. Garbage must be packed out. Leashed pets are permitted.

Reservations, fees: Reservations are not accepted. There is no fee for camping. A free campfire permit is required from the district office. Open June through October, weather permitting.

Directions: From Angels Camp, drive east on Highway 4 to Lake Alpine and continue for about nine miles to the campground on the left side of the road (just east of the Mokelumne River Bridge). Note: Trailers are not recommended because of the steep access road.

Contact: Stanislaus National Forest, Calaveras Ranger District, 209/795-1381, fax 209/795-6849.

185 BLOOMFIELD

🚶 ≋ 🏕 5⁰ 🚐 ⛺

Scenic rating: 7

in Stanislaus National Forest

Map 6.3, page 367

This is a primitive and little-known camp set at 7,800 feet near Ebbetts Pass. The North Fork Mokelumne River runs right by the camp, with good stream access for about a mile on each side of the camp. The access road continues south to Highland Lakes, a destination that provides car-top boating, fair fishing, and trailheads for hiking into the Carson-Iceberg Wilderness.

Campsites, facilities: There are 20 sites for tents or RVs up to 16 feet (no hookups).

Picnic tables and fire rings are provided. Drinking water and vault toilets are available. Garbage must be packed out. Facilities and supplies are available at Lake Alpine Lodge, 25 minutes away. Leashed pets are permitted.

Reservations, fees: Reservations are not accepted. Sites are $8 per night. A free campfire permit is required from the district office. Open June through October, weather permitting.

Directions: From Angels Camp, drive east on Highway 4 to Lake Alpine and continue for about 15 miles to Forest Road 8N01 on the right side of the road (1.5 miles west of Ebbetts Pass). Turn right and drive two miles to the campground on the right side of the road. Note: Access roads are rough and not recommended for trailers.

Contact: Stanislaus National Forest, Calaveras Ranger District, 209/795-1381, fax 209/795-6849.

186 PACIFIC VALLEY

Scenic rating: 7

in Stanislaus National Forest overlooking Pacific Creek

Map 6.3, page 367

This is a do-it-yourself special; that is, more of a general area for camping than a campground, set up for backpackers heading out on expeditions into the Carson-Iceberg Wilderness to the south. It is set at 7,600 feet along Pacific Creek, a tributary to the Mokelumne River. The landscape here is an open lodgepole forest with nearby meadow and a small stream. The trail from camp is routed south and reaches three forks within two miles. The best is routed deep into the wilderness, flanking Hiram Peak (9,760 feet), Airola Peak (9,938 feet), and Iceberg Peak (9,720 feet).

Campsites, facilities: There are 15 sites for tents or RVs up to 16 feet (no hookups). Picnic tables and fire grills are provided. Vault toilets are available. No drinking water is available. Garbage must be packed out. Leashed pets are permitted.

Reservations, fees: Reservations are not accepted. There is no fee for camping. A free campfire permit is required from the district office. Open June through October, weather permitting.

Directions: From Angels Camp, drive east on Highway 4 to Lake Alpine and continue for eight miles to a dirt road. Turn right (south) and drive about 0.5 mile to the campground. Note: Trailers are not recommended because of the rough roads.

Contact: Stanislaus National Forest, Calaveras Ranger District, 209/795-1381, fax 209/795-6849.

187 UPPER AND LOWER HIGHLAND LAKES

Scenic rating: 9

in Stanislaus National Forest

Map 6.3, page 367

This camp is set between Upper and Lower Highland Lakes, two beautiful alpine ponds that offer good fishing for small brook trout as well as spectacular panoramic views. The boat speed limit is 15 mph, and a primitive boat ramp is at Upper Highland Lake. Swimming is allowed, although the water is very cold. The elevation at this campground is 8,600 feet, with Hiram Peak (9,760 feet) looming to the nearby south. Several great trails are available from this camp. Day hikes include up Boulder Creek and Disaster Creek. For overnight backpacking, a trail that starts at the north end of Highland Lakes (a parking area is available) is routed east for two miles to Wolf Creek Pass, where it connects with the Pacific Crest Trail; from there, turn left or right—you can't lose. The access road is not recommended for trailers or large RVs.

Campsites, facilities: There are 35 sites for tents or RVs up to 16 feet (no hookups). Picnic tables and fire grills are provided. Drinking water and vault toilets are available. Garbage must be packed out. Leashed pets are permitted.
Reservations, fees: Reservations are not accepted. Sites are $8 per night. Open June through October, weather permitting.
Directions: From Angels Camp, drive east on Highway 4 to Arnold, past Lake Alpine, and continue for 14.5 miles to Forest Road 8N01 (one mile west of Ebbetts Pass). Turn right and drive 7.5 miles to the campground on the right side of the road. Note: The roads are rough and trailers are not recommended.
Contact: Stanislaus National Forest, Calaveras Ranger District, 209/795-1381, fax 209/795-6849.

188 PINE MARTEN

Scenic rating: 8

near Lake Alpine in Stanislaus National Forest
Map 6.3, page 367

Lake Alpine is a beautiful Sierra lake surrounded by granite and pines and set at 7,320 feet, just above where the snowplows stop in winter. This camp is on the northeast side, about a quarter mile from the shore. Fishing for rainbow trout is good in May and early June, before the summer crush. Despite the long drive to get here, the lake is becoming better known for its beauty, camping, and hiking. Lake Alpine has 180 surface acres and a 10-mph speed limit. A trailhead out of nearby Silver Valley Camp provides a two-mile hike to pretty Duck Lake and beyond into the Carson-Iceberg Wilderness.
Campsites, facilities: There are 32 sites for tents or RVs up to 27 feet (no hookups). Picnic tables and fire grills are provided. Drinking water and restrooms with flush toilets are available. A boat ramp is nearby. A grocery store, propane gas, and coin laundry are nearby. Some facilities are wheelchair-accessible. Leashed pets are permitted.

Reservations, fees: Reservations are not accepted. Sites are $18 per night, $5 per night for each additional vehicle. Open June to early October, weather permitting.
Directions: From Angels Camp, drive east on Highway 4 to Arnold and continue for 29 miles to Lake Alpine. Drive to the northeast end of the lake to the campground entrance on the right side of the road.
Contact: Stanislaus National Forest, Calaveras Ranger District, 209/795-1381, fax 209/795-6849.

189 SILVER VALLEY

Scenic rating: 8

on Lake Alpine in Stanislaus National Forest
Map 6.3, page 367

This is one of four camps at Lake Alpine. Silver Valley is on the northeast end of the lake at 7,400 feet in elevation, with a trailhead nearby that provides access to the Carson-Iceberg Wilderness. (For recreation information, see the previous listing, *Pine Marten*.)
Campsites, facilities: There are 21 sites for tents or RVs up to 16 feet (no hookups). Picnic tables and fire grills are provided. Drinking water and vault toilets are available. Some facilities are wheelchair-accessible. A boat launch, grocery store, and coin laundry are nearby. Leashed pets are permitted.
Reservations, fees: Reservations are not accepted. Sites are $18 per night. A free campfire permit is required. Open June through October, weather permitting.
Directions: From Angels Camp, drive east on Highway 4 to Arnold and continue for 29 miles to Lake Alpine. Drive to the northeast end of the lake to the campground entrance on the right side of the road. Turn right and drive 0.5 mile to the campground.
Contact: Stanislaus National Forest, Calaveras Ranger District, 209/795-1381, fax 209/795-6849.

190 LAKE ALPINE CAMPGROUND

🚶 🏊 🎣 🛶 🏕 ♿ 🚐 ⬆

Scenic rating: 8

on Lake Alpine in Stanislaus National Forest

Map 6.3, page 367   **BEST (**

This is the campground that is in the greatest demand at Lake Alpine, and it is easy to see why. It is very small, a boat ramp is adjacent to the camp, you can get supplies at a small grocery store within walking distance, and during the evening rise you can often see the jumping trout from your campsite. Lake Alpine is one of the prettiest lakes you can drive to, set at 7,303 feet amid pines and Sierra granite. A trailhead out of nearby Silver Valley Camp provides a two-mile hike to pretty Duck Lake and beyond into the Carson-Iceberg Wilderness.

Campsites, facilities: There are 25 sites for tents or RVs up to 27 feet (no hookups). Picnic tables and fire grills are provided. Drinking water, flush and vault toilets, and a boat launch are available. A grocery store, restaurant, coin showers, and a coin laundry are nearby. Some facilities are wheelchair-accessible. Leashed pets are permitted.

Reservations, fees: Reservations are not accepted. Sites are $18 per night. Open June through October, weather permitting.

Directions: From Angels Camp, drive east on Highway 4 to Arnold and continue for 29 miles to Lake Alpine. Just before reaching the lake turn right and drive 0.25 mile to the campground on the left.

Contact: Stanislaus National Forest, Calaveras Ranger District, 209/795-1381, fax 209/795-6849.

191 SILVER TIP

🚶 🏊 🎣 🛶 🏕 ♿ 🚐 ⬆

Scenic rating: 6

near Lake Alpine in Stanislaus National Forest

Map 6.3, page 367

This camp is just over a half mile from the shore of Lake Alpine at an elevation of 7,350 feet. Why then would anyone camp here when there are campgrounds right at the lake? Two reasons: One, those lakeside camps are often full on summer weekends. Two, Highway 4 is snowplowed to this campground entrance, but not beyond. So in big snow years when the road is still closed in late spring and early summer, you can park your rig here to camp, then hike in to the lake. In the fall, it also makes for a base camp for hunters. (See the previous listing, *Lake Alpine Campground*, for more information.)

Campsites, facilities: There are 23 sites for tents or RVs up to 27 feet (no hookups). Picnic tables and fire grills are provided. Drinking water and flush toilets are available. A boat launch is about a mile away. A grocery store, coin laundry, and coin showers are nearby. Some facilities are wheelchair-accessible. Leashed pets are permitted.

Reservations, fees: Reservations are not accepted. Sites are $18 per night. Open June to early October, weather permitting.

Directions: From Angels Camp, drive east on Highway 4 to Arnold and continue for 29 miles to Lake Alpine. A mile before reaching the lake (adjacent to the Bear Valley/Mount Reba turnoff), turn right at the campground entrance on the right side of the road.

Contact: Stanislaus National Forest, Calaveras Ranger District, 209/795-1381, fax 209/795-6849.

192 UNION RESERVOIR WALK-IN

🚶 🏊 🛶 ⛵ 5% ⛺

Scenic rating: 10

northeast of Arnold in Stanislaus National Forest

Map 6.3, page 367

Union Reservoir is set in Sierra granite at 6,850 feet. It's a beautiful and quiet lake that is kept that way with rules that mandate a 5-mph speed limit and walk-in camping only. Most of the sites provide lakeside views. Fishing is often good—trolling for kokanee salmon—but you need a boat. The setting is great, especially for canoes or other small boats. This camp was once a secret, but now it fills up quickly on weekends.

Campsites, facilities: There are 15 dispersed, primitive walk-in tent sites. Pit toilets are available. No drinking water is available. Garbage must be packed out. A boat ramp is available nearby. Leashed pets are permitted.

Reservations, fees: Reservations are not accepted. There is no fee for camping. Open June through September, weather permitting.

Directions: From Angels Camp, drive east on Highway 4 for about 32 miles to Spicer Reservoir Road. Turn right and drive east for about seven miles to Forest Road 7N75. Turn left and drive three miles to Union Reservoir. There are four designated parking areas for the walk-in camps along the road.

Contact: Stanislaus National Forest, Calaveras Ranger District, 209/795-1381, fax 209/795-6849; Northern California Power Agency, 209/728-1387.

193 SPICER RESERVOIR GROUP CAMP

🚶 🏊 🛶 ⛵ 🐕 ♿ ⛺

Scenic rating: 7

near Spicer Reservoir in Stanislaus National Forest

Map 6.3, page 367

This is one of two camps at Spicer Reservoir, a small but pretty body of water set at 6,300 feet and surrounded by canyon walls. Trails along much of the lake provide a nice day-hiking option. (See next listing, *Spicer Reservoir,* for more information.)

Campsites, facilities: There is one group site for tents or RVs up to 28 feet (no hookups) that can accommodate up to 60 people. Picnic tables and fire grills are provided. Drinking water, vault toilets, group facilities, and a primitive amphitheater are available. A boat ramp is available a mile away. Some facilities are wheelchair-accessible. Leashed pets are permitted.

Reservations, fees: Reservations are required at 209/295-4512. The camp is $120 per night. Open June through September, weather permitting.

Directions: From Angels Camp, drive east on Highway 4 for about 32 miles to Spicer Reservoir Road/Forest Road 7N01. Turn right, drive seven miles, bear right at a fork with a sharp right turn, and drive a mile to the campground at the west end of the lake.

Contact: Stanislaus National Forest, Calaveras Ranger District, 209/795-1381, fax 209/795-6849.

194 SPICER RESERVOIR

🚶 🏊 🛶 ⛵ 🐕 ♿ 🚐 ⛺

Scenic rating: 8

near Spicer Reservoir in Stanislaus National Forest

Map 6.3, page 367

Set at 6,300 feet, Spicer Reservoir isn't big by reservoir standards, covering only 227 acres, but it is quite pretty from a boat and is surrounded by canyon walls. The beauty is added to by good trout fishing. A boat ramp is available near the campground, and the lake speed limit is 10 mph. A trail links the east end of Spicer Reservoir to the Summit Lake trailhead, with the route bordering the north side of the reservoir. Note: This area can really get hammered with snow in big winters, so in the spring and early summer, always check for access conditions before planning a trip.

Campsites, facilities: There are 60 sites for tents or RVs up to 50 feet (no hookups). Picnic tables and fire grills are provided. Drinking water and vault toilets are available. Some facilities are wheelchair-accessible. A boat ramp is available nearby. Leashed pets are permitted.

Reservations, fees: Reservations are not accepted. Sites are $16 per night. Open June through October, weather permitting.

Directions: From Angels Camp, drive east on Highway 4 for about 32 miles to Spicer Reservoir Road/Forest Road 7N01. Turn right, drive seven miles, bear right at a fork with a sharp right turn, and drive a mile to the campground at the west end of the lake.

Contact: Stanislaus National Forest, Calaveras Ranger District, 209/795-1381, fax 209/795-6849.

195 SAND FLAT-STANISLAUS RIVER
🧍‍♂️🏊‍♂️🚣‍♂️🏕️♿🚐⛺

Scenic rating: 7

on the Clark Fork of the Stanislaus River in Stanislaus National Forest

Map 6.3, page 367

Sand Flat campground, at 6,200 feet, is only three miles (by vehicle on Clark Fork Road) from an outstanding trailhead for the Carson-Iceberg Wilderness. The camp is used primarily by late-arriving backpackers who camp for the night, get their gear in order, then head off on the trail. The trail is routed out of Iceberg

Meadow, with a choice of heading north to Paradise Valley (unbelievably green and loaded with corn lilies along a creek) and onward to the Pacific Crest Trail, or east to Clark Fork and upstream to Clark Fork Meadow below Sonora Peak. Two choices, both winners.

Campsites, facilities: There are 53 sites for tents or RVs up to 22 feet (no hookups) and 15 walk-in tent sites. Picnic tables and fire grills are provided. Drinking water and vault toilets are available. You can buy supplies in Dardanelle. Some facilities are wheelchair-accessible. Leashed pets are permitted.

Reservations, fees: Reservations are not accepted. Sites are $9 per night per vehicle. Open May to early October, weather permitting.

Directions: From Sonora, drive east on Highway 108 past the town of Strawberry to Clark Fork Road. Turn left on Clark Fork Road and drive six miles to the campground entrance on the right side of the road.

Contact: Stanislaus National Forest, Summit Ranger District, 209/965-3434, fax 209/965-3372.

196 CLARK FORK AND CLARK FORK HORSE
🧍‍♂️🚣‍♂️🏕️🐎♿🚐⛺

Scenic rating: 8

on the Clark Fork of the Stanislaus River in Stanislaus National Forest

Map 6.3, page 367

Clark Fork borders the Clark Fork of the Stanislaus River and is used by both drive-in vacationers and backpackers. A trailhead for hikers is 0.25 mile away on the north side of Clark Fork Road (a parking area is available here). From here the trail is routed up along Arnot Creek, skirting between Iceberg Peak on the left and Lightning Mountain on the right, for eight miles to Wolf Creek Pass and the junction with the Pacific Crest Trail. (For another nearby trailhead, see the previous entry, *Sand Flat-Stanislaus River*.)

Campsites, facilities: There are 88 sites for tents or RVs up to 40 feet, and at an adjacent area, 14 equestrian sites for tents or RVs up to 22 feet. No hookups. Picnic tables and fire grills are provided. Drinking water and flush toilets are available. At the equestrian site, no drinking water is available but there are water troughs. Some facilities are wheelchair-accessible. You can buy supplies in Dardanelle. Leashed pets are permitted.

Reservations, fees: Reservations are not accepted. Sites are $12–13 per night, horse camp fee is $7 per night, $5 per night for each additional vehicle. Open May through October, weather permitting.

Directions: From Sonora, drive east on Highway 108 past the town of Strawberry to Clark Fork Road. Turn left, drive five miles, turn right again, and drive 0.5 mile to the campground entrance on the right side of the road.

Contact: Stanislaus National Forest, Summit Ranger District, 209/965-3434, fax 209/965-3372.

197 FENCE CREEK

Scenic rating: 4

near the Middle Fork of the Stanislaus River in Stanislaus National Forest

Map 6.3, page 367

Fence Creek is a feeder stream to Clark Fork, which runs a mile downstream and joins with the Middle Fork Stanislaus River en route to Donnells Reservoir. The camp sits along little Fence Creek, 5,600 feet in elevation. Fence Creek Road continues east for another nine miles to an outstanding trailhead at Iceberg Meadow on the edge of the Carson-Iceberg Wilderness.

Campsites, facilities: There are 38 sites for tents or RVs up to 22 feet (no hookups). Picnic tables and fire grills are provided. Vault toilets are available. No drinking water is available. You can buy supplies in Pinecrest about 10 miles away. Leashed pets are permitted.

Reservations, fees: Reservations are not accepted. Sites are $8 per night. Open May to mid-October, weather permitting.

Directions: From Sonora, drive east on Highway 108 about 50 miles to Clark Ford Road. Turn left and drive a mile to Forest Road 6N06. Turn left again and drive 0.5 mile to the campground on the right.

Contact: Stanislaus National Forest, Summit Ranger District, 209/965-3434, fax 209/965-3372.

198 BOULDER FLAT

Scenic rating: 7

near the Middle Fork of the Stanislaus River in Stanislaus National Forest

Map 6.3, page 367

You want camping on the Stanislaus River? As you drive east on Highway 108, this is the first in a series of campgrounds along the Middle Fork Stanislaus. Boulder Flat is set at 5,600 feet and offers easy access off the highway. Here's another bonus: This stretch of river is stocked with trout.

Campsites, facilities: There are 21 sites for tents or RVs up to 22 feet (no hookups). Picnic tables and fire grills are provided. Drinking water and vault toilets are available. You can buy supplies in Dardanelle. Some facilities are wheelchair-accessible. Leashed pets are permitted.

Reservations, fees: Reservations are not accepted. Sites are $15–17 per night, $5 per night for each additional vehicle. Open May through October, weather permitting.

Directions: From Sonora, drive east on Highway 108 past the town of Strawberry to Clark Fork Road. At Clark Fork Road, continue east on Highway 108 for a mile to the campground on the left side of the road.

Contact: Stanislaus National Forest, Summit Ranger District, 209/965-3434, fax 209/965-3372.

199 BRIGHTMAN FLAT

Scenic rating: 7

on the Middle Fork of the Stanislaus River in Stanislaus National Forest

Map 6.3, page 367

This camp is on the Middle Fork of the Stanislaus River at 5,700 feet elevation, a mile east of Boulder Flat and two miles west of Dardanelle. (For recreation options, see the *Pigeon Flat* listing in this chapter.)

Campsites, facilities: There are 33 sites for tents or RVs up to 22 feet (no hookups). Picnic tables and fire grills are provided. Vault toilets and drinking water are available. You can buy supplies in Dardanelle. Some facilities are wheelchair-accessible. Leashed pets are permitted.

Reservations, fees: Reservations are not accepted. Sites are $12 per night, $5 per night for each additional vehicle. Open May through October, weather permitting.

Directions: From Sonora, drive east on Highway 108 past the town of Strawberry to Clark Fork Road. At Clark Fork Road continue east on Highway 108 for two miles to the campground entrance on the left side of the road.

Contact: Stanislaus National Forest, Summit Ranger District, 209/965-3434, fax 209/965-3372.

200 DARDANELLE

Scenic rating: 7

on the Middle Fork of the Stanislaus River in Stanislaus National Forest

Map 6.3, page 367

This Forest Service camp is within walking distance of supplies in Dardanelle and is also right alongside the Middle Fork Stanislaus River. This section of river is stocked with trout by the Department of Fish and Game. The trail to see Columns of the Giants is just 1.5 miles to the east out of Pigeon Flat.

Campsites, facilities: There are 28 sites for tents or RVs up to 28 feet (no hookups). Picnic tables and fire grills are provided. Drinking water and vault toilets are available. You can buy supplies in Dardanelle. Some facilities are wheelchair-accessible. Leashed pets are permitted.

Reservations, fees: Reservations are not accepted. Sites are $17–21 per night, $5 per night for each additional vehicle. Open May through October, weather permitting.

Directions: From Sonora, drive east on Highway 108 past Strawberry to Dardanelle and the campground on the left side of the road.

Contact: Stanislaus National Forest, Summit Ranger District, 209/965-3434, fax 209/965-3372.

201 PIGEON FLAT

Scenic rating: 7

on the Middle Fork of the Stanislaus River in Stanislaus National Forest

Map 6.3, page 367

The prime attraction at Pigeon Flat is the short trail to Columns of the Giants, a rare example of columnar hexagonal rock, similar to the phenomenon at Devils Postpile near Mammoth Lakes. In addition, the camp is adjacent to the Middle Fork Stanislaus River; trout are small here and get fished hard. Supplies are available within walking distance in Dardanelle. The elevation is 6,000 feet.

Campsites, facilities: There are nine walk-in tent sites. Picnic tables and fire grills are provided. Vault toilets are available. No drinking water is available. You can buy supplies in Dardanelle. Leashed pets are permitted.

Reservations, fees: Reservations are not accepted. Sites are $10 per night, $5 per night for each additional vehicle. Open May through October, weather permitting.

Directions: From Sonora, drive east on Highway 108 past the town of Strawberry to Dardanelle. Continue 1.5 miles east to the campground on the right side of the road, next to the Columns of the Giants Interpretive Site.

Contact: Stanislaus National Forest, Summit Ranger District, 209/965-3434, fax 209/965-3372.

202 EUREKA VALLEY

Scenic rating: 8

on the Middle Fork of the Stanislaus River in Stanislaus National Forest

Map 6.3, page 367

There are about a half-dozen campgrounds on this stretch of the Middle Fork Stanislaus River near Dardanelle, at 6,100 feet in elevation. The river runs along two sides of this campground, making it quite pretty. This stretch of river is planted with trout by the Department of Fish and Game, but it is hit pretty hard despite its relatively isolated location. A good short and easy hike is to Columns of the Giants, accessible on a 0.25-mile-long trail out of Pigeon Flat, a mile to the west.

Campsites, facilities: There are 28 sites for tents or RVs up to 22 feet (no hookups). Picnic tables and fire grills are provided. Drinking water and vault toilets are available. You can buy supplies in Dardanelle. Leashed pets are permitted.

Reservations, fees: Reservations are not accepted. Sites are $15 per night, $5 per night for each additional vehicle. Open May through October, weather permitting.

Directions: From Sonora, drive east on Highway 108 past the town of Strawberry to Dardanelle. Continue three miles east to the campground on the right.

Contact: Stanislaus National Forest, Summit Ranger District, 209/965-3434, fax 209/965-3372.

203 NIAGARA CREEK

Scenic rating: 6

in Stanislaus National Forest

Map 6.3, page 367

This camp is set beside Niagara Creek at 6,600 feet, high in Stanislaus National Forest on the western slopes of the Sierra. It provides direct access to a network of roads in national forest, including routes to Double Dome Rock and another to Eagle Meadows. So if you have a four-wheel-drive vehicle or dirt bike, this is the place to come.

Campsites, facilities: There are 10 sites for tents or RVs up to 22 feet (no hookups); some are walk-in sites. Picnic tables and fire grills are provided. A vault toilet is available. No drinking water is available. You can buy supplies in Pinecrest about 10 miles away. Leashed pets are permitted.

Reservations, fees: Reservations are not accepted. Sites are $6 per night. Open May through October, weather permitting.

Directions: From Sonora, drive east on Highway 108 to the town of Strawberry and continue for about 15 miles to Eagle Meadows Road/Forest Road 5N01 on the right. Turn right and drive 0.5 mile to the campground on the left.

Contact: Stanislaus National Forest, Summit Ranger District, 209/965-3434, fax 209/965-3372.

204 MILL CREEK

Scenic rating: 7

on Mill Creek in Stanislaus National Forest

Map 6.3, page 367

This pretty little camp is set along Mill Creek at 6,200 feet in elevation, high in Stanislaus National Forest, near a variety of outdoor recreation options. The camp is near the Middle Fork Stanislaus River, which is stocked with trout near Donnells. For hiking, there is an outstanding trailhead at Kennedy Meadow (east of Donnells).

For fishing, both Beardsley Reservoir (boat necessary) and Pinecrest Lake (shoreline prospects fair) provide two nearby alternatives.

Campsites, facilities: There are 18 sites for tents or RVs up to 22 feet (no hookups). Picnic tables and fire grills are provided. Vault toilets are available. No drinking water is available. Leashed pets are permitted.

Reservations, fees: Reservations are not accepted. Sites are $6 per night. Open May to mid-October, weather permitting.

Directions: From Sonora, drive east on Highway 108 to Strawberry. From Strawberry continue east on Highway 108 about 13 miles to Forest Road 5N21. Turn right on Forest Road 5N21 and drive 0.1 mile to the campground access road (Forest Road 5N26) on the left.

Contact: Stanislaus National Forest, Summit Ranger District, 209/965-3434, fax 209/965-3372.

205 NIAGARA CREEK OFF-HIGHWAY VEHICLE

Scenic rating: 6

on Niagara Creek in Stanislaus National Forest

Map 6.3, page 367

This small, primitive camp along Niagara Creek is designed primarily for people with off-highway vehicles. Got it? It is set on Niagara Creek near Donnells Reservoir. The elevation is 6,600 feet.

Campsites, facilities: There are 10 sites for tents or RVs up to 22 feet (no hookups). Picnic tables and fire grills are provided. A vault toilet is available. No drinking water is available. You can buy supplies in Pinecrest about 10 miles away. Leashed pets are permitted.

Reservations, fees: Reservations are not accepted. Sites are $6 per night. Open May through October, weather permitting.

Directions: From Sonora, drive east on Highway 108 to Strawberry and continue for about 15 miles to Eagle Meadows Road/Forest Road

5N01. Turn right and drive 1.5 miles to the campground on the left (just after crossing the bridge at Niagara Creek).

Contact: Stanislaus National Forest, Summit Ranger District, 209/965-3434, fax 209/965-3372.

206 BAKER

Scenic rating: 7

on the Middle Fork of the Stanislaus River in Stanislaus National Forest

Map 6.3, page 367

Baker lies at the turnoff for the well-known and popular Kennedy Meadow trailhead for the Emigrant Wilderness. The camp is set along the Middle Fork Stanislaus River, 6,200 feet elevation, downstream a short way from the confluence with Deadman Creek. The trailhead, with a nearby horse corral, is another two miles farther on the Kennedy Meadow access road. From here it is a 1.5-mile hike to a fork in the trail; right will take you two miles to Relief Reservoir, 7,226 feet, and left will route you up Kennedy Creek for five miles to pretty Kennedy Lake, just north of Kennedy Peak (10,716 feet).

Campsites, facilities: There are 44 sites for tents or RVs up to 22 feet (no hookups). Picnic tables and fire grills are provided. Drinking water and vault toilets are available. You can buy supplies in Dardanelle. Some facilities are wheelchair-accessible. Leashed pets are permitted.

Reservations, fees: Reservations are not accepted. Sites are $15 per night, $5 per night for each additional vehicle. Open May to mid-October, weather permitting.

Directions: From Sonora, drive east on Highway 108 past Strawberry to Dardanelle. From Dardanelle, continue 5.5 miles east to the campground on the right side of the road at the turnoff for Kennedy Meadow.

Contact: Stanislaus National Forest, Summit Ranger District, 209/965-3434, fax 209/965-3372.

207 DEADMAN

Scenic rating: 7

on the Middle Fork of the Stanislaus River in Stanislaus National Forest

Map 6.3, page 367

This is a popular trailhead camp and an ideal jump-off point for backpackers heading into the adjacent Emigrant Wilderness. The elevation is 6,200 feet. The camp is a short distance from Baker (see the previous listing, *Baker*, for hiking destinations).

Campsites, facilities: There are 17 sites for tents or RVs up to 22 feet (no hookups). Picnic tables and fire grills are provided. Drinking water and vault toilets are available. You can buy supplies in Dardanelle. Some facilities are wheelchair-accessible. Leashed pets are permitted.

Reservations, fees: Reservations are not accepted. Sites are $15 per night, $5 per night for each additional vehicle. Open May to early October, weather permitting.

Directions: From Sonora, drive east on Highway 108 past the town of Strawberry to Dardanelle. From Dardanelle, continue 5.5 miles east to the Kennedy Meadow turnoff. Drive a mile on Kennedy Meadow Road to the campground, which is opposite the parking area for Kennedy Meadow Trail.

Contact: Stanislaus National Forest, Summit Ranger District, 209/965-3434, fax 209/965-3372.

208 BOOTLEG

Scenic rating: 6

on the Walker River in Humboldt-Toiyabe National Forest

Map 6.3, page 367

Location is always a key, and easy access off U.S. 395, the adjacent West Walker River, and good trout stocks in summer make this a popular spot. (See the next listings, *Chris Flat* and *Sonora Bridge*, for more information.) Note that this camp is on the west side of the highway, and that anglers will have to cross the road to gain fishing access. The elevation is 6,600 feet.

Campsites, facilities: There are 63 sites for tents or RVs up to 35 feet (no hookups). Picnic tables and fire grills are provided. Drinking water and flush toilets are available. Leashed pets are permitted.

Reservations, fees: Reservations are not accepted. Sites are $15 per night, $5 per night for each additional vehicle. Open early May to mid-September, weather permitting.

Directions: From Carson City, drive south on U.S. 395 to Coleville and then continue south for 13 miles to the campground on the west side of the highway (six miles north of the junction of U.S. 395 and Highway 108).

Contact: Humboldt-Toiyabe National Forest, Bridgeport Ranger District, 760/932-7070, fax 760/932-5899.

209 CHRIS FLAT

Scenic rating: 7

on the Walker River in Humboldt-Toiyabe National Forest

Map 6.3, page 367

This is one of two campgrounds set along U.S. 395 next to the West Walker River, a pretty trout stream with easy access and good stocks of rainbow trout. The plants are usually made at two campgrounds, resulting in good prospects here at Chris Flat and west on Highway 108 at Sonora Bridge. The elevation is 6,600 feet.

Campsites, facilities: There are 15 sites for tents or RVs up to 30 feet (no hookups). Picnic tables and fire grills are provided. Drinking water (shut off during freezing temperatures) and vault toilets are available. Leashed pets are permitted.

Reservations, fees: Reservations are not

accepted. Sites are $15 per night, $5 per night for each additional vehicle. Open April to early November, weather permitting.

Directions: From Carson City, drive south on U.S. 395 to Coleville and then continue south for 15 miles to the campground on the east side of the road (four miles north of the junction of U.S. 395 and Highway 108).

Contact: Humboldt-Toiyabe National Forest, Bridgeport Ranger District, 760/932-7070, fax 760/932-5899.

210 SONORA BRIDGE

Scenic rating: 7

near the Walker River in Humboldt-Toiyabe National Forest

Map 6.3, page 367

The West Walker River is a pretty stream, flowing over boulders and into pools, and each year this stretch of river is well stocked with rainbow trout by the Department of Fish and Game. One of several campgrounds near the West Walker, Sonora Bridge is set at 6,800 feet, about a half mile from the river. The setting is in the transition zone from high mountains to high desert on the eastern edge of the Sierra Nevada.

Campsites, facilities: There are 23 sites for tents or RVs up to 35 feet (no hookups). Picnic tables and fire grills are provided. Drinking water and vault toilets are available. Leashed pets are permitted.

Reservations, fees: Reservations are not accepted. Sites are $13 per night, $5 per night for each additional vehicle. Open May through October, weather permitting.

Directions: From north of Bridgeport, at the junction of U.S. 395 and Highway 108, turn west on Highway 108 and drive one mile to the campground on the left.

Contact: Humboldt-Toiyabe National Forest, Bridgeport Ranger District, 760/932-7070, fax 760/932-5899.

211 LEAVITT MEADOWS

Scenic rating: 9

on the Walker River in Humboldt-Toiyabe National Forest

Map 6.3, page 367

While Leavitt Meadows sits right aside Highway 108, a little winding two-laner, there are several nearby off-pavement destinations that make this camp a winner. The camp is set in the high eastern Sierra, east of Sonora Pass at 7,000 feet in elevation, where Leavitt Creek and Brownie Creek enter the West Walker River. There is a pack station for horseback riding nearby. For four-wheel-drive owners, the most popular side trip is driving four miles west on Highway 108, then turning south and driving four miles to Leavitt Lake, where the trout fishing is sometimes spectacular, if you're trolling a gold Cripplure.

Campsites, facilities: There are 16 sites for tents or RVs up to 30 feet (no hookups). Picnic tables, food lockers, and fire grills are provided. Drinking water and vault toilets are available. Leashed pets are permitted.

Reservations, fees: Reservations are not accepted. Sites are $13 per night, $5 per night for each additional vehicle. Open April through October, weather permitting.

Directions: From the junction of Highway 108 and U.S. 395 north of Bridgeport, turn west on Highway 108 and drive approximately seven miles to the campground on the left side of the road.

Contact: Humboldt-Toiyabe National Forest, Bridgeport Ranger District, 760/932-7070, fax 760/932-5899.

212 OBSIDIAN

Scenic rating: 6

on Molybdenite Creek in Humboldt-Toiyabe National Forest

Map 6.3, page 367

This primitive, little-known camp at 7,800 feet in elevation is set up for backpackers, with an adjacent trailhead providing a jump-off point into the wilderness; wilderness permits are required. The trail here is routed up the Molybdenite Creek drainage and into the Hoover Wilderness.

Campsites, facilities: There are 14 sites for tents or RVs up to 30 feet (no hookups). Picnic tables and fire grills are provided. Vault toilets are available. No drinking water is available. Garbage must be packed out. Leashed pets are permitted.

Reservations, fees: Reservations are not accepted. Sites are $8 per night, $5 per night for each additional vehicle. Open June through October, weather permitting.

Directions: At the junction of U.S. 395 and Highway 108 (13 miles north of Bridgeport), drive south a short distance on U.S. 395 to an improved dirt road and a sign that says "Little Walker River Road." Turn west and drive four miles to the campground.

Contact: Humboldt-Toiyabe National Forest, Bridgeport Ranger District, 760/932-7070, fax 760/932-5899.

213 CASCADE CREEK

Scenic rating: 6

in Stanislaus National Forest

Map 6.3, page 367

This campground is set along Cascade Creek at an elevation of 6,000 feet. A Forest Service road about a quarter mile west of camp on the south side of the highway provides a side trip three miles up to Pikes Peak, at 7,236 feet.

Campsites, facilities: There are 14 sites for tents or RVs up to 22 feet (no hookups). Picnic tables and fire rings are provided. Pit and vault toilets are available. No drinking water is available. Supplies are available in Dardanelle. Leashed pets are permitted.

Reservations, fees: Reservations are not accepted. Sites are $8 per night. Open May through October, weather permitting.

Directions: From Sonora, drive east on Highway 108 to Strawberry and continue for 11 miles to the campground on the left side of the road.

Contact: Stanislaus National Forest, Summit Ranger District, 209/965-3434, fax 209/965-3372.

SAN FRANCISCO BAY AREA

© ROBERT HOLMES/CALTOUR

BEST CAMPGROUNDS

❮ Scenic Destinations
Steep Ravine Environmental Campsites, **page 477**

❮ Hikes with Views
Angel Island State Park Walk-In/Boat-In, **page 481**

❮ Island Campgrounds
Angel Island State Park Walk-In/Boat-In, **page 481**

It's ironic that many people who have chosen

to live in the Bay Area are often the ones who complain the most about it. We've even heard some say, "Some day I'm going to get out of here and start having a good time."

I wish I could take anyone who has ever had these thoughts on a little trip in my airplane and circle the Bay Area at 3,000 feet. What you see is that despite strips of roadways and pockets of cities where people are jammed together, most of the region is wild, unsettled, and beautiful. There is no metropolitan area in the world that offers better and more diverse recreation and open space so close to so many.

The Bay Area has 150 significant parks (including 12 with redwoods), 7,500 miles of hiking and biking trails, 45 lakes, 25 waterfalls, 100 miles of coast, mountains with incredible lookouts, bays with islands, and in all, 1.2 million acres of greenbelt with hundreds of acres being added each year with land bought by money earmarked from property taxes. The land has no limit. Enjoy it.

Along with the unique recreation possibilities here come unique campgrounds. There are boat-in camps at Tomales Bay, ferry-in camps on Angel

Island, and hike-in camps at Point Reyes National Seashore, the Marin Headlands, Sunol-Ohlone Wilderness, Butano Redwoods State Park, and Big Basin Redwoods State Park – along with a sprinkling of the more traditional drive-in sites at state, county, and regional parks throughout the region.

Note that proximity to a metropolitan area means two things: The demand is higher. So plan ahead. The second thing is that 85 percent of the park use occurs from 3 P.M. Friday to 5 P.M. Sunday, so if you visit at non-peak times it's like having the park to yourself. One shocker is that in spring and fall, there is a huge drop-off in use on weekdays, Sunday through Thursday.

There are many world-class landmarks to see while staying in the Bay Area. In San Francisco alone, there are the Golden Gate Bridge, Fisherman's Wharf, Alcatraz, Ghirardelli Square, Chinatown, AT&T ballpark, the Crissy Field waterfront, cable cars, Fort Point, the Cliff House and Ocean Beach, and Fort Funston.

In fact, instead of going far away for a vacation, residents might consider what so many do from all over the world: Stay and discover the treasures in your own backyard.

SAN FRANCISCO BAY AREA

MAP 7.1
page 469

MAP 7.2
page 470

MAP 7.3
page 471

MAP 7.4
page 472

see Sacramento
and Gold Country
page 390

see San
Joaquin
Valley
page 592

Camanche
Lake

San Joaquin River

Santa
Nella

San Luis
Reservoir

Stockton

Manteca

Rio
Vista

Pittsburg

Concord

Danville

Livermore

Fremont

San
Jose

Morgan
Hill

Gilroy

Santa
Cruz

Suisun
City

Suisun Bay

Vallejo

Richmond

Berkeley

Oakland

Hayward

Redwood
City

Woodside

Pescadero

San
Francisco
Bay

Petaluma

San
Rafael

San
Francisco

Pacifica

Bolinas

Olema

San Pablo
Bay

PACIFIC OCEAN

10 mi

10 km

© AVALON TRAVEL PUBLISHING, INC.

Map 7.1 Campgrounds 1-16 Pages 473-482

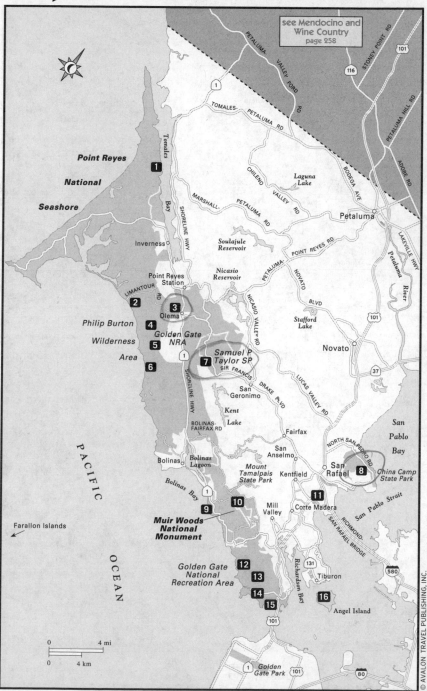

see Mendocino and
Wine Country
page 258

Point Reyes

National

Seashore

Tomales Bay

SHORELINE HWY

Inverness

LIMANTOUR RD

Point Reyes
Station

2

3

Olema

Philip Burton

4

Wilderness

5

Golden Gate
NRA

Area

6

Bolinas

Bolinas
Lagoon

Bolinas Bay

BOLINAS-
FAIRFAX RD

7

Samuel P.
Taylor SP

SIR FRANCIS

DRAKE BLVD

San
Geronimo

Kent
Lake

Fairfax

San
Anselmo

Mount
Tamalpais
State Park

Kentfield

9

10

**Muir Woods
National
Monument**

Golden Gate
National
Recreation Area

12

13

14

15

Mill
Valley

Corte Madera

11

San
Rafael

8

China Camp
State Park

San
Pablo
Bay

San Pablo Strait

NORTH SAN PEDRO RD

RICHMOND-
SAN RAFAEL BRIDGE

Richardson Bay

131

Tiburon

16

Angel Island

580

Farallon Islands

P A C I F I C

O C E A N

PETALUMA

VALLEY
FORD

RD

STONEY POINT RD

101

116

TOMALES-

PETALUMA

RD

CHILENO

VALLEY

RD

Laguna
Lake

MARSHALL-
PETALUMA
RD

Soulajule
Reservoir

Nicasio
Reservoir

POINT REYES RD

PETALUMA

NOVATO

BLVD

BODEGA AVE

PETALUMA HILL RD

ADOBE RD

Petaluma

LAKEVILLE HWY

Petaluma
River

Stafford
Lake

101

Novato

37

NICASIO VALLEY RD

LUCAS VALLEY RD

1

1

1

0 4 mi

0 4 km

Golden
Gate Park

1

101

80

Map 7.2 Campgrounds 17-20 Pages 482-484

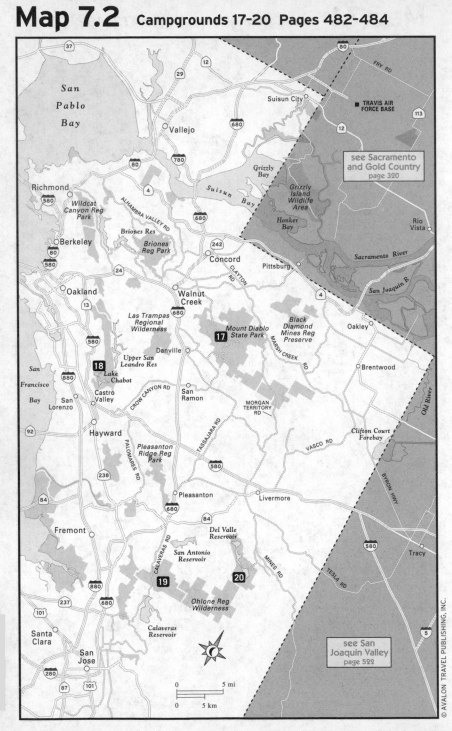

Map 7.3   Campgrounds 21-25 Pages 485-487

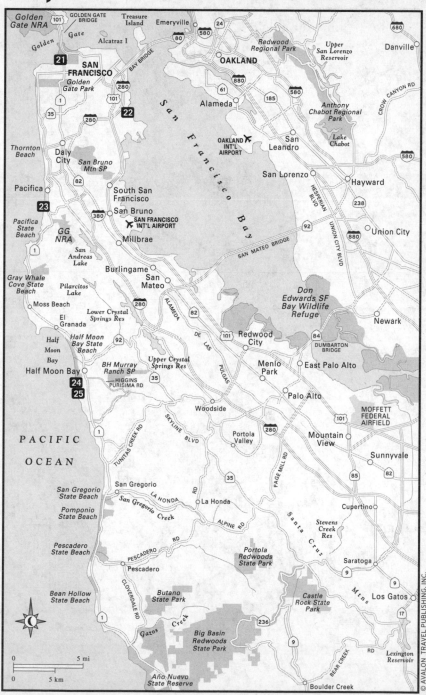

Map 7.4 Campgrounds 26-38 Pages 487-495

1 TOMALES BAY BOAT-IN

🏃 🏊 🛶 ⛟ 5% ⛰

Scenic rating: 10

on Tomales Bay

Map 7.1, page 469

Here is a little slice of paradise secreted away along the west shore of Tomales Bay. A series of dispersed boat-in camps are set along small, sandy coves along the bases of steep cliffs, set from just north of Indian Beach at Tomales Bay State Park on north all the way to Tomales Point. Note that boaters are required to bring portable toilets, and that reservations are often a necessity, especially on weekends. Tomales Bay is pretty, quiet, and protected from the coastal winds, and offers outstanding sea kayaking. Note that some spots that appear gorgeous during low tides can be covered by water during high tides, so pick your spot with care.

Campsites, facilities: There are 20 permits issued daily for dispersed boat-in tent sites along the shore of Tomales Bay. Permits must be obtained from the Bear Valley Visitor Center before camping; for directions to the visitors center, refer to the *Sky Camp Hike-In* listing. Pit toilets are available only at Marshall Beach and Tomales/Kehoe Beach. No drinking water or other facilities are available. Garbage must be packed out. Boaters must bring portable toilets. No wood-gathering. No pets are allowed.

Reservations, fees: Reservations are strongly recommended, available Monday through Friday at 415/663-8054. Sites are $15–40 per night. Open year-round, weather permitting.

Directions: Drive on U.S. 101 to Petaluma and the East Washington exit. Take that exit west and drive west (this street becomes Bodega Avenue) through Petaluma and continue to Highway 1. Turn left (south) on Highway 1 and drive 3.5 miles to the Miller County Park boat launch on the right (0.5 mile before Blakes Landing). Launch your boat and paddle across Tomales Bay to the boat-in campsites along the Point Reyes National Seashore.

Contact: Point Reyes National Seashore, 415/464-5100, fax 415/464-5149, www.nps .gov/pore.

2 COAST CAMP HIKE-IN

🏃 ⛰

Scenic rating: 7

in Point Reyes National Seashore

Map 7.1, page 469

This is a classic ocean-bluff setting, a hike-in camp set just above Santa Maria Beach on the Point Reyes National Seashore, providing an extended tour into a land of charm. It is a 2.8-mile hike to get here, the northernmost camp on Coast Trail. (The complete Coast Trail is a 19-mile trip that is one of the best hikes in the Bay Area.) From Coast Camp, the trail contours south along the bluffs above the beach for 1.4 miles to Sculptured Beach, where there is a series of odd geologic formations, including caves, tunnels, and sea stacks. A backcountry permit is required. Note: This camp is set on the edge of the area that burned in the 1995 wildfire.

Campsites, facilities: There are 12 individual and two group hike-in sites. Picnic tables and fire grills are provided. Drinking water is available intermittently; check for current status. Vault toilets are available. Charcoal or gas stoves are allowed, with backpacking stoves recommended for cooking. No wood fires permitted. Garbage must be packed out. No vehicles or pets are permitted.

Reservations, fees: Reservations are recommended (available Monday through Friday) and permits required from the Bear Valley Visitor Center at 415/663-8054; for directions to the visitors center, refer to the Sky Camp Hike-In listing. Sites are $15 per night, four-day maximum stay; $15–40 per night for group sites. Open year-round.

Directions: From U.S. 101 in Marin, take the Sir Francis Drake Boulevard/San Anselmo exit and drive about 20 miles to Highway 1 at Olema. Turn right on Highway 1 and drive a very short distance. Turn left at Bear Valley Road and drive north for two miles to Limantour Road. Turn left at Limantour Road and drive six miles to the access road for the Point Reyes Hostel. Turn left and drive 0.2 mile to the trailhead on the right side of the road. A parking area is a short distance ahead and to the right.

Contact: Point Reyes National Seashore, 415/464-5100, fax 415/464-5149, www.nps .gov/pore.

❸ OLEMA RANCH CAMPGROUND

Scenic rating: 4

in Olema

Map 7.1, page 469

If location is everything, then this 32-acre campground should be rated a 10. It is set in Olema, in a valley amid Marin's coastal foothills, an ideal jump-off spot for a Point Reyes adventure. It borders the Point Reyes National Seashore to the west and the Golden Gate National Recreation Area to the east, with Tomales Bay to the nearby north. There are several excellent trailheads available within a 10-minute drive along Highway 1 to the south. The campsites are small, tightly placed, and I have received complaint letters about the ambience of the place.

Campsites, facilities: There are 203 sites, some with full or partial hookups (20 and 30 amps), for tents or RVs of any length, and a large area for up to 175 tents. Picnic tables and fire rings are provided. Drinking water, restrooms with showers, dump station, coin laundry, post office, ATM, general store, firewood, ice, playground, video rentals, bicycle rentals, RV supplies, gasoline and propane, horseshoes, volleyball, shuffleboard, ping-pong, badminton, tetherball, Wi-Fi, modem access, arcade, meeting facilities, amphitheater, and a recreation hall (for groups of 25 or more only) are available. Some facilities are wheelchair-accessible. Leashed pets are permitted.

Reservations, fees: Reservations are accepted at 800/655-CAMP (800/655-2267). Sites are $25–38 per night, $2 per night for each additional vehicle, $3 per person per night for more than two people, $1 per pet per night. Weekly rates available. Some credit cards accepted. Open year-round.

Directions: From U.S. 101 in Marin, take the San Anselmo/Sir Francis Drake Boulevard exit and drive west for about 22 miles to Highway 1 at Olema. Turn north (right) on Highway 1 and drive 0.25 mile to the campground on the left.

Contact: Olema Ranch Campground, 415/663-8001, fax 415/663-8832, www .olemaranch.com.

❹ SKY CAMP HIKE-IN

Scenic rating: 7

in Point Reyes National Seashore

Map 7.1, page 469

Sky Camp is set on the western flank of Mount Wittenberg on Inverness Ridge at 1,025 feet, right at the edge of the area in Point Reyes National Seashore that burned in the 1995 wildfire. To reach the camp, take Bear Valley Trail from park headquarters and walk 0.2 mile to Mount Wittenberg Trail. Turn right (north) on Mount Wittenberg Trail and hike 2.2 miles to Sky Trail. Turn right and hike 0.6 mile to the campground. From here you get a dramatic view of the burned area and the adjacent Marin coast. No wood fires and no pets are permitted.

Campsites, facilities: There are 11 individual sites and a group site (walk-in only) which can accommodate up to 25 people. Permits must be obtained from the Bear Valley Visitor Center before camping. Pit toilets and fire grills (charcoal only, no wood fires) are provided. Drinking water is available intermittently;

check for current status. Garbage must be packed out. No vehicles or pets are allowed.

Reservations, fees: Reservations recommended in person or by phone at the Bear Valley Visitor Center from Monday through Friday at 415/663-8054. Permits are required. Sites are $15 per night, $15–40 per night for the group area (maximum of 25 people); four-day maximum stay. Open year-round.

Directions: From U.S. 101 in Marin, take the Sir Francis Drake Boulevard/San Anselmo exit and drive west for about 20 miles to Highway 1 at Olema. Turn north on Highway 1 and drive a very short distance to Bear Valley Road. Turn left at Bear Valley Road and drive north for 0.7 mile to the visitors center road on the left (signed "Seashore Information"). Turn left and drive to the visitors center parking lot and Bear Valley Trailhead.

Contact: Point Reyes National Seashore, 415/464-5100, fax 415/464-5149, www.nps .gov/pore.

⑤ GLEN CAMP HIKE-IN
🚶 ⛺

Scenic rating: 10

in Point Reyes National Seashore

Map 7.1, page 469

Glen Camp Hike-In is set in the coastal foothills of Point Reyes National Seashore and is surrounded by forest. The hike to it starts at the Bear Valley Visitor Center, where you can obtain your backcountry permits and hiking information, and is routed on popular Bear Valley Trail, a wide road made out of compressed rock. It is 1.6 miles to Divide Meadow, with a modest 215-foot climb, then another 1.6 miles through Bear Valley to Glen Trail. Turn left on Glen Loop Trail and hike 1.4 miles, with the trail lateraling in and out of two canyons to reach the camp. It is secluded and quiet. Get a map, a permit, and bring everything you need.

Campsites, facilities: There are 12 hike-in sites. Picnic tables and fire grills are provided. Pit toilets are available. Drinking water is available

intermittently; check for current status. Charcoal or gas stoves are allowed, with backpacking stoves recommended for cooking. No wood fires permitted. Garbage must be packed out. No vehicles or pets are permitted.

Reservations, fees: Reservations recommended by phone or in person at the Bear Valley Visitor Center from Monday through Friday at 415/663-8054. Permits are required. Sites are $15 per night, four-day maximum stay. Open year-round.

Directions: From U.S. 101 in Marin, take the Sir Francis Drake Boulevard/San Anselmo exit and drive west for about 20 miles to Highway 1 at Olema. Turn north on Highway 1 and drive a very short distance to Bear Valley Road. Turn left at Bear Valley Road and drive north for 0.7 mile to the visitors center road on the left (signed "Seashore Information"). Turn left and drive to the visitors center parking lot and Bear Valley Trailhead. It is a 4.6-mile hike to the camp.

Contact: Point Reyes National Seashore, 415/464-5100, fax 415/464-5149, www.nps .gov/pore.

⑥ WILDCAT CAMP HIKE-IN
🚶 ⛺

Scenic rating: 10

in Point Reyes National Seashore

Map 7.1, page 469

This backpack camp sits in a grassy meadow near a small stream that flows to the ocean, just above remote Wildcat Beach. From the Palomarin Trailhead, getting to this camp takes you on a fantastic 5.6-mile hike that crosses some of the Bay Area's most beautiful wildlands. The trail is routed along the ocean for about a mile, heads up in the coastal hills, turns left, and skirts past Bass Lake, Crystal Lake, and Pelican Lake and, ultimately, heads past Alamere Creek to this beautiful camp set on an ocean bluff. A fantastic side trip is to hike along the beach from Wildcat Camp on south, where you can get a full frontal view of Alamere Falls. It is a dramatic 40-foot free fall, one of the rare ocean bluff waterfalls anywhere.

Campsites, facilities: There are four individual and three group hike-in sites. Picnic tables and fire grills are provided. Vault toilets are available. Drinking water is available intermittently; check for current status. Charcoal or gas stoves are allowed, with backpacking stoves recommended for cooking. No wood fires permitted. Garbage must be packed out. No vehicles or pets are permitted.

Reservations, fees: Reservations are recommended (available Monday through Friday) and permits required from the Bear Valley Visitor Center at 415/663-8054; for directions to the visitors center, refer to the *Sky Camp Hike-In* listing. Sites are $15 per night, group areas are $30–40 per night; four-day maximum stay. Open year-round.

Directions: From U.S. 101 in Marin, take the Sir Francis Drake Boulevard/San Anselmo exit and drive about 20 miles west on Sir Francis Drake Boulevard to the town of Olema and Highway 1. Turn left on Highway 1 and drive 9.3 miles to Olema-Bolinas Road on the right (if the sign is missing—a common event—note that a white ranch house is opposite the turn). Turn right on Olema-Bolinas Road and drive 1.5 miles to Mesa Road. Turn right and drive six miles (past an area known as "The Towers" due to all the antennas) to the parking area and Palomarin Trailhead. It is a 5.6-mile hike to the campground on Coast Trail.

Contact: Point Reyes National Seashore, 415/464-5100, fax 415/464-5149, www.nps.gov/pore.

7 SAMUEL P. TAYLOR STATE PARK

Scenic rating: 9

near San Rafael

Map 7.1, page 469

This is a beautiful park, with campsites set amid redwoods, complete with a babbling brook running nearby. The park covers more than 2,700 acres of wooded countryside in the steep and rolling hills of Marin County. This features unique contrasts of coast redwoods and open grassland. Hikers will find 20 miles of hiking trails, a hidden waterfall, and some good mountain-biking routes on service roads. The paved bike path that runs through the park and parallels Lagunitas Creek is a terrific, easy ride. Trees include redwood, Douglas fir, oak, and madrone, and native wildflowers include buttercups, milkmaids, and Indian paintbrush. The section of the park on the north side of Sir Francis Drake has the best hiking in the park. Campsites are on the south side of the park, except for three sites on the north side.

Campsites, facilities: There are 25 sites for tents, 35 sites for tents or RVs up to 27 feet, two primitive sites for up to 10 people each, two group sites for 25 and 50 people, one hike-in/bike-in camp, and one equestrian site with corrals at Devil's Gulch Horse Camp. No hookups. Picnic tables, food lockers, and fire grills are provided. Drinking water, flush and pit toilets, and Wi-Fi are available. There are a small store and café two miles away in Lagunitas. Some facilities are wheelchair-accessible. Leashed pets are permitted in campsites only.

Reservations, fees: Reservations are accepted ($7.50 reservation fee) at 800/444-PARK (800/444-7275) or www.reserveamerica.com. Sites are $20–25 per night and $6 per night for each additional vehicle, primitive groups sites are $23 per night, group sites $75–150 per night, equestrian camp $50 per night, $3 per person per night for hike-in/bike-in site. Open year-round.

Directions: From U.S. 101 in Marin, take the Sir Francis Drake Boulevard exit and drive west for about 15 miles to the park entrance on the left side of the road.

Contact: Samuel P. Taylor State Park, 415/488-9897, fax 415/488-4315; Marin Sector, 415/898-4362, www.parks.ca.gov.

8 CHINA CAMP STATE PARK WALK-IN

🚶 🚴 🐎 ⛺

Scenic rating: 10

on San Pablo Bay near San Rafael

Map 7.1, page 469

This is one of the Bay Area's prettiest campgrounds. It is set in woodlands with a picturesque creek running past. The camps are shaded and sheltered. Directly adjacent to the camp is a meadow, marshland, and then San Pablo Bay. Deer can seem as tame as chipmunks. Hiking is outstanding here, either taking Shoreline Trail for a pretty walk near the edge of San Pablo Bay, or Bay View Trail for the climb up the ridge that borders the park, in the process gaining spectacular views of the bay and miles of charm. The landscape here includes an extensive intertidal salt marsh, and meadow and oak habitats. There are five miles of hiking trails, heavily used on spring and summer weekends. A sidelight is the China Camp Village, which depicts an early Chinese settlement.

Campsites, facilities: There are 30 walk-in tent sites and one hike-in/bike-in site. Picnic tables, food lockers, and fire grills are provided. Drinking water and a restroom with flush toilets and showers are available. Leashed pets are permitted at the campground and picnic areas.

Reservations, fees: Reservations are accepted ($7.50 reservation fee) at 800/444-PARK (800/444-7275) or www.reserveamerica.com. Sites are $20–25 per night, $5 per night for each additional vehicle, $2 per person per night for hike-in/bike-in site. Open year-round, weather permitting.

Directions: From San Francisco, drive north on U.S. 101 to San Rafael and take the North San Pedro Road exit. Drive east on North San Pedro Road for five miles to the Back Ranch Meadows Campground entrance on the right. Turn right and drive a short distance to the campground trailhead at the end of

the road. Reaching the sites requires a one- to five-minute walk.

Contact: China Camp State Park Walk-In, 415/456-0766, fax 415/456-1743; Marin Sector, 415/898-4362, www.parks.ca.gov.

9 STEEP RAVINE ENVIRONMENTAL CAMPSITES

🚶 🏊 📷 ♿ ⛺

Scenic rating: 10

in Mount Tamalpais State Park

Map 7.1, page 469   **BEST (**

This is one of the most remarkable spots on the California coast, with primitive cabins/wood shacks set on a bluff on Rocky Point overlooking the ocean. It is primitive but dramatic, with passing ships, fishing boats, lots of marine birds, occasionally even whales, and a chance for heart-stopping sunsets. There is an easy walk to the north down to Redrock Beach, which is secluded, and just across the road (with a short jog to the right) is a trailhead for Steep Ravine Trail on the slopes of Mount Tamalpais. After a while you'll feel like you're a million miles from civilization.

Campsites, facilities: There are seven walk-in sites for tents and 10 primitive cabins (also known as environmental sites), each with a wood stove, picnic table, and a flat wood surface for sleeping. At tent sites, picnic tables and fire grills are provided and pit toilets are available. Drinking water is nearby, and wood is available for purchase. No pets are permitted.

Reservations, fees: Reservations are accepted ($7.50 reservation fee) at 800/444-PARK (800/444-7275) or www.reserveamerica.com. Sites are $15 per night for tent sites, $75 per night for environmental cabins, one vehicle per cabin, five people maximum per site. Open year-round.

Directions: From U.S. 101 in Marin, take the Stinson Beach/Highway 1 exit. Drive west to the stoplight at the T intersection (Highway

1). Turn left on Highway 1 and drive about 11 miles to the gated access road on the left side of the highway at Rocky Point. (The gate lock combination will be provided when reservations are made, or by calling 415/388-2070 up to one week before your stay.)

Contact: Mount Tamalpais State Park, 415/388-2070; Marin Sector, 415/898-4362, www.parks.ca.gov.

10 PANTOLL CAMPGROUND WALK-IN AND ALICE EASTWOOD GROUP CAMPS

🥾 🚴 ⛵ 🐕 ⛺

Scenic rating: 9

in Mount Tamalpais State Park

Map 7.1, page 469

When camping at Pantoll, you are within close range of the divine, including some of the best hiking, best lookouts, and just plain best places to be anywhere in the Bay Area. The camp is set in the woods on the western slopes of Mount Tamalpais, which some say is a place of special power, with sensational hiking and trailheads. The walk to the Pantoll Campground can be as short as 100 feet, and as long as just over a quarter mile. This landscape is a mix of redwood groves, oak woodlands, and grasslands, providing both drop-dead beautiful views of the ocean nearby, as well as a trip into a lush redwood canyon with a stream. Steep Ravine Trail is routed out of camp to the west into a wondrous gorge filled with redwoods and a stream with miniature waterfalls. It is best seen after a good rain, when everything is dripping with moisture. Another great hike from this camp is on Matt Davis/Coast Trail, which provides beautiful views of the coast. Another must is the nearby drive to the East Peak Lookout, where the entire world seems within reach. This park provides more than 50 miles of trails for hiking and biking, which in turn link to a network of 200 miles of other trails.

Campsites, facilities: There are 16 walk-in tent sites, and two group sites for 10–75 people. Picnic tables, food lockers, and fire grills are provided. Drinking water, flush toilets, and Wi-Fi are available. Firewood is available for purchase. Leashed pets are permitted at campsites only.

Reservations, fees: Reservations are accepted ($7.50 reservation fee) for groups only at 800/444-PARK (800/444-7275) or www .reserveamerica.com. Sites are $15 per night, $75–150 per night for group sites. Open year-round.

Directions: From U.S. 101 in Marin, take the Stinson Beach/Highway 1 exit. Drive west to the stoplight at the T intersection for Highway 1. Turn left and drive about four miles uphill to the Panoramic Highway. Bear to the right on Panoramic Highway and continue for 5.5 miles to the Pantoll parking area. Turn left at the Pantoll parking area and ranger station. A 100- to 500-foot walk is required to reach the campground. To reach the group site, directions and the combination to the gate lock will be provided when reservations are made, or by calling 415/388-2070 up to one week before your stay.

Contact: Mount Tamalpais State Park, 415/388-2070; Marin Sector, 415/898-4362, www.parks.ca.gov.

11 MARIN RV PARK

🥾 🏊 ⛵ 🐕 ♿ 🚐 ⛺

Scenic rating: 2

in Greenbrae

Map 7.1, page 469

For out-of-towners with RVs, this can make an ideal base camp for Marin County adventures. To the west are Mount Tamalpais State Park, Muir Woods National Monument, Samuel P. Taylor State Park, and Point Reyes National Seashore. To the nearby east is the Loch Lomond Marina on San Pablo Bay, where fishing trips can be arranged for striped bass and sturgeon; phone Loch Lomond Bait Shop,

415/456-0321. The park offers complete sightseeing information and easy access to buses and ferry service to San Francisco.

Campsites, facilities: There are 89 sites with full hookups (30 and 50 amps) for tents or RVs. Restrooms with showers, coin laundry, modem access, swimming pool, dump station, and RV supplies are available. Some facilities are wheelchair-accessible. Leashed pets are permitted.

Reservations, fees: Reservations are recommended. Sites are $40 per night, $2 per person per night for more than two people. Six people maximum per site. Weekly and monthly rates available. Some credit cards accepted. Open year-round.

Directions: From the south: From the Golden Gate Bridge, drive north on U.S. 101 for 10 miles to Lucky Drive (south of San Rafael). Exit and turn left on Redwood Highway (no sign) and drive three blocks north to the park entrance on the right.

From the north: From San Rafael, drive south on U.S. 101 to the Lucky Drive exit (450A). Take that exit to the first light at Tamal Vista. Turn left and drive to the next stoplight and Wornum Avenue. Turn left at Wornum Avenue and drive under the freeway to Redwood Highway (frontage road). Turn left and drive four blocks north to the park entrance.

Contact: Marin RV Park, 415/461-5199 or 888/461-5199, fax 415/925-1584, www.marinrvpark.com.

12 HAYPRESS HIKE-IN

Scenic rating: 9

on Marin Headlands

Map 7.1, page 469

Haypress campground is set on the northern outskirts of Tennessee Valley at the north end of the Marin Headlands. Reaching this camp is not difficult, just a 0.75 mile hike, departing from one of Marin's most popular trailheads in Tennessee Valley. Yet in just 20–30 minutes, hikers can create a world that seemingly belongs just to them at this camp. This is a primitive backpacking-style campground where you must supply everything you need.

Campsites, facilities: There are five tent sites, with a maximum of four people per site. Picnic tables are provided. Portable toilets and food lockers are available. No drinking water is available. No fires are permitted; backpacking stoves required for cooking. No pets are allowed.

Reservations, fees: Reservations and permit required from visitors center before camping; no fee. All three sites can be reserved by groups of up to 12 from November through March. Open year-round, weather permitting, with a three-night maximum stay per season.

Directions: From U.S. 101 in Marin, take the Stinson Beach/Highway 1 exit. Drive 0.6 mile to Tennessee Valley Road. Turn left on Tennessee Valley Road and drive two miles until the road dead-ends at the parking area and trailhead. Take the trailhead for Tennessee Valley (see directions above and map/brochure) and hike 0.75 miles to the campground.

Contact: Marin Headlands Visitor Center, Golden Gate National Recreation Area, Building 948, Fort Barry, Sausalito, CA 94965, 415/331-1540, www.nps.gov/goga/camping. A map/brochure is available at the Marin Headlands Visitor Center or by contacting the Golden Gate National Recreation Area, Marin Headlands, at the address listed. A detailed hiking map of the area is available for a fee.

13 HAWKCAMP HIKE-IN

Scenic rating: 10

on Marin Headlands

Map 7.1, page 469

This is the most remote of the campgrounds on the Marin Headlands. It is high above Gerbode Valley, requiring a hike of 3.5 miles, climbing much of the way from the parking lot and trailhead at Tennessee Valley. It is a small campground, with three sites and room for no more than four people per site. After parking at Tennessee Valley, take the trailhead for the Old Marincello Vehicle Road/Bobcat Trail. This route climbs in a counterclockwise direction around Mount Vortac; after 1.7 miles you will reach a junction with Mount Vortac Trail. Do not turn at that junction. Continue straight on Bobcat Trail for 0.7 mile to a junction with Hawk Trail. Turn right and hike on the trail for one mile to Hawkcamp, set at an elevation of 750 feet. Below you to the southeast is Gerbode Valley.

Campsites, facilities: There are three tent sites, with a maximum of four people per site. Picnic tables and food lockers are provided and chemical toilets are available. No drinking water is available. No fires are permitted. Garbage must be packed out. Backpacking stoves required for cooking. No pets are allowed.

Reservations, fees: Reservations and permit required from the visitors center before camping; no fee. All three sites can be reserved by groups of up to 12 from November through March. Open year-round, weather permitting, with a three-night maximum stay per season.

Directions: From U.S. 101 in Marin, take the Stinson Beach/Highway 1 exit. Drive 0.6 mile and turn left on Tennessee Valley Road. Drive two miles until the road dead-ends at the parking area and trailhead. Take the trailhead for Old Marincello Vehicle Road/Bobcat Trail and hike 3.5 miles.

Contact: Marin Headlands Visitor Center, Golden Gate National Recreation Area, Building 948, Fort Barry, Sausalito, CA 94965, 415/331-1540, www.nps.gov/goga/camping. A map/brochure is available at the Marin Headlands Visitor Center or by contacting the Golden Gate National Recreation Area, Marin Headlands, at the address listed. A detailed hiking map of the area is available for a fee.

14 BICENTENNIAL WALK-IN

Scenic rating: 9

at Marin Headlands

Map 7.1, page 469

Of the four hike-in campgrounds set at the Marin Headlands, it is Bicentennial Walk-In that is the easiest to reach. It is only a 100-yard walk from the parking area near Battery Wallace, just northwest of the parking area. This is a small camp with space for just three tents, with a maximum of two people per site.

Campsites, facilities: There are three tent sites. No more than two people and one tent per site. Portable toilets and food lockers are available. Picnic tables are available 100 yards away at Battery Wallace. Drinking water is available one mile away at the Marin Headlands Visitor Center. Backpacking stoves required for cooking. Garbage must be packed out. No pets are allowed.

Reservations, fees: Reservations and permit required from the visitors center before camping; no fee. Open year-round, weather permitting, with a three-night maximum stay per season.

Directions: From San Francisco drive north on U.S. 101 over the Golden Gate Bridge, and into Marin to the Alexander Avenue exit. Take the Alexander Avenue exit and turn left underneath the highway. Take the wide paved road to the right (Conzelman Road, but there is no sign), and look for the Marin Headlands sign. Continue west for 3.5 miles (it becomes a one-way road) to the parking area on your left for Battery Wallace (on your right). Park and walk 100 yards north to the campground.

Contact: Marin Headlands Visitor Center, Golden Gate National Recreation Area, Building 948, Fort Barry, Sausalito, CA 94965, 415/331-1540, www.nps.gov/goga/camping. A map/brochure is available at the Marin Headlands Visitor Center or by contacting the Golden Gate National Recreation Area, Marin Headlands, at the address listed. A detailed hiking map of the area is available for a fee.

15 KIRBY COVE

Scenic rating: 10

on Marin Headlands

Map 7.1, page 469

Kirby Cove is nestled in a grove of cypress and eucalyptus trees in a stunning setting just west of the Golden Gate Bridge. It is one of the most beautiful campsites in any metropolitan area in North America. It is small and pristine, with space for just four sites and restricted parking. The view from lookouts near the camp are drop-dead beautiful—sweeping views of the Golden Gate Bridge, San Francisco Headlands, and the mouth of the bay opening to the Pacific Ocean.

Campsites, facilities: There are four sites for tents. No more than 10 people per site. Picnic tables, food lockers, and fire rings/barbecue pits are provided. It is recommended that you bring a backpacking stove because of occasional fire restrictions; wood collecting is not permitted. Pit toilets are available. No drinking water is available. Garbage must be packed out. No pets are allowed.

Reservations, fees: Reserve at 800/365-CAMP (800/365-2267) or http://reservations. nps.gov, $25 per night for up to three cars and 10 people. Open April to late October.

Directions: From San Francisco drive north on U.S. 101 over the Golden Gate Bridge and into Marin to the Alexander Avenue exit. Take the Alexander Avenue exit and turn left underneath the highway. Take the wide paved road to the right (Conzelman Road, but there is no sign), and look for the Marin Headlands sign. Continue west on Conzelman about 0.25 mile to Kirby Cove Road (the first turn on the left, a dirt road). Bear left and drive to the gate. When you get reservations, you will get the code for the gate. Unlock the gate and drive 0.9 mile to the campground.

Contact: Marin Headlands Visitor Center, Golden Gate National Recreation Area, Building 948, Fort Barry, Sausalito, CA 94965, 415/331-1540, www.nps.gov/goga/camping.

A map/brochure is available at the Marin Headlands Visitor Center or by contacting the Golden Gate National Recreation Area, Marin Headlands, at the address listed. A detailed hiking map of the area is available for a fee.

16 ANGEL ISLAND STATE PARK WALK-IN/BOAT-IN

Scenic rating: 10

on Angel Island

Map 7.1, page 469   BEST (

Camping at Angel Island is one of the unique adventures in the Bay Area; the only catch is that getting to the campsites requires a ferry boat ride and then a walk of 1–2 miles, or a kayak or boat trip from the mainland directly to the camp. The payoff comes at the end of the day, when all of the park's day visitors depart for the mainland, leaving the entire island to you. Plan far ahead because the sites can book up months in advance. The group camp is popular with kayakers because of beach access. From start to finish, it's a great trip, featuring a private campsite, often with spectacular views of San Francisco Bay, the San Francisco waterfront and skyline, Marin Headlands, and Mount Tamalpais. The tromp up to 798-foot Mount Livermore includes a short, very steep stretch, but in return furnishes one of the most spectacular urban lookouts in America. Be ready for cold, foggy weather at night in midsummer. The park features more than 13 miles of trails, including Perimeter Road, a must-do for all avid hikers, with bikes permitted on the park's fire road system. Angel Island has a stunning history, including being used from 1910 to 1940 to process thousands of immigrants as they entered America; historic tram tours are available.

Campsites, facilities: There are 10 hike-in sites, and one group hike-in/boat-in site for up to 20 people. Picnic tables, barbecues, and food lockers are provided. Drinking water and pit toilets are available. Garbage service is available. No pets are permitted. A seasonal café is on the island. No open wood campfires permitted; only charcoal allowed. Some facilities are wheelchair-accessible.

Reservations, fees: Reservations are accepted ($7.50 reservation fee) at 800/444-PARK (800/444-7275) or www.reserveamerica. com. Sites are $15–20 per night (limit eight people per site). To avoid park entrance fees, campers must check in at the Ayala Cove kiosk (at Angel Island) and show reservation vouchers to the ferry boat operator. Call the park at 415/435-1915 for group rates. Open year-round, with limited ferry service in winter.

Directions: Angel Island is in northern San Francisco Bay and can be reached by ferry from San Francisco and Oakland/Alameda; for schedule information, call 415/773-1188, www.blueandgoldfleet.com; and from Tiburon, for schedule information, call 415/435-2131, www.angelislandferry.com.

Contact: Angel Island State Park 415/435-1915, Marin District 707/769-5665 or fax 707/865-2046, www.parks.ca.gov; bike rentals, 415/897-0715; Sea Trek Ocean Kayaking, 415/488-1000; tram tours, 925/426-3058 or 415/897-0715.

17 MOUNT DIABLO STATE PARK

Scenic rating: 6

east of Oakland

Map 7.2, page 470

Mount Diablo, elevation 3,849 feet, provides one of the most all-encompassing lookouts anywhere in America, an awesome 360° on clear mornings. On crystal-clear days you can see the Sierra Nevada and its white, snowbound crest. Some claim to have seen Half Dome in Yosemite with binoculars. The drive to the summit is a must-do trip, and the weekend interpretive center right on top of the mountain is one of the best in the Bay Area. The camps at Mount Diablo are set in foothill/oak grassland country, with some shaded sites. Winter and spring are good times to visit, when the weather is still cool enough for good hiking trips. Most of the trails require long hikes, often including significant elevation gains and losses. No alcohol is permitted in the park. The park offers extensive but challenging hiking, biking, and horseback riding. A museum, visitors center, and gift shop is perched on the Diablo summit. Summers are hot and dry, and in late summer the park can be closed because of fire danger. In winter, snow occasionally falls on the peak—according to my logbook, during the first full moon in February.

Campsites, facilities: There are 64 sites in three campgrounds for tents or RVs up to 20 feet long (no hookups), five group sites for 20–50 people, and one group site for equestrian use. The equestrian site has hitching posts and a water trough. Picnic tables and fire grills are provided. Drinking water and flush and vault toilets are available. Showers are available at Juniper and Live Oak campgrounds. Leashed pets are permitted in campgrounds and picnic areas.

Reservations, fees: Reservations are accepted ($7.50 reservation fee) at 800/444-PARK (800/444-7275) or www.reserveamerica .com. Sites are $14–19 per night, $6 per night for each additional vehicle, group sites are $55–111 per night. Open year-round.

Directions: From Danville on I-680, take the Diablo Road exit. Turn east on Diablo Road and drive three miles to Mount Diablo Scenic Boulevard. Turn left and continue 3.5 miles (the road becomes South Gate Road) to the park entrance station. Register at the kiosk, obtain a park map, and drive to the designated campground.

Contact: Mount Diablo State Park, 925/837-2525 or 925/837-0904; Diablo Vista District, 707/769-5652, www.mdia.org or www.parks .ca.gov.

18 ANTHONY CHABOT REGIONAL PARK

🚶 🚵 🏊 🛶 🏕️ ♿ 🚐 ⛺

Scenic rating: 7

near Castro Valley

Map 7.2, page 470

The campground at Chabot Regional Park is set on a hilltop sheltered by eucalyptus, with good views and trails available. The best campsites are the walk-in units, requiring a walk of only a minute or so. Several provide views of Lake Chabot to the south 0.5 mile away. The 315-acre lake provides good trout fishing in the winter and spring, and a chance for huge but elusive largemouth bass. Huckleberry Trail is routed down from the campground (near walk-in site 20) to the lake at Honker Bay, a good fishing area. There is also a good 12-mile bike ride around the lake. In all, this 5,000-acre park includes 31 miles of hiking, biking, and riding trails. East Bay Skyline Trail runs the length of the park. Boat rentals are available, but no swimming or water-body contact is permitted. A weekend marksmanship range is available at the park, and a golf course is nearby.

Campsites, facilities: There are 53 sites for tents and small RVs, 12 sites with full hookups (30 amps) for RVs, and 10 walk-in sites for tents only. Picnic tables and fire grills are provided. Restrooms with flush toilets and showers, drinking water, dump station, amphitheater, small marina, boat rentals, snack bar, picnic area, bait and tackle, and naturalist-led campfire programs are available. No boat launch, and gas motors and inflatables are prohibited. Leashed pets are permitted.

Reservations, fees: Reservations are accepted at 510/562-2267 ($7 reservation fee). Sites are $18–25 per night, $6 per night for each additional vehicle, $2 per pet per night. Some credit cards accepted. Open year-round.

Directions: From I-580 in the Oakland hills, drive to the 35th Avenue exit. Take that exit, and at the stop sign, turn east on 35th Avenue and drive up the hill and straight across Skyline Boulevard, where 35th Avenue becomes Redwood Road. Continue on Redwood Road for eight miles to the park and Marciel Road (campground entrance road) on the right.

Contact: Regional Park Headquarters, 510/635-0135, ext. 2200, fax 510/569-4319; Anthony Chabot Regional Park, 510/639-4751; Chabot Equestrian Center, 510/569-4428, www.ebpark.org/parks.htm.

19 SUNOL REGIONAL WILDERNESS

🚶 🏕️ ⛺

Scenic rating: 7

south of Sunol

Map 7.2, page 470

This is a very primitive camp set in the Sunol Regional Wilderness, an outstanding park for off-season hiking, camping, wildlife-viewing, and wildflowers. The camps require walks of 25–50 yards, with wilderness-style camping also available requiring a hike of 3.4 miles or more. In the spring and early summer, it is one of the best of the 150 parks in the Bay Area to see wildflowers. It is also the home of more nesting golden eagles than anywhere else in the world, with a chance to see falcons and hawks as well. In addition, Alameda Creek in Little Yosemite forms several miniature pool-and-drop waterfalls in the spring and early summer. The Little Yosemite area is a scenic gorge about two miles upstream from the visitors center. The park is set in rolling oak/bay grasslands. Some backpack sites provide access to Ohlone Wilderness Trail. It is extremely quiet and secluded, with a nearby spring developed to provide drinking water. This is also one of the Bay Area's most popular parks to bring dogs. Dogs are allowed in the Ohlone Wilderness during the day, but not overnight. No alcohol is permitted in the park, and it is subject to confiscation. Bicycles and fires are prohibited at the trail and equestrian camps. Temporary closures can occur in late summer because of fire danger. Gates are locked at night; campers must arrive before dusk.

Campsites, facilities: There are four primitive sites for tents requiring walks of 25–50 yards, and a wilderness camp requiring hikes of 3.4 miles and longer. Picnic tables and fire grills are provided. Drinking water and vault toilets are available at the primitive sites. Picnic areas and naturalist programs are also available. Leashed pets are permitted in the campsites, but not overnight in the wilderness.

Reservations, fees: Reservations are required at 510/636-1684 ($7 reservation fee). Sites are $12 per night, $5 per night for each additional vehicle, $7 per person per night for trail camp, $2 per pet per night. Permit required for the wilderness camps. Some credit cards accepted. Open year-round, weather permitting.

Directions: In the East Bay on I-680, drive to Sunol and the Highway 84/Calaveras Road exit. Turn south on Calaveras and drive four miles to Geary Road. Turn left on Geary Road and drive two miles to the park entrance.

Contact: East Bay Regional Park District Headquarters, 510/635-0135, fax 510/569-4319; Sunol Regional Wilderness, 925/862-2244, www.ebparks.org/parks.htm.

20 DEL VALLE REGIONAL PARK

🏃 🏊 🛶 🎣 🐎 ♿ 🚐 ⛺

Scenic rating: 7

near Livermore

Map 7.2, page 470

Of the 65 parks in the East Bay Regional Park District, it is Del Valle that provides the greatest variety of recreation at the highest quality. Del Valle Reservoir is the centerpiece, a five-mile-long, narrow lake that fills a canyon with 16 miles of shoreline, providing a good boat launch for powerboating (10 mph speed limit) and good fishing for trout (stocked), striped bass, panfish, and catfish. Two swimming beaches are popular in summer. The park offers boat tours of the natural history and lake ecology of the area. The sites are somewhat exposed because of the grassland habitat, but they fill anyway on most weekends and three-day holidays. A trailhead south of the lake provides access to Ohlone Wilderness Trail, and for the well conditioned, there is the 5.5-mile butt-kicker of a climb to Murietta Falls, gaining 1,600 feet in 1.5 miles. Murietta Falls is the Bay Area's highest waterfall, 100 feet tall, though its thin, silvery wisp is difficult to view directly and rarely evokes much emotional response after such an intense climb. Riding trails are also available in this 4,000-acre park.

Campsites, facilities: There are 150 sites, including 21 with water and sewer hookups for tents or RVs of any length, and two walk-in group areas for up to 75 people each. Group camps require a walk of a 0.25–1 mile. Picnic tables and fire grills are provided. Drinking water, restrooms with flush toilets and showers, dump station, full marina, boat and sailboard rentals, seasonal campfire programs, swimming beaches, and a boat launch are available. Some facilities are wheelchair-accessible. Leashed pets are permitted.

Reservations, fees: Reservations are required ($7 reservation fee) at 510/636-1684. Sites are $18–25 per night, $6 per night for each additional vehicle, $2–3 per day boat launch fee, $2 per pet per night. Some credit cards accepted. Open year-round.

Directions: From I-580 east at Livermore, take the North Livermore Avenue exit and turn south (right if driving from San Francisco). Drive south and proceed through Livermore (road becomes South Livermore Avenue). Continue for 1.5 miles (the road then becomes Tesla Road) to Mines Road. Turn right on Mines Road and drive 3.5 miles to Del Valle Road. Continue straight on Del Valle Road for four miles to the park entrance.

Contact: Del Valle Regional Park, 925/373-0332; East Bay Regional Park District, 510/635-0135, www.ebparks.org/parks.htm.

21 ROB HILL GROUP WALK-IN
🏃 🐕 ⛺

Scenic rating: 8

in San Francisco Presidio

Map 7.3, page 471

Rob Hill Group Camp is a pretty spot set in a wooded area beneath cypress and eucalyptus canopy. It is well hidden in the Presidio in the San Francisco Headlands and is San Francisco's only campground with tent sites. Hiking is good in the vicinity. There are two group camps here—a great spot for a youth group camp. They are full all the time. Parking is limited. From the parking area, it is an uphill climb of 150 feet to the camp. Free shuttle service is available within the Presidio, which can connect you to Muni bus service.

Campsites, facilities: There are two group tent sites, each with sites for up to 30 people. Picnic tables, flush and portable toilets, stand-up grills, and a community fire circle are available. No drinking water is available. Generators and amplified music are prohibited. Leashed pets are permitted.

Reservations, fees: Reservations are required. Sites are $65 per night. Open April through October.

Directions: From the Peninsula, drive north on U.S. 101 into San Francisco and continue to Lombard Street. Get in the left lane and stay on Lombard (U.S. 101 and Doyle Drive go off to the right) and drive to Presidio Boulevard. Turn right on Presidio Boulevard and drive (it becomes Lincoln Boulevard) into the Presidio (past the Golden Gate Bridge toll plaza) to Kobbe Avenue. Turn left on Kobbe Avenue and drive to Washington Avenue. Turn right and drive to Central Magazine. Turn left and drive to the first service road on the right. Turn right at that service road and park. Walk up the hill 150 feet to the campsites on the right.

From Marin, take U.S. 101 south over the Golden Gate Bridge and get in the right lane to the toll plaza. Immediately after the toll plaza, look for Merchant Street. Turn right on Merchant Street and drive up the hill to the stop sign at Lincoln Boulevard. Turn right and drive to Kobbe Avenue. Turn left and drive to Washington Boulevard. Turn right and drive to Central Magazine Road. Turn left and drive to the first service road on the right. Turn right at that service road and park. Walk up the hill 150 feet to the campsites on the right.

Contact: The Presidio Trust/Rob Hill Camp information (reservations) 415/561-5444, www.presidio.gov or www.nps.gov/prsf.

22 CANDLESTICK RV PARK
🏃 🐕 ♿ 🚐 ⛺

Scenic rating: 6

in San Francisco

Map 7.3, page 471

This RV park is set adjacent to the old stadium that everybody calls Candlestick Park; although the name is now officially Monster Park. It is five miles from downtown San Francisco and an ideal destination for out-of-towners who want to explore the city without having to drive, because the park offers tours and inexpensive shuttles to the downtown area. In addition, there are good hiking opportunities along the shoreline of the bay. On summer afternoons, when the wind howls at 20–30 mph here, sailboarders rip by. Rates are higher, much higher, on 49er game days, and the stadium is usually packed with 60,000 or more people.

Campsites, facilities: There are 165 sites with full hookups (30 and 50 amps) for trailers or RVs up to 42 feet, and 24 tent sites. Some sites are pull-through. Restrooms with showers, coin laundry, modem access, grocery store, game room, motor-home washing, and propane are available. Shuttles and bus tours are also available. Some facilities are wheelchair-accessible. A security officer is posted at the entry station at night. Small leashed pets are permitted.

Reservations, fees: Reservations are

recommended at 800/888-CAMP (800/888-2267). Sites are $55–58 per night, $10 per night for each additional vehicle, $3 per person per night for more than two people. Rates are higher on 49er game days. Some credit cards accepted. Open year-round.

Directions: From San Francisco on U.S. 101, take the Monster Park exit to Gilman Road. Turn east on the stadium entrance road/Gilman Road and drive around the parking lot to the far end of the stadium (Gate 4).

Contact: Candlestick RV Park, 415/822-2299, fax 415/822-7638, www.sanfranciscorvpark .com.

23 SAN FRANCISCO RV RESORT

🏕 🏊 🎣 🐎 🎲 🚵 ♿ 🚐

Scenic rating: 8

in Pacifica

Map 7.3, page 471

This is one of the best RV parks in the Bay Area. It is set on the bluffs just above the Pacific Ocean in Pacifica, complete with beach access, nearby fishing pier, and sometimes excellent surf fishing. There is also a nearby golf course and the chance for dramatic ocean sunsets. The park is kept clean and in good shape, and though there is too much asphalt, the proximity to the beach overcomes it. It is only 20 minutes from San Francisco.

Campsites, facilities: There are 182 sites with full hookups (50 amps) for RVs up to 45 feet. No tents. Restrooms with showers, heated swimming pool, year-round spa, playground, game room, group facilities, cable TV, Wi-Fi, modem access, convenience store, coin laundry, and propane gas are available. Some facilities are wheelchair-accessible. Leashed pets are permitted, with some exceptions.

Reservations, fees: Reservations are recommended at 650/355-7093. Sites are $40–60 per night. Some credit cards accepted. Open year-round.

Directions: From San Francisco, drive south

on Highway 280 to Highway 1. Bear west on Highway 1 and drive into Pacifica to the Palmetto Drive exit. Take that exit and drive south to the stop sign (you will be on the west side of the highway). Continue straight ahead (the road becomes Palmetto Avenue) for about two blocks and look for the entrance to the park on the right side of the road at 700 Palmetto.

From the south, drive north on Highway 1 into Pacifica. Take the Manor Drive exit. At the stop sign, turn left on Oceana Avenue (you will be on the east side of the highway), and drive a block to another stop sign at Manor Drive. Turn left, drive a short distance over the highway to a stop sign at Palmetto Avenue. Turn left and drive about two blocks to the park on the right.

Contact: San Francisco RV Resort, 650/355-7093, fax 650/355-7102, www.sanfranciscorvresort.com.

24 HALF MOON BAY STATE BEACH

🏕 🚴 🏊 🎣 🐎 ♿ 🚐 ⛺

Scenic rating: 7

at Half Moon Bay

Map 7.3, page 471

In summer, this park often fills to capacity with campers touring Highway 1. The campground has level, grassy sites for tents, a clean parking area for RVs, and a state beach available just a short walk away. The feature here is four miles of broad, sandy beaches with three access points with parking. A visitors center is available. Side trips include Princeton and Pillar Point Marina, seven miles north on Highway 1, where fishing and whale-watching trips are possible. Typical weather is fog in summer, clear days in spring and fall, and wet and windy in the winter—yet occasionally there are drop-dead beautiful days in winter between storms, warm, clear, and windless. Temperatures range from lows in the mid-40s in winter to highs in the mid-60s in fall.

One frustrating point: The weekend traffic on Highway 1 up and down the coast here is often jammed, with absolute gridlock during festivals.

Campsites, facilities: There are 52 sites for tents or RVs up to 40 feet (no hookups), four hike-in/bike-in sites, and one group site (for up to 50 people) two miles north of the main campground. Picnic tables, food lockers, and fire grills are provided. Restrooms with flush toilets and coin showers, drinking water, Wi-Fi, pay telephone, and dump station are available. Some facilities are wheelchair-accessible. Leashed pets are permitted, except on the beach.

Reservations, fees: Reservations are required ($7.50 reservation fee) at 800/444-PARK (800/444-7275) or www.reserveamerica.com. Sites are $25 per night, $111 per night for group site, $3 per person per night for hike-in/bike-in sites, $6 per night for each additional vehicle. Open year-round.

Directions: Drive to Half Moon Bay to the junction of Highway 1 and Highway 92. Turn south on Highway 1 and drive two blocks to Kelly Avenue. Turn right on Kelly Avenue and drive 0.5 mile to the park entrance at the end of the road.

Contact: Half Moon Bay State Beach, 650/726-8820 or 650/726-8819; Santa Cruz District, 831/335-6318, www.parks.ca.gov.

25 PELICAN POINT RV PARK

Scenic rating: 7

in Half Moon Bay

Map 7.3, page 471

This park is in a rural setting on the southern outskirts of the town of Half Moon Bay, set on an extended bluff near the ocean. The sites consist of cement slabs with picnic tables. Note that half of the RV sites are monthly rentals. All facilities are available nearby, with restaurants available in Half Moon Bay and 10 miles north in Princeton at Pillar Point Har-

bor. The harbor has an excellent boat launch, a fish-cleaning station, party boat trips for salmon and rockfish and, in the winter, whale-watching trips.

Campsites, facilities: There are 75 sites with full hookups (30 and 50 amps) for RVs up to 40 feet. No tents. Picnic tables are provided. Restrooms with showers, coin laundry, propane gas, small store, clubhouse, and dump station are available. Leashed pets are permitted.

Reservations, fees: Reservations are accepted. Sites are $40–45 per night, $2 per night for each additional vehicle, $3.30 per person per night for more than two people, $1 per pet per night. Some credit cards accepted. Open year-round.

Directions: In Half Moon Bay, at the junction of Highway 1 and Highway 92, turn south on Highway 1 and drive 2.5 miles to Miramontes Point Road. Turn right and drive a short distance to the park entrance on the left.

Contact: Pelican Point RV Park, 650/726-9100.

26 MEMORIAL COUNTY PARK

Scenic rating: 8

near La Honda

Map 7.4, page 472

This beautiful 500-acre redwood park is set on the western slopes of the Santa Cruz Mountains, tucked in a pocket between the tiny towns of La Honda and Loma Mar. The park is known for its family camping areas and Tan Oak and Mount Ellen nature trails. The campground features access to a nearby network of 50 miles of trails, with the best hike along the headwaters of Pescadero Creek. In late winter, it is sometimes possible to see steelhead spawn (no fishing permitted, of course). The trails link with others in nearby Portola State Park and Sam McDonald County Park, providing access to a vast recreation land. A swimming hole on

Pescadero Creek next to the campground is popular during the summer. The camp is often filled on summer weekends, but the sites are spaced so it won't cramp your style.

Campsites, facilities: There are 156 sites for tents or RVs up to 35 feet, two group sites for tents or RVs up to 35 feet (no hookups) that can accommodate up to 75 people, and six areas for youth groups of up to 50 people. Picnic tables, food lockers, and fire grills are provided. Drinking water, restrooms with coin showers and flush toilets, amphitheater, picnic area, summer convenience store, visitors center, summer campfire programs, and firewood are available. A dump station is available from May through October. No pets are allowed.

Reservations, fees: Reservations are accepted for groups only at 650/363-4021. Sites are $19 per vehicle per night, $8 per night for each additional vehicle. Group sites are $130 per night, plus $5 per vehicle per stay. Open year-round.

Directions: From Half Moon Bay at the junction of Highway 1 and Highway 92, drive south on Highway 1 for 18 miles to the Pescadero Road exit. Turn left (east) on Pescadero Road and drive about 10.5 miles to the park entrance on the right.

Contact: Memorial County Park, 650/879-0212 or 650/879-0238; San Mateo County Parks and Recreation, 650/363-4021, www.sanmateocountyparks.org.

27 BUTANO STATE PARK

Scenic rating: 9

near Pescadero

Map 7.4, page 472

The campground at Butano is set in canyon filled with a redwood forest, so pretty and with such good hiking that it has become popular enough to make reservations a must. The reason for its popularity is a series of exceptional hikes, including one to the Año Nuevo Lookout (well, the lookout is now blocked by trees,

but there are glimpses of the ocean elsewhere along the way), Mill Ox Loop, and, for the ambitious, 11-mile Butano Rim Loop. The latter has a backpack camp with seven trail campsites (primitive with pit toilets available) requiring a 5.5-mile hike in the park's most remote area, where no drinking water is available. Creek water is within a half mile of the campsites; bring a water purifier.

Campsites, facilities: There are 20 sites for tents or RVs up to 24 feet (no hookups), 18 walk-in sites, and seven hike-in sites (5.5 miles, with pit toilets available). Picnic tables, food lockers, and fire grills are provided. Drinking water and restrooms with flush toilets are available. Leashed pets are permitted in campsites, picnic areas, and on paved roads.

Reservations, fees: Reservations are accepted ($7.50 reservation fee) at 800/444-PARK (800/444-7275) or www.reserveamerica.com. Sites are $25 per night, $10 per night for walk-in sites and hike-in trail sites, $6 per night for each additional vehicle. Note: Reservations are not available for hike-in trail sites and are available in summer only for walk-in sites. Open year-round.

Directions: Drive to Half Moon Bay and the junction of Highway 1 and Highway 92. Drive south on Highway 1 for 18 miles to the Pescadero Road exit. Turn left on Pescadero Road and drive three miles past the town of Pescadero to Cloverdale Road. Turn right and drive 4.5 miles to the park entrance on the left.

Contact: Butano State Park, 650/879-2040, fax 650/879-2173; Santa Cruz District, 831/335-6318, www.parks.ca.gov.

28 PORTOLA REDWOODS STATE PARK

Scenic rating: 9

near Skyline Ridge

Map 7.4, page 472

Portola Redwoods State Park is very secluded, since visitors are required to travel on an extremely slow and winding series of roads to reach it. The park features redwoods and a mixed evergreen and hardwood forest on the western slopes of the Santa Cruz Mountains, the headwaters of Pescadero Creek, and 18 miles of hiking trails. A literal highlight is a 300-foot-high redwood, one of the tallest trees in the Santa Cruz Mountains. In addition to redwoods, there are Douglas fir and live oak, as well as a riparian zone along the stream. A four-mile hike links up to nearby Pescadero Creek County Park (which, in turn, borders Memorial County Park). At times in the summer, a low fog will move in along the San Mateo coast, and from lookouts near Skyline, visitors can peer to the west at what seems like a pearlescent sea with little islands (hilltops) poking through (this view is available from the access road, not from campsites). Wild pigs are occasionally spotted here, with larger numbers at neighboring Pescadero Creek County Park.

Campsites, facilities: There are 52 sites for tents or RVs up to 24 feet (no hookups), four hike-in/bike-in sites, four walk-in sites, six hike-in backpack sites (three-mile hike), and four group sites for 25–50 people each. Picnic tables, storage lockers, and fire grills are provided. Drinking water, restrooms with flush toilets and coin showers, and firewood are available. There are nature hikes and campfire programs scheduled on weekends from Memorial Day through Labor Day. The nearest gas is 13 miles away. Leashed pets are permitted on paved surfaces only.

Reservations, fees: Reservations are accepted ($7.50 reservation fee) at 800/444-PARK (800/444-7275) or www.reserveamerica.com. Sites are $25 per night, $6 per night for each additional vehicle, $3 per person per night for hike-in/bike-in sites, $10 per person per night for walk-in sites and hike-in backpack sites, $111–224 per night for group sites. Open April through November.

Directions: From Palo Alto on I-280, turn west on Page Mill Road and drive (slow and twisty) to Skyline Boulevard/Highway 35.

Cross Skyline and continue west on Alpine Road (very twisty) for about three miles to Portola State Park Road. Turn left on Portola State Park Road and drive about three miles to the park entrance at the end of the road.

Contact: Portola Redwoods State Park, 650/948-9098; Santa Cruz District, 831/335-6318, www.parks.ca.gov.

29 BIG BASIN REDWOODS STATE PARK

🎿 🐕 ♿ 🚐 ⛺

Scenic rating: 10

near Santa Cruz

Map 7.4, page 472

Big Basin is one of the best state parks in California, featuring giant redwoods near the park headquarters, secluded campsites set in forest, and rare opportunities to stay in a tent cabin or a backpacking trail site. The park covers more than 18,000 acres of redwoods, much of it old-growth, including forest behemoths more than 1,000 years old. It is a great park for hikers, with four waterfalls making for stellar destinations. Sempervirens Falls, a long, narrow, silvery stream, is an easy 1.5-hour round-trip on Sequoia Trail. The famous Berry Creek Falls, a spectacular 70-foot cascade set in a beautiful canyon, is framed by redwoods. For hikers in good condition, figure two hours (4.7 miles) to reach Berry Creek Falls, five hours for the round-trip in and out, and six hours for the complete loop (12 miles) that extends into the park's most remote areas. Other waterfalls include Silver Falls and Golden Falls. There is also an easy nature loop trail near the park headquarters in the valley floor that is routed past several mammoth redwoods. This is California's oldest state park, established in 1902. It is home to the largest continuous stand of ancient coast redwoods south of Humboldt State Park in far Northern California. There are more than 80 miles of trails with elevations varying from 2,000 feet at the eastern Big Basin Rim on down to sea level. Rainfall averages 60 inches per year, most arriving from December through mid-March.

Campsites, facilities: There are 31 sites for tents or RVs up to 27 feet or trailers up to 24 feet (no hookups), 69 sites for tents only, 38 walk-in sites, 36 tent cabins (reservations required), two hike-in/bike-in sites, 52 hike-in campsites, and four group sites for 40–50 people. Picnic tables, food lockers, and fire grills are provided. Drinking water, restrooms with flush toilets and coin showers, dump station, firewood, and groceries are available. Some facilities are wheelchair-accessible. Leashed pets are allowed in campsites and on paved roads only.

Reservations, fees: Reservation are accepted ($7.50 reservation fee) at 800/444-PARK (800/444-7275) or www.reserveamerica. com. Sites are $25 per night for individual sites and walk-in sites, $6 per night for each additional vehicle, $10 per person for hike-in sites, $3 per person per night for hike-in/bike-in sites, $180–224 per night for group sites. Reserve tent cabins at 800/874-8368. Open year-round.

Directions: From Santa Cruz, turn north on Highway 9 and drive 12 miles to Boulder Creek and Highway 236 (signed Big Basin). Turn west on Highway 236 and drive nine miles to the park headquarters.

Contact: Big Basin Redwoods State Park, 831/338-8860 or 831/338-8861; Santa Cruz District, 831/335-6318, www.santacruzstate-parks.org or www.parks.ca.gov.

30 SANBORN-SKYLINE COUNTY PARK

🏃 🐕 🚶 ♿ 🚐 ⛺

Scenic rating: 8

near Saratoga

Map 7.4, page 472

This is a pretty camp set in redwood forest, semi-primitive, but like a world in a different orbit compared to the asphalt of San Jose and the rest of the Santa Clara Valley. These campgrounds get heavy use on summer weekends, of course. This is headquarters for a 3,688-acre park that stretches from the foothills of Saratoga up to the Skyline Ridge in the Santa Cruz Mountains. Fifteen miles of hiking trails are available, with a trailhead at camp. Most trails explore lush wooded slopes, with redwoods and tan oak. Dogs are prohibited at walk-in sites, but are allowed at the RV sites, the main park's grassy area, and day-use areas.

Campsites, facilities: There are 15 sites with full hookups (20 and 30 amps) for RVs up to 30 feet, a separate walk-in campground with 33 sites for tents, and a youth group area for up to 35 people. Picnic tables, food lockers, and fire pits are provided. Drinking water, restrooms with flush toilets and coin showers, dump station, a seasonal youth science center, and a one-mile nature trail are available. Some facilities are wheelchair-accessible. Leashed pets are permitted in RV campground and picnic areas only.

Reservations, fees: Reservations are required ($6 reservation fee) at 408/355-2201. Sites are $25 per night for RV sites, $10 per night for walk-in, $25 for youth group area for up to 30 people for first night and then $10 per night. Check-in required before sunset; gates are locked at dusk. Some credit cards accepted. RV sites open year-round, walk-in sites open April to mid-October.

Directions: From Highway 17 in San Jose, drive south for six miles to Highway 9/Saratoga Avenue. Turn west and drive to Saratoga, then continue on Highway 9 for two miles to Sanborn Road. Turn left and drive one mile to the park on the right. Walk-in sites require a 0.1- to 0.5-mile walk from the parking area.

Contact: Sanborn-Skyline County Park, 408/867-9959, www.parkhere.org.

31 JOSEPH D. GRANT COUNTY PARK

🥾 🚲 🛶 🐴 ♿ 🚐 ⛺

Scenic rating: 7

near San Jose

Map 7.4, page 472

Grant Ranch is a great, wild playland covering more than 9,000 acres in the foothills of nearby Mount Hamilton to the east. It features 52 miles of hiking trails (horses permitted), 20 miles of old ranch roads that are perfect for mountain biking, a pretty lake (Grant Lake), and miles of foothills, canyons, oaks, and grasslands. The campground is set amid oak grasslands, is shaded, and can be used as a base camp for planning the day's recreation. The best hikes are to Halls Valley, especially in the winter and spring when there are many secret little creeks and miniature waterfalls in hidden canyons; Hotel Trail; and Cañada de Pala Trail, which drops to San Felipe Creek, the prettiest stream in the park. Warm water fishing is available in the lake and several smaller ponds. A great side trip is the slow, curvy drive east to Lick Observatory for great views of the Santa Clara Valley. Wood fires are often banned in summer.

Campsites, facilities: There are 40 sites for tents or RVs up to 31 feet (no hookups). Picnic tables, food lockers, and fire pits are provided. Drinking water, restrooms with flush toilets and free showers, and dump station are available. Some facilities are wheelchair accessible. Leashed pets are permitted.

Reservations, fees: Reservations are recommended ($6 reservation fee) at 408/355-2201. Sites are $9–18 per night. Check-in required before sunset; gates are locked at dusk. Open year-round.

Directions: In San Jose at the junction of I-680 and U.S. 101, take I-680 north to the Alum Rock Avenue exit. Turn east and drive four miles to Mount Hamilton Road. Turn right and drive eight miles to the park headquarters entrance on the right side of the road.

Contact: Joseph D. Grant County Park, 408/274-6121, fax 408/270-4808, www.parkhere.org.

32 COTILLION GARDENS RV PARK

🏊 🐴 🛁 ♿ 🚐 ⛺

Scenic rating: 6

near Santa Cruz

Map 7.4, page 472

This is a pretty place with several possible side trips. It is set on the edge of the Santa Cruz Mountain redwoods, near Henry Cowell Redwoods State Park and the San Lorenzo River. The Santa Cruz Beach and Boardwalk is is only a few minutes away by car, and Monterey is 45 miles away. Other side trips include the steam engine ride along the San Lorenzo River out of Roaring Camp Train Rides in Felton and visiting Loch Lomond Reservoir near Ben Lomond for hiking, boat rentals, or fishing. A golf course is nearby. There is a mix of both overnighters and some long-term rentals at this park.

Campsites, facilities: There are 80 sites with full or partial hookups (30 amps) for RVs up to 36 feet, two sites for tents, and five camping cabins. One RV site is pull-through. Picnic tables and fire rings are provided. Restrooms with showers, dump station, cable TV, modem access, recreation room, heated seasonal swimming pool, and a convenience store are available. Some facilities are wheelchair-accessible. Leashed pets are permitted.

Reservations, fees: Reservations are recommended, but are not accepted for tent sites. RV sites are $41–45 per night, $30 per night for tent sites, plus $3 per person per night for more than two people. Call for cabin prices. Some credit cards accepted. Open year-round.

Directions: From Los Gatos, drive west on Highway 17 for 20 miles toward Santa Cruz to the Mount Hermon Road exit/Scotts Valley (second exit in Scotts Valley). Take the Mount Hermon Road exit to the stoplight at Mount Hermon Road. Turn right on Mount

Hermon Road and drive 3.5 miles to Felton and Graham Hill Road (Y intersection). Bear right onto Graham Hill Road, immediately move to the left lane, and drive 50 feet to Highway 9. Turn left on Highway 9 and drive 1.5 miles to the park on the left.

Contact: Cotillion Gardens RV Park, 831/335-7669.

33 HENRY COWELL REDWOODS STATE PARK

Scenic rating: 8

near Santa Cruz

Map 7.4, page 472

This state park near Santa Cruz has good hiking, good views, and a chance of fishing in the winter for steelhead. The 1,750-acre park features 20 miles of trails in the forest, where the old-growth redwoods are estimated at 1,400–1,800 years old. One great easy hike is a 15-minute walk to a lookout platform over Santa Cruz and the Pacific Ocean; the trailhead is near campsite 49. Another good hike is Eagle Creek Trail, a three-mile walk that heads along Eagle Creek and the San Lorenzo River, running through a classic redwood canyon. In winter, there is limited steelhead fishing in the San Lorenzo River. A side-trip option is taking the Roaring Camp Big Trees Railroad, which is adjacent to camp, 831/335-4400. Insider's tips: Poison oak is prevalent in this park and around the campground, so take precautions. Also, alcohol is prohibited in the campground, but not in the day-use area.

Campsites, facilities: There are 111 sites for tents or RVs up to 35 feet (no hookups), and one hike-in/bike-in site. Picnic tables and fire grills are provided. Drinking water, restrooms with flush toilets and coin showers, and Wi-Fi are available. Some facilities are wheelchair-accessible. A nature center, bookstore, and picnic area are nearby. Leashed pets are permitted, but must be kept inside tents or vehicles at night.

Reservations, fees: Reservations accepted mid-March through October ($7.50 reservation fee); reserve at 800/444-PARK (800/444-7275) or www.reserveamerica.com. Sites are $25 per night (maximum of eight people), $3 per person per night for hike-in, bike-in site. Open mid-February through November.

Directions: In Scotts Valley on Highway 17, take the Mount Hermon Road exit and drive west toward Felton to Lockwood Lane. Turn left on Lockwood Lane and drive about one mile to Graham Hill Road. Turn left on Graham Hill Road and drive 0.5 mile to the campground on the right.

Contact: Henry Cowell Redwoods State Park, 831/438-2396 or 831/335-4598, www.santacruzstateparks.org or www.parks.ca.gov.

34 SANTA CRUZ RANCH RV PARK

Scenic rating: 5

near Scotts Valley

Map 7.4, page 472

This camp is situated on 6.5 acres and is just a short hop from Santa Cruz and Monterey Bay. There are many side-trip options, making this a prime location for vacationers cruising the California coast. In Santa Cruz there are several quality restaurants, plus fishing trips and boat rentals at Santa Cruz Wharf, as well as the famous Santa Cruz Boardwalk and amusement park. Discount tickets for local attractions are available in the office. Note that most of the sites are filled with long-term renters; a few sites are set aside for overnight vacationers.

Campsites, facilities: There are 25 pull-through sites with full hookups (30 amps) for RVs up to 43 feet and five sites for tents. Picnic tables are provided. Restrooms with showers, cable TV, dump station, coin laundry, free Wi-Fi and modem access, recreation and meeting room, spa, and a seasonal heated swimming pool are available. No open fires. Leashed pets are permitted with approval.

Reservations, fees: Reservations are recommended. RV sites are $34–48 per night, tent sites are $26.10–29 per night, $2 per night for each additional vehicle. First pet is free and second pet is $1 per night. Weekly, monthly, and group rates available. Some credit cards accepted. Open year-round.

Directions: From Santa Cruz, at the junction of Highways 1 and 17, turn north on Highway 17 and drive three miles to the Mount Hermon/Big Basin exit. Take that exit north onto Mount Hermon Road and drive 0.5 mile to Scotts Valley Drive. Turn right and drive 0.7 mile to Disc Drive. Turn right and continue to 917 Disc Drive on the left.

Contact: Santa Cruz Ranch RV Park, 831/438-1288 or 800/546-1288, fax 831/438-2877, www.santacruzranchrv.com.

3 5 HENRY W. COE STATE PARK

👥 🚲 🛶 🐕 5% 🚐 ⛺

Scenic rating: 8

near Gilroy

Map 7.4, page 472

This is the Bay Area's backyard wilderness, with 87,000 acres of wildlands, including a 23,300-acre wilderness area. There are more than 100 miles of ranch roads and 300 miles of hiking trails, a remarkable network that provides access to 140 ponds and small lakes, hidden streams, and a habitat that is paradise for fish, wildlife, and wild flora. The best camping introduction is at drive-in campsites at park headquarters, set at a hilltop at 2,600 feet that is ideal for stargazing and watching meteor showers. That provides a taste. If you like it, then come back for the full meal. It is the wilderness hike-in and bike-in sites where you will get the full flavor of the park. Before setting out for the outback, always consult with the rangers here—the ambitious plans of many hikers cause them to suffer dehydration and

heatstroke. For wilderness trips, the best jump-off point is Coyote Creek or Hunting Hollow trailheads upstream of Coyote Reservoir near Gilroy. The park has excellent pond-style fishing but requires extremely long hikes (typically 10- to 25-mile round-trips) to reach the best lakes, including Mustang Pond, Jackrabbit Lake, Coit Lake, and Mississippi Lake. Expect hot weather in the summer; spring and early summer are the prime times. Even though the park may appear to be 120 square miles of oak foothills, the terrain is often steep, and making ridges often involves climbs of 1,500 feet. There are many great secrets to be discovered here, including Rooster Comb and Coyote Creek. At times on spring days, wild pigs seem to be everywhere. Golden eagles are also abundant. Bring a water purifier for hikes because there is no drinking water in the outback.

Campsites, facilities: There are 10 sites for tents and 10 sites for tents or RVs up to 24 feet (no hookups). There are also eight equestrian campsites, 82 hike-in/bike-in sites, and 10 group sites for 10–50 people. At the drive-in site at park headquarters, picnic tables and fire grills are provided. Drinking water and vault toilets are available. Leashed pets are permitted at the drive-in campgrounds only. At the horse camps, corrals and water troughs are available. At hike-in/bike-in sites, vault toilets are provided, but no drinking water is available. Garbage must be packed out at hike-in/bike-in camps.

Reservations, fees: Reservations are accepted ($7.50 reservation fee) at 800/444-PARK (800/444-7275) or www.reserveamerica.com. Sites are $12 per night, $5 per night for each additional vehicle, $30 per night for group sites. No reservation for hike-in/bike-in or horse sites, $14 per night for horse sites, $3 per person per night for hike-in/bike-in sites. For hike-in/bike-in or horse sites, a wilderness permit is required from park headquarters. Make reservations for group sites ($7.50 reservation fee) at 408/779-2728. Open year-round.

Morgan Hill on U.S. 101,
ne Avenue exit. Turn east
(including over the bridge
at Anderson Lake, then very twisty and narrow) to the park entrance.

Contact: Henry W. Coe State Park, 408/779-
2728, www.coepark.org or www.parks
.ca.gov.

36 UVAS CANYON COUNTY PARK

Scenic rating: 8

near Morgan Hill

Map 7.4, page 472

This lushly wooded park of 1,133 acres is
nestled on the eastern side of the Santa Cruz
Mountains. It has a stunning array of waterfalls that can be reached with short hikes,
including Triple Falls, Black Rock Falls,
and several others, making for stellar hikes
in winter and spring. In all, the park has six
miles of trails, including a self-guided interpretive trail. But Uvas is even better known
for its lake, Uvas Reservoir (5 miles away),
which provides some of the better bass and
crappie fishing in the Bay Area. Prospects are
best by far during the spring, when the lake
is also stocked with rainbow trout. Swimming and powerboating are prohibited. Note
that the gate to the campground is locked
at sunset.

Campsites, facilities: There are 25 sites for
tents only. There is a youth group area with
tent sites for up to 40 people. Picnic tables,
food lockers, and fire grills (charcoal fires
only) are provided; fires may be prohibited
during fire season. Drinking water and flush
toilets are available. There is a boat ramp at
the reservoir six miles away. Some facilities
are wheelchair-accessible. Leashed pets are
permitted.

Reservations, fees: Reservations are required
($6 reservation fee) at 408/355-2201. Sites
are $18 per night, and $25 per night for the

youth group site. Open year-round. Check-
in required before sunset; gates close at
sunset.

Directions: From U.S. 101 in San Jose, turn
west on Bernal Avenue and drive to Santa
Teresa Boulevard. Turn left (south) and
drive three miles to Bailey Avenue. Turn
right (west) on Bailey Avenue and drive 2.3
miles to McKean Road (McKean Road becomes Uvas Road 2.2 miles south of Bailey
Road). Drive south on McKean/Uvas Road
to Croy Road. Turn right on Croy Road and
drive 4.4 miles, through Sveadal, to the park
entrance.

Contact: Uvas Canyon County Park, 408/779-
9232, fax 408/779-3315, www.parkhere
.org; Coyote Discount Bait and Tackle,
408/463-0711.

37 MOUNT MADONNA COUNTY PARK

Scenic rating: 7

between Watsonville and Gilroy

Map 7.4, page 472

It's a twisty son-of-a-gun road to reach the
top of Mount Madonna, but the views on
clear days of Monterey Bay to the west and
Santa Clara Valley to the east always make
it worth the trip. In addition, a small herd
of white deer are kept protected in a pen
near the parking area for a rare chance to
see unique wildlife. This 3,688-acre park
is dominated by redwood forest, but at the
lower slopes of Mount Madonna the landscape changes to oak woodland, dense chaparral, and grassy meadows. Ohlone Indians
once lived here. There are many good hiking trails in the park; the best is Bayview
Loop. The 20-mile trail system includes a
one-mile self-guided nature trail. Elevation
in the park reaches 1,896 feet. Free programs
are offered at the amphitheater on Saturday evenings during the summer. Insider's
note: Campsite 105 at Valley View is the only

pull-through site. While no credit cards are accepted in person, there is a self-pay machine that accepts credit cards, a nice touch. The campsites are dispersed throughout four campgrounds.

Campsites, facilities: There are 118 sites with partial hookups (30 amps) for tents or RVs up to 31 feet and two group areas for up to 240 people. One site is pull-through. Five youth-group areas for 40–50 people each are also available; youth groups must have tax-exempt status. Picnic tables, food lockers, and fire pits are provided. Drinking water, restrooms with coin showers and flush toilets, dump station, seasonal live music, archery range, picnic areas, amphitheater, and visitors center are available. Some facilities are wheelchair-accessible. Leashed pets are permitted.

Reservations, fees: Reservations are accepted ($6 reservation fee) at 408/355-2201. Sites are $18–25 per night, $150–450 per night for group areas and $25 per night for youth group areas. Some credit cards accepted at self-serve machine. Open year-round.

Directions: From U.S. 101 in Gilroy, take the Hecker Pass Highway/Highway 152 exit west. Drive west seven miles to Pole Line Road and the park entrance on the right.

From Highway 1 in Watsonville, turn east onto Highway 152 and drive about 12 miles east to Pole Line Road and the park entrance on the left.

Contact: Call Mount Madonna County Park, 408/842-2341, fax 408/842-6642, www.parkhere.org.

38 COYOTE LAKE COUNTY PARK

Scenic rating: 7

near Gilroy

Map 7.4, page 472

Coyote Lake, a long, narrow lake set in a canyon just over the ridge east of U.S. 101, is a pretty surprise to newcomers. It covers 635 acres and is stocked with trout from late winter through spring; the lake also provides the top fishery for bass in the Bay Area. Other species are bluegill and crappie. Both powerboating and non-motorized boating are allowed; the boat launch is one mile north of the visitors center. Swimming is prohibited. Several campsites are set on a bluff with a lake view. The campground is nestled in oaks, among 796 acres of parkland, furnishing some much-needed shade. There are no longer hiking trails along the lakeshore, but more than 13 miles of multi-use trails (horses and mountain bikes are allowed) are available. Note: If you continue east about four miles on the access road that runs past the lake to the Coe State Park Hunting Hollow entrance, you'll come to two outstanding trailheads (one at a parking area, one at the Coyote Creek gate) into that park's wildlands. Wildlife, including deer and wild turkey, is abundant.

Campsites, facilities: There are 74 pull-through sites for tents or RVs up to 31 feet (no hookups). Picnic tables, food lockers, and fire pits are provided. Drinking water, flush toilets, and a boat ramp are available. A visitors center is also available. Some facilities are wheelchair-accessible. Leashed pets are permitted.

Reservations, fees: Reservations are required ($6 reservation fee) at 408/355-2201. Sites are $10–18 per night, $6 per day for boat launching. Some credit cards accepted. Open year-round.

Directions: Drive on U.S. 101 to Gilroy and Leavesley Road. Take that exit and drive east on Leavesley Road for 1.75 miles to New Avenue. Turn left on New Avenue and drive 0.6 mile to Roop Road. Turn right on Roop Road and drive three miles to Coyote Reservoir Road. Turn left on Coyote Reservoir Road and drive to the campground.

Contact: Coyote Lake County Park, 408/842-7800, fax 408/842-6439, www.parkhere.org; Coyote Discount Bait and Tackle, 408/463-0711.

MONTEREY
AND BIG SUR

COURTESY OF THE NATIONAL PARK SERVICE

BEST CAMPGROUNDS

⊂ Scenic Destinations
Manresa Uplands State Beach Walk-In, **page 504**

The scenic charm seems to extend to infinity
from the seaside towns of Santa Cruz, Monterey, Big Sur, and San Simeon. The primary treasure is the coast, which is rock-strewn and sprinkled with inshore kelp beds, where occasionally you can find sea otters playing Pop Goes the Weasel. The sea here is a color like no other, often more of a tourmaline than a straight green or blue.

From Carmel to Lucia alone, touring Big Sur on Highway 1 is one of the most captivating drives anywhere. The inland strip along Highway 1 provides access to state parks, redwoods, coastal streams, Los Padres National Forest, and the Ventana Wilderness. As you explore farther south on the Pacific Coast Highway, you will discover a largely untouched coast.

Most vacations to this region include several must-do trips, often starting in Monterey with a visit to Fisherman's Wharf and its domesticated sea lions, and then to the nearby Monterey Bay Aquarium.

From there, most head south to Big Sur to take in a few brush strokes of nature's canvas, easily realizing why this area is beloved around the world.

At first glance, however, it's impossible not to want the whole painting. That is where the campgrounds come in. They provide both the ideal getaway and a launch point for adventure.

At Big Sur, the campgrounds are what many expect: small hideaways in the big redwoods. The campgrounds are in a variety of settings, some near Big Sur River, others in the forest.

Other good opportunities are available in Los Padres National Forest and the adjacent Ventana Wilderness, which provides outstanding camping and hiking in the off-season, when the Sierra is buried in snow.

One note of caution: The state park campgrounds on Highway 1 are among the most popular in North America. Reservations far in advance are required all summer, even on weekdays. They are always the first to fill on the state's reservation system. So get the game wired to get your site.

During the summer, only the fog on the coast and the intense heat just 10 miles inland keep this region from attaining perfection.

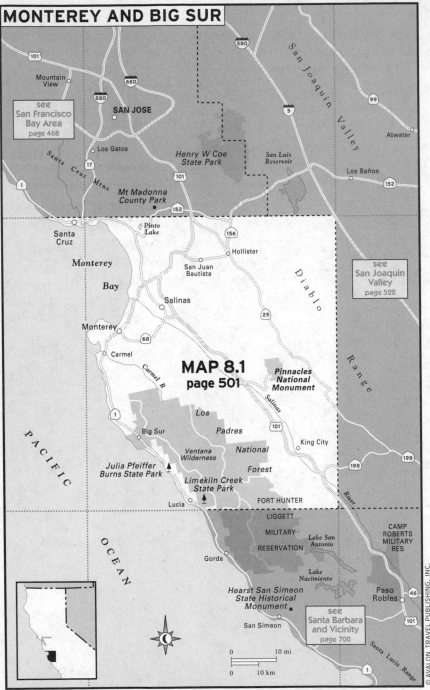

MONTEREY AND BIG SUR

Mountain View

101

680

880

SAN JOSE

580

San Joaquin Valley

99

5

Atwater

see
San Francisco
Bay Area
page 468

Los Gatos

Santa Cruz Mtns

17

1

*Henry W Coe
State Park*

*San Luis
Reservoir*

101

Los Baños

152

*Mt Madonna
County Park*

152

Santa
Cruz

*Pinto
Lake*

156

Monterey

Bay

*San Juan
Bautista*

Hollister

D i a b l o

see
San Joaquin
Valley
page 522

Salinas

25

Monterey

68

Carmel

**MAP 8.1
page 501**

*Pinnacles
National
Monument*

R a n g e

Carmel R

Los

Padres

Salinas

1

Big Sur

National

101

King City

*Ventana
Wilderness*

Forest

198

198

*Julia Pfeiffer
Burns State Park*

*Limekiln Creek
State Park*

Lucia

FORT HUNTER

River

P A C I F I C

LIGGETT

MILITARY

RESERVATION

*Lake San
Antonio*

CAMP
ROBERTS
MILITARY
RES

O C E A N

Gorda

*Lake
Nacimiento*

Paso
Robles

46

101

*Hearst San Simeon
State Historical
Monument*

see
Santa Barbara
and Vicinity
page 700

San Simeon

Santa Lucia Range

1

0   10 mi

0   10 km

© AVALON TRAVEL PUBLISHING, INC.

Map 8.1

Campgrounds 1-35
Pages 502-517

© AVALON TRAVEL PUBLISHING, INC.

BRIGHTON STATE BEACH

🏃 🚴 🏊 🎣 🐕 ♿ 🚐 ⛺

Scenic rating: 10

near Capitola

Map 8.1, page 501

This is one in a series of state park camps set on the bluffs overlooking Monterey Bay. They are among the most popular and in-demand state campgrounds in California. Reservations are a necessity. This camp is set near a forest of Monterey pine and live oak. The summer is often foggy and cool, especially in the morning. Beachcombing, swimming, and surf fishing for perch provide recreation options, and skiff rentals are available at the nearby Capitola Wharf. The San Lorenzo River enters the ocean nearby.

Campsites, facilities: There are 111 sites for tents or RVs up to 36 feet, three group sites, and four hike-in/bike-in sites. Some sites have partial hookups (30 amps). Picnic tables, fire rings, and food lockers are provided. Drinking water, restrooms with coin showers and flush toilets, and visitors center are available. Dump stations, propane gas, groceries, coin laundry, restaurant, and gas station are available within 2.5 miles. Some facilities are wheelchair-accessible. Leashed pets are permitted.

Reservations, fees: Reservations are recommended ($7.50 reservation fee) and can be made at 800/444-PARK (800/444-7275) or www.reserveamerica.com. Sites are $25–35 per night, $6 per night for each additional vehicle, $125 per night for group site, $5 per person per night for hike-in/bike-in site. Two-night maximum stay per month. Open year-round, weather permitting.

Directions: From Santa Cruz, drive south on Highway 1 for about five miles to the Park Avenue exit. Take that exit and turn right on Park Avenue and drive a short distance to McGregor Drive (a four-way stop). Turn left and drive a short distance to the park entrance on the right.

Contact: New Brighton State Beach, 831/464-6330 or 831/464-6329; California State Parks, Santa Cruz District, 831/335-6318, www.santacruzstateparks.org or www.parks.ca.gov.

2 SEACLIFF STATE BEACH

🏊 🎣 🐕 ♿ 🚐

Scenic rating: 10

near Santa Cruz

Map 8.1, page 501

Here is a very pretty spot on a beach along Monterey Bay. Beach walks are great, especially on clear evenings for dramatic sunsets. A visitors center is available in the summer. This is a popular layover for vacationers touring Highway 1 in the summer, but the best weather is from mid-August to early October. This is a popular beach for swimming and sunbathing, with a long stretch of sand backed by coastal bluffs. A structure called the "old cement ship" by many nearby provides some fascination, but visitors are no longer allowed to walk on it for safety reasons. It is actually an old concrete freighter, the *Palo Alto*. Fishing is often good adjacent to the ship.

Campsites, facilities: There are 25 sites with full hookups (30 amps) for RVs up to 40 feet, and an overflow area that can accommodate 21 RVs up to 34 feet (no hookups). No tents. Picnic tables and fire grills are provided. Drinking water, restrooms with flush toilets and coin showers, and picnic area are available. Propane gas, groceries, and a coin laundry are available nearby. Some facilities are wheelchair-accessible. Leashed pets are permitted in the camping area and on the beach.

Reservations, fees: Reserve ($7.50 reservation fee) at 800/444-PARK (800/444-7275) or www.reserveamerica.com. Sites are $35–44 per night, and $6 per night for each additional vehicle. Open year-round.

Directions: From Santa Cruz, drive south on Highway 1 about six miles to State Park Drive/Seacliff Beach exit. Take that exit, turn west (right), and drive a short distance to the park entrance.

Contact: Seacliff State Beach, 831/685-6442 or 831/685-6500; California State Parks, Santa Cruz District, 831/429-2851, fax 831/429-2876, www.santacruzstateparks.org or www.parks.ca.gov.

3 PINTO LAKE PARK

Scenic rating: 7

near Watsonville

Map 8.1, page 501

Pinto Lake can be a real find. Of the nine lakes in the nine Bay Area counties that offer camping, it is the only one where the RV campsites are actually near the lake. For the few who know about it, it's an offer that can't be refused. But note that no tent camping is permitted. The lake is best known as a fishing lake, with trout stocks and a small resident population of crappie and bluegill. Rainbow trout are stocked twice weekly in season. A 5-mph speed limit has been established for boaters, and no swimming or wading is permitted. The leash law for dogs is strictly enforced here.

Campsites, facilities: There are 28 sites with full hookups (30 amps) for RVs of any length. No tents. Picnic tables, cable TV, and barbecues are provided. A boat ramp, boat rentals, volleyball, softball field, and horseshoes are available nearby in the summer. Leashed pets are permitted. Most facilities are wheelchair-accessible. Open year-round.

Reservations, fees: Reservations are accepted. Sites are $25 per night, $2 per night per person for more than two people (children 12 and under are free), $2 per night for each additional vehicle, $2 per pet per night. Credit cards are not accepted.

Directions: From Santa Cruz, drive 17 miles south on Highway 1 to the exit for Watsonville/Gilroy-Highway 152. Take that exit onto Main Street, then immediately turn left

on Green Valley Road and drive 2.7 miles (0.5 mile past Holohan intersection) to the entrance for the lake and campground on the left.

From Monterey, drive north on Highway 1 to the Green Valley Road exit. Take that exit and turn right at the Green Valley Road and drive 2.7 miles (0.5 mile past the Holohan intersection) to the entrance for the lake and campground.

Contact: Pinto Lake Park, City of Watsonville, 831/722-8129, www.pintolake.com.

4 CASA DE FRUTA RV ORCHARD RESORT

Scenic rating: 3

near Pacheco Pass

Map 8.1, page 501

This 80-acre RV park has a festival-like atmosphere to it, with country music and dancing every weekend in the summer and barbecues on Sunday. The resort is also busy during the Gilroy Garlic Festival in July and the Hollister Independence Rally, a motorcycle event held nearby during the Fourth of July weekend. Huge, but sparse, San Luis Reservoir is 20 miles to the east.

Campsites, facilities: There are 300 sites with full hookups (30 amps) for RVs; some sites are pull-through. Tent sites are also available. Picnic tables are provided. Restrooms with flush toilets and showers, dump station, satellite TV, coin laundry, playground, swimming pool, wading pool, outdoor dance floor, horseshoes, volleyball courts, baseball diamonds, wine- and cheese-tasting room, candy factory, bakery, fruit stand, 24-hour restaurant, motel, gift shop, carousel, narrow-gauge train ride through animal park, and a minimart are available. Leashed pets are permitted. Some facilities are wheelchair-accessible.

Reservations, fees: Reservations are accepted at 800/548-3813. Sites are $30–36 per night, $2 per person per night for more than two people, $3 per pet per night. Some credit cards accepted. Open year-round.

Directions: Drive on U.S. 101 to the junction with Highway 152 (near Gilroy). Take Highway 152 east and drive 13 miles to Casa de Fruta Parkway. Take that exit and drive a short distance to the resort.

Contact: Casa de Fruta RV Orchard Resort, 408/842-9316 or 800/548-3813, www.casadefruta.com.

5 MANRESA UPLANDS STATE BEACH WALK-IN

Scenic rating: 10

south of Santa Cruz

Map 8.1, page 501   BEST (

This is a beautiful and extremely popular state park, with the campground set on uplands overlooking the Pacific Ocean. Many sites have ocean views; others are set back in a secluded grove of pine and cypress trees. The walk to the campsites is 20–150 yards from a vehicle-unloading zone. There is beach access for fishing, swimming, and surfing. Santa Cruz and Monterey are each a short drive away and offer endless recreation possibilities.

Campsites, facilities: There are 64 walk-in tent sites. Picnic tables, food lockers, and fire grills are provided. Drinking water, restrooms with flush toilets and coin showers, and firewood are available. Some facilities are wheelchair-accessible. Leashed pets are permitted in the campground and on the beach.

Reservations, fees: Reserve ($7.50 reservation fee) at 800/444-PARK (800/444-7275) or www.reserveamerica.com. Sites are $25 per night, $6 per night for each additional vehicle. Open April through October.

Directions: From Santa Cruz, drive 12 miles southeast on Highway 1 to the San Andreas Road exit. Take that exit south and drive five miles to Sand Dollar Drive. Turn right and drive a short distance to the park entrance

on the left. The parking area is about 1,000 yards from the camping area. A 20-minute unloading zone is available within 20–150 yards of the sites.

Contact: Manresa Uplands Beach State Park, 831/761-1795; California State Parks, Santa Cruz District, 831/335-6318, www.santacruzstateparks.org or www.parks.ca.gov.

6 SANTA CRUZ KOA

Scenic rating: 8

near Watsonville

Map 8.1, page 501

Bike rentals and nearby access to Manresa State Beach make this KOA campground a winner. The little log cabins are quite cute, and security is first class. For those who have been here, it is a popular layover spot and weekend vacation destination. The only downer is the amount of asphalt.

Campsites, facilities: There are 180 sites, including five pull-through, with full or partial hookups (30 and 50 amps) for RVs up to 40 feet, six sites for tents only, 50 camping cabins, and three camping lodges. Picnic tables and fire grills are provided. Restrooms with showers, two dump stations, free Wi-Fi, modem access, swimming pool, spa, playground, two recreation rooms, bicycle rentals, miniature golf, convenience store, and propane gas are available. Some facilities are wheelchair-accessible. Leashed pets are permitted.

Reservations, fees: Reservations are advised by calling 800/562-7701. Sites are $51.70–104.50 per night, $3– $6 per night per person for more than two people. Some credit cards accepted. Open year-round.

Directions: From Santa Cruz, drive 12 miles southeast on Highway 1. Take the San Andreas Road exit and head southwest for 3.5 miles to 1186 San Andreas Road.

Contact: Santa Cruz KOA, 831/722-0551, fax 831/722-0989, www.santacruzkoa.com or www.koa.com.

7 SUNSET STATE BEACH

Scenic rating: 9

near Watsonville

Map 8.1, page 501

On clear evenings, the sunsets here look as if they are imported from Hawaii. The camp is set on a bluff along Monterey Bay. While there are no ocean views from the campsites, the location makes for easy, short walks down to the beach for beautiful shoreline walks. The beachfront features pine trees, bluffs, and expansive sand dunes. Large agricultural fields border the park. This area was once a good spot for clamming, but they've just about been fished out. The best weather is in late summer and fall. Spring can be windy here, and early summer is often foggy. Reservations are often needed well in advance to secure a spot.

Campsites, facilities: There are 90 sites for tents or RVs up to 31 feet (no hookups), one hike-in/bike-in site, and one group site for up to 50 people. Picnic tables, food lockers, and fire grills are provided. Drinking water, restrooms with flush toilets and coin showers, Wi-Fi, and firewood are available. Some facilities are wheelchair-accessible. Leashed pets are permitted, except on the beach.

Reservations, fees: Reserve ($7.50 reservation fee) at 800/444-PARK (800/444-7275) or www.reserveamerica.com. Sites are $25 per night, $6 per night for each additional vehicle, $5 per person per night for hike-in/bike-in site, $224 per night for group site. Open year-round.

Directions: From Highway 1 near Watsonville, take the Riverside Drive exit toward the ocean to Beach Road. Drive 3.5 miles on Beach Road to the San Andreas Road exit. Turn right on San Andreas Road and drive about three miles to Sunset Beach Road. Turn left and drive a short distance to the park entrance.

Contact: Sunset State Beach, 831/763-7063; California State Parks, Santa Cruz District,

831/335-6318, www.santacruzstateparks.org or www.parks.ca.gov.

8 McALPINE LAKE AND PARK

Scenic rating: 5

near San Juan Bautista

Map 8.1, page 501

This is the only privately operated campground in the immediate region that has any spots for tenters. The camping cabins here look like miniature log cabins, quite cute and comfortable. In addition, the park has a 40-foot-deep lake stocked with trout, bass, bluegill, and catfish; no fishing license is required. The swimming pool was recently transformed into a trout-fishing pond. Other highlights of the park are its proximity to Mission San Juan Bautista and the relatively short drive to the Monterey-Carmel area.

Campsites, facilities: There are 40 sites for tents only, 27 sites with partial hookups (30 amps) for tents or RVs, 14 sites with full hookups (30 amps) for RVs, and four cabins. Picnic tables and fire grills are provided. Restrooms with flush toilets and showers, dump station, banquet facilities, fishing pond, bait and tackle, gold panning, coin laundry, propane gas, and groceries are available. Some facilities are wheelchair-accessible. Leashed pets are permitted.

Reservations, fees: Reservations are accepted. Sites are $27–35 per night, $3–5 per person per night for more than two people, $5 per night for each additional vehicle. Some credit cards accepted. Open year-round.

Directions: On U.S. 101, drive to the Highway 129 exit. Take Highway 129 west and drive 100 feet to Searle Road (frontage road). Turn left onto Searle Road and drive to the stop sign at Anzar. Turn left again on Anzar and drive under the freeway to the park entrance on the left (900 Anzar Road).

Contact: McAlpine Lake and Park,

831/623-4263, fax 831/623-4559, www
.mcalpinelake.com.

9 MONTEREY VACATION RV PARK

Scenic rating: 4

near San Juan Bautista

Map 8.1, page 501

This RV park has an ideal location for many vacationers. It's a 10-minute drive to San Juan Bautista, 15 minutes to winery tours, 30 minutes to the Monterey Bay Aquarium, and 40 minutes to Monterey's Fisherman's Wharf and Cannery Row. It's set in an attractive spot with some trees, but the nearby attractions are what make it a clear winner. The park is next to the old stagecoach trail where famous outlaw Joaquin Murrieta once ambushed travelers. Note that about half of the sites are occupied by long-term renters.

Campsites, facilities: There are 88 sites with full hookups (30 amps) for RVs up to 40 feet; many are pull-through. No tents. Picnic tables and barbecues are provided at some sites. Restrooms with flush toilets and showers, spa, swimming pool, coin laundry, recreation halls, modem access (in office), and propane gas are available. Some facilities are wheelchair-accessible. Leashed pets up to 40 pounds are permitted, with certain restrictions.

Reservations, fees: Reservations are recommended for three-day holiday weekends; $27–35 per night, $3 per person per night for more than two people, $1 per pet per night. Some credit cards accepted (except on discounts). Open year-round.

Directions: On U.S. 101, drive toward San Juan Bautista (between Gilroy and Salinas). The park is on U.S. 101 two miles south of the Highway 156/San Juan Bautista exit at 1400 Highway 101.

Contact: Monterey Vacation RV Park, 831/726-9118, fax 831/726-1841.

10 MISSION FARM RV PARK

Scenic rating: 4

near San Juan Bautista

Map 8.1, page 501

The primary appeal of this RV park is that it is within easy walking distance of San Juan Bautista. The park is set beside a walnut orchard. Golfing and fishing are nearby.

Campsites, facilities: There are 144 sites with full hookups (30 amps) for RVs up to 33 feet. No tents. Picnic tables are provided. Restrooms with flush toilets and showers, barbecue area, cable TV, coin laundry, and propane gas are available. Leashed pets are permitted; a dog run is available.

Reservations, fees: Reservations are recommended. Sites are $28–31 per night, $7 per person per night for more than two people, $1–2 per pet per night. Monthly rates available. Some credit cards accepted. Open year-round.

Directions: From U.S. 101 near San Juan Bautista, drive three miles east on U.S. 101/Highway 156. Merge onto Highway 156 East toward San Juan Bautista/Hollister and drive three miles to The Alameda. Turn right at The Alameda and drive one block to San Juan-Hollister Road. Turn left and drive 0.25 mile to the campground at 400 San Juan-Hollister Road.

Contact: Mission Farm RV Park, 831/623-4456.

11 CABANA HOLIDAY RV RESORT

Scenic rating: 3

near Salinas

Map 8.1, page 501

If Big Sur, Monterey, and Carmel are packed, this spot provides some overflow space. This is the artichoke capital of the world. It's about a half-hour drive from the Monterey area.

Campsites, facilities: There are 79 sites with full or partial hookups (30 and 50 amps) for RVs up to 40 feet; some sites are pull-through. Limited space for tents is available, and 21 cabins can be rented. Picnic tables are provided. Restrooms with showers, recreation room, swimming pool (heated and open mid-May to mid-October), playground, clubhouse, basketball court, and a coin laundry are available. Leashed pets are permitted. Some facilities are wheelchair-accessible.

Reservations, fees: Reservations are recommended. RV sites are $45 per night and tents are $20 per night. Some credit cards accepted. Open year-round.

Directions: From Salinas, drive north on U.S. 101 for seven miles to Highway 156 West. Take the exit for Highway 156 West and drive over the overpass 0.2 mile to the Prunedale Road exit. Take that exit to Prunedale North Road. Turn right and drive a short distance to the campground entrance on the left.

Contact: Cabana Holiday, 831/663-2886 or 800/541-0085 (reservations), fax 831/663-1660, www.reynoldsresorts.com.

🕿 FREMONT PEAK STATE PARK

🚶 🏕 🚻 ♿ 🚗 ⛰

Scenic rating: 7

near San Juan Bautista

Map 8.1, page 501

Most vacationers in this region are heading to Monterey Bay and the surrounding environs. That's why Fremont Peak State Park is missed by a lot of folks. It is on a ridge (2,900 feet) with great views of Monterey Bay available on the trail going up Fremont Peak (3,169 feet) in the Gavilan Range. An observatory with a 30-inch telescope at the park is open to the public on specified Saturday evenings. There are views of the San Benito Valley, Salinas Valley, and the Santa Lucia Moun-

tains. A picnic is held in the park each April to commemorate Captain John C. Frémont, his expeditions, and his raising of the U.S. flag in defiance of the Mexican government. Note: There is no access from this park to the adjacent Hollister Hills State Vehicular Recreation Area.

Campsites, facilities: There are 25 primitive sites for tents or RVs up to 25 feet (no hookups), and one group site for up to 50 people. Picnic tables and fire rings are provided. Drinking water and vault toilets are available. Some facilities are wheelchair-accessible. Leashed pets are permitted.

Reservations, fees: Reservations are accepted ($7.50 reservation fee) at 800/444-PARK (800/444-7275) or www.reserveamerica.com. Sites are $11–15 per night, $4 per night for each additional vehicle, $75 per night for group site. Open March through November.

Directions: From Highway 156 in San Juan Bautista, drive to San Juan Canyon Road. Turn south on San Juan Canyon Road (unsigned except for state park directional sign) and drive 11 miles (narrow, twisty, not recommended for vehicles longer than 25 feet) to the park.

Contact: Fremont Peak State Park, 831/623-4255; Monterey State Park District, Gavilan Sector, 831/623-4526; observatory, 831/623-2465, www.parks.ca.gov.

🕿 HOLLISTER HILLS STATE VEHICULAR RECREATION AREA

Scenic rating: 4

near Hollister

Map 8.1, page 501

This unique park was designed for off-highway-vehicle enthusiasts. It provides 80 miles of trails for motorcycles and 40 miles of trails for four-wheel-drive vehicles. Some of the trails are accessible directly from the campground. All trails close at sunset. Note that there is no direct access to Fremont Peak State Park, bordering directly to the west. Elevations at the park range 800–2,600 feet. Visitors are advised to always call in advance when planning a trip because the area is sometimes closed for special events. A sidelight is that a 288-acre area is set aside for hiking and mountain biking. In addition, a self-guided natural history walk is routed into Azalea Canyon and along the San Andreas Fault.

Campsites, facilities: There are four campgrounds with a total of 125 sites for tents or RVs of any length (no hookups), and group sites for up to 300 people. Picnic tables and fire rings are provided. Drinking water, restrooms with flush toilets and showers, and a camp store are available. Leashed pets are permitted.

Reservations, fees: Reservations are not accepted. Sites are $10 per night per vehicle. Call for group rates. Open year-round.

Directions: From Highway 156 west of Hollister, drive east to Union Road. Turn right (south) on Union Road and drive three miles to Cienega Road. Turn right (south) on Cienega Road and drive five miles to the park on the right.

Contact: Hollister Hills State Vehicular Recreation Area, 831/637-3874, District Office, 831/637-8186; Pit Stop, park store, 831/637-3138, www.parks.ca.gov.

14 MARINA DUNES RV PARK

Scenic rating: 4

near Monterey Bay

Map 8.1, page 501

This is a popular park for RV cruisers who are touring Highway 1 and want a layover spot near Monterey. This place fills the bill, open all year and in Marina, just a short drive from the many side-trip opportunities available in Monterey and Carmel. It is set in the sand dunes, about 300 yards from the ocean. Horseback riding, boat rentals, and golfing are nearby.

Campsites, facilities: There are 65 sites, most with full hookups (30 and 50 amps), for RVs of any length and 10 sites for tents. Picnic tables and barbecue grills are provided, and some sites have fireplaces. Restrooms with showers, drinking water, coin laundry, cable TV, Wi-Fi, modem access, recreation room, playground, meeting room, picnic area, RV supplies, gift shop, and propane are available. Leashed pets are permitted. Some facilities are wheelchair-accessible. Open year-round.

Reservations, fees: Reservations are recommended. Sites are $45–65 per night, $5 per night for each additional vehicle. Some credit cards accepted.

Directions: From Highway 1 in Marina, drive to the Reservation Road exit. Take that exit and drive west a short distance to Dunes Drive. Turn right on Dunes Drive and drive to the end of the road and the park entrance on the right.

Contact: Marina Dunes RV Park, 831/384-6914, fax 831/384-0285, www.marinadunesrv.com.

15 LAGUNA SECA RECREATION AREA

Scenic rating: 5

near Monterey

Map 8.1, page 501

This campground is just minutes away from the sights in Monterey and Carmel. It is situated in oak woodlands overlooking the world-famous Laguna Seca Raceway. There are three separate camping areas.

Campsites, facilities: There are 172 sites for tents or RV up to 40 feet; most sites have partial hookups (30 amps). A large overflow area is also available for RVs and tents. Picnic tables and fire pits are provided. Restrooms with showers, dump station, pond, rifle and pistol range, clubhouse, and group camping and meeting facilities are available. Some facilities are wheelchair-accessible. Leashed pets are permitted.

Reservations, fees: Reservations are accepted ($5 reservation fee) at 831/755-4895 or 888/588-2267. Sites are $22–30 per night, $10 per night for each additional vehicle, $2 per pet per night. Some credit cards accepted. Open year-round.

Directions: From Monterey and Highway 101, drive east on Highway 68 for 6.5 miles to the park entrance on the left.

Contact: Laguna Seca Recreation Area, 831/758-3604 or fax 831/758-6818, www .co.monterey.ca.us/parks.

16 CARMEL BY THE RIVER RV PARK

Scenic rating: 8

on the Carmel River

Map 8.1, page 501

Location, location, location. That's what vacationers want. Well, this park is set on the Carmel River, minutes away from Carmel, Cannery Row, the Monterey Bay Aquarium, golf courses, and the beach. Hedges and flowers separate each RV site.

Campsites, facilities: There are 35 sites with full hookups (50 amps) for RVs of any length. No tents. Restrooms with showers, cable TV, Wi-Fi, modem access (in office), recreational cabana, game room with pool tables, barbecue area, and river access are available. A convenience store, coin laundry, and propane gas are nearby. Some facilities are wheelchair-accessible. Leashed pets are permitted.

Reservations, fees: Reservations are accepted for two or more nights. Sites are $56 per night, $2–3 per person per night for more than two people, $3 per night for each additional vehicle, $3 per pet per night. Open year-round.

Directions: In Carmel on Highway 1 drive to Carmel Valley Road. Take Carmel Valley Road southeast and drive 4.5 miles to Schulte Road. Turn right and drive to the end of the road (27680 Schulte Road in Carmel).

Contact: Carmel by the River RV Park, 831/624-9329, fax 831/624-8416, www.carmelrv.com.

17 SADDLE MOUNTAIN RV PARK AND CAMPGROUND

Scenic rating: 6

near the Carmel River

Map 8.1, page 501

This pretty park is set about 100 yards from the Carmel River amid a grove of oak trees. The park offers hiking trails, and if you want to make a buyer's swing into Carmel, it's only a five-mile drive. Note: The Carmel River is reduced to a trickle most of the year.

Campsites, facilities: There are 25 tent sites and 25 sites with full hookups (30 amps) for RVs up to 40 feet. Picnic tables, food lockers, cable TV, Wi-Fi, and fire grills are provided. Restrooms with flush toilets and showers are available. A seasonal swimming pool, playground, horseshoe pits, basketball court, and a game room are available nearby. Some facilities are wheelchair-accessible. Leashed pets are permitted in the RV area only; check for current status of pet policy for campground.

Reservations, fees: Reservations are accepted for weekends only. Sites are $30–50 per night, $5 per person per night for more than two people, $5 per night for each additional vehicle. Group rates available. Open year-round.

Directions: In Carmel on Highway 1 drive to Carmel Valley Road. Take Carmel Valley Road southeast and drive 4.5 miles to Schulte Road. Turn right and drive to the park at the end of the road.

Contact: Saddle Mountain RV Park and Campground, 831/624-1617, www.saddle-mountaincamping.com.

18 PINNACLES CAMPGROUND

🏃 🏊 🐕 ♿ 🚙 🏕

Scenic rating: 7

near Pinnacles National Monument

Map 8.1, page 501

This is the only camp at the Pinnacles National Monument, where there are more than 30 miles of hiking trails and two sets of talus caves. The jagged pinnacles for which the park was named were formed by the erosion of an ancient volcanic eruption and are popular for rock climbing. Pinnacles National Monument is like a different planet, and condors can sometimes be seen flying in the monument and over the campground. It's a 24,000-acre park with volcanic clusters and strange caves, all great for exploring. This is a popular place for astronomy buffs, and ranger-led dark sky viewings are available occasionally. Campfire programs are held in the amphitheater most of the year. If you are planning to stay a weekend in the spring, arrive early on Friday evening to be sure you get a campsite. In the summer, beware of temperatures in the 90s and 100s. Also note that caves can be closed to access; always check with rangers. Note that a ban on wood fires is in effect. Duraflame logs are permitted as a substitute.

Campsites, facilities: There are 103 sites for tents, 36 sites with partial hookups (30 amps) for RVs, and 13 group sites. Picnic tables and fire grills are provided. Drinking water, restrooms with flush toilets and coin showers, dump station, amphitheater, convenience store, and a swimming pool are available. Some facilities are wheelchair-accessible. Although discouraged, leashed pets are permitted, except on trails.

Reservations, fees: Reservations ($7 reserva-tion fee) are available by phone, limited hours and days, and by website, and required for group sites. RV sites are $15–40 per person per night, $10–35 per night for a tent site, $5 per night for each additional vehicle, $3 per pet per stay. The group site is $7.50 per person per night with a minimum of $75. Some credit cards accepted. Open year-round, weather permitting.

Directions: From Hollister, drive south on Highway 25 for 32 miles to Highway 146 west (signed "Pinnacles"). Take Highway 146 and drive 2.5 miles to the campground.

Contact: Pinnacles Campground, 831/389-4462, www.pinncamp.com.

19 BOTTCHER'S GAP WALK-IN

🏃 🐕 🏕

Scenic rating: 6

in Los Padres National Forest

Map 8.1, page 501

Here is a surprise for all the Highway 1 cruis-ers who never leave the highway. Just inland is this little-known camp, set in beautiful, redwood-filled Palo Colorado Canyon It's a good jump-off spot for a hiking trip; the trail leading out of camp is routed all the way into the Ventana Wilderness. Compared to the RV parks near Monterey and Carmel, this place is truly a world apart. The elevation is 2,100 feet.

Campsites, facilities: There are 11 walk-in sites. Picnic tables and fire grills are pro-vided. Vault toilets are available. There is no drinking water. Leashed pets are permitted.

Reservations, fees: Reservations are not accepted. Sites are $12 per night. Open year-round.

Directions: From Carmel, drive south on Highway 1 for about 10 miles to Palo Colo-rado Road/County Road 5012. Turn left and drive nine miles to the campground.

Contact: Los Padres National Forest,

Monterey Ranger District, 831/385-5434, fax 831/385-0628; Parks Management Company, 805/434-1996.

20 WHITE OAKS
🏕 🎣 🐕 ⛺

Scenic rating: 7

on Chews Ridge in Los Padres National Forest

Map 8.1, page 501

This camp is set at 4,000 feet, near Anastasia Creek, and there's a surprisingly remote feel to the area despite its relative proximity to Carmel Valley. There is a good hike that starts about a mile from the camp and is routed into the Ventana Wilderness. Several backcountry trail camps are also available.

Campsites, facilities: There are seven sites for tents only. There is no drinking water. Picnic tables and fire grills are provided. Vault toilets are available. Leashed pets are permitted.

Reservations, fees: Reservations are not accepted. There is no camping fee. Open year-round, weather permitting.

Directions: From Highway 1 in Carmel, drive to Carmel Valley road. Turn east on Carmel Valley Road and drive about 22 miles to Tassajara Road/County Road 5007. Turn right (south) on Tassajara Road/County Road 5007 and drive eight miles to the campground on the left.

From Salinas, drive south on Highway 101 to Soledad. Continue south for approximately one mile to the exit for Arroyo Road. Take that exit and drive west on Arroyo Road (becomes Arroyo Seco Road) for 16.5 miles to Carmel Valley Road. Turn right and drive 17.5 miles to Tassajara Road. Turn left and drive eight miles to the campground on the left.

Contact: Los Padres National Forest, Monterey Ranger District, 831/385-5434, fax 831/385-0628.

21 ANDREW MOLERA STATE PARK WALK-IN
🏕 🏊 🚣 ⛺

Scenic rating: 7

in Big Sur

Map 8.1, page 501

Considering the popularity and grandeur of Big Sur, some campers might find it hard to believe that any primitive campgrounds are available. Believe it. This park offers walk-in sites amid some beautiful coastal terrain. One of the highlights is a great trail that leads one mile to a beautiful beach. It is part of a trail system that features miles of trails routed through meadows, along beaches, and to hilltops. The campsites here used to be overcrowded and too close together, but several years ago, the campground was reorganized to provide more privacy for campers.

Campsites, facilities: There are 24 sites for tents. Picnic tables, food lockers and fire grills are provided. Drinking water and flush toilets are available. Bring your own firewood. No pets allowed.

Reservations, fees: Reservations are not accepted. Sites are $10 per night. Open year-round, weather permitting.

Directions: From Carmel, drive 21 miles south on Highway 1 to the park camping lot on the right. Park and walk 150 yards to the camp.

Contact: Pfeiffer Big Sur State Park, 831/667-2315; California State Parks, Monterey District, 831/649-2836, www.parks.ca.gov.

22 BIG SUR CAMPGROUND AND CABINS
🏕 🏊 🚣 🏠 🐕 🚴 ♿ 🚐 ⛺

Scenic rating: 8

on the Big Sur River

Map 8.1, page 501

This camp is in the redwoods near the Big Sur River. Campers can stay in the redwoods, hike on great trails through the forest at nearby state parks, or explore nearby Pfeiffer Beach. Nearby Los Padres National Forest and Ventana Wilderness in the mountains to the east provide access to remote hiking trails with ridge-top vistas. Cruising Highway 1 south to Lucia and back offers endless views of breathtaking coastal scenery.

Campsites, facilities: There are 40 sites with partial hookups (20 and 30 amps) for RVs up to 36 feet, 40 sites with no hookups for tents or RVs, 15 cabins, and four tent cabins. Picnic tables and fire grills are provided. Restrooms with flush toilets and showers, drinking water, dump station, playground, basketball, inner-tube rentals, convenience store, and a coin laundry are available. Some facilities are wheelchair-accessible. Leashed pets are permitted at campsites. No pets in cabins.

Reservations, fees: Reservations are recommended. Sites are $30 per night, $4 per night for RV hookups, $4 per person per night for more than two people, $8 per night for each additional vehicle, $4 per pet per night. Some credit cards accepted. Open year-round.

Directions: From Carmel, drive 25 miles south on Highway 1 to the campground on the right side of the road (two miles north of the state park).

Contact: Big Sur Campground and Cabins, 831/667-2322.

23 PFEIFFER BIG SUR STATE PARK

🏃 🚴 🏊 🚣 🎣 🐕 ♿ 🚐 ⛺

Scenic rating: 10

in Big Sur

Map 8.1, page 501

This stretch of coast is one of the most beautiful anywhere. This is one of the most popular state parks in California, and it's easy to see why. You can have it all: fantastic coastal vistas along Highway 1, redwood forests and waterfalls in the Julia Pfeiffer Burns State Park (11.5 miles to the south), expansive beaches with elusive sea otters playing on the edge of kelp beds in Andrew Molera State Park (4.5 miles north), great restaurants such as Ventana Inn (a few miles south), and private, patrolled sites. Reservations are a necessity. Some campsites in this park are set along the Big Sur River. The park features 800 acres of alders, conifers, cottonwoods, maples, oaks, redwoods, sycamores, and willows, plus open meadows—just about everything, in other words. Wildlife includes raccoons, skunk, deer, squirrels, occasional bobcats and mountain lions, and many birds, among them water ouzels and belted kingfishers. Wild boar are spotted infrequently. A number of loop trails provide spectacular views of the Pacific Ocean and the Big Sur Gorge. Big Sur Lodge is within the park.

Campsites, facilities: There are 218 sites for tents or RVs up to 32 feet and trailers up to 27 feet, two hike-in or bike-in sites, and two group sites for up to 35 people. Picnic tables and fire grills are provided. Restrooms with flush toilets and showers, Wi-Fi, and drinking water are available. Groceries, a café, and propane gas are available nearby. Some facilities are wheelchair-accessible. Leashed pets are permitted in the campground only.

Reservations, fees: Reservations are accepted ($7.50 reservation fee) at 800/444-PARK (800/444-7275) or www.reserveamerica.com. Sites are $20–35 per night, $8 per night for each additional vehicle, $75 per night for group sites, $3 per person per night for hike-in/bike-in sites. Open year-round.

Directions: From Carmel, drive 26 miles south on Highway 1 to the park on the left (east side of highway).

Contact: Pfeiffer Big Sur State Park, 831/667-2315, fax 831/667-2886; California State Parks, Monterey District, 831/649-2836, www.parks.ca.gov.

24 CHINA CAMP
🚶 🏊 🏠 🚐 ⛺

Scenic rating: 6

on Chews Ridge in Los Padres National Forest

Map 8.1, page 501

A lot of folks might find it difficult to believe that a spot that feels so remote can be so close to the manicured Carmel Valley. But here it is, one of two camps on Tassajara Road at an elevation of 4,500 feet. This one has a trail out of camp that is routed into the Ventana Wilderness. Tassajara Hot Springs, a private facility, is seven miles away at the end of Tassajara Road.

Campsites, facilities: There are six sites for tents or RVs up to 20 feet (no hookups). Picnic tables and fire grills are provided. Vault toilets are available. No drinking water is available. Leashed pets are permitted.

Reservations, fees: No reservations are accepted. There is no camping fee. Open April through November, weather permitting.

Directions: From Highway 1 in Carmel, turn east on Carmel Valley Road and drive about 22 miles. Turn right (south) on Tassajara Road/County Road 5007 and drive 11 miles to the campground on the right.

From Salinas, drive south on Highway 101 to Soledad. Continue south for approximately one mile to the exit for Arroyo Road. Take that exit and drive west on Arroyo Road (becomes Arroyo Seco Road) for 16.5 miles to Carmel Valley Road. Turn right and drive 17.5 miles to Tassajara Road. Turn left and drive 11 miles to the campground on the right.

Contact: Los Padres National Forest, Monterey Ranger District, 831/385-5434, fax 831/385-0628.

25 RIVERSIDE CAMPGROUND AND CABINS
🚶 🏊 🛶 🏠 🚐 ⛺

Scenic rating: 8

on the Big Sur River

Map 8.1, page 501

This is one in a series of privately operated camps designed for Highway 1 cruisers touring the Big Sur area. This camp is set amid redwoods. Side trips include expansive beaches with sea otters playing on the edge of kelp beds (Andrew Molera State Park), redwood forests and waterfalls (Julia Pfeiffer Burns State Park), and several quality restaurants, including Nepenthe for those on a budget, and the Ventana Inn for those who can light cigars with $100 bills.

Campsites, facilities: There are 45 sites for tents or RVs up to 40 feet; 14 sites have partial hookups (20 amps). Cabins are also available. Picnic tables and fire pits are provided. Restrooms with coin showers, coin laundry, and firewood are available. A store is nearby. Leashed pets are permitted at campsites.

Reservations, fees: Reservations are recommended. Sites are $30 per night, $5 per person per night for more than two people, $10 per night for each additional vehicle, $5 per pet per night. Some credit cards accepted. Open April through October.

Directions: From Carmel, drive 22 miles south on Highway 1 to the campground on the right.

Contact: Riverside Campground and Cabins, tel./fax 831/667-2414, www.riversidecampground.com.

26 FERNWOOD PARK
🚶 🏊 🛶 🏠 🚐 ⛺

Scenic rating: 7

on the Big Sur River

Map 8.1, page 501

This RV park is on the banks of the Big Sur River in the redwoods of the beautiful

Big Sur coast. Many of the sites are set along the river. There also are eight tent cabins. A highlight is that there is live music on Saturday nights in season. You can crown your trip with a dinner at the Ventana Inn (first-class—bring your bank with you). The park is adjacent to Pfeiffer Big Sur State Park.

Campsites, facilities: There are 13 sites for tents only, 31 sites with partial hookups (30 amps) for RVs up to 36 feet, 11 tent cabins, and a motel. Fire grills and picnic tables are provided. Restrooms with showers, grocery store, restaurant, and a bar are available. Leashed pets are permitted.

Reservations, fees: Reservations are accepted. Sites are $27–30 per night, $5 per person per night for more than two people (to maximum of six), $5 per night for each additional vehicle, $5 per pet per night. Tent cabins are $60 per night, and $10 per person per night for more than two people. Discounts available in the off-season. Some credit cards accepted. Open year-round.

Directions: From Carmel, drive 26 miles south on Highway 1 to the campground on the right.

Contact: Fernwood Park, 831/667-2422, fax 831/667-2663, www.fernwoodbigsur.com.

27 VENTANA CAMPGROUNDS

Scenic rating: 10

in Big Sur

Map 8.1, page 501

This rustic camp has wooded sites and is set in an ideal location for many. The campsites are private and extremely beautiful, set in the redwoods with a small creek running through camp, with a few small waterfalls nearby. Premium side trips are available, highlighted by the beautiful beach at Andrew Molera State Park (a one-mile hike is necessary), the majestic redwoods, a creek hike, and a bluff-top waterfall in Julia Pfeiffer Burns State Park.

Campsites, facilities: There are 60 tent sites and 20 sites for tents or RVs up to 24 feet (no hookups). Picnic tables and fire rings are provided. A restroom with showers and flush toilets is available. A small store is nearby with firewood and ice. Some facilities are wheelchair-accessible. Leashed pets are permitted.

Reservations, fees: Reservations are accepted by telephone or website. Sites are $29–35 per night, $5 per person per night for more than two people, $5 per night for each additional vehicle, $5 per pet per night. Three-day minimum stay on holidays. Some credit cards accepted. Open March through October.

Directions: From Carmel, drive 30 miles south on Highway 1 to Big Sur and the campground entrance on the left, 0.5 mile past the post office.

Contact: Ventana Campground, 831/667-2712, www.ventanacampground.com.

28 ARROYO SECO

Scenic rating: 8

along Arroyo Seco River in Los Padres National Forest

Map 8.1, page 501

This pretty spot near the Arroyo Seco River is just outside the northern border of the Ventana Wilderness. The elevation is 900 feet. Arroyo Seco Group Camp is available to keep the pressure off this campground.

Campsites, facilities: There are 49 sites for tents or RVs up to 26 feet, plus a group site for 25–50 people. Picnic tables and fire grills are provided. Drinking water, restrooms with flush toilets and coin showers, and a dump station are available. Leashed pets are permitted.

Reservations, fees: Reservations are accepted ($9 reservation fee) for individual sites and required for group sites at 877/444-6777 or www.ReserveUSA.com. Sites are $20 per night, $5 per night for each additional vehicle, $50 per night for the group site. Open year-round.

Directions: Drive on U.S. 101 to the town of Greenfield and the Arroyo Seco Road/Elm Avenue exit. Turn west on Elm Avenue/Road G16 and drive six miles to Arroyo Seco Road. Turn left and drive 6.5 miles to Carmel Valley Road. Turn right and drive 3.5 miles to the campground.

Contact: Los Padres National Forest, Monterey Ranger District, 831/385-5434, fax 831/385-0628; Rocky Mountain Recreation Company, 831/674-5726.

29 SAN LORENZO COUNTY PARK

Scenic rating: 3

in King City

Map 8.1, page 501

A lot of folks cruising up and down the state on U.S. 101 can underestimate their travel time and find themselves caught out near King City, a small city about midpoint between Northern and Southern California. Well, don't sweat it, because San Lorenzo County Park offers a spot to overnight. It's set near the Salinas River, which isn't exactly the Mississippi, but it'll do. A museum complex captures the rural agricultural life of the valley. The park covers 200 acres, featuring playgrounds and ball fields.

Campsites, facilities: There are 99 sites with full or partial hookups (30 amps) for tents or RVs of any length; some sites are pull-through. Picnic tables and fire pits are provided. A dump station, restrooms with flush toilets and showers, picnic area, coin laundry, meeting facilities, playgrounds, horseshoes, volleyball, softball fields, walking trail, and computer kiosks are available. Leashed pets are permitted.

Reservations, fees: Reservations are accepted ($5 reservation fee) at 831/385-5964. Sites are $18–27 per night, $10 per night for each additional vehicle, $2 per pet per night. Off-season and group rates available. Open year-round.

Directions: From King City on U.S. 101, take the Broadway exit, turn onto Broadway, and drive to the park at 1160 Broadway.

Contact: San Lorenzo County Park, 831/385-5964, www.co.monterey.ca.us/parks.

30 ESCONDIDO

Scenic rating: 6

in Los Padres National Forest

Map 8.1, page 501

This is a prime jump-off spot for backpackers heading into the Ventana Wilderness. The camp is set at an elevation of 2,300 feet at a trailhead that connects to a network of other trails. The only catch is you have to plan on an often-steep climb of more than 1,000 feet to reach the ridge.

Campsites, facilities: There are nine sites for tents only. Picnic tables and fire grills are provided. Vault toilets and drinking water are available. Garbage must be packed out. Leashed pets are permitted.

Reservations, fees: Reservations are not accepted. There is no camping fee. Open April through November.

Directions: From U.S. 101 in King City, turn south on County Route G14 and drive 18 miles. Turn north on Mission Road and drive six miles. Turn left on Del Venturi-Milpitas Road/Indian Road and drive 20 miles to the campground on the left.

Contact: Los Padres National Forest, Monterey Ranger District, 831/385-5434, fax 831/385-0628.

31 MEMORIAL PARK

Scenic rating: 6

in Los Padres National Forest

Map 8.1, page 501

This is one of two backcountry camps in the area. The highlights are a trailhead and the vicinity of the Arroyo Seco River. The camp has a trailhead that provides access to the Ventana Wilderness trail network. The elevation is 2,000 feet, which gives hikers a nice head start on the climb. Be sure to pack plenty of drinking water for the trail and, even in spring, expect warm, dry conditions.

Campsites, facilities: There are eight sites for tents only. Picnic tables and fire grills are provided. Vault toilets are available. No drinking water is available. Garbage must be packed out. Leashed pets are permitted.

Reservations, fees: Reservations are not accepted. There is no camping fee. Open year-round.

Directions: From U.S. 101 in King City, turn south on County Route G14 and drive 18 miles. Turn north on Mission Road and drive six miles. Turn left on Del Venturi-Milpitas Road/County Road 4050 and drive 16 miles to the campground on the right.

Contact: Los Padres National Forest, Monterey Ranger District, 831/385-5434, fax 831/385-0628.

32 KIRK CREEK

Scenic rating: 8

in Los Padres National Forest near the Pacific Ocean

Map 8.1, page 501

This pretty camp is set along Kirk Creek as it empties into the Pacific Ocean. There is beach access through a footpath. Another trail from camp branches north through the Ventana Wilderness, which is sprinkled with little-used, hike-in, backcountry campsites. For gorgeous scenery without all the work, a quaint little café in Lucia provides open-air dining on a cliff-top deck, with a dramatic sweeping lookout over the coast.

Campsites, facilities: There are 33 sites for tents or RVs up to 30 feet (no hookups). Picnic tables and fire grills are provided. Drinking water and flush toilets are available. Leashed pets are permitted.

Reservations, fees: Reservations are not accepted. Sites are $20 per night. Open year-round.

Directions: From Monterey, drive south on Highway 1 to Lucia. From Lucia, continue south on Highway 1 for four miles to the campground on the right.

Contact: Parks Management Company, 805/434-1996, fax 805/434-1986; Los Padres National Forest, Monterey Ranger District, 831/385-5434, fax 831/385-0628.

33 LIMEKILN STATE PARK

Scenic rating: 9

south of Big Sur on the Pacific Ocean

Map 8.1, page 501

Limekiln State Park provides spectacular views of the Big Sur coast. This camp provides a great layover spot in the Big Sur area of Highway 1, with drive-in campsites set both near the beach and the redwoods—take your pick. Several hiking trails are nearby, including one that is routed past some historic lime kilns, which were used in the late 1800s to make cement and bricks. Want more? A short rock hop on a spur trail (just off the main trail) leads to dramatic 100-foot Limekiln Falls, a gorgeous waterfall. This camp was originally called Limekiln Beach Redwoods and was privately operated. It became a state park in 1995. One remaining problem: Parking is limited.

Campsites, facilities: There are 10 sites for tents and 18 sites for tents or RVs up to 24 feet (no hookups) and trailers up to 15 feet. Picnic tables and fire grills are provided. Drinking water, restrooms with showers and flush toilets, and firewood are available. Leashed pets are allowed, except on trails.

Reservations, fees: Reservations are accepted ($7.50 reservation fee) at 800/444-PARK (800/444-7275) or www.reserveamerica.com. Sites are $20–25 per night, $6 per night for each additional vehicle. Some credit cards accepted for reservations, but not at park. Open year-round, weather and road conditions permitting.

Directions: From Big Sur, drive south on Highway 1 for 32 miles (past Lucia) to the park on the left.

Contact: Limekiln State Park, 831/667-2403; California State Parks, Monterey District, 831/649-2836, www.parks.ca.gov.

34 NACIMIENTO

Scenic rating: 5

in Los Padres National Forest

Map 8.1, page 501

This little-known spot is set near the Nacimiento River at 1,600 feet elevation. Most campers will head up Nacimiento-Ferguson Road to camp on a Friday night and get up Saturday morning to head off on a hiking or backpacking trip in the nearby Ventana Wilderness.

Campsites, facilities: There are eight sites for tents or RVs up to 25 feet (no hookups). Picnic tables and fire grills are provided. Vault toilets are available. No drinking water is available. Leashed pets are permitted.

Reservations, fees: Reservations are not accepted. Sites are $10 per night. Open year-round.

Directions: From Monterey, drive south on Highway 1 to Lucia. From Lucia, continue south on Highway 1 for four miles to Nacimiento Road. Turn east (left) on Nacimiento Road and drive 11 winding miles to the campground on the right.

Contact: Parks Management Company,

805/434-1996, fax 805/434-1986; Los Padres National Forest, Monterey Ranger District, 831/385-5434, fax 831/385-0628.

35 PONDEROSA

Scenic rating: 4

in Los Padres National Forest

Map 8.1, page 501

As soon as you turn off Highway 1, you leave behind the crowds and enter a land that is largely unknown to people. This camp is set at 1,500 feet elevation in Los Padres National Forest, not far from the border of the Ventana Wilderness (good hiking and backpacking) and the Hunter Liggett Military Reservation (wild-pig hunting is allowed there with a permit). It is one in a series of small camps on Nacimiento-Ferguson Road.

Campsites, facilities: There are 23 sites for tents or RVs up to 35 feet. Picnic tables and fire grills are provided. Vault toilets and drinking water are available. Leashed pets are permitted.

Reservations, fees: Reservations are not accepted. Sites are $15 per night. Open year-round.

Directions: From Monterey, drive south on Highway 1 to Lucia. From Lucia, continue south on Highway 1 for four miles to Nacimiento-Ferguson Road. Turn left on Nacimiento-Ferguson Road and drive about 12 miles to the campground on the right.

Contact: Parks Management Company, 805/434-1996, fax 805/434-1986, www.campone.com; Los Padres National Forest, Monterey Ranger District, 831/385-5434, fax 831/385-0628.

SAN JOAQUIN VALLEY

© TED HOLZEM/MINTIER & ASSOCIATES

BEST CAMPGROUNDS

◖ White-Water Rafting
Lumsden, pages 534-535

The San Joaquin Valley is noted for its

searing weather all summer long. But that is also when the lakes in the foothills become something like a Garden of Eden for boating and water-sports enthusiasts. The region also offers many settings in the Sierra foothills, which can serve as launch points for short drives into the alpine beauty of Yosemite, Sequoia, and Kings Canyon National Parks.

Most of the campgrounds in this region are family-oriented. Many of them are on access roads to Yosemite. A bonus is that most have lower prices than their counterparts in the park, and are more hospitable to children.

The lakes are the primary recreation attraction, with the refreshing, clean water revered as a tonic against the valley heat all summer long. When viewed from the air, the closeness of these lakes to the Sierra Nevada mountain range is surprising to many. Their proximity to the high country results in cool, high-quality water – the product of snowmelt sent down river canyons on the western slope. Some of these lakes are among the best around for waterskiing and powerboat recreation, including Lake Don Pedro east of Modesto, Bass Lake near Oakhurst, Lake McClure near Merced, Pine Flat Lake east of Fresno, and Lake Kaweah near Visalia.

In addition, Lake Don Pedro, and Pine Flat Lake and Lake Kaweah in the nearby Sequoia and Kings Canyon region, are among the best fishing lakes in the entire Central Valley; some anglers rate Don Pedro as the number-one all-around fishing lake in the state. The Sierra rivers that feed these lakes (and others) also offer the opportunity to fly-fish for trout. In particular, the Kaweah and Kings Rivers boast many miles of ideal pocket water for fly fishers. While the trout on these streams are only occasionally large, the catch rates are often high and the rock-strewn beauty of the river canyons is exceptional.

SAN JOAQUIN VALLEY

see Sacramento and Gold Country
page 320

see Tahoe and the Northern Sierra
page 364

Jackson

Camanche Lake

Stockton

New Melones Res

Sonora

Manteca

Lake Tulloch

Don Pedro Reservoir

Modesto

Lake McClure

MAP 9.1
page 523

MAP 9.2
page 524

Yosemite

National

Park

Mono Lake

see Yosemite and Mammoth Lakes
page 552

see San Francisco Bay Area
page 468

Merced

Santa Nella

San

see Sequoia and Kings Canyon
page 606

Lakeshore

Kings Canyon National Park

Madera

Millerton Lake

Pine Flat Reservoir

San Luis Reservoir

Hollister

Joaquin

River

Kings

Fresno

see Monterey and Big Sur
page 500

King City

Lonoak

MAP 9.3
page 525

River

MAP 9.4
page 526

Hanford

Tulare

Los Padres NF

Lucia

FORT HUNTER LIGGETT MILITARY INSTALLATION

Coalinga

Priest Valley

Avenal

Earlimart

Lake San Antonio

Lake Nacimiento

San Simeon

Cholame

Blackwells Corner

No Campgrounds

MAP 9.5
page 527

PACIFIC

San Luis Obispo

Simmler

Bakersfield

OCEAN

Taft

see Santa Barbara and Vicinity
page 700

Los Padres National Forest

0   20 mi
0   20 km

© AVALON TRAVEL PUBLISHING, INC.

Map 9.1

Campgrounds 1-7
Pages 528-531

Map 9.2

Campgrounds 8-30

Pages 531-542

9.1

9.3

Copperopolis

Sonora

108

New Melones
Res

8
9

Jamestown

Stanislaus River

4

108

Lake
Tulloch

Tuolumne River

FERRETTI RD

12

Chinese
Camp

Groveland

14

Woodward
Reservoir

120

108

13

120

15 16
17

Escalon

10

Moccasin

18

120

Stanislaus

11

LA GRANGE RD

Stanislaus
National
Forest

Oakdale

Lake
Don Pedro

Riverbank

Coulterville

Modesto
Reservoir

19

Modesto

Waterford

20

21

La
Grange

132

23

24

Lake
McClure

26

132

22

Turlock
Lake

25

MERCED FALLS RD

Ceres

Hughson

Tuolumne River

99

49

Denair

Snelling

27

Lake
McSwain

Turlock

Merced
Falls

Delhi

Merced River

30

Winton

Yosemite
Lake

Bear
Lake

28

165

Livingston

99

Atwater

140

Owens
Lake

Mariposa
Lake

29

San Joaquin

Stevinson

Merced

Planada

140

River

140

Le Grand

Gustine

San Luis
NWR

Merced
National Wildlife
Refuge

59

99

San Joaquin River

Chowchilla

Los Banos

152

5

165

33 140

33

Map 9.3

Campground 31
Page 543

Map 9.4

Campgrounds 32-35
Pages 543-545

Map 9.5

Campgrounds 36-41
Pages 545-548

1 DOS REIS COUNTY PARK

Scenic rating: 6

on the San Joaquin River near Stockton

Map 9.1, page 523

This is a nine-acre county park that has a quarter mile of San Joaquin River frontage, boat ramp, and nearby access to the eastern Delta near Stockton. Note that tent camping is available on weekends and holidays only. The sun gets scalding hot here in the summer, branding everything in sight. That's why boaters make quick work of getting in the water, then cooling off with water sports. In the winter, this area often has zero visibility from tule fog.

Campsites, facilities: There are 26 sites with full hookups (20 and 30 amps) for RVs of any length and tents; some sites are pull-through. Picnic tables and fire grills are provided. Restrooms with showers, children's play area, horseshoe pits, and a boat ramp are available. A store, coin laundry, and propane gas are within three miles. Leashed pets are permitted with a limit of two.

Reservations, fees: Reservations are required at least two weeks in advance. Sites are $20 per night, $10 per night for each additional vehicle, $1 per pet per night. Open year-round.

Directions: From I-5 and Stockton, drive south to the Lathrop exit. Turn west on Lathrop and drive 1.5 blocks to Manthy Road. Turn north (right) and drive 0.5 mile to Dos Reis Road. Turn left and drive to the campground at the end of the road.

Contact: San Joaquin County Parks Department, 209/953-8800 or 209/331-7400, www.co.san-joaquin.ca.us/parks.

2 CASWELL MEMORIAL STATE PARK

Scenic rating: 7

on the Stanislaus River near Stockton

Map 9.1, page 523

Caswell Memorial State Park features shoreline frontage along the Stanislaus River, along with an additional 250 acres of parkland. The Stanislaus provides shoreline fishing for catfish on summer nights. Bass and crappie are also occasionally caught. Other recreation options here include an interpretive nature trail and swimming. Bird-watching is popular; look for red-shouldered and red-tail hawks. During warm months, bring mosquito repellent.

Campsites, facilities: There are 64 sites for tents or RVs up to 24 feet (no hookups), and one group site for up to 50 people. Picnic tables, food lockers, and fire grills are provided. Drinking water, flush toilets, showers, firewood, a swimming beach, and nature trails are available. Some facilities are wheelchair-accessible. Weekend interpretive programs and junior ranger programs are available in the summer. Leashed pets are permitted.

Reservations, fees: Reservations are accepted ($7.50 reservation fee) for the summer at 800/444-PARK (800/444-7275) or www.reserveamerica.com. Sites are $20 per night, and $6 per night for each additional vehicle; groups with up to 12 vehicles, $110 per night. Open year-round.

Directions: Drive on Highway 99 to Austin Road (1.5 miles south of Manteca). Turn south on Austin Road and drive four miles to the park entrance at the end of the road.

Contact: Caswell Memorial State Park, 209/599-3810; California State Parks, Four Rivers Sector, 209/826-1197, fax 209/826-0284, www.parks.ca.gov.

🛑 CARNEGIE STATE VEHICULAR RECREATION AREA

🐕 ♿ 🚐 ⛰️

Scenic rating: 2

near Tracy

Map 9.1, page 523

This is a major state-run OHV area, with mainly dirt bikes and all-terrain vehicles. Don't show up without one, or its equivalent. This area is barren, ugly, and extremely noisy on weekends. It can get hot, windy, and dusty as well. But that's just what dirt bikers want, and they have it all to themselves. The main campground fills on most weekends from October through May. The area covers 1,500 acres with challenging hill-type trail riding and a professionally designed motocross track. There is also a four-wheel-drive obstacle course. Elevations here rise to 1,800 feet, with summer temperatures peaking at 105°F. Winters are mild.

Campsites, facilities: There are 22 sites for tents or RVs of any length (no hookups). Picnic tables, shade ramadas, and fire rings are provided. Drinking water and flush toilets are available, but note that the drinking water (high in iron) might taste terrible, and you are advised to bring bottled water. Nearest supplies are 14 miles away. Some facilities are wheelchair-accessible. Leashed pets are permitted.

Reservations, fees: Reservations are not accepted. Sites are $10 per night. Open year-round, weather permitting.

Directions: From I-580 (south of Tracy), drive to Corral Hollow Road. Take that exit and drive west for six miles to the campground on the left.

Contact: Carnegie State Vehicular Recreation Area, 925/447-9027; Carnegie Sector Office, 925/447-0426, www.parks.ca.gov.

🔲 FRANK RAINES REGIONAL PARK

🚶 🐕 ♿ 🚐 ⛰️

Scenic rating: 4

near Modesto

Map 9.1, page 523

This park is primarily a riding area for folks with dirt bikes, all-terrain vehicles, and dune buggies who take advantage of the rough-terrain riding course available here. About 1,500 acres of the 2,000-acre park are reserved for OHV use. Deer and pig hunting in season are also a possibility. A side-trip option is to visit Minniear Park, directly to the east, which is a day-use wilderness park with hiking trails and a creek. This area is very pretty in the spring when the foothills are still green and many wildflowers are blooming.

Campsites, facilities: There are 34 sites with full hookups (50 amps) for RVs or tents, and 20 sites with no hookups for tents or RVs. Some sites are pull-through. Fire grills and picnic tables are provided. Restrooms with showers, drinking water, picnic area, baseball diamond, group facilities, nature trails, and a recreation hall are available. Some facilities are wheelchair-accessible. Leashed pets are permitted.

Reservations, fees: Reservations are not accepted. Sites are $15–23 per night, $5 per night for each additional vehicle, $3 per pet per night, extra fee for use of OHV area. Open year-round.

Directions: On I-5, drive to the Patterson exit (south of the junction of I-5 and I-580). Turn west on the Patterson exit and drive onto Diablo Grande Parkway. Continue a short distance under the freeway to Del Puerto Canyon Road. Turn west (right) and drive 16 miles to the park and the campground on the right.

Contact: Stanislaus County Parks and Recreation Department, 866/648-7275 or 209/525-6750, www.co.stanislaus.ca.us/ER/PARKS/Parks.htm.

5 SAN LUIS CREEK

🚶 🏊 🛶 ⛴ 🐕 🚐 ⛺

Scenic rating: 5

on San Luis Reservoir

Map 9.1, page 523

San Luis Creek Campground is near San Luis Reservoir. It is one in a series of camps operated by the state in the San Luis Reservoir State Recreation Area, adjacent to the reservoir and O'Neill Forebay, home of many of the biggest striped bass in California, including the world record for landlocked stripers.

Campsites, facilities: There are 53 sites with partial hookups (20 and 30 amps) for tents or RVs up to 35 feet, and two group sites for up to 30–60 people. Picnic tables and fire pits are provided. Drinking water, pit toilets, and a dump station are available. A boat ramp is nearby. Leashed pets are permitted.

Reservations, fees: Reservations are accepted ($7.50 reservation fee) at 800/444-PARK (800/444-7275) or www.reserveamerica.com. Sites are $20–25 per night, $6 per night for each additional vehicle, $66–135 per night for group sites. Open year-round.

Directions: Drive on Highway 152 to San Luis Reservoir (12 miles west of Los Banos) and the signed campground entrance road (15 miles west of Los Banos). Turn north and drive two miles to the campground on the left.

Contact: San Luis Reservoir State Recreation Area, 209/826-1196; Four Rivers Sector, 209/826-1197, fax 209/826-0284, www.parks.ca.gov.

6 MEDEIROS

🚶 🏊 🛶 ⛴ 🐕 🚐 ⛺

Scenic rating: 5

on O'Neill Forebay near Santa Nella

Map 9.1, page 523

This is a vast, primitive campground set on the stark expanse of foothill country on O'Neill Forebay and near San Luis Reservoir. Some of the biggest striped bass in California history

have been caught here at the forebay. It is best known for wind in the spring, hot weather in the summer, and low water levels in the fall. Striped-bass fishing is best in the fall when the wind is down and stripers will corral schools of bait fish near the lake surface. Sailboarding is decent. There's a large, developed, swimming beach on O'Neill Forebay, and boats can be launched four miles west of the campground at San Luis Creek. There used to be another boat ramp at Medeiros, but it's been closed since 9/11 and will not reopen. In addition to security concerns, there were problems with launching in low water conditions. The forebay can get congested on weekends and holidays; the reservoir is less crowded. The campground elevation is 225 feet. (See next listing, *Basalt*, for more information about San Luis.)

Campsites, facilities: There are 350 primitive sites for tents or RVs of any length (no hookups). Some shaded ramadas with fire grills and picnic tables are available. Drinking water and chemical toilets are available. A boat ramp is four miles away. Leashed pets are permitted.

Reservations, fees: Reservations are not accepted. Sites are $10 per night, and each additional vehicle is $6 per night. Boat launching is $6 per day. Open year-round.

Directions: Drive on Highway 152 to Highway 33 (about 10 miles west of Los Banos). Turn north (right) on Highway 33 and drive 0.25 mile to the campground entrance on the left.

Contact: San Luis Reservoir State Recreation Area, 209/826-1196; Four Rivers Sector, 209/826-1197, fax 209/826-0284, www.parks.ca.gov.

7 BASALT

🚶 🏊 🛶 ⛴ 🐕 ♿ 🚐 ⛺

Scenic rating: 5

on San Luis Reservoir

Map 9.1, page 523

San Luis Reservoir is a huge, man-made lake, covering 13,800 acres with 65 miles of shoreline, developed among stark foothills to provide a storage facility along the California Aqueduct. It fills by late winter and is used primarily by anglers, water-skiers, and sailboarders. When the Sacramento River Delta water pumps take the water, they also take the fish, filling this lake up with both. Striped-bass fishing is best in the fall when the stripers chase schools of bait fish on the lake surface. Spring and early summer can be quite windy, but that makes for good sailboarding. The adjacent O'Neill Forebay is the best recreation bet because of the boat launch and often good fishing. There is a visitors center at the Romero Overlook. The elevation is 575 feet. Summer temperatures can occasionally exceed 100°F, but evenings are usually pleasant. During winter, tule fog is common. Note that in spring and early summer, it can turn windy very quickly. Warning lights mark several spots at the reservoir and forebay.

Campsites, facilities: There are 79 sites for tents or RVs up to 30 feet (no hookups). Picnic tables and fire grills are provided. Drinking water, restrooms with flush toilets and coin showers, dump station, picnic areas, and a boat ramp are available. A store, coin laundry, gas station, restaurant, and propane gas are nearby (about 1.5 miles away). Some facilities are wheelchair-accessible. Leashed pets are permitted.

Reservations, fees: Reservations are accepted ($7.50 reservation fee) at 800/444-PARK (800/444-7275) or www.reserveamerica.com. Sites are $15–20 per night, and $6 per night for each additional vehicle. Boat launching is $6 per day. Open year-round.

Directions: Drive on Highway 152 to San Luis Reservoir (12 miles west of Los Banos) and the Basalt campground entrance road. Turn south on Basalt Road and drive 2.5 miles to the campground on the left.

Contact: San Luis Reservoir State Recreation Area, 209/826-1196; Four Rivers Sector, 209/826-1197, fax 209/826-0284, www.parks.ca.gov.

8 GLORY HOLE

Scenic rating: 7

at New Melones Reservoir

Map 9.2, page 524

Glory Hole encompasses both Big Oak and Ironhorse campgrounds. This is one of two major recreation areas on New Melones Reservoir in the Sierra Nevada foothills, a popular spot with a boat ramp nearby for access to outstanding waterskiing and fishing. (See the next entry, *Tuttletown Recreation Area*.) Campfire programs are often available at the amphitheater in summer. Camp hosts are usually on-site year-round.

Campsites, facilities: Big Oak has 55 sites for tents or RVs up to 40 feet (no hookups) and Ironhorse has 89 sites for tents or RVs of any length; 20 walk-in sites are for tents only. Picnic tables and fire grills are provided. Drinking water, restrooms with flush toilets and showers, marina, boat ramps, houseboat and boat rentals, swimming beach, amphitheater, and playground are available. Some facilities are wheelchair-accessible. Leashed pets are permitted.

Reservations, fees: Reservations are accepted at 877/444-6777 or www.ReserveUSA.com. Sites are $12–16 per night. Open year-round.

Directions: From Sonora, drive north on Highway 49 for about 15 miles (Glory Hole Market will be on the left side of the road) to Whittle Ranch Road. Turn left and drive five miles to the campground, with sites on both sides of the road.

Contact: U.S. Bureau of Reclamation, New Melones Visitor Center, 209/536-9094, fax 209/536-9652; New Melones Lake Marina, 209/785-3300; Glory Hole Sports, 209/736-4333.

9 TUTTLETOWN RECREATION AREA

☒ ☒ ☒ ☒ ☒ ☒ ☒ ☒

Scenic rating: 7

at New Melones Reservoir

Map 9.2, page 524

Here is a mammoth camping area set on the giant New Melones Reservoir in the Sierra Nevada foothills, a beautiful sight when the lake is full. The lake is set in the valley foothills between the historic mining towns of Angels Camp and Sonora. New Melones is one of California's top recreation lakes. All water sports are permitted. Waterskiing and houseboating are particularly popular. Tuttletown encompasses three campgrounds (Acorn, Manzanita, and Chamise) and two group camping areas (Oak Knoll and Fiddleneck). New Melones is a huge reservoir that covers 12,500 acres and offers more than 100 miles of shoreline and good fishing. The elevation is 1,085 feet. A boat ramp is near camp. Although the lake's main body is huge, the better fishing is well up the lake's Stanislaus River arm (for trout) and in its coves (for bass and bluegill), where there are submerged trees providing perfect aquatic habitat. Trolling for kokanee salmon also has become popular. The lake level often drops dramatically in the fall.

Campsites, facilities: At Acorn there are 69 sites for tents or RVs of any length (no hookups), at Chamise there are 36 tent sites, and at Manzanita there are 55 sites for tents or RVs of any length, 13 walk-in tent sites; Oak Knoll group site holds up to 80 people, and Fiddleneck group site up to 48 people. Picnic tables and fire grills are provided. Drinking water, restrooms with flush toilets and showers, dump station, playground, and a boat ramp are available. Some facilities are wheelchair-accessible. Leashed pets are permitted.

Reservations, fees: Reservations are accepted at 877/444-6777 or www.ReserveUSA.com. Sites are $12–16 per night, and the group fee is $128–$160 per night. Open year-round.

Directions: From Sonora, drive north on Highway 49 to Reynolds Ferry Road. Turn left and drive about two miles to the entrance road to the campgrounds.

Contact: U.S. Bureau of Reclamation, New Melones Visitor Center, 209/536-9094, fax 209/536-9652.

10 WOODWARD RESERVOIR COUNTY PARK

☒ ☒ ☒ ☒ ☒ ☒ ☒ ☒

Scenic rating: 7

near Oakdale

Map 9.2, page 524

This is one of the best sailing lakes in Northern California. Regattas are held through the year, and it is also very popular for sailboarding. Woodward's nickname, in fact, is "Windward Reservoir." Woodward Reservoir is a large lake covering 2,900 acres with 23 miles of shoreline, set in the rolling foothills just north of Oakdale. It is a good lake for both waterskiing and fishing, with minimal conflict between the two sports. All boating is allowed, and speedboats have the main lake body to let her rip. Trout fishing has improved and they are stocked here in winter. Bass fishing has been slow the past several years. Note that because this is one of the largest reservoirs near Modesto and Stockton, it gets lots of local traffic, especially on summer weekends. There are equestrian facilities at this park, and horse camping is permitted in undeveloped sites only.

Campsites, facilities: There are 155 sites, 114 with partial hookups and four with full hookups (30 amps), for RVs or tents. Picnic tables and fire grills are provided. Drinking water is available intermittently; check for current status. A dump station, picnic shelter, three boat ramps, dry boat storage, restrooms with flush toilets and showers, and some equestrian facilities are available. Some facilities are wheelchair-accessible. Leashed pets are permitted.

Reservations, fees: Reservations are not

accepted. Sites are $15–23 per night per vehicle, $7 per day boat launch fee, $3 per pet per night, $2 per horse per night. Holiday rates are higher. Open year-round.

Directions: Drive on Highway 120 to Oakdale (the road becomes Highway 108/120) and the junction with County Road J14/26 Mile Road. Turn left on 26 Mile Road and drive four miles to the park entrance at Woodward Reservoir (14528 26 Mile Road).

Contact: Woodward Reservoir County Park, 209/847-3304; Stanislaus County Parks, 209/525-6750, www.co.stanislaus.ca.us/ER/PARKS/Parks.htm; Woodward Marina, 209/847-3129.

11 THE RIVER'S EDGE

Scenic rating: 7

on the Stanislaus River

Map 9.2, page 524

New owners bought this place in 2004 and changed the name from Knights Ferry Resort. This is a privately run campground in the small historic town of Knights Ferry. The campground has a good number of trees. A nice touch is a restaurant overlooking the Stanislaus River. Side trips include tours of the covered bridge ("the longest west of the Mississippi") and several historic buildings and homes, all within walking distance of the park. River access and hiking trails are available at the east end of town. Two runs are available, the Goodwin Canyon Run, which is exciting, even scary and challenging, and the Knights Ferry Run, an easy float. Raft and canoe rentals are also available nearby. This resort is popular with rafters and canoeists.

Campsites, facilities: There are 14 sites with partial hookups (30 amps) for tents or RVs up to 40 feet. A community fire pit, restrooms with showers, and a restaurant are available. No pets permitted.

Reservations, fees: Reservations are required with a deposit. Sites are $35 per night. Some

credit cards accepted. Open April through October.

Directions: From Oakdale, drive east on Highway 108 for approximately 12 miles to Knight's Ferry and Kennedy Road. Turn left and drive to a bridge, cross the bridge, and continue a short distance to Sonora Road/Main Street. Turn left and drive to the campground entrance at the River's Edge Restaurant.

Contact: The River's Edge, 209/881-3349.

12 LAKE TULLOCH RV CAMPGROUND AND MARINA

Scenic rating: 7

on the south shore of Lake Tulloch

Map 9.2, page 524

This camp features tons of waterfront on Lake Tulloch, a dispersed tent area, and cabins with direct beach access. Unlike so many reservoirs in the foothill country, this one is nearly always full of water. In addition, it is a place where anglers and water-skiers live in harmony. That is because of the many coves and a six-mile-long arm with an enforced 5-mph speed limit. It's a big lake, shaped like a giant X with extended lake arms adding up to 55 miles of shoreline. The campground features mature oak trees that provide shade to most of the developed sites. A secret at Tulloch is that fishing is also good for crawdads. The elevation is 500 feet.

Campsites, facilities: There are 130 sites, including 31 boat sites and 72 with full or partial hookups (30 and 50 amps) for tents or RVs up to 40 feet, a large area for lakefront tent camping and self-contained RVs, and 10 waterfront cabins. Picnic tables and fire grills are provided. Drinking water, restrooms with flush toilets and showers, coin laundry, convenience store, dump station, playground, restaurant, volleyball, horseshoes, tetherball, ping-pong, swimming beach, marina, boat rentals, boat slips, fuel dock, and a boat launch are available. Some facilities are wheelchair-accessible. Leashed pets are permitted.

Reservations, fees: Reservations are accepted. The fee is $20–30 per night, $12 per night for each additional vehicle, and $1 per pet per night. Group rates are available. Boat launch fee is $5 per day. Some credit cards accepted. Open year-round.

Directions: From Manteca, drive east on Highway 120 (it becomes Highway 108/120) to Oakdale. Continue east for 13 miles to Tulloch Road on the left. Turn left and drive 4.6 miles to the campground entrance and gatehouse at the south shore of Lake Tulloch.

Contact: Lake Tulloch RV Campground and Marina, 209/881-0107 or 800/894-2267, www.laketullochcampground.com.

13 MOCCASIN POINT

🏊 🛶 🚤 ♿ 🚐 ⛺

Scenic rating: 7

at Lake Don Pedro

Map 9.2, page 524

This camp is at the northeastern end of Lake Don Pedro, adjacent to a boat ramp. Moccasin Point juts well into the lake, directly across from where the major Tuolumne River arm enters the lake. Don Pedro is a giant lake, with extended lake arms and nearly 13,000 surface acres and 160 miles of shoreline. It is one of the best boating and recreation lakes in California, but subject to drawdowns from midsummer through early fall. At different times, fishing is excellent for salmon, trout, or bass. Other species are redear sunfish, catfish, crappie, and bluegill. Houseboating and boat-in camping (bring sunscreen) provide options. The elevation is 800 feet.

Campsites, facilities: There are 50 sites for tents, 18 sites with full hookups (20 and 30 amps) for RVs of any length, and an overflow camping area. Some sites are pull-through. Picnic tables, food lockers, and barbecue units are provided at all sites. Drinking water, restrooms with showers, dump station, group

picnic area, fish-cleaning station, propane gas, ice, small store, boat ramp, motorboat and houseboat rentals, fuel, moorings, and bait and tackle are available. Some facilities are wheelchair-accessible. Ground fires are prohibited. No pets are permitted.

Reservations, fees: Reservations are accepted for a minimum of two nights, or three nights on holidays. Reservations ($6 reservation fee) can be made by telephone or website. Sites are $19–26 per night, $6 per night for each additional vehicle. Boat launching is $6 per day. Some credit cards accepted. Open year-round.

Directions: From Manteca, drive east on Highway 120 (it becomes Highway 108/120) for 30 miles to the Highway 120/Yosemite exit. Bear right on Highway 120 and drive 11 miles to Jacksonville Road. Turn left on Jacksonville Road and drive a short distance to the campground on the right.

Contact: Don Pedro Recreation Agency, 209/852-2396; Moccasin Point Marina, 209/989-2206, www.donpedrolake.com.

14 LUMSDEN BRIDGE

🎣 🏕 ⛺

Scenic rating: 7

on the Tuolumne River in Stanislaus National Forest

Map 9.2, page 524   **BEST (**

This is one of three camps along this immediate stretch of the Tuolumne River, one of the best white-water rafting rivers in California. Note that a permit is required for this activity; contact the Forest Service for details. The camp is set at 1,500 feet on the north side of the river, accessible just after crossing the Lumsden Bridge, hence the name. (See the next entry, *Lumsden,* for more information.) Note: At the time of publication, the access road to the campground was closed at South Fork campground, requiring a three-mile hike, bike, or OHV trip to reach Lumsden Bridge camp. Check for current status.

Campsites, facilities: There are nine sites for tents only. Picnic tables and fire grills are provided. Vault toilets are available. No drinking water is available. Garbage must be packed out. Leashed pets are permitted.

Reservations, fees: Reservations are not accepted. There is no camping fee. Open April through October, weather permitting.

Directions: From Groveland, drive east on Highway 120 for about eight miles (just under a mile beyond County Road J132) to Ferretti Road. Turn left on Ferretti Road and drive to Lumsden Road. Turn right and continue for 5.5 miles to the camp on the left side of the road. (The road is not recommended for RVs or trailers.)

Contact: Stanislaus National Forest, Groveland Ranger District, 209/962-7825, fax 209/962-7412.

15 LUMSDEN
🏊 🐕 ⛺

Scenic rating: 7

on the Tuolumne River in Stanislaus National Forest

Map 9.2, page 524   **BEST (**

This is one of the great access points for white-water rafting on the wild and scenic Tuolumne River and its premium stretch between Hetch Hetchy Reservoir in Yosemite and Don Pedro Reservoir in the Central Valley foothills. Unless you are an expert rafter, you are advised to attempt running this stretch of river only with a professional rafting company. Note that a permit is required for this activity; contact the Forest Service for details. The camp is set at 1,500 feet, just across the road from the river. The access road down the canyon is steep and bumpy. There are two other camps within a mile, South Fork and Lumsden Bridge.

Campsites, facilities: There are sites for tents only. Picnic tables and fire grills are provided. Vault toilets are available. No drinking water is available. Garbage must be packed out. Leashed pets are permitted.

Reservations, fees: Reservations are not accepted. There is no camping fee. Open April through October, weather permitting.

Directions: From Groveland, drive east on Highway 120 for about eight miles (just under a mile beyond County Road J132) to Ferretti Road. Turn left on Ferretti Road and drive to Lumsden Road. Turn right and continue for four miles to the camp on the left side of the road.

Contact: Stanislaus National Forest, Groveland Ranger District, 209/962-7825, fax 209/962-7412.

16 SOUTH FORK
🏊 🐕 ⛺

Scenic rating: 6

near the Tuolumne River in Stanislaus National Forest

Map 9.2, page 524

South Fork camp is 0.5 mile upstream from Lumsden and about a mile downstream from Lumsden Bridge. Why do I say "upstream" and "downstream" instead of east and west? Because this is a camp for white-water rafters, featuring the spectacular Tuolumne River and access to its most exciting stretches. You should attempt to run this river only with a professional rafting company; a Forest Service permit is required. The elevation is 1,500 feet. A Forest Service map is advised when visiting this area.

Campsites, facilities: There are eight sites for tents only. Picnic tables and fire grills are provided. Vault toilets are available. No drinking water is available. Garbage must be packed out. Leashed pets are permitted.

Reservations, fees: Reservations are not accepted. There is no camping fee. Open April through October, weather permitting.

Directions: From Groveland, drive east on Highway 120 for about eight miles (just under a mile beyond County Road J132) to Ferretti Road. Turn left on Ferretti and drive to Lumsden Road. Turn right and continue for five miles to the camp on the left side of the road.

Contact: Stanislaus National Forest, Groveland Ranger District, 209/962-7825, fax 209/962-7412.

17 LOST CLAIM

Scenic rating: 4

near the Tuolumne River in Stanislaus National Forest

Map 9.2, page 524

This is one in a series of easy-access camps off Highway 120 that provide overflow areas when all the sites are taken in Yosemite National Park to the east. A feeder stream to the Tuolumne River runs by the camp. The elevation is 3,100 feet.

Campsites, facilities: There are 10 sites for tents only. Picnic tables and fire grills are provided. Vault toilets and drinking water are available. A convenience store is nearby. Leashed pets are permitted.

Reservations, fees: Reservations are not accepted. Sites are $12 per night. Open May through Labor Day.

Directions: From Groveland, drive east on Highway 120 for 12 miles (four miles past the Groveland District Office) to the campground on the left side of the road. (The access road is not recommended for RVs or trailers.)

Contact: Stanislaus National Forest, Groveland Ranger District, 209/962-7825, fax 209/962-7412.

18 THE PINES

Scenic rating: 4

in Stanislaus National Forest

Map 9.2, page 524

The Pines camp is set at 3,200 feet in elevation on the western edge of Stanislaus National Forest, only 0.5 mile from the Groveland

District Office and about five miles from the Tuolumne River (see *Lumsden* listing in this chapter). A Forest Service road is routed south of camp for two miles, climbing to Smith Peak Lookout (3,877 feet) and providing sweeping views to the west of the San Joaquin Valley foothills.

Campsites, facilities: There are 11 sites for tents or RVs up to 22 feet (no hookups), and two group sites for up to 50 people each. Picnic tables and fire grills are provided. Drinking water and vault toilets are available. A convenience store is nearby. Leashed pets are permitted.

Reservations, fees: Reservations are required ($9 reservation fee) for the group sites only at 877/444-6777 or www.ReserveUSA.com. Sites are $12 per night, $65 per night for group site. Open late April through October, weather permitting.

Directions: From Groveland, drive east on Highway 120 for nine miles (about a mile past the County Road J132 turnoff) to the signed campground entrance road on the right. Turn right onto the campground entrance road and drive a short distance to the camp.

Contact: Stanislaus National Forest, Groveland Ranger District, 209/962-7825, fax 209/962-7412.

19 BLUE OAKS

Scenic rating: 7

at Lake Don Pedro

Map 9.2, page 524

Blue Oaks is between the dam at Lake Don Pedro and Fleming Meadows. The on-site boat ramp to the east is a big plus here. (See the next entry, *Fleming Meadows,* and the *Moccasin Point* listing in this chapter for more information.)

Campsites, facilities: There are 195 sites for tents or RVs of any length; some sites have partial hookups (20 and 30 amps) and one is pull-through. Group camping is available.

Picnic tables, food lockers, and barbecue units are provided. Drinking water, restrooms with flush toilets and showers, boat launch, fish-cleaning stations, and a dump station are available. Some facilities are wheelchair-accessible. A store, coin laundry, and propane gas are nearby at Fleming Meadows Marina. No ground fires are permitted. No pets are permitted.

Reservations, fees: Reservations are accepted ($6 reservation fee) by telephone or website with a two-night minimum; three-night minimum on holidays. Sites are $19–23 per night, $6 per night for each additional vehicle; group fee is $200 per night. Boat launching is $6 per day. Some credit cards accepted. Open Memorial Day weekend through Labor Day weekend.

Directions: From Manteca, take Highway 120 east to Oakdale (the road becomes Highway 120/108). Continue east on Highway 108 for 20 miles to La Grange Road/J59 (signed "Don Pedro Reservoir"). Turn right on La Grange Road and drive 10 miles to Bonds Flat Road. Turn left on Bonds Flat Road and drive 0.5 mile to the campground on the left.

Contact: Don Pedro Recreation Area, 209/852-2396, www.donpedrolake.com.

20 FLEMING MEADOWS

Scenic rating: 7

on Lake Don Pedro

Map 9.2, page 524

Fleming Meadows is set on the shore of Lake Don Pedro, just east of the dam. A boat ramp is available in the campground on the southeast side of the dam. A sandy beach and concession stand are here. This is a big camp at the foot of a giant lake, where hot weather, warm water, waterskiing, and bass fishing make for weekend vacations. Don Pedro has many extended lake arms, providing 160 miles of shoreline and nearly 13,000 surface acres when full. (See the *Moccasin Point* listing in this chapter for more information.)

Campsites, facilities: There are 172 sites for tents or RVs of any length, including 50 walk-in sites for tents, and 90 sites with full hookups (20 and 30 amps) for RVs. A few sites are pull-through. Picnic tables, food lockers, and barbecues are provided. Drinking water, restrooms with flush toilets and showers, and a dump station are available. A coin laundry, store, ice, snack bar, group picnic areas, restaurant, swimming lagoon, amphitheater, softball field, volleyball, bait and tackle, motorboat and houseboat rentals, boat ramp, mooring, boat storage, engine repairs, and propane gas are nearby. Some facilities are wheelchair-accessible. Ground fires are prohibited. No pets are permitted.

Reservations, fees: Reservations are accepted ($6 reservation fee) with a two-night minimum, and a three-night minimum on holidays. Sites are $19–26 per night, $6 per night for each additional vehicle. Boat launching is $6 per day. Some credit cards accepted. Open year-round.

Directions: From Manteca, take Highway 120 east to Oakdale (the road becomes Highway 120/108). Continue east on Highway 108 for 20 miles to La Grange Road/J59 (signed Don Pedro Reservoir). Turn right on La Grange Road and drive 10 miles to Bonds Flat Road. Turn left on Bonds Flat Road and drive 2.5 miles to the campground on the left.

Contact: Don Pedro Recreation Area, 209/852-2396; Lake Don Pedro Marina, 209/852-2369, www.donpedrolake.com.

21 MODESTO RESERVOIR REGIONAL PARK AND BOAT-IN

Scenic rating: 7

on Modesto Reservoir

Map 9.2, page 524

Modesto Reservoir is a big lake, at 2,800 acres with 31 miles of shoreline, set in the hot foothill country. That's good because it is a popular place in the summer. Waterskiing is excellent in the main lake body. Sandy swimming beaches are available, and swimming is popular. Anglers head to the southern shore of the lake, which is loaded with submerged trees and coves and is also protected by a 5-mph speed limit. Fishing for bass is good, though the fish are often small. Wildlife viewing is good and waterfowl hunting is available in season. The elevation is 200 feet.

Campsites, facilities: There are 145 sites with full hookups (30 amps) for RVs up to 36 feet and 36 tent sites. Picnic tables and fire grills are provided. Drinking water, restrooms with flush toilets and showers, dump station, two boat ramps, a store, snack bar, propane, gas, archery range, and radio-controlled glider field are available. Some facilities are wheelchair-accessible. No gas cans are permitted. No pets are allowed.

Reservations, fees: Reservations are not accepted. Sites are $15–23 per night, $2 surcharge per vehicle on holidays. Boat launching is $7 per day. Open year-round.

Directions: From Modesto, drive east on Highway 132 for 16 miles past Waterford to Reservoir Road. Turn left and drive to the campground at 18143 Reservoir Road.

Contact: Modesto Reservoir Regional Park, 209/525-6750, fax 209/525-6773; Modesto Marina, 209/874-1340, www.co.stanislaus.ca.us/ER/PARKS/Parks.htm.

22 TURLOCK LAKE STATE RECREATION AREA

Scenic rating: 6

east of Modesto

Map 9.2, page 524

This campground is on the shady south shore of the Tuolumne River, about one mile from Turlock Lake. Turlock Lake warms to 65–74°F in the summer, cooler than many Central Valley reservoirs, since the water entering this lake is released from the bottom of Don Pedro Res-

ervoir. It often seems just right for boating and all water sports on hot summer days. The lake covers 3,500 surface acres and offers 26 miles of shoreline. A boat ramp is available near the camp, making it ideal for boaters/campers. Bass fishing is fair in the summer. In the late winter and spring, the lake is quite cold, fed by snowmelt from the Tuolumne River. Trout fishing is good year-round as a result. The elevation is 250 feet. The park is bordered by ranches, orchards, and mining tailings along the river.

Campsites, facilities: There are 48 sites for tents or RVs up to 27 feet (no hookups), 15 sites for tents, and one hike-in/bike-in site. Picnic tables, fire grills, and food lockers are provided. Drinking water and restrooms with flush toilets and coin showers are available. A swimming beach and boat ramp are available nearby. The boat facilities are wheelchair-accessible. Leashed pets are permitted.

Reservations, fees: Reservations are accepted ($7.50 reservation fee) at 800/444-PARK (800/444-7275) or www.reserveamerica.com. Sites are $20 per night, $6 per night for each additional vehicle, $5 per person per night for hike-in/bike-in site. Boat launching is $6 per day. Open year-round.

Directions: From Modesto, drive east on Highway 132 for 14 miles to Waterford, then continue eight miles on Highway 132 to Roberts Ferry Road. Turn right (south) and drive one mile to Lake Road. Turn left and drive two miles to the campground on the left.

Contact: Turlock Lake State Recreation Area, 209/874-2056 or 209/874-2008, www.parks.ca.gov.

23 McCLURE: HORSESHOE BEND RECREATION AREA

Scenic rating: 7

on Lake McClure

Map 9.2, page 524

Lake McClure is a unique, horseshoe-shaped lake in the foothill country west of Yosemite.

It adjoins smaller Lake McSwain, connected by the Merced River. McClure is shaped like a giant H, with its lake arms providing 82 miles of shoreline, warm water for waterskiing, and fishing for bass (on the west half of the H near Cotton Creek) and for trout (on the east half of the H). There is a boat launch adjacent to the campground. It's one of four lakes in the immediate area; the others are Don Pedro Reservoir to the north and Modesto Reservoir and Turlock Lake to the west. The elevation is 900 feet.

Campsites, facilities: There are 110 sites for tents or RVs of any length, including 35 with partial hookups (30 amps). Picnic tables and barbecues are provided. Restrooms with showers, dump station, a boat ramp, fish-cleaning stations, picnic areas, swimming lagoon, store, and coin laundry are available. Some facilities are wheelchair-accessible. Leashed pets are permitted.

Reservations, fees: Reservations are accepted ($6 reservation fee) at 800/468-8889. Sites are $16–25 per night, $6–19 per night for each additional vehicle, $3 per pet per night. Boat launching is $6 per day. Some credit cards accepted. Open year-round.

Directions: From Modesto, drive east on Highway 132 for 31 miles to La Grange and then continue for about 17 miles (toward Coulterville) to the north end of Lake McClure and the campground entrance road on the right side of the road. Turn right and drive 0.5 mile to the campground.

Contact: Horseshoe Bend Recreation Area, 209/878-3452; Merced Irrigation District, 209/378-2521, www.lakemcclure.com.

24 BARRETT COVE RECREATION AREA

Scenic rating: 7

on Lake McClure

Map 9.2, page 524

Lake McClure is shaped like a giant H, with its lake arms providing 82 miles of shore-line. The lake is popular for water sports, including skiing, wakeboarding, houseboating, and fishing. Although swimming is not prohibited in the lake, you'll rarely see people swimming or playing along the shore, mainly because of the typically steep drop-offs. This camp is on the left side of the H, that is, on the western shore, within a park that provides a good boat ramp. This is the largest in a series of camps on Lake McClure. (See the previous entry, *Horseshoe Bend Recreation Area,* and the next entries, *McClure Point Recreation Area* and *Bagby Recreation Area,* for more information.)

Campsites, facilities: There are 275 sites for tents or RVs of any length, including 89 with full hookups (30 amps). Picnic tables and barbecues are provided. Restrooms with showers, boat ramps, dump station, swimming lagoon, and playground are available. A convenience store, coin laundry, marina, picnic areas, fish-cleaning stations, boat and houseboat rentals, and propane gas are also available on-site. Some facilities are wheelchair-accessible. Leashed pets are permitted.

Reservations, fees: Reservations are accepted ($6 reservation fee) at 800/468-8889. Sites are $16–25 per night, $6–19 per night for each additional vehicle, $3 per pet per night. Boat launching is $6 per day. Some credit cards accepted. Open year-round.

Directions: From Modesto, drive east on Highway 132 for 31 miles to La Grange and then continue for about eight miles (toward Coulterville) to Merced Falls Road. Turn right and drive three miles to the campground entrance on the left. Turn left and drive a mile to the campground on the left side of the road.

Contact: Barrett Cove Recreation Area, 209/378-2611; Merced Irrigation District, 209/378-2521, fax 209/378-2519, www.lakemcclure.com.

25 McCLURE POINT RECREATION AREA

🏊 🎣 🚗 🦌 🚐 ⛺

Scenic rating: 7

on Lake McClure

Map 9.2, page 524

McClure Point Recreation Area is the campground of choice for campers/boaters coming from the Turlock and Merced areas. It is a well-developed facility with an excellent boat ramp that provides access to the main body of Lake McClure. This is the best spot on the lake for waterskiing.

Campsites, facilities: There are 100 sites for tents or RVs up to 40 feet; 52 sites have partial hookups (30 amps). Picnic tables and barbecues are provided. Restrooms with showers, boat ramps, boat rentals, marina, fish-cleaning stations, picnic areas, swimming lagoon, and a coin laundry are available. A store is nearby. Leashed pets are permitted.

Reservations, fees: Reservations are accepted ($6 reservation fee) at 800/468-8889. Sites are $19–25 per night, $3 per pet per night. Boat launching is $6 per day. Open year-round.

Directions: From Turlock, drive east on County Road J16 for 19 miles to the junction with Highway 59. Continue east on Highway 59/County Road J16 for 4.5 miles to Snelling and bear right at Lake McClure Road. Drive approximately two miles to Lake McSwain Dam and continue for seven miles to the campground at the end of the road.

Contact: McClure Point and Bagby Recreation Area, 209/378-2521, fax 209/378-2519, www.lakemcclure.com.

26 BAGBY RECREATION AREA

🏊 🎣 🚗 🦌 🚐 ⛺

Scenic rating: 7

on upper Lake McClure

Map 9.2, page 524

This is the most distant and secluded camp on Lake McClure. It is set near the Merced River as it enters the lake, way up adjacent to the Highway 49 Bridge, nearly an hour's drive from the dam. Trout fishing is good in the area, and it makes sense; when the lake heats up in summer, the trout naturally congregate near the cool incoming flows of the Merced River.

Campsites, facilities: There are 30 sites for tents or RVs of any length, including 10 with partial hookups (30 amps). Drinking water, restrooms with flush toilets and coin showers, picnic areas, fish-cleaning stations, and a boat ramp are available. Leashed pets are permitted.

Reservations, fees: Reservations are accepted ($6 reservation fee) at 800/468-8889. Sites are $19–25 per night, $6–19 per night for each additional vehicle, $3 per pet per night. Boat launching is $6 per day. Open year-round.

Directions: From Turlock, drive east on County Road J16 for 19 miles to the junction with Highway 59. Continue east on Highway 59/County Road J16 for 4.5 miles to Snelling and Merced Falls Road (continue straight, well signed). Drive 0.5 mile to Hornitos Road. Turn right and drive eight miles (drive over the bridge) to Hornitos to a Y. Bear left at the Y in Hornitos (signed to Highway 49) and drive 10 miles to Highway 49. Turn left on Highway 49 and drive eight miles to the Bagby Bridge and entrance kiosk on the right.

Contact: McClure Point and Bagby Recreation Area, 209/378-2521, fax 209/378-2519, www.lakemcclure.com.

27 McSWAIN RECREATION AREA

🏊 🚤 🚐 🏠 🎣 🚗 🏕

Scenic rating: 7

near McSwain Dam on the Merced River

Map 9.2, page 524

Lake McSwain is actually the afterbay for adjacent Lake McClure, and this camp is near the McSwain Dam on the Merced River. Even though McClure and McSwain sit beside each other, each has its own identity. McSwain is low-key with a 10-mph speed limit. If you have a canoe or car-top boat, this lake is preferable to Lake McClure because waterskiing is not allowed. In terms of size, McSwain is like a puddle compared to the giant McClure, but unlike McClure, the water levels are kept up almost year-round at McSwain. The water is cold here and trout stocks are good in the spring. The lake is used primarily by anglers, and several fishing derbies are held here each year. The shoreline is favorable for swimming, and there is even a good sandy beach.

Campsites, facilities: There are 99 sites for tents or RVs up to 40 feet, including 65 with partial hookups (30 amps). The best access sites for large RVs are the pull-through sites in the G Loop. Picnic tables, barbecues, and electrical connections are provided. Drinking water, dump station, restrooms with showers, boat ramp, boat rentals, coin laundry, and a playground are available. A convenience store, marina, snack bar, fish-cleaning stations, picnic area, and propane gas are available nearby. Leashed pets are permitted.

Reservations, fees: Reservations are accepted ($6 reservation fee) at 800/468-8889. Sites are $19–25 per night, $3 per pet per night. Boat launching is $6 per day. Open year-round.

Directions: From Turlock, drive east on County Road J16 for 19 miles to the junction with Highway 59. Continue east on Highway 59/County Road J16 for 4.5 miles to Snelling. Continue straight ahead to Lake McClure Road and drive seven miles to the campground turnoff on the right.

Contact: Lake McSwain Recreation Area, 209/378-2521, fax 209/378-2519; Lake McSwain Marina, 209/378-2534, www .lakemcclure.com.

28 FISHERMAN'S BEND RIVER CAMPGROUND

🏊 🚤 🚐 🏠 🎣 ♿ 🚗 🏕

Scenic rating: 5

on the San Joaquin River

Map 9.2, page 524

This small, privately operated campground is set along the San Joaquin River on the southern outskirts of the San Joaquin Delta country. The park offers shaded sites and direct river access for boaters. This section of river provides fishing for catfish on hot summer nights. Although many of the sites are rented seasonally or longer, about 10 sites are usually available for overnight campers.

Campsites, facilities: There are 38 pull-through sites with full hookups (30 amps) for RVs of any length, and 20 sites for tents only. Picnic tables are provided. Drinking water, restrooms with showers, dump station, coin laundry, boat ramp, fish-cleaning station, seasonal swimming pool, playground, and modem access are available. Some facilities are wheelchair-accessible. Leashed pets are permitted, with certain restrictions.

Reservations, fees: Reservations are accepted at 800/862-3731. Sites are $17–30 per night, $3 per person per night for more than three people. Monthly rates available. Some credit cards accepted. Open year-round.

Directions: Drive on I-5 to the exit for Newman/Stuhr Road (south of the junction of I-5 and I-580). Take that exit and turn east on County Road J18/Stuhr Road and drive 6.5 miles to Hills Ferry Road. Turn left and drive a mile to River Road. Turn left on River Road and drive to 26836 River Road on the right.

Contact: Fisherman's Bend River Campground, 209/862-3731.

29 GEORGE J. HATFIELD STATE RECREATION AREA WALK-IN

Scenic rating: 5

near Newman

Map 9.2, page 524

This is a small state park set in the heart of the San Joaquin Valley, near the confluence of the Merced River and the San Joaquin River, well known for hot summer days and foggy winter nights. The park has many trees. Swimming is popular in the summer. Fishing is good for catfish in the summer here, and some folks will stay up late hoping a big channel catfish will take their bait. During the peak migration from late fall through winter and early spring, there can also be a good number of striped bass in the area. This park is more popular for day use than for camping. The campsites require a walk of about 100 feet. This campground may close during the winter; check current status before planning an off-season trip.

Campsites, facilities: There are 15 walk-in sites for tents, and a large group site for tents or RVs of any length. The group site has an electrical hookup (20 amps) and can accommodate up to 40 people. Picnic tables and fire grills are provided. Drinking water and flush toilets are available. Supplies can be obtained in Newman, five miles away. Leashed pets are permitted.

Reservations, fees: Reservations are accepted ($7.50 reservation fee) only for groups at 800/444-PARK (800/444-7275) or www.reserveamerica.com. Sites are $10–14 per night, $6 per night for each additional vehicle, $90 per night for group site. Open year-round, weather permitting.

Directions: Drive on I-5 to the exit for Newman/Stuhr Road (south of the junction of I-5 and I-580). Take that exit and turn east on County Road J18/Stuhr Road and drive to Newman and the junction with Highway 33. Continue straight on Stuhr Road for 1.5 miles to Hills Ferry Road. Turn left and drive three miles to the park entrance on the right (just past the bridge over the San Joaquin River).

Contact: George J. Hatfield State Recreation Area, 209/632-1852; Four Rivers Sector, 209/826-1197, fax 209/826-0284, www.parks.ca.gov.

30 CONNELL STATE RECREATION AREA

Scenic rating: 6

on the Merced River

Map 9.2, page 524

The weather gets scorching hot around these parts in the summer, and a lot of out-of-towners would pay a bunch for a little shade and a river to sit next to. That's what this park provides, with the Merced River flowing past, along with occasional mermaids on the beach. The park covers 70 acres and has many trees. Fishing is popular for catfish, black bass, and panfish. In high-water years the Merced River attracts salmon (in the fall); check current fishing regulations.

Campsites, facilities: There are 20 sites for tents or RVs up to 30 feet (no hookups), and two group sites for tents only for 25–50 people. Group sites have an electrical hookup (20 amps). Picnic tables, fire grills, and food lockers are provided. Drinking water, restrooms with flush toilets and coin showers, and a swimming beach are available. Firewood is available for purchase. Supplies can be obtained in Delhi, five miles away. Leashed pets are permitted.

Reservations, fees: Reservations are accepted ($7.50 reservation fee) at 800/444-PARK (800/444-7275) or www.reserveamerica.com. Sites are $15–20 per night, $6 per night for each additional vehicle, $53–111 per night for group sites. Open year-round.

Directions: From Modesto, drive south on Highway 99 to Delhi. Continue south for five miles to the South Avenue exit. Take that exit and turn east on South Avenue and drive 2.7 miles to Pepper Street. Turn right and drive one mile to McConnell Road. Turn right and drive a short distance to the park entrance at the end of the road.

Contact: McConnell State Recreation Area, 209/394-7755; Four Rivers Sector, 209/826-1197, fax 209/826-0284, www.parks.ca.gov.

31 LOS BANOS CREEK RESERVOIR

Scenic rating: 6

near Los Banos

Map 9.3, page 525

Los Banos Creek Reservoir is set in a long, narrow valley, covering 410 surface acres with 12 miles of shoreline. It provides a smaller, more low-key setting (a 5-mph speed limit is enforced) compared to the nearby giant, San Luis Reservoir. In spring, it can be quite windy and is a popular spot for sailboarding and sailing. It is also stocked with trout in late winter and spring, and some large bass have been caught here. The elevation is 330 feet. Although drinking water is available, campers are advised to bring their own water, as the water supply is limited here.

Campsites, facilities: There are 15 sites for tents or RVs up to 30 feet (no hookups). Picnic tables, drinking water, and fire grills are provided. Chemical toilets and picnic areas are available. A boat ramp is available nearby. Leashed pets are permitted.

Reservations, fees: Reservations are not accepted. The fee is $10 per night, and $6 per night for each additional vehicle. Boat launching is $6 per day. Open year-round, weather permitting.

Directions: Drive on Highway 152 to Volta Road (five miles west of Los Banos). Turn south on Volta Road and drive about a mile to Pioneer Road. Turn left on Pioneer Road and drive a mile to Canyon Road. Turn south

(right) onto Canyon Road and drive about five miles to the park.

Contact: San Luis Reservoir State Recreation Area, 209/826-1196; Four Rivers Sector, 209/826-1197, fax 209/826-0284, www.parks.ca.gov.

32 LOST LAKE

Scenic rating: 7

on lower San Joaquin River

Map 9.4, page 526

Lost Lake campground is part of a Fresno County park. It is set in the foothills of the San Joaquin Valley, at an elevation of about 500 feet, along the lower San Joaquin River. The campground is broken out into two areas, with about half along the river. Many think this park is quite pretty. There is a lot of wildlife at this park, especially birds and deer. A self-guided hiking trail is routed into a nature study area. Easy canoeing is a plus, with no powerboats permitted. Trout fishing is available; check fishing regulations.

Campsites, facilities: There are 42 sites for tents, with most accessible for self-contained RVs up to 36 feet, and one group site for up to 80 people. Picnic tables and barbecues are provided. Drinking water, flush toilets, dump station, volleyball, softball, and playground are available. A restaurant and store are two miles away in Friant. Leashed pets are permitted.

Reservations, fees: Reservations accepted for the group site only. Sites are $11 per night, $5 per night for each additional vehicle, and $80 per night for the group site. Open year-round.

Directions: From Fresno, drive north on Highway 41 for 24 miles to the first exit for Friant Road. Take that exit and drive 12 miles to the entrance road for Lost Lake. Turn left and drive a short distance to the campground.

Contact: Fresno County Parks Department, 559/488-3004, fax 559/488-1988.

33 VISALIA/FRESNO SOUTH KOA

🏊 🦌 🎣 🚐 ⛺

Scenic rating: 3

west of Visalia

Map 9.4, page 526

This is a layover spot for Highway 99 cruisers. If you're looking for a spot to park your rig for the night, you can't get too picky around these parts. Most campers here are on their way to or from Sequoia and Kings Canyon National Parks. The swimming pool is a great bonus during the summer. Grassy shaded sites are available. Golf and tennis are nearby. Note that a few of the sites are occupied by monthly renters.

Campsites, facilities: There are 48 pull-through sites with full or partial hookups (30 and 50 amps), 20 sites for tents or RVs with no hookups, 20 sites for tents only, and eight cabins. Restrooms with showers, seasonal heated swimming pool, laundry facilities, playground, recreation room, free Wi-Fi, dog walk, store, gift shop, dump station, and propane gas are available. Leashed pets are permitted, with certain restrictions.

Reservations, fees: Reservations are accepted at 800/562-0544. Sites are $25.75–39.75 per night, $5 per person per night for more than two people. Some credit cards accepted. Open year-round.

Directions: From Highway 99 near Visalia, take the Goshen Avenue exit and drive 0.2 mile to Betty Drive/County Road 332. Turn left and drive 0.5 mile to County Road 76. Turn left and drive 0.5 mile (becomes Avenue 308) to the campground.

Contact: Visalia-Fresno KOA, 559/651-0544, www.koa.com.

34 TRAVELER'S RV PARK

🚶 🏊 🏠 🎣 ♿ 🚐 ⛺

Scenic rating: 2

near Kettleman City

Map 9.4, page 526

Being stuck in Kings County looking for a place to park an RV is no picnic. Unless, that is, you are lucky enough to know about Traveler's RV Park. The spaces are wide open with long-distance views of the Sierra. It's the "only game in town." Visitors will find access to miles of open paths and roads for hiking or running. The restaurant is open 24 hours a day, and campers get a 10 percent discount. Some may remember this park as Kettleman City RV Park.

Campsites, facilities: There are 46 pull-through sites with full hookups (30 and 50 amps) for RVs up to 36 feet, and two tent sites. Picnic tables are provided. Restrooms with showers, coin laundry, playgrounds, swimming pool, dump station, dog run, tire and RV repair, and propane gas are available. A restaurant and snack bar are nearby. Leashed pets are permitted. Some facilities are wheelchair-accessible.

Reservations, fees: Reservations are accepted. Sites are $27–29 per night, $5 per night for each additional vehicle. Weekly and monthly rates available. Some credit cards accepted. Open year-round.

Directions: Drive on I-5 to the junction with Highway 41 (Kettleman Junction). Take Highway 41 north and drive 0.5 mile to Hubert Way. Turn left on Hubert Way and drive a short distance to Cyril Place. Turn right on Cyril Place and continue to the park entrance (30000 Cyril Place).

Contact: Traveler's RV Park, 559/386-0583.

35 SUN AND FUN RV PARK

Scenic rating: 2

near Tulare

Map 9.4, page 526

This RV park is just off Highway 99, exactly halfway between San Francisco and Los Angeles. Are you having fun yet? Anybody making the long drive up or down the state on Highway 99 will learn what a dry piece of life the San Joaquin Valley can seem in summer. That's why the swimming pool at this RV park can be a lifesaver. The park has a number of mature trees, providing an opportunity for shade. Note that most of the sites are filled with long-term renters, but a few spaces are reserved for overnight campers.

Campsites, facilities: There are 53 sites with full hookups (30 and 50 amps) for RVs of any length. No tents. Picnic tables and barbecues are provided at some sites. Restrooms with showers, drinking water, cable TV, modem access, dump station, playground, swimming pool, spa, coin laundry, dog runs, and a recreation room are available. Some facilities are wheelchair-accessible. A golf course, restaurant, and store are nearby. Leashed pets are permitted.

Reservations, fees: Reservations are accepted. Sites are $26 per night. Monthly rates available. Open year-round.

Directions: From Tulare, drive south on Highway 99 for three miles to the Avenue 200 exit. Take Avenue 200 west and drive a short distance to the park (1000 Avenue 200).

Contact: Sun and Fun RV Park, 559/686-5779.

36 COLONEL ALLENSWORTH STATE HISTORIC PARK

Scenic rating: 2

near Earlimart

Map 9.5, page 527

What you have here is the old town of Allensworth, which has been restored as a historical park dedicated to the African-American pioneers who founded it with Colonel Allen Allensworth. He was the highest-ranking army chaplain of his time. Allensworth is the sole town in California to be established, financed, and governed by African Americans. One museum is available at the school here and another is at the colonel's house with a 30-minute movie on the history of Allensworth. Tours are available by appointment. One frustrating element here is that railroad tracks run alongside the park and it can be disruptive. There can be other problems—very hot weather in the summer, and since it is an open area, the wind can blow dust and sand. Are we having fun yet? One nice touch is the addition of shade ramadas at some campsites. A history note: This small farming community was founded in 1908, but a drop in the water table led to its demise.

Campsites, facilities: There are 15 sites for tents or RVs up to 35 feet (no hookups). Picnic tables and fire grills are provided. Restrooms with flush toilets and coin showers, drinking water, dump station, a visitors center, and picnic area are available. A store and coin laundry are 12 miles away in Delano. Some facilities are wheelchair-accessible. Leashed pets are permitted.

Reservations, fees: Reservations are not accepted. Sites are $10 per night, and $5 per night for each additional vehicle. Open year-round.

Directions: From Fresno, drive south on Highway 99 about 60 miles to Earlimart and the Avenue 56 exit. Turn right (west) on Avenue 56 and drive seven miles to the Highway 43 turnoff. Turn left (south) on Highway 43 and drive two miles to Palmer Avenue. Turn right (and drive over the railroad tracks) to the park entrance.

Contact: Colonel Allensworth State Historic Park, 661/849-3433 or 661/634-3795, www .parks.ca.gov.

37 LOST HILLS RV PARK

Scenic rating: 2

near Kern National Wildlife Refuge

Map 9.5, page 527

The pickings can get slim around these parts when you're cruising on I-5, so if it's late, you'll likely be happy to find this camp (formerly known as Lost Hills KOA). The cabin that sleeps four is a nice plus. The nearby Kern National Wildlife Refuge, about a 15-minute drive away, offers a side-trip possibility. It's a waterfowl reserve that attracts ducks, geese, and other waterfowl in the fall and winter. An 18-hole golf course is also within 15 miles.

Campsites, facilities: There are 79 sites, all pull-through, with full hookups (30 and 50 amps) for RVs, nine sites for tents only, an overflow area with 20 sites for tents and self-contained RVs, and one cabin. Picnic tables are provided. Restrooms with showers, drinking water, swimming pool, coin laundry, store, modem access, and propane gas are available. Some facilities are wheelchair-accessible. Restaurants are nearby. Leashed pets are permitted, with certain restrictions.

Reservations, fees: Reservations are accepted at 661/797-2719. Sites are $28–31 per night, and $3 per person per night for more than two people. Some credit cards accepted. Open year-round.

Directions: Drive on I-5 to the junction with Highway 46 (41 miles south of Avenal near Lost Hills). Turn west on Highway 46 and drive a short distance to the park entrance on the south side of the road (near the Carl's Jr.).

Contact: Lost Hills RV Park, 661/797-2719.

38 BAKERSFIELD KOA

Scenic rating: 2

north of Bakersfield

Map 9.5, page 527

If you're stuck in the southern valley and the temperature makes you feel as if you're sitting in a cauldron, well, this spot provides a layover for the night near the town of Shafter. The closest golf course is eight miles away.

Campsites, facilities: There are 20 tent sites, 35 RV sites with full or partial hookups (30 and 50 amps), and two cabins. Picnic tables are provided. Restrooms with showers, drinking water, seasonal swimming pool, coin laundry, convenience store, dump station, and propane gas are available. Leashed pets are permitted. Some facilities are wheelchair-accessible.

Reservations, fees: Reservations are accepted at 800/562-1633. Sites are $28–35 per night, $2 per person per night for more than two people. Some credit cards accepted. Open year-round.

Directions: From Bakersfield, drive north on Highway 99 for 12 miles to the Shafter-Lerdo Highway exit. Take that exit and drive a mile west on Lerdo Highway to the park (5101 East Lerdo Highway in Shafter).

Contact: Bakersfield KOA, 661/399-3107, fax 661/399-8981, www.koa.com.

39 SELBY

Scenic rating: 6

at the Carrizo Plain National Monument, northeast of San Luis Obispo

Map 9.5, page 527

The Carrizo Plain is California's largest nature preserve, but because of its remote location, primitive setting, and lack of recreational lakes and streams, it remains largely unknown and is explored by few people. The feature attraction is to visit Soda Lake in the winter to see flocks of the endangered sandhill crane; the lake is a nesting area for these huge birds with seven-foot wingspans. Selby is a primitive camping area at the base of the Caliente Mountain Range, known for its scorching hot temperatures (hey, after all, "Caliente") during the summer. The top hiking destination in the region is Painted Rock, a 55-foot rock with Chumash pictographs. Other hiking trails are available.

Campsites, facilities: This is a primitive camping area with six designated sites for tents or RVs up to 25 feet (no hookups). Picnic tables, shade ramadas, and fire rings are provided. A chemical toilet is available. No drinking water is available. Garbage must be packed out. Nearest services are about 50 miles away. Leashed pets are permitted.

Reservations, fees: Reservations are not accepted. There is no fee for camping, but donations are encouraged. Open year-round.

Directions: From Bakersfield, drive west on Highway 58 for about 30 miles to McKittrick (where Highway 33 merges with Highway 58). Bear left on Highway 58/33, continuing through town, and drive west for approximately 10 miles to Seven-Mile Road. Turn west on Seven-Mile Road, and drive seven miles (six miles will be on gravel/dirt road) to Soda Lake Road. Turn left on Soda Lake Road and drive about six miles to the Selby camping area on your right.

Contact: Bureau of Land Management, Bakersfield Field Office, 661/391-6000, fax 661/391-6041.

40 KCL

Scenic rating: 6

at the Carrizo Plain National Monument, northeast of San Luis Obispo

Map 9.5, page 527

KCL is the name of the old ranch headquarters in the Carrizo, of which remains old broken-down outbuildings, a corral, and not much else. Note that the buildings are off-limits to visitors. At least there are some trees here (in comparison, there are none at nearby Selby camp). The Carrizo Plain is best known for providing a habitat for many rare species of plants, animals, and insects, in addition to furnishing the winter nesting sites at Soda Lake for the awesome migration of giant sandhill cranes. These birds are often spotted north of this area. This campground is popular with hunters and birders because of its easy access to Soda Lake Road for daily outings. Dispersed camping is allowed throughout the national monument.

Campsites, facilities: This is a primitive camping area with six sites for tents or RVs up to 25 feet (no hookups). Picnic tables and fire pits are provided. A pit toilet and corrals are available. No drinking water is available. Garbage must be packed out. The nearest services are about 50 miles away. Leashed pets are permitted.

Reservations, fees: Reservations are not accepted. There is no camping fee. Open year-round.

Directions: From Bakersfield, drive west on Highway 58 for about 30 miles to McKittrick (where Highway 33 merges with Highway 58). Bear left on Highway 58/33, continuing through town, and drive west for about 10 miles to Seven-Mile Road. Turn west on Seven-Mile Road, and drive seven miles (six miles will be on gravel/dirt road) to Soda Lake Road. Turn left on Soda Lake Road and drive 0.5 mile to the entrance of the Carrizo Plains National Monument. Continue about 15 miles to the KCL camping area on your right.

Contact: Bureau of Land Management, Bakersfield Field Office, 661/391-6000, fax 661/391-6041.

41 BUENA VISTA AQUATIC RECREATION AREA

Scenic rating: 6

near Bakersfield

Map 9.5, page 527

This is the showpiece of Kern County recreation. Buena Vista is actually two connected lakes fed by the West Side Canal: little Lake Evans to the west and larger Lake Webb to the east. Be certain to know the difference between the two: Lake Webb (875 acres) is open to all boating including personal watercraft, and fast boats towing skiers are a common sight in designated ski areas. The speed limit is 45 mph. Lake Evans (85 acres) is small, quiet, and has a strictly enforced 5-mph speed limit, an ideal lake for family water play and fishing. Swimming is prohibited at both lakes, but is allowed in the lagoons. Lake Webb is a catfish lake, while Lake Evans is stocked in season with trout, and also has bass, bluegill, catfish, and crappie. The elevation is 330 feet.

Campsites, facilities: There are 112 sites, some with full hookups (30 and 50 amps) for RVs or tents, and an overflow camping area. Picnic tables and fire grills are provided. Restrooms with flush toilets and showers, drinking water, playground, four boat ramps, store, dump station, and picnic shelters are available. Two swimming lagoons, marina, snack bar, fishing supplies, and groceries are available nearby. A PGA-rated golf course is two miles west. Some facilities are wheelchair accessible. Leashed pets are permitted.

Reservations, fees: Reservations are accepted at 661/868-7050 Monday through Friday. Sites are $26–39 per night, $7–15 per night for each additional vehicle, $4 per night per pet. Some credit cards accepted. Open year-round.

Directions: From I-5 just south of Bakersfield, take Highway 119 west and drive two miles to Highway 43. Turn south (left) on Highway 43 and drive two miles to the campground at road's end.

Contact: Buena Vista Aquatic Recreation Area, Kern County Parks, 661/868-7000, www.co.kern.ca.us/parks/index.htm; Buena Vista concession, 661/763-1770.

YOSEMITE AND MAMMOTH LAKES

COURTESY OF THE MAMMOTH LAKES VISITORS BUREAU

BEST CAMPGROUNDS

Some of nature's most perfect artwork and the most

profound natural phenomena imaginable have been created in Yosemite and the adjoining eastern Sierra near Mammoth Lakes.

Yosemite Valley is the world's greatest showpiece. It is also among the most highly visited and well-known destinations on earth. Many of the campgrounds listed in this section are within close driving proximity of Yosemite National Park. When it comes to cabin rentals in this region, the variety is extraordinary.

Anything in Yosemite, or in its sphere of influence, is going to be in high demand almost year-round, and the same is true near Mammoth Lakes.

Many family recreation opportunities exist at lake-based settings, including at Lake Alpine, Pinecrest Lake on the western slopes of the Sierra, and at June Lake, Silver Lake, Lake Mary, Twin Lakes, Convict Lake, and Rock Creek Lake on the eastern Sierra.

Of course, most visits to this region start with a tour of Yosemite Valley. It is framed by El Capitan, the Goliath of Yosemite, on one side and the three-spired Cathedral Rocks on the other. As you enter the valley, Bridalveil Falls comes to view, a perfect free fall over the south canyon rim, then across a meadow. To your left you'll see the two-tiered Yosemite Falls, and finally, Half Dome, the single most awesome piece of rock in the world.

The irony is that this is all most people ever see of the region, even though it represents but a fraction of the fantastic land of wonder, adventure, and unparalleled natural beauty. Though 24,000 people jam into five square miles of Yosemite Valley each summer day, the park is actually 90 percent wilderness. Other landmark areas you can reach by car include the Wawona Grove of Giant Sequoias, Tenaya Lake, Tuolumne Meadows, and Hetch Hetchy.

But that's still only scratching the surface. For those who hike, another world will open up: Yosemite has 318 lakes, dozens of pristine streams, the Grand Canyon of the Tuolumne River, Matterhorn Peak, Benson Lake (with the largest white-sand beach in the Sierra), and dozens of spectacular waterfalls.

If you explore beyond the park boundaries, the adventures just keep getting better. Over Tioga Pass, outside the park and just off Highway 120, are Tioga Lake, Ellery Lake, and Saddlebag Lake (10,087 feet), the latter of which is the highest lake in California accessible by car. To the east is Mono Lake and its weird tufa spires, which create a stark moonscape.

The nearby June Lake Loop and Mammoth Lakes area is a launch point to another orbit. Both have small lakes with on-site cabin rentals, excellent fishing, great hiking and mountain biking for all levels, and phenomenal skiing and winter sports. In addition, just east of Mammoth Lakes airport is a series of hot springs, including a famous spot on Hot Creek, something of a legend in these parts.

More hiking and fishing opportunities abound at Devils Postpile National Monument, where you can hike to Rainbow Falls. At nearby Agnew Meadows, you'll find a trail that hugs the pristine San Joaquin River up to Thousand Island Lake and leads to the beautiful view from Banner and Ritter Peaks in the Ansel Adams Wilderness. Horseback riding is also popular in this area, with pack trips available from Reds Meadow.

If you didn't already know, many of California's best lakes for a chance to catch giant rainbow and brown trout are in this region. They include Bridgeport Reservoir, Twin Lakes, June Lake, Convict Lake, and Crowley Lake in the eastern Sierra.

This region has it all: beauty, variety, and a chance at the hike or fish of a lifetime. There is nothing else like it.

YOSEMITE AND MAMMOTH LAKES

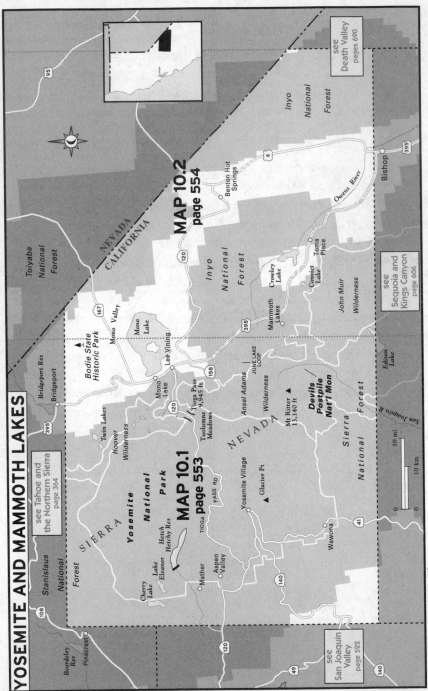

see Tahoe and the Northern Sierra page 364

see Death Valley pages 690

see Sequoia and Kings Canyon page 606

see San Joaquin Valley page 592

MAP 10.2 page 554

MAP 10.1 page 553

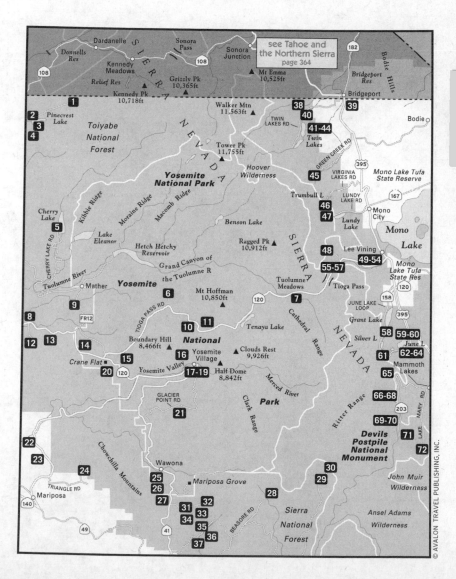

Map 10.2

Campgrounds 73-100
Pages 589-601

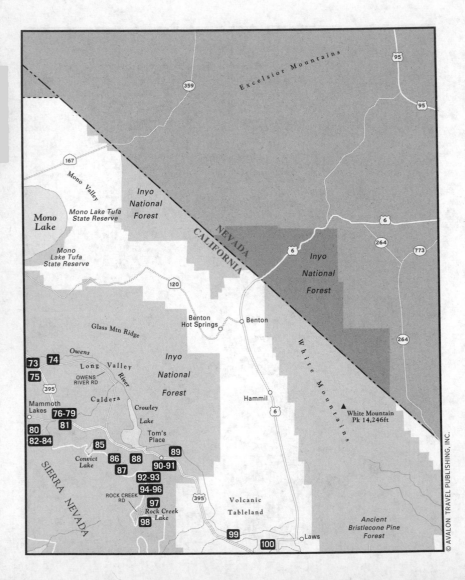

© AVALON TRAVEL PUBLISHING, INC.

1 HERRING RESERVOIR

Scenic rating: 8

at Herring Lake in Stanislaus National Forest

Map 10.1, page 553

This is a pretty little spot, a rustic campground set near Herring Creek as it enters Herring Lake, set at an elevation of 7,350 feet. There is no boat ramp, but hand-launched boats, such as canoes, rafts, prams, and float tubes, are ideal. The lake is shallow, with fair fishing for brook trout and rainbow trout. No horses are permitted here.

Campsites, facilities: There are 24 sites for tents or RVs up to 22 feet (no hookups). Fire rings are provided. Vault toilets are available. No drinking water is available. Garbage must be packed out. Leashed pets are permitted.

Reservations, fees: Reservations are not accepted. There is no camping fee, although donations are accepted. Open May through October, weather permitting.

Directions: From Sonora, drive east on Highway 108 for about 25 miles to Strawberry. Continue past Strawberry for two miles to Herring Creek Road/Forest Road 4N12. Turn right and drive seven miles to Hamill Canyon Road/Forest Road 4N12. Bear right and drive 0.25 mile to Herring Creek Reservoir. Continue another 0.25 mile (cross the bridge) and turn right and drive to the campground. The road is rough and not recommended for RVs or low-clearance vehicles.

Contact: Stanislaus National Forest, Summit Ranger District, 209/965-3434, fax 209/965-3372.

2 PINECREST

Scenic rating: 7

near Pinecrest Lake in Stanislaus National Forest

Map 10.1, page 553

This monster-sized Forest Service camp is set near Pinecrest Lake. A launch ramp is available, and a 20-mph speed limit is enforced on the lake. A trail circles the lake and also branches off to nearby Catfish Lake. In early summer, there is good fishing for stocked rainbow trout. The elevation is 5,600 feet. Winter camping is allowed near the Pinecrest Day-Use Area. (For details about Pinecrest Lake, see the listing for *Meadowview* in this chapter.)

Campsites, facilities: There are 200 sites for tents or RVs up to 40 feet (no hookups). Picnic tables and fire grills are provided. Drinking water and toilets are available. Garbage must be packed out. A grocery store, coin laundry, coin showers, boat ramp, and propane gas are nearby at Pinecrest Lake Resort. Some facilities are wheelchair-accessible. Leashed pets are permitted.

Reservations, fees: Reservations are required ($9 reservation fee) from mid-May to mid-September at 877/444-6777 or www.ReserveUSA.com. Sites are $19 per night. Open April through October, weather permitting.

Directions: From Sonora, drive east on Highway 108 for about 30 miles to the signed turn for Pinecrest Lake on the right. Turn right and drive to the access road (0.7 mile past the turnoff signed Pinecrest) for the campground. Turn right and drive a short distance to the campground.

Contact: Stanislaus National Forest, Summit Ranger District, 209/965-3434, fax 209/965-3372.

3 PIONEER TRAIL GROUP CAMP

Scenic rating: 8

near Pinecrest Lake in Stanislaus National Forest

Map 10.1, page 553

If you're going to Pinecrest Lake with a Scout troop, this is the spot, since it is set up specifically for groups. You get beautiful creek and lake views, with the camp set at an elevation of 5,700 feet. (For recreation information, see the next entry, *Meadowview*.)

Campsites, facilities: There are three group areas for tents or RVs up to 22 feet (no hookups) that can accommodate 50–100 people each. Picnic tables and fire grills are provided. Drinking water and vault toilets are available. Garbage must be packed out. A grocery store, coin laundry, boat ramp, coin showers, and propane gas are nearby. Some facilities are wheelchair-accessible. Leashed pets are permitted.

Reservations, fees: Reservations are required ($9 reservation fee) at 877/444-6777 or www.ReserveUSA.com. Sites are $55–70 per night. Open May through October, weather permitting.

Directions: From Sonora, drive east on Highway 108 for about 30 miles to the signed road for Pinecrest Lake. Turn right at the sign and drive 0.5 mile to the signed road for Pinecrest/Dodge Ridge Road. Turn right and drive about a mile to the campground entrance on the left.

Contact: Stanislaus National Forest, Summit Ranger District, 209/965-3434, fax 209/965-3372.

🄴 MEADOWVIEW

🚶 🚴 ⛴ 🎣 🛶 🐕 ♿ 🚐 ⛺

Scenic rating: 7

near Pinecrest Lake in Stanislaus National Forest

Map 10.1, page 553

No secret here, folks. This camp is one mile from Pinecrest Lake, a popular weekend vacation area (and there's a trail that connects the camp with the town). Pinecrest Lake is set at 5,621 feet, covers 300 acres and 2.5 miles of shoreline, has a sandy swimming beach, and has a 20-mph speed limit for boaters. The lake is the centerpiece of a fully developed family vacation area; boat rentals at the small marina are a big bonus. The lake is stocked with rainbow trout and also has a small resident population of brown trout. The easy hike around the lake is a popular walk. If you want something more ambitious, there is a cutoff on the north side of the lake that is routed one mile up to little Catfish Lake, which in reality is a set of shallow ponds surrounded by old-growth forest. The Dodge Ridge Ski Area is nearby, with many privately owned cabins in the area.

Campsites, facilities: There are 100 sites for tents or RVs up to 22 feet (no hookups). Picnic tables and fire grills are provided. Drinking water and flush toilets are available. A grocery store, coin laundry, boat ramp, boat rentals, coin showers, and propane gas are nearby. Garbage must be packed out. Some facilities are wheelchair-accessible. Leashed pets are permitted.

Reservations, fees: Reservations are not accepted. Sites are $14 per night. Open May through September, weather permitting.

Directions: From Sonora, drive east on Highway 108 for about 30 miles to the signed road for Pinecrest Lake. Turn right at the sign and drive 0.5 mile to Pinecrest/Dodge Ridge Road. Turn right and drive about 200 yards to the campground entrance on the right side of the road.

Contact: Stanislaus National Forest, Summit Ranger District, 209/965-3434, fax 209/965-3372.

🄵 CHERRY VALLEY AND BOAT-IN

🚶 ⛴ 🎣 🛶 🐕 🚐 ⛺

Scenic rating: 8

on Cherry Lake in Stanislaus National Forest

Map 10.1, page 553

Cherry Lake is a mountain lake surrounded by national forest at 4,700 feet in elevation, just outside the western boundary of Yosemite National Park. It is much larger than most people anticipate and provides much better trout fishing than anything in Yosemite. The camp is on the southwest shore of the lake, a very pretty spot, about a mile ride to the boat launch on the west side of the Cherry

Valley Dam. A bonus is that dispersed boat-in camping is allowed on the lake's east side. All water sports are allowed, yet because it takes a considerable drive to reach the lake, you won't find nearly the waterskiing traffic as at other regional lakes. Water levels can fluctuate here. The lake is bordered to the east by Kibbie Ridge; just on the other side are Yosemite Park and Lake Eleanor. Insider's tip: During periods of campfire restrictions, which is often most of the summer in this national forest, this campground is the only one in the area where campfires are permitted. A fire permit is required from the Forest Service.

Campsites, facilities: There are 45 sites for tents or RVs up to 22 feet (no hookups). Primitive boat-in camping is permitted on the lake's east side. Picnic tables and fire grills are provided. Drinking water and vault toilets are available. A boat ramp is nearby. Leashed pets are permitted.

Reservations, fees: Reservations are not accepted. Sites are $15 per night, $30 per night for double sites. There is no camping fee for boat-in sites. Open April through October, weather permitting.

Directions: From Groveland, drive east on Highway 120 for about 15 miles to Forest Road 1N07/Cherry Lake Road. Turn left and drive 20 miles to Cottonwood Road/Forest Road 1N04. Turn left and drive one mile to the campground entrance road. Turn right and drive one mile to the campground.

Contact: Stanislaus National Forest, Groveland Ranger District, 209/962-7825, fax 209/962-7412.

area and beyond, or for overnight backpacking trips. The day hike to Lukens Lake is an easy two-mile trip, the payoff being this pretty little alpine lake set amid a meadow, pines, and granite. Just about everybody who camps at White Wolf makes the trip. Backpackers (wilderness permit required) can make the overnight trip into the Ten Lakes Basin, set below Grand Mountain and Colby Mountain. Bears are common at this camp, and campers are required to secure food in the bearproof lockers. The elevation is 8,000 feet.

Campsites, facilities: There are 74 sites for tents or RVs up to 27 feet (no hookups). Tent cabins are also available. Picnic tables, food lockers, and fire grills are provided. Drinking water and flush toilets are available. Evening ranger programs are occasionally available. A small store with a walk-up window and limited items is nearby. Leashed pets are permitted in the campground, but not on trails.

Reservations, fees: Reservations are not accepted. Sites are $14 per night, plus $20 park entrance fee per vehicle. Open July to early September, weather permitting.

Directions: From Merced, drive east on Highway 140 to the Arch Rock entrance station. Continue east to the Big Oak Flat Road junction (0.5 mile before entering Yosemite Valley). Turn left and drive 14 miles to Tioga Road. Turn right and drive 15 miles to White Wolf Road on the left. Turn left and drive a mile to the campground entrance road on the right.

Contact: Yosemite National Park, 209/372-0200, for an automated menu of recorded information, www.nps.gov/yose.

6 WHITE WOLF

🚶 🛶 🐾 🚙 ⛺

Scenic rating: 8

in Yosemite National Park

Map 10.1, page 553

This is one of Yosemite National Park's prime mountain camps for people who like to hike, either for great day hikes in the immediate

7 TUOLUMNE MEADOWS

🚶 🛶 🐾 🚙 ⛺

Scenic rating: 8

in Yosemite National Park

Map 10.1, page 553   **BEST (**

This is Yosemite's biggest camp, and for the variety of nearby adventures, it might also be the best. It is set in the high country, at

8,600 feet, and can be used as a base camp for fishing, hiking, and horseback riding, or as a start-up point for a backpacking trip (wilderness permits required). This is one of the top trailheads in North America. There are two outstanding and easy day hikes from here, one heading north on the Pacific Crest Trail for the near-level walk to Tuolumne Falls and Glen Aulin, the other heading south up Lyell Fork (toward Donohue Pass), with good fishing for small brook trout. With a backpack (wilderness permit required), either route can be extended for as long as desired into remote and beautiful country. The campground is huge, and neighbors are guaranteed, but it is well wooded and feels somewhat secluded even with all the RVs and tents. There are lots of food-raiding bears in the area, so use of the food lockers is required.

Campsites, facilities: There are 304 sites for tents or RVs up to 35 feet (no hookups), four horse camps, and seven group sites that can accommodate 30 people each. There are also an additional 25 hike-in sites available for backpackers (no parking is available for backpacker campsites, often reserved for those hiking the Pacific Crest Trail, for which a wilderness permit is required). Picnic tables, fire grills, and food lockers are provided. Drinking water, flush toilets, and dump station are available. Showers and groceries are nearby. Leashed pets are permitted, except in group sites, horse camps, and backpacker sites.

Reservations, fees: Reservations are accepted at 800/436-PARK (800/436-7275) or http://reservations.nps.gov; half of the sites are available through reservations; the other half are first-come, first-served. Sites are $20 per night for individual sites, $5 per night per person for walk-in (backpack) sites, $25 per night for horse camp, and $40 per night for group sites, plus a $20 per vehicle park entrance fee. Open July to mid-September, weather permitting.

Directions: From Merced, drive east on Highway 140 to the Arch Rock entrance station. Continue east to the Big Oak Flat Road junction (0.5 mile before entering Yosemite Valley).

Turn left and drive 14 miles to Tioga Road. Turn right and drive 46 miles to the campground on the right side of the road.

From just south of Lee Vining at the junction of U.S. 395 and Highway 120, turn west and drive to the Tioga Pass entrance station for Yosemite National Park. Continue for about eight miles to the campground entrance on the left.

Contact: Yosemite National Park, 209/372-0200, for an automated menu of recorded information, www.nps.gov/yose.

❽ SWEETWATER

Scenic rating: 4

near the South Fork of the Tuolumne River in Stanislaus National Forest

Map 10.1, page 553

This camp is set at 3,000 feet, near the South Fork Tuolumne River, one of several camps along Highway 120 that provide a safety valve for campers who can't find space in Yosemite National Park to the east. Nearby, on the North Fork of the Tuolumne River, is a popular swimming area known as Rainbow Pools, with a waterfall and series of pools created by the river. Whitewater rafting and kayaking are also available a few miles from this camp; a Forest Service permit is required.

Campsites, facilities: There are 12 sites for tents or RVs up to 22 feet (no hookups). Picnic tables and fire grills are provided. Drinking water and vault toilets are available. Leashed pets are permitted.

Reservations, fees: Reservations are not accepted. Sites are $15 per night. Open April through October, weather permitting.

Directions: From Groveland, drive east on Highway 120 for about 15 miles (five miles past the Groveland District Office) to the campground on the left side of the road.

Contact: Stanislaus National Forest, Groveland Ranger District, 209/962-7825, fax 209/962-7412.

9 DIMOND "O"

Scenic rating: 7

in Stanislaus National Forest

Map 10.1, page 553

Dimond "O" is set at 4,400 feet in elevation on the eastern side of Stanislaus National Forest—just two miles from the western border of Yosemite National Park.

Campsites, facilities: There are 36 sites for tents or RVs up to 22 feet (no hookups). Picnic tables and fire grills are provided. Drinking water and vault toilets are available. Some facilities are wheelchair-accessible. Leashed pets are permitted.

Reservations, fees: Reservations are accepted ($9 reservation fee) at 877/444-6777 or www.ReserveUSA.com. Sites are $16 per night. Open April through October, weather permitting.

Directions: From Groveland, drive east on Highway 120 for 25 miles to Evergreen Road/ Forest Road 12. Turn left on Evergreen Road and drive six miles to the campground.

Contact: Stanislaus National Forest, Groveland Ranger District, 209/962-7825, fax 209/962-7412.

10 YOSEMITE CREEK

Scenic rating: 9

on Yosemite Creek in Yosemite National Park

Map 10.1, page 553   BEST (

This is the most remote drive-to camp in Yosemite National Park, a great alternative to camping in the valley or at Tuolumne Meadows, and the rough, curvy access road keeps many visitors away. It is set along Yosemite Creek at 7,659 feet, with poor trout fishing but a trailhead for a spectacular hike. If you arrange a shuttle ride, you can make a great one-way trip down to the north side of the Yosemite Canyon rim, skirting past the top of Yosemite Falls (a side trip to Yosemite Point

is a must!), then tackling the unbelievable descent into the valley, emerging at Camp 4 Walk-In. Note: The narrow entrance road is a remnant of "Old Tioga Road."

Campsites, facilities: There are 40 sites with no hookups for tents or small RVs. Picnic tables, food lockers (mandatory use), and fire grills are provided. Vault toilets are available. No drinking water is available. Leashed pets are permitted.

Reservations, fees: Reservations are not accepted. Sites are $10 per night, plus $20 park entrance fee per vehicle. A 14-day stay limit is enforced. Open July to early September, weather permitting.

Directions: From Merced, drive east on Highway 140 to the Arch Rock entrance station. Continue east to the Big Oak Flat Road junction (0.5 mile before entering Yosemite Valley). Turn left and drive 14 miles to Tioga Road. Turn right and drive about 30 miles (just beyond the White Wolf turnoff on the left) to Yosemite Creek Campground Road on the right. Turn right (RVs over 24 feet and trailers are not recommended) and drive five miles to the campground at the end of the road.

Contact: Yosemite National Park, 209/372-0200, for an automated menu of recorded information, www.nps.gov/yose.

11 PORCUPINE FLAT

Scenic rating: 6

near Yosemite Creek in Yosemite National Park

Map 10.1, page 553

Porcupine Flat, set at 8,100 feet, is southwest of Mount Hoffman, one of the prominent nearby peaks along Tioga Road in Yosemite National Park. The trailhead for a hike to May Lake, set just below Mount Hoffman, is about five miles away on a signed turnoff on the north side of the road. There are several little peaks above the lake where hikers can gain great views, including one of the back side of Half Dome.

Campsites, facilities: There are 52 sites for tents or RVs up to 35 feet (no hookups). There is limited RV space. Picnic tables, fire rings, and food lockers (mandatory use) are provided. Pit toilets are available. No drinking water is available. No pets are allowed.

Reservations, fees: Reservations are not accepted. Sites are $10 per night, plus $20 park entrance fee per vehicle. Open July to mid-October, weather permitting.

Directions: From Merced, drive east on Highway 140 to the Arch Rock entrance station. Continue east to the Big Oak Flat Road junction (0.5 mile before entering Yosemite Valley). Turn left and drive 14 miles to Tioga Road. Turn right and drive about 25 miles to the campground on the left side of the road (16 miles west from Tuolumne Meadows).

Contact: Yosemite National Park, 209/372-0200, for an automated menu of recorded information, www.nps.gov/yose.

12 MOORE CREEK GROUP CAMP
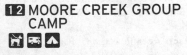

Scenic rating: 6

in Stanislaus National Forest

Map 10.1, page 553

This group camp is set at 3,100 feet, just past where the Sierra alpine zone takes over from foothill oak woodlands. It is near the access route (Highway 120) to the Crane Flat entrance station of Yosemite National Park.

Campsites, facilities: There is one group site for tents or RVs up to 30 feet (no hookups) that can accommodate up to 40 people. Picnic tables and fire grills are provided. No drinking water is available. No toilet is available and campers are required to bring a portable toilet with them. Garbage must be packed out. Leashed pets are permitted.

Reservations, fees: Reservations are required at Groveland Ranger District at 209/962-7825. There is no camping fee. Open year-round.

Directions: From Groveland, drive east on Highway 120 for about 12 miles to Buck Meadows Road. Turn right and drive 1.5 miles (the road becomes Forest Road 2S05) to the campground on the right.

Contact: Stanislaus National Forest, Groveland Ranger District, 209/962-7825, fax 209/962-7412.

13 YOSEMITE LAKES

Scenic rating: 6

on Tuolumne River at Groveland

Map 10.1, page 553

This is a 400-acre park set at 3,600 feet along the South Fork Tuolumne River in the Sierra foothills near Groveland. Its proximity to Yosemite National Park, just five miles from the west entrance station, make it ideal for many. The park is an affiliate of Thousand Trails, whose facilities usually are open only to members, but in this case, it is open to the general public on a limited basis. It is a family-oriented park with a large variety of recreation options and seasonal organized activities. Fishing and swimming are popular, and the river is stocked with trout. A plus is 24-hour security.

Campsites, facilities: There are 20 sites with full hookups (30 amps) for RVs of any length and 25 sites for tents available to the public (more sites available to Thousand Trails members only), and cabins, yurts, and a hostel. Picnic tables and fire rings are provided. Restrooms, drinking water, showers, flush toilets, fish-cleaning station, and coin laundry are available. A store, gas station, propane, and firewood are available. Kayak rentals, pedalboats, inner tubes, and bicycles are available for rent. Leashed pets are permitted.

Reservations, fees: Reservations are accepted at 800/533-1001. Sites are $37–39.50 per night for RVs, $29.50–32 per night for tents.

Some credit cards accepted. Open year-round, weather permitting.

Directions: Drive east on Highway 120 to Groveland. From Groveland, continue east for 18 miles to the entrance road (signed) for Yosemite Lakes on the right. Turn right and drive a short distance to the park.

Contact: Yosemite Lakes, 209/962-0121, www.stayatyosemite.com.

14 HODGDON MEADOW
🏕️ 🚐 ⛺

Scenic rating: 7

in Yosemite National Park

Map 10.1, page 553

Hodgdon Meadow is on the outskirts of Yosemite, just inside the park's borders at the Big Oak Flat (Highway 120) entrance station, at 4,900 feet in elevation. It is near a small feeder creek to the South Fork Tuolumne River. It is about a 20-minute drive on Highway 120 to a major junction, where a left turn takes you on Tioga Road and to Yosemite's high country, including Tuolumne Meadows, and where staying on Big Flat Road routes you toward Yosemite Valley (25 miles from the camp). Because of the presence of bears, use of food lockers is required.

Campsites, facilities: There are 105 sites for tents or RVs up to 24 feet (no hookups) and four group sites for 13–30 people each. Picnic tables, fire rings, and food lockers are provided. Drinking water and flush toilets are available. Leashed pets are permitted in the campground, but not in group camps or on trails.

Reservations, fees: Reservations are accepted at 800/436-PARK (800/436-7275) or http://reservations.nps.gov, and are required April to mid-October. Sites are $20 per night May through October, $14 remainder of year, group campsite $40 per night, plus $20 park entrance fee per vehicle. Open year-round, except for group sites.

Directions: From Groveland, drive east on Highway 120 to the Big Oak Flat entrance station for Yosemite National Park. Just after passing the entrance station, turn left and drive a short distance to the campground on the right.

Contact: Yosemite National Park, 209/372-0200, for an automated menu of recorded information, www.nps.gov/yose.

15 TAMARACK FLAT
🚶 🚐 ⛺

Scenic rating: 7

on Tamarack Creek in Yosemite National Park

Map 10.1, page 553

The road to this campground looks something like the surface of the moon. Then you arrive and find one of the few primitive drive-to camps in Yosemite National Park, at 6,300 feet in elevation. From the trailhead at camp, you can link up with El Capitan Trail and then hike across Ribbon Meadow on up to the north valley rim at El Capitan, 7,569 feet in elevation. This is the largest single piece of granite in the world, and standing atop it for both the sensation and the divine view is a breathtaking experience. From camp, Yosemite Valley is 23 miles away. Note that the use of food lockers is now required.

Campsites, facilities: There are 52 sites for tents or RVs up to 24 feet (no hookups). Note that the access road is difficult. Picnic tables, food lockers, and fire grills are provided. Vault toilets are available. No drinking water is available. No pets are allowed.

Reservations, fees: Reservations are not accepted. Sites are $10 per night, plus $20 park entrance fee per vehicle. Open June to early September.

Directions: From Merced, drive east on Highway 140 to the Arch Rock entrance station. Continue east to the Big Oak Flat Road junction (0.5 mile before entering Yosemite Valley). Turn left and drive 14 miles to Tioga Road. Turn right on Tioga Road and drive three miles to the campground entrance on the right side of the road. Turn right and drive 2.5 miles to the campground at the end of the road. Trailers and RVs are not advised.

Contact: Yosemite National Park, 209/372-0200, for an automated menu of recorded information, www.nps.gov/yose.

16 CAMP 4

Scenic rating: 8

in Yosemite Valley in Yosemite National Park

Map 10.1, page 553

The concept at Camp 4 was to provide a climber's bivouac near the base of El Capitan, and so it is. It has also worked as a walk-in alternative to drive-in camps that sometimes resemble combat zones. The sites here are jammed together, and six people will be placed in your site, whether you know them or not. Regardless, the camp is in a great location, within walking distance of Yosemite Falls. It has a view of Leidig Meadow and the southern valley rim, with Sentinel Rock directly across the valley. A trail is routed from camp to Lower Yosemite Fall. In addition, the trailhead for Yosemite Falls Trail is a short distance away, a terrible, butt-kicking climb up Columbia Rock to the rim adjacent to the top of the falls, but providing one of the most incredible views in all the world. Insider's note: After originally being named Camp 4, the park once renamed this campground as "Sunnyside Walk-In." The name was switched back to the original, because climbers never stopped calling it Camp 4.

Campsites, facilities: There are 35 walk-in tent sites. Six people are placed in each campsite, regardless of the number of people in each party. Picnic tables, fire pits, and food lockers (mandatory use) are provided. Drinking water and flush toilets are available. A parking area, showers, groceries, and a coin laundry are nearby. No pets are allowed.

Reservations, fees: Reservations are not accepted. Sites are $5 per person per night, plus $20 park entrance fee per vehicle. There

is a seven-day limit during the summer. Open year-round.

Directions: From Merced, drive east on Highway 140 to the Arch Rock entrance station. Continue east to the Big Oak Flat Road junction (0.5 mile before entering Yosemite Valley). Continue into Yosemite Valley, and drive past the chapel to a stop sign. Turn left, cross Sentinel Bridge, and drive one mile to another stop sign. Continue 1.5 miles and look for the large sign marking the parking area for Camp 4 Walk-In on the right (near the base of El Capitan).

Contact: Yosemite National Park, 209/372-0200, for an automated menu of recorded information, www.nps.gov/yose.

17 LOWER PINES

Scenic rating: 9

in Yosemite Valley in Yosemite National Park

Map 10.1, page 553

Lower Pines sits right along the Merced River, quite pretty, in the center of Yosemite Valley. Of course, the tents and RVs are jammed in quite close together. Within walking distance is the trail to Mirror Lake (a zoo on parade), as well as the trailhead at Happy Isles for the hike up to Vernal Fall and Nevada Fall. The park's shuttle bus picks up riders near the camp entrance.

Campsites, facilities: There are 60 sites for tents or RVs up to 40 feet, one double site for tents or RVs up to 40 feet and two group camps. No hookups. Fire rings, picnic tables, and food lockers (mandatory use) are provided. Drinking water and flush toilets are available. A grocery store, coin laundry, propane gas, recycling center, and horse and bike rentals are available nearby. Leashed pets are allowed.

Reservations, fees: Reservations are required at 800/436-PARK (800/436-7275) or http://reservations.nps.gov. Sites are $20 per night, $30 per night for double or group sites, plus $20 park entrance fee per vehicle.

There is a seven-day limit during the summer. Open late March through October, weather permitting.

Directions: From Merced, drive east on Highway 140 to the Arch Rock entrance station. Continue east to the Big Oak Flat Road junction (0.5 mile before entering Yosemite Valley). Continue into Yosemite Valley, drive past Curry Village (on the right) to the campground entrance on the left side of the road (just before Clarks Bridge).

Contact: Yosemite National Park, 209/372-0200, for an automated menu of recorded information, www.nps.gov/yose.

18 UPPER PINES

Scenic rating: 9

in Yosemite Valley in Yosemite National Park

Map 10.1, page 553

Of the campgrounds in Yosemite Valley, Upper Pines is the closest trailhead to paradise, providing you can get a campsite at the far south end of the camp. From here it is a short walk to Happy Isles trailhead and with it the chance to hike to Vernal Fall on Mist Trail (steep), or beyond to Nevada Fall (very steep) at the foot of Liberty Cap. But crowded this camp is, and you'd better expect it. People come from all over the world to camp here. Sometimes it appears as if they are from other worlds as well. The elevation is 4,000 feet.

Campsites, facilities: There are 238 sites for tents or RVs up to 35 feet (no hookups), 39 sites for tents or RVs up to 35 feet with partial hookups (30 amps), and 50 walk-in sites. Fire rings, picnic tables, and food lockers (mandatory use) are provided. Drinking water, flush toilets, and dump station are available. A grocery store, coin laundry, propane gas, recycling center, and horse and bike rentals are available nearby. Leashed pets are permitted in the campgrounds, but not on trails.

Reservations, fees: Reservations are required at 800/436-PARK (800/436-7275) or

http://reservations.nps.gov. Sites are $20 per night, plus $20 park entrance fee per vehicle. There is a seven-day limit during the summer. Open year-round.

Directions: From Merced, drive east on Highway 140 to the Arch Rock entrance station. Continue east to the Big Oak Flat Road junction (0.5 mile before entering Yosemite Valley). Continue into Yosemite Valley, drive past Curry Village (on the right) to the campground entrance on the right side of the road (just before Clarks Bridge).

Contact: Yosemite National Park, 209/372-0200, for an automated menu of recorded information, www.nps.gov/yose.

19 NORTH PINES

Scenic rating: 9

in Yosemite Valley in Yosemite National Park

Map 10.1, page 553

North Pines is set along the Merced River. A trail out of camp heads east and links with the paved road/trail to Mirror Lake, a virtual parade of people. If you continue hiking past Mirror Lake you will get astounding views of Half Dome and then leave the masses behind as you enter Tenaya Canyon. The elevation is 4,000 feet.

Campsites, facilities: There are 81 sites for tents or RVs up to 40 feet (no hookups). Picnic tables, fire grills, and food lockers (mandatory use) are provided. Drinking water and flush toilets are available. A grocery store, coin laundry, recycling center, propane gas, and horse and bike rentals are available nearby. Leashed pets are allowed.

Reservations, fees: Reservations are required at 800/436-PARK (800/436-7275) or http://reservations.nps.gov. Sites are $20 per night, plus $20 park entrance fee per vehicle. Open April through September, weather permitting.

Directions: From Merced, drive east on Highway 140 to the Arch Rock entrance station.

Continue east to the Big Oak Flat Road junction (0.5 mile before entering Yosemite Valley). Continue into Yosemite Valley, drive past Curry Village (on the right), continue past Upper and Lower Pines Campgrounds, and drive over Clarks Bridge to a junction at the horse stables. Turn left at the horse stables and drive a short distance to the campground on the right.

Contact: Yosemite National Park, 209/372-0200, for an automated menu of recorded information, www.nps.gov/yose.

20 CRANE FLAT

Scenic rating: 6

near Tuolumne Grove of Big Trees in Yosemite National Park

Map 10.1, page 553

Crane Flat is within a five-minute drive of the Tuolumne Grove of Big Trees and to the Merced Grove to the nearby west. This is the feature attraction in this part of Yosemite National Park, set near the western border in close proximity to the Big Oak Flat Entrance Station (Highway 120). The elevation is 6,200 feet. Yosemite Valley is about a 25-minute drive away.

Campsites, facilities: There are 166 sites for tents or RVs up to 35 feet (no hookups). Picnic tables, fire rings, and food lockers are provided. Drinking water and flush toilets are available. Groceries, propane gas, and a gas station are nearby. Leashed pets are allowed in the campground.

Reservations, fees: Reservations are required at 800/436-PARK (800/436-7275) or http://reservations.nps.gov. Sites are $20 per night, plus $20 park entrance fee per vehicle. Open June through September, weather permitting.

Directions: From Groveland, drive east on Highway 120 to the Big Oak Flat entrance station for Yosemite National Park. After passing through the entrance station, drive about 10 miles to the campground entrance road on the right. Turn right and drive 0.5 mile to the campground.

Contact: Yosemite National Park, 209/372-0200, for an automated menu of recorded information, www.nps.gov/yose.

21 BRIDALVEIL CREEK AND EQUESTRIAN AND GROUP CAMP

Scenic rating: 10

near Glacier Point in Yosemite National Park

Map 10.1, page 553   **BEST (**

There may be no better view in the world than the one from Glacier Point, looking down into Yosemite Valley, where Half Dome stands like nature's perfect sculpture. Then there are the perfect views of Yosemite Falls, Nevada Fall, Vernal Fall, and several hundred square miles of Yosemite's wilderness backcountry. This is the closest camp to Glacier Point's drive-to vantage point, but it is also the closest camp to the best day hikes in the entire park. Along Glacier Point Road are trailheads to Sentinel Dome (incredible view of Yosemite Falls) and Taft Point (breathtaking drop, incredible view of El Capitan), and McGurk Meadow (one of the most pristine spots on Earth). At 7,200 feet, the camp is more than 3,000 feet higher than Yosemite Valley. A good day hike out of camp leads you to Ostrander Lake, just below Horse Ridge.

Campsites, facilities: There are 110 sites for tents or RVs up to 35 feet (no hookups), three equestrian sites, and two group sites for 13–30 people each. Picnic tables, fire grills, and food lockers (mandatory use) are provided. Drinking water and flush toilets are available. Leashed pets are permitted, except in group sites.

Reservations, fees: Reservations are not accepted for individual sites, but they are required for equestrian sites and group sites at 800/436-PARK (800/436-7275) or http://reservations.nps.gov. Sites are $14 per night, $25

per night for equestrian site, $40 per night for group site, plus $20 park entrance fee per vehicle. A 14-day stay limit is enforced. Open July to early September, weather permitting. **Directions:** From Merced, drive east on Highway 140 to the Arch Rock entrance station. Continue east (past Big Oak Flat Road junction) to the junction with Wawona Road/ Highway 41 (just before Yosemite Valley). Turn right on Highway 41/Wawona Road and drive about 10 miles to Glacier Point Road. Turn left on Glacier Point Road and drive about five miles (a few miles past Badger Pass Ski Area) to Peregoy Meadow and the campground access road on the right. Turn right and drive a short distance to the campground.
Contact: Yosemite National Park, 209/372-0200, for an automated menu of recorded information, www.nps.gov/yose.

22 MERCED RECREATION AREA
🚶 🚴 🏊 ⛵ 🎣 🐕 ♿ 🚐 ⛺

Scenic rating: 8
on the Merced River east of Briceburg

Map 10.1, page 553   BEST (

What a spot: The campsites are along one of the prettiest sections of the Merced River, where you can enjoy great hiking, swimming, rafting, kayaking, and fishing, all on the same day. There are three campgrounds here: McCabe Flat, Willow Placer, and Railroad Flat. The access road out of camp leads downstream to the Yosemite Railroad Grade, which has been converted into a great trail. One of the best wildflower blooms anywhere in the Sierra foothills is found near here at Red Hills (just outside Chinese Camp), best usually in April. If you don't mind the cold water, swimming in the Merced River's pools can provide relief from summer heat. Evening fly-fishing is good in many of the same spots through July. But the true attraction on the Merced River is rafting and kayaking. An extraordinarily long stretch of river, 29 miles, can be run from the put-in at Red Bud Day-Use Area to the takeout at Bagby. A number of whitewater guide companies work this stretch of river.
Campsites, facilities: There are 21 walk-in tent sites and nine sites for tents or RVs up to 18 feet (no hookups). Picnic tables and fire grills are provided. Vault and pit toilets are available. No drinking water is available at the campsites (drinking water is available across from the Briceburg Bridge). Some facilities are wheelchair-accessible. Leashed pets are permitted. Supplies are available in Mariposa.
Reservations, fees: Reservations are not accepted. Sites are $10 per night. There is a 14-day limit. Open April through October, weather permitting.
Directions: From Merced, turn east on Highway 140 and drive 40 miles to Mariposa. Continue another 15 miles to Briceburg and the Briceburg Visitor Center on the left. Turn left at a road that is signed "BLM Camping Areas" (the road remains paved for about 150 yards). Drive over the Briceburg suspension bridge and turn left, traveling downstream on the road, parallel to the river. Drive 2.5 miles to McCabe Flat, 3.8 miles to Willow Placer, and 4.8 miles to Railroad Flat.
Contact: Bureau of Land Management, Folsom Field Office, 916/985-4474, fax 916/985-3259.

23 YOSEMITE-MARIPOSA KOA
🏊 🐕 🚸 ♿ 🚐 ⛺

Scenic rating: 7
near Mariposa

Map 10.1, page 553

A little duck pond, swimming pool, and proximity to Yosemite National Park make this one a winner. A shuttle bus service (fee) to the national park is a great bonus. The RV sites are lined up along the entrance road. A 10 P.M. "quiet time" helps ensure a good night's sleep. It's a one-hour drive to Yosemite Valley, and your best bet is to get there early to enjoy the spectacular beauty before the park is packed with people.

Campsites, facilities: There are 49 sites with full or partial hookups (30 and 50 amps) for RVs up to 40 feet, 26 tent sites, 12 cabins, and three lodges. Picnic tables and barbecues are provided; no wood fires. Restrooms with showers, dump station, Wi-Fi, telephone/modem access, coin laundry, convenience store, propane gas, recreation room, seasonal swimming pool, peewee golf, train caboose with arcade, and a playground are available. Some facilities are wheelchair accessible. Leashed pets are permitted in RV and tent sites only, with certain restrictions.

Reservations, fees: Reservations are accepted at 800/562-9391. Sites are $30–55 per night, $6 per person per night for more than two people, $5 per night for each additional vehicle, $2 per pet per night. Call for cabin and lodge prices. Some credit cards accepted. Open year-round.

Directions: From Merced, drive east on Highway 140 to Mariposa. Continue on Highway 140 for seven miles to Midpines and the campground entrance on the left at 6323 Highway 140.

Contact: Yosemite-Mariposa KOA, 209/966-2201, www.koa.com.

24 JERSEYDALE
🏃 🐾 5% 🚙 ⛺

Scenic rating: 5

in Sierra National Forest

Map 10.1, page 553

This little camp gets overlooked by many visitors shut out of nearby Yosemite National Park simply because they don't realize it exists. Jerseydale is set southwest of the national park in Sierra National Forest, with two good side trips nearby. If you continue north on Jerseydale Road to its end (about six miles), you will come to a Forest Service road/trailhead that provides access east along a portion of the South Fork of the Merced River, where there is often good fishing, swimming, and rafting. In addition, a dirt road from the camp is routed east for many miles into the Chowchilla Mountains.

Campsites, facilities: There are eight sites for tents or RVs up to 24 feet (no hookups). Picnic tables and fire grills are provided. Drinking water and vault toilets are available. Garbage must be packed out. Leashed pets are permitted.

Reservations, fees: Reservations are not accepted. There is no fee for camping. Open May through November.

Directions: From Mariposa, drive northeast on Highway 140 for about five miles to Triangle Road (if you reach Midpines, you have gone 1.5 miles too far). Turn right on Triangle Road and drive about six miles to Darrah and Jerseydale Road. Turn left and drive three miles to the campground on the left side of the road (adjacent to the Jerseydale Ranger Station).

Contact: Sierra National Forest, Bass Lake Ranger District, 559/877-2218, fax 559/877-3108.

25 WAWONA
🏃 🏊 🛶 🐾 🚗 ⛺

Scenic rating: 9

on the South Fork of the Merced River in Yosemite National Park

Map 10.1, page 553

Wawona is an attractive alternative to the packed camps in Yosemite Valley, providing you don't mind the relatively long drives to the best destinations. The camp is pretty, set along the South Fork of the Merced River, with the sites more spacious than at most other drive-to camps in the park. The nearest attraction is the Mariposa Grove of Giant Sequoias, but get your visit in by 9 A.M., because after that it turns into a zoo, complete with shuttle train. The best nearby hike is a strenuous 10-mile round-trip to Chilnualna Falls, the prettiest sight in the southern region of the park; the trailhead is at the east end of Chilnualna Road in North Wawona. It's a 45-minute drive to either Glacier Point or Yosemite Valley.

Campsites, facilities: There are 93 sites for tents or RVs up to 35 feet (no hookups), two group tent sites for 13–30 people each, and two horse camps. Picnic tables, fire grills, and food lockers (mandatory use) are provided. Drinking water and flush toilets are available. Leashed pets are permitted, but not in group sites, horse camps, or on trails. There are also some stock-handling facilities for camping with pack animals; call for further information. A grocery store, dump station, propane gas, gas station, post office, restaurant, and seasonal horseback-riding facilities are available nearby.

Reservations, fees: Reservations are required May to September, when individual sites are $20 per night. Reserve at 800/436-PARK (800/436-7275) or http://reservations.nps.gov. No reservations are needed from October to April, when individual sites are $14 per night. Year-round fees are $25 per night for horse camps, $40 per night for group tent sites, plus $20 park entrance fee per vehicle. A seven-day camping limit is enforced during the summer. Open year-round.

Directions: From Oakhurst, drive north on Highway 41 to the Wawona entrance of Yosemite National Park. Continue north on Highway 41 past Wawona (golf course on the left) and drive one mile to the campground entrance on the left.

Contact: Yosemite National Park, 209/372-0200, for an automated menu of recorded information, www.nps.gov/yose.

26 SUMMIT CAMP
Scenic rating: 5

in Sierra National Forest

Map 10.1, page 553

The prime attraction of tiny Summit Camp is its proximity to the Wawona entrance of Yosemite National Park. It sits along a twisty

Forest Service road, perched in the Chowchilla Mountains at 5,800 feet, about three miles from Big Creek. It's a little-known alternative when the park campgrounds at Wawona are packed.

Campsites, facilities: There are four primitive sites for tents or RVs up to 16 feet (no hookups). Picnic tables and fire grills are provided. Vault toilets are available. No drinking water is available. Garbage must be packed out. Leashed pets are permitted.

Reservations, fees: Reservations are not accepted. There is no fee for camping. Open June through October, weather permitting.

Directions: From Oakhurst, drive north on Highway 41 toward the town of Fish Camp and to the gravel Forest Road 5S09X a mile before Fish Camp on the left. Turn left and drive six twisty miles to the campground on the left side of the road. Trailers are not recommended.

Contact: Sierra National Forest, Bass Lake Ranger District, 559/877-2218, fax 559/877-3108.

27 SUMMERDALE
Scenic rating: 7

on the South Fork of the Merced River in Sierra National Forest

Map 10.1, page 553

You can't get much closer to Yosemite National Park. This camp is within a mile of the Wawona entrance to Yosemite, about a five-minute drive to the Mariposa Grove. If you don't mind its proximity to the highway, this is a pretty spot in its own right, set along Big Creek, a feeder stream to the South Fork Merced River. Some good swimming holes are in this area. The elevation is 5,000 feet.

Campsites, facilities: There are 30 sites for tents or RVs up to 24 feet (no hookups). Picnic tables and fire grills are provided. Drinking water and vault toilets are available. A grocery store is nearby (within one mile). Some facilities are wheelchair-accessible. Leashed pets are permitted.

Reservations, fees: Reservations are accepted ($9 reservation fee) at 877/444-6777 or www .ReserveUSA.com. Sites are $17 per night, $5 per night for each additional vehicle. Open May through October, weather permitting.

Directions: From Oakhurst, drive north on Highway 41 to Fish Camp and continue for one mile to the campground entrance on the left side of the road.

Contact: Sierra National Forest, Bass Lake Ranger District, 559/877-2218, fax 559/877-3108.

28 UPPER CHIQUITO
🏃 🐕 🚐 ⛺

Scenic rating: 7

on Chiquito Creek in Sierra National Forest

Map 10.1, page 553

Upper Chiquito is set at 6,800 feet on a major access road to Sierra National Forest and the western region of the Ansel Adams Wilderness, about 15 miles to the east. The camp is set on Upper Chiquito Creek. About a mile down the road (southwest) is a Forest Service spur road (turn north) that provides access to a trail that is routed up Chiquito Creek for three miles to gorgeous Chiquita Lake (another route with a longer drive and shorter hike is available out of Fresno Dome).

Campsites, facilities: There are 20 sites for tents or RVs up to 20 feet (no hookups). Picnic tables and fire grills are provided. Vault toilets are available. No drinking water is available. Garbage must be packed out. Leashed pets are permitted.

Reservations, fees: Reservations are not accepted. There is no fee for camping. Open June through September, weather permitting.

Directions: From Fresno, drive north on Highway 41 for 50 miles to Yosemite Forks and County Road 222. Turn right on County Road 222 (keeping to the right at each of two Y intersections) and drive six miles to

Pines Village and Beasore Road. Turn left onto Beasore Road and drive 16 miles to the campground.

Contact: Sierra National Forest, Bass Lake Ranger District, 559/877-2218, fax 559/877-3108.

29 CLOVER MEADOW
🏃 🐕 🚐 ⛺

Scenic rating: 8

in Sierra National Forest

Map 10.1, page 553

This is one of two excellent jump-off camps in the area for backpackers; the other is Granite Creek. The camp is set at 7,000 feet, adjacent to the Clover Meadow Ranger Station, where backcountry information is available. While a trail is available from camp heading east into the Ansel Adams Wilderness, most hikers drive about three miles farther northeast on Minarets Road to a trailhead for a five-mile hike to Cora Lakes.

Campsites, facilities: There are seven sites for tents or RVs up to 20 feet (no hookups). Picnic tables and fire grills are provided. Drinking water and vault toilets are available. Leashed pets are permitted.

Reservations, fees: Reservations are not accepted. There is no fee for camping. Open June through September, weather permitting.

Directions: From Fresno, drive north on Highway 41 for about 25 miles to North Fork Road/County Road 200. Turn right and drive northeast for 17.5 miles to Auberry Road/County Road 222. Turn left (north) and drive one mile to the town of North Fork and Mammoth Pool Road. Turn right and drive 1.5 miles to County Road 225 (still Mammoth Pool Road). Turn right and drive (the road eventually becomes Minarets Road) to the junction with Forest Road 4S81. Bear left (north) on Forest Road 4S81 and drive to the campground entrance road. Bear left (signed for Clover Meadow) and drive to the campground, adjacent to the Clover Meadow

Ranger Station. The total distance from North Fork to the entrance road is about 63 miles; it's 20 miles north of the well-signed Mammoth Pool Reservoir on Minarets Road.

Contact: Sierra National Forest, Bass Lake Ranger District, 559/877-2218, fax 559/877-3108.

30 GRANITE CREEK AND EQUESTRIAN CAMP

🏕 🏊 🚵 🐴 🔼

Scenic rating: 6

in Sierra National Forest

Map 10.1, page 553

This camp is a good jump-off point for backpackers since a trail from camp leads north for five miles to Cora Lakes in the Ansel Adams Wilderness, with the option of continuing to more remote wilderness. Note that nearby Clover Meadow camp (see previous listing) may be more desirable because it has both drinking water to tank up your canteens and a ranger station to obtain the latest trail information. In addition, the upper half of this campground is available for equestrians. The elevation is 6,900 feet.

Campsites, facilities: There are 20 sites for tents or RVs up to 20 feet (no hookups). Picnic tables and fire grills are provided. Vault toilets and a horse corral are available. No drinking water is available. Garbage must be packed out. Leashed pets are permitted.

Reservations, fees: Reservations are not accepted. There is no fee for camping. Open June through September, weather permitting.

Directions: From Fresno, drive north on Highway 41 for about 25 miles to North Fork Road/County Road 200. Turn right and drive northeast for 17.5 miles to Auberry Road/County Road 222. Turn left (north) and drive one mile to the town of North Fork and Mammoth Pool Road. Turn right and drive 1.5 miles to County Road 225 (still Mammoth Pool Road). Turn right and drive (the road eventually becomes Minarets Road) to

the junction with Forest Road 4S81. Bear left (north) on Forest Road 4S81 and drive to the campground entrance road. Turn left (signed for Granite Creek) and drive 3.5 miles to the campground. (The total distance from North Fork to the entrance road is about 66.5 miles; it's 23.5 miles north of Mammoth Pool Reservoir on the well-signed Minarets Road.)

Contact: Sierra National Forest, Bass Lake Ranger District, 559/877-2218, fax 559/877-3108.

31 BIG SANDY

🏊 🏕 🚗 🔼

Scenic rating: 7

on Big Creek in Sierra National Forest

Map 10.1, page 553

It's only six miles from the highway and just eight miles from the southern entrance to Yosemite National Park. Add that up: Right, when Wawona is full in southern Yosemite, this camp provides a much-needed option. It's a pretty camp set on Big Creek in the Sierra National Forest, one of two camps in the immediate area. The elevation is 5,800 feet. If you head into Yosemite for the tour of giant sequoias in Wawona, get there early, by 7:30 or 8:30 A.M., when the grove is still quiet and cool, and you will have the old, mammoth trees practically to yourself.

Campsites, facilities: There are 18 sites for tents or RVs up to 20 feet (no hookups). Picnic tables and fire grills are provided. Vault toilets are available. No drinking water is available. Leashed pets are permitted.

Reservations, fees: Reservations are not accepted. Site are $14 per night, $5 per night for each additional vehicle. Open from June through October, weather permitting.

Directions: From Oakhurst drive north on Highway 41 for 15 miles to Forest Road 6S07 (one mile before reaching Marriotts). Turn right on Forest Road 6S07 and drive about six miles (a slow, rough road) to the camp.

Contact: Sierra National Forest, Bass

Lake Ranger District, 559/877-2218, fax 559/877-3108.

32 FRESNO DOME
👫🛶🏕️🚗🏕️

Scenic rating: 7

on Big Creek in Sierra National Forest

Map 10.1, page 553

This camp is named after nearby Fresno Dome to the east, at 7,540 feet the dominating feature in the surrounding landscape. The trailhead for a mile hike to its top is two miles curving down the road to the east. This camp is set at 6,400 feet on Big Creek in Sierra National Forest, a good option to nearby Yosemite National Park.

Campsites, facilities: There are 15 sites for tents or RVs up to 20 feet (no hookups). Picnic tables and fire grills are provided. Pit toilets are available. No drinking water is available. Garbage must be packed out. Leashed pets are permitted.

Reservations, fees: Reservations are not accepted. Sites are $14 per night, $5 per night for each additional vehicle. Open June to mid-October, weather permitting.

Directions: From Oakhurst, drive north on Highway 41 approximately five miles to Sky Ranch Road/Forest Road 6S10. Turn right and drive 12 miles to the campground on the left.

Contact: Sierra National Forest, Bass Lake Ranger District, 559/877-2218, fax 559/877-3108.

33 KELTY MEADOW AND EQUESTRIAN CAMP
👫🏕️🚗🏕️

Scenic rating: 6

on Willow Creek in Sierra National Forest

Map 10.1, page 553

This primitive campground is often used by campers with horses. It is at Kelty Meadow by Willow Creek. Side-trip options feature nearby Fresno Dome, the Nelder Grove of giant sequoias and, of course, the southern entrance to nearby Yosemite National Park. The elevation is 5,800 feet.

Campsites, facilities: There are 11 sites for tents or RVs up to 20 feet. Fire grills and picnic tables are provided. Vault toilets and hitching posts are available. No drinking water is available. Leashed pets are permitted.

Reservations, fees: Reservations are required ($9 reservation fee) for equestrian sites at 877/444-6777 or www.ReserveUSA.com. Sites are $14 per night, $5 per night for each additional vehicle. Open June through October, weather permitting.

Directions: From Oakhurst on Highway 41, drive five miles north to Sky Ranch Road/Forest Road 6S10. Turn left (northeast) and drive approximately 10 miles to the campground.

Contact: Sierra National Forest, Bass Lake Ranger District, 559/877-2218, fax 559/877-3108.

34 NELDER GROVE
👫🏕️🚗🏕️

Scenic rating: 7

in Sierra National Forest

Map 10.1, page 553

Nelder Grove is a primitive spot, also pretty, yet it is a camp that is often overlooked. It is set amid the Nelder Grove of giant sequoias, the majestic mountain redwoods. There are two interpretive trails, each about a two-mile walk. Since the southern entrance to Yosemite National Park is just 10 miles away, Nelder Grove is overshadowed by Yosemite's Wawona Grove. The elevation is 5,300 feet. A good option.

Campsites, facilities: There are seven sites for tents or RVs up to 20 feet (no hookups). Picnic tables and fire grills are provided. Vault toilets are available. No drinking water is available. Garbage must be packed out. Leashed pets are permitted.

Yosemite and Mammoth Lakes **571**

Reservations, fees: Reservations are not accepted. There is no fee for camping. Open May through September, weather permitting.
Directions: From Fresno, drive north on Highway 41 for 46 miles to the town of Oakhurst. Continue north on Highway 41 for five miles to Sky Ranch Road/Forest Road 6S10. Turn right (northeast) and drive about eight miles to Forest Road 6S47Y. Turn left and drive a short distance to the campground.
Contact: Sierra National Forest, Bass Lake Ranger District, 559/877-2218, fax 559/877-3108.

35 SOQUEL

Scenic rating: 7

on the North Fork of Willow Creek in Sierra National Forest

Map 10.1, page 553

Soquel is at 5,400 feet in elevation on the North Fork of Willow Creek, an alternative to nearby Grey's Mountain in Sierra National Forest. When the camps are filled at Bass Lake, these two camps provide overflow areas as well as more primitive settings for those who are looking for more of a wilderness experience.
Campsites, facilities: There are 11 sites for tents or RVs up to 20 feet (no hookups). Picnic tables and fire grills are provided. Vault toilets are available. No drinking water is available. Leashed pets are permitted.
Reservations, fees: Reservations are accepted ($9 reservation fee) at 877/444-6777 or www .ReserveUSA.com. Sites are $14 per night, $5 per night for each additional vehicle. Open June through October, weather permitting.
Directions: From Fresno, drive north on Highway 41 for 46 miles to the town of Oakhurst. Continue north on Highway 41 for five miles to Sky Ranch Road/Forest Road 6S10. Turn right (east) and drive approximately five miles to Forest Road 6S40. Turn right and

drive about three-quarters of a mile to the campground.
Contact: Sierra National Forest, Bass Lake Ranger District, 559/877-2218, fax 559/877-3108.

36 TEXAS FLAT GROUP CAMP

Scenic rating: 5

on the North Fork of Willow Creek in Sierra National Forest

Map 10.1, page 553

If you are on your honeymoon, this definitely ain't the place. Unless you like the smell of horses, that is. It's a pretty enough spot, set along the North Fork of Willow Creek, but the camp is primitive and designed for groups with horses. This camp is 15 miles from the south entrance of Yosemite National Park and 15 miles north of Bass Lake. The elevation is 5,400 feet.
Campsites, facilities: There are four group sites for tents or RVs up to 20 feet (no hookups) that can accommodate 25–100 people each. Fire grills and picnic tables are provided. Vault toilets and a corral are available. No drinking water is available. Leashed pets are permitted.
Reservations, fees: Reservations are required ($9 reservation fee) at 877/444-6777 or www .ReserveUSA.com. Sites are $68–82 per night. Open June through November.
Directions: From Fresno, drive about 52 miles north on Highway 41 to Sky Ranch Road/ County Road 632. Turn right (east) on Sky Ranch Road/Forest Road 6S10 and drive approximately five miles to Forest Road 6S40. Turn right and drive about three-quarters of a mile to Forest Road 6S08. Turn left and drive 2.5 miles to Forest Road 6S38 and the campground.
Contact: Sierra National Forest, Bass Lake Ranger District, 559/877-2218, fax 559/877-3108.

37 GREY'S MOUNTAIN

Scenic rating: 7

on Willow Creek in Sierra National Forest

Map 10.1, page 553

This is a small, primitive campground to keep in mind when all the campgrounds are filled at nearby Bass Lake. It is one of a series of campgrounds on Willow Creek. The elevation is 5,400 feet, set just below Sivels Mountain to the east at 5,813 feet.

Campsites, facilities: There are 26 sites for tents or RVs up to 20 feet (no hookups). Picnic tables and fire grills are provided. Vault toilets are available. No drinking water is available. Leashed pets are permitted.

Reservations, fees: Reservations are not accepted. Sites are $14 per night, $5 per night for each additional vehicle. Open June through October, weather permitting.

Directions: From Oakhurst, drive north on Highway 41 for approximately five miles to Sky Ranch Road/Forest Road 6S10. Turn right and drive five miles to Forest Road 6S40. Turn right and drive 0.75 mile to Forest Road 6S08 and the camp.

Contact: Sierra National Forest, Bass Lake Ranger District, 559/877-2218, fax 559/877-3108.

38 BUCKEYE

Scenic rating: 8

near Buckeye Creek in Humboldt-Toiyabe National Forest

Map 10.1, page 553

Here's a little secret: A two-mile hike out of camp heads to the undeveloped Buckeye Hot Springs. That is what inspires campers to bypass the fishing at nearby Robinson Creek (three miles away) and Twin Lakes (six miles away). The camp feels remote and primitive, set at 7,000 feet on the eastern slope of the Sierra near Buckeye Creek. Another secret is that rainbow trout are planted at the little bridge that crosses Buckeye Creek near the campground. A trail that starts near camp is routed through Buckeye Canyon and into the Hoover Wilderness.

Campsites, facilities: There are 65 paved sites for tents or RVs up to 35 feet (no hookups). Picnic tables and fire grills are provided. Drinking water and vault and flush toilets are available. Some facilities are wheelchair-accessible. Leashed pets are permitted.

Reservations, fees: Reservations are not accepted. Sites are $13 per night, $5 per night for each additional vehicle. Open May through October, weather permitting.

Directions: On U.S. 395, drive to Bridgeport and the junction with Twin Lakes Road. Turn west and drive seven miles to Buckeye Road. Turn right (north) on Buckeye Road (dirt, often impassable when wet) and drive 3.5 miles to the campground.

Contact: Humboldt-Toiyabe National Forest, Bridgeport Ranger District, 760/932-7070, fax 760/932-5899; American Land and Leisure, 760/932-9888.

39 WILLOW SPRINGS RV PARK

Scenic rating: 6

near Bridgeport

Map 10.1, page 553

Willow Springs RV Park is set at 6,800 feet along U.S. 395, which runs along the eastern Sierra from Carson City south to Bishop and beyond to Lone Pine. The park is one mile from the turnoff to Bodie ghost town. A nice touch to the place is a central campfire that has been in place for more than 50 years. The country is stark here on the edge of the high Nevada desert, but there are many side trips that give the area life. The most popular destinations are to the nearby south: Mono Lake, with its tufa towers and incredible populations of breeding gulls and waterfowl, and the Bodie ghost town. For trout fishing, there's Bridgeport Reservoir to the north (good trolling) and downstream to the East Walker River (fly-fishing), both excellent destinations, as well as Twin Lakes to the west (huge brown trout).

Campsites, facilities: There are 25 sites with full hookups (30 amps) for RVs of any length. No tents. A motel is also available. Picnic tables are provided. Restrooms with showers, coin laundry, and nightly campfires are available. A restaurant is within walking distance. Leashed pets are permitted.

Reservations, fees: Reservations are accepted. Sites are $28 per night, $4 per person per night for more than two people. Open May through October.

Directions: From Bridgeport on U.S. 395, drive five miles south to the park, which is on the east side of the highway.

Contact: Willow Springs RV Park, 760/932-7725.

40 HONEYMOON FLAT

Scenic rating: 8

on Robinson Creek in Humboldt-Toiyabe National Forest

Map 10.1, page 553

The camp is set beside Robinson Creek at 7,000 feet in elevation, in the transition zone between the Sierra Nevada range to the west and the high desert to the east. It is easy to reach on the access road to Twin Lakes, only three miles farther. The lake is famous for occasional huge brown trout. However, the fishing at Robinson Creek is also often quite good, thanks to large numbers of trout planted each year.

Campsites, facilities: There are 35 sites with no hookups for tents or RVs up to 35 feet. Picnic tables and fire grills are provided. Drinking water, food lockers, and vault toilets are available. Some facilities are wheelchair-accessible. Leashed pets are permitted.

Reservations, fees: Reservations are accepted ($9 reservation fee) at 877/444-6777 or www.ReserveUSA.com. Sites are $13 per night, $5 per night for each additional vehicle. Open mid-April through October.

Directions: On U.S. 395, drive to Bridgeport and the junction with Twin Lakes Road. Turn west and drive eight miles to the campground.

Contact: Humboldt-Toiyabe National Forest, Bridgeport Ranger District, 760/932-7070, fax 760/932-5899; American Land and Leisure, 760/932-9888.

41 PAHA

Scenic rating: 8

near Twin Lakes in Humboldt-Toiyabe National Forest

Map 10.1, page 553

This is one in a series of camps near Robinson Creek and within close range of Twin Lakes. The elevation at the camp is 7,000 feet. (See the *Lower Twin Lake* and *Honeymoon Flat* listings in this chapter for more information.)

Campsites, facilities: There are 22 sites for tents or RVs up to 35 feet (no hookups). Picnic tables and fire grills are provided. Drinking water, flush toilets, and food lockers are available. Two boat launches, a store, coin showers, and a coin laundry are available nearby at Twin Lakes Resort. Leashed pets are permitted.

Reservations, fees: Reservations are accepted ($9 reservation fee) at 877/444-6777 or www.ReserveUSA.com. Sites are $15 per night, $5 per night for each additional vehicle. Open May through October, weather permitting.

Directions: On U.S. 395, drive to Bridgeport and the junction with Twin Lakes Road. Turn west and drive 10 miles to the campground.

Contact: Humboldt-Toiyabe National Forest, Bridgeport Ranger District, 760/932-7070, fax 760/932-5899; American Land and Leisure, 760/932-9888.

42 ROBINSON CREEK

Scenic rating: 9

near Twin Lakes in Humboldt-Toiyabe National Forest

Map 10.1, page 553

This campground, one of a series in the area, is set at 7,000 feet on Robinson Creek, not far from Twin Lakes. The campground is divided into two areas. (For recreation options, see the entries in this chapter for *Lower Twin Lake* and *Honeymoon Flat*.)

Campsites, facilities: There are 54 paved sites for tents or RVs up to 35 feet (no hookups). Picnic tables, food lockers, and fire grills are provided. Drinking water and flush and vault toilets are available. Some facilities are wheelchair-accessible. An amphitheater is nearby. Boat launches, a store, coin laundry, and coin showers are nearby at Twin Lakes Resort. Leashed pets are permitted.

Reservations, fees: Reservations are accepted ($9 reservation fee) at 877/444-6777 or www.ReserveUSA.com. Sites are $15 per night, $5 per night for each additional vehicle. Open mid-April through October, weather permitting.

Directions: On U.S. 395, drive to Bridgeport and the junction with Twin Lakes Road. Turn west and drive 10 miles to the campground.

Contact: Humboldt-Toiyabe National Forest, Bridgeport Ranger District, 760/932-7070, fax 760/932-5899; American Land and Leisure, 760/932-9888.

43 CRAGS CAMPGROUND

Scenic rating: 8

on Robinson Creek in Humboldt-Toiyabe National Forest

Map 10.1, page 553

Crags Campground is set at 7,100 feet in the Sierra, one of a series of campgrounds along Robinson Creek near Lower Twin Lake. While this camp does not offer direct access to Lower Twin, home of giant brown trout, it is very close. (See the entries in this chapter for *Lower Twin Lake* and *Honeymoon Flat*.)

Campsites, facilities: There are 52 sites for tents or RVs up to 45 feet (no hookups). Picnic tables, food lockers, and fire grills are provided. Drinking water and flush toilets are available. Some facilities are wheelchair-accessible. A boat launch (at Lower Twin Lake), store, a coin laundry, and coin showers are within a half mile. Leashed pets are permitted.

Reservations, fees: Reservations are accepted ($9 reservation fee) at 877/444-6777 or www.ReserveUSA.com. Sites are $15 per night, $5 per night for each additional vehicle. Open April through October, weather permitting.

Directions: On U.S. 395, drive to Bridgeport and the junction with Twin Lakes Road. Turn west and drive 11 miles to South Twin Road (just before reaching Lower Twin Lake). Turn left and drive over the bridge at Robinson Creek to another road on the left. Turn left and drive a short distance to the campground.

Contact: Humboldt-Toiyabe National Forest, Bridgeport Ranger District, 760/932-7070, fax 760/932-5899; American Land and Leisure, 760/932-9888.

44 LOWER TWIN LAKE

Scenic rating: 9

in Humboldt-Toiyabe National Forest

Map 10.1, page 553   BEST (

The Twin Lakes are actually two lakes, set high in the eastern Sierra at 7,000 feet. Each lake is unique. Lower Twin, known as the fishing lake, with a 5-mph speed limit, has a full resort, marina, boat ramp, and some of the biggest brown trout in the West. The state-record brown—26.5 pounds—was caught here in 1985. Of course, most of the trout are your typical 10- to 12-inch planted rainbow trout, but nobody seems to mind, with the chance of a true monster-sized fish always in the back of the minds of anglers. Upper Twin Lake, with a resort and marina, is a primary destination for boaters, personal watercraft, water-skiers, swimmers, and sailboarders. These lakes are very popular in summer. An option for campers is an excellent trailhead for hiking near Mono Village at the head of Upper Twin Lake. Here you will find Barney Lake Trail, which is routed up the headwaters of Robinson Creek, steeply at times, to Barney Lake, an excellent day hike.

Campsites, facilities: There are 15 paved sites for tents or RVs up to 35 feet (no hookups). Picnic tables and fire grills are provided. Drinking water, flush toilets, and food lockers are available. A boat launch, store, coin showers, and a coin laundry are available nearby. Leashed pets are permitted.

Reservations, fees: Reservations are accepted ($9 reservation fee) at 877/444-6777 or www.ReserveUSA.com. Sites are $15 per night, $5 per night for each additional vehicle. Open early May to mid-October, weather permitting.

Directions: On U.S. 395, drive to Bridgeport and the junction with Twin Lakes Road. Turn west and drive 11 miles to South Twin Road (just before reaching Lower Twin Lake). Turn left and drive over the bridge at Robinson Creek and to the campground entrance road on the right.

Contact: Humboldt-Toiyabe National Forest, Bridgeport Ranger District, 760/932-7070, fax 760/932-5899; American Land and Leisure, 760/932-9888.

45 GREEN CREEK

Scenic rating: 7

in Humboldt-Toiyabe National Forest

Map 10.1, page 553

This camp is ideal for backpackers or campers who like to fish for trout in streams. That is because it is set at 7,500 feet, with a trailhead

that leads into the Hoover Wilderness and to several high mountain lakes, including Green Lake, West Lake, and East Lake; the ambitious can hike beyond in remote northeastern Yosemite National Park. The camp is set along Green Creek, a fair trout stream with small rainbow trout.

Campsites, facilities: There are 11 sites for tents or RVs up to 35 feet and two group sites for tents or RVs of any length that can accommodate 25–30 people each. No hookups. Picnic tables and fire grills are provided. Drinking water and vault toilets are available. Leashed pets are permitted.

Reservations, fees: Reservations are not accepted for individual sites but are required ($9 reservation fee) for group sites at 877/444-6777 or www.ReserveUSA.com. Sites are $13 per night, $5 per night for each additional vehicle, and $42–50 per night for a group site. Open mid-May to early October, weather permitting.

Directions: From Bridgeport, drive south on U.S. 395 for four miles to Green Lakes Road (dirt). Turn right and drive seven miles to the campground.

Contact: Humboldt-Toiyabe National Forest, Bridgeport Ranger District, 760/932-7070, fax 760/932-5899; American Land and Leisure, 760/932-9888.

46 TRUMBULL LAKE

Scenic rating: 8

in Humboldt-Toiyabe National Forest

Map 10.1, page 553

This is a high-mountain camp (9,500 feet) at the gateway to a beautiful Sierra basin. Little Trumbull Lake is the first lake on the north side of Virginia Lakes Road, with Virginia Lakes set nearby, along with the Hoover Wilderness and access to many other small lakes by trail. A trail is available that is routed just north of Blue Lake, and then it leads west to Frog Lake, Summit Lake, and beyond into a remote area of Yosemite National Park. If you don't want to rough it, cabins, boat rentals, and a restaurant are available at Virginia Lakes Resort. No gas motors, swimming, and water/body contact is permitted at Virginia Lakes.

Campsites, facilities: There are 45 sites for tents or RVs up to 35 feet (no hookups). Picnic tables and fire grills are provided. Drinking water and vault toilets are available. A store is nearby at the resort. Some facilities are wheelchair-accessible. Leashed pets are permitted.

Reservations, fees: Reservations are accepted ($9 reservation fee) at 877/444-6777 or www.ReserveUSA.com. Sites are $13 per night, $5 per night for each additional vehicle. Open June through September, weather permitting.

Directions: From Bridgeport, drive south on U.S. 395 for 13.5 miles to Virginia Lakes Road. Turn right on Virginia Lakes Road and drive 6.5 miles to the campground entrance road.

Contact: Humboldt-Toiyabe National Forest, Bridgeport Ranger District, 760/932-7070, fax 760/932-5899; American Land and Leisure, 760/932-9888.

47 LUNDY CANYON CAMPGROUND

Scenic rating: 7

near Lundy Lake

Map 10.1, page 553

This camp is set high in the eastern Sierra at 7,800 feet in elevation along pretty Lundy Creek, the mountain stream that feeds Lundy Lake and then runs downhill, eventually joining other creeks on its trip to nearby Mono Lake. Nearby Lundy Lake is a long, narrow lake with good fishing for rainbow trout and brown trout. The water is clear and cold, even through the summer. There is a trailhead just west of the lake that is routed steeply up into the Hoover Wilderness to several small pretty lakes, passing two waterfalls about two miles in. A must-do side trip is visiting Mono Lake

and its spectacular tufa towers, best done at the Mono Lake Tufa State Reserve along the southern shore of the lake.

Campsites, facilities: There are 50 sites for tents or RVs up to 24 feet (no hookups). Picnic tables and fire rings are provided. Pit toilets are available. No drinking water is available. You can buy supplies in Lee Vining, 8.5 miles away. Leashed pets are permitted.

Reservations, fees: Reservations are not accepted. Sites are $8 per night, with a limit of two vehicles and six people per site. Monthly rates available. Open May through October.

Directions: From Lee Vining, drive north on U.S. 395 for seven miles to Lundy Lake Road. Turn left and drive a short distance to the campground.

Contact: Mono County Public Works, 760/932-5440, fax 760/932-5441.

48 SADDLEBAG LAKE

Scenic rating: 10

in Inyo National Forest

Map 10.1, page 553

This camp is set in spectacular high country above tree line, the highest drive-to camp and lake in California; Saddlebag Lake sits at 10,087 feet. The camp is about a quarter mile from the lake, within walking range of the little store, boat rentals, and a one-minute drive for launching a boat at the ramp. The scenery is stark; everything is granite, ice, or water, with only a few lodgepole pines managing precarious toeholds, sprinkled across the landscape on the access road. An excellent trailhead is available for hiking, with the best hike routed out past little Hummingbird Lake to Lundy Pass. A hiker's shuttle boat, which will ferry you across the lake, is a nice plus. Note that with the elevation and the high mountain pass, it can be windy and cold here, and some people find it difficult to catch their breath on simple hikes. In addition, RV users should note that level sites are extremely hard to come by.

Campsites, facilities: There are 20 sites for tents or RVs up to 40 feet (no hookups), and one group tent site for up to 25 people. Drinking water, fire grills, and picnic tables are provided. Vault toilets, boat rentals, and a primitive boat launch are available. A grocery store is nearby. Some facilities are wheelchair-accessible. Leashed pets are permitted.

Reservations, fees: Reservations are not accepted for individual sites, but are required ($9 reservation fee) for the group site at 877/444-6777 or www.ReserveUSA.com. Sites are $17 per night, $56 per night for the group site. Open early June to mid-October, weather permitting.

Directions: On U.S. 395, drive 0.5 mile south of Lee Vining and the junction with Highway 120. Turn west and drive about 11 miles to Saddlebag Lake Road. Turn right and drive 2.5 miles to the campground on the right.

From Merced, drive east on Highway 140 to the Arch Rock entrance station. Continue east to the Big Oak Flat Road junction (0.5 mile before entering Yosemite Valley). Turn left and drive 14 miles to Tioga Road. Turn right and drive about 65 miles (past Tuolumne Meadows) and through the Tioga Pass entrance station. Continue two miles to Saddlebag Lake Road. Turn left and drive 2.5 miles (rough road) to the campground on the right.

Contact: Inyo National Forest, Mono Basin Scenic Area Ranger Station and Visitor Center, 760/647-3044, fax 760/647-3046.

49 LOWER LEE VINING CAMP

Scenic rating: 7

near Lee Vining

Map 10.1, page 553

This former Mono County camp and its neighboring camps—Cattleguard, Moraine, Aspen, Big Bend, and Boulder—can be a godsend for vacationers who show up at Yosemite National Park and make the discovery that there are no sites left, a terrible experience

for some late-night arrivals. But these Forest Service campgrounds provide a great safety valve, even if they are extremely primitive, on the edge of timber. Lee Vining Creek is the highlight, flowing right past the campgrounds along Highway 120, bound for Mono Lake to the nearby east. It is stocked regularly during the fishing season. A must-do side trip is venturing to the south shore of Mono Lake to walk amid the bizarre yet beautiful tufa towers. There is good rock-climbing and hiking in the area. Although sunshine is the norm, be prepared for all kinds of weather: It can snow every month of the year here. Short but lively thunderstorms are common in early summer. Other nearby trips are available to Mammoth Lakes, June Lake, and Bodie State Park.

Campsites, facilities: There are 59 sites for tents or RVs up to 40 feet (no hookups). Picnic tables and fire rings are provided. Portable toilets are available. No drinking water is available. You can buy supplies in Lee Vining (about two miles away). Leashed pets are permitted.

Reservations, fees: Reservations are not accepted. Sites are $14 per night. Open May through October, weather permitting.

Directions: On U.S. 395, drive to just south of Lee Vining and the junction with Highway 120. Turn west on Highway 120 and drive about 2.5 miles. Turn left into the campground entrance.

Contact: Inyo National Forest, Mono Basin Scenic Area Ranger Station and Visitor Center, 760/647-3044, fax 760/647-3046.

50 CATTLEGUARD CAMP

Scenic rating: 7

near Lee Vining

Map 10.1, page 553

This camp is an alternative to Yosemite National Park. Though primitive, it has several advantages: It is quiet, gets more sun than the three neighboring camps (Lower Lee Vining,

Moraine, and Boulder), and provides the best views of Dana Plateau. (For more information, see the previous listing, *Lower Lee Vining Camp*.)

Campsites, facilities: There are 16 sites for tents or RVs up to 30 feet (no hookups). Picnic tables and fire rings are provided. Portable toilets are available. No drinking water is available. You can buy supplies in Lee Vining (about two miles away). Leashed pets are permitted.

Reservations, fees: Reservations are not accepted. Sites are $14 per night. Open May through October, weather permitting.

Directions: On U.S. 395, drive to just south of Lee Vining and the junction with Highway 120. Turn west on Highway 120 and drive about three miles. Turn left into the campground entrance.

Contact: Inyo National Forest, Mono Basin Scenic Area Ranger Station and Visitor Center, 760/647-3044, fax 760/647-3046.

51 MORAINE CAMP
🚶 🚣 🐕 🚐 ⛺

Scenic rating: 7

near Lee Vining

Map 10.1, page 553

This camp provides an alternative to Yosemite National Park. (For more information, see the *Lower Lee Vining Camp* listing in this chapter.)

Campsites, facilities: There are 30 sites for tents or RVs up to 30 feet (no hookups). Picnic tables and fire rings are provided. Portable toilets are available. There is no drinking water. You can buy supplies in Lee Vining (about two miles away). Leashed pets are permitted.

Reservations, fees: Reservations are not accepted. Sites are $14 per night. Open May through October, weather permitting.

Directions: On U.S. 395, drive to just south of Lee Vining and the junction with Highway 120. Turn west on Highway 120 and drive 3.5 miles to Poole Power Plant Road. Exit left

onto Poole Power Plant Road and drive 0.25 mile to the campground entrance at the end of the road.

Contact: Inyo National Forest, Mono Basin Scenic Area Ranger Station and Visitor Center, 760/647-3044, fax 760/647-3046.

52 BOULDER CAMP
🚶 🚣 🐕 🚐 ⛺

Scenic rating: 7

near Lee Vining

Map 10.1, page 553

This camp provides an alternative to Yosemite National Park. (For more information, see *Lower Lee Vining Camp* in this chapter.)

Campsites, facilities: There are 10 sites for tents or RVs up to 30 feet (no hookups). Picnic tables and fire rings are provided. Portable toilets are available. No drinking water is available. You can buy supplies in Lee Vining (about two miles away). Leashed pets are permitted.

Reservations, fees: Reservations are not accepted. Sites are $14 per night. Open May through October, weather permitting.

Directions: On U.S. 395, drive to just south of Lee Vining and the junction with Highway 120. Turn west on Highway 120 and drive 3.5 miles to Poole Power Plant Road. Exit left and then make a quick right on Poole Power Plant Road and drive 0.5 mile to the campground entrance on the left.

Contact: Inyo National Forest, Mono Basin Scenic Area Ranger Station and Visitor Center, 760/647-3044, fax 760/647-3046.

53 BIG BEND
🚣 🐕 ♿ 🚐 ⛺

Scenic rating: 8

on Lee Vining Creek in Inyo National Forest

Map 10.1, page 553

This camp is set in sparse but beautiful country along Lee Vining Creek at 7,800 feet elevation. Ancient pine trees are on site. It is an excellent bet for an overflow camp if Tuolumne Meadows in nearby Yosemite is packed. The view from the camp to the north features Mono Dome (10,614 feet) and Lee Vining Peak (11,691 feet).

Campsites, facilities: There are 17 sites for tents or RVs up to 30 feet (no hookups). Picnic tables and fire grills are provided. Drinking water and vault toilets are available. Some facilities are wheelchair-accessible. Leashed pets are permitted.

Reservations, fees: Reservations are not accepted. Sites are $17 per night. Open late April to mid-October, weather permitting.

Directions: On U.S. 395, drive to just south of Lee Vining and the junction with Highway 120. Turn west on Highway 120 and drive about 3.5 miles to Poole Power Plant Road and the signed campground access road on the right. Turn right and drive a short distance to the camp.

Contact: Inyo National Forest, Mono Basin Scenic Area Ranger Station and Visitor Center, 760/647-3044, fax 760/647-3046.

54 ASPEN

Scenic rating: 8

on Lee Vining Creek

Map 10.1, page 553

This high-country, primitive camp is set along Lee Vining Creek at 7,500 feet, on the eastern slopes of the Sierra just east of Yosemite National Park. Take the side trip to moonlike Mono Lake, best seen at the south shore's Tufa State Reserve.

Campsites, facilities: There are 58 sites for tents or RVs up to 40 feet (no hookups). Picnic tables and fire rings are provided. Portable toilets are available. Drinking water is available. You can buy supplies in Lee Vining. Leashed pets are permitted.

Reservations, fees: Reservations are not accepted. Sites are $14 per night. Open May through October, weather permitting.

Directions: On U.S. 395, drive to just south of Lee Vining and the junction with Highway 120. Turn west on Highway 120 and drive about 3.5 miles. Exit onto Poole Power Plant Road. Turn left and drive about four miles west to the campground on the left.

Contact: Inyo National Forest, Mono Basin Scenic Area Ranger Station and Visitor Center, 760/647-3044, fax 760/647-3046.

55 JUNCTION

Scenic rating: 7

near Ellery and Tioga Lakes in Inyo National Forest

Map 10.1, page 553

Which way do you go? From Junction, any way you choose, you can't miss. Two miles to the north is Saddlebag Lake, the highest drive-to lake (10,087 feet) in California. Directly across the road is Ellery Lake, and a mile to the south is Tioga Lake, two beautiful, pristine waters with trout fishing. To the east is Mono Lake, and to the west is Yosemite National Park. From camp, it is a one-mile hike to Bennetville, a historic camp. Take your pick. Camp elevation is 9,600 feet.

Campsites, facilities: There are 13 sites for tents or RVs up to 30 feet (no hookups). Picnic tables and fire grills are provided. Vault toilets are available. No drinking water is available. Some facilities are wheelchair-accessible. Leashed pets are permitted.

Reservations, fees: Reservations are not accepted. Sites are $11 per night. Open early June to mid-October, weather permitting.

Directions: On U.S. 395, drive to just south of Lee Vining and the junction with Highway 120. Turn west on Highway 120 and drive about 10 miles to Saddlebag Road and the campground on the right side of the road.

From Merced, drive east on Highway 140 to the Arch Rock entrance station. Continue east to the Big Oak Flat Road junction (0.5 mile before entering Yosemite Valley). Turn left and drive 14 miles to Tioga Road. Turn right and drive about 65 miles (past Tuolumne Meadows) and through the Tioga Pass entrance station. Continue two miles to Saddlebag Lake Road and the campground on the left side of the road.

Contact: Inyo National Forest, Mono Basin Scenic Area Ranger Station and Visitor Center, 760/647-3044, fax 760/647-3046.

56 TIOGA LAKE

Scenic rating: 9

in Inyo National Forest

Map 10.1, page 553

Tioga Lake is a dramatic sight, with gemlike blue waters encircled by Sierra granite at 9,700 feet in elevation. Together with adjacent Ellery Lake, it makes a pair of gorgeous waters with near-lake camping, trout fishing (stocked with rainbow trout), and access to Yosemite National Park and Saddlebag Lake. Conditions here are much like those at neighboring Ellery. The only downers: It can get windy here (no foolin'!) and the camps fill quickly from the overflow crowds at Tuolumne Meadows. (See next listing, *Ellery Lake,* for more information.)

Campsites, facilities: There are 13 sites for tents or RVs up to 30 feet (no hookups). Picnic tables and fire grills are provided. Drinking water and vault toilets are available. Some facilities are wheelchair-accessible. Leashed pets are permitted.

Reservations, fees: Reservations are not accepted. Sites are $17 per night. Open early June to mid-October, weather permitting.

Directions: On U.S. 395, drive to just south of Lee Vining and the junction with Highway 120. Turn west on Highway 120 and drive about 11 miles (just past Ellery Lake) to the campground on the left side of the road.

From Merced, drive east on Highway 140 to the Arch Rock entrance station. Continue east to the Big Oak Flat Road junction (0.5

mile before entering Yosemite Valley). Turn left and drive 14 miles to Tioga Road. Turn right and drive about 65 miles (past Tuolumne Meadows) and through the Tioga Pass entrance station. Continue one mile to the campground entrance road on the right side of the road.

Contact: Inyo National Forest, Mono Basin Scenic Area Ranger Station and Visitor Center, 760/647-3044, fax 760/647-3046.

57 ELLERY LAKE

Scenic rating: 9

in Inyo National Forest

Map 10.1, page 553

Ellery Lake offers all the spectacular beauty of Yosemite but is two miles outside park borders. That means it is stocked with trout by the Department of Fish and Game (no lakes in Yosemite are planted, hence the lousy fishing). Just like neighboring Tioga Lake, here are deep-blue waters set in rock in the 9,500-foot elevation range, one of the most pristine highway-access lake settings anywhere. Although there is no boat ramp, boats with small motors are allowed and can be hand-launched. Nearby Saddlebag Lake, the highest drive-to lake in California, is a common side trip. Whenever Tuolumne Meadows fills in Yosemite, this camp fills shortly thereafter. Camp elevation is 9,500 feet.

Campsites, facilities: There are 12 sites for tents or RVs up to 30 feet (no hookups). Picnic tables and fire grills are provided. Drinking water and vault toilets are available. A grocery store is nearby. Some facilities are wheelchair-accessible. Leashed pets are permitted.

Reservations, fees: Reservations are not accepted. Sites are $15 per night. Open early June to mid-October, weather permitting.

Directions: On U.S. 395, drive to just south of Lee Vining and the junction with Highway 120. Turn west on Highway 120 and drive about 10 miles to the campground on the left side of the road.

From Merced, drive east on Highway 140 to the Arch Rock entrance station. Continue east to the Big Oak Flat Road junction (0.5 mile before entering Yosemite Valley). Turn left and drive 14 miles to Tioga Road. Turn right and drive about 65 miles (past Tuolumne Meadows) and through the Tioga Pass entrance station. Continue four miles to the campground entrance road on the right.

Contact: Inyo National Forest, Mono Basin Scenic Area Ranger Station and Visitor Center, 760/647-3044, fax 760/647-3046.

58 SILVER LAKE

Scenic rating: 9

in Inyo National Forest

Map 10.1, page 553

Silver Lake is set at 7,200 feet, an 80-acre lake in the June Lake Loop with Carson Peak looming in the background. Boat rentals, fishing for trout at the lake, a beautiful trout stream (Rush Creek) next to the camp, and a nearby trailhead for wilderness hiking and horseback riding (rentals available) are the highlights. The camp is largely exposed and vulnerable to winds, the only downer. Within walking distance to the south is Silver Lake, always a pretty sight, especially when afternoon winds cause the lake surface to sparkle in crackling silvers. The lake speed limit is 10 mph. Swimming is not recommended because of the rocky shoreline. Just across the road from the camp is a great trailhead for the Ansel Adams Wilderness, with a two-hour hike available that climbs to pretty Agnew Lake overlooking the June Lake basin; wilderness permit required for overnight use.

Campsites, facilities: There are 63 sites for tents or RVs up to 32 feet (no hookups). Picnic tables and fire grills are provided. Drinking water, flush toilets, and horseback-riding facilities are available. A grocery store, coin laundry, motorboat rentals, boat ramp, bait, café, boat fuel, and propane gas are avail-able nearby. Some facilities are wheelchair-accessible. Leashed pets are permitted.

Reservations, fees: Reservations are accepted ($9 reservation fee) at 877/444-6777 or www.ReserveUSA.com. Sites are $15 per night, $4 per night for each additional vehicle. Open late April to early November, weather permitting.

Directions: From Lee Vining on U.S. 395, drive south for six miles to the first Highway 158 north/June Lake Loop turnoff. Turn west (right) and drive nine miles (past Grant Lake) to Silver Lake. Just as you arrive at Silver Lake (a small store is on the right), turn left at the campground entrance.

Contact: Inyo National Forest, Mono Basin Scenic Area Ranger Station and Visitor Center, 760/647-3044, fax 760/647-3046.

59 OH! RIDGE

Scenic rating: 8

on June Lake in Inyo National Forest

Map 10.1, page 553

This is the largest of the campgrounds on June Lake. However, it is not the most popular since it is not right on the lakeshore, but back about a quarter mile or so from the north end of the lake. Regardless, it has the best views of the lake, with the ridge of the high Sierra providing a backdrop. The lake is a good one for trout fishing. The elevation is 7,600 feet.

Campsites, facilities: There are 148 sites for tents or RVs up to 40 feet (no hookups). Picnic tables and fire grills are provided. Drinking water, flush toilets, and a swimming beach are available. A grocery store, coin laundry, boat ramp, boat and tackle rentals, moorings, and propane gas are available nearby. Some facilities are wheelchair-accessible. Leashed pets are permitted.

Reservations, fees: Reservations are accepted ($9 reservation fee) at 877/444-6777 or www.ReserveUSA.com. Sites are $15 per night, $4 per night for each additional vehicle.

Open late April to early November, weather permitting.

Directions: From Lee Vining, drive south on U.S. 395 (past the first Highway 158/June Lake Loop turnoff) to June Lake Junction (a gas station/store is on the west side of the road) and Highway 158 south. Turn west on Highway 158 south and drive two miles to Oh! Ridge Road. Turn right and drive a mile to the campground access road (signed). Turn left and drive to the campground.

Contact: Inyo National Forest, Mono Basin Scenic Area Ranger Station and Visitor Center, 760/647-3044, fax 760/647-3046.

60 PINE CLIFF RESORT

Scenic rating: 7

at June Lake

Map 10.1, page 553

You found "kid heaven" at Pine Cliff Resort. This camp is in a pretty setting along the north shore of June Lake (7,600 feet in elevation), the feature lake among four in the June Lake Loop. The campsites are nestled in pine trees, designed so each site accommodates different-sized rigs and families, and the campground is set about a quarter mile from June Lake. This is the only camp at June Lake Loop that has a swimming beach available. The landscape is a pretty one, with the lake set below snowcapped peaks. The bonus is that June Lake gets large numbers of trout plants each summer, making it extremely popular with anglers. Of the lakes in the June Lake Loop, this is the one that has the most of everything—the most beauty, the most fish, the most developed accommodations and, alas, the most people. This resort has been operated as a family business for more than 50 years.

Campsites, facilities: There are 154 sites with full hookups (20 and 30 amps) for RVs, 17 sites with partial hookups (20 and 30 amps) for tents or RVs, and 55 sites for tents; a few sites are pull-through. There are also 14 rental trailers. Picnic tables and fire rings are provided. Restrooms with flush toilets and showers, drinking water, coin laundry, basketball, volleyball, tetherball, horseshoes, convenience store, and propane gas are available. Some facilities are wheelchair-accessible. A primitive boat ramp, fish-cleaning facilities, and fuel are available nearby. Leashed pets are permitted, with a maximum of two pets per site.

Reservations, fees: Reservations are recommended. Sites are $14–24 per night, $5 per night for each additional vehicle. The first pet is free, and the second pet is $1 per night. Open mid-April through October.

Directions: From Lee Vining, drive south on U.S. 395 (passing the first Highway 158 north/June Lake Loop turnoff) to June Lake Junction (a sign is posted for "June Lake Village") and Highway 158 south. Turn right (west) on Highway 158 south and drive two miles to North Shore Drive (a sign is nearby for Pine Cliff Resort). Turn right and drive 0.5 mile to Pine Cliff Road. Turn left and drive 0.5 mile to the resort store on the right (route is well signed).

Contact: Pine Cliff Resort, 760/648-7558.

61 GULL LAKE

Scenic rating: 8

in Inyo National Forest

Map 10.1, page 553

Little Gull Lake, just 64 acres, is the smallest of the lakes on the June Lake Loop, but to many it is the prettiest. It is set at 7,600 feet, just west of June Lake and, with Carson Peak looming on the Sierra crest to the west, it is a dramatic and intimate setting. The lake is stocked with trout each summer, providing good fishing. A boat ramp is on the lake's southwest corner. Insider's tip: There is a rope swing at Gull Lake that youngsters love.

Campsites, facilities: There are 11 sites for tents or RVs up to 30 feet (no hookups).

Drinking water, fire grills, and picnic tables are provided, and flush toilets are available. A grocery store, coin laundry, boat ramp, and propane gas are available nearby. Some facilities are wheelchair-accessible. Leashed pets are permitted.

Reservations, fees: Reservations are not accepted. Sites are $15 per night, $4 per night for each additional vehicle. Open late April to early November, weather permitting.

Directions: From Lee Vining, drive south on U.S. 395 (past the first Highway 158/June Lake Loop turnoff) to June Lake Junction (a gas station/store is on the west side of the road) and Highway 158. Turn west on Highway 158 and drive three miles to the campground entrance on the right side of the road.

Contact: Inyo National Forest, Mono Basin Scenic Area Ranger Station and Visitor Center, 760/647-3044, fax 760/647-3046.

62 REVERSED CREEK

🥾 🚴 🚤 🐎 ♿ 🚐 ⛺

Scenic rating: 6

in Inyo National Forest

Map 10.1, page 553

This camp is set at 7,600 feet near pretty Reversed Creek, the only stream in the region that flows toward the mountains, not away from them. It is a small, tree-lined stream that provides decent trout fishing. The campsites are sheltered and set in a grove of aspen, but close enough to the road so you can still hear highway traffic. There are also cabins available for rent near here. Directly opposite the camp, on the other side of the road, is Gull Lake and the boat ramp. Two miles to the west, on the west side of the road, is the trailhead for the hike to Fern Lake on the edge of the Ansel Adams Wilderness, a little butt-kicker of a climb.

Campsites, facilities: There are 17 sites for tents or RVs up to 30 feet (no hookups). Picnic tables and fire grills are provided. Drinking water and flush toilets are available. A grocery

store, coin laundry, and propane gas are nearby. Boating is available at nearby Silver Lake, two miles away. Some facilities are wheelchair-accessible. Leashed pets are permitted.

Reservations, fees: Reservations are not accepted. Sites are $15 per night, $4 per night for each additional vehicle. Open mid-May through October, weather permitting.

Directions: From Lee Vining, drive south on U.S. 395 (past the first Highway 158/June Lake Loop turnoff) to June Lake Junction (a gas station/store is on the west side of the road) and Highway 158 south. Turn right (west) on Highway 158 south and drive three miles to the campground on the left side of the road (across from Gull Lake).

Contact: Inyo National Forest, Mono Basin Scenic Area Ranger Station and Visitor Center, 760/647-3044, fax 760/647-3046.

63 JUNE LAKE

🚣 🚴 🚤 🐎 🚐 ⛺

Scenic rating: 9

in Inyo National Forest

Map 10.1, page 553

June Lake gets the highest use of all the lakes in the June Lakes Loop, and it has the best swimming, best fishing, and best sailboarding. There are three campgrounds at pretty June Lake; this is one of the two operated by the Forest Service (the other is Oh! Ridge). This one is on the northeast shore of the lake at 7,600 feet in elevation, a pretty spot with all supplies available just two miles to the south in the town of June Lake. The nearest boat launch is north of town. This is a good lake for trout fishing, receiving high numbers of stocked trout each year. A 10-mph speed limit is enforced.

Campsites, facilities: There are 28 sites for tents or RVs up to 32 feet (no hookups). Picnic tables and fire grills are provided. Drinking water, restrooms with flush toilets and coin showers, and a boat ramp are available. A grocery store, coin laundry, boat and tackle rentals, moorings, and propane gas are available nearby. Leashed pets are permitted.

Reservations, fees: Reservations are accepted ($9 reservation fee) at 877/444-6777 or www.ReserveUSA.com. Sites are $15 per night, $4 per night for each additional vehicle. Open late April to early November, weather permitting.

Directions: From Lee Vining, drive south on U.S. 395 (passing Highway 158 North) for 20 miles (six miles past Highway 158 north) to June Lake Junction (a sign is posted for "June Lake Village") and Highway 158 south. Turn west (right) on Highway 158 south and drive two miles to June Lake. Turn right (signed) and drive a short distance to the campground.

Contact: Inyo National Forest, Mono Basin Scenic Area Ranger Station and Visitor Center, 760/647-3044, fax 760/647-3046.

64 HARTLEY SPRINGS
🚶 🐾 🚐 ⛺

Scenic rating: 8

in Inyo National Forest

Map 10.1, page 553

Even though this camp is only a five-minute drive from U.S. 395, those five minutes will take you into another orbit. It is set in a forest of Jeffrey pine and has the feel of a remote, primitive camp, set in a high-mountain environment at an elevation of 8,400 feet. About two miles to the immediate north at elevation 8,611 feet is Obsidian Dome "Glass Flow," a craggy geologic formation that some people enjoy scrambling around and exploring; pick your access point carefully.

Campsites, facilities: There are 20 sites for tents or RVs up to 40 feet (no hookups). Picnic tables and fire grills are provided. Vault toilets are available. No drinking water is available. Garbage must be packed out. Leashed pets are permitted.

Reservations, fees: Reservations are not accepted. There is no fee for camping.

Open late May to early November, weather permitting.

Directions: From Lee Vining, drive south on U.S. 395 (passing the first Highway 158/June Lake Loop turnoff) for 10 miles to June Lake Junction. Continue south on U.S. 395 for six miles to Glass Creek Road (a dirt road on the west side of the highway). Turn west (right) and drive two miles to the campground entrance road on the left.

Contact: Inyo National Forest, Mono Basin Scenic Area Ranger Station and Visitor Center, 760/647-3044, fax 760/647-3046.

65 AGNEW MEADOWS AND EQUESTRIAN CAMP
🚶 🏊 🐾 🚐 ⛺

Scenic rating: 9

in Inyo National Forest

Map 10.1, page 553   BEST (

This is a perfect camp to use as a launching pad for a backpacking trip or day of fly-fishing for trout. It is set along the Upper San Joaquin River at 8,400 feet, with a trailhead for the Pacific Crest Trail available near the camp. From here you can hike seven miles to the gorgeous Thousand Island Lake, a beautiful lake sprinkled with islands set below Banner and Ritter Peaks in the spectacular Minarets. For day hikes, another choice is walking River Trail, which is routed from Agnew Meadows along the San Joaquin, providing excellent fishing, though the trout are small.

Campsites, facilities: There are 21 sites for tents or RVs up to 45 feet, and four group sites for tents or RVs that can accommodate 10–20 people each. No hookups. Picnic tables and fire grills are provided. Drinking water, vault toilets, and horseback-riding facilities are available (three family sites have hitching racks where horse camping is permitted). Supplies can be obtained at Red's Meadow store. Leashed pets are permitted.

Reservations, fees: Reservations are not accepted for individual sites, but are required ($9 reservation fee) for equestrian sites and group sites at 877/444-6777 or www.ReserveUSA .com. Sites are $16–20 per night for individual sites, $30–50 per night for equestrian and group sites, plus $4–7 per person Reds Meadow/ Agnew Meadows access fee. Open mid-June to mid-September, weather permitting.

Directions: On U.S. 395, drive to Mammoth Junction/Highway 203. Turn west on Highway 203 and drive four miles, through the town of Mammoth Lakes to Minaret Road (still Highway 203). Turn right and drive five miles to Minaret Station (past the Mammoth Mountain Ski Area). Continue for 2.6 miles to the campground entrance road on the right. Turn right and drive just under a mile to the campground. Note: The access road to the group sites is steep and narrow.

Access note: Noncampers are required to use a shuttle bus (fee) from the shuttle bus terminal at Mammoth Mountain Main Lodge Gondola Station 7 A.M.–7:30 P.M. Space available for leashed dogs, bikes, and backpacks.

Contact: Inyo National Forest, Mammoth Ranger Station and Visitor Center, 760/924-5500, fax 760/924-5547.

tables and fire grills are provided. Drinking water, vault toilets, and horseback-riding facilities are available. Limited supplies are available at a small store, or buy full supplies in Mammoth Lakes. Leashed pets are permitted.

Reservations, fees: Reservations are not accepted. Sites are $16 per night, plus $4–7 per person Reds Meadow/Agnew Meadows access fee. Open mid-June to mid-September, weather permitting.

Directions: On U.S. 395, drive to Mammoth Junction/Highway 203. Turn west on Highway 203 and drive four miles, through the town of Mammoth Lakes to Minaret Road (still Highway 203). Turn right and drive five miles to Minaret Station (past the Mammoth Mountain Ski Area). Continue for 5.1 miles to the campground on the right.

Access note: Noncampers are required to use a shuttle bus (fee) from the shuttle bus terminal at Mammoth Mountain Main Lodge Gondola Station 7 A.M.–7:30 P.M. Space available for leashed dogs, bikes, and backpacks.

Contact: Inyo National Forest, Mammoth Ranger Station and Visitor Center, 760/924-5500, fax 760/924-5547.

66 PUMICE FLAT

Scenic rating: 8

on the San Joaquin River in Inyo National Forest

Map 10.1, page 553

Pumice Flat (7,700 feet in elevation) provides roadside camping within short range of several adventures. A trail out of camp links with the Pacific Crest Trail, where you can hike along the Upper San Joaquin River for miles, with excellent access for fly-fishing, and head north into the Ansel Adams Wilderness. Devils Postpile National Monument is just two miles south, along with the trailhead for Rainbow Falls.

Campsites, facilities: There are 17 sites for tents or RVs up to 45 feet (no hookups). Picnic

67 UPPER SODA SPRINGS

Scenic rating: 8

on the San Joaquin River in Inyo National Forest

Map 10.1, page 553

This is a premium location within earshot of the Upper San Joaquin River and within minutes of many first-class recreation options. The river is stocked with trout at this camp, with several good pools within short walking distance. Farther upstream, accessible by an excellent trail, are smaller wild trout that provide good fly-fishing prospects. Devils Postpile National Monument, a massive formation of ancient columnar jointed rock, is only three miles to the south. The Pacific Crest Trail passes right by the camp, providing a trailhead for access to numerous lakes in the Ansel Adams Wilderness. The elevation is 7,700 feet.

Campsites, facilities: There are 29 sites for tents or RVs up to 36 feet (no hookups). Picnic tables and fire grills are provided. Drinking water, flush toilets, and horseback-riding facilities are available. Limited supplies can be obtained at Red's Meadow store. Leashed pets are permitted.

Reservations, fees: Reservations are not accepted. Sites are $16 per night, plus $4–7 per person Reds Meadow/Agnew Meadows access fee. Open mid-June to mid-September, weather permitting.

Directions: On U.S. 395, drive to Mammoth Junction/Highway 203. Turn west on Highway 203 and drive four miles, through the town of Mammoth Lakes to Minaret Road (still Highway 203). Turn right and drive five miles to Minaret Station (past the Mammoth Mountain Ski Area). Continue for 5.1 miles to the campground entrance road on the right. Turn right and drive 0.25 mile to the campground.

Access note: Noncampers are required to use a shuttle bus (fee) from the shuttle bus terminal at Mammoth Mountain Main Lodge Gondola Station 7 A.M.–7:30 P.M. Space is available for leashed dogs, bikes, and backpacks.

Contact: Inyo National Forest, Mammoth Ranger Station and Visitor Center, 760/924-5500, fax 760/924-5547.

68 PUMICE FLAT GROUP CAMP
🕺 🛶 🐕 🚐 ⛺

Scenic rating: 6

on the San Joaquin River in Inyo National Forest

Map 10.1, page 553

Pumice Flat Group Camp is set at 7,700 feet in elevation near the Upper San Joaquin River, adjacent to Pumice Flat. (For recreation information, see *Pumice Flat* listing in this chapter.)

Campsites, facilities: There are four group sites for tents or RVs up to 45 feet (no hookups) that can accommodate 20–50 people each. Picnic tables and fire grills are provided. Drinking water, flush toilets, and horseback-riding facilities are available. You can buy supplies in Mammoth Lakes. Leashed pets are permitted.

Reservations, fees: Reservations are required ($9 reservation fee) at 877/444-6777 or www.ReserveUSA.com. Sites are $50–110 per night per group, plus $4–7 per person Reds Meadow/Agnew Meadows access fee. Open mid-June to mid-September, weather permitting.

Directions: On U.S. 395, drive to Mammoth Junction/Highway 203. Turn west on Highway 203 and drive four miles, through the town of Mammoth Lakes to Minaret Road (still Highway 203). Turn right and drive five miles to Minaret Station (past the Mammoth Mountain Ski Area). Continue for 5.1 miles to the campground on the left side of the road.

Access note: Noncampers are required to use a shuttle bus (fee) from the shuttle bus terminal at Mammoth Mountain Main Lodge Gondola Station 7 A.M.–7:30 P.M. Space is available for leashed dogs, bikes, and backpacks.

Contact: Inyo National Forest, Mammoth Ranger Station and Visitor Center, 760/924-5500, fax 760/924-5547.

69 MINARET FALLS
🕺 🛶 🏕 ♿ 🚐 ⛺

Scenic rating: 8

on the San Joaquin River in Inyo National Forest

Map 10.1, page 553

This camp has one of the prettiest settings of the series of camps along the Upper San Joaquin River and near Devils Postpile National Monument. It is set at 7,600 feet near Minaret Creek, across from where beautiful Minaret Falls pours into the San Joaquin River. Devils Postpile National Monument, one of the best examples in the world of hexagonal, columnar jointed rock, is less than a mile from camp, where there is also a trail to awesome Rainbow Falls. The Pacific Crest Trail runs right through this area as well, and if you hike to the south, there is excellent streamside fishing access.

Campsites, facilities: There are 28 sites for tents or RVs up to 47 feet (no hookups). Picnic tables and fire grills are provided. Drinking water and vault toilets are available. Horseback-riding facilities are available nearby. You can buy limited supplies at Red's Meadow store, or all supplies in Mammoth Lakes. Some facilities are wheelchair-accessible. Leashed pets are permitted.

Reservations, fees: Reservations are not accepted. Sites are $16 per night, plus $4–7 per person Reds Meadow/Agnew Meadows access fee. Open mid-June to mid-September, weather permitting.

Directions: On U.S. 395, drive to Mammoth Junction/Highway 203. Turn west on Highway 203 and drive four miles, through the town of Mammoth Lakes to Minaret Road (still Highway 203). Turn right and drive five miles to Minaret Station (past the Mammoth Mountain Ski Area). Continue for six miles to the campground entrance road on the right. Turn right and drive 0.25 mile to the campground.

Access note: Noncampers are required to use a shuttle bus from the shuttle bus terminal at Mammoth Mountain Main Lodge Gondola Station 7 A.M.–7:30 P.M. Space is available for leashed dogs, bikes, and backpacks.

Contact: Inyo National Forest, Mammoth Ranger Station and Visitor Center, 760/924-5500, fax 760/924-5547.

70 DEVILS POSTPILE NATIONAL MONUMENT

🏃 🦌 ♿ 🚐 ⛺

Scenic rating: 9

near the San Joaquin River

Map 10.1, page 553

Devils Postpile is a spectacular and rare example of hexagonal, columnar jointed rock that looks like posts, hence the name. The camp is set at 7,600 feet in elevation and provides nearby access for the easy hike to the Postpile. Guided walks are offered during the summer; call for details. If you keep walking, it is a 2.5-mile walk to Rainbow Falls, a breathtaking 101-foot cascade that produces rainbows in its floating mist, seen only from the trail alongside the waterfall looking downstream. The camp is also adjacent to the Middle Fork San Joaquin River and the Pacific Crest Trail.

Campsites, facilities: There are 21 sites for tents or RVs up to 25 feet (no hookups). Picnic tables, food lockers, and fire grills are provided. Drinking water and flush toilets are available. Some facilities are wheelchair-accessible. Leashed pets are permitted.

Reservations, fees: Reservations are not accepted. Sites are $14 per night, plus $4–7 per person Reds Meadow/Devils Postpile access fee. Open mid-June to mid-October, weather permitting, with a two-week maximum stay. Note: National Parks Pass and Golden Passport are not accepted.

Directions: On U.S. 395, drive to Mammoth Junction/Highway 203. Turn west on Highway 203 and drive four miles, through the town of Mammoth Lakes to Minaret Road (still Highway 203). Turn right and drive five miles to Minaret Station (past the Mammoth Mountain Ski Area). Continue for nine miles to the campground entrance road on the right.

Access note: Noncampers are required to use a shuttle bus from the shuttle bus terminal at Mammoth Mountain Main Lodge Gondola Station 7 A.M.–7:30 P.M. Space is available for leashed dogs, bikes, and backpacks.

Contact: Devil Postpile National Monument, 760/934-2289, www.nps.gov/depo.

71 RED'S MEADOW

🏃 〰️ 🏠 🚐 ⛺

Scenic rating: 6

in Inyo National Forest

Map 10.1, page 553

Red's Meadow has long been established as one of the best outfitters for horseback-riding trips. To get the feel of it, three-mile round-trip rides are available to Rainbow Falls. Multiday trips into the Ansel Adams Wilderness on the Pacific Crest Trail are also available. A small restaurant is a bonus here, always a must-stop for long-distance hikers getting a shot to chomp their first hamburger in weeks, something like a bear finding a candy bar, quite a sight for the drive-in campers. The nearby Devils Postpile National Monument, Rainbow Falls, Minaret Falls, and San Joaquin River provide recreation options. The elevation is 7,600 feet.

Campsites, facilities: There are 56 sites for tents or RVs up to 30 feet (no hookups). Picnic tables, food lockers, and fire grills are provided. Drinking water, flush toilets, horseback riding, and natural hot springs are available. You can buy limited supplies at a small store. Leashed pets are permitted.

Reservations, fees: Reservations are not accepted. Sites are $16 per night, plus $4–7 per person Reds Meadow/Agnew Meadows access fee. Open mid-June to mid-September, weather permitting.

Directions: On U.S. 395, drive to Mammoth Junction/Highway 203. Turn west on Highway 203 and drive four miles, through the town of Mammoth Lakes to Minaret Road (still Highway 203). Turn right and drive five miles to Minaret Station (past the Mammoth Mountain Ski Area). Continue for 7.4 miles to the campground entrance on the left.

Access note: Noncampers are required to use a shuttle bus from the shuttle bus terminal at Mammoth Mountain Main Lodge Gondola Station 7 A.M.–7:30 P.M. Space available for leashed dogs, bikes, and backpacks.

Contact: Inyo National Forest, Mammoth Ranger Station and Visitor Center, 760/924-5500, fax 760/924-5547.

72 LAKE GEORGE

🏃 🚣 🚐 🏠 🚐 ⛺

Scenic rating: 8

in Inyo National Forest

Map 10.1, page 553

The sites here have views of Lake George, a beautiful lake in a rock basin set below the spectacular Crystal Crag. Lake George is at 9,000 feet in elevation, a small lake fed by creeks coming from both Crystal Lake and TJ Lake. TJ Lake is only about a 20-minute walk from the campground, and Crystal Lake is about a 45-minute romp; both make excellent short hiking trips. Trout fishing at Lake George is decent—not great, not bad, but decent. Swimming is not allowed, but boats with small motors are permitted.

Campsites, facilities: There are 16 sites for tents or RVs up to 25 feet (no hookups). Picnic tables and fire grills are provided. Drinking water and flush toilets are available. A grocery store, coin laundry, coin showers, primitive boat launch, and propane gas are available nearby. Leashed pets are permitted.

Reservations, fees: Reservations are not accepted. Sites are $16 per night with a seven-day limit. Open mid-June to mid-September, weather permitting.

Directions: From Lee Vining on U.S. 395, drive south for 25 miles to Mammoth Junction and Highway 203/Minaret Summit Road. Turn west on Highway 203 and drive four miles to Lake Mary Road. Continue straight through the intersection and drive four miles to Lake Mary Loop Drive. Turn left and drive 0.3 mile to Lake George Road. Turn right and drive 0.5 mile to the campground.

Contact: Inyo National Forest, Mammoth Ranger Station and Visitor Center, 760/924-5500, fax 760/924-5547.

73 GLASS CREEK
🥾🛶🏕️♿🚐⛺

Scenic rating: 5

in Inyo National Forest

Map 10.2, page 554

This primitive camp is set along Glass Creek at 7,600 feet, about a mile from Obsidian Dome to the nearby west. A trail follows Glass Creek past the southern edge of the dome, a craggy, volcanic formation that tops out at 8,611 feet in elevation. That trail continues along Glass Creek, climbing to the foot of San Joaquin Mountain for a great view of the high desert to the east. Insider's tip: The Department of Fish and Game stocks Glass Creek with trout just once each June, right at the camp.

Campsites, facilities: There are 50 sites for tents or RVs up to 40 feet (no hookups). Picnic tables and fire grills are provided. Vault toilets are available. No drinking water is available. Some facilities are wheelchair-accessible. Leashed pets are permitted.

Reservations, fees: Reservations are not accepted. There is no fee for camping. Open late April to early November, weather permitting.

Directions: From Lee Vining, drive south on U.S. 395 (past the first Highway 158/June Lake Loop turnoff) for 11 miles to June Lake Junction. Continue south on U.S. 395 for six miles to a Forest Service road (Glass Creek Road). Turn west (right) and drive 0.25 mile to the camp access road on the right. Turn right and continue 0.5 mile to the main camp at the end of the road. Two notes: 1. A primitive area with large RV sites can be used as an overflow area on the right side of the access road. 2. If arriving from the south on U.S. 395, a direct left turn to Glass Creek Road is impossible. Heading north you will pass the CalTrans Crestview Maintenance Station on the right. Continue north, make a U-turn when possible, and follow the above directions.

Contact: Inyo National Forest, Mono Basin Scenic Area Ranger Station and Visitor Center, 760/647-3044, fax 760/647-3046.

74 BIG SPRINGS
🥾🛶〽️🏕️🚐⛺

Scenic rating: 5

on Deadman Creek in Inyo National Forest

Map 10.2, page 554

Big Springs, at 7,300 feet, is set on the edge of the high desert on the east side of U.S. 395. The main attractions are Deadman Creek, which runs right by the camp, and Big Springs, which is set just on the opposite side of the river. There are several hot springs in the area, best reached by driving south on U.S. 395 to the Mammoth Lakes Airport and turning left on Hot Creek Road. As with all hot springs, use at your own risk.

Campsites, facilities: There are 26 sites for tents or RVs up to 40 feet (no hookups). Picnic tables and fire grills are provided. Vault toilets are available. No drinking water is available. Leashed pets are permitted.

Reservations, fees: Reservations are not accepted. There is no fee for camping. Open late April through early November, weather permitting.

Directions: From Lee Vining, drive south on U.S. 395 (past the first Highway 158/June Lake Loop turnoff) to June Lake Junction. Continue south for about seven miles to Owens River Road. Turn east (left) and drive two miles to a fork. Bear left at the fork and drive 0.25 mile to the camp on the left side of the road.

Contact: Inyo National Forest, Mono Basin Scenic Area Ranger Station and Visitor Center, 760/647-3044, fax 760/647-3046.

75 DEADMAN/OBSIDIAN FLAT GROUP
🥾🛶🏕️🚐⛺

Scenic rating: 5

on Deadman Creek in Inyo National Forest

Map 10.2, page 554

This little-known camp is set at 7,800 feet along little Deadman Creek. It is primitive and dusty in the summer, cold in the early summer and fall. From camp, hikers can drive west for three miles to the headwaters of Deadman Creek and to a trailhead for a route that runs past San Joaquin Mountain and beyond to little Yost Lake, a one-way hike of four miles.

Campsites, facilities: There are 30 sites for tents or RVs up to 30 feet. A group camp for tents or RVs of any length can accommodate up to 50 people at nearby Obsidian Flat. No hookups. Picnic tables and fire grills are provided. Vault toilets are available. No drinking water is available. Garbage must be packed out. Leashed pets are permitted.

Reservations, fees: Reservations are not accepted for individual sites but are required ($9 reservation fee) for the group camp at 877/444-6777 or www.ReserveUSA.com. There is no camping fee for individual sites; the group camp is $20 per night. Open late May to early November, weather permitting.

Directions: From Lee Vining, drive south on U.S. 395 (past the first Highway 158/June Lake Loop turnoff) to June Lake Junction. Continue south for 6.5 miles to a Forest Service road (Deadman Creek Road) on the west (right) side of the road. Turn west (right) and drive two miles to the camp access road on the right. Turn right and drive 0.5 mile to the camp. Note: If you are arriving from the south on U.S. 395 and you reach the CalTrans Crestview Maintenance Station on the right, you have gone one mile too far; make a U-turn when possible and return for access.

Contact: Inyo National Forest, Mono Basin Scenic Area and Visitor Center, 760/647-3044, fax 760/647-3046.

76 PINE GLEN
🚶 🐕 🚐 ⛺

Scenic rating: 6

in Inyo National Forest

Map 10.2, page 554

This is a well-situated base camp for several side trips. The most popular is the trip to Devils Postpile National Monument, with a shuttle ride from the Mammoth Ski Area. Other nearby trips include exploring Inyo Craters, Mammoth Lakes, and the hot springs at Hot Creek east of Mammoth Lakes Airport. The elevation is 7,800 feet.

Campsites, facilities: There are 11 sites (used as overflow from Old Shady Rest and New Shady Rest campgrounds) and five group sites for tents or RVs up to 55 feet (no hookups) that can accommodate 25–30 people each. Picnic tables and fire grills are provided. Drinking water, flush toilets, and a dump station are available. A grocery store, coin laundry, propane gas, and horseback-riding facilities are nearby in Mammoth Lakes. Leashed pets are permitted.

Reservations, fees: Reservations are not accepted for individual sites but are required ($9 reservation fee) for group sites at 877/444-6777 or www.ReserveUSA.com. Sites are $15 per night, and group sites are $35–50 per night. Open late May through September, weather permitting.

Directions: From Lee Vining on U.S. 395, drive south for 25 miles to Mammoth Junction and Highway 203/Minaret Summit Road. Turn west on Highway 203 and drive about three miles to the Mammoth Lakes Visitor Center. Just past the visitor center, turn right on Old Sawmill Road and drive a short distance to the campground on the right.

Contact: Inyo National Forest, Mammoth Ranger Station and Visitor Center, 760/924-5500, fax 760/924-5547.

77 NEW SHADY REST
🚶 🐕 🚣 🚐 ⛺

Scenic rating: 6

in Inyo National Forest

Map 10.2, page 554

This easy-to-reach camp is set at 7,800 feet, not far from the Mammoth Mountain Ski Area. The surrounding Inyo National Forest provides many side-trip opportunities, including Devils Postpile National Monument (by shuttle available from near the Mammoth

Mountain Ski Area), Upper San Joaquin River, and the Inyo National Forest backcountry trails, streams, and lakes.

Campsites, facilities: There are 95 sites for tents or RVs up to 38 feet (no hookups). Picnic tables and fire grills are provided. Drinking water and flush toilets are available. A dump station, playground, grocery store, coin laundry, and propane gas are available nearby. Leashed pets are permitted.

Reservations, fees: Reservations are accepted ($9 reservation fee) at 877/444-6777 or www .ReserveUSA.com. Sites are $15 per night with a 14-day limit. Open mid-May through October, weather permitting.

Directions: From Lee Vining on U.S. 395, drive south for 25 miles to Mammoth Junction and Highway 203/Minaret Summit Road. Turn west on Highway 203 and drive about three miles to the Mammoth Lakes Visitor Center. Just past the visitors center, turn right on Old Sawmill Road and drive a short distance to the campground on the right.

Contact: Inyo National Forest, Mammoth Ranger Station and Visitor Center, 760/924-5500, fax 760/924-5547.

78 OLD SHADY REST

Scenic rating: 6

in Inyo National Forest

Map 10.2, page 554

Names such as "Old Shady Rest" are usually reserved for mom-and-pop RV parks. The Forest Service respected tradition in officially naming this park what the locals have called it all along. Like New Shady Rest, this camp is near the Mammoth Lakes Visitor Center, with the same side trips available. It is one of three camps in the immediate vicinity. The elevation is 7,800 feet.

Campsites, facilities: There are 51 sites for tents or RVs up to 55 feet (no hookups). Picnic tables and fire grills are provided. Drinking water and flush toilets are available. A dump station, playground, grocery store, coin laundry, and propane gas are available nearby. Leashed pets are permitted.

Reservations, fees: Reservations are accepted ($9 reservation fee) at 877/444-6777 or www .ReserveUSA.com. Sites are $15 per night with a 14-day limit. Open mid-June to early September, weather permitting.

Directions: From Lee Vining on U.S. 395, drive south for 25 miles to Mammoth Junction and Highway 203/Minaret Summit Road. Turn west on Highway 203 and drive about three miles to the Forest Service Visitor Center. Just past the visitors center, turn right and drive 0.3 mile to the campground on the left.

Contact: Inyo National Forest, Mammoth Ranger Station and Visitor Center, 760/924-5500, fax 760/924-5547.

79 MAMMOTH MOUNTAIN RV PARK

Scenic rating: 6

near Mammoth Lakes

Map 10.2, page 554

This RV park is just across the street from the Forest Service Visitor Center. Got a question? Someone there has got an answer. This camp is open year-round, making it a great place to stay for a ski trip.

Campsites, facilities: There are 185 sites, some with full hookups (50 amps), for tents or RVs up to 45 feet. Two cabins are also available. Picnic tables are provided. Fire pits are provided at some sites. Restrooms with showers, drinking water, cable TV, modem access, dump station, coin laundry, heated year-round swimming pool, seasonal recreation room, playground, RV supplies, and a spa are available. Some facilities are wheelchair-accessible. Supplies can be obtained in Mammoth Lakes, 0.25 mile away. Leashed pets are permitted, with certain restrictions.

Reservations, fees: Reservations are accepted at 800/582-4603. Sites are $21–40 per night,

$3 per person per night for more than two people, $2 per night for each additional vehicle, $3 per pet per night. Some credit cards accepted. Open year-round.

Directions: From Lee Vining on U.S. 395, drive south for 25 miles to Mammoth Junction and Highway 203. Turn west on Highway 203 and drive three miles to the park on the left.

From Bishop, drive 40 miles north on Highway 395 to Mammoth Lakes exit. Turn west on Highway 203, go under the overpass, and drive three miles to the park on the left.

Contact: Mammoth Mountain RV Park, 760/934-3822, fax 760/934-1896, www .mammothrv.com.

80 TWIN LAKES

Scenic rating: 8

in Inyo National Forest

Map 10.2, page 554

From Twin Lakes, you can look southwest and see pretty Twin Falls, a wide cascade that runs into the head of upper Twin Lake. There are actually two camps here, one on each side of the access road, at 8,600 feet. Lower Twin Lake is a favorite for fly fishers in float tubes. Powerboats, swimming, and sailboarding are not permitted. Use is heavy at the campground. Often there will be people lined up waiting for another family's weeklong vacation to end so theirs can start. Excellent hiking trails are in the area.

Campsites, facilities: There are 94 sites for tents or RVs up to 40 feet (no hookups). Picnic tables and fire grills are provided. Drinking water, flush toilets, and a boat launch are available. A grocery store, coin laundry, coin showers, and propane gas are available nearby. Some facilities are wheelchair-accessible. Leashed pets are permitted.

Reservations, fees: Reservations are accepted ($9 reservation fee) at 877/444-6777 or www .ReserveUSA.com. Sites are $14 per night.

Open mid-May to late October, weather permitting.

Directions: From Lee Vining on U.S. 395, drive south for 25 miles to Mammoth Junction and Highway 203/Minaret Summit Road. Turn west on Highway 203 and drive four miles to Lake Mary Road. Continue straight through the intersection and drive 2.3 miles to Twin Lakes Loop Road. Turn right and drive 0.5 mile to the campground.

Contact: Inyo National Forest, Mammoth Ranger Station and Visitor Center, 760/924-5500, fax 760/924-5547.

81 SHERWIN CREEK

Scenic rating: 7

in Inyo National Forest

Map 10.2, page 554

This camp is set along little Sherwin Creek, at 7,600 feet in elevation, a short distance from the town of Mammoth Lakes. If you drive a mile east on Sherwin Creek Road, then turn right at the short spur road, you will find a trailhead for a hike that is routed up six miles to Valentine Lake in the John Muir Wilderness, set on the northwest flank of Bloody Mountain.

Campsites, facilities: There are 87 sites for tents or RVs up to 34 feet (no hookups), and 15 walk-in sites for tents only. Picnic tables and fire grills are provided. Drinking water and flush toilets are available. Leashed pets are permitted.

Reservations, fees: Reservations are accepted ($9 reservation fee) at 877/444-6777 or www .ReserveUSA.com. Sites are $15 per night. Open early May to mid-September, weather permitting.

Directions: From Lee Vining on U.S. 395, drive south for 25 miles to Mammoth Junction and Highway 203/Minaret Summit Road. Turn west on Highway 203 and drive about three miles to the Mammoth Lakes Visitor Center and continue a short distance to Old Mammoth Road. Turn left and drive about a

mile to Sherwin Creek. Turn south and drive two miles on largely unpaved road to the campground on the left side of the road.
Contact: Inyo National Forest, Mammoth Lakes Visitor Center, 760/924-5500, fax 760/924-5547.

82 LAKE MARY

Scenic rating: 9

in Inyo National Forest

Map 10.2, page 554

Lake Mary is the star of the Mammoth Lakes region. Of the 11 lakes in the area, this is the largest and most developed. It provides a resort, boat ramp, and boat rentals, and it receives the highest number of trout stocks. No water/body contact, including swimming, is allowed, and the speed limit is 10 mph. It is set at 8,900 feet in a place of incredible natural beauty, one of the few spots that literally has it all. Of course, that often includes quite a few other people. If there are too many for you, an excellent trailhead is available at nearby Coldwater camp that routes you up to Emerald Lake.
Campsites, facilities: There are 48 sites for tents or RVs up to 30 feet (no hookups). Picnic tables, food lockers, and fire grills are provided. Drinking water and flush toilets are available. A grocery store, coin laundry, and propane gas are nearby. Leashed pets are permitted.
Reservations, fees: Reservations are not accepted. Sites are $16 per night with a 14-day limit. Open early June to mid-September, weather permitting.
Directions: Take U.S. 395 to Mammoth Junction and Highway 203. Turn west on Highway 203 and drive through the town of Mammoth Lakes to the junction of Minaret Road/Highway 203 and Lake Mary Road. Continue straight through the intersection and drive 3.6 miles to Lake Mary Loop Drive. Turn right and drive 0.5 mile to the campground entrance.

Contact: Inyo National Forest, Mammoth Ranger Station and Visitor Center, 760/924-5500, fax 760/924-5547.

83 PINE CITY

Scenic rating: 7

near Lake Mary in Inyo National Forest

Map 10.2, page 554

This camp is at the edge of Lake Mary at an elevation of 8,900 feet. This camp is popular for both families and fly fishers with float tubes. Swimming is not permitted.
Campsites, facilities: There are 10 sites for tents or RVs up to 40 feet (no hookups). Picnic tables and fire grills are provided. Drinking water and flush toilets are available. A grocery store, coin laundry, boat launch, boat rentals, and propane gas are available nearby. Some facilities are wheelchair-accessible. Leashed pets are permitted.
Reservations, fees: Reservations are not accepted. Sites are $16 per night. Open early June to mid-September.
Directions: Take U.S. 395 to Mammoth Junction and Highway 203. Turn west on Highway 203 and drive through the town of Mammoth Lakes to the junction of Minaret Road/Highway 203 and Lake Mary Road. Continue straight through the intersection and drive 3.6 miles to Lake Mary Loop Drive. Turn left and drive 0.25 mile to the campground.
Contact: Inyo National Forest, Mammoth Ranger Station and Visitor Center, 760/924-5500, fax 760/924-5547.

84 COLDWATER

Scenic rating: 7

on Coldwater Creek in Inyo National Forest

Map 10.2, page 554

While this camp is not the first choice of many simply because there is no lake view, it has a special attraction all its own. First, it is a two-minute drive from the campground to Lake Mary, where there is a boat ramp, rentals, and good trout fishing. Second, at the end of the campground access road is a trailhead for two outstanding hikes. From the Y at the trailhead, if you head right, you will be routed up Coldwater Creek to Emerald Lake, a great little hike. If you head to the left, you will have a more ambitious trip to Arrowhead, Skelton, and Red Lakes, all within three miles. The elevation is 8,900 feet.

Campsites, facilities: There are 78 sites for tents or RVs up to 50 feet (no hookups). Picnic tables and fire grills are provided. Drinking water, flush toilets, and horse facilities are available. You can buy supplies in Mammoth Lakes. Leashed pets are permitted.

Reservations, fees: Reservations are accepted ($9 reservation fee) at 877/444-6777 or www.ReserveUSA.com. Sites are $16 per night, with a 14-day limit. Open mid-June to mid-September.

Directions: From Lee Vining on U.S. 395, drive south for 25 miles to Mammoth Junction and Highway 203/Minaret Summit Road. Turn west on Highway 203 and drive four miles to Lake Mary Road. Continue straight through the intersection and drive 3.6 miles to Lake Mary Loop Drive. Turn left and drive 0.6 mile to the camp entrance road.

Contact: Inyo National Forest, Mammoth Ranger Station and Visitor Center, 760/924-5500, fax 760/924-5547.

85 CONVICT LAKE

Scenic rating: 7

in Inyo National Forest

Map 10.2, page 554   BEST (

After driving in the stark desert on U.S. 395 to get here, it is always astonishing to clear the rise and see Convict Lake (7,583 feet) and its gemlike waters set in a mountain bowl beneath a back wall of high, jagged wilderness peaks. The camp is right beside Convict Creek, about a quarter mile from Convict Lake. Both provide very good trout fishing, including some rare monster-sized brown trout below the Convict Lake outlet. Fishing is often outstanding in Convict Lake, with a chance of hooking a 10- or 15-pound trout. The lake speed limit is 10 mph, and although swimming is allowed, it is not popular because of the cold, often choppy water. A trail is routed around the lake, providing a nice day hike. A bonus is an outstanding resort with a boat launch, boat rentals, cabin rentals, small store, restaurant, and bar. Horseback rides and hiking are also available, with a trail routed along the north side of the lake, then along upper Convict Creek (a stream crossing is required about three miles in), and into the John Muir Wilderness. This is the most popular camp in the Mammoth area and it is frequently full. While the lake rates a 10 for scenic beauty, the camp itself is in a stark desert setting, out of sight of the lake, plus it can get windy and cold here because of the exposed sites.

Campsites, facilities: There are 88 sites for tents or RVs up to 40 feet (no hookups). Rental cabins are also available through the Convict Lake Resort. Picnic tables and fire grills are provided. Drinking water and flush toilets are available. A dump station, boat ramp, store, restaurant, and horseback-riding facilities are available nearby. Some facilities are wheelchair-accessible. Leashed pets are permitted.

Reservations, fees: Reservations are accepted ($9 reservation fee) at 877/444-6777 or www .ReserveUSA.com. Sites are $16 per night. For cabin reservations, phone 760/934-3880 or 800/992-2260. Open mid-April through October, weather permitting; cabins open year-round.

Directions: From Lee Vining on U.S. 395, drive south for 31 miles (five miles past Mammoth Junction) to Convict Lake Road (adjacent to Mammoth Lakes Airport). Turn west (right) on Convict Lake Road and drive three miles to Convict Lake. Cross the dam and drive a short distance to the campground entrance road on the left. Turn left and drive 0.25 mile to the campground.

From Bishop, drive north on U.S. 395 for 35 miles to Convict Lake Road. Turn west (left) and drive three miles to the lake and campground.

Contact: Inyo National Forest, Mammoth Ranger Station and Visitor Center, 760/924-5500, fax 760/924-5547; Convict Lake Resort and Cabins, 800/992-2260.

86 McGEE CREEK RV PARK
🧗 🚣 🐕 🚐 ⛺

Scenic rating: 6
near Crowley Lake
Map 10.2, page 554

This is a popular layover spot for folks visiting giant Crowley Lake. Crowley Lake is still one of the better lakes in the Sierra for trout fishing, with good prospects for large rainbow trout and brown trout, though the 20-pound brown trout that once made this lake famous are now mainly a legend. McGee Creek runs through the campground, and trout fishing is popular. Several trout ponds are also available; call for fees. Beautiful Convict Lake provides a nearby side-trip option. It is also about nine miles to Rock Creek Lake, a beautiful high-mountain destination. The elevation is 7,000 feet.

Campsites, facilities: There are 40 sites with full, partial, or no hookups (50 amps) for tents or RVs up to 40 feet; some sites are pull-through. Picnic tables and fire pits are provided. Drinking water and restrooms with showers and flush toilets are available. Leashed pets are permitted.

Reservations, fees: Reservations are accepted. Sites are $19–29 per night, $3 per person per night for more than two people. Weekly and monthly rates available. Open late April through September, weather permitting.

Directions: From the junction of U.S. 395 and Highway 203 (the Mammoth Lakes turnoff), drive south on U.S. 395 for eight miles to the turnoff for McGee Creek Road. Take that exit and look for the park entrance on the left.

Contact: McGee Creek RV Park, 760/935-4233.

87 GEE CREEK
🧗 🚣 🐕 🛖 ♿ 🚐 ⛺

Scenic rating: 7
in Inyo National Forest
Map 10.2, page 554

This is a Forest Service camp at an elevation of 7,600 feet, set along little McGee Creek, a good location for fishing and hiking. There are few trees here. The stream is stocked with trout, and a trailhead is just up the road. From here you can hike along upper McGee Creek and into the John Muir Wilderness.

Campsites, facilities: There are 28 sites for tents or RVs up to 25 feet (no hookups). Picnic tables and fire grills are provided. Drinking water, flush toilets, and shade structures are available. Horseback-riding facilities are available nearby. Some facilities are wheelchair-accessible. Leashed pets are permitted.

Reservations, fees: Reservations are accepted at 877/444-6777 or www.ReserveUSA.com. Sites are $17 per night, $5 per night for each additional vehicle. Open mid-May to mid-October, weather permitting.

Directions: From Mammoth Lakes at the junction of U.S. 395 and Highway 203, drive south on U.S. 395 for 8.5 miles to McGee Creek Road (signed). Turn right (toward the Sierra) and drive 1.5 miles on a narrow, windy road to the campground.

Contact: Inyo National Forest, White Mountain Ranger District, 760/873-2500, fax 760/873-2563; McGee Creek Pack Station, 760/935-4324.

88 CROWLEY LAKE

Scenic rating: 5

near Crowley Lake

Map 10.2, page 554

This large BLM camp is across U.S. 395 from the south shore of Crowley Lake. For many, Crowley is the trout-fishing capital of the eastern Sierra, with the annual opener (the last Saturday in April) a great celebration. Though the trout fishing can go through a lull in midsummer, it can become excellent again in the fall when the lake's population of big brown trout heads up to the top of the lake and the mouth of the Owens River. This is a large lake with 45 miles of shoreline. In the summer, water sports include swimming, waterskiing, wakeboarding, personal watercraft riding, and sailboarding. The surroundings are fairly stark; the elevation is 6,800 feet.

Campsites, facilities: There are 47 sites for tents or RVs of any length (no hookups). Picnic tables and fire grills are provided. Vault toilets are available. No drinking water is available. A grocery store, boat ramp, boat rentals, and horseback-riding facilities are nearby. Floating chemical toilets are available on the lake. Leashed pets are permitted.

Reservations, fees: Reservations are not accepted. Sites are $5 per night, and season passes are available for $300. Open late April through October, weather permitting.

Directions: Drive on U.S. 395 to the Crowley Lake Road exit (30 miles north of Bishop). Take that exit west (toward the Sierra) to Crowley Lake Road. Turn right on Crowley Lake Road and drive northwest for three miles to the campground entrance on the left (well signed).

Contact: Bureau of Land Management, Bishop Field Office, 760/872-4881, fax 760/872-5050; McGee Creek Pack Station, 760/935-4324.

89 TUFF

Scenic rating: 5

near Crowley Lake in Inyo National Forest

Map 10.2, page 554

Easy access off U.S. 395 makes this camp a winner, though it is not nearly as pretty as those up Rock Creek Road to the west of Tom's Place. The fact that you can get in and out of here quickly makes it ideal for campers planning fishing trips to nearby Crowley Lake. The elevation is 7,000 feet.

Campsites, facilities: There are 34 sites for tents or RVs up to 45 feet (no hookups). Picnic tables and fire grills are provided. Drinking water and flush toilets are available. Some facilities are wheelchair-accessible. Leashed pets are permitted.

Reservations, fees: Reservations are accepted ($9 reservation fee) at 877/444-6777 or www .ReserveUSA.com. Sites are $17 per night, $5 per night for each additional vehicle. Open late April to mid-October, weather permitting.

Directions: From Mammoth Lakes at the junction of U.S. 395 and Highway 203, drive south on U.S. 395 for 15.5 miles (one mile north of Tom's Place) to Rock Creek Road. Turn left (east) on Rock Creek Road and drive 0.5 mile to the campground.

Contact: Inyo National Forest, White Mountain Ranger District, 760/873-2500, fax 760/873-2563.

90 FRENCH CAMP

Scenic rating: 5

on Rock Creek near Crowley Lake in Inyo National Forest

Map 10.2, page 554

French Camp is just a short hop from U.S. 395 and Tom's Place, right where the high Sierra turns into high plateau country. Side-trip opportunities include boating and fishing on giant Crowley Lake and, to the west on Rock

Creek Road, visiting little Rock Creek Lake 10 miles away. The elevation is 7,500 feet.

Campsites, facilities: There are 86 sites for tents or RVs up to 35 feet (no hookups). Picnic tables and fire grills are provided. Drinking water, flush toilets, and a dump station are available. Leashed pets are permitted.

Reservations, fees: Reservations are accepted ($9 reservation fee) at 877/444-6777 or www .ReserveUSA.com. Site are $17 per night, $5 per night for each additional vehicle. Open late April through October, weather permitting.

Directions: From Mammoth Lakes at the junction of U.S. 395 and Highway 203, drive south on U.S. 395 for 15 miles to Tom's Place and Rock Creek Road. Turn right (toward the Sierra) at Rock Creek Road and drive 0.25 mile to the campground on the right.

Contact: Inyo National Forest, White Mountain Ranger District, 760/873-2500, fax 760/873-2563.

91 HOLIDAY
🏃 🏊 🐕 🎣 ♿ 🚐 ⛺

Scenic rating: 5

near Crowley Lake in Inyo National Forest

Map 10.2, page 554

There's a story behind every name. The story here is that this camp is open only on holiday weekends as an overflow camp. It is near Rock Creek, not far from Crowley Lake. The elevation is 7,500 feet, with surroundings far more stark than the camps to the west on Rock Creek Road.

Campsites, facilities: There are 35 sites for tents or RVs up to 16 feet (no hookups); the sites can also be used as a group camp for up to 70 people. Picnic tables and fire grills are provided. Drinking water and flush toilets are available. Some facilities are wheelchair-accessible. Leashed pets are permitted.

Reservations, fees: Reservations are not accepted for individual sites, but are required for the group site at 760/935-4339. Sites are

$17 per night. Call for group rates. Opened as necessary.

Directions: From Mammoth Lakes at the junction of U.S. 395 and Highway 203, drive south on U.S. 395 for 15 miles south to Tom's Place and Rock Creek Road. Turn right (toward the Sierra) and drive 0.5 mile to the campground on the left.

Contact: Inyo National Forest, White Mountain Ranger District, 760/873-2500, fax 760/873-2563.

92 ASPEN GROUP CAMP
🏃 🏊 🐕 🎣 ♿ 🚐 ⛺

Scenic rating: 7

near Crowley Lake in Inyo National Forest

Map 10.2, page 554

This small group campground set on Rock Creek is used primarily as a base camp for anglers and campers heading to nearby Crowley Lake or venturing west to Rock Creek Lake. The elevation at the camp is 8,100 feet.

Campsites, facilities: There is one group camp for tents or RVs up to 25 feet (no hookups) that can accommodate up to 25 people. Picnic tables and fire grills are provided. Drinking water and flush toilets are available. Limited supplies are available in Tom's Place, three miles away. Some facilities are wheelchair-accessible. Leashed pets are permitted.

Reservations, fees: Reservations are required ($9 reservation fee) at 877/444-6777 or www .ReserveUSA.com. The group fee is $55 per night. Open mid-May to mid-October, weather permitting.

Directions: From Mammoth Lakes at the junction of U.S. 395 and Highway 203, drive south on U.S. 395 for 15 miles south to Tom's Place and Rock Creek Road. Turn right (toward the Sierra) at Rock Creek Road and drive three miles to the campground.

Contact: Inyo National Forest, White Mountain Ranger District, 760/873-2500, fax 760/873-2563.

93 IRIS MEADOW

Scenic rating: 5

near Crowley Lake in Inyo National Forest

Map 10.2, page 554

Iris Meadow, at 8,300 feet elevation on the flank of Red Mountain (11,472 feet), is the first in a series of five Forest Service camps set near Rock Creek Canyon on the road leading from Tom's Place up to pretty Rock Creek Lake. A bonus is that some of the campsites are next to the creek. Rock Creek is stocked with trout, and nearby Rock Creek Lake also provides fishing and boating for hand-launched boats. This camp also has access to a great trailhead for wilderness exploration.

Campsites, facilities: There are 14 sites for tents or RVs up to 30 feet (no hookups). Picnic tables and fire grills are provided. Drinking water and flush toilets are available. Limited supplies are available in Tom's Place, three miles away. Some facilities are wheelchair-accessible. Leashed pets are permitted.

Reservations, fees: Reservations are not accepted. Sites are $18 per night, $5 per night for each additional vehicle. Open late May to mid-September, weather permitting.

Directions: From Mammoth Lakes at the junction of U.S. 395 and Highway 203, drive south on U.S. 395 for 15 miles to Tom's Place and Rock Creek Road. Turn right (toward the Sierra) at Rock Creek Road and drive three miles to the campground.

Contact: Inyo National Forest, White Mountain Ranger District, 760/873-2500, fax 760/873-2563.

94 BIG MEADOW

Scenic rating: 8

near Crowley Lake in Inyo National Forest

Map 10.2, page 554

This is a smaller, quieter camp in the series of campgrounds along Rock Creek. Some of the campsites are along the creek. Beautiful Rock Creek Lake provides a nearby side trip. The elevation is 8,600 feet. In the fall, turning aspens here make for spectacular colors.

Campsites, facilities: There are 11 sites for tents or RVs up to 22 feet (no hookups). Picnic tables and fire grills are provided. Drinking water and flush toilets are available. Limited supplies are available in Tom's Place, four miles away. Some facilities are wheelchair-accessible. Leashed pets are permitted.

Reservations, fees: Reservations are not accepted. Sites are $18 per night, $5 per night for each additional vehicle. Open early May to mid-September.

Directions: From Mammoth Lakes at the junction of U.S. 395 and Highway 203, drive south on U.S. 395 for 15 miles south to Tom's Place and Rock Creek Road. Turn right (toward the Sierra) at Rock Creek Road and drive four miles to the campground.

Contact: Inyo National Forest, White Mountain Ranger District, 760/873-2500, fax 760/873-2563.

95 PALISADE

Scenic rating: 8

near Crowley Lake in Inyo National Forest

Map 10.2, page 554

This shoe might just fit. Palisade, a tiny campground, provides a pretty spot along Rock Creek at 8,600 feet in elevation, with many side-trip options. The closest is fishing for small trout on Rock Creek and at pretty Rock Creek Lake up the road to the west. Another option is horseback riding, and horse rentals are in the area. The area is loaded with aspens. Some of the campsites are directly on the creek.

Campsites, facilities: There are five sites for tents or RVs up to 30 feet (no hookups); this campground can also be used as a group site for up to 30 people. Picnic tables and fire grills are provided. Drinking water and flush toilets are available. Horseback-riding facilities are available nearby. Limited supplies are available in Tom's Place, five miles away. Leashed pets are permitted.

Reservations, fees: Reservations are accepted at 760/935-4339. Sites are $18 per night, $5 per night for each additional vehicle. The group price is $85 per night. Open mid-May to mid-September, weather permitting.

Directions: From Mammoth Lakes at the junction of U.S. 395 and Highway 203, drive south on U.S. 395 for 15 miles south to Tom's Place and Rock Creek Road. Turn right (toward the Sierra) at Rock Creek Road and drive five miles to the campground.

Contact: Inyo National Forest, White Mountain Ranger District, 760/873-2500, fax 760/873-2563; Rock Creek Pack Station, 760/935-4493; Recreation Resource Management, 760/935-4339.

96 EAST FORK

Scenic rating: 8

near Crowley Lake in Inyo National Forest

Map 10.2, page 554

This is a beautiful, popular campground set along East Fork Rock Creek at 9,000 feet elevation. The camp is only three miles from Rock Creek Lake, where there's an excellent trailhead. Mountain biking is popular in this area, and Lower Rock Creek and Sand Canyon have two of the most difficult and desirable trails around; they're suggested for experienced riders only.

Campsites, facilities: There are 133 sites for tents or RVs up to 35 feet (no hookups). Picnic tables and fire grills are provided. Drinking water and flush toilets are available. Limited supplies are available in Tom's Place and at Rock Creek Lakes Resort. Leashed pets are permitted.

Reservations, fees: Reservations are accepted ($9 reservation fee) at 877/444-6777 or www.ReserveUSA.com. Sites are $17 per night, $5

per night for each additional vehicle. Open mid-May through October.

Directions: From Mammoth Lakes at the junction of U.S. 395 and Highway 203, drive south on U.S. 395 for 15 miles south to Tom's Place and Rock Creek Road. Turn right (toward the Sierra) at Rock Creek Road and drive five miles to the campground access road on the left.

Contact: Inyo National Forest, White Mountain Ranger District, 760/873-2500, fax 760/873-2563.

97 PINE GROVE UPPER AND LOWER

Scenic rating: 8

near Crowley Lake in Inyo National Forest

Map 10.2, page 554

Pine Grove is one of the smaller camps in the series of campgrounds along Rock Creek. Of the five camps in this canyon, this one is the closest to Rock Creek Lake, just a two-mile drive away (Rock Creek Lake Campground is closer, of course). The aspens here are stunning in September, when miles of mountains turn to shimmering golds. Some of the campsites are along the creek. The elevation is 9,300 feet.

Campsites, facilities: There are 23 sites for tents or RVs up to 16 feet (no hookups). Picnic tables and fire grills are provided. Drinking water and flush toilets are available. Horseback-riding facilities are available nearby. Limited supplies can be obtained in Tom's Place and at Rock Creek Lakes Resort. Leashed pets are permitted.

Reservations, fees: Reservations are not accepted. Sites are $17 per night, $5 per night for each additional vehicle. Open mid-May through mid-October.

Directions: From Mammoth Lakes at the junction of U.S. 395 and Highway 203, drive south on U.S. 395 for 15 miles south to Tom's Place and Rock Creek Road. Turn right (toward the

Sierra) at Rock Creek Road and drive seven miles to the campground.

Contact: Inyo National Forest, White Mountain Ranger District, 760/873-2500, fax 760/873-2563.

98 ROCK CREEK LAKE

🚶🏻 🚴 🏊 ⛵ 🎣 🛶 🐎 🚍 ⛺

Scenic rating: 9

in Inyo National Forest

Map 10.2, page 554

Rock Creek Lake, set at an elevation of 9,600 feet, is a small but beautiful lake that features cool, clear water, small trout, and a great trailhead for access to the adjacent John Muir Wilderness, with 50 other lakes within a two-hour hike. The setting is drop-dead beautiful, hence the high rating for scenic beauty, but note that the campsites are set closely together, side by side, in a paved parking area. This 63-acre lake has a 5-mph speed limit and swimming is allowed. The lake is stocked with Alpers trout, and they are joined by resident brown trout in the 10–16-pound class. At times, especially afternoons in late spring, winds out of the west can be cold and pesky at the lake. If this campground is full, the nearby Mosquito Flat walk-in campground provides an option. Note that Mosquito Flat has a limit of one night and is designed as a staging area for wilderness backpacking trips, with tent camping only. Insider's tip: Rock Creek Lakes Resort has mouth-watering homemade pie available in the café.

Campsites, facilities: There are 26 sites for tents or RVs up to 22 feet (no hookups), and one group tent site for up to 50 people; some of the sites require a short walk-in. Picnic tables and fire grills are provided. Drinking water, flush toilets, an unimproved boat launch, and boat rentals are available. Horseback-riding facilities and a café are nearby. Limited supplies can be obtained in Tom's Place and at

Rock Creek Lakes Resort. Leashed pets are permitted.

Reservations, fees: Reservations are accepted for individual sites and required ($9 reservation fee) for group sites at 877/444-6777 or www.ReserveUSA.com. Sites are $18 per night, $5 per night for each additional vehicle, $55 per night for a group site. Open mid-May through October, weather permitting.

Directions: From the junction of U.S. 395 and Highway 203 (the Mammoth Lakes turnoff), drive 15 miles south on U.S. 395 to Tom's Place. Turn right (toward the Sierra) at Rock Creek Road and drive seven miles to the campground.

Contact: Inyo National Forest, White Mountain Ranger District, 760/873-2500, fax 760/873-2563; Rock Creek Pack Station, 760/935-4493.

99 PLEASANT VALLEY

🚶🏻 🏊 🎣 🐎 ♿ 🚍 ⛺

Scenic rating: 7

near Pleasant Valley Reservoir

Map 10.2, page 554

Pleasant Valley County Campground is set near long, narrow Pleasant Valley Reservoir, created by the Owens River. A 15-minute walk from camp will take you to the lake. It is east of the Sierra range in the high desert plateau country; the elevation is 4,200 feet. That makes it available for year-round fishing, and trout are stocked. The Owens River passes through the park, providing wild trout fishing, with most anglers practicing catch-and-release fly-fishing. This is also near a major jump-off point for hiking, rock-climbing, and wilderness fishing at the Bishop Pass area to the west.

Campsites, facilities: There are 200 sites for tents or RVs of any length (no hookups). Picnic tables and fire grills are provided. Drinking water (hand-pumped well water) and vault toilets are available. Groups can be accommodated. Some facilities are wheelchair-accessible. Leashed pets are permitted.

Reservations, fees: Reservations are not accepted. Sites are $10 per night per vehicle. Open year-round.

Directions: Drive on U.S. 395 to Pleasant Valley Road (seven miles north of Bishop) on the east side of the road. Turn northeast and drive one mile to the park entrance.

Contact: Inyo County Parks Department, 760/878-0272 or 760/873-5577, www.395.com/inyo/campgrounds.

100 HIGHLANDS RV PARK

Scenic rating: 3

near Bishop

Map 10.2, page 554

This is a privately operated RV park near Bishop that is set up for U.S. 395 cruisers. There is a casino in town. A great side trip is up two-lane Highway 168 to Lake Sabrina.

The elevation is 4,300 feet. Note that a few sites are occupied by long-term renters.

Campsites, facilities: There are 103 sites with full hookups (30 and 50 amps) for RVs of any length; many sites are pull-through. No tents. Picnic tables and cable TV are provided. Drinking water, restrooms with flush toilets and showers, dump station, social room with pool table, modem access (in office), propane gas, ice, fish-cleaning station, and coin laundry are available. You can buy groceries nearby (about three blocks away). Leashed pets are permitted.

Reservations, fees: Reservations are recommended. Sites are $33 per night, $1 per person per night for more than two people. Weekly and monthly rates available. Some credit cards accepted. Open year-round.

Directions: From Bishop, drive two miles north on U.S. 395/North Sierra Highway to the campground on the right (east side of road) at 2275 North Sierra Highway.

Contact: Highlands RV Park, 760/873-7616.

SEQUOIA AND KINGS CANYON

BEST CAMPGROUNDS

《 Scenic Destinations
Sabrina, page 636

《 Hikes with Views
Canyon View, **page 649**
Whitney Trailhead Walk-In,
    page 666

《 Family Destinations
Dorst Creek, page 652

《 White-Water Rafting
Kirch Flat, page 640
Fairview, **page 671**
Hobo, **page 682**

There is no place on earth like the high Sierra, from

Mount Whitney north through Sequoia and Kings Canyon National Parks. This is a paradise filled with deep canyons, high peaks, and fantastic natural beauty, and sprinkled with groves of the largest living things in the history of the earth – giant sequoias.

Though the area is primarily known for the national parks, the campgrounds available span a great variety of settings. The most popular spots, though, are in the vicinity of Sequoia and Kings Canyon National Parks, or on the parks' access roads.

Sooner or later, everyone will want to see the biggest tree of them all – the General Sherman Tree, estimated to be 2,300-2,700 years old and with a circumference of 102.6 feet. It is in the Giant Forest at Sequoia National Park. To stand in front of it is to know true awe. That said, I find the Grant Grove and the Muir Grove even more enchanting.

These are among the highlights of a driving tour through both parks. A must for most is taking in the view from Moro Rock – parking and then making the 300-foot walk up a succession of stairs to reach the 6,725-foot summit. Here you can scan a series of mountain rims and granite peaks, highlighted by the Great Western Divide.

The drive out of Sequoia and into Kings Canyon features rim-of-the-world-type views as you first enter the Kings River canyon. You then descend to the bottom of the canyon, right along the Kings River, gaze up at the high glacial-carved canyon walls, and drive all the way out to Cedar Grove, the end of the road. The canyon rises 8,000 feet from the river to Spanish Peak, making it the deepest canyon in the continental United States.

Crystal Cave is another point of fascination. Among the formations are adjoined crystal columns that look like the sound pipes in the giant organ at the Mormon Tabernacle. Lights are placed strategically for perfect viewing.

This is only a start. Bears, marmots, and deer are abundant and are commonly seen in Sequoia, especially at Dorst Creek Campground. If you drive up to Mineral King and take a hike, it can seem like the marmot capital of the world.

But this region also harbors many wonderful secrets having nothing to do with the national parks. One of them, for instance, is the Muir Trail Ranch near Florence Lake. The ranch is set in the John Muir Wilderness and requires a trip by foot, boat, or horse to reach it. Other unique launch points for trips into the wilderness lie nearby.

On the western slopes of the Sierra, pretty lakes with good trout fishing include Edison, Florence, and Hume Lakes. Hidden spots in Sierra National Forest provide continual fortune hunts, especially up the Dinkey Creek drainage above Courtright Reservoir. On the eastern slopes, a series of small streams offers good vehicle access; here, too, you'll encounter the beautiful Rock Creek Lake, Sabrina and South Lakes (west of Bishop), and great wilderness trailheads at the end of almost every road.

The remote Golden Trout Wilderness on the southwest flank of Mount Whitney is one of the most pristine areas in California. Yet it is lost in the shadow of giant Whitney, elevation 14,497.6 feet, the highest point in the continental United States, where hiking has become so popular that reservations are required at each trailhead for overnight use, and quotas are enforced to ensure an undisturbed experience for each visitor.

In the Kernville area, there are campgrounds along the Kern River. Most choose this canyon for one reason: the outstanding white-water rafting and kayaking.

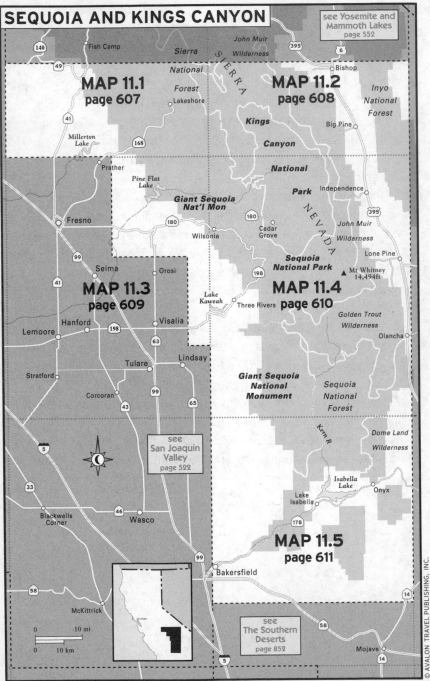

SEQUOIA AND KINGS CANYON

see Yosemite and Mammoth Lakes page 552

Fish Camp

Sierra

SIERRA

John Muir Wilderness

Bishop

MAP 11.1
page 607

National

Forest

Lakeshore

MAP 11.2
page 608

Inyo

National

Forest

Big Pine

Kings

Millerton Lake

Canyon

Prather

National

Independence

Pine Flat Lake

Giant Sequoia Nat'l Mon

Park

Fresno

Wilsonia

Cedar Grove

NEVADA

John Muir

Wilderness

Lone Pine

Selma

Orosi

Sequoia National Park

Mt Whitney 14,494ft

MAP 11.3
page 609

Lake Kaweah

Three Rivers

MAP 11.4
page 610

Golden Trout Wilderness

Hanford

Visalia

Olancha

Lemoore

Tulare

Lindsay

Giant Sequoia National Monument

Sequoia National Forest

Stratford

Corcoran

see San Joaquin Valley page 522

Kern R

Dome Land Wilderness

Blackwells Corner

Wasco

Isabella Lake

Onyx

Lake Isabella

MAP 11.5
page 611

Bakersfield

McKittrick

0   10 mi

0   10 km

see The Southern Deserts page 852

Mojave

© AVALON TRAVEL PUBLISHING, INC.

Map 11.1

Campgrounds 1–39
Pages 612–629

11.2

11.3

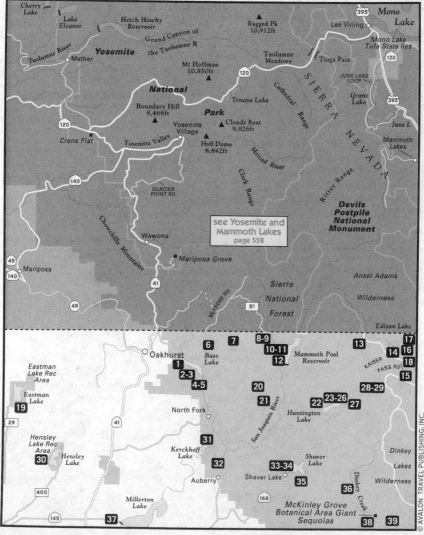

© AVALON TRAVEL PUBLISHING, INC.

Map 11.3

Campgrounds 66-74
Pages 639-643

Map 11.4

Campgrounds 75-130
Pages 643-668

11.2
11.3
11.5

1 2
3 4
5

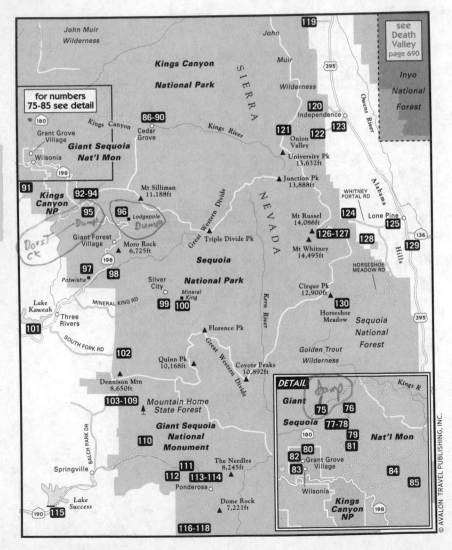

Map 11.5

Campgrounds 131-170
Pages 668-686

1 CRANE VALLEY GROUP AND RECREATION POINT GROUP

🏃 🏊 🎣 🚐 🏠 🐕 🚙 ⛺

Scenic rating: 8

on Bass Lake in Sierra National Forest

Map 11.1, page 607

This is a group camp at Bass Lake. Bass Lake is a long, narrow, mountain lake set in the Sierra foothills at 3,400 feet. It's especially popular in the summer for waterskiing, personal watercraft riding, and swimming.

Campsites, facilities: There are 14 group sites for tents only that can accommodate 30–50 people each at Recreation Point and seven group sites for tents or RVs up to 45 feet (no hookups) that can accommodate 30–50 people each at Crane Valley Camp. Picnic tables and fire grills are provided at both camps. Drinking water and flush toilets are available at Recreation Point. Vault toilets are available at Crane Valley. No drinking water is available. A store is nearby. Leashed pets are permitted.

Reservations, fees: Reservations are required ($9 reservation fee) at 877/444-6777 or www.ReserveUSA.com. Sites are $30–75 per night. Open year-round.

Directions: From Fresno, drive north on Highway 41 to Oakhurst and continue 2.5 miles to Yosemite Forks and Bass Lake Road/County Road 222. Turn right at Bass Lake Road and drive four miles to the campground.

Contact: Sierra National Forest, Bass Lake Ranger District, 559/877-2218, fax 559/877-3108.

2 FORKS

🏃 🏊 🎣 🚐 🏠 🐕 ♿ 🚙 ⛺

Scenic rating: 8

on Bass Lake in Sierra National Forest

Map 11.1, page 607

Bass Lake is set in a canyon. It's a long, narrow, deep lake that is popular for fishing in the spring and waterskiing in the summer. It's a pretty spot, set at 3,500 feet in the Sierra National Forest. This is one of several camps at the lake. Boats must be registered at the Bass Lake observation tower after launching.

Campsites, facilities: There are 31 sites for tents or RVs up to 40 feet (no hookups). Picnic tables and fire grills are provided. Drinking water and flush toilets are available. A store, dump station, and coin laundry are nearby. Some facilities are wheelchair-accessible. Leashed pets are permitted.

Reservations, fees: Reservations are accepted ($9 reservation fee) at 877/444-6777 or www.ReserveUSA.com. Sites are $19 per night, $5 per night for each additional vehicle. Open May through October.

Directions: From Fresno, drive north on Highway 41 to Oakhurst and continue 2.5 miles to Yosemite Forks and Bass Lake Road/County Road 222. Turn right at Bass Lake Road and drive six miles (staying right at two forks) to the campground (on the south shore of Bass Lake). Note: The road is narrow and curvy.

Contact: Sierra National Forest, Bass Lake Ranger District, 559/877-2218, fax 559/877-3108; California Land Management, 559/642-3212.

3 LUPINE-CEDAR BLUFFS

🏃 🏊 🎣 🚐 🏠 🐕 ♿ 🚙 ⛺

Scenic rating: 8

on Bass Lake in Sierra National Forest

Map 11.1, page 607

This is the camping headquarters at Bass Lake and the only camp open year-round, except for the group camp. Bass Lake is a popular vacation spot, a pretty lake, long and narrow, covering 1,200 acres when full and surrounded by national forest. The elevation is 3,500 feet. Most of the campgrounds are filled on weekends and three-day holidays. Fishing is best in the spring for rainbow trout and largemouth bass, and by mid-June water-skiers have usually taken over. Boats must be registered at the Bass Lake observation tower after launching.

Campsites, facilities: There are 113 sites for tents or RVs up to 35 feet (no hookups), and several double sites. Picnic tables and fire grills are provided. Drinking water and flush toilets are available. Some facilities are wheelchair-accessible. Groceries, coin showers, and a boat ramp are available within two miles. Leashed pets are permitted.

Reservations, fees: Reservations are accepted ($9 reservation fee) at 877/444-6777 or www.ReserveUSA.com. Sites are $19 per night, $38 per night for double sites, $5 per night for each additional vehicle. Open year-round.

Directions: From Fresno, drive north on Highway 41 to Oakhurst and continue 2.5 miles to Yosemite Forks and Bass Lake Road/County Road 222. Turn right at Bass Lake Road and drive eight miles (staying right at two forks) to the campground (on the south shore of Bass Lake).

Contact: Sierra National Forest, Bass Lake Ranger District, 559/877-2218, fax 559/877-3108.

4 SPRING COVE

Scenic rating: 8

on Bass Lake in Sierra National Forest

Map 11.1, page 607

This is one of the several camps beside Bass Lake, a long, narrow reservoir in the Sierra foothill country. A bonus here is that the shoreline is quite sandy nearly all around the lake. That makes for good swimming and sunbathing. Expect hot weather in the summer. Boats must be registered at the Bass Lake observation tower after launching. The elevation is 3,400 feet.

Campsites, facilities: There are 63 sites for tents or RVs up to 35 feet (no hookups). Picnic tables and fire grills are provided. Drinking water and flush toilets are available. Groceries and a boat ramp are available nearby. Some facilities are wheelchair-accessible. Leashed pets are permitted.

Reservations, fees: Reservations are accepted ($9 reservation fee) at 877/444-6777 or www.ReserveUSA.com. Sites are $19 per night. Open May through August.

Directions: From Fresno, drive north on Highway 41 to Oakhurst and continue 2.5 miles to Yosemite Forks and Bass Lake Road/County Road 222. Turn right at Bass Lake Road and drive 8.5 miles (staying right at two forks) to the campground (on the south shore of Bass Lake).

Contact: Sierra National Forest, Bass Lake Ranger District, 559/877-2218, fax 559/877-3108.

5 WISHON POINT

Scenic rating: 9

on Bass Lake in Sierra National Forest

Map 11.1, page 607

This camp on Wishon Point is the smallest, and many say the prettiest, of the camps at Bass Lake. The elevation is 3,400 feet.

Campsites, facilities: There are 47 sites for tents or RVs up to 30 feet (no hookups). Some sites are pull-through. Picnic tables and fire grills are provided. Drinking water and flush toilets are available. Groceries and a boat ramp are nearby. Some facilities are wheelchair-accessible. Leashed pets are permitted.

Reservations, fees: Reservations are accepted ($9 reservation fee) at 877/444-6777 or www.ReserveUSA.com. Sites are $19 per night. Open June through September.

Directions: From Fresno, drive north on Highway 41 to Oakhurst and continue 2.5 miles to Yosemite Forks and Bass Lake Road/County Road 222. Turn right at Bass Lake Road and drive nine miles (staying right at two forks) to the campground (on the south shore of Bass Lake).

Contact: Sierra National Forest, Bass Lake Ranger District, 559/877-2218, fax 559/877-3108.

6 CHILKOOT

𐀀𐀀 𐀀𐀀 𐀀𐀀 𐀀𐀀

Scenic rating: 7

near Bass Lake in Sierra National Forest

Map 11.1, page 607

A lot of people have heard of Bass Lake, but only the faithful know about Chilcoot Creek. That's where this camp is, but it's just two miles from Bass Lake. It provides a primitive option to use either as an overflow area for Bass Lake or for folks who don't want to get jammed into one of the Bass Lake campgrounds on a popular weekend. The elevation is 4,600 feet.

Campsites, facilities: There are 14 sites for tents or RVs up to 20 feet (no hookups). Picnic tables and fire grills are provided. Vault toilets are available. No drinking water is available. Groceries and a coin laundry are available at Bass Lake. Leashed pets are permitted.

Reservations, fees: Reservations are accepted ($9 reservation fee) at 877/444-6777 or www .ReserveUSA.com. Sites are $14 per night, $5 per night for each additional vehicle. Open May through August.

Directions: From Fresno, drive north on Highway 41 to Oakhurst and continue 2.5 miles to Yosemite Forks and Bass Lake Road/County Road 222. Turn right at Bass Lake Road and drive six miles to the town of Bass Lake and Beasore Road. Turn left at Beasore Road and drive 4.5 miles to the campground.

Contact: Sierra National Forest, Bass Lake Ranger District, 559/877-2218, fax 559/877-3108.

7 GAGGS CAMP

𐀀𐀀 𐀀𐀀 5% 𐀀𐀀 𐀀𐀀

Scenic rating: 7

in Sierra National Forest

Map 11.1, page 607

The masses are not exactly beating a hot trail to this camp. It's a small, remote, and primitive spot, set along a little creek at 5,700 feet, deep in the interior of Sierra National Forest. A Forest Service map is advisable. With that in hand, you can make the three-mile drive to Little Shuteye Pass, where the road is often gated in the winter (the gate is open when the look-out station is staffed); from here it is a three-mile trip to Shuteye Peak, 8,351 feet, where there is a drop-dead gorgeous view of the surrounding landscape.

Campsites, facilities: There are 12 sites for tents or RVs up to 16 feet (no hookups). Picnic tables and fire grills are provided. Vault toilets are available. No drinking water is available. Garbage must be packed out. Leashed pets are permitted.

Reservations, fees: Reservations are not accepted. Sites are $14 per night, $5 per night for each additional vehicle. Open June through October, weather permitting.

Directions: From Fresno, drive north on Highway 41 for about 25 miles to North Fork Road/County Road 200. Turn right and drive northeast for 17.5 miles to Auberry Road/County Road 222. Turn left (north) and drive one mile to the town of North Fork and Mammoth Pool Road. Turn right and drive 0.5 mile to Malum Ridge Road/County Road 274. Turn left (north) and drive 4.5 miles to Central Camp Road/Forest Road 6S42. Turn right and drive 11.5 miles (narrow, dirt road) to the campground on the right.

Contact: Sierra National Forest, Bass Lake Ranger District, 559/877-2218, fax 559/877-3108.

8 SODA SPRINGS

𐀀𐀀 𐀀𐀀 𐀀𐀀 𐀀𐀀 𐀀𐀀 𐀀𐀀 𐀀𐀀

Scenic rating: 7

on the West Fork of Chiquito Creek in Sierra National Forest

Map 11.1, page 607

Soda Springs is set at 4,400 feet on West Fork Chiquito Creek, about five miles from Mammoth Pool Reservoir. It is used primarily as an overflow area if the more developed camps with drinking water have filled up. As long as you remember that the camp is primitive, it is a good overflow option.

Campsites, facilities: There are 18 sites for tents or RVs up to 20 feet (no hookups). Picnic tables and fire grills are provided. Vault toilets are available. No drinking water is available. A store and boat ramp are nearby. Leashed pets are permitted.

Reservations, fees: Reservations are not accepted. The fee is $14 per night, $5 per night for each additional vehicle. Open April through October, weather permitting.

Directions: From Fresno, drive north on Highway 41 for about 25 miles to North Fork Road/County Road 200. Turn right and drive northeast for 17.5 miles to Auberry Road/County Road 222. Turn left (north) and drive one mile to the town of North Fork and Mammoth Pool Road. Turn right and drive 1.5 miles to County Road 225 (still Mammoth Pool Road). Turn right and drive 35 miles (the road becomes Minarets Road/Forest Road 81) to the campground.

Contact: Sierra National Forest, Bass Lake Ranger District, 559/877-2218, fax 559/877-3108.

9 LOWER CHIQUITO
🐕 🚙 ⛺

Scenic rating: 7

on Chiquito Creek in Sierra National Forest

Map 11.1, page 607

Lower Chiquito is a primitive, little-known, pretty camp in Sierra National Forest, about eight miles from Mammoth Pool Reservoir. Mosquitoes can be abundant in summer. The elevation is 4,900 feet, with a very warm climate in summer. Note that Lower Chiquito is a long distance (a twisting, 30- to 40-minute drive) from Upper Chiquito, despite the similarity in names and streamside settings along the same creek.

Campsites, facilities: There are seven sites for tents or RVs up to 20 feet (no hookups). Picnic

tables and fire grills are provided. Vault toilets are available. No drinking water is available. Leashed pets are permitted.

Reservations, fees: Reservations are not accepted. Sites are $14 per night, $5 per night for each additional vehicle. Open May through September, weather permitting.

Directions: From the town of North Fork (south of Bass Lake), drive east on Mammoth Pool Road/County Road 225 (it becomes Minarets Road/Forest Road 4S81). Bear left (north, still Minarets Road/Forest Road 4S81) and drive to Forest Road 6S71. Turn left on Forest Road 6S71 and drive three miles to the campground. (The distance is about 40 miles from North Fork.)

Contact: Sierra National Forest, Bass Lake Ranger District, 559/877-2218, fax 559/877-3108.

10 PLACER
🏃 🏊 🚣 🚙 🐕 ⛺

Scenic rating: 7

near Mammoth Pool Reservoir on Chiquito Creek in Sierra National Forest

Map 11.1, page 607

This little camp is just three miles from Mammoth Pool Reservoir. With Forest Road access and a pretty setting along Chiquito Creek, it is one of the better campgrounds used as an overflow area for Mammoth Pool visitors. The elevation is 4,100 feet. (For more information, see the *Mammoth Pool* listing in this chapter.)

Campsites, facilities: There are eight sites for tents only. Picnic tables and fire grills are provided. Vault toilets are available. No drinking water is available. Leashed pets are permitted.

Reservations, fees: Reservations are accepted ($9 reservation fee) at 877/444-6777 or www.ReserveUSA.com. Sites are $14 per night. Open April through October.

Directions: From Fresno, drive north on Highway 41 for about 25 miles to North

Fork Road/County Road 200. Turn right and drive northeast for 17.5 miles to Auberry Road/County Road 222. Turn left (north) and drive one mile to the town of North Fork and Mammoth Pool Road. Turn right and drive 1.5 miles to County Road 225 (still Mammoth Pool Road). Turn right and drive about 37 miles (the road becomes Minarets Road/Forest Road 81) to a junction. Bear right (still Mammoth Pool Road) and drive one mile to the campground on the right. The drive from North Fork takes 1.5–2 hours.

Contact: Sierra National Forest, Bass Lake Ranger District, 559/877-2218, fax 559/877-3108.

11 SWEETWATER

Scenic rating: 6

near Mammoth Pool Reservoir on Chiquito Creek in Sierra National Forest

Map 11.1, page 607

Sweetwater is small and primitive, but if the camp at Mammoth Pool Reservoir is filled up, this spot provides an alternative. It is set on Chiquito Creek, just a mile from the lake. The elevation is 3,800 feet. (See the next listing, *Mammoth Pool,* for more information.)

Campsites, facilities: There are 10 sites for tents or RVs up to 20 feet (no hookups). Picnic tables and fire grills are provided. Vault toilets are available. No drinking water is available. A store and boat ramp are within 1.5 miles. Leashed pets are permitted.

Reservations, fees: Reservations are accepted ($9 reservation fee) at 877/444-6777 or www.ReserveUSA.com. Sites are $14 per night. Open April through October.

Directions: From Fresno, drive north on Highway 41 for about 25 miles to North Fork Road/County Road 200. Turn right and drive northeast for 17.5 miles to Auberry Road/County Road 222. Turn left (north) and drive one mile to the town of North Fork and Mammoth Pool Road. Turn right and drive

1.5 miles to County Road 225 (still Mammoth Pool Road). Turn right and drive about 37 miles (the road becomes Minarets Road/Forest Road 81) to a junction. Bear right (still Mammoth Pool Road) and drive 1.5 miles to the campground on the right. The drive from North Fork takes 1.5–2 hours.

Contact: Sierra National Forest, Bass Lake Ranger District, 559/877-2218, fax 559/877-3108.

12 MAMMOTH POOL

Scenic rating: 7

near Mammoth Pool Reservoir in Sierra National Forest

Map 11.1, page 607

Mammoth Pool was created by a dam in the San Joaquin River gorge, a steep canyon, resulting in a long, narrow lake with steep, high walls. The lake seems much higher than its official elevation of 3,330 feet, but that is because of the high ridges. This is the only drive-in camp at the lake, though there is a boat-in camp, China Camp, on the lake's upper reaches. Trout fishing can be good in the spring and early summer, with waterskiing dominant during warm weather. All water sports are allowed during part of the season, but get this: Water sports are restricted from May 1 to June 15 because of deer migrating across the lake—that's right, swimming—but the campgrounds here are still open. Note that the water level can drop significantly by late summer.

Campsites, facilities: There are 47 sites for tents or RVs up to 30 feet (no hookups). Picnic tables and fire grills are provided. Drinking water and vault toilets are available. A store and boat ramp are within a mile. Leashed pets are permitted.

Reservations, fees: Reservations are accepted ($9 reservation fee) at 877/444-6777 or www.ReserveUSA.com. Sites are $15 per night, $5 per night for each additional vehicle. Open May through October.

Directions: From Fresno, drive north on Highway 41 for about 25 miles to North Fork Road/County Road 200. Turn right and drive northeast for 17.5 miles to Auberry Road/County Road 222. Turn left (north) and drive one mile to the town of North Fork and Mammoth Pool Road. Turn right and drive 1.5 miles to County Road 225 (still Mammoth Pool Road). Turn right and drive about 37 miles (the road becomes Minarets Road/Forest Road 81) to a junction. Bear right (still Mammoth Pool Road) and drive three miles to Mammoth Pool Reservoir and the campground. The drive from North Fork takes 1.5–2 hours.
Contact: Sierra National Forest, Bass Lake Ranger District, 559/877-2218, fax 559/877-3108.

13 SAMPLE MEADOW
🚶 🐕 🚐 ⛺

Scenic rating: 7

on Kaiser Creek in Sierra National Forest
Map 11.1, page 607

This is a pretty, secluded spot set at 7,800 feet along Kaiser Creek, with nearby trailheads available for backpackers. While there is a trail out of camp, most will drive a mile down Forest Road 80 to the Rattlesnake Parking Area. From here, one trail is routed three miles southwest to Kaiser Ridge and Upper and Lower Twin Lakes in the Kaiser Wilderness, a great hike. Another trail is routed north for three miles to Rattlesnake Creek, and then enters the western slopes of the Ansel Adams Wilderness, with this section featuring a series of canyons, streams, and very few people.
Campsites, facilities: There are 16 sites for tents or RVs up to 16 feet (no hookups). Picnic tables and fire grills are provided. Vault toilets are available. No drinking water is available. Garbage must be packed out. Leashed pets are permitted.
Reservations, fees: Reservations are not

accepted. There is no camping fee. Open June through October, weather permitting.
Directions: From Fresno, drive east on Highway 168 to Shaver Lake, and then continue 21 miles to Huntington Lake and Kaiser Pass Road/Forest Road 80. Bear right on Forest Road 80 and drive eight miles to a fork with Forest Road 7505. Turn left on Forest Road 7505 and drive 3.5 miles to a fork with the campground entrance road. Bear left at the campground entrance road and drive 0.25 mile to the campground. The road is narrow and curvy, with blind turns.
Contact: Sierra National Forest, High Sierra Ranger District, 559/855-5355, fax 559/855-5375.

14 PORTAL FOREBAY
🚶 🏊 ⛵ 🐕 🚐 ⛺

Scenic rating: 8

on Forebay Lake in Sierra National Forest
Map 11.1, page 607

This small, primitive camp is set along the shore of little Forebay Lake at 7,200 feet. The camp is pretty and provides a good hiking option, with a trailhead near the camp that is routed up Camp 61 Creek and then to Mono Creek, with a ford of Mono Creek required about two miles in. Another side trip is visiting Mono Hot Springs about five miles to the east, just off the road to Lake Edison.
Campsites, facilities: There are 11 sites for tents or RVs up to 16 feet (no hookups). Picnic tables and fire grills are provided. Vault toilets are available. No drinking water is available. Garbage must be packed out. Groceries are available nearby at Mono Hot Springs. Leashed pets are permitted.
Reservations, fees: Reservations are not accepted. Sites are $12 per night. Open June through September.
Directions: From Fresno, drive east on Highway 168 to Shaver Lake, and then continue 21 miles to Huntington Lake and Kaiser Pass Road/Forest Road 80. Bear right on Forest

Road 80 and drive eight miles to a fork with Forest Road 5. Stay right at the fork on Forest Road 80 and continue five miles to the campground entrance on the left. The road is narrow and curvy, with blind turns.

Contact: Sierra National Forest, High Sierra Ranger District, 559/855-5355, fax 559/855-5375; California Land Management, 559/893-2111.

15 BOLSILLO
🏕️ 🛶 🐕 5% ⛰️

Scenic rating: 4

on Bolsillo Creek in Sierra National Forest

Map 11.1, page 607

This tiny camp has many first-class bonuses. It is set at 7,400 feet along Bolsillo Creek, just three miles by car to Mono Hot Springs and seven miles to Lake Edison. A trailhead out of camp provides the chance for a three-mile hike south, climbing along Bolsillo Creek and up to small, pretty Corbett Lake on the flank of nearby Mount Givens, 10,648 feet.

Campsites, facilities: There are three tent sites. Picnic tables and fire grills are provided. Drinking water and vault toilets are available. Garbage must be packed out. You can buy supplies in Mono Hot Springs. Leashed pets are permitted.

Reservations, fees: Reservations are not accepted. There is no camping fee. Open June through October, weather permitting.

Directions: From Fresno, drive east on Highway 168 to Shaver Lake, then continue 21 miles to Huntington Lake and Kaiser Pass Road/Forest Road 80. Bear right on Forest Road 80 and drive eight miles to a fork with Forest Road 5. Stay right on Forest Road 80 and drive seven miles (two miles past Portal Forebay) to the campground entrance on the right. The road is narrow and curvy with blind turns, and RVs and trailers are not recommended.

Contact: Sierra National Forest, High Si-

erra Ranger District, 559/855-5355, fax 559/855-5375.

16 MONO HOT SPRINGS
🏕️ 🏊 🛶 🎿 🎣 🐕 🚐 ⛰️

Scenic rating: 8

on the San Joaquin River in Sierra National Forest

Map 11.1, page 607

The campground is set in the Sierra at 7,400 feet in elevation along the San Joaquin River directly adjacent to the Mono Hot Springs Resort. The hot springs are typically 104°F, with public pools (everybody wears swimming suits) available just above the river on one side, and the private resort (rock cabins available) with its private baths on the other. A small convenience store and excellent restaurant are available at the lodge. The best swimming lake in the Sierra Nevada, Dorris Lake, is a 15-minute walk past the lodge; the lake is clear, clean, and yet not too cold, with walls on one side for fun jumps into deep water. The one downer: The drive in to the campground is long, slow, and hellacious, with many blind corners in narrow sections.

Campsites, facilities: There are 26 sites for tents or RVs up to 16 feet (no hookups). Picnic tables and fire grills are provided. Vault toilets are available. Drinking water is not available. You can buy supplies in Mono Hot Springs. Leashed pets are permitted.

Reservations, fees: Reservations are accepted at 877/444-6777 ($9 reservation fee) or www.ReserveUSA.com. Sites are $16 per night, $32 per night for double site, $5 per night for additional vehicle. Open May to mid-October, weather permitting.

Directions: From the town of Shaver Lake, drive east on Highway 168 for 21 miles to Kaiser Pass Road. Bear northeast on Kaiser Pass Road/Forest Road 80 (slow and curvy) to Mono Hot Springs Campground Road (signed). Turn left and drive a short distance to the campground.

Contact: Sierra National Forest, High Sierra Ranger District, 559/855-5355, fax 559/855-5375; California Land Management, 559/893-2111.

17 VERMILLION
🚶 🏊 🛶 ⛵ 🐕 🚐 ⛺

Scenic rating: 8

on Lake Edison in Sierra National Forest

Map 11.1, page 607

Lake Edison is a premium vacation destination. It is a large, high-mountain camp set just a few miles from the border of the John Muir Wilderness. The elevation is 7,700 feet. A 15-mph speed limit on the lake guarantees quiet water, and trout fishing is often quite good in early summer, with occasionally huge brown trout hooked. Swimming is allowed. A day-trip option is to hike the trail from the camp out along the north shore of Lake Edison for five miles to Quail Meadows, where it intersects with the Pacific Crest Trail in the John Muir Wilderness. A lodge at the lake provides meals and supplies, with a hikers' boat shuttle available to the head of the lake. Hang out here for long and you are bound to see JMT hikers taking a break. Note that the drive in is long and extremely twisty on a narrow road. Also note that the lake level can drop dramatically here by late summer.

Campsites, facilities: There are 31 sites for tents or RVs up to 16 feet (no hookups). Picnic tables and fire grills are provided. Drinking water and vault toilets are available. A boat ramp, boat rentals, bait and tackle, horseback-riding facilities, convenience store, and restaurant are nearby. Leashed pets are permitted.

Reservations, fees: Reservations are accepted ($9 reservation fee) at 877/444-6777 or www.ReserveUSA.com. Sites are $16 per night, $5 per night for each additional vehicle. Open June through September.

Directions: From the town of Shaver Lake, drive east on Highway 168 for 21 miles to Kaiser Pass Road. Bear northeast on Kaiser Pass Road/Forest Road 80 (slow and curvy) to Mono Hot Springs (the road becomes Edison Lake Road). Continue on Kaiser Pass/Edison Lake Road for five miles to the campground. It is about 0.25 mile from the west shore of Lake Edison.

Contact: Sierra National Forest, High Sierra Ranger District, 559/855-5355, fax 559/855-5375; California Land Management, 559/893-2111.

18 MONO CREEK
🚶 🏊 🛶 🐕 🚐 ⛺

Scenic rating: 6

near Lake Edison in Sierra National Forest

Map 11.1, page 607

Here's a beautiful spot in the forest near Mono Creek that makes for an overflow campground when the camps at Mono Hot Springs and Lake Edison are filled. The camp is set at 7,400 feet about three miles from Lake Edison, via a twisty and bumpy road. Edison has good evening trout fishing and a small restaurant. For side trips, the Mono Hot Springs Resort is three miles away (slow, curvy, and bumpy driving), and there are numerous trails nearby into the backcountry. A camp host is on-site.

Campsites, facilities: There are 14 sites for tents or RVs up to 16 feet (no hookups). Picnic tables and fire grills are provided. Vault toilets are available. Drinking water is not available. Limited supplies and small restaurants are available at Lake Edison and Mono Hot Springs. Leashed pets are permitted.

Reservations, fees: Reservations are accepted ($9 reservation fee) at 877/444-6777 or www.ReserveUSA.com. Sites are $16 per night, $32 per night for double site, $5 per night for each additional vehicle. Open June to mid-October, weather permitting.

Directions: From the town of Shaver Lake, drive east on Highway 168 for 21 miles to Kaiser Pass Road. Bear northeast on Kaiser Pass Road/Forest Road 80 (slow and curvy) to Mono Hot Springs (the road becomes Edison

Lake Road). Continue on Kaiser Pass/Edison Lake Road for three miles to the campground on the left.

Contact: Sierra National Forest, High Sierra Ranger District, 559/855-5355, fax 559/855-5375; California Land Management, 559/893-2111.

19 CODORNIZ RECREATION AREA

Scenic rating: 6

on Eastman Lake

Map 11.1, page 607

Eastman Lake provides relief on your typical 90- and 100-degree summer day out here. It is tucked in the foothills of the San Joaquin Valley at an elevation of 650 feet and covers 1,800 surface acres. Shade shelters have been added at 12 of the more exposed campsites, a big plus. The warm water in summer makes it a good spot for a dip, and it is thus a favorite for waterskiing, swimming, and, in the spring, for fishing. Swimming is best at the large beach on the west side. The DFG has established a trophy bass program here, and fishing can be good in the appropriate season for rainbow trout, catfish, bluegill, and redear sunfish. Check fishing regulations, posted on all bulletin boards. The lake is also a designated "Watchable Wildlife" site; it is home to 163 species of birds and a nesting pair of bald eagles. A small area near the upper end of the lake is closed to boating to protect a bald eagle nest site. Some may remember the problem that Eastman Lake had with hydrilla, an invasive weed. The problem has been largely solved, and a buoy line has been placed at the mouth. No water activities are allowed upstream of this line. Mild winter temperatures are a tremendous plus at this lake.

Campsites, facilities: There are 62 sites for tents or RVs of any length (some have full hookups/50 amps and one is pull-through), three group sites for up to 200 people, three equestrian sites, and one group equestrian site. Picnic tables and fire grills are provided. Drinking water, flush toilets with showers, dump station, playground, volleyball court, Frisbee golf course, and a boat ramp are available. An equestrian staging area is available for overnight use, and there are seven miles of hiking, biking, and equestrian trails. Leashed pets are permitted.

Reservations, fees: Reservations are accepted ($9 reservation fee) at 877/444-6777 or www.ReserveUSA.com. Sites are $14–22 per night, $55–75 per night for group sites, and $8–25 per night for equestrian sites. Open year-round.

Directions: Drive on Highway 99 to Chowchilla and the Avenue 26 exit. Take that exit and drive east for 17 miles to County Road 29. Turn left (north) on County Road 29 and drive eight miles to the lake.

Contact: U.S. Army Corps of Engineers, Sacramento District, Eastman Lake, 559/689-3255, fax 559/689-3408.

20 ROCK CREEK

Scenic rating: 6

in Sierra National Forest

Map 11.1, page 607

Drinking water is the big bonus here. It's easier to live with than the no-water situation at Fish Creek, the other camp in the immediate area. It is also why this camp tends to fill up on weekends. A side trip is the primitive road that heads southeast out of camp, switchbacks as its heads east, and drops down the canyon near where pretty Aspen Creek feeds into Rock Creek. The elevation at camp is 4,300 feet. (For the best camp in the immediate region, see the *Mammoth Pool* listing.)

Campsites, facilities: There are 18 sites for tents or RVs up to 32 feet (no hookups). Picnic tables and fire grills are provided. Drinking water and vault toilets are available. Leashed pets are permitted.

Reservations, fees: Reservations are accepted ($9 reservation fee) at 877/444-6777 or www.ReserveUSA.com. Sites are $15 per night, $30 per night for a double site. Open April through October, weather permitting.

Directions: From Fresno, drive north on Highway 41 for about 25 miles to North Fork Road/County Road 200. Turn right and drive northeast for 17.5 miles to Auberry Road/County Road 222. Turn left (north) and drive one mile to the town of North Fork and Mammoth Pool Road. Turn right and drive 1.5 miles to County Road 225 (still Mammoth Pool Road). Turn right and drive about 25 miles (the road becomes Minarets Road/Forest Road 81) to the campground on the right.

Contact: Sierra National Forest, Bass Lake Ranger District, 559/877-2218, fax 559/877-3108.

21 FISH CREEK

Scenic rating: 6

in Sierra National Forest

Map 11.1, page 607

This is a small, primitive camp set along Fish Creek at 4,600 feet in the Sierra National Forest. It's a nearby option to Rock Creek, both set on the access road to Mammoth Pool Reservoir.

Campsites, facilities: There are seven sites for tents or RVs up to 16 feet (no hookups). Picnic tables and fire grills are provided. Vault toilets are available. No drinking water is available. Leashed pets are permitted.

Reservations, fees: Reservations are accepted ($9 reservation fee) at 877/444-6777 or www.ReserveUSA.com. Sites are $14 per night. Open April through October, weather permitting.

Directions: From Fresno, drive north on Highway 41 for about 25 miles to North Fork Road/County Road 200. Turn right and drive northeast for 17.5 miles to Auberry Road/County Road 222. Turn left (north) and drive one mile to the town of North Fork and

Mammoth Pool Road. Turn right and drive 1.5 miles to County Road 225 (still Mammoth Pool Road). Turn right and drive about 21 miles (the road becomes Minarets Road/Forest Road 81) to the campground on the right.

Contact: Sierra National Forest, Bass Lake Ranger District, 559/877-2218, fax 559/877-3108.

22 UPPER AND LOWER BILLY CREEK

Scenic rating: 8

on Huntington Lake in Sierra National Forest

Map 11.1, page 607

Huntington Lake is at an elevation of 7,000 feet in the Sierra Nevada. These camps are at the west end of the lake along the north shore, where Billy Creek feeds the lake. Of these two adjacent campgrounds, Lower Billy Creek is smaller than Upper Billy and has lakeside sites available. The lake is four miles long and 0.5 mile wide, with 14 miles of shoreline, several resorts, boat rentals, and a trailhead for hiking into the Kaiser Wilderness.

Campsites, facilities: Upper Billy has 44 sites for tents or RVs up to 30 feet. Lower Billy has 13 sites for tents or RVs up to 30 feet. No hookups. Picnic tables and fire grills are provided. Drinking water and vault toilets are available at both camps; Upper Billy also has flush toilets available. A small store is nearby. Leashed pets are permitted.

Reservations, fees: Reservations are accepted ($9 reservation fee) at 877/444-6777 or www.ReserveUSA.com. Sites are $17 per night, $5 per night for each additional vehicle. Open June through September, weather permitting.

Directions: From Fresno, drive east on Highway 168 to Shaver Lake, then continue 21 miles to Huntington Lake and Huntington Lake Road. Turn left on Huntington Lake Road and drive about five miles to the campgrounds on the left.

Contact: Sierra National Forest, High Sierra Ranger District, 559/855-5355, fax 559/855-5375; California Land Management, 559/893-2111.

23 CATAVEE

🚶 🏊 🚣 🛥️ 🏕️ ♿ 🚐 ⛺

Scenic rating: 7

on Huntington Lake in Sierra National Forest

Map 11.1, page 607

Catavee is one of three camps in the immediate vicinity, set on the north shore at the eastern end of Huntington Lake. The camp sits near where Bear Creek enters the lake. Huntington Lake is a scenic, High Sierra Ranger District lake at 7,000 feet, where visitors can enjoy fishing, hiking, and sailing. Sailboat regattas take place here regularly during the summer. All water sports are allowed. Nearby resorts offer boat rentals and guest docks, and a boat ramp is nearby. Tackle rentals and bait are also available. A trailhead near camp offers access to the Kaiser Wilderness.

Campsites, facilities: There are 23 sites for tents or RVs up to 30 feet (no hookups). Picnic tables and fire grills are provided. Drinking water and flush toilets are available. Horseback-riding facilities and a small store are nearby. Some facilities are wheelchair-accessible. Leashed pets are permitted.

Reservations, fees: Reservations are accepted ($9 reservation fee) at 877/444-6777 or www .ReserveUSA.com. Sites are $17 per night, $5 per night for each additional vehicle. Open June through October, weather permitting.

Directions: From Fresno, drive east on Highway 168 to Shaver Lake, then continue 21 miles to Huntington Lake and Huntington Lake Road. Turn left on Huntington Lake Road and drive one mile (just past Kinnikinnick) to the campground on the right.

Contact: Sierra National Forest, High Sierra Ranger District, 559/855-5355, fax 559/855-5375; California Land Management, 559/893-2111.

24 KINNIKINNICK

🚶 🏊 🚣 🛥️ 🏕️ ♿ 🚐 ⛺

Scenic rating: 7

on Huntington Lake in Sierra National Forest

Map 11.1, page 607

Flip a coin; there are three camps in the immediate vicinity on the north shore of the east end of Huntington Lake and, with a boat ramp nearby, they are all favorites. Kinnikinnick is set between Catavee and Deer Creek Campgrounds. The elevation is 7,000 feet.

Campsites, facilities: There are 27 sites for tents or RVs up to 40 feet (no hookups). Picnic tables and fire grills are provided. Drinking water and vault toilets are available. Horseback-riding facilities and a store are available nearby. Some facilities are wheelchair-accessible. Leashed pets are permitted.

Reservations, fees: Reservations are accepted ($9 reservation fee) at 877/444-6777 or www .ReserveUSA.com. Sites are $19 per night, $5 per night for each additional vehicle. Open June through October, weather permitting.

Directions: From Fresno, drive east on Highway 168 to Shaver Lake, then continue 21 miles to Huntington Lake and Huntington Lake Road. Turn left on Huntington Lake Road and drive one mile to the campground on the right.

Contact: Sierra National Forest, High Sierra Ranger District, 559/855-5355, fax 559/855-5375; California Land Management, 559/893-2111.

25 DEER CREEK

🚶 🏊 🚣 🛥️ 🏕️ ♿ 🚐 ⛺

Scenic rating: 8

on Huntington Lake in Sierra National Forest

Map 11.1, page 607

This is one of the best camps at Huntington Lake, set near lakeside at Bear Cove with a boat ramp nearby. It is on the north shore of the lake's eastern end. Huntington Lake is four miles long and 0.5 mile wide, with 14 miles of shoreline, several resorts, boat rentals, and a trailhead for hiking into the Kaiser Wilderness. Two other campgrounds are nearby.

Campsites, facilities: There are 28 sites for tents or RVs up to 40 feet (no hookups). Picnic tables and fire grills are provided. Drinking water and flush toilets are available. Some facilities are wheelchair-accessible. A store and propane gas are nearby. Leashed pets are permitted.

Reservations, fees: Reservations are accepted ($9 reservation fee) at 877/444-6777 or www.ReserveUSA.com. Sites are $19–21 per night, $5 per night for each additional vehicle. Open June through October, weather permitting.

Directions: From Fresno, drive east on Highway 168 to Shaver Lake, then continue 21 miles to Huntington Lake and Huntington Lake Road. Turn left on Huntington Lake Road and drive one mile to the campground entrance road on the left.

Contact: Sierra National Forest, High Sierra Ranger District, 559/855-5355, fax 559/855-5375.

26 COLLEGE

Scenic rating: 7

on Huntington Lake in Sierra National Forest

Map 11.1, page 607

College is a beautiful site along the shore of the northeastern end of Huntington Lake, at 7,000 feet elevation. This camp is close to a small store in the town of Huntington Lake.

Campsites, facilities: There are 11 sites for tents or RVs up to 30 feet (no hookups). Picnic tables and fire grills are provided. Drinking water and flush and vault toilets are available. Horseback-riding facilities, store, and propane gas are available nearby. Leashed pets are permitted.

Reservations, fees: Reservations are accepted ($9 reservation fee) at 877/444-6777 or www.ReserveUSA.com. Sites are $17 per night, $5

per night for each additional vehicle. Open June through October, weather permitting.

Directions: From Fresno, drive east on Highway 168 to Shaver Lake, then continue 21 miles to Huntington Lake and Huntington Lake Road. Turn left on Huntington Lake Road and drive 0.5 mile to the campground.

Contact: Sierra National Forest, High Sierra Ranger District, 559/855-5355, fax 559/855-5375; California Land Management, 559/893-2111.

27 RANCHERIA

Scenic rating: 8

on Huntington Lake in Sierra National Forest

Map 11.1, page 607

This is the granddaddy of the camps at Huntington Lake, and also the easiest to reach. It is along the shore of the lake's eastern end. A bonus here is nearby Rancheria Falls National Recreation Trail, which provides access to beautiful Rancheria Falls. Another side trip is the 15-minute drive to Bear Butte (the access road is across from the campground entrance) at 8,598 feet, providing a sweeping view of the lake below. The elevation at camp is 7,000 feet.

Campsites, facilities: There are 149 sites for tents or RVs up to 40 feet (no hookups). Picnic tables and fire grills are provided. Drinking water and flush and vault toilets are available. A store and propane gas are available nearby. Leashed pets are permitted.

Reservations, fees: Reservations are accepted ($9 reservation fee) at 877/444-6777 or www.ReserveUSA.com. Sites are $17 per night, $5 per night for each additional vehicle. Open year-round, weather permitting.

Directions: From Fresno, drive east on Highway 168 to Shaver Lake, then continue 20 miles to Huntington Lake and the campground on the left.

Contact: Sierra National Forest, High Sierra Ranger District, 559/855-5355, fax

559/855-5375; California Land Management, 559/893-2111.

28 BADGER FLAT

Scenic rating: 7

on Rancheria Creek in Sierra National Forest

Map 11.1, page 607

This camp is a good launching pad for backpackers. It is set at 8,200 feet along Rancheria Creek. The trail leading out of the camp is routed into the Kaiser Wilderness to the north and Dinkey Lakes Wilderness to the south.

Campsites, facilities: There are 15 sites for tents or RVs up to 22 feet (no hookups). Fire grills and picnic tables are provided. Vault toilets and horseback-riding facilities are available. No drinking water is available. Leashed pets are permitted.

Reservations, fees: Reservations are not accepted. Sites are $12 per night. Open June through October, weather permitting.

Directions: From Fresno, drive east on Highway 168 to Shaver Lake, then continue 21 miles to Huntington Lake and Kaiser Pass Road/Forest Road 80. Turn right and drive four miles to the campground.

Contact: Sierra National Forest, High Sierra Ranger District, 559/855-5355, fax 559/855-5375.

29 BADGER FLAT GROUP AND HORSE CAMP

Scenic rating: 7

on Rancheria Creek in Sierra National Forest

Map 11.1, page 607

Badger Flat is a primitive site along Rancheria Creek at 8,200 feet, about five miles east of Huntington Lake. It is a popular horse camp and a good jump-off spot for wilderness trekkers. A trail that passes through camp provides two options: Head south for three miles to enter the Dinkey Lakes Wilderness, or head north for two miles to enter the Kaiser Wilderness.

Campsites, facilities: There is one group site for tents or RVs up to 30 feet (no hookups) that can accommodate up to 100 people. Picnic tables and fire grills are provided. Vault toilets and horse facilities are available. No drinking water is available. A store is nearby. Leashed pets are permitted.

Reservations, fees: Reservations are required ($9 reservation fee) at 877/444-6777 or www.ReserveUSA.com. The fee is $250 per night. Open June through October, weather permitting.

Directions: From Fresno, drive east on Highway 168 to Shaver Lake, then continue 21 miles to Huntington Lake and Kaiser Pass Road/Forest Road 80. Turn right and drive five miles to the campground on the right.

Contact: Sierra National Forest, High Sierra Ranger District, 559/855-5355, fax 559/855-5375; California Land Management, 559/893-2111.

30 HIDDEN VIEW

Scenic rating: 5

north of Fresno on Hensley Lake

Map 11.1, page 607

Hensley Lake is popular with water-skiers and personal watercraft users in spring and summer, and it has good prospects for bass fishing as well. Hensley covers 1,500 surface acres with 24 miles of shoreline and, as long as water levels are maintained, makes for a wonderful water playland. Swimming is good, with the best spot at Buck Ridge on the east side of the lake, where there are picnic tables and trees for shade. The reservoir was created by a dam on the Fresno River. A nature trail is also here. The elevation is 540 feet.

Campsites, facilities: There are 55 sites for tents or RVs of any length, some with electric hookups (30 amps), and two group sites for

25–100 people. Picnic tables and fire grills are provided. Restrooms with flush toilets and showers, drinking water, dump station, playground, and a boat ramp are available. Some facilities are wheelchair accessible. Leashed pets are permitted.

Reservations, fees: Reservations are accepted at 877/444-6777 or www.ReserveUSA.com. Sites are $14–20 per night, $50 per night for group sites. Boat launching is free for campers. Open year-round.

Directions: From Madera, drive northeast on Highway 145 for about six miles to County Road 400. Bear left on County Road 400 and drive to County Road 603 below the dam. Turn left and drive about two miles on County Road 603 to County Road 407. Turn right on County Road 407 and drive 0.5 mile to the campground.

Contact: U.S. Army Corps of Engineers, Sacramento District, Hensley Lake, 559/673-5151, fax 559/673-2044.

31 SMALLEY COVE

Scenic rating: 7

on Kerckhoff Reservoir near Madera

Map 11.1, page 607

Kerckhoff Reservoir can get so hot that it might seem you could fry an egg on the rocks. Campers should be certain to have some kind of tarp they can set up as a sun screen. The lake is small and remote, and the use of boat motors more than five horsepower is prohibited. Most campers bring rafts or canoes, and there is a good swimming beach near the picnic area and campground. Fishing is not so good here. The elevation is 1,000 feet.

Campsites, facilities: There are five sites for tents or RVs up to 30 feet (no hookups). Picnic tables and fire grills are provided. Drinking water and vault toilets are available. Five group picnic sites are available. You can buy supplies in Auberry. Some facilities are wheelchair-accessible. Leashed pets are permitted.

Reservations, fees: Reservations are not accepted. Sites are $10 per night, $3 per night for each additional vehicle, $7 per night for additional RV, $1 per pet per night. Open year-round.

Directions: From Fresno, take Highway 41 north for three miles to the exit for Highway 168 east. Take that exit and drive east on Highway 168 for about 22 miles to Auberry Road. Turn left (north) and drive 2.8 miles to Powerhouse Road. Turn left and drive 8.5 miles to the campground.

Contact: PG&E Land Services, 916/386-5164, fax 916/386-5388, www.pge.com/recreation.

32 TRAILHEAD WALK-IN, EQUESTRIAN, AND GROUP CAMP

Scenic rating: 8

on the San Joaquin River

Map 11.1, page 607

Not many folks know about this spot. It's a primitive setting, but it has some bonuses. For one thing, there's access to the San Joaquin River if you drive to the fishing access trailhead at the end of the road. From there, you get great views of the San Joaquin River Gorge. The camp is a trailhead for two excellent hiking and equestrian trails. Note that the terrain is steep and can be difficult to traverse. Also, this area has poison oak and rattlesnakes. And one more thing: It can get very hot here in summer. Are we having fun yet? The setting is primarily oaks, gray pine, and chapparal. Beautiful wildflower displays are highlights in the late winter and spring.

Campsites, facilities: There are five sites for tents only and two group sites for tents only that can accommodate up to 15 people each. Drinking water, vault toilets, and a hitching post are available. Bring your own firewood. You can buy supplies in Auberry. Leashed pets are permitted.

Reservations, fees: Reservations are not accepted for individual sites but are required for group sites at 559/855-3492. There is no camping fee, but donations are encouraged. Open year-round.

Directions: From Fresno, take Highway 41 north for three miles to the exit for Highway 168 east. Take that exit and drive east on Highway 168 for about 22 miles to Auberry Road. Turn left and drive 2.8 miles to Powerhouse Road. Turn left and drive two miles to Smalley Road (signed "Smalley Road and San Joaquin River Gorge Management Area"). Turn left and drive four miles to the campground on the right.

Contact: San Joaquin River Gorge Management Area, 559/855-3492; Bureau of Land Management, Bakersfield Field Office, 661/391-6000, fax 661/391-6041.

33 CAMP EDISON

Scenic rating: 8

on Shaver Lake

Map 11.1, page 607

Camp Edison is the best camp at Shaver Lake, set on a peninsula along the lake's western shore, with a boat ramp and marina. The lake is at an elevation of 5,370 feet in the Sierra, a pretty area that has become popular for its calm, warm days and cool water. Boat rentals and bait and tackle are available at the marina. Newcomers with youngsters will discover that the best area for swimming and playing in the water is on the east side of the lake. Though more distant, this part of the lake offers sandy beaches rather than rocky drop-offs.

Campsites, facilities: There are 252 sites for RVs or tents; some sites have full or partial hookups (20, 30, and 50 amps). During the summer season, 45 tent trailers also are available. Picnic tables, fire rings, and barbecues are provided. Restrooms with flush toilets and pay showers, drinking water, cable TV,

Wi-Fi, general store, dump station, coin laundry, marina, boat ramp, and horseback-riding facilities are available. Some facilities are wheelchair-accessible. Leashed pets are permitted.

Reservations, fees: Reservations are recommended. Sites are $24–45 per night, $6 per night for each additional vehicle, $6 per day for boat launching, $5 per pet per night. Tent trailers are $75 per night. Group and long-term rates available. Open year-round with limited winter services.

Directions: From Fresno, take the exit for Highway 41 north and drive north on Highway 41 to the exit for Highway 180 east. Take that exit and drive east on Highway 180 to Highway 168 east. Take that exit and drive east on Highway 168 to the town of Shaver Lake. Continue one mile on Highway 168 to the campground entrance road on the right. Turn right and drive to the campground on the west shore of Shaver Lake.

Contact: Camp Edison, Southern California Edison, 559/841-3134, fax 559/841-3193, www.sce.com/campedison.

34 DORABELLE

Scenic rating: 7

on Shaver Lake in Sierra National Forest

Map 11.1, page 607

This is one of the few Forest Service camps in the state that is set up more for RVers than for tenters. The camp is along a long cove at the southwest corner of the lake, well protected from winds out of the northwest. Shaver Lake is a popular lake for vacationers, and waterskiing and wakeboarding are extremely popular. It is well stocked with trout and kokanee salmon. Boat rentals and bait and tackle are available at the nearby marina. The elevation is 5,400 feet.

Campsites, facilities: There are 68 sites for tents or RVs up to 40 feet (no hookups). Picnic tables and fire grills are provided. Drinking

water and vault toilets are available. A store is nearby. Leashed pets are permitted.

Reservations, fees: Reservations are accepted ($9 reservation fee) at 877/444-6777 or www.ReserveUSA.com. Sites are $17 per night, $5 per night for each additional vehicle. Open May through September, weather permitting.

Directions: From Fresno, drive east on Highway 168 to Dorabelle Road (on the right just as you enter the town of Shaver Lake). Turn right on Dorabelle Road and drive one mile to the campground at the southwest end of Shaver Lake.

Contact: Sierra National Forest, High Sierra Ranger District, 559/855-5355, fax 559/855-5375; California Land Management, 559/893-2111.

35 SWANSON MEADOW

Scenic rating: 4

near Shaver Lake in Sierra National Forest

Map 11.1, page 607

This is the smallest and most primitive of the camps near Shaver Lake; it is used primarily as an overflow area if lakeside camps are full. It is about two miles south of Shaver Lake at an elevation of 5,600 feet.

Campsites, facilities: There are eight sites for tents or RVs up to 30 feet (no hookups). Picnic tables and fire grills are provided. Vault toilets are available. No drinking water is available. A store is nearby. Leashed pets are permitted.

Reservations, fees: Reservations are not accepted. Sites are $13 per night, $5 per night for each additional vehicle. Open May through October, weather permitting.

Directions: From Fresno, drive east on Highway 168 to Dinkey Creek Road (on the right just as you enter the town of Shaver Lake). Turn right and drive three miles to the campground entrance road on the left. Turn left and drive a short distance to the campground.

Contact: Sierra National Forest, High

Sierra Ranger District, 559/855-5355, fax 559/855-5375; California Land Management, 559/893-2111.

36 DINKEY CREEK AND GROUP CAMP

Scenic rating: 7

in Sierra National Forest

Map 11.1, page 607

This is a huge Forest Service camp set along Dinkey Creek at 5,700 feet, well in the interior of Sierra National Forest. It is a popular camp for anglers who take the trail and hike upstream along the creek for small-trout fishing in a pristine setting. Backpackers occasionally lay over here before driving on to the Dinkey Lakes Parking Area, for hikes to Mystery Lake, Swede Lake, South Lake, and others in the nearby Dinkey Lakes Wilderness.

Campsites, facilities: There are 128 sites for tents or RVs up to 35 feet (no hookups), and one group site for up to 50 people. Picnic tables and fire grills are provided. Drinking water, flush and vault toilets, and horseback-riding facilities are available nearby. You can buy supplies in Dinkey Creek. Leashed pets are permitted.

Reservations, fees: Reservations are accepted for individual sites and required for the group site ($9 reservation fee) at 877/444-6777 or www.ReserveUSA.com. Sites are $20 per night, $5 per night for each additional vehicle, $140 per night for the group site. Open May through September, weather permitting.

Directions: From Fresno, drive east on Highway 168 to Dinkey Creek Road (on the right just as you enter the town of Shaver Lake). Turn right and drive 13 miles to the campground. A map of Sierra National Forest is advised.

Contact: Sierra National Forest, High Sierra Ranger District, 559/855-5355, fax 559/855-5375.

37 MILLERTON LAKE STATE RECREATION AREA

Scenic rating: 6

near Madera

Map 11.1, page 607

As the temperature gauge goes up in the summer, the value of Millerton Lake increases at the same rate. The lake is set at 578 feet in the foothills of the San Joaquin Valley, and the water is like gold here. The campground and recreation area are set on a peninsula along the north shore of the lake; there are sandy beach areas on both sides of the lake with boat ramps available near the campgrounds. It's a big lake, with 43 miles of shoreline, from a narrow lake inlet extending to an expansive main lake body. The irony at Millerton is that when the lake is filled to the brim, the beaches are covered, so ideal conditions are actually when the lake level is down a bit, typically from early summer on. Fishing can be good here in spring for bass. Catfish are popular for shoreliners on summer evenings. Waterskiing is very popular in summer, of course. Anglers head upstream, water-skiers downstream. The lake's south side has a huge day-use area. During winter, boat tours are available to view bald eagles. A note of history: The original Millerton County Court-house, built in 1867, is in the park.

Campsites, facilities: There are 148 sites, 26 with full hookups, for tents or RVs up to 36 feet, three boat-in sites, and two group sites for 45–75 people. Picnic tables and fire grills are provided. Drinking water, restrooms with flush toilets and coin showers, dump station, picnic areas, full-service marina, snack bar, boat rentals, and boat ramps are available. Some facilities are wheelchair-accessible. You can buy supplies in Friant. Leashed pets are permitted.

Reservations, fees: Reservations are accepted ($7.50 reservation fee) at 800/444-7275 or www.reserveamerica.com. Sites are $25–34 per night, $7 per night for each additional vehicle, $11 for boat-in sites, $90–168 per night for group sites. Boat launching is $7 per day. Open year-round.

Directions: Drive on Highway 99 to Madera at the exit for Highway 145 East. Take that exit east and drive on Highway 145 for 22 miles (six miles past the intersection with Highway 41) to the park entrance on the right.

Contact: Millerton Lake State Recreation Area, 559/822-2332, fax 559/822-2319, www.parks.ca.gov.

38 GIGANTEA

Scenic rating: 7

on Dinkey Creek in Sierra National Forest

Map 11.1, page 607

This primitive campground is set along Dinkey Creek adjacent to the McKinley Grove Botanical Area, which features a little-known grove of giant sequoias. The campground is set on a short loop spur road, and day visitors are better off stopping at the McKinley Grove Picnic Area. The elevation is 6,400 feet.

Campsites, facilities: There are 11 sites for tents or RVs up to 35 feet (no hookups). Picnic tables and fire grills are provided. Vault toilets are available. No drinking water is available. Garbage must be packed out. You can buy supplies in Dinkey Creek. Leashed pets are permitted.

Reservations, fees: Reservations are not accepted. Sites are $13 per night. Open May through September, weather permitting.

Directions: From Fresno, drive east on Highway 168 to Dinkey Creek Road (on the right just as you enter the town of Shaver Lake). Turn right and drive 13 miles to McKinley Grove Road/Forest Road 40. Turn right and drive 6.5 miles to the campground.

Contact: Sierra National Forest, High Sierra Ranger District, 559/855-5355, fax 559/855-5375.

39 BUCK MEADOW
🏃 🐕 🚐 ⛺

Scenic rating: 7

on Deer Creek in Sierra National Forest

Map 11.1, page 607

This is one of the three little-known, primitive camps in the area. It's set at 6,800 feet along Deer Creek, about seven miles from Wishon Reservoir, a more popular destination.

Campsites, facilities: There are 10 sites for tents or RVs up to 35 feet (no hookups). Picnic tables and fire grills are provided. Vault toilets are available. No drinking water is available. Garbage must be packed out. Leashed pets are permitted.

Reservations, fees: Reservations are not accepted. Sites are $13 per night, $5 per night for each additional vehicle. Open June through September.

Directions: From Fresno, drive east on Highway 168 to Dinkey Creek Road (on the right just as you enter the town of Shaver Lake). Turn right and drive 13 miles to McKinley Grove Road (Forest Road 40). Turn right and drive eight miles to the campground.

Contact: Sierra National Forest, High Sierra Ranger District, 559/855-5355, fax 559/855-5375.

40 JACKASS MEADOWS
🏃 🚣 🏊 🛶 🚐 🦌 ♿ 🚐 ⛺

Scenic rating: 7

on Florence Lake in Sierra National Forest

Map 11.2, page 608

Jackass Meadows is a pretty spot adjacent to Florence Lake, near the Upper San Joaquin River. There are good canoeing, rafting, and float-tubing possibilities, all high-Sierra style, and swimming is allowed. The boat speed limit is 15 mph. The elevation is 7,200 feet. The lake is remote and can be reached only after a long, circuitous drive on a narrow road and many blind turns. A trailhead at the lake offers access to the wilderness and the John Muir Trail. A hikers' water taxi is available.

Campsites, facilities: There are 44 sites for tents or RVs up to 20 feet (no hookups). Picnic tables and fire grills are provided. Vault toilets are available. There is no drinking water. A boat launch, fishing boat rentals, and wheelchair-accessible fishing pier is available nearby. Leashed pets are permitted.

Reservations, fees: Reservations are accepted at 877/444-6777 ($9 reservation fee) or www .ReserveUSA.com. Sites are $16 per night, $32 per night for a double site, $5 per night for each additional vehicle. Open June to mid-October, weather permitting.

Directions: From the town of Shaver Lake, drive east on Highway 168 for 21 miles to Kaiser Pass Road. Bear northeast on Kaiser Pass Road/Forest Road 80 (slow and curvy) to a junction (left goes to Mono Hot Springs and Lake Edison) with Florence Lake Road. Bear right at the junction and drive seven miles to the campground.

Contact: Sierra National Forest, High Sierra Ranger District, 559/855-5355, fax 559/855-5375; California Land Management, 559/893-2111.

41 TRAPPER SPRINGS
🏃 🚣 🏊 🛶 🚐 🦌 ♿ 🚐 ⛺

Scenic rating: 8

on Courtright Reservoir in Sierra National Forest

Map 11.2, page 608

Trapper Springs is on the west shore of Courtright Reservoir, set at 8,200 feet on the west slope of the Sierra. Courtright is a great destination, with excellent camping, boating, fishing, and hiking into the nearby John Muir Wilderness. A 15-mph speed limit makes the lake ideal for fishing, canoeing, and rafting. Swimming is allowed, but the water is very cold. The lake level can drop dramatically by late summer. A trailhead a mile north of camp by car heads around the north end of the lake to a fork; to the left it is routed into the Dinkey Lakes Wilderness, and to the right it is routed to the head of the lake, then follows Dusy Creek in a long climb into spectacular country in the John Muir Wilderness. There are two driving routes to this lake, one from Shaver Lake and the other from Pine Flat Reservoir; both are very long, slow, and twisty drives.

Campsites, facilities: There are 75 sites for tents or RVs up to 35 feet (no hookups). Picnic tables and fire grills are provided. Drinking water and vault toilets are available. A boat ramp is nearby. Some facilities are wheelchair-accessible. Leashed pets are permitted.

Reservations, fees: Reservations are not accepted. Sites are $18 per night, $9 per night for additional RV, $3 per night for each additional vehicle, $1 per pet per night. Open June through October.

Directions: From Fresno, drive east on Highway 168 to Dinkey Creek Road (on the right just as you enter the town of Shaver Lake). Turn right and drive 13 miles to McKinley Grove Road/Forest Road 40. Turn right and drive 14 miles to Courtright Road. Turn left (north) and drive 12 miles to the campground entrance road on the right.

Contact: Sierra National Forest, High Sierra Ranger District, 559/855-5355, fax 559/855-5375; PG&E Land Services, 916/386-5164, fax 916/386-5388, www.pge.com/recreation.

42 MARMOT ROCK WALK-IN
🖐️🚴‍♀️⛵🛶🐕⛺

Scenic rating: 8

on Courtright Reservoir in Sierra National Forest

Map 11.2, page 608

Courtright Reservoir is in the high country at 8,200 feet. Marmot Rock Walk-In is set at the southern end of the lake, with a boat ramp nearby. This is a pretty Sierra lake that provides options for boaters and hikers. Trout fishing can also be good here. Boaters must

observe a 15-mph speed limit, which makes for quiet water. There are two driving routes to this lake, one from Shaver Lake and the other from Pine Flat Reservoir; both are very long, slow, and twisty drives.

Campsites, facilities: There are 15 walk-in sites for tents only. Picnic tables and fire grills are provided. Vault toilets and drinking water are available. A boat ramp is available nearby. Leashed pets are permitted.

Reservations, fees: Reservations are not accepted. Sites are $16 per night, $3 per night for each additional vehicle, $1 per pet per night. Open June through September.

Directions: From Fresno, drive east on Highway 168 to Dinkey Creek Road (on the right just as you enter the town of Shaver Lake). Turn right and drive 13 miles to McKinley Grove Road/Forest Road 40. Turn right and drive 14 miles to Courtright Road. Turn left (north) and drive 10 miles to the campground entrance road on the right (on the south shore of the lake). Park and walk a short distance to the campground.

Contact: PG&E Land Services, 916/386-5164, fax 916/386-5388, www.pge.com/recreation; Sierra National Forest, High Sierra Ranger District, 559/855-5355, fax 559/855-5375.

43 WISHON VILLAGE RV RESORT
🖐️🚴‍♀️⛵🛶🐕🚐⛺

Scenic rating: 7

near Wishon Reservoir

Map 11.2, page 608

This privately operated mountain park is set near the shore of Wishon Reservoir, about one mile from the dam. Trout stocks often make for good fishing in early summer, and anglers with boats love the 15-mph speed limit, which keeps personal watercraft off the water. Backpackers and hikers can find a great trailhead at the south end of the lake at Coolidge Meadow, where a trail awaits that is routed to the Woodchuck Creek drainage and numerous lakes in the John Muir Wilderness. The elevation is 6,500 feet.

Campsites, facilities: There are 97 sites with full hookups (50 amps) for RVs up to 60 feet, and 26 sites for tents. A rental trailer is also available. Picnic tables and fire pits are provided. Restrooms with coin showers, drinking water, and Sunday church service are available. Coin laundry, ice, boat ramp, motorboat rentals, bait and tackle, boat slips, volleyball, horseshoes, and propane gas are available nearby. Leashed pets are permitted.

Reservations, fees: Reservations are recommended. RV sites are $33 per night, $23 per night for tent sites, $3 per person per night for more than two people, $2 per pet per night. Weekly and monthly rates available. Open May through October.

Directions: From Fresno, drive east on Highway 168 to Dinkey Creek Road (on the right just as you enter the town of Shaver Lake). Turn right and drive 13 miles to McKinley Grove Road (Forest Road 40). Turn right and drive 15 miles to the park (66500 McKinley Grove Road/Forest Road 40).

Contact: Wishon Village RV Resort, 559/865-5361, www.wishonvillage.com.

44 LILY PAD

Scenic rating: 7

near Wishon Reservoir in Sierra National Forest

Map 11.2, page 608

This is the smallest of the three camps at Wishon Reservoir. It is set along the southwest shore at 6,500 feet, about a mile from both the lake and a good boat ramp. A 15-mph speed limit ensures quiet water, making this an ideal destination for families with canoes or a raft. The conditions at this lake are similar to those at Courtright Reservoir. There are two driving routes to this lake, one from Shaver Lake and the other from Pine

Flat Reservoir; both are very long, slow, and twisty drives.

Campsites, facilities: There are 11 sites for tents or RVs up to 35 feet (no hookups), and four hike-in sites. Picnic tables and fire grills are provided. Drinking water and vault toilets are available. Groceries, boat rentals, boat ramp, and propane gas are available nearby. Leashed pets are permitted.

Reservations, fees: Reservations are not accepted. Sites are $16 per night, $7 per night for additional RV, $3 per night for each additional vehicle, $1 per pet per night. Open May through October, weather permitting.

Directions: From Fresno, drive east on Highway 168 to Dinkey Creek Road (on the right just as you enter the town of Shaver Lake). Turn right and drive 13 miles to McKinley Grove Road (Forest Road 40). Turn right and drive 16 miles to the campground on the right.

Contact: Sierra National Forest, High Sierra Ranger District, 559/855-5355, fax 559/855-5375; PG&E Land Services, 916/386-5164, www.pge.com/recreation.

45 UPPER KINGS RIVER GROUP CAMP

Scenic rating: 8

on Wishon Reservoir

Map 11.2, page 608

Wishon Reservoir is a great place for a camping trip. When the lake is full, which is not often enough, the place has great natural beauty, set at 6,400 feet and surrounded by national forest. The fishing is fair enough on summer evenings, and a 15-mph speed limit keeps the lake quiet. Swimming is allowed, but the water is very cold. A side-trip option is hiking from the trailhead at Woodchuck Creek, which within the span of a one-day hike takes you into the John Muir Wilderness and past three lakes—Woodchuck, Chimney, and Marsh. There are two driving routes to this lake, one from Shaver Lake and the other from Pine Flat Reservoir; both are very long, slow, and twisty drives.

Campsites, facilities: There is a group site for tents or RVs up to 40 feet (no hookups) that can accommodate up to 50 people. Picnic tables and fire grills are provided. Drinking water and vault toilets are available. Leashed pets are permitted.

Reservations, fees: Reservations are required at 916/386-5164. Sites are $150 per night. Open June to early October, weather permitting.

Directions: From Fresno, drive east on Highway 168 to Dinkey Creek Road (on the right just as you enter the town of Shaver Lake). Turn right and drive 13 miles to McKinley Grove Road/Forest Road 40. Turn right and drive to the Wishon Dam. The campground is near the base of the dam.

Contact: PG&E Land Services, 916/386-5164, fax 916/386-5388, www.pge.com/recreation.

46 HORTON CREEK

Scenic rating: 7

near Bishop

Map 11.2, page 608

This is a little-known, primitive BLM camp set along Horton Creek, northwest of Bishop. It can make a good base camp for hunters in the fall, with wild, rugged country to the west. The elevation is 4,975 feet.

Campsites, facilities: There are 53 sites for tents or RVs up to 30 feet (no hookups). Picnic tables and fire grills are provided. Pit toilets and garbage containers are available. No drinking water is available. Leashed pets are permitted.

Reservations, fees: Reservations are not accepted. Sites are $5 per night and there is a 14-day stay limit. Open early May through October, weather permitting.

Directions: Drive on U.S. 395 to Sawmill Road (eight miles north of Bishop). Turn left (northwest, toward the Sierra) and drive a very short distance to Round Valley Road. Turn right and drive approximately five miles to the campground entrance on the left.

Contact: Bureau of Land Management, Bishop Field Office, 760/872-4881, fax 760/872-5050.

47 BROWN'S MILLPOND CAMPGROUND

Scenic rating: 6

near Bishop

Map 11.2, page 608

This privately operated camp is adjacent to the Millpond Recreation Area, which offers ball fields, playgrounds, and a swimming lake. No powerboats are allowed. There are opportunities for sailing, archery, tennis, horseshoe games, and fishing.

Campsites, facilities: There are 75 sites for tents or RVs of any length; some sites have partial hookups (30 amps). Picnic tables and fire grills are provided. Restrooms with flush toilets and coin showers, drinking water, and coin laundry are available. Leashed pets are permitted.

Reservations, fees: Reservations are accepted. Sites are $17–20 per vehicle per night. Open March through October.

Directions: Drive on U.S. 395 to a road signed "Millpond/County Park" (seven miles north of Bishop). Turn southwest (toward the Sierra) at that road (Ed Powers Road) and drive 0.2 mile to Sawmill Road. Turn right and drive 0.8 mile to Millpond Road. Turn left and drive a short distance to the campground.

Contact: Brown's Millpond Campground, 760/873-5342, www.brownscampgrounds.com/millpond.html.

48 BROWN'S TOWN

Scenic rating: 5

near Bishop

Map 11.2, page 608

This privately operated campground is one of several in the vicinity of Bishop. It's all shade and grass, and it's next to the golf course.

Campsites, facilities: There are 150 sites with no hookups for tents or RVs of any length and 44 sites with partial hookups (30 amps) for tents or RVs. Some sites are pull-through. Picnic tables are provided, and fire grills are provided at most sites. Restrooms with flush toilets and coin showers, drinking water, cable TV at 10 sites, dump station, museum, convenience store, and a snack bar are available. Leashed pets are permitted.

Reservations, fees: Reservations are accepted. Sites are $17–22 per night, $1 per person per night for more than two people. One-vehicle limit per site. Fourteen-day stay limit per season. Some credit cards accepted. Open March through Thanksgiving, weather permitting.

Directions: Drive on U.S. 395 to Schober Lane (one mile south of Bishop) and the campground entrance. Turn northwest (toward the Sierra) and into the campground.

Contact: Brown's Town, 760/873-8522, www .brownscampgrounds.com/browns.html.

49 FORKS

Scenic rating: 7

near South Lake in Inyo National Forest

Map 11.2, page 608

After a visit here, it's no mystery how the Forest Service named this camp. It is at the fork in the road, which gives you two options: You can turn south on South Lake Road and drive along the South Fork of Bishop Creek up to pretty South Lake, or you can keep driving on Highway 168 to another beautiful lake, Lake Sabrina, where hikers will find a trailhead that offers access to the John Muir Wilderness. The elevation is 7,800 feet.

Campsites, facilities: There are nine sites for tents or RVs up to 22 feet (no hookups). Picnic tables and fire grills are provided. Drinking water and vault toilets are available. Supplies are available in Bishop. Leashed pets are permitted.

Reservations, fees: Reservations are not accepted. Sites are $16 per night. Open late April through October, weather permitting.

Directions: Drive on U.S. 395 to Bishop and Highway 168. Turn west (toward the Sierra) on Highway 168 and drive 14 miles to South Lake Road. Turn left and drive 0.25 mile to the campground entrance on the right.

Contact: Inyo National Forest, White Mountain Ranger District, 760/873-2500, fax 760/873-2563; Rainbow Pack Outfitters, 760/872-8803.

50 BIG TREES

Scenic rating: 8

on Bishop Creek in Inyo National Forest

Map 11.2, page 608

This is a small Forest Service camp on Bishop Creek at 7,500 feet in elevation. This section of the stream is stocked with small trout by the Department of Fish and Game. Both South Lake and Lake Sabrina are about 10 miles away.

Campsites, facilities: There are nine sites for tents or RVs up to 30 feet (no hookups). Picnic tables and fire grills are provided. Drinking water and flush toilets are available. Horseback-riding facilities are available approximately seven miles away. Supplies are available in Bishop. Leashed pets are permitted.

Reservations, fees: Reservations are not accepted. Sites are $16 per night. Open late April through October, weather permitting.

Directions: Drive on U.S. 395 to Bishop and Highway 168. Turn west (toward the Sierra)

on Highway 168 and drive 11 miles to the campground access road on the left. Turn left and drive two miles on a dirt road to the campground.
Contact: Inyo National Forest, White Mountain Ranger District, 760/873-2500, fax 760/873-2563; Rainbow Pack Outfitters, 760/872-8803.

51 BISHOP PARK

Scenic rating: 6

near Lake Sabrina in Inyo National Forest

Map 11.2, page 608

Bishop Park Camp is one in a series of camps along Bishop Creek. This one is set just behind the summer community of Aspendell. It is about two miles from Lake Sabrina, an ideal day trip or jump-off spot for a backpacking expedition into the John Muir Wilderness. The elevation is 8,400 feet.
Campsites, facilities: There are 21 sites for tents or RVs up to 22 feet (no hookups), and a group tent site for up to 25 people. Picnic tables and fire grills are provided. Drinking water and flush toilets are available. Horseback-riding facilities are available nearby. Supplies are available in Bishop. Some facilities are wheelchair-accessible. Leashed pets are permitted.
Reservations, fees: Reservations are not accepted for the family sites, but are required for the group site. Reservations are accepted ($9 reservation fee) at 877/444-6777 or www .ReserveUSA.com. Sites are $16 per night, $45 per night for group site. Open mid-May to mid-October, weather permitting.
Directions: Drive on U.S. 395 to Bishop and Highway 168. Turn west (toward the Sierra) on Highway 168 and drive 15 miles to the campground.
Contact: Inyo National Forest, White Mountain Ranger District, 760/873-2500, fax 760/873-2563; Rainbow Pack Outfitters, 760/872-8803.

52 INTAKE AND INTAKE WALK-IN

Scenic rating: 7

on Sabrina Creek in Inyo National Forest

Map 11.2, page 608

This small camp, set at 8,200 feet at a tiny reservoir on Bishop Creek, is about three miles from Lake Sabrina where a trailhead leads into the John Muir Wilderness. Nearby North Lake and South Lake provide side-trip options. All three are beautiful alpine lakes.
Campsites, facilities: There are eight sites for tents or RVs up to 22 feet (no hookups), and seven walk-in tent sites. Picnic tables and fire grills are provided. Drinking water and flush toilets are available. Supplies are available in Bishop. Leashed pets are permitted.
Reservations, fees: Reservations are not accepted. Sites are $16 per night. The walk-in sites are open year-round, weather permitting. Drive-in sites are open April through October, weather permitting.
Directions: Drive on U.S. 395 to Bishop and Highway 168. Turn west (toward the Sierra) on Highway 168 and drive 14.5 miles to the campground entrance.
Contact: Inyo National Forest, White Mountain Ranger District, 760/873-2500, fax 760/873-2563.

53 FOUR JEFFREY

Scenic rating: 8

near South Lake in Inyo National Forest

Map 11.2, page 608

The camp is set on the South Fork of Bishop Creek at 8,100 feet, about four miles from South Lake. If you can arrange a trip in the fall, make sure you visit this camp. The fall colors are spectacular, with the aspen trees exploding in yellows and oranges. It is also the last camp on South Lake Road to be closed in the fall, and though nights are cold, it is well worth the trip. This is by far the largest of the Forest Service camps in the vicinity. There are three lakes in the area: North Lake, Lake Sabrina, and South Lake. South Lake is stocked with trout and has a 5-mph speed limit.

Campsites, facilities: There are 106 sites for tents or RVs up to 25 feet (no hookups). Picnic tables and fire grills are provided. Drinking water, vault toilets, and a dump station are available. Some facilities are wheelchair-accessible. Horseback-riding facilities are available nearby. A café, small store, and fishing-boat rentals are available at South Lake. Supplies are available in Bishop. Leashed pets are permitted.

Reservations, fees: Reservations are accepted at 877/444-6777 ($9 reservation fee) or www.ReserveUSA.com. Sites are $16 per night. Open mid-April through October, weather permitting.

Directions: Drive on U.S. 395 to Bishop and Highway 168. Turn west (toward the Sierra) on Highway 168 and drive 14 miles to South Lake Road. Turn left and drive 0.5 mile to the campground.

Contact: Inyo National Forest, White Mountain Ranger District, 760/873-2500, fax 760/873-2563; Rainbow Pack Outfitters, 760/872-8803.

54 CREEKSIDE RV PARK

🏊 🐕 🚐 ⛺

Scenic rating: 7

on the South Fork of Bishop Creek

Map 11.2, page 608

This privately operated park in the high country is set up primarily for RVs. A lot of folks are surprised to find it here. The South Fork of Bishop Creek runs through the park. A bonus here is a fishing pond stocked with Alpers trout. North, Sabrina, and South Lakes are in the area. The elevation is 8,300 feet.

Campsites, facilities: There are 45 sites with full or partial hookups (20 and 30 amps) for RVs up to 40 feet, and four sites for tents.

Fourteen rental trailers are also available. Restrooms with flush toilets and coin showers, drinking water, convenience store, propane, horseshoes, and fish-cleaning facilities are available. Leashed pets are permitted.

Reservations, fees: Reservations are accepted. Sites are $35 per night, $1 per person per night for more than two people, $5 per night for each additional vehicle, $5 per pet per night. Open May through October. Some credit cards accepted.

Directions: Drive on U.S. 395 to Bishop and Highway 168. Turn west (toward the Sierra) on Highway 168 and drive 14 miles to South Lake Road. Turn left and drive two miles to the campground entrance on the left (1949 South Lake Road).

Contact: Creekside RV Park, 760/873-4483.

55 NORTH LAKE

🥾 🏊 🐕 ⛺

Scenic rating: 8

on Bishop Creek near North Lake in Inyo National Forest

Map 11.2, page 608

North Lake is a beautiful Sierra lake set at an elevation of 9,500 feet, with good trout fishing much of the season and surrounded by beautiful aspens. No motors are allowed on this 13-acre lake. The camp is set on the North Fork of Bishop Creek near North Lake and close to a trailhead that offers access to numerous lakes in the John Muir Wilderness and eventually connects with the Pacific Crest Trail. There is also an outstanding trailhead that leads to several small alpine lakes in the nearby John Muir Wilderness for day hikes, or all the way up to Bishop Pass and Dusy Basin.

Campsites, facilities: There are 11 sites for tents only. Picnic tables and fire grills are provided. Drinking water and vault toilets are available. Horseback-riding facilities are available nearby. Supplies are available in Bishop. Leashed pets are permitted.

Reservations, fees: Reservations are not accepted. Sites are $16 per night. Open mid-May through September, weather permitting.
Directions: Drive on U.S. 395 to Bishop and Highway 168. Turn west (toward the Sierra) on Highway 168 and drive 17 miles to Forest Road 8S02 (signed "North Lake"). Turn right (north) on Forest Road 8S02 and drive two miles to the campground.
Contact: Inyo National Forest, White Mountain Ranger District, 760/873-2500, fax 760/873-2563; Bishop Pack Outfitters, 760/872-8803.

56 SABRINA

Scenic rating: 8

near Lake Sabrina in Inyo National Forest

Map 11.2, page 608   BEST (

You get the best of both worlds at this camp. It is set at 9,000 feet on Bishop Creek, just 0.5 mile from 200-acre Lake Sabrina, a beautiful high Sierra lake. A 10-mph boat speed limit is in effect. Sabrina is stocked with trout, including some big Alpers trout. Trails nearby are routed into the high country of the John Muir Wilderness. Take your pick. Whatever your choice, it's a good one. By the way, Sabrina is pronounced "Sa-bry-na," not "Sa-bree-na."
Campsites, facilities: There are 18 sites for tents or RVs up to 30 feet (no hookups). Picnic tables and fire grills are provided. Drinking water and vault toilets are available. A boat ramp and boat rentals are available nearby. Supplies are available in Bishop. Leashed pets are permitted.
Reservations, fees: Reservations are not accepted. Sites are $16 per night. Open mid-May through October, weather permitting.
Directions: Drive on U.S. 395 to Bishop and Highway 168. Turn west (toward the Sierra) on Highway 168 and drive 17 miles (signed "Lake Sabrina" at a fork) to the campground.
Contact: Inyo National Forest, White Mountain Ranger District, 760/873-2500,

fax 760/873-2563; Bishop Pack Outfitters, 760/873-4785.

57 BAKER CREEK CAMPGROUND

Scenic rating: 4

near Big Pine

Map 11.2, page 608

Because this is a county-operated RV park, it is often overlooked by campers who consider only camps on reservations systems. That makes this a good option for cruisers touring the eastern Sierra on U.S. 395. It's ideal for a quick overnighter, with easy access from Big Pine. The camp is set along Baker Creek at 4,000 feet in the high plateau country of the eastern Sierra. An option is fair trout fishing during the evening bite on the creek.
Campsites, facilities: There are 70 sites for tents or RVs up to 40 feet (no hookups). Picnic tables and fire grills are provided. Vault toilets and hand-pumped well water are available. You can buy supplies about 1.5 miles away in Big Pine. Leashed pets are permitted.
Reservations, fees: Reservations are not accepted. The fee is $10 per vehicle per night. Open year-round, weather permitting.
Directions: Drive on U.S. 395 to Big Pine and Baker Creek Road. Turn west (toward the Sierra) on Baker Creek Road and drive a mile to the campground.
Contact: Inyo County Parks Department, 760/878-0272 or 760/763-5577, www.395.com/inyo/campgrounds.

58 GLACIER VIEW

Scenic rating: 4

near Big Pine

Map 11.2, page 608

This is one of two county camps near the town of Big Pine, providing U.S. 395 cruisers with two options. The camp is set along the Big Pine Canal at 3,900 feet. It is owned by the county but operated by a concessionaire, Brown's, which runs five small campgrounds in the area: Glacier View, Keough Hot Springs, Millpond, Brown's Owens River, and Brown's Town.

Campsites, facilities: There are 40 sites for tents or RVs of any length; some sites have partial hookups (30 amps) and/or are pull-through. Picnic tables and fire grills are provided. Restrooms with flush toilets and coin showers and drinking water are available. Supplies are available in Big Pine. Leashed pets are permitted.

Reservations, fees: Reservations are not accepted. Sites are $10–15 per vehicle per night. Open year-round.

Directions: Drive on U.S. 395 to the park entrance (0.5 mile north of Big Pine) on the southeast side of the road. Turn east (away from the Sierra) and enter the park.

Contact: Inyo County Parks Department, 760/872-6911 or 760/873-5577, www.395 .com/inyo/campgrounds.

59 PALISADE GLACIER AND CLYDE GLACIER GROUP CAMP

Scenic rating: 8

on Big Pine Creek in Inyo National Forest

Map 11.2, page 608

This is a trailhead camp set at 7,600 feet, most popular for groups planning to rock-climb the Palisades. This climbing trip is for experienced mountaineers only; it's a dangerous expedition where risk of life can be included in the bargain. Safer options include exploring the surrounding John Muir Wilderness.

Campsites, facilities: There are two group sites for tents or RVs up to 35 feet (no hookups) that can accommodate up to 35 people each. Picnic tables and fire grills are provided. Drinking water and vault toilets are available. Some facilities are wheelchair-accessible. Leashed pets are permitted.

Reservations, fees: Reservations are required ($9 reservation fee) at 877/444-6777 or www .ReserveUSA.com. Sites are $50 per night. Open mid-April to mid-October.

Directions: Drive on U.S. 395 to Big Pine and Crocker Street/Glacier Lodge Road. Turn west (toward the Sierra) and drive nine miles (it becomes Glacier Lodge Road) to the campground on the left.

Contact: Inyo National Forest, White Mountain Ranger District, 760/873-2500, fax 760/873-2563.

60 BIG PINE CREEK

Scenic rating: 8

in Inyo National Forest

Map 11.2, page 608

This is another good spot for backpackers to launch a multiday trip. The camp is set along Big Pine Creek at 7,700 feet, with trails near the camp that are routed to the numerous lakes in the high country of the John Muir Wilderness.

Campsites, facilities: There are 36 sites for tents or RVs up to 22 feet (no hookups). Picnic tables and fire grills are provided. Drinking water and vault toilets are available. Some facilities are wheelchair-accessible. Leashed pets are permitted.

Reservations, fees: Reservations are not accepted. Sites are $16 per night. Open early May through October, weather permitting.

Directions: Drive on U.S. 395 to Big Pine and Crocker Street/Glacier Lodge Road. Turn west (toward the Sierra) and drive nine miles (it becomes Glacier Lodge Road) to the campground.

Contact: Inyo National Forest, White Mountain Ranger District, 760/873-2500, fax 760/873-2563.

61 UPPER SAGE FLAT

Scenic rating: 8

on Big Pine Creek in Inyo National Forest

Map 11.2, page 608

This is one in a series of Forest Service camps in the area set up primarily for backpackers taking off on wilderness expeditions. Several trails are available near the camp that lead into the John Muir Wilderness. The trail is routed west past several lakes to the base of the Palisades, and beyond to John Muir Trail. Even starting at 7,600 feet, expect a steep climb.

Campsites, facilities: There are 21 sites for tents or RVs up to 35 feet (no hookups). Picnic tables and fire grills are provided. Drinking water and vault toilets are available. Some facilities are wheelchair-accessible. Leashed pets are permitted.

Reservations, fees: Reservations are accepted (with a $9 reservation fee) at 877/444-6777 or www.ReserveUSA.com. Sites are $16 per night. Open mid-April through October, weather permitting.

Directions: Drive on U.S. 395 to Big Pine and Crocker Street/Glacier Lodge Road. Turn west (toward the Sierra) and drive 8.5 miles (it becomes Glacier Lodge Road) to the campground.

Contact: Inyo National Forest, White Mountain Ranger District, 760/873-2500, fax 760/873-2563.

62 SAGE FLAT

Scenic rating: 8

on Big Pine Creek near Big Pine in Inyo National Forest

Map 11.2, page 608

This camp, like the others in the immediate vicinity, is set up primarily for backpackers who are getting ready to head out on multi-day expeditions into the nearby John Muir Wilderness. The trail is routed west past several lakes to the base of the Palisades, and beyond to John Muir Trail. Your hike from here will begin with a steep climb from the trailhead at 7,600 feet elevation. The camp is set along Big Pine Creek, which is stocked with small trout.

Campsites, facilities: There are 21 sites for tents or RVs up to 35 feet (no hookups). Picnic tables and fire grills are provided. Drinking water and vault toilets are available. Leashed pets are permitted.

Reservations, fees: Reservations are not accepted. Sites are $16 per night. Open mid-April through October, weather permitting.

Directions: Drive on U.S. 395 to Big Pine and Crocker Street/Glacier Lodge Road. Turn west (toward the Sierra) and drive eight miles (it becomes Glacier Lodge Road) to the campground.

Contact: Inyo National Forest, White Mountain Ranger District, 760/873-2500, fax 760/873-2563.

63 TINNEMAHA CAMPGROUND

Scenic rating: 6

near Big Pine

Map 11.2, page 608

This primitive, little-known (to out-of-towners) county park campground is on Tinnemaha Creek at 4,400 feet. The creek is stocked with Alpers trout. Horse camping is allowed; but call ahead.

Campsites, facilities: There are 55 sites for tents or RVs of any length (no hookups). Picnic tables and fire grills are provided. Vault toilets are available. Limited drinking water is available. Stream water is available and must be boiled or pump-filtered before use. Leashed pets are permitted.

Reservations, fees: Reservations are not accepted. Sites are $10 per vehicle per night. Open year-round.

Directions: Drive on U.S. 395 to Tinnemaha Creek Road (seven miles south of Big Pine and 19.5 miles north of Independence). Turn west (toward the Sierra) on Fish Springs Road and drive 0.5 mile to Tinnemaha Creek Road. Turn west (left) and drive two miles to the park on the right.

Contact: Inyo County Parks Department, 760/878-0272 or 760/873-5577, www.395.com/inyo/campgrounds.

64 TABOOSE CREEK CAMPGROUND

Scenic rating: 4

near Big Pine

Map 11.2, page 608

The eastern Sierra is stark country, but this little spot provides a stream (Taboose Creek) and some trees near the campground. There is an opportunity for trout fishing—fair, not spectacular. The easy access off U.S. 395 is a bonus. The elevation is 3,900 feet.

Campsites, facilities: There are 56 sites for tents or RVs up to 40 feet (no hookups). Picnic tables and fire grills are provided. Drinking water (hand-pumped from a well) and vault toilets are available. Supplies are available in Big Pine or Independence. Leashed pets are permitted.

Reservations, fees: Reservations are not accepted. The fee is $10 per vehicle per night. Open year-round.

Directions: Drive on U.S. 395 to Taboose Creek Road (11 miles south of Big Pine and 14 miles north of Independence). Turn west (toward the Sierra) on Taboose Creek Road and drive 2.5 miles to the campground (straight in).

Contact: Inyo County Parks Department, 760/878-0272 or 760/873-5577, www.395.com/inyo/campgrounds.

65 GRANDVIEW

Scenic rating: 6

near Big Pine in Inyo National Forest

Map 11.2, page 608

This is a primitive and little-known camp, and the folks who find this area earn their solitude. It is in the White Mountains east of Bishop at 8,600 feet along White Mountain Road. The road borders the Ancient Bristlecone Pine Forest to the east and leads north to jump-off spots for hikers heading up Mount Barcroft (13,023 feet) or White Mountain (14,246 feet, the third-highest mountain in California). A trail out of the camp leads up to an old mining site.

Campsites, facilities: There are 26 sites for tents or RVs up to 22 feet (no hookups). Picnic tables and fire grills are provided. Vault toilets are available. No drinking water is available. Garbage must be packed out. Leashed pets are permitted.

Reservations, fees: Reservations are not accepted. There is no camping fee. Open year-round.

Directions: From Big Pine on U.S. 395, turn east on Highway 168 and drive 13 miles. Turn north on White Mountain/Bristlecone Forest Road (Forest Road 4S01) and drive 5.5 miles to the campground.

Contact: Inyo National Forest, White Mountain Ranger District, 760/873-2500, fax 760/873-2563.

66 ISLAND PARK AND DEER CREEK POINT GROUP

Scenic rating: 7

on Pine Flat Lake

Map 11.3, page 609

These are two of four Army Corps of Engineer campgrounds available at Pine Flat Lake, a popular lake set in the foothill country east of Fresno. When Pine Flat is full, or close to full, it is very pretty. The lake is 21 miles long with 67 miles of shoreline and 4,270 surface acres. Right—a big lake with unlimited potential. Because the temperatures get warm in spring here, then smoking hot in summer, the lake is like Valhalla for boating and water sports. The fishing for white bass is often excellent in late winter and early spring and, after that, conditions are ideal for water sports. The elevation is 1,000 feet.

Campsites, facilities: There are 52 sites for tents or RVs of any length (no hookups), 60 overflow sites (at Island Park), and two group sites for 50 people each for tents or RVs up to 45 feet. Picnic tables and fire grills are provided. Restrooms with flush toilets and coin showers, drinking water, pay telephone, boat ramp, fish-cleaning station, and dump station are available. Some facilities are wheelchair-accessible. There is a seasonal store at the campground entrance. Boat rentals are available within five miles. Leashed pets are permitted.

Reservations, fees: Reservations ($9 reservation fee) are accepted for individual sites and required for the group sites at 877/444-6777 or www.ReserveUSA.com. Sites are $16 per night, $75 per night for group site. Boat launching is $3 per day. Open year-round.

Directions: From Fresno, drive east on Highway 180 for 17.5 miles to Trimmer Springs Road. Turn left and drive eight miles to the town of Piedra. Continue on Trimmer Springs Road for one mile to Pine Flat Road. Turn right and drive 0.25 mile to the park entrance (signed "Island Park").

Contact: U.S. Army Corps of Engineers, Sacramento District, Pine Flat Field Office, 559/787-2589, fax 559/787-2773.

67 LAKERIDGE CAMPING AND BOATING RESORT

Scenic rating: 7

on Pine Flat Lake

Map 11.3, page 609

Pine Flat Lake is a 20-mile-long reservoir with seemingly unlimited recreation po-

tential. It is an excellent lake for all water sports. It is in the foothills east of Fresno at 970 feet elevation, covering 4,912 surface acres with 67 miles of shoreline. The lake's proximity to Fresno has made it a top destination for boating and water sports. Fishing for white bass can be excellent in the spring and early summer. There are also rainbow trout, largemouth bass, smallmouth bass, bluegill, catfish, and black crappie. Note: A downer is that there are only a few sandy beaches, and the lake level can drop to as low as 20 percent full.

Campsites, facilities: There are 107 sites with full or partial hookups (30 amps) for tents or RVs up to 36 feet. Picnic tables and barbecue grills are available at some sites. Restrooms with showers, modem access, coin laundry, ice, horseshoes, and pay phone are available. A convenience store and boat and houseboat rentals are nearby. Leashed pets are permitted.

Reservations, fees: Reservations are recommended at 877/787-2260. Sites are $20–25 per night, $2.50 per pet per night. Some credit cards accepted. Open year-round.

Directions: From Fresno, drive east on Highway 180 for 17.5 miles to Trimmer Springs Road. Turn left and drive eight miles to the town of Piedra. Continue on Trimmer Springs Road for four miles to Sunnyslope Road. Turn right and drive one mile to the resort on the right.

Contact: Lakeridge Camping and Boating Resort, 559/787-2260, fax 559/787-2354; marina, 559/787-2506.

68 KIRCH FLAT

Scenic rating: 6

on the Kings River in Sierra National Forest

Map 11.3, page 609   BEST (

Kirch Flat is on the Kings River, about five miles from the head of Pine Flat Lake. This campground is a popular take-out spot for rafters and kayakers running the Middle Kings, putting in at Garnet Dike dispersed camping area and then making the 10-mile, Class III run downstream to Kirch Flat. The camp is set in the foothill country at 1,100 feet in elevation, where the temperatures are often hot and the water cold.

Campsites, facilities: There are 17 sites for tents or RVs up to 22 feet (no hookups), and one group camp for up to 50 people. Picnic tables and fire grills are provided. Vault toilets are available. No drinking water is available. Leashed pets are permitted.

Reservations, fees: Reservations are not accepted for individual sites, but are required for the group site at 559/855-5355. There is no fee for individual sites, and the group site is $50 per night. Open year-round.

Directions: From Fresno, drive east on Highway 180 for 17.5 miles to Trimmer Springs Road. Turn left and drive 28 miles to Trimmer. Continue east on Trimmer Springs Road (along the north shore of Pine Flat Lake) and drive 18 miles to the campground on the right.

Contact: Sierra National Forest, High Sierra Ranger District, 559/855-5355, fax 559/855-5375.

69 BLACK ROCK

Scenic rating: 7

on Black Rock Reservoir in Sierra National Forest

Map 11.3, page 609

Little Black Rock Reservoir is a little-known spot that can provide a quiet respite compared to the other big-time lakes and camps in the region. The camp is set near the outlet stream on the west end of the lake, created from a small dam on the North Fork Kings River at 4,200 feet elevation.

Campsites, facilities: There are 10 sites for tents only. Picnic tables and fire grills are provided. Vault toilets are available. There is no

drinking water. Garbage must be packed out. Leashed pets are permitted.

Reservations, fees: Reservations are not accepted. Sites are $12 per night. Open year-round.

Directions: From Fresno, drive east on Highway 180 for 17.5 miles to Trimmer Springs Road. Turn left and drive 28 miles to Trimmer. Continue east on Trimmer Springs Road (along the north shore of Pine Flat Lake) and drive 18 miles to Black Road. Turn left and drive 10 miles to the campground.

Contact: Sierra National Forest, High Sierra Ranger District, 559/855-5355, fax 559/855-5375; PG&E Land Services, 916/386-5164, fax 916/386-5388, www.pge.com/recreation.

70 CAMP 4 1/2

Scenic rating: 7

on the Kings River in Sequoia National Forest

Map 11.3, page 609

I found five sites here, not "four and a half." This Sequoia National Forest campground is small, primitive, and usually hot. The elevation is 1,000 feet. It is one in a series of camps just east of Pine Flat Lake along the Kings River, primarily used for rafting access. (See *Kirch Flat* and *Mill Creek Flat* listings in this chapter for more information.)

Campsites, facilities: There are five sites for tents only. Picnic tables and fire grills are provided. Vault toilets are available. No drinking water is available. Garbage must be packed out. Leashed pets are permitted.

Reservations, fees: Reservations are not accepted. There is no fee for camping. Open year-round.

Directions: From Fresno, drive east on Highway 180 for 17.5 miles to Trimmer Springs Road. Turn left and drive 28 miles to Trimmer. Continue east on Trimmer Springs Road (along the north shore of Pine Flat Lake) and drive 18 miles (it becomes Forest Road

11S12) to Forest Road 12S01 (crossing the river). Take Forest Road 12S01 for one mile (along the river) to a dirt road on the right (at the junction of the second bridge). Turn right (still Forest Road 12S01) and drive 0.7 mile to the campground. Not advised for trailers or large RVs.

Contact: Sequoia National Forest, Hume Lake Ranger District, 559/338-2251, fax 559/338-2131.

71 CAMP 4
🏕 🏊 🚣 🛶 🐾 ⛺

Scenic rating: 7

on the Kings River in Sequoia National Forest

Map 11.3, page 609

This is one in a series of camps set on the Kings River upstream from Pine Flat Lake, a popular access point for rafters and kayakers. The Kings River is well known for providing some of the best rafting and kayaking water in California. The weather gets so hot that many take a dunk in the river on purpose; non-rafters had better bring a cooler stocked with ice and drinks. Camp 4 is a mile from Mill Creek Flat.

Campsites, facilities: There are five sites for tents only. Picnic tables and fire grills are provided. Vault toilets are available. No drinking water is available. Garbage must be packed out. Leashed pets are permitted.

Reservations, fees: Reservations are not accepted. There is no fee for camping. Open year-round.

Directions: From Fresno, drive east on Highway 180 for 17.5 miles to Trimmer Springs Road. Turn left and drive 28 miles to Trimmer. Continue east on Trimmer Springs Road (along the north shore of Pine Flat Lake) and drive 18 miles (it becomes Forest Road 11S12) to Forest Road 12S01 (crossing the river). Take Forest Road 12S01 for one mile (along the river) to a dirt road on the right (at the junction of the second bridge). Turn right (still Forest Road 12S01) and drive

1.5 miles to the campground (on the south side of the river). Not advised for trailers and large RVs.

Contact: Sequoia National Forest, Hume Lake Ranger District, 559/338-2251, fax 559/338-2131.

72 MILL CREEK FLAT
🏕 🚣 🐾 ⛺

Scenic rating: 7

on the Kings River in Sequoia National Forest

Map 11.3, page 609

This camp is on the Kings River at the confluence of Mill Creek. It's a small, primitive spot that gets very hot in the summer. The elevation is 1,100 feet. Rafters sometimes use this as an access point for trips down the Kings River. This is best in spring and early summer, when melting snow from the high country fills the river with water.

Campsites, facilities: There are five sites for tents only. Picnic tables and fire grills are provided. Vault toilets are available. No drinking water is available. Garbage must be packed out. Leashed pets are permitted.

Reservations, fees: Reservations are not accepted. There is no fee for camping. Open year-round.

Directions: From Fresno, drive east on Highway 180 for 17.5 miles to Trimmer Springs Road. Turn left and drive 28 miles to Trimmer. Continue east on Trimmer Springs Road (along the north shore of Pine Flat Lake) and drive 18 miles (it becomes Forest Road 11S12) to Forest Road 12S01 (crossing the river). Take Forest Road 12S01 for one mile (along the river) to a dirt road on the right (at the junction of the second bridge). Turn right (still Forest Road 12S01) and drive 2.5 miles to the campground (on the south side of the river). Not advised for trailers and large RVs.

Contact: Sequoia National Forest, Hume Lake Ranger District, 559/338-2251, fax 559/338-2131.

7.3 PINE FLAT RECREATION AREA

🥾 🏊 〰️ ⤵️ 🐕 ♿ 🚐 ⛺

Scenic rating: 7

near Pine Flat Lake

Map 11.3, page 609

This is a county park that is open all year, set below the dam of Pine Flat Lake, actually not on the lake at all. As a county park campground, it is often overlooked by out-of-towners.

Campsites, facilities: There are 52 pull-through sites for tents or RVs of any length (no hookups). Fire grills and picnic tables are provided. Restrooms with flush toilets, drinking water, dump station, and a wheelchair-accessible fishing area are available. A store, coin laundry, and propane gas are nearby (within a mile). Leashed pets are permitted.

Reservations, fees: Reservations are not accepted. Sites are $11 per night, $5 per night for each additional vehicle. Open year-round.

Directions: From Fresno, drive east on Highway 180 for 17.5 miles to Trimmer Springs Road. Turn left and drive eight miles to the town of Piedra. Continue on Trimmer Springs Road for one mile to Pine Flat Road. Turn right and drive three miles to the campground on the right.

Contact: Fresno County Parks Department, 559/488-3004, fax 559/488-1988.

7.4 CHOINUMNI

🥾 〰️ 🐕 🚐 ⛺

Scenic rating: 7

on lower Kings River

Map 11.3, page 609

This campground is set in the San Joaquin foothills on the Kings River, a pretty area. Since the campground is operated by Fresno County, it is off the radar scope of many visitors. Fishing, rafting, canoeing, and hiking are popular. The elevation is roughly 1,000 feet,

surrounded by a landscape of oak woodlands and grassland foothills. The park is roughly 33 miles east of Fresno.

Campsites, facilities: There are 36 sites for tents or RVs of any length (no hookups), and one group site for up to 75 people. Some sites are pull-through. Picnic tables and fire rings are provided. Drinking water, flush toilets, and dump station are available. Canoe rentals are available nearby. No facilities within 10 miles. Leashed pets are permitted.

Reservations, fees: Reservations are accepted for the group site only. Sites are $11 per night, $5 per night for each additional vehicle, $80 per night for the group site. Open year-round.

Directions: From Fresno, drive east on Highway 180 for 17.5 miles to Piedra Road. Turn left on Piedra Road and drive eight miles to Trimmer Springs Road. Turn right on Trimmer Springs Road and drive one mile to Pine Flat Road. Turn right and drive 100 yards to the camp entrance on the right.

Contact: Fresno County Parks Department, 559/488-3004, fax 559/488-1988.

7.5 PRINCESS

🐕 🚐 ⛺

Scenic rating: 7

on Princess Meadow in Giant Sequoia National Forest

Map 11.4, page 610

This mountain camp is at 5,900 feet. It is popular because of its proximity to both Hume Lake and the star attractions at Kings Canyon National Park. Hume Lake is just four miles from the camp and the Grant Grove entrance to Kings Canyon National Park is only six miles away to the south, while continuing on Highway 180 to the east will take you into the heart of Kings Canyon.

Campsites, facilities: There are 90 sites for tents or RVs up to 22 feet (no hookups). Picnic tables and fire grills are provided. Drinking water, vault toilets, and a dump station are available. A store is four miles away at Hume Lake. Leashed pets are permitted.

Reservations, fees: Reservations are accepted ($9 reservation fee) at 877/444-6777 or www .ReserveUSA.com. Sites are $15 per night, $30 per night for a double site, $5 per night for each additional vehicle, plus $20 per vehicle national park entrance fee. Prices are higher on holiday weekends. Open May through September, weather permitting.

Directions: From Fresno, drive east on Highway 180 for 55 miles to the Big Stump Entrance Station at Sequoia and Kings Canyon National Parks. Continue 1.5 miles to a junction (signed left for Grant Grove). Turn left and drive 1.5 miles to Grant Grove Village, then continue for 4.5 miles to the campground on the right.

Contact: Sequoia National Forest, Hume Lake Ranger District, 559/338-2251, fax 559/338-2131.

76 HUME LAKE

Scenic rating: 8

in Giant Sequoia National Forest

Map 11.4, page 610

For newcomers, Hume Lake is a surprise: a pretty lake, with great summer camps for teenagers. Canoeing and kayaking are excellent, and so is the trout fishing, especially near the dam. Swimming is allowed. A 5-mph speed limit is in effect on this 85-acre lake, and only electric motors are permitted. Another surprise is the adjacent religious camp center. The nearby entrances to Kings Canyon National Park add a bonus. The elevation is 5,200 feet.

Campsites, facilities: There are 60 tent sites and 14 sites for tents or RVs up to 22 feet (no hookups). Picnic tables and fire grills are provided. Drinking water and flush toilets are available. A store, café, bicycle rentals, and boat rentals are nearby. Leashed pets are permitted.

Reservations, fees: Reservations are accepted ($9 reservation fee) at 877/444-6777 or www .ReserveUSA.com. Sites are $17 per night, $5 per night for each additional vehicle, plus $20 per vehicle national park entrance fee. Rates are higher on holiday weekends. Open May to early September, weather permitting.

Directions: From Fresno, drive east on Highway 180 for 55 miles to the Big Stump Entrance Station at Sequoia and Kings Canyon National Parks. Continue 1.5 miles to a junction (signed left for Grant Grove). Turn left and drive six miles to the Hume Lake Road junction. Turn right and drive three miles to Hume Lake and the campground entrance road. Turn right and drive 0.25 mile to the campground on the left.

Contact: Sequoia National Forest, Hume Lake Ranger District, 559/338-2251, fax 559/338-2131.

77 ASPEN HOLLOW GROUP CAMP

Scenic rating: 6

near Hume Lake in Sequoia National Forest

Map 11.4, page 610

This large group camp is set at 5,200 feet about a mile south of Hume Lake near a feeder to Tenmile Creek, the inlet stream to Hume Lake. Entrances to Kings Canyon National Park are nearby.

Campsites, facilities: This is a group camp for tents or RVs of any length (no hookups) that can accommodate up to 100 people. Picnic tables and fire grills are provided. Drinking water and vault toilets are available. A store is nearby. Some facilities are wheelchair-accessible. Leashed pets are permitted.

Reservations, fees: Reservations are required ($9 reservation fee) at 877/444-6777 or www .ReserveUSA.com. The fee is $165 per night, plus $20 per vehicle national park entrance fee. Open May to early September, weather permitting.

Directions: From Fresno, drive east on Highway 180 for 55 miles to the Big Stump Entrance Station at Sequoia and Kings Canyon National Parks. Continue 1.5 miles to a junction (signed left for Grant Grove). Turn left and drive six miles to the Hume Lake Road junction. Turn right and drive three miles to Hume Lake and the campground entrance road. Turn right and drive around Hume Lake. Continue south one mile (past the lake) to the campground entrance road.

Contact: Sequoia National Forest, Hume Lake Ranger District, 559/338-2251, fax 559/338-2131.

78 LOGGER FLAT GROUP CAMP

🏊 🚶 ♿ 🚐 ⛺

Scenic rating: 7

on Tenmile Creek in Giant Sequoia National Forest

Map 11.4, page 610

This is the group-site alternative to Landslide campground. This camp is set near the confluence of Tenmile Creek and Landslide Creek at 5,300 feet in elevation, about two miles upstream from Hume Lake. (For more information, see the next entry, *Landslide*.)

Campsites, facilities: This is one group campsite for tents or RVs of any length (no hookups) that can accommodate up to 50 people. Picnic tables and fire grills are provided. Drinking water and vault toilets are available. A store is nearby. Some facilities are wheelchair-accessible. Leashed pets are permitted.

Reservations, fees: Reservations are required ($9 reservation fee) at 877/444-6777 or www.ReserveUSA.com. The fee is $82.50 per night, plus $20 per vehicle national park entrance fee. Open May to early September, weather permitting.

Directions: From Fresno, drive east on Highway 180 for 55 miles to the Big Stump Entrance Station at Sequoia and Kings Canyon National Parks. Continue 1.5 miles to a

junction (signed left for Grant Grove). Turn left and drive six miles to the Hume Lake Road junction. Turn right and drive three miles to Hume Lake and the campground entrance road. Turn right and drive around Hume Lake to Tenmile Road. Continue south three miles to the campground entrance on the right.

Contact: Sequoia National Forest, Hume Lake Ranger District, 559/338-2251, fax 559/338-2131.

79 LANDSLIDE

🏊 🚶 🚐 ⛺

Scenic rating: 7

on Landslide Creek in Giant Sequoia National Forest

Map 11.4, page 610

If you want quiet, you got it; few folks know about this camp. If you want a stream nearby, you got it; Landslide Creek runs right beside the camp. If you want a lake nearby, you got it; Hume Lake is just to the north. If you want a national park nearby, you got it; Kings Canyon National Park is nearby. Add it up: You got it. The elevation is 5,800 feet.

Campsites, facilities: There are eight sites for tents only and one site for RVs up to 22 feet (no hookups). Picnic tables and fire grills are provided. Drinking water and vault toilets are available. A store is nearby. Leashed pets are permitted.

Reservations, fees: Reservations are not accepted. Sites are $13 per night, $26 per night for a double site, $5 per night for each additional vehicle, plus $20 per vehicle national park entrance fee. Open May through September, weather permitting.

Directions: From Fresno, drive east on Highway 180 for 55 miles to the Big Stump Entrance Station at Sequoia and Kings Canyon National Parks. Continue 1.5 miles to a junction (signed left for Grant Grove). Turn right at Generals Highway and drive three miles to Hume Lake Road/Tenmile Road

(Forest Road 13S09). Turn left and drive about seven miles (past Tenmile campground) to the campground on the left.

Contact: Sequoia National Forest, Hume Lake Ranger District, 559/338-2251, fax 559/338-2131.

80 CRYSTAL SPRINGS

Scenic rating: 5

in Kings Canyon National Park

Map 11.4, page 610

Directly to the south of this camp is the General Grant Grove and its giant sequoias. But continuing on Highway 180 provides access to the interior of Kings Canyon National Park, and this camp makes an ideal jump-off point. From here you can drive east, passing Cedar Grove Village, cruising along the Kings River, and finally coming to a dead-end loop, taking in the drop-dead gorgeous landscape of one of the deepest gorges in North America. One of the best hikes, but also the most demanding, is the 13-mile round-trip to Lookout Peak, out of the Cedar Grove Village area. It involves a 4,000-foot climb to 8,531 feet, and with it, a breathtaking view of Sierra ridges, Cedar Grove far below, and Kings Canyon.

Campsites, facilities: There are 50 sites for tents or RVs up to 22 feet (no hookups). Picnic tables and fire grills are provided. Drinking water and flush toilets are available. Evening ranger programs are often available in the summer. Some facilities are wheelchair-accessible. A store and horseback-riding facilities are nearby. Showers are available in Grant Grove Village during the summer season. Leashed pets are permitted, except on trails.

Reservations, fees: Reservations are not accepted. Sites are $18 per night, plus $20 per vehicle national park entrance fee. Open mid-May to mid-September, weather permitting.

Directions: From Fresno, drive east on Highway 180 for 55 miles to the Big Stump Entrance Station at Sequoia and Kings Canyon National Parks. Continue 1.5 miles to a junction (signed left for Grant Grove). Turn left and drive 1.5 miles to Grant Grove Village, then continue for 0.7 mile to the campground entrance on the right.

Contact: Sequoia and Kings Canyon National Parks, 559/565-3341; Grant Grove Visitor Center, 559/565-4307, www.nps.gov/seki.

81 TENMILE

Scenic rating: 7

on Tenmile Creek in Giant Sequoia National Forest

Map 11.4, page 610

This is one of three small, primitive campgrounds along Tenmile Creek south (and upstream) of Hume Lake. RV campers are advised to use the lower campsites because they are larger. This one is about four miles from the lake at 5,800 feet in elevation. It provides an alternative to camping in nearby Kings Canyon National Park.

Campsites, facilities: There are 13 sites for tents or RVs up to 22 feet (no hookups). Picnic tables and fire grills are provided. Vault toilets are available. No drinking water is available. Some facilities are wheelchair-accessible. Leashed pets are permitted.

Reservations, fees: Reservations are not accepted. Sites are $13 per night, $26 per night for a double site, plus $20 per vehicle for national park entrance fee. Camping fees are higher on holiday weekends. Open May to mid-September, weather permitting.

Directions: From Fresno, drive east on Highway 180 for 55 miles to the Big Stump Entrance Station at Sequoia and Kings Canyon National Parks. Continue 1.5 miles to a junction (signed left for Grant Grove). Turn right at Generals Highway and drive three miles to Hume Lake Road/Tenmile Road (Forest Road 13S09). Turn left and drive about five miles to the campground on the left.

Contact: Sequoia National Forest, Hume

Lake Ranger District, 559/338-2251, fax 559/338-2131.

82 AZALEA

Scenic rating: 7

in Kings Canyon National Park

Map 11.4, page 610

This camp is tucked just inside the western border of Kings Canyon National Park. It is set at 6,600 feet, near the General Grant Grove of giant sequoias. (For information on several short, spectacular hikes among the giant sequoias, see the next listing, *Sunset.*) Nearby Sequoia Lake is privately owned; no fishing, no swimming, no trespassing. To see the spectacular Kings Canyon, one of the deepest gorges in North America, re-enter the park on Highway 180.

Campsites, facilities: There are 110 sites for tents or RVs up to 30 feet (no hookups). Picnic tables and fire grills are provided. Drinking water and flush toilets are available. Evening ranger programs are often available. A store and horseback-riding facilities are nearby. Showers are available in Grant Grove Village during the summer. Some facilities are wheelchair-accessible. Leashed pets are permitted, except on trails.

Reservations, fees: Reservations are not accepted. Sites are $18 per night, plus $20 per vehicle national park entrance fee. Open year-round.

Directions: From Fresno, drive east on Highway 180 for 55 miles to the Big Stump Entrance Station at Sequoia and Kings Canyon National Parks. Continue 1.5 miles to a junction (signed left for Grant Grove). Turn left and drive 1.5 miles to Grant Grove Village, then continue for 0.7 mile to the campground entrance on the left.

Contact: Sequoia and Kings Canyon National Parks, 559/565-3341; Grant Grove Visitor Center, 559/565-4307; Grant Grove Horse Stables, 559/335-9292, www.nps.gov/seki.

83 SUNSET

Scenic rating: 7

in Kings Canyon National Park

Map 11.4, page 610

This is the biggest of the camps that are just inside the Sequoia National Park boundaries at Grant Grove Village, 6,600 feet in elevation. The nearby General Grant Grove of giant sequoias is the main attraction. There are many short, easy walks among the sequoias, each breathtakingly beautiful. They include Big Stump Trail, Sunset Trail, North Grove Loop, General Grant Tree, Manzanita and Azalea Loop, and Panoramic Point and Park Ridge Trail. Seeing the General Grant Tree is a rite of passage for newcomers; after a half-hour walk you arrive at a sequoia that is approximately 1,800 years old, 107 feet in circumference, and 267 feet tall.

Campsites, facilities: There are 157 sites for tents or RVs up to 30 feet (no hookups). Picnic tables and fire grills are provided. Drinking water and flush toilets are available. Some facilities are wheelchair-accessible. In the summer, evening ranger programs are often available. A store and horseback-riding facilities are nearby. Showers are available in Grant Grove Village during the summer. Leashed pets are permitted, except on trails.

Reservations, fees: Reservations are not accepted. Sites are $18 per night, plus $20 per vehicle national park entrance fee. Open late May to mid-September, weather permitting.

Directions: From Fresno, drive east on Highway 180 for 55 miles to the Big Stump Entrance Station at Sequoia and Kings Canyon National Parks. Continue 1.5 miles to a junction (signed left for Grant Grove). Turn left (still Highway 180) and drive one mile to the campground entrance (0.5 mile before reaching Grant Grove Village).

Contact: Sequoia and Kings Canyon National Parks, 559/565-3341; Grant Grove Visitor Center, 559/565-4307, www.nps.gov/seki.

84 BUCK ROCK

🐕 🚐 ⛺

Scenic rating: 4

near Big Meadows Creek in Giant Sequoia
National Monument

Map 11.4, page 610

This is a remote camp that provides a little-
known option to nearby Sequoia and Kings
Canyon National Parks. If the national parks
are full and you're stuck, this camp provides an
insurance policy. The elevation is 7,500 feet.

Campsites, facilities: There are nine primitive
sites for tents or RVs up to 16 feet (no hookups). Picnic tables and fire grills are provided.
Vault toilets are available. No drinking water
is available. Leashed pets are permitted.

Reservations, fees: Reservations are not
accepted. There is no fee for camping, but
there is a $20 per vehicle national park en-
trance fee. Open May to early September,
weather permitting.

Directions: From Fresno, drive east on
Highway 180 for 55 miles to the Big Stump
Entrance Station at Sequoia and Kings Canyon National Parks. Continue 1.5 miles to a
junction (signed left for Grant Grove). Turn
right at Generals Highway and drive about
five miles to Big Meadows Road/Forest Road
14S11. Turn left on Big Meadows Road and
drive five miles to the campground entrance
road on the left. Turn left and drive a short
distance to the campground.

Contact: Sequoia National Forest, Hume
Lake Ranger District, 559/338-2251, fax
559/338-2131.

85 BIG MEADOWS

🚶 🛶 🐕 🚐 ⛺

Scenic rating: 7

on Big Meadows Creek in Giant Sequoia
National Monument

Map 11.4, page 610

This primitive, high-mountain camp (7,600
feet) is beside little Big Meadows Creek. Back-

packers can use this as a launching pad, with
the nearby trailhead (one mile down the road
to the west) leading to the Jennie Lake Wilderness. Kings Canyon National Park, only a
12-mile drive away, is a nearby side trip.

Campsites, facilities: There are 40 sites along
Big Meadows Creek and Big Meadows Road
for tents or RVs up to 22 feet (no hookups).
Picnic tables and fire grills are provided. Vault
toilets are available. No drinking water is available. Leashed pets are permitted.

Reservations, fees: Reservations are not
accepted. There is no fee for camping, but
there is a $20 per vehicle national park en-
trance fee. Open May to early October,
weather permitting.

Directions: From Fresno, drive east on
Highway 180 for 55 miles to the Big Stump
Entrance Station at Sequoia and Kings Canyon National Parks. Continue 1.5 miles to a
junction (signed left for Grant Grove). Turn
right at Generals Highway and drive about
five miles to Big Meadows Road/Forest Road
14S11. Turn left on Big Meadows Road and
drive five miles to the camp.

Contact: Sequoia National Forest, Hume
Lake Ranger District, 559/338-2251, fax
559/338-2131.

86 SENTINEL

🚶 🛶 🏠 🐕 ♿ 🚐 ⛺

Scenic rating: 8

in Kings Canyon National Park

Map 11.4, page 610

This camp provides an alternative to nearby
Sheep Creek (see next listing). They both tend
to fill up quickly in the summer. It's a short
walk to Cedar Grove Village, the center of activity in the park. The elevation is 4,600 feet.
Hiking and trout fishing are excellent in the
vicinity. The entrance road provides stunning
rim-of-the-world views of Kings Canyon, and
then drops to right along the Kings River.

Campsites, facilities: There are 82 sites for
tents or RVs up to 30 feet (no hookups). Picnic

tables and fire grills are provided. Restrooms with flush toilets and drinking water are available. Some facilities are wheelchair-accessible. A store, coin showers, coin laundry, and snack bar are nearby. Leashed pets are permitted.

Reservations, fees: Reservations are not accepted. Sites are $18 per night, plus $20 per vehicle national park entrance fee. Open late April through mid-November, weather permitting.

Directions: From Fresno, drive east on Highway 180 for 55 miles to the Big Stump Entrance Station at Sequoia and Kings Canyon National Parks. Continue 1.5 miles to a junction (signed left for Grant Grove). Turn left and drive 32 miles to the campground entrance on the left (near Cedar Grove Village).

Contact: Sequoia and Kings Canyon National Parks, 559/565-3341; Cedar Grove Visitor Center, 559/565-3793, www.nps.gov/seki.

87 SHEEP CREEK

Scenic rating: 8

in Kings Canyon National Park

Map 11.4, page 610

This is one of the camps that always fills up quickly on summer weekends. It's a pretty spot and just a short walk from Cedar Grove Village. The camp is set along Sheep Creek at 4,600 feet.

Campsites, facilities: There are 111 sites for tents or RVs up to 30 feet (no hookups). Picnic tables and fire grills are provided. Restrooms with flush toilets and drinking water are available. A store, coin laundry, snack bar, and coin showers are available nearby. Leashed pets are permitted.

Reservations, fees: Reservations are not accepted. Sites are $18 per night, plus $20 per vehicle national park entrance fee. Open late April to mid-November.

Directions: From Fresno, drive east on Highway 180 for 55 miles to the Big Stump

Entrance Station at Sequoia and Kings Canyon National Parks. Continue 1.5 miles to a junction (signed left for Grant Grove). Turn left and drive 31.5 miles to the campground entrance on the left (near Cedar Grove Village).

Contact: Sequoia and Kings Canyon National Parks, 559/565-3341; Cedar Grove Visitor Center, 559/565-3793, www.nps.gov/seki.

88 CANYON VIEW

Scenic rating: 8

in Kings Canyon National Park

Map 11.4, page 610   BEST (

This is another of several camps in the Cedar Grove Village area of the Kings Canyon National Park. The elevation is 4,600 feet. The access road leads to dramatic views of the deep Kings River Canyon, one of the deepest gorges in North America. One of the best hikes here, but also one of the most demanding, is the 13-mile round-trip to Lookout Peak out of the Cedar Grove Village area. It involves a 4,000-foot climb to 8,531 feet, and with it, a breathtaking view of Sierra ridges, Cedar Grove far below, and Kings Canyon.

Campsites, facilities: There are 23 sites for tents only. Picnic tables and fire grills are provided. Drinking water and flush toilets are available. Coin showers, store, snack bar, and a coin laundry are nearby. Leashed pets are permitted.

Reservations, fees: Reservations are not accepted. Sites are $18 per night, plus $20 per vehicle national park entrance fee. Open late May through September, weather permitting.

Directions: From Fresno, drive east on Highway 180 for 55 miles to the Big Stump Entrance Station at Sequoia and Kings Canyon National Parks. Continue 1.5 miles to a junction (signed left for Grant Grove). Turn left and drive 32.5 miles to the campground entrance (0.5 mile past the ranger station, near Cedar Grove Village).

Contact: Sequoia and Kings Canyon National Parks, 559/565-3341; Cedar Grove Visitor Center, 559/565-3793, www.nps.gov/seki.

89 CANYON VIEW GROUP CAMP

Scenic rating: 8

in Kings Canyon National Park

Map 11.4, page 610

If it weren't for this spot, large groups wishing to camp together in Kings Canyon National Park would be out of luck. Reservations are a must. The elevation is 4,600 feet.

Campsites, facilities: There are nine tent-only group sites; five sites accommodate groups of 7–19 per site, and four sites accommodate groups of 20–40 per site. Picnic tables and fire grills are provided. Drinking water and flush toilets are available. A store, coin laundry, coin showers, and snack bar are nearby. Leashed pets are permitted.

Reservations, fees: Reservations are not accepted for five sites that accommodate 7–19 people each. Reservations are required for four sites that accommodate 20–40 people each. Reservations are accepted at 559/565-4335 from November through April, and 559/565-3792 from May through October. Sites are $35–40 per night, plus $20 per vehicle national park entrance fee. Open June through September, weather permitting.

Directions: From Fresno, drive east on Highway 180 for 55 miles to the Big Stump Entrance Station at Sequoia and Kings Canyon National Parks. Continue 1.5 miles to a junction (signed left for Grant Grove). Turn left and drive 32.5 miles to the campground entrance (0.5 mile past the ranger station, near Cedar Grove Village).

Contact: Sequoia and Kings Canyon National Parks, 559/565-3341; Cedar Grove Visitor Center, 559/565-3793, www.nps.gov/seki.

90 MORAINE

Scenic rating: 8

in Kings Canyon National Park

Map 11.4, page 610

This is one in a series of camps in the Cedar Grove Village area of Kings Canyon National Park. This camp is used only as an overflow area. Hikers should drive past the Cedar Grove Ranger Station to the end of the road at Copper Creek, a prime jump-off point for a spectacular hike. The elevation is 4,600 feet.

Campsites, facilities: There are 120 sites for tents or RVs up to 30 feet (no hookups). Picnic tables and fire grills are provided. Drinking water and flush toilets are available. Coin showers, store, snack bar, and a coin laundry are nearby. Leashed pets are permitted.

Reservations, fees: Reservations are not accepted. Sites are $18 per night, plus $20 per vehicle national park entrance fee. Open June through September, weather permitting.

Directions: From Fresno, drive east on Highway 180 for 55 miles to the Big Stump Entrance Station at Sequoia and Kings Canyon National Parks. Continue 1.5 miles to a junction (signed left for Grant Grove). Turn left and drive 33 miles to the campground entrance (one mile past the ranger station, near Cedar Village).

Contact: Sequoia and Kings Canyon National Parks, 559/565-3341; Cedar Grove Visitor Center, 559/565-3793, www.nps.gov/seki.

91 ESHOM CREEK

Scenic rating: 7

on Eshom Creek in Giant Sequoia National Monument

Map 11.4, page 610

The campground at Eshom Creek is just two miles outside the boundaries of Sequoia

National Park. It is well hidden and a considerable distance from the crowds and sights in the park interior. It is set along Eshom Creek at an elevation of 4,800 feet. Many campers at Eshom Creek hike straight into the national park, with a trailhead at Redwood Saddle (just inside the park boundary) providing a route to see the Redwood Mountain Grove, Fallen Goliath, Hart Tree, and Hart Meadow in a sensational loop hike.

Campsites, facilities: There are 23 sites for tents or RVs up to 22 feet (no hookups), and five group sites for up to 12 people each. Picnic tables and fire grills are provided. Drinking water and vault toilets are available. Leashed pets are permitted.

Reservations, fees: Reservations are not accepted. Sites are $15 per night, $5 per night for each additional vehicle, $30 per night for group site. Camping fees are higher on holiday weekends. Open May to early October, weather permitting.

Directions: Drive on Highway 99 to Visalia and the exit for Highway 198 east. Take that exit and drive east on Highway 198 for 11 miles to Highway 245. Turn left (north) on Highway 245 and drive 18 miles to Badger and County Road 465. Turn right and drive eight miles to the campground.

Contact: Sequoia National Forest, Hume Lake Ranger District, 559/338-2251, fax 559/338-2131.

92 FIR GROUP CAMPGROUND
🏃 🚴 🐕 🚐 ⛺

Scenic rating: 6

near Stony Creek in Giant Sequoia National Monument

Map 11.4, page 610

This is the second of two large group camps in the area set along Stony Creek.

Campsites, facilities: This is a group camp for tents or RVs up to 45 feet (no hookups) that can accommodate up to 100 people. Picnic tables and fire grills are provided. Drinking water and vault toilets are available. A store and coin laundry are nearby. Leashed pets are permitted.

Reservations, fees: Reservations are required at 877/444-6777 ($9 reservation fee) or www .ReserveUSA.com. The fee is $165 per night, plus $20 per vehicle national park entrance fee. Fees are higher on holiday weekends. Open late May to early September, weather permitting.

Directions: From Fresno, drive east on Highway 180 for 55 miles to the Big Stump Entrance Station at Sequoia and Kings Canyon National Parks. Continue 1.5 miles to a junction (signed left for Grant Grove). Turn right at Generals Highway and drive about 14 miles to the campground entrance on the left.

Contact: Sequoia National Forest, Hume Lake Ranger District, 559/338-2251, fax 559/338-2131.

93 STONY CREEK
🏃 🚴 🐕 🚐 ⛺

Scenic rating: 6

in Giant Sequoia National Monument

Map 11.4, page 610

Stony Creek Camp provides a good option if the national park camps are filled. It is set at creekside at 6,400 feet elevation. Sequoia and Kings Canyon National Parks are nearby.

Campsites, facilities: There are 49 sites for tents or RVs up to 22 feet (no hookups). Picnic tables and fire grills are provided. Drinking water and flush toilets are available. A store and coin laundry are nearby. Leashed pets are permitted.

Reservations, fees: Reservations are accepted ($9 reservation fee) at 877/444-6777 or www .ReserveUSA.com. Sites are $17 per night, $5 per night for each additional vehicle, plus $20 per vehicle national park entrance fee. Fees are higher on holiday weekends.

Open May to early September, weather permitting.

Directions: From Fresno, drive east on Highway 180 for 55 miles to the Big Stump Entrance Station at Sequoia and Kings Canyon National Parks. Continue 1.5 miles to a junction (signed left for Grant Grove). Turn right at Generals Highway and drive about 13 miles to the campground entrance on the right.

Contact: Sequoia National Forest, Hume Lake Ranger District, 559/338-2251, fax 559/338-2131.

94 COVE GROUP CAMP

Scenic rating: 6

near Stony Creek in Giant Sequoia National Monument

Map 11.4, page 610

This large group camp is beside Stony Creek. The elevation is 6,500 feet.

Campsites, facilities: This is a group camp for tents or RVs up to 22 feet (no hookups) that can accommodate up to 50 people. Picnic tables and fire grills are provided. Drinking water and vault toilets are available. A store and coin laundry are available nearby. Leashed pets are permitted.

Reservations, fees: Reservations are required at 877/444-6777 or www.ReserveUSA.com ($9 reservation fee). The fee is $82.50 per night, plus $20 per vehicle national park entrance fee. Open May to early September, weather permitting.

Directions: From Fresno, drive east on Highway 180 for 55 miles to the Big Stump Entrance Station at Sequoia and Kings Canyon National Parks. Continue 1.5 miles to a junction (signed left for Grant Grove). Turn right at Generals Highway and drive about 14 miles to the campground entrance on the left (just past Fir Group Campground).

Contact: Sequoia National Forest, Hume Lake Ranger District, 559/338-2251, fax 559/338-2131.

95 DORST CREEK

Scenic rating: 7

on Dorst Creek in Sequoia National Park

Map 11.4, page 610   BEST (

Things that go bump in the night swing through Dorst all summer long. That's right, Mr. Bear (a whole bunch of them) makes food raids like a UPS driver on a pick-up route. There are so many bears raiding food here that some years rangers keep a running tally posted on the bulletin board. That's why keeping your food in a bearproof locker is not only a must, it's the law. The camp is set on Dorst Creek at 6,700 feet, near a trail that is routed into the backcountry and through Muir Grove. It is one in a series of big, popular camps in Sequoia National Park.

Campsites, facilities: There are 204 sites for tents or RVs up to 30 feet (no hookups) and five group sites for 12–50 people each. Picnic tables and fire grills are provided. Drinking water, flush toilets, and dump station are available. Some facilities are wheelchair-accessible. A store, coin showers, and a coin laundry are eight miles away. Leashed pets are permitted.

Reservations, fees: Reservations are accepted at 800/365-CAMP (800/365-2267) or http://reservations.nps.gov. Sites are $20 per night (includes reservation fee), plus $20 per vehicle national park entrance fee, $40–60 per night for group sites. Open Memorial Day through Labor Day.

Directions: From Fresno, drive east on Highway 180 for 55 miles to the Big Stump Entrance Station at Sequoia and Kings Canyon National Parks. Continue 1.5 miles to a junction (signed left for Grant Grove). Turn right at Generals Highway and drive about 25.5 miles to the campground entrance on the right.

Contact: Sequoia and Kings Canyon National Parks, 559/565-3341; Lodgepole Visitor Center, 559/565-4436, www.nps.gov/seki.

96 LODGEPOLE

Scenic rating: 8

on the Marble Fork of the Kaweah River in Sequoia National Park

Map 11.4, page 610

This giant, pretty camp on the Marble Fork of the Kaweah River is typically crowded. A bonus here is an excellent trailhead nearby that leads into the backcountry of Sequoia National Park. The elevation is 6,700 feet. For information on backcountry permits, phone the Mineral King Ranger Station, 559/565-3135.

Campsites, facilities: There are 214 sites for tents or RVs up to 40 feet (no hookups). Picnic tables and fire grills are provided. Restrooms with flush toilets, drinking water, dump station, gift shop, and evening ranger programs are available. A store, deli, coin showers, and a coin laundry are nearby. Leashed pets are permitted.

Reservations, fees: Reservations are accepted at 800/365-CAMP (800/365-2267) or http://reservations.nps.gov. Sites are $18–20 per night (includes reservation fee), plus $20 per vehicle national park entrance fee. Open year-round, with limited winter services.

Directions: From Fresno, drive east on Highway 180 for 55 miles to the Big Stump Entrance Station at Sequoia and Kings Canyon National Parks. Continue 1.5 miles to a junction (signed left for Grant Grove). Turn right at Generals Highway and drive about 25 miles to Lodgepole Village and the turnoff for Lodgepole Campground. Turn left and drive 0.25 mile (past Lodgepole Village) to the campground.

Contact: Sequoia and Kings Canyon National Parks, 559/565-3341, www.nps.gov/seki.

97 POTWISHA

Scenic rating: 7

on the Marble Fork of the Kaweah River in Sequoia National Park

Map 11.4, page 610

This pretty spot on the Marble Fork of the Kaweah River is one of Sequoia National Park's smaller drive-to campgrounds. By looking at maps, newcomers may think it is a very short drive farther into the park to see the General Sherman Tree, Giant Forest, and the famous trailhead for the walk up Moro Rock. Nope. It's a slow, twisty drive, but with many pullouts for great views. A few miles east of the camp, visitors can find Buckeye Flat and a trail that is routed along Paradise Creek.

Campsites, facilities: There are 42 sites for tents or RVs up to 30 feet (no hookups). Picnic tables and fire grills are provided. Drinking water, flush toilets, dump station, and evening ranger programs are available. Some facilities are wheelchair-accessible. Leashed pets are permitted.

Reservations, fees: Reservations are not accepted. Sites are $18 per night, plus $20 per vehicle national park entrance fee. Open year-round.

Directions: From Visalia, drive east on Highway 198 for 36 miles to the Ash Mountain entrance station to Sequoia and Kings Canyon National Parks. Continue into the park (the road becomes Generals Highway) and drive four miles to the campground on the left. Vehicles of 22 feet or longer are not advised on Generals Highway from Potwisha to Giant Forest Village and are advised to use Highway 180 through the Big Stump entrance station.

Contact: Sequoia and Kings Canyon National Parks, 559/565-3341, www.nps.gov/seki.

98 BUCKEYE FLAT

🥾 🛶 🛁 🐕 ⛺

Scenic rating: 8

on the Middle Fork of the Kaweah River in Sequoia National Park

Map 11.4, page 610

In any big, popular national park such as Sequoia, the smaller the campground, the better. Well, Buckeye Flat is one of the smaller ones here, set on the Middle Fork of the Kaweah River with a trail just south of camp that runs beside pretty Paradise Creek.

Campsites, facilities: There are 28 tent sites. Picnic tables and fire grills are provided. Drinking water and flush toilets are available. Leashed pets are permitted.

Reservations, fees: Reservations are not accepted. Sites are $18 per night, plus $20 per vehicle national park entrance fee. Open mid-April to mid-September, weather permitting.

Directions: From Visalia, drive east on Highway 198 for 36 miles to the Ash Mountain entrance station to Sequoia and Kings Canyon National Parks. Continue into the park (the road becomes Generals Highway) and drive 6.2 miles to the turnoff (across from Hospital Rock) for Buckeye Flat Campground. Turn right and drive 0.6 mile to the campground. Vehicles of 22 feet or longer are not advised on Generals Highway from Potwisha to Giant Forest Village and are advised to use Highway 180 through the Big Stump entrance station.

Contact: Sequoia and Kings Canyon National Parks, 559/565-3341, www.nps.gov/seki.

99 ATWELL MILL

🥾 🐕 ⛺

Scenic rating: 7

on Atwell Creek in Sequoia National Park

Map 11.4, page 610

This small, pretty camp in Sequoia National Park is on Atwell Creek near the East Fork of the Kaweah River, at an elevation of 6,650 feet. While the road in is paved, it is slow and twisty, with many blind turns. The terrain in this canyon is open and dry, overlooking the East Fork Kaweah River well below. A trail at camp is routed south for a mile down to the Kaweah River, then climbs out of the canyon and along Deer Creek for another two miles through the East Fork Grove, an outstanding day hike.

Campsites, facilities: There are 21 tent sites; no RVs or trailers are permitted. Picnic tables and fire grills are provided. Drinking water and pit toilets are available. A small store is nearby. Leashed pets are permitted.

Reservations, fees: Reservations are not accepted. Sites are $12 per night, plus $20 per vehicle park entrance fee. Open late May to mid-October, weather permitting.

Directions: From Visalia, drive east on Highway 198 for 36 miles to the town of Three Rivers. Continue east for three miles to Mineral King Road. Turn right on Mineral King Road and drive 19 miles (slow, steep, narrow, and twisty, with blind curves) to the campground. RVs and trailers are not recommended.

Contact: Sequoia and Kings Canyon National Parks, 559/565-3341, www.nps.gov/seki.

100 COLD SPRINGS

🥾 🛶 🐕 ⛺

Scenic rating: 9

on the East Fork of the Kaweah River in Sequoia National Park

Map 11.4, page 610

This high-country camp at Sequoia National Park is set at 7,500 feet on the East Fork of the Kaweah River. There is a stellar hiking trail from here, with the trailhead just west of the camp. The hike is routed south along Mosquito Creek, climbing over the course of about three miles to the pretty Mosquito Lakes, a series of four small, beautiful lakes set on the north flank of Hengst Peak

(11,127 feet). At road's end, there are two wilderness trailheads for sensational hikes, including one routed out to the Great Western Divide.

Campsites, facilities: There are 40 tent sites. Picnic tables and fire grills are provided. Drinking water and pit toilets are available. A store is nearby. Leashed pets are permitted.

Reservations, fees: Reservations are not accepted. Sites are $12 per night, plus $20 per vehicle national park entrance fee. Open May to September.

Directions: From Visalia, drive east on Highway 198 for 36 miles to the town of Three Rivers. Continue east for three miles to Mineral King Road. Turn right on Mineral King Road and drive 23 miles (slow, steep, narrow, and twisty, with blind curves) to the campground. RVs and trailers are not recommended.

Contact: Sequoia and Kings Canyon National Parks, 559/565-3341, www.nps.gov/seki.

101 HORSE CREEK

Scenic rating: 6

on Lake Kaweah

Map 11.4, page 610

Lake Kaweah is a big lake, covering nearly 2,000 acres with 22 miles of shoreline. This camp is set on the southern shore of the lake. In the spring when the lake is full and the surrounding hills are green, you may even think you have found Valhalla. With such hot weather in the San Joaquin Valley, it's a boater's heaven, ideal for water-skiers. In spring, when the water is too cool for water sports, anglers can have the lake to themselves with good bass fishing. Other species include trout, catfish, and crappie. By early summer, it's crowded with personal watercraft and ski boats. The lake level fluctuates and flooding is a potential problem in some years. Another problem is that the water level

drops a great deal during late summer, as thirsty farms suck up every drop they can get, killing prospects of developing beaches for swimming and wading. The elevation is 300 feet.

Campsites, facilities: There are 80 sites for tents or RVs up to 30 feet (no hookups). Picnic tables and fire grills are provided. Restrooms with flush toilets and showers, drinking water, playground, and a dump station are available. Some facilities are wheelchair-accessible. Two paved boat ramps are available at Kaweah Recreation Area and Lemon Hill Recreation Area. A store, coin laundry, boat and water-ski rentals, ice, snack bar, restaurant, gas station, and propane gas are available nearby. Leashed pets are permitted.

Reservations, fees: Reservations are accepted ($9 reservation fee) at 877/444-6777 or www.ReserveUSA.com. Sites are $16 per night. Some credit cards accepted. Open year-round.

Directions: From Visalia, drive east on Highway 198 for 25 miles to Lake Kaweah's south shore and the camp on the left.

Contact: U.S. Army Corps of Engineers, Lake Kaweah, 559/597-2301, fax 559/597-2468.

102 SOUTH FORK

Scenic rating: 7

on the South Fork of the Kaweah River in Sequoia National Park

Map 11.4, page 610

The smallest developed camp in Sequoia National Park might just be what you're looking for. It is set at 3,650 feet on the South Fork of the Kaweah River, just inside the southwestern border of Sequoia and Kings Canyon National Parks. While it is technically in the park, it is nothing like at the Giant Forest. Instead, the road in is twisty and slow, the landscape open and hot. A trail heads east from the camp and traverses Dennison Ridge, eventually leading to Hockett

Lakes, a long, demanding overnight trip. This is black-bear habitat so proper food storage is required.

Campsites, facilities: There are 13 sites for tents only. Picnic tables and fire grills are provided. Vault toilets are available. No drinking water is available. Leashed pets are permitted, except on trails.

Reservations, fees: Reservations are not accepted. Sites are $12 per night from May through October, no fee in other months, $20 per vehicle national park entrance fee. Open year-round.

Directions: From Visalia, drive east on Highway 198 for 35 miles to South Fork Road (one mile before reaching the town of Three Rivers). Turn right on South Fork Road and drive 13 miles to the campground (the road is dirt for the last four miles).

Contact: Sequoia and Kings Canyon National Parks, 559/565-3341, www.nps.gov/seki.

103 BALCH PARK

Scenic rating: 6

near Mountain Home State Forest

Map 11.4, page 610

Balch Park is surrounded by Mountain Home State Forest and Giant Sequoia National Monument. A nearby grove of giant sequoias is a feature attraction. The elevation is 6,500 feet. Two stocked fishing ponds are also available.

Campsites, facilities: There are 71 sites for tents or RVs up to 40 feet (no hookups); some sites are pull-through. Picnic tables and fire grills are provided. Drinking water and flush toilets and vault toilets are available. Some facilities are wheelchair-accessible. Leashed pets are permitted.

Reservations, fees: Reservations are not accepted. Sites are $16 per night, $5 per night for each additional vehicle, $3 per pet per night. Open May to late October.

Directions: From Porterville, drive east on

Highway 190 for 19 miles (a mile past the town of Springville) to Balch Park Road. Turn left (north) at Balch Park Road and drive three miles to Bear Creek Road. Turn east (right) and drive 15 miles (extremely slow and curvy) to the campground (RVs not recommended).

Alternate route for RV drivers: After turning north onto Balch Park Road, drive 40 miles (long and curvy) to the park.

Contact: Balch Park, Tulare County, 559/733-6291, www.co.tulare.ca.us.

104 HIDDEN FALLS WALK-IN

Scenic rating: 7

on the Tule River in Mountain Home State Forest

Map 11.4, page 610

This small, quiet camp, set at 5,900 feet along the Tule River near Hidden Falls, is one of the prettier camps in Mountain Home State Forest. It is remote and overlooked by all but a handful of insiders who know its qualities.

Campsites, facilities: There are eight walk-in sites for tents only. Picnic tables and fire grills are provided. Drinking water and pit toilets are available. Leashed pets are permitted.

Reservations, fees: Reservations are not accepted. There is no fee for camping. Open mid-May to early October, weather permitting.

Directions: From Porterville, drive east on Highway 190 for 19 miles (a mile past the town of Springville) to Balch Park Road. Turn left (north) at Balch Park Road and drive about 23 miles to the Mountain Home State Forest sign. Continue on Balch Park Road (the road is long and twisty) and follow the signs to the State Forest Headquarters (where free forest maps are available). The campgrounds are well signed from this point.

Contact: Mountain Home State Forest, 559/539-2321 (summer) or 559/539-2855 (winter).

105 MOSES GULCH

🏃 🏕 🐕 ⛺

Scenic rating: 7

on the Tule River in Mountain Home State
Forest

Map 11.4, page 610

Obscure Moses Gulch sits on the Tule River
in a canyon below Moses Mountain (9,331
feet) to the nearby north. A trailhead at the
eastern end of the state forest provides access
both north and south along the North Fork of
the Middle Fork Tule River for a scenic hike.
The elevation here is 5,400 feet. Mountain
Home State Forest is surrounded by Sequoia
National Forest. The cost? Free.

Campsites, facilities: There are 10 sites for
tents only. Picnic tables and fire grills are provided. Drinking water and vault toilets are
available. Leashed pets are permitted.

Reservations, fees: Reservations are not
accepted. There is no fee for camping. Open
mid-May through September, weather
permitting.

Directions: From Porterville, drive east on
Highway 190 for 19 miles (a mile past the
town of Springville) to Balch Park Road. Turn
left (north) at Balch Park Road and drive about
23 miles to the Mountain Home State Forest
sign. Continue on Balch Park Road (the road
is long and twisty) and follow the signs to the
State Forest Headquarters (where free forest
maps are available). The campgrounds are well
signed from this point.

Contact: Mountain Home State Forest,
559/539-2321 (summer) or 559/539-2855
(winter).

106 FRAZIER MILL

🏃 🐕 ♿ 🚐 ⛺

Scenic rating: 5

in Mountain Home State Forest

Map 11.4, page 610

Abundant old-growth sequoias are the prime
attraction at this remote camp. The Wishon

Fork of the Tule River is the largest of the
several streams that pass through this forest.
You can't beat the price.

Campsites, facilities: There are 49 sites for
tents, with a few of these sites also for RVs up
to 35 feet (no hookups). Picnic tables and fire
grills are provided. Drinking water and vault
toilets are available. Some facilities are wheelchair-accessible. Leashed pets are permitted.

Reservations, fees: Reservations are not
accepted. There is no fee for camping. Open
from mid-May to early October, weather
permitting.

Directions: From Porterville, drive east on
Highway 190 for 19 miles (a mile past the
town of Springville) to Balch Park Road.
Turn left (north) at Balch Park Road and
drive about 23 miles to the Mountain Home
State Forest sign. Continue on Balch Park
Road (the road is long and twisty) and follow the signs to the State Forest Headquarters (where free forest maps are available).
The campgrounds are well signed from this
point.

Contact: Mountain Home State Forest,
559/539-2321 (summer) or 559/539-2855
(winter).

107 SHAKE CAMP

🏃 🐕 ♿ 🚐 ⛺

Scenic rating: 6

in Mountain Home State Forest

Map 11.4, page 610

This is a little-known spot for horseback riding. Horses can be rented for the day, hour, or
night. The camp is set at 6,500 feet and there's
a trailhead here for trips into the adjoining
Sequoia National Forest and beyond to the
east into the Golden Trout Wilderness. Hikers
should note that the Balch Park Pack Station,
a commercial outfitter, is nearby, so you can
expect horse traffic on the trail.

Campsites, facilities: There are 11 sites for
tents or RVs up to 20 feet (no hookups).
Picnic tables and fire grills are provided.

Drinking water and vault toilets are available. A public pack station with corrals is nearby. Some facilities are wheelchair-accessible. Leashed pets are permitted.

Reservations, fees: Reservations are not accepted. There is no fee for camping. Open mid-May to early October, weather permitting.

Directions: From Porterville, drive east on Highway 190 for 19 miles (a mile past the town of Springville) to Balch Park Road. Turn left (north) at Balch Park Road and drive about 23 miles to the Mountain Home State Forest sign. Continue on Balch Park Road (the road is long and twisty) and follow the signs to the State Forest Headquarters (where free forest maps are available). The campgrounds are well signed from this point.

Contact: Mountain Home State Forest, 559/539-2321 (summer) or 559/539-2855 (winter).

108 HEDRICK POND

Scenic rating: 6

in Mountain Home State Forest

Map 11.4, page 610

Mountain Home State Forest is highlighted by giant sequoias, and Hedrick Pond provides a fishing opportunity, as it's stocked occasionally in summer with rainbow trout. This camp is set at 6,200 feet, one of five campgrounds in the immediate region. (See the next listing, *Methuselah Group Camp*, for recreation options.)

Campsites, facilities: There are 14 sites for tents or RVs up to 20 feet (no hookups). Picnic tables and fire grills are provided. Drinking water and vault toilets are available. Some facilities are wheelchair-accessible. Leashed pets are permitted.

Reservations, fees: Reservations are not accepted. There is no fee for camping. Open from mid-May through October, weather permitting.

Directions: From Porterville, drive east on Highway 190 for 19 miles (a mile past the town of Springville) to Balch Park Road. Turn left (north) at Balch Park Road and drive about 23 miles to the Mountain Home State Forest sign. Continue on Balch Park Road (the road is long and twisty) and follow the signs to the State Forest Headquarters (where free forest maps are available). The campgrounds are well signed from this point.

Contact: Mountain Home State Forest, 559/539-2321 (summer) or 559/539-2855 (winter).

109 METHUSELAH GROUP CAMP

Scenic rating: 6

in Mountain Home State Forest

Map 11.4, page 610

This is one of the few group campgrounds anywhere in California that is free to users. But hey: Remember to bring water. The elevation is 5,900 feet. Mountain Home State Forest is best known for its remoteness, old-growth giant sequoias (hence the name of this camp, Methuselah), trails that provide access to small streams, and horseback trips into the surrounding Sequoia National Forest.

Campsites, facilities: This is one group site for tents or RVs up to 20 feet (no hookups) that can accommodate 20–100 people. Fire grills and picnic tables are provided. Vault toilets are available. No drinking water is available. Leashed pets are permitted. Garbage must be packed out.

Reservations, fees: Reservations are required. There is no fee for camping. Open mid-May to early October, weather permitting.

Directions: From Porterville, drive east on Highway 190 for 19 miles (a mile past the town of Springville) to Balch Park Road. Turn left (north) at Balch Park Road and drive about 23 miles to the Mountain Home State Forest sign. Continue on Balch Park Road (the road is long and twisty) and follow the signs to the State Forest Headquarters (where free forest maps are available). The campgrounds are well signed from this point.

Contact: Mountain Home State Forest, 559/539-2321 (summer) or 559/539-2855 (winter).

110 WISHON

Scenic rating: 8

on the Tule River in Giant Sequoia National Monument

Map 11.4, page 610

Wishon Camp is set at 3,900 feet on the Middle Fork of the North Fork Tule River, just west of the Doyle Springs Summer Home Tract. Just down the road to the east, on the left side, is a parking area for a trailhead. The hike here is routed for a mile to the Tule River and then runs along the stream for about five miles, to Mountain Home State Forest.

Campsites, facilities: There are 39 sites for tents or RVs up to 22 feet (no hookups). Picnic tables and fire grills are provided. Drinking water and vault toilets are available. Leashed pets are permitted.

Reservations, fees: Reservations are accepted ($9 reservation fee) at 877/444-6777 or www.ReserveUSA.com. Sites are $15 per night, $5 per night for each additional vehicle. Fees are higher on holiday weekends. Open year-round.

Directions: From Porterville, drive east on Highway 190 for 25 miles to County Road 209/Wishon Drive. Turn left at County Road 208/Wishon Drive and drive 3.5 miles (narrow, curvy—RVs not advised).

Contact: Sequoia National Forest and Giant Sequoia National Monument, Tule River/Hot Springs Ranger District, 559/539-2607, fax 559/539-2067.

111 BELKNAP

Scenic rating: 7

on the South Fork of Middle Fork Tule River in Giant Sequoia National Monument

Map 11.4, page 610

The groves of sequoias in this area are a highlight wherever you go. This camp is set on the South Fork of the Middle Fork Tule River near McIntyre Grove and Belknap Camp Grove; a trail from camp is routed east for three miles through Wheel Meadow Grove to the junction with Summit National Recreation Trail at Quaking Aspen camp. The elevation is 5,000 feet.

Campsites, facilities: There are 15 sites for tents only. Picnic tables and fire grills are provided. Drinking water and vault toilets are available. A store is nearby. Leashed pets are permitted.

Reservations, fees: Reservations are accepted ($9 reservation fee) at 877/444-6777 or www.ReserveUSA.com. Sites are $15 per night, $5 per night for each additional vehicle. Fees are higher on holiday weekends. Open mid-April to mid-November.

Directions: From Porterville, drive east on Highway 190 for 34 miles to Camp Nelson and Nelson Drive. Turn right on Nelson Drive and continue one mile to the camp.

Contact: Sequoia National Forest and Giant Sequoia National Monument, Tule River/Hot Springs Ranger District, 559/539-2607, fax 559/539-2067.

112 COY FLAT

Scenic rating: 4

in Giant Sequoia National Monument

Map 11.4, page 610

Coy Flat is set between Coy Creek and Bear Creek, small forks of the Tule River, at 5,000 feet in elevation. The road out of camp is routed five miles (through Rogers'

Camp, which is private property) to the Black Mountain Grove of redwoods, with some giant sequoias set just inside the border of the neighboring Tule River Indian Reservation. From camp, a hiking trail (Forest Trail 31S31) is routed east for two miles through the Belknap Camp Grove of sequoias and then turns and heads south for four miles to Slate Mountain, where it intersects with Summit National Recreation Trail, a steep butt-kicker of a hike that tops out at over 9,000 feet.

Campsites, facilities: There are 20 sites for tents or RVs up to 22 feet (no hookups). Picnic tables and fire grills are provided. Drinking water and vault toilets are available. Leashed pets are permitted.

Reservations, fees: Reservations are accepted ($9 reservation fee) at 877/444-6777 or www.ReserveUSA.com. Sites are $15 per night, $5 per night for each additional vehicle. Camping fees are higher for holiday weekends. Open from mid-April to mid-November.

Directions: From Porterville, drive east on Highway 190 for 34 miles to Camp Nelson and Coy Flat Road. Turn right on Coy Flat Road and drive one mile to the campground.

Contact: Sequoia National Forest and Giant Sequoia National Monument, Tule River/Hot Springs Ranger District, 559/539-2607, fax 559/539-2067.

113 QUAKING ASPEN

Scenic rating: 4

in Giant Sequoia National Monument

Map 11.4, page 610

Quaking Aspen sits at a junction of Forest Service roads at 7,000 feet in elevation, near the headwaters of Freeman Creek. A trailhead for Summit National Recreation Trail runs right through camp; it's a popular trip on horseback, heading deep into Sequoia National Forest. Another trailhead is 0.5 mile away on Forest Road 21S50. This hike is

routed east along Freeman Creek and reaches the Freeman Grove of sequoias in four miles. This camp is in the vicinity of the Sequoia National Forest fire, named the McNalley Fire, which burned more than 100,000 acres to the east of this area in the summer of 2002. The fire started in the Kern River Canyon and then burned up the Kern Canyon north to Forks of the Kern and the surrounding environs. While 11 groves of giant sequoias here were saved, much of the surrounding forest several miles to the east of the camps was burned.

Campsites, facilities: There are 32 sites for tents or RVs up to 24 feet (no hookups). Picnic tables and fire grills are provided. Drinking water and vault toilets are available. A store is nearby. Leashed pets are permitted. Some facilities are wheelchair-accessible.

Reservations, fees: Reservations are accepted ($9 reservation fee) at 877/444-6777. Sites are $15 per night, $5 per night for each additional vehicle. Fees are higher on holiday weekends. Open May to mid-November, weather permitting.

Directions: From Porterville, drive east on Highway 190 for 34 miles to Camp Nelson. Continue east on Highway 190 for 11 miles to the campground on the right.

Contact: Sequoia National Forest and Giant Sequoia National Monument, Tule River/Hot Springs Ranger District, 559/539-2607, fax 559/539-2067.

114 QUAKING ASPEN GROUP CAMP

Scenic rating: 4

at the headwaters of the South Fork of the Middle Fork Tule River in Giant Sequoia National Monument

Map 11.4, page 610

For groups, here is an alternative to nearby Peppermint. (See the *Peppermint* entry in this chapter for recreation options.) The elevation is 7,000 feet. (For details about this area, refer to the previous listing, *Quaking Aspen*.)

Campsites, facilities: There are seven group sites for tents or RVs up to 24 feet (no hookups) that can accommodate 12–50 people each. Picnic tables and fire grills are provided. Drinking water and vault toilets are available. A lodge with limited supplies is nearby. Some facilities are wheelchair-accessible. Leashed pets are permitted.

Reservations, fees: Reservations are required ($9 reservation fee) at 877/444-6777 or www.ReserveUSA.com. Sites are $22.50–95 per night, depending on group size. Open mid-May to mid-November.

Directions: From Porterville, drive east on Highway 190 for 34 miles to Camp Nelson. Continue east on Highway 190 for 11 miles to the campground on the right.

Contact: Sequoia National Forest and Giant Sequoia National Monument, Tule River/Hot Springs Ranger District, 559/539-2607, fax 559/539-2067.

115 TULE

Scenic rating: 7

on Lake Success

Map 11.4, page 610

Lake Success is a big lake with many arms, providing 30 miles of shoreline and making the place seem like a dreamland for boaters on hot summer days. The lake is set in the foothill country, at an elevation of 650 feet, where day after day of 100-degree summer temperatures are common. That is why boating, waterskiing, and personal watercraft are so popular—anything to get wet. In the winter and spring, fishing for trout and bass is good, including the chance for largemouth bass. No beaches are developed for swimming because of fluctuating water levels, though the day-use area has a decent sloped stretch of shore that is good for swimming. Lake Success is much shallower than most reservoirs, and

the water can fluctuate from week to week, with major drawdowns during the summer. The wildlife area along the west side of the lake is worth exploring, and there is a nature trail below the dam. The campground is the centerpiece of the Tule Recreation Area.

Campsites, facilities: There are 104 sites for tents or RVs up to 35 feet; some sites have electrical hookups (30 and 50 amps). Picnic tables and fire grills are provided. Restrooms with flush toilets and showers, dump station, picnic areas, and a playground are available. A store, marina, boat ramp, houseboat, boat and water-ski rentals, bait and tackle, propane gas, restaurant, and gas station are available nearby. Leashed pets are permitted.

Reservations, fees: Reservations are accepted at 877/444-6777 or www.ReserveUSA.com. Sites are $16–21 per night. Open year-round.

Directions: Drive on Highway 65 to Porterville and the junction with Highway 190. Turn east on Highway 190 and drive eight miles to Lake Success and the campground entrance on the left.

Contact: U.S. Army Corps of Engineers, Sacramento District, 559/784-0215, fax 559/784-5469; Success Marina, 559/781-2078.

116 HOLEY MEADOW GROUP CAMP

Scenic rating: 7

on Double Bunk Creek in Giant Sequoia National Monument

Map 11.4, page 610

Holey Meadow is set at 6,400 feet on the western slopes of the Sierra, near Redwood and Long Meadow. Parker Pass is a mile to the west, and if you drive on the Forest Service road over the pass, continue southwest (four miles from camp) to Cold Springs Saddle, and then turn east on the Forest

Service spur road, it will take you two miles to Starvation Creek and the Starvation Creek Grove.

Campsites, facilities: There is a group site for tents or RVs up to 16 feet (no hookups) that can accommodate up to 60 people. Fire grills and picnic tables are provided. Vault toilets are available. There is no drinking water; water is available 2.5 miles away at Redwood Meadow campground. Leashed pets are permitted.

Reservations, fees: Reservations are required at 877/444-6777 ($9 reservation fee) or www .ReserveUSA.com. The camp is $90 per night. Open June to October.

Directions: Drive on Highway 99 to Earlimart (about eight miles north of Delano) and the exit for Avenue 56/County Road J22. Take that exit east and drive 39 miles to the town of California Hot Springs and Parker Pass Road/ County Road M50. Turn left on Parker Pass Road and drive 12 miles to Western Divide Highway/County Road M107. Turn left on Western Divide Highway and drive 0.5 mile to the campground entrance.

Contact: Sequoia National Forest and Giant Sequoia National Monument, Tule River/Hot Springs Ranger District, 559/539-2607, fax 559/539-2067.

117 REDWOOD MEADOW

👫 🐕 🚻 ♿ 🚐 ⛺

Scenic rating: 7

near Parker Meadow Creek in Giant Sequoia National Monument

Map 11.4, page 610

The highlight here is the 1.5-mile Trail of the Hundred Giants, which is routed through a grove of giant sequoias and is accessible for wheelchair hikers. This is the site where President Clinton proclaimed the Giant Sequoia National Monument in 2000. The camp is set near Parker Meadow Creek at 6,100 feet elevation. Despite its remoteness, this has become a popular place.

Campsites, facilities: There are 15 sites for tents or RVs up to 16 feet (no hookups). Picnic tables and fire grills are provided. Drinking water and vault toilets are available. Leashed pets are permitted.

Reservations, fees: Reservations are accepted ($9 reservation fee) at 877/444-6777 or www .ReserveUSA.com. Sites are $15 per night, $5 per night for each additional vehicle. Camping fees are higher on holiday weekends. Open from June to October, weather permitting.

Directions: Drive on Highway 99 to Earlimart (about eight miles north of Delano) and the exit for Avenue 56/County Road J22. Take that exit east and drive 39 miles to the town of California Hot Springs and Parker Pass Road/County Road M50. Turn left on Parker Pass Road and drive 12 miles to Western Divide Highway/County Road M107. Turn left on Western Divide Highway and drive three miles to the campground entrance.

Contact: Sequoia National Forest and Giant Sequoia National Monument, Tule River/Hot Springs Ranger District, 559/539-2607, fax 559/539-2067.

118 LONG MEADOW GROUP CAMP

👫 🛶 🐕 🚐 ⛺

Scenic rating: 8

in Giant Sequoia National Monument

Map 11.4, page 610

Long Meadow is set on little Long Meadow Creek at an elevation of 6,000 feet, within a mile of the remote Cunningham Grove of redwoods to the east. Note that Redwood Meadow is just one mile to the west, where the Trail of the Hundred Giants is a feature attraction.

Campsites, facilities: There is one group site for tents or RVs up to 16 feet (no hookups) that can accommodate up to 25 people. Picnic tables and fire grills are provided. Vault toilets are available. No drinking water is available. Leashed pets are permitted.

Reservations, fees: Reservations are required ($9 reservation fee) at 877/444-6777 or www .ReserveUSA.com. The site is $50 per night. Open June through September.

Directions: Drive on Highway 99 to Earlimart (about eight miles north of Delano) and the exit for Avenue 56/County Road J22. Take that exit east and drive 39 miles to the town of California Hot Springs and Parker Pass Road/ County Road M50. Turn left on Parker Pass Road and drive 12 miles to Western Divide Highway/County Road M107. Turn left on Western Divide Highway and drive four miles to the campground entrance.

Contact: Sequoia National Forest and Giant Sequoia National Monument, Tule River/Hot Springs Ranger District, 559/539-2607, fax 559/539-2067.

119 GOODALE CREEK

Scenic rating: 6

near Independence

Map 11.4, page 610

This obscure BLM camp is set along little Goodale Creek at 4,000 feet. It is a good lay-over spot for U.S. 395 cruisers heading north. In hot summer months, snakes are occasionally spotted near this campground.

Campsites, facilities: There are 62 sites for tents or RVs up to 30 feet (no hookups). Picnic tables and fire rings are provided. Pit toilets are available. No drinking water is available. Leashed pets are permitted.

Reservations, fees: Reservations are not accepted. Sites are $5 per night; season passes are $300. Open early April through October, weather permitting.

Directions: Drive on U.S. 395 to Aberdeen Road (12 miles north of Independence). Turn west (toward the Sierra) on Aberdeen Road and drive two miles to the campground on the left.

Contact: Bureau of Land Management, Bishop Field Office, 760/872-4881, fax 760/873-5050.

120 OAK CREEK

Scenic rating: 6

in Inyo National Forest

Map 11.4, page 610

Oak Creek is in a series of little-known camps west of Independence that provide a jump-off spot for backpackers. This camp is set at 5,000 feet, with a trail from camp that is routed west (and up) into the California Bighorn Sheep Zoological Area, a rugged, stark region well above the tree line. Caution: Plan on a terrible, long, butt-kicker of a climb up to the Sierra crest; stay on the trail.

Campsites, facilities: There are 22 sites for tents or RVs up to 28 feet (no hookups). Picnic tables and fire grills are provided. There is no drinking water. Vault toilets are available. Garbage must be packed out. Some facilities are wheelchair-accessible. Supplies and a coin laundry are available in Independence. Leashed pets are permitted.

Reservations, fees: Reservations are not accepted. There is no fee for camping, but donations are encouraged. Open year-round, with a 14-day stay limit.

Directions: Drive on U.S. 395 to North Oak Creek Drive (two miles north of Independence). Turn west (toward the Sierra) at North Oak Creek Drive and drive three miles to the campground on the right.

Contact: Inyo National Forest, Mount Whitney Ranger District, 760/876-6200, fax 760/876-6202; Interagency Visitor Center, 760/876-6222.

121 ONION VALLEY

Scenic rating: 8

in Inyo National Forest

Map 11.4, page 610

Onion Valley is one of the best trailhead camps for backpackers in the Sierra. The camp is set at 9,200 feet, and from here it's a 2,600-foot climb over the course of about three miles to awesome Kearsarge Pass (11,823 feet). From there you can camp at the Kearsarge Lakes, explore the Kearsarge Pinnacles, or join the John Muir Trail and venture to your choice of many High Sierra Ranger District lakes. A wilderness map and a free wilderness permit (if obtained from the ranger station) are your passports to the high country from this camp. Note: Bears frequent this camp almost every night of summer. Do not keep your food in your vehicle. Many cars have been severely damaged by bears. Use bearproof food lockers at the campground and parking area, or use bearproof food canisters (required). For backpackers, trailhead reservations are required.

Campsites, facilities: There are 29 sites for tents or RVs up to 16 feet (no hookups). Picnic tables and fire grills are provided. Drinking water and vault toilets are available. Leashed pets are permitted.

Reservations, fees: Reservations are accepted ($9 reservation fee) at 877/444-6777 or www .ReserveUSA.com. Sites are $13 per night. Open late May through September, weather permitting.

Directions: Drive on U.S. 395 to Independence and Market Street. Turn west (toward the Sierra) at Market Street (becomes Onion Valley Road) and drive 15 miles to the campground at the road's end.

Contact: Inyo National Forest, Mount Whitney Ranger District, 760/876-6200, fax 760/876-6202; Interagency Visitor Center, 760/876-6222.

122 GRAY'S MEADOW

Scenic rating: 6

on Independence Creek in Inyo National Forest

Map 11.4, page 610

Gray's Meadow is one of two adjacent camps that are set along Independence Creek. The creek is stocked with small trout by the Department of Fish and Game. The highlight in the immediate area is the trailhead at the end of the road at Onion Valley Camp. For U.S. 395 cruisers looking for a spot, this is a pretty alternative to the camps in Bishop.

Campsites, facilities: There are 52 sites for tents or RVs up to 34 feet (no hookups). Picnic tables and fire grills are provided. Drinking water and flush toilets are available. Supplies and a coin laundry are available in Independence. Leashed pets are permitted.

Reservations, fees: Reservations are accepted ($9 reservation fee) at 877/444-6777 or www .ReserveUSA.com. Sites are $12–13 per night. Open March through October, with a 14-day stay limit.

Directions: Drive on U.S. 395 to Independence and Market Street. Turn west (toward the Sierra) at Market Street (becomes Onion Valley Road) and drive five miles to the campground on the right.

Contact: Inyo National Forest, Mount Whitney Ranger District, 760/876-6200, fax 760/876-6202; Interagency Visitor Center, 760/876-6222.

123 INDEPENDENCE CREEK CAMPGROUND

Scenic rating: 4

in Independence

Map 11.4, page 610

This unpublicized county park is often overlooked among U.S. 395 cruisers. It is set at 3,900 feet just outside of Independence, which is spiraling downward into something resembling a ghost town. True to form, maintenance is sometimes lacking here. Independence Creek runs through the campground and a museum is within walking distance. At the rate it's going, the whole town could be a museum.

Campsites, facilities: There are 25 sites for

tents or RVs up to 40 feet (no hookups). Picnic tables and fire grills are provided. Drinking water and vault toilets are available. Some facilities are wheelchair-accessible. Supplies and a coin laundry are available in Independence. Leashed pets are permitted.

Reservations, fees: Reservations are not accepted. Sites are $10 per vehicle per night. Open year-round.

Directions: Drive on U.S. 395 to Independence and Market Street. Turn west (toward the Sierra) at Market Street and drive one mile (outside the town limits) to the campground.

Contact: Inyo County Parks Department, 760/878-0272 or 760/873-5577, www.395 .com/inyo/campgrounds.

124 LONE PINE AND LONE PINE GROUP

🥾 🏊 🐴 🚐 🏕

Scenic rating: 8

near Mount Whitney in Inyo National Forest

Map 11.4, page 610

This is an alternative for campers preparing to hike Mount Whitney or start the John Muir Trail. It is set at 6,000 feet, 2,000 feet below Whitney Portal (the hiking jump-off spot), providing a lower-elevation location for hikers to acclimate themselves to the altitude. The camp is set on Lone Pine Creek, with decent fishing and spectacular views of Mount Whitney. Because of its exposure to the east, there are also beautiful sunrises, especially in fall.

Campsites, facilities: There are 43 sites for tents or RVs up to 35 feet (no hookups), and one group site for up to 15 people. Picnic tables and fire grills are provided. Drinking water and pit toilets are available. Supplies are available in Lone Pine. Leashed pets are permitted.

Reservations, fees: Reservations are accepted ($9 reservation fee) at 877/444-6777 or www .ReserveUSA.com. Sites are $14 per night, $45 per night for the group site. Open year-round, with a 14-day stay limit.

Directions: Drive on U.S. 395 to Lone Pine and Whitney Portal Road. Turn west (toward the Sierra) on Whitney Portal Road and drive six miles to the campground on the left.

Contact: Inyo National Forest, Mount Whitney Ranger District, 760/876-6200, fax 760/876-6202; Interagency Visitor Center, 760/876-6222.

125 PORTAGEE JOE CAMPGROUND

🏊 🐴 🚐 🏕

Scenic rating: 4

near Lone Pine

Map 11.4, page 610

This small, little-known county park provides an option for both Mount Whitney hikers and U.S. 395 cruisers. It is about five miles from Diaz Lake, set on a small creek at 3,750 feet, near the base of Mount Whitney. Very few out-of-towners know about this spot, a nice insurance policy if you find yourself stuck for a campsite in this region.

Campsites, facilities: There are 15 sites for tents or RVs of any length (no hookups). Picnic tables and fire grills are provided. Vault toilets and drinking water are available. Supplies and a coin laundry are available in Lone Pine. Leashed pets are permitted.

Reservations, fees: Reservations are not accepted. Sites are $10 per vehicle per night. Open year-round.

Directions: Drive on U.S. 395 to Lone Pine and Whitney Portal Road. Turn west (toward the Sierra) on Whitney Portal Road and drive one mile to Tuttle Creek Road. Turn left (south) at Tuttle Creek Road and drive 0.1 mile to the campground on the right.

Contact: Inyo County Parks Department, 760/878-0272 or 760/873-5577, www.395 .com/inyo/campgrounds.

126 WHITNEY TRAILHEAD WALK-IN

🏃 🐕 ⛺

Scenic rating: 9

in Inyo National Forest

Map 11.4, page 610   BEST ☾

If Whitney Portal is full (common for this world-class trailhead), this camp at 8,300 feet can be reached by hiking in 0.25 mile. Reservations for the summit hike are required. That accomplished, this hike-in camp is an excellent spot for spending a day to become acclimated to the high altitude. The trailhead to the Mount Whitney summit (14,497.6 feet) is nearby. Mount Whitney is the beginning of the 211-mile John Muir Trail, which ends in Yosemite Valley. Food-raiding bears are a common problem here. Campers are required to use bearproof food lockers or food canisters. For information on backcountry permits, phone the ranger district.

Campsites, facilities: There are 10 walk-in tent sites. Picnic tables and fire grills are provided. Drinking water and pit toilets are available. Supplies are available in Lone Pine. Leashed pets are permitted.

Reservations, fees: Reservations are not accepted. Sites are $8 per night. Open mid-May to late October, with a one-night stay limit.

Directions: Drive on U.S. 395 to Lone Pine and Whitney Portal Road. Turn west (toward the Sierra) and drive 13 miles to the parking lot at Whitney Portal. Park and hike 0.25 mile to the campground.

Contact: Inyo National Forest, Mount Whitney Ranger District, 760/876-6200, fax 760/876-6202; Interagency Visitor Center, 760/876-2222.

127 WHITNEY PORTAL AND WHITNEY PORTAL GROUP

🏃 🐕 ♿ 🚐 ⛺

Scenic rating: 9

near Mount Whitney in Inyo National Forest

Map 11.4, page 610

This camp is home to a world-class trailhead. It is regarded as the number-one jump-off spot for the hike to the top of Mount Whitney, the highest spot in the continental United States, 14,497.6 feet, as well as the start of the 211-mile John Muir Trail from Mount Whitney to Yosemite Valley. Hikers planning to scale the summit must have a wilderness permit, available by reservation at the Forest Service office in Lone Pine. The camp is at 8,000 feet, and virtually everyone staying here plans to make the trek to the Whitney summit, a climb of 6,500 feet over the course of 10 miles. The trip includes an ascent over 100 switchbacks (often snow-covered in early summer) to top Wotan's Throne and reach Trail Crest (13,560 feet). Here you turn right and take Summit Trail, where the ridge is cut by huge notch windows providing a view down more than 10,000 feet to the little town of Lone Pine and the Owens Valley. When you sign the logbook on top, don't be surprised if you see my name in the registry. A plus at the campground is watching the JMT hikers arrive who are just finishing the trail from north to south—that is, from Yosemite to Whitney. There is no comparing the happy look of success when they drop their packs for the last time, head into the little store, and pick a favorite refreshment for celebration.

Campsites, facilities: There are 44 sites for tents or RVs up to 30 feet (no hookups), and three group sites for up to 15 people each. Picnic tables and fire grills are provided. Drinking water and vault toilets are available. Some facilities are wheelchair-accessible. Supplies are available in Lone Pine. Leashed pets are permitted.

Reservations, fees: Reservations are accepted ($9 reservation fee) at 877/444-6777 or www .ReserveUSA.com. Sites are $16 per night, $45 per night for a group site. Stays are limited to seven days. Open late May to mid-October, with a 14-day stay limit.

Directions: Drive on U.S. 395 to Lone Pine and Whitney Portal Road. Turn west (toward the Sierra) on Whitney Portal Road and drive 13 miles to the campground on the left.

Contact: Inyo National Forest, Mount Whitney Ranger District, 760/876-6200, fax 760/876-6202; Interagency Visitor Center, 760/876-2222.

128 TUTTLE CREEK

Scenic rating: 4

near Mount Whitney

Map 11.4, page 610

This primitive BLM camp is set at the base of Mount Whitney along Tuttle Creek at 5,120 feet and is shadowed by several impressive peaks (Mount Whitney, Lone Pine Peak, and Mount Williamson). It is often used as an overflow area if the camps farther up Whitney Portal Road are full. Note: This campground is often confused with a small county campground also on Tuttle Creek Road just off Whitney Portal Road.

Campsites, facilities: There are 85 sites for tents or RVs up to 30 feet (no hookups). Picnic tables and fire rings are provided. Pit toilets are available. No drinking water. Supplies are available in Lone Pine. Leashed pets are permitted.

Reservations, fees: Reservations are not accepted. Sites are $5 per night; season passes are $300. Open early March through October.

Directions: Drive on U.S. 395 to Lone Pine and Whitney Portal Road. Turn west (toward the Sierra) on Whitney Portal Road and drive 3.5 miles to Horseshoe Meadow Road. Turn left and drive 1.5 miles to Tuttle Creek Road and the campground entrance (a dirt road) on the right.

Contact: Bureau of Land Management, Bishop Field Office, 760/872-4881, fax 760/873-5050.

129 DIAZ LAKE

Scenic rating: 6

near Lone Pine

Map 11.4, page 610

Diaz Lake is set at 3,650 feet in the Owens Valley. It is sometimes overlooked by visitors to nearby Mount Whitney. It's a small lake, just 85 acres, and it is popular for trout fishing in the spring, when a speed limit of 15 mph is enforced. The lake is stocked with Alpers trout. May through October, when hot weather takes over and the speed limit is bumped to 35 mph, you can say *adios* to the anglers and *hola* to waterskiers. Diaz Lake is extremely popular for waterskiing and swimming and it is sunny most of the year. A 20-foot limit is enforced for boats. A nine-hole golf course is nearby.

Campsites, facilities: There are 200 sites for RVs of any length or tents; some have partial hookups. Picnic tables and fire grills are provided. Restrooms with flush toilets and solar shower, drinking water (from a well), playground, and a boat ramp are available. Supplies and a coin laundry are available in Lone Pine. Leashed pets are permitted.

Reservations, fees: Group reservations are accepted at 760/876-5656. Sites are $10–14 per vehicle per night. Open year-round.

Directions: Drive on U.S. 395 to the Diaz Lake entrance (three miles south of Lone Pine) on the west side of the road.

Contact: Inyo County Parks Department, 760/878-0272 or 760/873-5577, www.395 .com/inyo/campgrounds.

130 HORSESHOE MEADOW WALK-IN AND EQUESTRIAN

🚶 🐴 ⛺

Scenic rating: 8

near the John Muir Wilderness in Inyo National Forest

Map 11.4, page 610

Horseshoe Meadow features three trailhead camps, remote and choice, for backpackers heading into the adjacent John Muir Wilderness and Golden Trout Wilderness. The three camps are Cottonwood Pass Walk-In, Cottonwood Lakes Walk-In, and Horseshoe Meadow Equestrian. The camps are set at 10,000 feet near the wilderness border, one of the highest trailheads and drive-to campgrounds in the state. Several trails lead out of camp. The best heads west through Horseshoe Meadow and along a creek, then rises steeply for four miles to Cottonwood Pass, where it intersects with the Pacific Crest Trail. From here backpackers can hike north on PCT to Chicken Spring Lake to set up camp, a rewarding overnighter, or drop into Big Whitney Meadow in the Golden Trout Wilderness. Some use this camp as a starting point to climb Mount Whitney from its back side (via Guitar Lake). Trailhead reservations are required. Food-raiding bears mean that campers are required to use bearproof food lockers or bearproof food canisters. The drive in is one of the most spectacular anywhere, with the access road following a cliff edge much of the way, with a 6,000-foot drop to the Owens Valley below. You will also pass fantastic volcanics, the site of many movie settings, including *Star Trek* with Captain Kirk (can you remember the episode? My kids, Jeremy and Kris, could, and they simulated a scene playing on the rocks here).

Campsites, facilities: Cottonwood Pass has 18 walk-in sites, Cottonwood Lakes has 12 walk-in sites, and Horseshoe Meadow Equestrian has 10 sites. No hookups. Picnic tables and fire grills are provided. Drinking water and vault toilets are available. A pack station and horse facilities are also available at the equestrian camp; campers are encouraged to pack out all livestock waste. Leashed pets are permitted.

Reservations, fees: Reservations are not accepted. Sites are $6 per night for walk-in sites, $12 per night for equestrian sites. Open late May to mid-October, with a one-night stay limit.

Directions: Drive on U.S. 395 to Lone Pine and Whitney Portal Road. Turn west (toward the Sierra) on Whitney Portal Road and drive 3.5 miles to Horseshoe Meadows Road. Turn left on Horseshoe Meadows Road and drive 19 miles to the end of the road (nearly a 7,000-foot climb) and the parking area. Park and walk a short distance to the campground.

Contact: Inyo National Forest, Mount Whitney Ranger District, 760/876-6200, fax 760/876-6202.

131 PEPPERMINT

🚶 🎣 🐴 🚐 ⛺

Scenic rating: 2

on Peppermint Creek in Giant Sequoia National Monument

Map 11.5, page 611

This is one of two primitive campgrounds at Peppermint Creek, but a road does not directly connect the two camps. Several backcountry access roads snake throughout the area, as detailed on a Forest Service map, and exploring them can make for some self-styled fortune hunts. For the ambitious, hiking the two-mile trail at the end of nearby Forest Road 21S05 leads to a fantastic lookout at The Needles (8,245 feet). The camp elevation is 7,100 feet. This camp is in the immediate vicinity of the Sequoia National Forest fire, named the McNalley Fire, which burned more than 100,000 acres in the summer of 2002. The fire started in the Kern River Canyon and then burned up the Kern Canyon north to Forks of the Kern. While 11 groves of giant sequoias here were saved, much of the surrounding forest right up to the edge of Peppermint was burned.

Campsites, facilities: There are 19 sites for tents or RVs up to 24 feet (no hookups). Picnic tables and fire rings are provided. Vault toilets are available. No drinking water is available. Garbage must be packed out. A lodge with limited supplies is nearby. Leashed pets are permitted.

Reservations, fees: Reservations are not accepted. There is no fee for camping. A fire permit is required. Open May through September.

Directions: From Porterville, drive east on Highway 190 for 34 miles to Camp Nelson. Continue east on Highway 190 for 15 miles to the campground entrance road.

Contact: Sequoia National Forest and Giant Sequoia National Monument, Tule River/Hot Springs Ranger District, 559/539-2607, fax 559/539-2067.

132 LOWER PEPPERMINT
🧍 🛶 🐕 🚐 ⛺

Scenic rating: 2

in Giant Sequoia National Monument

Map 11.5, page 611

This is a little-known camp in Sequoia National Forest, set along Peppermint Creek at 5,300 feet. This area has a vast network of backcountry roads, which are detailed on a Forest Service map. This camp is in the immediate vicinity of the Sequoia forest fire, named the McNalley Fire, which burned more than 100,000 acres in the summer of 2002. The fire started in the Kern River Canyon and then burned up the Kern Canyon north to Forks of the Kern. While 11 groves of giant sequoias here were saved, much of the surrounding forest right up to the edge of Lower Peppermint was burned.

Campsites, facilities: There are 17 sites for tents or RVs up to 22 feet (no hookups). Picnic tables and fire grills are provided. Drinking water and vault toilets are available. Leashed pets are permitted.

Reservations, fees: Reservations are not accepted. Sites are $14 per night. Open June through September.

Directions: From Bakersfield, drive east on Highway 178 for 40 miles to the town of Lake Isabella and Highway 155/Burlando Way. Turn left (north) and drive 10 miles to Kernville Sierra Way. Turn (north) and drive 24 miles to Johnsondale and Forest Road 22S82/Lloyd Meadow Road. Turn right and drive about 10.5 miles (paved road) to the campground.

Contact: Sequoia National Forest and Giant Sequoia National Monument, Tule River/Hot Springs Ranger District, 559/539-2607, fax 559/539-2067.

133 LIMESTONE
🧍 🛶 🐕 🚐 ⛺

Scenic rating: 1

on the Kern River in Sequoia National Forest

Map 11.5, page 611

Set deep in the Sequoia National Forest at 3,800 feet, Limestone is a small campground along the Kern River, fed by snowmelt from Mount Whitney. This stretch of the Kern is extremely challenging and sensational for white-water rafting, with cold water and many of the rapids rated Class IV and Class V—for experts with guides only. The favored put-in is at the Johnsondale Bridge, and from here it's a 21-mile run to Kernville. The river pours into Isabella Lake many miles later. Two sections are unrunnable: Fairview Dam (Mile 2.5) and Salmon Falls (Mile 8). For nonrafters, South Creek Falls provides a side trip, one mile to the west. This campground was one of two burned in the McNalley Fire in the summer of 2002. The fire started near Road's End Lodge (which burned down), 16 miles up the Kern River Highway. Other campgrounds to the south were not burned. Even though the canyon has been blackened and left with tree skeletons from the start of the fire on north past Forks of the Kern, the river can still provide an outstanding rafting and kayaking experience. The sight of the damage from the fire, however, is shocking.

Campsites, facilities: There are 22 sites for tents or RVs up to 30 feet (no hookups). Picnic tables and fire grills are provided. Vault toilets are available. No drinking water is available. Supplies and a coin laundry are available in Kernville. Leashed pets are permitted.

Reservations, fees: Reservations are not accepted. Sites are $13 per night, $5 per night for each additional vehicle. Open April through November, weather permitting.

Directions: From Bakersfield, drive east on Highway 178 for about 40 miles to the town of Lake Isabella and Highway 155/Burlando Way. Turn left (north) and drive 10 miles to Kernville and the Kern River Highway/Sierra Way. Turn left on the Kern River Highway and drive 19 miles (two miles past Fairview) to the campground entrance.

Contact: Sequoia National Forest, Kern River Ranger District, Kernville Office, 760/376-3781, fax 760/376-3795.

134 LEAVIS FLAT

Scenic rating: 7

on Deer Creek in Giant Sequoia National Monument

Map 11.5, page 611

Leavis Flat is just inside the western border of Sequoia National Forest along Deer Creek, at an elevation of 3,000 feet. The highlight here is the adjacent California Hot Springs.

Campsites, facilities: There are nine sites for tents or RVs up to 16 feet (no hookups). Picnic tables and fire grills are provided. Drinking water and vault toilets are available. A store, coin laundry, and propane gas can be found nearby. Leashed pets are permitted.

Reservations, fees: Reservations are accepted ($9 reservation fee) at 877/444-6777 or www.ReserveUSA.com. Sites are $15 per night, $5 per night for each additional vehicle. Camping fees are higher on holiday weekends. Open year-round.

Directions: Drive on Highway 99 to Earlimart (about eight miles north of Delano) and the exit for Avenue 56/County Road J22. Take that exit east and drive 39 miles to the town of California Hot Springs and the campground.

Contact: Sequoia National Forest and Giant Sequoia National Monument, Tule River/Hot Springs Ranger District, 559/539-2607, fax 559/539-2067.

135 WHITE RIVER

Scenic rating: 7

in Giant Sequoia National Monument

Map 11.5, page 611

White River is set at 4,000 feet, on the White River near where little Dark Canyon Creek enters it. A trail from camp follows downstream along the White River to the west for three miles, dropping into Ames Hole and Cove Canyon. The region's hot springs are about a 10-minute drive away to the north.

Campsites, facilities: There are 12 sites for tents or RVs up to 16 feet (no hookups). Picnic tables and fire grills are provided. Drinking water and vault toilets are available. Leashed pets are permitted.

Reservations, fees: Reservations are accepted ($9 reservation fee) at 877/444-6777 or www.ReserveUSA.com. Sites are $15 per night, $5 per night for each additional vehicle. Camping fees are higher on holiday weekends. Open May through September.

Directions: Drive on Highway 99 to Delano and the exit for Highway 155. Take that exit and drive east for about 40 miles to Jack Ranch Road (just west of Glennville). Turn left on Jack Ranch Road and drive about four miles to

White River Road/Sugarloaf Drive. Turn right and drive 1.5 miles to Forest Road 24S05. Bear left and drive 0.75 mile to Idlewild, and continue (on this dirt road) for six miles to the campground.

Contact: Sequoia National Forest and Giant Sequoia National Monument, Tule River/Hot Springs Ranger District, 559/539-2607, fax 559/539-2067.

136 FROG MEADOW
🏃🐕5%🚐🔺

Scenic rating: 6

near Giant Sequoia National Monument

Map 11.5, page 611

This small, primitive camp, set near Tobias Creek at 7,500 feet, is in the center of a network of Forest Service roads that explore the surrounding Sequoia National Forest. The nearby feature destination is the Tobias Peak Lookout (8,284 feet), two miles directly south of the camp.

Campsites, facilities: There are 10 sites for tents or RVs up to 16 feet (no hookups). Picnic tables and fire grills are provided. Vault toilets are available. No drinking water is available. Leashed pets are permitted. Garbage must be packed out.

Reservations, fees: Reservations are not accepted. There is no fee for camping. Open June through September, weather permitting.

Directions: Drive on Highway 99 to Delano and the exit for Highway 155. Take that exit and drive east for about 40 miles to Jack Ranch Road (just west of Glennville). Turn left on Jack Ranch Road and drive about four miles to White River Road/Sugarloaf Drive. Turn right on Sugarloaf Drive and drive 4.5 miles to Guernsey Mill/Sugarloaf Drive. Continue on Sugarloaf Road/Forest Road 23S16 for about seven miles to Forest Road 24S50 (a dirt road). Turn left on Forest Road 24S50 and drive four miles to Frog Meadow and the campground. The route is

long, slow, and circuitous. A map of Sierra National Forest is required.

Contact: Sequoia National Forest and Giant Sequoia National Monument, Tule River/Hot Springs Ranger District, 559/539-2607, fax 559/539-2067.

137 FAIRVIEW
🏃🛶🎣🐕♿🚐🔺

Scenic rating: 1

on the Kern River in Sequoia National Forest

Map 11.5, page 611   BEST (

Fairview is one of six campgrounds set on the Upper Kern River above Isabella Lake and adjacent to the Kern River, one of the prime rafting and kayaking rivers in California. This camp sits at 3,500 feet. Many of the rapids are rated Class IV and Class V—for experts with guides only. The favored put-in is at the Johnsondale Bridge, and from here it's a 21-mile run to Kernville. The river eventually pours into Isabella Lake. Two sections are unrunnable, Fairview Dam (Mile 2.5) and Salmon Falls (Mile 8). This campground was one of two burned in the McNalley Fire in the summer of 2002. The first started near Road's End Lodge (which burned down), 16 miles up the Kern River Highway. Other campgrounds to the south of that were not burned. Even though the canyon has been blackened and left with tree skeletons from the start of the fire on north past Forks of the Kern, the river can still provide an outstanding rafting experience. The sight of the damage from the fire, however, is shocking.

Campsites, facilities: There are 55 sites for tents or RVs up to 45 feet (no hookups). Picnic tables and fire grills are provided. Drinking water and vault toilets are available. Some facilities are wheelchair-accessible. Supplies and a coin laundry are available in Kernville. Leashed pets are permitted.

Reservations, fees: Reservations are accepted ($9 reservation fee) at 877/444-6777 or www

.ReserveUSA.com. Sites are $15 per night, $5 per night for each additional vehicle. Camping fees are higher on holiday weekends. Open April through October, weather permitting.

Directions: From Bakersfield, drive east on Highway 178 for about 40 miles to the town of Lake Isabella and Highway 155/Burlando Way. Turn left (north) and drive 10 miles to Kernville and the Kern River Highway/Sierra Way. Turn left on the Kern River Highway and drive 18 miles to the town of Fairview. Continue to the north end of town to the campground entrance.

Contact: Sequoia National Forest, Kern River Ranger District, Kernville Office, 760/376-3781, fax 760/376-3795.

138 HORSE MEADOW

Scenic rating: 8

on Salmon Creek in Sequoia National Forest

Map 11.5, page 611

This is a little-known spot set along Salmon Creek at 7,600 feet. It is a region known for big meadows, forests, backcountry roads, and plenty of horses. It is just west of the Dome Land Wilderness, and there is a series of three public pastures for horses in the area, as well as trails ideal for horseback riding. From camp, one such trail follows along Salmon Creek to the west to Salmon Falls, a favorite for the few who know of it. A more popular overnight trip is to head to a trailhead about five miles east, which provides a route to Manter Meadows in the Dome Lands.

Campsites, facilities: There are 41 sites for tents or RVs up to 22 feet (no hookups). Picnic tables and fire grills are provided. Drinking water and vault toilets are available. Garbage must be packed out. Leashed pets are permitted.

Reservations, fees: Reservations are not accepted. Sites are $10 per night, $5 per night

for each additional vehicle. Open June through October, weather permitting.

Directions: From Bakersfield, drive east on Highway 178 for about 40 miles to the town of Lake Isabella and Highway 155/Burlando Way. Turn left (north) and drive 10 miles to Kernville and the Kern River Highway/Sierra Way. Turn left on the Kern River Highway for about 20 miles to Sherman Pass Road (signed "Highway 395/Black Rock Ranger Station"). Make a sharp right on Sherman Pass Road and drive about 6.5 miles to Cherry Hill Road/Forest Road 22S12 (there is a green gate with a sign that says "Horse Meadow/Big Meadow"). Turn right and drive about four miles (the road becomes dirt) and continue for another three miles (follow the signs) to the campground entrance road.

Contact: Sequoia National Forest, Kern River Ranger District, Kernville Office, 760/376-3781, fax 760/376-3795.

139 GOLDLEDGE

Scenic rating: 7

on the Kern River in Sequoia National Forest

Map 11.5, page 611

This is another in the series of camps on the Kern River north of Isabella Lake. This one is set at 3,200 feet.

Campsites, facilities: There are 37 sites for tents or RVs up to 30 feet (no hookups). Picnic tables and fire grills are provided. Drinking water and vault toilets are available. Supplies and a coin laundry are available in Kernville. Leashed pets are permitted.

Reservations, fees: Reservations are accepted ($9 reservation fee) at 877/444-6777 or www.ReserveUSA.com. Sites are $15 per night, $5 per night for each additional vehicle. Camping fees are higher on holiday weekends. Open May through August.

Directions: From Bakersfield, drive east on Highway 178 for about 40 miles to the town of Lake Isabella and Highway 155/ Burlando Way. Turn left (north) and drive 10 miles to Kernville and the Kern River Highway/Sierra Way. Turn left on the Kern River Highway and drive 10 miles to the campground.

Contact: Sequoia National Forest, Kern River Ranger District, Kernville Office, 760/376-3781, fax 760/376-3795.

140 HOSPITAL FLAT

Scenic rating: 8

on the North Fork of the Kern River in Sequoia National Forest

Map 11.5, page 611

It's kind of like the old shell game, trying to pick the best of the campgrounds along the North Fork of the Kern River. This one is seven miles north of Isabella Lake. The elevation is 2,800 feet. (For information on rafting on the Kern River, see the *Fairview* listing in this chapter.)

Campsites, facilities: There are 40 sites for tents or RVs up to 30 feet (no hookups), and one group site for up to 30 people. Picnic tables and fire grills are provided. Drinking water and vault toilets are available. Some facilities are wheelchair-accessible. Supplies and a coin laundry are available in Kernville. Leashed pets are permitted.

Reservations, fees: Reservations are accepted for individual sites and required for the group site ($9 reservation fee) at 877/444-6777 or www.ReserveUSA.com. Sites are $15 per night, $5 per night for each additional vehicle, $75 per night for the group site. Camping fees are higher on holiday weekends. Open May through August.

Directions: From Bakersfield, drive east on Highway 178 for about 40 miles to the town of Lake Isabella and Highway 155/ Burlando Way. Turn left (north) and drive 10 miles to Kernville and the Kern River Highway/Sierra Way. Turn left on the Kern

River Highway and drive 6.5 miles to the campground.

Contact: Sequoia National Forest, Kern River Ranger District, Kernville Office, 760/376-3781, fax 760/376-3795.

141 CAMP 3

Scenic rating: 9

on the North Fork of the Kern River in Sequoia National Forest

Map 11.5, page 611

This is the second in a series of camps along the Kern River north of Isabella Lake (in this case, five miles north of the lake). If you don't like this spot, Hospital Flat is just two miles upriver and Headquarters is just one mile downriver. The camp elevation is 2,800 feet.

Campsites, facilities: There are 52 sites for tents or RVs up to 30 feet (no hookups), and two group sites for up to 30 people. Picnic tables and fire grills are provided. Drinking water and vault toilets are available. Some facilities are wheelchair-accessible. A store and a coin laundry are available in Kernville. Leashed pets are permitted.

Reservations, fees: Reservations are accepted for individual sites and required for the group sites ($9 reservation fee) at 877/444-6777 or www.ReserveUSA.com. Sites are $15 per night, $5 per night for each additional vehicle, $75 per night for a group site. Camping fees are higher on holiday weekends. Open May through August.

Directions: From Bakersfield, drive east on Highway 178 for about 40 miles to the town of Lake Isabella and Highway 155/ Burlando Way. Turn left (north) and drive 10 miles to Kernville and the Kern River Highway/Sierra Way. Turn left on the Kern River Highway and drive five miles to the campground.

Contact: Sequoia National Forest, Kern River Ranger District, Kernville Office, 760/376-3781, fax 760/376-3795.

142 HEADQUARTERS

🎣 🛶 🚣 🏕 ♿ 🚐 ⛺

Scenic rating: 8

on the North Fork of the Kern River in Sequoia National Forest

Map 11.5, page 611

As you head north from Isabella Lake on Sierra Way, this is the first in a series of Forest Service campgrounds from which to take your pick, all of them set along the North Fork of the Kern River. The North Fork Kern is best known for offering prime white water for rafting and kayaking. The elevation is 2,800 feet.

Campsites, facilities: There are 44 sites for tents or RVs up to 27 feet (no hookups). Picnic tables and fire grills are provided. Drinking water and vault toilets are available. Some facilities are wheelchair-accessible. Supplies and a coin laundry are available in Kernville. Leashed pets are permitted.

Reservations, fees: Reservations are accepted ($9 reservation fee) at 877/444-6777 or www .ReserveUSA.com. Sites are $15 per night, $5 per night for each additional vehicle. Camping fees are higher on holiday weekends. Open year-round.

Directions: From Bakersfield, drive east on Highway 178 for about 40 miles to the town of Lake Isabella and Highway 155/Burlando Way. Turn left (north) and drive 10 miles to Kernville and the Kern River Highway/Sierra Way. Turn left on the Kern River Highway and drive three miles to the campground.

Contact: Sequoia National Forest, Kern River Ranger District, Kernville Office, 760/376-3781, fax 760/376-3795.

143 PANORAMA

🚶 🐕 🚐 ⛺

Scenic rating: 7

in Giant Sequoia National Monument

Map 11.5, page 611

This pretty spot is set at 7,200 feet in elevation in a region of Sequoia National Forest filled with a network of backcountry roads. This camp is set in an inconspicuous spot and is easy to miss. A good side trip is to drive two miles south, turn left, and continue a short distance to a trailhead on the right side of the road for Portuguese Peak (a Forest Service map is strongly advised). From here, it's a one-mile butt-kicker to the top of Portuguese Peak, 7,914 feet in elevation.

Campsites, facilities: There are 10 sites for tents or RVs up to 16 feet (no hookups). Picnic tables and fire grills are provided. Vault toilets are available. No drinking water is available. Garbage must be packed out. Leashed pets are permitted.

Reservations, fees: Reservations are not accepted. There is no fee for camping. Open June through August.

Directions: Drive on Highway 99 to Delano and the exit for Highway 155. Take that exit and drive east for about 40 miles to Jack Ranch Road (just west of Glennville). Turn left on Jack Ranch Road and drive about four miles to White River Road/Sugarloaf Drive. Turn right on Sugarloaf Drive and drive 4.5 miles to Guernsey Mill/Sugarloaf Drive. Continue on Sugarloaf Road/Forest Road 23S16 for about six miles to the campground (paved all the way).

Contact: Sequoia National Forest and Giant Sequoia National Monument, Tule River/Hot Springs Ranger District, 559/539-2607, fax 559/539-2067.

144 CEDAR CREEK

🎣 🏕 ⛺

Scenic rating: 7

in Sequoia National Forest

Map 11.5, page 611

This is a little-known Forest Service camp set at 4,800 feet on the southwest flank of Sequoia National Forest, right along little Cedar Creek, with easy access off Highway 155. Greenhorn Mountain Park and Alder Creek provide nearby alternatives.

Campsites, facilities: There are 10 sites for tents only. Picnic tables and fire grills are provided. There is no drinking water. Vault toilets are available. Garbage must be packed out. Leashed pets are permitted.

Reservations, fees: Reservations are not accepted. There is no fee for camping. Open year-round.

Directions: Drive on Highway 99 to Delano and the exit for Highway 155. Take that exit and drive east on Highway 155 for 41 miles to Glennville. Continue east for nine miles to the campground.

Contact: Sequoia National Forest, Kern River Ranger District, Lake Isabella Office, 760/379-5646, fax 760/379-8597.

145 GREENHORN MOUNTAIN PARK

🚶‍♂️ 🎿 🐕 🚐 ⛺

Scenic rating: 7

near Shirley Meadows

Map 11.5, page 611

This county campground is near the Shirley Meadows Ski Area, a small ski park open on weekends in winter when there is sufficient snow. Greenhorn Mountain Park covers 160 acres, set at 6,000 feet in elevation. The region is filled with a network of Forest Service roads, detailed on a map of Sequoia National Forest. Isabella Lake is a 15-minute drive to the east.

Campsites, facilities: There are 70 sites for tents or RVs up to 24 feet (no hookups). Fourteen cabins are also available as a group rental. Picnic tables and fire pits or fire rings are provided. Drinking water is available intermittently; check for current status. Restrooms with flush toilets and showers are available. Leashed pets are permitted.

Reservations, fees: No reservations accepted, except for groups of at least 40 people. Sites are $14 per night. Open spring through fall, weather permitting.

Directions: From Bakersfield, drive east on Highway 178 for about 40 miles to the town of Lake Isabella and Highway 155/Burlando Way. Turn left (north) and drive six miles to Wofford Heights. Turn left (west) on Highway 155 and drive 10 miles to the park on the left.

Contact: Kern County Parks, 661/868-7000, www.co.kern.ca.us/parks/.

146 ALDER CREEK

🚶‍♂️ 🎿 🐕 🚐 ⛺

Scenic rating: 7

in Sequoia National Forest

Map 11.5, page 611

This primitive camp is just inside the western border of Sequoia National Forest, an obscure spot that requires traversing a very twisty and, at times, rough road. It is set at 3,900 feet, just 0.25 mile upstream from where Alder Creek meets Slick Rock Creek. There is a trail out of the camp that runs north for two miles along Slick Rock Creek.

Campsites, facilities: There are 13 sites for tents or RVs up to 20 feet (no hookups). Picnic tables and fire grills are provided. Vault toilets are available. No drinking water is available. Garbage must be packed out. Leashed pets are permitted.

Reservations, fees: Reservations are not accepted. There is no fee for camping. Open May through October.

Directions: Drive on Highway 99 to Delano and the exit for Highway 155. Take that exit and drive east on Highway 155 for 41 miles to Glennville. Continue east for eight miles to Alder Creek Road. Turn right on Alder Creek Road and drive three miles to the campground.

Contact: Sequoia National Forest, Kern River Ranger District, Lake Isabella Office, 760/379-5646, fax 760/379-8597.

147 EVANS FLAT AND EQUESTRIAN CAMP

🚶 🐴 ⛴ ⛺

Scenic rating: 4

in Sequoia National Forest

Map 11.5, page 611

Evans Flat is an obscure campground in the southwest region of Sequoia National Forest, about 10 miles west of Isabella Lake, with no other camps in the vicinity. You have to earn this one, but if you want solitude, Evans Flat can provide it. It is set at 6,100 feet, with Woodward Peak 0.5 mile to the east. A natural spring is east of camp within walking distance.

Campsites, facilities: There are 20 sites for tents or RVs up to 20 feet (no hookups). Fire grills and picnic tables are provided. A vault toilet is available. No drinking water is available. Garbage must be packed out. Four corrals with water troughs (though water for the troughs is not always available) and a pasture area are provided for horses. Leashed pets are permitted.

Reservations, fees: Reservations are not accepted. There is no fee for camping. Open May through October.

Directions: From Bakersfield, drive east on Highway 178 for about 40 miles to the town of Lake Isabella and Highway 155. Turn left (north) and drive six miles to Wofford Heights. Turn left (west) on Highway 155 and drive seven miles to Rancheria Road. Turn left and drive 8.3 miles (first paved, then dirt) to the campground.

Contact: Sequoia National Forest, Greenhorn Ranger District, 760/379-5646, fax 760/379-8597.

148 RIVERNOOK CAMPGROUND

🏊 🚣 ⛴ 🐴 ♿ ⛴ ⛺

Scenic rating: 7

on the North Fork of the Kern River

Map 11.5, page 611

This is a large, privately operated park set near Isabella Lake a few miles from the head of the lake. Boat rentals are available at one of the nearby marinas. An optional side trip is to visit Keysville, the first town to become established on the Kern River during the gold rush days. The elevation is 2,665 feet.

Campsites, facilities: There are 30 pull-through sites with full hookups (30 and 50 amps) for RVs, 41 sites with partial hookups for RVs, and 59 sites for tents. Picnic tables, fire rings, and drinking water are provided. Restrooms with flush toilets and showers, three dump stations, and cable TV are available. Leashed pets are permitted. Some facilities are wheelchair-accessible.

Reservations, fees: Reservations are recommended. Sites are $25–35 per night, $5 per person per night for more than two people. Some credit cards accepted. Open year-round.

Directions: From Bakersfield, drive east on Highway 178 for about 40 miles to the town of Lake Isabella and Highway 155/Burlando Way. Turn left (north) and drive 10 miles to Kernville and the Kern River Highway/Sierra Way. Turn left on Sierra Way and drive 0.5 mile to the park entrance (14001 Sierra Way).

Contact: Rivernook Campground, 760/376-2705, fax 760/376-2595.

149 LIVE OAK NORTH AND SOUTH

🏊 🚣 ⛴ 🐴 ⛴ ⛺

Scenic rating: 8

on Isabella Lake

Map 11.5, page 611

This is one of two camps set in the immediate area on Isabella Lake's northwest side; the other is Tillie Creek. Live Oak is on the west side of the road, Tillie Creek on the eastern, lake side of the road. (For recreation information, see the next listing, *Tillie Creek.*)

Campsites, facilities: There are 150 sites for tents or RVs up to 30 feet (no hookups) and one group site for up to 100 people. Picnic tables and fire grills are provided. Drinking water and restrooms with coin showers and flush toilets are available. Supplies are available in nearby Wofford Heights. Leashed pets are permitted.

Reservations, fees: Reservations ($9 reservation fee) are accepted for individual sites, and required for the group site at 877/444-6777 or www.ReserveUSA.com. Sites are $17 per night, $5 per night for each additional vehicle, $250 per night for group site for up to 100 people. Open May through September.

Directions: From Bakersfield, drive east on Highway 178 for about 40 miles to the town of Lake Isabella and Highway 155. Turn left (north) and drive six miles to the campground entrance road on the left (0.5 mile before reaching Wofford Heights).

Contact: Sequoia National Forest, Kern River Ranger District, Lake Isabella Office, 760/379-5646, fax 760/379-8597.

150 TILLIE CREEK

Scenic rating: 9

on Isabella Lake

Map 11.5, page 611

This is one of two camps (the other is Live Oak) near where Tillie Creek enters Isabella Lake, set on the northwest shore of the lake near the town of Wofford Heights. Isabella Lake is a large lake, and with it comes a dynamic array of campgrounds, marinas, and facilities. It is set at 2,650 feet in the foothills east of Bakersfield, fed by the Kern River, and dominated by water sports of all kinds.

Campsites, facilities: There are 159 sites for tents or RVs up to 45 feet and four group sites for tents or RVs up to 45 feet that can accommodate 60–150 people each. No hookups. Picnic tables and fire grills are provided. Drinking water and restrooms with showers and flush toilets are available. Dump station, playground, amphitheater, and a fish-cleaning station are available nearby. Some facilities are wheelchair-

accessible. Supplies are nearby in Wofford Heights. Leashed pets are permitted.

Reservations, fees: Reservations ($9 reservation fee) are accepted for individual sites and required for group sites at 877/444-6777 or www.ReserveUSA.com. Sites are $17 per night, $5 per night for each additional vehicle, $125–220 per night for group sites. Open year-round.

Directions: From Bakersfield, drive east on Highway 178 for about 40 miles to the town of Lake Isabella and Highway 155. Turn left (north) and drive five miles to the campground (0.5 mile before reaching Wofford Heights).

Contact: Sequoia National Forest, Kern River Ranger District, Lake Isabella Office, 760/379-5646, fax 760/379-8597.

151 CAMP 9

Scenic rating: 8

on Isabella Lake

Map 11.5, page 611

This campground is primitive and sparsely covered, but it has several bonus features. It is set along the northeast shore of Isabella Lake, known for good boating, waterskiing in the summer, and fishing in the spring. Other options include great rafting and kayaking waters along the North Fork of the Kern River (north of the lake), a good bird-watching area at the South Fork Wildlife Area (along the east side of the lake), and an off-highway-motorcycle park across the road from this campground. The elevation is 2,650 feet.

Campsites, facilities: There are 109 primitive sites for tents or RVs of any length (no hookups), and two group sites that can accommodate 40 people each. Drinking water, flush and vault toilets, dump station, boat launch, and a fish-cleaning station are available. Supplies and a coin laundry are available nearby in Kernville. Some facilities are wheelchair-accessible. Leashed pets are permitted.

Reservations, fees: Reservations are not

accepted. Sites are $10 per night, $5 per night for each additional vehicle, $60 per night for a group site. Open year-round.

Directions: From Bakersfield, drive east on Highway 178 for about 40 miles to the town of Lake Isabella and Highway 155. Turn right (south) and drive six miles to the campground entrance on the right (on the northeast shore of Isabella Lake). The campground entrance is just south of the small airport at Lake Isabella.

Contact: Sequoia National Forest, Kern River Ranger District, Lake Isabella Office, 760/379-5646, fax 760/379-8597.

152 HUNGRY GULCH

Scenic rating: 9

near Isabella Lake in Sequoia National Forest

Map 11.5, page 611

Hungry Gulch is on the western side of Isabella Lake, but across the road from the shore. Nearby Boulder Gulch camp, directly across the road, is an alternative. There are no boat ramps in the immediate area. (For details about Isabella Lake, see the *Pioneer Point* listing in this chapter.)

Campsites, facilities: There are 78 sites for tents or RVs up to 30 feet (no hookups). Picnic tables and fire grills are provided. Drinking water and restrooms with coin showers and flush toilets are available. A playground is available nearby. Supplies and a coin laundry are available in Lake Isabella. Leashed pets are permitted.

Reservations, fees: Reservations are accepted ($9 reservation fee) at 877/444-6777 or www .ReserveUSA.com. Sites are $17 per night, $5 per night for each additional vehicle. Open April through September.

Directions: From Bakersfield, drive east on Highway 178 for about 40 miles to the town of Lake Isabella and Highway 155. Turn left (north) and drive four miles on Highway 155 to the campground.

Contact: Sequoia National Forest, Kern River Ranger District, Lake Isabella Office, 760/379-5646, fax 760/379-8597.

153 BOULDER GULCH

Scenic rating: 8

on Isabella Lake

Map 11.5, page 611

Boulder Gulch lies fairly near the western shore of Isabella Lake, across the road from Hungry Gulch. Take your pick. Isabella is one of the biggest lakes in Southern California and a prime destination point for Bakersfield area residents. Fishing for trout and bass is best in the spring. The lake is stocked with trout in winter, and other species are bluegill, catfish, and crappie. By the dog days of summer, when people are bow-wowin' at the heat, water-skiers take over, along with folks just looking to cool off. Like a lot of lakes in the valley, Isabella is subject to drawdowns. The elevation is 2,650 feet. (For more information, see the *Pioneer Point* listing in this chapter.)

Campsites, facilities: There are 78 sites for tents or RVs up to 45 feet (no hookups). Picnic tables and fire grills are provided. Restrooms with flush toilets and coin showers, drinking water, playground, and a fish-cleaning station are available. Supplies and a coin laundry are available in the town of Lake Isabella. Leashed pets are permitted.

Reservations, fees: Reservations are accepted ($9 reservation fee) at 877/444-6777 or www .ReserveUSA.com. Sites are $17 per night, $5 per night for each additional vehicle. Open April through September.

Directions: From Bakersfield, drive east on Highway 178 for about 40 miles to the town of Lake Isabella and Highway 155. Turn left (north) and drive four miles to the campground entrance.

Contact: Sequoia National Forest, Kern River Ranger District, Lake Isabella Office, 760/379-5646, fax 760/379-8597.

154 FRENCH GULCH GROUP CAMP

🏊 🎣 🛶 🐾 🚗 ⛺

Scenic rating: 9

on Isabella Lake

Map 11.5, page 611

This is a large group camp on Isabella Lake at the southwest end of the lake about two miles north of Pioneer Point and the spillway. (For recreation information, see the next listing, *Pioneer Point.*) The elevation is 2,700 feet.

Campsites, facilities: There is one large group site for tents or RVs of any length (no hookups) that can accommodate up to 100 people. Picnic tables and fire grills are provided. Drinking water and restrooms with flush toilets and solar-heated showers are available. A store, coin laundry, and propane gas are nearby. Leashed pets are permitted.

Reservations, fees: Reservations are required ($9 reservation fee) at 877/444-6777 or www .ReserveUSA.com. The fee is $250 per night. Open year-round.

Directions: From Bakersfield, drive east on Highway 178 for about 40 miles to the town of Lake Isabella and Highway 155. Turn left (north) and drive three miles to the campground entrance on the right.

Contact: Sequoia National Forest, Kern River Ranger District, Lake Isabella Office, 760/379-5646, fax 760/379-8597.

155 PIONEER POINT

🏊 🎣 🛶 🐾 🚶 🚗 ⛺

Scenic rating: 9

on Isabella Lake in Sequoia National Forest

Map 11.5, page 611

Isabella Lake is one of the largest freshwater lakes in Southern California, and with it comes a dynamic array of campgrounds, marinas, and facilities. It is set at 2,650 feet in the foothills east of Bakersfield, fed by the Kern River, and dominated by boating sports of all kinds. This camp is at the lake's southwest corner, between the spillway and the main dam, with a boat ramp available a mile to the east. Another camp, Main Dam, is nearby. Isabella is a first-class lake for waterskiing, but in the spring and early summer sailboarding is also excellent, best just east of the Auxiliary Dam. Boat rentals of all kinds are available at several marinas.

Campsites, facilities: There are 78 sites for tents or RVs up to 30 feet (no hookups). Picnic tables and fire grills are provided. Drinking water and restrooms with coin showers and flush toilets are available. A playground and a fish-cleaning station are available nearby. A boat ramp is three miles from camp. Supplies and a coin laundry are available in the town of Lake Isabella. Leashed pets are permitted.

Reservations, fees: Reservations are accepted ($9 reservation fee) at 877/444-6777 or www .ReserveUSA.com. The fee is $17 per night, $5 per night for each additional vehicle. Open year-round.

Directions: From Bakersfield, drive east on Highway 178 for about 40 miles to the town of Lake Isabella and Highway 155. Turn left (north) and drive 2.5 miles north on Highway 155 to the campground.

Contact: Sequoia National Forest, Kern River Ranger District, Lake Isabella Office, 760/379-5646, fax 760/379-8597.

156 KEYESVILLE SPECIAL MANAGEMENT AREA

🏍 🎣 🛶 🐾 🚗 ⛺

Scenic rating: 5

on the Kern River near Lake Isabella

Map 11.5, page 611

The Keyesville area originally was developed in the 1850s during the California gold rush; gold was first discovered in this area in 1851. Very few historical buildings remain, however, since much of the old town of Keyesville was comprised of tents and small shacks along trails. Today, this camp is used primarily by OHV enthusiasts and miners and is an alternative to the more crowded and developed campgrounds around Lake Isabella. The Kern River runs through this 7,133-acre BLM area and campsites are available near the river; dispersed camping is also allowed. The Sequoia National Forest borders this area to the north and west. Keyesville has multi-use trails and specific areas for recreational mining and OHV use. Hunting is allowed in season. Fishing for trout or bass is another option. Swimming is not recommended because of the swift water, undercurrents, and obstacles. A free permit is required for whitewater rafting and is available at the forest service office in Lake Isabella, 760/379-5646.

Campsites, facilities: There are several sites for tents or RVs up to 30 feet (no hookups); dispersed camping is also available. Picnic tables and fire rings are provided. Vault toilets are available. There is no drinking water. Garbage must be packed out. Leashed pets are permitted.

Reservations, fees: Reservations are not accepted. There is no fee for camping. A 14-day stay limit for every 30 days is enforced; 28 camping days maximum per year. Open year-round.

Directions: From Bakersfield, drive east on Highway 178 for approximately 40 miles to the town of Lake Isabella and Highway 155. Turn left (north) on Highway 155 and drive one mile to Keyesville Road. Turn left and drive 0.5 mile to the Special Management Area entrance.

Contact: Bureau of Land Management, Bakersfield Field Office, 661/391-6000, fax 661/391-6041.

157 MAIN DAM

Scenic rating: 8

on Isabella Lake

Map 11.5, page 611

This camp is on the south shore of Isabella Lake, just east of Pioneer Point and within a

mile of a boat ramp. The elevation is 2,500 feet. This camp is used as an overflow area and is only open on holiday weekends. (For recreation information, see the *Pioneer Point* listing in this chapter.)

Campsites, facilities: There are 82 sites for tents or RVs up to 45 feet (no hookups). Picnic tables and fire grills are provided. Drinking water and flush and vault toilets are available. A dump station is available nearby. Supplies and a coin laundry are available in the town of Lake Isabella. Leashed pets are permitted.

Reservations, fees: Reservations are not accepted. Sites are $15 per night, $5 per night for each additional vehicle. Open May to September, holiday weekends only.

Directions: From Bakersfield, drive east on Highway 178 for about 40 miles to the town of Lake Isabella and Highway 155. Turn left (north) and drive 1.5 miles to the campground.

Contact: Sequoia National Forest, Kern River Ranger District, Lake Isabella Office, 760/379-5646, fax 760/379-8597.

158 AUXILIARY DAM

Scenic rating: 8

on Isabella Lake

Map 11.5, page 611

This primitive camp was designed to be an overflow area if other camps at Isabella Lake are packed. It's the only camp directly on the shore of the lake, and many people like it. In addition, a boat ramp is just a mile east for good lake access, and the sailboarding prospects adjacent to the campground are the best of the entire lake. The winds come up and sail right over the dam, creating a steady breeze in the afternoon that is not gusty. The elevation is 2,650 feet.

Campsites, facilities: There are a number of primitive, undesignated sites for tents or RVs of any length (no hookups). Drinking water and restrooms with flush toilets and coin showers are available. Supplies and a coin laundry are available in the town of Lake Isabella. Some facilities are wheelchair-accessible. Leashed pets are permitted.

Reservations, fees: Reservations are not accepted. Sites are $5 per night per vehicle from May through September or $35 for a season pass. There is no fee for camping from October through April. Open year-round.

Directions: From Bakersfield, drive east on Highway 178 for about 40 miles to the town of Lake Isabella. Continue east on Highway 178 for one mile to the campground entrance.

Contact: Sequoia National Forest, Kern River Ranger District, Lake Isabella Office, 760/379-5646, fax 760/379-8597.

159 PARADISE COVE

Scenic rating: 6

on Isabella Lake

Map 11.5, page xxx

Paradise Cove is on the southeast shore of Isabella Lake at 2,600 feet in elevation. A boat ramp is about two miles away to the west, near the South Fork Picnic Area. While the camp is not directly at the lakeshore, it does overlook the broadest expanse of the lake. This part of the lake is relatively undeveloped compared to the areas near Wofford Heights and the dam.

Campsites, facilities: There are 58 sites for tents and a primitive area for up to 80 RVs of any length (no hookups). Picnic tables and fire grills are provided at some sites. Drinking water, restrooms with flush toilets and coin showers, and a fish-cleaning station are available. Some facilities are wheelchair-accessible. Supplies, dump station, and a coin laundry are available in Mountain Mesa. Leashed pets are permitted.

Reservations, fees: Reservations are accepted ($9 reservation fee) at 877/444-6777 or www .ReserveUSA.com. Sites are $12–17 per night, $5 per night for each additional vehicle. Open year-round.

Directions: From Bakersfield, drive east on Highway 178 for about 40 miles to the town of Lake Isabella. Continue east on Highway 178 for six miles to the campground entrance.

Contact: Sequoia National Forest, Kern River Ranger District, Lake Isabella Office, 760/379-5646, fax 760/379-8597.

160 KOA LAKE ISABELLA

Scenic rating: 4

on Isabella Lake

Map 11.5, page xxx

This KOA camp provides a good, clean option to the Forest Service camps on the southern end of Isabella Lake, Southern California's largest lake. It is set in South Fork Valley (elevation 2,600 feet), east of the lake off Highway 178. The nearest boat ramp is at South Fork Picnic Area (about a five-minute drive to the west), where there is also a good view of the lake.

Campsites, facilities: There are 70 sites with full or partial hookups (30 amps) for tents or RVs up to 40 feet; some sites are pull-through. Picnic tables are provided, along with fire rings at some sites. Restrooms with flush toilets and showers, drinking water, playground, seasonal swimming pool, coin laundry, recreation room, pub, convenience store, dump station, firewood, and propane gas are available. Leashed pets are permitted.

Reservations, fees: Reservations are accepted. Sites are $23–38 per night for RVs, $4 per person per night for more than three people. Some credit cards accepted. Open year-round.

Directions: From Bakersfield, drive east on Highway 178 for about 40 miles to the town of Lake Isabella. Continue east on Highway 178 for 10 miles to the campground entrance on the left (well signed).

Contact: KOA Lake Isabella, 760/378-2001 or 800/562-2085, www.koa.com.

161 SANDY FLAT

Scenic rating: 6

on the Kern River in Sequoia National Forest

Map 11.5, page 611

This camp is opened as an overflow camp if Hobo is filled. It is about a mile from Hobo. It is a low-use campground, with less shade than Hobo; some sites are shaded, others, well, nope. It is used primarily as a boat launch area for kayakers and rafters. Fishing is fair for catfish, bass, and rainbow trout. The river is stocked with trout in the summer.

Campsites, facilities: There are 35 sites for tents or RVs up to 24 feet (no hookups). Fire rings and picnic tables are provided. Vault toilets and drinking water are available. Leashed pets are permitted.

Reservations, fees: Reservations are not accepted. Sites are $15 per night, $5 per night for each additional vehicle. Open May through September.

Directions: From Bakersfield, drive east on Highway 178 for 35 miles to Borel Road (five miles from Lake Isabella). Turn right (south) at Borel Road and drive 0.3 mile to Old Kern Canyon Road. Turn right and drive one mile to the campground on your right.

Contact: Sequoia National Forest, Kern River Ranger District, Lake Isabella Office, 760/379-5646, fax 760/379-8597.

162 HOBO

Scenic rating: 7

on the Kern River in Sequoia National Forest

Map 11.5, page 611   BEST (

The secret is out about Hobo: It is set adjacent to a mineral hot springs, that is, an open-air springs, with room for about 10 people at once. The camp is also situated along the lower Kern River, about 10 miles downstream of the dam at Isabella Lake. Rafters sometimes use this camp as a put-in spot for an 18-mile run to the takeout at Democrat Picnic Area, a challenging Class IV run. The elevation is 2,300 feet.

Campsites, facilities: There are 35 sites for tents or RVs up to 24 feet (no hookups). Fire grills and picnic tables are provided. Drinking water, vault toilets, and showers are available. Leashed pets are permitted.

Reservations, fees: Reservations are accepted ($9 reservation fee) at 877/444-6777 or www .ReserveUSA.com. The fee is $14 per night for the first vehicle, $5 per night for each additional vehicle. Open year-round.

Directions: From Bakersfield, drive east on Highway 178 for 35 miles to Borel Road (five miles from Lake Isabella). Turn right (south) at Borel Road and drive 0.3 mile to Old Kern Road. Turn right and drive two miles to the campground on your right.

Contact: Sequoia National Forest, Kern River Ranger District, Lake Isabella Office, 760/379-5646, fax 760/379-8597.

163 BRECKENRIDGE

Scenic rating: 7

in Sequoia National Forest

Map 11.5, page 611

This is a popular spot for people to visit with sport utility vehicles. It is a tiny, primitive camp set at 6,600 feet near Breckenridge Mountain (a good lookout here) in a little-traveled southwest sector of the Sequoia National Forest. From camp, it's a two-mile drive south up to the lookout, with sweeping views afforded in all directions. There are no other camps in the immediate area.

Campsites, facilities: There are eight tent sites. Picnic tables and fire grills are provided. Vault toilets are available. No drinking water is available. Garbage must be packed out. Leashed pets are permitted.

Reservations, fees: Reservations are not accepted. There is no fee for camping. Open May through September.

Directions: From Bakersfield, drive east on Highway 178 for about 40 miles to the town of Lake Isabella and Lake Isabella Boulevard. Turn right (south) on Lake Isabella Boulevard and drive two miles to a Y intersection with Kern River Canyon Road and Caliente Bodfish Road. Bear left on Caliente Bodfish Road and drive nine miles to the town of Havilah. Continue on Caliente Bodfish Road for two miles to Forest Road 28S06. Turn right and drive about 10 miles to the campground.

Contact: Sequoia National Forest, Kern River Ranger District, Lake Isabella Office, 760/379-5646, fax 760/379-8597.

164 KERN RIVER CAMPGROUND

🛶 🚐 🎣 ♿ 🚻 ♿ 🚐 ⛺

Scenic rating: 7

at Lake Ming

Map 11.5, page 611

The campground is set at Lake Ming, a small but exciting place. The lake covers just 205 surface acres, and with the weather so hot, the hot jet boats can make it a wild affair here. It's become a popular spot for southern valley residents, only a 15-minute drive from Bakersfield. It is so popular for water sports that every year, beginning in March, the lake is closed to the public one weekend per month for private boat races and waterskiing competitions. The lake is restricted to sailing and sailboarding on the second weekend of every month and on Tuesday and Thursday afternoons. All other boating, including waterskiing, is permitted on the remaining days. All boats are required to have a permit; boaters may buy one at the park. Swimming is not allowed because there is a parasite in the water that has been known to cause swimmer's itch. Yikes. The lake is stocked with rainbow trout in the winter months, and they join a sprinkling of bluegill, catfish, crappie, and bass. The elevation is 450 feet. Maximum stay is 10 days.

Campsites, facilities: There are 50 sites for tents or RVs up to 28 feet. Picnic tables and fire rings are provided. Restrooms with flush toilets and coin showers, drinking water, dump station, playground, concession stand, picnic area, and a boat ramp are available. Some facilities are wheelchair-accessible. A store is nearby. Leashed pets are permitted.

Reservations, fees: Reservations are not accepted. Sites are $22 per night, $4 per night per pet. Discounts available in winter. Open year-round.

Directions: From Bakersfield, drive east on Highway 178 for 11 miles to Alfred Harrell Highway. Turn left (north) on Alfred Harrell Highway and drive four miles to Lake Ming Road. Turn right on Lake Ming Road and follow the signs to the campground on the right, 0.25 mile west of the lake.

Contact: Kern County Parks and Recreation Department, 661/868-7000, www.co.kern .ca.us/parks/.

165 TROY MEADOWS

🚶 🛶 🎣 🐕 🚻 ♿ 🚐 ⛺

Scenic rating: 7

on Fish Creek in Sequoia National Forest

Map 11.5, page 611

Obscure? Yes, but what the heck, it gives you an idea of what is possible out in the boondocks. The camp is set at 7,800 feet right along Fish Creek. Black Rock Ranger Station is available two miles northwest. You are advised to stop there before any backcountry trips. Note that off-highway vehicles (OHVs) are allowed in this area. Also note that Jackass National Recreation Trail is a short drive to the east; it runs north aside Jackass Creek to its headwaters just below Jackass Peak (9,245 feet). Note: At the time of publication this campground was closed for renovations, but was expected to reopen for the 2007 season; call for current status.

Campsites, facilities: There are 73 sites for tents or RVs up to 60 feet (no hookups). Picnic tables and fire grills are provided. Drinking

water and vault toilets are available. Garbage must be packed out. Some facilities are wheelchair-accessible. Leashed pets are permitted.

Reservations, fees: Reservations are not accepted. Sites are $10 per night. Open June through October, weather permitting.

Directions: Drive on U.S. 395 to Ninemile Canyon Road (four miles north of the town of Pearsonville, 48 miles south of Lone Pine). Turn west on Ninemile Canyon Road and drive 31 miles (the road becomes Sherman Pass Road) to the campground.

Contact: Sequoia National Forest, Kern River Ranger District, Kernville Office, 760/376-3781, fax 760/376-3795.

166 FISH CREEK

Scenic rating: 8

in Sequoia National Forest

Map 11.5, page 611

This is a pretty spot set at the confluence of Fish Creek and Jackass Creek. The elevation is 7,500 feet. The nearby trails are used by off-highway vehicles, which can make this a noisy campground during the day.

Campsites, facilities: There are 40 sites for tents or RVs up to 24 feet (no hookups). Picnic tables and fire grills are provided. Drinking water and vault toilets are available. Garbage must be packed out. Leashed pets are permitted.

Reservations, fees: Reservations are not accepted. Sites are $10 per night. Open June through October, weather permitting.

Directions: Drive on U.S. 395 to Ninemile Canyon Road (four miles north of the town of Pearsonville, 48 miles south of Lone Pine). Turn west on Ninemile Canyon Road and drive 28 miles (the road becomes Sherman Pass Road) to the campground.

Contact: Sequoia National Forest, Kern River Ranger District, Kernville Office, 760/376-3781, fax 760/376-3795.

167 KENNEDY MEADOW

Scenic rating: 8

on the South Fork of the Kern River in Sequoia National Forest

Map 11.5, page 611

This is a pretty Forest Service campground set amid piñon pine and sage country, with the Pacific Crest Trail running by the camp. That makes it a great trailhead camp, as well as a refreshing stopover for PCT through-hikers. A highlight is the nearby South Fork Kern River, which provides fishing for rainbow trout. The camp receives moderate use and is a lifesaver for PCT through-hikers.

Campsites, facilities: There are 38 sites for tents or RVs up to 30 feet (no hookups). Picnic tables and fire rings are provided. Drinking water (seasonal) and vault toilets are available. Garbage must be packed out. Leashed pets are permitted.

Reservations, fees: Reservations are not accepted. The fee is $10 per night. Open year-round, weather permitting.

Directions: Drive on U.S. 395 to Ninemile Canyon Road (four miles north of the town of Pearsonville, 48 miles south of Lone Pine). Turn west on Ninemile Canyon Road and drive 21 miles to a small store. Bear right at the store (still Ninemile Canyon Road) and continue for three miles to the campground.

Contact: Sequoia National Forest, Kern River Ranger District, Kernville Office, 760/376-3781, fax 760/376-3795.

168 LONG VALLEY

Scenic rating: 5

near the Dome Land Wilderness

Map 11.5, page 611

This one is way out there. It's set at road's end in Long Valley, a mile from the border of the Dome Land Wilderness to the east, and the camp is used primarily as a jump-off spot for hikers. A trail from camp leads 2.5 miles west, climbing along a small stream and reaching the South Fork of the Kern River, in rugged and remote country. The elevation is 5,200 feet.

Campsites, facilities: There are 13 tent sites. Picnic tables and fire grills are provided. Vault toilets are available. No drinking water is available. Garbage must be packed out. Leashed pets are permitted.

Reservations, fees: No reservations are accepted. There is no camping fee, but donations are encouraged. Open year-round.

Directions: Drive on U.S. 395 to Ninemile Canyon Road (four miles north of the town of Pearsonville, 48 miles south of Lone Pine). Turn west on Ninemile Canyon Road and drive 11 miles to the BLM Work Station and Cane Brake Road. Turn left on Cane Brake Road (the dirt road opposite the BLM station) and drive six miles to Long Valley Road. Turn right and drive eight miles to the campground entrance road on the left. Turn left and drive one mile to the campground.

Contact: Bureau of Land Management, Bakersfield Field Office, 661/391-6000, fax 661/391-6041.

169 CHIMNEY CREEK
🚶 🐕 5% 🚐 ⛺

Scenic rating: 5

on the Pacific Crest Trail

Map 11.5, page 611

This BLM camp is set at 5,900 feet along the headwaters of Chimney Creek, on the southern flank of Chimney Peak (7,990 feet) two miles to the north. This is a trailhead camp for the Pacific Crest Trail, one of its relatively obscure sections. The PCT heads north from camp and in 10 miles it skirts the eastern border of Dome Land Wilderness.

Campsites, facilities: There are 36 sites for tents or RVs up to 25 feet (no hookups). Picnic tables and fire grills are provided. Vault toilets are available. No drinking water is available.

Garbage must be packed out. Leashed pets are permitted.

Reservations, fees: Reservations are not accepted. There is no fee for camping, but donations are encouraged. Open year-round.

Directions: Drive on U.S. 395 to Ninemile Canyon Road (four miles north of the town of Pearsonville, 48 miles south of Lone Pine). Turn west on Ninemile Canyon Road and drive 11 miles to the BLM Work Station and Cane Brake Road. Turn left on Cane Brake Road (the dirt road opposite the BLM station) and drive three miles to the camp on the left.

Contact: Bureau of Land Management, Bakersfield Field Office, 661/391-6000, fax 661/391-6041.

170 WALKER PASS WALK-IN
🚶 🐕 5% 🚐 ⛺

Scenic rating: 6

on the Pacific Crest Trail southwest of Death Valley National Park

Map 11.5, page 611

Long-distance hikers on the Pacific Crest Trail (PCT) treat this camp as if they were arriving at Valhalla. That's because it is set right on the trail and, better yet, drinking water is available. Out here in the desert there aren't many places where you can act like a camel and suck up all the liquid you can hold. The camp is set at 5,200 feet, southwest of Death Valley National Park. And if you guessed it was named for Joe Walker, the West's greatest trailblazer and one of my heroes, well, right you are. If you arrive by car instead of on the PCT, use this spot as a base camp. Because of its desert remoteness, very few hikers start trips from this location.

Campsites, facilities: There are two sites for tents or RVs up to 20 feet (no hookups) with limited parking and nine walk-in sites for tents only. Picnic tables and fire rings are provided. Drinking water (spring through fall) and pit toilets are available. Hitching racks and corrals are available. Garbage must be packed out. Leashed pets are allowed.

Reservations, fees: Reservations are not accepted. There is no fee for camping, but donations are encouraged. A 14-day stay limit is enforced. Open year-round.

Directions: From Bakersfield, drive east on Highway 178 for about 40 miles to the town of Lake Isabella. Continue east on Highway 178 to Onyx and continue 14 miles to Walker Pass and the right side of the road (where a sign is posted for the Pacific Crest Trail). Park and walk 0.25 mile to the campground.

Contact: Bureau of Land Management, Bakersfield Field Office, 661/391-6000, fax 661/391-6041.

DEATH VALLEY

What good are Death Valley, the Panamint Range,

and the nearby desert environs? The answer is that this country is good for looking at. On a fall evening, you can take a seat on a ridge, overlooking hundreds of square miles of landscape, and just watch. Every few minutes, you'll find, the view changes. It is like watching the face of someone you care for, one minute joyous, the next pensive, then wondrous, then mysterious.

The desert is like this, always changing the way it looks, just as the sunlight changes. The reason is that as the sun passes through the sky, its azimuth is continuously changing. In turn, that causes a continuous transformation in the way sunlight is refracted through the atmosphere and across the vast landscape. So, especially at dawn and dusk in spring and fall, the desert looks different from minute to minute. For those who appreciate this subtlety, the desert calls for them in a way that many others do not understand.

There are other appeals. It is often warm even on the fringe of winter, the wildflowers are small but can be spectacular in spring, and the highways – and everything else – are wide open, at times without another soul for miles in all directions. This region is huge, with Death Valley the largest national park in the lower 48 states, yet there are only nine campgrounds. Because of the sparse nature of the land, campers should arrive self-contained; that is, equipped with everything they need.

Some of the highlights include the lowest point in the United States, 282 feet below sea level, at Badwater in Death Valley National Park. Yet also in the park is Telescope Peak, towering at 11,049 feet. Crazy? Oh yeah.

When viewed from a distance, in between is a vast terrain that seems devoid of vegetation. The sub-sea-level salt flats indeed can seem like a bunch of nothing. But they are linked to barren, rising mountains, Eureka Dunes, and surrounding vastness everywhere.

Camping is good at the developed campsites but better if you strike out on your own and create your own site, do-it-yourself style. One key is to never camp at a water source or in the bottom of ravines. Instead, always camp a good distance from water sources and on shelves or flat spots above ravines. This is why: 1. If you camp at a water source, you may unintentionally block it from use by wildlife. In their case, it may be life or death, and yet you are in their way, so keep at wide berth from water sources at night. 2. Never camp at the bottom of ravines in the desert because you can drown. What? Yep. Thunderstorms with tremendous short-term rainfall are common in the desert. If the runoff is blocked, the water can back itself up like a small lake, and then suddenly break through with the force of a small flood. In turn, if you are camped at the bottom of a ravine, you can find yourself in the path of a surprise torrent of water, right in the middle of the desert, the driest place in the state.

Of course, summer is well known for the blazing temperatures, over 100°F about every day and occasionally hitting 120°F and up.

But that is not when people visit here. They visit in fall, winter, and spring. And if you see somebody sitting on an overlooking ridge at dusk, watching the changing colors of the landscape as if it were created from the palette of an artist, well, don't be surprised. When it comes to beautiful views, the changing colors of the emotion of the land, it doesn't get any better than this.

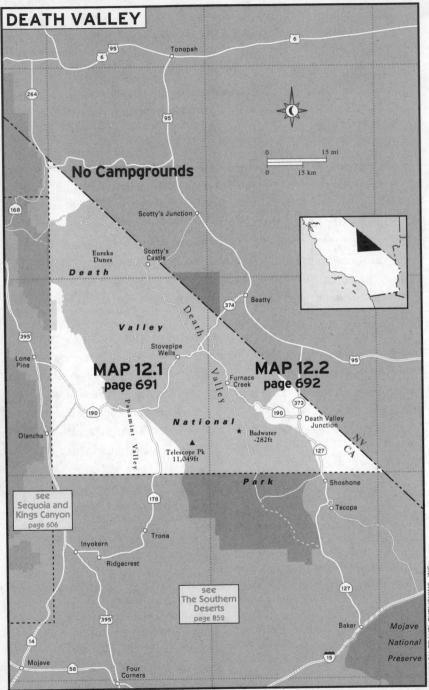

DEATH VALLEY

No Campgrounds

Tonopah

6
95
6

264

95

168

Scotty's Junction

Eureka
Dunes

Death

Scotty's
Castle

Beatty

374

Valley

Stovepipe
Wells

395

Lone
Pine

MAP 12.1
page 691

Death

Furnace
Creek

MAP 12.2
page 692

95

190

373

Valley

190

Death Valley
Junction

Olancha

National

★ Badwater
-282ft

▲ Telescope Pk
11,049ft

127

NV
CA

Park

Shoshone

see
Sequoia and
Kings Canyon
page 606

178

Tecopa

Inyokern

Trona

Ridgecrest

127

see
The Southern
Deserts
page 852

Baker

Mojave

395

National

14

15

Preserve

Mojave

58

Four
Corners

0   15 mi
0   15 km

Map 12.1

Campgrounds 1-6
Pages 693-695

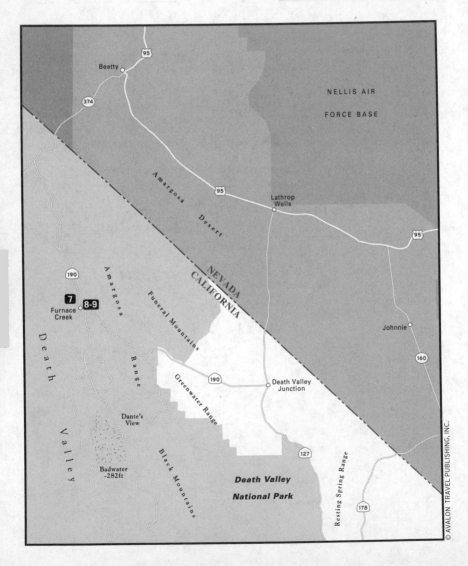

Map 12.2

Campgrounds 7-9
Pages 695-696

12.1

1 2

Beatty

95

374

NELLIS AIR
FORCE BASE

Amargosa

Desert

95

Lathrop
Wells

95

NEVADA
CALIFORNIA

190

Amargosa

7 8-9

Furnace
Creek

Funeral Mountains

Johnnie

160

190

Death Valley
Junction

Range

Greenwater Range

Dante's
View

D
e
a
t
h

Black Mountains

127

Resting Spring Range

V
a
l
l
e
y

Badwater
-282ft

**Death Valley
National Park**

178

© AVALON TRAVEL PUBLISHING, INC.

1 MESQUITE SPRING
🚶 🐕 ♿ 🚐 ⛺

Scenic rating: 7

in Death Valley National Park

Map 12.1, page 691

Mesquite Spring is the northernmost and often the prettiest campground in Death Valley, providing you time it right. If you are a lover of desert beauty, then you must make this trip in late winter or early spring, when all kinds of tiny wildflowers can bring the stark valley floor to life. The key is soil moisture, courtesy of rains in November and December. The elevation is 1,800 feet. Mesquite Spring Campground is within short range of two side trips. It is five miles (past the Grapevine Entrance Station) to Ubehebe Crater, a scenic point, and four miles to Scotty's Castle, a historic building, where tours are available.

Campsites, facilities: There are 30 sites for tents or RVs up to 30 feet (no hookups). Picnic tables and fire grills are provided. Drinking water, flush toilets, and a dump station are available. Some facilities are wheelchair-accessible. Leashed pets are permitted.

Reservations, fees: Reservations are not accepted. Sites are $12 per night, plus a $20 park entrance fee that is valid for seven days. Visitors may pay the entrance fee and obtain a park brochure at the Furnace Creek, Grapevine, Stovepipe Wells, or Beatty Ranger Stations.

Directions: From Furnace Creek Visitor Center, drive north on Highway 190 for 19 miles to Scotty's Castle Road. Turn right (east) and drive 33 miles (just before the Grapevine entrance station and three miles before reaching Scotty's Castle) to the campground entrance road on the left. Turn left and drive two miles to the campground.

Contact: Death Valley National Park, 760/786-3200, fax 760/786-3283, www.nps.gov/deva.

2 STOVEPIPE WELLS
🚶 🏊 🐕 ♿ 🚐 ⛺

Scenic rating: 4

in Death Valley National Park

Map 12.1, page 691

Stovepipe Wells is on the major highway through Death Valley. The RV sites consist of an enormous asphalt area with sites simply marked on it. There is no shelter or shade. But note: Get fuel here because prices are usually lower than at Furnace Creek. An unusual trail is available off the highway within a short distance; look for the sign for the Mosaic Canyon Trail parking area. From here you can take the easy one-mile walk up a beautiful canyon, where the walls are marble and seem as if they are polished. Rock scramblers can extend the trip for another mile. The elevation is at sea level on the edge of a large expanse of Death Valley below sea level.

Campsites, facilities: There are 18 sites for tents only and 200 sites for RVs of any length (no hookups). Picnic tables and fire rings are provided at the tent sites. Drinking water, restrooms with flush toilets and coin showers, dump station, swimming pool (extra fee), camp store, and gasoline are available. Some facilities are wheelchair-accessible. Leashed pets are permitted at campsites only.

Reservations, fees: Reservations are not accepted. Sites are $12 per night, plus a $20 park entrance fee per vehicle that is valid for seven days. Open mid-October to mid-April.

Directions: In Stovepipe Wells Village, drive west on Highway 190 to the signed entrance (just before the general store) on the right.

Contact: Death Valley National Park, 760/786-3200, fax 760/786-3283, www.nps.gov/deva.

3 EMIGRANT

Scenic rating: 4

in Death Valley National Park

Map 12.1, page 691

The key here is the elevation, and Emigrant, at 2,100 feet, is out of the forbidding subzero elevations of Death Valley. That makes it one of the more habitable camps. From the camp a good side trip is to drive south 21 miles on Emigrant Canyon Road, then turn east on Upper Wildrose Canyon Road for seven miles, the last two miles a rough dirt road. That done, you come to the trailhead for Wildrose Peak, on the left side of the road at the parking area for the Charcoal Kilns. The trail here climbs 4.2 miles to the peak, with awesome views in the last two miles; the last mile is a butt-kicker.

Campsites, facilities: There are 10 sites for tents only. Picnic tables and fire rings are provided. Drinking water and flush toilets are available. Campfires are not permitted during the summer. Leashed pets are permitted at campsites only.

Reservations, fees: No reservations are accepted and there is no camping fee; however, there is a $10 park entrance fee per vehicle that is valid for seven days. Open year-round.

Directions: In Stovepipe Wells Village, drive eight miles southwest on Highway 190 to the campground on the right.

Contact: Death Valley National Park, 760/786-3200, fax 760/786-3283, www .nps.gov/deva.

4 WILDROSE

Scenic rating: 4

in Death Valley National Park

Map 12.1, page 691

Wildrose is set on the road that heads out to the primitive country of the awesome Panamint Range, eventually coming within range of Telescope Peak, the highest point in Death Valley National Park (11,049 feet). The elevation at the camp is 4,100 feet.

Campsites, facilities: There are 23 sites for tents or RVs up to 25 feet (no hookups). Picnic tables and fire rings are provided. Drinking water (April through November only) and pit toilets are available. Campfires are not permitted during the summer. Leashed pets are permitted at campsites only.

Reservations, fees: No reservations are accepted and there is no camping fee; however, there is a $20 park entrance fee per vehicle that is valid for seven days. Open year-round.

Directions: From Stovepipe Wells Village, drive south on Highway 190 for eight miles to Emigrant Canyon Road (just past the Emigrant rest area). Turn left (east) on Emigrant Canyon Road and drive 22 miles to the campground entrance on the left.

Contact: Death Valley National Park, 760/786-3200, fax 760/786-3283, www .nps.gov/deva.

5 THORNDIKE

Scenic rating: 4

in Death Valley National Park

Map 12.1, page 691

This is one of Death Valley National Park's little-known camps. It is set in the high country at 7,500 feet. It's free, of course. Otherwise the park service would have to actually send somebody out to tend to the place. Nearby are century-old charcoal kilns that were built by Chinese laborers and tended by Shoshone workers. The trailhead that serves Telescope Peak (11,049 feet), the highest point in Death Valley, can be found in nearby Mahogany Flat.

Campsites, facilities: This backcountry campground is accessible only by foot or high-clearance vehicle; it has six sites for tents. Picnic tables and fire rings are provided. Pit toilets are available. No drinking water is available. Campfires are not permitted in the summer. Garbage must be packed out. Leashed pets are permitted at campsites only.

Reservations, fees: No reservations are accepted and there is no camping fee; however, there is a $20 park entrance fee per vehicle that is valid for seven days.

Directions: In Death Valley at Stovepipe Wells Village, drive south on Highway 190 for eight miles to Emigrant Canyon Road (just past the Emigrant rest area). Turn left (east) on Emigrant Canyon Road and drive 21 miles to Wildrose Canyon Road. Turn left and drive nine miles to the camp. (The road becomes extremely rough; high-clearance vehicle is required.)

Contact: Death Valley National Park, 760/786-3200, fax 760/786-3283, www .nps.gov/deva.

6 MAHOGANY FLAT FOUR-WHEEL DRIVE

Scenic rating: 5

in Death Valley National Park

Map 12.1, page 691

This is one of two primitive, hard-to-reach camps (the other is Thorndike) set in the Panamint Range high country. It is one of the few shaded camps, offering beautiful piñon pines and junipers. What makes it popular, however, is the trail to Telescope Peak leading out from camp. Only the ambitious and well conditioned should attempt the climb, a seven-mile trip one-way with breathtaking (literally) views of both Panamint Valley and Death Valley. The elevation at the campground is 8,200 feet and Telescope Peak tops out at 11,049 feet, which translates to a climb of 2,849 feet.

Campsites, facilities: There are 10 sites for tents only. Picnic tables and fire rings are provided. Pit toilets are available. No drinking water is available. Campfires are not permitted during the summer. Garbage must be packed

out. The campground is accessible only by foot or four-wheel-drive vehicle. Leashed pets are permitted at campsites only.

Reservations, fees: No reservations are accepted and there is no camping fee; however, there is a $20 park entrance fee per vehicle that is valid for seven days. Open year-round, weather permitting.

Directions: From Stovepipe Wells Village, drive south on Highway 190 for eight miles to Emigrant Canyon Road (just past the Emigrant rest area). Turn left (east) on Emigrant Canyon Road and drive 21 miles to Wildrose Canyon Road. Turn left and drive nine miles (passing Thorndike campground) to the end of the road and the camp.

Contact: Death Valley National Park, 760/786-3200, fax 760/786-3283, www .nps.gov/deva.

7 FURNACE CREEK

Scenic rating: 5

in Death Valley National Park

Map 12.2, page 692

This is a well-developed national park site that provides a good base camp for exploring Death Valley, especially for newcomers. The nearby visitors center includes Death Valley Museum and offers maps and suggestions for hikes and drives in this unique wildland. The elevation is 190 feet below sea level. This camp offers shady sites, a rarity in Death Valley. It's open all year, but keep in mind that the daytime summer temperatures commonly exceed 120°F, making this area virtually uninhabitable in the summer.

Campsites, facilities: There are 136 sites for tents or RVs up to 35 feet (no hookups), and two group sites for up to 10 vehicles and 40 people each. Picnic tables and fire rings are provided. Drinking water, flush toilets, dump station, and evening ranger programs are available. Campfires are not permitted during the summer. Some facilities are wheelchair-accessible. Leashed pets are permitted at campsites only.

Reservations, fees: Reservations are recommended mid-October through mid-April at 800/365-CAMP (800/365-2267) or at www .reservationsnps.gov. Sites are $18 per night (includes reservation fee), plus a $20 park entrance fee per vehicle that is valid for seven days. Group sites are $50 per night. Open year-round.

Directions: From Furnace Creek Ranch, drive one mile north on Highway 190 to the signed campground entrance on the left.

Contact: Death Valley National Park, 760/786-3200, fax 760/786-3283, www .nps.gov/deva.

8 TEXAS SPRING

Scenic rating: 2

in Death Valley National Park

Map 12.2, page 692

Although this camp is slightly more protected than Sunset camp, there's limited shade and no shelter. The lower half of the campground is for tents only. It is open only in winter. The upper end of the camp has trails that provide access to the historic springs and a viewing area. The nearby visitors center, which features the Death Valley Museum, offers maps and suggestions for hikes and drives. The lowest point in the United States, Badwater, set 282 feet below sea level, is to the southwest. This camp has one truly unique feature: bathrooms that are listed on the National Historic Register.

Campsites, facilities: There are 92 sites for tents or RVs of any length (no hookups). Picnic tables and fire rings are provided. Drinking water, flush toilets, and a dump station are available. Campfires are not permitted in the summer. Some facilities are wheelchair-accessible. Leashed pets are permitted.

Reservations, fees: No reservations are accepted. Sites are $12 per night, plus a $20

park entrance fee per vehicle that is valid for seven days. Open mid-October to mid-April.

Directions: From Furnace Creek Ranch, drive south on Highway 190 for 0.25 mile to the signed campground entrance on the left.

Contact: Death Valley National Park, 760/786-3200, fax 760/786-3283, www .nps.gov/deva.

9 SUNSET

Scenic rating: 4

in Death Valley National Park

Map 12.2, page 692

This camp is another enormous section of asphalt where the campsites consist of white lines for borders. Sunset is one of several options for campers in the Furnace Creek area of Death Valley, with an elevation of 190 feet below sea level. It is advisable to make your first stop at the nearby visitors center for maps and suggested hikes (according to your level of fitness) and drives. Don't forget your canteen—and if you're backpacking in Death Valley, never set up a wilderness camp within 100 yards of water.

Campsites, facilities: There are 1,000 sites for RVs of any length (no hookups). Drinking water, flush toilets, and a dump station are available. Campfires are not permitted in the summer. Some facilities are wheelchair-accessible. Leashed pets are permitted at campsites.

Reservations, fees: No reservations are accepted. Sites are $10 per night, plus a $20 park entrance fee per vehicle that is valid for seven days. Open mid-October through mid-April.

Directions: From Furnace Creek Ranch, turn south on Highway 190 and drive 0.25 mile to the signed campground entrance and turn left into the campground.

Contact: Death Valley National Park, 760/786-3200, fax 760/786-3283, www.nps .gov/deva.

SANTA BARBARA AND VICINITY

COURTESY OF THE SANTA BARBARA CONFERENCE & VISITORS BUREAU AND FILM COMMISSION/GREG PETERSON

BEST CAMPGROUNDS

❰ Scenic Destinations
Gaviota State Park, **page 721**
El Capitán State Beach, **page 722**
Santa Rosa Island Boat-In, **page 744**

❰ Family Destinations
Gaviota State Park, **page 721**
El Capitán State Beach, **page 722**

❰ Boat-In Campgrounds
Santa Rosa Island Boat-In, **page 744**

❰ Fishing
North Shore/South Shore San Antonio, **pages 707-708**
Cachuma Lake Recreation Area, **page 732**

❰ Waterskiing
Lake Nacimiento Resort, **page 708**

❰ Island Campgrounds
San Miguel Island Boat-In and Hike-In, **page 743**
Santa Rosa Island Boat-In, **page 744**
Santa Cruz Island Boat-In, **page 744**
Anacapa Island Boat-In and Hike-In, **page 745**

For many, this region of the California coast is like a dream, the best place to live on earth. Visitors, picking one or several of the dozens of campgrounds in the region, can get a taste of why it is so special. What you will likely find, however, is that a taste will only whet your appetite. That's how it is here. Many keep coming back for more. Some eventually even move here.

The region is a unique mix of sun-swept sand beaches that stretch 200 miles and surprise inland coastal forests. The coast offers a series of stunning state beaches, where getting a campsite reservation can feel like winning the lottery. If you have a dream trip in mind in which you cruise the coast highway the entire length, you'd better have the reservation system wired from the start. These campsites go fast and are filled every night of the vacation season. There are many highlights on the coast: San Simeon, Hearst Castle, all the state beaches, the stunning towns of Cambria, Goleta, and Cayucos, and the Coast Highway that provides a route through all of it.

Yet as popular as the coast is, just inland lie many remote, hidden campsites and destinations. Los Padres National Forest spans a matrix of canyons with small streams, mountaintop lookouts, and wilderness trailheads. In fact, rangers reviewing the text for this book requested that I remove one of the trails highlighted from a campground because it was too primitive and difficult for most visitors to successfully follow to its end at a mountaintop. The landscape is a mix of pine, deep canyons, chaparral, and foothills.

Two of California's best recreation lakes also provide major destinations — Lake Nacimiento and San Antonio Reservoir. Nacimiento is one of the top family-oriented lakes for water sports, and it also provides sensational fishing for white bass and largemouth bass in the spring. San Antonio is a great lake for bass, at times even rating as one of the best in America, and tours to see bald eagles are also popular in the winter. Cachuma Lake and Lake Casitas near Santa Barbara have produced some of the largest bass caught in history.

The ocean is dramatic here, the backdrop for every trip on the Coast Highway, and it seems to stretch to forever. Maybe it does. For many visiting here, forever is how long they wish to stay.

SANTA BARBARA AND VICINITY

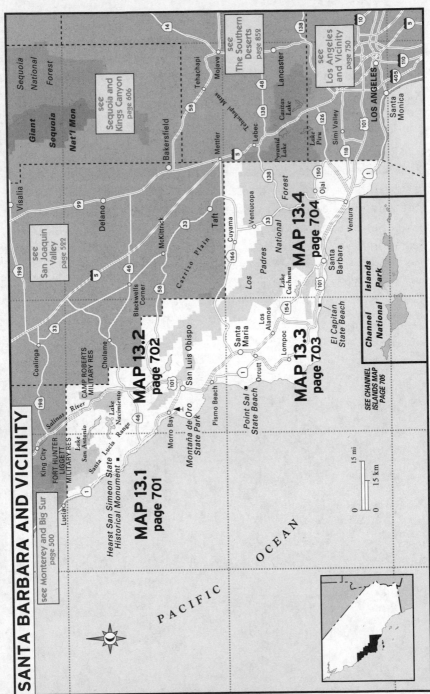

see Monterey and Big Sur
page 500

Sequoia
National
Forest

*Giant
Sequoia
Nat'l Mon*

see
Sequoia and
Kings Canyon
page 606

see
The Southern
Deserts
page 852

see
Los Angeles
and Vicinity
page 750

LOS ANGELES

Santa
Monica

Tehachapi

Mojave

Lancaster

Bakersfield

Tehachapi Mtns

Lebec

Casitas
Lake

Pyramid
Lake

Lake
Piru

Simi Valley

Ojai

Mettler

Visalia

Delano

McKittrick

Taft

Ventucopa

Cuyama

Ventura

Santa
Barbara

Lake
Cachuma

El Capitan
State Beach

Carrizo Plain

Blackwells
Corner

San Joaquin
Valley
page 592

Coalinga

King City

Salinas   River

Santa   Lucia   Range

Lake
Nacimiento

Lake
San Antonio

FORT HUNTER
LIGGETT
MILITARY RES

Lucia

CAMP ROBERTS
MILITARY RES

Cholame

San Luis Obispo

Morro Bay

Montaña de Oro
State Park

Pismo Beach

Santa
Maria

Los
Alamos

Lompoc

Orcutt

Point Sal
State Beach

Hearst San Simeon State
Historical Monument

**MAP 13.1
page 701**

**MAP 13.2
page 702**

**MAP 13.3
page 703**

**MAP 13.4
page 704**

Los   Padres   National   Forest

Channel
Islands
National
Park

SEE CHANNEL
ISLANDS MAP
PAGE 705

PACIFIC   OCEAN

15 mi

15 km

0

0

Map 13.1

Campgrounds 1-3
Pages 706-707

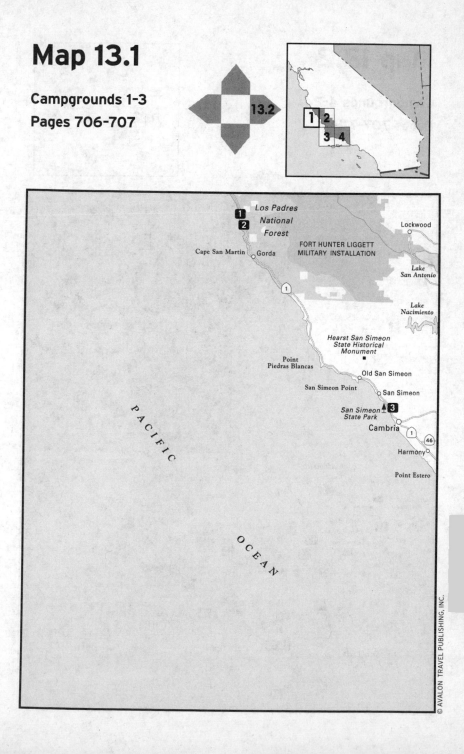

13.2

1 2
3 4

Los Padres
National
Forest

Lockwood

Cape San Martin Gorda

FORT HUNTER LIGGETT
MILITARY INSTALLATION

Lake
San Antonio

1

Lake
Nacimiento

Hearst San Simeon
State Historical
Monument

Point
Piedras Blancas

Old San Simeon

San Simeon Point

San Simeon

San Simeon
State Park

3

Cambria

1

46

Harmony

Point Estero

PACIFIC

OCEAN

Map 13.2

Campgrounds 4-24
Pages 707-718

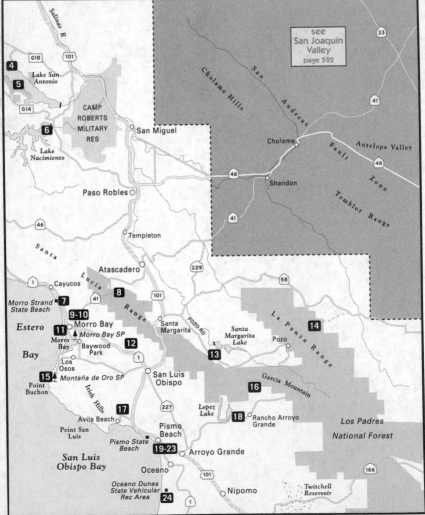

Map 13.3

Campgrounds 25-34
Pages 718-723

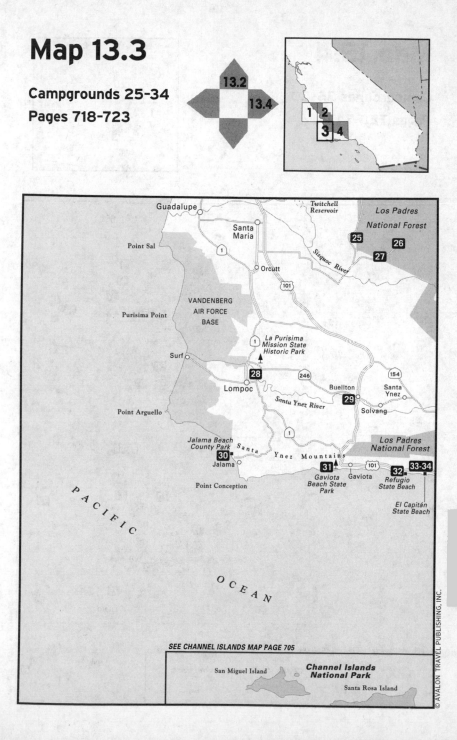

Map 13.4

Campgrounds 35-80

Pages 723-743

13.3

1 2
3 4

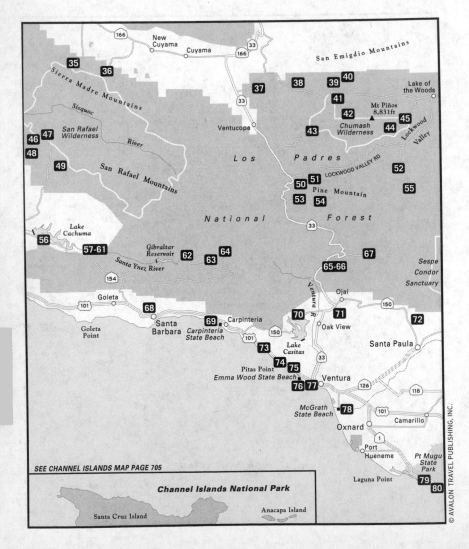

166

New Cuyama

Cuyama

33

166

San Emigdio Mountains

35

36

Sierra Madre Mountains

Sisquoc

37

33

38

39 40

41

Lake of the Woods

42

Mt Piños 8,831ft

45

San Rafael Wilderness

River

Ventucopa

43

Chumash Wilderness

44

Lockwood Valley

46 47

48

49

San Rafael Mountains

Los   Padres

LOCKWOOD VALLEY RD

52

50 51

Pine Mountain

55

53 54

National   Forest

33

Lake Cachuma

56

57-61

Gibraltar Reservoir

62

63 64

Santa Ynez River

65-66

67

Sespe Condor Sanctuary

154

Goleta

101

68

Ventura R.

Ojai

71

150

Goleta Point

Santa Barbara

69

Carpinteria

70

Oak View

72

Carpinteria State Beach

101

150

Lake Casitas

Santa Paula

73

33

Pitas Point

74

94 75

Emma Wood State Beach

Ventura

126

118

76 77

McGrath State Beach

78

101

Camarillo

Oxnard

1

Port Hueneme

Pt Mugu State Park

SEE CHANNEL ISLANDS MAP PAGE 705

Laguna Point

79 80

Channel Islands National Park

Santa Cruz Island

Anacapa Island

© AVALON TRAVEL PUBLISHING, INC.

CHANNEL
ISLANDS DETAIL Campgrounds 81-85 Pages 743-746

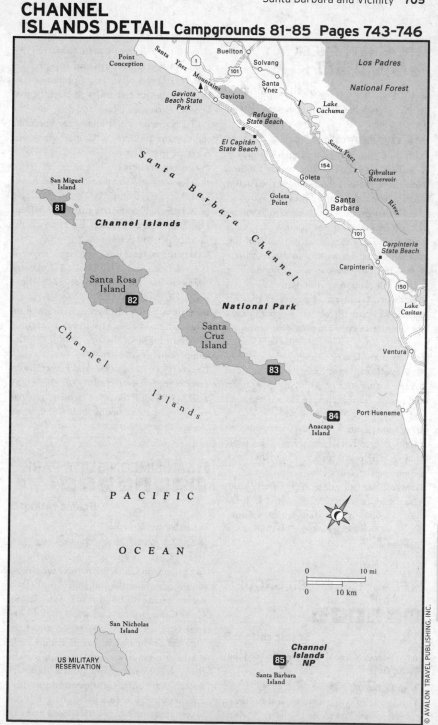

Point
Conception

Buellton

Solvang

Santa Ynez Mountains

1

101

Santa
Ynez

Los Padres

National Forest

Gaviota
Beach State
Park

Gaviota

Refugio
State Beach

Lake
Cachuma

Santa Ynez

El Capitán
State Beach

154

Gibraltar
Reservoir

San Miguel
Island

Santa Barbara Channel

Goleta

Goleta
Point

River

81

Channel Islands

Santa
Barbara

101

Santa Rosa
Island

82

National Park

Carpinteria
State Beach

Carpinteria

150

Lake
Casitas

C h a n n e l

Santa
Cruz
Island

83

Ventura

I s l a n d s

84

Port Hueneme

Anacapa
Island

P A C I F I C

O C E A N

0   10 mi

0   10 km

San Nicholas
Island

*Channel
Islands
NP*

85

US MILITARY
RESERVATION

Santa Barbara
Island

© AVALON TRAVEL PUBLISHING, INC.

1 PLASKETT CREEK

🧍 🏊 ⛵ 🦌 🚐 ⛺

Scenic rating: 8

in Los Padres National Forest overlooking the Pacific Ocean

Map 13.1, page 701

This is a premium coastal camp for Highway 1 cruisers, set at an elevation of just 100 feet along little Plaskett Creek above the Pacific Ocean. The campground provides access to Sand Dollar Beach. It gets overlooked by many for two reasons: It is not listed with a reservation service, and it is farther south of Big Sur than most are willing to drive. A little café in Lucia provides open-air dining with a dramatic lookout over the coast.

Campsites, facilities: There are 45 sites for tents or RVs up to 30 feet (no hookups). Picnic tables and fire grills are provided. Drinking water and flush toilets are available. Leashed pets are permitted.

Reservations, fees: Reservations are not accepted. Sites are $22 per night, $5 per night per person for bicyclists, $5 per person per extra vehicle. Open year-round.

Directions: From Monterey, drive south on Highway 1 to Lucia. From Lucia, continue south on Highway 1 for 9.5 miles to the campground on the left.

Contact: Los Padres National Forest, Monterey Ranger District, 831/385-5434, fax 831/385-0628; Parks Management Company, 805/434-1996, fax 805/434-1986, www.campone.com.

2 PLASKETT CREEK GROUP CAMP

🧍 🏊 ⛵ 🦌 🚐 ⛺

Scenic rating: 8

in Los Padres National Forest overlooking the Pacific Ocean

Map 13.1, page 701

This is one of two prime coastal camps in the immediate area along Highway 1, which is one of the prettiest drives in the West. The camp is for small groups and is set beside little Plaskett Creek. For a premium day trip, drive north five miles to Nacimiento-Ferguson Road, turn east, and drive into Los Padres National Forest and to the border of the Ventana Wilderness. Coastal views and hikes are first-class.

Campsites, facilities: There are three group sites for tents or RVs up to 30 feet (no hookups) that can accommodate up to 40 people each. Picnic tables and fire grills are provided. Drinking water and vault toilets are available. Leashed pets are permitted.

Reservations, fees: Reservations are required ($9 reservation fee) at 877/444-6777 or www.ReserveUSA.com. Groups sites are $80 per night. Open year-round.

Directions: From Monterey, drive south on Highway 1 to Lucia. From Lucia, continue south on Highway 1 for 9.5 miles to the campground on the left.

Contact: Los Padres National Forest, Monterey Ranger District, 831/385-5434, fax 831/385-0628; Parks Management Company, 805/434-1996, fax 805/434-1986, www.campone.com.

3 SAN SIMEON STATE PARK

🧍 🚴 🏊 ⛵ 🦌 ♿ 🚐 ⛺

Scenic rating: 9

in San Simeon State Park

Map 13.1, page 701

Hearst Castle is only five miles northeast, so San Simeon Creek is a natural for visitors planning to take the tour; for a tour reservation, phone 800/444-4445. San Simeon Creek Campground is set across the highway from the ocean, with easy access under the highway to the beach. San Simeon Creek, while not exactly the Mississippi, runs through the campground and adds a nice touch. Washburn Campground provides another option at this park; though it has better views, the sites are exposed and can be windy. It is one mile inland on a plateau overlooking the Pacific Ocean and Santa Lucia Mountains. The best hike in the area is from Leffingwell Landing to Moonstone Beach, featuring sweeping views of the coast from ocean bluffs and a good chance to see passing whales. There are three preserves in the park, including a wintering site for monarch butterfly populations, and it has an archaeological site dating from more than 5,800 years ago. In the summer, junior ranger programs and interpretive programs are available.

Campsites, facilities: At San Simeon Creek Camp, there are 115 sites for tents or RVs up to 35 feet (no hookups), 10 sites for tents only, and two hike-in/bike-in sites. Picnic tables and fire grills are provided. Drinking water, dump station, and restrooms with flush toilets and coin showers are available. At Washburn Camp, there are 70 sites for tents or RVs up to 31 feet (no hookups). Picnic tables and fire grills are provided. Drinking water, chemical flush toilets, and firewood are available. Some facilities are wheelchair-accessible. A grocery store, coin laundry, gas station, restaurants, and propane gas are two miles away in Cambria. Leashed pets are permitted in the campgrounds only.

Reservations, fees: Reservations are accepted ($7.50 reservation fee) at 800/444-PARK (800/444-7275) or www.reserveamerica.com. Sites are $20–25 per night at San Simeon Creek, $11–15 per night at Washburn, $3 per night for each additional vehicle, $2 per person per night for hike-in/bike-in sites. Open year-round.

Directions: From Cambria, drive two miles north on Highway 1 to San Simeon Creek Road. Turn east and drive 0.2 mile to the park entrance on the right.

Contact: San Simeon State Park, 805/927-2035, www.parks.ca.gov.

◢ NORTH SHORE SAN ANTONIO

🏃 🚴 🏊 🛶 🚤 🐕 🚐 ⛰

Scenic rating: 7

on Lake San Antonio

Map 13.2, page 702	BEST ☾

Lake San Antonio makes a great year-round destination for adventure. It is a big, warm-water lake, long and narrow, set at an elevation of 780 feet in the foothills north of Paso Robles. The camp features four miles of shoreline camping, with the bonus of primitive sites along Pleyto Points. The lake is 16 miles long, covers 5,500 surface acres, and has 60 miles of shoreline and average summer water temperatures in the 70s, making it an ideal place for fun in the sun. It is one of the top lakes in California for bass fishing, best in spring and early summer. It is also good for striped bass, catfish, crappie, sunfish, and bluegill. It provides the best wintering habitat in the region for bald eagles, and eagle-watching tours are available from the south shore of the lake. Of course, the size of the lake, along with hot temperatures all summer, make waterskiing and water sports absolutely first-class. Note that boat rentals are not available here, but at South Shore. Equestrian trails are also available.

Campsites, facilities: There are 200 sites with no hookups for tents or RVs of any length, 24 sites with full or partial hookups (30 amps) for tents or RVs of any length, and up to 1,800 primitive dispersed sites near the shoreline. Mobile home rentals are also available. Fire grills and picnic tables are provided. Restrooms with showers, drinking water, dump station, boat ramp, hitching posts, a general store, volleyball, and fishing licenses are available. Leashed pets are permitted.

Reservations, fees: Reservations are not accepted. Sites are $23–25 per night, $15 per night for each additional vehicle, $2 per pet per night. Boat launching is $6 per day. Off-season discounts available. Some credit cards accepted. Open year-round.

Directions: On U.S. 101, drive to the Jolon Road/G14 exit (just north of King City). Take that exit and turn south on Jolon Road and drive 27 miles to Pleyto Road (curvy road). Turn right and drive three miles to the North Shore entrance of the lake. Note: When arriving from the south or east on U.S. 101 near Paso Robles, it is faster to take the G18/Jolon Road exit.

Contact: North Shore, 805/472-2311, www .lakesanantonio.net or www.co.monterey .ca.us/parks.

5 SOUTH SHORE SAN ANTONIO

🥾 🚴 🏊 🎣 🛶 🐴 🏕 🚐 ⛺

Scenic rating: 7

on Lake San Antonio

Map 13.2, page 702   **BEST (**

Harris Creek, Redondo Vista, and Lynch are the three campgrounds set near each other along the south shore of Lake San Antonio, a 16-mile reservoir that provides good bass fishing in the spring and waterskiing in the summer. There are also 26 miles of good biking and hiking trails in the park. There are a museum and visitors center available at the park's administration building. In the winter, the Monterey County Department of Parks offers a unique eagle-watching program here, which includes boat tours. (See the previous entry, *North Shore,* for more details about the lake.) Note that South Shore has boat rentals, laundry facilities, and a playground.

Campsites, facilities: There are three campgrounds here: Redondo has 173 sites with no hookups for tents or RVs and 86 sites with full hookups (30 amps) for tents or RVs; Lynch has 52 sites for tents and 54 sites with partial hookups for tents or RVs; Harris Creek has 88 sites for tents and 26 sites with partial hookups for tents or RVs. Mobile-home rentals are also available. Picnic tables and fire grills are provided. Drinking water and flush toilets

are available. Restrooms with showers, dump station, marina, boat ramp, boat rentals, boat slips, bait and tackle, playground, recreation room, coin laundry, general store, and fishing licenses are available nearby. Leashed pets are permitted.

Reservations, fees: Reservations are accepted for 15 sites only at 888/588-2267. Sites are $27 per night, $15 per night for each additional vehicle, $2 per pet per night. Boat launching is $6 per day. Some credit cards accepted. Off-season discounts available. Group reservations at 805/472-2311. Open year-round.

Directions: From the north, on U.S. 101 (just north of King City), take the Jolon Road/G14 exit. Turn south on Jolon Road and drive 21 miles to Lockwood and Interlake Road (G14). Turn right and drive 18 miles to San Antonio Lake Road. Turn left and drive three miles to the South Shore entrance of the lake.

From the south, drive on U.S. 101 to Paso Robles and the 24th Street exit (G14 west). Take that exit and drive 14 miles to Lake Nacimiento Drive. Turn right and drive across Lake Nacimiento Dam to Interlake Road. Turn left and drive seven miles to Lake San Antonio Road. Turn right and drive three miles to the South Shore entrance.

Contact: South Shore, 805/472-2311, www .lakesanantonio.net or www.co.monterey .ca.us/parks.

6 LAKE NACIMIENTO RESORT

🏊 🎣 🛶 🏕 🐴 🚐 ⛺

Scenic rating: 8

at Lake Nacimiento

Map 13.2, page 702   **BEST (**

This is the only game in town at Nacimiento, and the management plays it well. It's an outstanding operation, with headquarters for a great fishing or water-sports trip. The fishing for white bass and largemouth bass can be incredible. And the water play is also great, with such a big lake, 70-degree temperatures, and some of the best waterskiing in California. The lake has 165 miles of shoreline with an incredible number of arms, many ideal for bass fishing. Nacimiento hosts about 25 fishing tournaments per year. Not only is bass fishing good, but there are also opportunities for trout (in cool months) and bluegill and catfish (in warm months). The resort has a lakeview restaurant open during the summer, and the campsites provide limited tree cover with pines and oaks. Two camps are on the lake's shore, and the rest are set back about three-quarters of a mile from the lake. Lakeview lodging is also available.

Campsites, facilities: There are a series of campgrounds with 297 sites with no hookups for tents or RVs of any length, 40 sites with full hookups for RVs up to 35 feet, and 12 group sites for 15–40 people each. Nineteen lodges, eight trailers, and two mobile homes are also available for rent. Picnic tables and fire grills are provided. Drinking water, restrooms with showers and flush toilets, dump station, boat ramp, boat docks, boat rentals, playground, seasonal swimming pool, seasonal restaurant, coin laundry, a general store, fishing licenses, swimming beaches, basketball and volleyball courts, and horseshoe pits are available. Leashed pets are permitted.

Reservations, fees: Reservations are accepted. Sites are $30–40 per vehicle per night, $10 per pet per night. Some credit cards accepted. Open year-round.

Directions: On U.S. 101, drive to Paso Robles and the 24th Street/Lake Nacimiento exit. Take that exit, turn west on 24th Street (becomes Lake Nacimiento Drive/G14) and drive for nine miles. Bear right on Lake Nacimiento Drive and continue for seven miles to the resort entrance on the left. Note: If you cross the Lake Nacimiento dam, you've gone too far.

Contact: Lake Nacimiento Resort, 805/238-

3256 or 800/323-3839, www.nacimientoresort.com.

7 MORRO STRAND STATE BEACH

Scenic rating: 7

near Morro Bay

Map 13.2, page 702

A ton of Highway 1 cruisers plan to stay overnight at this state park. It is set along the ocean near Morro Bay, right on the beach, a pretty spot year-round. The park features a three-mile stretch of beach that connects the southern and northern entrances to the state beach. Fishing, jogging, sailboarding, and kite flying are popular. Side trips include the Morro Bay Wildlife Refuge, the Museum of Natural History, or an ocean-fishing trip out of Morro Bay. (See the *Morro Bay State Park* listing in this chapter for more information.)

Campsites, facilities: There are 76 sites for tents or RVs up to 24 feet (no hookups). Picnic tables and fire grills are provided. Drinking water and flush toilets are available. Cold, outdoor showers are also available. Supplies and a coin laundry are available in Morro Bay. Leashed pets are permitted, but not on the beach.

Reservations, fees: Reservations are accepted ($7.50 reservation fee) at 800/444-PARK (800/444-7275) or www.reserveamerica.com. Sites are $20–35 per night, $5 per night for each additional vehicle. Open year-round.

Directions: On Highway 1, drive to Morro Bay. Take the Yerba Buena Street/Morro Strand State Beach exit. Turn west on Yerba Buena Street and drive one block to the campground.

Contact: Morro Strand State Beach, 805/772-8812; San Luis Obispo Coast District, 805/927-2065, www.parks.ca.gov.

8 CERRO ALTO

Scenic rating: 7

near San Luis Obispo

Map 13.2, page 702

This camp is set near Morro Creek, which runs most of the year but can disappear in late summer in dry years. Some sites are along the creek, nicely spaced, with sycamore and bay trees peppering the hillside. There are numerous hiking and mountain-biking trails. The best of these is Cerro Alto Trail, which is accessible from camp and then is routed four miles up to Cuesta Ridge for sweeping views of Morro Bay.

Campsites, facilities: There are 22 sites for tents or RVs up to 30 feet (no hookups). Picnic tables and fire grills are provided. Drinking water and vault toilets are available. A camp host and pay phone are nearby. Some facilities are wheelchair-accessible. Leashed pets permitted.

Reservations, fees: Reservations are not accepted. Sites are $18 per night. Open year-round, weather permitting.

Directions: From U.S. 101 at Atascadero, take the Highway 41 west exit. Drive west on Highway 41 for eight miles to the campground on the left.

Contact: Los Padres National Forest, Santa Lucia Ranger District, 805/925-9538, fax 805/961-5781.

9 RANCHO COLINA RV PARK

Scenic rating: 6

in Morro Bay

Map 13.2, page 702

This privately operated RV park is one of several camping options in the Morro Bay area. Folks who park here typically stroll the boardwalk, exploring the little shops. (For recreation, see the entry for Morro Bay State Park in this chapter.) About 20 percent of the sites here are long-term rentals.

Campsites, facilities: There are 57 sites with full hookups (30 amps) for RVs up to 40 feet. No tents. Picnic tables are provided. Restrooms with showers, laundry facilities, and a recreation room are available. You can buy supplies nearby. Leashed pets are permitted.

Reservations, fees: Reservations are accepted. Sites are $30 per night. Monthly rates available. Some credit cards accepted. Open year-round.

Directions: From Morro Bay on Highway 1, drive one mile east on Atascadero Road/Highway 41 to the park at 1045 Atascadero Road.

Contact: Rancho Colina RV Park, 805/772-8420.

10 MORRO DUNES TRAVEL TRAILER PARK AND RESORT CAMPING

Scenic rating: 6

in Morro Bay

Map 13.2, page 702

A wide array of side-trip possibilities and great natural beauty make Morro Bay an attractive destination. Most visitors will walk the boardwalk, try at least one of the coastal restaurants, and then head to Morro Bay State Park for hiking or sea kayaking. Other folks will head straight to the port for fishing, or just explore the area before heading north to San Simeon for the Hearst Castle tour. (See next listing, *Morro Bay State Park,* for more information.)

Campsites, facilities: There are 178 sites with full or partial hookups (30 amps) for RVs of any length, and 48 sites for tents. Some sites are pull-through. Picnic tables and fire grills are provided. Restrooms with showers, drinking water, cable TV, Wi-Fi, modem access, coin laundry, general store, clubhouse, RV storage, RV supplies and repair, recreation hall, group facilities, horseshoes, basketball, firewood, ice, and a dump station are available. Propane gas, a golf course, a playground, and boat rentals are nearby. Leashed pets are permitted. Some facilities are wheelchair-accessible.

Reservations, fees: Reservations are accepted. RV sites are $27.50–31.90 per night, tent sites are $23.10 per night, $1 per person per night for more than two people, $1 per pet per night. Weekly and monthly rates are available during the winter. Some credit cards accepted. Open year-round.

Directions: Drive on Highway 1 to Morro Bay and the exit for Highway 41. Take that exit and turn west on Atascadero Road/Highway 41 and drive 0.5 mile to 1700 Embarcadero/Atascadero Road.

Contact: Morro Dunes Travel Trailer Park and Resort Camping, 805/772-2722, fax 805/772-2372, www.morrodunes.com.

11 MORRO BAY STATE PARK

Scenic rating: 9

in Morro Bay

Map 13.2, page 702

Reservations are strongly advised at this popular campground. This is one of the premium stopover spots for folks cruising north on Highway 1. The park offers a wide range of activities and exhibits covering the natural and cultural history of the area. The park features lagoon and natural bay habitat. The most prominent feature is Morro Rock. A "morro" is a small volcanic peak, and there are nine of them along the local coast. The top hike at the park climbs one of them, Black Hill, and rewards hikers with sensational coastal views. The park has a marina and golf course, with opportunities for sailing, fishing, and bird-watching. Activities include beach walks, kayaking in Morro Bay, ocean fishing on a party boat, and touring Hearst Castle.

Campsites, facilities: There are 95 sites for tents or RVs up to 31 feet (no hookups), 27 sites with partial hookups (15 and 30 amps) for RVs up to 35 feet, five hike-in/bike-in sites,

and two group sites for 25–35 people. Picnic tables, food lockers, and fire rings are provided. Restrooms with flush toilets and coin showers, drinking water, dump station, Wi-Fi, museum exhibits, nature walks, and interpretive programs are available. A coin laundry, grocery store, propane gas, boat ramp, mooring, boat rentals, gas stations, and food service are available in Morro Bay. Some facilities are wheelchair-accessible. Leashed pets are permitted, but not on the beach.

Reservations, fees: Reservations are accepted ($7.50 reservation fee) at 800/444-PARK (800/444-7275) or www.reserveamerica.com. Sites are $20–34 per night, $5 per person per night for hike-in/bike-in sites, $66–111 per night for group sites. Open year-round.

Directions: On Highway 1, drive to Morro Bay and take the exit for Los Osos-Baywood Park/Morro Bay State Park. Turn south and drive one mile to State Park Road. Turn right and drive one mile to the park entrance on the right.

Contact: Morro Bay State Park, 805/772-7434; San Luis Obispo Coast District, 805/927-2065, www.parks.ca.gov.

12 EL CHORRO REGIONAL PARK

Scenic rating: 6

near San Luis Obispo

Map 13.2, page 702

North of Morro Bay on the way to San Simeon and Hearst Castle, this can be a prime spot for RV travelers. Note that the campground isn't in the state park reservation system, which means there are times when coastal state parks can be jammed full and this regional park may still have space. Morro Bay, six miles away, provides many possible side trips. The park has full recreational facilities, including a golf course, volleyball, horseshoe pits, softball fields, hiking trails, and botanical gardens. Note that there's a men's prison about four miles away. For some people, this can be a real turnoff.

Campsites, facilities: There are 63 sites for tents or RVs up to 40 feet and some undesignated overflow sites; 44 sites have full hookups and the remaining sites have no hookups. Some primitive sites are pull-through. Fire grills and picnic tables are provided. Restrooms with flush toilets and showers, drinking water, playground, picnic area, off-leash dog area, and recreational facilities are available. Supplies and a coin laundry are nearby in San Luis Obispo. Leashed pets are permitted.

Reservations, fees: Reservations are accepted for groups only (minimum of six campsites). Sites are $18–27 per night, $9 per night for each additional vehicle, $2 per pet per night. Weekly rates available. Two-week maximum stay. Some credit cards accepted. Open year-round.

Directions: From San Luis Obispo, drive 4.5 miles north on Highway 1 to the park entrance on the right side of the highway.

Contact: El Chorro Regional Park, 805/781-5930, www.slocountyparks.com.

13 SANTA MARGARITA KOA
🛶 🐕 🚴 🚐 ⛺

Scenic rating: 6

near Santa Margarita Lake

Map 13.2, page 702

Santa Margarita Lake should have a sign at its entrance that proclaims, "Fishing Only!" That's because the rules here do not allow waterskiing or any water contact, including swimming, wading, using float tubes, and sailboarding. The excellent prospects for bass fishing, along with the prohibitive rules, make this lake a favorite among anglers. Santa Margarita Lake covers nearly 800 acres, most of it long and narrow and set in a dammed-up valley in the foothill country at an elevation of 1,300 feet, just below the Santa Lucia Mountains. Horseback riding is available nearby.

Campsites, facilities: There are 54 sites for tents or RVs up to 40 feet; most have full or partial hookups (30 amps) and one is pull-through. Eleven cabins are also available. Picnic tables and fire grills are provided. Restrooms with flush toilets and showers, drinking water, modem access, seasonal swimming pool, playground, coin laundry, convenience store, dump station, and propane gas are available. Leashed pets are permitted.

Reservations, fees: Reservations are accepted at 800/562-5619. Sites are $24–35 per night, $3–4 per person per night for more than two people. Some credit cards accepted. Open year-round.

Directions: From San Luis Obispo, drive north on U.S. 101 for eight miles to the Highway 58/Santa Margarita exit. Take that exit and drive through the town of Santa Margarita to Estrada. Turn right on Estrada and drive eight miles (Estrada becomes Pozo Road) to Santa Margarita Lake Road. Turn left and drive 0.5 mile to the campground on the right.

Contact: Santa Margarita KOA, 805/438-5618, fax 805/438-3576, www.koa.com.

14 LA PANZA
🚶 🐕 🚙 ⛺

Scenic rating: 3

in Los Padres National Forest

Map 13.2, page 702

This primitive spot sits at 2,200 feet in the La Panza Range, an oak woodland area that is crisscrossed by numerous off-highway-vehicle and hiking trails and small streams. Some of the trails are not maintained. The Machesna Mountain Wilderness is to the south. Water is scarce.

Campsites, facilities: There are 15 sites for tents or RVs up to 16 feet (no hookups). Picnic tables and fire grills are provided. Vault toilets are available. There is no drinking water. Garbage must be packed out. Leashed pets are permitted.

Reservations, fees: Reservations are not accepted. There is no camping fee. An

Adventure Pass ($30 annual fee) or a $5 daily fee per parked vehicle is required. Open year-round.

Directions: From San Luis Obispo, drive eight miles north on U.S. 101. Turn east on Highway 58 and drive four miles (two miles past Santa Margarita). Turn southeast on Pozo Road and drive for 16 miles to the town of Pozo and Pozo Grade Road. Turn right and drive five miles to Red Hill Road. Turn right and drive one mile to the camp on the left.

Contact: Los Padres National Forest, Santa Lucia Ranger District, 805/925-9538, fax 805/961-5781.

15 MONTAÑA DE ORO STATE PARK
🏃 🚴 🛶 🐾 🚐 ⛺

Scenic rating: 9

near Morro Bay

Map 13.2, page 702

This sprawling chunk of primitive land includes coastline, 8,500 acres of foothills, and 1.373-foot Valencia Peak. The name means "Mountain of Gold," named for the golden wildflowers that bloom here in the spring. The camp is perched near a bluff, and while there are no sweeping views from campsites, they await nearby. Bluffs Trail is one of the best easy coastal walks anywhere, offering stunning views of the ocean and cliffs and, in the spring, tons of wildflowers over the course of just 1.5 miles. Another hiking option at the park is to climb Valencia Peak, a little butt-kicker of an ascent that tops out at 1,373 feet, providing more panoramic coastal views. These are the two best hikes among 50 miles of trails for horses, mountain bikers, and hikers, with trails accessible right out of the campground.

Campsites, facilities: There are 48 sites for tents or RVs up to 27 feet (no hookups), four walk-in (50–150-yard walk) environmental sites, four equestrian sites, and two group equestrian sites for up to 50 people and 25 horses. Picnic tables and fire grills are provided, but fires are not allowed at the environmental sites. Vault toilets are available. Drinking water is available only at the main campground; stock water is available at the equestrian campground. There is limited corral space and single-site equestrian camps with two stalls each. Garbage from equestrian and environmental sites must be packed out. Supplies and a coin laundry are available five miles away in the town of Los Osos. Leashed pets are permitted, except at the environmental sites and on trails.

Reservations, fees: Reservations are accepted ($7.50 reservation fee) at 800/444-PARK (800/444-7275) or www.reserveamerica.com. Sites are $11–15 per night, $25–30 for equestrian sites, $3 per night for each additional vehicle, $75 per night for group sites. Open year-round.

Directions: From Morro Bay, drive two miles south on Highway 1. Turn on South Bay Boulevard and drive four miles to Los Osos. Turn right on Los Osos Valley Road and drive five miles (it becomes Pecho Valley Road) to the park.

Contact: Montaña de Oro State Park, 805/528-0513; San Luis Obispo Coast District, 805/927-2065, www.parks.ca.gov.

16 HI MOUNTAIN
🏃 🐾 🚐 ⛺

Scenic rating: 4

in Los Padres National Forest

Map 13.2, page 702

At an elevation of 2,800 feet, this camp is on the edge of the Santa Lucia Wilderness. You can reach the Hi Mountain Lookout if you continue driving 1.5 miles past the campground. The Lookout has awesome 360-degree views from the 3,180-foot summit.

Campsites, facilities: There are 11 sites for tents or RVs up to 16 feet (no hookups). Note that trailers are not recommended. Picnic tables and fire grills are provided. Vault toilets are available. There is no drinking water. Garbage must be packed out. Leashed pets are permitted.

Reservations, fees: No reservations are accepted. There is no camping fee, and an Adventure Pass is not required. Open year-round (road may be closed during heavy rains).

Directions: From San Luis Obispo, drive eight miles north on U.S. 101. Turn east on Highway 58 and drive four miles (four miles past Santa Margarita) to Pozo Road/Santa Margarita Lake. Turn right (southeast) and drive 16 miles to the town of Pozo and Hi Mountain Road. Turn right on Hi Mountain Road (next to the Pozo fire station) and drive four miles to the campground.

Contact: Los Padres National Forest, Santa Lucia Ranger District, 805/925-9538, fax 805/961-5781.

17 AVILA HOT SPRINGS SPA AND RV PARK

Scenic rating: 6

on San Luis Obispo Bay

Map 13.2, page 702

The hot mineral pool here is a featured attraction. This is a natural mineral hot springs with an artesian well that produces water directly into the spas at 104°F. A pizza kitchen and snack bar are available as well. Nearby recreation options include Avila State Beach and Pismo State Beach.

Campsites, facilities: There are 21 sites with full hookups for RVs, 17 tent sites in three areas, and 21 cabins. Some sites are pull-through. Picnic tables and fire grills (at some sites) are provided. Restrooms with showers, cable TV, heated swimming pool, hot mineral pool, spa, dump station, recreation room, arcade, pizza kitchen, and group barbecue pits are available. An 18-hole golf course is nearby. Leashed pets are permitted. Some facilities are wheelchair-accessible.

Reservations, fees: Reservations are accepted

at 805/595-2359. Sites are $45 per night, $5 per night for each additional vehicle. Some credit cards accepted. Open year-round.

Directions: From San Luis Obispo, drive south on U.S. 101 for nine miles to the Avila Beach Drive exit. Take that exit and drive a short distance to the park at 250 Avila Beach Drive.

Contact: Avila Hot Springs Spa and RV Park, 805/595-2359, www.avilahotsprings.com.

18 LOPEZ LAKE RECREATION AREA

Scenic rating: 7

near Arroyo Grande

Map 13.2, page 702

Lopez Lake has become an example of how to do something right, with specially marked areas set aside exclusively for waterskiing, personal watercraft, and sailboarding, and the rest of the lake designated for fishing and low-speed boating. There are also full facilities for swimming, with a big swimming beach and two giant water slides, a children's wading pool, and a nice beach area. Another bonus is the scenic boat tours available on Saturdays, which get plenty of takers. A 25-mile trail system provides opportunities for biking, hiking, and horseback riding. That makes it perfect for just about everyone and, with good bass fishing, the lake has become very popular, especially on spring weekends when the bite is on. Other species include trout, bluegill, crappie, and catfish. Lopez Lake is set amid oak woodlands southeast of San Luis Obispo. The lake is shaped something like a horseshoe, has 940 surface acres with 22 miles of shoreline when full, and gets excellent weather most of the year. Features of the park in summer are ranger-led hikes and campfire shows. Many campsites overlook the lake or are nestled among oaks.

Campsites, facilities: There are 143 sites with full hookups (20 and 30 amps) for tents or RVs, 211 sites for tents, an overflow site with no hookups for tents or RVs of any length, and six group sites for 50–100 people each. Picnic tables and fire rings are provided. Restrooms with showers, playground, children's wading pool, coin laundry, convenience store, ice, snack bar, marina, boat ramp, mooring, boat fuel (dry land fueling only), tackle, boat rentals, and water slides are available. Some facilities are wheelchair-accessible. Leashed pets are permitted.

Reservations, fees: Reservations are required by phone or website. Sites are $18–27 per night, $9 per night for each additional vehicle, $96–192 per night for a group site, $2 per dog per night. Boat launching is $6 per day. Group rates available. Two-week maximum stay in summer. Some credit cards accepted. Open year-round.

Directions: From Arroyo Grande on U.S. 101, take the Grand Avenue exit. Turn east and drive through Arroyo Grande to Lopez Drive. Turn left (northeast) on Lopez Drive and drive 10 miles to the park.

Contact: Lopez Lake Recreation Area, 805/788-2381; Lopez Lake Marina, 805/489-1006, www.slocountyparks.com.

19 PISMO STATE BEACH: NORTH BEACH

🚶 🚴 🏊 🏕 ♿ 🚐 ⛺

Scenic rating: 7

in Pismo State Beach

Map 13.2, page 702

Pismo State Beach is nationally renowned for its beaches, dunes, and, in the good old days, clamming. The adjacent tree-lined dunes make for great walks or, for kids, great rolls. The beach is popular with bird-watchers, and the habitat supports the largest wintering colony of monarch butterflies in the United States. Plan on a reservation and having plenty of company in summer. This is an exceptionally popular state beach, either as an ultimate destination or as a stopover for folks cruising Highway 1. There are four

restaurants and ATV rentals within two blocks. A trolley service provides a shuttle to the surrounding community. The clamming on minus low tides was legendary. Poaching has devastated the clamming here, with no legal clams taken for years.

Campsites, facilities: There are 103 sites for tents or RVs up to 36 feet (no hookups). Fire grills and picnic tables are provided. Restrooms with showers and flush toilets, drinking water, Wi-Fi, and a dump station are available. Horseback-riding facilities, grocery store, ATV rentals, restaurants, coin laundry, and propane gas are nearby. Some facilities are wheelchair-accessible. Leashed pets are permitted at the campground and on the beach.

Reservations, fees: Reservations are accepted ($7.50 reservation fee) at 800/444-PARK (800/444-7275) or www.reserveamerica.com. Sites are $20–25 per night, and $6 per night for each additional vehicle. Open year-round.

Directions: On Highway 1 in Pismo Beach, take the North Beach/State Campground exit (well signed) and drive to the park entrance.

Contact: Pismo State Beach, 805/773-2334, www.parks.ca.gov.

20 PISMO COAST VILLAGE RV RESORT

🚶 🚴 🏊 🏕 🐕 ♿ 🚐

Scenic rating: 7

in Pismo Beach

Map 13.2, page 702

This big-time RV park gets a lot of use by Highway 1 cruisers. Set near the ocean, its location is a plus. Pismo Beach is well known for its sand dunes and beautiful coastal frontage.

Campsites, facilities: There are 400 sites with full hookups (30 and 50 amps) for RVs up to 40 feet. No tents. Picnic tables, fire rings, and satellite TV are provided. Restrooms with showers, modem access, Wi-Fi, playgrounds, heated swimming pool, coin laundry, convenience store, firewood, ice, recreation room, propane gas, seasonal recreation programs, restaurant, RV supplies and repair, bicycle rentals, and a nine-hole miniature golf course are available. Leashed pets are permitted, with restrictions on certain breeds. Some facilities are wheelchair-accessible.

Reservations, fees: Reservations are accepted at 888/RV-BEACH (888/782-3224). Sites are $34–47 per night. Group discounts available in the off-season. Some credit cards accepted. Open year-round.

Directions: In Pismo Beach, drive on Highway 1/Pacific Coast Highway to the park at 165 South Dolliver Street/Highway 1.

Contact: Pismo Coast Village, 805/773-1811, fax 805/773-1507, www.pismocoastvillage.com.

21 LE SAGE RIVIERA

Scenic rating: 6

near Pismo State Beach

Map 13.2, page 702

This is a year-round RV park that can serve as headquarters for folks who are interested in visiting several nearby attractions, including neighboring Pismo State Beach and Lopez Lake, 10 miles to the east. The park is set on the ocean side of Highway 1, 250 yards from the beach. Note that many sites are filled with seasonal renters.

Campsites, facilities: There are 60 sites with full hookups (30 and 50 amps) for RVs up to 55 feet; many are pull-through. No tents. Picnic tables are provided. Restrooms with showers, drinking water, and coin laundry are available. Stores, restaurants, and golf courses are nearby. Some facilities are wheelchair-accessible. Leashed pets are permitted with certain restrictions.

Reservations, fees: Reservations are accepted. Sites are $25–55 per night, $3 per night for each additional vehicle. Holiday rates are higher. Winter discount. Some credit cards accepted. Open year-round.

Directions: In Pismo Beach on Highway 1, drive south on Highway 1 for 0.5 mile to the park on the right (west side) to 319 North Highway 1 (in Grover Beach).

Contact: Le Sage Riviera, 805/489-5506, fax 805/489-2103.

22 OCEANO MEMORIAL PARK AND CAMPGROUND

Scenic rating: 7

in Oceano

Map 13.2, page 702

This San Luis Obispo county park is extremely busy during the summer and busy the rest of the year. The location is a bonus; it's set within a quarter mile of the Pismo State Beach entrance, the site of great sand dunes and wide-open ocean frontage. Oceano has a fishing lagoon.

Campsites, facilities: There are 22 sites for tents or RVs up to 40 feet (full hookups). No pull-through sites. Picnic tables and fire grills are provided. Drinking water, restrooms with coin showers and flush toilets, basketball court, horseshoes, athletic field, and picnic area are available. A playground, coin laundry, grocery store, and propane gas are available nearby. Leashed pets are permitted.

Reservations, fees: Reservations are not accepted. RV sites are $23–27 per night, $18 per night for tents, $9 per night for each additional vehicle, $2 per pet per night. Weekly rates are available. Four-week maximum stay. Open year-round.

Directions: From Pismo Beach, drive south on U.S. 101 to the Pismo Beach/Grand Avenue exit west to Highway 1. Take that exit and turn south on Highway 1 and drive 1.5 miles to Pier Avenue. Turn right on Pier Avenue and drive a short distance to Norswing. Turn left and drive to the end of the street and

Mendel Avenue. Turn right and drive to Air Park Drive. Turn right and drive to the park on the right.

Contact: Oceano Memorial Park and Campground, 805/781-5930, fax 805/781-1102, www.slocountyparks.com.

23 PISMO STATE BEACH: OCEANO
🏃 🚴 🏊 🛶 🎣 🐕 ♿ 🚐 ⛰

Scenic rating: 6

in Pismo State Beach

Map 13.2, page 702

This is a prized state beach campground, with Pismo Beach and its sand dunes and coastal frontage a centerpiece for the state park system. Its location on the central coast on Highway 1, as well as its beauty and recreational opportunities, makes it extremely popular. It fills to capacity most nights, and reservations are usually a necessity. (For more information on Pismo State Beach, see *North Beach* listing in this chapter.)

Campsites, facilities: There are 40 sites for tents or RVs up to 31 feet (no hookups), 42 sites with partial hookups for trailers and RVs up to 36 feet. Picnic tables and fire grills are provided. Drinking water and restrooms with flush toilets and coin showers are available. Horseback-riding facilities, grocery store, coin laundry, dump station, restaurants, and gas stations are nearby. Some facilities are wheelchair accessible, including a fishing overlook at Oceano Lagoon. Leashed pets are permitted at the campground and beach.

Reservations, fees: Reservations are accepted ($7.50 reservation fee) at 800/444-PARK (800/444-7275) or www.reserveamerica.com. Sites are $20–34 per night, $5 per night for additional vehicle. Open year-round.

Directions: From Pismo Beach, drive two miles south on Highway 1 to Pier Avenue. Turn right and drive 0.2 mile to the campground entrance.

Contact: Pismo State Beach, 805/473-7220, www.parks.ca.gov.

24 OCEANO DUNES STATE VEHICULAR RECREATION AREA
🏃 🏊 🛶 🏕 🚐 ⛰

Scenic rating: 6

south of Pismo Beach

Map 13.2, page 702

This is "national headquarters" for all-terrain vehicles (ATVs)—you know, those three- and four-wheeled motorcycles that turn otherwise normal people into lunatics. The camps are along one to three miles of beach and 1,500 acres of open sand dunes, and since not many make the walk to the campsites, four-wheel drives or ATVs are needed for access. The area covers 3,600 acres, including 5.5 miles of beach open for vehicles and 1,500 acres of sand dunes available for OHVs. They roam wild on the dunes here; that's the law, so don't go planning a quiet stroll. If you don't like 'em, you are strongly advised to go elsewhere. If this is your game, have fun and try to keep from killing yourself. Each fall, the "National Sand Drags" are held here. More than one million people visit here each year. High tides can limit access. A beach towing service for RVs and trailers is available. Activities include swimming, surfing, surf fishing, horseback riding, and bird- and nutcase-watching.

Campsites, facilities: There are 1,000 sites for tents or RVs of any length (no hookups). Chemical and vault toilets are provided. There is no drinking water. Drinking water, horseback-riding facilities, grocery store, coin laundry, restaurants, gas stations, Wi-Fi, and a dump station are available nearby. Leashed pets are permitted at the campground and beach.

Reservations, fees: Reservations are accepted ($7.50 reservation fee) at 800/444-PARK (800/444-7275) or www.reserveamerica.com.

Sites are $10 per night per vehicle. Open year-round.

Directions: Drive on U.S. 101 to Arroyo Grande and take the Grand Avenue exit. Turn left (toward the beach) on Grand Avenue and drive four miles until the road ends at the North Entrance beach camping area. The South Entrance is one mile south. To get there from Highway 1, take Pier Avenue.

Contact: Oceano Dunes, 805/473-7230, fax 805/473-7234, www.parks.ca.gov.

25 COLSON CANYON
🥾 🐕 5% ⛺

Scenic rating: 6

in Los Padres National Forest

Map 13.3, page 703

Colson is set just a mile from the western border of Los Padres National Forest, making it far easier to reach than other Forest Service camps in this region. The camp is named after the canyon in which it sits, Colson Canyon. This area really has just two seasons when you should visit, spring and fall. In the summer, it's hot and dry, with no water available, and is scarcely fit for habitation. The elevation is 2,100 feet.

Campsites, facilities: There are five tent sites. Picnic tables and fire grills are provided. No toilet is available (because of vandalism), so bring your own portable toilet. There is no drinking water. Garbage must be packed out. Leashed pets are permitted.

Reservations, fees: Reservations are not accepted. There is no camping fee, and an Adventure Pass is not required. Open year-round.

Directions: From U.S. 101 in Santa Maria, take the Betteravia Road exit east and drive eight miles to a fork with Santa Maria Mesa Road. Bear left at the fork and drive southeast on Santa Maria Mesa Road to Tepusquet Road. Turn left on Tepusquet Road and drive 6.5 miles to Colson Canyon Road. Turn right

on Colson Canyon Road/Forest Road 11N04 and drive four miles to the campground on the left. Colson Canyon Road can be impassable when wet.

Contact: Los Padres National Forest, Santa Lucia Ranger District, 805/925-9538, fax 805/961-5781.

26 WAGON FLAT
🥾 🐕 5% ⛺

Scenic rating: 6

on the North Fork of La Brea Creek in Los Padres National Forest

Map 13.3, page 703

Not many folks know about this obscure spot, and if it's a hot, late-summer day, they're probably better off for it. The camp is set at an elevation of 1,400 feet, pretty in spring, but in summer often a hot, dry region of Los Padres National Forest. The bright spot is little La Brea Creek, which runs by the camp.

Campsites, facilities: There are three sites for tents. Picnic tables and fire grills are provided. Vault toilets are available. Drinking water is not available. Garbage must be packed out. Leashed pets are permitted.

Reservations, fees: Reservations are not accepted. There is no camping fee. An Adventure Pass ($30 annual fee or $5 daily pass) per parked vehicle is required. Open year-round, road conditions permitting.

Directions: From U.S. 101 in Santa Maria, take the Betteravia Road exit east and drive eight miles to a fork with Santa Maria Mesa Road. Bear left at the fork and drive southeast on Santa Maria Mesa Road to Tepusquet Road. Turn left on Tepusquet Road and drive 6.5 miles to Colson Canyon Road. Turn right on Colson Canyon Road/Forest Road 11N04 and drive seven miles to La Brea Canyon Road. Turn left and drive four miles to the campground. Note: In the winter and spring, multiple stream crossings are required and a high-clearance vehicle may be necessary; Colson Canyon Road can become impassable.

Contact: Los Padres National Forest, Santa Lucia Ranger District, 805/925-9538, fax 805/961-5781.

27 BARREL SPRINGS

Scenic rating: 7

in Los Padres National Forest

Map 13.3, page 703

This small, primitive camp sits at 1,000 feet in elevation along La Brea Creek and is shaded by the oaks in La Brea Canyon. It is named after nearby Barrel Springs, which forms a small creek and feeds into La Brea Creek.

Campsites, facilities: There are six tent sites. Picnic tables and fire grills are provided. Vault toilets are available. There is no drinking water. Garbage must be packed out. Leashed pets are permitted.

Reservations, fees: Reservations are not accepted and there is no camping fee. An Adventure Pass ($30 annual fee or $5 daily pass) per parked vehicle is required. Open year-round, but access roads may be closed during and after heavy rains.

Directions: From U.S. 101 in Santa Maria, take the Betteravia Road exit east and drive eight miles to a fork with Santa Maria Mesa Road. Bear left at the fork and drive southeast on Santa Maria Mesa Road to Tepusquet Road. Turn left on Tepusquet Road and drive 6.5 miles to Colson Canyon Road. Turn right on Colson Canyon Road/Forest Road 11N04 and drive eight miles to the campground. Note: In the winter and spring, multiple stream crossings are required and a high-clearance vehicle may be neccessay; Colson Canyon Road can become impassable.

Contact: Los Padres National Forest, Santa Lucia Ranger District, 805/925-9538, fax 805/961-5781.

28 RIVER PARK

Scenic rating: 4

in Lompoc

Map 13.3, page 703

Before checking in here you'd better get a lesson in how to pronounce Lompoc. It's "Lom-Poke." If you arrive and say, "Hey, it's great to be in Lom-Pock," they might just tell ya to get on back to the other cowpokes. The camp is set next to the lower Santa Ynez River, which looks quite a bit different than it does up in Los Padres National Forest. A small fishing lake within the 45-acre park is stocked with trout and catfish. A camp host and resident ranger are on-site. Side-trip possibilities include the nearby La Purisima Mission State Historic Park and Jalama Beach.

Campsites, facilities: There are 33 sites for RVs up to 40 feet (full hookups), a group camping area for tents or RVs, and an open area for up to five tents. No pull-through sites. Picnic tables and barbecues are provided. Restrooms with flush toilets and coin showers, drinking water, dump station, fishing pond, fitness, trail, sand volleyball, horseshoes, group facilities, and a playground are available. Supplies and a coin laundry are nearby. Leashed pets are permitted with certain restrictions.

Reservations, fees: Reservations are not accepted for family sites but are required for groups at 805/875-8036. Sites are $5–15 per night, $10 per night for each additional vehicle, $5 per night for hike-in/bike-in sites, $1 per pet per night. Group fees are $5 per night per tent, $10 per night per RV, with a $25 minimum. Weekly rates available. Some credit cards accepted. Open year-round.

Directions: In Lompoc, drive to the junction of Highway 246 and Sweeney Road at the southwest edge of town and continue to the park at 401 East Highway 246.

Contact: Lompoc Parks and Recreation Department, 805/875-8100, fax 805/736-5195, www.ci.lompoc.ca.us.

29 FLYING FLAGS RV RESORT AND CAMPGROUND

Scenic rating: 3

near Solvang

Map 13.3, page 703

This is one of the few privately operated parks in the area that welcomes tenters as well as RVers. Nearby side trips include the Santa Ynez Mission, just east of Solvang. The town of Solvang is of interest. It was originally a small Danish settlement that has expanded since the 1920s yet managed to keep its cultural heritage intact through the years. The town is exceptionally clean, an example of how to do something right. Wineries and casinos are nearby.

Campsites, facilities: There are 256 sites with full or partial hookups (30 and 50 amps) for RVs of any length and 100 sites for tents. Most sites are pull-through. Picnic tables are provided. Restrooms with showers, cable TV, playground, heated swimming pool, spa, coin laundry, convenience store, dump station, ice, recreation room, modem access, free Wi-Fi, arcade, five clubhouses, group facilities, and propane gas are available. A nine-hole golf course, boat launch, and boat rentals are nearby. Some facilities are wheelchair-accessible. Leashed pets are permitted with certain restrictions.

Reservations, fees: Reservations are accepted by phone or website. Sites are $21–46 per night, $3 per person per night for more than two people, $5 per night for each additional vehicle, $1 per pet per night for more than two dogs. Holiday rates are higher. Monthly rates available. Open year-round. Some credit cards accepted.

Directions: From Santa Barbara, drive 45 miles north on U.S. 101 to Highway 246. Turn west (left) on Highway 246 and drive about a half mile to Avenue of the Flags (a four-way stop). Turn left on Avenue of the Flags and drive about one block to the campground entrance on the left at 180 Avenue of the Flags.

Contact: Flying Flags RV Resort and Campground, 805/688-3716, fax 805/688-9245, www.flyingflags.com.

30 JALAMA BEACH COUNTY PARK

Scenic rating: 8

near Lompoc on the Pacific Ocean

Map 13.3, page 703

This is a pretty spot set where Jalama Creek empties into the ocean, about five miles north of Point Conception and just south of Vandenberg Air Force Base. The area is known for its sunsets and beachcombing. The camp is so popular that a waiting list is common in summer. Activities include surfing, sailboarding, and fishing for perch, cabezon, kelp bass, and halibut.

Campsites, facilities: There are 117 sites for tents or RVs up to 40 feet, and two group sites for 7–15 vehicles each. Some sites have electrical (30 amps) hookups. Picnic tables and fire pits are provided. Restrooms with flush toilets and showers, drinking water, dump station, general store, snack bar, bait and tackle, picnic area, firewood, and ice are available. Note that the nearest gas station is 20 miles away. Leashed pets are permitted, but a vaccination certificate is required. Some facilities are wheelchair-accessible.

Reservations, fees: Reservations are not accepted for individual sites. Sites are $18–25 per night, $8 per night for each additional vehicle, $144 per night for a group site, $3 per pet per night. Weekly rates available in the off-season. Some credit cards accepted. Open year-round.

Directions: From Lompoc, drive about five miles south on Highway 1. Turn southwest on Jalama Road and drive 14 miles to the park.

Contact: Jalama Beach County Park, 805/736-

6316, fax 805/735-8020 or 805/736-3504, www.santabarbaraparks.org.

31 GAVIOTA STATE PARK

Scenic rating: 10

near Santa Barbara

Map 13.3, page 703   BEST (

This is the granddaddy, the biggest of the three state beaches along U.S. 101 northwest of Santa Barbara. Spectacular and beautiful, the park covers 2,700 acres, providing trails for hiking and horseback riding, as well as a mile-long stretch of stunning beach frontage. Gaviota means "seagull" and was first named by the soldiers of the Portola Expedition in 1769, who learned why you always wear a hat (or a helmet) when they are passing overhead. The ambitious can hike the beach to get more seclusion. Trails to Gaviota Overlook (1.5 miles) and Gaviota Peak (3.2 miles one-way) provide lookouts with drop-dead gorgeous views of the coast and Channel Islands. Want more? There is also a 0.5-mile trail to the hot springs. This park is known for being windy and for shade being hard to find. Unfortunately, a railroad trestle crosses above the day-use parking lot. You know what that means? Of course you do. It means trains run through here day and night, and with them, noise. This is a popular beach for swimming and surf fishing, as well as boat launching and fishing from the pier.

Campsites, facilities: There are 41 sites for tents or RVs up to 30 feet (no hookups) and an area for hike-in/bike-in sites. Picnic tables and fire grills are provided. Restrooms with flush toilets and coin showers, drinking water, summer lifeguard service, and a boat hoist (two-ton maximum weight) are available. Some facilities are wheelchair-accessible. A convenience store (open summer only) is nearby. Leashed pets are permitted at campsites.

Reservations, fees: Reservations are not accepted. Sites are $20–25 per night, $8 per night for each additional vehicle, $3 per person per night for hike-in/bike-in sites. Boat launching is $8 per day. One-week maximum stay in summer and two-week maximum in winter. Open year-round.

Directions: From Santa Barbara, drive north on U.S. 101 for 30 miles to the Gaviota State Beach exit. Take that exit and turn west and drive a short distance to the park entrance.

Contact: Gaviota State Park, Channel Coast District 805/968-1033, www.parks.ca.gov.

32 REFUGIO STATE BEACH

Scenic rating: 9

near Santa Barbara

Map 13.3, page 703

Refugio State Beach is the smallest of the three beautiful state beaches along U.S. 101 north of Santa Barbara. The others are Gaviota and El Capitan, which also have campgrounds. Palm trees planted close to Refugio Creek provide a unique look to this beach and campground. This is a great spot for family campers with bikes, with a paved two-mile bike trail connecting Refugio campground with El Capitan. Fishing is often good in this area of the coast. As with all state beaches and private camps on the Coast Highway, reservations are strongly advised and often a necessity throughout the vacation season.

Campsites, facilities: There are 67 sites for tents or RVs up to 30 feet (no hookups), one hike-in/bike-in site, and three group sites for tents or RVs that can accommodate up to 80 people and 25 vehicles. Picnic tables and fire grills are provided. Restrooms with flush toilets and coin showers, drinking water, summer lifeguard service, summer convenience store, and food services are available. Some facilities are wheelchair-accessible. Leashed pets are permitted at campsites.

Reservations, fees: Reservations are accepted ($7.50 reservation fee) at 800/444-PARK (800/444-7275) or www.reserveamerica.com.

Sites are $25–35 per night, $8 per night for each additional vehicle, $3 per night per person for hike-in/bike-in sites, $125–180 per night for the group site. One-week maximum stay in summer and two-week maximum in winter. Open year-round, weather permitting.
Directions: From Santa Barbara, drive northwest on U.S. 101 for 23 miles to the Refugio State Beach exit. Take that exit and turn west (left) and drive a short distance to the campground entrance.
Contact: Refugio State Beach 805/968-1711, Channel Coast District 805/968-1033, www.parks.ca.gov.

33 EL CAPITAN CANYON

Scenic rating: 8

near Goleta

Map 13.4, page 703

El Capitan Canyon is a unique campground where you do not bring your own tent, but rather rent permanent safari tents or cabins on-site. The tent cabins are situated on 12-by-14-foot wood platforms, and they come fully furnished with beds and linens. The safari tents are heated and have electricity. The park covers 65 acres in the coastal foothills north of Santa Barbara and offers visitors the best of both worlds: There are 2,200 acres of public land near the camp with backcountry hiking and mountain-biking trails, or for those who prefer the sand and surf, beach access is within walking distance and ocean kayaking and deep-sea fishing trips can be booked at the resort. In the summer live entertainment is available, including a concert series and the "Blues and Barbecue" event every Saturday night. Dogs are strictly prohibited in a mission here to stop the spread of nonnative plants; this in turn has inspired a return of native habitat and the birds and wildlife that rely on it.
Campsites, facilities: There are 26 tent cabins and 96 cabins. No RVs are allowed. Picnic tables and fire pits are provided. Restrooms

with flush toilets and showers, drinking water, heated swimming pool, children's playground, live music (on Saturday nights), volleyball, horseshoes, convenience store, horseback-riding facilities, massage service, free use of bicycles, and firewood are available. Some facilities are wheelchair-accessible. Pets are not allowed.
Reservations, fees: Reservations are recommended at 866/352-2729. The fee is $185–345 per night for a tent cabin. Discounts are available in the off-season. Some credit cards accepted. Open year-round.
Directions: From Santa Barbara, drive about 20 miles northwest on U.S. 101 to the El Capitán State Beach exit. Go straight on the frontage road paralleling the freeway for about 100 yards. Turn right at the sign for El Capitan Canyon on the mountain side of the freeway.
Contact: El Capitan Canyon, 805/685-3887, fax 805/968-6772, www.elcapitancanyon.com.

34 EL CAPITÁN STATE BEACH

Scenic rating: 10

near Santa Barbara

Map 13.3, page 703   BEST (

This is one in a series of beautiful state beaches along the Santa Barbara coast. El Capitán has a sandy beach and rocky tidepools. The water is warm, the swimming good. A stairway descends from the bluffs to the beach, a beautiful setting, and sycamores and oaks line El Capitán Creek. A paved, two-mile bicycle trail is routed to Refugio State Beach, a great family trip. This is a perfect layover for Coast Highway vacationers, and reservations are usually required to assure a spot. Refugio State Beach to the north is another camping option.
Campsites, facilities: There are 130 sites for tents or RVs up to 40 feet, one hike-in/bike-in site, two group sites for tents or RVs that can accommodate 50–125 people each, and three group sites for tents only that

can accommodate 50–125 people each. No hookups. Picnic tables and fire grills are provided. Restrooms with flush toilets and coin showers, drinking water, summer lifeguard service, and a summer convenience store are available. Leashed pets are permitted in the campgrounds, but not on the beach. Some facilities are wheelchair-accessible.

Reservations, fees: Reservations are accepted ($7.50 reservation fee) at 800/444-PARK (800/444-7275) or www.reserveamerica.com. Sites are $25 per night, $8 per night for each additional vehicle, $3 per person per night for hike-in/bike-in sites, $111–280 per night for group sites. One-week maximum stay in summer and two-week maximum in winter. Open year-round, weather permitting.

Directions: From Santa Barbara, drive north on U.S. 101 for 20 miles to the El Capitán State Beach exit. Turn west (left) and drive a short distance to the campground entrance.

Contact: El Capitán State Beach 805/968-1711, Channel Coast District 805/968-1033, www.parks.ca.gov.

35 BATES CANYON
🐕 🏕️

Scenic rating: 7

in Los Padres National Forest

Map 13.4, page 704

This camp is on the northeast flank of the Sierra Madre, along a small stream in Bates Canyon, at 2,900 feet in elevation. Note that the primitive access road out of camp to the south is often gated; it leads to the Sierra Madre Ridge, where a road contours right along the ridge on the border of the San Rafael Wilderness, passing from peak to peak.

Campsites, facilities: There are six tent sites. Picnic tables and fire grills are provided. Vault toilets are available. There is no drinking water. Garbage must be packed out. Leashed pets are permitted.

Reservations, fees: Reservations are not accepted and there is no camping fee. An Adventure Pass ($30 annual fee or $5 daily pass) per parked vehicle is required. Open year-round. Note that access roads can be closed during and after heavy rains.

Directions: From Santa Maria, drive east on Highway 166 for 50 miles to Cottonwood Canyon Road. Turn right on Cottonwood Canyon Road and drive southwest for 7.5 miles to the campground.

Contact: Los Padres National Forest, Santa Lucia Ranger District, 805/925-9538, fax 805/961-5781.

36 ALISO PARK
🥾 🐕 🏕️ ♿ 🚐 🏕️

Scenic rating: 6

in Los Padres National Forest

Map 13.4, page 704

This primitive, quiet camp is set at the foot of the Sierra Madre at 3,200 feet, directly below McPherson Peak (5,749 feet). It is just inside the northeast boundary of Los Padres National Forest, making it easily accessible from Highway 166.

Campsites, facilities: There are 10 sites for tents or RVs up to 28 feet (no hookups). Picnic tables and fire grills are provided. Pit toilets are available. Drinking water is not available. Garbage must be packed out. Some facilities are wheelchair accessible. Leashed pets are permitted.

Reservations, fees: Reservations are not accepted and there is no camping fee. An Adventure Pass ($30 annual fee or $5 daily pass) per parked vehicle is required. Open year-round.

Directions: From Santa Maria, drive east on Highway 166 for 59 miles to Aliso Canyon Road/Forest Road 10N04. Turn right on Aliso Canyon Road/Forest Road 10N04 and drive south about six miles to the campground at the end of the road.

Contact: Los Padres National Forest, Mount Piños Ranger District, 661/245-3731, fax 661/245-1526.

37 BALLINGER

🏠 🚐 ⛺

Scenic rating: 3

in Los Padres National Forest

Map 13.4, page 704

Ballinger Camp is right inside the boundary of Los Padres National Forest in the Mount Piños Ranger District, just six miles east of Highway 33. During the week, this camp receives very little use. On weekends, it gets moderate, even heavy use at times, from OHV owners. Note that the California "green sticker" is required to ride OHVs here. The camp is set at an elevation of 3,000 feet.

Campsites, facilities: There are 20 sites for tents or RVs up to 32 feet (no hookups). Picnic tables and fire grills are provided. Vault toilets are available. No drinking water is available. Garbage must be packed out. Leashed pets are permitted.

Reservations, fees: Reservations are not accepted and there is no camping fee. An Adventure Pass ($30 annual fee or $5 daily pass) per parked vehicle is required. Open year-round.

Directions: From Maricopa, drive southwest on Highway 166 about 14 miles to Highway 33. Turn south on Highway 33 and drive about 3.5 miles to Ballinger Canyon Road/Forest Road 9N10. Turn left (east) and drive three miles to the campground.

Contact: Los Padres National Forest, Mount Piños Ranger District, 661/245-3731, fax 661/245-1526.

38 VALLE VISTA

🏠 🚐 ⛺

Scenic rating: 8

in Los Padres National Forest

Map 13.4, page 704

The view of the southern San Joaquin Valley and the snow-capped Sierra is the highlight of this primitive camp. It is set at 4,800 feet, near the boundary of Los Padres National Forest. Visitors have an opportunity to view condors here, and you can usually spot a few buzzards, er, turkey vultures, circling around. If you don't bring your own water, they might just start circling you. Little-known fact: This camp sits exactly on the border of Kern County and Ventura County.

Campsites, facilities: There are seven sites for tents or RVs up to 22 feet (no hookups). Picnic tables and fire grills are provided. Pit toilets are available. No drinking water is available. Garbage must be packed out. Leashed pets are permitted.

Reservations, fees: Reservations are not accepted and there is no camping fee. An Adventure Pass ($30 annual fee or $5 daily pass) per parked vehicle is required. Open year-round.

Directions: From Maricopa, drive south on Highway 166 about nine miles to Cerro Noroeste Road. Turn left and drive 12 miles to the campground on the left.

Contact: Los Padres National Forest, Mount Piños Ranger District, 661/245-3731, fax 661/245-1526.

39 CABALLO

🐕 🚐 ⛺

Scenic rating: 4

in Los Padres National Forest

Map 13.4, page 704

Caballo is set at 5,850 feet on a small creek that is the headwaters for Santiago Creek, on the northern flank of Mount Abel. The creek flows only about 10 days a year, usually before the opening of the campground, so do not count on it for water. It is one of several primitive camps in the immediate area—a take-your-pick offer. But it's an offer not many folks even know about.

Campsites, facilities: There are six sites for tents or RVs up to 16 feet (no hookups). Picnic tables and fire grills are provided. Pit toilets are available. No drinking water is available.

Garbage must be packed out. Leashed pets are permitted.

Reservations, fees: Reservations are not accepted and there is no camping fee. An Adventure Pass ($30 annual fee or $5 daily pass) per parked vehicle is required. Open early May through October, weather permitting.

Directions: Drive on I-5 to just south of Lebec to the Frazier Park exit. Take that exit and drive west on Frazier Mountain Road to the town of Lake of the Woods and Cuddy Valley Road. Continue straight on Cuddy Valley Road for six miles to Mil Potrero Highway (signed "Pine Mountain Club"). Turn right and drive 10 miles to Forest Road 9N27. Turn right and drive a short distance to the campground. Note: To reach Marian campground, continue for another mile.

Contact: Los Padres National Forest, Mount Piños Ranger District, 661/245-3731, fax 661/245-1526.

40 MARIAN

Scenic rating: 4

in Los Padres National Forest

Map 13.4, page 704

Marian is extremely primitive, set on the outskirts of Los Padres National Forest at 6,600 feet in elevation, between Brush Mountain to the immediate northwest and San Emigdio Mountain to the immediate southeast. A primitive route out of camp leads three miles to the San Emigdio summit, 7,495 feet in elevation. A network of Forest Service roads provides access to a number of other camps in the area, as well as to Mount Abel (8,286 feet) and Mount Piños (8,831 feet). If the access gate is locked, reaching this camp requires a two-mile hike; nearby Toad Spring and Caballo are smaller but more easily accessible. Note that not only is no drinking water available, but there are no toilets either.

Campsites, facilities: There are five sites for tents or RVs up to 16 feet (no hookups). Picnic tables and fire grills are provided. No drinking water or toilets are available, so bring your own. Garbage must be packed out. Leashed pets are permitted.

Reservations, fees: Reservations are not accepted and there is no camping fee. An Adventure Pass ($30 annual fee or $5 daily pass) per parked vehicle is required. Open early May through October, weather permitting.

Directions: Drive on I-5 to just south of Lebec to the Frazier Park exit. Take that exit and drive west on Frazier Mountain Road to the town of Lake of the Woods and Cuddy Valley Road. Continue straight on Cuddy Valley Road for six miles to Mil Potrero Highway (signed "Pine Mountain Club"). Turn right and drive 10 miles to Forest Road 9N27. Turn right and drive one mile (passing Caballo campground) to the camp. Note: Four-wheel-drive or high-clearance vehicles are recommended.

Contact: Los Padres National Forest, Mount Piños Ranger District, 661/245-3731, fax 661/245-1526.

41 TOAD SPRINGS

Scenic rating: 8

in Los Padres National Forest

Map 13.4, page 704

Toad Springs is set at 5,700 feet near Apache Saddle, on the northwest flank of Mount Abel (8,286 feet). It is at the head of Quatal Canyon with a spectacular badlands landscape. No water or toilets are available, so forget this one for your honeymoon. Note that a landslide destroyed a primitive trail (about a mile out of camp) that once was routed south out of camp for six miles to Mesa Springs and a trail camp. It is considered too dangerous for use.

Campsites, facilities: There are five sites for tents or RVs up to 16 feet (no hookups). Picnic tables and fire grills are provided. No drinking water or toilet is available, so bring your own. Garbage must be packed out. Leashed pets are permitted.

Reservations, fees: Reservations are not accepted and there is no camping fee. An Adventure Pass ($30 annual fee or $5 daily pass) per parked vehicle is required. Open early May through October, weather permitting.

Directions: Drive on I-5 to just south of Lebec to the Frazier Park exit. Take that exit and drive west on Frazier Mountain Road to the town of Lake of the Woods and Cuddy Valley Road. Continue straight on Cuddy Valley Road for six miles to Mil Potrero Highway (signed "Pine Mountain Club"). Turn right and drive 10 miles to the campground on the left.

Contact: Los Padres National Forest, Mount Piños Ranger District, 661/245-3731, fax 661/245-1526.

42 CAMPO ALTO
👣 🐕 5% ♿ 🚙 ⛺

Scenic rating: 6

in Los Padres National Forest

Map 13.4, page 704

Campo Alto means "High Camp," and you'll find that the name fits when you visit here. The camp is set high (8,250 feet) on Cerro Noroeste/Mount Abel in Los Padres National Forest. Don't show up thirsty, as there's no drinking water. About half a mile from camp there is a trailhead on the southeast side of the road. From here, you can hike two miles to Grouse Mountain, and in another mile, reach remote, hike-in Sheep Camp.

Campsites, facilities: There are 17 sites for tents or RVs up to 22 feet (no hookups). Picnic tables and fire grills (stoves) are provided. Pit toilets are available. No drinking water is available. Garbage must be packed out. Some facilities are wheelchair accessible. Leashed pets are permitted.

Reservations, fees: Reservations are not accepted and there is no camping fee. An Adventure Pass ($30 annual fee or $5 daily pass) per parked vehicle is required. Open May through October, weather permitting.

Directions: Drive on I-5 to just south of Lebec to the Frazier Park exit. Take that exit and drive west on Frazier Mountain Road to the town of Lake of the Woods and Cuddy Valley Road. Continue straight on Cuddy Valley Road and drive six miles to Mil Potrero Highway (signed "Pine Mountain Club"). Turn right and drive nine miles to Cerro Noroeste Road (Forest Road 9N07). Turn left and drive nine miles to the campground.

Contact: Los Padres National Forest, Mount Piños Ranger District, 661/245-3731, fax 661/245-1526.

43 NETTLE SPRINGS
👣 🐕 🚙 ⛺

Scenic rating: 4

in Los Padres National Forest

Map 13.4, page 704

This remote camp borders the Chumash Wilderness, set near the end of a Forest Service road in Apache Canyon. A mile east of camp, via the access road, is a primitive trailhead on the left side. This trail is routed four miles to Mesa Springs and a trail camp. The elevation is 4,400 feet.

Campsites, facilities: There are 11 sites for tents or RVs up to 22 feet (no hookups). Picnic tables and fire grills are provided. Pit toilets and drinking water are available. Garbage must be packed out. Leashed pets are permitted.

Reservations, fees: Reservations are not accepted and there is no camping fee. An Adventure Pass ($30 annual fee or $5 daily pass) per parked vehicle is required. Open year-round.

Directions: From Maricopa, drive 14 miles south on Highway 166 to the Highway 33 exit. Turn south on Highway 33 and drive about 13 miles to Apache Canyon Road (Forest Road 8N06). Turn left and drive about 11 miles to the campground. Note: The last 10 miles are rough and high-clearance vehicles are advised.

Contact: Los Padres National Forest, Mount Piños Ranger District, 661/245-3731, fax 661/245-1526.

44 MOUNT PIÑOS

Scenic rating: 7

in Los Padres National Forest

Map 13.4, page 704

This camp is set at 7,800 feet, one of three camps on the eastern flank of Mount Piños (8,831 feet). This is one of the few places on earth where it is possible to see flying California condors, the largest bird in North America. Note that a once-popular drive to the top of Mount Piños for beautiful and sweeping views is now closed after being recognized as a Chumash holy site. There's access to the Mount Piños summit trail 2.5 miles away on Mil Potrero Highway at the Chula Vista parking area. From there it's about two miles to the summit, which is a designated botanical area. July and August usually are the best months for wildflower displays. McGill provides a nearby camping alternative.

Campsites, facilities: There are 19 sites for tents or RVs up to 16 feet (no hookups). Picnic tables and fire grills are provided. Pit toilets and drinking water are available. Some facilities are wheelchair accessible. Leashed pets are permitted.

Reservations, fees: Reservations are not accepted. Sites are $14 per night. Open late May through October, weather permitting.

Directions: Drive on I-5 to just south of Lebec to the Frazier Park exit. Take that exit and drive west on Frazier Mountain Road to the town of Lake of the Woods and Cuddy Valley Road. Continue straight on Cuddy Valley Road and drive about six miles to Mount Piños

Highway. Bear left and drive five miles (the road name changes several times, but stay on the main road) to the campground.

Contact: Los Padres National Forest, Mount Piños Ranger District, 661/245-3731, fax 661/245-1526.

45 GILL

Scenic rating: 6

near Mount Piños in Los Padres National Forest

Map 13.4, page 704

The camp is set at 7,400 feet, about four miles from the top of nearby Mount Piños. Although the road is closed to the top of Mount Piños, there are numerous hiking and biking trails in the area that provide spectacular views. On clear days, there are vantage points to the high Sierra, the San Joaquin Valley, and Antelope Valley.

Campsites, facilities: There are 73 sites for tents or RVs up to 16 feet (no hookups), and two group sites for 60 and 80 people. Picnic tables and fire grills are provided. Pit toilets are available. There is no drinking water. Some facilities are wheelchair-accessible. Leashed pets are permitted.

Reservations, fees: Reservations are required ($9 group reservation fee) for group sites at 877/444-6777 or www.ReserveUSA.com. Sites are $14 per night, $75 per night for a group site. Open late May through October, weather permitting.

Directions: Drive on I-5 to just south of Lebec to the Frazier Park exit. Take that exit and drive west on Frazier Mountain Road to the town of Lake of the Woods and Cuddy Valley Road. Continue straight on Cuddy Valley Road and drive about six miles to Mount Piños Highway. Bear left and drive about five miles to the campground on the right.

Contact: Los Padres National Forest, Mount Piños Ranger District, 661/245-3731, fax 661/245-1526.

46 DAVY BROWN

🏃 🏊 🚣 🐕 🚐 ⛺

Scenic rating: 7

on Davy Brown Creek in Los Padres National Forest

Map 13.4, page 704

This is a pretty spot, set along little Davy Brown Creek at 2,100 feet, deep in Los Padres National Forest. The border of the San Rafael Wilderness and an excellent trailhead are just two miles down the road (along Davy Brown Creek) to the northeast at Nira (see next listing, *Nira*, for hiking options).

Campsites, facilities: There are 13 sites for tents or RVs up to 25 feet (no hookups). Picnic tables and fire grills are provided. Vault toilets are available. No drinking water is available. Garbage must be packed out. Leashed pets are permitted.

Reservations, fees: Reservations are not accepted and there is no camping fee. An Adventure Pass ($30 annual fee or $5 daily pass) per parked vehicle is required. Open year-round.

Directions: From U.S. 101 in Santa Barbara, take Highway 154 and drive northeast for 22 miles to Armour Ranch Road. Turn right on Armour Ranch Road and drive 1.5 miles to Happy Canyon Road. Turn right on Happy Canyon Road/County Route 3350 and drive 11 miles to Cachuma Saddle. Continue straight (north) on Sunset Valley/Cachuma Road/Forest Road 8N09 for four miles to the campground.

Contact: Los Padres National Forest, Santa Lucia Ranger District, 805/925-9538, fax 805/961-5781.

47 NIRA

🏃 🏊 🚣 🐕 ♿ 🚐 ⛺

Scenic rating: 8

on Manzana Creek in Los Padres National Forest

Map 13.4, page 704

Nira is a premium jump-off spot for backpackers, set at 1,000 feet along Manzana Creek, on the border of the San Rafael Wilderness. A primary wilderness trailhead is available, routed east into the San Rafael Wilderness through Lost Valley, along Fish Creek, and to Manzana Creek (and beyond), all in just six miles, with a series of hike-in camps available as the trail enters the wilderness interior. Today's history lesson? This camp was originally an NRA (National Recovery Act) camp during the Depression, hence the name Nira.

Campsites, facilities: There are 11 sites for tents or RVs up to 16 feet (no hookups). Picnic tables and fire grills are provided. Vault toilets and horse-hitching posts are available. No drinking water is available. Garbage must be packed out. Some facilities are wheelchair accessible. Leashed pets are permitted.

Reservations, fees: Reservations are not accepted and there is no camping fee. An Adventure Pass ($30 annual fee or $5 daily pass) per parked vehicle is required. Open year-round, but access roads may be closed during and after heavy rains.

Directions: From U.S. 101 in Santa Barbara, take Highway 154 northeast and drive 22 miles to Armour Ranch Road. Turn right on Armour Ranch Road and drive 1.5 miles to Happy Canyon Road. Turn right on Happy Canyon Road and drive 11 miles to Cachuma Saddle. Continue straight (north) on Sunset Valley/Cachuma Road/Forest Road 8N09 for six miles to the campground.

Contact: Los Padres National Forest, Santa Lucia Ranger District, 805/925-9538, fax 805/961-5781.

48 FIGUEROA

🏃 🐕 🚐 ⛺

Scenic rating: 7

in Los Padres National Forest

Map 13.4, page 704

This is one of the more attractive camps in Los Padres National Forest. It is set at 3,500 feet beneath an unusual stand of oak and huge manzanita trees and offers a view of the Santa Ynez Valley. Nearby attractions include the Piño Alto Picnic Area, 2.5 miles away, offering a panoramic view of the adjacent wildlands with a 0.5-mile, wheelchair-accessible nature trail. An exceptional view is also available from the nearby Figueroa fire lookout. Though it requires a circuitous 10-mile ride around Figueroa Mountain to get there, Nira to the east provides the best trailhead for the San Rafael Wilderness in this area.

Campsites, facilities: There are 32 sites for tents or RVs up to 25 feet (no hookups). Picnic tables and fire grills are provided. Drinking water and vault toilets are available. Garbage must be packed out. Leashed pets are permitted.

Reservations, fees: Reservations are not accepted and there is no camping fee. An Adventure Pass ($30 annual fee or $5 daily pass) per parked vehicle is required. Open year-round.

Directions: Drive on Highway 154 to Los Olivos and Figueroa Mountain Road. Turn northeast on Figueroa Mountain Road and drive 12.5 miles to the campground.

Contact: Los Padres National Forest, Santa Lucia Ranger District, 805/925-9538, fax 805/961-5781.

49 CACHUMA

Scenic rating: 6

near Cachuma Creek in Los Padres National Forest

Map 13.4, page 704

This camp is set at 2,200 feet along one of the major streams that feeds Cachuma Lake, just 10 miles downstream. A dirt road south of the camp follows the creek to the lake.

Campsites, facilities: There are six tent sites. Picnic tables and fire grills are provided. Vault toilets and drinking water are available. Garbage must be packed out. Leashed pets are permitted.

Reservations, fees: Reservations are not accepted and there is no camping fee. An Adventure Pass ($30 annual fee or $5 daily pass) per parked vehicle is required. Open year-round.

Directions: From U.S. 101 in Santa Barbara, take Highway 154 and drive northeast for 22 miles to Armour Ranch Road. Turn right on Armour Ranch Road and drive 1.5 miles to Happy Canyon Road. Turn right on Happy Canyon Road/County Route 3350 and drive 9.5 miles to the campground.

Contact: Los Padres National Forest, Santa Barbara Ranger District, 805/967-3481, fax 805/967-7312.

50 OZENA

Scenic rating: 7

in Los Padres National Forest

Map 13.4, page 704

This camp is set at 3,660 feet, about a mile from Reyes Creek and about 3.5 miles from Reyes Creek campground, the premium campground in this area. This camp gets light use and is known primarily by the locals. A Forest Service map is recommended.

Campsites, facilities: There are 10 sites for tents or RVs up to 22 feet (no hookups). Picnic tables and fire grills are provided. Vault toilets are available. No drinking water is available. Garbage must be packed out. You can buy groceries and propane gas about 30 minutes away in Ojai or Frazier Park. Leashed pets are permitted.

Reservations, fees: Reservations are not accepted and there is no camping fee. An Adventure Pass ($30 annual fee or $5 daily pass) per parked vehicle is required. Open year-round.

Directions: From Ojai, drive north on Highway 33 for 36 miles to Lockwood Valley Road. Turn right on Lockwood Valley Road and drive 1.5 miles to the campground on the right.

Contact: Los Padres National Forest, Mount Piños Ranger District, 661/245-3731, fax 661/245-1526.

51 REYES CREEK FAMILY AND EQUESTRIAN CAMP

Scenic rating: 7

in Los Padres National Forest

Map 13.4, page 704

This developed Forest Service camp sits at the end of an old spur, Forest Road 7N11. The camp is set at 3,960 feet along Reyes Creek, which is stocked with trout in early summer. The Piedra Blanca/Gene Marshall Trail is routed out of camp to the south and climbs three miles to Upper Reyes backpack camp, and beyond, up a ridge and down to Beartrap Creek and several trail camps along that creek. In all, the trail covers approximately 20 miles.

Campsites, facilities: There are 30 sites for tents or RVs up to 22 feet (no hookups). Picnic tables and fire grills are provided. Pit toilets, drinking water, and a corral are available. Garbage must be packed out. Some facilities are wheelchair accessible. A small store, bar, and café are nearby. Leashed pets are permitted.

Reservations, fees: Reservations are not accepted and there is no camping fee. An Adventure Pass ($30 annual fee or $5 daily pass) per parked vehicle is required. Open year-round.

Directions: From Ojai, drive north on Highway 33 for 36 miles to Lockwood Valley Road. Turn right on Lockwood Valley Road (Ozena Road) and drive about 3.5 miles to Forest Road 7N11. Turn right and drive about 1.5 miles to the village of Camp Scheideck and a T intersection. Bear left at the T intersection and drive 0.25 mile to the campground.

Contact: Los Padres National Forest, Mount Piños Ranger District, 661/245-3731, fax 661/245-1526.

52 PINE SPRINGS

Scenic rating: 6

near San Guillermo Mountain in Los Padres National Forest

Map 13.4, page 704

This primitive camp is set at 5,800 feet in elevation on a short spur road that dead-ends on the east flank of San Guillermo Mountain (6,569 feet). Pine Springs feeds the tiny headwaters of Guillermo Creek at this spot. This is a quiet spot. It gets little use, primarily in the fall by hunters.

Campsites, facilities: There are 12 sites for tents or RVs up to 22 feet (no hookups). Picnic tables and fire grills are provided. Pit toilets and drinking water are available. Garbage must be packed out. Leashed pets are permitted.

Reservations, fees: Reservations are not accepted and there is no camping fee. An Adventure Pass ($30 annual fee or $5 daily pass) per parked vehicle is required. Open early May through October, weather permitting.

Directions: Drive on I-5 to just south of Lebec to the Frazier Park exit. Take that exit and drive west on Frazier Mountain Road to the town of Lake of the Woods and Lockwood Valley Road. Turn left on Lockwood Valley Road (take the left fork) and drive about 12 miles to Grade Valley Road (Forest Road 7N03). Turn left and drive 3.5 miles to Forest Road 7N03A. Turn right and drive one mile to the campground.

Contact: Los Padres National Forest, Mount Piños Ranger District, 661/245-3731, fax 661/245-1526.

53 PINE MOUNTAIN

Scenic rating: 6

in Los Padres National Forest

Map 13.4, page 704

Pine Mountain, along with nearby Reyes Peak campground (0.25 mile to the east; see next entry), is a tiny, primitive campground in a pretty setting with a few trailheads close at hand. The two best nearby hikes lead to springs. A trail is routed out of camp and into Boulder Canyon for a mile down the mountain, where it meets another trail that turns left and heads a quarter mile to McGuire Spring Trail camp (piped spring water is available there). It's advisable to obtain a Forest Service map. A popular launch area for hang gliders is 1.5 miles west of the campground. The elevation is 6,700 feet.

Campsites, facilities: There are six tent sites. Picnic tables and fire grills are provided. Pit toilets and drinking water are available. Garbage must be packed out. Leashed pets are permitted.

Reservations, fees: Reservations are not accepted and there is no camping fee. An Adventure Pass ($30 annual fee or $5 daily pass) per parked vehicle is required. Open April to early November, weather permitting.

Directions: From Ojai, drive north on Highway 33 for 33 miles to Reyes Peak Road. Turn right on Pine Mountain/Reyes Peak Road and drive five miles to the campground on the left.

Contact: Los Padres National Forest, Ojai Ranger District, 805/646-4348, fax 805/646-0484.

54 REYES PEAK
Scenic rating: 6

in Los Padres National Forest

Map 13.4, page 704

Reyes Peak is a primitive camp set at 6,800 feet. Three short hikes in the immediate vicinity lead to trail camps. The closest is from a trailhead just to the west of camp, which provides an easy, 0.5-mile hike north to Raspberry Spring (a backcountry camp is available there). A popular launch area for hang gliders is 0.5-half mile from camp. Nearby Pine Mountain campground (see previous entry) provides an alternative for camping.

Campsites, facilities: There are six tent sites. Picnic tables and fire grills are provided. Vault toilets and drinking water are available. Garbage must be packed out. Leashed pets are permitted.

Reservations, fees: Reservations are not accepted and there is no camping fee. An Adventure Pass ($30 annual fee or $5 daily pass) per parked vehicle is required. Open April to early November, weather permitting.

Directions: From Ojai, drive north on Highway 33 for 33 miles to Reyes Peak Road. Turn right on Reyes Peak Road and drive 5.5 miles to the campground.

Contact: Los Padres National Forest, Ojai Ranger District, 805/646-4348, fax 805/646-0484.

55 THORN MEADOWS FAMILY AND EQUESTRIAN CAMP
Scenic rating: 7

on Piru Creek in Los Padres National Forest

Map 13.4, page 704

The reward at Thorn Meadows is a small, quiet spot along Piru Creek at 5,000 feet, deep in Los Padres National Forest. A trail out of camp leads three miles up to Thorn Point, a magnificent 6,935-foot lookout. It is by far the best view in the area, worth the 2,000-foot climb, and on a clear day you can see the Channel Islands.

Campsites, facilities: There are five sites for tents or RVs up to 16 feet (no hookups). Picnic tables and fire grills are provided. Pit toilets, drinking water and a double split corral are available. Garbage must be packed out. Leashed pets are permitted.

Reservations, fees: Reservations are not accepted and there is no camping fee. An Adventure Pass ($30 annual fee or $5 daily pass) per parked vehicle is required. Open early May through October, weather permitting.

Directions: Drive on I-5 to just south of Lebec and the Frazier Park exit. Take that exit and drive west on Frazier Mountain Road to the town of Lake of the Woods and Lockwood Valley Road. Turn left on Lockwood Valley Road and drive about 12 miles to Mutau Flat Road (Forest Road 7N03/Grade Valley Road). Turn left and drive seven miles to Forest Road 7N03B. Turn right and drive one mile to the campground.

Contact: Los Padres National Forest, Mount Piños Ranger District, 661/245-3731, fax 661/245-1526.

56 CACHUMA LAKE RECREATION AREA

Scenic rating: 7

near Santa Barbara

Map 13.4, page 704 — **BEST**

Cachuma has become one of the best lakes in America for fishing big bass, and the ideal climate makes it a winner for camping as well. Cachuma is set at 750 feet in the foothills northwest of Santa Barbara, a big, beautiful lake covering 3,200 acres. In low-rain years the drawdowns are so significant that you'd hardly recognize the place. The rules are perfect for fishing: No waterskiing, personal watercraft, swimming, canoeing, kayaking, or sailboarding is permitted; for fishing boats there is a 5-mph speed limit in the coves and a 40-mph limit elsewhere. After fishing, picnicking and camping come in a distant second and third in popularity, respectively.

Campsites, facilities: There are 420 sites for tents or RVs of any length, and nine group areas for 8–30 vehicles. Some sites have full or partial hookups (30 amps) and/or are pull-through. Yurts are also available. Picnic tables and fire pits are provided. Drinking water, restrooms with flush toilets and coin showers, and coin laundry are available. Playground, general store, propane gas, seasonal swimming pool, full-service marina, fishing piers, bait and tackle, boat ramp, mooring, boat fuel, boat and water bike rentals, bicycle rentals, nature cruises, miniature golf, dump station, group facilities,

RV storage, gas station, ice, and a snack bar are available nearby. Watercraft under 10 feet and inflatables under 12 feet are prohibited on the lake. Leashed pets are permitted, but they must be kept at least 50 feet from the lake.

Reservations, fees: Reservations are accepted only for groups and yurts at 805/686-5050. Sites are $18–25 per night, $8 per night for each additional vehicle, $144–540 per night for group sites, $3 per pet per night. Some credit cards accepted. Open year-round.

Directions: From Santa Barbara, drive 18 miles north on Highway 154 to the campground entrance on the right.

Contact: Cachuma Lake Recreation Area, Santa Barbara County, 805/686-5054; Cachuma Marina and Boat Rentals, 805/688-4040; Cachuma Boat Tours, 805/686-5050, www.cachuma.com.

57 FREMONT

Scenic rating: 7

near the Santa Ynez River in Los Padres National Forest

Map 13.4, page 704

As you travel west to east, Fremont is the first in a series of Forest Service campgrounds near the Santa Ynez River. This one is just inside the boundary of Los Padres National Forest at 900 feet in elevation, nine miles east of Cachuma Lake to the west.

Campsites, facilities: There are 15 sites for tents or RVs up to 22 feet (no hookups). Picnic tables and fire grills are provided. Drinking water and flush toilets are available. Some facilities are wheelchair-accessible. Groceries are available within two miles and propane gas is available at Cachuma Lake nine miles away. Leashed pets are permitted.

Reservations, fees: Reservations are accepted at 877/444-6777 ($9 group reservation fee) or www.ReserveUSA.com. Sites are $15 per night, $5 per night for each additional vehicle. Open early April to late October.

Directions: From Santa Barbara, drive northwest on Highway 154 for about 10 miles to Paradise Road/Forest Road 5N18. Turn right on Paradise Road/Forest Road 5N18 and drive 2.5 miles to the campground on the right.

Contact: Los Padres National Forest, Santa Barbara Ranger District, 805/967-3481, fax 805/967-7312; Rocky Mountain Recreation Company, 805/521-1319.

58 LOS PRIETOS
🏃 🎣 ♿ 🚐 ⛺

Scenic rating: 7
near the Santa Ynez River in Los Padres National Forest

Map 13.4, page 704

Los Prietos is set across from the Santa Ynez River at an elevation of 1,000 feet, just upstream from nearby Fremont campground to the west. There are several nice hiking trails nearby; the best starts near the Los Prietos Ranger Station, heading south for two miles to Wellhouse Falls (get specific directions and a map at the ranger station). River access is available 0.25 mile away at the White Rock day-use area.

Campsites, facilities: There are 37 sites for tents or RVs up to 22 feet (no hookups). Picnic tables and fire grills are provided. Drinking water and flush toilets are available. Some facilities are wheelchair-accessible. Leashed pets are permitted.

Reservations, fees: Reservations are accepted at 877/444-6777 ($9 group reservation fee) or www.ReserveUSA.com. The fee is $15 per night, $5 per night for each additional vehicle. Open early April to late October.

Directions: From Santa Barbara, take Highway 154 and drive 10 miles northeast to Paradise Road/Forest Road 5N18. Turn right on Paradise Road/Forest Road 5N18 and drive 3.8 miles to the campground.

Contact: Los Padres National Forest, Santa Barbara Ranger District, 805/967-3481, fax 805/967-7312.

59 UPPER OSO FAMILY AND EQUESTRIAN CAMP
🏃 🎣 ♿ 🚐 ⛺

Scenic rating: 7
near the Santa Ynez River in Los Padres National Forest

Map 13.4, page 704

This is one of the Forest Service campgrounds in the Santa Ynez Recreation Area. It is set in Oso Canyon at 1,100 feet, one mile from the Santa Ynez River. This is a prime spot for equestrians, with horse corrals available at adjacent campsites. Note that at high water this campground can become inaccessible. A mile north of camp is the Santa Cruz trailhead for a hike that is routed north up Oso Canyon for a mile, then three miles up to Happy Hollow, and beyond that to a trail camp just west of Little Pine Mountain, elevation 4,508 feet. A trailhead into the San Rafael Wilderness is nearby, and once on the trail, you'll find many primitive sites in the backcountry.

Campsites, facilities: There are 25 sites for tents or RVs up to 22 feet (no hookups). Picnic tables and fire grills are provided. Drinking water and flush toilets are available. Some facilities are wheelchair-accessible. Many sites have horse corrals. Leashed pets are permitted.

Reservations, fees: Reservations are accepted ($9 group reservation fee) at 877/444-6777 or www.ReserveUSA.com. Sites are $15 per night, $20 per night for equestrian sites, $5 per night for each additional vehicle. Open year-round, weather permitting.

Directions: From Santa Barbara, take Highway 154 and drive 10 miles northeast to Paradise Road/Forest Road 5N18. Turn right on Paradise Road/Forest Road 5N18 and drive six miles to Upper Oso Road. Turn left on Upper Oso Road and drive one mile to the campground at the end of the road.

Contact: Los Padres National Forest, Santa Barbara Ranger District, 805/967-3481, fax 805/967-7312.

60 PARADISE

Scenic rating: 7

near the Santa Ynez River in Los Padres National Forest

Map 13.4, page 704

Here is yet another option among the camps along the Santa Ynez River. As you drive east it is the second camp you will come to, just after Fremont. Trout are usually planted upriver of the campground during the spring. The best hiking trailheads nearby are at Upper Oso Camp and the Sage Hill Group Campground. Cachuma Lake is six miles to the west.

Campsites, facilities: There are 15 sites for tents or RVs up to 22 feet. Picnic tables and fire grills are provided. Drinking water and flush toilets are available. Some facilities are wheelchair-accessible. Groceries are available nearby. Leashed pets are permitted.

Reservations, fees: Reservations are accepted ($9 reservation fee) at 877/444-6777 or www .ReserveUSA.com. Sites are $15 per night, $5 per night for each additional vehicle. Open year-round.

Directions: From Santa Barbara, take Highway 154 and drive 10 miles northeast to Paradise Road/Forest Road 5N18. Turn right on Paradise Road/Forest Road 5N18 and drive three miles to the campground on the right.

Contact: Los Padres National Forest, Santa Barbara Ranger District, 805/967-3481, fax 805/967-7312.

61 SAGE HILL GROUP AND EQUESTRIAN CAMP

Scenic rating: 7

on the Santa Ynez River in Los Padres National Forest

Map 13.4, page 704

This is another in the series of camps along the Santa Ynez River in Los Padres National Forest. This one, set at 2,000 feet, was designed for large groups as well as equestrians, with horse corrals available next to one group site. A 3.5-mile loop trail starts at the back end of Sage Hill Group Camp. The first mile is a self-guided interpretive trail.

Campsites, facilities: There are five group areas for tents or RVs up to 32 feet (no hookups) that can accommodate 25–50 people each. Picnic tables and fire grills are provided. Drinking water and flush toilets are available. Horse corrals are in one group site. Some facilities are wheelchair-accessible. Leashed pets are permitted.

Reservations, fees: Reservations are required ($9 reservation fee) at 877/444-6777 or www .ReserveUSA.com. Sites are $75–100 per night. Open year-round, weather permitting.

Directions: From Santa Barbara, take Highway 154 and drive 10 miles northeast to Paradise Road/Forest Road 5N18. Turn right on Paradise Road/Forest Road 5N18 and drive five miles to the ranger station and the campground entrance road. Turn left and drive 0.5 mile to the campground.

Contact: Los Padres National Forest, Santa Barbara Ranger District, 805/967-3481, fax 805/967-7312.

62 MONO HIKE-IN

Scenic rating: 7

on Mono Creek in Los Padres National Forest

Map 13.4, page 704

Not many folks know about this spot. The camp is small and primitive, at elevation 1,500 feet on little Mono Creek. Also note that Little Caliente Hot Springs is one mile northeast of the campground. Mono Creek is a feeder to Gibraltar Reservoir, a long, narrow lake with no direct access available.

Campsites, facilities: There are three tent sites. Picnic tables and fire grills are provided. Vault toilets and drinking water are available. Garbage must be packed out. Leashed pets are permitted.

Reservations, fees: Reservations are not accepted and there is no camping fee. An Adventure Pass ($30 annual fee or $5 daily pass) per parked vehicle is required. Open year-round, weather permitting.

Directions: From U.S. 101 in Santa Barbara, take Highway 154 and drive northeast for eight miles to East Camino Cielo/Forest Road 5N12. Turn right on East Camino Cielo/Forest Road 5N12 and drive 18 miles to the end of the paved road at Camuesa Road/Forest Road 5N15 (a dirt road). Continue on Camuesa Road for five miles to the old Juncal Campground (closed). Turn left (still on Forest Road 5N15) and drive seven miles to the parking area for Mono Hike-In. Park and hike approximately 100 yards to the campground.

Contact: Los Padres National Forest, Santa Barbara Ranger District, 805/967-3481, fax 805/967-7312.

63 P-BAR FLAT

Scenic rating: 7

on the Santa Ynez River in Los Padres National Forest

Map 13.4, page 704

The best thing or the worst thing, depending on how you look at it, about P-Bar Flat is a trailhead that is routed north into the remote wildlands of Los Padres National Forest. The camp is very small and primitive, set at 1,800 feet along the Santa Ynez River. The trail starts by heading up Horse Canyon along a creek, but eventually it is routed 10 miles to Hildreth Peak, elevation 8,066 feet, a 6,000-foot butt-kicker of a climb. A lot of guys in prison get less punishment.

Campsites, facilities: There are four tent sites. Picnic tables and fire grills are provided. Vault toilets and drinking water are available. Garbage must be packed out. Leashed pets are permitted.

Reservations, fees: Reservations are not accepted and there is no camping fee. An Adventure Pass ($30 annual fee or $5 daily pass) per parked vehicle is required. Open year-round, weather permitting.

Directions: From U.S. 101 in Santa Barbara, take Highway 154 and drive northeast for eight miles to East Camino Cielo/Forest Road 5N12. Turn right on East Camino Cielo/Forest Road 5N12 and drive 18 miles to the end of the paved road at Camuesa Road/Forest Road 5N15 (a dirt road). Continue on Camuesa Road for five miles to the old Juncal Campground (closed). Turn left (still on Forest Road 5N15) and drive four miles to the campground.

Contact: Los Padres National Forest, Santa Barbara Ranger District, 805/967-3481, fax 805/967-7312.

64 MIDDLE SANTA YNEZ

Scenic rating: 7

on the Santa Ynez River in Los Padres National Forest

Map 13.4, page 704

There are four camps bordering the Santa Ynez River between Gibraltar Reservoir to the west and little Jameson Lake to the east. Look them over and pick the one you like best. This one is set at an elevation of 1,500 feet, about a half mile east of P-Bar Flat (see the previous listing, *P-Bar Flat*, for a trailhead there).

Campsites, facilities: There are 13 tent sites. Picnic tables and fire grills are provided. Vault toilets and drinking water are available. Garbage must be packed out. Leashed pets are permitted.

Reservations, fees: No reservations are accepted and there is no camping fee. An Adventure Pass ($30 annual fee or $5 daily pass) per parked vehicle is required. Senior discount available. Open year-round, weather permitting.

Directions: From U.S. 101 in Santa Barbara, take Highway 154 and drive northeast for eight miles to East Camino Cielo/Forest Road 5N12. Turn right on East Camino Cielo/

Forest Road 5N12 and drive 18 miles to the end of the paved road at Camuesa Road/Forest Road 5N15 (a dirt road). Continue on Camuesa Road for five miles to the old Juncal Campground (closed). Turn left (still on Forest Road 5N15) and drive three miles to the campground.

Contact: Los Padres National Forest, Santa Barbara Ranger District, 805/967-3481, fax 805/967-7312.

65 HOLIDAY GROUP CAMP

Scenic rating: 7

on Matilija Creek in Los Padres National Forest

Map 13.4, page 704

This group site, set at 2,000 feet, is near the North Fork of the Matilija. It's only three miles uphill from Matilija Reservoir.

Campsites, facilities: There is one group site for tents or RVs up to 22 feet (no hookups) that can accommodate up to 75 people. Picnic tables and fire grills are provided. Drinking water and vault toilets are available. Garbage must be packed out. Leashed pets are permitted.

Reservations, fees: Reservations are required ($9 reservation fee) at 877/444-6777 or www.ReserveUSA.com. The fee is $70 per night. Open year-round.

Directions: From Ojai, drive northwest on Highway 33 for nine miles to the campground entrance on the right.

Contact: Los Padres National Forest, Ojai Ranger District, 805/646-4348, fax 805/646-0484; Rocky Mountain Recreation, 805/640-1977.

66 WHEELER GORGE

Scenic rating: 7

on Matilija Creek in Los Padres National Forest

Map 13.4, page 704

This developed Forest Service camp is set at 2,000 feet and is one of the more popu-lar spots in the area. The North Fork of the Matilija runs beside the camp and provides some fair trout fishing in the spring and good swimming holes in early summer. Interpretive programs are also available, a nice plus, and a nature trail is adjacent to the campground.

Campsites, facilities: There are 70 sites for tents or RVs up to 35 feet (no hookups), including six double sites. Picnic tables and fire grills are provided. Pit toilets are available. Drinking water is available intermittently; check for current status. Garbage must be packed out. Leashed pets are permitted. Some facilities are wheelchair-accessible.

Reservations, fees: Reservations are accepted ($9 reservation fee) at 877/444-6777 or www.ReserveUSA.com. Sites are $20 per night, $5 per night for each additional vehicle. Open year-round.

Directions: From Ojai, drive northwest on Highway 33 for 8.5 miles to the campground entrance on the left.

Contact: Los Padres National Forest, Ojai Ranger District, 805/646-4348, fax 805/646-0484; Rocky Mountain Recreation, 805/640-1977.

67 ROSE VALLEY

Scenic rating: 8

in Los Padres National Forest

Map 13.4, page 704

The short walk to Rose Valley Falls, a 300-foot waterfall that provides a happy surprise, makes this camp a sure-thing winner in late winter and spring. The walk to the waterfall is just 0.5-mile round-trip; note that there are two views of it, a long-distance view of the entire waterfall, and then at the base, a view of just the lower tier. It is one of the scenic highlights in this section of Los Padres National Forest. The camp is set at 3,400 feet next to Rose Valley Creek, about two miles from Sespe Creek. If this campground is full, there is another campground, Middle Lion, two miles beyond Rose Valley camp.

Campsites, facilities: There are nine sites for tents or RVs up to 30 feet (no hookups). Picnic tables and fire grills are provided. Vault toilets are available. There is no drinking water. Horseback-riding facilities are available nearby. Garbage must be packed out. Some facilities are wheelchair-accessible. Leashed pets are permitted.

Reservations, fees: Reservations are not accepted and there is no camping fee. An Adventure Pass ($30 annual fee or $5 daily pass) per parked vehicle is required. Open year-round, weather permitting.

Directions: From Ojai, drive north on Highway 33 for 15 miles to Sespe River Road/Rose Valley Road. Turn right on Sespe River Road/Rose Valley Road and drive 5.5 miles to the campground entrance.

Contact: Los Padres National Forest, Ojai Ranger District, 805/646-4348, fax 805/646-0484.

68 SANTA BARBARA SUNRISE RV PARK

Scenic rating: 3

in Santa Barbara

Map 13.4, page 704

Motor-home cruisers get a little of two worlds here. For one thing, the park is close to the beach; for another, the downtown shopping area isn't too far away, either. This is the only RV park in Santa Barbara.

Campsites, facilities: There are 33 sites with full hookups (20, 30 and 50 amps) for RVs of any length. Several sites are pull-through. Restrooms with showers, cable TV, free Wi-Fi, and a coin laundry are available. A grocery store, golf course, tennis courts, and propane gas are nearby. Leashed pets are permitted.

Reservations, fees: Reservations are recommended. Sites are $45 per night, $5 per person per night for more than two people, $5 per

night for each additional vehicle, $5 per pet per night. Some credit cards accepted. Open year-round.

Directions: In Santa Barbara on U.S. 101 northbound, drive to the Salinas Street exit. Take that exit and drive to the park (well signed) at 516 South Salinas Street, near the highway exit.

In Santa Barbara on U.S. 101 southbound, drive to the Milpas Street exit. Take that exit and turn left on Milpas Street. Drive under the freeway to Carpinteria Street. Turn right and drive 0.5 mile to Salinas Street. Turn right and drive 0.5 mile to the park on the right.

Contact: Santa Barbara Sunrise RV Park, 805/966-9954 or 800/345-5018, fax 805/966-7950.

69 CARPINTERIA STATE BEACH

Scenic rating: 8

near Santa Barbara

Map 13.4, page 704

First, plan on reservations, and then, plan on plenty of neighbors. This state beach is one pretty spot, and a lot of folks cruising up the coast like the idea of taking off their boots here for awhile. This is an urban park; that is, it is within walking distance of downtown, restaurants, and shopping. You can love it or hate it, but this camp is almost always full. It features one mile of beach. Harbor seals can be seen December through May, along with an occasional passing gray whale. Tidepools here are protected and contain starfish, sea anemones, crabs, snails, octopus, and sea urchins. In the summer, the visitors center features a living tidepool exhibit. Other state beaches to the nearby north are El Capitán State Beach and Refugio State Beach, both with campgrounds.

Campsites, facilities: There are 65 sites with no hookups for tents, 79 sites with full or partial hookups (30 amps) for RVs up to 30 feet, 29 sites with partial hookups for RVs up to 35 feet, 38 sites with no hookups for RVs up to 21 feet, one hike-in/bike-in site, and seven group sites that can accommodate 25–65 people each. Picnic tables and fire rings are provided. Drinking water, restrooms with flush toilets and coin showers, and a picnic area are available. A convenience store, coin laundry, restaurants, and propane gas are nearby in the town of Carpinteria. Some facilities are wheelchair-accessible. Leashed pets are permitted, except on the beach.

Reservations, fees: Reservations are accepted ($7.50 reservation fee) at 800/444-PARK (800/444-7275) or www.reserveamerica.com. Sites are $25–44 per night, $8 per night for each additional vehicle, $5 per person per night for hike-in/bike-in site, $90–224 per night for group sites. Open year-round, except for group sites.

Directions: From Santa Barbara, drive south on U.S. 101 for 12 miles to Carpinteria and the Casitas Pass Road exit. Take that exit and turn right on Casitas Pass Road and drive about a block to Carpinteria Avenue. Turn right and drive a short distance to Palm Avenue. Turn left and drive about six blocks to the campground at the end of Palm Avenue.

Contact: Carpinteria State Beach, 805/684-2811; Channel Coast District, 805/968-1033, www.parks.ca.gov.

70 LAKE CASITAS RECREATION AREA

🚴 🏊 🚤 🛶 🐎 🎣 ♿ 🚐 ⛺

Scenic rating: 7

north of Ventura

Map 13.4, page 704

Lake Casitas is known as one of Southern California's world-class fish factories, with more 10-pound bass produced here than anywhere and including the former state record, a bass that weighed 21 pounds, 3 ounces. Other fish species include catfish, crappie, and sunfish. Fishing at night is permitted on select weekends. The ideal climate in the foothill country gives the fish a nine-month growing season and provides excellent weather for camping. Casitas is north of Ventura at an elevation of 567 feet in the foothills bordering Los Padres National Forest. The lake has 32 miles of shoreline with a huge number of sheltered coves, covering 2,710 acres. The lake is managed primarily for anglers. Waterskiing, personal watercraft, and swimming are not permitted, and only boats between 11 and 26 feet are allowed on the lake. Canoes and kayaks are allowed. The park holds many special events, including the Ojai Wine Festival and the Ojai Renaissance Festival.

Campsites, facilities: There are 400 sites for tents or RVs of any length and a group site for a minimum of 10 vehicles; some sites have full or partial hookups (30 and 50 amps) and/or are pull-through. Trailer rentals are also available. Picnic tables and fire rings are provided. Restrooms with flush toilets and showers, drinking water, two dump stations, playgrounds, general store, picnic areas, propane, ice, snack bar, water playground, bike rentals, and a full-service marina (including boat ramps, boat rentals, slips, fuel, tackle, and bait) are available. Some facilities are wheelchair-accessible. Leashed pets are permitted, except on the lake or boats.

Reservations, fees: Reservations are accepted ($7.50 reservation fee, $65 fee for group sites) at 805/649-1122. Sites are $19–50 per night, $10 per night for each additional vehicle, $2.50 per pet per night. The fee for the group site is $19 per vehicle per night with a two-night, 10-vehicle minimum. Some credit cards accepted. Open year-round.

Directions: From Ventura, drive north on Highway 33 for 10.5 miles to Highway 150/Baldwin Road. Turn left (west) on Highway 150 and drive three miles to Santa Ana Road. Turn left and drive to the lake and campground entrance at 11311 Santa Ana Road.

Contact: Lake Casitas Recreation Area, 805/649-2233, fax 805/649-4661; Lake Casitas Marina, 805/649-2043; Nature Cruises, 805/682-4726, ext. 654, www.lakecasitas .info.

71 CAMP COMFORT PARK

Scenic rating: 4

on San Antonio Creek north of Ventura

Map 13.4, page 704

This Ventura County park gets missed by many. It's set in a residential area in the Ojai Valley foothill country at 1,000 feet. San Antonio Creek runs through the park and there are shade trees. Lake Casitas Recreation Area is 10 miles away.

Campsites, facilities: There are 15 sites with full hookups (30 and 50 amps) for tents or RVs up to 34 feet; some sites have electrical hookups. Picnic tables and fire pits are provided. Restrooms with flush toilets and showers, drinking water, coin laundry, picnic areas, group facilities, clubhouse, and a playground are available. Supplies are nearby. Leashed pets are permitted in the campground only.

Reservations, fees: Reservations are accepted ($20 reservation fee). Sites are $37 per night, $1 per pet per night. Open year-round.

Directions: From Ventura, take Highway 33 north to North Creek Road. Turn right and drive 4.5 miles to the park at 11969 North Creek Road.

Contact: Camp Comfort Park, 805/654-3951; http://gsa.countyofventura.org/parks/.

72 FAR WEST RESORT

Scenic rating: 7

on Santa Paula Creek east of Ventura

Map 13.4, page 704

Far West Resort is set near little Santa Paula Creek in the foothill country adjacent to Steckel County Park. For those who want a well-developed park with a lot of amenities, the shoe fits. Note that at one time the two campgrounds, Far West Resort and Steckel County Park, were linked. No more, and for good reason. Far West Resort is a tight ship where the gates close at 10 P.M. and quiet time assures campers of a good night's sleep. It is a good place to bring a family. Steckel County Park, on the other hand, has a campground with so many problems that I removed it from the book. Steckel is a beautiful place gone bad, crime-ridden and scary for most visitors, with partying, fights, and loud noise. So what do you do? Go next door to Far West where the inmates aren't running the asylum, and the days are fun and nights are peaceful.

Campsites, facilities: There are 72 sites with full or partial hookups (20, 30, and 50 amps) for RVs of any length, and a tent area for up to 400 people. Picnic tables and fire rings are provided. Restrooms with flush toilets and showers, drinking water, coin laundry, modem access, Wi-Fi, dump station, clubhouse, petting zoo, video room, RV storage, and horseshoes are available. Supplies are nearby. Leashed pets are permitted.

Reservations, fees: Reservations are accepted for RV sites and required for the tent area. Sites are $26.50 per night for RVs, $16 per night for tents, $3 per night for each additional vehicle, $1 per pet per night, $3 per person per night for group sites. Weekly, monthly, and group rates available. Some credit cards accepted. Open year-round for RVs; tent sites closed in winter.

Directions: From Ventura, drive east on Highway 126 for 14 miles to Highway 150. Turn northwest on Highway 150 and drive five miles to the resort entrance on the right.

Contact: Far West Resort, 805/933-3200.

73 HOBSON COUNTY PARK

Scenic rating: 6

north of Ventura on the Pacific Ocean

Map 13.4, page 704

This county park is at the end of Rincon Parkway, kind of like a crowded cul-de-sac, with easy access to the beach and many side-trip possibilities. There is a great reef here for exploring at low tides. Emma Wood State Beach, San

Buenaventura State Beach, and McGrath State Beach are all within 11 miles of the park.

Campsites, facilities: There are 31 sites for tents or RVs up to 34 feet; some sites have full hookups, including cable TV. Picnic tables and fire pits are provided. Restrooms with flush toilets and coin showers, drinking water, and a snack bar are available. Leashed pets are permitted, but not on the beach.

Reservations, fees: Reservations are not accepted. Sites are $27–40 per night, $1 per pet per night. Open year-round.

Directions: From Ventura, drive northwest on U.S. 101 for three miles to the State Beaches exit. Take that exit and turn north on West Pacific Highway and drive five miles to the campground on the left.

Contact: Ventura County Parks Department, 805/654-3951; http://gsa.countyofventura .org/parks/.

74 FARIA COUNTY PARK

Scenic rating: 7

north of Ventura on the Pacific Ocean

Map 13.4, page 704

This county park provides a possible base of operations for beach adventures, including surf fishing. It is set along the ocean, with Emma Wood State Beach, San Buenaventura State Beach, and McGrath State Beach all within 10 miles of the park.

Campsites, facilities: There are 42 sites for tents or RVs up to 34 feet; some sites have full hookups (30 amps), including cable TV. Picnic tables and fire pits are provided. Restrooms with flush toilets and coin showers, drinking water, and a snack bar are available. Leashed pets are permitted.

Reservations, fees: Reservations are not accepted. Sites are $27–40 per night, $1 per pet per night. Open year-round.

Directions: From Ventura, drive north on U.S. 101 for three miles to the State Beaches exit. Take that exit and turn north on West

Pacific Highway and drive four miles to the campground.

Contact: Ventura County Parks Department, 805/654-3951; http://gsa.countyofventura .org/parks/.

75 RINCON PARKWAY

Scenic rating: 5

north of Ventura on the Pacific Ocean

Map 13.4, page 704

This is basically an RV park near the ocean, where the sites are parking end-to-end along old Highway 1. It is not quiet. Passing trains across the highway vie for noise honors with the surf. Emma Wood State Beach, San Buenaventura State Beach, and McGrath State Beach are all within 10 miles. Two activities you can do here are surf fish and watch great sunsets.

Campsites, facilities: There are 127 sites for RVs up to 34 feet (no hookups). No tents. Supplies are available nearby. Leashed pets are allowed, but not on the beach.

Reservations, fees: Reservations are not accepted. Sites are $21 per night per vehicle. Open year-round.

Directions: From Ventura, drive northwest on U.S. 101 for three miles to the State Beaches exit. Take that exit and turn north on West Pacific Highway and drive 4.5 miles to the campground on the left.

Contact: Ventura County Parks Department, 805/654-3951; http://gsa.countyofventura .org/parks/.

76 EMMA WOOD STATE BEACH

Scenic rating: 8

north of Ventura on the Pacific Ocean

Map 13.4, page 704

This is more of a parking lot than a campground with individual sites. And oh, what a place to camp: It is set along the ocean, a pretty spot with tidepools full of all kinds of little marine critters waiting to be discovered. It is also just a short drive from the town of Ventura and the Mission San Buenaventura. One downer, a big one for many: noise from passing trains. Another downer: no toilets at night, so you must have a self-contained vehicle. The gate closes at 10 P.M. and reopens at 6 A.M.

Campsites, facilities: There are 90 sites for RVs up to 40 feet (no hookups). No tents. Chemical toilets are available for day use only. No drinking water is available. Supplies and a coin laundry are three miles away. Leashed pets are permitted, but not on the beach.

Reservations, fees: Reservations are not accepted. Sites are $20 per night, $8 per night for each additional vehicle. Open year-round, weather and tides permitting.

Directions: From Ventura drive north on U.S. 101 for three miles to the State Beaches exit. Take that exit, drive under the freeway, and continue less than a mile to the park entrance on the left.

Contact: Emma Wood State Beach 805/648-4807, Ventura Sector 805/648-4127, Channel Coast District 805/968-1033, www.parks .ca.gov.

🟥 77 EMMA WOOD STATE BEACH: VENTURA RIVER GROUP CAMP
🚴 🏊 ⛴ 🐾 🚐 ⛺

Scenic rating: 1

at Emma Wood State Beach near Ventura

Map 13.4, page 704

This is an extremely noisy area and the campsites are also downright ugly. It is set near the freeway and railroad tracks, and you get a lot of noise from both. It's not popular either. What you have here is mainly a dry riverbed. It is saved somewhat by a freshwater marsh at the southwest end of the beach that attracts red-tailed hawks, songbirds, and raccoons.

Campsites, facilities: There are four group

tent sites for up to 30 people each, one group site for RVs of any length that can accommodate up to 50 people, and five hike-in/bike-in sites. Picnic tables and fire rings are provided. Drinking water, chemical toilets, and cold showers are available. Leashed pets are permitted in the campground, but not on the beach. Supplies are within one mile.

Reservations, fees: Reservations are required ($7.50 reservation fee) for the group sites at 800/444-PARK (800/444-7275) or www .reserveamerica.com. The fee is $66–186 per night, $5 per person per night for hike-in/ bike-in sites. Open year-round.

Directions: On U.S. 101 in Ventura, take the Main Street exit and turn west. Drive one mile on Main Street to the campground on the left.

Contact: Emma Wood State Beach 805/648-4807, Ventura Sector 805/648-4127, Channel Coast District 805/968-1033, www.parks .ca.gov.

🟥 78 McGRATH STATE BEACH
🚶 🚴 🏊 ⛴ 🐾 ♿ 🚐 ⛺

Scenic rating: 9

south of Ventura on the Pacific Ocean

Map 13.4, page 704

This is a pretty spot just south of Ventura Harbor. Campsites are about 400 yards from the beach. This park features two miles of beach frontage, as well as lush riverbanks and sand dunes along the ocean shore. That gives rise to some of the best bird-watching in California. The north tip of the park borders the Santa Clara River Estuary Natural Preserve, where the McGrath State Beach Nature Trail provides an easy walk (wheelchair-accessible) along the Santa Clara River as it feeds into the estuary and then into the ocean. Rangers caution all considering swimming here to beware of strong currents and rip tides; they can be deadly. Note that the park and campground can close on short notice during winter because of river floodings; check status before planning a trip here. Ventura Harbor and the Channel Islands National Park Visitor Center are nearby side trips.

Campsites, facilities: There are 174 sites for tents or RVs up to 30 feet (no hookups); 29 of the sites can be used as group sites. There is also a hike-in/bike-in site. Picnic tables and fire grills are provided. Restrooms with flush toilets and coin showers, drinking water, and a dump station are available. A lifeguard service is provided in summer. Supplies and a coin laundry are nearby. Some facilities are wheelchair-accessible. Leashed pets are permitted in campsites only.

Reservations, fees: Reservations are accepted ($7.50 reservation fee) for individual sites at 800/444-PARK (800/444-7275) or www.reserveamerica.com. Sites are $20–25 per night, $8 per night for each additional vehicle, $5 per person per night for hike-in/bike-in site. For group prices and reservations, phone 805/648-3918. Open year-round, weather and river conditions permitting.

Directions: Drive on U.S. 101 to south of Ventura and the Seaward exit. Take that exit and drive to the stoplight and Harbor Boulevard. Turn west on Harbor Boulevard and drive four miles to the park (signed).

Contact: McGrath State Beach, 805/654-4744; Ventura Sector, 805/648-4127; Channel Coast District, 805/968-1033, www.parks.ca.gov.

79 POINT MUGU STATE PARK: THORNHILL BROOME, LA JOLLA VALLEY, AND LA JOLLA CANYON

Scenic rating: 7

in Point Mugu State Park

Map 13.4, page 704

Point Mugu State Park is known for its rocky bluffs, sandy beaches, rugged hills, and uplands. There are two major river canyons

and wide grassy valleys sprinkled with sycamores, oaks, and a few native walnut trees. Of the campgrounds at Point Mugu, Thornhill Broome campground is more attractive than Big Sycamore (see next listing) for many visitors because it is on the ocean side of the highway (Big Sycamore is on the north side of the highway). It is a 2.5-mile walk to reach La Jolla Valley. While the beachfront is pretty and you can always just lie there in the sun and pretend you're a beached whale, the park's expanse on the east side of the highway in the Santa Monica Mountains provides more recreation. That includes two stellar hikes, the 9.5-mile Big Sycamore Canyon Loop and the 7-mile La Jolla Valley Loop. In all, the park covers 14,980 acres, far more than the obvious strip of beachfront. The park has more than 70 miles of hiking trails and five miles of ocean shoreline. Swimming, body surfing, and surf fishing are available on the beach.

Campsites, facilities: There are 65 primitive sites at Thornhill Broome for tents or RVs up to 31 feet (no hookups), one group site at La Jolla Canyon Group Walk-In for up to 50 people, and 10 environmental walk-in sites and one hike-in group camp for up to 25 people at La Jolla Valley and Group Walk-In. Picnic tables and fire rings are provided at some sites; no open fires are allowed at the environmental walk-in sites. Drinking water and chemical toilets are available at Thornhill Broome. Drinking water, flush toilets, and showers are available at La Jolla Canyon. La Jolla Valley has chemical toilets but no water and no fires; camp stoves are allowed. Supplies can be obtained nearby. Some facilities are wheelchair-accessible. Leashed pets are permitted, but not at the La Jolla Valley campground or on trails. Note that nearby Big Sycamore has a dump station and nature center.

Reservations, fees: Except for environmental sites, reservations are accepted ($7.50 reservation fee) at 800/444-PARK (800/444-7275) or www.reserveamerica.com. Sites are $16 per night at Thornhill Broome, $10 per night for each additional vehicle, $3 per person per night for environmental sites and group site at La Jolla Valley, $111 per night for group site at La Jolla Canyon. Open year-round, but subject to closure during inclement weather and fire season.

Directions: From Oxnard, drive 15 miles south on Highway 1 to the camp entrance: on the right for Thornhill Broome, on the left for La Jolla Canyon Group and La Jolla Valley.

Contact: California State Parks, Angeles District 818/880-0350, www.parks.ca.gov.

80 POINT MUGU STATE PARK: BIG SYCAMORE CANYON

🥾 🚲 🏊 ⛵ 🐴 ♿ 🚐 ⛺

Scenic rating: 6

in Point Mugu State Park

Map 13.4, page 704

While this camp is across the highway from the ocean, it is also part of Point Mugu State Park, which covers 14,980 acres. That gives you plenty of options. One of the best is taking the Big Sycamore Canyon Loop, a long hiking route with great views that starts right at the camp. In all, it's a 9.5-mile loop that climbs to a ridge top and offers beautiful views of nearby canyons and long-distance vistas of the coast. Note: The front gate closes at 10 P.M. and reopens at 7 A.M.

Campsites, facilities: There are 55 sites for tents or RVs up to 31 feet (no hookups), and one hike-in/bike-in site. Picnic tables and fire grills are provided. Restrooms with flush toilets and coin showers, drinking water, and a dump station are available. A weekend nature center is within walking distance. Supplies can be obtained nearby. Some facilities are wheelchair-accessible. Leashed pets are permitted at campsites and on the beach, but not on trails.

Reservations, fees: Reservations are accepted ($7.50 reservation fee) at 800/444-PARK (800/444-7275) or www.reserveamerica.com. Sites are $25 per night, $10 per night for each additional vehicle, $3 per person per night for hike-in/bike-in site. Open year-round.

Directions: From Oxnard, drive south on Highway 1 for 16 miles to the camp on the left.

Contact: California State Parks, Angeles District 818/880-0350, www.parks.ca.gov.

81 SAN MIGUEL ISLAND BOAT-IN AND HIKE-IN

🥾 🛶 🚣 5% ⛰

Scenic rating: 10

in Channel Islands National Park

Channel Islands Detail Map, page 705 **BEST (**

There is no camping trip like this one anywhere in America. It starts with a three-hour boat ride, after which you arrive at San Miguel Island, the most unusual of the five Channel Islands. It is small, distant, and extremely rugged, and it is home to unique birds and much wildlife, including elephant seals and the largest sea lion rookery in California (on the south side of the island). Only rarely do people take advantage of this island paradise, limited to no more than 75 people at any one time on the entire island. To reach the campground start from Cuyler Harbor, where you will be dropped off, and then hike up Nidever Canyon and take the left fork. Bring plenty of water, warm clothes, and be prepared for the chance of fog and wind; the boat typically will not return to pick you up for several days. That's why camping here is like staking out your own personal island wilderness.

Campsites, facilities: There are nine primitive tent sites. Picnic tables and food lockers are provided. Pit toilets and windbreaks are available. No drinking water is available, and garbage must be packed out. No open fires are allowed; bring a camp stove for cooking. No pets are permitted.

Reservations, fees: Reserve by calling Island Packers, 805/642-1393, or Truth Aquatics, 805/962-1127, at Sea Landing in Santa Barbara. After arranging transportation, you must obtain a camping reservation at 800/365-CAMP (800/365-2267) or http://reservations .nps.gov. Sites are $15 per night. There is a fee for round-trip boat transportation. Open year-round, weather permitting.

Directions: Drive on U.S. 101 to south of Ventura and the Seaward exit. Take that exit and turn west on Seaward Avenue and drive about one mile until you merge onto Harbor Boulevard. Bear left on Harbor Boulevard and drive about two miles to Spinnaker Drive. Turn right and drive a short distance to the harbor. The boat ride is at least three hours each way.

Contact: Channel Islands National Park Visitor Information Line, 805/658-5730; Sea Landing, 805/963-3564, www.nps.gov/chis/.

82 SANTA ROSA ISLAND BOAT-IN
🏃 🏊 🛶 5% ⛺

Scenic rating: 10

in Channel Islands National Park

Channel Islands Detail Map, page 705 **BEST**

Santa Rosa, the second-largest of the Channel Islands (the largest is Santa Cruz), is 10 miles wide and 15 miles long, and it holds many mysteries and adventures. A camping trip to Santa Rosa Island, available Friday through Sunday, will be an unforgettable experience even for those who think they've seen it all. The island is beautiful in the spring, when its grasslands turn emerald green and are sprinkled with wildflowers. There are many good hikes; the best are the Cherry Canyon Trail into the island's interior, and the Lobo Canyon Trail descending to a Chumash village site and tidepools. Because the boat ride to Santa Rosa is approximately three hours, longer than the trip to Santa Cruz, this island often receives fewer visitors than its nearby neighbor, which makes it even more special. Bring warm clothes because of the chance of fog and wind. A huge bonus is drinking water at the camp.

Campsites, facilities: There are 15 primitive tent sites. Picnic tables and windbreaks are provided. Drinking water and pit toilets are available. No open fires are allowed; bring a camp stove for cooking. Garbage must be packed out. No pets are permitted.

Reservations, fees: Reserve transportation by calling Island Packers, 805/642-1393, or Truth Aquatics, 805/962-1127, at Sea Landing in Santa Barbara. After arranging transportation, you must obtain a camping reservation at 800/365-CAMP (800/365-2267) or http://reservations.nps.gov. Sites are $15 per night. A fee is charged for round-trip boat transportation. Open year-round, weather permitting.

Directions: Drive on U.S. 101 to south of Ventura and the Seaward exit. Take that exit and turn west on Seaward Avenue and drive about one mile until you merge onto Harbor Boulevard. Bear left on Harbor Boulevard and drive about two miles to Spinnaker Drive. Turn right and drive a short distance to the harbor. The boat ride is about three hours each way.

Contact: Channel Islands National Park Visitor Information Line, 805/658-5730; Sea Landing, 805/963-3564, www.nps.gov/chis/.

83 SANTA CRUZ ISLAND BOAT-IN
🏃 🏊 🛶 🛶 5% ⛺

Scenic rating: 10

in the Channel Islands

Channel Islands Detail Map, page 705 **BEST**

This is the largest of the Channel Islands, perfect for camping and multiday visits. It covers 96 square miles, features a 2,450-foot mountain (Devil's Peak), and boasts an incredible array of flora and fauna, sheltered canyons, and sweeping ocean views. Kayaking through sea caves is outstanding, but can be dangerous, so use caution. The camp is set in a eucalyptus grove in a valley, with trailheads near camp that hikers can take to the surrounding ridgeline. A great hike is from Pelican Bay to Prisoner's Harbor, a three-miler that is routed along the coast to a beautiful beach. The hike is on Nature Conservancy property and requires a permit. The

application for a permit is available at www. nature.org/wherewework/northamerica/states/ californiapreserves/art6335.html.
Campsites, facilities: There are 40 primitive tent sites. Picnic tables are provided. Pit toilets and drinking water are available. No open fires are allowed; bring a camp stove for cooking. Garbage must be packed out. No pets are permitted.
Reservations, fees: Reserve transportation by calling Island Packers, 805/642-1393, or Truth Aquatics, 805/962-1127, at Sea Landing in Santa Barbara. After arranging transportation, you must obtain a camping reservation at 800/365-CAMP (800/365-2267) or http://reservations.nps.gov. Sites are $15 per night. A fee is charged for round-trip boat transportation. Open year-round, weather permitting.
Directions: Drive on U.S. 101 to south of Ventura and the Seaward exit. Take that exit and turn west on Seaward Avenue and drive about one mile until you merge onto Harbor Boulevard. Bear left on Harbor Boulevard and drive about two miles to Spinnaker Drive. Turn right and drive a short distance to the harbor. The boat ride is about one hour each way.
Contact: Channel Islands National Park Visitor Information Line, 805/658-5730; Sea Landing, 805/963-3564, www.nps .gov/chis/.

84 ANACAPA ISLAND BOAT-IN AND HIKE-IN

Scenic rating: 10

in Channel Islands National Park

Channel Islands Detail Map, page 705 **BEST**

Little Anacapa, long and narrow, is known for its awesome caves, cliffs, and sea lion rookeries that range near huge kelp beds. After landing on the island, you face a 154-step staircase trail that leaves you perched on an ocean bluff. From there, it is a 0.5-mile hike to the camp. Other trails venture past Inspiration Point and

Cathedral Cove and provide vast views of the channel. The inshore waters are an ecological preserve loaded with marine life and seabirds and, with the remarkably clear water, this island makes a great destination for snorkeling and sea kayaking. Of the Channel Islands, the boat ride here is the shortest, only 50 minutes.
Campsites, facilities: There are seven primitive tent sites. Picnic tables are provided. Pit toilets are available. No drinking water is available. Garbage must be packed out. No open fires are allowed; bring a camp stove for cooking. No pets are permitted.
Reservations, fees: Reserve transportation by calling Island Packers, 805/642-1393, or Truth Aquatics, 805/962-1127, at Sea Landing in Santa Barbara. After arranging transportation, you must obtain a camping reservation at 800/365-CAMP (800/365-2267) or http://reservations.nps.gov. Sites are $15 per night. A fee is charged for round-trip boat transportation. Open year-round, weather permitting.
Directions: Drive on U.S. 101 to south of Ventura and the Seaward exit. Take that exit and turn west on Seaward Avenue and drive about one mile until you merge onto Harbor Boulevard. Bear left on Harbor Boulevard and drive about two miles to Spinnaker Drive. Turn right and drive a short distance to the harbor. The boat ride is about 50 minutes each way.
Contact: Channel Islands National Park Visitor Information Line, 805/658-5730; Sea Landing, 805/963-3564, www.nps .gov/chis/.

85 SANTA BARBARA ISLAND BOAT-IN AND HIKE-IN

Scenic rating: 10

in Channel Islands National Park

Channel Islands Detail Map, page 705

This is a veritable dot of an island, well to the south of the four others that make up the

Channel Islands. It is best known for its five miles of hiking trails, solitude, snorkeling, swimming, and excellent viewing of marine mammals. It is a breeding ground for elephant seals, with dolphins, sea lions, and whales (in the winter) all common in the area. The snorkeling can be wonderful, as you dive amid playful seals. The only negative is the long boat ride, four hours from the mainland. After landing, it is a steep hike to the campground (no stairs up the bluff), covering about a half mile. Most campers treat this as a wilderness backpacking experience with a long boat ride instead of a long hike.

Campsites, facilities: There are 10 primitive tent sites. Picnic tables are provided. Pit toilets are available. No drinking water is available. Garbage must be packed out. No open fires are allowed; bring a camp stove for cooking. No pets are permitted.

Reservations, fees: Reserve transportation by calling Island Packers, 805/642-1393, or Truth Aquatics, 805/962-1127, at Sea Landing in Santa Barbara. After arranging transportation, you must obtain a camping reservation at 800/365-CAMP (800/365-2267) or http://reservations.nps.gov. Sites are $15 per night. A fee is charged for round-trip boat transportation. Open year-round, weather permitting.

Directions: Drive on U.S. 101 to south of Ventura and the Seaward exit. Take that exit and turn west on Seaward Avenue and drive about one mile until you merge onto Harbor Boulevard. Bear left on Harbor Boulevard and drive about two miles to Spinnaker Drive. Turn right and drive a short distance to the harbor. The boat ride is about four hours each way.

Contact: Channel Islands National Park Visitor Information Line, 805/658-5730; Sea Landing, 805/963-3564, www.nps.gov/chis/.

LOS ANGELES AND VICINITY

BEST CAMPGROUNDS

Hikes with Views
Manker Flats, page 774
Mount San Jacinto State Park:
 Wilderness Walk-In Camps, page 803

Family Destinations
Serrano, page 795

Boat-In Campgrounds
Catalina Island Boat-In, page 765

Fishing
Hermit Gulch, page 766

Waterskiing
Lake Piru Recreation Area, page 754
Lake Perris State Recreation
 Area, page 786
Lake Elsinore Campground
 and Recreation Area, page 789

Island Campgrounds
Parson's Landing Hike-In, page 763
Two Harbors, page 763
Little Harbor Hike-In, page 764
Catalina Island Boat-In, page 765

The stereotypical image of the region you see on

TV – the blonde in a convertible, the surfer with the movie-star jawline – is so flawed as to be ridiculous, pathetic, and laughable. And while there is some classic beach, lifeguards and all, the surrounding area for recreation spans some of the best opportunities in California.

In fact, there are more campgrounds in this region than any other in California's 16 geographic regions except for three: Tahoe/North Sierra, Sequoia and Kings Canyon, and Shasta and Trinity. It stuns some to learn that Los Angeles and its nearby forests provide more campgrounds than even the Yosemite area, and three times as many as the San Francisco Bay Area and its 1.2 million acres of greenbelt.

But for those of us who know this landscape, it does not come as a surprise. The area has a tremendous range of national forests, canyons, mountains, lakes, coast, and islands. In fact, there are so many hidden gems that it is like a giant fortune hunt for those who love the outdoors.

While most people first think of the coast, the highways, and the beaches when envisioning this region, it is the opportunities for camping and hiking in the national forests that surprise most. Angeles National Forest and San Bernardino National Forest provide more than one million acres, 1,000 miles of trails, and dozens of hidden campgrounds, including remote sites along the Pacific Crest Trail that make perfect launch points for weekend trips.

The mountaintop views are incredible, probably best from Mount Baldy (10,064 feet), Mount San Jacinto (10,834 feet), and Mount San Gorgonio (11,490 feet). A series of great campgrounds are nestled on the flanks of all three of these destinations. It is only a start.

Even more famous is the region's top recreation lake, Big Bear, for fishing and boating. Though the region is known for its high population, and Big Bear is no exception on weekends, the relatively few people on weekdays, especially Monday to Thursday mornings, can be stunning to discover. Other top lakes include Arrowhead, Castaic, and several smaller reservoirs.

Yet this is not even the best of it. Look over the opportunities and take your pick. People? What people?

LOS ANGELES AND VICINITY

MAP 14.1 page 751

MAP 14.2 page 752

MAP 14.3 page 753

see The Southern Deserts page 852

see San Diego and Vicinity page 814

see Santa Barbara and Vicinity page 700

Joshua Tree National Park

Anza-Borrego Desert State Park

San Bernardino National Forest

San Bernardino

Cleveland National Forest

Cleveland NF

Angeles National Forest

Los Padres National Forest

Joshua Tree

Yucca Valley

Palm Springs

Beaumont

Redlands

Riverside

Murrieta

Temecula

Vista

San Juan Capistrano

Laguna Beach

Irvine

Anaheim

Corona

Lake Mathews

Long Beach

Pasadena

Mt Baldy 10,064ft

Cajon Junction

Victorville

Adelanto

Barstow

Lancaster

Palmdale

Lebec

Fillmore

Simi Valley

Thousand Oaks

Ojai

Ventura

Casitas

Pyramid Lake

Casitas Lake

Lake Piru

Redondo Beach

Rancho Palos Verdes

Avalon

Two Harbors

Santa Catalina Island

LOS ANGELES

PACIFIC OCEAN

10 mi
10 km

© AVALON TRAVEL PUBLISHING, INC.

Map 14.1

Campgrounds 1-26
Pages 754-766

14.2

1 2 3

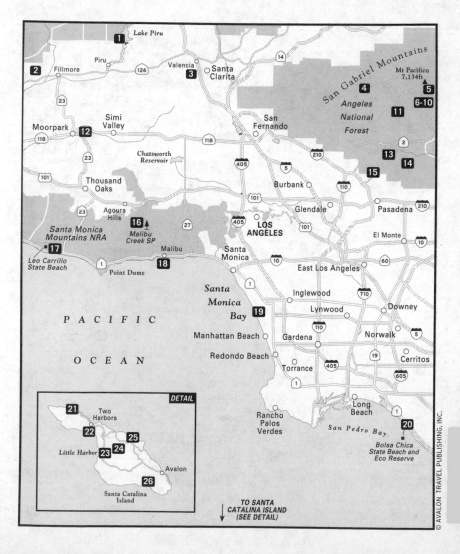

Lake Piru

1

Piru

2 Fillmore

126

Valencia

3 Santa Clarita

14

San Gabriel Mountains

Mt Pacifico 7,134ft

4

5

6-10

Angeles National Forest

11

23

Simi Valley

San Fernando

Moorpark

118

12

Chatsworth Reservoir

118

2

13

14

23

210

405

5

15

101

Thousand Oaks

Burbank

110

101

23

Agoura Hills

Glendale

Pasadena

210

Santa Monica Mountains NRA

16

Malibu Creek SP

27

405

LOS ANGELES

101

El Monte

10

17

Leo Carrillo State Beach

1

Malibu

18

Santa Monica

10

East Los Angeles

60

Point Dume

Santa Monica Bay

1

Inglewood

710

Downey

19

Lynwood

Norwalk

5

110

PACIFIC

Manhattan Beach

Gardena

OCEAN

Redondo Beach

19

Cerritos

Torrance

405

605

1

DETAIL

21

Two Harbors

Long Beach

1

22

25

Rancho Palos Verdes

San Pedro Bay

20

Little Harbor

23 **24**

Bolsa Chica State Beach and Eco Reserve

Avalon

26

Santa Catalina Island

TO SANTA CATALINA ISLAND (SEE DETAIL)

© AVALON TRAVEL PUBLISHING, INC.

Map 14.2

Campgrounds 27-80
Pages 766-793

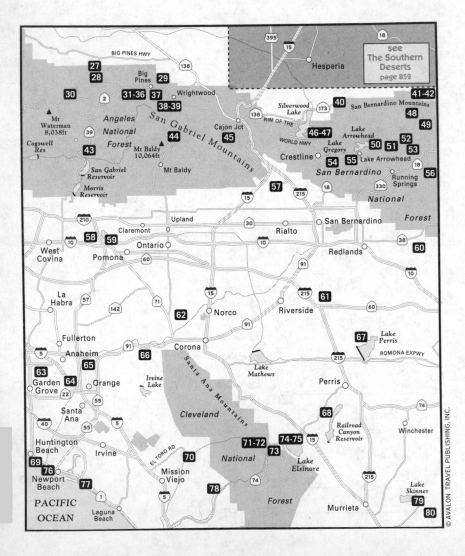

Map 14.3

Campgrounds 81-116
Pages 793-809

1 LAKE PIRU RECREATION AREA

Scenic rating: 7

on Lake Piru

Map 14.1, page 751   **BEST (**

Things can get crazy at Lake Piru, but it's usually a happy crazy, not an insane crazy. Lake Piru is shaped like a teardrop and covers 1,200 acres when full and is set at an elevation of 1,055 feet. This is a lake set up for waterskiing, with lots of fast boats. All others be forewarned: The rules prohibit boats under 12 feet or over 26 feet, as well as personal watercraft. Canoes and kayaks over eight feet are permitted in a special-use area. Bass and trout fishing can be quite good in the spring before the water-skiers take over. From Memorial Day weekend through Labor Day weekend, there is a designated swimming area, safe from the boats. The tent sites here consist of roughly 40-by-40 foot areas amid trees.

Campsites, facilities: There are 235 sites with partial hookups (30 and 50 amps) for tents or RVs up to 40 feet, seven sites with full hookups (30 and 50 amps) for RVs, and one group camp with no hookups for tents or RVs that can accommodate 4–12 vehicles. Fire pits and picnic tables are provided. Restrooms with flush toilets and showers, drinking water, dump station, convenience store, coin laundry, picnic area, boat storage, propane, fish-cleaning station, seasonal snack bar, ice, full-service marina, boat ramp, temporary mooring, boat rentals, and bait and tackle are available. Some facilities are wheelchair-accessible. Leashed pets are permitted, but not in the lake.

Reservations, fees: Reservations are accepted ($7 reservation fee) for individual sites and required for group sites ($20 reservation fee and $50 key charge) at 805/521-1572. Sites are $19–42 per night, $2 per pet per night. Group sites are $96 minimum per night for up to four vehicles (with a two-night minimum),

and $24 per night for each additional vehicle. Holiday rates are higher. Some credit cards accepted. Open year-round.

Directions: From Ventura, drive east on Highway 126 for about 30 miles to the Lake Piru Recreation Area/Piru Canyon Road exit. Take that exit and drive northeast on Piru Canyon Road for about six miles to the campground at the end of the road.

Contact: Lake Piru Recreation Area, 805/521-1500; Lake Piru Marina, 805/521-1231, www.lake-piru.org.

2 KENNEY GROVE PARK AND GROUP CAMPGROUND

Scenic rating: 4

near Fillmore

Map 14.1, page 751

A lot of folks miss this spot, a park tucked away among orchards, coast live oaks, and eucalyptus groves, with several group campgrounds. This is a privately leased facility on Ventura County property. It's just far enough off the highway to allow for some privacy.

Campsites, facilities: This is a group camp with 33 sites with partial hookups (30 amps) for RVs up to 40 feet and 18 sites for tents. No pull-through sites. Picnic tables and fire pits are provided. Drinking water, restrooms with flush toilets and showers, amphitheater, softball field, horseshoes, and a playground are available. Supplies and a coin laundry are nearby. Leashed pets are permitted.

Reservations, fees: Reservations are required and a minimum of five sites must be reserved. Sites are $17 per night for tents, $20 per night for RVs, $1 per pet per night. Open year-round.

Directions: From Ventura, drive east on Highway 126 for 22 miles to Old Telegraph Road (before the town of Fillmore). Turn left on Old Telegraph Road and drive 0.6 mile to 7th Street. Turn left (northwest) and drive 0.3 mile to North Oak Avenue. Turn right and drive one-half mile to the park on the left.

Contact: Kenney Grove, tel./fax 805/524-0750.

3 VALENCIA TRAVEL VILLAGE

Scenic rating: 6

in Valencia

Map 14.1, page 751

This huge RV park is in the scenic San Fernando foothills, just five minutes from Six Flags Magic Mountain. Lake Piru and Lake Castaic are only 15 minutes away. The camp was built on a 65-acre horse ranch.

Campsites, facilities: There are 379 sites with full or partial hookups (30 and 50 amps) for RVs; most are pull-through. No tents. Picnic tables and fire pits (some sites) are provided. A market, two heated swimming pools, spa, lounge, video and games arcade, playground, shuffleboard, horseshoes, volleyball courts, coin laundry, Wi-Fi, modem access, propane, and dump station are available. Some facilities are wheelchair-accessible. Leashed pets are permitted.

Reservations, fees: Reservations are recommended at 888/LUV-TORV (888/588-8678). Sites are $49 per night, $2 per person per night for more than two people. Weekly and monthly rates are available. Some credit cards accepted. Open year-round.

Directions: Drive on I-5 to Santa Clarita and Highway 126 west/Henry Mayo Road. Take that exit and drive west on Highway 126 for one mile to the camp on the left.

Contact: Valencia Travel Village, 661/257-3333.

4 MESSENGER FLATS

Scenic rating: 7

near Mount Gleason in Angeles National Forest

Map 14.1, page 751

Messenger Flats is an ideal camp for many, two miles west of Mount Gleason (6,502 feet). The Pacific Crest Trail is routed just north of the camp, featuring a two-mile hike with a climb of 600 feet to reach Gleason's summit. The camp is at 5,500 feet, set in a flat area about two miles east of an electronic transmitter at Mount Gleason.

Campsites, facilities: There are 10 tent sites. Picnic tables and fire grills are provided. Drinking water and vault toilets are available. Garbage must be packed out. Some facilities are wheelchair-accessible. Two horse corrals are also available. Leashed pets are permitted.

Reservations, fees: Reservations are not accepted. Sites are $8 per night. Open year-round, weather permitting.

Directions: From Pasadena, drive north on I-210 for four miles to the exit for Highway 2/Angeles Crest Highway. Take that exit and drive north on Highway 2 for nine miles to Angeles Forest Highway/County Road N3. Turn left on Angeles Forest Highway and drive 12 miles to Mill Creek Summit and Santa Clara Divide Road/Forest Road 3N17. Turn left and drive 12 miles to the campground (the last mile is unpaved).

Contact: Angeles National Forest, Los Angeles River Ranger District, 818/899-1900, fax 818/896-6727.

5 MOUNT PACIFICO

Scenic rating: 7

on the Pacific Crest Trail in Angeles National
Forest

Map 14.1, page 751

This is one of the great primitive camps in
Angeles National Forest. It is set near the top
of Mount Pacifico at an elevation of 7,134 feet,
with the Pacific Crest Trail located 0.5 mile
from camp. The views are outstanding, especially to the north of the sparse Antelope Valley and beyond. From here, the PCT is routed
through a series of ravines and draws and up
short ridges, pleasant but not inspiring.

Campsites, facilities: There are seven tent
sites. Picnic tables and fire grills are provided.
Vault toilets are available. No drinking water
is available. Garbage must be packed out.
Leashed pets are permitted.

Reservations, fees: Reservations are not
accepted. An Adventure Pass ($30 annual fee or
$5 daily pass per vehicle) is required. Open mid-
May to mid-November, weather permitting.

Directions: From Pasadena, drive north on
I-210 for four miles to the exit for Highway
2/Angeles Crest Highway. Take that exit and
drive north on Highway 2 for nine miles to
Angeles Forest Highway/County Road N3.
Turn left on Angeles Forest Highway and drive
about 12 miles to the intersection with Santa
Clara Divide Road/Forest Road 3N17 (look
for the Mill Creek Summit sign). Turn right
(east) and drive about six miles to Mount Pacifico Road. Turn left on the dirt road and drive
four miles to the campground. High-clearance
vehicles are recommended.

Note that at Mill Creek Summit, the gate
is locked from November 15 to May 15 and it
will be necessary to hike from the gate. When
Santa Clara Divide Road is impassable because
of weather conditions, it will be necessary to
hike from Alder Saddle.

Contact: Angeles National Forest, Los Angeles River Ranger District, 818/899-1900, fax
818/896-6727.

6 HORSE FLATS

Scenic rating: 7

near the San Gabriel Wilderness in Angeles
National Forest

Map 14.1, page 751

This is one of several options in the immediate area: Chilao, Bandido Group Camp,
and Coulter Group Camp are the other three.
Horse Flats is set at 5,700 feet along a national
recreation trail (Silver Moccasin Trail) and is
about two miles by trail to the Chilao Visitor Center. Two trails into the San Gabriel
Wilderness are nearby.

Campsites, facilities: There are 25 sites for tents
or RVs up to 22 feet (no hookups). Picnic tables
and fire pits are provided. Vault toilets, hitching
rails, and horse corrals are available. No drinking water is available. Some facilities are wheelchair-accessible. Leashed pets are permitted.

Reservations, fees: Reservations are not
accepted. Sites are $12 per night. Open April
through November, weather permitting.

Directions: From Pasadena, drive north on
I-210 for four miles to the exit for Highway
2/Angeles Crest Highway. Take that exit and
drive northeast on Highway 2 for 30 miles to
Santa Clara Divide Road/Forest Road 3N17
at Three Points (signed). Turn left and drive
three miles to Horse Flats Road. Turn left and
drive one mile to the campground.

Contact: Angeles National Forest, Los Angeles River Ranger District, 818/899-1900,
fax 818/896-6727; Chilao Visitor Center,
626/796-5541.

7 BANDIDO GROUP CAMP

Scenic rating: 6

near the Pacific Crest Trail in Angeles National
Forest

Map 14.1, page 751

This is a base camp for groups preparing to
hike off into the surrounding wilderness. A

trail out of the camp heads east and intersects with the Pacific Crest Trail a little over two miles away at Three Points, a significant PCT junction. Before heading out visitors must check in and register with the rangers at the Los Angeles River Ranger District office, two miles west of Three Points on Highway 2. The elevation is 5,840 feet.

Campsites, facilities: There is one group camp for tents or RVs up to 40 feet (no hookups) that accommodates up to 120 people. Picnic tables and fire rings are provided. There is no drinking water. Vault toilets, corrals, and water troughs are available. Leashed pets are permitted.

Reservations, fees: Reservations are required at 818/899-1900. The camp is $100 per night with a 60-person maximum, $200 per night with 120-person maximum. Open April to mid-November, weather permitting.

Directions: From Pasadena, drive north on I-210 for four miles to the exit for Highway 2/Angeles Crest Highway. Take that exit and drive northeast on Highway 2 for 30 miles to Santa Clara Divide Road/Forest Road 3N17 at Three Points (signed). Turn left and drive two miles to the campground on the left.

Contact: Angeles National Forest, Los Angeles River Ranger District, 818/899-1900, fax 818/896-6727; Chilao Visitor Center, 626/796-5541.

8 CHILAO CAMPGROUND

Scenic rating: 6

near the San Gabriel Wilderness in Angeles National Forest

Map 14.1, page 751

This popular trailhead camp gets a lot of use. And it's easy to see why, with the Chilao Visitor Center nearby (have any questions—here's where you ask them) and a national recreation trail running right by the camp. Access to the Pacific Crest Trail is three miles north at Three Points (five miles if hiking the Silver Moccasin Trail), and parking is avail-

able there. An Adventure Pass is required to park at all trailheads. The elevation is 5,300 feet. Note: There is frequent bear activity, so use precautions.

Campsites, facilities: There are 84 sites for tents or RVs up to 28 feet (no hookups), with one site for RVs up to 36 feet. Picnic tables and fire rings are provided. Drinking water and vault toilets are available. Some facilities are wheelchair-accessible. Leashed pets are permitted.

Reservations, fees: Reservations are not accepted. Sites are $12 per night. Open April to mid-November, weather permitting.

Directions: From Pasadena, drive north on I-210 for four miles to the exit for Highway 2/Angeles Crest Highway. Take that exit and drive northeast on Highway 2 for 27 miles to the campground entrance road (signed) on the left.

Contact: Angeles National Forest, Los Angeles River Ranger District, 818/899-1900, fax 818/896-6727; Chilao Visitor Center, 626/796-5541.

9 COULTER GROUP CAMP

Scenic rating: 6

near the San Gabriel Wilderness in Angeles National Forest

Map 14.1, page 751

This is a popular group camp set near both a visitors center and a trailhead for the Pacific Crest Trail. Access to the PCT is 3.5 miles north at Three Points (5.5 miles if hiking the Silver Moccasin Trail), and parking is available there. An Adventure Pass is required to park at the trailheads. The elevation is 5,300 feet. It is close to Chilao Campground.

Campsites, facilities: There is one group site for up to 50 people (no hookups). Four picnic tables, a barbecue pit, fire ring, vault toilet, and drinking water are available. Some facilities are wheelchair-accessible. Leashed pets are permitted.

Reservations, fees: Reservations are required

at 818/899-1900. The camp is $100 per night. Open April to mid-November, weather permitting.

Directions: From Pasadena, drive north on I-210 for four miles to the exit for Highway 2/Angeles Crest Highway. Take that exit and drive northeast on Highway 2 for 27 miles to the campground entrance road on the left (enter through the Litle Pines Loop at Chilao Campground).

Contact: Angeles National Forest, Los Angeles River Ranger District, 818/899-1900, fax 818/896-6727.

10 SULPHUR SPRINGS WALK-IN
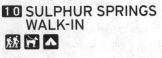

Scenic rating: 6

near the Pacific Crest Trail in Angeles National Forest

Map 14.1, page 751

This walk-in camp is on the South Fork of Little Rock Creek, a short distance from a trailhead for the Pacific Crest Trail. It is set at 5,300 feet amid pines and is a popular jump-off point for hikes. It formerly was a drive-in camp, but the road washed out and future plans for fixing the road were uncertain at the time of publication. The nearby Chilao Visitor Center is a must-stop for newcomers.

Campsites, facilities: There are seven sites for tents only. Picnic tables and stoves are provided. Pit toilets are available. There is no drinking water. Leashed pets are permitted.

Reservations, fees: Reservations are not accepted. Sites are $8 per night. Open April to mid-November, weather permitting.

Directions: From Pasadena, drive north on I-210 for four miles to the exit for Highway 2/Angeles Crest Highway. Take that exit and drive northeast on Highway 2 for 30 miles to Santa Clara Divide Road/Forest Road 3N17 at

Three Points. Turn left on Santa Clara Divide Road/Forest Road 3N17 and drive 4.5 miles to Alder Saddle. Bear right (north), onto the pavement, and drive one mile to the Pacific Crest Trail (100 yards before the road closure gate). Park your vehicle and walk east (downhill) on the Pacific Crest Trail for 0.75 mile to the camp.

Contact: Angeles National Forest, Los Angeles River Ranger District, 818/899-1900, fax 818/896-6727; Chilao Visitor Center, 626/796-5541.

11 MONTE CRISTO

Scenic rating: 7

on Mill Creek in Angeles National Forest

Map 14.1, page 751

This is a Forest Service camp on Mill Creek at 3,600 feet, just west of Iron Mountain. The camp is situated under sycamore trees, which provide great color in the fall. In most years Mill Creek flows six months out of the year.

Campsites, facilities: There are 19 sites for tents or RVs up to 30 feet (no hookups). Picnic tables and fire grills are provided. Vault toilets are available. There is no drinking water. Some facilities are wheelchair-accessible. Leashed pets are permitted.

Reservations, fees: Reservations are not accepted. Sites are $8 per night. Open year-round.

Directions: From Pasadena, drive north on I-210 for four miles to the exit for Highway 2/Angeles Crest Highway. Take that exit and drive northeast on Highway 2 for nine miles to Angeles Forest Highway/County Road N3. Turn left on Angeles Forest Highway and drive about ten miles to the campground on the right.

Contact: Angeles National Forest, Los Angeles River Ranger District, 818/899-1900, fax 818/896-6727.

12 OAK PARK

Scenic rating: 3

in Simi Valley near Moorpark

Map 14.1, page 751

One of the frustrations of trying to find a camp for the night is that so many state and national park campgrounds are full from reservations, especially at the state beaches. The county parks often provide a safety valve, and Oak Park certainly applies. But not always, and that's the catch. This is an oft-overlooked county park set in the foothill country of Simi Valley. The park has many trails offering good hiking possibilities. The camp is somewhat secluded, more so than many expect. The catch? Sometimes the entire campground is rented to a single group. Note: Gates close at dusk and reopen at 8 A.M.

Campsites, facilities: There are 16 sites with partial hookups (20 and 30 amps) for RVs, a group area for up to 13 RVs, and a large tent area with no hookups that can accommodate up to 140 people. Picnic tables and fire pits are provided. Restrooms with flush toilets, drinking water, group facilities, clubhouse, and a dump station are available. Horseshoe pits, a playground, and basketball and volleyball courts are available nearby. Supplies and a coin laundry are within two miles. Leashed pets are permitted.

Reservations, fees: Reservations are accepted. Sites are $10 per night for tents, $12–25 per night for RVs, $5 per person per night for more than two people, $17–20 per night per vehicle for group RV site, $1 per pet per night. Open year-round, except Christmas Day.

Directions: From Ventura, drive south on U.S. 101 to Highway 23. Turn north on Highway 23 (which becomes Highway 123 East) and drive about three miles to the Collins Street exit. Continue straight through the intersection (it becomes Old Los Angeles Avenue) and drive 1.5 miles to the park entrance on the left.

Contact: Oak Park, 805/527-6886, www .ventura.org/gsa/parks.

13 VALLEY FORGE HIKE-IN

Scenic rating: 8

on the San Gabriel River in Angeles National Forest

Map 14.1, page 751

Valley Forge is a good camp for anglers or hikers who are looking for a short backpacking trip. A 2.5-mile hike is required to reach this campground. For hikers, a national recreation trail passes close to the camp. For anglers, there are small but feisty native trout. The elevation is 3,500 feet.

Campsites, facilities: There are 12 tent sites. Picnic tables and fire rings are provided. Vault toilets are available. No drinking water is available. Stream water can be used if it is boiled or pump-filtered. Garbage must be packed out. Leashed pets are permitted.

Reservations, fees: Reservations are not accepted. There is no fee for camping. Adventure Pass ($30 annual fee or $5 daily fee per vehicle) is required. Open year-round, weather permitting.

Directions: From Pasadena, drive north on I-210 for four miles to the exit for Highway 2/ Angeles Crest Highway. Take that exit and drive north on Highway 2 for 14 miles to Mount Wilson Road. Turn right on Mount Wilson Road, then immediately turn left into the parking lot. Access the Gabrielino National Recreation Trail, which is located behind the restrooms, and hike 2.5 miles to the campground.

Contact: Angeles National Forest, Los Angeles River Ranger District, 818/899-1900, fax 818/896-6727.

14 WEST FORK HIKE-IN

Scenic rating: 8

on the West Fork of the San Gabriel River in Angeles National Forest

Map 14.1, page 751

It takes a circuitous drive and a four- to five-mile hike to reach this camp, but for backpackers it is worth it. The camp is on the West Fork of the San Gabriel River amid pine woodlands, with two national recreation trails intersecting at the campground. The canyon is deep and the river is beautiful. The elevation is 3,100 feet.

Campsites, facilities: There are seven tent sites. Picnic tables and fire rings are provided. Vault toilets are available. No drinking water is available. Stream water can be used if it is boiled or pump-filtered. Garbage must be packed out. Leashed pets are permitted.

Reservations, fees: Reservations are not accepted. There is no fee for camping. Adventure Pass ($30 annual fee or $5 daily fee per parked vehicle) is required. Open year-round.

Directions: From Pasadena, drive north on I-210 for four miles to the exit for Highway 2/ Angeles Crest Highway. Take that exit and drive north on Highway 2 for 14 miles to Mount Wilson Road. Turn right on Mount Wilson Road, then immediately turn left into the parking lot. Access the Gabrielino National Recreation Trail, which is located behind the restrooms, and hike five miles to the campground.

Contact: Angeles National Forest, Los Angeles River Ranger District, 818/899-1900, fax 818/896-6727.

15 MILLARD

🥾 🐕 ⛺

Scenic rating: 8

near Millard Falls in Angeles National Forest

Map 14.1, page 751

This tiny, pretty camp, set near a creek amid oak and alder woodlands, is best known as the launching point for some excellent hikes. The best is the 0.5-mile hike to Millard Falls, where you actually rock-hop your way upstream to the 60-foot waterfall, a drop-dead beautiful sight. On weekends, there can be lots of foot traffic through the campground with hikers on their way to the falls. Another trail out of camp leads to Inspiration Point and continues to San Gabriel Peak. It's a short walk to the campsites.

Campsites, facilities: There are five tent sites. Picnic tables and fire pits are provided. Vault toilets are available. No drinking water is available, but stream water may be boiled or filtered. Garbage must be packed out. Leashed pets are permitted.

Reservations, fees: Reservations are not accepted. There is no fee for camping. Adventure Pass ($30 annual fee or $5 daily fee per parked vehicle) is required. Open year-round.

Directions: From Pasadena, drive north on I-10 to the exit for Lake Avenue. Take that exit north and drive 3.5 miles to Loma Alta Drive. Turn left (west) at Loma Alta Drive and drive one mile to Chaney Trail Road (at the flashing yellow light). Turn right at Chaney Trail and drive 1.5 miles (keep left at the fork) to the parking lot for the campground. It is a short walk on a fire road to the campground. Note: A gate is locked at Chaney Trail from 8 P.M. to 6 A.M., preventing drive-in access approximately 1.5 miles from the campground.

Contact: Angeles National Forest, Los Angeles River Ranger District, 818/899-1900, fax 818/896-6727.

16 MALIBU CREEK STATE PARK

🥾 🚴 🏊 🛶 🐴 ♿ 🚙 ⛺

Scenic rating: 9

near Malibu

Map 14.1, page 751

If you plan on staying here, be sure to get your reservation in early. This 6,600-acre state park is just a few miles out of Malibu between Highway 1 and U.S. 101, two major thoroughfares for vacationers. Despite its popularity, the park manages to retain a natural setting, with miles of trails for hiking, biking, and horseback riding, and inspiring scenic views. The park offers 15 miles of streamside trail through oak and sycamore woodlands and also some chaparral covered slopes. It is an ideal spot for a break on a coastal road trip. This park was once used as a setting for the filming of some movies and TV shows, including *Planet of the Apes* and *M*A*S*H*.

Campsites, facilities: There are 62 sites for tents or RVs up to 30 feet (no hookups) and a group tent site for up to 60 people. Picnic tables are provided. No wood fires are permitted in the summer, but propane and charcoal barbecues are allowed. Drinking water and restrooms with flush toilets and coin showers are available. Some facilities are wheelchair-accessible. Leashed pets are permitted, but only in the campground area.

Reservations, fees: Reservations are accepted ($7.50 reservation fee) at 800/444-PARK (800/444-7275) or www.reserveamerica.com. Sites are $25 per night, $8 per night for each additional vehicle, $120 per night for group site. Open year-round.

Directions: From U.S. 101: Drive on U.S. 101 to the exit for Las Virgenes Canyon Road (on the western border of Calabasas). Take that exit south and drive on Las Virgenes Canyon Road/County Road N1 for four miles to the park entrance on the right.

From Highway 1: Drive on Highway 1 to Malibu and Malibu Canyon Road. Turn north on Malibu Canyon Road and drive north for 5.5 miles (the road becomes Las Virgenes Canyon Road/County Road N1) to the park entrance on the left.

Contact: Malibu Creek State Park, 818/880-0367, fax 818/706-3869, www.parks.ca.gov.

17 LEO CARRILLO STATE PARK

Scenic rating: 8

north of Malibu

Map 14.1, page 751

The camping area at this state park is set in a canyon, and reservations are essential during the summer and on weekends the remainder of the year. Large sycamore trees shade the campsites. The Nicholas Flat Trail pro-

vides an excellent hike to the Willow Creek Overlook for beautiful views of the beach. In addition, a pedestrian tunnel provides access to a wonderful coastal spot with sea caves, tunnels, tidepools, and patches of beach. This park features 1.5 miles of beach for swimming, surfing, and surf fishing. In the summer, lifeguards are posted at the beach. Many will remember a beach camp that was once popular here. Well, that sucker is gone, wiped out by a storm.

Campsites, facilities: There are 127 sites for tents or RVs up to 31 feet (no hookups), one hike-in/bike-in area for up to 24 people, and one group tent site for up to 50 people. Picnic tables and fire rings are provided. Restrooms with flush toilets and coin showers, drinking water, a dump station, a seasonal visitors center, Wi-Fi, summer programs, and a summer convenience store are available. Some facilities are wheelchair-accessible. Leashed pets are permitted. Front gates close at 10 P.M. and reopen at 7 A.M.

Reservations, fees: Reservations are recommended ($7.50 reservation fee) at 800/444-PARK (800/444-7275) or www.reserveamerica.com. Sites are $20–25 per night, $10 per night for each additional vehicle, $3 per person per night for hike-in/bike-in site, $120 per night for group tent site. Open year-round.

Directions: From Santa Monica, drive north on Highway 1 for 28 miles to the park entrance (signed) on the right.

From Oxnard, drive south on Highway 1 for 20 miles to the park entrance (signed) on the left.

Contact: California State Parks, Angeles District 818/880-0350 or fax 818/880-6165, www.parks.ca.gov.

18 MALIBU BEACH RV PARK

Scenic rating: 7

in Malibu

Map 14.1, page 751

This is one of the few privately developed RV parks in the region that provides some sites for tent campers as well. It's one of the nicer spots in the area, set on a bluff overlooking the Pacific Ocean, near both Malibu Pier (for fishing) and Paradise Cove. Each site has a view of either the ocean or adjacent mountains. Sites with ocean views are charged a small premium. Whale-watching is best in March and April, and then again in October and November. Dolphin-watching is popular year-round.

Campsites, facilities: There are 35 sites for tents, and 140 sites with full or partial hookups (30 and 50 amps) for RVs; some sites are pull-through. Picnic tables and barbecue grills are provided. Restrooms with showers, spa, recreation room, playground, coin laundry, Wi-Fi, modem access, dog walk area, propane gas, ice, cable TV, dump station, and a convenience store are available. Some facilities are wheelchair-accessible. Leashed pets are permitted, except in the tent area, and certain breeds are prohibited.

Reservations, fees: Reservations are recommended at 800/622-6052. Sites are $29.12–77.28 for RV sites, $5 per person per night for tent sites (four-person maximum per site), $10 per night for each additional vehicle, $5 per person per night for more than two people, $3 per night per pet. Some credit cards accepted. Open year-round.

Directions: Drive on Pacific Coast Highway/Highway 1 to the Malibu area. The park is two miles north of the intersection of Highway 1 and Malibu Canyon Road on the east side of the road.

Contact: Malibu Beach RV Park, 310/456-6052, www.maliburv.com.

19 DOCKWEILER BEACH RV PARK

Scenic rating: 6

near Manhattan Beach on the Pacific Ocean

Map 14.1, page 751

This layover spot for coast cruisers is just a hop from the beach and the Pacific Ocean. There is access to a 26-mile-long coastal bike path.

Campsites, facilities: There are 117 sites with full hookups (20, 30, and 50 amps) for RVs up to 37 feet. No tents. Picnic tables and barbecue grills are provided. Restrooms with flush toilets and showers, dump station, and coin laundry are available. Some facilities are wheelchair-accessible. You can buy supplies nearby. Leashed pets are permitted, with a two-dog limit.

Reservations, fees: Reservations are accepted ($7 reservation fee) at 310/322-4951 or 800/950-7275. Sites are $24–32 per night, $2 per pet per night. Open year-round. Some credit cards accepted.

Directions: From Santa Monica and the junction of I-405 and I-10, take I-405 south and drive 12 miles to the exit for Imperial Highway west. Take that exit and drive west on Imperial Highway for four miles to the park (signed) on the left.

Contact: Dockweiler Beach RV Park, Los Angeles County, 310/322-7036.

20 BOLSA CHICA STATE BEACH

Scenic rating: 7

near Huntington Beach

Map 14.1, page 751

This state beach extends three miles from Seal Beach to Huntington Beach City Pier. A bikeway connects it with Huntington State Beach, seven miles to the south. Across the road from Bolsa Chica is the 1,000-acre Bolsa Chica Ecological Preserve, managed by the Department of Fish and Game. The campground consists of basically a beachfront parking lot, but a popular one at that. A great little walk is available at the adjacent Bolsa Chica State Reserve, a 1.5-mile loop that provides an escape from the parking lot and entry into the 530-acre nature reserve, complete with egrets, pelicans, and many shorebirds. Lifeguard service is available during the summer. This camp has a seven-day maximum stay during the summer and a 14-day maximum stay during the winter. Surf fishing is popular here for perch, cabezon, small sharks, and croaker. There are also occasional runs of grunion, a small fish that spawns in hordes on the sandy beaches of Southern California.

Campsites, facilities: There are 56 sites with full hookups (30 and 50 amps) available in a parking lot configuration for RVs up to 48 feet. No tents. Fire rings are provided. Restrooms with flush toilets and coin showers, drinking water, Wi-Fi, dump station, picnic areas, bicycle trail, volleyball, basketball, and food service (seasonal) are available. Some facilities are wheelchair-accessible, including a paved ramp for wheelchair access to the beach. Leashed pets are permitted at campsites.

Reservations, fees: Reservations are accepted ($7.50 reservation fee) at 800/444-PARK (800/444-7275) or www.reserveamerica.com. Sites are $29–39 per night, $10 per night for each additional vehicle. Open year-round.

Directions: Drive on Highway 1 to the park entrance (1.5 miles north of Huntington Beach).

Contact: Bolsa Chica State Beach, 714/846-3460; Huntington State Beach, 714/536-1454, www.parks.ca.gov.

21 PARSON'S LANDING HIKE-IN
🚶 🏊 🛶 5% 🏕

Scenic rating: 10

on Catalina Island

Map 14.1, page 751   BEST (

This primitive campground is one of five on Catalina Island. It is set on the island's northern end, seven miles from the island's isthmus and the village of Two Harbors. If you want to try and avoid the crowds, this is the area to

visit; forget Avalon and head instead to Two Harbors.

Campsites, facilities: There are eight tent sites, each for up to six campers. Picnic tables, barbecue and fire rings, and a locker with firewood and 2.5 gallons of drinking water are provided. Chemical toilets are available. There are no sun shades, so bring your own. Pets are not permitted.

Reservations, fees: Reservations are required at 310/510-8368. Sites are $12 per person per night, $6 per person per night for ages 11 and under, plus $9 first night for wood and water. A fee is charged for the ferry ride to Avalon at Catalina Island from Newport Beach, Long Beach, or San Pedro. Check in at the Two Harbors visitor information booth to validate your camping permit and obtain locker key for water and wood. Open year-round, weather permitting, with a 10-day maximum stay.

Directions: Take ferry boat ride to Avalon. From Avalon, take shuttle bus to Two Harbors. At Two Harbors, check in at the visitor information booth to validate your camping permit and obtain locker key for water and wood. From Two Harbors, hike seven miles to campsites. Note: A shuttle boat is sometimes available from Two Harbors to Emerald Bay; from Emerald Bay, it is a 1.5-mile hike to the campground.

Contact: For ferry information, camp reservations, or general information: Avalon, 310/510-2800; Two Harbors, 310/510-0303, www.scico.com.

22 TWO HARBORS
🚶 🏊 🛶 5% 🏕

Scenic rating: 10

on Catalina Island

Map 14.1, page 751   BEST (

This campground is only 0.25 mile away from the village of Two Harbors. Nearby attractions include the Two Harbors Dive Station with snorkeling equipment, paddleboard rentals, and scuba tank fills to 3,000 psi. There are guided tours of the island and a scheduled bus service between Two Harbors and Avalon; the bus stops at all the interior campgrounds. An excellent hike is the nine-mile round-trip from Two Harbors to Emerald Bay, featuring a gorgeous coast and pretty valleys. A 0.25-mile hike is required to reach this campground.

Campsites, facilities: There are 42 sites for tents, three group sites for up to 25 people each, and 13 tent cabins for up to six people each. Picnic tables and fire grills are provided. Drinking water, sun shades (at most sites), cold showers, and chemical toilets are available. Tent cabin sites also include cots, camp stove, and lantern. Firewood, charcoal, and propane are sold at the ranger station and can also be ordered in advance. A general store, restaurant and saloon, snack bar, tennis courts, volleyball, coin laundry, and hot showers are available in the town of Two Harbors. Pets are not permitted.

Reservations, fees: Reservations are required at 310/510-8368. For groups of at least 20 people, reserve at 310/510-2800, extension 1412. Sites are $12 per person per night, $6 per night for ages 11 and under. A fee is charged for the round-trip ferry ride to Avalon at Catalina Island from Newport Beach, Long Beach, or San Pedro. Check in at the visitor information booth to validate your camping permit and obtain locker key for water and wood. Open year-round, weather permitting, except for tent cabins, which are open April to October. Maximum stay is 10 days.

Directions: Take ferry boat ride to Avalon. From Avalon, take shuttle bus to Two Harbors. At Two Harbors, check in at the visitor information booth to validate your camping permit and obtain locker key for water and wood. From Two Harbors, hike 0.25 mile to campground.

Contact: For ferry information, camp reservations, or general information: Avalon, 310/510-2800; Two Harbors, 310/510-0303, www.scico.com.

23 LITTLE HARBOR HIKE-IN

Scenic rating: 10

on Catalina Island

Map 14.1, page 751   **BEST**

There is plenty to do here: You can swim, dive, fish, or go for day hikes. There are two sandy beaches near this camp. One is great for swimming and snorkeling, and the other has surf for boogie boarding. A Native American historic site is nearby. Two Harbors has several excellent hikes, including the nine-mile excursion to Emerald Bay. Of course, you could always take the shuttle bus. Many folks consider this to be the pick of the campgrounds on the island. It is a gorgeous place—small wonder that some big Hollywood flicks have been shot here.

Campsites, facilities: There are 16 tent sites. Picnic tables and fire rings are provided. Drinking water, cold showers, sun shades (at most sites), pay telephone, shuttle bus service, and chemical toilets are available. Wood, charcoal, and propane are available from the ranger station, and it is recommended that you order in advance. Kayak and snorkel gear rentals are available in Two Harbors. Pets are not permitted.

Reservations, fees: Reservations are required at 310/510-8368. The fee is $12 per person per night, $6 per person per night for ages 11 and under. A fee is charged for the round-trip ferry ride to Avalon at Catalina Island from Newport Beach, Long Beach, or San Pedro. Check in at the visitor information booth to validate your camping permit and obtain locker key for water and wood. Open year-round, weather permitting, with a maximum stay of 10 days.

Directions: Take ferry boat ride to Avalon. From Avalon, take shuttle bus (or hike or bike) to Little Harbor. From Little Harbor, hike 6.8 miles to the campground. The campground is about 16 miles from Avalon.

Contact: For ferry information, camp reservations, or general information: Avalon, 310/510-2800; Two Harbors, 310/510-0303; Wet Spot Rentals, 310/510-2229, www.scico .com.

24 BLACK JACK HIKE-IN
🏃 🏊 🛶 5% ⛺

Scenic rating: 7

on Catalina Island

Map 14.1, page 751

This camp is named after Mount Black Jack (2,008 feet), the island's highest point, and it is a great place to hunker down for a spell. It's also the site of the old Black Jack Mine. This is the least-popular campground on the island, viewed by most as a stopover site, not a base camp. From Black Jack Junction (accessible by shuttle bus), it is a 1.5-mile hike to the camp. Note that shuttle bus service is limited from October to mid-June. The camp is set at 1,500 feet in elevation. The camp is nine miles from Avalon and 11.8 miles from Two Harbors. If you stand in just the right spot, you can see the mainland, but Los Angeles will seem like a million miles away.

Campsites, facilities: There are 11 tent sites with a maximum of six campers per site. Drinking water, picnic tables, fire rings, cold showers, and a locker with firewood are provided. Chemical toilets are available. A pay phone is available nearby. Propane, charcoal, and other rental equipment are available April through October. Pets are not permitted.

Reservations, fees: Reservations are required at 310/510-8368. The fee is $12 per person per night, $6 per person per night for ages 11 and under. A fee is charged for the round-trip ferry ride to Avalon at Catalina Island from Newport Beach, Long Beach, or San Pedro. Check in at the visitor information booth to validate your camping permit and obtain locker key for water and wood. Open year-round, weather permitting, with a maximum stay of 10 days.

Directions: Take ferry boat ride to Avalon.

From Avalon, take the shuttle bus to Black Jack Junction. Depart the bus and hike one mile to the campground.

Contact: For ferry information, camp reservations, or general information: Avalon, 310/510-2800; Two Harbors, 310/510-0303, www.scico.com.

25 CATALINA ISLAND BOAT-IN
🏃 🏊 🛶 🚤 🐎 5% ⛺

Scenic rating: 10

on Catalina Island

Map 14.1, page 751   BEST (

Here is one of the most unusual and best camping experiences in California: the 11 boat-in sites at Catalina Island. These primitive camps are on the north shore of the island, between Avalon and Two Harbors. You reach them by private boat or by renting a kayak and paddling there. There are no overnight powerboat rentals on the island. A ranger checks each boat-in site daily and collects any fees. There are no moorings, so you must anchor your boat and use a dinghy to reach shore. Since these sites are primitive, they have no toilets, no drinking water, no fire rings, and no sun shade. That means you must plan your trip carefully.

Campsites, facilities: There are 17 primitive boat-in sites for tents. Picnic tables are provided. There are no toilets; bring your own or buy waste-disposal bags from the ranger. There is no drinking water or shade. No campfires or beach fires are allowed; charcoal and propane stoves are permitted. Garbage must be packed out. Kayak rentals are available in Avalon or Two Harbors. No moorings. Leashed pets are permitted.

Reservations, fees: Reservations are accepted at 310/510-8368. Sites are $12 per person per night, $6 per night for ages 11 and under. Fishing license is required if fishing. Open year-round, weather permitting, with a maximum stay of 10 days.

Directions: Boat-in or take ferry boat ride to Avalon. From Avalon or Two Harbors, rent kayak and paddle to campsite or reach the camp by private boat.

Contact: For ferry information, camp reservations, or general information: Avalon, 310/510-2800; Two Harbors, 310/510-0303, www.campingcatalinaisland.com.

26 HERMIT GULCH

Scenic rating: 10

on Catalina Island

Map 14.1, page 751   BEST (

This is the closest campground to the town of Avalon, the gateway to Catalina. Reaching the camp requires a 1.5-mile hike up Avalon Canyon. If you're making a tourist trip, there are a ton of things to do here: Visit Avalon's underwater city park, play the nine-hole golf course, rent a bicycle, or visit the famous casino. Scenic tours, glass-bottomed boat tours, and Wrigley Memorial and Botanical Gardens are available. Fishing can be excellent, including angling for white seabass, yellowtail, and, in the fall, even marlin. The best hiking experience in the Avalon area is found by taking the shuttle bus to the Airport in the Sky and from there hiking along Empire Landing Road. The route traces the island's curving, hilly northern shore, providing great views of secluded beaches, coves, and rock formations, and a chance to see wildlife, at times even buffalo. Note that free hiking permits are required. Also, if cycling outside of Avalon, a $50 permit is required! Taxi service is available in Avalon, but it is expensive.

Campsites, facilities: There are 42 sites for tents and eight tent cabins. Picnic tables, fire rings, and barbecue pits are provided. Restrooms with flush toilets and coin showers, drinking water, ice, lockers, playground, coin microwave, vending machines, and a pay phone are available. Some camping equipment is available for rent.

Groups can be accommodated. Wood fires are not allowed. Pets are not permitted.

Reservations, fees: Reservations are required at 310/510-8368. Sites are $12 per night, $6 per person per night for ages 11 and under. The fee for tent cabins is $40 per night, plus $6–12 per person. A fee is charged for the round-trip ferry ride to Avalon at Catalina Island from Newport Beach, Long Beach, or San Pedro. Check in at the visitor information booth to validate your camping permit and obtain locker key for water and wood. Open year-round, weather permitting, with a maximum stay of 10 days.

Directions: Take ferry boat ride to Avalon. In Avalon at Sumner Avenue, walk up Avalon Canyon (follow the "Avalon Canyon Road" sign) for 1.5 miles to the campground. The camp is across from the picnic area.

Contact: For ferry information, camp reservations, or general information: Avalon, 310/510-2800; Two Harbors, 310/510-0303, www.scico.com.

27 SYCAMORE FLATS

Scenic rating: 7

on Big Rock Creek in Angeles National Forest

Map 14.2, page 752

Sycamore Flats is a developed camp just inside the northern boundary of Angeles National Forest, set at 4,200 feet on the southwest flank of Pinyon Ridge. While there are no trails leading out from this camp, a trailhead is at South Fork, which is two miles to the south.

Campsites, facilities: There are 11 sites for tents or RVs up to 18 feet (no hookups). Picnic tables and fire grills are provided. Vault toilets are available. There is no drinking water. Garbage must be packed out. Leashed pets are permitted. There is no drinking water in dry years.

Reservations, fees: Reservations are not accepted. There is no fee for camping. Adventure Pass ($30 annual fee or a $5 daily fee per vehicle) is required. Open year-round, weather permitting.

Directions: From Palmdale (at the junction of Highway 14 and Highway 138), take Highway 138 southeast and drive about 10 miles to Pearblossom and Longview Road. Turn south (right) and drive a short distance to Avenue W/Valyermo Road. Turn left on Avenue W/Valyermo Road and drive about 20 miles into the national forest (past the ranger station) to Big Rock Road. Turn right on Big Rock Road and drive about two miles to the campground entrance.

Contact: Angeles National Forest, Santa Clara/Mojave Rivers Ranger District, 661/296-9710, fax 661/296-5847.

28 SOUTH FORK
🏃 🏊 🐕 🚐 🏕

Scenic rating: 7

on Big Rock Creek in Angeles National Forest

Map 14.2, page 752

This is an excellent trailhead camp set at 4,500 feet along South Fork Creek. One trail climbs 2.2 miles to the west to Devils Punchbowl County Park, topping out at Devils Chair (the trail includes a steep descent and climb). There are two other options. You can hike south along Big Rock Creek, and another hike heads east on High Desert National Recreation Trail (also called Manzanita Trail).

Campsites, facilities: There are 21 sites for tents or RVs up to 16 feet (no hookups). Picnic tables and fire rings are provided. Vault toilets are available. No drinking water is available. Garbage must be packed out. Leashed pets are permitted.

Reservations, fees: Reservations are not accepted. An Adventure Pass ($30 annual fee or a $5 daily fee per vehicle) is required. Open year-round, weather permitting.

Directions: From Palmdale (at the junction of Highway 14 and Highway 138), take Highway 138 southeast and drive about 10

miles to Pearblossom and Longview Road. Turn south (right) and drive a short distance to Avenue W/Valyermo Road. Turn left on Avenue W/Valyermo Road and drive about 20 miles into the national forest (past the ranger station) to Big Rock Road. Turn right on Big Rock Road and drive about two miles up the canyon (past the Sycamore Flat campground entrance) to the South Fork campground entrance.

Contact: Angeles National Forest, Santa Clara/Mojave River Ranger District, 661/296-9710, fax 661/296-5847.

29 TABLE MOUNTAIN
🐕 🚐 🏕

Scenic rating: 6

in Angeles National Forest

Map 14.2, page 752

This is a family campground that accommodates both tents and RVs. The road leading in is a paved two-lane county road, easily accessible by any vehicle. The nearby Big Pines Visitor Information Center, one mile to the south, can provide maps and information on road conditions. The camp elevation is 7,200 feet. A rough road for four-wheel-drive rigs is available out of camp that leads north along the Table Mountain Ridge.

Campsites, facilities: There are 115 sites for tents or RVs up to 32 feet (no hookups). Picnic tables and fire pits are provided. Drinking water, vault toilets and a reservable amphitheater are available. Leashed pets are permitted.

Reservations, fees: Reservations are accepted ($9 reservation fee) at 877/444-6777 or www.ReserveUSA.com. Sites are $13 per night. Open May through November, weather permitting.

Directions: Drive on I-15 to Cajon Junction (north of San Bernardino) and the exit for Highway 138 west. Take that exit and drive west on Highway 138 to Angeles Crest Highway/Highway 2. Turn west on Angeles Crest

Highway and drive five miles to Wrightwood, then continue for three miles to Big Pines and Table Mountain Road. Turn right on Table Mountain Road and drive one mile to the campground.

Contact: Angeles National Forest, Santa Clara/Mojave Rivers Ranger District, 661/296-9710, fax 661/296-5847; Big Pines Visitor Center, 760/249-3504.

30 BUCKHORN

Scenic rating: 9

near Snowcrest Ridge in Angeles National Forest

Map 14.2, page 752

This is a prime jump-off spot for backpackers in Angeles National Forest. The camp is set at 6,300 feet among huge pine and cedar trees, along a small creek near Mount Waterman (8,038 feet). A great day hike begins here, a tromp down to Cooper Canyon and the PCT; hikers will be rewarded by beautiful Cooper Falls on this three-hour round-trip. Want a weekend trip? Got it: The Burkhart National Recreational Trail descends into Caruthers Canyon where hikers can access the High Desert National Recreational Trail and head east to Devil's Punchbowl County Park to Vincent's Gap and the Pacific Crest Trail.

Campsites, facilities: There are 38 sites for tents or RVs up to 18 feet (no hookups). Picnic tables and fire pits are provided. Drinking water and vault toilets are available. Leashed pets are permitted.

Reservations, fees: Reservations are not accepted. Sites are $12 per night. Open April to mid-November, weather permitting.

Directions: From Pasadena, drive north on I-210 for four miles to the exit for Highway 2/Angeles Crest Highway. Take that exit and drive northeast on Highway 2 for 35 miles to the signed campground entrance.

Contact: Angeles National Forest, Los Ange-

les River Ranger District, 818/899-1900, fax 818/896-6727.

31 JACKSON FLAT GROUP CAMP WALK-IN

Scenic rating: 4

near the Pacific Crest Trail in Angeles National Forest

Map 14.2, page 752

This is a good spot for a group to overnight, assess themselves, and get information before heading out into the surrounding wildlands. The camp is set in the Angeles National Forest high country at 7,500 feet, near the end of a short spur road. It takes a 200-yard walk to reach this campground from the parking area. There are two nature trails and an observation deck on site. The Pacific Crest Trail passes just north of camp and can be reached by a short connecting link trail.

Campsites, facilities: There are five group tent sites for 30–40 people each. Picnic tables and fire pits are provided. Drinking water and flush and vault toilets are available. Leashed pets are permitted.

Reservations, fees: Reservations are required ($9 reservation fee) at 877/444-6777 or www.ReserveUSA.com. Sites are $85–100 per night. Open June through October, weather permitting.

Directions: Drive on I-15 to Cajon Junction (north of San Bernardino) and the exit for Highway 138 west. Take that exit and drive west on Highway 138 to Angeles Crest Highway/Highway 2. Turn west on Angeles Crest Highway and drive five miles to Wrightwood, then continue for three miles to Big Pines. Bear left (still on Angeles Crest Highway) and drive two miles to a Forest Service road (opposite the sign for Grassy Hollow Campground). Turn right and drive one mile to the campground parking lot. Walk 200 yards to the campground.

Contact: Angeles National Forest, Santa Clara/

Mojave Rivers Ranger District, 661/296-9710, fax 661/296-5847.

32 CABIN FLAT HIKE-IN
🧍 🛶 🐕 5% ⛰

Scenic rating: 7

on Prairie Fork Creek in Angeles National Forest

Map 14.2, page 752

It takes a six-mile trek to get here, but that done, you're guaranteed solitude along little Prairie Fork Creek, deep in the Angeles National Forest. Along the way, you will pass several other camps, including Guffy and Lupine. A short trail runs beside the stream for about a quarter mile. The elevation is 5,300 feet. The campground area is closed to vehicles to protect the yellow-legged frog.

Campsites, facilities: There are 12 sites for tents or RVs up to 16 feet (no hookups). Picnic tables and fire pits are provided. Vault toilets are available. There is no drinking water. Garbage must be packed out. Leashed pets are permitted.

Reservations, fees: Reservations are not accepted. There is no fee for camping. Adventure Pass ($30 annual fee or a $5 daily fee per vehicle) is required. Open mid-May through November, weather permitting.

Directions: From I-15 near Cajon, take Highway 138 west. Turn west on Angeles Crest Highway/Highway 2 and drive five miles to Wrightwood. Continue for three miles to Big Pines. Bear left and continue on Angeles Crest Highway for 1.5 miles to Blue Ridge Road. Turn left (opposite Inspiration Point) on Blue Ridge Road and drive five miles to Guffy Campground. From Guffy, you can hike, bike, or ride a horse for six miles to Cabin Flat Campground.

Contact: Angeles National Forest, Santa Clara/Mojave Rivers Ranger District, 661/296-9710, fax 661/296-5847.

33 APPLE TREE
🐕 ⛰

Scenic rating: 6

near Jackson Lake in Angeles National Forest

Map 14.2, page 752

This is one of four camps set on Big Pines "Highway" near Jackson Lake. This "lake" is more of a pond and is about a half mile to the west, just up the road. Lake and Peavine Camps are between Apple Tree and Jackson Lake, while Mountain Oak is just beyond the lake. Any questions? Rangers can answer them at the nearby Big Pines Visitor Information Center and ski complex. The elevation is 6,200 feet.

Campsites, facilities: There are eight tent sites. Picnic tables and fire rings are provided. Vault toilets are available. There is no drinking water. Garbage must be packed out. Leashed pets are permitted.

Reservations, fees: Reservations are not accepted. There is no fee for camping. Adventure Pass ($30 annual fee or a $5 daily fee per vehicle) is required. Open year-round, weather permitting.

Directions: Drive on I-15 to Cajon Junction (north of San Bernardino) and the exit for Highway 138 west. Take that exit and drive west on Highway 138 to Angeles Crest Highway/Highway 2. Turn west on Angeles Crest Highway and drive five miles to Wrightwood, and then continue for three miles to Big Pines and Big Pines Highway/County Road N4. Bear right on Big Pines Highway and drive two miles to the campground.

Contact: Angeles National Forest, Santa Clara/Mojave Rivers Ranger District, 661/296-9710, fax 661/296-5847.

34 MOUNTAIN OAK

Scenic rating: 4

near Jackson Lake in Angeles National Forest

Map 14.2, page 752

This is one of four camps within a mile of little Jackson Lake on Big Pines Highway. The others are Lake, Peavine, and Apple Tree. This camp is about a quarter mile northwest of the lake. The elevation is 6,200 feet.

Campsites, facilities: There are 17 sites for tents or RVs up to 18 feet (no hookups). Picnic tables and fire pits are provided. Vault and flush toilets are available. There is no drinking water. Groceries and propane gas are nearby. Leashed pets are permitted.

Reservations, fees: Reservations are accepted ($9 reservation fee) at 877/444-6777 or www.ReserveUSA.com. Sites are $12 per night. Open May through November, weather permitting.

Directions: Drive on I-15 to Cajon Junction (north of San Bernardino) and the exit for Highway 138 west. Take that exit and drive west on Highway 138 to Angeles Crest Highway/Highway 2. Turn west on Angeles Crest Highway and drive five miles to Wrightwood, and then continue for three miles to Big Pines and Big Pines Highway/County Road N4. Bear right on Big Pines Highway and drive three miles to the campground.

Contact: Angeles National Forest, Santa Clara/Mojave Rivers Ranger District, 661/296-9710, fax 661/296-5847.

35 LAKE

Scenic rating: 8

on Jackson Lake in Angeles National Forest

Map 14.2, page 752

This is a pretty setting on the southeast shore of little Jackson Lake. Of the four camps within a mile, this is the only one right beside the lake. The elevation is 6,100 feet.

Campsites, facilities: There are eight sites for tents or RVs up to 18 feet (no hookups). Picnic tables and fire pits are provided. Vault toilets are available. There is no drinking water. Leashed pets are permitted. Some facilities are wheelchair-accessible.

Reservations, fees: Reservations are accepted ($9 reservation fee) at 877/444-6777 or www.ReserveUSA.com. Sites are $12 per night. Open May through November, weather permitting.

Directions: Drive on I-15 to Cajon Junction (north of San Bernardino) and the exit for Highway 138 west. Take that exit and drive west on Highway 138 to Angeles Crest Highway/Highway 2. Turn west on Angeles Crest Highway and drive five miles to Wrightwood, and then continue for three miles to Big Pines and Big Pines Highway/County Road N4. Bear right on Big Pines Highway and drive 2.5 miles to the campground.

Contact: Angeles National Forest, Santa Clara/Mojave Rivers Ranger District, 661/296-9710, fax 661/296-5847.

36 PEAVINE

Scenic rating: 4

near Jackson Lake in Angeles National Forest

Map 14.2, page 752

This tiny camp is one of four in the immediate area, just 0.5 mile east of little eight-acre Jackson Lake. This area is popular for snow play in the winter. The elevation is 6,100 feet.

Campsites, facilities: There are four tent sites. Picnic tables and fire pits are provided. Vault toilets are available. There is no drinking water. Garbage must be packed out. A store and propane gas are nearby. Leashed pets are permitted.

Reservations, fees: Reservations are not accepted. There is no fee for camping. Adventure Pass ($30 annual fee or a $5 daily fee per vehicle) is required. Open year-round, weather permitting.

Directions: Drive on I-15 to Cajon Junction (north of San Bernardino) and the exit for Highway 138 west. Take that exit and drive west on Highway 138 to Angeles Crest Highway/Highway 2. Turn west on Angeles Crest Highway and drive five miles to Wrightwood, and then continue for three miles to Big Pines and Big Pines Highway/County Road N4. Bear right on Big Pines Highway and drive and drive 2.7 miles to the campground.

Contact: Angeles National Forest, Santa Clara/Mojave Rivers Ranger District, 661/296-9710, fax 661/296-5847.

37 BLUE RIDGE

Scenic rating: 8

on the Pacific Crest Trail in Angeles National Forest

Map 14.2, page 752

Blue Ridge is set high in Angeles National Forest at 8,000 feet and makes a jump-off spot for a multiday backpacking trip. The Pacific Crest Trail runs right alongside the camp. Guffy, also aside the PCT, provides an option two miles to the southeast. Note that some of the surrounding area is closed to vehicles to protect the yellow-legged frog.

Campsites, facilities: There are eight sites for tents or RVs up to 20 feet. Picnic tables and fire rings are provided. Vault toilets are available. No drinking water is available. Garbage must be packed out. Leashed pets are permitted.

Reservations, fees: Reservations are not accepted. There is no fee for camping. Adventure Pass ($30 annual fee or a $5 daily fee per vehicle) is required. Open May through November, weather permitting.

Directions: Drive on I-15 to Cajon Junction (north of San Bernardino) and the exit for Highway 138 west. Take that exit and drive west on Highway 138 to Angeles Crest Highway/Highway 2. Turn west on Angeles Crest

Highway and drive five miles to Wrightwood, and then continue for three miles to Big Pines. Bear left (still on Angeles Crest Highway) and drive 1.5 miles to Blue Ridge Road (adjacent to Inspiration Point). Turn left on Blue Ridge Road and drive three miles to the campground.

Contact: Angeles National Forest, Santa Clara/Mojave Rivers Ranger District, 661/296-9710, fax 661/296-5847.

38 LUPINE WALK-IN

Scenic rating: 7

on Prairie Fork Creek in Angeles National Forest

Map 14.2, page 752

This little-known, hard-to-reach camp, set at 6,500 feet along Prairie Fork Creek, is now a walk-in camp. It is closed to vehicles in order to protect the yellow-legged frog. A challenging butt-kicker hike on a primitive trail starts here. The trail leads from the camp over Pine Mountain Ridge, down into a canyon, and then winds to the east up Dawson Peak—long, difficult, and completed by few.

Campsites, facilities: There are 11 sites for tents only. Picnic tables and fire pits are provided. Vault toilets are available. No drinking water is available. Garbage must be packed out. Leashed pets are permitted.

Reservations, fees: Reservations are not accepted. There is no fee for camping. Adventure Pass ($30 annual fee or a $5 daily fee per vehicle) is required. Open May through November, weather permitting.

Directions: Drive on I-15 to Cajon Junction (north of San Bernardino) and the exit for Highway 138 west. Take that exit and drive west on Highway 138 to Angeles Crest Highway/Highway 2. Turn west on Angeles Crest Highway and drive five miles to Wrightwood, and then continue for three miles to Big Pines. Bear left (still on Angeles

Crest Highway) and drive 1.5 miles to Blue Ridge Road (adjacent to Inspiration Point). Turn left on Blue Ridge Road and drive five miles to the locked gate. From here, you can hike, bike, or ride a horse for three miles to the campground.

Contact: Angeles National Forest, Santa Clara/ Mojave Rivers Ranger District, 661/296-9710, fax 661/296-5847.

39 GUFFY HIKE-IN

Scenic rating: 7

on the Pacific Crest Trail in Angeles National Forest

Map 14.2, page 752

A short trail right out of this camp connects with the Pacific Crest Trail, making Guffy a backpacker's special. The camp and access road are closed to vehicles in order to protect the yellow-legged frog. The elevation is 8,300 feet.

Campsites, facilities: There are six tent sites. Picnic tables and fire rings are provided. Vault toilets are available. No drinking water is available. Garbage must be packed out. Leashed pets are permitted.

Reservations, fees: Reservations are not accepted. An Adventure Pass ($30 annual fee or a $5 daily fee per vehicle) is required. Open May through November, weather permitting.

Directions: From I-15 near Cajon, take Highway 138 west. Turn west on Angeles Crest Highway/Highway 2 and drive five miles to Wrightwood. Continue for three miles to Big Pines. Bear left and continue on Angeles Crest Highway for 1.5 miles to Blue Ridge Road. Turn left (opposite Inspiration Point) on Blue Ridge Road and park. From here, you can hike, bike, or ride a horse six miles to the campground.

Contact: Angeles National Forest, Santa Clara/ Mojave Rivers Ranger District, 661/296-9710, fax 661/296-5847.

40 MOJAVE RIVER FORKS REGIONAL PARK

Scenic rating: 5

near Silverwood Lake

Map 14.2, page 752

Full hookups are a bonus for RV drivers, as is the park's proximity to Silverwood Lake—which is only nine miles away but does not have any sites with hookups. The sites here are well spaced, but the nearby "river" is usually dry. The elevation at this 840-acre park is 3,200 feet.

Campsites, facilities: There are 25 sites with full hookups (20 and 30 amps) for RVs up to 40 feet, 25 sites with no hookups for RVs, 30 sites for tents only, and four group sites for 200–300 people each. Several sites are pull-through. Picnic tables and fire grills are provided. Restrooms with flush toilets and showers, drinking water, and a dump station are available. Leashed pets are permitted.

Reservations, fees: Reservations are accepted for group sites only. Sites are $10–20 per night, $5 per night for each additional vehicle, $1 per pet per night. Some credit cards accepted. Campers must show proof of current vehicle registration and insurance. Open year-round.

Directions: Drive on I-15 to Cajon Junction (north of San Bernardino) and the exit for Highway 138/Silverwood. Take that exit east and drive nine miles to a fork with Highway 173. Bear left at the fork on Highway 173 and drive six miles to the park on the right.

Contact: Mojave River Forks Regional Park, 760/389-2322, www.co.san-bernardino .ca.us/parks.

41 BIG PINE FLATS

Scenic rating: 6

in San Bernardino National Forest

Map 14.2, page 752

This is a favorite staging area for OHV users, with many OHV trails nearby. It is a pretty spot set at 6,800 feet in San Bernardino National Forest and provides a little of both worlds: You are surrounded by wildlands near Redondo Ridge, yet you're not a long drive (about 45 minutes) from Big Bear Lake to the south. Any questions? The firefighters at Big Pine Flats Fire Station, just across the road, can answer them.

Campsites, facilities: There are 17 sites for tents or RVs up to 32 feet (no hookups). Picnic tables and fire grills are provided. Vault toilets are available. No drinking water is available. Leashed pets are permitted.

Reservations, fees: Reservations are not accepted. Sites are $16 per night. Open mid-May to mid-October.

Directions: Drive on Highway 30 to the junction with Highway 330 (east of San Bernardino near Highland). Take Highway 330 north (signed "Mountain Resorts") and drive 35 miles to the dam on Big Bear Lake and a fork with Highway 38. Continue straight on Highway 38 and drive about four miles to the town of Fawnskin and Rim of the World Highway. Turn left and drive seven miles (after 0.5 mile it becomes Forest Road 3N14, a dirt road) to Big Pine Flats Fire Station and the campground on the right.

Contact: San Bernardino National Forest, Mountaintop Ranger District, Big Bear Ranger Station/Discovery Center, 909/382-2790, fax 909/866-1781.

42 BIG PINE GROUP AND EQUESTRIAN

Scenic rating: 3

in San Bernardino National Forest

Map 14.2, page 752

This camp is adjacent to the Big Pine Flats Fire Station and is used by equestrians and OHV riders. A trailhead for the Pacific Crest Trail is about two miles to the southeast of the camp via Forest Road 3N14. The elevation is 6,700 feet.

Campsites, facilities: There is one group camp for tents or RVs up to 32 feet (no hookups) that can accommodate up to 60 people. Picnic tables and fire grills are provided. Vault toilets and drinking water are available. Horse facilities include corrals and water troughs. Leashed pets are permitted.

Reservations, fees: Reservations are required ($9 reservation fee) at 877/444-6777 or www.ReserveUSA.com. The camp is $65 per night. Open mid-May to mid-November.

Directions: Drive on Highway 30 to the junction with Highway 330 (east of San Bernardino near Highland). Take Highway 330 north (signed "Mountain Resorts") and drive 35 miles to the dam on Big Bear Lake and a fork with Highway 38. Continue straight on Highway 38 and drive about four miles to the town of Fawnskin and Rim of the World Highway. Turn left and drive seven miles (after 0.5 mile it becomes Forest Road 3N14, a dirt road) to Forest Road 3N16. Turn left and drive 0.25 mile to the campground on the right.

Contact: San Bernardino National Forest, Mountain Top Ranger District, Big Bear Ranger Station/Discovery Center, 909/382-2790, fax 909/866-1781.

43 COLDBROOK

Scenic rating: 5

on the North Fork of the San Gabriel River in Angeles National Forest

Map 14.2, page 752

Note: At the time of publication, this campground was closed, but expected to reopen; check for current status before planning a trip. This roadside camp is set along the North Fork San Gabriel River, with little Crystal Lake to the north. A secret waterfall is hidden off the road, about three miles north on Soldier Creek. To find it, park at the deep bending turn in the road at Soldier Creek, then hike uphill for less than a mile. It's just like a treasure hunt, and it's always a welcome surprise to find the waterfall. The elevation is 3,300 feet. Note that there is some damage from a 2002 wildfire and a 2005 flood.

Campsites, facilities: There are 20 sites for tents or RVs up to 22 feet (no hookups). Picnic tables and fire rings are provided. Vault toilets are available. No drinking water is available. Garbage must be packed out. Leashed pets are permitted.

Reservations, fees: Reservations are not accepted. Sites are $12 per night, $5 per night for each additional vehicle. Open year-round.

Directions: Drive on I-210 to Azusa and the exit for Azusa Canyon and San Gabriel Canyon Road/Highway 39. Take that exit and drive north on San Gabriel Canyon Road for 18 miles to the campground entrance.

Contact: Angeles National Forest, San Gabriel River Ranger District, 626/335-1251, fax 626/914-3790.

44 MANKER FLATS
🏞 🐴 🚐 ⛺

Scenic rating: 7

near Mount Baldy in Angeles National Forest

Map 14.2, page 752   **BEST** (

This camp is best known for its proximity to Mount Baldy and the nearby trailhead to reach San Antonio Falls. The trail to San Antonio Falls starts at an elevation of 6,160 feet, 0.3 mile up the road on the left. From here, it's a 1.5-mile saunter on a ski park maintenance road to the waterfall, a pretty 80-footer. The wild and ambitious can continue six more miles and climb to the top of Mount Baldy (10,064 feet) for breathtaking 360-degree views. Making this all-day butt-kicker is like a baptism for Southern California hikers.

Campsites, facilities: There are 21 sites for tents or RVs up to 16 feet (no hookups). Picnic tables and fire grills are provided. Drinking water and flush toilets are available. Leashed pets are permitted. There is no drinking water in dry years.

Reservations, fees: Reservations are not accepted. Sites are $12 per night, $5 per night for each additional vehicle. Open May through September.

Directions: Drive on I-10 to Ontario and the exit for Highway 83. Take that exit and drive north on Highway 83 to Mount Baldy Road. Continue north on Mount Baldy Road for nine miles to the campground.

Contact: Angeles National Forest, San Gabriel River Ranger District, 626/335-1251, fax 626/914-3790.

45 APPLE WHITE
🏞 🐴 ♿ 🚐 ⛺

Scenic rating: 5

near Lytle Creek in San Bernardino National Forest

Map 14.2, page 752

Nothing like a little insiders' know-how, especially at this camp, set at 3,300 feet near Lytle Creek. You can reach the Middle Fork of Lytle Creek by driving north from Fontana via Serra Avenue to the Lytle Creek area. To get to the stretch of water that is stocked with trout by the Department of Fish and Game, turn west on Middle Fork Road, which is 1.5 miles before the campground at Apple White. The first mile upstream is stocked repeatedly every other week in spring and early summer.

Campsites, facilities: There are 44 sites for tents or RVs up to 30 feet (no hookups). Picnic tables and fire grills are provided. Restrooms with flush toilets and drinking water are available. A store is nearby. Leashed pets are permitted. Some facilities are wheelchair-accessible.

Reservations, fees: Reservations are not accepted. Sites are $10 per night, double sites are $15 per night, $3 per night for each additional vehicle. Open year-round.

Directions: Drive to Ontario and the junction of I-10 and I-15. Take I-15 north and drive 11 miles to the Sierra Avenue exit. Take that exit and turn left, go under the freeway, and continue north (into the national forest) for about nine miles to the campground on the right.

Contact: San Bernardino National Forest, Front Country Ranger District, Lytle Creek Ranger Station, 909/382-2850, fax 909/887-8197.

46 SILVERWOOD LAKE STATE RECREATION AREA: MESA

Scenic rating: 6

on Silverwood Lake

Map 14.2, page 752

The Old Fire did extensive damage to this park in 2003. The prettiest part of the recreation area was destroyed by fire, along with damage to a section of this campground. Sites 1–13 were burned and there is no shade, so bring your own. This state park campground is on the west side of Silverwood Lake at 3,355 feet in elevation, bordered by San Bernardino National Forest to the south and high desert to the north. The hot weather and proximity to San Bernardino make it a winner with boaters, who have 1,000 surface acres of water and 13 miles of shoreline to explore. All water sports are allowed. It's a great lake for waterskiing (35-mph speed limit), water sports (5-mph speed limit in major coves), and sailboarding, with afternoon winds usually strong in the spring and early summer. Note that the quota on boats is enforced, with a maximum of 166 boats per day, and that boat-launch reservations are required on summer weekends and holidays. There are also designated areas for boating, waterskiing, and fishing to reduce conflicts. Fishing varies dramatically according to season, with trout planted in the cool months, and largemouth bass, bluegill, striped bass, catfish, and crappie caught the rest of the year. A large sandy swimming beach is available on the lake's southeast side at the Sawpit Recreation Area. The park also has a modest trail system with both nature and bike trails. Note that because of the 2003 wildfire, Miller Canyon is accessible only by

foot. It is off-limits during bald eagle nesting season. A bonus is that there are also some hike-in/bike-in campsites.

Campsites, facilities: There are 131 sites for tents or RVs up to 22 feet (no hookups), with a few for RVs of any length, and four hike-in/bike-in sites. Some sites are pull-through. Picnic tables and fire rings (fire restriction may be in effect) are provided. Restrooms with flush toilets and coin showers, drinking water, Wi-Fi, dump station, boat ramp, marina, boat rentals, and small store are available. Some facilities are wheelchair-accessible. Leashed pets are permitted.

Reservations, fees: Reservations are accepted ($7.50 reservation fee) at 800/444-PARK (800/444-7275) or www.reserveamerica.com. Sites are $20–25 per night, $8 per night for each additional vehicle, $2 per night per person for hike-in/bike-in sites. Open year-round.

Directions: Drive on I-15 to Cajon Junction (north of San Bernardino) and the exit for Highway 138 east. Take that exit and drive east on Highway 138 for 12 miles to the park entrance on the right.

Contact: Silverwood Lake State Recreation Area, 760/389-2303 or 760/389-2281; Silverwood Lake Marina, 760/389-2299, www.parks.ca.gov.

47 SILVERWOOD LAKE STATE RECREATION AREA: WEST FORK GROUP CAMPS

Scenic rating: 4

at Silverwood Lake

Map 14.2, page 752

A catastrophic fire in 2003 destroyed a good part of this group camp area, along with what many consider to be the prettiest part of the state recreation area. The Old Fire burned one of the group camps and the equestrian camp here. There are now two group camps at this site, located about 2.5 miles from the lake. There is extensive burn damage evident in this area, and work is ongoing to repair some of the damage. (For information on Silverwood Lake, see the listing for *Mesa*.) These group campgrounds are about 2.5 miles from the lake.

Campsites, facilities: There are two group camps for RVs of any length (no hookups) or tents that can accommodate up to 100 people each. Picnic tables and fire rings (fire restriction may be in effect) are provided. Restrooms with flush toilets and coin showers and drinking water are available. Some facilities are wheelchair-accessible. Shaded picnic areas, fishing, hiking, swimming, boating, food service, and a store are available nearby. A dump station is available at Mesa campground. Leashed pets are permitted.

Reservations, fees: Reservations are required ($7.50 reservation fee) at 800/444-PARK (800/444-7275) or www.reserveamerica .com. The camp is $200 per night. Open April through October.

Directions: Drive on I-15 to Cajon Junction (north of San Bernardino) and the exit for Highway 138 east. Take that exit and drive east on Highway 138 for 12 miles to the park entrance on the right.

Contact: Silverwood Lake State Recreation Area, 760/389-2303 or 760/389-2281, www .parks.ca.gov.

48 IRONWOOD GROUP CAMP
🐴 🔺

Scenic rating: 7

in San Bernardino National Forest

Map 14.2, page 752

This is a primitive and isolated group camp. It is set at 6,700 feet, nestled in huge pines amid an old-growth forest, and also close to a creek near a meadow. The last two miles of the access road can be rough going for cars.

Campsites, facilities: There is one group camp for tents only that can accommodate up to 25 people and five cars (no trailers or RVs). Picnic tables and fire grills are provided. Vault toilets are available. No drinking water is available.

Garbage must be packed out. Leashed pets are permitted.

Reservations, fees: Reservations are required ($9 reservation fee) at 877/444-6777 or www .ReserveUSA.com. The camp is $65 per night. Open mid-May to mid-October.

Directions: From San Bernardino, drive east on Highway 30 to the junction with Highway 330 (east of San Bernardino near Highland). Take Highway 330 north (signed "Mountain Resorts") and drive 35 miles to the dam on Big Bear Lake and a fork with Highway 38. Continue straight on Highway 38 and drive about four miles to the town of Fawnskin and Rim of the World Highway. Turn left and drive six miles (after 0.5 mile it becomes Forest Road 3N14, a dirt road) to Forest Road 3N97. Turn left and drive two miles to the campground.

Contact: San Bernardino National Forest, Mountain Top Ranger District, Big Bear Ranger Station/Discovery Center, 909/382-2790, fax 909/866-1781.

49 FISHERMAN'S HIKE-IN
🎎 🛶 🐴 5% 🔺

Scenic rating: 10

on Deep Creek in San Bernardino National Forest

Map 14.2, page 752

Get here and you join the 5 Percent Club. Fisherman's Hike-In is a secluded, wooded campground set deep in San Bernardino National Forest at 5,400 feet. Deep Creek, a designated Wild and Scenic River, runs alongside providing stream trout fishing and a beautiful setting. It's worth the significant effort required to get here. Once here, you will find a primitive route along the creek (which looks more like a deer trail than a hiking trail) that anglers use to tromp along the stream. The trout are small but well colored, and the first cast into the head of a pool often results in a strike. Remember, it is catch-and-release fishing only in this area.

Campsites, facilities: There are four tent sites. Picnic tables and fire grills are provided. Vault toilets are available. No drinking water is available. Garbage must be packed out. Leashed pets are permitted.

Reservations, fees: Reservations are required ($9 reservation fee) at 877/444-6777 or www .ReserveUSA.com. Sites are $10 per night. Open year-round, weather permitting.

Directions: From San Bernardino, drive east on Highway 30 to the junction with Highway 330 (east of San Bernardino near Highland). Take Highway 330 north (signed "Mountain Resorts") and drive to Running Springs and the junction with Highway 18. Turn east on Highway 18 and drive to Green Valley Road. Turn left on Green Valley Road and drive three miles to Forest Road 3N16 (a dirt road). Turn left and drive four miles (you will cross two creeks that vary in depth depending on season; high clearance is recommended but is typically not necessary) to the campground (one mile past the town of Green Valley Lake) to an intersection with Forest Road 3N34. Bear left on Forest Road 3N34 and drive west for 1.3 miles to Forest Service Trail 2W07 on your left. Park and take this hiking trail for 2.5 miles southwest to Deep Creek. The campground is on the other side of the creek.

Contact: San Bernardino National Forest, Mountaintop Ranger District, Arrowhead Ranger Station, 909/382-2782, fax 909/337-1104.

National Forest is well worth exploring; a hike along the stream to fish for small trout (catch-and-release only) or see a unique set of small waterfalls is highly recommended.

Campsites, facilities: There are 27 sites for tents or RVs up to 22 feet (no hookups). Picnic tables and fire rings are provided. Drinking water and flush toilets are available. Some facilities are wheelchair-accessible. A store is nearby. Leashed pets are permitted.

Reservations, fees: Reservations are accepted ($9 reservation fee) at 877/444-6777 or www .ReserveUSA.com. Sites are $16 per night, $5 per night for each additional vehicle. Open May through September.

Directions: Drive on Highway 30 to San Bernardino and the Waterman exit. Take that exit and drive north on Waterman Avenue until it becomes Highway 18. Continue on Highway 18/Rim of the World Highway and drive 17 miles to Highway 173. Turn left on Highway 173 and drive north for 1.6 miles to the stop sign. Turn right (still on Highway 173) and drive 2.9 miles to Hospital Road. Turn right and continue 0.1 mile to the top of the small hill. Turn left just past the hospital entrance and continue a short distance to the campground.

Contact: San Bernardino National Forest, Mountaintop Ranger District, Arrowhead Ranger Station, 909/382-2782, fax 909/337-1104.

50 NORTH SHORE

Scenic rating: 8

on Lake Arrowhead in San Bernardino National Forest

Map 14.2, page 752

Of the two camps at Lake Arrowhead, this one is preferable. It is set at 5,300 feet near the northeastern shore of the lake, which provides decent trout fishing in the spring and early summer from a boat. Note that this is a private lake, and there is no shore access. To the nearby north, Deep Creek in San Bernardino

51 TENT PEG GROUP

Scenic rating: 10

near the Pacific Crest Trail in San Bernardino National Forest

Map 14.2, page 752

This camp would be a lot easier to reach with a helicopter than a vehicle. But that's why Tent Peg is a well-loved camp for the few who book it: It's a primitive camp for groups at 5,400 feet, complete with trailhead. A rough jeep road heads out of camp to the west and down into Deep Creek. In addition, there is a trailhead for a three-mile hike down the canyon to the south to Fisherman's Hike-In campground, set along Deep Creek. The trout are small but willing, in a beautiful setting (catch-and-release only).

Campsites, facilities: There is one group camp that will accommodate 10–25 people and five vehicles. Picnic tables and fire grills are provided. Vault toilets are available. No drinking water is available. A store is approximately five miles away. Leashed pets are permitted.

Reservations, fees: Reservations are required ($9 reservation fee) at 877/444-6777 or www.ReserveUSA.com. The camp is $60 per night. Open mid-May through October.

Directions: From San Bernardino, drive east on Highway 30 to the junction with Highway 330 (east of San Bernardino near Highland). Take Highway 330 north (signed "Mountain Resorts") and drive to Running Springs and the junction with Highway 18. Turn east on Highway 18 and drive to Green Valley Road. Turn left on Green Valley Road and drive three miles to Forest Road 3N16 (a dirt road). Turn left and drive four miles (you will cross two creeks that vary in depth depending on season; high clearance is recommended but is typically not necessary) to the campground (one mile past the town of Green Valley Lake) to an intersection with Forest Road 3N34. Bear left on Forest Road 3N34 and drive one mile to the campground on the left.

Contact: San Bernardino National Forest, Mountaintop Ranger District, Arrowhead Ranger Station, 909/382-2782, fax 909/337-1104.

a developed Forest Service camp set at a fork in the road at 6,200 feet. A challenging jeep road and motorcycle trail is available from here, heading west into Deep Creek Canyon. Note that Tent Peg Group Camp is just 0.5 mile to the west on Forest Road 3N34 (hiking trails are available there).

Campsites, facilities: There are 29 sites for tents or RVs up to 16 feet (no hookups). Picnic tables and fire rings are provided. Drinking water and vault toilets are available. Leashed pets are permitted.

Reservations, fees: Reservations are accepted ($9 reservation fee) at 877/444-6777 or www.ReserveUSA.com. Sites are $16 per night. Open mid-May through October.

Directions: From San Bernardino, drive east on Highway 30 to the junction with Highway 330 (east of San Bernardino near Highland). Take Highway 330 north (signed "Mountain Resorts") and drive to Running Springs and the junction with Highway 18. Turn east on Highway 18 and drive to Green Valley Road. Turn left on Green Valley Road and drive three miles to Forest Road 3N16 (a dirt road). Turn left and drive four miles (you will cross two creeks that vary in depth depending on season; high clearance is recommended but is typically not necessary) to an intersection. Bear left at the intersection and drive a very short distance to the campground entrance on the right.

Contact: San Bernardino National Forest, Mountaintop Ranger District, Arrowhead Ranger Station, 909/382-2782, fax 909/337-1104.

52 CRAB FLATS

Scenic rating: 4

near Crab Creek in San Bernardino National Forest

Map 14.2, page 752

Four-wheel-drive cowboys and dirt-bike enthusiasts often make this a base camp, known as a staging area for off-highway vehicles. It is

53 GREEN VALLEY

Scenic rating: 7

near Green Valley Lake in San Bernardino National Forest

Map 14.2, page 752

This camp sits along pretty Green Valley Creek at an elevation of 7,000 feet. Little Green Valley Lake is a mile to the west; it is privately owned, but public access is allowed. It's quiet and intimate at this lake, and kayaks and rowboats can be rented. The lake is stocked with trout by the Department of Fish and Game and it is also a good spot to take a flying leap and belly flop when water levels are high enough.

Campsites, facilities: There are 38 sites for tents or RVs up to 22 feet (no hookups). Picnic tables and fire grills are provided. Drinking water and flush toilets are available. A store and coin laundry are nearby. Leashed pets are permitted.

Reservations, fees: Reservations are accepted ($9 reservation fee) at 877/444-6777 or www .ReserveUSA.com. Sites are $16 per night, $5 per night for each additional vehicle. Open May through October.

Directions: From San Bernardino, take Highway 30 east to the junction with Highway 330 (east of San Bernardino near Highland). Take Highway 330 north (signed "Mountain Resorts") and drive to Running Springs and the junction with Highway 18. Turn east on Highway 18 and drive to Green Valley Lake Road. Turn left on Green Valley Lake Road and drive five miles to the campground (one mile past the town of Green Valley Lake).

Contact: San Bernardino National Forest, Mountaintop Ranger District, Arrowhead Ranger Station, 909/382-2782, fax 909/337-1104.

54 CAMP SWITZERLAND

Scenic rating: 7

near Lake Gregory

Map 14.2, page 752

Well, it really doesn't look much like Switzerland, but this camp is set in a wooded canyon at 4,500 feet below the dam at little Lake Gregory. Since it is well below the dam, there are no lake views or even much of a sense that the lake is nearby. Yet it is only a short distance away. Lake Gregory covers just 120 acres, and while no privately owned boats are permitted here, boats can be rented at the marina. No gas motors are

permitted at the lake, but electric motors are allowed. Trout and steelhead are stocked. It is surrounded by the San Bernardino National Forest. A large swimming beach is available on the south shore (about three-quarters of a mile away) with a water slide and dressing rooms.

Campsites, facilities: There are 40 sites with full or partial hookups (30 amps) for tents or RVs up to 25 feet and a few sites for any length. Some sites are pull-through. Two cabins are also available. Picnic tables are provided. Restrooms with flush toilets and coin showers and drinking water are available. Campfires are now allowed. A store and propane gas are nearby. Leashed pets are permitted, with some restrictions.

Reservations, fees: Reservations are accepted. Sites are $27–32 per night, $3–5 per night for more than two people, $5 per night for each additional vehicle, $6 per pet per night. Open year-round, weather permitting.

Directions: Drive on Highway 30 to San Bernardino and the Waterman Avenue exit. Take that exit and drive north on Waterman Avenue until it becomes Highway 18. Continue on Highway 18 (two miles east of the junction of Highway 30 and Highway 259). Turn north on Highway 18/Rim of the World Highway and drive 14 miles to Crestline/Highway 138. Turn north (left) on Highway 138 and drive two miles to Lake Drive. Continue straight and drive three miles to the campground entrance (signed, just past the fire station, below the dam at the north end of Lake Gregory).

Contact: Camp Switzerland, 909/338-2731.

55 DOGWOOD

Scenic rating: 6

near Lake Arrowhead in San Bernardino National Forest

Map 14.2, page 752

So close, but yet so far—that's the paradox between Lake Arrowhead and Dogwood. The lake is just a mile away, but there is no public access. The lake is ringed by gated trophy homes. The elevation is 5,600 feet. Any questions? The rangers at the Arrowhead Ranger Station, about 1.5 miles down the road to the east, can answer them.

Campsites, facilities: There are 94 sites for tents or RVs up to 40 feet (no hookups); some sites have partial hookups (30 amps). Picnic tables and fire grills are provided. Drinking water, restrooms with flush toilets and coin showers, and a dump station are available. Some facilities are wheelchair-accessible. A store is nearby. Leashed pets are permitted.

Reservations, fees: Reservations are accepted ($9 reservation fee) at 877/444-6777 or www.ReserveUSA.com. Sites are $24–29 per night, $5 per night for each additional vehicle. Open mid-May through October.

Directions: Drive on Highway 30 to San Bernardino and Highway 18 (two miles east of the junction of Highway 30 and Highway 215). Turn north on Highway 18 and drive 15 miles to Rim of the World Highway. Continue on Highway 18 for 0.3 mile to the road immediately after Daley Canyon Road. Turn left and make an immediate right on the Daley Canyon access road. Drive a short distance to the campground entrance on the left.

Contact: San Bernardino National Forest, Mountaintop Ranger District, Arrowhead Ranger Station, 909/382-2782, fax 909/337-1104.

56 SHADY COVE GROUP AND WALK-IN
🥾 🐕 🏕️

Scenic rating: 7

near the Children's Forest in San Bernardino National Forest

Map 14.2, page 752

The highlight here is the adjacent short looped trail that is routed through the Chil-

dren's Forest. The camp is excellent for Boy Scout and Girl Scout troops. The walk to the camp is about 100 yards. The elevation is 7,500 feet.

Campsites, facilities: There are three group sites for tents only for up to 30 people each; two sites are walk-in. Picnic tables and fire grills are provided. Drinking water and vault toilets are available. Some facilities are wheelchair-accessible. Note: The camp is gated for safety; groups are given a combination. Leashed pets are permitted.

Reservations, fees: Reservations are required. The group sites are $60 per night. Open May to mid-October, weather permitting.

Directions: From San Bernardino and Highway 330, drive north on Highway 330 to the town of Running Springs. Continue just past Running Springs to Keller Peak Road (just past Deer Lick Fire Station). Turn right (south) on Keller Peak Road and drive four miles to the Children's Forest. Bear left to the parking area. The walk-in sites are 100 yards from the parking area.

Contact: San Bernardino National Forest, Mountaintop Ranger District, Arrowhead Ranger Station, 909/382-2782, fax 909/337-1104.

57 GLEN HELEN REGIONAL PARK
🥾 🏊 🛶 🐕 ♿ 🚐 🏕️

Scenic rating: 4

near Cajon Pass

Map 14.2, page 752

The centerpieces of Glen Helen Regional Park are two lakes. The San Bernardino County park covers 1,340 acres in the rolling hills at the mouth of Cajon Pass. Hiking trails are nearby. The ponds are stocked with trout in winter and with catfish in summer, and bass are also occasionally caught. Both lakes are set up for shore-fishing, with no boats allowed on the lakes, except for those little pedal boats, and no lake swimming or water contact is permitted. Two 350-foot water slides, a lagoon pool, and sandy beaches are a great bonus. A major obtrusive problem is the location of the campground, set just across the street from the park, near both the freeway and railroad tracks. That's right, drivers in passing cars can actually see you, and at night, passing trains feel and sound like the world is ending. The Hyundai Pavilion within the park is the largest outdoor amphitheater in the United States and can accommodate up to 65,000 people at major events. A OHV park is four miles away.

Campsites, facilities: There are 47 sites for tents or RVs of any length, and two group sites for 50–200 people. Some sites are pull-through and one site has partial hookups. Picnic tables and fire rings are provided. Restrooms with flush toilets and showers, drinking water, and a dump station are on site. Some facilities are wheelchair-accessible. A swimming lagoon, water park, picnic area with shelters, bait and tackle, pedal boat rentals, volleyball, horseshoes, and water slides are available nearby on-site. A snack bar is available on weekends. A store and gas station are a 0.5 mile away. Leashed pets are permitted.

Reservations, fees: Reservations are accepted at 909/887-7540. Sites are $13–18 per night, $5 per night for each additional vehicle, $1 per pet per night. A fee is charged for fishing. Youth group rates available. Must show proof of vehicle registration, insurance and driver's license. Maximum 14-day stay in any 30-day period. Group sites are $3 per person per night ($10 reservation fee). Open year-round.

Directions: From San Bernardino, drive north on I-215 for nine miles to the exit for Devore Road. Take that exit and turn west on Devore Road and drive one mile (crossing the railroad tracks) to the campground and the park (adjacent to the interchange for I-15 and I-215).

Contact: Glen Helen Regional Park, 909/887-7540, fax 909/887-1359; Hyundai Pavilion, 909/880-6500 or 909/88-MUSIC (909/886-8742), www.co.san-bernardino .ca.us/parks.

58 LOS ANGELES/POMONA/ FAIRPLEX KOA
🏊 🏕 ♿ 🚐 ⛺

Scenic rating: 4

in Pomona

Map 14.2, page 752

This is what you might call an urban RV park. Then again, the L.A. County Fairgrounds are right across the street, and there's something going on there every weekend. Frank G. Bonnelli Regional Park, which includes Puddingstone Lake, is only 15 minutes away.

Campsites, facilities: There are 159 pull-through sites with full hookups (50 amps) for RVs, 27 sites with partial hookups for RVs, and 11 tent sites. Two cabins are also available. Restrooms with showers, heated pool and spa, convenience store, dump station, dog walk, and coin laundry are available. Some facilities are wheelchair-accessible. Leashed pets are permitted, with certain restrictions.

Reservations, fees: Reservations are accepted. Sites are $34–37.50 per night, $25 per night for tent sites, $3 per night for each additional vehicle, $4 per person per night for more than two people. Some credit cards accepted. Open year-round.

Directions: Drive on I-10 to the exit for Fairplex Drive (five miles west of Pomona). Take that exit north (toward the mountain) and drive two miles to McKinley Avenue. Turn right on McKinley Avenue and drive one mile to White Avenue. Turn left and drive about 0.5 mile (0.2 mile south of Arrow Street) to the park on the right (2200 North White Avenue).

Contact: Los Angeles/Pomona/Fairplex KOA, 909/593-8915, www.koa.com.

59 EAST SHORE RV PARK

🛶 🎣 🚤 🏕 ⚓ ♿ 🚐 ⛺

Scenic rating: 7

at Puddingstone Lake

Map 14.2, page 752

Considering how close Puddingstone Lake is to so many people, the quality of fishing and waterskiing might be a surprise to newcomers. The lake covers 250 acres and is an excellent recreation facility. For the most part, rules permit waterskiing and personal watercraft between 10 A.M. and sunset, making it an excellent lake for fishing for bass and trout (in season) during the morning and evening. All water sports are allowed here, with specific days and hours for powerboating and personal watercraft. A ski beach is available on the north shore, and there is a large, sandy swimming beach on the southwest shore about a mile away. The lake is just south of Raging Waters in San Dimas and is bordered to the south by Bonnelli Regional Park; there are also a golf course and equestrian facilities adjacent to the park.

Campsites, facilities: There are 519 sites with full hookups (20, 30, and 50 amps) for RVs of any length, 25 walk-in sites for tents, and three group tent sites. Some sites are pull-through. Restrooms with showers, cable TV, modem access, recreation room, swimming pools, general store, playground, basketball, volleyball, horseshoes, propane gas delivery, 24-hour ranger service, and coin laundry are available. A hot-tub facility is nearby. Leashed pets are permitted at RV sites, but not at tent sites. Some facilities are wheelchair-accessible.

Reservations, fees: Reservations are accepted. Sites are $37–44 per night for RV sites for up to two people, $24 per night for up to three people at tent sites, $2 per person per night for additional people, $8 per person per night for the group tent sites, $2 per pet per night. Monthly and seasonal rates available. Some credit cards accepted. Open year-round.

Directions: Drive on I-10 to the exit for Fairplex Drive (five miles west of Pomona). Take that exit north to Via Verde (the first traffic light). Turn left on Via Verde and drive to the first stop sign at Campers View. Turn right on Campers View and drive into the park.

Contact: East Shore RV Park, 909/599-8355 or 800/809-3778, www.eastshorervpark.com.

60 YUCAIPA REGIONAL PARK

🥾 🛶 🎣 🏕 ⚓ ♿ 🚐 ⛺

Scenic rating: 7

near Redlands

Map 14.2, page 752

This is a great family-oriented county park, complete with water slides and paddleboats for the kids and fishing access and hiking trails for adults. Three lakes are stocked weekly with catfish in the summer and trout in the winter, the closest thing around to an insurance policy for anglers. Spectacular scenic views of the Yucaipa Valley, the San Bernardino Mountains, and Mount San Gorgonio are possible from the park. The park covers 885 acres in the foothills of the San Bernardino Mountains. A one-acre swimming lagoon and two water slides make this a favorite for youngsters. The Yucaipa Adobe and Mousley Museum of Natural History is nearby.

Campsites, facilities: There are 26 sites for RVs of any length and nine sites for tents. All sites have full hookups (20, 30, and 50 amps) and/or are pull-through. Picnic tables and fire rings are provided at most sites. Drinking water and restrooms with flush toilets and showers are available, and shade ramadas are available at tent sites. A seasonal swimming lagoon and water slides, fishing ponds, seasonal paddleboat and aquacycle rentals, pay phone, seasonal snack bar, picnic shelters, playground, volleyball (bring net), horseshoes, group facilities, bait shop, and dump station are available nearby. The water slide is open Memorial Day weekend through Labor Day weekend. Some facilities are wheelchair-accessible. Leashed pets are permitted.

Reservations, fees: Reservations are accepted ($2 reservation fee). Sites are $18 per night for tent sites, $27 per night per vehicle for RV sites, $1 per pet per night. Weekly and youth group rates available. Some credit cards accepted. Additional charges apply for fishing, swimming, and use of the water slide. Proof of vehicle registration required for campers. Maximum 14-day stay in any 30-day period. Open year-round.

Directions: Drive on I-10 to Redlands and the exit for Yucaipa Boulevard. Take that exit and drive east on Yucaipa Boulevard to Oak Glen Road. Turn left and continue two miles to the park on the left.

Contact: Yucaipa Regional Park, 909/790-3127, fax 909/790-3121, www.co.san-bernardino.ca.us/parks.

61 RANCHO JURUPA PARK

Scenic rating: 4

near Riverside

Map 14.2, page 752

Lord, it gets hot in the summertime, but there is shade and grass here at this 200-acre park. The setting is along the Santa Ana River, amid cottonwood trees and meadows. This Riverside County park stocks trout and catfish in a three-acre fishing lake. Hiking, cycling and equestrian trails are also available in the park. Shaded picnic sites are a plus. Summer visitors will find that the nearest lake for swimming and water sports is Lake Perris, about a 20-minute drive away. The elevation is 780 feet.

Campsites, facilities: There are 67 sites with full or partial hookups (30 and 50 amps) for tents or RVs of any length. Picnic tables and fire grills are provided. Drinking water, flush toilets with showers, and a dump station are available. Some facilities are wheelchair-accessible. Leashed pets are permitted.

Reservations, fees: Reservations are accepted ($6.50 reservation fee) for the individual sites and required ($12 reservation fee) for the group camp at 800/234-7275. Sites are $18–20 per night, $144 per night for the group camp, $1 per pet per night. Weekly rates available. A fishing fee is charged. Some credit cards accepted. Open year-round, with a maximum 14-day stay in a 28-day period.

Directions: Drive on I-215 to Riverside and Highway 60. Take Highway 60 east and drive seven miles to Rubidoux Boulevard. Turn left on Rubidoux Boulevard and drive 0.5 mile to Mission Boulevard. Turn left on Mission Boulevard and drive about one mile to Crestmore Road. Turn right and drive 1.5 miles to the park gate on the left (4800 Crestmore Road).

Contact: Rancho Jurupa Park, 951/684-7032, fax 951/955-4305, www.riversidecounty parks.org.

62 PRADO REGIONAL PARK

Scenic rating: 6

on Prado Park Lake near Corona

Map 14.2, page 752

Prado Park Lake is the centerpiece of a 2,280-acre recreation-oriented park that features hiking trails, an equestrian center, athletic fields, shooting range, dog-training facility, and 36-hole golf course. The lake is small and used primarily for paddling small boats and fishing, which is best in the winter and early spring when trout are planted, and then in early summer for catfish and bass. Gas motors, inflatables, sailboarding, swimming, and water/body contact are not permitted. The shooting facility, the site of the 1984 Olympic shooting venue, is outstanding.

Campsites, facilities: There are 75 sites with full hookups (30 and 50 amps) for RVs of any length, 15 tent sites, and nine group sites. Most sites are pull-through. Picnic tables and fire rings are provided. Restrooms with showers, coin laundry, pay phone, snack bar, picnic area, playground, group facilities, boat ramp, and bait shop are available. A playing field with softball, soccer, and horseshoes is on-site. Some facilities are wheelchair-accessible. Leashed pets are permitted.

Reservations, fees: Reservations accepted with a $2 reservation fee, and a $10 reservation fee for group sites. Sites are $22 per night, $5 per night for each additional vehicle, $1 per pet per night. Group sites are $3 per person per night for up to 50 people, and $2 per person per night for more than 50 people. Weekly rates available. A fee is charged for fishing. Campers must show proof of vehicle registration and insurance. Some credit cards accepted. Open year-round, with a maximum 14-day stay in a 30-day period.

Directions: Drive on Highway 91 to Highway 71 (west of Norco and Riverside). Take Highway 71 north and drive four miles to Highway 83/Euclid Avenue. Turn right on Euclid Avenue and drive one mile to the park entrance on the right.

Contact: Prado Regional Park, 909/597-4260, fax 909/393-8428, www.co.san-bernardino .ca.us/parks.

63 TRAVELERS WORLD RV PARK

Scenic rating: 1

near Disneyland

Map 14.2, page 752

This is one of the most popular RV parks for visitors to Disneyland and other nearby attractions. It is easy to see why, with the park just a half mile from Disneyland. A shuttle service is available to Disneyland for a fee.

Campsites, facilities: There are 335 sites with full hookups (20, 30, and 50 amps) for tents or RVs up to 40 feet; some sites are pull-through. Picnic tables and fire grills are provided. Restrooms with showers, cable TV, modem access, playground, adult lounge/game room, heated swimming pool, coin laundry, convenience store, dump station, ice, recreation room, RV wash rack, and propane gas are available. Leashed pets are permitted. Some facilities are wheelchair-accessible.

Reservations, fees: Reservations are recommended. Sites are $32–38 per night, $3 per person per night for more than two people, $3 per night for each additional vehicle, $2 per pet per night. Some credit cards accepted. Open year-round.

Directions: Drive on I-5 to Anaheim and the exit for Ball Road. Take that exit and drive on Ball Road for about one block to the park on the left at 333 West Ball Road.

Contact: Travelers World RV Park, 714/991-0100, fax 714/991-4939.

64 C. C. CAMPERLAND

Scenic rating: 1

near Disneyland

Map 14.2, page 752

Camperland is nine blocks south of Disneyland, and that right there is the number-one appeal. The Crystal Cathedral is one mile away, and Knott's Berry Farm is also close by. An outdoor sink for washing dishes and a pet restroom are bonuses.

Campsites, facilities: There are 70 sites with full hookups (30 and 50 amps) for tents or RVs up to 40 feet. No pull-through sites. Picnic tables are provided. Restrooms with showers, swimming pool, coin laundry, dump station, and ice are available. Leashed pets are permitted with certain restrictions, except in the tent area.

Reservations, fees: Reservations are accepted. Sites are $36–56 per night for RVs, $28–34 per night for tents, $3 per person per night for more than two people, $3 per night for each additional vehicle, $3 per pet per night. Some credit cards accepted. Open year-round.

Directions: Drive on I-5 to Garden Grove and the exit for Harbor Boulevard/Anaheim south. Take that exit and drive south on Harbor Boulevard for 1.5 miles to the park on the left (12262 Harbor Boulevard).

Contact: C. C. Camperland, 714/750-6747, www.cccamperland.com.

65 ORANGELAND RV PARK

🏊 🐕 ♿ 🚐

Scenic rating: 1

near Disneyland

Map 14.2, page 752

This park is about three miles east of Disneyland. If the other RV parks near Disneyland are filled, this is a useful alternative. Note that about half of the sites are filled with long-term renters.

Campsites, facilities: There are 203 sites for RVs of any length (full hookups); some sites are pull-through. No tents. Picnic tables and fire grills are provided. Restrooms with showers, playground, heated swimming pool, spa, exercise room, coin laundry, convenience store, modem access, Wi-Fi, car wash, shuffleboard court, billiards, dump station, ice, and a recreation room are available. Some facilities are wheelchair-accessible. Leashed pets are permitted, with certain restrictions.

Reservations, fees: Reservations are recommended. Sites are $55–75 per night, $1 per pet per night. Monthly rates available. Some credit cards accepted. Open year-round.

Directions: Drive on I-5 to Anaheim and the exit for Katella Avenue. Take that exit east for Katella Avenue and drive two miles (passing Anaheim Stadium and the Santa Ana River) to Struck Avenue. Turn right and drive 200 yards to the park on the right (1600 West Struck Avenue).

Contact: Orangeland RV Park, 714/633-0414, fax 714/633-9012, www.orangeland.com.

66 CANYON RV PARK GROUP CAMPGROUND

🥾 🚴 🏊 🚣 🐕 ♿ 🚐

Scenic rating: 6

near Yorba Linda

Map 14.2, page 752

The group campground is set in a mature grove of cottonwood and sycamore trees, with natural riparian wildland areas and open spaces nearby. It is near the Santa Ana River (swimming or wading at the lake or creek is prohibited). The Santa Ana River Bicycle Trail runs through this park, which runs from Orange in Riverside County to Huntington Beach and the Pacific Ocean. Side-trip possibilities include Chino Hills State Park to the north, Cleveland National Forest to the south, and Lake Matthews to the southeast. The park is also close to Disneyland and Knott's Berry Farm. Canyon RV Park is a private group campground operating under a long-term lease from Orange County. It is at Featherly Regional Park.

Campsites, facilities: There are 140 sites with full hookups (30 and 50 amps) for RVs up to 40 feet, and a youth group area. No tents are allowed, except in the youth group area. Nine cabins are also available. Picnic tables and fire pits are provided. Restrooms with flush toilets and showers, Wi-Fi, modem access, two dump stations, seasonal swimming pool, horseshoes, firewood, ice, and two playgrounds are available. A visitors center and two amphitheaters are on-site. A convenience store, coin laundry, and propane are also available. Restaurants are nearby. Leashed pets are permitted, with some restrictions. Some facilities are wheelchair-accessible.

Reservations, fees: Reservations are accepted by phone, fax, or website. Sites are $35 per night, $5 per night for each additional vehicle, $1 per person per night for more than two people, $1 per pet per night. Call for youth-group rates. Some credit cards accepted. Open year-round.

Directions: Drive on I-5 to Highway 91 in Anaheim. Take Highway 91 east and drive 13 miles to the exit for Gypsum Canyon Road. Take that exit to Gypsum Canyon Road. Turn left, drive under the freeway, and drive about one block to the park entrance on the left.

Contact: Canyon RV Park, 714/637-0210, fax 714/637-9317, www.canyonrvpark.com or www.ocparks.com.

67 LAKE PERRIS STATE RECREATION AREA

🚶 🚴 🏊 🛶 🛶 🎣 🐕 🏕 ♿ 🚐 ⛺

Scenic rating: 7

on Lake Perris

Map 14.2, page 752   **BEST (**

Lake Perris is a great recreation lake with first-class fishing for spotted bass, and many fishing records have been set here. In the summer, it's an excellent destination for boating and water sports. It is set at 1,500 feet in Moreno Valley, just southwest of the Badlands foothills. The lake has a roundish shape, covering 2,200 acres, with an island that provides a unique boat-in picnic site. There are large ski beaches on the northeast and southeast shores and a designated sailing cove on the northwest side, an ideal spot for various watersports; inflatables are not permitted. Swimming is also excellent, but it's allowed only at the developed beaches a short distance from the campground. The recreation area covers 8,300 acres and includes 10 miles of paved bike trails, including a great route that circles the lake, 15 miles of equestrian trails, and five miles of hiking trails. Summer campfire and junior ranger programs are available. There is also a special area for scuba diving, and a rock-climbing area is just south of the dam.

Campsites, facilities: There are 177 sites for tents only, 254 sites with partial hookups (30 amps) for tents or RVs up to 31 feet, seven primitive horse camps with corrals and water troughs, and six group sites with no hookups for 25–100 people each. Picnic tables and fire grills are available. Restrooms with flush toilets and coin showers, drinking water, Wi-Fi, dump station, playground, convenience store, two swimming beaches, boat launch, and fishing boat rentals are available. Some facilities are wheelchair-accessible. Leashed pets are permitted, with certain restrictions, except at the beach or in the water.

Reservations, fees: Reservations are accepted ($7.50 reservation fee) for individual sites at 800/444-PARK (800/444-7275) or www.reserveamerica.com. Sites are $15–28 per night, $21 per night for equestrian sites, $8 per night for each additional vehicle, $120 per night for group sites. Reserve group sites at 951/940-5611 and equestrian sites at 951/940-5600. Open year-round.

Directions: From Riverside, drive southeast on Highway 215/60 for about five miles to the 215/60 split. Bear south on 215 at the split and drive six miles to Ramona Expressway. Turn left (east) and drive 3.5 miles to Lake Perris Drive. Turn left and drive 0.75 mile to the park entrance.

Contact: Lake Perris State Recreation Area, 951/657-0676, or Lake Perris Marina, 951/657-2179, www.parks.ca.gov.

68 PALM VIEW RV PARK

🏊 🐕 🏕 🚐 ⛺

Scenic rating: 5

near Lake Elsinore

Map 14.2, page 752

This privately operated RV park is in a quiet valley at 700 feet elevation and has a duck pond. The sites are fairly rustic, with some shade trees. The park's recreation area offers basketball, volleyball, horseshoes, tetherball, and a playground. For you wonderful goofballs, bungee jumping and parachuting are available in the town of Perris. Note that most of the sites are occupied by long-term renters.

Campsites, facilities: There are 41 sites with full hookups (30 amps) for RVs, nine tent sites, and a group tent area that can accommodate up to 200 people. Some sites are pull-through. Picnic tables and fire rings are provided. Restrooms, dump station, recreation area, modem access, seasonal swimming pool, coin laundry, playground, convenience store, ice, and firewood are available. Leashed pets are permitted.

Reservations, fees: Reservations are accepted. Sites are $25–28 per night. The group area is

$5 per person per night. Monthly rates available. Open year-round.

Directions: Drive to the junction of I-15 and Highway 74. At that junction, take Highway 74/Central Avenue and drive east on Highway 74 for 4.5 miles to River Road. Turn right (south) and drive one mile to the park on the left (22200 River Road).

Contact: Palm View RV Park, 951/657-7791, fax 951/657-7673.

69 SUNSET VISTA RV PARK

Scenic rating: 7

in Huntington Beach

Map 14.2, page 752

This RV park is operated by the city of Huntington Beach. This park is a helpful layover for Highway 1 cruisers. Bolsa Chica State Beach provides an alternative spot to park an RV. The best nearby adventure is the short loop walk at Bolsa Chica State Reserve (see the *Bolsa Chica State Beach* listing in this chapter for more information).

Campsites, facilities: There are 46 sites with partial hookups (30 and 50 amps) for RVs up to 40 feet. Fire rings are provided. Drinking water, outdoor cold showers, flush toilets, and dump station are available. Supplies are available within a mile. Leashed pets are allowed.

Reservations, fees: Reservations are accepted by mail or in person. Sites are $45 per night. Some credit cards accepted. Open October through May.

Directions: Drive on I-405 to Huntington Beach and the exit for Beach Boulevard. Take that exit west and drive on Beach Boulevard to Highway 1/Pacific Coast Highway. Turn right (north) and drive approximately one mile to 1st Street. Turn left and drive a short distance to the park entrance.

Contact: Huntington Beach, Parks Department, 714/536-5286.

70 O'NEILL REGIONAL PARK AND EQUESTRIAN CAMP

Scenic rating: 6

near Cleveland National Forest

Map 14.2, page 752

This Orange County park is just far enough off the main drag to get missed by most of the RV cruisers on I-5. It is set near Trabuco Canyon, adjacent to Cleveland National Forest to the east. About 70 percent of the campsites are set under a canopy of sycamore and oak, and in general, the park is heavily wooded. The park covers 3,800 acres and features 18 miles of trails, including those accessible by equestrians. Several roads near this park lead to trailheads into Cleveland National Forest. Occasional mountain-lion warnings are posted by rangers. The elevation is 1,000 feet.

Campsites, facilities: There are 79 sites for tents and RVs of any length (no hookups), six equestrian sites for up to two horses per site, and two group camping areas for 20–130 people each. A few sites are pull-through. Picnic tables and fire rings are provided. Restrooms with flush toilets and showers, drinking water, playground, picnic area, amphitheater, horseshoes, firewood, and a dump station are available. Horse corral, water faucets, and an arena are available at equestrian sites. An interpretive center is open on weekends. A store is nearby. Some facilities are wheelchair-accessible. Leashed pets are permitted.

Reservations, fees: Reservations are accepted for individual sites ($12 reservation fee), and required for group sites ($25 reservation fee). Reservations are not accepted for equestrian sites. Sites are $15 per night, $5 per night for each additional vehicle, $2 per pet per night, $3 per night per horse. The group site is $15 per vehicle per night, plus a $12 processing fee. Some credit cards accepted. Open year-round.

Directions: From I-5 in Laguna Hills, take the County Road S18/El Toro Road exit and drive east (past El Toro) for 7.5 miles. Turn right onto Live Oak Canyon Road/County Road S19 and drive about three miles to the park on the right.

Contact: O'Neill Regional Park, 949/923-2260 or 949/923-2256, www.ocparks.com.

71 FALCON GROUP CAMPS

Scenic rating: 4

in the Santa Ana Mountains in Cleveland National Forest

Map 14.2, page 752

At an elevation of 3,300 feet, Falcon is near the trailheads for the San Juan and Chiquito Trails, which both lead into the backcountry and the Santa Ana Mountains. There are three group campgrounds here, with limited parking at Lupine and Yarrow Campgrounds.

Campsites, facilities: There are three group sites for tents or RVs (no hookups). Sage Camp accommodates 30 people and RVs up to 40 feet, Lupine Camp accommodates 40 people and RVs up to 20 feet, and Yarrow Camp accommodates 70 people and RVs up to 30 feet. Picnic tables and fire rings are provided. Drinking water and vault toilets are available. A store is within five miles. Leashed pets are permitted.

Reservations, fees: Reservations are required ($9 reservation fee) at 877/444-6777 or www.ReserveUSA.com. Sites are $50–100 per night. Open year-round, weather permitting.

Directions: Drive on I-15 to Lake Elsinore and the Central exit to Highway 74 west. Take that exit and drive west on Highway 74 for 12 miles (the road becomes Grand Avenue for a couple of miles in Lake Elsinore, then bears right) to Forest Road 6S05 (Long Canyon Road). Turn right and drive approximately 4.5 miles to the campground entrance on the left

Contact: Cleveland National Forest, Trabuco Ranger District, 951/736-1811, fax 951/736-3002.

72 BLUE JAY

Scenic rating: 4

in the Santa Ana Mountains in Cleveland National Forest

Map 14.2, page 752

The few hikers who know of this spot like it and keep coming back, provided they time their hikes when temperatures are cool. The trailheads to San Juan Trail and Chiquito Trail (which is accessed from the San Juan Trail), both of which lead into the backcountry and the Santa Ana Mountains, are adjacent to the camp. A Forest Service map is strongly advised. The elevation is 3,400 feet.

Campsites, facilities: There are 50 sites for tents or RVs up to 20 feet (no hookups). Picnic tables and fire rings are provided. Drinking water and vault toilets are available. A store is within five miles. Leashed pets are permitted.

Reservations, fees: Reservations are not accepted. Sites are $15 per night. Open year-round, weather permitting.

Directions: Drive on I-15 to Lake Elsinore and the Central exit to Highway 74 west. Take that exit and drive west on Highway 74 for 12 miles (the road becomes Grand Avenue for a couple of miles in Lake Elsinore, then bears right) to Forest Road 6S05 (Long Canyon Road). Turn right and drive approximately four miles to Falcon Group Camp on the left

Contact: Cleveland National Forest, Trabuco Ranger District, 951/736-1811, fax 951/736-3002.

73 EL CARISO NORTH CAMPGROUND

Scenic rating: 5

near Lake Elsinore in Cleveland National Forest

Map 14.2, page 752

This pretty, shaded spot at 2,600 feet is just inside the border of Cleveland National Forest with Lake Elsinore to the east. On the drive in there are great views to the east, looking down at Lake Elsinore and across the desert country. Hikers should head west to the Upper San Juan Campground.

Campsites, facilities: There are 18 sites for tents or RVs up to 32 feet (no hookups). Picnic tables and fire rings are provided. Drinking water and vault toilets are available. Leashed pets are permitted.

Reservations, fees: Reservations are not accepted. Sites are $15 per night. Open year-round, weather permitting.

Directions: Drive on I-15 to Lake Elsinore and the Central exit to Highway 74 west. Take that exit and drive west on Highway 74 for 12 miles (the road becomes Grand Avenue for a couple of miles in Lake Elsinore, then bears right) to the campground on the right.

Drive on I-5 to San Juan Capistrano and Highway 74/Ortega Highway. Turn east on the Ortega Highway and drive 24 miles northeast (into national forest) to the campground.

Contact: Cleveland National Forest, Trabuco Ranger District, 951/736-1811, fax 951/736-3002.

74 LAKE ELSINORE WEST MARINA AND RV RESORT

🛶 ⚓ 🚐 🐕 ♿ 🚙

Scenic rating: 7

on Lake Elsinore

Map 14.2, page 752

This privately operated RV park has 1,000 feet of lake frontage and boat rentals are nearby. Note that about a third of the sites are occupied by long-term renters. (For information about Lake Elsinore, see the next listing, *Lake Elsinore Campground and Recreation Area.*)

Campsites, facilities: There are 195 sites with full hookups (50 amps) for RVs up to 40 feet. No tents. Picnic tables and cable TV are provided. Restrooms with showers, dump station, horseshoe pit, clubhouse, modem access, convenience store, group facilities, propane,

and a boat ramp are available. Some facilities are wheelchair-accessible. Leashed pets are permitted, with some restrictions.

Reservations, fees: Reservations are accepted at 800/328-6844. Sites are $40 per night, $3–5 per person per night for more than two people, $1 per pet per night. Some credit cards accepted. Open year-round.

Directions: Drive to the junction of I-15 and Highway 74. At that junction, take Highway 74 west/Central Avenue and drive west for four miles to the entrance to the park on the left (32700 Riverside Drive).

Contact: Lake Elsinore West Marina, 951/678-1300 or 800/328-6844, fax 951/678-6377, www.lakeelsinoremarina.com.

75 LAKE ELSINORE CAMPGROUND AND RECREATION AREA

🥾 🚲 ⚓ 🛶 🚐 🐕 ♿ 🚙 ⛺

Scenic rating: 7

on Lake Elsinore

Map 14.2, page 752   BEST (

The weather is hot and dry enough in this region to make the water in Lake Elsinore more valuable than gold. Elsinore is a huge, wide lake, where water-skiers, personal-watercraft riders, and sailboarders can find a slice of heaven. This camp is set along the north shore, where there are also several trails for hiking, biking, and horseback riding. There is a designated area near the campground for swimming and water play; a gently sloping lake bottom is a big plus here. Fishing has improved greatly in recent years and the lake is stocked with trout and striped bass. Other fish species include channel catfish, crappie, and bluegill. Night fishing is available. Anglers have a chance to fish for Whiskers, a very special catfish. It is a hybrid channel catfish that was stocked in 2000. It is a genetic cross between a blue and channel catfish, meaning that Whiskers could grow to more than 100 pounds. If you catch Whiskers, it's worth $200 in prize money; call the 24-hour hotline at 909/245-9976. If you like thrill sports, hang gliding and parachuting are also available at the lake and, as you scan across the water, you can often look up and see these daredevils soaring overhead. The recreation area covers 3,300 acres and has 15 miles of shoreline. The elevation is 1,239 feet. While the lake is huge when full, in low-rain years Elsinore's water level can be subject to extreme and erratic fluctuations. Boaters planning to visit this lake should call first to get the latest on water levels and quality.

Campsites, facilities: There are nine primitive sites and 185 sites for tents or RVs up to 40 feet; several sites have full hookups (30 amps). Fire pits are provided. Picnic tables are provided at some sites. Restrooms with flush toilets and showers, drinking water, picnic area, and a dump station are available. Supplies and coin laundry are nearby. Some facilities are wheelchair-accessible. Leashed pets are permitted.

Reservations, fees: Reservations are accepted at 800/416-6992. Sites are $25–30 per night, $5 per pet per night. Some credit cards accepted. Open year-round.

Directions: Drive to the junction of I-15 and Highway 74. At that junction, take Highway 74 west/Central Avenue. Drive a short distance on Central Avenue to Collier. Turn right on Collier and drive 0.25 mile to Riverside Drive. Turn left and drive approximately 1.5 miles to the campground on the left.

Contact: Lake Elsinore Campground, 951/471-1212; City of Lake Elsinore, 951/674-3124, fax 951/245-9308.

76 NEWPORT DUNES WATERFRONT RESORT

🚲 🏊 🛶 🛥️ 🏕️ 🐕 🚶 ♿ 🚐 ⛺

Scenic rating: 9

in Newport Beach

Map 14.2, page 752

This five-star resort is set in a pretty spot on the bay, with a beach, boat ramp, and storage

area providing bonuses. The resort received the "Mega Park of the Year Award 2003" from the California Travel Parks Association. It is situated on 100 acres of Newport Bay beach, beautiful and private, without public access. It features one mile of beach and a swimming lagoon, beachfront sites, and 24-hour security. A one-mile promenade circles the resort and is popular for cycling and inline skating. Nearby to the west is Corona del Mar State Beach, and to the south, Crystal Cove State Park. The park is five minutes' walking distance from Balboa Island and is next to the largest estuary in California, the Upper Newport Bay Ecological Reserve.

Campsites, facilities: There are 382 sites with full hookups (30 and 50 amps) for tents or RVs up to 50 feet. Cottages are also available. Picnic tables are provided. Restrooms with showers, heated swimming pool and spa, waveless saltwater lagoon, 440-slip marina, satellite TV, Wi-Fi, organized activities, beach volleyball, coin laundry, market, waterfront restaurant, café, fitness center, game room/video arcade, group facilities, dog run, playground, RV and boat storage, RV and boat wash, and marina with boat launch ramp are available. Some facilities are wheelchair-accessible. Boat, kayak, sailboard, and bicycle rentals are available, along with lessons for various water sports. Leashed pets are permitted, with some restrictions, but not in the cottages.

Reservations, fees: Reservations are accepted up to two years in advance (except for July 4) at 800/765-7661. Tent sites are $69–70 per night, RV sites are $89–220 per night, $8 per night for each additional vehicle, $2 per pet per night. Monthly rates available. Some credit cards accepted. Open year-round.

Directions: Drive on I-405 to the exit for Highway 55. Take that exit south and drive on Highway 55 to Highway 73. Turn south on Highway 73 and drive three miles to the Jamboree Road exit. Take that exit, turn right, and drive south on Jamboree Road for five miles to Back Bay Drive. Turn right and drive a short distance to the resort on the left.

Contact: Newport Dunes Waterfront

Resort, 949/729-3863, fax 949/729-1133, www .newportdunes.com.

77 CRYSTAL COVE STATE PARK HIKE-IN AND HORSE CAMP

🚶 🚴 ♒ ⚓ ⛺

Scenic rating: 9

south of Corona del Mar on the Pacific Ocean

Map 14.2, page 752

First, get this straight: This park does not provide beach camping. The campsites require hikes of 3.5–4.5 miles. That known, this place is very special. This is a gorgeous park that covers 2,200 acres, featuring 3.5 miles of coast and a 1,140-acre underwater park that is popular with scuba divers and snorkelers. The inland acreage is popular with mountain bikers and hikers, and the beach is popular with swimmers and surfers. Of the hike-in camps, the two Moro camps are the most popular. The two Moro camps have a ridge-top vantage point and beautiful views of the ocean. Deer Canyon Camp is sheltered by a grove of oaks and offers privacy, but no views. El Moro Canyon is shady and tree-lined. Note that El Moro Creek flows only in the wet season. The camps are rarely full. Most of the park's backcountry is grass hills and some foothill woodlands. Guided nature hikes are available.

Campsites, facilities: There are 32 hike-in/bike-in and equestrian sites at three environmental campgrounds: Lower Moro, Upper Moro, and Deer Canyon (horses are not allowed at Lower Moro). Picnic tables are provided. Pit toilets are available. No drinking water is available. No fires are permitted. Bring a backpacking stove for cooking. No pets are permitted.

Reservations, fees: Reservations are accepted ($7.50 reservation fee) at 800/444-PARK (800/444-7275) or www.reserveamerica .com. Sites are $11–15 per night, $10 per night for each additional vehicle. Registration at the visitors center is required. Open year-round.

Directions: Drive on Highway 1 to the park entrance (three miles south of Corona del Mar) on the east side of the highway. Register at the visitors center. The Moro camps require a 3.5- to four-mile walk. The Deer Canyon Camp requires a 4.5-mile walk.

Contact: Crystal Cove State Park, 949/494-3539; Orange Coast District, Central Sector, 949/492-0802, www.crystalcovestatepark.com or www.parks.ca.gov.

78 CASPERS WILDERNESS PARK FAMILY, GROUP, AND EQUESTRIAN CAMP

🚶 🚴 🏇 ♿ 🚐 ⛺

Scenic rating: 6

on the San Juan Creek

Map 14.2, page 752

This is an 8,500-acre protected wilderness preserve that is best known for coastal stands of live oak and magnificent stands of California sycamore. Highway 74 provides access to this regional park. It is a popular spot for picnics, day hikes, horseback riding, and cycling. Since the campground is not listed with any of the computer-based reservation services, it is overlooked by most out-of-town travelers. A highlight is 30 miles of trails. Much of the land is pristine and protected in its native state. It is bordered to the south by the San Juan Creek and to the east by the Cleveland National Forest and the San Mateo Canyon Wilderness, adding to its protection.

Campsites, facilities: There are 42 sites with partial hookups (no electrical) for tents or RVs of any length, 23 equestrian sites, six group sites for 40–60 people each, and 13 sites in an overflow area for tents and RVs. Picnic tables, fire pits, and barbecues are provided. Drinking water, restrooms with flush toilets and showers, dump station, corrals, stables, amphitheater, museum with interpretive programs, and a playground are available. Pets are not allowed. Some facilities are wheelchair-accessible.

Reservations, fees: Reservations are required

at 800/600-1600. Sites are $13–15 per night, $3 per night per horse. Some credit cards accepted. Open year-round.

Directions: Drive on I-5 to San Juan Capistrano and Highway 74/Ortega Highway. Turn east on Ortega Highway and drive 7.5 miles northeast to the signed park entrance on the left.

Contact: Caspers Wilderness Park, Orange County, 949/923-2210, fax 949/728-0346, www.ocparks.com.

79 LAKE SKINNER RECREATION AREA

Scenic rating: 7

on Lake Skinner

Map 14.2, page 752

Lake Skinner is set within a Riverside County park at an elevation of 1,470 feet in sparse foothill country, where the water can sparkle, and it covers 1,200 surface acres. There is a speed limit of 10 mph and only four-stroke engines are allowed. Unlike nearby Lake Elsinore, which is dominated by fast boats and water-skiers, no water-contact sports are permitted here; hence no waterskiing, no swimming, no sailboarding. However, a half-acre swimming pool is available in the summer. Afternoon winds make for great sailing, and you can count on consistent midday breezes. The fishing can be good. Many fish are stocked at this lake, including trophy-sized bass and trout, along with catfish and bluegill. The fishing records here include a 39.5-pound striped bass, 33-pound catfish, and 14-pound, 8-ounce largemouth bass. The recreation area also provides hiking trails.

Campsites, facilities: There are 213 sites for tents or RVs of any length, an overflow area, and three group camping areas; many sites have full or partial hookups (50 amps) and/or are pull-through. Picnic tables and fire grills are provided. Restrooms with flush toilets and coin showers, drinking water, playground, convenience store, picnic area, group facili-

ties, ice, bait, dump station, swimming pool (in the summer), boat ramp, marina, mooring, boat rentals, and propane gas are available. Leashed pets are permitted. Some facilities are wheelchair-accessible.

Reservations, fees: Reservations are accepted ($6.50 reservation fee) at 800/234-7275. Sites are $17–20 per night, $12 per night for overflow area, $192–216 per night for group sites, $1 per pet per night. Open year-round. Some credit cards accepted.

Directions: Drive on I-15 to Temecula and the exit for Rancho California. Take that exit and drive northeast 9.5 miles to the park entrance on the right.

Contact: Lake Skinner Recreation Area, 951/926-1541, www.riversidecountyparks .org.

80 INDIAN OAKS TRAILER RANCH

Scenic rating: 5

near Temecula

Map 14.2, page 752

This campground is on 21 acres in the Temecula Valley. The highlight of the ranch is a spring-fed lake with swimming beach and paddleboat rentals. Catch-and-release fishing is allowed at no charge, and no fishing license is required. The lake is stocked with catfish, bluegill, and largemouth bass. Shaded campsites are available and there is plenty of open space. Horseback-riding facilities are across the road from the campground. Nearby attractions are golf courses, hot-air balloon rides, wineries, a casino, and Old Town Temecula.

Campsites, facilities: There are 29 tent sites and 17 sites with full or partial hookups (30 amps) for RVs up to 40 feet. One site is pull-through. Picnic tables and fire pits are provided at the tent sites and some of the RV sites. Drinking water, coin laundry, snack bar, dump station, picnic area, propane, playground, group facilities, paddleboat rentals, horseshoes, shuffleboard, billiards, and organized activities are available. Some facilities are wheelchair-accessible. Leashed pets are permitted.

Reservations, fees: Reservations are recommended. Sites are $20 per night for a tent site and $25–35 per night for an RV site. Weekly and monthly rates are available. Some credit cards accepted. Open year-round.

Directions: From Temecula, drive north on I-15 to the exit for Rancho California Road. Take that exit and drive east on Rancho California Road for 15 miles to East Benton Road. Turn right and drive three miles to the ranch on the right.

Contact: Indian Oaks Trailer Ranch, 951/302-5399.

81 HANNA FLAT

Scenic rating: 8

near Big Bear Lake in San Bernardino National Forest

Map 14.3, page 753

This is one of the largest, best maintained, and most popular of the Forest Service camps in the Big Bear Lake District (Serrano Campground is the most popular). All the trees and vegetation provide seclusion for individual sites. There is great forest scenery with many hardwood trees, including oak and mountain mahogany. The camp is set at 7,000 feet on the slopes on the north side of Big Bear Lake, just under three miles from the lake. Big Bear is a beautiful mountain lake covering more than 3,000 acres, with 22 miles of shoreline and often excellent trout fishing and waterskiing. A trailhead for the Pacific Crest Trail is a mile by road north of the camp.

Campsites, facilities: There are 88 sites for tents or RVs up to 32 feet (no hookups). Picnic tables and fire grills are provided. Drinking water and flush toilets are available. Some facilities are wheelchair-accessible. Leashed pets are permitted.

Reservations, fees: Reservations are accepted ($9 reservation fee) at 877/444-6777 or www .ReserveUSA.com. Sites are $20 per night, $5 per night for each additional vehicle. Open May through September.

Directions: Drive on Highway 30 to the junction with Highway 330 (east of San Bernardino near Highland). Take Highway 330 north (signed "Mountain Resorts") and drive 28 miles (Highway 330 becomes Highway 18/Rim of the World Highway) to the Big Bear Lake Dam and a fork with Highway 38 and Highway 18. Continue straight on Highway 38 and drive approximately four miles to the town of Fawnskin and Rim of the World Highway. Turn left and drive three miles (after 0.5 mile, it becomes Forest Road 3N14, a dirt road) to the campground on the left.

Contact: San Bernardino National Forest, Mountaintop Ranger District, Big Bear Ranger Station/Discovery Center, 909/382-2790, fax 909/866-1781.

82 HOLCOMB VALLEY

Scenic rating: 7

near the Pacific Crest Trail in San Bernardino National Forest

Map 14.3, page 753

This camp is set near the Holcomb Valley Historic Area, at 7,400 feet in the mountains about four miles north of Big Bear Lake. On the way in on Van Dusen Canyon Road you will pass a trailhead for the Pacific Crest Trail (two miles southeast of the camp). From here you can make the two-mile climb southwest to Bertha Peak, 8,198 feet, overlooking Big Bear to the south.

Campsites, facilities: There are 22 sites for tents or RVs up to 32 feet (no hookups). Picnic tables and fire grills are provided. Pit toilets are available. No drinking water is available. Leashed pets are permitted.

Reservations, fees: Reservations are not accepted. Sites are $12 per night. Open year-round.

Directions: Drive on Highway 30 to the junction with Highway 330 (east of San Bernardino near Highland). Take Highway 330 north (signed "Mountain Resorts") and drive 28 miles (Highway 330 becomes Highway 18/Rim of the World Highway) to the Big Bear Lake Dam and a fork with Highway 38 and Highway 18. Continue straight on Highway 38 and drive about 10 miles to Van Dusen Canyon Road/Forest Road 3N09. Turn left and drive three miles (a dirt road) to Forest Road 3N16. Turn left and drive to the campground on the right.

Contact: San Bernardino National Forest, Mountaintop Ranger District, Big Bear Ranger Station/Discovery Center, 909/382-2790, fax 909/866-1781.

83 TANGLEWOOD GROUP CAMP

🚶 🏕 ♿ 🚐 ⛺

Scenic rating: 4

on the Pacific Crest Trail in San Bernardino National Forest

Map 14.3, page 753

This primitive group camp is off an old spur road with the trailhead for the Pacific Crest Trail—the primary highlight. It is set at 7,400 feet in a flat but wooded area northeast of Big Bear Lake. It is about a 10- to 15-minute drive from Big Bear City.

Campsites, facilities: There is one group campsite for tents or RVs up to 32 feet (no hookups) that can accommodate up to 40 people. Picnic tables and fire grills are provided. Vault toilets are available. No drinking water is available. Some facilities are wheelchair-accessible. Leashed pets are permitted.

Reservations, fees: Reservations are required ($9 reservation fee) at 877/444-6777 or www.ReserveUSA.com. The camp is $65 per night. Open mid-May through September.

Directions: Drive on Highway 30 to the junction with Highway 330 (east of San Bernardino near Highland). Take Highway 330

north (signed "Mountain Resorts") and drive 28 miles (Highway 330 becomes Highway 18/Rim of the World Highway) to the Big Bear Lake Dam and a fork with Highway 38 and Highway 18. Continue straight on Highway 38 and drive about 10 miles to Van Dusen Canyon Road/Forest Road 3N09. Turn left (dirt road) and drive four miles to Forest Road 3N16. Turn right and drive 1.7 miles to Forest Road 3N79. Turn right and drive 0.5 mile to the campground. Trailers are not recommended.

Contact: San Bernardino National Forest, Mountaintop Ranger District, Big Bear Ranger Station/Discovery Center, 909/382-2790, fax 909/866-1781.

84 GRAY'S PEAK GROUP CAMP

🏕 🚐 ⛺

Scenic rating: 4

near Big Bear Lake in San Bernardino National Forest

Map 14.3, page 753

The appeal of this primitive group camp is its proximity to Big Bear Lake, with the camp just three miles northwest of the lake, set at 7,200 feet. Gray's Peak (7,952 feet) is about a mile south of the camp, but there is no direct access to the peak. The drive is not recommended for trailers or large RVs.

Campsites, facilities: There is one group campsite for tents and RVs up to 16 feet (no hookups) that can accommodate up to 40 people. Picnic tables and fire grills are provided. Vault toilets are available. No drinking water is available. Leashed pets are permitted.

Reservations, fees: Reservations are required ($9 reservation fee) at 877/444-6777 or www.ReserveUSA.com. The camp is $65 per night. Open mid-May to mid-October.

Directions: Drive on Highway 30 to the junction with Highway 330 (east of San Bernardino near Highland). Take Highway 330 north (signed "Mountain Resorts") and drive 28 miles (Highway 330 becomes Highway 18/ Rim of the World Highway) to the Big Bear Lake Dam and a fork with Highway 38 and Highway 18. Continue straight on Highway 38 and drive about four miles to the town of Fawnskin and Rim of the World Highway. Turn left and drive 1.2 miles (after 0.5 mile, it becomes Forest Road 3N14, a dirt road) to Forest Road 2N13. Turn left and drive about a mile to the campground on the right.

Contact: San Bernardino National Forest, Mountaintop Ranger District, Big Bear Ranger Station/Discovery Center, 909/382-2790, fax 909/866-1781.

85 SERRANO

Scenic rating: 8

on Big Bear Lake in San Bernardino National Forest

Map 14.3, page 753   BEST (

This campground opened in the 1990s and became the first National Forest campground to offer state-of-the-art restrooms and hot showers. That is why it costs more to camp here. Regardless, it has since become the most popular campground in the region. Location is also a big plus, as this is one of the few camps at Big Bear within walking distance of the lakeshore. It covers 60 acres, a big plus. Another bonus is a paved trail that is wheelchair-accessible. Want more? Big Bear is the jewel of Southern California lakes, the Lake Tahoe of the South, with outstanding trout fishing and waterskiing. All water sports are allowed. The lake is stocked with trout and catfish, and it also has large-and smallmouth bass, crappie, bluegill, and sunfish. Swimming is excellent at this lake with large, sandy beaches around the shoreline. However, the water is cold. A trailhead for the Pacific Crest Trail is nearby, and Canada is only 2,200 miles away. The elevation is 6,800 feet.

Campsites, facilities: There are 132 sites for tents or RVs up to 35 feet; some sites have full hookups (30 amps). Picnic tables and fire rings are provided. Restrooms with flush toilets and coin showers, drinking water, and a dump station are available. Some facilities are wheelchair-accessible. A store is nearby. Leashed pets are permitted.

Reservations, fees: Reservations are accepted ($9 reservation fee) at 877/444-6777 or www .ReserveUSA.com. Sites are $24–34 per night, $48 per night for double sites. Open April through November.

Directions: Drive on Highway 30 to the junction with Highway 330 (east of San Bernardino near Highland). Take Highway 330 north (signed "Mountain Resorts") and drive 28 miles (Highway 330 becomes Highway 18/ Rim of the World Highway) to the Big Bear Lake Dam and a fork with Highway 38 and Highway 18. Continue straight on Highway 38 and drive about 2.5 miles to Fawnskin and North Shore Lane (signed "Serrano Campground"). Turn right on North Shore Lane and drive to the campground entrance.

Contact: San Bernardino National Forest, Mountaintop Ranger District, Big Bear Ranger Station/Discovery Center, 909/382-2790, fax 909/866-1781.

86 HOLLOWAY'S MARINA AND RV PARK

Scenic rating: 6

on Big Bear Lake

Map 14.3, page 753

This privately operated RV park (no tent sites) is a good choice at Big Bear Lake with boat rentals, ramp, and full marina available. Big Bear is the jewel of Southern California's lakes, covering more than 3,000 surface acres with 22 miles of shoreline. Its cool waters make for excellent trout fishing, and yet, by summer, it has heated up enough to make for superb waterskiing. A bonus in the summer is that a breeze off the lake keeps the temperature in the mid-80s. Note that about one-third of the sites are occupied by long-term renters. (For details about the lake, see the previous listing, *Serrano*.)

Campsites, facilities: There are 116 sites with full hookups (30 and 50 amps) for RVs up to 40 feet. No tents. Picnic tables and fire grills are provided. Restrooms with flush toilets and showers, drinking water, dump station, cable TV, convenience store, ice, propane gas, coin laundry, playground, and a full marina with boat rentals are on the premises. Leashed pets are permitted.

Reservations, fees: Reservations are accepted at 800/448-5335. Sites are $45–55 per night, $5 per night for each additional vehicle. Monthly rates available. Some credit cards accepted. Open year-round, weather permitting.

Directions: Drive on Highway 30 to the junction with Highway 330 (east of San Bernardino near Highland). Take Highway 330 north (signed "Mountain Resorts") and drive 28 miles (Highway 330 becomes Highway 18/Rim of the World Highway) to the Big Bear Lake Dam and a fork with Highway 38 and Highway 18. Turn left on Highway 18 and drive three miles to Edgemoor Road. Turn left at Edgemoor Road and drive 0.25 mile to the park entrance on the left.

Contact: Holloway's Marina and RV Park, 909/866-5706 or 800/448-5335, fax 909/866-5436, www.800bigbearboating.com.

87 BLUFF MESA GROUP CAMP

Scenic rating: 7

near Big Bear Lake in San Bernardino National Forest

Map 14.3, page 753

Bluff Mesa Group Camp is one of several camps south of Big Bear Lake. A highlight here is the trailhead (signed on the access road on the way in) for the 0.5-mile walk to the Champion Lodgepole Pine, the largest

lodgepole pine in the world: 400 years old, 112 feet tall, with a circumference of 20 feet. Many Forest Service roads are available nearby for self-planned side trips. The elevation is 7,600 feet.

Campsites, facilities: There is one group campsite for tents or RVs up to 20 feet (no hookups) that can accommodate up to 40 people. Picnic tables and fire grills are provided. Vault toilets are available. No drinking water is available. Leashed pets are permitted.

Reservations, fees: Reservations are required ($9 reservation fee) at 877/444-6777 or www.ReserveUSA.com. The fee is $60 per night. Open mid-May to mid-October.

Directions: Drive on Highway 30 to the junction with Highway 330 (east of San Bernardino near Highland). Take Highway 330 north (signed "Mountain Resorts") and drive 28 miles (Highway 330 becomes Highway 18/Rim of the World Highway) to the Big Bear Lake Dam and a fork with Highway 38 and Highway 18. Turn right at Highway 18 and drive about four miles to Mill Creek Road. Turn right on Mill Creek Road and drive about 1.5 miles to the sign at the top of the hill and Forest Road 2N10. Turn right on Forest Road 2N10 and drive three miles (dirt road) to Forest Road 2N86. Turn right on Forest Road 2N86 and drive 0.25 mile to the campground.

Contact: San Bernardino National Forest, Mountaintop Ranger District, Big Bear Ranger Station/Discovery Center, 909/382-2790, fax 909/866-1781.

88 BOULDER GROUP CAMP

Scenic rating: 6

near Big Bear Lake in San Bernardino National Forest

Map 14.3, page 753

This is a primitive camp at 7,500 feet elevation, just far enough away from some prime attractions to make you wish you could move the camp to a slightly different spot. The headwaters of Metcalf Creek are hidden in the forest on the other side of the road, tiny Cedar Lake is about a half-mile drive north, and Big Bear Lake is about two miles north. You get the idea.

Campsites, facilities: There is one group campsite for tents and RVs up to 20 feet (no hookups) that can accommodate up to 40 people. Picnic tables and fire grills are provided. Vault toilets are available. No drinking water is available. A store and coin laundry are nearby. Leashed pets are permitted.

Reservations, fees: Reservations are required ($9 reservation fee) at 877/444-6777 or www .ReserveUSA.com. The camp is $60 per night. Open mid-May to mid-October.

Directions: Drive on Highway 30 to the junction with Highway 330 (east of San Bernardino near Highland). Take Highway 330 north (signed "Mountain Resorts") and drive 28 miles (Highway 330 becomes Highway 18/Rim of the World Highway) to the Big Bear Lake Dam and a fork with Highway 38 and Highway 18. Turn right at Highway 18 and drive about four miles to Mill Creek Road. Turn right on Mill Creek Road and drive about 1.5 miles to the sign at the top of the hill and Forest Road 2N10. Turn right on Forest Road 2N10 and drive about two miles to the campground entrance road (Forest Road 2M10B). Turn right and drive to the camp.

Contact: San Bernardino National Forest, Mountaintop Ranger District, Big Bear Ranger Station/Discovery Center, 909/382-2790, fax 909/866-1781.

89 PINEKNOT

Scenic rating: 6

near Big Bear Lake in San Bernardino National Forest

Map 14.3, page 753

This popular, developed Forest Service camp is set just east of Big Bear Lake Village (on the southern shore of the lake) about two miles from the lake. It is a popular spot for mountain biking, with several ideal routes available. Of the camps at Big Bear, this is the closest to supplies. The elevation is 7,000 feet. (For details about the lake, see the *Serrano* listing in this chapter.)

Campsites, facilities: There are 52 sites for tents or RVs up to 35 feet (no hookups). Picnic tables and fire grills are provided. Drinking water and flush toilets are available. Some facilities are wheelchair-accessible. A store and coin laundry are nearby. Leashed pets are permitted.

Reservations, fees: Reservations are accepted ($9 reservation fee) at 877/444-6777 or www .ReserveUSA.com. Sites are $19 per night. Open May to mid-October.

Directions: Drive on Highway 30 to the junction with Highway 330 (east of San Bernardino near Highland). Take Highway 330 north (signed "Mountain Resorts") and drive 28 miles (Highway 330 becomes Highway 18/Rim of the World Highway) to the Big Bear Lake Dam and a fork with Highway 38 and Highway 18. Turn right at Highway 18 and drive about six miles to Summit Boulevard. Turn right and drive through the parking area to the road on the left (just before the gate to the ski area). Turn left and drive 0.25 mile to the campground on the right.

Contact: San Bernardino National Forest, Mountaintop Ranger District, Big Bear Ranger Station/Discovery Center, 909/382-2790, fax 909/866-1781.

90 BUTTERCUP GROUP CAMP

Scenic rating: 5

near the town of Big Bear Lake in San Bernardino National Forest

Map 14.3, page 753

This is a forested camp designed for large groups looking for a developed site near Big

Bear Lake. It is about four miles from the southeast side of the lake, just outside the Snow Summit Ski Area. The elevation is 7,000 feet.

Campsites, facilities: There is one group campsite for tents or RVs up to 25 feet (no hookups) that can accommodate up to 40 people. Picnic tables and fire rings are provided. Drinking water and vault toilets are available. A store and coin laundry are nearby. Leashed pets are permitted.

Reservations, fees: Reservations are required ($9 reservation fee) at 877/444-6777 or www .ReserveUSA.com. The camp is $90 per night. Open mid-May to mid-October.

Directions: Drive on Highway 30 to the junction with Highway 330 (east of San Bernardino near Highland). Take Highway 330 north (signed "Mountain Resorts") and drive 28 miles (Highway 330 becomes Highway 18/ Rim of the World Highway) to the Big Bear Lake Dam and a fork with Highway 38 and Highway 18. Turn right at Highway 18 and drive about six miles to Summit Boulevard. Turn right and drive through the parking area to the road on the left (just before the gate to the ski area). Turn left and drive 0.5 mile (past Pineknot Camp) to the campground on the right.

Contact: San Bernardino National Forest, Mountaintop Ranger District, Big Bear Ranger Station/Discovery Center, 909/382-2790, fax 909/866-1781.

91 JUNIPER SPRINGS GROUP CAMP

Scenic rating: 3

in San Bernardino National Forest

Map 14.3, page 753

This is a little-known group camp, set at 7,700 feet in a desertlike area about 10 miles east of Big Bear Lake. It is little known because there are not a lot of reasons to camp here. You need to be creative. Got a Scrabble game? Want to watch the junipers grow? Or maybe watch the features of the land change colors as the day passes? You get the idea.

Campsites, facilities: There is one group camp for tents and RVs up to 20 feet (no hookups) that can accommodate up to 40 people. Picnic tables and fire grills are provided. Vault toilets are available. No drinking water is available. Leashed pets are permitted.

Reservations, fees: Reservations are required ($9 reservation fee) at 877/444-6777 or www .ReserveUSA.com. The camp is $60 per night. Open year-round.

Directions: Drive on I-10 to Redlands and Highway 38. Take Highway 38 northeast and drive about 40 miles (1.5 miles past Onyx Summit) to Forest Road 2N01 on the right. Turn right (dirt road) and drive three miles to a Forest Service road (opposite the sign on the left posted Forest Road 2N04). Turn right and drive into the campground.

Contact: San Bernardino National Forest, Mountaintop Ranger District, Big Bear Ranger Station/Discovery Center, 909/382-2790, fax 909/866-1781.

92 COUNCIL GROUP CAMP

Scenic rating: 5

near Jenks Lake and the San Gorgonio Wilderness in San Bernardino National Forest

Map 14.3, page 753

This is a group camp in a pretty wooded area 0.5 mile from little Jenks Lake (there is a nice, easy walk around the lake) and a few miles north of the northern border of the San Gorgonio Wilderness. There are several other camps in the area.

Campsites, facilities: There is one group campsite for tents or RVs up to 22 feet (no hookups) that can accommodate up to 50 people. Picnic tables and fire rings are provided. Drinking water and vault toilets are available. Some facilities are wheelchair-accessible. Leashed pets are permitted.

Reservations, fees: Reservations are required ($9 reservation fee) at 877/444-6777 or www.ReserveUSA.com. The camp is $130 per night. Open May to mid-November.

Directions: Drive on I-10 to Redlands and Highway 38. Take Highway 38 northeast and drive 26 miles to the campground on the left, just past the Barton Flats Visitor Center.

Contact: San Bernardino National Forest, Mountaintop Ranger District, Big Bear Ranger Station/Discovery Center, 909/382-2790, fax 909/866-1781.

93 BARTON FLATS

🚶 🐕 ♿ 🚐 ⛺

Scenic rating: 7

near Jenks Lake in San Bernardino National Forest

Map 14.3, page 753

This is one of the more developed Forest Service camps in San Bernardino National Forest. The camp is set at 6,500 feet, about two miles from Jenks Lake, a small, pretty lake with good hiking and a picnic area. Barton Creek, a small stream, runs nearby, although it may be waterless in late summer. The San Gorgonio Wilderness, one mile to the south, is accessible via Forest Service roads to the wilderness area trailhead. Permits are required for overnight camping within the wilderness boundaries and are available at Forest Service ranger stations. For those driving in on Highway 38, stop at the Mill Creek Ranger Station in Redlands.

Campsites, facilities: There are 52 sites for tents or RVs of any length (no hookups). Picnic tables and fire grills are provided. Drinking water and restrooms with coin showers and flush toilets are available. Some facilities are wheelchair-accessible. Leashed pets are permitted.

Reservations, fees: Reservations are accepted

($9 reservation fee) at 877/444-6777 or www.ReserveUSA.com. Sites are $20 per night, $40 per night for multifamily sites, $5 per night for each additional vehicle. Open May to mid-November.

Directions: Drive on I-10 to Redlands and Highway 38. Take Highway 38 northeast and drive 27.5 miles to the campground on the left.

Contact: San Bernardino National Forest, Mountaintop Ranger District, Big Bear Ranger Station/Discovery Center, 909/382-2790, fax 909/866-1781.

94 SAN GORGONIO

🚶 🐕 ♿ 🚐 ⛺

Scenic rating: 7

near the San Gorgonio Wilderness in San Bernardino National Forest

Map 14.3, page 753

San Gorgonio is one in a series of Forest Service camps along Highway 38 and about 2.5 miles from Jenks Lake. (See the previous listing, *Barton Flats,* for details.) The elevation is 6,500 feet.

Campsites, facilities: There are 53 sites for tents or RVs of any length (no hookups). Picnic tables and fire grills are provided. Drinking water and restrooms with flush toilets and coin showers are available. Leashed pets are permitted. Some facilities are wheelchair-accessible.

Reservations, fees: Reservations are accepted ($9 reservation fee) at 877/444-6777 or www.ReserveUSA.com. Sites are $20 per night, $40 per night for multifamily sites, $5 per night for each additional vehicle. Open mid-May to mid-October.

Directions: Drive on I-10 to Redlands and Highway 38. Take Highway 38 northeast and drive 28 miles to the campground.

Contact: San Bernardino National Forest, Mountaintop Ranger District, Big Bear Ranger Station/Discovery Center, 909/382-2790, fax 909/866-1781.

95 OSO AND LOBO GROUP

Scenic rating: 6

near the San Gorgonio Wilderness in San Bernardino National Forest

Map 14.3, page 753

Oso and Lobo Group Camps are set directly adjacent to each other at 6,600 feet elevation. The camps are about three-quarters of a mile from the Santa Ana River. Little Jenks Lake is two miles away to the west, and the northern border of the San Gorgonio Wilderness is just a few miles to the south.

Campsites, facilities: There are two group sites for tents or RVs of any length (no hookups) that can accommodate 75–100 people each. Picnic tables and fire grills are provided. Drinking water and flush toilets are available. Leashed pets are permitted.

Reservations, fees: Reservations are required ($9 reservation fee) at 877/444-6777 or www .ReserveUSA.com. The fee is $190–250 per night. Open May to mid-October, weather permitting.

Directions: From I-10 in Redlands, drive 29 miles east on Highway 38 to the campground entrance road on the left.

Contact: San Bernardino National Forest, Mountaintop Ranger District, Big Bear Ranger Station/Discovery Center, 909/382-2790, fax 909/866-1781.

96 SOUTH FORK

Scenic rating: 7

near the Santa Ana River in San Bernardino National Forest

Map 14.3, page 753

This is an easy-access Forest Service camp just off Highway 38, set at 6,400 feet near the headwaters of two rivers, the South Fork River and the Santa Ana River. It is part of the series of camps in the immediate area, just north of the San Gorgonio Wilderness. This one is a four-mile drive from little Jenks Lake. (See the *Barton Flats* listing in this chapter for more details.)

Campsites, facilities: There are 24 sites for tents or RVs up to 25 feet (no hookups). Picnic tables and fire rings are provided. Drinking water and vault toilets are available. Leashed pets are permitted.

Reservations, fees: Reservations are accepted ($9 reservation fee) at 877/444-6777 or www .ReserveUSA.com. Sites are $15 per night, $5 per night for each additional vehicle. Open mid-May through September.

Directions: Drive on I-10 to Redlands and Highway 38. Take Highway 38 northeast and drive 29.5 miles to the campground entrance road.

Contact: San Bernardino National Forest, Mountaintop Ranger District, Big Bear Ranger Station/Discovery Center, 909/382-2790, fax 909/866-1781.

97 HEART BAR FAMILY AND SKYLINE GROUP CAMPS

Scenic rating: 4

in San Bernardino National Forest

Map 14.3, page 753

It's a good thing there is drinking water at this camp. Why? Because Heart Bar Creek often isn't much more than a trickle and can't be relied on for water. The camp is set at 6,900 feet near Big Meadows and Aspen Grove. A challenging butt-kicker of a hike has a trailhead about a half mile away to the north off a spur road, midway between the camp and the fire station. The trail here is routed along Wildhorse Creek to Sugarloaf Mountain (9,952 feet, about 8–9 miles one-way to the top). Insider's note: Just past the midway point on the trail to Sugarloaf Mountain is a trail camp on Wildhorse Creek.

Campsites, facilities: There are 95 sites for tents or RVs up to 40 feet (no hookups), and one group tent site for up to 25 people. Picnic tables and fire grills are provided. Drinking water and vault toilets are available. Some facilities are wheelchair-accessible. Leashed pets are permitted.

Reservations, fees: Reservations are accepted ($9 reservation fee) for individual sites and required for the group site at 877/444-6777 or www.ReserveUSA.com. Sites are $15 per night, $30 per night for multifamily sites, $70 per night for the group site. Open mid-May to early October.

Directions: Drive on I-10 to Redlands and Highway 38. Take Highway 38 northeast and drive 33.5 miles to Forest Road 1N02. Turn right and drive one mile to the campground.

Contact: San Bernardino National Forest, Mountaintop Ranger District, Big Bear Ranger Station/Discovery Center, 909/382-2790, fax 909/866-1781.

98 HEART BAR EQUESTRIAN GROUP AND WILD HORSE EQUESTRIAN

🏃 🐕 🚙 ⛰️

Scenic rating: 5

in San Bernardino National Forest

Map 14.3, page 753

You might not meet Mr. Ed here, but bring an apple anyway. Heart Bar is a horse camp on Heart Bar Creek, less than a mile east of Heart Bar Family Camp. Wild Horse is just 0.1 mile before Heart Bar Family Camp. A good trail that leads into the San Gorgonio Wilderness starts four miles down the road at Fish Creek Meadows. It is routed west for three miles to Fish Creek and then up Grinnell Mountain to the north peak of the Ten Thousand Foot Ridge. A wilderness permit is required. The elevation is 7,000 feet.

Campsites, facilities: Heart Bar has one group campsite for tents or RVs up to 22 feet (no hookups) and can accommodate up to 65 people. Wild Horse has 11 equestrian sites, including two double sites. Picnic tables and fire grills are provided. Flush toilets are avail-

able. No drinking water is available. Water is available for horses. Heart Bar has 46 corrals. Leashed pets are permitted.

Reservations, fees: Reservations are required ($9 reservation fee) at 877/444-6777 or www.ReserveUSA.com. Sites are $20 per night for equestrian sites at Wild Horse and $250 per night for the group camp at Heart Bar. Open May to early October.

Directions: Drive on I-10 to Redlands and Highway 38. Take Highway 38 northeast and drive 33.5 miles to Forest Road 1N02. Turn right and drive a mile to the Heart Bar Group Campground on the right. Continue for 0.1 mile to the Wild Horse camp on the left. To reach Heart Bar Group Equestrian Campground, continue another 0.1 mile.

Contact: San Bernardino National Forest, Mountaintop Ranger District, Big Bear Ranger Station/Discovery Center, 909/382-2790, fax 909/866-1781.

99 COON CREEK CABIN GROUP CAMP

🏃 🐕 ⛰️

Scenic rating: 4

on the Pacific Crest Trail in San Bernardino National Forest

Map 14.3, page 753

Backpackers call this the "Coon Creek jump-off" because it is set on the Pacific Crest Trail at 8,200 feet and provides a "jump-off" for a trek on the PCT. The camp is set on Coon Creek, but the creek often runs dry by summer. Note that in the off-season the access road, Forest Road 1N02, can be gated; campers must hike or cross-country ski to the camp.

Campsites, facilities: There is one group camp for tents only for up to 40 people and 10 vehicles (no trailers or RVs). Picnic tables and fire grills are provided. Vault toilets are available. No drinking water is available. Leashed pets are permitted.

Reservations, fees: Reservations are required ($9 reservation fee) at 877/444-6777 or www

.ReserveUSA.com. The camp is $70–77 per night. Open year-round.
Directions: Drive on I-10 to Redlands and Highway 38. Take Highway 38 northeast and drive 33.5 miles to Forest Road 1N02. Turn right and drive five miles to the campground entrance (dirt road).
Contact: San Bernardino National Forest, Mountaintop Ranger District, Big Bear Ranger Station/Discovery Center, 909/382-2790, fax 909/866-1781.

100 BOGART PARK/FAMILY, GROUP, AND EQUESTRIAN

Scenic rating: 4

in Cherry Valley

Map 14.3, page 753

This county park is overlooked by many vacationers on I-10, and it is as pretty as it gets for this area. There are two miles of horse trails and some hiking trails for a recreation option during the cooler months. It covers 414 acres of Riverside County foothills set at the north end of Cherry Valley. The elevation is 2,800 feet. Bears frequent this area, so store your food properly and avoid scented products.
Campsites, facilities: There are 26 sites for tents or RVs up to 40 feet (no hookups), a group campground for tents that can accommodate up to 100 people, and a group equestrian campground. Fire grills and picnic tables are provided. Drinking water and flush toilets are available. The equestrian camp has corrals and water troughs. Supplies are available in Beaumont. Some facilities are wheelchair-accessible. Leashed pets are permitted.
Reservations, fees: Reservations are accepted and required for group sites ($6.50–12 reservation fee) at 800/234-7275. Sites are $12 per night, $120 per night for the group equestrian camp, $144 per night for the group camp, $1 per night per pet or horse. Open year-round, but closed on Tuesday and Wednesday.

Directions: Drive on I-10 to Beaumont and the exit for Beaumont Avenue. Take that exit north and drive four miles to Brookside. Turn right and drive 0.5 mile to Cherry Avenue. Turn left at Cherry Avenue and drive to the park on the right (9600 Cherry Avenue).
Contact: Bogart Park, 951/845-3818; Riverside County Parks, 800/234-7275, www.riversidecountyparks.org.

101 PINE RANCH RV PARK

Scenic rating: 2

in Banning

Map 14.3, page 753

Banning may not seem like a hotbed of civilization at first glance, but this clean, comfortable park is a good spot to make camp while exploring some of the area's hidden attractions, including Agua Caliente Indian Canyons and the Lincoln Shrine. It is set at 2,400 feet, 22 miles from Palm Springs. A good side trip is to head south on curving "Highway" 240 up to Vista Point in the San Bernardino National Forest.
Campsites, facilities: There are 106 sites with full hookups (30 and 50 amps) for RVs; many sites are pull-through. No tents. Picnic tables and fire grills are provided. Restrooms with showers, cable TV, playground, heated swimming pool, coin laundry, Wi-Fi, dump station, ice, horseshoes, and propane gas are available. Leashed pets are permitted, with certain restrictions.
Reservations, fees: Reservations are accepted for groups only. Sites are $29 per night, $2 per person per night for more than two people, $1 per night for each additional vehicle. Some credit cards accepted. Open year-round.
Directions: Drive on I-10 to Banning and the exit for Highway 243. Take that exit south and take 8th Street south for one block to Lincoln. Turn left on Lincoln and drive two blocks to San Gorgonio. Turn right and drive one mile to the park (1455 South San Gorgonio Avenue).

Contact: Pine Ranch RV Park, 951/849-7513, fax 951/849-7998.

102 MOUNT SAN JACINTO STATE PARK: WILDERNESS WALK-IN CAMPS

🥾 ⛰️

Scenic rating: 10

near Mount San Jacinto

Map 14.3, page 753   BEST (

This is one of the most spectacular getaways in the western United States. It includes a tram ride that will take you from 2,643 feet to 8,516 feet, with stunning views across the desert, especially heart-breaking sunsets. On clear days, you can see the Salton Sea 50 miles to the south. From the tram, you then hike up to 2.75 miles to the camps, set at 9,100 feet, an ideal launch point for the hike to the Mount San Jacinto summit, at 10,834 feet the second-highest peak in Southern California. From Round Valley Camp, it is a 7.5-mile round-trip (just add another mile round-trip from Tamarack Valley Camp). On clear days from the summit, you can see 100 miles, including the Channel Islands, Mexico, and Nevada. On summer weekends, these campgrounds are often filled for dates more than a month in advance. Insider's tip: Be prepared for all types of weather conditions; weather can turn cold/rainy/snowy/windy quickly here. Snow camping is allowed.

Campsites, facilities: There are 28 tent sites (200 people maximum) at Round Valley and 13 tent sites (80 people maximum) at Tamarack Valley. Groups are limited to 15 people. Pit toilets are available. No drinking water is available. There is seasonal stream water that must be boiled or pump-filtered before use. No campfires are permitted. Bring a camp stove (propane or gas) for cooking. Garbage must be packed out. No firearms or wheels are permitted. Horses are allowed, but bring weed-free feed and water for the horses. Pets are not permitted.

Reservations, fees: There is no fee for camping. Free camping permit required and can be obtained at the park office or by mail at Mount San Jacinto State Park, P.O. Box 308, Idyllwild, CA 92549 (include a stamped, self-addressed envelope). A fee is charged for the tram ride. Open year-round, except when the tram is closed for maintenance.

Directions: From Banning, drive east on I-10 for 12 miles to the Highway 111/Palm Springs exit. Take that exit to Highway 111 and drive south nine miles to Tramway Road. Turn right and drive three miles to the parking area for Palm Springs Aerial Tramway. Ride the tram to Mountain Station. Hike 2.25 miles to Round Valley Camp, or continue from Round Valley Camp for another 0.5 mile to Tamarack Valley Camp.

Contact: Mount San Jacinto State Park, 951/659-2607, www.parks.ca.gov; Palm Springs Aerial Tramway, 818/515-8726 or 760/325-1391, www.pstramway.com.

103 BLACK MOUNTAIN GROUP CAMP

🥾 🐕 🚙 ⛰️

Scenic rating: 6

near Mount San Jacinto in San Bernardino National Forest

Map 14.3, page 753

This is a beautiful scenic area, particularly to the north on the edge of the San Jacinto Wilderness and to the east of Mount San Jacinto State Park. The camp is set at 7,500 feet and is within a mile of a trailhead for the Pacific Crest Trail. Here you can turn southeast and hike along Fuller Ridge for another mile to the border of Mount San Jacinto State Park. Note that Black Mountain Lookout is just a two-mile drive, close to Boulder Basin Camp.

Campsites, facilities: There is one group camp for tents and RVs up to 16 feet (no hookups) that can accommodate up to 100 people. Picnic tables and fire rings are provided. Drinking water and vault toilets are available. Leashed pets are permitted.

Reservations, fees: Reservations are required ($9 reservation fee) at 877/444-6777 or www .ReserveUSA.com. The camp is $60–120 per night. Open May to mid-October.

Directions: Drive on I-10 to Banning and Highway 243/Pinesto Palms Scenic Highway. Turn south on Pinesto Palms Scenic Highway and drive about 15 miles to Forest Road 4S01. Turn left on Forest Road 4S01 and drive eight miles (a narrow dirt road) to the campground on the right. Trailers are not advised.

Contact: San Bernardino National Forest, San Jacinto Ranger District, 909/382-2921, fax 951/659-2107.

104 BOULDER BASIN
🏃 🐕 🚍 🔺

Scenic rating: 8

near the San Jacinto Wilderness in San Bernardino National Forest

Map 14.3, page 753

This camp is on the top of the world for these parts: 7,300 feet, adjacent to the Black Mountain Fire Lookout with great views in all directions and highlighted by Tahquitz Peak (8,828 feet) 10 miles to the southeast. Boulder Basin is also near the San Jacinto Wilderness (to the northeast) and makes a good trailhead camp for hikers. A trail starting at Black Mountain Lookout leads west, dropping steeply into a canyon and also into a designated scenic area.

Campsites, facilities: There are 34 sites for tents or RVs up to 15 feet (no hookups). Note that trailers and RVs are not recommended. Picnic tables and fire rings are provided. Drinking water and vault toilets are available. Leashed pets are permitted.

Reservations, fees: Reservations are accepted ($9 reservation fee) at 877/444-6777 or www .ReserveUSA.com. Sites are $10 per night. Open May to mid-October.

Directions: Drive on I-10 to Banning and Highway 243/Pinesto Palms Scenic Highway. Turn south on Pinesto Palms Scenic Highway and drive about 15 miles to Forest Road 4S01/ Black Mountain Road. Turn left and drive six miles (a narrow dirt road) to the campground on the right. RVs not advised.

Contact: San Bernardino National Forest, San Jacinto Ranger District, 909/382-2921, fax 951/659-2107.

105 DARK CANYON
🏃 🛶 🐕 🚍 🔺

Scenic rating: 7

in the San Jacinto Mountains in San Bernardino National Forest

Map 14.3, page 753

This pretty setting is on the slopes of the San Jacinto Mountains at 5,800 feet in elevation. Hikers can drive to the Seven Pines Trailhead less than a mile north of camp at the end of Forest Road 4S02. The trail leads east for three miles into Mount San Jacinto State Park to Deer Springs, where there is a trail camp and a junction with the Pacific Crest Trail. A wilderness permit is required.

Campsites, facilities: There are 17 sites for tents or RVs up to 17 feet (no hookups). Picnic tables and fire grills are provided. Drinking water and vault toilets are available. Leashed pets are permitted.

Reservations, fees: Reservations are accepted ($9 reservation fee) at 877/444-6777 or www .ReserveUSA.com. Sites are $12 per night. Open May to mid-October.

Directions: Drive on I-10 to Banning and Highway 243/ Pinesto Palms Scenic Highway. Turn south on Pinesto Palms Scenic Highway and drive about 13 miles to Forest Road 4S02. Turn left on Forest Road 4S02 and drive three miles (narrow paved road) to the campground.

Contact: San Bernardino National Forest, San Jacinto Ranger District, 909/382-2921, fax 951/659-2107.

106 MARION MOUNTAIN

Scenic rating: 7

in San Bernardino National Forest

Map 14.3, page 753

You get good lookouts and a developed campground at this spot. Nearby Black Mountain is a good side trip that includes a drive-to scenic lookout point. In addition, there are several trailheads in the area. The best one starts near this camp and heads up the slopes to Marion Mountain and east into adjacent Mount San Jacinto State Park. The elevation is 6,400 feet.

Campsites, facilities: There are 24 sites for tents or RVs up to 15 feet (no hookups). Picnic tables and fire grills are provided. Drinking water and vault toilets are available. Leashed pets are permitted.

Reservations, fees: Reservations are accepted ($9 reservation fee) at 877/444-6777 or visit www.ReserveUSA.com. Sites are $10 per night. Open May to mid-October.

Directions: Drive on I-10 to Banning and Highway 243/ Pinesto Palms Scenic Highway. Turn south on Pinesto Palms Scenic Highway and drive about 13 miles south to Forest Road 4S02. Turn left on Forest Road 4S02 and drive two miles (narrow paved road) to the campground.

Contact: San Bernardino National Forest, San Jacinto Ranger District, 909/382-2921, fax 951/659-2107.

107 FERN BASIN

Scenic rating: 7

near Mount San Jacinto State Park in San Bernardino National Forest

Map 14.3, page 753

This is a nearby alternative to Stone Creek (you'll pass it on the way in) and Dark Canyon (another three miles in). Marion Mountain Trailhead is accessible within one-half mile of the campground by driving east on Forest Road 4S02.

Campsites, facilities: There are 22 sites for tents or RVs up to 15 feet (no hookups). Picnic tables and fire rings are provided. Drinking water and vault toilets are available. Leashed pets are permitted.

Reservations, fees: Reservations are accepted ($9 reservation fee) at 877/444-6777 or www .ReserveUSA.com. Sites are $10 per night. Open May to mid-October

Directions: Drive on I-10 to Banning and Highway 243/ Pinesto Palms Scenic Highway. Turn south on Pinesto Palms Scenic Highway and drive about 13 miles south to Forest Road 4S02. Turn left on Forest Road 4S02 and drive one mile (narrow paved road) to the campground on the left.

Contact: San Bernardino National Forest, San Jacinto Ranger District, 909/382-2921, fax 951/659-2107.

108 MOUNT SAN JACINTO STATE PARK: STONE CREEK

Scenic rating: 7

in Mount San Jacinto State Park

Map 14.3, page 753

This is a wooded camp set in Mount San Jacinto State Park. The elevation is 5,900 feet, 0.25 mile off the main road along Stone Creek, just outside the national forest boundary. It is less than a mile from Fern Basin and less than three miles from Dark Canyon. The best trailhead in the immediate area is Seven Pines Trail out of Marion Mountain Camp, one-half mile from this camp.

Campsites, facilities: There are 26 sites for tents, and 21 sites for tents or RVs up to 24 feet (no hookups). Picnic tables and fire rings are provided. Drinking water and vault toilets are available. Some facilities are wheelchair-accessible. Supplies and coin laundry are three miles away in Pine Cove. Leashed pets are permitted.

Reservations, fees: Reservations are accepted ($7.50 reservation fee) at 800/444-PARK (800/444-7275) or www.reserveamerica.com. Sites are $11–15 per night, $5 per night for each additional vehicle. Open year-round.

Directions: Drive on I-10 to Banning and Highway 243/Idyllwild Panoramic Highway. Turn south on Idyllwild Panoramic Highway and drive about 13 miles south to the park entrance on the left.

Contact: Mount San Jacinto State Park, 951/659-2607; Inland Empire District, 951/443-2423, www.parks.ca.gov.

109 GOLDEN VILLAGE PALMS RV RESORT

Scenic rating: 5

in Hemet

Map 14.3, page 753

This RV resort is for those ages 55 and over. It is the biggest RV park in Southern California. The grounds are lush, with gravel pads for RVs. It is set near Diamond Valley Lake, about 10 miles south, a new lake that is the largest reservoir in Southern California. A golf course is nearby, Lake Hemet is 20 miles east, and winery tours are available in Temecula, a 30-minute drive. About 250 of the 1,019 sites are rented on a year-round basis.

Campsites, facilities: There are 1,019 sites with full hookups (50 amps) for RVs up to 45 feet; some sites are pull-through. No tent sites. Restrooms with flush toilets and showers, drinking water, cable TV, modem access, Wi-Fi, business services, three heated swimming pools, three spas, recreation room, fitness center, billiard room, coin laundry, large clubhouse, banquet and meeting rooms, organized activities, pavilion, church services, library, ballroom, shuffleboard, nine-hole putting green, volleyball courts, and horseshoe pits are available. A day-use area with propane barbecues is also available. Leashed pets are permitted.

Reservations, fees: Reservations are accepted at 800/323-9610. Sites are $36–50 per night, $10 per person per night for more than two people. Weekly, monthly, and annual rates available. Open year-round.

Directions: Drive to the junction of I-215 and Highway 74 (near Perris). At that junction, take Highway 74 east and drive 14 miles to Hemet (the highway becomes Florida Avenue in Hemet) and continue to the resort on the left.

Contact: Golden Village Palms RV Resort, 951/925-2518, www.goldenvillagepalms .com.

110 CASA DEL SOL RV PARK RESORT

Scenic rating: 3

in Hemet

Map 14.3, page 753

Hemet is a retirement town, so if you want excitement, the four lakes in the area are the best place to look for it: Lake Perris to the northwest, Diamond Valley Lake and Lake Skinner to the south, and Lake Hemet to the east. The elevation at this 20-acre resort is 1,575 feet. Note that many of the sites are taken by year-round or long-term rentals.

Campsites, facilities: There are 358 sites with full hookups (30 and 50 amps) for RVs up to 40 feet. No tents. Restrooms with flush toilets and showers, drinking water, cable TV, telephone and modem access, ice, library, heated swimming pool, spa, recreation room, exercise room, billiard room, shuffleboard courts, golf driving cage, dog runs, and coin laundry are available. Leashed pets are permitted.

Reservations, fees: Reservations are accepted at 888/925-2516. Sites are $32 per night, $2.50 per person per night for more than two people. Weekly and monthly rates available. Some credit cards accepted. Open year-round.

Directions: Drive to the junction of I-215 and Highway 74 (near Perris). At that junction,

take Highway 74 east and drive 15 miles to Hemet (the highway becomes Florida Avenue in Hemet) and drive to Kirby Avenue. Turn right (south) on Kirby Avenue and drive a half block to the resort (2750 West Acacia Avenue).
Contact: Casa del Sol RV Park Resort, 951/925-2515, www.casadelsolrvpark.com.

111 MOUNTAIN VALLEY RV RESORT

Scenic rating: 3

in Hemet

Map 14.3, page 753

This is one of three RV parks in the Hemet area. Four lakes in the area provide side-trip possibilities: Lake Perris to the northwest, Lake Skinner and Diamond Valley Lake to the south, and Lake Hemet to the east. Golf courses are nearby.

Campsites, facilities: There are 170 sites with full hookups (30 and 50 amps) for RVs up to 40 feet. No tents or campers. Restrooms with flush toilets and showers, cable TV, drinking water, a fireside room, heated swimming pool, enclosed spa, fitness center, golf driving cage, card-access laundry, billiards room, meeting room, group facilities, computer kiosk, Wi-Fi, and telephone hookups are available. Some facilities are wheelchair-accessible. A store and propane gas are nearby. Leashed pets are permitted, with some breeds prohibited.

Reservations, fees: Reservations are accepted at 800/926-5593. Sites are $33 per night, $5 per person per night for more than two people, $2 per pet per night. Weekly, monthly, and annual rates available. Some credit cards accepted. Open year-round.

Directions: Drive to the junction of I-215 and Highway 74 (near Perris). At that junction, take Highway 74 east and drive 15 miles to Hemet (the highway becomes Florida Avenue in Hemet) and continue to South Lyon Avenue. Turn right on South Lyon Avenue and

drive to the park at the corner of Lyon and South Acacia (235 South Lyon).
Contact: Mountain Valley RV Resort, 951/925-5812, www.mountainvalleyrvp.com.

112 IDYLLWILD COUNTY PARK

Scenic rating: 6

near San Bernardino National Forest

Map 14.3, page 753

This Riverside County park covers 202 acres, set at 5,300 feet and surrounded by Mount San Jacinto State Park, San Jacinto Wilderness, and the San Bernardino National Forest lands. That provides plenty of options for visitors. The park has equestrian trails and an interpretive trail. The top hike in the region is the ambitious climb up the western slopes to the top of Mount San Jacinto (10,804 feet), a terrible challenge of a butt-kicker that provides one of the most astounding views in all the land. (The best route, however, is out of Palm Springs, taking the aerial tramway, which will get you to 8,516 feet in elevation before hiking out the rest.)

Campsites, facilities: There are 83 sites for tents or RVs up to 40 feet (no hookups). Fire grills and picnic tables are provided. Drinking water and restrooms with flush toilets and coin showers are available. A store, coin laundry, and propane gas are nearby. Leashed pets are permitted. Some facilities are wheelchair-accessible. There is no drinking water in dry years.

Reservations, fees: Reservations are accepted ($6.50 reservation fee) at 800/234-PARK (800/234-7275). Sites are $17 per night, $1 per pet per night. Some credit cards accepted. Open year-round.

Directions: Drive on I-10 to Banning and Highway 243/Idyllwild Panoramic Highway. Turn south on Idyllwild Panoramic Highway and drive to Idyllwild and Riverside County

Playground Road. Turn west on Riverside County Playground Road and drive 0.5 mile (follow the signs) to the park entrance on the right.

Contact: Idyllwild County Park, 951/659-2656, www.riversidecountyparks.org.

113 MOUNT SAN JACINTO STATE PARK: IDYLLWILD

Scenic rating: 8

in Mount San Jacinto State Park

Map 14.3, page 753

This is a prime spot for hikers and one of the better jump-off points for trekking in the area, set at 5,400 feet. There are no trails from this campground. But 0.5 mile north is Deer Spring Trail, which is connected with the Pacific Crest Trail and then climbs on to Mount San Jacinto (10,834 feet) and its astounding lookout.

Campsites, facilities: There are 11 sites for tents only, 10 sites for tents or RVs up to 18 feet, eight sites for RVs only up to 24 feet, and three hike-in/bike-in sites. Two of the sites have full hookups. Fire grills and picnic tables are provided. Drinking water, restrooms with flush toilets and coin showers, and Wi-Fi are available. Supplies and coin laundry (100 yards) are nearby. Leashed pets are permitted. Some facilities are wheelchair-accessible.

Reservations, fees: Reservations are accepted ($7.50 reservation fee) at 800/444-PARK (800/444-7275) or www.reserveamerica. com. Sites are $15–29 per night, $5 per night for each additional vehicle, $3 per person per night for hike-in/bike-in site. Open year-round.

Directions: In Idyllwild, drive to the north end of town on Highway 243 to the park entrance on the left (next to the fire station). Note: From I-10 in Banning, take the A Street exit onto Highway 243. Drive south for 23.8 miles to the campground on the right, just before Idyllwild.

From I-10 in Banning, take the A Street exit onto Highway 243. Drive south on Highway 243 for 23.8 miles to the campground on the right, just before the town of Idyllwild.

Contact: Mount San Jacinto State Park, 951/659-2607; Inland Empire District, 951/443-2423, www.parks.ca.gov.

114 LAKE HEMET

Scenic rating: 7

near Hemet

Map 14.3, page 753

Lake Hemet covers 420 acres, is set at 4,340 feet, and sits near San Bernardino National Forest just west of Garner Valley. Many campsites have lake views. It provides a good camping/fishing destination, with large stocks of trout each year, and yep, catch rates are good. The lake also has bass, bluegill, and catfish. Boating rules prohibit boats under 10 feet, canoes, sailboats, inflatables, and swimming—no swimming or wading at Lake Hemet. The boat speed limit is 10 mph.

Campsites, facilities: There are 275 sites for RVs up to 40 feet, and two group sites for tents or RVs that can accommodate up to 100 people each. Some sites have full hookups (20 amps) or are pull-through. Picnic tables and fire rings are provided. Restrooms with flush toilets and coin showers, drinking water, dump station, playground, boat ramp, boat rentals, convenience store, coin laundry, and propane gas are available. Some facilities are wheelchair-accessible. Leashed pets are permitted.

Reservations, fees: Reservations are accepted for groups only. Sites are $17–21 per vehicle per night, $1–2.50 per person per night for more than two people, $1 per pet per night. Some credit cards accepted. Open year-round.

Directions: From Palm Desert, drive southwest on Highway 74 for 33 miles (near Lake Hemet) to the campground entrance on the left. For directions if arriving from the west (several options), phone 951/659-2680, ext. 2.

Contact: Lake Hemet, 951/659-2680, www .lakehemet.org.

115 HURKEY CREEK PARK

Scenic rating: 5

near Lake Hemet

Map 14.3, page 753

This large Riverside County park is just east (across the road) of Lake Hemet, beside Hurkey Creek (which runs in winter and spring). The highlight, of course, is the nearby lake, known for good fishing in the spring. No swimming is permitted. The camp elevation is 4,800 feet. The park covers 59 acres.

Campsites, facilities: There are 130 sites and five group sites for tents or RVs up to 40 feet (no hookups) that can accommodate up to 100 people each. Fire grills and picnic tables are provided. Drinking water, restrooms with flush toilets and coin showers, a playground and picnic areas are available. Some facilities are wheelchair-accessible. A dump station is available at nearby Lake Hemet. Leashed pets are permitted.

Reservations, fees: Reservations are accepted for individual sites and required for the group areas ($6.50–12 reservation fee) at 800/234-PARK (800/234-7275). Sites are $17 per night, $1 per pet per night. Group sites are $160 per night for up to 40 people, plus $4 per person per night for more than 40 people. Some credit cards accepted. Open year-round.

Directions: From Palm Desert, drive southwest on Highway 74 for 32 miles (near Lake Hemet) to the campground entrance on the right.

Contact: Hurkey Creek Park, 951/659-2050, www.riversidecountyparks.org.

116 ANZA RV RESORT

Scenic rating: 4

near Anza

Map 14.3, page 753

This is a year-round RV park set at 4,100 feet, with many nearby recreation options. Lake Hemet is 16 miles away, with hiking, motorbiking, and jeep trails nearby in San Bernardino National Forest. Pacific Crest Trail hikers are welcome to clean up and to arrange for food and mail pick-up. Note that most sites are filled with long-term renters.

Campsites, facilities: There are 116 sites for tents and RVs; many have full hookups (30 and 50 amps) and some sites are pull-through. Picnic tables are provided. Restrooms with showers, catch-and-release fishing pond, horseshoe pits, coin laundry, convenience store, dump station, ice, recreation room, modem access, and propane gas are available. Leashed pets are permitted, with certain restrictions.

Reservations, fees: Reservations are accepted. Sites are $18–20 per night, $1 per person per night for more than two people. Open year-round.

Directions: From Palm Desert, drive west on Highway 74 for 24 miles to Highway 371. Turn left on Highway 371 and drive west to the town of Anza and Kirby Road. Turn left on Kirby Road and drive 3.5 miles to the campground on the left at Terwilliger Road (look for the covered wagon out front).

Contact: Anza RV Resort, 951/763-4819, fax 951/763-0619.

SAN DIEGO AND VICINITY

© JOANNE DIBONA/SAN DIEGO CVB

San Diego was picked as one of the best regions

to live in America in an unofficial vote at a national conference for the Outdoors Writers Association of America.

It is easy to understand why: the weather, the ocean and beaches, the lakes and the fishing, Cleveland National Forest, the state parks, the mountains, the hiking, biking, and water sports. What more could anyone ask for? For many, the answer is you don't ask for more, because it does not get any better than this.

The weather is near perfect. It fits a warm coastal environment with an azure-tinted sea that borders foothills and mountains. In a relatively small geographic spread, you get it all.

The ocean here is warm and beautiful, with 70 miles of beaches and often sensational fishing offshore for albacore, yellowtail, and marlin. The foothills provide canyon settings for many lakes, including Lower Otay, Morena, Barrett, El Capitan, Cuyamaca, San Vicente, Hodges, Henshaw, and several more – with some of the biggest lake-record bass ever caught in the world.

Cleveland National Forest provides a surprise for many – remote mountains with canyons, hidden streams, small campgrounds, and a terrain with a forest of fir, cedar, and hardwoods such as oak. A landmark is Palomar

Mountain, with several campgrounds at Palomar State Park and nearby in national forest. This is a great family destination. Long-distance views, stargazing, and watching meteor showers are all among the best anywhere in the state from the 5,000-foot ridges and lookouts set on the edge of Anza-Borrego Desert to the nearby east.

For more urban pursuits, San Diego's Mission Bay Park offers a fantastic network of recreation, with trails for biking and inline skating, and beaches and boating access.

Everywhere you go, you will find campgrounds and parks, primitive to deluxe. Some of the more remote sections of Cleveland National Forest, as well as Cuyamaca Rancho State Park, provide access to wild lands and primitive campsites. There are developed RV parks in the San Diego area that cost as much as fine hotel rooms in other parts of the state, and they're worth it, like silver dollars in a sea of pennies.

The region is one of the few that provides year-round recreation at a stellar level.

If you could live anywhere in America, where would it be? Well, that's what makes it so special to explore and visit, camping along the way.

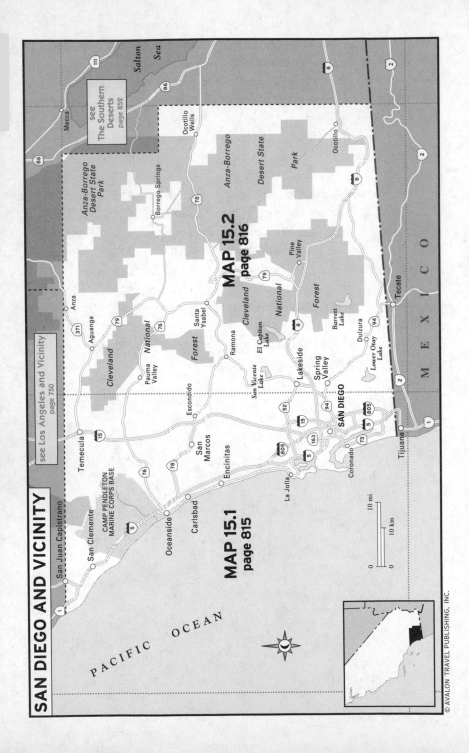

SAN DIEGO AND VICINITY

see Los Angeles and Vicinity
page 750

see
The Southern
Deserts
page 852

Salton
Sea

Mecca

Anza-Borrego
Desert State
Park

Borrego Springs

Ocotillo
Wells

Anza-Borrego

Desert State

Park

Ocotillo

Anza

Aguanga

Santa
Ysabel

Cleveland

National

Forest

Pine
Valley

Cleveland

National

Forest

Tecate

MAP 15.2
page 816

Temecula

Pauma
Valley

Ramona

San Vicente
Lake

El Capitan
Lake

Lakeside

Spring
Valley

Barrett
Lake

Dulzura

Lower Otay
Lake

Escondido

San
Marcos

Encinitas

SAN DIEGO

Coronado

Tijuana

Oceanside

Carlsbad

La Jolla

CAMP PENDLETON
MARINE CORPS BASE

San Clemente

San Juan Capistrano

MAP 15.1
page 815

10 mi

10 km

0

0

PACIFIC OCEAN

M E X I C O

Map 15.1

Campgrounds 1-16
Pages 817-825

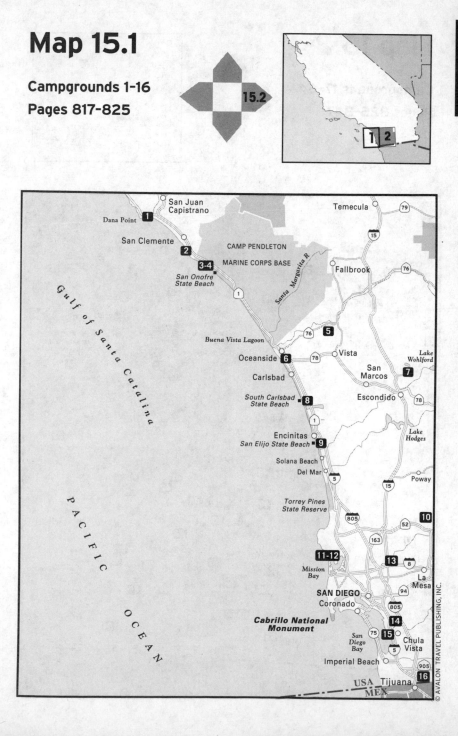

Map 15.2

Campgrounds 17-64
Pages 825-847

◼1 DOHENY STATE BEACH
🏃 🚵 🏊 🎣 🏕 🐕 ♿ 🚍 ⛰

Scenic rating: 8

on Dana Point Harbor

Map 15.1, page 815

Some campsites are within steps of the beach. Yet this state beach is right in town, set at the entrance to Dana Point Harbor. It is a pretty spot with easy access off the highway. Reservations are needed to guarantee a site at this popular campground. A lifeguard service is available in the summer, and campfire and junior ranger programs are also available. A day-use area has a lawn with picnic area and volleyball courts. Bonfire rings are set up on the beach. Surfing is popular, but note that it is permitted at the north end of the beach only. San Juan Capistrano provides a nearby side trip, just three miles away.

Campsites, facilities: There are 115 sites for tents or RVs up to 35 feet (no hookups), and one hike-in/bike-in site. Picnic tables and fire grills are provided. Drinking water, restrooms with flush toilets and coin showers, dump station, Wi-Fi, aquarium, and seasonal snack bar are available. Propane gas and gasoline are nearby. Some facilities are wheelchair-accessible. Leashed pets are permitted in campground only, not on the beach.

Reservations, fees: Reservations are accepted ($7.50 reservation fee) at 800/444-PARK (800/444-7275) or www.reserveamerica.com. The fee is $20–40 per night, $10 per night for each additional vehicle, $3 per person per night for hike-in/bike-in site (photo ID required). Open year-round.

Directions: Drive on I-5 to the exit for Pacific Coast Highway/Camino de las Ramblas (three miles south of San Juan Capistrano). Take that exit and drive to Dana Point/Harbor Drive (second light). Turn left and drive one block to the park entrance. Doheny State Beach is about one mile from I-5.

Contact: Doheny State Beach, 949/496-6172; Orange Coast District, San Clemente Sector, 949/492-0802, www.parks.ca.gov.

◼2 SAN CLEMENTE STATE BEACH
🏃 🚵 🏊 🎣 🏕 🐕 ♿ 🚍 ⛰

Scenic rating: 8

near San Clemente

Map 15.1, page 815

The campground at San Clemente State Beach is set on a bluff, not on a beach. A few campsites here have ocean views. Surfing is popular on the north end of a one-mile beach. The beach here is popular for swimming, body surfing, and skin diving. Of the three local state beaches that provide easy access and beachfront camping, this one offers full hookups. The others are Doheny State Beach to the north and San Onofre State Beach to the south. A feature at this park is a two-mile long interpretive trail, along with hike-in/bike-in campsites. Surfing camp is held here during the summer.

Campsites, facilities: There are 160 sites, 56 with full hookups (30 amps), for tents or RVs up to 40 feet, two hike-in/bike-in sites, and one group site with no hookups for tents or RVs for up to 50 people and 20 vehicles. Picnic tables and fire grills are provided. Restrooms with flush toilets and coin showers, dump station, Wi-Fi, summer lifeguard service, and summer programs are available. A store, coin laundry, and propane gas are nearby. Some facilities are wheelchair-accessible. Leashed pets are permitted in the campground only.

Reservations, fees: Reservations are accepted ($7.50 reservation fee) at 800/444-PARK (800/444-7275) or www.reserveamerica.com. The fee is $20–39 per night, $10 per night for each additional vehicle, $186 per night for the group site, $3 per person per night for hike-in/bike-in site. Open year-round.

Directions: From I-5 in San Clemente, take the Avenida Calafia exit. Drive west for a short distance to the park entrance on the left.

Contact: San Clemente State Beach, 949/492-3156 or 949/492-3281; Orange Coast District, 949/492-0802, www.parks.ca.gov.

3 SAN ONOFRE STATE BEACH: BLUFF AREA

🚶 🚴 🏊 ⛵ 🎣 🐕 ♿ 🚐 ⛺

Scenic rating: 7

near San Clemente

Map 15.1, page 815

This camp may appear perfect at first glance, but nope, it is very noisy. Both the highway and train tracks are within very close range; you can practically feel the ground rumble, and that's not all: With Camp Pendleton just on the other side of the freeway, there is considerable noise from helicopters and other operations. Too bad. This is one of three parks set along the beach near San Clemente, just off the busy Coast Highway. The campground is set on top of a 90-foot bluff. This state beach covers more than 3,000 acres, featuring 3.5 miles of sandy beaches and access trails on the neighboring bluffs. This area is one of the most popular in California for surfing, with this state beach also good for swimming. The shadow of the San Onofre Nuclear Power Plant is nearby. Other state beaches in the area are San Clemente State Beach and Doheny State Beach, both situated to the north.

Campsites, facilities: There are 176 sites for tents or RVs up to 30 feet (no hookups), and one group site for up to 50 people. Picnic tables and fire rings are provided. Drinking water, flush toilets, and cold outdoor showers are available. A store, coin laundry, and propane gas are available within about five miles. Some facilities are wheelchair accessible. Leashed pets are permitted at the campground and beach, but must stay on designated trails to access the beach.

Reservations, fees: Reservations are accepted ($7.50 reservation fee) at 800/444-PARK (800/444-7275) or www.reserveamerica.com. The fee is $20–25 per night, $10 per night for each additional vehicle, $175 per night for the group site. Open March through October, weather permitting.

Directions: From San Clemente, drive south on I-5 for three miles to the Basilone Road exit. Take that exit and drive south on Basilone Road for two miles to the park.

Contact: San Onofre State Beach, 949/492-4872; Orange Coast District Office, 949/492-0802 or 909/366-8500, www.parks.ca.gov.

4 SAN ONOFRE STATE BEACH: SAN MATEO

🚶 🎣 🐕 ♿ 🚐 ⛺

Scenic rating: 9

near San Clemente

Map 15.1, page 815

This state beach is considered one of the best surf breaks in the United States—it's well known as the outstanding Trestles Surfing Area. The camp is set inland and includes a nature trail, featuring a marshy area where San Mateo Creek meets the shoreline. Although this is a state beach, the camp is relatively far from the ocean; it is a 1.5-mile walk to the beach. But it sure is a lot quieter than the nearby option, Bluff Area campground.

Campsites, facilities: There are 159 sites for tents or RVs up to 35 feet; 67 sites have partial hookups (30 amps). Picnic tables and fire grills are provided. A dump station and restrooms with coin showers and flush toilets are available. A store, propane gas, and coin laundry are nearby. Leashed pets are permitted. Some facilities are wheelchair-accessible.

Reservations, fees: Reservations are accepted ($7.50 reservation fee) at 800/444-PARK (800/444-7275) or www.reserveamerica.com. The fee is $20–39 per night, $10 per night for each additional vehicle. Open year-round.

Directions: Drive on I-5 to the southern end of San Clemente and the Cristianitos Road exit. Take that exit and drive east on Cristianitos Road for 1.5 miles to the park entrance on the right.

Contact: San Onofre State Beach, 949/492-4872; Orange Coast District Office, 949/492-0802 or 909/366-8500, www.parks.ca.gov.

⑤ GUAJOME COUNTY PARK

Scenic rating: 5

in Oceanside

Map 15.1, page 815

Guajome means "home of the frog" and, yep, so it is with little Guajome Lake and the adjacent marsh, both of which can be explored with a delightful two-mile hike. The lake provides a bit of fishing for warm-water species, mainly sunfish and catfish. Swimming is prohibited. Because of the wetlands, a huge variety of birds stop here on their migratory journeys, making this a favorite area for bird-watching. A historic adobe house in the park is a must-see. The park covers 557 acres and features several miles of trails for hiking and horseback riding and a nearby museum with antique gas and steam engines and farm engines.

Campsites, facilities: There are 35 sites with full hookups (30 amps) for tents or RVs up to 45 feet; a few sites are pull-through. Picnic tables and fire grills are provided. Drinking water, restrooms with flush toilets and showers, dump station, and a playground are available. An enclosed pavilion and gazebo can be reserved for groups. A store and propane gas are nearby. Leashed pets are permitted.

Reservations, fees: Reservations are accepted ($3 reservation fee) at 858/565-3600. Sites are $16 per night, $1 per pet per night. Some credit cards accepted. Open year-round.

Directions: From Oceanside, drive east on Highway 76/Mission Avenue for seven miles to Guajome Lakes Road. Turn right (south) on Guajome Lakes Road and drive to the entrance.

Contact: San Diego County Parks Department, Guajome County Park, 760/724-4489, fax 760/945-5152, www.sdparks.org.

⑥ PARADISE BY THE SEA RV RESORT

Scenic rating: 7

in Oceanside

Map 15.1, page 815

This is a classic oceanfront RV resort, but no tenters need apply. It's an easy walk to the beach. The main coastal rail line runs adjacent to the resort, so expect some noise. For boaters, Oceanside Marina to the immediate north is the place to go. Oceanside is an excellent headquarters for deep-sea fishing, with charter trips available; contact Helgren's Sportfishing, 760/722-2133, to arrange charters. Legoland is four miles from the resort, and the Wave Waterpark and Mission San Luis Rey are seven miles away. Camp Pendleton, a huge Marine Corps training complex, is to the north.

Campsites, facilities: There are 102 sites with full hookups (30 amps) for RVs up to 40 feet; a few sites are pull-through. No tents. Picnic tables are provided. Restrooms, flush toilets, showers, cable TV, Wi-Fi, heated swimming pool, spa, clubhouse, banquet room, coin laundry, RV supplies, and a convenience store are available. Boat rentals are nearby. Leashed pets are permitted, with certain breeds prohibited.

Reservations, fees: Reservations are recommended. Sites are $39–50 per night, $3 per person per night for more than two people, $15 per night for each additional vehicle, $1.50 per pet per night. Ninety-day limit per stay. Some credit cards accepted. Open year-round.

Directions: Drive on I-5 to Oceanside and the Oceanside Boulevard exit. Take that exit and drive west on Oceanside Boulevard for 0.5 mile to South Coast Highway. Turn left on South Coast Highway and drive to the park on the right (1537 South Coast Highway).

Contact: Paradise by the Sea RV Resort, 760/439-1376, fax 760/439-1919, www.paradisebythesearvresort.com.

7 DIXON LAKE RECREATION AREA

🚶 🛶 🚐 🎣 ♿ 🚙 ⛺

Scenic rating: 7

near Escondido

Map 15.1, page 815

Little Dixon Lake is the centerpiece of a regional park in the Escondido foothills. The camp is set at an elevation of 1,405 feet, about 400 feet above the lake's shoreline. No private boats or swimming are permitted, and a 5-mph speed limit for rental boats keeps things quiet. The water is clear, with fair bass fishing (25 lb. 1 oz. bass caught in 2006) in the spring and trout fishing in the winter and early spring. Catfish are stocked in the summer, trout in winter and spring. In the summer, the lake is open at night for fishing for catfish. A pretty and easy hike is Jack Creek Nature Trail, a one-mile walk to a seasonal 20-foot waterfall. Note that no wood fires are permitted, but charcoal and gas are allowed.

Campsites, facilities: There are 45 sites for tents or RVs up to 35 feet; 11 sites have full hookups (30 amps). A cabin is also available. Picnic tables, fire grills, and food lockers are provided. Drinking water, restrooms with flush toilets and showers, picnic shelters, boat rentals, bait, ice, snack bar, and a playground are available. Some facilities are wheelchair accessible. No pets are allowed.

Reservations, fees: Reservations are accepted ($5 reservation fee) at 760/741-3328. Sites are $20–25 per night. Groups can be accommodated. Some credit cards accepted. Open year-round.

Directions: Drive on I-15 to the exit for El Norte Parkway (four miles north of Escondido). Take that exit northeast and drive four miles to La Honda Drive. Turn left and drive about one mile to Dixon Lake.

Contact: Dixon Lake Recreation Area, City of Escondido, 760/839-4680, www .dixonlake.com.

8 SOUTH CARLSBAD STATE BEACH

🚶 🚴 🏊 🛶 🎣 🐎 ♿ 🚙 ⛺

Scenic rating: 9

near Carlsbad

Map 15.1, page 815

No reservation? Then likely you can forget about staying here. This is a beautiful state beach and, as big as it is, the sites go fast to the coastal cruisers who reserved a spot. The campground is set on a bluff, with half the sites overlooking the ocean. The nearby beach is accessible by a series of stairs. This is a phenomenal place for scuba diving and snorkeling, with a nearby reef available. This is also a popular spot for surfing and body surfing. Legoland is one mile away.

Campsites, facilities: There are 222 sites for tents or RVs up to 35 feet (no hookups). Picnic tables and fire rings are provided. Drinking water, restrooms with flush toilets and coin showers, Wi-Fi, and a dump station are available. A lifeguard service is provided in summer. Some facilities are wheelchair-accessible. Supplies and a coin laundry are available in Carlsbad. Leashed pets are permitted, but not on the beach.

Reservations, fees: Reservations are accepted ($7.50 reservation fee) at 800/444-PARK (800/444-7275) or www.reserveamerica .com. Sites are $25–35 per night, $10 per night for each additional vehicle. Open year-round, with limited facilities in the winter.

Directions: Drive on I-5 to Carlsbad and the exit for Palomar Airport Road. Take that exit and drive west for 0.3 mile to Carlsbad Boulevard South. Turn south on Carlsbad Boulevard South and drive three miles to Poinsettia Avenue and the park entrance on the right.

Contact: South Carlsbad State Beach, 760/438-3143; San Diego Coast District, 619/688-3260, www.parks.ca.gov.

9 SAN ELIJO STATE BEACH

Scenic rating: 9

in Cardiff by the Sea

Map 15.1, page 815

As with South Carlsbad State Beach, about half the sites here overlook the ocean—that is, these are bluff-top campgrounds. The swimming and surfing are good here, with a reef nearby for snorkeling and diving. What more could you ask for? Well, for one thing, how about not so many trains? Yep, train tracks run nearby and the trains roll by several times a day. So much for a chance at tranquility. Regardless, it is a beautiful beach just north of the small town of Cardiff by the Sea. As at all state beaches, reservations are usually required to get a spot between Memorial Day weekend and Labor Day weekend. Nearby San Elijo Lagoon at Solana Beach is an ecological preserve. Though this is near a developed area, there are numerous white egrets, as well as occasional herons and other marine birds.

Campsites, facilities: There are 144 sites for tents or RVs up to 22 feet (no hookups), 26 sites for tents or RVs up to 24 feet (full hookups), and one hike-in/bike-in site. Picnic tables and fire rings are provided. Drinking water, restrooms with flush toilets and coin showers, Wi-Fi, coin laundry, dump station, and a small store are available. A lifeguard service is available in the summer. Some facilities are wheelchair-accessible. Leashed pets are permitted, but not on the beach.

Reservations, fees: Reservations are accepted ($7.50 reservation fee) at 800/444-PARK (800/444-7275) or www.reserveamerica.com. Sites are $25–44 per night, $10 per night for each additional vehicle, $3 per person per night for hike-in/bike-in site. Open year-round.

Directions: Drive on I-5 to Encinitas and the Encinitas Boulevard exit. Take that exit and drive west on Encinitas Boulevard for one mile to U.S. 101 (South Coast Highway). Turn south (left) on U.S. 101 and drive two miles to the park on the right.

Contact: San Elijo State Beach, 760/753-5091; San Diego Coast District, 619/688-3260 or 760/720-7005, www.parks.ca.gov.

10 SANTEE LAKES RECREATION PRESERVE

Scenic rating: 6

near Santee

Map 15.1, page 815

This is a 190-acre park built around a complex of seven lakes. Some campsites are lakefront. The park is best known for its fishing. The lakes are stocked with large numbers of trout and catfish, with fantastic lake records including a 39-pound catfish, 13-pound rainbow trout, 13.9-pound largemouth bass, and 2.5-pound bluegill. Rowboats, pedal boats, kayaks, and canoes are available for rent. So how many lakes can you boat on? Answer: Only one, Lake 5. Fishing is now allowed on all lakes, and float tubing is permitted on four lakes for campers only. No swimming or water/body contact is allowed here, and no private motorized boats are permitted. This small regional park is 20 miles east of San Diego. It receives more than 100,000 visitors per year. The camp is set at 400 feet. The Carlton Oaks Country Club is 0.5-mile away and open to the public.

Campsites, facilities: There are 300 sites with full hookups (50 amps) for RVs of any length, and tents are allowed at some sites. Some sites are pull-through. Picnic tables are provided and some sites have barbecue grills. Restrooms with flush toilets and showers, drinking water, dump station, boat rentals, playground, seasonal swimming pool, general store, picnic area, amphitheater, RV storage, recreation center, Wi-Fi, pay phone, propane, and coin laundry are available. Some facilities are wheelchair-accessible. Leashed pets are permitted in the campground.

Reservations, fees: Reservations are accepted by website or at 619/596-3141. Sites are

$32–42 per night, $2 per night for each additional vehicle, $1 per pet per night. Weekly and monthly rates available. Some credit cards accepted. Open year-round.

Directions: Drive on I-8 to El Cajon and Highway 67. Take the Highway 67 exit north (toward Santee) and drive one mile to Bradley Avenue. Take that exit and drive a short distance to Bradley Avenue. Turn left and drive one mile to Cuyamaca Street. Turn right and drive 1.6 miles to Mission Gorge Road. Turn left (west) and drive 0.3 mile to Fanita Parkway. Turn right and drive a short distance to the campground entrance on the left at 9310 Fanita Parkway.

Contact: Santee Lakes Recreation Preserve, Padre Dam Municipal Water District, 619/596-3141, www.santeelakes.com.

11 CAMPLAND ON THE BAY

Scenic rating: 6

on Mission Bay

Map 15.1, page 815

No kidding, this is one of the biggest campgrounds on this side of the galaxy. The place has a prime location: The park overlooks Kendall Frost Wildlife Preserve and is set on Mission Bay, a beautiful spot and a boater's paradise; it includes a private beach. Waterskiing, sailboarding, and ocean access for deep-sea fishing are preeminent. SeaWorld, just north of San Diego, offers a premium side trip. There used to be numerous complaints about poor communications and customer services support, as well as staff shortages and safety issues. These problems appear to have been addressed by management, and the situation has improved.

Campsites, facilities: There are more than 558 sites, most with full or partial hookups (30 and 50 amps) for tents or RVs up to 45 feet. Picnic tables and fire pits are provided. Restrooms with flush toilets and showers, drinking water, cable TV, phone and modem access, Wi-Fi,

swimming pools, spa, recreation hall, arcade, playground, café, dump station, coin laundry, grocery store, amphitheater, RV and boat storage, RV supplies, propane gas, boat ramp, marina, boat docks, water toy rentals, boat and bike rentals, and organized activities and events are available. Leashed pets are permitted, with certain restrictions.

Reservations, fees: Reservations are accepted up to two years in advance at 800/422-9386 ($25 site guarantee fee); tent sites are $39–84 per night, RV sites are $46–249.90 per night; $7 per night for each additional vehicle or boats and trailers, $3 per night per pet. Weekly rates are available during the winter. Some credit cards accepted. Open year-round.

Directions: Drive on I-5 south to San Diego and the Balboa-Garnet exit. Take that exit to Mission Bay Drive and drive to Grand Avenue. Turn right and drive one mile to Olney Street. Turn left on Olney Street and drive to Pacific Beach Drive. Turn left and drive a short distance to the campground entrance.

From northbound I-5 in San Diego, take the Grand-Garnet exit. Stay in the left lane to Grand Avenue. Turn left on Grand Avenue and drive to Olney Street. Turn left on Olney Street and continue as above.

Contact: Campland on the Bay, 800/422-9386, administration office, 858/581-4200, www.campland.com.

12 SANTA FE PARK RV RESORT

Scenic rating: 3

in San Diego

Map 15.1, page 815

This resort is a short drive from a variety of side trips, including the San Diego Zoo, SeaWorld, the historic San Diego Mission and Presidio Park, golf courses, beaches, sportfishing, and Tijuana.

Campsites, facilities: There are 129 sites with full hookups (20 and 30 amps) for RVs up to 40 feet. No tent camping is allowed. Picnic tables and barbecues are provided. Restrooms with flush toilets and showers, drinking water, playground, heated swimming pool, spa, dump station, satellite TV, Wi-Fi, recreation room, mini theater, fitness center, and coin laundry are available. Some facilities are wheelchair-accessible. Leashed pets under 25 pounds are permitted, with some restrictions.

Reservations, fees: Reservations are accepted by website or at 800/959-3787. Sites are $41–59 per night, $2 per pet per night. Weekly and monthly rates available. Some credit cards accepted. Open year-round.

Directions: Drive on I-5 south to San Diego and Exit 23 for Balboa-Garnet. Take that exit, get in the left lane, and drive a short distance to the second stoplight and Damon Street. Turn left and drive 0.25 mile to Santa Fe Street. Turn left and drive 1.4 miles to the resort on the right (5707 Santa Fe Street).

On northbound I-5, drive to Exit 23 for Grand-Garnet. Take that exit and continue as it feeds to East Mission Bay Drive. Continue through four traffic signals to Damon Street. Turn right and drive 0.25 mile to Santa Fe Street. Turn left and drive 1.4 miles to the resort on the right (5707 Santa Fe Street). Note: Disregard the "Not a through street" sign on Santa Fe.

Contact: Santa Fe Park RV Resort, 858/272-4051 or 800/959-3787, fax 858/272-2845, www.santafeparkrvresort.com.

13 MISSION TRAILS REGIONAL PARK

Scenic rating: 7

near San Diego

Map 15.1, page 815

Kumeyaay Lake and its campground are the centerpiece of this more than 6,000-acre park, which is only eight miles northeast of downtown San Diego. The park includes chaparral,

oak woodland, mountains, and grasslands. Fishing is permitted for bass, bluegill, crappie, catfish, and carp; catch-and-release fishing is recommended. There are more than 40 miles of trails for hiking, biking, and horseback riding. Bird-watching is good in this park. Interpretive programs and organized activities are available.

Campsites, facilities: There are 46 sites for tents or RVs up to 40 feet (no hookups). Picnic tables, tent pads, and fire boxes are provided. Restrooms with flush toilets and solar-heated showers, dump station, amphitheater, picnic area, and firewood are available. Alcoholic beverages are prohibited. Some facilities are wheelchair-accessible. Leashed pets are permitted.

Reservations, fees: Reservations are accepted at www.mtrp.org/campground. The fee is $14 per night, $4 per night for each additional vehicle, $3 per pet per night. Open year-round Friday through Monday; campground closed Tuesday through Thursday.

Directions: From I-8 in San Diego, take the Mission Gorge/Fairmount exit. Turn north on Mission Gorge Road and drive 6.5 miles to the northern (Kumeyaay Lake) entrance and Father Junipero Serra Trail. Turn left on Father Junipero Serra Trail and drive 0.2 mile to the lake and campground on the right.

Contact: Mission Trails Regional Park, City of San Diego 619/668-2748, Visitors Center 619/668-3281, www.sandiego.gov.

14 SAN DIEGO METROPOLITAN KOA

Scenic rating: 2

in Chula Vista

Map 15.1, page 815

This is one in a series of parks set up primarily for RVs cruising I-5. Chula Vista is between Mexico and San Diego, allowing visitors to make side trips east to Lower Otay Lake, north to the San Diego attractions, south to Tijuana, or "around the corner" on Highway 75 to Silver Strand State Beach. Nearby San Diego Bay is beautiful, with excellent water-skiing (in designated areas), sailboarding, and a great swimming beach.

Campsites, facilities: There are 208 sites for RVs of any length (no hookups), 48 sites for tents, and 27 cabins. Many sites are pull-through. Picnic tables and barbecue grills are provided. Restrooms with flush toilets and showers, drinking water, modem access, Wi-Fi, playground, dump station, coin laundry, heated swimming pool, spa, bike rentals, propane gas, seasonal organized activities, and convenience store are available. Some facilities are wheelchair-accessible. Leashed pets are permitted.

Reservations, fees: Reservations are accepted at 800/762-KAMP (800/762-5267). Sites are $30–49 per night for tents, $38–67 per night for RVs, $5 per night for each additional vehicle, $4 per person per night for more than two people. Some credit cards accepted. Open year-round.

Directions: Drive on I-5 to Chula Vista and the exit for E Street. Take that exit and drive east on E Street for three miles to 2nd Avenue. Turn left (north) on 2nd Avenue and drive 0.75 mile to the park on the right (111 North 2nd Avenue).

Contact: San Diego Metropolitan KOA, 619/427-3601, fax 619/427-3622, www.koa .com.

sailboarding are also excellent. Bike paths are nearby.

Campsites, facilities: There are 237 sites with full hookups (30 and 50 amps) for RVs. Some sites are pull-through. No tents. Picnic tables and cable TV are provided. Restrooms with flush toilets and showers, drinking water, Wi-Fi, modem access, fitness center, play-grounds, heated swimming pool and spa, game room, two waterfront restaurants, marina, fishing pier, free boat launch, coin laundry, propane gas, bicycle rentals, car rentals, picnic area, meeting rooms, and general store are available. Some facilities are wheelchair-accessible. Leashed pets up to 20 pounds are permitted, with certain restrictions.

Reservations, fees: Reservations are accept-ed at 800/770-2878 or at www.chulavistarv .com. Sites are $41.50–54.50 per night, $3 per night per additional person for more than two people, $3 per night for each additional vehicle, $1 per pet per night. Boat slips are $16–20 per day. Weekly and monthly rates are available. Some credit cards accepted. Open year-round.

Directions: Drive on I-5 to Chula Vista and the exit for J Street/Marina Parkway. Take that exit, turn left, and drive 0.5 mile west to Sandpiper Way. Turn left and drive a short distance to the park on the left (460 Sand-piper Way).

Contact: Chula Vista RV Resort, 619/422-0111, fax 619/422-8872, www.chulavistarv .com.

15 CHULA VISTA RV RESORT

Scenic rating: 6

in Chula Vista

Map 15.1, page 815

This RV park is about 50 yards from San Diego Bay, a beautiful, calm piece of water where waterskiing is permitted in designated areas. An excellent swimming beach is avail-able, and conditions in the afternoon for

16 LA PACIFICA RV RESORT

Scenic rating: 1

in San Ysidro

Map 15.1, page 815

This RV park is less than two miles from the Mexican border. Note that many sites are filled with long-term renters, but some sites are available for overnight use.

Campsites, facilities: There are 177 sites with full hookups (30 and 50 amps) for RVs up to 40 feet. No tents. Many sites are pull-through. Picnic tables are provided at most sites. Restrooms with flush toilets and showers, heated swimming pool, whirlpool, clubhouse, video and book library, cable TV, phone and modem hookups, Wi-Fi, recreation room, dump station, coin laundry, and propane gas are available. All facilities are wheelchair-accessible. Leashed pets under 20 pounds are permitted.

Reservations, fees: Reservations are accepted at 888/786-6997. The fee is $40 per night. Weekly and monthly rates available. Some credit cards accepted. Open year-round.

Directions: From the San Diego area, drive south on I-5 to San Ysidro and the exit for Dairymart Road. Take that exit east to Dairymart Road and drive a short distance to San Ysidro Boulevard. Turn left and drive to the park on the left (1010 San Ysidro Boulevard).

Contact: La Pacifica RV Resort, 619/428-4411, fax 619/428-4413.

17 DRIPPING SPRINGS

Scenic rating: 7

near the Agua Tibia Wilderness in Cleveland National Forest

Map 15.2, page 816

This is one of the premium Forest Service camps available, set just inside the national forest border near Vail Lake and adjacent to the Agua Tibia Wilderness. Dripping Springs Trail is routed south out of camp, starting at 1,600 feet and climbing near the peak of Agua Tibia Mountain, 4,779 feet.

Campsites, facilities: There are 33 sites for tents or RVs up to 22 feet (no hookups). Equestrian sites are available. Picnic tables and fire rings are provided. There is no drinking water. Vault toilets are available. Supplies are available nearby in Temecula. Leashed pets are permitted.

Reservations, fees: Reservations are not accepted. The fee is $12 per night. Open June through February. Closed March through May for protection of an endangered species, the arroyo southwestern toad.

Directions: From I-15 in Temecula, drive 11 miles southeast on Highway 79 to the campground.

Contact: Cleveland National Forest, Palomar Ranger District, 760/788-0250, fax 760/788-6130.

18 OAK GROVE

Scenic rating: 4

near Temecula Creek in Cleveland National Forest

Map 15.2, page 816

Oak Grove camp is on the northeastern fringe of Cleveland National Forest at 2,800 feet. Easy access from Highway 79 makes this a popular camp. The Palomar Observatory is five miles up the mountain to the west, but there is no direct way to reach it from the campground and it cannot be viewed from camp. Lake Henshaw is about a half-hour drive to the south. A boat ramp and boat rentals are available there.

Campsites, facilities: There are 81 sites for tents or RVs up to 27 feet (no hookups). Picnic tables and fire grills are provided. Drinking water and flush toilets are available. Propane gas and groceries are nearby. Leashed pets are permitted.

Reservations, fees: Reservations are not accepted. Sites are $15–23 per night. Open year-round.

Directions: Drive on I-15 to the Highway 79 exit. Take that exit and drive south on Highway 79 to Aguanga. Continue southeast on Highway 79 for 6.5 miles to the camp entrance.

Contact: Cleveland National Forest, Palomar Ranger District, 760/788-0250, fax 760/788-6130.

19 PALOMAR MOUNTAIN STATE PARK

👣 🚴 🛶 🎣 ♿ 🚐 ⛺

Scenic rating: 8

near the Palomar Observatory

Map 15.2, page 816

This is one of the best state parks in Southern California for hiking. It is also one of the friendliest. In fact, in 2004 Reserve America named Palomar as one of the top 100 family campgrounds in the United States. It features 14 miles of trails, including several loop trails, often featuring long-distance views. Yet forest covers much of this park, one of the few sites in this Southern California region with a Sierra Nevada–like feel to it. This camp offers hiking trails and some fishing in Doane Pond (state fishing laws are in effect here—great for youngsters learning to fish). There are numerous excellent hikes, including Boucher Trail (four miles) and Lower Doane Valley Trail (three miles). The view from Boucher Lookout is stunning, at 5,438 feet looking out over the valley below. This developed state park is a short drive from the Palomar Observatory (not part of the park). There are four other campgrounds in the immediate area that are a short distance from the observatory. At the Palomar Observatory you'll find the 200-inch Hale Telescope, America's largest telescope. This is a private, working telescope, run by the California Institute of Technology. Observatory tours are available, and the telescope can be viewed (but not used) by the public. The campground elevation is 4,700 feet.

Campsites, facilities: There are 31 sites for tents or RVs up to 27 feet (no hookups) and trailers up to 24 feet, three group sites for 15–25 people, and one hike-in/bike-in site. Picnic tables, fire grills, and food lockers are provided. Drinking water and restrooms with flush toilets and coin showers are available. Some facilities are wheelchair-accessible. Leashed pets are permitted in the campground, but not on trails.

Reservations, fees: Reservations are accepted ($7.50 reservation fee) at 800/444-PARK (800/444-7275) or www.reserveamerica.com. Sites are $15–20 per night, $6 per night for each additional vehicle, $3 per person per night for hike-in/bike-in site, $60–90 per night for group sites. Fishing license required for fishing pond; buy before arrival. Open year-round.

Directions: Drive on I-15 to the Highway 76 exit (east of Oceanside). Take that exit and drive east on Highway 76 for approximately 25 miles to County Road S6 (which brings you to the top of Palomar Mountain). At the top of the mountain, turn left, drive about 50 feet to State Park Road/County Road S7. Turn left on State Park Road/County Road S7 and drive about 3.5 miles to the park entrance.

Contact: Palomar Mountain State Park 760/742-3462, Colorado Desert District 760/767-5311, Palomar Observatory 760/742-2119, www.parks.ca.gov.

20 FRY CREEK

👣 🎣 ⛺

Scenic rating: 6

near the Palomar Observatory in Cleveland National Forest

Map 15.2, page 816

A small, seasonal stream, Fry Creek, runs near the camp. The elevation is 5,200 feet. On a clear night, you can see forever from Palomar Mountain. Literally. That's because the Palomar Observatory, just a short distance from this forested camp, houses America's largest telescope. With the 200-inch Hale Telescope, it is possible for scientists to see 100 billion galaxies. It is open to public touring (check for current hours), but you cannot touch the telescope.

Campsites, facilities: There are 20 tent sites. No RVs or trailers are allowed. Picnic tables and fire rings are provided. Drinking water and flush toilets are available. A store and coin showers are available nearby. Leashed pets are permitted.

Reservations, fees: Reservations are not

accepted. Sites are $12 per night. Open May through November, weather permitting.

Directions: Drive on I-15 to the Highway 76 exit (east of Oceanside). Take that exit and drive east on Highway 76 for 25 miles to County Road S6 (which brings you to the top of Palomar Mountain). Turn left on County Road S6 and drive about nine miles to the campground entrance on the left. The road is not recommended for trailers.

Contact: Cleveland National Forest, Palomar Ranger District, 760/788-0250, fax 760/788-6130.

21 OBSERVATORY

Scenic rating: 4

near the Palomar Observatory in Cleveland National Forest

Map 15.2, page 816

This popular Forest Service camp is used primarily as a layover spot for campers visiting the nearby Palomar Observatory, housing the largest telescope in America. There are four other camps in the immediate area. The elevation is 4,800 feet. The trailhead for Observatory Trail starts at this camp. This two-hour hike from the campground to the observatory includes one short, steep climb through woodlands, highlighted by a vista deck with a beautiful view of Mendenhall Valley, and then onward to the top and to the viewing area to catch a glimpse of the telescope. Tours are available, but the telescope itself is not available to the public for use.

Campsites, facilities: There are 42 sites for tents or RVs up to 27 feet (no hookups). Picnic tables and fire grills are provided. Drinking water and restrooms with flush toilets and coin showers are available. Some facilities are wheelchair accessible. Leashed pets are permitted.

Reservations, fees: Reservations are not accepted. Sites are $15 per night, double sites are $23 per night. Open May through November.

Directions: Drive on I-15 to the Highway 76 exit (east of Oceanside). Take that exit and drive east on Highway 76 for 25 miles to County Road S6 (which brings you to the top of Palomar Mountain). Turn left on County Road S6 and drive about 8.5 miles to the campground entrance on the right. The road is not recommended for trailers.

Contact: Cleveland National Forest, Palomar Ranger District, 760/788-0250, fax 760/788-6130.

22 INDIAN FLATS

Scenic rating: 6

near the Pacific Crest Trail in Cleveland National Forest

Map 15.2, page 816

Indian Flats is a remote campground, set at 3,600 feet just north of Pine Mountain. The Pacific Crest Trail passes only two miles down the road to the south. A two-mile hike south on the PCT will take you down into a canyon and the home of Agua Caliente Creek.

Campsites, facilities: There are 17 sites for tents (no hookups). Picnic tables and fire grills are provided. Vault toilets are available. There is no drinking water. Leashed pets are permitted.

Reservations, fees: Reservations are not accepted. Sites are $5 per night. Open June through February, closed March through May for protection of an endangered species, the arroyo southwestern toad.

Directions: From El Cajon, drive east on I-8 to Highway 79 (near Descanso Junction). Turn north on Highway 79 and drive to the town of Warner Springs. Continue two miles on Highway 79 to Forest Road 9S05. Turn right on Forest Road 9S05 and drive six miles to the campground.

Contact: Cleveland National Forest, Palomar Ranger District, 760/788-0250, fax 760/788-6130.

23 CRESTLINE GROUP CAMP

Scenic rating: 4

near the Palomar Observatory in Cleveland National Forest

Map 15.2, page 816

This Forest Service camp is designed expressly for large groups. (For adventure information, see the *Palomar Mountain State Park* listing in this chapter.) The elevation is 4,800 feet.

Campsites, facilities: There is one group campsite for tents only for up to 50 people. Picnic tables and fire grills are provided. Drinking water and vault toilets are available. A store is nearby. Leashed pets are permitted.

Reservations, fees: Reservations are required ($9 reservation fee) at 877/444-6777 or www .ReserveUSA.com. The site is $75 per night. Open May through November.

Directions: Drive on I-15 to the Highway 76 exit (east of Oceanside). Take that exit and drive east on Highway 76 for 25 miles to County Road S6 (which brings you to the top of Palomar Mountain). Turn left on County Road S6 and drive about 6.5 miles to the campground at the junction of County Roads S6 and S7. The road is not recommended for trailers.

Contact: Cleveland National Forest, Palomar Ranger District, 760/788-0250, fax 760/788-6130.

24 OAK KNOLL CAMPGROUND

Scenic rating: 5

near the Palomar Observatory

Map 15.2, page 816

The camp is set at 3,000 feet in San Diego County foothill country among giant old California oaks. It is at the western base of Palomar Mountain, and to visit the Palomar Observatory and its awesome 200-inch telescope requires a remarkably twisty 10-mile drive up the mountain (the telescope is not open to the public, but the observatory is open). The campground management suggests you bring your telescope or borrow one of theirs for nighttime stargazing. A good side trip is driving to the Boucher Lookout in Palomar Mountain State Park. Trailheads for excellent hikes on Palomar Mountain include Observatory Trail (starting at Observatory) and Doane Valley Loop (starting in Palomar Mountain State Park).

Campsites, facilities: There are 46 sites for tents or RVs up to 30 feet; many sites have full or partial hookups (30 amps). Picnic tables and fire barrels are provided. Drinking water, restrooms with flush toilets and coin showers, dump station, library, video arcade, Wi-Fi, recreation hall, pavilion, seasonal activities, playground, swimming pool, baseball diamond, horseshoes, basketball court, coin laundry, propane gas, and convenience store are available. Leashed pets are permitted, with certain restrictions.

Reservations, fees: Reservations are accepted. Sites are $25–35 per night, $5 per person per night for more than two people, $3 per night for each additional vehicle, $2 per pet per night. Monthly rates available. Open year-round.

Directions: Drive on I-15 to the Highway 76 exit (east of Oceanside). Take that exit and drive east on Highway 76 for 21 miles to South Grade Road/County Road S6. Turn left and drive a short distance to the campground on the left.

Contact: Oak Knoll Campground, 760/742-3437, www.oakknoll.net.

25 VERN WHITAKER HORSE CAMP

Scenic rating: 5

in Anza-Borrego Desert State Park

Map 15.2, page 816

This camp is popular during spring and fall, with lighter use during the winter. The draw for equestrian campers are the 30 miles of horse trails. Campers are expected to clean up after their horses, and garbage bins are available for manure.

Campsites, facilities: There are 10 equestrian sites for tents or RVs up to 24 feet (no hookups). Picnic tables and fire grills are provided. Restrooms with flush toilets, an outdoor shower, drinking water, picnic areas, group gathering area, horse-washing station, and horse corrals are available. Leashed pets are permitted in the campground, but not on trails or in wilderness.

Reservations, fees: Reservations are accepted ($7.50 reservation fee) at 800/444-PARK (800/444-7275) or www.reserveamerica.com. Sites are $20 per night, which includes two horses, $2 per additional horse per night. Open October through May.

Directions: From Julian, at the junction of Highway 78 and Highway 79, drive east on Highway 78 (steep and curvy) for 19.5 miles to Yaqui Pass Road/County Road 53. Turn left (north) and drive eight miles to Palm Canyon Drive. Turn left and drive to Borrego Springs and bear right (at the traffic circle) onto northbound Borrego Springs Road. Drive four miles on Borrego Springs Road to Henderson Canyon Road. Bear right and drive a short distance to the campground entrance road (look for the metal sign). Turn left and continue four miles to the camp. Note: Part of the last four miles are on a private road; please respect the property owner's rights.

Contact: Anza-Borrego Desert State Park, 760/767-4205; Colorado Desert District, 760/767-5311, fax 760/767-3427, www.parks .ca.gov.

26 ARROYO SALADO PRIMITIVE CAMP AREA
🏃 🐕 🚐 ⛺

Scenic rating: 5

in Anza-Borrego Desert State Park

Map 15.2, page 816

This camp is a primitive spot set along (and named after) an ephemeral stream, the Arroyo Salado. About eight miles to the west is the trailhead for Thimble Trail, which is routed south into a wash in the Borrego Badlands. The elevation is 880 feet.

Campsites, facilities: This is a primitive, open camping area for tents or small RVs of any length (no hookups). Vault toilets are available. No drinking water is available. Fires are allowed in metal containers. Garbage and ashes must be packed out. Open fires are not allowed. Leashed pets are permitted in the campground, but not on trails or in wilderness.

Reservations, fees: Reservations are not accepted. There is no fee for camping. Open year-round.

Directions: From Julian, at the junction of Highway 78 (steep and curvy) and Highway 79, drive east on Highway 78 for 19.5 miles to Yaqui Pass Road/County Road S3. Turn left (north) and drive eight miles to Borrego Springs and Palm Canyon Drive. Turn right on Palm Canyon Drive (becomes Highway 522) and drive 20 miles (past Fonts Point) to the campground entrance on the right.

Contact: Anza-Borrego Desert State Park, 760/767-4205; Colorado Desert District, 760/767-5311, fax 760/767-3427, www.parks .ca.gov.

27 BORREGO PALM CANYON
🏃 🐕 ♿ 🚐 ⛺

Scenic rating: 4

in Anza-Borrego Desert State Park

Map 15.2, page 816

This is one of the best camps in Anza-Borrego Desert State Park, with two excellent hikes available. The short hike into Borrego Palm Canyon is like being transported to another world, from the desert to the tropics, complete with a small waterfall, a rare sight in these parts. Panorama Overlook Trail also starts here. An excellent visitors center is available, offering an array of exhibits and a slide show. The elevation is 760 feet. Anza-Borrego Desert

State Park is one of the largest state parks in the continental United States, covering more than 600,000 acres and with 500 miles of dirt roads. The park is appropriately named for the desert bighorn sheep (*borrego* in Spanish) that live in the mountains.

Campsites, facilities: There are 65 sites for tents or RVs up to 25 feet (no hookups), 52 sites with full hookups (30 amps) for RVs up to 35 feet, and five group tent sites for up to 24 people each. Picnic tables and fire grills are provided. Drinking water, restrooms with flush toilets and showers, and dump station are available. Some facilities are wheelchair-accessible. A store, coin laundry, and propane gas are nearby. Leashed pets are permitted.

Reservations, fees: Reservations are accepted ($7.50 reservation fee) at 800/444-PARK (800/444-7275) or www.reserveamerica.com. Sites are $12–26 per night, $53 per night for group sites. Open year-round.

Directions: From Julian, at the junction of Highway 78 and Highway 79, drive east on Highway 78 (steep and curvy) for 19.5 miles to Yaqui Pass Road/County Road S3. Turn left (north) and drive eight miles to Borrego Springs and Palm Canyon Drive. Turn left (west) and drive 4.5 miles to the campground entrance road on the right.

Contact: Anza-Borrego Desert State Park, 760/767-4205; Colorado Desert District, 760/767-5311, fax 760/767-3427, www.parks .ca.gov.

28 WOODS VALLEY KAMPGROUND

Scenic rating: 5

near Lake Wohlford

Map 15.2, page 816

This privately operated park is situated on 20 acres and is popular with families. Lake Wohlford is about 10 miles to the south and has a lake speed limit of 5 mph. The lake is stocked with rainbow trout, brown trout, steelhead,

channel catfish, and blue catfish. Insider's tip: A bald eagle winters at Lake Wohlford.

Campsites, facilities: There are 59 sites for RVs of any length, and 30 sites for tents. Many of the RV sites have partial hookups and some have full hookups (30 amps). Picnic tables and fire barrels are provided. Drinking water, restrooms with flush toilets and showers, dump station, coin laundry, swimming pool, catch-and-release fishing pond, small animal farm, playground, volleyball, horseshoes, recreation hall, group facilities, and supplies are available. Leashed pets are permitted, with some dogs prohibited.

Reservations, fees: Reservations are accepted. Sites are $31–45 per night, $3 per night for each additional vehicle, $3 per pet per night. Monthly rates available. Open year-round.

Directions: From San Diego, drive north on I-15 to the Escondido area and take the Via Rancho Parkway exit and continue to Via Rancho Parkway. Turn right (name changes to Bear Valley Parkway) and drive approximately nine miles to a T intersection and Valley Parkway. Turn right on Valley Parkway and drive approximately six miles (name changes to Valley Center Road) to Woods Valley Road. Turn right and drive 2.2 miles to the park on the left.

Contact: Woods Valley Kampground, 760/749-2905, www.woodsvalley.com.

29 LAKE HENSHAW RESORT

Scenic rating: 7

near Santa Ysabel

Map 15.2, page 816

Lake Henshaw is the biggest lake in San Diego County, with 25 miles of shoreline, yet it has only one camp. It's a good one, with the cabin rentals a big plus. The camp is on the southern corner of the lake, at 2,727 feet near Cleveland National Forest. Swimming, water/body contact, canoes, and rafts are not permitted and a 10-mph speed limit is in effect. The fishing is best for catfish, especially in the summer, and at times decent for bass, with the lake-record bass weighing 14 pounds, four ounces. Other fish species are trout, bluegill, and crappie. Like many reservoirs, Lake Henshaw is sometimes plagued by low water levels. A mobile home park is also on the premises.

Campsites, facilities: There are 139 sites for tents or RVs of any length (no hookups), and 25 sites with full hookups (20 amps) for tents or RVs of any length. Picnic tables and fire pits are provided. Restrooms with flush toilets and showers, cabins, swimming pool, spa, picnic area, clubhouse, playground, dump station, coin laundry, propane gas, boat and motor rentals, boat launch, bait and tackle, café, and convenience store are available. Some facilities are wheelchair-accessible. A golf course is 10 miles away. Leashed pets are permitted.

Reservations, fees: Reservations are not accepted. Sites are $18–23 per night, $2 per pet per night, and $7.50 per person per day for lake use. Boat launching is $5 per day. Some credit cards accepted. Open year-round.

Directions: From Santa Ysabel, drive seven miles north on Highway 79 to Highway 76. Turn east on Highway 76 and drive four miles to the campground on the left.

Contact: Lake Henshaw Resort, 760/782-3487 or 760/782-3501.

30 CULP VALLEY PRIMITIVE CAMP AREA
🏕 🐕 🚐 ⛺

Scenic rating: 4

near Peña Springs in Anza-Borrego Desert State Park

Map 15.2, page 816

Culp Valley is set near Peña Springs, which is more of a mudhole than springs. A 600-yard hike takes you to an overlook of Hellhole Canyon and an eastern view of the Borrego Valley. The elevation at this campground is 3,400 feet.

Campsites, facilities: This is a primitive, open

camping area for tents or small RVs of any length (no hookups). Vault toilets are available. No drinking water is available. Fires are permitted in metal containers. Garbage and ashes must be packed out. Leashed pets are permitted in the campground, but not on trails.

Reservations, fees: Reservations are not accepted. There is no fee for camping. Open year-round.

Directions: From Julian, at the junction of Highway 78 and Highway 79, drive east on Highway 78 (steep and curvy) for 10 miles to Highway S2. Turn left (north) and drive 16 miles to Highway S22/Borrego Salton Seaway. Turn right (east) and drive 10 miles to the campground entrance road on the left.

Contact: Anza-Borrego Desert State Park, 760/767-4205; Colorado Desert District, 760/767-5311, fax 760/767-3427, www.parks.ca.gov.

31 STAGECOACH TRAILS RV PARK
🏕 🏊 🐕 ♿ 🚐 ⛺

Scenic rating: 6

near Julian

Map 15.2, page 816

You want space? You got space. That includes 600,000 acres of public lands bordering this RV campground, making Stagecoach Trails Resort ideal for those who love horseback riding and hiking. Ninety corrals and two round pens at the campground let you know right away that this camp is very horse-friendly. It is more than a horse camp, however, with amenities for various types of campers. The resort provides the perfect jumping-off place for trips into neighboring Anza-Borrego Desert State Park and onto the Pacific Crest Trail, which is 2.5 miles away. The resort's name comes from its proximity to the old Wells Fargo Butterfield Stage Route. While the scenic rating merits a 6, if the rating were based purely on cleanliness, professionalism, and friendliness, this resort would rate a 10.

Campsites, facilities: There are 250 sites with full hookups (30 amps) for RVs of any length, and a large dispersed camping area for tents. Most RV sites are pull-through. Picnic tables and fire rings are provided. Drinking water, restrooms with flush toilets and showers, a heated pool, ninety horse corrals, a roping area, guided horseback riding, convenience store, ATM, coin laundry, group facilities, horseshoe pits, shuffleboard, 24-hour security, and propane gas are available. Some facilities are wheelchair-accessible. Leashed pets are permitted.

Reservations, fees: Reservations are accepted at 877/TWO-CAMP (877/896-2267). Sites are $30 per night, $5 per person per night for more than two people, $5 per night per horse. Some credit cards accepted. Open year-round.

Directions: From Santa Ysabel, turn north on Highway 79 and drive 14 miles to County Road S2/San Felipe Road. Turn right and drive 17 miles to Highway 78. Turn right (west, toward Julian) and drive 0.3 mile to County Road S2 (Great Southern Overland Stage Route). Turn left and drive four miles to the resort on the right (at Mile Marker 21 on Road S2). Note: There are various ways to get here. Since equestrian campers towing horse trailers and other campers may need alternate directions, and those not towing rigs might want shortcut directions, call the resort for driving details.

Contact: Stagecoach Trails Park, 760/765-2197, www.stagecoachtrails.com.

32 YAQUI PASS PRIMITIVE CAMP AREA

Scenic rating: 1

in Anza-Borrego Desert State Park

Map 15.2, page 816

This extremely primitive area is set beside rough Yaqui Pass Road at an elevation of 1,730 feet. The camping area is a large, open, sloping area of asphalt, where it is darn near impossible to get an RV level. The trailhead for Kenyon Loop Trail is to the immediate south. This spot is often overlooked because the Tamarisk Grove camp nearby provides shade, drinking water, and a feature trail.

Campsites, facilities: This is an primitive, open camping area for tents or small RVs of any length (no hookups). No drinking water or toilets are available. No open fires are allowed. Garbage must be packed out. Leashed pets are permitted, but not on trails or in wilderness.

Reservations, fees: No reservations are accepted and there are no fees. Open year-round.

Directions: From Julian, at the junction of Highway 78 and Highway 79, drive east on Highway 78 (steep and curvy) for 19.5 miles to Yaqui Pass Road/County Road S3. Turn left (north) and drive 2.5 miles to the campground entrance on the right.

Contact: Anza-Borrego Desert State Park, 760/767-4205; Colorado Desert District, 760/767-5311, fax 760/767-3427, www.parks .ca.gov.

33 YAQUI WELL PRIMITIVE CAMP AREA

Scenic rating: 2

in Anza-Borrego Desert State Park

Map 15.2, page 816

This camp is used primarily as an overflow area if the more developed Tamarisk Grove camp is full. Cactus Loop Trail, a 2.5-mile loop hike that passes seven varieties of cacti, starts at Tamarisk Grove. The elevation is 1,400 feet.

Campsites, facilities: This is a primitive, open camping area for tents or small RVs of any length (no hookups). Vault toilets are available. No drinking water is available. Fires are permitted in metal containers. Garbage and ashes must be packed out. Open fires are not permitted. Leashed pets are permitted, but not on trails or in wilderness.

Reservations, fees: No reservations are accepted and there are no fees. Open year-round.

Directions: From Julian, at the junction of Highway 78 and Highway 79, drive east on Highway 78 (steep and curvy) for 19.5 miles to Yaqui Pass Road/County Road S3. Turn left (north) and drive a short distance to the campground entrance road on the left.

Contact: Anza-Borrego Desert State Park, 760/767-4205; Colorado Desert District, 760/767-5311, fax 760/767-3427, www.parks .ca.gov.

34 OCOTILLO WELLS STATE VEHICLE RECREATION AREA

👫 🚲 🐕 🚻 ♿ 🚐 ⛺

Scenic rating: 4

in Ocotillo Wells

Map 15.2, page 816

This can be a wild place, a giant OHV camp where the population of Ocotillo Wells can go from 100 to 5,000 overnight, no kidding. Yet if you arrive when there is no off-road event, it can also be a lonely, extremely remote destination. Some locals call the OHV crowd "escapees" and watch stunned as they arrive every February for two or three weeks. OHV events are held here occasionally as well. Mountain bikers also use these trails. One great side note is that annually there is "Desert Cleanup Day," when OHV users will clean up the place; date changes every year. The non-OHV crowd can still use this camp, but most come in the winter on weekdays, when activity is lower. The landscape is barren desert, dry as an iguana's back. A few shade ramadas are provided on-site. The area covers 72,000 acres, ranging from below sea level to an elevation of 400 feet. It is adjacent to Anza-Borrego Desert State Park, another 600,000 acres of wildlands. The wash-and-ridge terrain includes a butte with dunes, a sand bowl, a blow sand dune, and springs. After wet winters, the blooms of wildflowers can be excellent. While this area is well known as a wild play area for the OHV crowd, it is also a place where on most days you can literally disappear and see no one. All drivers should watch for soft ground. Many vehicles get stuck here and have to be towed out. Also, dispersed camping is allowed in most of these state park lands.

Campsites, facilities: There are 60 dispersed primitive sites for tents or RVs of any length (no hookups). Picnic tables and fire rings are provided. Chemical toilets and shade ramadas are available. There is no drinking water. A coin-shower building is available near the ranger station, and another is 3.5 miles east at Holmes Camp. A store, restaurants, propane, and auto supplies are available four miles away in Ocotillo Wells. A gas station is seven miles from the ranger station. Leashed pets are permitted.

Reservations, fees: No reservations are accepted and there is no fee, with a 30-day maximum stay per year. Open year-round.

Directions: From Julian, at the junction of Highway 78 and Highway 79, drive east on Highway 78 for 31.5 miles to Ranger Station Road. Turn left and drive 0.25 mile to the ranger station. (Note: For an alternative route, advisable for big rigs, that avoids curvy sections of Highway 78, see the detour route detailed in the *Stagecoach Trails RV Park* listing in this chapter.)

Contact: Ocotillo Wells SVRA, 760/767-5391, fax 760/767-4951, www.parks.ca.gov.

35 TAMARISK GROVE

👫 🐕 ♿ 🚐 ⛺

Scenic rating: 5

in Anza-Borrego Desert State Park

Map 15.2, page 816

This is the number-one campground in Anza-Borrego Desert State Park, and it is easy to see why: Big tamarisk trees provide shade, and the park provides limited drinking water (recommended that you bring your own water as a backup). It is one of three camps in the immediate area, so if this camp is full, primitive Yaqui Well to the immediate west and Yaqui Pass to the north on Yaqui Pass Road provide alternatives. Cactus Loop Trail, with the trailhead just north of camp, provides a hiking option. This is a 1.5-mile loop that passes seven varieties of cacti, some as tall as people. The elevation is 1,400 feet at this campground.

Campsites, facilities: There are 27 sites for tents or RVs up to 21 feet (no hookups). Picnic tables and fire grills are provided. Restrooms with flush toilets and coin showers and limited drinking water are available. Some facilities are wheelchair-accessible. Leashed pets are permitted in the campground, but not on trails or in wilderness.

Reservations, fees: Reservations are accepted ($7.50 reservation fee) at 800/444-PARK (800/444-7275) or www.reserveamerica.com. Sites are $12–17 per night, $6 per night for each additional vehicle. Open October through May.

Directions: From Julian, at the junction of Highway 78 and Highway 79, drive east on Highway 78 (steep and curvy) for 19.5 miles to Yaqui Pass Road/County Road S3. Turn left (north) and drive 0.5 mile to the campground on the right.

Contact: Anza-Borrego Desert State Park, 760/767-4205; Colorado Desert District, 760/767-5311, fax 760/767-3427, www.parks.ca.gov.

36 PINEZANITA RV PARK AND CAMPGROUNDS
🏊 🐕 🚐 ⛺

Scenic rating: 6

near Julian

Map 15.2, page 816

Set at an elevation of 4,680 feet in dense pine and oak, this camp has had the same owners, the Stanley family, for more than 30 years. The fishing pond is a great attraction for kids (no license is required); no swimming allowed. The pond is stocked with bluegill and catfish, some of which are 12 inches or longer. Two possible side trips include Lake Cuyamaca, five miles to the south, and William Heise

County Park, about 10 miles to the north as the crow flies. Note that while the 2003 wildfires burned the area adjacent to the park, Pinezanita itself sustained no damage.

Campsites, facilities: There are 210 sites with full or partial hookups (30 and 50 amps) for RVs, 32 sites for tents, and three cottages. Picnic tables and fire rings are provided. Restrooms with flush toilets and showers, drinking water, a general store, ice, propane, bait and tackle, fishing pond, and dump station are available. Leashed pets are permitted, but not in the cottages.

Reservations, fees: Reservations are accepted. Sites are $24 per night per vehicle, $2 per night per person for more than two people, $4–6 per night for hookups, and $2 per night per pet. Some credit cards accepted. Open year-round.

Directions: From El Cajon, drive east on I-8 to Highway 79 (near Descanso Junction). Turn north on Highway 79 and drive 20 miles to Julian and the campground on the left.

Contact: Pinezanita RV Park and Campgrounds, 760/765-0429, www.pinezanita.com.

37 WILLIAM HEISE COUNTY PARK
🏊 🐕 🥾 🚐 ⛺

Scenic rating: 6

near Julian

Map 15.2, page 816

This is a beautiful county park, set at 4,200 feet, that offers hiking trails and a playground, all amid pretty woodlands with a mix of oak and pine. A great hike starts right at camp (at the tent camping area), signed "Nature Trail." It joins Canyon Oak Trail and, after little more than a mile, links with Desert View Trail. Here you will reach an overlook with a beautiful view of the Anza-Borrego Desert and the Salton Sea. The park features more than 900 acres of mountain forests of oak, pine, and cedar. A popular equestrian trail is Kelly

Ditch Trail, which is linked to Cuyamaca Rancho State Park and Lake Cuyamaca. The vast Anza-Borrego Desert State Park lies to the east, and the historic mining town of Julian is five miles away. Julian is known for its Apple Day Festival each fall. Note: The wildfires of 2003 damaged some of this area and several trails were still closed at the time of publication; check for current status.

Campsites, facilities: There are 20 sites for tents or RVs up to 40 feet with partial hookups (30 amps), 37 sites for tents or RVs up to 40 feet (full hookups), 42 sites for tents only, two group sites for up to 30 people each, and four cabins. Picnic tables and fire grills are provided. Restrooms with flush toilets and showers, drinking water, coin laundry, dump station, picnic areas, and a playground are available. Supplies are available five miles away in Julian. Leashed pets are permitted.

Reservations, fees: Reservations are accepted ($3 reservation fee) at 858/565-3600. Sites are $12–18 per night, group sites are $25–50 per night, $1 per pet per night. Some credit cards accepted. Open year-round.

Directions: From El Cajon, drive east on I-8 to Highway 79 (near Descanso Junction). Turn north on Highway 79 and drive to Julian and Highway 78. Turn west (left) on Highway 78 and drive to Pine Hills Road. Turn left (south) on Pine Hills Road and drive two miles to Frisius Drive. Turn left (south) on Frisius Drive and drive two miles to the park.

Contact: San Diego County Parks Department, 760/765-0650, www.sdparks.org.

38 FISH CREEK
Scenic rating: 3
in Anza-Borrego Desert State Park
Map 15.2, page 816

This primitive camp is set just inside the eastern border of Anza-Borrego Desert State Park at the foot of the Vallecito Mountains to the west. This is the closest camp to the Ocotillo Wells State Vehicular Recreation Area, which is 12 miles to the north. RVs are not recommended because of the steep access road. Note that the Elephant Tree Discovery Trail is a few miles north of camp.

Campsites, facilities: There are eight sites for tents. Vault toilets and Wi-Fi are available and some sites have picnic tables and fire rings. No drinking water is available. Garbage must be packed out. Leashed pets are permitted.

Reservations, fees: Reservations are not accepted. There is no fee for camping. Open year-round.

Directions: From Julian, at the junction of Highway 78 and Highway 79, drive east on Highway 78 (steep and curvy) for 34 miles to Ocotillo Wells and Split Mountain Road. Turn right (south) and drive seven miles to the campground access road. Drive two miles to the campground entrance on the left.

Contact: Anza-Borrego Desert State Park, 760/767-4205; Colorado Desert District, 760/767-5311, fax 760/767-3427, www.parks.ca.gov.

39 DOS PICOS COUNTY PARK
Scenic rating: 4
near Ramona
Map 15.2, page 816

Dos Picos means "two peaks" and is the highlight of a landscape featuring old groves of oaks and steep, boulder-strewn mountain slopes. Some of the oaks are 300 years old. The park covers 78 acres and has a nature trail. As a county park, this camp is often missed. The park is quite picturesque, with plenty of shade trees and a small pond. Fishing is allowed in the pond, but swimming is prohibited. Several nearby recreation options are in the area, including Lake Poway and Lake Sutherland. The elevation is 1,500 feet. Note that this park was partially damaged by the Cedar Fire of 2003, although the campground is intact.

Campsites, facilities: There are two sites with

full hookups (30 amps), 61 sites with partial hookups, 11 sites with no hookups, one youth group area for up to 25 people, and a caravan area for tents or RVs. Picnic tables and fire grills are provided. Restrooms with flush toilets and showers, drinking water, dump station, playground, horseshoes, and soccer field are available. Supplies and a coin laundry are one mile away in Ramona. Leashed pets are permitted.

Reservations, fees: Reservations are accepted ($3 reservation fee) at 858/565-3600. Sites are $12–16 per night, $25 per night for the group area, $225 per night for the caravan area, $1 per pet per night. Some credit cards accepted. Open year-round.

Directions: Drive on I-8 to El Cajon and the exit for Highway 67. Take that exit and drive north on Highway 67 for 22 miles to Mussey Grade Road. Turn right (a sharp turn) on Mussey Grade Road and drive two miles to the park.

Contact: San Diego County Parks Department, Dos Picos County Park, 760/789-2220, fax 760/789-8435, www.sdparks.org.

40 CUYAMACA RANCHO STATE PARK: PASO PICACHO

🚶 🚴 🛶 🏇 ♿ 🚐 ⛺

Scenic rating: 2

in Cuyamaca Rancho State Park

Map 15.2, page 816

This camp is set at 4,900 feet in Cuyamaca Rancho State Park, best known for Cuyamaca Peak, 6,512 feet. Stonewall Peak Trail is accessible from across the street. This is a five-mile (sun-exposed) round-trip, featuring the climb to the summit at 5,730 feet. There are long-distance views from here, highlighted by the Salton Sea and the Anza-Borrego State Desert. It's the most popular hike in the park, a fair to moderate grade, and completed by a lot of families. Another, more ambitious, hike is the trail up to Cuyamaca Peak, starting at the southern end of the campground, a 6.5-mile round-trip

tromp (alas, on a paved road; at least it's closed to traffic) with a climb of 1,600 feet in the process. The view from the top is breathtaking, with the Pacific Ocean and Mexico visible to the west and south, respectively. Cuyamaca means "The Rain Beyond."

Campsites, facilities: There are 85 sites for tents or RVs up to 30 feet long and 10 feet tall (no hookups), five cabins, a nature den cabin, four wood cabins, two group tent sites for up to 60 people each, and one hike-in/bike-in site. Fire grills and picnic tables are provided. Restrooms with flush toilets and coin showers, drinking water, Wi-Fi, and dump station are available. Supplies are available nearby in Cuyamaca. Leashed pets are permitted.

Reservations, fees: Reservations are accepted ($7.50 reservation fee) at 800/444-PARK (800/444-7275) or www.reserveamerica.com. Sites are $15–20 per night, $350 per night for group sites, $50 per night for nature den cabin, $45 per night for cabins, $3 per person per night for hike-in/bike-in site. Open year-round.

Directions: From El Cajon, drive east on I-8 to Highway 79 (near Descanso Junction). Turn north (left) and drive 13.5 miles to the park entrance on the left.

Contact: Cuyamaca Rancho State Park, 760/765-0755, fax 760/765-3021, www.parks.ca.gov.

41 VALLECITO COUNTY PARK

🏇 🤸 🚐 ⛺

Scenic rating: 3

near Anza-Borrego Desert State Park

Map 15.2, page 816

This county park in the desert gets little attention in the face of the other nearby attractions. This is a 71-acre park built around a sod reconstruction of the historic Vallecito Stage Station. It was part of the Butterfield Overland Stage from 1858 to 1861. The route carried mail and passengers from Missouri to San Francisco in 25 days, covering 2,800 miles. Vallecito means "little valley." It provides a quiet alternative to some of the busier campgrounds in the desert. One bonus is that it is usually 10° cooler here than at Agua Caliente. A covered picnic area is a big plus. Other nearby destinations include Agua Caliente Hot Springs, Anza-Borrego Desert State Park to the east, and Lake Cuyamaca and Cuyamaca Rancho State Park about 35 miles away. The elevation is 1,500 feet.

Campsites, facilities: There are 44 sites for tents or RVs up to 40 feet (no hookups), one group area for up to 15 RVs, and one youth camping area for up to 35 people. Picnic tables, fire rings, and barbecues are provided. Drinking water, flush toilets, and a playground are available. Leashed pets are permitted.

Reservations, fees: Reservations are available ($3 reservation fee) at 858/565-3600. Sites are $12 per night, $75 per night for the group area, $25 per night for the youth group area, $1 per pet per night. Some credit cards accepted. Open Labor Day weekend through Memorial Day weekend; closed June, July, and August.

Directions: From El Cajon, drive east on I-8 for about 75 miles to the town of Ocotillo (the first town after crossing from San Diego County to Imperial County) and County Road S2/Imperial Highway. Turn north (left) on County Road S2/Imperial Highway and drive 30 miles to the park entrance.

Contact: San Diego County Parks Department, 858/694-3049, fax 858/495-5841, www .sdparks.org.

42 AGUA CALIENTE REGIONAL PARK
🏃 🏊 ♨️ 🚴 ♿ 🚐 ⛺

Scenic rating: 3
near Anza-Borrego Desert State Park

Map 15.2, page 816

This is a popular park in winter. It has two naturally fed pools: A large outdoor ther-

mal pool is kept at its natural 90°F, and an indoor pool is heated to 102°F and outfitted with jets. Everything is hot here. The weather is hot, the coffee is hot, and the water is hot. And hey, that's what "Agua Caliente" means—hot water, named after the nearby hot springs. Anza-Borrego Desert State Park is also nearby. If you would like to see some cold water, Lake Cuyamaca and Cuyamaca Rancho State Park are about 35 miles away. The elevation is 1,350 feet. The park covers 910 acres with several miles of hiking trails.

Campsites, facilities: There are 106 sites with full or partial hookups (30 amps) for RVs up to 40 feet, 35 sites with no hookups for tents or RVs, and a group area for up to 100 people. Picnic tables and fire grills are provided. Restrooms with flush toilets and showers, drinking water, outdoor and indoor pools, picnic area, and a playground with horseshoes and shuffleboard are available. Groceries and propane gas are nearby. Some facilities are wheelchair-accessible. No pets are allowed.

Reservations, fees: Reservations are accepted ($3 reservation fee) at 858/565-3600. Sites are $14–18 per night, and the group area is $75 per night. Some credit cards accepted. Open Labor Day weekend through Memorial Day weekend; closed June, July, and August.

Directions: From El Cajon, drive east on I-8 about 75 miles to the town of Ocotillo (the first town after crossing from San Diego County to Imperial County) and County Road S2/Imperial Highway. Turn north (left) on County Road S2/Imperial Highway and drive 25 miles to the park entrance.

From Julian, take Highway 78 east and drive 12 miles to County Road S2/San Felipe Road. Turn right on County Road S2/San Felipe Road and drive 21 miles south to the park entrance.

Contact: San Diego County Parks Department, 858/694-3049, fax 858/495-5841, www .sdparks.org.

43 CUYAMACA RANCHO STATE PARK: GREEN VALLEY

🏃 🚵 🛶 🐴 ♿ 🚐 ⛺

Scenic rating: 3

in Cuyamaca Rancho State Park

Map 15.2, page 816

Green Valley is the southernmost camp in Cuyamaca Rancho State Park, which was 98 percent burned in the Cedar Fire of 2003; parts of the park are still closed because of fire damage. It is set at 3,900 feet, with Cuyamaca Peak (6,512 feet) looming overhead to the northwest. A trailhead is available (look for the picnic area) at the camp for an easy five-minute walk to Green Valley Falls, and it can be continued out to the Sweetwater River in a 1.5-mile round-trip. The park covers 25,000 acres with trails for hiking, mountain biking, and horseback riding.

Campsites, facilities: There are 81 sites for tents or RVs up to 30 feet long and 10 feet tall (no hookups), and one hike-in/bike-in site. Picnic tables and fire grills are provided. Restrooms with flush toilets and coin showers, drinking water, Wi-Fi, and dump station are available. Some facilities are wheelchair-accessible. A store and propane gas are nearby. Leashed pets are permitted.

Reservations, fees: Reservations are accepted ($7.50 reservation fee) at 800/444-PARK (800/444-7275) or www.reserveamerica.com. Sites are $15–20 per night, $6 per night for each additional vehicle, $3 per person per night for hike-in/bike-in site. Open year-round.

Directions: From El Cajon, drive east on I-8 to Highway 79 (near Descanso Junction). Turn north (left) on Highway 79 and drive seven miles to the campground entrance on the left (near Mile Marker 4).

Contact: Cuyamaca Rancho State Park, 760/765-0755, fax 760/765-3021, www.parks.ca.gov.

44 LAGUNA

🏃 🐕 ♿ 🚐 ⛺

Scenic rating: 4

near Little Laguna Lake in Cleveland National Forest

Map 15.2, page 816

Laguna is set on Little Laguna Lake, one of the few lakes in America where "Little" is part of its official name. That's because for years everybody always referred to it as "Little Laguna Lake," and it became official. Yep, it's a "little" lake all right, a relative speck, and the lake can occasionally dry up. The camp is on its eastern side at an elevation of 5,550 feet. A trailhead for the Pacific Crest Trail is a mile north on the Sunrise Highway. Big Laguna Lake, which is actually a pretty small lake, is one mile to the west.

Campsites, facilities: There are 103 sites for tents, and 73 sites for tents or RVs up to 50 feet (no hookups). Picnic tables and fire grills are provided. Drinking water and restrooms with flush toilets and coin showers are available. A store and propane gas are available nearby. Some facilities are wheelchair-accessible. Leashed pets are permitted.

Reservations, fees: Reservations are accepted ($9 reservation fee) at 877/444-6777 or www.ReserveUSA.com. Sites are $15 per night. Open year-round.

Directions: From San Diego, drive east on I-8 about 50 miles to the Laguna Junction exit for the Sunrise Highway. Turn north on the Sunrise Highway and drive 11 miles to the town of Mount Laguna. Continue north on Sunrise Highway for 2.5 miles to the campground entrance road on the left.

Contact: Cleveland National Forest, Descanso Ranger District, 619/445-6235, fax 619/445-1753; Laguna Mountain Visitor Center, 619/473-8547.

45 EL PRADO GROUP CAMP

Scenic rating: 3

in Cleveland National Forest

Map 15.2, page 816

El Prado Group Camp is directly adjacent to Laguna and is an alternative to nearby Horse Heaven Group Camp. Five separate group sites are available. The elevation is 5,500 feet.

Campsites, facilities: There are five group sites for tents or RVs up to 27 feet (no hookups) that can accommodate 30–50 people each. Picnic tables and fire grills are provided. Drinking water and vault toilets are available. You can buy supplies in Mount Laguna. Leashed pets are permitted.

Reservations, fees: Reservations are required ($9 reservation fee) at 877/444-6777 or www .ReserveUSA.com. Sites are $45–75 per night. Open Memorial Day weekend to mid-October, weather permitting.

Directions: From San Diego, drive east on I-8 about 50 miles to the Laguna Junction exit for the Sunrise Highway. Turn north on the Sunrise Highway and drive 11 miles to the town of Mount Laguna. Continue north on Sunrise Highway for 2.5 miles to the campground entrance road on the left.

Contact: Cleveland National Forest, Descanso Ranger District, 619/445-6235, fax 619/445-1753.

46 HORSE HEAVEN GROUP CAMP

Scenic rating: 3

near the Pacific Crest Trail in Cleveland National Forest

Map 15.2, page 816

Horse Heaven is set on the northeastern border of Cleveland National Forest at 5,500 feet, near Mount Laguna in the Laguna Recreation Area. The Pacific Crest Trail passes near the camp. Laguna and El Prado Group Camp

provide nearby options. Side-trip possibilities include visiting Little Laguna Lake to the immediate west and Desert View Picnic Area to the south at Mount Laguna.

Campsites, facilities: There are three group sites for tents or RVs up to 27 feet (no hookups) that can accommodate 40–100 people each. Picnic tables and fire grills are provided. Drinking water and vault toilets are available. You can buy supplies in Mount Laguna. Leashed pets are permitted.

Reservations, fees: Reservations are accepted ($9 reservation fee) at 877/444-6777 or www .ReserveUSA.com. Sites are $60–150 per night. Open Memorial Day weekend through Labor Day weekend.

Directions: From San Diego, drive east on I-8 about 50 miles to the Laguna Junction exit for the Sunrise Highway. Turn north on the Sunrise Highway and drive 11 miles to the town of Mount Laguna. Continue north on Sunrise Highway for two miles to the campground entrance road on the left.

Contact: Cleveland National Forest, Descanso Ranger District, 619/445-6235, fax 619/445-1753.

47 VACATIONER RV RESORT

Scenic rating: 2

near El Cajon

Map 15.2, page 816

This well-maintained resort is 25 minutes from San Diego, 40 minutes from Mexico. Discount tickets to area attractions such as the San Diego Zoo, SeaWorld, and the Wild Animal Park are available. There is the very real chance of getting highway noise if you have a site at the back of the park. The RV sites are on asphalt and gravel, and there are many shade trees. The elevation is 260 feet.

Campsites, facilities: There are 150 sites with full hookups (30 and 50 amps) for RVs up to 40 feet, including 20 pull-through sites. No tent camping is allowed. Restrooms with flush toilets and showers, drinking water, coin laundry, recreation room, horseshoe pits, telephone and modem access, Wi-Fi, heated swimming pool, spa, satellite TV, free video library, RV storage, and a picnic area with barbecues are available. A store is nearby. Some facilities are wheelchair-accessible. Leashed pets up to 20 pounds are permitted, with certain restrictions.

Reservations, fees: Reservations are accepted at 866/490-5844. Sites are $40 per night, $2 per person per night for more than two people, $5 per night for each additional vehicle, $2 per pet per night. Some credit cards accepted. Open year-round.

Directions: From El Cajon, drive east on I-8 for three miles to the Greenfield Drive exit. Take that exit, turn north and drive 100 feet to East Main Street. Turn left (west) and drive 0.5 mile to the park on the left.

Contact: Vacationer RV Resort, 866/490-5844 or 619/442-0904, fax 619/442-4378.

48 RANCHO LOS COCHES RV PARK

Scenic rating: 2

near Lake Jennings

Map 15.2, page 816

This is not your typical RV park. This place has plenty of charm and a private setting. There is an abundance of history here, too. The park land was once the smallest Mexican land grant of the 19th century. The former ranch was also once a station for the Jackass Mail and Butterfield Stage routes. Windmill House, built in 1925, is featured prominently on the property and is a local historic landmark. Nearby Lake Jennings provides an option for boaters and anglers and also has a less developed camp on its northeast shore. Vista Point on the southeastern side of the lake provides a side trip. (For more information, see the next listing, *Lake Jennings County Park.*) Casinos are nearby.

Campsites, facilities: There are 142 sites with full hookups (30 and 50 amps) for RVs up to 45 feet and four tent areas. Restrooms with flush toilets and showers, drinking water, cable TV, dump station, heated swimming pool, spa, recreation hall, horseshoes, table tennis, Wi-Fi, and coin laundry are available. A store and gas station are one mile away. Leashed pets are permitted.

Reservations, fees: Reservations are accepted by website or at 800/630-0448. Sites are $39 per night for RVs, $25 per night for tents, $3 per person per night for more than two people. Weekly and monthly rates available. Open year-round.

Directions: From El Cajon, drive east on I-8 to the Los Coches Road exit. Take that exit, and drive under the freeway to Highway 8 Business Route. Turn right on Highway 8 Business Route and drive 0.25 mile to the park entrance on the left (13468 Highway 8 Business).

Contact: Rancho Los Coches RV Park, 619/443-2025, fax 619/443-8440, www .rancholoscochesrv.com.

49 LAKE JENNINGS COUNTY PARK

Scenic rating: 6

on Lake Jennings

Map 15.2, page 816

Lake Jennings, at 108 acres, is a nice little backyard fishing hole and recreation area set at 700 feet, with easy access from I-8. Most people come here for the fishing; the lake is stocked with trout and catfish. It has quality prospects for giant catfish, as well as largemouth bass, bluegill, and in cool months, rainbow trout. The lake record blue catfish is 60 pounds. Note that while shore fishing is available on a daily basis, boats are permitted on the lake from November through August, Friday through Sunday. Night fishing is allowed on weekends during the summer. A fishing permit is required. The highlights here are evening picnics, summer catfishing, and a boat ramp and rentals. Swimming and water/body contact are prohibited. Miles of hiking trails are routed through chaparral-covered hills. Only one camp is available right at the lake, and this is it. Note that though some of this park was damaged in the Cedar Fire of 2003, the campground was unaffected.

Campsites, facilities: There are 30 sites with full hookups (30 amps) for RVs up to 35 feet, 35 sites with partial hookups (20 amps) for RVs up to 25 feet, 25 tent sites, and a youth group area for up to 35 people. Some sites are pull-through. Picnic tables and fire grills are provided. Restrooms with flush toilets and showers, drinking water, nature trail, clubhouse, horseshoes, and dump station are available. A store is nearby. Leashed pets are permitted.

Reservations, fees: Reservations are accepted at 858/565-3600. Sites are $14–18 per night, $25 per night for the group area, $1 per pet per night. Open year-round.

Directions: From San Diego, drive east on I-8 for 21 miles to Lake Jennings Park Road. Turn north (left) on Lake Jennings Park Road and drive one mile to the park entrance.

Contact: San Diego County Parks Department, 858/694-3049, fax 858/495-5841, www .sdparks.org; Lake Jennings Entrance Station, 619/443-2004; boat rentals, 619/443-9503.

50 WOODED HILL GROUP
🏃 🐕 🚐 ⛺

Scenic rating: 4

near the Pacific Crest Trail in Cleveland National Forest

Map 15.2, page 816

This camp is set on the southern flank of Mount Laguna. The Pacific Crest Trail is within one mile of Burnt Rancheria Campground, a mile up the road to the northwest. The elevation is 6,000 feet.

Campsites, facilities: There is one group site for tents or RVs up to 27 feet (no hookups) that can accommodate up to 100 people. Picnic tables and fire grills are provided. Drink-

ing water and vault toilets are available. A store is nearby. Leashed pets are permitted.

Reservations, fees: Reservations are required ($18 reservation fee) at 877/444-6777 or www .ReserveUSA.com. Sites are $165 per night. Open Memorial Day weekend to Labor Day weekend.

Directions: From San Diego, drive east on I-8 about 50 miles to the Laguna Junction exit for the Sunrise Highway. Turn north on the Sunrise Highway and drive about eight miles to the campground entrance road on the left.

Contact: Cleveland National Forest, Descanso Ranger District, 619/445-6235, fax 619/445-1753.

51 BURNT RANCHERIA
🏃 🐕 ♿ 🚐 ⛺

Scenic rating: 6

near the Pacific Crest Trail in Cleveland National Forest

Map 15.2, page 816

Burnt Rancheria is set high on the slopes of Mount Laguna in Cleveland National Forest, at an elevation of 6,000 feet. Remodeled in 2005, it is quiet and private with large, roomy sites. The Pacific Crest Trail is approximately one mile from camp. Desert View Picnic Area, a mile to the north, provides a good side trip. Wooded Hill Group Campground is one mile away.

Campsites, facilities: There are 58 sites for tents or RVs up to 50 feet (no hookups), and 51 sites for tents only. Picnic tables and fire grills are provided. Vault and flush toilets and coin showers are available. Drinking water is available. Some facilities are wheelchair-accessible. Supplies are nearby in Mount Laguna. Leashed pets are permitted.

Reservations, fees: Reservations are accepted ($9 reservation fee) at 877/444-6777 or www.ReserveUSA.com. Sites are $15 per night. Open May through October, weather permitting.

Directions: From San Diego, drive east on I-8

about 50 miles to the Laguna Junction exit for the Sunrise Highway. Turn north on the Sunrise Highway and drive about 10 miles north to the campground entrance road on the right.
Contact: Cleveland National Forest, Descanso Ranger District, 619/445-6235, fax 619/445-1753.

52 MOUNTAIN PALM SPRINGS PRIMITIVE CAMP AREA
🏃 🏕 🚗 ⛰

Scenic rating: 4

in Anza-Borrego Desert State Park

Map 15.2, page 816

A plus for this camping area is easy access from County Road S2, but no water is a giant minus. Regardless of pros and cons, only hikers will get the full benefit of the area. A trail leads south to Bow Willow Creek (and Bow Willow) and onward into Bow Willow Canyon. The Carrizo Badlands Overlook is on the southeast side of Sweeney Pass, about a 10-minute drive south on County Road S2. The elevation is 760 feet.

Campsites, facilities: This is a primitive, open camping area for tents or RVs of any length (no hookups). Vault toilets are available. No drinking water is available. Fires are permitted in metal containers. Garbage and ashes must be packed out. Leashed pets are permitted, but not on trails or in wilderness.

Reservations, fees: Reservations are not accepted. There is no fee for camping. Open year-round.

Directions: From El Cajon, drive east on I-8 for about 75 miles to the town of Ocotillo (the first town after crossing from San Diego County to Imperial County) and County Road S2/Imperial Highway. Turn north (left) on County Road S2/Imperial Highway and drive 27.5 miles to the campground entrance road on the left (about 0.5 mile past the Bow Willow campground turnoff). Turn left and continue 0.75 mile to the camp.

Contact: Anza-Borrego Desert State Park,

760/767-4205; Colorado Desert District, 760/767-5311, fax 760/767-3427, www.parks .ca.gov.

53 CIBBETS FLAT
🏃 🏕 🚗 ⛰

Scenic rating: 4

on Troy Canyon Creek in Cleveland National Forest

Map 15.2, page 816

Cibbets Flat is at the southern flank of the Laguna Mountains near Troy Canyon Creek, and Kitchen Creek runs adjacent to the camp. It is an obscure, fairly remote camp and staging area for the Pacific Crest Trail. A trailhead for the PCT is a mile southeast of camp, mostly used by hikers heading north across the Laguna Mountains. The elevation is 4,200 feet.

Campsites, facilities: There are 25 sites for tents or RVs up to 27 feet (no hookups). Picnic tables and fire grills are provided. Drinking water and vault toilets are available. Leashed pets are permitted.

Reservations, fees: Reservations are not accepted. Sites are $10 per night. Open year-round.

Directions: From El Cajon, drive east on I-8 for about 50 miles to Boulder Oaks, then continue a short distance to the exit for Kitchen Creek/Cameron Station. Turn north on Kitchen Creek Road and drive 4.5 miles to the campground entrance on the right.

Contact: Cleveland National Forest, Descanso Ranger District, 619/445-6235, fax 619/445-1753.

54 COTTONWOOD
🏃 🏕 🚗 ⛰

Scenic rating: 4

in the McCain Valley Recreation Area

Map 15.2, page 816

This camp is set on the western edge of the McCain Valley Recreation Area. Like most

Bureau of Land Management camps, it is little known and little used. It is occasionally frequented by backcountry horseback riders. The elevation is 4,000 feet.

Campsites, facilities: There are 29 sites for tents or RVs up to 35 feet (no hookups). Picnic tables and fire grills are provided. Drinking water and vault toilets are available. Two group horse corrals are also available. Leashed pets are permitted.

Reservations, fees: Reservations are not accepted. Sites are $6 per night. Open year-round.

Directions: From El Cajon, drive east on I-8 for 70 miles to the Boulevard/Campo exit. Take that exit right, then at the frontage road, turn left immediately and drive east (just south of the interstate) for two miles to McCain Valley Road. Turn left on McCain Valley Road and drive about 13 miles to the campground.

Contact: Bureau of Land Management, El Centro Field Office, 760/337-4400, fax 760/337-4490.

55 BOW WILLOW
🖾 🐎 🚐 🏕

Scenic rating: 4

near Bow Willow Canyon in Anza-Borrego Desert State Park

Map 15.2, page 816

Bow Willow Canyon is a rugged setting that can be explored by hiking the trail that starts at this camp. A short distance east of the camp, the trail forks to the south to Rockhouse Canyon. For a good side trip, drive back to County Road S2 and head south over Sweeney Pass for the view at the Carrizo Badlands Overlook.

Campsites, facilities: There are 16 sites for tents or RVs up to 24 feet (no hookups). Picnic tables, fire rings, and shade ramadas are provided. Limited drinking water and vault toilets are available. Leashed pets are permitted in the campground, but not on trails.

Reservations, fees: Reservations are not

accepted. Sites are $7 per night. Open year-round.

Directions: From El Cajon, drive east on I-8 about 75 miles to the town of Ocotillo (the first town after crossing from San Diego County to Imperial County) and County Road S2/Imperial Highway. Turn north (left) on County Road S2/Imperial Highway and drive 27 miles to the gravel campground entrance road on the left.

Contact: Anza-Borrego Desert State Park, 760/767-4205; Colorado Desert District, 760/767-5311, fax 760/767-3427, www.parks .ca.gov.

56 BOBCAT MEADOWS
🖾 🐎 🚐 🏕

Scenic rating: 6

in Cleveland National Forest

Map 15.2, page 816

This camp, along with nearby Corral Canyon, caters primarily to OHV users. The camp is shaded with live oaks and is a 10-minute drive from Corral Canyon camp. This camp is similar, but it has no water. The more spacious sites and privacy can make up for that. The elevation is 3,800 feet.

Campsites, facilities: There are 20 sites for tents or RVs up to 27 feet (no hookups). Fire pits are provided. Vault toilets are available. No drinking water is available. Garbage must be packed out. Leashed pets are permitted.

Reservations, fees: Reservations are not accepted and there is no camping fee. Adventure Pass ($30 annual fee or $5 daily fee per parked vehicle) is required. Open year-round.

Directions: From El Cajon, drive east on I-8 to Pine Valley, then continue east for four miles to Buckman Springs Road. Take the Buckman Springs off-ramp, turn right (south) on Buckman Springs Road, and drive 3.6 miles to Corral Canyon Road, marked by a sign "Camp Morena." Turn right and drive 6.2 miles (the road becomes Forest Service Road

17S04) to Four Corners Trailhead. Bear left (Forest Service Road 17S04) and drive a mile to the campground on the left.

Contact: Cleveland National Forest, Descanso Ranger District, 619/445-6235, fax 619/445-1753.

57 CORRAL CANYON
🏃 🐕 🚐 ⛺

Scenic rating: 6

in Cleveland National Forest

Map 15.2, page 816

This is a primitive camp set adjacent to a network of OHV trails leading 24 miles into the Corral Canyon area, hence the name. Most of the routes lead into a chaparral landscape. The camp is set at 3,500 feet and is primarily used by the OHV crowd. The availability of drinking water at this campground is a big plus.

Campsites, facilities: There are 20 sites for tents or RVs up to 27 feet (no hookups). Picnic tables and fire rings are provided. Drinking water and vault toilets are available. Garbage must be packed out. Leashed pets are permitted.

Reservations, fees: Reservations are not accepted and there is no camping fee. Adventure Pass ($30 annual fee or $5 daily fee per parked vehicle) is required. Open year-round.

Directions: From El Cajon, drive east on I-8 to Pine Valley, then continue east for four miles to Buckman Springs Road. Take the Buckman Springs off-ramp, turn right (south) on Buckman Springs Road, and drive 3.6 miles to Corral Canyon Road, marked by a sign "Camp Morena." Turn right and drive 6.2 miles (the road becomes Forest Service Road 17S04) to the Four Corners Trailhead. Continue straight on Corral Canyon Road for one mile to the campground on the right.

Contact: Cleveland National Forest, Descanso Ranger District, 619/445-6235, fax 619/445-1753.

58 BOULDER OAKS EQUESTRIAN
🏃 🐕 🚐 ⛺

Scenic rating: 4

near Lake Morena in Cleveland National Forest

Map 15.2, page 816

Boulder Oaks is easy to reach, just off I-8, yet it is a very small camp with an important trailhead for the Pacific Crest Trail running right by it. This camp also is designed as a trailhead camp for equestrians. The elevation is 3,300 feet, set in the southern end of Cleveland National Forest and the Laguna Mountains. This campground is closed March 1 to approximately mid-June to protect the breeding activity of the arroyo southwestern toad, an endangered species.

Campsites, facilities: There are 19 sites for tents or RVs up to 27 feet (no hookups) and 17 equestrian sites. Picnic tables and fire grills are provided. Drinking water and vault toilets are available. Leashed pets are permitted.

Reservations, fees: Reservations are accepted ($9 reservation fee) at 877/444-6777 or www .ReserveUSA.com. Sites are $12–24 per night for equestrian sites, $10 per night for individual sites. Open mid-June through February.

Directions: From El Cajon, drive east on I-8 to Pine Valley, then continue east for four miles to Buckman Springs Road. Take the Buckman Springs off-ramp, turn right (south) on Buckman Springs Road, and drive a short distance to a four-way stop sign at Old Highway 80. Turn left and drive 2.5 miles to the campground.

Contact: Cleveland National Forest, Descanso Ranger District, 619/445-6235, fax 619/445-1753.

59 LARK CANYON OHV
🏃 🐕 🚐 ⛺

Scenic rating: 5

in the McCain Valley Recreation Area

Map 15.2, page 816

This is a small camp that few know of, set at 4,000 feet in the McCain Valley National

Cooperative and Recreation Area. It is near a popular off-highway-vehicle area. Many dirt bikers use it as their base camp.

Campsites, facilities: There are 15 sites for tents or RVs up to 35 feet (no hookups). Picnic tables and fire grills are provided. Vault toilets are available. Drinking water is available. Garbage must be packed out. Leashed pets are permitted.

Reservations, fees: Reservations are not accepted. The fee is $6 per night. Open year-round.

Directions: From El Cajon, drive east on I-8 for 70 miles to the Boulevard/Campo exit. Take that exit right, then at the frontage road, turn left immediately and drive east (just south of the interstate) for two miles to McCain Valley Road. Turn left at McCain Valley Road and drive three miles to the campground.

Contact: Bureau of Land Management, El Centro Field Office, 760/337-4400, fax 760/337-4490.

60 SWEETWATER SUMMIT REGIONAL PARK

Scenic rating: 7

near Sweetwater Reservoir in Bonita

Map 15.2, page 816

This regional park overlooks the Sweetwater Reservoir in Bonita. The campground is set right on the summit, overlooking the Sweetwater Valley. This camp has equestrian sites with corrals for the horses. There are 15 miles of trails for hiking, mountain biking, and horseback riding in the park. There are several golf courses nearby and it is 15 minutes from Tijuana. The Chula Vista Nature Center is nearby on the shore of south San Diego Bay.

Campsites, facilities: There are 46 sites with partial hookups (20 amps) for tents or RVs up to 45 feet, including 15 equestrian sites with corrals. Picnic tables and fire grills are provided. Restrooms with flush toilets and showers, drinking water, covered pavilion, and dump station are available. Leashed pets are permitted.

Reservations, fees: Reservations are accepted ($3 reservation fee) at 858/565-3600 or 877/565-3600. Sites are $16 per night, $2 per horse per night, $1 per pet per night. Open year-round.

Directions: From San Diego, drive south on I-805 for 10 miles to Bonita Road. Turn east on Bonita Road and drive to San Miguel Road. Bear right on San Miguel Road and drive two miles to the park entrance on the left.

Contact: San Diego County Parks Department, Sweetwater Summit Regional Park, 619/472-7572, fax 619/472-7571, www.sdparks.org.

61 LAKE MORENA COUNTY PARK

Scenic rating: 7

near Campo

Map 15.2, page 816

Lake Morena is like a silver dollar in a field of pennies if you like to fish, but there is no swimming or powerboating allowed. Yes, Lake Morena is out in the boondocks, but it's well worth the trip. If you like to fish for bass, don't miss it. The county park camp is set on the southern shore at an elevation of 3,200 feet. The landscape is chaparral, oak woodlands, and grasslands, and the campsites are set in a grove of oaks. When full, the lake covers 1,500 surface acres, but water levels can fluctuate wildly here. Catch rates for bass can be excellent, and some bass are big; the lake record for largemouth bass weighed 19 pounds, three ounces, and the lake record for trout weighed nine pounds, six ounces. Boat rentals are available nearby; motor boats are allowed only on Fridays and Saturdays. The lake is just south of Cleveland National Forest and only seven or eight miles from the California/Mexico border.

The Pacific Crest Trail passes through the park, and the surrounding national forest has hiking and horseback-riding trails. San Diego is about a 45-minute drive from the campground.

Campsites, facilities: There are 86 sites and a group area for tents or RVs of any length; many sites have full hookups (30 amps). Ten cabins are also available. Picnic tables and fire grills are provided. Restrooms with flush toilets and showers and drinking water are available. A store, boat ramp, and rowboat rentals are nearby. Leashed pets are permitted.

Reservations, fees: Reservations are accepted ($3 reservation fee) at 858/565-3600 or 877/565-3600. Sites are $12–16 per night, $25–50 per night for the group area, $1 per pet per night, $5 per day for boat launching. Open year-round.

Directions: From El Cajon, drive east on I-8 to Pine Valley, then continue east for four miles to the exit for Buckman Springs Road/County Road S1. Take that exit, turn south (right), and drive 5.5 miles to Oak Drive. Turn right (south) on Oak Drive and drive 1.5 miles to Lake Morena Drive. Turn left on Lake Morena Drive and drive to the park entrance on the right.

Contact: San Diego County Parks Department, Lake Morena County Park, 619/579-4101, fax 619/478-5327, www.sdparks.org.

62 LAKE MORENA RV PARK

Scenic rating: 6

near Campo

Map 15.2, page 816

This camp is near the southern side of Lake Morena, a great lake for fishing and off-season vacations. It is one of three camps near the lake and the best for RVs. Lake Morena, at 3,200 feet, is a large reservoir in the San Diego County foothills and is known for big bass. It is also known for fluctuating water levels. Swimming is prohibited at this lake.

(See the previous listing, *Lake Morena County Park*, for information on Lake Morena.)

Campsites, facilities: There are 41 sites with full or partial hookups (30 and 50 amps) for RVs up to 40 feet. No tents. Picnic tables are provided. Restrooms with flush toilets and showers, dump station, nine-hole pitch-and-putt golf course, propane gas, and coin laundry are available. Some facilities are wheelchair-accessible. Leashed pets are permitted.

Reservations, fees: Reservations are recommended. Sites are $28 per night. Some credit cards accepted. Open year-round.

Directions: From El Cajon, drive east on I-8 to Buckman Springs Road. Take the Buckman Springs off-ramp, turn right (south) on Buckman Springs Road, and drive 5.5 miles to Oak Drive. Turn right on Oak Drive and drive 1.5 miles to Lake Morena Drive. Turn left on Lake Morena Drive and drive a short distance to the park on the right (2330 Lake Morena Drive).

Contact: Lake Morena RV Park, 619/478-5677, fax 619/478-5031.

63 POTRERO COUNTY PARK

Scenic rating: 3

near the Mexican border

Map 15.2, page 816

If you are looking for a spot to hole up for the night before getting through customs, this is the place. This park covers 115 acres, set at an elevation of 2,300 feet. It is a broad valley peppered with coastal live oaks amid grassy meadows and rocky foothills. The average summer high temperature is in the 90-degree range, and the average winter low is 34 degrees. There is occasional light snowfall in the winter. Potrero means "pasturing place." Some of the summer grazers are rattlesnakes, occasionally spotted here. Side trips include the railroad museum and century-old historic stone store in Campo and the Mexican community of Tecate. In fact, it is just a heartbeat away from the customs inspection station in Tecate. A good side trip is to the nearby Tecate Mission Chapel, where you can pray that the guards do not rip your vehicle up in the search for contraband. Insider's tip: In the spring you may hear the evening call of the Pacific tree frog.

Campsites, facilities: There are 39 sites with partial hookups (20, 30, and 50 amps) for RVs up to 45 feet, 10 tent sites, and a group site for up to 45 people. Picnic tables and fire grills are provided. Restrooms with flush toilets and showers, drinking water, playground, and dump station are available. Picnic areas, ball fields, and a dance pavilion are available. You can buy supplies in Potrero. Leashed pets are permitted.

Reservations, fees: Reservations are accepted ($3 reservation fee) at 858/565-3600 or 877/565-3600. Sites are $10–12 per night, $25–50 per night for the group site, $1 per pet per night. Open year-round.

Directions: From El Cajon, drive east on Highway 94 for 42 miles (near the junction of Highway 188) to Potrero Valley Road. Turn north on Potrero Valley Road and drive one mile to Potrero Park Road. Turn right (east) on Potrero Park Road and drive one mile to the park entrance.

Contact: San Diego County Parks Department, 619/478-5212, fax 619/478-2060, www.sdparks.org.

64 OUTDOOR WORLD RETREAT

Scenic rating: 4

in Boulevard

Map 15.2, page 816

This retreat sits on 163 acres and has hiking trails. The elevation is 3,800 feet. The town of Boulevard is centrally situated for a wide variety of recreation possibilities. About 10 miles to the north is Mount Laguna, with hiking trails available. About 30 minutes to the south is the nearest point of entry to Mexico at Tecate. Fishing at Lake Morena or Lake Cuyamaca is also a possibility, as is soaking in nearby hot springs. A casino is four miles away. A train museum is available in Campo, about 16 miles away.

Campsites, facilities: There are 151 sites with full or partial hookups (20, 30, and 50 amps) for tents or RVs up to 45 feet, a primitive tent camping area, and a group camping area for up to 1,000 people. Some sites are pull-through. Picnic tables and fire rings are provided at some sites. A clubhouse, restrooms with showers, horseshoes, volleyball court, coin laundry, gift shop, general store, Wi-Fi, group campfire area, and organized activities and classes are available. Golf carts are allowed. Some facilities are wheelchair-accessible. Leashed pets are permitted, with some breeds prohibited.

Reservations, fees: Reservations are accepted by website or at 888/703-0009. Sites are $20–33 per night, $3 per person per night for more than two people, $3 per night for each additional vehicle, $3 per night per pet. Weekly, monthly, and group rates available. Some credit cards accepted. Open year-round.

Directions: From El Cajon, drive east on I-8 for approximately 50 miles (past Alpine) to the Crestwood/Live Oak Springs Road exit. Take that exit and turn east and drive 0.5 mile to Church Street. Turn right and drive 4.2 miles to Highway 94. Turn left (east) and drive 1.1 miles to the resort on the right.

Contact: Outdoor World Retreat, 619/766-4480, www.outdoorworldrvpark.com.

THE SOUTHERN DESERTS

© ROBERT HOLMES/CALTOUR

BEST CAMPGROUNDS

☾ Waterskiing
Los Alamos, **page 868**
Moabi Regional Park, **page 880**
Havasu Landing Resort and Casino, **page 881**

There is no region so vast in California – yet with fewer people – than the broad expanse of Anza-Borrego Desert State Park, Joshua Tree National Park, Mojave National Preserve, Salton Sea, and endless BLM land. And yet the area is best loved not for the desert, but for the boating, water sports, and recreation of the Colorado River. Each of these respective areas has distinct qualities, separate and special, yet they are also joined at the edges.

What often attracts people to this region for the first time is a party at the Colorado River. On big weekends, it can even seem as if there is a party within close vicinity of every boat ramp on the river. The weather is hot, the boats are fast, and the body oil can flow as fast as the liquid refreshments. Campgrounds are available throughout this region for the best access to the water.

The rest of the area is far different.

Anza-Borrego (covered in the *San Diego and Vicinity* chapter) is so big that it seems to stretch to forever. That is because it does. The park covers 600,000 acres, the largest state park in California. The landscape features virtually every type of desert terrain, but most obvious are canyons, badlands, and barren ridges. In spring, the blooming cholla can be impressive. This is habitat for the endangered desert bighorn, and seeing one can be the highlight of a lifetime of wildlife-viewing.

Joshua Tree National Park, on the other hand, features a sweeping desert landscape edged by mountains, peppered with the peculiar Joshua tree. It is best known by most as the place where the high desert (Mojave Desert, 4,000 feet elevation) meets the low desert (Colorado Desert). This transition creates the setting for a diversity in vegetation and habitat. The strange piles of rocks often appear to have been left there by an ancient prehistoric giant, as if chipped, chiseled, and then left in rows and piles.

The national park is far different than Mojave National Preserve. The highlights here are the Kelso Dunes, a series of volcanic cliffs and a forest of Joshua trees. It is remote and explored by relatively few visitors. The Mojave is a point of national significance because it is where three major landscapes join: the Sonoran Desert, the Colorado Desert, and the Mojave Desert.

The Salton Sea and the endless BLM desert land provide one of the most distinct (and strange) lakes and terrain on earth. The Salton Sea, created in an accident from a broken dike, is one of the largest inland seas in the world. The BLM's desert land is under BLM control only because no other agency wanted it.

Throughout this country, campgrounds are sprinkled in most of the best spots. Some are extremely remote. Some consist of nothing but flat parking areas. Some are simple staging areas for OHV riders, and some serve as a base camp for a weekend party. Somewhere amid all this, a place like no other, you will likely be able to find a match for your desires.

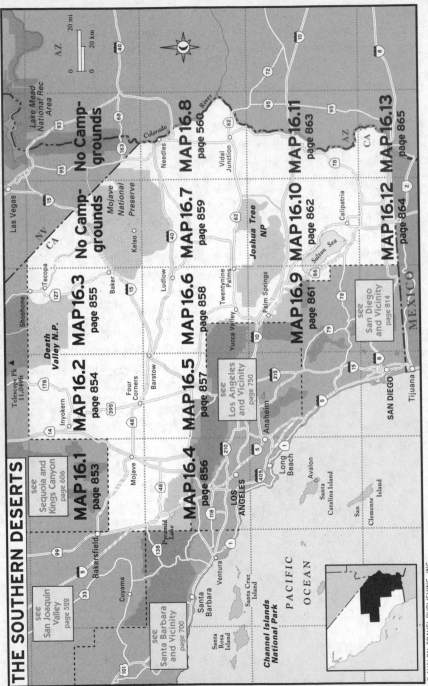

THE SOUTHERN DESERTS

Map 16.1

**Campgrounds 1-3
Pages 866-867**

16.2

16.4

1	2	3		
4	5	6	7	8
		9	10	11
			12	13

Johnsondale

**Giant
Sequoia
National
Monument**

Sequoia

Fairview

National

Forest

Posey

Riverkern

Kernville

155

Woody

Glennville

Alta
Sierra

Wofford
Heights

178

Onyx

Weldon

*Sequoia
National
Forest*

Isabella Lake

Lake Isabella

River

Bodfish

178

*Sequoia
National
Forest*

Lake Ming

Kern

178

see
Sequoia and
Kings Canyon
page 606

58

Lamont

Arvin

S I E R R A

N E V A D A

Aqueduct

Los Angeles

14

Tehachapi

*Brite Valley
Aquatic Rec Area* 1 2

58

3

99

Cummings Mtn
7,760ft

Double Mtn
7,981ft

Mojave

5

14

58

© AVALON TRAVEL PUBLISHING, INC.

Map 16.2

Campground 4
Pages 867-868

16.1 16.3
16.5

1 2 3
4 5 6 7 8
9 10 11
12 13

Death Valley National Park

Little Lake

CHINA LAKE

395

NAVAL WEAPONS

CENTER

Pearsonville

Trona

Slate Range

Inyokern 178

178

395 Ridgecrest

14

CHINA LAKE

NAVAL WEAPONS

CENTER

Red Rock Canyon State Park
4

El Paso Mountains

395

Mojave Desert

58

© AVALON TRAVEL PUBLISHING, INC.

Map 16.3

Campground 5
Pages 868

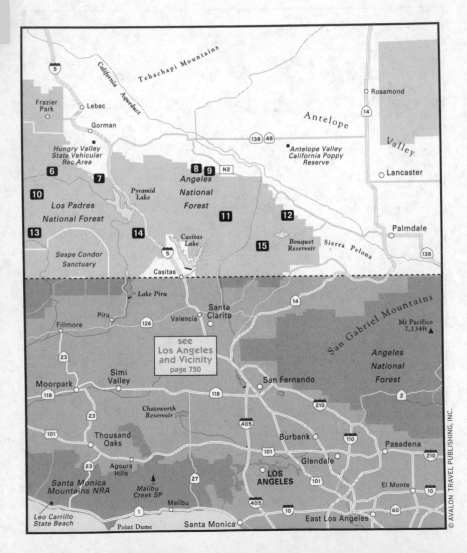

Map 16.5

Campgrounds 16-21
Pages 872-875

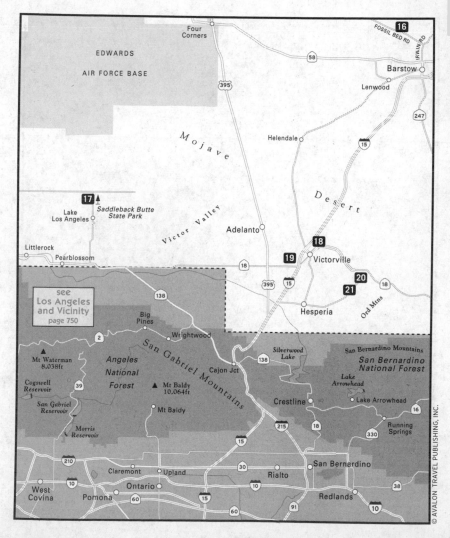

Map 16.6

Campgrounds 22-26
Pages 875-878

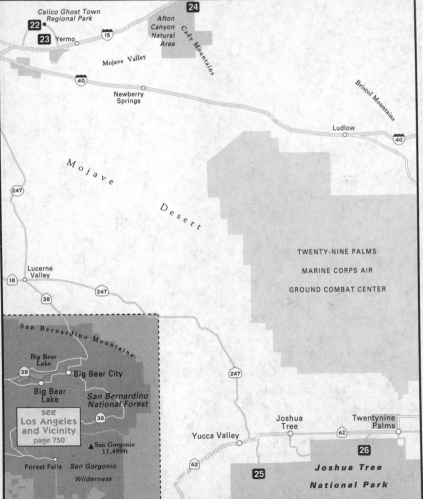

© AVALON TRAVEL PUBLISHING, INC.

Map 16.7

Campgrounds 27-29
Pages 878-879

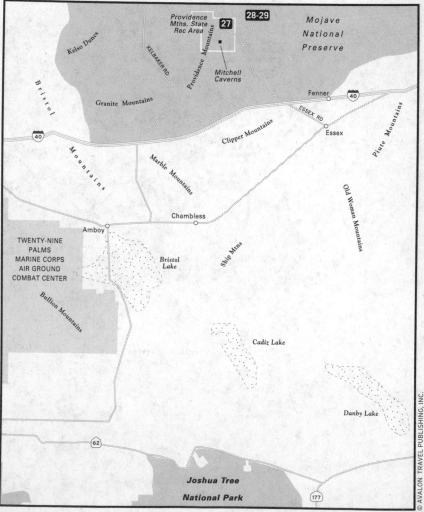

Providence Mths. State Rec Area

27

28-29

Mojave National Preserve

Kelso Dunes

KELBAKER RD

Providence Mountains

Mitchell Caverns

Fenner

40

ESSEX RD

Essex

Piute Mountains

Bristol

Granite Mountains

40

Clipper Mountains

Mountains

Marble Mountains

Old Woman Mountains

Chambless

Amboy

Ship Mtns

TWENTY-NINE PALMS MARINE CORPS AIR GROUND COMBAT CENTER

Bristol Lake

Bullion Mountains

Cadiz Lake

Danby Lake

62

Joshua Tree National Park

177

Map 16.8

Campgrounds 30-37
Pages 879-883

© AVALON TRAVEL PUBLISHING, INC.

Map 16.9

Campgrounds 38-51
Pages 883-889

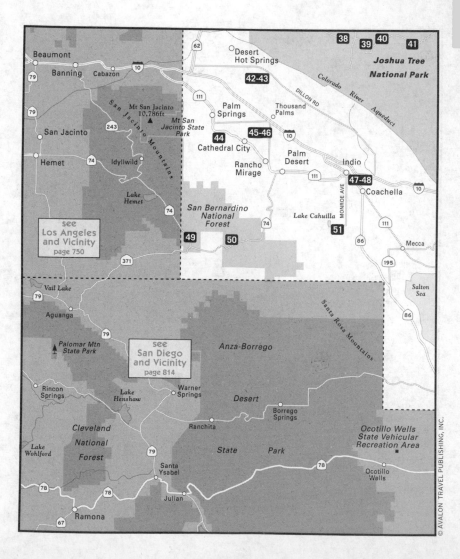

Beaumont

Banning Cabazon

San Jacinto

Hemet

Idyllwild

San Jacinto Mountains

Mt San Jacinto
10,786ft ▲

Mt San
Jacinto State
Park

Lake
Hemet

see
**Los Angeles
and Vicinity**
page 750

62

Desert
Hot Springs

42-43

Palm
Springs

Thousand
Palms

44

45-46

Cathedral City

Rancho
Mirage

Palm
Desert

San Bernardino
National
Forest

49

50

Lake Cahuilla

DILLON RD

Colorado River Aqueduct

38 **39** **40** **41**

**Joshua Tree
National Park**

Indio

47-48

Coachella

MONROE AVE

51

Mecca

Salton
Sea

Vail Lake

Aguanga

Palomar Mtn
State Park

Rincon
Springs

Lake
Henshaw

Warner
Springs

see
**San Diego
and Vicinity**
page 814

Anza-Borrego

Santa Rosa Mountains

Desert

Borrego
Springs

Cleveland

National

Forest

Lake
Wohlford

Ranchita

Santa
Ysabel

Julian

Ramona

State   Park

Ocotillo Wells
State Vehicular
Recreation Area

Ocotillo
Wells

16.6

16.10

1 2 3
4 5 6 7 8
9 10 11
12 13

Map 16.10

Campgrounds 52-63
Pages 889-895

Map 16.11

Campgrounds 64-70
Pages 895-899

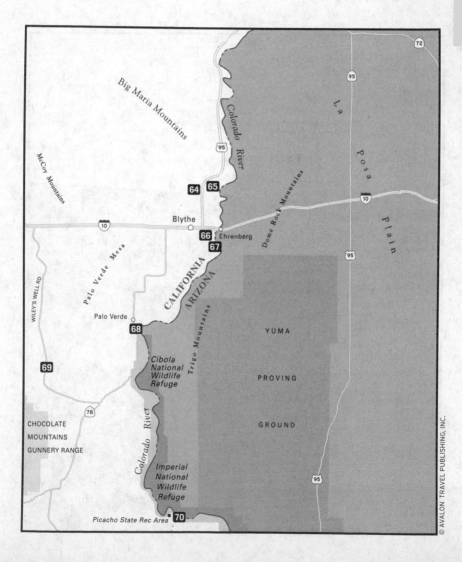

Map 16.12

Campground 71
Page 899

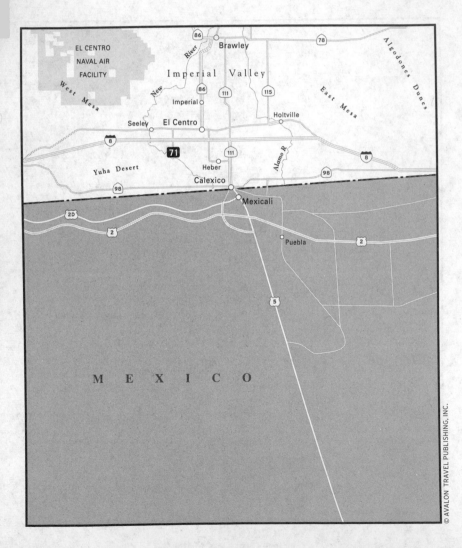

Map 16.13

Campgrounds 72-75
Pages 899-901

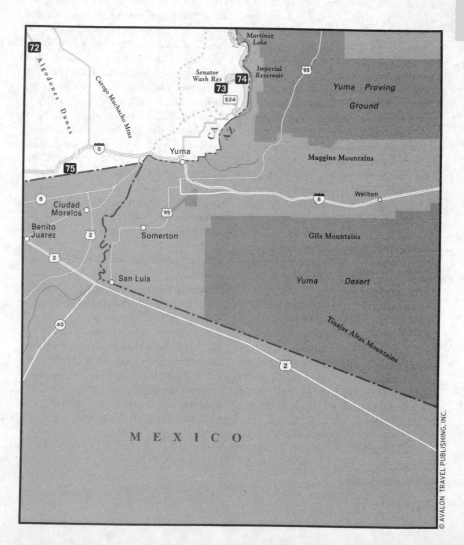

❶ BRITE VALLEY AQUATIC RECREATION AREA

Scenic rating: 7

at Brite Lake

Map 16.1, page 853

Brite Valley Lake is a speck of a water hole (90 acres) on the northern flank of the Tehachapi Mountains in Kern County, at an elevation of 4,000 feet. No gas motors are permitted on the lake, so it's perfect for canoes, kayaks, or inflatables. No swimming is permitted. Use is moderate, primarily by picnickers and anglers. The lake is stocked with trout in the spring and catfish in the summer. Other species include bluegill. A golf course is nearby.

Campsites, facilities: There are 12 sites with partial hookups (20 amps) for RVs of any length and a tent camping area. Picnic tables and fire grills are provided. Drinking water, restroom with flush toilets and showers, dump station, playground, reservable picnic pavilions, and a fish-cleaning station are available. Supplies are available about eight miles away in Tehachapi. Leashed pets are permitted.

Reservations, fees: Reservations are not accepted. Sites are $15–20 per night for each vehicle. Boat launching is $3 per day. Open late April to late October.

Directions: From Bakersfield, drive east on Highway 58 for 40 miles toward the town of Tehachapi. Take the Highway 202 exit and drive three miles west to Banducci Road. Turn left and drive for about one mile to the park on the right.

Contact: Tehachapi Valley Recreation and Parks District, 661/822-3228, fax 661/823-8529.

❷ INDIAN HILL RANCH AND RV PARK

Scenic rating: 7

near Tehachapi

Map 16.1, page 853

This is a unique park with two seasonal ponds stocked with largemouth bass and catfish. Crappie and bluegill are other fish species. The campground is open year-round and offers spacious, private sites with oak trees and a view of Brite Valley. A bonus is the hiking trails in the park. The elevation is 5,000 feet. Although this area is known for being windy, this campground is somewhat sheltered from the wind.

Campsites, facilities: There are 46 sites for RVs; many have full hookups and nearly half are pull-through. Tents are allowed with RVs only. Picnic tables and fire pits are provided. Restroom with flush toilets and showers (seasonal), dump station, coin laundry, Wi-Fi, propane, and two stocked fishing ponds are available. Small leashed pets are permitted, with certain restrictions.

Reservations, fees: Reservations are accepted. Sites are $20–40 per night. Monthly and group rates available. Some credit cards accepted. Open year-round, with some sites closed from November to mid-May.

Directions: Drive on Highway 58 to Tehachapi and Exit 148 for Tehachapi/Highway 202. Take that exit to Tucker Road. Turn right and drive south one mile to Highway 202/Valley Boulevard. Turn right (west) and drive four miles to Banducci Road. Turn left and drive 0.75 mile to Arosa Road. Turn left and drive 1.7 miles to the park at 18061 Arosa Road.

Contact: Indian Hill Ranch and RV Park, 661/822-6613, www.indianhillranch.com.

3 TEHACHAPI MOUNTAIN PARK

🚶 🏕 🐕 ♿ 🚐 ⛺

Scenic rating: 6

southwest of Tehachapi

Map 16.1, page 853

This county park is overlooked by most out-of-towners. It is a pretty spot covering 5,000 acres, set on the slopes of the Tehachapi Mountains, with elevations in the park ranging from 5,500 to 7,000 feet. The roads to the campgrounds are steep, but the sites are flat. Trails for hikers and equestrians are available, but no horses are allowed at the campground. An interpretive trail, Nuooah Nature Trail, is available. This park is popular not only in spring, but also in winter, with the elevations sometimes high enough to get snow (chains often required for access). The park lies eight miles southwest of the town of Tehachapi on the southern side of Highway 58 between Mojave and Bakersfield. Woody's Peak, at almost 8,000 feet, overlooks the park from its dominion in the Tehachapi Mountains, the dividing line between the San Joaquin Valley and the Los Angeles Basin.

Campsites, facilities: There are 61 sites for tents or RVs of any length (no hookups), a group campsite for up to 40 people, and group lodging with 10 cabins for a minimum of 40 people. Picnic tables and fire grills are provided. Drinking water (natural spring) and chemical toilets are available. Some facilities are wheelchair-accessible. Leashed pets are permitted.

Reservations, fees: Reservations are accepted for the group site and group cabins only. Sites are $14 per night per vehicle, $275 per night for the group site, and $2 per pet per night. Reserve group site and cabins at 661/868-7002. Open year-round, weather permitting.

Directions: In Tehachapi, take Tehachapi Boulevard to the Cury Street exit. Take that exit south and drive about three miles to Highline Road. Turn right on Highline Road and drive two miles to Water Canyon Road. Turn left on Water Canyon Road and drive three miles to the park.

Contact: Kern County Parks Department, info line, 661/868-7000, www.co.kern.ca.us/parks/index.htm.

4 RED ROCK CANYON STATE PARK

🚶 🏕 🐕 ♿ 🚐 ⛺

Scenic rating: 8

near Mojave

Map 16.2, page 854

This unique state park is one of the prettiest spots in the region year-round. What makes it worthwhile in any season is the chance to see wondrous geologic formations, most of them tinted red. The park also has paleontology sites, as well as remnants of some 1890s-era mining operations. A great, easy hike is the two-mile walk to Red Cliffs Natural Preserve, where there are awesome 300-foot cliffs and columns, painted red by the iron in the soil. Part of this area is closed from February through June to protect nesting raptors. For those who don't hike, a must is driving up Jawbone Canyon Road to see Jawbone and Last Chance Canyons. Hikers have it better. The park also has excellent wildflower blooms from March through May. A primitive OHV trail also is available; check regulations. The elevation is 2,600 feet.

Campsites, facilities: There are 50 sites for tents or RVs up to 30 feet (no hookups). Picnic tables and fire grills are provided. Drinking water, pit toilets, dump station, picnic area, seasonal exhibits, seasonal campfire program, and a seasonal nature trail are available. In spring and fall, nature walks led by rangers are available. Some facilities are wheelchair-accessible. Leashed pets are permitted in the campground only.

Reservations, fees: Reservations are not accepted. Sites are $12 per night, and $5 for each additional vehicle. Open year-round.

Directions: Drive on Highway 14 to the town of Mojave (50 miles east of the Los Angeles Basin area). Continue northeast on Highway 14 for 25 miles to the park entrance on the left.

Contact: Red Rock Canyon State Park, Mojave Desert Information Center, 661/942-0662, fax 661/940-7327, www.parks.ca.gov.

5 TECOPA HOT SPRINGS PARK

Scenic rating: 3

north of Tecopa

Map 16.3, page 855

This Inyo County campground is out there in no-man's-land, and if it weren't for the hot springs and the good rockhounding, all you'd see around here would be a few skeletons. Regardless, it's quite an attraction in the winter, when the warm climate is a plus and the nearby mineral baths are worth taking a dunk in. Rockhounds will enjoy looking for amethysts, opals, and petrified wood in the nearby areas. The elevation is 1,500 feet. Nobody gets here by accident.

Campsites, facilities: There are 250 sites for tents or RVs of any length (with partial hookups of 30 amps). Some sites are pull-through. Picnic tables and fire grills are provided. Restrooms with flush toilets and showers and a dump station are available. There is no drinking water. Groceries and propane gas are available within 10 miles. Leashed pets are permitted.

Reservations, fees: Reservations are accepted. Sites are $14–17 per vehicle per night. Weekly and monthly rates are available. Open year-round.

Directions: From Baker, drive north on Highway 127 for 58 miles to a county road signed "Tecopa Hot Springs" (south of the junction of Highway 178 and Highway 127). Turn right (east) and drive five miles to the park and campground entrance.

Contact: Tecopa Hot Springs Park, 760/852-4481, Inyo County Parks and Recreation, 760/873-5577.

6 KINGS

Scenic rating: 5

near Piru Creek in Los Padres National Forest

Map 16.4, page 856

The Hungry Valley State Vehicular Recreation Area is just five miles to the east. Figure it out: Right, this is a primitive but well-placed camp for four-wheel-drive and off-highway vehicles. The camp is near Piru Creek, off a short spur road, so it feels remote yet is close to one of California's top off-road areas.

Campsites, facilities: There are seven sites for tents or RVs up to 16 feet (no hookups). Picnic tables and fire grills are provided. Vault toilets are available. No drinking water is available. Garbage must be packed out. Leashed pets are permitted.

Reservations, fees: No reservations are accepted and there is no camping fee. An Adventure Pass ($30 annual fee or $5 daily fee) per parked vehicle is required. Open year-round.

Directions: Drive on I-5 to south of Gorman and the Gorman-Hungry Valley Road exit (the northern exit for the Hungry Valley Recreation Area). Take that exit and turn south on Hungry Valley Road (Forest Road 8N01) and drive six miles to Gold Hill Road (Forest Road 8N01). Turn right and drive six miles to Forest Road 18N01A. Turn left and drive 0.75 mile to the campground.

Contact: Los Padres National Forest, Mount Piños Ranger District, 661/245-3731, fax 661/245-1526.

7 LOS ALAMOS

Scenic rating: 4

near Pyramid Lake in Angeles National Forest

Map 16.4, page 856   BEST (

Los Alamos is set at an elevation of 2,600 feet near the southern border of the Hungry Valley State Vehicular Recreation Area and about 2.5 miles north of Pyramid Lake. Pyramid Lake is a big lake, covering 1,300 acres with 20 miles of shoreline, and is extremely popular for waterskiing and fast boating (35 mph speed limit), as well as for sailboarding (best at the northern launch point), fishing (best in the spring and early summer and in the fall for striped bass), and swimming. A lifeguard is on duty at the boat launch area during the summer season.

Campsites, facilities: There are 93 sites and three group sites for tents or RVs up to 40 feet (no hookups) that can accommodate up to 25 people each. Picnic tables and fire pits are provided. Drinking water and flush toilets are available. A boat ramp is at the Emigrant Landing Picnic Area. Leashed pets are permitted. Some facilities are wheelchair-accessible.

Reservations, fees: Reservations are not accepted for individual sites, but are required for group sites at 661/248-6725. Sites are $14 per night, $65 per night for a group site. Open year-round.

Directions: Drive on I-5 to eight miles south of Gorman and the Smokey Bear Road exit. Take the Smokey Bear Road exit and drive west about three-quarters of a mile and follow the signs to the campground.

Contact: Angeles National Forest, Santa Clara/Mojave Rivers Ranger District, 661/296-9710, fax 661/296-5847; Recreation Resource Management, 661/248-6725.

8 SAWMILL
🚶 🐕 5% 🚐 ⛺

Scenic rating: 7

on the Pacific Crest Trail in Angeles National Forest

Map 16.4, page 856

This is a classic hiker's trailhead camp. It is set at 5,200 feet, right on the Pacific Crest Trail and just one mile from the junction with Burnt Peak Canyon Trail. For a good day hike, head southeast on the Pacific Crest Trail for one mile to Burnt Peak Canyon Trail, turn right (southwest), and hike just over a mile to Burnt Peak, elevation 5,788 feet. Note that this camp

is inaccessible after the first snow. Nearby Upper Shake provides an alternative.

Campsites, facilities: There are eight sites for tents or RVs up to 16 feet (no hookups). Note that RVs are not recommended. Picnic tables and fire pits are provided. Vault toilets are available. No drinking water is available. Garbage must be packed out. Leashed pets are permitted.

Reservations, fees: No reservations are accepted and there is no camping fee. An Adventure Pass ($30 annual fee or $5 daily pass per parked vehicle) is required. Open May through October, weather permitting.

Directions: Drive on I-5 to the Tehachapis near the small town of Castaic and Lake Hughes Road. Turn northeast on Lake Hughes Road and drive 27 miles to the town of Lake Hughes and Pine Canyon Road/County Road N2. Turn left on Pine Canyon Road and drive 10 miles to Bushnell Summit Road. Turn left and drive two miles to the campground on the left.

Contact: Angeles National Forest, Santa Clara/Mojave Rivers Ranger District, 661/296-9710, fax 661/296-5847.

9 UPPER SHAKE
🚶 🐕 🚐 ⛺

Scenic rating: 7

on the Pacific Crest Trail in Angeles National Forest

Map 16.4, page 856

Upper Shake, like nearby Sawmill, is right on the Pacific Crest Trail. The elevation is 4,400 feet. Hikers who plan on heading to Burnt Peak are better off departing from Sawmill (less than two miles to the west). This camp is used primarily as a jump-off point for those heading east on the PCT; Lake Hughes is the nearest destination, less than four miles away, and a mile after that is Lake Elizabeth. The camp is inaccessible after the first snow.

Campsites, facilities: There are 18 sites for tents or RVs up to 22 feet (no hookups). Picnic tables and fire pits are provided. Vault toilets are available. No drinking water is available.

Garbage must be packed out. Leashed pets are permitted.

Reservations, fees: No reservations are accepted and there is no camping fee. An Adventure Pass ($30 annual fee or $5 daily pass per parked vehicle) is required. Open May through October, weather permitting.

Directions: Drive on I-5 to the Tehachapis near the small town of Castaic and Lake Hughes Road. Turn northeast on Lake Hughes Road and drive 27 miles to the town of Lake Hughes and Pine Canyon Road/County Road N2. Turn left on Pine Canyon Road and drive about 5.5 miles to the entrance road on the left.

Contact: Angeles National Forest, Santa Clara/Mojave Rivers Ranger District, 661/296-9710, fax 661/296-5847.

10 TWIN PINES AND DUTCHMAN

Scenic rating: 6

on Alamo Mountain in Los Padres National Forest

Map 16.4, page 856

Twin Pines Camp is set at 6,600 feet on Alamo Mountain, a small, remote, and primitive spot—no picnic tables, no toilets, no drinking water. Dutchman Campground is nearby at 6,800 feet. These spots are best known by four-wheel-drive enthusiasts rumbling around the area. The big attraction here is access to Miller Jeep Trail, a gnarly black-diamond route that can bend metal and alter minds. This camp also provides an alternative to the Hungry Valley State Vehicular Recreation Area to the nearby northeast.

Campsites, facilities: There are five tent sites at Twin Pines and eight primitive sites at Dutchman. Picnic tables and fire grills are provided. Pit toilets are available. No drinking water is available. Garbage must be packed out. Leashed pets are permitted.

Reservations, fees: No reservations are accepted and there is no camping fee. An Adventure Pass ($30 annual fee or $5 daily

fee per parked vehicle) is required. Open early May through October, weather permitting.

Directions: Drive on I-5 to south of Gorman and the Gorman-Hungry Valley Road exit (the northern exit for the Hungry Valley Recreation Area). Take that exit and turn south on Hungry Valley Road (Forest Road 8N01) and drive six miles to Gold Hill Road (Forest Road 8N01). Turn right and drive 13 miles to Twin Pines campground. To reach Dutchman, at Twin Pines campground, turn right at Forest Road 7N01 and drive three miles to the campground.

Contact: Los Padres National Forest, Mount Piños Ranger District, 661/245-3731, fax 661/245-1526.

11 COTTONWOOD

Scenic rating: 5

near the Warm Springs Mountain Lookout in Angeles National Forest

Map 16.4, page 856

Cottonwood Camp is set at 2,680 feet in remote Angeles National Forest along a small stream. The camp is on the north flank of Warm Springs Mountain. A great side trip is to the Warm Springs Mountain Lookout (4,023 feet), about a five-mile drive. Drive south on Forest Road 7N09 for three miles, turn right (west) on Forest Road 6N32, and drive for 1.5 miles to Forest Road 7N13. Turn left (south) and drive a mile to the summit.

Campsites, facilities: There are 22 sites for tents or RVs up to 22 feet (no hookups). Picnic tables and fire pits are provided. Vault toilets are available. No drinking water is available. Garbage must be packed out. Supplies are available less than four miles away in the town of Lake Hughes. Leashed pets are permitted.

Reservations, fees: No reservations are accepted and there is no camping fee. An Adventure Pass ($30 annual fee or $5 daily pass per parked vehicle) is required. Open year-round.

Directions: Drive on I-5 to the Tehachapis near the small town of Castaic and Lake Hughes

Road. Turn northeast on Lake Hughes Road and drive 27 miles to the campground on the right.

Contact: Angeles National Forest, Santa Clara/ Mojave Rivers Ranger District, 661/296-9710, fax 661/296-5847.

12 SPUNKY
👫 🛶 🏕 ⛰

Scenic rating: 7

in Angeles National Forest
Map 16.4, page 856

Note: At the time of publication, this campground was closed because of storm damage. Check for current status before planning a trip. Spunky Camp is set at 3,300 feet elevation amid good tree cover, much of it large oaks. The campsites are open in a peaceful setting. The highlight is hiking, with the Pacific Crest Trail passing just 1.5 miles east of the camp. In addition, many campers will hike up the canyon behind the campground. The creek runs during the winter. Nearby Elizabeth Lake, 10 miles to the west, provides swimming, fishing, sailing, sailboarding, and low-speed powerboating, with a 10-horsepower maximum on motors.

Campsites, facilities: There are 10 tent sites. Picnic tables and fire pits are provided. Pit toilets are available. No drinking water is available. A restaurant, gas station, and minimart are available one mile away in Green Valley. Leashed pets are permitted.

Reservations, fees: Reservations are not accepted. There is no camping fee. An Adventure Pass ($30 annual fee or $5 daily pass per parked vehicle) is required. Open year-round.

Directions: From the junction of I-5 and Highway 14, take Highway 14 to Santa Clarita and the exit for Valencia Boulevard. Take that exit east and drive two miles to Bouquet Canyon Road. Turn left on Bouquet Canyon Road and drive 19 miles to Spunky Canyon Road. Turn left and drive four miles to the campground on the right.

Contact: Angeles National Forest, Santa Clara/ Mojave Rivers Ranger District, 661/296-9710, fax 661/296-5847.

13 HALF MOON
👫 🏕 🚐 ⛰

Scenic rating: 7

near Piru Creek in Los Padres National Forest
Map 16.4, page 856

Half Moon is a primitive camp set along Piru Creek at 4,700 feet. Adjacent to camp, Forest Road 7N13 follows the creek for a few miles, then dead-ends at a trailhead that continues along more remote stretches of this little stream. Hikers should also consider the trail to nearby Thorn Point for a beautiful lookout (see the entry for *Thorn Meadows Family and Equestrian Camp* in the *Santa Barbara and Vicinity* chapter for more information).

Campsites, facilities: There are 10 sites for tents or RVs up to 22 feet (no hookups). Picnic tables and fire grills are provided. Pit toilets are available. No drinking water is available. Garbage must be packed out. Leashed pets are permitted.

Reservations, fees: No reservations are accepted and there is no camping fee. An Adventure Pass ($30 annual fee or $5 daily fee per parked vehicle) is required. Open early May through October, weather permitting.

Directions: Drive on I-5 to just south of Lebec and the Frazier Park exit. Take that exit and drive west on Frazier Mountain Road to the town of Lake of the Woods and Lockwood Valley Road. Turn left on Lockwood Valley Road and drive about 12 miles to Grade Valley Road (Forest Road 7N03). Turn left and drive 11 miles to the campground on the left. High-clearance or four-wheel-drive vehicles are recommended; access requires crossing a creek in which the current can be fairly fast and high, especially in the spring.

Contact: Los Padres National Forest, Mount Piños Ranger District, 661/245-3731, fax 661/245-1526.

14 OAK FLAT

Scenic rating: 3

near Pyramid Lake in Angeles National Forest

Map 16.4, page 856

Oak Flat is just a short drive from Pyramid Lake, at 2,800 feet near the southwestern border of Angeles National Forest. Pyramid is surrounded by national forest, quite beautiful, and is a favorite destination for folks with powerboats, especially those towing waterskiers. The lake covers 1,300 acres and has 20 miles of shoreline. Water sports are popular in the summer, and fishing for striped bass can be good in the spring and fall. Other species are largemouth bass, catfish, crappie, and bluegill. (For more information on Pyramid Lake, see the *Los Alamos* listing in this chapter.)

Campsites, facilities: There are 27 sites for tents or RVs up to 18 feet (no hookups). Picnic tables and fire pits are provided. Vault toilets are available. No drinking water is available. Garbage must be packed out. Leashed pets are permitted.

Reservations, fees: No reservations are accepted and there is no camping fee. An Adventure Pass ($30 annual fee or $5 daily fee per parked vehicle) is required. Open year-round.

Directions: Drive on I-5 to six miles north of Castaic to Templin Highway. Take Templin Highway west and drive three miles to the campground.

Contact: Angeles National Forest, Santa Clara/Mojave Rivers Ranger District, 661/296-9710, fax 661/296-5847.

15 STREAMSIDE

Scenic rating: 7

on Bouquet Canyon Creek in Angeles National Forest

Map 16.4, page 856

Note: At the time of publication, this campground was closed because of storm damage; check current status before planning a trip. Streamside Camp sits along pretty Bouquet Canyon Creek at an elevation of 2,500 feet. This stream is typically stocked with trout in late spring and early summer. The creek and campgrounds are just downstream of Bouquet Reservoir, which provides stream flows in warm weather. Rangers advise not to drink the water from Bouquet Canyon Creek under any circumstances. Also, a warning to hikers is that this area has plenty of poison oak.

Campsites, facilities: There are nine tent sites. Picnic tables and fire pits are provided. Vault toilets are available. No drinking water is available. Leashed pets are permitted.

Reservations, fees: Reservations are not accepted and there is no camping fee. An Adventure Pass ($30 annual fee or $5 daily pass per parked vehicle) is required. Open year-round.

Directions: From the junction of I-5 and Highway 14, take Highway 14 to Santa Clarita and the exit for Valencia Boulevard. Take that exit east and drive two miles to Bouquet Canyon Road. Turn left on Bouquet Canyon Road and drive about 14 miles to the campground on the left.

Contact: Angeles National Forest, Santa Clara/Mojave Rivers Ranger District, 661/296-9710, fax 661/296-5847.

16 OWL CANYON

Scenic rating: 3

near Barstow

Map 16.5, page 857

The primary attraction of Owl Canyon camp is that the surrounding desert is sprinkled with exposed fossils of ancient animals. Guess they couldn't find any water, heh, heh. Well, if people try hiking here without a full canteen, there may soon be some human skeletons out here, too. Actually, rangers tell us that the general public is unlikely to spot fossils here because it takes some basic scientific knowledge to identify them. The sparse BLM land out here is kind of like an ugly dog you learn to love: After a while, when you look closely, you learn it has a heart of gold. This region is best visited in the spring and fall, of course, when hiking allows a fresh, new look at what may appear to some as a wasteland. The beauty is in the detail of it—tiny critters and tiny flowers seen against the unfenced vastness, with occasional fossils yet to be discovered. The elevation is 2,600 feet.

Campsites, facilities: There are 31 sites for tents or RVs of any length (no hookups). Picnic tables and fire grills are provided. Vault toilets are available. There is no drinking water. Leashed pets are permitted.

Reservations, fees: Reservations are not accepted. Sites are $6 per night. Open year-round.

Directions: Drive on I-15 to Barstow to the exit for 1st Street. Take that exit and drive north on 1st Street (crossing the Mojave River Bridge) for 0.75 mile to Irwin Road. Turn left and drive eight miles to Fossil Bed Road. Turn left and drive two miles to the campground on the right.

Contact: Bureau of Land Management, Barstow Field Office, 760/252-6000, fax 760/252-6099.

17 SADDLEBACK BUTTE STATE PARK

Scenic rating: 8

near Lancaster

Map 16.5, page 857

This 3,000-acre park was originally established to preserve ancient Joshua trees. In fact, it used to be called Joshua Tree State Park, but folks kept getting it confused with Joshua Tree National Park, so it was renamed. The terrain is sparsely vegetated and desertlike, with excellent hiking trails up the nearby buttes. The best hike is Saddleback Loop, a five-mile trip that features a 1,000-foot climb to Saddleback Summit at

3,651 feet. On rare clear days, there are fantastic views in all directions, including the Antelope Valley California Poppy Preserve, the surrounding mountains, and the Mojave Desert. On the typical hazy day, the poppy preserve might as well be on the moon; you can't even come close to seeing it. The elevation is 2,700 feet.

Campsites, facilities: There are 30 sites for tents or RVs up to 30 feet (no hookups). A group camp is available for up to 30 people. Picnic tables, shade ramadas, and fire grills are provided. Drinking water, flush toilets, and dump station are available. A visitors center is nearby. Some facilities are wheelchair-accessible. Leashed pets are permitted in the campground only.

Reservations, fees: Reservations are not accepted for individual sites, but the group camp may be reserved ($7.50 reservation fee) at 800/444-PARK (800/444-7275) or www.reserveamerica.com. Sites are $12 per night, $5 per night for each additional vehicle, $66 per night for the group site. Open year-round.

Directions: Drive north on Highway 14 to Lancaster and the exit for Avenue J. Take that exit and drive east on Avenue J for 17 miles to the park entrance on the right.

Or drive south on Highway 14 to Lancaster to the exit for 20th Street west. Take that exit, turn left, and drive to Avenue J. Turn east on Avenue J and drive 17 miles to the park entrance on the right.

Contact: Saddleback Butte State Park, Mojave Desert Information Center, 661/942-0662, fax 661/940-7327, www.parks.ca.gov.

18 SHADY OASIS VICTORVILLE KOA

Scenic rating: 3

near Victorville

Map 16.5, page 857

Most long-distance trips on I-15 are grueling endurance tests with drivers making the mistake of trying to get a decent night's sleep at a roadside rest stop. Why endure the torture, especially with a KOA way out here, in Victorville of all places? Where the heck is Victorville? If you are exhausted and lucky enough to find the place, you won't be making any jokes about it.

Campsites, facilities: There are 136 sites, many with full or partial hookups (30 amps), some pull-through, for tents or RVs of any length, and eight cabins. Picnic tables and fire grills are provided. Drinking water, restrooms with flush toilets and showers, recreation room, seasonal heated swimming pool, playground, modem access, convenience store, propane gas, and a coin laundry are available. Some facilities are wheelchair-accessible. Leashed pets are permitted.

Reservations, fees: Reservations are accepted at 800/KOA-3319 (800/562-3319); $24–40 per night, $2 per person for more than two people, $1 per night for each additional vehicle. Some credit cards accepted. Open year-round.

Directions: Drive on I-15 to Victorville and Stoddard Wells Road (north of Victorville). Turn south on Stoddard Wells Road and drive a short distance to the campground (16530 Stoddard Wells Road).

Contact: Shady Oasis Victorville KOA, 760/245-6867, fax 760/243-2108, www.koa.com.

19 DESERT WILLOW RV PARK

🏊 🐴 ♿ 🚐

Scenic rating: 2

in Hesperia

Map 16.5, page 857

This is an RV park for I-15 cruisers looking to make a stop. Silverwood Lake, a 1,000-acre recreation lake with fishing, boating, and water sports, is 18 miles to the south. The elevation is 3,200 feet.

Campsites, facilities: There are 176 sites with full hookups (30 and 50 amps) for RVs; some sites are pull-through. No tents. Note that only

17 sites are available for overnight campers. Restrooms with showers, cable TV hookups, ice, coin laundry, propane gas, swimming pool, indoor spa, and library are on the premises. Some facilities are wheelchair-accessible. Leashed pets are permitted.

Reservations, fees: Reservations are accepted at 800/900-8114. Sites are $35 per night, $5 per person for more than two people, $1 per pet per night. Monthly rates available. Open year-round.

Directions: Drive on I-15 to Hesperia and Exit 143. Take that exit to Main Street. Turn west and drive to the park on the right (12624 Main Street West).

Contact: Desert Willow RV Park, 760/949-0377, fax 760/949-4334.

20 MOJAVE NARROWS REGIONAL PARK

🚶 🛶 🚐 🐴 🎣 ♿ 🚌 ⛺

Scenic rating: 7

on the Mojave River

Map 16.5, page 857

Almost no one except the locals knows about this little county park. It is like an oasis in the Mojave Desert. There are actually two small lakes here: the larger Horseshoe Lake and Pelican Lake. No private boats are allowed and rental rowboats and pedal boats are available on weekends. Swimming and water/body contact are prohibited. It is set at 2,000 feet and provides a few recreation options, including a pond stocked in season with trout and catfish, horseback-riding facilities, and equestrian trails. Hiking includes a wheelchair-accessible trail. The Mojave River level fluctuates here, almost disappearing in some years in summer and early fall. One of the big events of the year here, the Huck Finn Jubilee, is on Father's Day in June. Note: The gate closes each evening.

Campsites, facilities: There are 110 sites for tents or RVs of any length; seven pull-through, 42 with full hookups (15 and 30 amps). Fourteen group areas are also available. Picnic tables and barbecue grills are provided. Drinking water, restrooms with flush toilets and showers, dump station, snack bar, playground, picnic shelters, bait, boat rentals, horse rentals, and horseback-riding facilities are available. A store, propane gas, and coin laundry are available three miles from the campground. Leashed pets are permitted.

Reservations, fees: Reservations accepted for RVs and groups. Sites are $22 per night, $1 per night per pet, $5 per day fishing fee. Weekly and group rates available. Some credit cards accepted. Open year-round.

Directions: Drive on I-15 to Victorville and the exit for Bear Valley Road. Take that exit and drive east on Bear Valley Road for six miles to Ridgecrest. Turn left on Ridgecrest, drive three miles, and make a left into the park.

Contact: Mojave Narrows Regional Park, 760/245-2226, www.co.san-bernardino.ca.us/parks/mojave.htm.

21 HESPERIA LAKE CAMPGROUND

Scenic rating: 5

in Hesperia

Map 16.5, page 857

This is a slightly more rustic alternative to Desert Willow RV Park in Hesperia. There is a small lake/pond for recreational fishing and there is a small fishing fee, but no fishing license is required. Boating and swimming are not allowed, but youngsters usually get a kick out of feeding the ducks and geese that live at the pond.

Campsites, facilities: There are 58 sites with partial hookups (20, 30, and 50 amps) for tents or RVs up to 40 feet, and two group areas for tents. Picnic tables and fire pits are provided. Drinking water, restrooms with flush toilets and showers, a playground, horseshoe pits, and a fishing pond are available. Some facilities are wheelchair-accessible. Leashed pets are permitted in the camp, with certain restrictions, but not around the lake.

Reservations, fees: Reservations are accepted at 800/521-6332. Sites are $20 per night, $2 per night per pet. Some credit cards accepted. Open year-round.

Directions: Drive on I-15 to Hesperia and the exit for Main Street. Take that exit and drive east on Main Street for 9.5 miles (the road curves and becomes Arrowhead Lake Road) to the park on the left.

Contact: Hesperia Lake Campground, 760/244-5951 or 800/521-6332.

22 CALICO GHOST TOWN REGIONAL PARK

Scenic rating: 4

near Barstow

Map 16.6, page 858

Let me tell you about this ghost town: There are probably more people here now than there have ever been. In the 1880s and 1890s it was a booming silver mine town, and there are still remnants of that. Alas, it now has lots of restaurants and shops. Recreation options include riding on a narrow-gauge railroad, touring what was once the largest silver mine in California, and watching an old-style melodrama with villains and heroes. This is a 480-acre park with self-guided tours, hiking trails, gold panning, summer entertainment, and museum, with festivals held through the year. Whatever you do, don't take any artifacts you may come across, such as an old nail, a jar, or anything; you will be doomed with years of bad luck. No foolin'. A park representative told us the story of a man from the East Coast who nabbed a beautiful rock on his visit. He then was plagued with years of bad luck, including broken bones, disappointment in his love life, and several family deaths. In desperation, he flew back to California and returned the rock to its rightful place.

Campsites, facilities: There are 252 sites for tents and RVs up to 45 feet; 104 sites have full or partial hookups (20, 30, and 50 amps) and some sites are pull-through. There are also three group camping areas, six cabins, and a bunkhouse. Fire pits are provided. Restrooms with flush toilets and showers, drinking water, and three dump stations are available. Pay phone, restaurants, and shops are on-site. Groceries, propane gas, and laundry facilities are available 10 miles away. Leashed pets are permitted.

Reservations, fees: Reservations are accepted ($2 reservation fee) at 800/TO-CALICO (800/862-2542). Sites are $18–22 per night, $1 per night per pet. Some credit cards accepted. Open year-round.

Directions: From Barstow, drive northeast on I-15 for seven miles to the exit for Ghost Town Road. Take that exit and drive north on Ghost Town Road for three miles to the park on the left.

Contact: Calico Ghost Town Regional Park, San Bernardino County, 760/254-2122, fax 760/254-2047, www.calicotown.com.

23 BARSTOW CALICO KOA

Scenic rating: 3

near Barstow

Map 16.6, page 858

Don't blame us if you end up way out here. Actually, for vacationers making the long-distance grind of a drive on I-15, this KOA can seem like the promised land. It has received awards for its cleanliness, and a nightly quiet time ensures that you have a chance to get rested. Vegetation screening between sites enhance privacy. But hey, as long as you're here, you might as well take a side trip to Calico Ghost Town, about three miles to the northeast at the foot of the Calico Mountains. A unique side trip is the Calico Early Man Site, about five miles to the north; tours are available. Primitive stone tools are believed to have been discovered here in 1942. Rockhounding, hiking, and an outlet mall are other nearby options. The elevation is 1,900 feet.

Campsites, facilities: There are 78 sites with full

or partial hookups (30 and 50 amps) for tents or RVs of any length; many are pull-through. Picnic tables and fire grills are provided. Drinking water, restrooms with flush toilets and showers, dump station, modem access, playground, heated swimming pool, recreation room, convenience store, propane gas, ice, and coin laundry are available. Some facilities are wheelchair-accessible. Leashed pets are permitted.

Reservations, fees: Reservations are accepted at 800/KOA-0059 (800/562-0059). Sites are $20–33 per night, $2.50 per person per night for more than two people. Some credit cards accepted. Open year-round.

Directions: From Barstow, drive northeast on I-15 for seven miles to the exit for Ghost Town Road. Take that exit and drive left under the freeway to a frontage road at the Shell gas station. Turn left at the frontage road and drive 0.25 mile to the campground on the right.

Contact: Barstow/Calico KOA, 760/254-2311, fax 760/254-2247, www.koa.com.

24 AFTON CANYON

Scenic rating: 6

near Barstow in the East Mojave National Scenic Area

Map 16.6, page 858

This camp is set at 1,400 feet elevation in a desert riparian habitat along the Mojave River. This is one of several Bureau of Land Management tracts near the Mojave National Preserve. Side-trip options include the Rainbow Basin Natural Area (about an hour's drive), Soda Springs, and the Calico Early Man Site. Remember, rivers in the desert are not like rivers in cooler climates. There are no fish worth eating.

Campsites, facilities: There are 22 sites for tents or RVs up to 30 feet (no hookups). Picnic tables and fire rings are provided. Vault toilets are available. Drinking water is available intermittently, so bring your own water. Leashed pets are permitted.

Reservations, fees: Reservations are not

accepted. Sites are $6 per night. Open year-round.
Directions: From Barstow, drive east on I-15 for 37 miles to Afton Road. Turn right (south) and drive three miles to the campground. Note: Four-wheel drive or high-clearance vehicles are recommended since the access road can be rough and have washouts.
Contact: Bureau of Land Management, Barstow Field Office, 760/252-6000, fax 760/252-6099.

25 BLACK ROCK CANYON AND HORSE CAMP

Scenic rating: 4

in Joshua Tree National Park

Map 16.6, page 858

This is the fanciest darn public campground this side of the desert. Why, it actually has drinking water. The camp is set at the mouth of Black Rock Canyon, 4,000 feet elevation, which provides good winter hiking possibilities amid unique (in other words, weird) rock formations, which are about a half-hour drive from the campground. Show up in summer and you'll trade your gold for a sip of water. The camp is set near the excellent Black Rock Canyon Visitor Center and a trailhead for a four-mile round-trip hike to a rock wash. If you scramble onward, the route continues all the way to the top of Eureka Peak, 5,518 feet, an 11-mile round-trip. But hey, why not just drive there?
Campsites, facilities: There are 100 sites for tents or RVs up to 35 feet (no hookups), and 15 equestrian sites for up to six people and four horses per site. Picnic tables and fire grills are provided. Drinking water, flush toilets, and a dump station are available. Some facilities are wheelchair-accessible. The horse camp has hitching posts and a water faucet and no tents are allowed. Leashed pets are permitted, but not on trails.
Reservations, fees: Reservations are accepted

at 800/365-CAMP (800/365-2267) or at http://reservations.nps.gov. Sites are $10 per night, plus $15 park entrance fee per vehicle. Open year-round, weather permitting.
Directions: From the junction of I-10 and Highway 62 near Palm Springs, drive northeast on Highway 62 for 22.5 miles to Yucca Valley and Joshua Lane. Turn right (south) on Joshua Lane and drive about five miles to the campground.
Contact: Joshua Tree National Park, 760/367-5500, fax 760/367-6392; Black Rock Nature Center, 760/367-3001, www.nps.gov/jotr.

26 INDIAN COVE CAMPGROUND

Scenic rating: 4

in Joshua Tree National Park

Map 16.6, page 858

This is one of the campgrounds near the northern border of Joshua Tree National Park. The vast desert park, covering 1,238 square miles, is best known for its unique granite formations and scraggly-looking trees. If you had to withstand the summer heat here, you'd look scraggly too. Drinking water is available at the Indian Cove Ranger Station.
Campsites, facilities: There are 101 sites for tents or RVs up to 35 feet (no hookups), and a group camp with 13 sites for tents only for up to 60 people. Drinking water is available at the Indian Cove Ranger Station. Vault toilets, picnic tables, and fire grills are provided. Gas, groceries, and laundry services are available in Twentynine Palms (7 miles) or Joshua Tree (12 miles). Leashed pets are permitted, but not on trails.
Reservations, fees: Reservations are accepted at 800/365-CAMP (800/365-2267) or at http://reservations.nps.gov. Sites are $10 per night, $20–35 per night for group sites, plus $15 per vehicle park entrance fee. Open year-round.
Directions: From the junction of I-10 and

Highway 62 near Palm Springs, drive northeast on Highway 62 for 22 miles to Yucca Valley, continue to the small town of Joshua Tree, and then continue nine miles to Indian Cove Road. Turn right and drive three miles to the campground.

Contact: Joshua Tree National Park, 760/367-5500, fax 760/367-6392, www.nps.gov/jotr.

27 PROVIDENCE MOUNTAINS STATE RECREATION AREA

🎿 🐕 �30 🏕️

Scenic rating: 8

near Mitchell Caverns

Map 16.7, page 859

This remote desert park, set at 4,300 feet, offers guided tours of Mitchell Caverns ($2–4 tour fee, discounts available). These tours are available daily from early September through Memorial Day weekend, and on weekends from Memorial Day to early September. It's a good idea to make a reservation for the tour at 760/928-2586. The cavern tours are the reason most people visit and camp at this park. The caverns are classic limestone formations. There are additional recreational opportunities. From the campground Nina Mora Overlook Trail is a short (0.25-mile) walk to a lookout of the Marble Mountains and the valley below. Another short hike with a great view is the steep, one-mile hike (one-way) on Crystal Springs Trail, the best of the bunch. Another hike is Mary Beale, an interpretive trail accessible from the visitors center, a one-mile loop.

Campsites, facilities: There are six sites for tents or RVs up to 31 feet (no hookups). Picnic tables and fire grills are provided. Drinking water and flush toilets are available. A pay phone is available nearby. Leashed pets are permitted in the campground only.

Reservations, fees: Reservations are not accepted. Sites are $12 per night, $5 per night for each additional vehicle. Open year-round.

Directions: Drive on I-40 to Essex Road (near

Essex, 116 miles east of Barstow). Take that road and drive north on Essex Road for 16 miles to the park at road's end.

Contact: Providence Mountains State Recreation Area, 760/928-2586; Mojave Desert Information Center, 661/942-0662, fax 661/940-7327, www.parks.ca.gov.

28 MID HILLS

🎿 🐕 🚐 🏕️

Scenic rating: 4

in the Mojave National Preserve

Map 16.7, page 859

This is a primitive campground set among the junipers and piñon trees in a mountainous area at 5,600 feet. It is one of two little-known camps in the vast desert that is now managed by the National Park Service. About two-thirds of the campsites were burned in the 2005 Hackberry Fire; most of the piñon and juniper trees burned as well. There is an eight-mile one-way trail that starts across from the entrance to Mid Hills and is routed down to the Hole-in-the-Wall Campground. It a pleasant walk in spring and fall.

Campsites, facilities: There are 26 sites for tents or RVs up to 22 feet (no hookups). Picnic tables and fire grills are provided. Drinking water and vault toilets are available. Leashed pets are permitted.

Reservations, fees: Reservations are not accepted. Sites are $12 per night. Open year-round.

Directions: Drive on I-40 to Essex Road (near Essex, 116 miles east of Barstow). Take that exit and drive north on Essex Road for 10 miles to Black Canyon Road. Turn north and drive nine miles (at Hole-in-the-Wall campground, the road becomes dirt) and continue seven miles to Wild Horse Canyon Road. Turn left and drive two miles (rough, dirt road) to the campground on the right.

Contact: Mojave National Preserve, Baker Information Center, 760/733-4040, fax 760/733-4027, www.nps.gov/moja.

29 HOLE-IN-THE-WALL (AND BLACK CANYON GROUP AND HORSE CAMP)

Scenic rating: 6

in the Mojave National Preserve

Map 16.7, page 859

This is the largest and best-known of the camps in the vast Mojave National Preserve. There are three camps: a family camp across the street from a group camp and an equestrian camp. All are set at 4,400 feet in elevation. An interesting side trip is to the Mitchell Caverns in the nearby Providence Mountains State Recreation Area.

Campsites, facilities: There are 35 sites for tents or RVs of any length (no hookups), one group site for up to 50 people, and an equestrian camp. Picnic tables and fire grills are provided. Drinking water, vault toilets, and a dump station are available. Leashed pets are permitted.

Reservations, fees: Reservations are not accepted. Sites are $12 per night. Make reservations for group camp and horse camp at 760/928-2572; $25 per night, including horse corral if needed. Open year-round.

Directions: Drive on I-40 to Essex Road (near Essex, 116 miles east of Barstow). Take that exit and drive north on Essex Road for 10 miles to Black Canyon Road. Turn north and drive nine miles to the campgrounds.

Contact: Mojave National Preserve, 760/733-4040, fax 760/733-4027, www.nps.gov/moja.

30 RAINBO BEACH RV AND MOBILE HOME RESORT

Scenic rating: 6

on the Colorado River

Map 16.8, page 860

The big bonus here is the full marina, making this resort on the Colorado River the headquarters for boaters and water-skiers. And headquarters it is, with tons of happy folks who are extremely well lubed, both inside and out. This resort boasts 800 feet of river frontage. A 70-site mobile home park is adjacent to the RV park. (For boating details, see the next listing, *Needles Marina Park*.)

Campsites, facilities: There are 64 sites with full hookups (30 and 50 amps) for RVs, a grassy area for tents, and three park-model cabins. Some sites are pull-through. Picnic tables are provided. Restrooms with showers, coin laundry, heated swimming pool, spa, recreation room, and a restaurant are available. A boat dock is available nearby. Leashed pets are permitted.

Reservations, fees: Reservations are accepted. Sites are $25–28 per night, and $16 per night for tents. Seasonal rates available. Some credit cards accepted. Open year-round.

Directions: Drive on I-40 to Needles and River Road. Turn north on River Road and drive 1.5 miles to the resort on the right.

Contact: Rainbo Beach RV and Mobile Home Resort, 760/326-3101, fax 760/326-5085.

31 NEEDLES MARINA PARK

Scenic rating: 6

on the Colorado River

Map 16.8, page 860

Bring your suntan lotion and a beach towel. This section of the Colorado River is a big tourist spot where the body oil and beer can flow faster than the river. There are a ton of hot bodies and hot boats, and waterskiing dominates the adjacent calm-water section of the Colorado River. However, note that upstream of the Needles-area put-in is the prime area for waterskiing. Downstream is the chance for canoeing or kayaking. Meanwhile, there's also an 18-hole golf course adjacent to the camp, but most folks head for the river. Compared to the surrounding desert, this park is almost a golden paradise. A mobile home park is adjacent to the RV park.

Campsites, facilities: There are 158 sites with full hookups (30 and 50 amps) for tents or RVs, and six cabins. Some sites are pull-through. Picnic tables are provided. Restrooms with flush toilets and showers, drinking water, heated pool, spa, recreation room, Wi-Fi, modem access, playground, picnic area, boat ramp, boat slips, store, gas, and laundry facilities are available. Leashed pets are permitted.

Reservations, fees: Reservations are accepted. Sites are $30–32 per night, $3.50 per night for air conditioning, $2.50 per pet per night. Some credit cards accepted. Open year-round.

Directions: Drive on I-40 to Needles and the exit for J Street. Take that exit and drive to Broadway. Turn left on Broadway and drive 0.75 mile to Needles Highway. Turn right (north) on Needles Highway and drive 0.5 mile to the park on the left.

Contact: Needles Marina Park, 760/326-2197, fax 760/326-4125, www.needlesmarinapark .com.

32 NEEDLES KOA

Scenic rating: 2

near the Colorado River

Map 16.8, page 860

At least you've got the Needles KOA out here, complete with swimming pool, where you can get a new start. Side trips include venturing to the nearby Colorado River or heading north to Lake Mead. Of course, you could always go to Las Vegas. Nah.

Campsites, facilities: There are 93 pull-through sites with full hookups (30 and 50 amps), and 18 pull-through sites with partial hookups (30 and 50 amps) for tents or RVs of any length. Five cabins are also available. Restrooms with flush toilets and showers, drinking water, recreation room, swimming pool, playground, store, snack bar, propane gas, and coin laundry are available. Some facilities are wheelchair-accessible. Leashed pets are permitted.

Reservations, fees: Reservations are accepted at 800/562-3407. Sites are $22–32 per night, $2 per person per night for more than two

people. Some credit cards accepted. Open year-round.

Directions: Drive on I-40 to Needles and the exit for West Broadway. Take that exit to Needles Highway. Turn northwest on Needles Highway and drive 0.75 mile to National Old Trails Highway. Turn left and drive one mile to the park on the right (5400 National Old Trails Highway).

Contact: Needles KOA, 760/326-4207, fax 760/326-6329, www.koa.com.

33 MOABI REGIONAL PARK

Scenic rating: 7

on the Colorado River

Map 16.8, page 860   BEST (

Campsites are situated in the main area of the park along 2.5 miles of shoreline peninsula. One of the features here is 24 group areas. The adjacent Colorado River provides the main attraction, the only thing liquid around these parts that isn't contained in a can or bottle. The natural response when you see it is to jump in the water and everybody does so, with or without a boat. You'll see lots of wild and crazy types having the times of their lives on the water. The boating season is a long one here, courtesy of that desert climate. Fishing is good here for catfish, smallmouth bass, bluegill, striped bass, and sometimes crappie.

Campsites, facilities: There is a large grassy area for tents and more than 600 sites for RVs or tents—155 with full or partial hookups (20, 30, and 50 amps), and a few are pull-through. There are also 24 group camping areas. Picnic tables and fire grills are provided at most sites. Restrooms with flush toilets and showers, coin laundry, store, ice, dump station, covered picnic area, marina, bait, and a boat ramp are available. Volleyball, basketball, horseshoes, and putting green are also available. An 18-hole golf course is nearby. Some facilities are wheelchair-accessible. Leashed pets are permitted.

Reservations, fees: Reservations are accepted. Sites are $15–35 per night per vehicle, $1 per night per pet. Long-term rates available in the winter, with limit of five months. Some credit cards accepted. Open year-round.

Directions: From Needles, drive east on I-40 for 11 miles to Park Moabi Road. Turn left on Park Moabi Road and continue 0.5 mile to the park entrance at the end of the road.

Contact: Moabi Regional Park Marina, 760/326-3831, fax 760/326-3272; San Bernardino County, 760/326-4777, www.co.san-bernardino.ca.us/parks/moabi.htm.

34 HAVASU LANDING RESORT AND CASINO

🏊 🛥 ⛴ 🐾 🚐 🅰

Scenic rating: 6

on western shore of Lake Havasu

Map 16.8, page 860   **BEST (**

Situated on the western shore of Lake Havasu, this full-service resort is run by the Chemehuevi Indian Tribe. It even includes a casino with slot machines and a card room. The resort is situated in a desert landscape in the Chemehuevi Valley. A boat shuttle operates from the resort to the London Bridge and Havasu City, Arizona. A mobile-home park is within the resort and an airstrip is nearby. Some of the RV sites are rented for the entire winter. Permits are required for off-road vehicles and can be obtained at the resort. This is one of the most popular boating areas in the southwestern United States. The lake is 45 miles long, covers 19,300 acres, and is at the low elevation of 482 feet. Havasu was created when the Parker Dam was built across the Colorado River.

Campsites, facilities: There are 180 sites with full hookups (30 and 50 amps) for RVs up to 35 feet, three large tent camping areas, and mobile home and RV rentals. Picnic tables, restrooms with flush toilets and showers, a dump station, a coin laundry, picnic areas, a restaurant and lounge, a casino, 24-hour security, 24-hour marina with gas dock, bait and tackle, a general store and deli, boat launches, boat slips, a fish-cleaning room, dry storage, a boat shuttle, and a boat launch and retrieval service are available. An airport is nearby. Leashed pets are permitted.

Reservations, fees: Reservations are accepted at 800/307-3610. Sites are $25–$30 per night for RV sites, $15–$20 per night for tent sites, $2 per person per night for more than two people, and $6 per night for each additional vehicle. Holiday rates are higher. Weekly and monthly rates are available. A boat-launch fee is charged. Some credit cards accepted. Two ATMs are on-site. Open year-round.

Directions: From Needles, drive south on Highway 95 for 19 miles to Havasu Lake Road. Turn left and drive 17.5 miles to the resort on the right.

From Blythe, drive north on Highway 95 for 79 miles to Havasu Lake Road. Turn right and drive 17.5 miles to the resort on the right.

Contact: Havasu Landing Resort and Casino, 760/858-4593 or 800/307-3610, www.havasulanding.com. For general information about Lake Havasu, contact the Lake Havasu Tourism Bureau, 928/453-3444 or 800/2-HAVASU (800/242-8278), www.golakehavasu.com; Lake Havasu Area Chamber of Commerce, 928/855-4115, www.havasuchamber.com.

35 BLACK MEADOW LANDING

🏊 🛥 ⛴ 🐾 🚐 🅰

Scenic rating: 6

south of Lake Havasu on the Colorado River

Map 16.8, page 860

This area of the Colorado River attracts a lot of people so reservations are highly recommended. Hot weather, warm water, and proximity to Las Vegas make this one of the top camping and boating hot spots in the West. Vacationers are here year-round, although fewer people use it in the late winter. Black Meadow Landing is a large resort with hundreds of RV sites, lodging, and a long list of amenities. Once you arrive, everything you need for a stay should be available within the resort.

Campsites, facilities: There are 350 sites with full hookups (30 amps) for RVs up to 40 feet and tent camping is available. Park-model cabins, kitchen cabins, and a motel are also available. Restrooms with flush toilets and showers, drinking water, picnic tables, picnic areas, horseshoe pit, a restaurant, a convenience store, a recreation room (winter only), bait and tackle, propane, a full-service marina, a boat launch, boat slips, boat and RV storage, a swimming lagoon, and a five-hole golf course are available. Leashed pets are permitted.

Reservations, fees: Reservations are accepted at 800/7-HAVASU (800/742-8278). Sites are $25–$52 per night, $6 per person per night for more than two people, $25 per night for tent sites, and $6 per night for each additional vehicle. Monthly rates are available. Some credit cards accepted. Open year-round.

Directions: From Southern California, take I-10 east to Blythe and turn north on U.S. 95. Continue to Vidal Junction at the intersection of U.S. 95 and Highway 62. Turn east on Highway 62 and drive to Earp and Parker Dam Road. Continue straight on Parker Dam Road and drive to a Y intersection and Black Meadow Landing Road (near Parker Dam). Bear left on Black Meadow Landing Road and drive approximately nine miles to the resort at the end of the road.

From Northern California, drive to Barstow and I-40. Turn east on I-40 and drive to Needles. Continue east on I-40 to Arizona Highway 95. Drive south on Arizona Highway 95 to Lake Havasu City. Continue south to the Parker Dam turnoff. Turn west and drive across the dam to a Y intersection and Black Meadow Landing Road. Bear right on Black Meadow Landing Road and drive approximately nine miles to the resort at the end of the road. Note: Towed vehicles are not allowed to cross the dam.

Contact: Black Meadow Landing, 760/663-4901, www.blackmeadowlanding.com. For general information about the Colorado River and Lake Havasu, contact the Lake Havasu Tourism Bureau, 928/453-3444 or 800/2-HAVASU (800/242-8278), www.golakehavasu.com; Lake Havasu Area Chamber of Commerce, 928/855-4115, www.havasuchamber.com.

36 RIVERLAND RESORT

Scenic rating: 6

on the Colorado River near Parker Dam

Map 16.8, page 860

This resort is in the middle of a very popular boating area, particularly for waterskiing. Summer is the busiest time here because of the sunshine and warm water. In the winter, even though temperatures can get pretty cold, around 40°F at night, the campground fills with retirees from the snow and rain country. Even though the resort is way out there on the Colorado River, there are plenty of services, including a convenience store, swimming beach, and full-service marina. Insider's tip: One of the best spots for catfish is a few miles down the road below Parker Dam.

Campsites, facilities: There are 60 sites with full hookups (50 amps) for RVs up to 40 feet. Picnic tables are provided. Tent camping and park-model cabins are available. Restrooms with flush toilets and showers, drinking water, cable television, Wi-Fi, a convenience store, a coin laundry, a full-service marina, a boat launch, boat slips, boat and RV storage, a swimming beach, a fishing pier, bait, a recreation room (winter only), and horseshoe pits are available. An ATM is within five miles and an 18-hole golf course is seven miles away. Leashed pets are permitted.

Reservations, fees: Reservations are accepted at 760/663-3733. Sites are $26 per night, $2 per person per night in summer, and $2 per pet per night. Monthly rates are available. Some credit cards accepted. Open year-round.

Directions: From Southern California, take I-10 east to Blythe and turn north on U.S. 95.

Continue to Vidal Junction at the intersection of U.S. 95 and Highway 62. Turn east on Highway 62 and drive to Earp and Parker Dam Road. Continue straight on Parker Dam Road and drive five miles to the resort on the right.
Contact: RiverLand Resort, 760/663-3733.

37 LOST LAKE RESORT

Scenic rating: 6

on the Colorado River in Parker Valley

Map 16.8, page 860

If you're looking for a remote spot on the Colorado River, this is it. This is kind of like an oasis in the middle of the desert. Direct access to the Colorado River is provided, and this is one of the few places around that sell fishing licenses for this stretch of the Colorado River. The Parker Valley section of the river is part of the Colorado River Indian Reservation, and the tribe requires that all anglers obtain a permit. One of the best spots for big catfish, including large flathead catfish and channel catfish, is below Parker Dam. If you catch a razorback sucker, a rare event, it must be released. It is an endangered species. Note that about half of the sites are filled with long-term or permanent renters.

Campsites, facilities: There are 150 sites with full hookups (30 amps). Tent camping is available. Picnic tables are provided at most sites. Restrooms with flush toilets, showers, a coin laundry, a convenience store, a café, recreation room (winter only), boat and RV storage, a boat launch, bait and tackle, fishing licenses, and a full-service marina are available. Leashed pets are permitted.

Reservations, fees: Reservations are accepted at 760/664-4413. Sites are $30 per night per vehicle. Monthly rates are available in winter. Some credit cards accepted. Open year-round.

Directions: From Southern California, take I-10 east to Blythe and turn north on U.S. 95. Drive for 31 miles to the resort on the right.

Contact: Lost Lake Resort, 760/664-4413.

38 HIDDEN VALLEY

Scenic rating: 7

in Joshua Tree National Park

Map 16.9, page 861

This is one of California's top campgrounds for rock-climbers. Set at 4,200 feet in the high desert country, this is one of several camping options in the area. A trailhead is available two miles from camp at Barker Dam, an easy one-mile loop that features the Wonderland of Rocks. The hike takes you next to a small lake with magical reflections of rock formations off its surface. The RV sites here are snatched up quickly and this campground fills almost daily with rock-climbers.

Campsites, facilities: There are 45 sites for tents or RVs up to 25 feet (no hookups). Picnic tables and fire grills are provided. Vault toilets are available. No drinking water is available. Leashed pets are permitted.

Reservations, fees: No reservations are accepted. Sites are $5 per night, and $15 park entrance fee per vehicle. Open year-round.

Directions: From the junction of I-10 and Highway 62 near Palm Springs, drive northeast on Highway 62 for 22 miles to Yucca Valley, then continue to the small town of Joshua Tree and Park Boulevard. Turn south on Park Boulevard and drive 14 miles to the campground on the left.

Contact: Joshua Tree National Park, 760/367-5500, fax 760/367-6392, www.nps.gov/jotr.

39 RYAN

Scenic rating: 4

in Joshua Tree National Park

Map 16.9, page 861

This is one of the high desert camps in the immediate area (see also the *Jumbo Rocks* listing in this chapter). Joshua Tree National Park is a forbidding paradise: huge, hot, and waterless (most of the time). The unique rock formations look as if some great artist made them with a chisel. The elevation is 4,300 feet. The best hike in the park starts here—a three-mile round-trip to Ryan Mountain is a 1,000-foot climb to the top at 5,470 feet. The view is simply drop-dead gorgeous, not only of San Jacinto, Tahquitz, and San Gorgonio peaks, but of several beautiful rock-studded valleys as well as the Wonderland of Rocks.

Campsites, facilities: There are 31 sites for tents or RVs up to 25 feet (no hookups). Picnic tables and fire grills are provided. Vault toilets are available. No drinking water is available. Hitching posts are available (bring water for the horses). Leashed pets are permitted.

Reservations, fees: Reservations are accepted for equestrian sites only at 760/367-5541. Sites are $5 per night, and there is a $15 park entrance fee per vehicle. Open year-round.

Directions: From the junction of I-10 and Highway 62 near Palm Springs, drive northeast on Highway 62 to Twentynine Palms and Utah Trail. Turn right (south) on Utah Trail and drive about 20 miles to the campground entrance on the left.

Contact: Joshua Tree National Park, 760/367-5500, fax 760/367-6392, www.nps.gov/jotr.

40 SHEEP PASS GROUP CAMP
🏃 🐕 🚐 ⛺

Scenic rating: 4

in Joshua Tree National Park

Map 16.9, page 861

Several campgrounds are in this stretch of high desert. Ryan campground (see previous listing), just a couple of miles down the road, has an excellent trailhead for a trek to Ryan Mountain, the best hike in the park. Temperatures are routinely over 100°F here in the summer. (For details on this area, see the *White Tank* listing in this chapter.)

Campsites, facilities: There are six group camps for tents or RVs up to 25 feet (no hookups) that can accommodate 20–50 people each. Picnic tables and fire grills are provided. Vault toilets are available. No drinking water is available. Leashed pets are permitted.

Reservations, fees: Reservations are accepted at 800/365-CAMP (800/365-2267) or at http://reservations.nps.gov. Sites are $20–35 per night, plus $15 park entrance fee per vehicle. Open year-round.

Directions: From the junction of I-10 and Highway 62 near Palm Springs, drive northeast on Highway 62 to Twentynine Palms and Utah Trail. Turn right (south) on Utah Trail and drive about 16 miles to the campground on the left.

Contact: Joshua Tree National Park, 760/367-5500, fax 760/367-6392, www.nps.gov/jotr.

41 JUMBO ROCKS
🏃 🐕 🚐 ⛺

Scenic rating: 4

in Joshua Tree National Park

Map 16.9, page 861

Joshua Tree National Park covers more than 1,238 square miles. It is striking high-desert country with unique granite formations that seem to change color at different times of the day. This camp is one of the higher ones in the park at 4,400 feet, with adjacent boulders and rock formations that look as if they have been strewn about by an angry giant. It is a popular site for rock-climbing.

Campsites, facilities: There are 125 sites for tents or RVs up to 35 feet (no hookups). Picnic tables and fire grills are provided. Vault toilets are available. No drinking water is available. Leashed pets are permitted.

Reservations, fees: Reservations are not accepted. Sites are $5, and there is a $15 park entrance fee per vehicle. Open year-round.

Directions: From the junction of I-10 and Highway 62 near Palm Springs, drive northeast on Highway 62 to Twentynine Palms and Utah Trail. Turn right (south) on Utah Trail and drive about nine miles to the campground on the left side of the road.
Contact: Joshua Tree National Park, 760/367-5500, fax 760/367-6392, www.nps.gov/jotr.

42 SAM'S FAMILY SPA

Scenic rating: 3

near Palm Springs

Map 16.9, page 861

Hot mineral pools attract swarms of winter vacationers to the Palm Springs area. The therapeutic pools are partially enclosed. This 50-acre park, set 13 miles outside of Palm Springs, provides an alternative to the more crowded spots. And this is one of the few parks in the area that allows tent campers. A mobile-home park is adjacent to the RV park. The elevation of Sam's Family Spa is 1,000 feet. (For information on the tramway ride to Desert View west of Palm Springs, or the hike to Mount San Jacinto, see the next listing, *Sky Valley Resort.*)
Campsites, facilities: There are 170 sites for tents and RVs up to 42 feet (with full hookups of 30 and 50 amps). Four mobile-home rentals and a motel are also available. Picnic tables are provided. There is a separate area with barbecues. Restrooms with showers, playground, heated swimming pool, heated wading pool, four hot mineral pools, sauna, Wi-Fi, coin laundry, and a convenience store are available. Some facilities are wheelchair-accessible. Leashed pets are permitted in the campground only.
Reservations, fees: Reservations are accepted online only; no telephone reservations. Sits are $38 per night. Weekly and monthly rates available. Some credit cards accepted. Open year-round.
Directions: Drive on I-10 to the Palm Springs

Area and the Palm Drive exit (to Desert Hot Springs). Take that exit and drive north on Palm Drive for about two miles to Dillon Road. Turn right (east) on Dillon Road and drive 4.5 miles to the park on the right (70–875 Dillon Road).
Contact: Sam's Family Spa, 760/329-6457, fax 760/329-8267, www.samsfamilyspa.com.

43 SKY VALLEY RESORT

Scenic rating: 2

near Palm Springs

Map 16.9, page 861

This 140-acre park is much like a small town, complete with RV homes, an RV park, and park-model rentals and seasonal restaurants. One of the best adventures in California is just west of Palm Springs, taking the aerial tram up from Chino Canyon to Desert View, a ride/climb of 2,600 feet for remarkable views to the east across the desert below. An option from there is hiking the flank of Mount San Jacinto, including making the ascent to the summit (10,804 feet), a round-trip butt-kicker of nearly 12 miles. Golf courses are nearby.
Campsites, facilities: There are 618 sites with full hookups (30 amps) for RVs up to 42 feet. No tents allowed. Restrooms with showers, cable TV, four swimming pools, nine natural hot mineral whirlpools, two laundry rooms, two large recreation rooms, fitness centers, children's playroom, seasonal grocery store, chapel program, seasonal tennis and golf lessons, business center with modem access, Wi-Fi, social director, shuffleboard, tennis, horseshoes, crafts room, and walking paths are available. Propane gas is nearby. Some facilities are wheelchair-accessible. Leashed pets are permitted.
Reservations, fees: Reservations are accepted at 888/893-7727 or by website. Sites are $38–39.50 per night, $5 per person per night for more than two people. Monthly rates

available. Some credit cards accepted. Open year-round.

Directions: Drive on I-10 to the Palm Springs area and the Palm Drive exit (to Desert Hot Springs). Take that exit and drive north on Palm Drive for three miles to Dillon Road. Turn right on Dillon Road and drive 8.5 miles to the park on the right (74–711 Dillon Road).

Contact: Sky Valley Resort, 760/329-2909, fax 760/329-9473, www.skyvalleyresort.com.

44 HAPPY TRAVELER RV PARK

Scenic rating: 1

in Palm Springs

Map 16.9, page 861

Are we having fun yet? They are at Happy Traveler, which is within walking distance of Palm Springs shopping areas and restaurants. The Palm Springs Air Museum has a collection of World War II aircraft. A casino is one mile away.

Campsites, facilities: There are 130 sites with full hookups (30 and 50 amps) for RVs up to 40 feet. No tents or tent trailers. Picnic tables are provided. Restrooms with showers, cable TV, swimming pool, spa, clubhouse, shuffleboard, propane, seasonal activities, and coin laundry are available. Leashed pets are permitted.

Reservations, fees: Reservations are accepted. Sites are $35.50 per night. Monthly rates available. Credit cards are not accepted. Open year-round.

Directions: Drive on I-10 to Palm Springs and Highway 111/Palm Canyon Drive. Take Palm Canyon Drive and drive 12 miles south to Mesquite Avenue. Turn right on Mesquite Avenue and drive to the park on the left (211 West Mesquite).

Contact: Happy Traveler RV Park, 760/325-8518, fax 760/778-6708, www.happytravelerrv.com.

45 OUTDOOR RESORT OF PALM SPRINGS

Scenic rating: 6

near Palm Springs

Map 16.9, page 861

This is considered a five-star resort, beautifully landscaped, huge, and offering many activities: swimming pools galore, 27-hole golf course, tons of tennis courts, spas, and on and on. The 137-acre park is four miles from Palm Springs. Note that this is a lot-ownership park with lots for sale. About a quarter of the sites are available for rent to vacationers. One of the best adventures in California is just west of Palm Springs, taking the aerial tram up from Chino Canyon to Desert View, a ride/climb of 2,600 feet for remarkable views to the east across the desert below.

Campsites, facilities: There are 1,213 sites with full hookups (50 amps) for RVs up to 45 feet. No tent camping. RV rentals are also available. Restrooms with showers, eight swimming pools, spas, 14 lighted tennis courts, 27-hole golf course, two clubhouses, a snack bar, café, a beauty salon, coin laundry, Wi-Fi, modem access, convenience store, shuffleboard, and planned activities are available. Some facilities are wheelchair-accessible. Leashed pets are permitted.

Reservations, fees: Reservations are accepted at 800/843-3131 (California only). Sites are $60–70 per night, $1 per pet per night with a two-pet maximum. RV rentals are $85–115 per night. Some credit cards accepted. Open year-round.

Directions: Drive on I-10 to the Palm Springs area and continue to Cathedral City and the exit for Date Palm Drive. Take that exit and drive south on Date Palm Drive for two miles to Ramon Road. Turn left and drive to the resort on the right (69–411 Ramon Road).

Contact: Outdoor Resort, 760/324-4005, www.outdoorresort.com.

46 PALM SPRINGS OASIS RV PARK

Scenic rating: 2

in Cathedral City

Map 16.9, page 861

This popular wintering spot is for RV cruisers looking to hole up in the Palm Springs area for awhile. Palm Springs is only six miles away. This is a seniors-only park, meaning that you need to be at the magic age of 55 or above to qualify for a stay.

Campsites, facilities: There are 140 sites with full hookups (30 and 50 amps) for RVs up to 45 feet. No tents. Restrooms with showers, cable TV, Wi-Fi, modem access, two swimming pools, spa, tennis courts, coin laundry, and propane gas are available. An 18-hole golf course is adjacent to the park. Some facilities are wheelchair-accessible. Children and people under age 55 are not allowed. Leashed pets are permitted, with a two-pet maximum.

Reservations, fees: Reservations are accepted. Sites are $41 per night, $2 per person per night for more than two people. Weekly and monthly rates available. Some credit cards accepted. Open year-round.

Directions: Drive on I-10 to the Palm Springs area and continue to Cathedral City and the exit for Date Palm Drive. Take that exit and drive south on Date Palm Drive for four miles to Gerald Ford Drive and the park on the left corner (36–100 Date Palm Drive).

Contact: Palm Springs Oasis RV Park, 760/328-4813 or 800/680-0144, fax 760/328-8455.

47 INDIAN WELLS RV PARK

Scenic rating: 2

in Indio

Map 16.9, page 861

Indio is a good-sized town midway between the Salton Sea to the south and Palm Springs to the north, which is about 20 miles away. In the summer, it is one of the hottest places in America. In the winter, it is a favorite for "snowbirds," that is, RV and trailer owners from the snow country who migrate south for the winter. About half of the sites are filled with long-term renters.

Campsites, facilities: There are 381 sites with full hookups (50 amps) for RVs up to 45 feet; most are pull-through. No tents. Restrooms with showers, cable TV, Wi-Fi, three swimming pools, two therapy pools, horseshoes, basketball, volleyball, shuffleboard courts, putting green, planned activities, ice, dog run, picnic area, and coin laundry are available. Some facilities are wheelchair-accessible. Leashed pets are permitted, with a maximum of two.

Reservations, fees: Reservations are accepted at 800/789-0895. Sites are $41 per night, $2.50 per person per night for more than two people. Weekly and monthly rates available. Some credit cards accepted. Open year-round.

Directions: Drive on I-10 to Indio and the exit for Jefferson Street. Take that exit, stay in the right lane, and drive to the light at Jefferson. Turn right at Jefferson and drive south for three miles to the park on the left (47–340 Jefferson Street).

Contact: Indian Wells RV Park, 760/347-0895, fax 760/775-1147.

48 OUTDOOR RESORTS INDIO

Scenic rating: 7

in Indio

Map 16.9, page 861

For owners of tour buses, motor coaches, and lavish RVs, it doesn't get any better than this in Southern California. Only RVers in Class A motor homes are allowed here. This resort bills itself as the "ultimate RV resort" and has been featured on the Travel Channel and in the *Wall Street Journal*. About 25 percent of the sites are available for rent; the other sites are owned by RVers. This park is set close to golf, shopping, and restaurants. Jeep tours of the surrounding desert canyons and organized recreation events are available.

Campsites, facilities: There are 419 sites with full hookups (50 amps) for Class A motor homes with a minimum length of 28 feet. No trailers or pickup-truck campers. Restrooms with showers, cable TV, Wi-Fi, modem access, swimming pools, tennis courts, sauna, spas, massage service, hair salon, café, fitness center, clubhouse, coin laundry, and an 18-hole golf course are available. Some facilities are wheelchair-accessible. Leashed pets are permitted, with a two-pet maximum.

Reservations, fees: Reservations are accepted. The winter rates are $60–70 per night, summer rates are $40–50 per night, $5 per night for electricity. Some credit cards accepted. Open year-round.

Directions: Drive on I-10 to Indio and the exit for Indio Boulevard/Jefferson Street. Take that exit, stay in the right lane, and drive to the light at Jefferson. Turn right at Jefferson and drive south for three miles to Avenue 48. Turn left and drive 0.25 mile to the park on the left side of the road (80–394 Avenue 48).

Contact: Outdoor Resorts Indio, 760/775-7255 or 800/892-2992 (outside California), www.outdoor-resorts-indio.com.

49 TOOL BOX SPRING
Scenic rating: 5

in San Bernardino National Forest

Map 16.9, page 861

This is a lightly used campground well off the beaten track. More like off the beaten universe. That makes it perfect for people who want to be by themselves when they go camping. Ramona Trail begins at the campground, heads out to the north, and provides a 3.5-mile one-way hike, with a 1,500-foot loss and then gain in elevation. In the winter, call for road conditions to determine accessibility. The elevation is 6,500 feet.

Campsites, facilities: There are six tent sites as well as disbursed camping. Picnic tables and fire grills are provided. Vault toilets are available. Drinking water is available intermittently; check for current status. Garbage must be packed out. Leashed pets are permitted.

Reservations, fees: No reservations accepted and there is no camping fee. An Adventure Pass ($30 annual fee or $5 daily pass per parked vehicle) is required. Open year-round, but subject to closure during fire season.

Directions: From Hemet, drive east on Highway 74 into San Bernardino National Forest and continue just past Lake Hemet to Forest Road 6S13. Turn right on Forest Road 6S13 (paved, then dirt) and drive four miles to a fork. Bear left at the fork and continue on Forest Road 6S13 for 4.5 miles to the camp on the left.

Contact: San Bernardino National Forest, San Jacinto Ranger District, 909/382-2921, fax 951/659-2107.

50 PINYON FLAT
Scenic rating: 6

near Cahuilla Tewanet Vista Point in San Bernardino National Forest

Map 16.9, page 861

The Cahuilla Tewanet Vista Point is just two miles east of the camp and provides a good, easy side trip, along with a sweeping view to the east of the desert on clear days. A primitive trail is available two miles away to the southeast via Forest Road 7S01 off a short spur road (look for it on the left side of the road). This hike crosses a mix of sparse forest and high-desert terrain for 10 miles, passing Cactus Spring five miles in. Desert bighorn sheep are sometimes spotted in this area. The elevation is 4,000 feet.

Campsites, facilities: There are 18 sites for tents or RVs up to 15 feet (no hookups). Picnic tables and fire rings are provided. Drinking water and vault toilets are available. Some facilities are wheelchair-accessible. Leashed pets are permitted.

Reservations, fees: Reservations are not accepted. Sites are $8 per night. Open year-round.

Directions: Drive on I-10 to Palm Springs and Highway 111. Turn south on Highway 111 and drive to Rancho Mirage and Highway 74. Turn right (south) on Highway 74 and drive 14 miles (a slow, twisty road) to the campground on the right.

Contact: San Bernardino National Forest, San Jacinto Ranger District, 909/382-2921, fax 951/659-2107.

51 LAKE CAHUILLA COUNTY PARK

Scenic rating: 7

near Indio

Map 16.9, page 861

Lake Cahuilla covers just 135 acres, but those are the most loved 135 acres for miles in all directions. After all, water out here is as scarce as polar bears. This 710-acre Riverside County park provides large palm trees and a 10-acre beach and water-play area. In the winter it is stocked with trout, and in the summer, with catfish. Other species include largemouth and striped bass, crappie, and carp to 30 pounds. No swimming is allowed. Only car-top boats are permitted (no gas motors), and a speed limit of 10 mph is enforced. An equestrian camp is also available, complete with corrals. Equestrian and hiking trails are available on nearby public land. Morrow Trail is popular, and the trailhead is near the park's ranger station. A warning: The wind can really howl through here, and temperatures well over 100°F are typical in the summer.

Campsites, facilities: There are 55 sites with partial hookups (30 and 50 amps) and 10 sites with no hookups for RVs, a primitive camping area with no hookups for tents or RVs, and a large group area with horse corrals. Maximum RV length is 45 feet. Fire grills and picnic tables are provided. Restrooms with showers, dump station, seasonal swimming pool, and a primitive (hand-launch) beach boat launch are available. No gas motors are allowed. Some facilities are wheelchair-accessible. Leashed pets are permitted.

Reservations, fees: Reservations are accepted ($7.50 reservation fee) at 800/234-PARK (800/234-7275). Sites are $13–18 per night, $1 per pet per night. Weekly rates are available during the winter. Maximum stay is two weeks. Some credit cards accepted. Open year-round, closed Tuesday, Wednesday, and Thursday from May through October.

Directions: Drive on I-10 to Indio and the exit for Monroe Street. Take that exit and drive south on Monroe Street to Avenue 58. Turn right (west) and drive two miles to the park at the end of the road.

Contact: Lake Cahuilla County Park, 760/564-4712, fax 760/564-2506, www.riversidecountyparks.org.

52 BELLE

Scenic rating: 4

in Joshua Tree National Park

Map 16.10, page 862

This camp is at 3,800 feet in rocky high country. It is one of six camps in the immediate area. (For more details, see the next listing, *White Tank*.)

Campsites, facilities: There are 18 sites for tents or RVs up to 35 feet (no hookups). Picnic tables and fire grills are provided. Vault toilets are available. No drinking water is available. Leashed pets are permitted.

Reservations, fees: No reservations are

accepted. Sites are $5 per night, and there is a $15 park entrance fee per vehicle. Open year-round.

Directions: From the junction of I-10 and Highway 62 near Palm Springs, drive northeast on Highway 62 to Twentynine Palms and Utah Trail. Turn right (south) on Utah Trail and drive eight miles to Pinto Basin Road. Turn left (heading toward I-10) and drive about 1.5 miles to the campground on the left.

Contact: Joshua Tree National Park, 760/367-5500, fax 760/367-6392, www.nps.gov/jotr.

53 WHITE TANK
🚶 🐕 🚐 ⛺

Scenic rating: 4

in Joshua Tree National Park

Map 16.10, page 862

Joshua Tree National Park is a unique area where the high and low desert meet. Winter is a good time to explore the beautiful boulder piles and rock formations amid scraggly Joshua trees. There are several trails in the area, with the best near Black Rock Campground, Hidden Valley, and Cottonwood. The elevation is 3,800 feet.

Campsites, facilities: There are 15 sites for tents or RVs up to 25 feet (no hookups). Picnic tables and fire grills are provided. Vault toilets are available. No drinking water is available. Leashed pets are permitted.

Reservations, fees: No reservations are accepted. Sites are $5 per night, and there is $15 park entrance fee per vehicle. Open year-round.

Directions: From the junction of I-10 and Highway 62 near Palm Springs, drive northeast on Highway 62 to Twentynine Palms and Utah Trail. Turn right (south) on Utah Trail and drive eight miles to Pinto Basin Road. Turn left (heading toward I-10) and drive three miles to the campground on the left.

Contact: Joshua Tree National Park,

760/367-5500, fax 760/367-6392, www.nps.gov/jotr.

54 COTTONWOOD
🚶 🐕 ♿ 🚐 ⛺

Scenic rating: 4

in Joshua Tree National Park

Map 16.10, page 862

If you enter Joshua Tree National Park at its southern access point, this is the first camp you will reach. The park visitors center, where maps are available, is a mandatory stop. This park is vast, high-desert country, highlighted by unique rock formations, occasional scraggly trees, and vegetation that manages to survive the bleak, roasting summers. This camp is set at 3,000 feet. A trailhead is available here for an easy one-mile nature trail, where small signs have been posted to identify different types of vegetation. You'll notice, however, that they all look like cacti (the plants, not the signs, heh, heh).

Campsites, facilities: There are 62 sites for tents or RVs up to 35 feet (no hookups), and a group campground with three sites for 15–20 people each. Picnic tables and fire grills are provided. Drinking water and flush toilets are available. Some facilities are wheelchair-accessible. Leashed pets are permitted.

Reservations, fees: Reservations are accepted for group sites only at 800/365-CAMP (800/365-2267). Sites are $10 per night, and group sites are $25 per night. Park entrance fee is $15 per vehicle. Open year-round.

Directions: From Indio, drive east on I-10 for 35 miles to the exit for Pinto Basin Road/Twentynine Palms (near Chiriaco Summit). Take that exit and drive north for seven miles (entering the park) to the campground on the right.

Contact: Joshua Tree National Park, 760/367-5500, fax 760/367-6392, www.nps.gov/jotr.

55 HEADQUARTERS

Scenic rating: 5

in the Salton Sea State Recreation Area

Map 16.10, page 862

This is the northernmost camp on the shore of the giant Salton Sea, one of the campgrounds at the Salton Sea State Recreation Area. Salton Sea is a vast, shallow, and unique lake, the center of a 360-square mile basin and one of the world's inland seas. Salton Sea was created in 1905 when a dike broke, and in turn, the basin was flooded with saltwater. The lake is 35 miles long, but it has an average depth of just 15 feet. It is set at the recreation area headquarters, just south of the town of Desert Beach at an elevation of 227 feet below sea level. Fishing for tilapia is popular, and it is also one of Southern California's most popular boating areas. Because of the low altitude, atmospheric pressure allows high performance for many ski boats. If winds are hazardous, a red beacon on the northeast shore of the lake will flash. If you see it, get to the nearest shore. The Salton Sea is about a three-hour drive from Los Angeles. Use is moderate year-round, but lowest in the summer because of temperatures that can hover in the 110°F range for days.

Campsites, facilities: There are 25 sites with no hookups for tents or RVs, 15 with full hookups (30 amps) for RVs up to 40 feet, and several hike-in/bike-in sites. Picnic tables, fire grills, and shade ramadas are provided. Drinking water, restrooms with flush toilets and coin showers, dump station, fish cleaning station, and visitors center with Wi-Fi access are available. A store is within two miles. Some facilities are wheelchair-accessible. Leashed pets are permitted in the campgrounds and on roadways only.

Reservations, fees: Reservations are accepted ($7.50 reservation fee) at 800/444-PARK (800/444-7275) or www.reserveamerica.com. Sites are $12–23 per night, and $2 per person per night for hike-in/bike-in sites. Boat launching is $3 per day. Open year-round.

Directions: From the Los Angeles area, take I-10 east to Indio and the exit for the Highway 86 Expressway. Take that exit and drive south for 12 miles to 66th Avenue. Turn left and drive less than one mile to Mecca and Highway 111. Turn right (south) on Highway 111 and drive 12 miles to the entrance on the right.

Contact: Salton Sea State Recreation Area, 760/393-3052 or 760/393-3059, www.parks.ca.gov.

56 MECCA BEACH

Scenic rating: 4

in the Salton Sea State Recreation Area

Map 16.10, page 862

This is one of the camps set in the Salton Sea State Recreation Area on the northeastern shore of the lake. The big attractions here are the waterfront sites, which are not available at nearby Headquarters campground (see previous listing).

Campsites, facilities: There are 110 sites, 10 with full hookups (30 amps) for tents or RVs of any length, and several hike-in/bike-in sites. Picnic tables and fire grills are provided. Drinking water, restrooms with flush toilets and showers, amphitheater, and a fish cleaning station are available. A dump station is one mile north of Headquarters campground and a store is within 3.5 miles. Leashed pets are permitted in the campgrounds and roadways only.

Reservations, fees: Reservations are accepted ($7.50 reservation fee) at 800/444-PARK (800/444-7275) or www.reserveamerica.com. Sites are $12–23 per night, $3 per person per night for hike-in/bike-in sites. Boat launching is $3 per day. Open year-round.

Directions: From the Los Angeles area, take I-10 east to Indio and the exit for the Highway 86 Expressway. Take that exit and drive south for 12 miles to 66th Avenue. Turn left and drive less than one mile to Mecca and Highway 111. Turn right (south) on Highway 111 and drive 12.5 miles to the entrance on the right.

Contact: Salton Sea State Recreation Area,

760/393-3052 or 760/393-3059, www.parks
.ca.gov.

57 CORVINA BEACH

🚶 🚲 🏊 ⛵ 🚤 🐕 ♿ 🚗 ⛺

Scenic rating: 5

in the Salton Sea State Recreation Area

Map 16.10, page 862

This is by far the biggest of the campgrounds on
the Salton Sea. The campground is actually more
of an open area on hard-packed dirt, best for
parking an RV. (For details about the Salton Sea,
see the *Headquarters* listing in this chapter.)

Campsites, facilities: There are 250 primitive
sites in an open area for tents or RVs of any
length (no hookups) and some hike-in/bike-in
sites. Drinking water and chemical toilets are
available. Fires are permitted in metal containers only. A store and gas station are available
within five miles. Leashed pets are permitted
in the campground and on roadways only.

Reservations, fees: Reservations are not
accepted. Sites are $7 per night, $2 per person per night for hike-in/bike-in sites. Boat
launching is $3 per day. Open year-round.

Directions: From the Los Angeles area, take
I-10 east to Indio and the exit for the Highway
86 Expressway. Take that exit and drive south
for 12 miles to 66th Avenue. Turn left and
drive less than one mile to Mecca and Highway
111. Turn right (south) on Highway 111 and
drive 14 miles to the entrance on the right.

Contact: Salton Sea State Recreation Area,
760/393-3052 or 760/393-3059, www.parks
.ca.gov.

58 CORN SPRINGS

🚶 🐕 🚗 ⛺

Scenic rating: 4

in BLM desert

Map 16.10, page 862

Just think: If you spend a night here, you
can say to darn near anybody, "I've camped

someplace you haven't." I don't know whether
to offer my condolences or congratulations,
but Corn Springs offers a primitive spot in the
middle of nowhere in desert country. A 0.5-mile
interpretive trail here can easily be walked in
tennis shoes. It is divided into 11 stops with different vegetation, wildlife habitat, and cultural
notes at each stop. The side trip to Joshua Tree
National Park to the north (40-minute drive to
closest entrance) is also well worth the adventure, as is the aerial tram ride available west of
Palm Springs (one-hour drive there) for an incredible view of the desert. On the other hand,
if it's a summer afternoon, tell me, just how do
you spend the day here when it's 115°F?

Campsites, facilities: There are nine sites for
tents or RVs up to 22 feet (no hookups) and
one group site for tents or RVs (one or two
only) up to 22 feet that can accommodate
up to 25 people. Picnic tables and fire grills
are provided. Drinking water, shade ramadas,
and vault toilets are available. Leashed pets
are permitted.

Reservations, fees: Reservations are not
accepted. Sites are $6 per night. Open
year-round.

Directions: From Indio, drive east on I-10
for 60 miles to the Corn Springs Road exit.
Take that exit to Old Chuckwalla Valley Road.
Turn right (south) onto Old Chuckwalla Valley Road and drive 0.5 mile to Corn Springs
Road. Turn right and drive 10 miles on a dirt
road to the campground on the left.

Contact: Bureau of Land Management, Palm
Springs Field Office, 760/251-4800, fax
760/251-4899.

59 SALT CREEK PRIMITIVE AREA

🚶 🚲 🏊 ⛵ 🚤 🐕 ♿ 🚗 ⛺

Scenic rating: 4

in the Salton Sea State Recreation Area

Map 16.10, page 862

Waterfront campsites are a bonus at this
campground, even though the campground

consists of just an open area on hard-packed dirt. Birding hikes are available during winter months. Several trails leave from camp, or nearby the camp, and head 1–2 miles to the Bat Cave Buttes, which are in the Durmid Hills on Bureau of Land Management property. There are bats in the numerous caves to explore, although the nearby OHV traffic has reduced their numbers. From the buttes, which are up to 100 feet above sea level, hikers can see both the north and south ends of the Salton Sea simultaneously. This is the only easily accessible place to view both shores of the Salton Sea. Many people believe the buttes are the southernmost point of the San Andreas Fault; the fault does not exist above ground south of here. (For details on the Salton Sea State Recreation Area, see the *Headquarters* listing in this chapter.)

Campsites, facilities: There are 200 primitive sites for tents or RVs of any length (no hookups) and several hike-in/bike-in sites. Drinking water and chemical toilets are available. Fires are permitted in metal containers only. Leashed pets are permitted in the campgrounds and on roadways only.

Reservations, fees: Reservations are not accepted. Sites are $7 per night, $2 per person per night for hike-in/bike-in sites. Open year-round.

Directions: From the Los Angeles area, take I-10 east to Indio and the exit for the Highway 86 Expressway. Take that exit and drive south for 12 miles to 66th Avenue. Turn left and drive less than one mile to Mecca and Highway 111. Turn right (south) on Highway 111 and drive 17.5 miles to the entrance on the right.

Contact: Salton Sea State Recreation Area, 760/393-3052 or 760/393-3059, www.parks. ca.gov.

60 FOUNTAIN OF YOUTH SPA

Scenic rating: 4

near the Salton Sea

Map 16.10, page 862

Natural artesian steam rooms are the highlight here, but close inspection reveals that nobody seems to be getting any younger. This is a vast private park on 90 acres, set near the Salton Sea. Though this park has 1,000 sites for RVs, almost half of the sites have seasonal renters. This park is popular with snowbird campers and about 2,000 people live here during the winter. (See the *Red Hill Marina County Park* listing in this chapter for side-trip options.)

Campsites, facilities: There are 835 sites with full hookups (30 and 50 amps) and 165 sites with no hookups for tents or RVs. Restrooms with flush toilets and showers, cable TV, natural artesian steam rooms, swimming pools, artesian mineral water spa, three freshwater spas, recreation halls, dump stations, fitness room, library, picnic areas, nine-hole golf course, horseshoes, organized activities, craft and sewing room, Wi-Fi, modem access, coin laundry, barber shop, beauty parlor, masseur, church services, propane gas, and groceries are available. Some facilities are wheelchair-accessible. Leashed pets are permitted.

Reservations, fees: No reservations accepted. Winter rates are $15–29 per night, summer rates are $15–24 per night, $1 per person per night for more than two people. Weekly and monthly rates available. Some credit cards accepted. Open year-round.

Directions: From the Los Angeles area, take I-10 east to Indio and the exit for the Highway 86 Expressway. Take that exit and drive south for 12 miles to Avenue 62. Turn right and drive less than one mile to Mecca and Highway 111. Turn left (south) on Highway 111 and drive 44 miles to Hot Mineral Spa Road. Turn left (north) on Hot Mineral Spa Road and drive approximately four miles to Coachella Canal Road. Turn right and drive approximately 1.5 miles to the park on the left.

From Calipatria, drive north on Highway 111 to Niland, and then continue north for 15 miles to Hot Mineral Spa Road. Turn right (north) on Hot Mineral Spa Road and drive approximately four miles to Coachella Canal Road. Turn right and drive about 1.5 miles to the park on the left.

Contact: Fountain of Youth Spa, 888/8000-SPA (888/800-0772) or 760/354-1340, fax 760/354-1558, www.foyspa.com.

61 BOMBAY BEACH

🚶 🚲 ⛵ 🎣 🛶 🐕 ♿ 🚐 ⛺

Scenic rating: 5

in the Salton Sea State Recreation Area

Map 16.10, page 862

All in all, this is a strange-looking place, with the Salton Sea, a vast body of water, surrounded by stark, barren countryside. This camp is set in a bay along the northeastern shoreline, where a beach and nature trails are available. The campground is a flat, open area. Nearby to the south is the Wister Waterfowl Management Area. The Salton Sea is California's unique saltwater lake set below sea level, with fishing for tilapia a possibility.

Campsites, facilities: There are 200 sites for tents or RVs of any length (no hookups) and several hike-in/bike-in sites. Drinking water and chemical toilets are available. Fires are permitted in metal containers only. A store, restaurant, marina, and boat launch are available nearby in Bombay Beach. Leashed pets are permitted.

Reservations, fees: Reservations are not accepted. Sites are $7 per night, $2 per person per night for hike-in/bike-in sites. Open year-round.

Directions: From the Los Angeles area, take I-10 east to Indio and the exit for the Highway 86 Expressway. Take that exit and drive south for 12 miles to 66th Avenue. Turn left and drive less than one mile to Mecca and Highway 111. Turn right (south) on Highway

111 and drive 25 miles to the campground entrance on the right.

From Calipatria, drive north on Highway 111 to Niland, then continue north 18 miles to the entrance on the left.

Contact: Salton Sea State Recreation Area, 760/393-3052 or 760/393-3059, www.parks.ca.gov.

62 RED HILL MARINA COUNTY PARK

⛵ 🛶 🚤 🐕 🚐 ⛺

Scenic rating: 3

near the Salton Sea

Map 16.10, page 862

It's called Red Hill Marina, but you won't find a marina here; it washed away in the mid-1970s. This county park is near the south end of the Salton Sea, one of the weirdest places on earth. Set 228 feet below sea level, it's a vast body of water covering 360 square miles, 35 miles long, but with an average depth of just 15 feet. It's an extremely odd place to swim, as you bob around effortlessly in the highly saline water. Note that swimming is not recommended in this park because of the muddy shore. Fishing is often good for corvina in spring and early summer. Hundred of species of birds stop by this area as they travel along the Pacific Flyway. Several wildlife refuges are in the immediate area, including two separate chunks of the Imperial Wildfowl Management Area, to the west and south, and the huge Wister Waterfowl Management Area, northwest of Niland. (For side-trip options, see the previous listing, *Bombay Beach*.)

Campsites, facilities: There are 40 sites for RVs or tents; some sites have partial hookups. Picnic tables, cabanas, and barbecue pits are provided. Restrooms with flush toilets and showers, a concession stand, beer, bait, fishing and hunting licenses and a boat launch are available. The water at this park is not certified for drinking. Leashed pets are permitted.

Reservations, fees: Reservations are not

accepted. Sites are $7–12 per night, $2 per night for each additional vehicle, with a 14-day limit. Open year-round.

Directions: From Mecca, drive south on Highway 111 to Niland, and continue to Sinclair Road. Turn right and drive 3.5 miles to Garst Road. Turn right and drive 1.5 miles to the end of Garst Road at Red Hill Road. Turn left on Red Hill Road and drive to the park at the end of the road.

From El Centro, drive north on Highway 111 to Brawley and Highway 78/Main Street. Turn west (left) on Highway 78/Main Street and drive a short distance to Highway 111. Turn right (north) and drive to Calipatria. Continue north on Highway 111 just outside of Calipatria to Sinclair Road. Turn left on Sinclair Road and drive to Garst Road. Turn right and drive 1.5 miles to where it ends at Red Hill Road. Turn left at Red Hill Road and drive to the end of the road and the marina and the campground.

Contact: Red Hill Marina, tel./fax 760/348-2310; Imperial County, 760/482-4384.

Campsites, facilities: There are 20 tent sites and 24 sites with full hookups (50 amps) for RVs up to 45 feet. Picnic tables and fire grills are provided. There is no drinking water. Restrooms with flush toilets and showers, a boat ramp, and a dump station are available. A store, coin laundry, and propane gas are available within five miles. Leashed pets are permitted.

Reservations, fees: Reservations are not accepted. Sites are $7–12 per night, $2 per night for each additional vehicle. Open year-round.

Directions: From El Centro, drive north on Highway 111 to Brawley and Highway 78/Main Street. Turn west (left) on Highway 78/Main Street and drive a short distance to Highway 111. Turn right (north) on Highway 111 and drive four miles to Rutherford Road (well signed). Turn right (east) and drive two miles to the park entrance on the right.

Contact: Wiest Lake County Park, tel./fax 760/344-3712; Imperial County, 760/482-4384.

63 WIEST LAKE COUNTY PARK

Scenic rating: 4

on Wiest Lake

Map 16.10, page 862

This is a developed county park along the southern shore of Wiest Lake, which adjoins the Imperial Wildfowl Management Area to the north. Wiest Lake is just 50 acres, set 110 feet below sea level, and a prized area with such desolate country in the surrounding region. Waterskiing and sailboarding can be excellent, although few take advantage of the latter. Swimming is allowed when lifeguards are on duty. The lake is most popular for fishing, with trout planted in winter and catfish in summer. The lake also has bass and bluegill. The Salton Sea, about a 20-minute drive to the northwest, is a worthy side trip.

64 MIDLAND LONG TERM VISITOR AREA

Scenic rating: 4

west of Blythe

Map 16.11, page 863

Like its neighbor to the south (Mule Mountain), this camp is attractive to snowbirds, rockhounds (geodes and agates can be collected), and stargazers. The campground is on the southwest slope of the Big Maria Mountains, a designated wilderness, set at an elevation of 250 feet. The campsites are situated on flattened desert pavements consisting of alluvium. The desert landscape is extremely stark.

Campsites, facilities: There are numerous dispersed sites for tents or RVs of any length (no hookups). No drinking water or toilets are available. A dump station is nearby and is available from mid-September to mid-April. Leashed pets are permitted.

Reservations, fees: Reservations are not accepted. The fee is $30 for 14 nights, $140 per season. Fees charged from September 15 to April 15. Summer is free, with a 14-day limit. Open year-round.

Directions: From Blythe, drive east on I-10 a short distance to Lovekin Boulevard. Turn left and drive about eight miles to the campground on the right.

Contact: Bureau of Land Management, Palm Springs Field Office, 760/251-4800, fax 760/251-4899.

65 MAYFLOWER COUNTY PARK

Scenic rating: 6

on the Colorado River

Map 16.11, page 863

The Colorado River is the fountain of life around these parts and, for campers, the main attraction of this county park. It is a popular spot for waterskiing. There is river access here in the Blythe area. Fishing is good for channel and flathead catfish, striped bass, large- and smallmouth bass, bluegill, and crappie. This span of water is flanked by agricultural lands, although there are several developed recreation areas on the California side of the river south of Blythe near Palo Verde.

Campsites, facilities: There are 25 tent sites and 152 sites for RVs of any length (with partial hookups of 30 and 50 amps). Picnic tables and fire grills are provided. Drinking water, restrooms with flush toilets and free showers, dump station, and a boat ramp are available. Leashed pets are permitted.

Reservations, fees: Reservations are not accepted. Sites are $16–18 per night, $2 boat launch fee, $1 per night per pet. Monthly rates available. Some credit cards accepted. Open year-round.

Directions: Drive on I-10 to Blythe and Highway 95. Take Highway 95 north (it becomes Intake Boulevard) and drive 3.5 miles to 6th Avenue. Turn right at 6th Avenue and drive 2.5 miles to Colorado River Road. Bear left and drive 0.5 mile to the park entrance.

Contact: Mayflower County Park, 760/922-4665; Riverside County, 760/922-9177, www.riversidecountyparks.org.

66 RIVIERA RV RESORT

Scenic rating: 6

near the Colorado River

Map 16.11, page 863

This RV park is set up for camper-boaters who want to hunker down for awhile along the Colorado River and cool off. Access to the park is easy off I-10, and a marina is available, both big pluses for those showing up with trailered boats. Swimming lagoons are another bonus. A golf course is within 10 miles. Note that about half of the sites are rented year-round.

Campsites, facilities: There are 287 sites for RVs of any length (with full hookups of 30 and 50 amps); some sites are pull-through. Tents are allowed, and seven park-model cabins are available. Picnic tables are provided. Restrooms with showers, heated swimming pool, spa, cable TV, Wi-Fi, modem access, coin laundry, telephone room, convenience store, card room, 24-hour security, RV and boat storage, arcade, recreation center, boat ramps, boat fuel, and propane gas are available. Some facilities are wheelchair accessible. Leashed pets are permitted, with certain restrictions.

Reservations, fees: Reservations are accepted at 800/RV-DESTINY (800/783-3784). Sites are $35–39 per night on weekends, $29 per night Sunday through Thursday, $2 per person for more than two people, $10 per night for each additional vehicle. Tent sites are $20 per night. Holiday rates are higher. Monthly rates available. Some credit cards accepted. Open year-round.

Directions: Drive on I-10 to Blythe and continue east for two miles to the exit for Riviera Drive. Take that exit east and drive two miles to the park on the right (14100 Riviera Drive).

Contact: Riviera RV Resort, 760/922-5350, fax 760/922-6540, www.reynoldsresorts .com.

67 DESTINY McINTYRE RV RESORT

Scenic rating: 3

on the Colorado River

Map 16.11, page 863

This RV park sits on the outskirts of Blythe on the Colorado River, with this stretch of river providing good conditions for boating, waterskiing, and other water sports. A swimming lagoon is a big plus, along with riverfront beach access. Fishing is an option, with a variety of fish providing fair results, including striped bass, largemouth bass, and catfish roaming the area.

Campsites, facilities: There are 40 tent sites and 160 sites with full hookups (30 and 50 amps) for RVs of any length, including 11 pull-through sites. Picnic tables and fire rings are provided. Drinking water, restrooms with flush toilets and showers, dump station, propane gas, store, bait, ice, and a boat ramp and boat fuel are available. Some facilities are wheelchair-accessible. Leashed pets are permitted November through April only.

Reservations, fees: Make reservations at 800/RV-DESTINY (800/783-3784). Sites are $19–37 per night on weekends, $25 per night Sunday through Thursday from November through March, $10–25 per night for a tent site, $4 per person per night for more than two people, $10 per night for each additional

vehicle. Monthly rates available. Some credit cards accepted. Open year-round.

Directions: Drive on I-10 to Blythe to the exit for Intake Boulevard south. Take that exit and drive south on Intake Boulevard for 6.5 miles to the junction with 26th Avenue (it takes off to the right) and the park entrance on the left. Turn left and enter the park.

Contact: Destiny McIntyre RV Resort, 760/922-8205, fax 760/922-5695, www .destinyrv.com/mcintyrervresort.htm.

68 PALO VERDE COUNTY PARK

Scenic rating: 5

near the Colorado River

Map 16.11, page 863

This is the only game in town, with no other camp around for many miles. It is set near a bend in the Colorado River, not far from the Cibola National Wildlife Refuge. A boat ramp is available at the park, making it a launch point for adventure. This stretch of river is a good one for powerboating and waterskiing. The best facilities for visitors are available here and on the west side of the river between Palo Verde and Blythe, with nothing available on the east side of the river.

Campsites, facilities: There are 20 sites for tents or RVs of any length (no hookups). Picnic tables, fire rings, restrooms with flush toilets, and shade ramadas are available. No drinking water. A boat ramp is available. A store, coin laundry, and propane gas are available in Palo Verde. Leashed pets are permitted.

Reservations, fees: Reservations are not accepted. There is no fee for camping. Open year-round.

Directions: Drive on I-10 to Highway 78 (two miles west of Blythe). Take Highway 78 south and drive about 20 miles (three miles past Palo Verde) to the park entrance road on the east side.

Contact: Palo Verde County Park, Imperial County, 760/482-4384.

69 MULE MOUNTAIN LONG TERM VISITOR AREA

Scenic rating: 4

west of Blythe

Map 16.11, page 863

Mule Mountain is out in the middle of nowhere, but rockhounds and stargazers have found it anyway; it's ideal for both activities. There are two campgrounds, Coon Hollow and Wiley's Well, along with dispersed camping. Rockhounding, in particular, can be outstanding with several geode and agate beds nearby. Hobby rock-collecting is permitted. Commercial rock-poaching is not. The site, ideal for winter camping, attracts snowbirds and is set in a desert landscape at an elevation of 150 feet. Bradshaw Trail runs east to west through the visitors area.

Campsites, facilities: There are 28 sites at Coon Hollow and 14 sites at Wiley's Well for tents or RVs up to 35 feet (no hookups). Picnic tables and fire grills are provided. Vault toilets are available. No drinking water is available. A dump station is nearby, halfway between the two campgrounds, and is available mid-September to mid-April. Leashed pets are permitted.

Reservations, fees: Reservations are not accepted. Sites are $30 for 14 nights, $140 per season, with a 14-day stay limit every 28 days. Open year-round.

Directions: From Blythe, drive west on I-10 about 15 miles to Wiley's Well Road. Turn left (south) and drive about nine miles (the road turns to dirt) to Wiley's Well. Continue another three miles to reach Coon Hollow. Dispersed camping is allowed once you pass the sign that indicates you're in the visitors center.

Contact: Bureau of Land Management, Palm Springs Field Office, 760/251-4800, fax 760/251-4899, www.blm.gov.

70 PICACHO STATE RECREATION AREA

Scenic rating: 6

near Taylor Lake on the Colorado River

Map 16.11, page 863

To get here, you really have to want it. Picacho State Recreation Area is way out there, requiring a long drive north out of Winterhaven on a spindly little road. The camp is on the southern side of Taylor Lake on the Colorado River. The park is the best deal around for many miles, though, with boat ramps, waterskiing, good bass fishing, and occasionally, crazy folks having the time of their lives. The sun and water make a good combination. This recreation area includes eight miles of the lower Colorado River. Park wildlife includes wild burros and bighorn sheep, with thousands of migratory waterfowl on the Pacific Flyway occasionally taking up residence. More than 100 years ago, Picacho was a gold-mining town with a population of 2,500 people. Visitors should always carry extra water and essential supplies.

Campsites, facilities: There are 58 sites for tents or RVs up to 35 feet (no hookups), two group sites for up to 100 people, and two boat-in campsites. Picnic tables and fire grills are provided. Drinking water, pit toilets, dump station, solar showers, and two boat launches are available. Some facilities are wheelchair-accessible. Leashed pets are permitted.

Reservations, fees: Reservations are accepted for group sites only at 760/996-2963. Sites are $10 per night. Group sites are $37.50 per night for up to 12 vehicles. Boat-in group sites are $22.50 per night for up to 15 people, and $1.50 per person per night for additional people. Open year-round.

Directions: From El Centro, drive east on I-8 to Winterhaven and the exit for Winterhaven/4th Avenue. Take that exit to Winterhaven Drive. Turn left on Winterhaven Drive and drive 0.5 mile to County Road S24/Picacho Road. Turn right and drive 24 miles (crossing rail tracks, driving under a railroad bridge, and over the American Canal, the road becoming dirt for the last 18 miles) to the campground. The road is not suitable for large RVs. The drive takes 1–2 hours from Winterhaven. In summer, thunderstorms can cause flash flooding, making short sections of the road impassable.

Contact: Picacho State Recreation Area, c/o Salton Sea State Recreation Area, 760/393-3059 or 760/996-2963 (reservations), www.parks.ca.gov.

71 RIO BEND RV AND GOLF RESORT

Scenic rating: 5

near El Centro

Map 16.12, page 864

This resort is set at 50 feet below sea level near Mount Signal, about a 20-minute drive south of the Salton Sea. For some, this region is a godforsaken wasteland, but hey, that makes arriving at this park all the more like coming to a mirage in the desert. This resort is a combination RV park and year-round community with park models for sale. Management does what it can to offer visitors recreational options, including a nine-hole golf course. It's hot out here, sizzling most of the year, but dry and cool in the winter, the best time to visit.

Campsites, facilities: There are 500 sites for RVs of any length, 67 with full or partial hookups (30 and 50 amps); some sites are pull-through. No tents. Picnic tables are provided. Cable TV and restrooms with showers are available. A convenience store, café, heated swimming pool, spa, shuffleboard, volleyball, horseshoes, two small stocked lakes for catch-and-release fishing, nine-hole golf course, library, pool table, club room, organized activities, and modem access are available on a seasonal basis. Some facilities are wheelchair-accessible. A small store is nearby. Leashed pets are permitted.

Reservations, fees: Reservations are accepted. Sites are $27–38 per night, $3 per person for more than two people. Weekly, monthly, and annual rates available. Some credit cards accepted. Open year-round.

Directions: From El Centro, drive west on I-8 for seven miles to the Drew Road exit. Take that exit and drive south on Drew Road for 0.25 mile to the park on the right (1589 Drew Road).

Contact: Rio Bend RV and Golf Resort, 760/352-7061 or 800/545-6481, www.riobendrvgolfresort.com.

72 IMPERIAL SAND DUNES RECREATION AREA

Scenic rating: 1

east of Brawley

Map 16.13, page 865

Gecko, Roadrunner, and Midway campgrounds are three of the many camping options at Imperial Sand Dunes Recreation Area. There isn't a tree within a million miles of this camp. People who wind up here all have the same thing in common: They're ready to ride across the dunes in their dune buggies or off-highway vehicles. The dune season is on a weather-permitting basis. Note that several areas are off-limits to motorized vehicles and camping because of plant and habitat protection; hiking in these areas is allowed. There are opportunities for hiking on this incredible moonscape. Other recreation options include watching the sky and waiting for a cloud to show up. A gecko, by the way, is a harmless little lizard. I've had them crawl on the sides of my tent. Nice little fellows.

Campsites, facilities: There are numerous dispersed sites for tents or RVs of any length (no hookups). Vault toilets and a trash bin are available. No drinking water is available. A few sites have camping pads. Leashed pets are permitted.

Reservations, fees: Reservations are not

accepted. Sites are $25 per week, $90 per season, with a 14-day stay limit every 28 days. Open year-round.

Directions: From Brawley, drive east on Highway 78 for 27 miles to Gecko Road. Turn south on Gecko Road and drive three miles to the campground entrance on the left. To reach Roadrunner Camp, continue for two miles to the campground at the end of the road.

Contact: Bureau of Land Management, El Centro Field Office, 760/337-4400, fax 760/337-4490. For more information on closed areas, contact the Imperial Sand Dunes ranger station at 760/344-3919 (closed in the summer).

73 SENATOR WASH RECREATION AREA

Scenic rating: 6

near Senator Wash Reservoir

Map 16.13, page 865

Senator Wash Reservoir Recreation Area features two campgrounds, named (surprise) Senator Wash South Shore and Senator Wash North Shore. This recreation area is approximately 50 acres, with many trees of various types and several secluded camping areas. At Senator Wash North Shore (where there are fewer facilities than at South Shore), campsites are both on the water as well as further inland. Gravel beaches provide access to the reservoir. Boat ramps are nearby. This spot provides boating, fishing, OHV riding, wildlife-viewing, and opportunities for solitude and sightseeing.

Campsites, facilities: There are numerous dispersed sites for tents or RVs of any length (no hookups). No drinking water is available. At South Shore, there are restrooms with flush toilets, outdoor showers, and drinking water. A buoyed swimming area and boat ramp providing boat-in access to campsites at North Shore is available about 0.25 mile from South Shore. At North Shore, there are two vault

toilets, but no drinking water; boat ramp is approximately 0.25 mile away. Some facilities are wheelchair-accessible. No camping at the boat ramp. Leashed pets are permitted.

Reservations, fees: Reservations are not accepted. Sites are $5 per night. There is a year-round maximum 14-day limit for every 28 days. Open year-round.

Directions: Drive on I-8 to Yuma, Arizona, and the exit for 4th Avenue. Take that exit and drive to Imperial Highway/County Road S24. Turn north and drive 22 miles to Senator Wash Road. Turn left and drive about three miles south to Mesa Campground. Turn left and drive 200 yards to the South Shore Campground access road on the right. Turn right and drive to the reservoir and campground.

Contact: Bureau of Land Management, Yuma Field Office, 928/317-3200, fax 928/317-3250.

74 SQUAW LAKE

Scenic rating: 6

near the Colorado River

Map 16.13, page 865

Take your pick. There are two camps near the Colorado River in this area (the other is Senator Wash). This one is near Squaw Lake, created by the nearby Imperial Dam on the Colorado River. These sites provides opportunities for swimming, fishing, boating, and hiking, featuring direct boat access to the Colorado River. Wildlife includes numerous waterfowl, as well as quail, coyotes, and reptiles. A speed limit of 5 mph is enforced on the lake; no wakes permitted. The no-wake zone ends at the Colorado River.

Campsites, facilities: There are 125 sites for RVs of any length (no hookups) and dispersed sites for tents. Picnic tables and barbecue grills are provided. Four restrooms with flush toilets and outdoor showers are available. Drinking water is available at a central location. Two boat ramps are nearby. Some facilities are wheelchair-accessible. Leashed pets are permitted.

Reservations, fees: Reservations are not accepted. Sites are $5 per night. There is a year-round maximum 14-day limit for every 28 days. Open year-round.

Directions: Drive on I-8 to Yuma, Arizona, and the exit for 4th Avenue. Take that exit and drive to Imperial Highway/County Road S24. Turn north and drive 22 miles to Senator Wash Road. Turn left and drive about four miles (well signed) to the lake and campground on the right.

Contact: Bureau of Land Management, Yuma Field Office, 928/317-3200, fax 928/317-3250.

75 MIDWAY

Scenic rating: 6

in the Imperial Sand Dunes Recreation Area

Map 16.13, page 865

This is off-highway-vehicle headquarters, a place where people bring their three-wheelers, four-wheelers, and motorcycles. That's because a large area has been set aside just for this type of recreation. Good news is that this area has become more family-oriented because of increased enforcement, eliminating much of the lawlessness and lunatic behavior of the past. As you drive in,

you will enter the Buttercup Recreation Area, which is part of the Imperial Sand Dunes Recreation Area. You camp almost anywhere you like, and nobody beefs. Note that several areas are off-limits to motorized vehicles and camping because of plant and habitat protection; hiking in these areas is allowed. (See *Imperial Sand Dunes Recreation Area* listing in this chapter for more options.)

Campsites, facilities: There are several primitive sites for tents or RVs of any length (no hookups). Vault toilets and a trash bin are available. No drinking water is available. Leashed pets are permitted.

Reservations, fees: Reservations are not accepted. Sites are $25 per week, $90 per season. Open year-round, weather permitting.

Directions: From El Centro, drive east on I-8 for about 40 miles to Gray's Wells Road (signed Sand Dunes). Take that exit and drive (it bears to the right) to a stop sign. Continue straight on Gray's Wells Road and drive three miles to another stop sign. To reach Buttercup Recreation Area, turn left and drive a short distance. To reach Midway, continue straight on Gray's Wells Road for 1.5 miles (the road turns from pavement to dirt and then dead-ends); camping is permitted anywhere in this region.

Contact: Bureau of Land Management, El Centro Field Office, 760/337-4400, fax 760/337-4490. For more information on closed areas, contact the Imperial Sand Dunes ranger station at 760/344-3919.

RESOURCES

© KEN DECAMP

NATIONAL FORESTS

The Forest Service provides many secluded camps and allows camping anywhere except where it is specifically prohibited. If you ever want to clear the cobwebs from your head and get away from it all, this is the way to go.

Many Forest Service campgrounds are quite remote and have no drinking water. You usually don't need to check in or make reservations, and sometimes, there is no fee. At many Forest Service campgrounds that provide drinking water, the camping fee is often only a few dollars, with payment made on the honor system. Because most of these camps are in mountain areas, they are subject to winter closure because of snow or mud.

Dogs are permitted in national forests with no extra charge and no hassle. Leashes are required for all dogs in some places. Always carry documentation of current vaccinations.

National Forest Adventure Pass

Angeles, Cleveland, Los Padres, and San Bernardino National Forests require an Adventure Pass for each parked vehicle. Daily passes cost $5; annual passes are available for $30. You can buy Adventure Passes at national forest offices in Southern California and dozens of retail outlets and online vendors. The new charges are use fees, not entrance fees. Holders of Golden Age and Golden Access (not Golden Eagle) cards can buy the Adventure Pass at a 50 percent discount at national forest offices only, or at retail outlets for the retail price. A Golden Eagle passport is honored in lieu of an Adventure Pass.

When you buy an annual Adventure Pass, you can also buy an annual second-vehicle Adventure Pass for $5. Major credit cards are accepted at most retail and online outlets and at some forest service offices. You can buy Adventure Passes by telephone at 909/382-2622, -2623, -2621, or by mail at San Bernardino National Forest, Pass Program Headquarters, 602 S. Tippecanoe Avenue, San Bernardino, CA 92408-2607. Checks should be made payable to USDA Forest Service.

You will not need an Adventure Pass while traveling through these forests, nor when you've paid other types of fees such as camping or ski pass fees. However, if you are camping in these forests and you leave the campground in your vehicle and park outside the campground for recreation, such as at a trailhead, day-use area, near a fishing stream, etc., you will need an Adventure Pass for your vehicle. You also need an Adventure Pass if camping at a no-fee campground. More information about the Adventure Pass program, including a listing of retail and online vendors, can be obtained at website www.fsadventurepass.org.

National Forest Reservations

Some of the more popular camps, and most of the group camps, are on a reservation system. Reservations can be made up to 240 days in advance, and up to 360 days in advance for groups. To reserve a site call 877/444-6777 or visit the website www.reserveusa.com. The reservation fee is usually $9 for a campsite in a national forest, and major credit cards are accepted. Holders of Golden Age or Golden Access passports receive a 50 percent discount for campground fees, except for group sites.

National Forest Maps

National Forest maps are among the best you can get for the price. They detail all backcountry streams, lakes, hiking trails, and logging roads for access. They cost $7 or more, and they can be obtained in person at forest service offices or by contacting U.S. Forest Service, Attn: Map Sales, P.O. Box 8268, Missoula, MT 59807, 406/329-3024, fax 406/329-3030, or visit www.fs.fed.us/recreation/nationalforeststore. Major credit cards are accepted if ordering by telephone.

Forest Service Information

Forest Service personnel are most helpful for obtaining camping or hiking trail information. Unless you are buying a map or Adventure Pass, it is advisable to phone in advance to get the best service. For specific information on a national forest, contact the following offices:

USDA Forest Service
Pacific Southwest Region
1323 Club Drive
Vallejo, CA 94592
707/562-USFS (707/562-8737)
fax 707/562-9130
www.fs.fed.us/r5

Angeles National Forest
701 North Santa Anita Avenue
Arcadia, CA 91006
626/574-1613
fax 626/574-5233
www.fs.fed.us/r5/angeles

Cleveland National Forest
10845 Rancho Bernardo Road, No. 200
San Diego, CA 92127-2107
858/673-6180
fax 858/673-6192
www.fs.fed.us/r5/cleveland

Eldorado National Forest
100 Forni Road
Placerville, CA 95667
530/622-5061
fax 530/621-5297
www.fs.fed.us/r5/eldorado

Humboldt-Toiyabe National Forest
1200 Franklin Way
Sparks, NV 89431
775/331-6444
fax 775/355-5399
www.fs.fed.us/r4/htnf

Inyo National Forest
351 Pacu Lane, Suite 200
Bishop, CA 93514
760/873-2400
fax 760/873-2458
www.fs.fed.us/r5/inyo

Klamath National Forest
1312 Fairlane Road
Yreka, CA 96097-9549
530/842-6131
fax 530/841-4571
www.fs.fed.us/r5/klamath

Lake Tahoe Basin Management Unit
35 College Drive
South Lake Tahoe, CA 96150
530/543-2600
fax 530/543-2693
www.fs.fed.us/r5/ltbmu

Lassen National Forest
2550 Riverside Drive
Susanville, CA 96130
530/257-2151
fax 530/252-6448
www.r5.fs.fed.us/r5/lassen

Los Padres National Forest
6755 Hollister Avenue, Suite 150
Goleta, CA 93117
805/968-6640
fax 805/961-5729
www.fs.fed.us/r5/lospadres

Mendocino National Forest
825 North Humboldt Avenue
Willows, CA 95988
530/934-3316
fax 530/934-7384
www.fs.fed.us/r5/mendocino

Modoc National Forest
800 West 12th Street
Alturas, CA 96101
530/233-5811
fax 530/233-8709
www.fs.fed.us/r5/modoc

Plumas National Forest
P.O. Box 11500
159 Lawrence Street
Quincy, CA 95971
530/283-2050
fax 530/283-7746
www.fs.fed.us/r5/plumas

San Bernardino National Forest
602 South Tippecanoe Avenue
San Bernardino, CA 92408-2607
909/382-2600
fax 909/383-5770
www.fs.fed.us/r5/sanbernardino

Sequoia National Forest
Giant Sequoia National Monument
1839 South Newcomb Street
Porterville, CA 93257
559/784-1500
fax 559/781-4744
www.fs.fed.us/r5/sequoia

Shasta-Trinity National Forest
3644 Avtech Parkway
Redding, CA 96002
530/226-2500
fax 530/226-2470
www.fs.fed.us/r5/shastatrinity

Sierra National Forest
1600 Tollhouse Road
Clovis, CA 93611
559/297-0706
fax 559/294-4809
www.fs.fed.us/r5/sierra

Six Rivers National Forest
1330 Bayshore Way
Eureka, CA 95501
707/442-1721
fax 707/442-9242
www.fs.fed.us/r5/sixrivers

Stanislaus National Forest
19777 Greenley Road
Sonora, CA 95370
209/532-3671
fax 209/533-1890
www.fs.fed.us/r5/stanislaus

Tahoe National Forest
631 Coyote Street
Nevada City, CA 95959
530/265-4531
fax 530/478-6109
www.fs.fed.us/r5/tahoe

STATE PARKS

The California State Parks system provides many popular camping spots in spectacular settings. These campgrounds include drive-in numbered sites, tent spaces, and picnic tables, with showers and bathrooms provided nearby. Reservations are often necessary during the summer. Although many parks are well known, there are still some little-known gems in the state parks system where campers can enjoy seclusion, even in the summer.

State park fees have increased significantly since 2002, but camping in a state park is still a good deal. Many of the campgrounds along the California coastline are particularly popular in summer and require planning to secure a campsite.

State Park Reservations

Most of the state park campgrounds are on a reservation system, and campsites can be booked up to seven months in advance at these parks. There are also hike-in/bike-in sites at many of the parks, and they are available on a first-come, first-served basis. Reservations can be made by telephone or online by phoning 800/444-PARK (800/444-7275) or visiting the website www.reserveamerica.com. The reservation fee is usually $7.50 for a campsite. Major credit cards are accepted for reservations but are generally not accepted in person at the parks.

Camping discounts of 50 percent are available for holders of the Disabled Discount Pass, and free camping is allowed for holders of the Disabled Veteran/Prisoner of War Pass.

For general information about California State Parks, contact:

California Department of Parks and Recreation
Public Information Office
P.O. Box 942896
1416 9th Street
Sacramento, CA 94296
916/653-6995 or 800/777-0369
fax 916/653-6995
www.parks.ca.gov

NATIONAL PARKS

California's national parks are natural wonders, varying from the spectacular yet crowded Yosemite Valley to the remote and rugged Lava Beds National Monument. Reservations for campsites are available five months in advance for many of the national parks in California. In addition to campground fees, expect to pay a park entrance fee ranging $10–20 per vehicle, or as low as $5 per person for hike-in/bike-in (you can buy an annual National Parks Pass that waives entrance fees). This entrance fee is valid for seven days. For an additional fee, a Golden Eagle sticker can be added to the National Parks Pass, thereby eliminating entrance fees at sites managed by the U.S. Fish and Wildlife Service, the U.S. Forest Service, and the Bureau of Land Management. Various discounts are available for holders of Golden Age and Golden Access passports, including a 50 percent reduction of camping fees (group camps not included) and a waiver of park entrance fees.

For Yosemite National Park reservations,

call 800/436-PARK (800/436-7275) or visit http://reservations.nps.gov. Major credit cards accepted.

For all other national parks, call 800/365-CAMP (800/365-2267) or visit http://reservations.nps.gov. Major credit cards are accepted.

National Park Service
Pacific West Region
One Jackson Center
1111 Jackson Street, Suite 700
Oakland, CA 94607
510/817-1304
www.nps.gov

Cabrillo National Monument
1800 Cabrillo Memorial Drive
San Diego, CA 92106-3601
619/557-5450
fax 619/226-6311
www.nps.gov/cabr

Channel Islands National Park
1901 Spinnaker Drive
Ventura, CA 93001
805/658-5730
fax 805/658-5799
www.nps.gov/chis

Death Valley National Park
P.O. Box 579
Death Valley, CA 92328-0579
760/786-3200
fax 760/786-3283
www.nps.gov/deva

Devils Postpile National Monument
P.O. Box 3999
Mammoth Lakes, CA 93546
760/934-2289 (summer only)
fax 760/934-8896 (summer only)
www.nps.gov/depo
For year-round information, contact Sequoia and Kings Canyon National Parks (see listing).

Golden Gate National Recreation Area
Fort Mason, Building 201
San Francisco, CA 94123-0022
415/561-4700
fax 415/561-4710
www.nps.gov/goga

Joshua Tree National Park
74485 National Park Drive
Twentynine Palms, CA 92277-3597
760/367-5500
fax 760/367-6392
www.nps.gov/jotr

Lassen Volcanic National Park
P.O. Box 100
Mineral, CA 96063-0100
530/595-4444
fax 530/595-3262
www.nps.gov/lavo

Lava Beds National Monument
1 Indian Well Headquarters
Tulelake, CA 96134
530/667-2282
fax 530/667-2737
www.nps.gov/labe

Mojave National Preserve
2701 Barstow Road
Barstow, CA 92311
760/733-4040 (information)
fax 760/252-6174
www.nps.gov/moja

Pinnacles National Monument
5000 Highway 146
Paicines, CA 95043
831/389-4485
fax 831/389-4489
www.nps.gov/pinn

Point Reyes National Seashore
Point Reyes Station, CA 94956-9799
415/464-5100
fax 415/464-5149
www.nps.gov/pore

Redwood National and State Parks
1111 2nd Street
Crescent City, CA 95531
707/464-6101
fax 707/464-1812
www.nps.gov/redw

Santa Monica Mountains National Recreation Area
401 West Hillcrest Drive
Thousand Oaks, CA 91360
805/370-2301
fax 805/370-1850
www.nps.gov/samo

Sequoia and Kings Canyon National Parks
47050 Generals Highway
Three Rivers, CA 93271-9651
559/565-3341
www.nps.gov/seki

Smith River National Recreation Area
P.O. Box 228
Gasquet, CA 95543
707/457-3131
fax 707/457-3794
www.fs.fed.us/r5/sixrivers

Whiskeytown National Recreation Area
P.O. Box 188
Whiskeytown, CA 96095
530/246-1225 or 530/242-3400
fax 530/246-5154
www.nps.gov/whis

Yosemite National Park
P.O. Box 577
Yosemite National Park, CA 95389
209/372-0200 for 24-hour recorded message
www.nps.gov/yose

U.S. ARMY CORPS OF ENGINEERS AND RESERVATIONS

Some of the family camps and most of the group camps operated by the U.S. Army Corps of Engineers are on a reservation system. Reservations can be made up to 240 days in advance, and up to 360 days in advance for groups. To reserve a site, call 877/444-6777 or visit the website www.reserveusa.com. The reservation fee is usually $9, and major credit cards are accepted. Holders of Golden Age or Golden Access passports receive a 50 percent discount for campground fees, except for group sites.

South Pacific Division
333 Market Street
San Francisco, CA 94105
415/977-8272
fax 415/977-8316
www.spn.usace.army.mil

Sacramento District
1325 J Street
Sacramento, CA 95814
916/557-5100
www.spk.usace.army.mil

Los Angeles District
915 Wilshire Boulevard, Suite 980
Los Angeles, CA 90017-3401
213/452-3908
fax 213/452-4209
www.spl.usace.army.mil

BUREAU OF LAND MANAGEMENT

Most of the BLM campgrounds are primitive and in remote areas. Often, there is no fee charged for camping. Holders of Golden Age or Golden Access passports receive a 50 percent discount, except for group camps, at BLM fee campgrounds.

Bureau of Land Management
California State Office
2800 Cottage Way, Suite W-1834
Sacramento, CA 95825-1886
916/978-4400
fax 916/978-4416
www.blm.gov/ca

California Desert District Office
22835 Calle San Juan de los Lagos
Moreno Valley, CA 92553
951/697-5200
fax 951/697-5299
www.blm.gov/ca/cdd

Alturas Field Office
708 West 12th Street
Alturas, CA 96101
530/233-4666
fax 530/233-5696
www.blm.gov/ca/alturas

Arcata Field Office
1695 Heindon Road
Arcata, CA 95521-4573
707/825-2300
fax 707/825-2301
www.blm.gov/ca/arcata

Bakersfield Field Office
3801 Pegasus Drive
Bakersfield, CA 93308
661/391-6000
fax 661/391-6040
www.blm.gov/ca/bakersfield

Barstow Field Office
2601 Barstow Road
Barstow, CA 92311
760/252-6000
fax 760/252-6099
www.blm.gov/ca/barstow

Bishop Field Office
351 Pacu Lane, Suite 100
Bishop, CA 93514
760/872-5000
fax 760/872-5050
www.blm.gov/ca/bishop

Eagle Lake Field Office
2950 Riverside Drive
Susanville, CA 96130
530/257-0456
fax 530/257-4831
www.blm.gov/ca/eaglelake

El Centro Field Office
1661 South 4th Street
El Centro, CA 92243
760/337-4400
fax 760/337-4490
www.blm.gov/ca/elcentro

Folsom Field Office
63 Natoma Street
Folsom, CA 95630
916/985-4474
fax 916/985-3259
www.blm.gov/ca/folsom

Hollister Field Office
20 Hamilton Court
Hollister, CA 95023
831/630-5000
fax 831/630-5055
www.blm.gov/ca/hollister

Palm Springs/South Coast Field Office
P.O. Box 581260
North Palm Springs, CA 92258-1260
760/251-4800
fax 760/251-4899
www.blm.gov/ca/palmsprings

Redding Field Office
355 Hemsted Drive
Redding, CA 96002
530/224-2100
fax 530/224-2172
www.blm.gov/ca/redding

Ridgecrest Field Office
300 South Richmond Road
Ridgecrest, CA 93555
760/384-5400
fax 760/384-5499
www.blm.gov/ca/ridgecrest

Ukiah Field Office
2550 North State Street
Ukiah, CA 95482
707/468-4000
fax 707/468-4027
www.blm.gov/ca/ukiah

OTHER VALUABLE RESOURCES
State Forests
Jackson Demonstration State Forest
802 North Main Street
Fort Bragg, CA 95437
707/964-5674
fax 707/964-0941

Mountain Home Demonstration State Forest
P.O. Box 517
Springville, CA 93265
559/539-2321 (summer)
559/539-2855 (winter)

County/Regional Park Departments

Del Norte County Parks
840 9th Street, Suite 11
Crescent City, CA 95531
707/464-7230
fax 707/464-5824
www.co.del-norte.ca.us

East Bay Regional Park District
P.O. Box 5381
Oakland, CA 94605-0381
510/562-PARK (510/562-7275)
or 510/544-2200
fax 510/635-3478
www.ebparks.org

Humboldt County Parks
1106 2nd Street
Eureka, CA 95501
707/445-7651
fax 707/445-7409
www.co.humboldt.ca.us/

Marin Municipal Water District
220 Nellen Avenue
Corte Madera, CA 94925
415/945-1455
fax 415/927-4953
www.marinwater.org

Midpeninsula Regional Open Space District
330 Distel Circle
Los Altos, CA 94022-1404
650/691-1200
fax 650/691-0485
www.openspace.org

Pacific Gas and Electric Company
Corporate Real Estate/Recreation
5555 Florin-Perkins Road, Room 100
Sacramento, CA 95826
916/386-5164
fax 916/923-7044
www.pge.com/recreation

Sacramento County Regional Parks
3711 Branch Center Road
Sacramento, CA 95827
916/875-6961
fax 916/875-6050
www.sacparks.net

San Diego County Parks and Recreation Department
2454 Heritage Park Row
San Diego, CA 92110
858/694-3049
fax 619/260-6492
www.co.san-diego.ca.us/parks

San Luis Obispo County Parks Department
1087 Santa Rosa Street
San Luis Obispo, CA 93408
805/781-5930
fax 805/781-1102
www.slocountyparks.org

San Mateo County Parks and Recreation Department
455 County Center, 4th floor
Redwood City, CA 94063-1646
650/363-4020
fax 650/599-1721
www.eparks.net

Santa Barbara County Parks and Recreation Department
610 Mission Canyon Road
Santa Barbara, CA 93105
805/568-2461
fax 805/568-2459
www.sbparks.com

Santa Clara County Parks Department
298 Garden Hill Drive
Los Gatos, CA 95032-7669
408/355-2200
fax 408/355-2290
www.parkhere.org

Sonoma County Regional Parks
2300 County Center Drive, Suite 120-A
Santa Rosa, CA 95404
707/565-2041
fax 707/579-8247
www.sonoma-county.org/parks

State and Federal Offices
U.S. Fish and Wildlife Service
1849 C Street NW
Washington, DC 20240
www.fws.gov

U.S. Geological Survey
Branch of Information Services
P.O. Box 25286, Bldg. 810, MS 306,
Federal Center
Denver, CO 80225
888/ASK-USGS (888/275-8747)
or 303/202-4700
www.usgs.gov

California Department of Fish and Game
1416 9th Street, 12th floor
Sacramento, CA 95814
916/445-0411
www.dfg.ca.gov

Information Services
Lake County Visitor Information Center
P.O. Box 1025
6110 East Highway 20
Lucerne, CA 95458
707/274-5652 or 800/525-3743
fax 707/274-5664
www.lakecounty.com

Mammoth Lakes Visitors Bureau
P.O. Box 48
437 Old Mammoth Road, Suite Y
Mammoth Lakes, CA 93546
888/GO-MAMMOTH (888/466-2666)
or 760/934-2712
fax 760/934-7066
www.visitmammoth.com

Mount Shasta Visitors Bureau
300 Pine Street
Mount Shasta, CA 96067
530/926-4865 or 800/926-4865
fax 530/926-0976
www.mtshastachamber.com

The Nature Conservancy of California
201 Mission Street, 4th floor
San Francisco, CA 94105-1832
415/777-0487
fax 415/777-0244
www.nature.org/california

Plumas County Visitors Bureau
550 Crescent Street
P.O. Box 4120
Quincy, CA 95971
530/283-6345 or 800/326-2247
fax 530/283-5465
www.plumascounty.org

Shasta Cascade Wonderland Association
1699 Highway 273
Anderson, CA 96007
530/365-7500 or 800/474-2782
fax 530/365-1258
www.shastacascade.com

Map Companies
Map Link
30 South La Patera Lane, Unit 5
Goleta, CA 93117
805/692-6777 or 800/962-1394
fax 805/692-6787 or 800/627-7768
www.maplink.com

Olmsted and Bros. Map Company
P.O. Box 5351
Berkeley, CA 94705
tel./fax 510/658-6534

Tom Harrison Maps
2 Falmouth Cove
San Rafael, CA 94901-4465
tel./fax 415/456-7940 or 800/265-9090
www.tomharrisonmaps.com

U.S. Forest Service
Attn: Map Sales
P.O. Box 8268
Missoula, MT 59807
406/329-3024
fax 406/329-3030
www.fs.fed.us/recreation/nationalforeststore

U.S. Geological Survey
Branch of Information Services
P.O. Box 25286, Federal Center
Denver, CO 80225
303/202-4700 or 888/ASK-USGS
(888/275-8747)
fax 303/202-4693
www.usgs.gov

Index

Acknowledgments

U.S. Forest Service

Matt Mathes, Pacific Region Headquarters

Jerry Reponen, Los Angeles River Ranger District, Angeles National Forest

Patrick Hersey, San Gabriel Ranger District, Angeles National Forest

Kirsten Johansen, Santa Clara-Mojave Ranger District, Angeles National Forest

Ann Carey, Descanso Ranger District, Cleveland National Forest

Jeff Wells, Palomar Ranger District, Cleveland National Forest

Jake Rodriguez, Trabuco Ranger District, Cleveland National Forest

Billy Brown, Amador Ranger District, Eldorado National Forest

Pete Robinson, Georgetown Ranger District, Eldorado National Forest

Nancy Platt, Christy Schroeder, and Fay Buel, Pacific Ranger District, Eldorado National Forest

Joyce Pratt, Placerville Ranger District, Eldorado National Forest

Eric Pignata, Bridgeport Ranger District, Humboldt-Toiyabe National Forest

Mike May, Carson Ranger District, Humboldt-Toiyabe National Forest

Kitty VanStelle, Mammoth Lakes Ranger Station and Visitor Center, Inyo National Forest

Cathie Morgan and Adam Smith, Mono Basin Scenic Area and Visitor Center, Inyo National Forest

Kendrah Madrid, Mount Whitney Ranger District, Inyo National Forest

Carol Puryear, Britta Suppes, and John Louth, White Mountain Ranger District, Inyo National Forest

Susan Reynolds, Goosenest Ranger District, Klamath National Forest

Veronica Selvage, Happy Camp and Oak Knoll Ranger Districts, Klamath National Forest

Charlie Krause, Scott River and Salmon River Ranger Districts, Klamath National Forest

Barbara Jackson, Almanor Ranger District, Lassen National Forest

Mario Guajardo, Eagle Lake Ranger District, Lassen National Forest

Mary Lou Schmierer, Hat Creek Ranger District, Lassen National Forest

Nicole Karres, Monterey Ranger District, Los Padres National Forest

Rick Howell, Mount Pinos Ranger District, Los Padres National Forest

Joe Sigorino, Ojai Ranger District, Los Padres National Forest

Jim Lopez, Santa Barbara Ranger District, Los Padres National Forest

Helen Tarbet, Santa Lucia Ranger District, Los Padres National Forest

Tony Kanownik, Covelo Ranger District, Mendocino National Forest

Gary Hayton, Grindstone Ranger District, Mendocino National Forest

Ray Linnet, Red Bluff Recreation Area, Mendocino National Forest

Debbie McIntosh, Upper Lake Ranger District, Mendocino National Forest

Jean Breakfield, Big Valley Ranger District, Modoc National Forest

Stephen Riley, Devil's Garden Ranger District, Modoc National Forest

Mike Kegg, Doublehead Ranger District, Modoc National Forest

Kathy Kempa, Warner Mountain Ranger District, Modoc National Forest

Pandora Valle and Bill Benson, Beckwourth Ranger District, Plumas National Forest

Mary August, Feather River Ranger District, Plumas National Forest

Judy Abrams, Mount Hough Ranger District, Plumas National Forest

Jonathan Cook-Fisher and Audrey Scranton, Mountaintop Ranger Station, San Bernardino National Forest

Roman Rodriguez, San Jacinto Ranger District, San Bernardino National Forest

Carol Hallacy, Hume Lake Ranger District, Sequoia National Forest

Sherry Montgomery, Kern River Ranger District, Kernville, Sequoia National Forest

Geri Adams, Kern River Ranger District, Lake Isabella, Sequoia National Forest

Carol Zeigler, Tule River-Hot Springs Ranger District, Sequoia National Forest

Cindy Beckstead, Big Bar Ranger District, Shasta-Trinity National Forest

Pat Smith, Hayfork Ranger District, Shasta-Trinity National Forest

Les Lloyd, McCloud Ranger District, Shasta-Trinity National Forest

Don Lee, Mount Shasta Ranger District, Shasta-Trinity National Forest

Cathy Southwick, Shasta Lake Ranger District, Shasta-Trinity National Forest

Marla Peckinpah, Mary Ellen Grigsby, and Steve Gut, Weaverville Ranger District, Shasta-Trinity National Forest

Judy Hanevold, Yolla Bolly Ranger District, Shasta-Trinity National Forest

Patrice Yakovetic and Linda McPhail, Bass Lake Ranger District, Sierra National Forest

Debbie Arndt, High Sierra Ranger District, Sierra National Forest

Jim Lasell, Lower Trinity Ranger District, Six Rivers National Forest

Vonnie Harding and Dave Williams, Orleans Ranger District, Six Rivers National Forest

Karey Dean, Six Rivers National Forest, Smith River National Recreation Area

Diane Arthur, Calaveras Ranger District, Stanislaus National Forest

Jan Cargill, Groveland Ranger District, Stanislaus National Forest

Bill Seib, Mi-Wok Ranger District, Stanislaus National Forest

Walt Moneski, Summit Ranger District, Stanislaus National Forest

Jan Welsh, American River Ranger District, Foresthill Ranger Station, Tahoe National Forest

Susanne Johnson, Lake Tahoe Basin Management Unit, Tahoe National Forest

Ricardo Buitron, Sierraville Ranger District, Tahoe National Forest

Lydia Olson and Heather Newell, Yuba River Ranger District, North, Tahoe National Forest

Rene Smith, Yuba River Ranger District, South, Tahoe National Forest

U.S. Army Corps of Engineers

Linda Clapp, Lake Sonoma Recreation Area, San Francisco District

Phil Deffenbaugh, Lake Kaweah, Sacramento District

Tom Ehrke, Hensley Lake, Sacramento District

Hector Galvan, Island Park and Deer Creek Point Campgrounds, Sacramento District

Kathy Guynes, Englebright Lake, Sacramento District

Denice Hogan, Black Butte Lake, Sacramento District

Joanne Jackson, Cordoniz Recreation Area, Sacramento District

Valerie Mavis, Lake Mendocino, San Francisco District

Donna Nelson, Acorn and Oak Knoll Campgrounds, Sacramento District

Dwayne Urquhart, Tule Campground, Sacramento District

Dale Verner, Martis Creek Lake, Sacramento District

Bureau of Land Management

Claude Singleton, Alturas Field Office
Clarence Killingsworth, Arcata Field Office
Steve Larsen and Kenneth Hock,
  Bakersfield Field Office
Bob Raver, Barstow Field Office
Jeff Yanez, Bishop Field Office
Susan Richey and Terry Knight,
  Carson City Field Office
Jim Hunt, Eagle Lake Field Office
Dallas Meeks, El Centro Field Office
Lou Cutajar, Folsom Field Office
Mona Daniels, Palm Springs Field Office
Mike Hoffman, Redding Field Office
Beth Lefebvre, Ukiah Field Office
Mirabella Lopez and Mark Lowans,
  Yuma Field Office

National Parks

Yvonne Menard, Channel Islands National
  Park
Terry Baldino and Alicia Alvarado, Death
  Valley National Park
Shanda Ochs, Lassen Volcanic National
  Park
Mike Wagman, Sequoia and Kings Canyon
  National Parks
Brent Gordon and Michele Woods, Yosemite
  National Park
Kale Bowling-Schaff, Lava Beds National
  Monument
Pete Lundberg, Devils Postpile National
  Monument
Ina Webb, Pinnacles National Monument
Linda Slater, Mojave National Preserve
Erin Foley, Golden Gate National
  Recreation Area
Susan Davis, Susan Doniger, Celia Riechel,
  and Debbie Wiest, Redwood National
  and State Parks
John Dell'Osso, Point Reyes National
  Seashore
Tricia Ford, Whiskeytown National
  Recreation Area

State Parks

Ruth Coleman, Roy Stearns, and Balenda
  Gray, Sacramento Headquarters
Ellen Absher, Mount San Jacinto State Park
John Arnold, Half Moon Bay State Beach
Ryan Banovitz, Bolsa Chica State Beach
Jill Bazemore, Emma Wood State Beach
Steven Bier, Salton Sea State Recreation
  Area
Avis Boutell and Star Sandoval, Bay Area
  Sector
Lynda Burman, Indian Grinding Rock State
  Historic Park
Joshua Bynum, Crystal Cove State Park
Kathy Dolinar and Kent Miller, Ocotillo
  Wells State Vehicular Recreation Area
Robert Carpenter, Henry Cowell Redwoods
  State Park
Brandon Carroll, Big Basin Redwoods State
  Park
Eric Carter, Prairie Creek Redwoods State
  Park
Taya Chase, Jeanette Fenske, and Liz
  Hamman, Humboldt Redwoods State
  Park
Joni Coombe, Pfeiffer Big Sur State Park
Suzanne Downing, San Juan Bautista
  Section
Donna Galyean, Humboldt Lagoons State
  Park
Dave Garcia, Limekiln State Park
Michael Grant, Butano State Park
Balenda Gray, Sacramento Headquarters
Greg Hall, Tolowa Dunes State Park
Ted Hannibal, Hollister Hills State Vehicular
  Recreation Area
John Hardcastle, Benbow Lake State
  Recreation Area
Kathy Hernandez, Folsom Lake State
  Recreation Area
Jacque Hoffman, Fort Ross State Historic
  Park
Laura Itogawa, Cuyamaca Rancho State
  Park
Travis Johnson, Palomar Mountain State Park

Gary Kinney, Seacliff State Beach
Nathan Kogen and Mike Selbo, Sunset State
    Beach
Lawani Kolley, Sierra District
John Kolsrud, Austin Creek State Recreation
    Area
Mike Lair, China Camp State Park
Sheri Larue, Malakoff Diggins State Historic
    Park
William Lutton, Turlock Lake State
    Recreation Area
Valerie Marshall, Mendocino District
Dan Martin, Woodson Bridge State
    Recreation Area
Melissa McGee, Standish-Hickey State
    Recreation Area
Maria Mendez, Colusa-Sacramento River
    State Recreation Area
Bill Mentzer, Marin Sector
Lynn Mochizuki, Point Mugu State Park
Javier Morales, Patrick's Point State Park
Cecelia Moreno, Auburn State Recreation
    Area
Dan Murray and Alison Strachan, Channel
    Coast District
Sean Nichols and Mark Pupich, Grover Hot
    Springs State Park
Jerelyn Oliveira, Colonel Allensworth State
    Historic Park
Denise Peterson, Brannan Island State
    Recreation Area
Shirley Plumhuf, McArthur-Burney Falls
    State Park
Christa Quick, Angeles District
Mary Rafuse, Castle Crags State Park
Kellen Riley, San Simeon State Park
Carol Schmal, South Carlsbad State Beach
Rachel Shaw, San Elijo State Beach
Dan Smith, Samuel P. Taylor State Park
Jason Smith, Sonoma Coast State Beach
Shannon Stalder, Grizzly Creek Redwoods
    State Park
Mike Stanley, Portola Redwoods State Park
Erin Steinart, Bothe-Napa Valley State Park
Veneta Stewart, Donner Memorial State Park

Sarah Straws and Bob Young, Calaveras Big
    Trees State Park
Katie Sundvall, Richardson Grove State
    Park
Debborah Tanner, Four Rivers Sector
Theresa Tate, New Brighton State Beach
Charlie Thompson, Sinkyone Wilderness
    State Park
Bob Thornton, Andrew Molera State Park
Jennifer Tustison, Orange Coast District
Mckeena Vanrillaer, Salt Point State Park
John Verhoeven, Fremont Peak State Park
Tony Villareal, Pismo State Beach/Oceano
    Dunes State Vehicular Recreation Area
Karen Vreeland, Millerton Lake State
    Recreation Area
Shelley Waltman-Derr, Clear Lake State
    Park
Melissa Weaver, San Luis Reservoir State
    Recreation Area
Kathy Williams, Silverwood Lake State
    Recreation Area
Bob Williamson, Carnegie State Vehicular
    Recreation Area
Susan Wilson, Morro Bay State Park
Adam Wollter, Sugarloaf Ridge State Park
Tyson Young, Caswell Memorial State Park

State Forests

Wayne Connor, Boggs Mountain
    Demonstration State Forest
Lois Kauffman, LaTour Demonstration State
    Forest
Alan Frame, Mountain Home Demonstration
    State Forest

Other

Randy Akana, Siskiyou County Public Works
Doug Allen, Edward Ancheta, Mike Ekdao,
    John Heenan, Theresa Nance, Fred
    Griggs, and Reggie Zapata, Santa Clara
    County Parks
Joe Anderson, Napa Valley Exposition
Marian Ardohain and Amy Tischman,
    Merced Irrigation District

Steve Benson, Huntington Beach City Parks

Tim Bolla, Richard Chandler, and Marilea Linne, Solano County Parks

Christopher Burdette, The Presidio Trust

Cheryl Bynum and Martha Martinez, Imperial County Parks

Dolores Canali, Cindy Donald, Duane Forest, Randal Higgins, Ruben Rodriguez, and Susan Storey, Riverside County Parks

Julie Cloherty, San Diego County Parks

Peggy Davidson, Nevada Irrigation District

Anna Diaz and Ann Springer, San Luis Obispo County Parks

Brent Doan, Lake Casitas Municipal Water District

Joy Feller, Nevada County Fairgrounds

Irene Flores, Karen Montanye, Juisa Powell, and Mary Sheehan, San Bernardino Regional Parks

Pam Gallo, Ventura County Parks

Clay Garland, Santa Barbara County Parks

Colleen Ghiglia, Lompoc Parks and Recreation

Patty Guida, New Melones Visitors Center, U.S. Bureau of Reclamation

Michelle Gilroy and Dennis Redfern, California Department of Fish & Game

Sherie Harral, Shasta Dam, U.S. Bureau of Reclamation

José Gutierrez, Sacramento Municipal Utility District

Heidi Gutnecht, City of San Diego

Chuck Hamilton and Ychelle Tillemans, Inyo County Parks

David Haverty and Donna LaGraffe, Sonoma County Regional Parks

Darlene Hennings, Placer County Facilities Services

Connie Jackson, Marty Johnson, and Danae Schmidt, Stanislaus County Parks and Recreation

Sara Johnston and Karen White, United Water Conservation District

Tracy Kves, Northern California Power Agency

Cynthia McDonald, Joy Vandell, Ross Jackson, and Mike Drury, Pacific Gas and Electric

Kathy McGadden, Greg Smith, and Jim Spreng, Monterey County Parks

Bill Minor, Humboldt County Public Works

Janet Morrison, Fresno County Parks

Dave Moore, San Mateo County Parks

Julie Ola, Alpine County Public Works Department

John Parsons, Stancy Perich, and John Wilbanks, Kern County Parks and Recreation

Don Pearson, Eldorado Irrigation District

Pam Phelps, City of Escondido

Christina Phillips, Hoopa Valley Tribal Council

Neil Pilegard, Tulare County Parks and Recreation

Patty Sereni, Napa County Fairgrounds

Ron Slimm, Orange County Parks

Alicia Smolke, San Joaquin County Parks

Pat Sotelo, Livermore Area Recreation and Park District

Laurie Swanson, Tahoe City Public Utilities District

Sue Vanderschans, Turlock Irrigation District

Roberta Warden, El Dorado Irrigation District

Amy Welch, Mono County Public Works

Jerry Wright, Yolo County Parks

www.moon.com

For helpful advice on planning a trip, visit www.moon.com for the **TRAVEL PLANNER** and get access to useful travel strategies and valuable information about great places to visit. When you travel with Moon, expect an experience that is uncommon and truly unique.

MOON CALIFORNIA CAMPING

Avalon Travel Publishing
An Imprint of
Avalon Publishing Group, Inc.

AVALON
publishing group incorporated

1400 65th Street, Suite 250
Emeryville, CA 94608, USA
www.moon.com

Senior Research Editor: Stephani Stienstra
Research Editors: Pamela S. Padula,
    Kathie Morgan
Editor and Series Manager: Sabrina Young
Acquisitions Manager: Rebecca K. Browning
Copy Editor: Ellie Behrstock
Graphics Coordinator: Nicole Schultz
Production Coordinator: Nicole Schultz
Interior Designer: Darren Alessi
Map Editor: Kevin Anglin
Cartographers: Suzanne Service
    and Kat Bennett
Proofreader: Deana Shields
Indexer: Greg Jewett

ISBN-10: 1-56691-831-6
ISBN-13: 978-1-56691-831-2
ISSN: 1531-8109

Printing History
1st Edition – 1987
15th Edition – February 2007
5 4 3 2 1

Keeping Current

We are committed to making this book the most accurate and enjoyable camping guide to the state. You can rest assured that every campground in this book has been carefully reviewed in an effort to keep this book as up-to-date as possible. However, by the time you read this book, some of the fees listed herein may have changed and campgrounds may have closed unexpectedly.

If you have a favorite gem you'd like to see included in the next edition, or see anything that needs updating, clarification, or correction, please drop us a line. Send your comments via email to feedback@moon.com, or use the address above.